Nineteenth-Century
Literature Criticism

Guide to Gale Literary Criticism Series

For criticism on	Consult these Gale series
Authors now living or who died after December 31, 1999	*CONTEMPORARY LITERARY CRITICISM (CLC)*
Authors who died between 1900 and 1999	*TWENTIETH-CENTURY LITERARY CRITICISM (TCLC)*
Authors who died between 1800 and 1899	*NINETEENTH-CENTURY LITERATURE CRITICISM (NCLC)*
Authors who died between 1400 and 1799	*LITERATURE CRITICISM FROM 1400 TO 1800 (LC)* *SHAKESPEAREAN CRITICISM (SC)*
Authors who died before 1400	*CLASSICAL AND MEDIEVAL LITERATURE CRITICISM (CMLC)*
Authors of books for children and young adults	*CHILDREN'S LITERATURE REVIEW (CLR)*
Dramatists	*DRAMA CRITICISM (DC)*
Poets	*POETRY CRITICISM (PC)*
Short story writers	*SHORT STORY CRITICISM (SSC)*
Literary topics and movements	*HARLEM RENAISSANCE: A GALE CRITICAL COMPANION (HR)* *THE BEAT GENERATION: A GALE CRITICAL COMPANION (BG)*
Asian American writers of the last two hundred years	*ASIAN AMERICAN LITERATURE (AAL)*
Black writers of the past two hundred years	*BLACK LITERATURE CRITICISM (BLC)* *BLACK LITERATURE CRITICISM SUPPLEMENT (BLCS)*
Hispanic writers of the late nineteenth and twentieth centuries	*HISPANIC LITERATURE CRITICISM (HLC)* *HISPANIC LITERATURE CRITICISM SUPPLEMENT (HLCS)*
Native North American writers and orators of the eighteenth, nineteenth, and twentieth centuries	*NATIVE NORTH AMERICAN LITERATURE (NNAL)*
Major authors from the Renaissance to the present	*WORLD LITERATURE CRITICISM, 1500 TO THE PRESENT (WLC)* *WORLD LITERATURE CRITICISM SUPPLEMENT (WLCS)*

ISSN 0732-1864

Volume 143

Nineteenth-Century Literature Criticism

Criticism of the
Works of Novelists, Philosophers, and Other
Creative Writers Who Died between 1800
and 1899, from the First Published Critical
Appraisals to Current Evaluations

Russel Whitaker
Project Editor

THOMSON
GALE

Detroit • New York • San Francisco • San Diego • New Haven, Conn. • Waterville, Maine • London • Munich

THOMSON

GALE

Nineteenth-Century Literature Criticism, Vol. 143

Project Editor
Russel Whitaker

Editorial
Jessica Bomarito, Kathy D. Darrow, Jeffrey W. Hunter, Jelena O. Krstović, Michelle Lee, Ellen McGeagh, Joseph Palmisano, Linda Pavlovski, Thomas J. Schoenberg, Lawrence J. Trudeau

Data Capture
Francis Monroe, Gwen Tucker

Indexing Services
Synapse, the Knowledge Link Corporation

Rights and Acquisitions
Lori Hines, Emma Hull, Shalice Shah-Caldwell

Imaging and Multimedia
Dean Dauphinais, Robert Duncan, Leitha Etheridge-Sims, Lezlie Light, Michael Logusz, Dan Newell, Kelly A. Quin, Denay Wilding

Composition and Electronic Capture
Kathy Sauer

Manufacturing
Rhonda Williams

Product Manager
Janet Witalec

LIBRARY OF CONGRESS CATALOG CARD NUMBER 84-643008

ISBN 0-7876-6931-8
ISSN 0732-1864

Printed in the United States of America
10 9 8 7 6 5 4 3 2 1

Contents

Preface vii

Acknowledgments xi

Literary Criticism Series Advisory Board xiii

Preface

Since its inception in 1981, *Nineteenth-Century Literature Criticism* (*NCLC*) has been a valuable resource for students and librarians seeking critical commentary on writers of this transitional period in world history. Designated an "Outstanding Reference Source" by the American Library Association with the publication of is first volume, *NCLC* has since been purchased by over 6,000 school, public, and university libraries. The series has covered more than 450 authors representing 33 nationalities and over 17,000 titles. No other reference source has surveyed the critical reaction to nineteenth-century authors and literature as thoroughly as *NCLC*.

Scope of the Series

NCLC is designed to introduce students and advanced readers to the authors of the nineteenth century and to the most significant interpretations of these authors' works. The great poets, novelists, short story writers, playwrights, and philosophers of this period are frequently studied in high school and college literature courses. By organizing and reprinting commentary written on these authors, *NCLC* helps students develop valuable insight into literary history, promotes a better understanding of the texts, and sparks ideas for papers and assignments. Each entry in *NCLC* presents a comprehensive survey of an author's career or an individual work of literature and provides the user with a multiplicity of interpretations and assessments. Such variety allows students to pursue their own interests; furthermore, it fosters an awareness that literature is dynamic and responsive to many different opinions.

Every fourth volume of *NCLC* is devoted to literary topics that cannot be covered under the author approach used in the rest of the series. Such topics include literary movements, prominent themes in nineteenth-century literature, literary reaction to political and historical events, significant eras in literary history, prominent literary anniversaries, and the literatures of cultures that are often overlooked by English-speaking readers.

NCLC continues the survey of criticism of world literature begun by Thomson Gale's *Contemporary Literary Criticism* (*CLC*) and *Twentieth-Century Literary Criticism* (*TCLC*).

Organization of the Book

An *NCLC* entry consists of the following elements:

- The **Author Heading** cites the name under which the author most commonly wrote, followed by birth and death dates. Also located here are any name variations under which an author wrote, including transliterated forms for authors whose native languages use nonroman alphabets. If the author wrote consistently under a pseudonym, the pseudonym will be listed in the author heading and the author's actual name given in parenthesis on the first line of the biographical and critical information. Uncertain birth or death dates are indicated by question marks. Single-work entries are preceded by a heading that consists of the most common form of the title in English translation (if applicable) and the original date of composition.

- The **Introduction** contains background information that introduces the reader to the author, work, or topic that is the subject of the entry.

- A **Portrait of the Author** is included when available.

- The list of **Principal Works** is ordered chronologically by date of first publication and lists the most important works by the author. The genre and publication date of each work is given. In the case of foreign authors whose works have been translated into English, the list will focus primarily on twentieth-century translations, selecting those works most commonly considered the best by critics. Unless otherwise indicated, dramas are dated by first performance, not first publication. Lists of **Representative Works** by different authors appear with topic entries.

■ Reprinted **Criticism** is arranged chronologically in each entry to provide a useful perspective on changes in critical evaluation over time. The critic's name and the date of composition or publication of the critical work are given at the beginning of each piece of criticism. Unsigned criticism is preceded by the title of the source in which it appeared. All titles by the author featured in the text are printed in boldface type. Footnotes are reprinted at the end of each essay or excerpt. In the case of excerpted criticism, only those footnotes that pertain to the excerpted texts are included. Criticism in topic entries is arranged chronologically under a variety of subheadings to facilitate the study of different aspects of the topic.

■ A complete **Bibliographical Citation** of the original essay or book precedes each piece of criticism.

■ Critical essays are prefaced by brief **Annotations** explicating each piece.

■ An annotated bibliography of **Further Reading** appears at the end of each entry and suggests resources for additional study. In some cases, significant essays for which the editors could not obtain reprint rights are included here. Boxed material following the further reading list provides references to other biographical and critical sources on the author in series published by Thomson Gale.

Indexes

Each volume of *NCLC* contains a **Cumulative Author Index** listing all authors who have appeared in a wide variety of reference sources published by Thomson Gale, including *NCLC*. A complete list of these sources is found facing the first page of the Author Index. The index also includes birth and death dates and cross references between pseudonyms and actual names.

A **Cumulative Nationality Index** lists all authors featured in *NCLC* by nationality, followed by the number of the *NCLC* volume in which their entry appears.

A **Cumulative Topic Index** lists the literary themes and topics treated in the series as well as in *Classical and Medieval Literature Criticism, Literature Criticism from 1400 to 1800, Twentieth-Century Literary Criticism,* and the *Contemporary Literary Criticism* Yearbook, which was discontinued in 1998.

An alphabetical **Title Index** accompanies each volume of *NCLC*, with the exception of the Topics volumes. Listings of titles by authors covered in the given volume are followed by the author's name and the corresponding page numbers where the titles are discussed. English translations of foreign titles and variations of titles are cross-referenced to the title under which a work was originally published. Titles of novels, dramas, nonfiction books, and poetry, short story, or essay collections are printed in italics, while individual poems, short stories, and essays are printed in roman type within quotation marks.

In response to numerous suggestions from librarians, Thomson Gale also produces an annual paperbound edition of the *NCLC* cumulative title index. This annual cumulation, which alphabetically lists all titles reviewed in the series, is available to all customers. Additional copies of this index are available upon request. Librarians and patrons will welcome this separate index; it saves shelf space, is easy to use, and is recyclable upon receipt of the next edition.

Citing *Nineteenth-Century Literature Criticism*

When citing criticism reprinted in the Literary Criticism Series, students should provide complete bibliographic information so that the cited essay can be located in the original print or electronic source. Students who quote directly from reprinted criticism may use any accepted bibliographic format, such as University of Chicago Press style or Modern Language Association style.

The examples below follow recommendations for preparing a bibliography set forth in *The Chicago Manual of Style,* 14th ed. (Chicago: The University of Chicago Press, 1993); the first example pertains to material drawn from periodicals, the second to material reprinted from books:

Guerard, Albert J. "On the Composition of Dostoevsky's *The Idiot.*" *Mosaic: A Journal for the Interdisciplinary Study of Literature* 8, no. 1 (fall 1974): 201-15. Reprinted in *Nineteenth-Century Literature Criticism.* Vol. 119, edited by Lynn M. Zott, 81-104. Detroit: Gale, 2003.

Berstein, Carol L. "Subjectivity as Critique and the Critique of Subjectivity in Keats's *Hyperion.*" In *After the Future: Postmodern Times and Places,* edited by Gary Shapiro, 41-52. Albany, N. Y.: State University of New York Press, 1990. Reprinted in *Nineteeth-Century Literature Criticism.* Vol. 121, edited by Lynn M. Zott, 155-60. Detroit: Gale, 2003.

The examples below follow recommendations for preparing a works cited list set forth in the *MLA Handbook for Writers of Research Papers,* 5th ed. (New York: The Modern Language Association of America, 1999); the first example pertains to material drawn from periodicals, the second to material reprinted from books:

Guerard, Albert J. "On the Composition of Dostoevsky's *The Idiot.*" *Mosaic: A Journal for the Interdisciplinary Study of Literature* 8. 1 (fall 1974): 201-15. Reprinted in *Nineteenth-Century Literature Criticism.* Ed. Lynn M. Zott. Vol. 119. Detroit: Gale, 2003. 81-104.

Berstein, Carol L. "Subjectivity as Critique and the Critique of Subjectivity in Keats's *Hyperion.*" *After the Future: Postmodern Times and Places.* Ed. Gary Shapiro. Albany, N. Y.: State University of New York Press, 1990. 41-52. Reprinted in *Nineteeth-Century Literature Criticism.* Ed. Lynn M. Zott. Vol. 121. Detroit: Gale, 2003. 155-60.

Suggestions are Welcome

Readers who wish to suggest new features, topics, or authors to appear in future volumes, or who have other suggestions or comments are cordially invited to call, write, or fax the Product Manager:

Product Manager, Literary Criticism Series
Thomson Gale
27500 Drake Road
Farmington Hills, MI 48331-3535
1-800-347-4253 (GALE)
Fax: 248-699-8054

Acknowledgments

The editors wish to thank the copyright holders of the criticism included in this volume and the permissions managers of many book and magazine publishing companies for assisting us in securing reproduction rights. We are also grateful to the staffs of the Detroit Public Library, the Library of Congress, the University of Detroit Mercy Library, Wayne State University Purdy/Kresge Library Complex, and the University of Michigan Libraries for making their resources available to us. Following is a list of the copyright holders who have granted us permission to reproduce material in this volume of *NCLC*. Every effort has been made to trace copyright, but if omissions have been made, please let us know.

COPYRIGHTED MATERIAL IN *NCLC*, VOLUME 143, WAS REPRODUCED FROM THE FOLLOWING PERIODICALS:

American Book Collector, v. 22, February, 1972. Copyright © 1972 by The American Book Collector, Inc. Reproduced by permission of the publisher.—*Annual Report of the Library Company of Philadelphia for the Year 1990.* 1991. Reproduced by permission.—*Ariel,* v. 9, July, 1978 for "Beatrice Cenci and Shelley's Vision of Moral Responsibility" by James D. Wilson. Copyright © 1978 The Board of Governors, The University of Calgary, Calgary, Alberta. Reproduced by permission of the publisher and the Literary Estate of the author.—*CLA Journal,* v. xiii, September, 1969; v. XVII, December 1973. Copyright © 1969, 1973 by The College Language Association. Both used by permission of The College Language Association.—*Comparative Drama,* v. 19, fall, 1985. Copyright © 1985 by *Comparative Drama.* Reproduced by permission.—*Drama Survey,* v. 4, summer, 1965 for "The Structure of *The Cenci*" by Charles L. Adams. Copyright © 1965 by The Bolingbroke Society, Inc. Reproduced by permission of the author.—*Essays in Literature,* v. 5, spring, 1978. Copyright © 1978 by Western Illinois University. Reproduced by permission.—*European Romantic Review,* v. 6, winter, 1996 for "Finding an Audience: Beatrice Cenci, Percy Shelley, and the Stage" by Ginger Strand and Sarah Zimmerman. Copyright © 1996 by Logos Press. Reproduced by permission of the respective authors and Taylor & Francis, Ltd. at www.tandf.co.uk/journals.—*Journal of Dramatic Theory and Criticism,* v. 5, fall 1990 for "The Harmony of the Horrorscape: A Perspective on the *Cenci*" by Daniel Davy. Copyright © 1990 by the Joyce and Elizabeth Hall Center for the Humanities and the Department of Theatre and Film at the University of Kansas, Lawrence, Kansas 66045, U.S.A. Reproduced by permission of the author.—*Keats-Shelley Journal,* v. 13, winter, 1964; v. 32, 1983; v. 47, 1998. Copyright © The Keats-Shelley Association of America, Inc. 1964 and renewed 1992, 1983, 1998. All reproduced by permission.—*MELUS,* v. 26, spring 2001. Copyright, MELUS: The Society for the Study of Multi-Ethnic Literature of the United States, 2001. Reproduced by permission.—*Prospects: An Annual of American Cultural Studies,* v. 19. Copyright © 1994 Cambridge University Press. All rights reserved. Reprinted with the permission of Cambridge University Press.—*Nineteenth-Century Contexts,* v. 15, 1991 for "Reflection in a 'Many-Sided Mirror': Shelley's *The Cenci* Through the Post-Revolutionary Prism" by Suzanne Ferriss. Copyright © 1991 by INCS. Reproduced by permission of the author and Taylor & Francis, Ltd. at http://www.tandf.co.uk/journals.—*Studies in Black Literature,* v. 5, summer, 1974. Copyright © 1974 by the editor. Reproduced by permission.—*Studies in Romanticism,* v. 23, fall, 1984; v. 25, fall, 1986; v. 33, fall, 1994; v. 39, summer, 2000. Copyright © 1984, 1986, 1994, 2000 by the Trustees of Boston University. All reproduced by permission.—*Tennessee Studies in Literature,* v. 24, 1979. Copyright © 1979 by The University of Tennessee Press. Reproduced by permission of The University of Tennessee Press.—*Unisa English Studies,* v. 28, April, 1990 for "Religion and Patriarchy in Shelley's *The Cenci*" by Alan M. Weinberg. Copyright © 1990. All rights reserved. Reproduced by permission of the author.—*University of Mississippi Studies in English,* n.s. v. 2, 1981. Copyright © 1981 The University of Mississippi. Reproduced by permission.—*Wordsworth Circle,* v. 19, spring, 1988. Copyright © 1988 by Marilyn Gaull. Reproduced by permission of the editor.

COPYRIGHTED MATERIAL IN *NCLC*, VOLUME 143, WAS REPRODUCED FROM THE FOLLOWING BOOKS:

Alston, David. From "The Fallen Meteor: Hugh Miller and Local Tradition," in *Hugh Miller and the Controversies of Victorian Science.* Edited by Michael Shortland. Oxford at the Clarendon Press, 1996. Reproduced by permission of Oxford University Press.—Barcus, James E. From "Unsigned Review, *The Literary Gazette, and Journal of Belles Lettres, Arts, Sciences,*" in *Shelley: The Critical Heritage.* Edited by James E. Barcus. Routledge & Kegan Paul, 1975. Copyright © 1975 by James E. Barcus. Reproduced by permission of the publisher.—Botstein, Leon. From "History, Rhetoric, and the Self: Robert Schumann and Music-Making German-Speaking Europe, 1800-1860," in *Schumann and His World.* Edited

PHOTOGRAPHS AND ILLUSTRATIONS APPEARING IN *NCLC*, VOLUME 143, WERE RECEIVED FROM THE FOLLOWING SOURCES:

Thomson Gale Literature Product Advisory Board

The members of the Thomson Gale Literature Product Advisory Board—reference librarians from public and academic library systems—represent a cross-section of our customer base and offer a variety of informed perspectives on both the presentation and content of our literature products. Advisory board members assess and define such quality issues as the relevance, currency, and usefulness of the author coverage, critical content, and literary topics included in our series; evaluate the layout, presentation, and general quality of our printed volumes; provide feedback on the criteria used for selecting authors and topics covered in our series; provide suggestions for potential enhancements to our series; identify any gaps in our coverage of authors or literary topics, recommending authors or topics for inclusion; analyze the appropriateness of our content and presentation for various user audiences, such as high school students, undergraduates, graduate students, librarians, and educators; and offer feedback on any proposed changes/enhancements to our series. We wish to thank the following advisors for their advice throughout the year.

Hugh Miller
1802-1856

Scottish nonfiction writer, essayist, journalist, folklorist, autobiographer, and editor.

INTRODUCTION

Miller is best known for nonfiction works that critics describe as "literary natural history." Such books as *The Old Red Sandstone; or, New Walks in an Old Field* (1841) and *Foot-prints of the Creator; or The Asterolepis of Stromness* (1849) reflect both Miller's studies as a scientist, particularly in the field of geology, and his skills as an engaging prose stylist. These works, along with Miller's autobiography, *My Schools and Schoolmasters* (1854), reveal their author as one of the most remarkable figures in nineteenth-century Scottish letters.

BIOGRAPHICAL INFORMATION

Miller was born in Cromarty into a line of Scottish seafaring men. When he was five, his father died at sea, and Miller was subsequently raised by Harriet Roy, his father's second wife. Miller's stepmother and his uncles Alexander and James all imparted their strong religious values to Miller. Miller's family also instilled in him a love of reading. An intelligent but easily bored student, Miller was forced to leave school at the age of fifteen because of disciplinary problems. Between February 1820 and November 1822, he worked as an apprentice stonemason to his mother's brother-in-law, David Wright. His work as a stonemason in the subsequent years led to the publication of his first book, *Poems, Written in the Leisure Hours of a Journeyman Mason* (1829). That same year, he also published *Letters on the Herring Fishing in the Moray Firth,* a work that utilizes the detailed and highly descriptive prose style for which he later became known. While pursuing his literary interests, Miller met a member of the Cromarty women's literary society, Lydia Mackenzie Fraser. They loved each other but Miller refused to marry her so long as he remained a stonemason and thus a member of the working class. While continuing to write, publishing newspaper articles that revealed his special interest in geology, Miller became an accountant at the Commercial Bank in Cromarty, a position that provided him with sufficient income to marry Fraser. He found the routine of the position unpleasant, however, and began corre-

sponding with geologists such as Sir Roderick Murchison and Louis Agassiz. Murchison later suggested to Miller that he undertake publishing a reference work that compiled his geological observations, advice which Miller eventually followed. In 1839, Miller was offered the opportunity to be the editor for *The Witness,* a Free Church of Scotland newspaper founded by the Reverend Robert A. Candlish. Under Miller's editorial guidance, it developed into a publication concerned with a variety of subjects, including literature and science. Miller's journalistic writings, some of which were posthumously collected in *Essays: Historical and Biographical, Political and Social, Literary and Scientific* (1862), illustrate Miller's interest in social reform and church policies. Miller's outspokenness in many of his articles caused tension between him and the Free Church of Scotland. Candlish unsuccessfully tried to replace Miller, who remained at the newspaper until his death. As a consequence of his years as a stonemason, Miller came to suffer from a malady common to workers in that occupation, in which stone and dust collects in the lungs. As his physical health declined, Miller also began to experience a deteriorating mental stability whose manifestations included frequent nightmares, delirium, and sleepwalking. Miller died of a self-inflicted gunshot wound in 1856. His suicide note indicated that he believed his sleepwalking was evidence of a diseased mind.

MAJOR WORKS

Miller's religious faith and his fascination with the natural history of Scotland provided the subject matter for much of his writing. Miller was a defender of the Bible as the ultimate source of knowledge pertaining to both the supernatural and the natural worlds, and he was thus an opponent of evolutionary theory. His attempts to reconcile geology and religion were combined with a passion for history and literature, giving works such as *The Old Red Sandstone* and *Foot-prints of the Creator* the broad scope and highly readable prose style that made them best-sellers in his lifetime. The combination of literary writing, scientific observation, and deeply held spiritual beliefs are also present in his autobiography, *My Schools and Schoolmasters*. In this work Miller represents himself as someone who raised himself above his working-class origins through hard work, religious faith, and intellectual pursuits. Because of this emphasis on personal development, some critics have viewed Miller's autobiography as an early example of the self-help book.

CRITICAL RECEPTION

A groundbreaking figure in the history of the sciences, Miller's works on natural history "were to be found in the remotest log-hut of the Far West, and on both sides of the Atlantic ideas of the nature and shape of geology were largely drawn from them" according to geologist Archibald Geikie. Modern critics still continue to study Miller's geological works, largely considering them seminal to the development of literary natural history as a genre. In addition to his legacy in natural history, Miller's works reflect the cultural changes in nineteenth-century Scottish society, specifically those deriving from the debate over the theory of evolution versus biblical doctrine. Although Miller's contributions to folklore are not as well recognized as his work in the sciences, some scholars such as David Alston consider Miller's importance as a folklorist to be significant, praising his thorough examination of the folklore and beliefs of a small geographical area. In addition, his political writings for *The Witness* illuminate various issues of reform that are vital to an understanding of mid-nineteenth-century Scottish society. They also, as George Rosie maintains, cover a wide variety of subjects pertaining to countries outside the British Isles—from parliamentary proceedings in Canada, to the introduction of the guillotine in Constantinople. For their complex mingling of scientific, personal, religious, and sociopolitical themes, and for their engaging and highly readable style, Miller's works continue to be esteemed by scientists and literary scholars alike.

PRINCIPAL WORKS

Letters on the Herring Fishing in the Moray Firth (letters) 1829

Poems, Written in the Leisure Hours of a Journeyman Mason (poetry) 1829

Scenes and Legends of the North of Scotland; or, The Traditional History of Cromarty (folklore) 1835

The Whiggism of the Old School, as Exemplified by the Past History and Present Policies of the Church of Scotland (journalism) 1839

The Old Red Sandstone; or, New Walks in an Old Field (nonfiction) 1841; revised as *The Old Red Sandstone; or, New Walks in an Old Field, to Which Is Appended a Series of Geological Papers Read before the Royal Physical Society of Edinburgh* 1858

Foot-prints of the Creator; or The Asterolepis of Stromness (nonfiction) 1849

*My Schools and Schoolmasters; or The Story of My Education (autobiography) 1854

The Testimony of the Rocks; or, Geology and Its Bearings on the Two Theologies (nonfiction) 1857

The Cruise of the Betsey; or, A Summer Ramble among the Fossilferous Deposits of the Hebrides, with Rambles of a Geologist; or, Ten Thousand Miles of the Fossilferous Deposits of Scotland (nonfiction) 1858

Sketch-book of Popular Geology: Being a Series of Lectures Delivered before the Philosophical Institution of Edinburgh (lectures) 1859; expanded as *Popular Geology: A Series of Lectures Read before the Philosophical Institution of Edinburgh, with Descriptive Sketches from a Geologist's Portfolio* 1860

†The Headship of Christ, and the Rights of the Christian People (essays) 1861

Essays: Historical and Biographical, Political and Social, Literary and Scientific (essays) 1862

Tales and Sketches (folklore and sketches) 1863

Edinburgh and Its Neighborhood, Geological and Historical, with the Geology of the Bass Rock (essays) 1864

Leading Articles on Various Subjects (essays) 1870

Works. 13 vols. (autobiography, essays, folklore, nonfiction, and journalism) 1870-79

*This work has also been published under the titles *An Autobiography: My Schools and Schoolmasters; or, The Story of My Education* and *My Schools and Schoolmasters; or, The Story of My Education: An Autobiography.*

†This work has also been published under the title *The Witness Papers: Headship of Christ and the Rights of the Christian People, A Collection of Essays, Historical and Descriptive Sketches, and Personal Portraitures.*

CRITICISM

John M. Clarke (essay date January 1903)

SOURCE: Clarke, John M. "Hugh Miller and His Centenary." *New England Magazine* n.s. 27, no. 5 (January 1903): 551-63.

[*In the following essay, Clarke assesses Miller's reputation in his native Scotland and in America on the one hundredth anniversary of his birth.*]

The people of Scotland have just been celebrating with unbounded enthusiasm the one hundredth anniversary of the birth of Hugh Miller.

In America Miller's name is not very familiar to the younger generation, but to those in the prime of life who, thirty or forty years ago, were reading with susceptible minds, it recalls diverse impressions: the story of a remarkable life, telling with wonderful beauty and cleverness of the rise from humblest beginnings to a conspicuous and influential climacteric; the scientific investigations of a geologist among the rocks and fossils of the Old Red Sandstone and the lavas of the Bass Rock; fulminations against a crude form of the doctrine of evolution presented by Robert Chambers's anonymous but striking book, "Vestiges of Creation"; an occasional glimpse of activity in ecclesiastical politics gathered from a chance allusion to his editorship of a powerful newspaper; and finally the tragic end of a brilliant life wrecked by long continued overwork.

Carlyle, not always a genial critic, characterized Miller's writings as luminous, memorable, wholesome, strong, fresh and breezy; Dean Buckland is credited with saying that he would give his left hand to possess Miller's powers of description; Dickens thought him "a delightful writer"; all quite superfluous expressions to the lover of fine English and lucid portrayal who has read *My Schools and Schoolmasters,* or *The Scenes and Legends of the North of Scotland,* or to the geologist of to-day who, in the attempt to produce popularizations of his science, has lost the combination in the *Old Red Sandstone, Footprints of the Creator* and *Rambles of a Geologist.*

Miller has been dead nearly fifty years but his books are still read without lessening fervor and even those which embodied his scientific investigations have not grown old nor useless, as is the usual fate of the publications in a growing science. Scotland has done well to remember with so much ardor the centenary of his birth.

Among the deep gashes which the waters of ocean and land working together have made in the east coast of Scotland, and just at the edge of the Highlands, is the Cromarty firth, a noble harbor where all the navies of the world could ride in security protected from the storms without and sentinelled by two noble headlands fronting the greater Moray firth and known as the "Sutors." Along the south side of this embayment, on a spit of land which is the remodelled beach of an ancient and greater firth, nestles the venerable and quaint village of Cromarty, where Hugh Miller was born on the tenth of October, 1802. Here all his early life was spent, and his writings are redolent of the town, its natural beauties, its inhabitants, its superstitions, traditions and history. The traveller who reaches this remote and peaceful spot, not by railway, for Cromarty does not reckon this among its conveniences, but by the little steam ferry which crosses the firth at a very oblique angle from the nearest station, Invergordon, wanders up gray walled and narrow streets around the base of the hill and soon comes upon a low, long house with straw thatched roof, grouted walls, and gables facing the street. This house, built by his great-grandfather, is the spot where Miller was born. One must stoop low on entering to avoid a crushing blow to hat and head and lower yet to pass from room to room of this little biggin. The low-ceiled rooms of the second story look out through diminutive windows where the thatch is carefully cut away, into the little court in front, and behind upon the larger and more pretentious structure erected by Miller's father in the days of a brief prosperity, but never occupied by him.

Miller's father was a sailor engaged in trade along the coast, but, like his ancestors for many generations, he went down with his ship, leaving Hugh, a little boy of five years, and two girls still younger to the charge of the desolate widow. Not long after, both sisters died together of scarlet fever and the little fellow was left alone with his mother. The mother had two brothers, "Uncle Sandy" and "Uncle James," serious minded and sagacious workmen, the one a carpenter, the other a saddler, and these took upon themselves the guidance of the boy Hugh. No part of Miller's autobiography is more pleasing than the tender thread of gratitude to these uncles which he has woven throughout his narrative, but it was "Uncle Sandy's" keen powers of observation, retentive mind and minute familiarity with all the traditions of the countryside which seem most to have aroused his interest in nature and shaped the bent of his zeal. But both concerned themselves deeply in his education and planned for him—for the boy had early showed more than usual mental acumen—a distinguished career in some one of the professions. So the little lad was entered at the "Dames' school," across the way from the thatched home, where two maiden sisters dealt out the mysteries of a written and printed language. Miller tells how useless and perfunctory it all seemed to him, this learning how to spell words and range them in sentences, until one day, of a sudden, he made the tremendous discovery that there were stories under these words, the story of Benjamin and Samuel, of David and of Daniel, that, as he says, "the art of reading was the art of finding stories in books." A new world had opened, and now his whetted appetite could not be sated on scripture tales alone. There followed those immortal tales, "Jack the Giant-killer," "Bluebeard," "Sindbad the Sailor," (and right here in telling this story the distinguished author breaks out vigorously: "Those intolerable nuisances, the useful knowledge books, had not yet arisen, like tenebrious stars, on the educational horizon to darken the world and shed their blighting influence on the opening intellect of the youthhood") and soon after Pope's translation of the "Odyssey" and "Iliad," and "Pilgrim's Progress"; thenceforward everything that the little town could be made to produce. Presently he was entered at the parish school, which, fronting on the shore near the east base of the sand spit, commands the whole length of the firth to the Sutors, and from the windows of this school every sailing craft which in line of business or in stress of weather entered the firth was seen and registered by the boys. There probably never was a school where the scholars knew and could draw so well upon their slates the lines and rigging of every variety of schooner, carvel and smack.

But the boy was learning more outside than within school. His teachers were not sympathetic and he himself was becoming wayward. The hills invited him and days which were due to the school were spent, usually with some of his companions of whom he was the acknowledged leader in all kinds of mischief, in the seacaves along the rocky shore of the southern Sutor or among the woods and glens of Cromarty hill. His school career terminated violently. Commanded to spell the word *awful* he spelt with the broad pronunciation to which he was used, *aw*-w-f-u-l. "No," said the master, "a-w, *aw*, f-u-l, *awful*. Spell it again." This seemed to him preposterous, to put another *aw* in the middle of the word and he refused. The hand to hand encounter which followed was a fierce and bloody one and both master and pupil retired from the conflict sadly battered, Miller, however, never to return.

Casting about now for a life's work he decided, greatly against the wishes of his uncles, to apprentice himself to a stone mason.

At that day a mason had to quarry as well as hew and lay his stone, and the work was arduous and severe but, the day's work done, there were the long northern eve-

nings free for other devices. So this future geologist and man of letters bound himself for three years to a master mason to quarry and hew stone during the day, while his long evenings were devoted to the most careful study of the best masters of English prose and poetry. He served his time and became skilful at his trade, but he likewise became accomplished at his diversion, and though Scotsmen easily break out into verse and he set up no claim to fine poetic diction, yet subsequently he published a volume of verse produced during this period, *Poems Written in the Leisure Hours of a Journeyman Mason,* his first book and only attempt in this line.

It was during this period, however, that his eyes were beginning to see into the secrets of the rocks. As the stone quarries where he wrought and the stone he hewed were for the most part of the Old Red Sandstone formation, he saw how similar it was in its structure to the sands of the beach where he had roamed so often with Uncle Sandy and his boy friends. It is a rather curious coincidence that the Old Red Sandstone which fringes the Cromarty hill was actually deposited in an ancient lagoon or embayment not vastly unlike the present Cromarty firth, and it was by this, his only means of comparison, that the young geologist was enabled to interpret the rock beds. He had seen on the Cromarty beaches that some of the sand deposits had been blown about by the wind and in these the grains looked unlike those which had simply been washed over by the water, and he searched for similar differences in the sand grains of the Old Red. He saw the rippled surfaces, the marks left by rills and wave borne pebbles, and these simple observations gradually led him into a world of new interest and endeavor. The little hints he caught he must interpret for himself. There were for him but few side lights and no books which served to solve his problems for him. His finer discoveries of the fossils in the rocks, the vast shoals of bizarre fishes, seem not to have been made during this time of his apprenticeship.

When he had served his period he betook himself to Edinburgh where he wrought at his trade in the neighborhood as long as his health permitted, but his lungs had begun to fill up with rock dust and he was compelled, on the verge of consumption, to abandon his work. Then followed a period of rest and slow convalescence spent about the beloved hills of Cromarty, and that was the time most fertile in additions to his own and the world's knowledge of the geology of his home country.

Miller was superior in all his undertakings and as a stone mason he wrought better, more artistically and intelligently than his fellows. On the Conon River, up back of Dingwall, is still standing a farm wall of his handiwork even yet pointed out as a model of such coarse construction; the parish churchyard and the burying ground of old St. Regulus at Cromarty hold examples of his mortuary sculpture, done when, as an itinerant sculptor he "wandered from one country burying ground to another, recording on his tablets of stone the tears of the living and the worth of the dead," and they are notable for the chastity of their style in contrast to the usual horrid and grewsome decoration of contemporary designers. The pediment of a dial still standing in one of the Cromarty gardens is a fine example of his achievement which shows not only his manual facility but the elevation of his standard of taste.

It would have been fortunate for geological science and well for Miller had some happy turn of the wheel made it possible for him to continue his study of the rocks without interruption, but it was not thus ordered and at no period in his life was he at liberty to pursue his chosen science save in the intervals of pressing necessary work. His achievements therefore as a geologist must be looked upon as little short of marvellous. One must pause a moment here to consider the conditions which surrounded him.

Geology in the period from 1830-1845, when his first results were achieved, was a little known science outside of a few centres of learning. It was, however, a very widely misunderstood and misinterpreted science; in a country so given over to controversial theology as Scotland, it was especially regarded as fraught with danger to the standards of the Church. One could not enter this field save at some cost to his standing in a conservative community. The Old Red Sandstone had been heard of before, but it had been regarded an unimportant local formation without evidences of ancient life. As his problems developed, the few books that could give this seeker any light seem not to have come his way. Miller had, indeed, to build up his own science from his own observations, and how well he did this is shown in many ways. Not alone are his conclusions as to the origin of the Old Red Sandstone vital facts today, but his keen insight foresaw and suggested peculiar features of its origin which in these latest years have started special trains of important investigation. He found that the rocks were filled with myriads of strange creatures which he believed and demonstrated to be fishes, though nothing like some of them had ever before been seen and he had naught with which to compare them except the fishes he knew in the waters of Cromarty. Yet such were his synthetic powers that he was able to reconstruct them with an accuracy that seems to-day, in the light of fuller knowledge, astonishing. Huxley, who long afterward brought to bear upon these Old Red fishes his brilliant and finely trained powers, remarked: "The more I study the fishes of the Old Red the more I am struck with the patience and sagacity manifested in Hugh Miller's researches and by the natural insight which in his case seems to have supplied the place of special anatomical knowledge."

The young stone mason, however, unable because of impaired health to continue the laborious toil of his business and not successful in obtaining enough mortuary sculpture to meet the demands of living, was now turned into another line of activity. In 1834 a branch of the Commercial Bank of Scotland was established in Cromarty and to him was offered the position of accountant therein; so after a preliminary training at Linlithgow he entered upon the career of a bank clerk.

Just at the close of his period of enforced leisure, Miller had completed the manuscript of his delightful *Scenes and Legends of the North of Scotland,* his first prose work, which has now run through fourteen editions. No more enjoyable reading could come into the hands of young or old. Miller's mother was a Highlander and from her he seems to have imbibed the Highland fondness for, and in some measure the awe of, the mysterious in nature. The ancient superstitions of Cromarty are laughed at, but not too heartily; tales of times which had no historian are told with interest, pathos and humor, and all are set forth in pure and forcible English. The pen of the young author had at last found its function in masterly prose.

For five years Miller served as bank clerk in his native town. They were years not of conspicuous mark in his career but of quiet assimilation and especially of keen furtherance of his geological studies. But his fertile mind toward the end of this time had become afire with interest in the ecclesiastical condition of the country. It is bootless for us to exclaim, as has been often done in this latter day, how much more would have been accomplished for science if Miller had kept free of entanglement in a theological controversy. To the writer, at least, it is not altogether clear that he could have rendered a greater service to science than by the very means which circumstances threw in his way. His church was in peril and it was his conviction, as he has said, that the country possessed "no other institution half so valuable as the church or in which the people had so large a stake." Disruption in the established church of Scotland was impending. Growth of democratic ideas in church government had developed increasing hostility to the intrusion of ministers upon livings, contrary to the wishes of the parish communions. Where the church is an establishment, church polity is state politics. The Cromarty bank clerk began the new episode in his career with a virile and cogent pamphlet on the burning question of intrusion addressed to Lord Brougham and opposing the position of the establishment, which attracted attention throughout the land. He became at once a marked man, and though he had even claimed to be thoroughly an "establishment man," he was immediately invited by the organized opposition party to take the editorship of their newspaper, the Edinburgh *Witness.* In 1839 his editorial work began, in 1843 occurred the Disruption and the establishment of the Free Church, in which movement he was unquestionably the largest lay factor. The *Witness,* under his editorship, became a mighty influence throughout Scotland; to it he gave the best years of his endeavor until his calamitous death in 1856. It was far from being simply an ecclesiastical organ, championing at every cost the interest of the Free Church; its columns teemed with pregnant editorials on all matters of public moment, of social and educational interest, and of his paper he modestly says that none other in Scotland had so wide a circulation among the men who had received a university education. In it he published what, when subsequently gathered together, made his best and most widely known books, **Schools and Schoolmasters, Old Red Sandstone, Footprints of the Creator, Cruise of the Betsey** and **Rambles of a Geologist,** and through this paper and these books his name became known and honored, not alone in Scotland, but among all English-speaking people.

"What we more especially owe to Miller," says Sir Archibald Geikie, speaking for the geologists, "is the awakening of a widespread interest in the methods and results of scientific inquiry. More than any other author of his day he taught men to recognize that beneath the technicalities and jargon that are too apt to conceal the meaning of the facts and inferences which they express, there lie the most vital truths in regard to the world in which we live. He clothed the dry bones of science with living flesh and blood. He made the aspects of past ages to stand out once more before us, as his vivid imagination conceived that they must once have been. He awakened an enthusiasm for geological questions such as had never before existed, and this wave of popular appreciation which he set in motion has never ceased to pulsate throughout the English-speaking population of the world. His genial ardor and irresistible eloquence swept away the last remnants of the barrier of orthodox prejudice against geology in this country. The present generation can hardly realize the former strength of that bigotry or appreciate the merit of the service rendered in the breaking of it down. The well-known satirical criticism of the poet Cowper[1] expressed a prevalent feeling among the orthodox of his day, and this feeling was still far from extinct when Miller began to write. No one, however, could doubt his absolute orthodoxy, and when the cause of the science was espoused by him, the voices of the objectors were finally silenced. There was another class of cavaliers who looked on geology as a mere collecting of minerals, a kind of laborious trifling concealed under a cover of uncouth technical terms. Their view was well expressed by Wordsworth when he singled out for contemptuous scorn the enthusiast—

> Who with pocket hammer smites the edge
> Of luckless rock or prominent stone,
>   Detaching by the stroke

> A chip or splinter, to resolve his doubts,
> And with that ready answer satisfied,
> The substance classes by some barbarous name
> And hurries on: He thinks himself enriched,
> Wealthier and doubtless wiser than before.

"But a champion had now arisen who, as far as might be, discarding technicalities, made even the dullest reader feel that the geologist is the historian of the earth, that he deals with a series of chronicles as real and as decipherable as those that record human events and that they can be made not only intelligible, but attractive as the subjects of simple and elegant prose."

Without education, except in the schools of which he had so charmingly written, Miller had risen to a position of the widest influence throughout Scotland, but notwithstanding this distinction he ever maintained the reticence and modesty of the country lad. He declined to stand for election as Lord Rector of Marischal College at Aberdeen and for the vacant professorship of Natural History in Edinburgh University, but he was satisfied to feel that, as he expressed it, "after a hard spent day he had not been an altogether unprofitable servant."

Sixteen years of arduous and amazingly productive toil as editor of the *Witness* told upon his health. He had suffered much from headaches, his nerves had become frayed with persistent overtaxing. Edinburgh streets in 1856 were filled with desperadoes and highwaymen, and he grew fearsome lest an inroad should be made upon his precious geological collections. He had got in the way of going about armed, had become somnambulistic, and one black night, toiling and overstrained till almost dawn with the proof sheets of his **Testimony of the Rocks,** the mind broke down, and in the darkness his life abruptly ended.

On August 22, 1902 (the exigencies of Scottish weather justified the change in date) a great throng entered Cromarty from all Britain, with representatives from Canada, the United States and Italy. The sun shone bright and warm upon the flag-decked buildings, the American colors being here and there intertwined with the multifold British flags and Scotia's yellow. The occasion was well supported; back of it appeared such names as Lords Balfour, Kelvin, Lister, Sir Archibald Geikie, Sir Norman Lockyer, Right Hon. James Bryce, Professors Masson, Bonney, Lapworth, Joly, Sollas.

On the hilltop just west of the town stands a fine shaft surmounted by a statue of Miller, and the pediment graced by sculptured bay leaves and "Pterichthys." At the foot of this shaft gathered a mighty throng of 2,000 people, who had come to do homage to the man, and here addresses were delivered by the provost of the town, Mr. Junor; by the member of Parliament, Mr. Bignold, representing local interest and pride; by Rev. Dr. Rainy, principal of the Free Church College, Edinburgh, on behalf of the church for which this life had done so profound a service, and by Sir Archibald Geikie and the delegate from the Geological Society of America, speaking for the science which he loved and to which he had given much. The public halls of the little town could not accommodate all who wished to sit down to the luncheon that followed, but the 250 who succeeded in gaining access to this function were regaled with a flow of distinguished eloquence and rare tributes from Sir Thomas Hanbury, Dr. John Horne of the Geological Survey of Scotland, Dr. Macadam Muir of the Glasgow Cathedral, Dr. Andrew Carnegie, Professor Middleton of Oxford, Sir James Grant, president of the Royal Society of Canada, and others. Thereafter in the Free Church (most appropriate spot!) Sir Archibald Geikie paid the tribute of all geologists to Miller's memory in a delightful and elegant address. It was an additional pleasure to all present at these ceremonies to be able to meet the only surviving child of Hugh Miller, Mrs. Miller Mackay of Lochinver.

A committee of the townspeople, represented by the provost, Mr. Junor, and Mr. John Bain as secretary, had brought about this celebration, partly in the hope that with the tributes laid on Miller's shrine might come to the town of his birth a more substantial memorial to his services—a public library and a museum of his scientific remains. The success of this project, through the devotion of Miller's admirers, the assiduity of his townsfolk and the munificence of Dr. Carnegie is assured.

Note

1. This is in the "Task," and runs thus:

> "Some drill and bore
> The solid earth and from the strata there
> Extract a register, by which we learn
> That He who made it and revealed its date
> To Moses was mistaken in its age."

W. M. Mackenzie (essay date 1905)

SOURCE: Mackenzie, W. M. "Literary Style." In *Hugh Miller: A Critical Study,* pp. 25-50. London: Hodder and Stoughton, 1905.

[In the following excerpt, Mackenzie analyzes Miller's prose style and the literary models that influenced his development as a writer.]

So far, then, have we been able to follow Miller in the careful training of himself for literary achievement. Without exactly playing "the sedulous ape," he studies

closely the general form, the tones and turns of expression characterising a well-defined group of writers, and shapes his own performance accordingly. It need not, therefore, be pronounced either futile or pedantic to endeavour to trace out more closely some of the affinities of Miller's style with the materials he so used. No analysis, indeed, can cumulatively explain the total result: style is a compound, not a mere literary mixture. Short of that, however, we can surely work to fuller knowledge and a clearer definition of the constituents, and so open the way to a keener appreciation of the whole.

Happily Miller has left us in no doubt as to his models and standards. He is confessedly of the Augustans, the men of Queen Anne's time, and the prose-writers who derived from them. He did not make literature of the vernacular as Burns did; that was possible only for a poet. He sought his models where every educated Scotsman did till the time of the Carlyle fashion, and was the last notable exponent in a dying mode. When Baron Hume declared that he excelled in "that classical style" with which his contemporaries had lost touch, Hugh modestly explained that he owed the merit "chiefly to accident; to having kept company with the older English writers—the Addisons, Popes, and Robertsons of the last century." And he goes on to say, "the tone of these earlier writers I have, I daresay, contrived in some measure to catch." The selection here is evidently summary, and the list may be easily extended by further testimony, both circumstantial and explicit.

Thus Miller's prose taken generally, is of the "middle style," the peculiar achievement of the eighteenth century writers, "familiar but not coarse, and elegant but not ostentatious"—Johnson's characterisation—which, if it never rises to the convoluted sublimity of the earlier men, never, on the other hand, sinks to the commonplace of colloquialism. It cannot be held that it is a style capable of the effects which have been drawn in modern times from a critical return to more archaic sources; but then, on the other hand, it is not, for ordinary purposes, so dangerous a medium, nor does it run such a risk of affectation and painful artificiality. For use in scientific exposition its fitness is unquestionable.

Miller had an early and close acquaintance with the *Spectator* papers. After their manner the unborn *Egotist* was conceived. Plainly his notion of "correctness" meant to a large degree a following of Addison whom he "had known so long, and, in his true poems, his prose ones, had loved so much." But his more serious range of subjects, and his more serious and direct treatment of them, were bound to react upon his forms of expression. It is with Addison in his graver moods that he has most in common. It is probably, in the main, owing to his influence that Miller's prose is predominantly loose rather than periodic. The following sentences, for example, where the main thought is stated at the outset, and the rest is attached as elaboration or development, are typical:—"The moon, nearly at full, was riding high overhead in a troubled sky, pouring its light by fits, as the clouds passed, on the grey ruins, and the mossy, tilt-like hillocks, which had been raised ages before over the beds of the sleepers. The deep, dark shadows of the tombs seemed stamped upon the sward, forming, as one might imagine, a kind of general epitaph upon the dead, but inscribed, like the handwriting on the wall, in the characters of a strange tongue."

But while Miller thus far resembles Addison, he does so with a difference. His sentences are more closely and correctly compacted; probably he owed this feature to the example of precisian purity in the Scotch writers of whom Robertson, mentioned above, is one. Rarely indeed does he get caught, as Addison was so often, in the peculiar fault of the loose style, a huddling together of explanatory clauses, or a careless arrangement with an incongruous result. He is also much more metaphorical in language. Intermittently, indeed, we have short lyric-like embellishments, the graftings of a poetic fancy—Spencer grants him "a large amount of poetry"—on the stouter stem of prose. Where Addison seeks a pathetic relief in Orientalised or barbaric imaginings, Miller supplies it direct from natural impressions or homely reflection. The free use of metaphor, too, on the part of the disciple results in a more vivid, if less insinuating effect. His prose is felt in consequence to have more "blood and juice."

Nor is there anything of the "gentle satirist": indeed it is but a Thackerayan hallucination with respect to Addison, whose satire has more conspicuously the note of cynical malice, daintily as it is disguised. But this was foreign to Miller's nature. If he dislikes a man or an opinion, he says so, with literary grace and satiric phrase it may be, but at least with no ambiguity. Setting aside his occasional viciousness, and lack of humorous toleration towards men and things outwith his sympathies, we may, for continuous ease and grace of diction, compare Miller more closely with Goldsmith than with any other. From Goldsmith he illustrates and quotes with exceptional frequency, especially in his earlier works where such influences as we have been considering will, naturally, be more apparent. Many passages indeed, in their balanced rhythm and sententious movement, almost seem modelled on analogous trains of thought from the earlier writer's pen.

Ultimately it is possible to trace this balanced, antithetical fashion to the judicial Johnson, whose customary syntactical suit it had become. There is occasionally, too, in Miller something of the Johnsonian rotundity of phrase, of which the neatest example is his turning out a familiar saying in the form, "Absence, though it rather strengthens than diminishes a true attachment," etc. We note the same ponderous influence in the way in which our author, though as careful of his transitions and culminations as a De Quincey could have wished, approaches detail over the shoulder of some comprehensive principle thereby to be illustrated or concretely embodied. The second letter on the *Herring Fishery in the Moray Firth* (1829) opens thus: "Dr Currie, the elegant and philosophical biographer of Burns, has remarked that knowledge, which some have defined to be power and others happiness, may with safety be considered as motion. He has said that it raises men to an eminence from whence they take within the sphere of their vision a large portion of the globe, and discover advantage at a great distance on its surface." And thus loftily we are introduced to a narrative of how the Cromarty fishermen, suffering from the failure of the fishing in their own firth, turned to account what they were hearing of its success at Wick by sailing thither to participate. The trick is, of course, older than Johnson; may in fact be dubbed the "classical" or grand style of literary attack; and was in form congenial to Miller's thought procedure. But it was the "great moralist" who gave it vogue as a literary pattern. It is allied with a grandiose style of reference to authors as the "learned," the "philosophical," the "ingenious" and so forth. In Miller's case, however, the sharpness of controversy and the practice of the inductive method in science, gradually filed down these formalisms very considerably.

Miller has been specifically praised for his descriptive powers. In landscape his success seems to be due to a certain architectural power, careful selection of detail and the elegance of language in which the whole is presented. But he does not paint on such a large canvas as Carlyle, nor with such interpretative insight. In fact his general method may be reduced to a simple formula. There is first a broad mapping out of his subject with the eye of the builder and geologist—the geological structure of landscape he rightly held should be studied with as much care by the painter as the anatomical structure of the body—then a dabbing in of the bolder colours, directed usually again by the geological interest, since "The colouring of the landscape is well-nigh as intimately connected with its geology as the drawing"; and finally a filling in of striking features clearly located or merely picturesquely grouped. Emphasis upon one or other of these essentials gives variety to the general method.

A fondness for colour indeed distinguishes most of Miller's landscapes. As a young man he had practised painting, and the highly varied programme of his purposes at twenty-six includes quite a number of contemplated pictures. A similar descriptive tendency was remarked by Ruskin of Sir Walter Scott. Thus, for Miller, the southern shore of the Moray Firth with its numerous little towns is "a belt of purple speckled with pearls."

This characteristic touch may be exemplified from almost any relevant portion of his work. The practice was deliberately cultivated for geological reasons.

In the following it is almost absent, while we have, however, a favourable instance of the other qualities remarked upon. Moreover, such success with valley portraiture is rare in literature. We are looking at Shenstone's Leasowes. Attention is first fixed on a hill of the Lower Coal Measures, a "huge blister of millstone grit. . . . Let the reader imagine it of soft, swelling outline, and ample base, with the singularly picturesque trap range full in front, some four miles away, and a fair rural valley lying between. Let him further imagine the side hill furrowed by a transverse valley, opening at right angles into the great front valley, and separating a-top into two forks, or branches, that run up, shallowing as they go, to near the hill-top. Let him, in short, imagine this great valley a broad right line, and the transverse forked valley a gigantic letter Y resting on it. And the forked valley on the hill-side—this gigantic letter Y—is the Leasowes. The picturesqueness of such a position can be easily appreciated. The forked valley, from head to gorge, is a reclining valley, partaking along its bottom of the slope of the eminence on which it lies, and thus possessing, what is by no means common among the valleys of England, true downhill watercourses, along which the gathered waters may leap in a chain of cascades; and commanding in its upper recesses, though embraced and sheltered on every side by the surrounding hill, extending prospects to the country below. It thus continues the scenic advantages of both hollow and rising ground—the quiet seclusion of the one, and the expansive landscapes of the other. The broad valley into which it opens is rich and well wooded. Just in front of the opening we see a fine sheet of water, about twenty acres in extent, the work of the monks; immediately to the right stand the ruins of the abbey; immediately to the left, the pretty, compact town of Hales Owen lies grouped around its fine old church and spire; a range of green, swelling eminences rises beyond; beyond these, fainter in the distance, and considerably bolder in the outline, ascends the loftier range of the trap hills—one of the number roughened by the tufted woods, and crowned by the obelisk at Hagley; and, over all, blue and shadowy on the far horizon, sweeps the undulating line of the mountains of Cambria."

What we, trained in a later school, miss in such descriptions is the human interest. There is no attempt to connect the external manifestations with the springs of emotion in the way Carlyle, even in a phrase, could do so happily; as of St Edmondsbury "looking out right pleasantly, from its hill-slope, towards the rising sun." Admirably perceived and represented though they are, Miller's pictures usually leave us cold, and unaffected by any feelings other than those of interest and admira-

tion. They, too often, as in the present case, lack individuality of impression; so that corner of country must have looked to any intelligent observer, albeit ungifted to describe and group its features in orderly sequence.

Miller himself speaks of his elaborate description of the Leasowes rather deprecatingly as simply "hard anatomy." These asides of "self-criticism" are never astray. But with his limited resources he is scarcely able to escape such a result. Colour which he uses so freely elsewhere as a relief is here practically absent; then his landscapes are always as we have noted—as was also the case with Scott—absolutely objective and divorced from the personal impression; while the only bit of his technique so far not referred to is the atmospheric, which is curiously confined to the effects of a rich sunset—in the present instance not permissible. The result, as he perceives, is a certain hardness, which indeed, in some degree, is a quality of all his landscape work.

The same lack of sympathetic insight is felt in his personal portraits. Individual externals are keenly discerned and clearly reproduced. "Click-clack was a rough-looking fellow, turned of forty, of about five feet ten, with a black, unshaven beard, like a shoe-brush stuck under his nose, which was red as a coal, and attired in a sadly-breached suit of Aberdeen grey, topped by a brimless hat, that had been borrowed, apparently, from some obliging scarecrow." This much, vivid and exact, our author can do by skilful choice and arrangement of material. But all through the sketch we feel that the note of "inwardness" is wanting, only to be supplied indeed by that neutral humour which Miller, whose fun is usually rather grim, did not possess. There is, in consequence, a defect of sympathy, the place of which is taken by strong ethical and religious prejudices, narrowly limiting his treatment of character. Humour of narration he certainly has, where the matter is indifferent or of slight importance. But character and conduct are always for Miller too serious things to be treated otherwise than at the bar of judgment. The result is sentence or sentimentalism. This defect is less apparent where his method gets a freer field in the admirable reconstructions from tradition "of a bygone state of society" in a little Scotch town. It is most palpable in his tales, where it is the chief reason for that lack of dramatic power, noted by Mr Carruthers with respect to *Scenes and Legends,* and referred to by Mrs Miller in her preface to *Tales and Sketches.* It is for this reason that so many of these stop short of only the highest excellence.

As for the use he makes of the "red" glow of the setting sun, it is so frequent as to become a mannerism. Scores of examples might be cited. Proximately it may be due to a morbid fondness for lonely evening walks in lugubrious places; but the fact that his imaginary meetings with Ferguson and Burns also take place in romantic situations, "fronting the setting sun," and "in strong red light," respectively, suggests for such a predilection a sentimental basis.

The power of grasping and grouping detail was particularly useful to the geologist. The clearness and effectiveness of his scientific exposition have always been recognised for a distinction as meritorious as it is rare. Subordinately, of course, it is further due to a readiness in concrete familiar illustration. The flattered head of *Cephalaspis* is like "a saddler's cutting-knife"; the markings on the mail covering of *Osteolepis* "lie as thickly as the circular perforations in a lace veil"; the dorsal fins of *Cheiracanthus* are like "two lug-sails stiffly extended." Viewed from the Cromarty Firth, the "lofty promontory" of the Black Isle resembles "a huge spear thrust horizontally into the sea, a ponderous mass of granitic gneiss, of about a mile in length, forming the head, and a rectilinear line of the Old Red Sandstone, more than ten miles in length, forming the shaft." This aptness of homely and pungent illustration at times, it is true, but forged fetters for the mind. He was determined, as we shall see, to have the central nucleus of the Highlands set in a "frame" of Old Red Sandstone, and he fought to the end against surrendering his besetting simile.

But while the details are thus picturesquely conceived, his powerful handling of them seems due to that synoptic habit of mind which we have already noticed as a feature of his literary method. He confesses himself "altogether deficient in the cleverness that can promptly master isolated details, when in ignorance of their bearing on the general scheme to which they belong." This remark, applicable all round, has place in an account of how he finally mastered book-keeping as a bank clerk. It is the secret of his power of scientific exposition.

Summarily Miller's style may be truthfully said to answer to Arnold's quasi-definition of the "classical" as "perfect in lucidity, measure, and propriety." But I cannot conceive how Bayne[1] can speak of it as "artless," or Sir Henry Craik (*English Prose*, vol. v.) as "natural," or, least of all, Mr McCarthy as "spontaneous" (*History of Our Own Time*, iv. 229). As a style it is, as we have seen, highly figurative and allusive; the transitions and openings are carefully managed; the total effect, without verbosity, is melodious in a high degree. This last, again, is a strong Addisonian note. But Miller was a most laborious writer. He corrected and corrected again. "Chalmers remarked of him that, when he did go off, he was a great gun, and the reverberation of his shot was long audible, but he required a deal of time to load" (Bayne). Never was a style—easy to read, however hard in the writing, graceful and perspicuous—less the man, solidly and largely built, inelegant of dress and gait, and of mental habit laborious and comprehensive; whose speech, too, was not the "undefiled English" he wrote, but the "Cromarty Scotch," with a vowel system exemplified in the utterance, "the exe hed been bussy in the gleds." Dr McCosh records that in conversation "his thoughts came out tumbling with a freshness, an originality, and a power, which somewhat disappeared" in his formally written work. As a journalist, again, he took several proofs; while the crowning test was a *viva-voce* reading. He had no ear for pitch—was quite unmusical, in fact—but possessed a splendid perception of rhythm. To this quality he obviously attached supreme importance, presumably for Plato's reason that "rhythm and harmony find their way into the secret places of the soul, on which they mightily fasten." He avoids all harsh collocations of words and syllables, and in this endeavour his vocabulary never seems to fail him. The unbroken melody is apt to cloy; one misses the sure idiomatic grip, unattainable by Scotch writers primly handling their English as they would a foreign tongue; our later prose has become more daring and changeful in experiment. But for calm, polished excellence, for the dry light of the courtly Augustan utterance refracted through the rich mind of a parochial genius, Miller's prose work is eminently worthy of a niche in the literary temple. That was his earliest and his ever dominant ambition, and he would be a captious, clannish critic indeed who could raise his voice in dissent.

The *Poems of a Journeyman Mason* present a striking contrast to his prose. The two possess scarcely a feature in common. The poems have but rarely any imaginative interest, and sink under a weight of moral judgment and religious profession. Cold print unsealed Miller's eyes to their defects. He published them in a fit of pique at editorial neglect—"It would have been a greatly wiser act . . . had I put them into the fire instead." His narrow conception of poetic value may be judged from the pronouncement that Byron, Ovid, and Moore "fearfully misused the talents that God gave them"; and that "the Langhorns, Wartons, Kirke-Whites, Shelleys, Keatses—shall I venture to say it?—Byrons" (mark the grouping), "are flowers of the spring, to be read in careless youth if there is to be any appreciation!" The epilogue to the book of verse is apologetic—the serious pieces are recommended for their seriousness, while the lighter pieces, "though wild and fanciful, are not immoral." Not thus, however, is the volume to be saved from the aesthetic judgment, which may be expressed in one of his own lines: "O, it is drear, fearfully drear." Plainly Miller was right when he decided that for his type of thinking "the accomplishment of verse was too narrow." Carlyle and Ruskin, minds cast in the same mould, had to learn the same lesson.

Note

1. Peter Bayne in *Life and Letters of Hugh Miller*, which is referred to throughout.

George Rosie (essay date 1981)

SOURCE: Rosie, George. "Hugh Miller: A Biography."
In *Hugh Miller: Outrage and Order,* pp. 13-87. Edinburgh: Mainstream Publishing, 1981.

[In the following excerpt, Rosie discusses Miller's editorship of the Witness.*]*

Sturm Und Drang

The first issue of Hugh Miller's *Witness* made its appearance on the streets of Edinburgh on 15 January 1840 (under a slogan coined by John Knox: "I am in the place where I am demanded of conscience to speak the truth, and therefore the truth I speak, impugn it whoso list"). From the outset Miller made it plain he meant business. "We enter upon our labours at a period emphatically momentous," he wrote in his first, very wordy, editorial, "at the commencement, it is probable, of one of the most important eras, never forgotten by a country, which influences for ages the conditions and character of the people, and from which the events of their future history take colour and form." Miller went on to contrast the luke-warm, limp-wristed policies of the "moderates" inside the Church of Scotland, with the energy of the "evangelicals". "Here, then, on a distinction as obvious as it is important we take our stand. The cause of the unchanged party in the Church is that of the Church itself;—it is that of the people of Scotland, and the people know it . . ."

While the first issue of *The Witness* (like many issues thereafter) was dominated by Church affairs, Miller found space for much else. He carried reports,—on the opening of the provincial parliament in Upper Canada, fresh riots in Valencia, the draft constitution for the state of Hanover, more honours for the Prince Albert of Saxe-Coburg, the "cruel diseases" that were ravaging the Turkish fleet, the health of the Princess of Denmark, the build-up of "certain armaments" in Russia, and the fact that the authorities in Constantinople had introduced the guillotine to the intense curiosity of Turkish execution enthusiasts (and the apparent indifference of the condemned men).

The first issue was also liberally peppered with advertisements for, among other things, church meetings, religious tracts, useful books, temperance medals, and Mr Thalberg's "Third and Farewell Concert" to take place at the Assembly Halls and which was due to be strummed on "Erard's New Patent Grand Piano Forte brought from London expressly for the occasion". In addition, there were less edifying items for sale such as old whiskey, sherry from the butt, the newest style in "dress vests", straw-hat pressing machines, pennypostage letter-weighters, plus "an automatic singing bird, Chinese juggler, and a transparent clock with the invisible movement" (the last three items available from the Royal Bazaar at 19 Princes Street).

Interestingly, the first issue of *The Witness* also carried an advertisement for the *Scottish Standard,* a pro-Patronage newspaper which was launched on the same day as Hugh Miller's *Witness*. The publishers confidently expected that the *Scottish Standard* would satisfy "long cherished expectations felt and acknowledged by all classes and parties in the country; for it is a fact, lamented over on the one side, and boasted on the other, that the Conservative Newspapers, both in number and circulation fall greatly behind those which advocate the Destructive principle . . ." The *Scottish Standard,* their owners promised, would be devoted to "the support of the British Constitution in Church and State". This proved to be a very creaky platform in the Edinburgh of 1840; within a year the *Scottish Standard* had flopped, and Miller was able to report with some relish that it had been "converted into a cravat for the *Edinburgh Evening Post*".

In fact, Miller took to the knockabout world of periodical journalism like a duck to water. For months he produced *The Witness* almost single-handed (sometimes with the help of his wife Lydia, who joined him in April 1840) working deep into the night, churning out reams of copy to fill the papers gaping maw. That first year he wrote a dazzling range and variety of articles from fiercely polemic pieces on Church politics (some of them enormously long) to crisp political commentary on the Navy estimates, capital punishment, the Edinburgh savings banks, the copyright bill, and the Queen's marriage. He also cooked up long, discursive pieces on, for example, China and the Chinese, and reviewed books such as Darwin's masterpiece *The Voyage of the Beagle*. (Miller waxed lyrical over Darwin's ability to combine "high literary abilities and fine taste to many extensive acquirements as a man of science".)

Miller seldom hesitated to weigh in on foreign affairs. He was appalled at the oppression and torture of Jews in Rhodes and Damascus, claimed that it was the Roman Catholic hierarchy in Damascus that was whipping up the anti-semitism, and looked forward to the day when the Jews would give up their benighted religion and become good Christians (i.e. Presbyterians). He was equally appalled at the behaviour of the British mercenaries in Spain who had "burnt villages, and cut throats, and shot and stabbed a great many human creatures who never did them any harm, and who, but for their exertion as man-slayers, would have still been alive . . ." There was nothing, Miller pronounced, "very fine in the idea of a man-butcher hired to destroy life at the rate of 1s per day".

But for a man who was so patently and sincerely agitated by injustice and the miserable conditions of working people, Miller kept some of his deepest bile for political radicals like the Socialists and the Chartists. Socialist pamphlets he found "detestably obscene" and "horribly blasphemous" while the participants of a Chartist rally on Glasgow Green were "dirty, squalid and depressed . . . entirely broken men". So far as Miller was concerned the Chartist movement was a dangerous fraud, and he was convinced that "the worst friends of the people are those who drive their claims too far. Popular license is but despotism in its first stage—a great truth confirmed by the history of almost every European country." As for one man one vote: "Universal suffrage in the present state of public morals would ruin the country," he cried, "the masses are not fit for it."[1]

The Witness was an odd, but vigorous mix of radicalism, church infighting, philosophical comment, foreign news, decent reporting, book reviews, and small ads. And it worked! Miller's editorial recipe proved highly successful (to the delight of the evangelical party in the Church of Scotland). In 1841—having seen off the conservative *Scottish Standard*—Miller was boasting that the circulation of *The Witness* was climbing fast and had now reached "third place in point of circulation among the long-established newspapers in Edinburgh". By the beginning of 1842, *The Witness* circulation (which had started at 700) was heading towards 2,000, making it second only to *The Scotsman* (which then had a circulation of 2,577). Nine other Edinburgh papers (*Courant, Advertiser, Journal, Chronicle, Mercury, Post, Observer, Pilot* and *Messenger*) were all selling well below *The Witness*. "With such a circulation," he announced to the traders and merchants of Edinburgh, "Advertisers must see that by employing our columns they are promoting their own interests."

But the main thrust of *The Witness* was to champion the evangelical party in the long confrontation between the British state and the Church of Scotland over who should appoint parish ministers. By 1843 the argument was coming to a head, and Chalmers and the evangelicals had decided that they could no longer put up with the high-handed arrogance of the British establishment (or for that matter, with the hand-wringing feebleness of the "moderates" in the Church of Scotland). In the weeks before the General Assembly of the Church, due to be held on 18 May 1843, they let it be known that they planned to "disrupt" the Church by walking out, and setting up their own "Free" Church of Scotland. It was a momentous occasion for Scottish religious and political life, and the question buzzing round Edinburgh was how many ministers would throw up their livelihoods to follow Chalmers and the evangelicals? The establishment and the moderates were completely convinced it would be a mere handful. Others were not so sure.

When the day came Hugh Miller was there with his notebook, waiting in the gallery of the Church of St Andrew & St George in George Street, Edinburgh. The atmosphere was electric, and there was a huge crowd of people outside, pressing against the church doors in a struggle to get in. After the procession of dignitaries had descended from the High Church of St Giles the moderator, the Rev Dr Welsh started off with a "deeply impressive prayer" which the back of the Church could not hear because of the noise from outside. Welsh then read out a formal statement which had been signed by 120 ministers and 74 church elders stating that a great, and intolerable infringement of the Church's constitution had been perpetrated, and that men of principle could stand for it no longer. He threw the document down on the table, and with Chalmers beside him, led the procession of four hundred or so ministers and elders out of the building and out of the establishment.

With the great men gone, Miller observed, "There suddenly glided into the front rows a small party of men who no-one knew, obscure, mediocre, blighted-looking men" who reminded Miller of the "thin and blasted corn of Pharoah's vision, and, like them too, seemed typical of a time of famine and destitution". In disgust, Miller left the Assembly to the "moderates" and followed the procession of determined evangelicals down the hill to the ramshackle Tanfield Hall in Canonmills, where they held the first General Assembly of the Free Church of Scotland. It was no empty gesture. About one-third of the Church's ministers walked out at the Disruption, cutting themselves off from state funds, their wages, their homes, their security, and risking their families in hard times in a poor country.

The years between 1840 and 1844 were hard going for Miller. The fledgling paper had to be nursed then coaxed to success, there were battles to be fought and campaigns to be won. It was, from all accounts, an exhausting business, and Miller never shook off the silicosis which he contracted working as a stone-mason in the quarries and building sites of Easter Ross and the Black Isle. But his idea of a holiday seems to have been to take off with his notepad to gather material for a book (with which he would then fill his free time). In the summer of 1844 Miller abandoned *The Witness* for a few weeks to cruise around the "small isles" (i.e. the Inner Hebrides) with his old friend John Swanson, then Free Church minister for the small isles. Swanson was one of the hundreds of Church of Scotland ministers who threw up their livings and homes at the Disruption. In his case he found himself with a widely scattered, but extremely pious flock, but with no permanent church building, and a Laird who refused to give him a site to build on. The Free Church had resorted to spending some of their scarce cash on a small yacht (called *Betsey*) in which Swanson and a crew of one sailed from island to island, tending his charges. Pleasant enough for much of the summer, perhaps, but a nasty, and sometimes near-lethal business in the Hebridean autumn and winter, when the westerly gales made the reef-strewn coast a nightmare. (*The Betsey* came close to being lost twice; once when Hugh Miller was on board).

In the middle of July 1844 Miller met up with Swanson at Tobermory on Mull, and for the next few weeks sailed the bound of Swanson's parish, flitting between Mull, Eigg, Skye, Rum and Pabba. And not in luxury; the cabin he and Swanson shared he describes as "the size of a common bed and just lofty enough under the beams to permit a man of 5ft 11ins to stand erect in his night cap". Miller was particularly fascinated by the beautiful and distinctly weird island of Eigg, situated between the southeast of Skye and the mainland at Ardnamurchan. Eigg was the island where Swanson had been the parish minister, and where, till the Disruption, he had expected to end his days. Miller was impressed by his friend's fluency in Gaelic (a language he had to learn the hard way), his oratory, and the loyalty he inspired among the population of the island. Although all that Swanson could offer the people was a dingy, peat-roofed cabin for a church, his services were invariably packed to the doors and beyond. Swanson seems to have had the characteristic zeal of the best of the evangelicals, and confirmed Miller's view that "Presbyterianism without the animating life is a poor shrunken thing. Without the vitality of evangelism it is nothing."

Miller was so intrigued by the geology, history, and people of Eigg (whom he describes as "an active, middle-sized race, with well-developed heads, acute intellects and singularly warm feelings") that he returned to the little island with Swanson the following year (1845). In his short book *The Cruise of the Betsey* Miller gives some insight into the poverty of much of the Inner Hebrides. The two men had dropped in to visit one of Swanson's parishioners, an old woman who had been bed-ridden for ten years, and Miller was outraged by what he found. "Scarce ever before had I seen so miserable a hovel," he wrote. "It was hardly larger than the cabin of the *Betsey,* and a thousand times less comfortable . . . The low chinky door opened direct into the one wretched apartment of the hovel, which we found lighted chiefly by holes in the roof . . . Within a foot of the bedridden woman's head there was a hole in the turf-wall, which was, we saw, usually stuffed with a bundle of rags . . . The little hole in the wall had formed the poor creature's only communication with the face of the external world for ten weary years."

Miller noticed that, on leaving, Swanson had slipped the woman a few coins. "I learned that not during the ten years in which she had been bed-ridden had she received a single farthing from the proprietor, nor, indeed, had any of the poor of the island, and that the parish had no session funds. I saw her husband a few days after,—an old, worn-out man, with famine written legibly in his hollow cheek and eye, and on the shrivelled frame, that seemed lost in his tattered dress; and he reiterated the same sad story. They had no means of living, he said, save through the charity of their poor neighbours, who had so little to spare; for the parish or the proprietor had never given them anything. He had once, he added, two fine boys, both sailors, who had helped them; but the one had perished in a storm off the Mull of Cantyre [Kintyre], and the other had died of fever when on a West India voyage; and though their poor girl was very dutiful, and staid in their crazy hut to take care of them in their helpless old age, what other could she do in a place like Eigg than just share with them their sufferings?"

The wretchedness of the rural poor, the living and working conditions of farm labourers, fisherman, Highland crofters, was something which haunted Miller. Some of his finest, most powerful essays are on the subject; *Peasant Properties, The Cottages of Our Hinds, The Bothy System, The Highlands, the Scotch Poor Law, Pauper Labour, The Felons of the Country,* and the superb *Sutherland As It Was And Is; Or How A Country May Be Ruined.* There was something about their mute suffering, their patience and silence that moved Miller more deeply than the squalor of the Edinburgh and Glasgow working class, who were turbulent, vocal, and often downright dangerous.

In the autumn of that same year (1845) Miller took eight weeks off from *The Witness* to wander in England, the "sister kingdom" which he had never visited. His account of his journey, called *First Impressions of England and Its People,* is one of the most interesting and least known of nineteenth century travel books. Despite choosing an autumn which was "ungenial and lowering" and a progress bedevilled by "indifferent health and consequent languor" Miller's account of England and the English is perceptive, lively, and studded with passages of power and insight. Putting up at mainly second class railway hotels, coaching inns and lodgings, Miller wandered down over the border to Newcastle, Durham, York, Manchester, Wolverhampton, Dudley, Stourbridge, Droitwitch, Birmingham, Stratford, Olney, London, Harrow, Liverpool, and then back to Edinburgh via Glasgow.

Inevitably perhaps, the constant theme in *First Impressions* is a comparison between the Scots and the English, from which the Scots come rather badly. One Sunday evening in Manchester, he watched the day-trippers spill off the train and noted, "There was not much actual drunkenness among the crowd . . . not a tithe of what I would have witnessed on a similar occasion in my own country." He put this down to the very different Sabbath habits of the two nations. "With the humble Englishman trained to no regular habit of church-going, Sabbath is a pudding-day, a clean-shirt day, a day for lolling on the green opposite the sun . . . or, if in the neighbourhood of a railway, for taking a short trip to some country inn, famous for its cakes and ale; but to the humble Scot become English in his Sabbath views, the day is, in the most cases, a time of sheer recklessness and dissipation."

He was also much taken by English women, finding that "The English type of face and person seems particularly well adapted to the female countenance and figure; and the proportion of pretty women to the population—women with clear, fair complexions, well-turned arms, soft features and fine busts—seems very great."

But as a shrewd observer of rural people, he thought that the country English were distinctly less intellectual and curious than their Scottish equivalents. He had no hesitation "in affirming that their minds lie much more profoundly asleep than those of the common people of Scotland. We have no class north of the Tweed that corresponds with the class of ruddy, round-faced, vacant English, so abundant in the rural districts." The ordinary Scot, he felt, was "a naturally more inquisitive, more curious being, than the common Englishman; he asks many more questions, and accumulates much larger hoards of fact".

But what the ordinary Englishman lacked in curiosity and intellectual drive, Miller found he more than made up with stubborn independence. They possessed, he thought, "much of that natural independence which the Scotchman wants; and village Hampdens—men quite ready to do battle on behalf of their civil rights with the lord of the manor as the Scot with a foreign enemy— are comparatively common characters". The paradox was that the English possessed a much greater intellectual "range" than the Scots. "There is an order of the English mind to which Scotland has not attained," he felt, "our first men stand in the second rank, not a foot's breadth behind the foremost of England's second rank men; but there is a front rank of British intellect in which there stands no Scotchman . . . Scotland has produced no Shakespeare; Burns and Sir Walter Scott united would fall short of the stature of the giant of Avon. Of Milton we have not even a representative."

Like most Scots, Miller relished the range and diversity of England (and of the four days he spent in London, two were devoted to wandering about the British Museum in a state of ecstasy). But he was fearful for the English establishment, and particularly for the powerful Church of England, which he thought was being eaten away from within by the "white ants" of "Puseyism", the Anglo-Catholic, High-Church revival, being led by the Oxford Movement (whose best propagandist was Edward Bouvier Pusey). The High-Church medievalists were taking over the upper reaches of English society,

Miller concluded, "with whose Conservative leanings the servile politics of Puseyism agreed well . . . Schools had been erected in which the rising generation might at once be shown the excellence, and taught the trick of implicit submission to authority . . ." This disabling reactionary ecclesiasticism, he thought, would lead the Church of England into "antagonism to the tendencies of the age" and render the institution irrelevant, and in danger of withering away.

Back in Scotland, some of the larger egos in the Free Church were becoming increasingly irritated by Hugh Miller, particularly at his racy turn of phrase, his capacity of aggravation and trouble, his scant respect for many Free Church dignitaries, and his determination to run *The Witness* his own way. One such enemy was the Rev Dr Robert Candlish (who had recommended Miller for the job in the first place) who now felt that there was a positive lack of "taste or tact" in the way Hugh Miller was handling important and delicate matters, and that it was time *The Witness* was merged with one or two other Free Church newspapers, and tightly run by a proper editorial board instead of the vague committee who took an overview of Miller's work.

Falling foul of an accomplished church politician like Robert Candlish was no joke. Miller knew that everything he had worked for was under threat, and he moved swiftly. In January 1847 he had printed, very quietly, a pamphlet marked "Strictly Private and Confidential" which he circulated to the entire editorial committee of *The Witness*. Miller's memorandum (for that's what it was) is a beautiful piece of pre-emptive bureaucracy. He quoted from letters which Candlish had thought were private, accused him of being out of touch with the Free Church members outside Edinburgh, rubbished the notion of running *The Witness* via a committee of professional churchmen, and pointed out that the main reason the paper seemed to be flagging was that he was obliged to print so many long and boring articles on Church affairs (such as "Dr Candlish's speech on education") and that many of *those* were inserted at the last minute by bumbling meddlers. He ended with a flourish: "My faults have no doubt been many; but they have not been faults of principle; nor have they lost me the confidence of that portion of the people of Scotland to which I belong and which I represent. And possessing their confidence, I do not now feel myself justified in retiring from my post."

The handiest memo-shuffler in IBM could have done no better. Candlish was crushed. And when he tried to back away, and suggested that all his communications to Miller and to other Free Church brass should be "superseded, set aside, buried and held as non-existent", Miller would have none of it. He refused to let Candlish off the hook. He was in a foul temper at the way

Candlish had tried to undermine his position by "private" letters to the Committee, then had complained when Miller laid his hands on a few. "The man who has let his neighbour understand, in strict secrecy, that he intends bleeding him for his benefit by sending a ball through him in the evening, has no reason to complain that his neighbour betrays his confidence by blabbing to the police," Miller wrote.

The speed with which Miller had moved to outflank Candlish convinced Thomas Chalmers for one that the idea of the committee running the day-to-day affairs of *The Witness* was a nonsense. He promptly convened a special meeting, delivered a fierce pro-Miller harangue, and then settled the matter by asking the sheepish churchmen, "which of you could direct Hugh Miller?" Having seen the way Miller disposed of Candlish none of them offered to try, the whole idea was dropped, and Miller's position was never challenged again. But Candlish's attempted *coup* did leave a sour taste in Miller's mouth, and thereafter he never quite trusted the divines of the Free Church in the same way. But it is entirely likely that the whole business did *The Witness* nothing but good; Miller lost some of his preoccupation with Free Church affairs, cut back on the coverage, and replaced it with general features, literature, and more popular science.

The obverse of Hugh Miller's enthusiasm for the Free Church of Scotland was a naked anti-Catholicism which flared up from time to time and did him no credit. While Miller never came near the mindless ranting of many of his compatriots (some of whom despaired of the soft line on Catholics Miller took in *The Witness,* and started their own anti-Catholic sheet called *The Rock*), a few of Miller's leaders and articles on Catholics and Catholicism were downright vicious. In September 1850, for example, he ran a long piece on *The Cowgate Flock,* the immigrant Irish who were flooding into Edinburgh's Cowgate in the 1840s. "They eschew cleanliness for that is a Protestant virtue," Miller wrote caustically. "They hate to be seen in unpatched garments because these are often the accompaniments of a mind defiled with deadly heresy. Rather than toil themselves, they not infrequently prefer living on the labour of others, especially Protestants."

He did identify the root differences between Protestantism and the Roman church. "Her name is mystery," he wrote of the Catholic Church, "and the power which she wields is not moral but mystical. The change she effects on those on whom she acts is not a moral or a spiritual reformation, but a mystic transformation . . ." But transformation or no, he thought, Catholicism was bad news. "The experience of the ages has demonstrated that wherever Popery comes, there too come beggary and wretchedness;—there the intellect is paralysed, ge-nius droops, industry is smitten, learning takes flight, commerce decays, every source of wealth and natural greatness dries up, and nothing is left but a universal wreck."

But Miller was even more contemptuous of Catholicism in the Anglo-Catholic form reviving under the Oxford Movement of the aggressive Edward Pusey. To Miller "Puseyism" represented everything that he loathed and despised in religious life. He saw it as an abomination, neither Protestant nor properly Catholic, but a shadowy, obscure, elusive thing, dangerous because it was fast becoming the religion of the politically-powerful English upper classes, and probably a stalking horse for the Roman church. Miller filled many columns of *The Witness* with attacks on Puseyism, but was at his most scathing after encountering it at first hand on his trip through England. He was repelled by a High-Church Cathedral service in York Minster. "The coldly-read or fantastically-chanted prayers, common-placed by the twice-a-day repetition of the centuries—the mechanical responses—the correct inanity of the choristers who had not even the life of music in them—the total want of lay attendance . . . all conspired to show that the Cathedral service of the English Church does not represent a living devotion, but a devotion that perished centuries ago."

In lying down with the dead, Miller thought, the Church of England were putting themselves in some peril and "in dressing out their clerical brethren in the cerements of Popery and setting them a-walking, could hardly have foreseen that many of them were to become the actual ghosts which they had decked them to simulate". What particularly incensed Miller about the High-Church revival in England was its incessant, and sometimes effective, hostility to science. He shared the alarm expressed by Charles Lyell that the classes in chemistry and botany, astronomy, geology and mineralogy at Oxford University could hardly raise half a dozen students, when fifteen years previously they had been heavily over-subscribed. "The medieval miasma, originated in the bogs and fens of Oxford, has been blown aslant over the face of the country," he wrote bitterly, "and not only religious but scientific truth is to experience, it would seem, the influence of its poisonous blights and rotting mildew".

By the late 1840s Hugh Miller was one of Edinburgh's literary lions, and like most of the species, was greatly stalked by polite society. The Duke of Argyll, for example, was a keen science buff, and continually invited Miller to Inverary Castle to discuss Higher Things (an invitation that Miller politely declined). Socially, Miller seems to have been both genuinely shy and something of a showman. Why else would a respectable Edinburgh intellectual and churchman dress himself up in a tweed plaid (as Miller invariably did) and pound the streets of the Capital like an upland shepherd? Why else would he spend happy hours posing as a stonemason for the calotype photographs of his friends David Octavius Hill and Robert Adamson? He enjoyed giving little drawing-room lectures on fossils and geology to the ladies of Edinburgh, or creating a *frisson* of dread in them with his tales of North Highland ghosts, or hard times in the Black Isle. He took huge delight in challenging his (mainly bookish) friends to wrestling, jumping over burns, or putting heavy stones, knowing full well that he would win. According to David Masson, another of Miller's simple-minded conceits was to entice his friends to try on his broad-brimmed hat, then falling about laughing as it slipped down over their noses. A large head, it was generally thought, was a mark of superiority.

There was, however, a darker side to Miller's success as a literary man and celebrity as a newspaper editor. He quickly became convinced that the enemies he made through his pugnacious articles and leaders in *The Witness* were a physical threat, and were likely to set some of Edinburgh's foot-pads or cut-purses on him. This seems very unlikely, but Miller took the notion seriously. By the early 1840s he had taken to carrying a loaded handgun around with him. One evening Miller walked past two of his friends in the Meadows of Edinburgh without recognising them. As a joke one of them shouted after him, "There goes that rascally editor of *The Witness*", and was horrified to find himself looking down the barrel of a cocked revolver. An embarrassed Hugh Miller later explained to his friends that he expected to be attacked any day, and the revolver was his defence.

Note

1. In the course of his editorship, Miller regularly showed flashes of a latent Scottish nationalism, which ran counterpoint to his British patriotism. Reporting on the instigation of an early proto-nationalist movement called The Scottish Association, he wrote that "it is one thing to acquiesce in the Union (of 1707) and quite another to acquiesce in the treatment which Scotland almost ever since that event, has been receiving at the hands of the English. And the present is a most favourable time for the country to take its stand against further aggression." But Miller warned that it would not be easy as "it is one of the inevitable effects of treatment such as that to which Scotland has been subjected by the English, to produce disunion and diversity of opinion in the injured country". And on another instance he made the point that "It has been the tendency of English misgovernment and aggression to render us a divided people."

Lynn L. Merrill (essay date 1989)

SOURCE: Merrill, Lynn L. "Hugh Miller and Evocative Geology." In *The Romance of Victorian Natural History,* pp. 236-54. New York: Oxford University Press, 1989.

[*In the following essay, Merrill maintains that Miller's* The Old Red Sandstone *appealed to Victorian readers because of its attention to the particulars of natural description.*]

> Where can be seen an intenser delight than that of children picking up new flowers and watching new insects, or hoarding pebbles and shells? . . . Every botanist who has had children with him in the woods and the lanes must have noticed how eagerly they joined him in his pursuits, how keenly they searched out plants for him, how intently they watched while he examined them, how they overwhelmed him with questions. . . . Having gained due familiarity with the simpler properties of inorganic objects, the child should by the same process be led on to a like exhaustive examination of the things it picks up in its daily walks, the less complex facts they present being alone noticed at first: in plants, the color, number and forms of the petals and shapes of the stalks and leaves; in insects, the numbers of the wings, legs, and antennae, and their colors. As they become fully appreciated and invariably observed, further facts may be successively introduced.[1]
>
> HERBERT SPENCER, "Education: Intellectual, Moral, and Physical," 1861

In the natural history prose of Philip Henry Gosse and Charles Kingsley, several common traits display themselves repeatedly: particularity of details, fascination with natural facts, vivification of nature whether organic or not, imaginative journeys through apertures of scale, and joy in nature's boundless variety. But the two naturalists were friends, and both took much of their pleasure at the seaside. Is it merely for those reasons that their works exhibit definite stylistic similarities? On the contrary, the language used by Gosse and Kingsley expresses common Victorian responses to natural history. They are not isolated eccentrics, but type specimens of the naturalist species. Their natural history discourse is thoroughly representative. This becomes clear if one looks at other writers completely outside the Gosse-Kingsley mold.

For example, *The Old Red Sandstone: or, New Walks in an Old Field,* by the Scots geologist Hugh Miller (1802-1856), takes its natural history rambles in an entirely different realm from that treated by *The Romance of Natural History, Evenings at the Microscope,* or *Glaucus.* Nevertheless, within what at first appears to be an unpromising area of inquiry—one dusty stratum or formation of ancient rock—Miller discovers many of the same rewards that lured Gosse and Kingsley to marine biology and microscopy. And in its prose, although somewhat more scientific and theoretical than Gosse's or Kingsley's, *The Old Red Sandstone* exploits many of the same motifs and devices.

Miller's book is worth looking at, first of all, simply as a cultural phenomenon. Published in 1841 (in book form), *The Old Red Sandstone* became a best-seller almost immediately. Lynn Barber, who devotes a chapter of her natural history survey to Miller, declares that after 1841 "Miller's name was known in every Victorian parlour."[2] She quotes Archibald Geikie, the geologist, as saying that Miller's books "were to be found in the remotest log-hut of the Far West, and on both sides of the Atlantic ideas of the nature and shape of geology were largely drawn from them."[3] Certainly references to Miller abound in the books by other naturalists; indeed, he takes on the status of a sort of Olympian god of natural history. Charles Kingsley mentions Miller several times in *Glaucus,* praising *The Old Red Sandstone* as the best possible example of "induction learnt from a narrow field of objects."[4] And Herbert Spencer, while maintaining in 1861 that "science excites poetry rather than extinguishes it," cites Miller as a prime practitioner of poetic science.[5]

Hugh Miller rose to such prominence for several reasons. First, he was a self-taught, working-class geologist who learned the science while toiling away at hard labor in stone quarries; such successes of working-class diligence of course appealed to the Victorians. (Recall how fond Kingsley and Samuel Smiles were of praising self-taught naturalists, such as Smiles' biographical subjects, Thomas Edward and Robert Dick.) Second, Miller, curiously enough, was a devoted Christian naturalist, just like Gosse and Kingsley. His was a geology wholly consistent with Christian doctrine. In the disturbing world of post-Lyellian geology, Miller's *Old Red Sandstone* "charmed everyone with the beauty and vigor of its knowledgeable creationist assertions," long after most geologists had renounced creationist ideas.[6] Two other Miller works were even more reassuring: *Footprints of the Creator* (1849) and *The Testimony of the Rocks* (1857). Third, Hugh Miller, the humble Scotsman, inherited the mantle of geologic glory from Charles Lyell, keeping geology before the public during the 1840s.[7] This was the decade when Adam Sedgwick became influential and when Ruskin advocated the study of geological landscapes in *Modern Painters*; these were "years of triumph" for geology.[8] Busily opening up vistas of vanished worlds, geologists, or more specifically paleontologists, were creating a sensation for the reading public. As Charles Kingsley maintained in *Glaucus,*

it is a question whether Natural History would have ever attained its present honors, had not Geology arisen, to connect every other branch of Natural History with problems as vast and awful as they are captivating to the imagination.[9]

Miller's fame rode on just such "vast and awful" speculations.

Finally, Hugh Miller became one of the most beloved of Victorian naturalists because of the power of his style. Among his peers, the naturalists and geologists of his day, Miller was held in high esteem, both for the thoroughness of his knowledge and for the gracefulness of his descriptions. Roderick Murchison called his style "beautiful and poetical," and William Buckland claimed that he "would give his left hand to possess such powers of description as this man."[10] Twentieth-century critics who deal with Miller agree. Lynn Barber calls Miller's style "lucid," full of apt similes,[11] and Julian M. Drachman goes so far as to proclaim that Miller "was one of the very finest literary masters who have ever undertaken to write on scientific subjects."[12]

It is true that in some sections of *The Old Red Sandstone* Miller's style is gripping; some of his descriptions of landscape are Ruskinian in intensity, and his imaginative recreations of past eras are vivid. But frankly, for the modern reader, *The Old Red Sandstone* is a daunting book. Packed with lengthy notes, figures, lists, and technical details of fossil fish anatomy, Miller's book makes for heavy slogging. I cannot agree with Lynn Barber, who says that "reading it today, one can still understand why" *Sandstone* "was a best-seller."[13] On the contrary, I find it difficult to picture large numbers of people enjoying many sections of the book. The really interesting question about *The Old Red Sandstone* is not why the descriptive set-pieces appealed to people, but why even the seemingly tedious technical portions appealed. I would suggest this explanation: that the exhaustive technical descriptions in chapter after chapter of the book, those that to a modern eye seem numbing in their detail, were embraced by Victorian readers as a fabulous treasure-store of material facts. *The Old Red Sandstone* captivated the Victorian imagination, in part, because it fairly bristled with particulars.

In the context of nineteenth-century natural history, of course, ever-multiplying particulars were a never-ending source of delight. To Lewes, Gosse, Kingsley, and so many others, particulars were the emblems of nature's unlimited bounty, best appreciated by the sharp, focused eye, the eye of literal or figurative microscopic vision. Miller, in fact, employs this aid, saying of the ichthyolites in his favorite formation that it does not "lessen the wonder that their nicer ornaments should yield their beauty only to the microscope."[14] And, like other naturalists of his time, Miller made a conscious attempt to refine his sight. He reports that after some practice he has "now learned to look at rocks with another eye" (p. 129), and notes also how, in making collections of rock, "the eye becomes practised in such researches" (p. 132), making his labors pay off. Like other naturalists, Miller becomes obsessed with the multiplicity of nature—that close examination of nature will yield more and more details that can be brought to light. When Miller realizes that nodules within the Old Red Sandstone formation have fossils inside them, he breaks open all he can find, until they are, in his words, "laid open":

> I set myself carefully to examine. The first nodule I laid open contained a bituminous-looking mass, in which I could trace a few pointed bones and a few minute scales. The next abounded in rhomboidal and finely-enamelled scales, of much larger size and more distinct character. I wrought on with the eagerness of a discoverer entering for the first time a *terra incognita* of wonders. Almost every fragment of clay, every splinter of sandstone, every limestone nodule, contained its organism,—scales, spines, plates, bones, entire fish . . .
>
> (p. 130)

Here is the same sense of wonder, and the same delight in minuteness, that one finds in Gosse and so many other Victorian naturalists.

Since Miller perceives dusty rocks as a wonderful *terra incognita,* he takes the value of all he finds within that land for granted. Each fragment, each splinter, each outline and angle and pattern is important. And all these minute details are reported at length—resulting in passages that I think are detailed to a fault. Collecting specimens until "half my closet walls are covered with the peculiar fossils of the Lower Old Red Sandstone" (p. 57), Miller reports on every characteristic of them. Fossil fish scales, somewhat incredibly, are painstakingly described:

> Each scale consists of a double plate,—an inner and an outer. The structure of the inner is not peculiar to the family or the formation: it is formed of a number of concentric circles, crossed by still minuter radiating lines,—the one described, and the other proceeding from a common centre. . . . All scales that receive their accessions of growth equally at their edges exhibit internally a corresponding character. The outer plate presents an appearance less common. It seems relieved into ridges that drop adown it like sculptured threads, some of them entire, some broken, some straight, some slightly waved . . .
>
> (p. 99)

The effect of page after page of such description can well be imagined.

Two points should be made about the passage quoted above. The first is that, obviously, structural examination of fish scales belongs more to the province of sci-

ence than to that of natural history. *The Old Red Sandstone* is a mixture of both. Far more than *Glaucus* or *The Romance of Natural History,* Miller's book aims to understand the laws governing its subject. It is often quite theoretical, speculating about geological causes and effects: Why did this species disappear? How did this come to be so well fossilized? In fact, Miller's book survives today mostly for geologists who appreciate its contribution to the geological understanding of an important stratigraphic member.[15]

The second point to be made about the passage is that Miller's technical descriptions frequently metamorphose into evocative descriptions. Far from being a dispassionate scientist, Miller displays an appreciation for the aesthetic features of minutiae that rivals even that of Gosse or Kingsley. Thus Miller's work, as its emphasis on microscopic vision and collecting indicates, also fits within the definition of natural history I have suggested.

While seeking to comprehend them, Miller nonetheless sees the fossils as quite beautiful, and portrays them as such. And although the quoted passage is mostly technical and devoid of emotion, toward the end it begins to exhibit Miller's sense of beauty, expressed in his typical figurative language. The outer plate of the scale has ridges "like sculptured threads," the implication being that they are not only minutely detailed—some straight and some wavy—but also that they are finely wrought, like tiny works of art. Other passages from *The Old Red Sandstone* make more explicit Miller's perception of beauty. One fossil fish, *Diplacanthus,* has "spines" on its fins, which "are of singular beauty" (p. 112). Besides their singularity, so esteemed in Victorian natural history, they each resemble "a bundle of rods, or rather, like a Gothic column, the sculptured semblance of a bundle of rods." Again, these curious objects are perceived as valuable natural works of art.

Another fish, the *Osteolepis,* turns up in the sandstone breathtakingly preserved as fossils that are also works of art. (Yet while giving the reader an aesthetic appreciation of the fossils, Miller is equally concerned with giving accurate scientific details, such as correct species names—often obtained in consultation with other experts, such as Agassiz or Murchison.) *Osteolepis* is a completely armored fish, sporting "plaited mail" on its head, "scaly mail" on its body, and fins with "mail of parallel and jointed bars" (p. 115). Likening the scales to armored mail is one Gossean touch, but Miller goes even further, stating that the "entire suit glittered with enamel." And that striking enamel is rife with detail, since "every plate, bar, and scale, was dotted with microscopic points." These points, or dots, remind Miller of the "circular perforations in a lace veil," an exquisite example of artistry.

Moving on to the next type of fish, the *Cheirolepis,* Miller finds that "an entirely different style obtains" (p. 115). In these fossils, Miller finds that

> the enamelled scales and plates glitter with minute ridges, that show like thorns in a December morning varnished with ice. Every ray of the fins presents its serrated edge; every occipital plate and bone its sculptured prominences; every scale its bunch of prickle-like ridges.

Whereas the first species of fossil presented, to the magnified vision, an effect "of lightness and beauty," the *Cheirolepis* appears more formidable. Miller succeeds at imbuing the primitive, ancient creature with a savage life; one can vividly imagine this glittering armored fish swimming in mysterious seas. And significantly, every detail of the fossil, if examined closely, generates more details: the fin has rays, which in turn have serrated edges, and so on.

The joyful discovery of particularities within particularities runs throughout **The Old Red Sandstone.** Learning to see ever more precise details of rocks and fossils has a scientific point, since the details facilitate classification and therefore understanding, but compiling them partakes of the old-fashioned pleasures of natural history. And since nature's variety is endless, there is always more to see. For example, while poking around in broken rock that contains the fossil fish, *Cephalaspis,* Miller notes that

> some of the specimens which exhibit this creature are exceedingly curious. In one a coprolite still rests in the abdomen; and a common botanist's microscope shows it thickly speckled over with minute scales, the indigestible exuviae of fish on which the animal had preyed. In the abdomen of another we find a few minute pebbles, . . . which had been swallowed by the creature attached to its food.

(p. 77)

In part, these details are "wonderful" because they enable "us" (like Gosse, Kingsley, and so many other Victorian naturalists, Miller uses the first-person plural pronoun as a means of including the reader and dramatizing the hunt) to understand how these ancient fish lived. But the minute scales inside the coprolite, inside the stomach, inside the abdomen, inside the *Cephalaspis,* again reveal the naturalist's pleasantly dizzy sensation of confronting details that recede to infinity.

Geology and paleontology (or "oryctology," the older name that Miller uses, p. 136) add the dimension of *time* to the naturalist's contemplation of objects scattered throughout *space,* and for this reason, Miller says, "geology, of all the sciences, addresses itself most powerfully to the imagination" (p. 57). What Miller calls the "wonders of geology" appeal to us because they "exercise every faculty of the mind,—reason, memory,

imagination" (p. 119). God's infinite variety in nature, where truth is always more wonderful than fiction, is revealed to the geologist in layers of time, each containing objects infinitely individuated. Miller at one point in his researches worries that the teeth of one fish he describes are too bizarre to be believed. His colleague Louis Agassiz reassures him:

> Do not be deterred, if you have examined minutely, by any dread of being deemed extravagant. The possibilities of existence run so deeply into the extravagant, that there is scarcely any conception too extraordinary for nature to realize.

(p. 78)

This is the faith of the naturalist: optimism about nature's endless extravagance.

Miller always keeps before the reader the motif of discovery. He speaks of himself as a "sort of Robinson Crusoe of geology" (p. 137). In part, he means that he was cut off from professional contacts for years, because of his class, but Miller is a Robinson Crusoe of geology also in the sense that he has a whole new world to explore in the layers of the Old Red Sandstone. What he finds in that world is, invariably, an "amazing multiplicity of being" (p. 227), "myriads" of creatures and forms that are "innumerable" and "multitudinous." The realm that he has stumbled upon is rich beyond comprehension: one two-mile section of shoreline bounded by the Old Red Sandstone is so complex that "years of examination and inquiry would fail to exhaust it" (p. 209). Since the lost world now represented by the Old Red Sandstone is dauntingly intricate, Miller opens his account of it with a personal anecdote that shows how he came to it in all innocence and ignorance and gradually learned about it. The lesson—quite overtly stated—is that the reader can, too.

The opening chapter of Miller's book invites one to begin a voyage of discovery. The very first sentence is Miller's "advice to young working men desirous of bettering their circumstances"; they should not bother with what "is misnamed pleasure" (presumably drinking and the like) but rather pursue "study" (p. 33). Putting faith in the chimera of Chartism in hopes of gaining the right to vote, says Miller, is a waste of time. How much better to "learn to make right use of your eyes: the commonest things are worth looking at,—even stones and weeds, and the most familiar animals." Heeding this familiar naturalist's injunction will lead to happiness. Miller can attest to that with a "simple narrative" (p. 35) of his own life. Twenty years ago he had gone off to work in a stone quarry, fearful about the rigors of such a life. Almost immediately, however, this healthful outdoor labor opens Miller's eyes to the world around him. He notices birds, the "prospect" around him, clear air, a waveless bay, and pleasant wooded slopes.

Most important of all, Miller discovers what is hidden inside some of the rocks being quarried:

> In the course of the first day's employment I picked up a nodular mass of blue limestone, and laid it open by a stroke of the hammer. Wonderful to relate, it contained inside a beautifully finished piece of sculpture—one of the volutes, apparently, of an Ionic capital.
>
> (p. 39)

Amazed, he wondered: "Was there another such curiosity in the whole world?" He soon realizes that the entire area of sedimentary deposits around the quarry is "a richer scene of wonder than I could have fancied in even my dreams" (p. 40). The layers of rock are, Miller realizes, like leaves in a book or "a herbarium," with "the pictorial records of a former creation in every page" (p. 40). Paging through this book of nature, the incipient geologist finds himself

> lost in admiration and astonishment, . . . my very imagination paralysed by an assemblage of wonders that seemed to outrival in the fantastic and the extravagant even its wildest conceptions.
>
> (p. 41)

Brought face to face with this "assemblage of wonders," Miller embarks on a voyage of discovery through time and space. Unlike Wallace or Bates, Miller did not need to journey to remote jungles of Malaysia or the Amazon to encounter natural curiosities; they are amply entombed in the rock beneath his feet. He thinks of himself ever after as a typical rambling naturalist, picking up flotsam from the shore, saying of his life: "I have been an explorer of caves and ravines, a loiterer along sea-shores, a climber among rocks, a labourer in quarries. My profession was a wandering one" (p. 42). Interestingly, when Miller finds his first belemnite fossil (part of an extinct cuttle-fish), he compares it to a strange stone brought home by a relative from Java; both are exotic curios, but Miller's exotic locale is the ordinary landscape of Britain.

After opening thus on a personal note, *The Old Red Sandstone* proceeds to the enumeration of countless scales, ribs, prickles, tubercules, spines, fins, and bones of vanished fish. Chapter after chapter catalogues these features, but they are enlivened by similes and fresh metaphors—spines that "run deep into the body, as a ship's masts run deep into her hulk" (p. 113), a *Coccosteus* shaped either like "a boy's kite" or like an "ancient one-sided shovel which we see sculptured on old tombstones" (p. 74), or the head-plates of a fish that are "burnished like ancient helmets" (p. 98). Along with the details of specimens, Miller includes extremely precise descriptions of geological strata and rock types, since they are the sets against which the fish—the *dramatis personae* (p. 65) of the story—come alive. Miller himself realizes that the thoroughness of his report may

overwhelm the unsuspecting reader: "I am particular, at the risk, I am afraid, of being tedious, in thus describing the geology of this northern country" (p. 56). He continues to be particular because the truth of his subject only exists in particulars. Only if one can amass all the facts can one discover the truth about them.

The facts—fragments of fish, plants, and other organisms—are strewn throughout the Old Red Sandstone and its attendant rocks like pieces of a puzzle. Miller is fond of telling stories of how those pieces have been reconstructed, and their meaning deciphered. He applauds Cuvier as a master of the craft of reconstructing bits of bone; they were to him clear "signs," though "incomprehensible to every one else" (p. 153). The current master of the art, though, is the ichthyologist whom Miller unabashedly reveres: Louis Agassiz. Miller tells the dramatic story of how Agassiz daringly reconstructed "the huge crustacean of Balruddery." Murchison, Buckland, and several other authorities had been baffled by the collection of "fragments of scaly rhombs, of scaly crescents, of scaly circles, with scaly parallelograms attached to them." No one would "hazard a conjecture" about their nature (p. 154).

Agassiz, however, "glanced over the collection" with a masterful eye. One strange specimen stood out; "his eye brightened as he contemplated it" (p. 154). Miller dramatically recounts Agassiz's revelation:

> "I will tell you," he said, turning to the company,—"I will tell you what these are,—the remains of a huge lobster." He arranged the specimens in the group before him with as much apparent ease as I have seen a young girl arranging the pieces of ivory or mother-of-pearl in an Indian puzzle. A few broken pieces completed the lozenge-shaped shield; two detached specimens placed on its opposite sides furnished the claws; two or three semi-rings with serrated edges composed the jointed body; the compound figure, which but a minute before had so strongly attracted his attention, furnished the terminal flap; and there lay the huge lobster before us, palpable to all.
>
> (pp. 154, 156)

The scene radiates the joy of discovery and conveys the incredible sensation of having an extinct and hardly even suspected animal loom up suddenly, "palpable to all." Agassiz solves the puzzle with exceptional skill, but Miller's description of the problem as being an "Indian puzzle" is not unusual. Like most Victorian naturalists, he perceives nature as a mosaic made up of infinite pieces, which fit together in surprising ways. Miller finds such surprises everywhere he looks, albeit usually without such theatrical fanfare. Who but Miller, or another Victorian naturalist perhaps, would take the trouble to count, and then recount for a reader, how many fossil organisms reside in "a single cubic inch" of shale from the Eathie Lias? Miller had the patience to tally there "about eighty molluscous organisms, mostly ammonites, and minute striated scallops" (p. 194).

Gradually, Hugh Miller shifts his focus away from the particularities of the fish and other fossils and toward the longer view—the scenery, or, as he calls it, the "physiognomy" (p. 201) of landscape. At this point, especially in chapter XI, Miller demonstrates his formidable descriptive powers for scenery. Very much like the Ruskin and Gosse passages with which I ended Chapter 6, Miller's descriptions of scenery depend on a hypothetical traveler who walks through the varying countryside. One long passage illustrates how differing rock types affect the manifestation of terrain. At first, "the traveller passes through a mountainous region of gneiss" (p. 201). Here the hills are "bulky" but "shapeless," and somewhat somber: they "raise their huge backs so high over the brown dreary moors" that stretch away at their feet. The traveler then "pursues his journey" and

> enters a district of micaceous schist. The hills are no longer truncated, or the moors unbroken: the heavy ground-swell of the former landscape has become a tempestuous sea, agitated by powerful winds and conflicting tides. The picturesque and somewhat fantastic outline is composed of high sharp peaks, bold craggy domes, steep broken acclivities, and deeply serrated ridges; and the higher hills seem as if set round with a framework of props and buttresses, that stretch out on every side like the roots of an ancient oak.
>
> (p. 202)

Noteworthy here, as in the selections from Gosse and Ruskin, is the energy invested in the landforms. They seem almost to have life—the gneiss hills raising their backs and the mica hills moving as if agitated by inner anxiety. The animation of the landscape is accompanied by formal precision; Miller is careful to tell that the ridges are "deeply serrated," and that the acclivities are "steep" and "broken."

From the mica landscape, the traveler "passes on, and the landscape varies" (p. 202). At times the hills become "naked skeletons," sterile and foreboding. Other rocks shape the landscape into soft, swelling forms, over which streams "linger." These differences Miller characterizes as "styles" (p. 202) of scenery, each with its own "peculiarities" (p. 204). Miller's schema is reminiscent of Ruskin in *Modern Painters*; Miller also notes the slaty crystalline rocks and then looks at the resultant landscapes with a painter's eye. It is even reminiscent of Ruskin's attempts, in *The Poetry of Architecture,* to link human societies and their styles with landscape.

Later in this scenery chapter, Miller guides the geological novice on an exploration of a certain "rocky trench" (p. 210) cut into the sandstone. "Will the reader," he asks, be willing to devote just a few minutes to walking about in this "solitary recess"? The answer is—of course. "We pass onwards," then, into the "denuded hollow" (p. 210). The stream-cut ravine is a window

into geological time, but Miller equally appreciates the natural profusion of forms that live along the rock. In a passage that would do Ruskin justice—one that Millais would be proud to capture in paint, perhaps as a background for Ophelia's downstream glide—Miller views the undergrowth with an artist's eye:

> We enter along the bed of the stream. A line of mural precipices rises on either hand,—here advancing in ponderous overhanging buttresses, there receding into deep damp recesses, tapestried with ivy, and darkened with birch and hazel. A powerful spring, charged with lime, comes pouring by a hundred different threads over the rounded brow of a beetling crag, and the decaying vegetation around it is hardening into stone. The cliffs vary their outline at every step, as if assuming in succession all the various combinations of form that constitute the wild and picturesque; and the pale hues of the stone seem, when brightened by the sun, the very tints a painter would choose to heighten the effect of his shades, or to contrast most delicately with the luxuriant profusion of bushes and flowers that wave over the higher shelves and crannies.
>
> (p. 211)

This is a natural tangle that seems an example of Carlylean "Natural Supernaturalism," because every element within the description seems alive or sensitive, in most cases fairly bursting with energy. The spring is "powerful," "charged," and does not merely flow but "comes pouring" over the rock. The buttresses "advance" and "overhang" the visitor. The crag has a "brow" like a face, and it "beetles" overhead.

Besides being vibrant, the seemingly small slice of scenery is visually crowded and complex. The stream moves through a "hundred" little channels, the cliffs constantly "vary their outline," and overlapping, changeable hues of dappled light and shade cover the stone. The cliff face is riddled with crannies, in which grow countless bushes and flowers. Miller continues his artist's metaphors, since the precipices seem to him "murals" and the luxuriant vegetation forms "tapestries." The very stone itself has chosen the exact "tints a painter would choose." How like Ruskin—who, in a famous "word painting" passage from *Modern Painters IV* (part V, chapter XI, section 6), notes how in one scene "on the broken rocks of the foreground . . . the mosses seem to set themselves consentfully and deliberately to the task of producing the most exquisite harmonies of colour in their power." The mosses "gather over" the rock "in little brown bosses, like small cushions of velvet made of mixed threads of dark ruby silk." Ruskin, too, looks at nature and sees a preexistent work of art, here mosses forming a beautifully "embroidered" cushion.

Miller continues his description, keeping it charged with a nearly personified energy. The banks become "steeper and more inaccessible," and the dell "wilder and more deeply wooded." The stream, restless, "frets and toils at our feet" (p. 211). Flowers multiply in an even "richer profusion . . . a thick mantling of ivy and honeysuckle." And the water unceasingly churns "foam, which, flung from the rock, incessantly" revolves in the stream's eddy (p. 212). Just when the rambler begins to feel claustrophobic, even slightly threatened by nature's demonstrated relentless fecundity, Miller changes tactics. "Mark now the geology of the ravine" (p. 212), he instructs. For this lush abundance of nature extends not only throughout the present—in space—but also backwards, throughout time. The rocks themselves, on close inspection, are found to be "a place of sepulture . . . where the dead lie by myriads" (p. 212). The river "brawls along," but Miller finds that

> it is through a vast burial-yard that it has cut its way,—a field of the dead so ancient, that the sepulchres of Thebes and Luxor are but of the present day in comparison,—resting-places for the recently departed, whose funerals are just over. These mouldering strata are charged with remains, scattered and detached as those of a churchyard, but not less entire in their parts,—occipital bones, jaws, teeth, spines, scales,—the dust and rubbish of a departed creation.
>
> (pp. 217-218)

To the consideration of these departed multitudes Miller now turns.

As he opens chapter XII, Miller shifts from the present to the past, attempting to pass "from the dead to the living" (p. 219), and reanimate the fossils now quiescent in the rock. From "consideration of the Old Red Sandstone as it exists in *space,*" Miller changes to the description of the rock in previous "*time,*—during the succeeding periods of its formation, and when its existences lived and moved as the denizens of primeval oceans" (p. 219). In this imaginative sweep, the geologist encompasses what Tennyson calls the "terrible Muses,"[16] terrible to think about: the wastes of time and space. Literary Victorians frequently dwelled upon such vastness, as did Carlyle who spoke of the "two grand fundamental world-enveloping Appearances, SPACE and TIME." Miller proves himself especially adept at invoking the power of time. In the most famous and most vivid passages of *The Old Red Sandstone* Miller achieves what Carlyle hoped for in *Sartor Resartus*: a magician's hat that would enable one to travel backward in time (chapter VIII, book III). As Herr Teufelsdröckh says, "Had we but the Time-annihilating Hat, to put on for once only, we should see ourselves in a World of Miracles."

A world of miracles, most assuredly, is what Hugh Miller finds. In his mind's eye, the beautiful but static fossils come alive again. For Miller, successive geologic eras become acts within a play; when each is over, the "curtain rises, and the scene is new" (p. 245). Amazingly, with Miller as a guide, the reader is invited to imagine himself walking through the forests of the past, breathing in "the rank stream of decaying vegetation" that "forms a thick blue haze" of "carbonic acid gas" (p. 257). Through the "ancient forest," Miller confidently says, "we pursue our walk" (p. 249). It is indeed, as Barber maintains, "precisely as a field naturalist setting out on an exploring expedition that he enters the geological past."[17]

The ancient geologic scenes in Hugh Miller's imagination exhibit the same qualities of particularity and boundless variety found in his contemporary landscapes. His assemblage of Silurian organisms is especially striking. These creatures lived in the period before the Old Red Sandstone fish appeared, the period so thoroughly documented by Sir Roderick Murchison in his 1838 scientific tome, *The Silurian System.* Rocks from the Silurian era show life to have existed on "four distinct platforms," all of them teeming with multifarious creatures. Miller scans each story of Siluria:

> Life abounded on these platforms, and in shapes the most wonderful. The peculiar encrinites of the group rose in miniature forests, and spread forth their sentient petals by millions and tens of millions amid the waters; vast ridges of corals, peopled by their innumerable builders,—numbers without number,—rose high amid the shallows; the chambered shells had become abundant,—the simpler testacea still more so; extinct forms of the graptolite or sea-pen existed by myriads.
>
> (p. 221)

Here no less than in the "denuded hollow" of the stream's ravine, nature teems with wonderfully autonomous forms. Petals are "sentient," and coral skeletons are "peopled" with living tenants. Everywhere Miller looks, nature is without limits: curious and strange organisms swim and wave by "millions," "myriads," "numbers without number." Life abounds. And even better, nature in its endless multiplication creates enduring monuments, works of meticulous beauty, "in shapes the most wonderful": chambered shells, vast ridges of coral, miniature petrified forests.

But these creatures pass away, and the history of the Old Red Sandstone period opens, Miller surmises, like the first scene in *The Tempest*—"amid thunders and lightnings, the roar of the wind" (p. 224). Fish take command of the seas, "which literally swarmed with life," including "miniature forests of algae, and . . . waters darkened by immense shoals of fish" (p. 226). Mysterious catastrophes at times overtake the ichthyolites. Miller envisions one such period, of disease or volcanic upheaval, and its aftermath:

> The period of death passed, and over the innumerable dead there settled a soft muddy sediment, that hid them from the light, bestowing upon them such burial as a November snowstorm bestows on the sere and blighted vegetation of the previous summer and autumn. For an

unknown space of time, represented in the formation by a deposit about fifty feet in thickness, the waters of the depopulated area seem to have remained devoid of animal life. A few scales and plates then begin to appear.

(p. 231)

These dreary, almost incomprehensible wastes of time and death Miller finds awesome to contemplate. The stretches of time are not entirely wastes, however, for nature continues its generation. With the naturalist's faith in variety, as well as the Christian's in God, Miller summarizes the process:

The process went on. Age succeeded age, and one stratum covered up another. Generations lived, died, and were entombed in the ever-growing depositions. Succeeding generations pursued their instincts by myriads, happy in existence, over the surface which covered the broken and perishing remains of their predecessors.

(p. 233)

Not only does God experiment, quite joyously it seems, with "an inexhaustible variety of design expatiated freely within the limits of the ancient type" (p. 233), but the animals themselves, although doomed to perish, enjoy themselves while alive. Like Gosse's microscopic animalcules, they are "happy in existence."

The assumption of happy fulfillment on the part of each minute creature rescues Miller's contemplation of the ages from despair. The spectacle can continue with its pageantry of form:

The curtain rises, and the scene is new. The myriads of the lower formation have disappeared, and we are surrounded, on an upper platform, by the existences of a later creation. There is sea all around, as before; and we find beneath a dark-coloured muddy bottom, thickly covered by a dwarf vegetation. . . . Forms of life essentially different career through the green depths, or creep over the ooze. Shoals of *Cephalaspides,* with their broad arrow-like heads and their slender angular bodies, feathered with fins, sweep past like clouds of cross-bow bolts in an ancient battle. We see the distinct gleam of scales, but the forms are indistinct and dim. . . . A huge crustacean, of uncouth proportions, stalks over the weedy bottom, or burrows in the hollows of the banks.

(p. 245)

Again, the paleontological panorama is graphically animated and convincing, thanks to Miller's characteristic devices: subjective plurality ("we see"), figurative language ("like clouds of cross-bow bolts"), and active, concrete diction. Within a sensory setting, of ooze, a weedy bottom, green light, and gleaming scales, mysterious fish and other creatures "career," "sweep," and "stalk."

With such charged description, Miller succeeds in evoking an air of portentous mystery. Readers feel irresistibly drawn into the remote geological past, as they

might be drawn into the jungle of the present by Darwin or Wallace or Bates. In the final few pages of his book, Miller rises to a crescendo of detail and drama, as he imagines the sea receding to make way for the thick vegetable riot on land that will eventually compact into coal. The transition from sea to land Miller achieves by projecting himself into a boat that approaches the shore. He thus conflates a change of time with one of space:

The water is fast shallowing. Yonder passes a broken branch, with the leaves still unwithered; and there floats a tuft of fern. Land, from the masthead! land! land!—a low shore thickly covered with vegetation. Huge trees of wonderful form stand out far into the water. There seems no intervening beach. A thick hedge of reeds, tall as the mast of pinnaces, runs along the deeper bays, like water-flags at the edge of a lake. A river of vast volume comes rolling from the interior, darkening the water for leagues with its slime and mud.

(p. 255)

Here the panoply of botanical forms, on a gigantic scale, is comparable only to deliberate works of art. Trees have "bright and glossy stems" that "seem rodded like Gothic columns," and their leaves are ranged in tiers, each resembling "a coronal wreath or an ancient crown."

As usual in Miller's scientific fantasies, the sheer quantity—not to mention diversity—of natural forms astonishes. Like the cubic inch of shale packed with mollusks, the jungle of bygone eons is crammed with curious specimens. The growth of the "vegetable kingdom" displays "amazing luxuriance" (p. 257). Organisms appear, "strangely-formed" (p. 256). Especially odd is one that swoops suddenly into view:

But what monster of the vegetable world comes floating down the stream,—now circling round in the eddies, now dancing on the ripple, now shooting down the rapid? It resembles a gigantic star-fish, or an immense coach-wheel divested of the rim.

(p. 256)

This truly bizarre plant, set off well by Miller's interrogative introduction, looks like some Rotifer or diatom that Philip Gosse might have sighted, but enlarged to monstrous size. Like a gigantic Rotifer, it displays ingenious appurtenances—cylinders, prickles, and "lance-like shoots."

In fact, one of the most interesting features of Miller's culminating sequence is his mention of the microscope. In O'Brien's story "The Diamond Lens," the protagonist longed to enter the microscopic world, temporarily deluded into thinking that the beautiful creatures there were compatible with his own size. Likewise, in the example I cited previously from Alfred Russel Wallace, the Malay people became terrified when looking through a microscope, assuming that the insects there illuminated had actually grown gigantic. For Hugh Miller, too, the wonders of nature on a microscopic scale can seem as tangible as those on a normal human scale. Size ranges are even interchangeable:

> And then these gigantic reeds!—are they not mere varieties of the common horse-tail of our bogs and morasses, magnified some sixty or a hundred times? Have we arrived at some such country as the continent visited by Gulliver, in which he found thickets of weeds and grass tall as woods of twenty years' growth, and lost himself amid a forest of corn fifty feet in height? The lesser vegetation of our own country,—reeds, mosses, and ferns,—seems here as if viewed through a microscope: the dwarfs have sprung up into giants.
>
> (p. 256)

Since the "lesser vegetation" of England did spring up, figuratively, into giants during the Fern Craze, it is appropriate that Miller points out how they literally reigned as giants in the past. The change of scale from gigantic to microscopic actually did take place in this instance. As Kingsley would say, nothing is impossible to nature.

As the author of such powerful passages as these, Hugh Miller captivated Victorian readers. They followed his geological narratives with rapt attention. They were willing even to follow him through the minute intricacies of serrated fish scales, if they were presented as astonishing particularities. So beloved did Miller become that his legions of admirers were stunned to learn that he had died by his own hand. In 1856, the last year of his life, Miller became increasingly agitated and fearful that robbers would break into and despoil his collections. He began to have hallucinations. After one especially terrifying vision, Hugh Miller scribbled a note to his wife saying that he could not bear the horror of his dream; what the horror was, he did not say. Then he shot himself.[18] Perhaps all the sepulchral imagery of his geology books presaged his embrace of death. In any case, the circumstances created a most difficult situation for his admirers: suicide was a sin. A public outcry insisted that Miller be spared that stigma. Was it not unthinkable that such a hero could have deliberately killed himself? Indeed it was. Miller was declared temporarily insane at the time of his death and granted Christian burial.

Hugh Miller advanced the science of geology by his patient research and careful speculation. But he advanced the cause of natural history as well, since geology, his chosen science, was for him preeminently an aesthetic and evocative study. Miller's widow remarked on this in her introduction to his posthumous volume, ***Popular Geology***: "My dear husband, did, indeed, bring to his science all that fondness, while he found in it much of that kind of enjoyment, which we are wont to associate

exclusively with the love of art."[19] Miller himself, puzzling about the antagonism sometimes found between science and poetry, unequivocally declared them brothers. Along with its particularities of crinoid and fish scale, geology can claim the evocative sweep—the poetry—of nature's variety in time. Just before his own death, Miller thought about that terrible Muse of poetry:

> The stony science, with buried creations for its domains, and half an eternity charged with its annals, possesses its realms of dim and shadowy fields, in which troops of fancies already walk like disembodied ghosts in the old fields of Elysium, and which bid fair to be quite dark and uncertain enough for all the purposes of poesy for centuries to come.[20]

Firm in his conception of the poetry of the "stony science," Hugh Miller garnered a wide audience for his works, an audience appreciative of this clear thinker whose "relation to nature and the knowledge of nature" was yet "above all a personal and emotional one."[21] Personal, artistic, emotional responses to rocks and fossil fish—these mark Miller as a naturalist, and ***The Old Red Sandstone*** as natural history discourse.

Notes

1. Herbert Spencer, "Education: Intellectual, Moral, and Physical," in *The Humboldt Library of Popular Science Literature,* Nos. 1-12 (New York: The Humboldt Publishing Co., n.d.), p. 284.

2. Lynn Barber, *The Heyday of Natural History: 1820-1870* (Garden City, NY: Doubleday and Company, Inc., 1980), p. 230.

3. Barber, p. 236.

4. Charles Kingsley, *Glaucus; or, the Wonders of the Shore* (London: Macmillan and Company, Limited, 1903), p. 218.

5. Spencer, p. 271.

6. Dennis R. Dean, "'Through Science to Despair': Geology and the Victorians," in *Victorian Science and Victorian Values: Literary Perspectives,* ed. James Paradis and Thomas Postlewait, Annals of the New York Academy of Sciences, vol. 360 (New York: The New York Academy of Sciences, 1981), p. 120.

7. Barber, p. 225.

8. Dean, p. 120.

9. Kingsley, *Glaucus,* p. 11.

10. Both quoted in Barber, p. 230.

11. Barber, p. 231.

12. Julian M. Drachman, *Studies in the Literature of Natural Science* (New York: The Macmillan Company, 1930), p. 131.

13. Barber, p. 231.

14. Hugh Miller, *The Old Red Sandstone; or, New Walks in an Old Field* (London: J. M. Dent and Co., n.d.), p. 114. Further page citations are made within the text.

15. A selection from *The Old Red Sandstone* is among those anthologized in one recent collection of geological literature, *Language of the Earth,* ed. Frank H. T. Rhodes and Richard O. Stone (New York: Pergamon Press, 1981). Miller's selection, however, is included not for its scientific value, but rather in the section "Geologists Are Also Human," pp. 36-41.

16. Noted in Dean, p. 115. Try as I might, I have been unable to track down the source of this particular quotation. However, Tennyson was fascinated by astronomy and geology, and recollections of the poet by those who knew him prove that he often mused on the vastness of geological time. For example, William Allingham quotes Tennyson as exclaiming: "Look at that hill (pointing to the one before the large window), it's four hundred millions of years old;—think of that!" In Norman Page, ed., *Tennyson: Interviews and Recollections* (Totowa, NJ: Barnes & Noble Books, 1983), p. 53. Another acquaintance reported of the poet: "This led him to speak of prehistoric things, and of the wonders which geology had brought to light. He referred to the period of the Weald, when there was a mighty estuary, like that of the Ganges, where we then stood; and when gigantic lizards, the iguanodon, etc., were the chief of living things." In Page, p. 180.

17. Barber, p. 231.

18. Carroll Lane Fenton and Mildred Adams Fenton, *Giants of Geology* (Garden City, NY: Doubleday & Company, Inc., 1952), p. 212.

19. From the Introductory Résumé to Hugh Miller, *Popular Geology: A Series of Lectures Read Before the Philosophical Institution of Edinburgh, With Descriptive Sketches from a Geologist's Portfolio* (Boston: Gould and Lincoln, 1859), p. 12.

20. Miller, *Popular Geology,* p. 127.

21. Drachman, p. 132.

Harry Hanham and Michael Shortland (essay date 1995)

SOURCE: Hanham, Harry and Michael Shortland. Introduction to *Hugh Miller's Memoir: From Stonemason to Geologist,* edited by Michael Shortland, pp. 1-86. Edinburgh: Edinburgh University Press, 1995.

[*In the following excerpt, Hanham and Shortland discuss Miller's autobiography and its relationship to the emerging field of self-help literature.*]

AUTOBIOGRAPHICAL CAREERS

MILLER AND PRINCIPAL BAIRD

Miller had been experimenting with prose before the **Poems** appeared. The task he had set himself was to reconcile the easy colloquial style of his own juvenile stories with the classical style of the eighteenth century, which he considered the only acceptable style for a writer of serious prose. By 1829 he had already written a number of experimental stories and articles, some of which were later published in the *Inverness Courier.*[1] But it was several years before his prose style settled down. Told in October 1834 that old Baron Hume the jurist had commended the excellence of his 'classical style', Miller responded at once (unusual for him). The response, to Miss Dunbar, raises, like Miller's expressed hope that his **Poems** would bring him employment, questions about his own sincerity:

> I owe my merit chiefly to accident;—to my having kept company with the older English writers,—the Addisons, Popes, and Robertsons of the last century at a time when I had no opportunity of becoming acquainted with the authors of the present time.[2]

Was Hugh Miller really too poor and isolated to have had access to current authors, or is this a piece of self-dramatising? Obviously the latter since Miller in his memoir describes provincial Scottish culture as rich, vibrant and accessible. Presumably one of his objects in presenting himself to Miss Dunbar in this manner was to attract patronage, another to legitimise his rejection of modernity. Miller's chosen subject was the life of his native Cromarty. He had a wealth of anecdote and story to draw on, and every few weeks a new incident in the bay or out at sea, or in one of the neighbouring parishes, could be added to his stock. Moreover, life in Cromarty was highly routinised, as it usually is in small towns; thus any new or unusual event stood out clearly against its background.

Miller was soon diverted from his Cromarty stories by outside intervention. The Reverend George Husband Baird, who happened to be in Inverness in the summer of 1829, asked to see the stonemason-poet. Baird, then sixty-eight years old, had been Principal of the University of Edinburgh since 1793. He was by any reckoning an undistinguished occupant of the office, having risen to it not by contributing to learning but by having married the Lord Provost's daughter. Nevertheless, Baird had been on good terms with both Robert Burns and Sir Walter Scott, and had edited some verses of the eighteenth-century shepherd-poet Michael Bruce.[3] He was, moreover, known by repute all over Scotland as a firm supporter of the extension of Highland education.[4]

Some months later, Miller described his meeting with Baird to a woman who had taken an interest in his career:

On the Saturday after the last of my letters on the Herring Fishery had appeared in the Courier, I received a note from my friend the Editor stating that Principal Baird who was then at Inverness was desirous of having some conversation with me. He added further that . . . such an opportunity ought not to be neglected. I accordingly went to Inverness and was introduced to the Principal. At first I felt how justly I could appreciate the feeling of the Jewish Spies 'We were as grasshoppers before them,' but the singular kindness of the reverend gentleman soon restored me to a proper confidence. He related to me anecdotes of some of the eminent literati of both the past and the present age. he had been the friend and correspondent of Burns, and the editor of the poems of Michael Bruce. The offers he made me were startling. He proposed that I should accompany him to Edinburgh; he asked me whether I did not stand in need of money, adding that his purse and credit were heartily at my service; he said he would introduce me, if I desired it, to Professor Wilson, as a suitable writer for Blackwoods Magazine; he informed me, too, that he belonged to a Committee of the General Assembly formed for the purpose of making some alterations in the sacred poetry of the Church and some additions to it; and then asked me whether I would not become a contributor. I was much flattered by his expressing it as his opinion that my writings betrayed few of the faults incident to an imperfect education; and by his requesting me to state to him by letter the manner in which I had attained my skill in the art of composition. This request as it fell in with a previously formed intention of writing a memoir of 'Four years of the life of a Journeyman-Mason' has furnished me with employment for the greater part of . . . last winter.[5]

The main point of Baird's offer of sponsorship in Edinburgh was to enable Miller to become a more skilful writer. In suggesting that Miller compose a letter explaining how he came to write so well in spite of the deficiencies of his education, Baird clearly had in mind a brief, analytical account that might be useful in his efforts to promote rural education. Miller chose instead to see in the request an excuse for writing his autobiography, a project he had already been contemplating. The autobiography took the form of two letters to Principal Baird, but its whole character suggests that Miller had mapped out much of the plan well in advance. In a later account of the meeting, Miller misleadingly describes Baird as requesting something approximating a full-fledged autobiography.[6]

To judge by the surviving correspondence, Miller failed to give Baird a clear answer to his offer of help. Indeed, Baird regarded the first installment of the autobiography, however lengthy, as non-responsive, and gently said so in his letter of thanks:

But you say nothing in your letter as to my suggestion when at Inverness of giving your busy hours to your profession here during the winter, and your leisure hours to reading books, and playing your pen, and extending your acquaintance with the living as well as with the dead world of literature.[7]

To this query Miller returned a lengthy and ingenious answer: he had found a way of combining literature and stonecutting in the north of Scotland. He could not be sure of his reception in Edinburgh, and might find it impossible there to preserve the economic independence that gave him a sense of security as a writer:

I have at present several pieces of work on hand mostly tombstones which will keep me busy for the greater part of the winter; and I have besides some prospect of procuring employment next spring in the churchyards of Inverness; where I trust I shall hardly meet with any very formidable rivalry in the art of inscription cutting. . . .

From my engagements here and at Inverness I cannot avail myself of your kind invitation to spend the winter at Edinburgh, but I appreciate its value, and feel grateful for your kindness. My acquaintance with the dead world of literature is very imperfect, and it is still more so with the living; instead, however, of regretting this I think it best to congratulate myself on the much pleasure which from this circumstance there yet remains for me to enjoy. If I live eight or ten years longer, and if my taste for reading continues I shall, I trust, pass through a great many paradises of genius. Half the creations of Scott are still before me, and more than half those of every other modern poet. But though I can appreciate the value of an opportunity of perusing the works of such authors, there are opportunities of a different kind to be enjoyed in Edinburgh, which from a rather whimsical bent of mind I would value more highly. My curiosity is never more active than when it has the person of a great man for its object, nor have I felt more delight in anything whatever than in associating in my mind when that curiosity was gratified my newly acquired idea of the personal appearance of such a man, with the ideas I had previously entertained of his character and genius. When I resided in the vicinity of Edinburgh I have sauntered for whole hours opposite the house of Sir Walter Scott in the hope of catching a glimpse of his person, and several times when some tall robust man has passed me in the streets, I have enquired of my companions whether that was not Prof. Wilson. But perhaps I am more ambitious now than I was five years ago. Perhaps I would not be satisfied with merely seeing such men, and I am yet aware that I have not yet done any thing which entitles me to the notice of the eminent though in one instance I have been so fortunate as to attract it. I must achieve at least a little of what I have hoped to achieve before I go to Edinburgh. But even this intention must not be followed up with too great eagerness. . . . I must be careful least by acquiring too exclusive a bent towards literary pursuit I contract a distaste for those employments which though not very pleasing in themselves are in my case at least intimately connected with happiness. I do not think I could be happy without being independent, and I cannot be independent except as a mechanic.[8]

Thinking now about the manner in which Baird approached Miller, there is nothing strange about Miller's ready response. Miller, who had steadfastly refused help from his uncles, seems once again to have feared a kind of intellectual take-over, a complete possession and domestication. Baird, to his credit, did not lose interest in Miller after this stiff-necked rebuff. Whenever Miller was in central Scotland, Baird welcomed him to his home; and for the rest of his life, Miller was an occasional visitor and correspondent. Indeed, one of Miller's most interesting letters describes a visit to Baird when the old man was prostrate with illness and grief at the extravagance (Miller suggests criminal extravagance) of his son.

What did Baird think of Miller's manuscript? He never saw it complete, since the second installment was lost on the way to Edinburgh. His reaction to the first part, however, was not more than polite. Acknowledging receipt of the manuscript, which was accompanied by a copy of Miller's letters on the herring fishery, he wrote:

> Believe me that both of these have at once confirmed and increased my estimate of the claims which I had previously conceived you to possess on public estimation.
>
> I shall wait with anxiety for Chapter second of your life, detailing your intellectual and poetical history from the time of your 'finishing your school education,' and your 'boyish waywardness.' Chapter first resembles the deep dark cavern into which you and your young friend took the desperate, downward, twelve feet leap;—Chapter second will resemble, I doubt not, that cavern as it afterwards appeared 'crusted on with a white stone resembling marble.' I have a telescopic view of this result similar to what you had when looking to the sea and opposite coast from the cavern's inmost extremity.[9]

Nor did Baird's tone change on reflection. A later letter simply says, 'I am gratified at learning that you are obligingly proceeding with your interesting autobiography.'[10] Two years later Baird wrote to ask whether Miller had any objection to the first part of his manuscript 'being referred to in one of the literary journals, and parts of it printed therein?'[11]

Baird's query about publication sent Miller back to his manuscript again. He was of two minds about its quality, and began to show it to his friends with a view to publication. The only other reaction to Miller's autobiography that has been preserved is outspoken. Miss Dunbar of Boath was belatedly shown the two parts of the manuscript in 1833 and responded candidly. She found it exciting reading, but intensely disliked the evidence it gave of obstinacy and willfulness. 'I was often angry with you', she observes. She also found the references to prostitutes towards the end of the narrative distasteful.

> Every page, every paragraph has to me an interest, a novelty, a freshness, in both the things told and the manner of telling them, that I never found in any work of the kind before. I devoured it, and yet prolonged the perusal of it for several days; and am now sorry that it is done. . . . How did Principal Baird receive the manuscript, and what is he to do with it? I was often angry with you in the course of the narrative. Why were you so very wayward, when you could have been so much otherwise? Why did you so cruelly disappoint your excellent uncles when you could so easily have more than realised their most sanguine anticipations? How much pain have you not given to hearts that were fond and proud of you. . . . Your dreams, your digressions, your anecdotes, your descriptions, have all a rare interest, and your style I deem beautifully correct,—but there is one objectionable passage [about prostitutes]. The fact it conveys is strikingly illustrative, but you have sufficiently established your argument without it; and it is not in accordance with the pure character of the rest.[12]

Did Principal Baird see in the narrative the deficits of character that Miss Dunbar saw? If so, one can understand why he did not press the wayward and headstrong mechanic to move south. Miller would clearly come to Edinburgh in his own good time, but not before. The old man was prepared to be polite and wait. As for Miller, he took Miss Dunbar's comments as encouraging, and began to plan revisions. 'I am glad you like my memoir', he wrote:

> It is a simple story of little promise; what indeed could be expected from the subject of it; but I have formed a plan regarding it which may convert it into a very readable sort of thing. I am not vain enough to think that it can have much interest as a memoir of the life and education of an obscure mechanic, but I have seen a good deal of character as exhibited both in classes and individuals, and from a rather peculiar point of observation, and the study of character is perhaps of all others the most popular. What I purpose therefore is to recast the whole narrative, and break it into chapters, to add a great deal and subtract a little, to occupy in it as I have done in life the part rather of one who has observed than of one who has acted, and then, if I have succeeded to the satisfaction of my friends and of myself, to commit it to the Press.[13]

The proposed revisions took many more years. The *Scenes and Legends* demanded attention in 1833 and gave Miller great trouble until its publication in 1835. Miller simply never found the time to return to the memoirs until they became the basis for *My Schools and Schoolmasters* in 1854, nearly a quarter-century later.

But we may well wonder why it was that Miller had already been mapping out an autobiography. For he was also at work on the first stages of the *Scenes and Legends.* Are we to use what we know about Miller's relations with his parents to help us? If so, it seems reasonable to conclude that the two projects, the autobiography (that is, the memoir published here) and the *Scenes and Legends* reflect his different loyalties to his father and mother. The memoir, which, like *My Schools and*

Schoolmasters, makes almost no mention of mother, sisters or womenfolk, stands for the active side of Miller's life, the life dedicated to the emulation of his father. The **Scenes and Legends,** by contrast—a work of the Highlands, rather than the Lowlands—belong to the fairy-tale world of his mother. Indeed, Lydia Miller attributes the latter book directly to her influence: 'From his mother Hugh undoubtedly drew almost all the materials for his **Scenes and Legends**'.[14] Neither work is exclusively father or mother oriented. But if we regard the two books as forming part of a single process of composition, we can understand both the masculine tone of the first autobiography and its concentration on a relatively narrow range of topics. Hugh Miller is a storyteller in both books, but in the first autobiography he plays down the miraculous, which figures so strongly in the **Scenes and Legends.**

While at work on his letters for Principal Baird, Miller received a letter from Isaac Forsyth of Elgin, who had helped him to publish his poems. His reply to Forsyth constitutes a sort of supplement to the letters to Baird, explaining his position generally and trying—on the whole vainly—to integrate his work on the **Scenes and Legends** with what he had recently finished writing in the memoir. It is reproduced in Appendix I, pp. 231-4.

SELF-MADE MEN

The working-class autobiography came into being in parallel with the formation of working-class conscience. At the beginning of the nineteenth century agricultural labourers, factory workers, artisans, sailors and the vast population of the marginally employed did not recognise themselves as belonging to the same economic and social class. Millhands did not feel any solidarity with farmers, nor stonemasons to wheelwrights. But by the 1820s, an immense change had occurred. Inspired by such writers as Thomas Paine, radicals founded corresponding societies and trade unions, as well as a vibrant and outspoken press—all of which, in E. P. Thompson's classic formulation, 'made' the working class.[15] In this context of unprecedented self-awareness, the working-class autobiography became a means both of self-expression and of contributing to political and social identity.[16]

The earliest working-class autobiographies appear uncertain of their audience and their own idiom. On occasion they touch on a harsh truth or two, but rudimentary political analysis and lengthy descriptions of village life were typically held together with the kind of serviceable but unsightly filler that builders call 'clunch'. In a vituperative survey of ten recently published autobiographies, the *Quarterly Review* in 1827 deplored the autobiographical urge that seemed to encourage 'every driveller to do his Memorabilia', resulting in a 'mania for this garbage of Confessions, and Recollections, and

Reminiscences'.[17] Not until the 1840s did the possibilities of working-class autobiography begin to be explored in depth and with literary distinction.

Autobiographies of working-class poets seem to have developed somewhat earlier than political autobiographies. This may be attributable to the support of Robert Southey, the poet laureate, who went to considerable lengths to encourage working-class poets to publish both their verses and their life stories.[18] While such poetry was often treated with condescension, the lives of poets, even 'persons in humble life and of defective education', were judged capable of producing interesting memoirs.[19] The Lancashire weaver-poet Samuel Bamford's *Passages in the Life of a Radical* (1844) met with such commercial success that he recounted his childhood in another volume four years later.[20] In 1848 Alexander Somerville's well-known *Autobiography of a Working Man* appeared in weekly installments in the *Manchester Examiner* before publication in book form under the authorship of 'One Who Has Whistled at the Plough'.

The Society for the Diffusion of Useful Knowledge, which drew much of its inspiration from the Scottish tradition of the 'lad o' pairts', took as its working credo that there were working men all over the country anxious to improve themselves. One of its publications, George Lillie Craik's *The Pursuit of Knowledge under Difficulties* (1830), attempted to tell the story of successful self-made men through the ages.[21] Despite its dullness the most successful volume in 'The Library of Entertaining Knowledge', it prefigured Samuel Smiles's much better-known *Self-Help* of a generation later.[22] *Chambers's Edinburgh Journal* also took an interest in the careers of self-made men, because the Chambers brothers considered it their mission to supply working men with useful as well as entertaining knowledge.[23]

Miller, who was constantly on the look-out for yardsticks by which to measure his own achievements, was surely aware that he was working in one of the boldest and most innovative literary modes. The one first-rate model that Hugh Miller might have learned from, he probably had not seen. This was the short autobiography of William Gifford, first editor of the *Quarterly Review,* which appeared as a preface to his edition of Juvenal in 1802 and was later printed in a popular collection of memoirs and letters.[24] Gifford, like Miller, was the son of a seaman who died when he was young, and he too had been brought up in a remote country town. Having developed literary tastes, Gifford's boyhood ambition was to become a schoolmaster, but he was instead bound by his guardian as assistant to a sailor and then as apprentice to a shoemaker. When his literary abilities became apparent in his early twenties, he was rescued from his apprenticeship by a perceptive surgeon and in due course sent to Oxford. Much of the appeal of Gifford's autobiography is that it is the story of a man already successful and accustomed to writing with a certain polish. Concise and elegant, there is nothing about it of the working man trying to make good, nor for that matter of the self-made man risen to eminence who is 'studious to conceal the poverty of his early childhood'.[25]

In his memoir, Gifford was anxious to explain how his translation of Juvenal had come to be written and why it had taken him so long to complete. He did not need to establish his credentials: he already had powerful friends from his Anti-Jacobin days and was a literary lion in his own right. Miller, by contrast, was still working as a stonemason in the graveyard at Cromarty. His was the voice of the working men whom the Society for the Diffusion of Useful Knowledge was trying to reach.

Miller seems to have set greater store on the anecdotes and reminiscences of his old school friends than on those of published writers. When his schoolmate Alexander Finlay wrote to him from Jamaica in 1836, reporting that he had made good as the proprietor of the Twickenham Park Estate at Spanish Town, Miller was able to reply with a comprehensive account of their old classmates. Five had died, three had become shopkeepers, one an unsuccessful painter, one a clergyman, and one a broken-down and disreputable failure. Of all their classmates, only Miller himself, John Swanson the minister, and Alexander Finlay the West Indian proprietor had in any sense made good.[26] Both were, in different ways, important to Miller.

John Swanson was Miller's lifelong friend and, towards the end of Miller's life, one of the few people he regularly visited. *The Cruise of the Betsey* is the record of a sojourn with Swanson, who, as minister of the Small Isles, used a small sailing craft to visit his isolated parishioners. Alexander Finlay, having dropped out of Miller's life for many years, suddenly re-emerged with the letter from Jamaica in 1836: he had come across an article by Miller in *Chambers's Edinburgh Journal.* Miller's response shows him at his most informal, rejoicing in the chance to relive his childhood and astoundingly well-informed about his schoolmates (see Appendix II, pp. 235-9).

Hugh Miller's correspondence is full of enquiries about the careers of working-class writers. He was particularly interested in the career of Allan Cunningham, a stonemason like himself, who had settled in London where he supervised the workshops of Sir Francis Chantrey, the distinguished sculptor, and wrote prolifically on the side. Miller also enquired avidly about his contemporaries in the north of Scotland. A minor writer for the *Inverness Courier* named James Calder he discovered to be the parish schoolmaster at Canisbay in Caithness, but Calder was reluctant to write about himself. Miss Dunbar of Boath's protégé, John Strahan, the weaver-poet of Forres, was more forthcoming. The two men were linked by the interest of Miss Dunbar and by the fact that both had published a volume of poems in 1829. Miller rather liked the poems in Strahan's *Walter and Emma: a Tale of Bothwell Bridge, and Other Poems.* But Strahan's career mattered more to Miller than his poetry, and with the help of Miss Dunbar he succeeded in extracting from Strahan an autobiography that paralleled his own. This narrative which offers us a glimpse of a different type of working-class career from Miller's, appears as Appendix III, pp. 240-5.

The memoir that Miller wrote for Baird clearly determined the shape of his career as a writer: autobiography became his principal literary form. The memoir, as we have seen, was reworked as ***My Schools and Schoolmasters.*** ***The Old Red Sandstone*** is the story of Miller's discovery of the fossils of the old red sandstone. ***First Impressions of England*** and ***The Cruise of the Betsey*** record the events of two of Miller's summer holidays. Only in ***The Foot-prints of the Creator*** and some of his last works did Miller move away from autobiography, and even then not very far.

As a literary figure, then, Miller must be considered primarily as a man who found in his own experiences sufficient material for a considerable number of books. Indeed, critics who have seen him primarily as a man of science or as a churchman have missed a key to Miller's life. Miller was a man devoted to the maintenance of his personal integrity, and he could maintain it only by constantly refreshing himself from the springs of his own personal experience.

The price that he paid for using autobiography as his medium was considerable. Though always direct and honest in his writing, Miller increasingly cast his work in didactic form. The habit took hold with his articles on geology for *Chambers's Edinburgh Journal* (see Appendix IV), which were overtly aimed at encouraging working men to take up scientific pursuits. By the time of ***My Schools and Schoolmasters,*** Miller was writing as an established man of letters anxious to lend a helping hand. When he was not thinking about himself as an institution, his writing was still as unforced and natural as in his first autobiography. But ***My Schools and Schoolmasters*** suffers from Miller's greater acquaintance with self-improvement books like *The Pursuit of Knowledge under Difficulties.* It is still a remarkable book, but one wishes for more spontaneity, more of the directness of youth. One is conscious of reading a Georgian story dressed up in Victorian clothes. There is even some bowdlerisation of the first autobiography: prostitutes, for instance, no longer 'disfigure' Miller's pages.[27]

More serious for Miller was the distortion of his own history. He was driven to present himself as a Scottish 'lad o' pairts' who by dint of his own exertions had risen from obscurity in society to move on his own terms among the rich and the great. *The Old Red Sandstone* opens with an exhortation to the working man to follow him and become a geologist. *My Schools and Schoolmasters* is dressed up as a textbook of self-help. And the publisher of a cheap edition of Miller's works had no doubt about how he should advertise them:

> To the higher and more cultivated classes of society he appeals by the purity and elegance of his style, as well as by his remarkable powers of description, and his profound knowledge of the marvels of nature. To the humbler classes and the working man, the story of his life—himself originally a working man in the strictest sense of the word, pushing his way upward to the distinguished position which he attained . . . cannot fail to prove of special value.[28]

Miller's autobiographical writings demonstrate very clearly that he chose the 'lad o' pairts' motif, less because it corresponded to the facts of his career than because it supplied him with a useful disguise. Like the great plaid he wore out-of-doors (as much, one suspects, from desire to flout the conventions of dress as from habit), the trappings of the 'lad o' pairts' gave him, so he thought, the greatest possible individual freedom.

Much is explained if we approach Miller at the time of his memoir not as an artisan determined to do well in the world but as a shy, sensitive man of quite unusual diffidence. To be an artisan was to be capable of enjoying an obscure and independent life outside the normal conventions of polite society. Hence Miller's declaration in refusing Principal Baird's offer to bring him to Edinburgh, that 'I do not think I could be happy without being independent, and I cannot be independent except as a mechanic'.[29] To be a mechanic may not have been gratifying in itself, but it did assure Miller effective independence.

There were also pressing psychological reasons why Miller chose to remain a mechanic. Miller suffered from an acute case of what he called 'Diffidence'. When in 1834 Miss Dunbar of Boath reproached him for not visiting her at Forres, Miller pleaded not pressure of work (as he had done on previous occasions) but that same diffidence:

> I shall . . . give you a full view of what you are yet only acquainted with in part. In a case like the present it is policy to be candid;—Is it not partial views and half glimpses that convert bushes and stones into ghosts and witches?

> There are a few excellent people in Cromarty whose company I deem very agreeable and whose friendship I value very highly, but whose thresholds without a spe-

cial invitation I never cross. Why? Just because diffidence tells me that I am a poor mechanic, regarded with a kind perhaps, but still a compassionate feeling, and that if I but take the slightest commonest liberty of social intercourse it is at the peril of being deemed forward and obtrusive. Well, I receive an invitation and accept of it. I come in contact with persons whom I like very much; the better feelings are awakened within me; the intellectual machine is set a working; and I communicate my ideas as they rise. 'You chattering blockhead,' says diffidence, the moment I return home, 'what right pray had *you* to engross so much of the conversation tonight? You are a pretty fellow to be sure to set up for a Sir Oracle!—Well you had better take care next time. Next time comes, and I am exceedingly taciturn. 'Pray Mr Block,' says diffidence, the instant she catches me alone, 'what fiend tempted you to go and eat the Lady's bread and butter to night, when you had determined prepense not to tender her so much as a single idea in return? A handsome piece of furniture truly to be stuck up at the side of a tea table!—Perhaps, however, you were too good for your company and wished to make them feel that you thought so.'[30]

Contemporaries, encountering a tall, physically powerful, and determined man, found it hard to believe in Miller's diffidence. Determination, recklessness, even ferocity, perhaps—but not diffidence. In his years as a banker in Cromarty he took to carrying pistols to protect his firm's money and the habit persisted after he finally moved to Edinburgh. His friends never knew, when they met him in an out-of-the-way place, whether to expect a cheerful welcome or a pair of pistols at the ready.

When Miller did finally thrust diffidence aside and give up being a mechanic, he was fortified by the example of his cousin George Munro. It was Munro's career that had first encouraged him to turn stonemason, and it was again Munro who emboldened him to give up stonemasonry. When Miller went south to become a banker, he found Munro already established nearby as an engineer of high repute. George Munro also seemed to have discovered the secret of personal independence, never worrying about what people thought about him. While Hugh Miller brooded and fretted lest people think he was merely an ignorant mechanic, George Munro went gaily about his business.

Miller never attained such gaiety. The independence he sought through autobiography—from the pressures of his childhood, the conflicting values of his parents, the values of his workmates—was, alas, only a paper independence. Miller remained bound all his life to his childhood, his parents, even his workmates.

Notes

1. For example, 'Antiquities at Cromarty' (*Inverness Courier,* 29 April 1829), 'A Noble Smuggler' (*Inverness Courier,* 13 May 1829), and 'Gipseys' (*Inverness Courier,* 23 September 1829).

2. Miller to Miss Dunbar of Boath, 25 October 1834, *LB* [Hugh Miller's *Letterbook,* Library of New College, Edinburgh] 114.

3. D. B. Horn, *A Short History of the University of Edinburgh,* Edinburgh, 1967, p. 102.

4. For more about Baird (1761-1840), see Alexander Grant, *The Story of the University of Edinburgh during its First Three Hundred Years,* 2 vols, London, 1882, II, pp. 270-1.

5. Miller to Mrs Allardyce, 12 February 1830, *LB,* 15.

6. [Hugh Miller] *My Schools [and Schoolmasters; or The Story of My Education,* Edinburgh, 1910] p. 448.

7. Baird to Miller, 4 November 1829, *LB,* 2.

8. Miller to Baird, 9 December 1829, *LB,* 5.

9. Baird to Miller, 4 November 1829, *LB,* 2.

10. Baird to Miller, 6 January 1830, *LB,* 9.

11. Baird to Miller, 14 February 1832, *LB,* 44.

12. Miss Dunbar to Miller, [January/February 1833?], *LB,* 51.

13. Miller to Miss Dunbar, 12 March 1833, *LB,* 52.

14. Bayne, [*The Life and Letters of*] *Hugh Miller,* [2 vols, London, 1871] I, p. 17.

15. E. P. Thompson, *The Making of the English Working Class,* Harmondsworth, 1977.

16. The variety and number of working-class autobiographies is indicated by the first volume of John Burnett, David Vincent, and David Mayall (eds), *The Autobiography of the Working Class: an Annotated Critical Bibliography,* 3 vols, Brighton, 1984-9.

17. Pages 149 and 164 of [James Lockhart], 'Autobiography', *Quarterly Review,* 35, 1827, pp. 149-65

18. The same year that Lockhart's review appeared, John Jones, a 'poor, humble, uneducated domestic', wrote to Southey seeking encouragement for his poetry. Southey not only responded immediately but arranged to publish Jones' verses and autobiography, and studies of other working-class poets, including the shoemaker James Woodhouse and 'the milkwoman of Bristol', Ann Yearsley. See John Jones, *Attempts in Verse . . . with an Introductory Essay . . . by Robert Southey,* London, 1831, pp. 1 and 171-80.

19. Page 81 of [T. H. Lister], 'Attempts at Verse', *Edinburgh Review,* 54, 1831, pp. 69-84.

20. Bamford's *Passages* appeared in parts between 1840 and 1844 before publication in two volumes in 1844; his *Early Days* was printed in 1848-9.

21. G. L. Craik, *The Pursuit of Knowledge under Difficulties; Illustrated by Anecdotes,* 2 vols, London, 1830-1.

22. Smiles claimed to have been greatly influenced by Craik's book. See his *Autobiography,* London, 1905, pp. 325-6. On the popularity of *The Pursuit of Knowledge* and its many editions, see David Vincent's brilliant work, *Bread, Knowledge and Freedom: A Study of Nineteenth-century Working Class Autobiography,* London, 1981, p. 144.

23. In radical circles, too, working men were enjoined to create a literature of their own, to help them acquire social and economic justice, as well as cultural recognition. See Martha Vicinus, *The Industrial Muse: A Study of Nineteenth Century British Working-class Literature,* London, 1974.

24. William Gifford (ed.), *The Satires of Decimus Junius Juvenalis,* London, 1802; John Nichols, *Illustrations of the Literary History of the Eighteenth Century, Consisting of Authentic Memoirs and Original Letters of Eminent Persons,* 6 vols, London, 1817-31, 6, pp. 14-28.

25. Anon., 'Gifford's Translation of Juvenal', *Monthly Review,* 40, 1803, 1-21, p. 2.

26. See Alexander Finlay to Miller, 14 August 1836, *LB,* 173 and Miller to Finlay, 15 October 1836, *LB,* 174.

27. *My Schools,* p. 326.

28. Leaflet issued by William P. Nimmo, Miller's Edinburgh publisher, c. 1869.

29. Miller to Baird, 9 December [1829], *LB,* 5.

30. Miller to Miss Dunbar of Boath, [March 1833], *LB,* 56.

James G. Paradis (essay date 1996)

SOURCE: Paradis, James G. "The Natural Historian as Antiquary of the World: Hugh Miller and the Rise of Literary Natural History." In *Hugh Miller and the Controversies of Victorian Science,* edited by Michael Shortland, pp. 122-49. Oxford: Clarendon Press, 1996.

[*In the following essay, Paradis examines* Scenes and Legends, The Old Red Sandstone *and* Footprints of the Creator.]

GEOLOGICAL AESTHETICS

Standing in the Newcastle town museum on his English ramble during the rainy autumn of 1845, Hugh Miller reflected upon the extensive geological fragments and Anglo-Roman antiquities, collected from the countryside near Hadrian's Wall:

As I passed, in the geologic apartment, from the older Silurian to the newer Tertiary, and then on from the newer Tertiary to the votive tablets, sacrificial altars, and sepulchral memorials of the Anglo-Roman gallery, I could not help regarding them as all belonging to one department. The antiquities piece on in natural sequence to the geology; and it seems but rational to indulge in the same sort of reasonings regarding them. They are fossils of an extinct order of things, newer than the Tertiary,—of an extinct race,—of an extinct religion

(Miller 1855, p. 35).

Geological and antiquarian objects shared the medium of rock, the substance that Miller knew intimately from his youth on the northern Scottish seacoast and his years as quarrier, stonemason, and monument cutter. Its shapes, compositions, and uses had been the preoccupations of his early years as an itinerant laborer, and we see Miller here fascinated with the inscribing forces that give meaning to the rock, forces now fossilized in the rubble of extinction.

Passing by rail on to Durham, Miller finds himself at dusk in a downpour peering at the great gloomy cathedral. Among the glistening tombstones, the familiar objects of his prior craft, he pauses before an ancient blue limestone slab of a thousand years, its carved face worn to a mound, the folds of its robe now but a few faint ridges. And then, peering still closer, Miller finds 'an immensely earlier sepulture' older by three times as many years as there are days in the thousand years of the tombstone (1855, p. 39). Nature inscribes much more indelibly than art her monuments of the dead, he observes, as he finds the tiny zoophyte fossils of *Cyathophyllum fungites* embedded at every angle in the stone. 'Never was there epitaph of human composition so scrupulously just to the real character of the dead', he concludes. Here, we see Miller in his true element, standing in the eroding rain in the presence of the artefact, the fossil remnant, and the darkening cathedral.

If Miller's view that geological and antiquarian inquiry lay on a historical continuum drew on his special insight as a craftsman of stone, the association of the two pursuits had many precedents. Older natural history writers like Gilbert White regarded natural history and antiquities as part of a common background of the 'productions' of remote times, the natural and cultural states interpenetrating one another (1876, p. 3). In the 'advertisement' to his *Natural History,* White advocated the pursuit of '*parochial history*', which, he held, 'ought to consist of natural productions, as well as antiquities' (1876, p. 3). White's correspondent, Thomas Pennant, was not only a prolific zoologist, but also an indefatigable antiquary, who published an assortment of county histories and travel guides (1774-6, 1796). Both White and Pennant viewed organic life and ancient artefacts as constituting a local world that enframed the ordinary workings of human life, a richly suggestive association

that has largely gone unremarked in historical studies of natural history.[1]

For geological enterprises, the association of natural history with antiquities had a special appropriateness, given the significance of structure, medium, and process in the world of rock (Rudwick 1979). As Charles Lyell noted, 'minerals, rocks or organic remains . . . when well examined and explained afford data to the geologist, as do coins, medals, and inscriptions to the historian' (1830-3, 1, p. 4). This convergence of historical methodologies and interests was likely to place the holiday observer of old fortresses beside the investigator of oceanside geological columns, and the two of them in the distant view of the Romantic seeker after sublime landscapes—likely, indeed, to place the contents all three species of gaze in the pages of such popular travel volumes as Pennant's *Tour of Scotland* (1774-6), Charles Cordiner's *Remarkable Ruins and Romantic Prospects of North Britain* (1795), or Miller's own **First Impressions of England** (1855). Thus, in his introduction, Miller observed: 'The art, so peculiar to the present age, of deciphering the ancient hieroglyphics sculptured on the rocks of our country, . . . will be comparatively a common accomplishment half a generation hence . . . when the hard names of the science shall have become familiar enough no longer to obscure its poetry' (1855, pp. x-xi). The views of the antiquary, geologist, and poet converge, Miller declares, because the mind is an instinctive metaphorist and allegorist, inscribing upon 'one set of figures made palpable to the senses another visible but to the imagination, and thus blends the ideal with the actual' (1855, p. xi).

It is not too difficult to detect in Miller's summons to metaphor-making a direct reference to problems that concerned scientific language, as outlined by Wordsworth in his preface of 1800 to the second edition of the *Lyrical Ballads.* Wordsworth, in a widely-known declaration, had contrasted the language of poetry with that of the sciences, on the grounds that poetry was an immediate, instinctive form of aesthetic perception, whereas the sciences were the constructs of sustained intellectual labour.[2] But the poet, Wordsworth noted, might well eventually follow the steps of the man of science: 'carrying sensation into the midst of the objects of the science itself. The remotest discoveries of the Chemist, the Botanist, or the Mineralogist, will be as proper objects of the Poet's art as any upon which it can be employed, if the time should ever come when these things shall be familiar to us . . .' (1932, p. 795). For Miller, that era had dawned, justifying a new kind of literary natural history based on an imaginative colouring of natural subjects. This new literary mode was to go beyond the received tradition of loosely associating the materials of natural history and antiquity; it was to blend them by means of metaphor and myth.

In Miller's writings, then, we find several developments that alter the natural history tradition as Miller received it from White and others. These developments were largely, if not consistently, in keeping with the strong aesthetic programme of the Romantic movement, which Miller, I argue, applied to the content of geology by means of his extended metaphor of the earth as monument.[3] From childhood onwards, Miller had immersed himself in literary culture. In the years he was labouring as a stonemason and writing his **Poems** (1829a), he was reading landscape poets like Cowper and Thomson, as well as the Romantic poets themselves—including Coleridge, Wordsworth, Scott, and Byron. This vigorous pursuit of literary culture was the preoccupation of his first stay in Edinburgh in 1824 (Bayne 1871, 1, pp. 141-4). Miller associated literary culture with his own intense religious convictions, another acquisition of these early years. Romance, he wrote to his friend William Ross, was the shadow of religion; the man of faith originated in the 'romantic man', living in 'an ideal world of his own creation' (Bayne 1871, 1, p. 230-1). In the apology at the end of the **Poems,** Miller spoke of the poet's world as a 'paradise of imagination', and of the ancient Scottish epics of Macpherson's Ossian with their rhapsodic natural scenes as the companions of his wandering life as a stonemason (1829a, p. 262). The recreation of the natural world in the language of aesthetic perception thus had a distinctive religious intensity in Miller's natural history works. Speaking autobiographically in 1838 in a fragment in *Chambers's Edinburgh Journal,* Miller recalled his first contemplation of a fossil he had found as a youth along the seashore: 'It filled my imagination with visions of the remote past, that teemed with wild poetry, and invested the subject of my studies with an obscure and terrible sublimity that filled the whole mind' (1838, p. 138; Shortland 1995, p. 253). In works such as **The Old Red Sandstone** and **The Footprints of the Creator,** Miller infused the immense landscapes of the remote past, constructed of geological and organic artefacts, with this intense emotion of the sublime.[4]

A second distinctive element of Miller's natural history writing is its frank and thorough enframing of geological exposition with self-reflective, experiential prose. This use of personal reflection places the content of geology into a psychological context of the self. As the two realms of narrative merge, natural history sometimes threatens to become autobiography. Such a juxtaposition also connects the physical realms of the remote geological landscape with the psychical realms of myth and dream, a connection Miller frankly exploits in the profuse antiquarian and mythological imagery of **The Old Red Sandstone.** Miller's natural history thus blends narratives of the self with the narratives of geological artefact in ways that, as Beer has observed in her study of Darwin (1983, pp. 5, 9), recast inherited mythologies into new forms. In his early **Poems,** Miller referred to his verses as transcripts of 'strange fancies and exploded opinions', which he compared to 'those limestone rocks that abound with the remains of animals of which the Zoologist gives us no account, or to those vaults which contain mummies of the Egyptian kings, concerning whom history is silent' (1829a, pp. 262-3). Miller's natural history, in transcribing these cryptic histories of obscure organisms of the remote past, blends them with a variety of personal myths, dreams, and legends, a combination that energizes his work as a whole.

Miller's natural history ultimately makes the narrative and aesthetical principles in natural objects an intellectual issue, upon which he builds an ontological argument. As Miller reflects upon his geological experience of the Scottish Old Red Sandstone and its organisms, he also engages this experience artistically through the gaze of a skilled craftsman in stone. Miller thus discovers a world structure that he believes to be the product of art. He sees an idealized world of emotion and form existing in the artefacts of remotest antiquity. This insight becomes the source of a natural supernaturalism, by which Miller asserts that the deity has artistically intervened in the shaping of natural history. The geological and fossil remnants of the earth, like the antiquities found across the ancient Scottish landscape, are manifestations of artistic process. We can recognize in this argument, which permeates Miller's natural history opus, a Romantic variant of Paley's Enlightenment argument from design. In **The Testimony of the Rocks** (1858, p. 253), Miller acknowledges the connection of his work with that of Paley. In the same passage, he also links his aesthetic argument with Thomas Carlyle's idea of natural supernaturalism in *Sartor Resartus* (Carlyle 1833-4). The aesthetically constructed nature—which Miller's experience as artisan gives him both authority and vision to see—can only have originated in the creative processes of mind. Geological and paleontological process thus become artistic narrative, accommodating both a dynamical view of natural form and the creationist principle. In Miller's natural history works, then, we have an interesting example of a detailed field natural history grounded in a Romantic aesthetic theory of development.[5]

THE OSSIANIC LANDSCAPE

Antiquarianism, like natural history, had inspired an extensive tradition of field observation in England and Scotland. Its practitioners ranged from highly-trained specialists to the casual amateur. Like natural history, it was an ambulatory, observational practice, most frequently carried out on a local, county scale but often inspiring lengthy journeys to remote places. Around country towns and city centres throughout the British Isles, antiquarians scoured the countryside for monuments, Roman remains and records. Operating beyond the margins of memory, clusters of adepts exchanged correspondence and maintained communication with each another about old monuments, records and artefacts. Sir Walter Scott, whose entire corpus of work, from the poetic narratives through the historical romances, brimmed with Scottish antiquities and tales, captured the type in his Waverley novel, *The Antiquary,* first published in 1816. The eccentric hero, old Mr Jonathan Oldbuck, who, Scott claimed, was based on an older man who had introduced him to Shakespeare, was an encyclopedia of antiquarian desiderata. Oldbuck maintained 'correspondence with most of the virtuosi of his time, who, like himself, measured decayed entrenchments, made plans of ruined castles, read illegible inscriptions, and wrote essays on medals in proportion of twelve pages to each letter of the legend' (Scott 1829, p. 21). Oldbuck's den was a sea of historical remnants, 'A chaos of maps, engravings, scraps of parchment, bundles of papers, pieces of old armour, swords, dirks, helmets, and Highland targets . . . busts, and Roman lamps and paterae, intermingled with one or two bronze figures' (Scott 1829, pp. 32-3). This chaos of objects, most of which had little meaning outside the knowledge of its possessor, was the stuff of interpretation. The landscape was aswarm with narrative, each artefact with a tale for its adept.

Antiquarianism also flourished at the grand level of cultural enquiry. One of the celebrated ventures of the eighteenth century was James Stuart and Nicholas Revett's two-year investigation and measurement of Grecian architecture and sculpture. This project, published as *The Antiquities of Athens and other Monuments of Greece* (1762-1816), decisively demonstrated that antiquarian investigation could deliver a serious product. Appearing over a period of nearly sixty years, the four main volumes of the *Antiquities* placed before the British and Continental eye the accurately measured and exquisitely engraved architectural and sculptural remains of classical Athens, including the Temple of Jupiter and the Parthenon itself. The two architects, supported by the Society of Dilettanti, lived in Turkish-occupied Athens and travelled to each field location to measure and sketch objects of interest. The aim of this remarkable field project was accuracy and preservation. The three-dimensional lithographs, all accurately proportioned, studiously refrained from filling in missing elements. Complete physical descriptions, detailed two-dimensional design plans and accurate measurements of architectural and sculptural details made this project a *tour de force* of realistic physical description and a model for any profession. Published in giant elephant folio, it gave material evidence of the artistic and architectural superiority of Classic culture over that of the Romans or, for that matter, that of contemporary England.[6] The appearance of the first volume of the *Antiquities* in 1762 touched off a sensation in English intellectual and artistic circles and inspired an architectural revival in London (Jenkyns 1980, pp. 5-6). The second

volume, published in 1787, a year after Stuart's death, brought before the eyes of the British and Continental public the first accurate documentation—and perhaps the finest engravings ever—of the Parthenon.

Nineteenth-century antiquarianism, fuelled by Romantic quest, gave rise to such grand progresses and orientalist collecting ventures as the Napoleonic expedition to Egypt in 1798 and the controversial exploits of Robert Bruce, the seventh Lord Elgin. Such international adventures glamorized antiquarian interests, capturing such artefacts as the Rosetta stone and the sculptures from the frieze of the Parthenon. These antiquities, soon famous and bitterly contested, joined the river of artefactual and natural objects streaming in from the colonies to early nineteenth-century England, often passing through the London Society of Antiquaries, to the chambers of the British Museum, and considerably raising the status of that institution. The same celebrated artefacts also came before the public eye in dazzling, detailed publications of the architectural remains salvaged from the ruins of time. Such volumes, often elaborately produced, became in their turn memorials of memorials that were among the finest sculptured art known to history (Stuart and Revett 1787, 1816).[7] In the Egyptian, as in the Greek antiquities, the widespread recognition that the Egyptian past had reached an unsuspected aesthetic pinnacle became more clear with each volume of the publication, under Edme Jomard, of the celebrated twenty-four volume *Description de l'Égypte* (1809-28). The *Description,* which included some 900 plates, gave detailed accounts and drawings of colossal buildings of Egyptian dynasties, drawings of an astonishing variety of antiquarian remains, including the Rosetta stone and its three texts, and accounts of modern Egypt and its natural history (Anderson and Fawzy 1987; Iversen 1961, pp. 127-32).

Edward Said has argued that these publications were decisive moments in the colonial interpretive control of the idea of the Orient (Said 1979, pp. 83-8). More broadly, such antiquarian projects provided a means of colonizing the past. Aestheticizing the past by celebrating its mystery and beauty opened its artefacts to new cultural uses and interpretations. The nostalgic quest for lost civilizations and ancient artefacts discovered objects that could be infused with transcendental significance. The memorials of the Sphinx, like the obelisks with their mysterious inscriptions, readily lent themselves to the emblematic literary tradition, which assigned symbolic status to material objects, treating them as objectified ideas—esoteric sources of sacred truths (Iversen 1961, pp. 57-87). Natural productions, once historicized and made sufficiently remote, served similar purposes. The Renaissance emblematic writer, Francis Quarles, observed, 'Before letters God was known by Hieroglyphicks; and, indeed, what are the Heavens, the Earth, nay every creature, but Hieroglyphicks and

Emblems of his Glory' (Iversen 1961, p. 83). The Rosetta stone, time's most famous artefact, was invested with ages of speculative interest in the hieratic mysteries of hieroglyphics. Thomas Champillion, in translating the hieratic text in 1822, forced the artefactual object to yield up its narrative mysteries. The scholar assumed new hermeneutic power. The pregnant imagery of the earth as hieroglyphic was widely assimilated by Romantics like Carlyle, Emerson, and Thoreau, who saw the earth as sleeve of the divine and could find 'epiphany in a fact' (Abrams 1971, pp. 412-13).

Well before the French expeditionary *Description,* in British works of local history and touring, antiquity and natural history emerged out of the cultural substratum in a common topological framework. In the cabinets of travel, such as Hans Sloane's immense collection—the nucleus of the British Museum—'Antiquity' was one of the 'natural kingdoms' (Stearn 1981, p. 6). Volumes reproducing the cabinets of travel likewise evolved a descriptive blend of castles, ancient ruins, Druidical remnants, burial monuments, noteworthy flora and fauna and spectacular landscapes. Although often banal, this literature created a rich tradition of engravings visualizing the natural as artifice and converting landscape to architecture (Rudwick 1976). Antiquity, natural history and landscape are here abstracted as shape, mass, proportion and substance, so drawing attention to their shared architectural features.

Thomas Pennant's *A Tour of Scotland, and Voyage to the Hebrides,* for example, illustrated numerous architectural and natural structures, including a Druidical circle of immense stones near Keswick, a Roman 'Head of Jupiter', a giant basking shark being harvested in Lochranza Bay off the Island of Arran, the ruined abbey and obelisk crosses in Oransay and Islay, and a striking series of geological illustrations of Fingal's Cave in the Hebrides (Pennant 1774-6, Vol. 1). This cave, as discussed at length in Michael Shortland's study of caves and cultural interpretation (1994), provided for the British traveller a shrine at which to worship the obscure forces of the sublime (see also Rudwick 1976, p. 173). The plates, contributed by Joseph Banks, were presented as rivals to the classical reproductions of Greece—very likely with the celebrated first volume of Stuart and Revett in mind. Banks's series measured and illustrated the massive cathedral-like cavern of Fingal's Cave and the astonishing natural basalt colonnades on Staffa and nearby islands (Pennant 1774-6, 1, pp. 161-9). Banks, somewhat bombastically, compared the titanic architecture of the Hebrides with that of classical Athens, so celebrated among his contemporaries: 'Compared to this, what are cathedrals and palaces built by men! Mere models or playthings, imitations as diminutive as his works will always be when compared to those of Nature. . . . Is not this the school where the art [of architecture] was originally studied, and what

has been added to this by the whole Grecian School? (Pennant 1774-6, 1, p. 262). Beside the architecture of Nature, the Athens of Stuart and Revett clearly shrank.

Scotland, as Pennant and others demonstrated, was a rich site for antiquarian speculation. Scottish history, full of struggle and cultural conflict, had left behind a theatre of ruined castles, fortifications, Celtic artefacts, and ancient texts. The dramatic landscape of mountains and coasts, combined with this history of ancient resistance to conquest, had left an extensive remains of sublime objects and ruins, dubbed by Archibald Geikie the 'Ossianic Landscape', in reference to James Macpherson's rhapsodic Ossianic fragments of the 1760s (1905, pp. 114-15). Such a landscape, which mingled artistic and topographical elements, was visible in *Antiquities and Scenery of the North of Scotland,* by the Reverend Charles Cordiner of Banff, published as a supplement to Pennant's two-volume *Tour of Scotland.* Expanding upon Pennant's work with a rich combination of antiquarian and geological illustrations from the Scottish north, including coastal rock arches, volcanic cones, and extensive northern obelisks, Cordiner wrote of an ancient, unrecorded 'Caledonian' culture of mathematical genius and high artistic achievement (1780). Developing this theme in a second much expanded work, *Remarkable Ruins and Romantic Prospects of North Britain,* Cordiner linked the ruins of the highlands with Ossianic remnants, invoking the themes of 'hieroglyphical representations' and 'Caledonian obelisks', and explicitly linking these with Egyptian origins, sacred mysteries, and mystical truths (1795, Vol. 1). This work, first published serially, contained over 100 plates engraved by Peter Mazell, covering dramatic landscape scenes such as Loch Ness, the cascade in Glen Quoich, and coastal heights in Ross-shire, the 'high and horrible' cliffs and 'yawning caverns' of the 'Ord of Caithness', as well as antiquities and zoology of Scotland. The result was a visual *tour de force,* in which the morphological remnants of the Earth were invested with iconographical significance.

As the descriptive language of geology and antiquity mingled, geological objects were frequently referred to as 'monuments'. This thematic use of the ruin of landscape, Nicolson has shown at length, was vigorously pursued by the cosmologist-theologian Thomas Burnet in the late seventeenth century. Burnet's epic images of the earth and its geological features as a damaged paradise presented the earth and the remnants of ancient civilizations as declining into sublime and colossal ruin (Nicolson 1959, pp. 219-23, *passim*; Willey 1961). The image of ruin and deep time, however, also suggested a prior state of original completeness that a methodologically inclined student could recapture by supplying the missing elements (Gould 1987). The adept contemplating a geological or antiquarian fragment—say a piece of Paley's watch—could reconstruct a whole, given a model by which to work analogically.

For Burnet, an earlier state of the Earth saw it home to the Biblical Garden of Eden, but a geologist like James Hutton, working a century later, judged it more of a curiosity inviting an intensely scholarly reconstruction. No one before Hutton, Geikie observed, 'had ever seen so clearly the abundant and impressive proofs of [the] remote antiquity recorded in the rocks of the earth's crust' (1905, p. 200). Although Hutton appropriated the Enlightenment metaphor of the machine for his 'system' of the Earth, the more powerful, underlying metaphor of his *Theory of the Earth* was that of long, sustained decay of the emerging landscape, giving rise to a 'succession of worlds' (1795, 1, pp. 3-6, 200, 371-6). Such a geological landscape, the product of massive, unseen forces acting over immense periods of time, could be 'seen' only through the mind's subtle reconstructions of the processes of decay (1795, pp. 180-4). Hutton was a patient gatherer of facts, a scholar who wandered and reflected in the mountains, glens, river valleys, and along the seacoasts, finding in the contemporary landscape the 'ruins of an older world . . . visible in the present structure of our planet'. (Geikie 1871, p. 53; Allen 1976, pp. 55-6). His indirect, meandering treatise, half-finished, citing lengthy passages of other works, doubling back on itself, was antiquarian in spirit, to the frustration of many (Davies 1969, p. 178). This imagery of ruin was applied to life forms by William Buckland, who suggested in *Geology and Mineralogy* that the organic, like the geological world, was a 'system of perpetual destruction, followed by continual renovation' (Buckland 1837, 1, p. 105). The entire second volume of Buckland's work was devoted to the visual reconstruction of fossil remains (see Rudwick 1992).

Geological and antiquarian interests converged in many cultural quarters, as artists, antiquarians and naturalists alike mingled the languages of geological, paleontological and archeological structure (Rudwick 1979; 1976, pp. 178-81). In the frontispiece to the first volume of his *Principles of Geology,* Lyell suggestively illustrated geological process by reference to the columns of the Temple of Serapis at Pozzuoli. Changes in land elevations relative to the sea were illustrated by the etchings of the bivalve *Lithodomus* upon the marble (1830-3, 1, pp. 449-54). In the temple, geological, organic and antiquarian artefacts were bound together in a Romantic conflict between human artistic desire and the irresistible processes of time and decay. This sense of geological process undermining civilization was present through much of Lyell's *Principles*—although it vanishes in his *Elements of Geology* (1838)—as Lyell lingered over the antiquarian debris of the destroyed cities, Herculaneum and Pompeii. Reflecting on the French Napoleonic expedition, Lyell suggested that the same enthusiasm applied to Herculaneum might have 'snatched from oblivion some of the lost works of the Augustan age' (1830-3, 1, p. 357). Thus, while Lyell had no doubt caught the reconstructive antiquarian fever of Cuvier (Rudwick 1979), both Cuvier and Lyell were no doubt feeling the powerful Romantic pull back into antiquity of the *Description de l'Égypte*.[8]

The idea of antiquity suggested ruin, the transitory nature of existence and the redemptive in memory. William Wordsworth was the great poet of this Romantic view, using hundreds of architectural remnants and monuments, such as the dilapidated abbey in 'Tintern Abbey', the pile of stones in 'Michael' and the ruined cottage in *The Excursion,* on which he inscribed the narratives of obscure but unforgotten people (Wordsworth 1932, pp. 91, 232, 410). Journeys to Scotland moved Wordsworth to memorialize in numerous poems the isolated, forlorn, yet enduring figures against the dramatic sweep of a giant land and its immense forces.[9] Much of Wordsworth's great memorial poem *The Excursion* takes place in churchyards and among ancient remnants of Celtic culture. For Wordsworth, art and its artefacts testified to the human spirit that persisted through the irretrievable losses of time. In inscribing thoughts of the dead by means of art upon material form, the memorial act, Wordsworth noted in his 'Essay on Epitaphs', gave testimony to the permanent and the deep spiritual yearnings of humanity. Found among the artefacts of all peoples, no matter how ancient, the monument and its epitaph embodied a principle of immortality in the human soul (1974).

PORTAL TO THE PAST

The young Hugh Miller, although firmly rooted in village fishing culture, was also immersed in a literary culture that mingled landscape, folk tale, magic, and myth—not to mention autobiography. Like the recurrent boy figure in Wordsworth's poems, bounding like a deer and haunted by the cataract, the child of the autobiographical *My Schools and Schoomasters* lived within a physical world of gigantic spaces animated by the elements. The Hill of Cromarty, Miller's 'true school and favorite play-ground', was a 'wild paradise' of sweeping slopes of hawthorn, rock strawberry, blocks of green hornblende, and veins of milk-white quartz, all hanging above the great German Ocean (1854, pp. 55, 57). This childhood experience in the world of elements was intensified by the Millers' literary interests in the tales and myths populating the surrounding landscape. Uncle Sandy, the mentor of these early days who introduced him to natural history, possessed intellectual gifts and interests that considerably shaped Miller's own, if we are to judge by Miller's later life: 'He was a keen local antiquary; knew a good deal about architectural styles of the various ages, at a time when these subjects were little studied or known, and possessed more traditionary lore, picked up chiefly in his country journeys, than any man I ever knew' (1854, p. 34). A great deal of this culture and several of these tales found their way into Miller's own *Scenes and Legends.*

Miller's pathway to natural history writing, as has been often noted, was indirect. His first volume, the *Poems,* interesting but not vivid, received a disappointing reception, which Miller seemed to anticipate in his rather apologetic title, dedication, and afterword (1829a, pp. 1-7, 261-8). This reception, however, did not deter Miller from his literary ambitions, which he turned quickly toward the productions of his prose. His letters on the herring fishery were published in the *Inverness Courier* in the summer of 1829 and collected as a pamphlet the same year by Robert Carruthers, the editor (Miller 1829b). These five letters, which Miller regarded as his first efforts as a natural history writer (Miller 1854, pp. 418-19) bear a strong resemblance to some of the general letters of Gilbert White's *Natural History and Antiquities of Selborne* (1789), which had undergone a significant revival in the 1820s (Allen 1976, pp. 99-100). Miller's *Letters,* an excerpt of which appeared in *Chambers's* in August 1832, are vivid and colorful and revealed—both to Miller and to others—how, once free of the technical restrictions of poetic form, he was able to integrate into fluent narrative a stunning range of myth, lyrical landscape, folk tale, legend, local colour and natural history. It was this pattern that he adopted in his first prose volume, *Scenes and Legends.*

By the time of Miller's second visit to Edinburgh and Linlithgow in 1834-5, Edinburgh had become a prolific theatre of natural history publishing and was afire with publication schemes (Sheets-Pyenson 1981). It had been in Edinburgh in 1826 that James Audubon, then an unknown, poorly educated American artist, had found the crucial support for his *Birds of America* (Audubon 1967, pp. 245-51). Its descriptive complement, the *Ornithological Biography,* was also published in Edinburgh in five volumes between 1831 and 1839. Two editions of the four-volume *American Ornithology* (1809-14) of Audubon's rival, the flamboyant Paisley poet and packman, Alexander Wilson, who had emigrated to America in 1793, appeared in Edinburgh in 1831 as volumes 68-71 of *Constable's Miscellany.* A variety of works such as the 'catechisms' of Oliver and Boyd's natural history series were also published in Edinburgh and aimed at the broad participatory culture associated with militant field observation (Rhind 1832). *Chambers's Edinburgh Journal,* which featured natural history pieces as part of its format, had attained a circulation of 50,000 by June of 1832, its first year of publication.

During his stay near Edinburgh in 1834-5, Miller would have heard about much of this activity from Sir Thomas Dick Lauder (1784-1848), one of his early patrons. Lauder furnished Miller both a model of the aspiring

natural history writer and a direct link to the Edinburgh natural history publishing world. His country seat was at Relugas in Morayshire, across the Moray Firth from Cromarty. Like Miller, he was a northern Scot, familiar with highland traditions and coastal village fishing culture in the region of Elgin, Banff, and Inverness. In addition to publishing a noteworthy geological paper on the Parallel Roads of Glen Roy in 1818, Lauder published in 1829 an unusual work of natural history, which he called *The Great Floods* of August, 1829 (Lauder 1873).[10] Lauder's *Floods* described the aftermath of two catastrophic floods produced by north-eastern storms off of the North Sea in the summer of 1829. Thousands of acres of land in Morayshire, including considerable portions of his own estate, Fountainhall, at Relugas were destroyed. Travelling by horseback, Lauder collected oral histories, first-hand descriptions, numerous anecdotes, and dozens of maps, illustrations, topographical sketches, and tables of rainfall to produce a detailed, energetic local history, filled with northern traditions and antiquities. This volume, cited in Lyell's *Principles* (1830-3, 1, p. 230) for its decisive demonstrations of climatic erosion, was also massive in its scope, treating numerous river basins and their watersheds. 'The hand of God appeared to be at work', Lauder observed, 'and I felt that He had only to pronounce dread fiat, and millions of such worlds as that we inhabit would cease to exist' (Lauder 1873, p. 52). The Huttonian metaphor of a succession of worlds had threatened to become a contemporary fact.

In 1832 Lauder moved from his country seat at Relugas to the Grange, a mansion near Edinburgh, partly to edit a new natural history series, the *Miscellany of Natural History.* This series was conceived as an aggressive rival to the newly established illustrated series, *The Naturalist's Library,* begun in Edinburgh in 1833 by William Lizars, the engraver who had helped Audubon launch his *Birds of America* project (Sheets-Peynson 1981). The first volume of Sir Thomas's series, titled *Parrots,* contained a striking frontispiece engraving of Audubon and began with Lauder's biographical sketch of Audubon; the second volume, titled *The Feline Species,* began with Lauder's biographical sketch of Cuvier (Lauder 1833, 1834). Although Lauder's ambitious natural history project failed after only two volumes, it preoccupied him with assembling biographies of naturalists like Cuvier and Audubon, as well as with the close study of the natural history writings of Buffon, Cuvier, Goldsmith and Alexander Wilson at the time of his closest personal association with Miller, when Miller was working on his own *Scenes and Legends.* When Miller went to Linlithgow in November 1834 to train for his appointment as clerk at the Cromarty Commercial Bank, he was a frequent guest of Lauder at the Grange and had use of Lauder's library (Bayne 1871, II, pp. 11-20). Before his visit to Edinburgh, Miller had expressed a new enthusiasm for natural history writing.

He had been introduced in early 1834 to the Highland *Guide* of the Anderson brothers, George and Peter, of Inverness (Anderson and Anderson 1834). This work, which Miller praised for its 'admirable digests of the Natural History, Antiquities, and Geology of the country', gave him a detailed local framework in which to orient his already extensive geological and paleontological findings (Miller 1841, p. 124). In March 1834, he had written to his friend Miss Dunbar, who had introduced him to Sir Thomas, that there was 'no study so universally favourite as natural history', adding 'I question whether Sir Thomas had any thought, twenty years ago of coming before the public as the editor of a work on natural history' (Bayne 1871, I, pp. 367, 369).

In framing his new work about his native Cromarty, Miller drew on Gilbert White's *Selborne* as a model. White's volume, he observed in a letter to Sir Thomas before his trip to Edinburgh, was immensely popular, despite Selborne's 'obscurity':

> The very local title of the work has not in the least militated against its interest. But why? Partly it would seem from the very pleasing manner in which it is written; partly because the natural history of even a single parish may be regarded as the natural history of the whole country in which that parish is included. And may not the germ of a similar popularity be found, if the writer do not fail in his part, in the traditional history of a Scotch village.
>
> (Miller to Lauder, LB 54, 21 March 1833).

Miller's 'traditional history' thus took its departure from Gilbert White's concept of 'parochial history'. Cromarty was to be the new Selborne. A year after Miller had returned to Cromarty from this second stay in Edinburgh, he dedicated *Scenes and Legends* to Lauder, calling himself '*protégé*' to the 'poet and painter of the Morayshire floods' (Miller 1835, pp. vi-vii). In the same dedication, he included the passage on White he had written to Lauder in March of 1833 (1829b, p. vii).

Miller's *Scenes and Legends* (1835), however, has less in common with the detailed natural descriptions of White than with the local colour, legend and provincial antiquarianism of Washington Irving's *Sketch Book of Geoffrey Crayon* (1819-20), with which it was compared by commentators (Bayne 1871, II, pp. 51, 116). *Scenes and Legends* is more a natural history of people in their traditional, legendary and physical settings. It locates human origins in the physical and psychical spaces of the past—the places Miller associated with his own origins. Miller narrates old tales, local stories and pagan myths, as well as accounts of Presbyterians' struggles against state-sanctioned Episcopacy, antiquarian accounts of monuments and obelisks along the Moray Firth, and spectacular scenes of 'sublime' landscapes. It is a literary omnibus, a historical 'vista into the past' (Miller 1835, p. vi).

To travel to this world, Miller describes his habit of mentally reconstructing, with the aid of his own 'little professional knowledge' of stonemasonry, the scattered remains of ruined cathedrals and castles. 'And thus have I pieced the fragments together, repairing every broken wall, and rebuilding every ruined tower, until the edifice has risen before me as an exhalation, and the deep-ribbed arches have interposed between me and the sky' (1835, p. 12). This restorative habit of mind, Miller continues, has sustained his interest in the decaying traditions and superstitions of Cromarty, which he speaks of as 'exploded' beliefs and compares to extinct animals, so long dead and so broken and scattered that not even Cuvier could have made them whole. Still, he notes, he is compelled to construct 'at least a ruin of them', before they are dissipated forever by the rational mind of the nineteenth century (1835, pp. 14-15).

In Chapter 4, Miller discovers the metaphorical portal to what might be called 'deep time' and his future works of natural history. Taking us to the summit of the Southern Sutor that towers above Cromarty, he looks out across the great bays and headlands at the massive rock formations themselves. Quite unexpectedly, in a shift in perception, he seems to penetrate through the ahistorical, 'pictorial' image of landscape to focus on the substratum itself.

> Let us survey the landscape a second time;—not merely in its pictorial aspect, nor as connected with the commoner associations which link it to its present inhabitants, but as *antiquaries of the world,*—as students of these wonderful monuments of nature, on which she has traced her hieroglyphical inscriptions of plants and animals that impart to us the history, not of a former age, but of a former creation
>
> (1835, p. 48).[11]

It can be his service, he suggests, to unlock the mystery of what has long since unfolded in some remote past. In this interpretive role of antiquary, Miller assumes new powers that draw on his own special insight. As monument and emblematic object the landscape is transformed into both architecture and enigma. It becomes a realm open to interpretation, a structure with a hermeneutic meaning. This view of the natural world is similar to the emblematic vision of Carlyle, who made extensive reference to physical nature as hieroglyphic (1833-4). Miller, however, has the knowledge and artistic power to turn the physical content of this new landscape into the substance of natural history.

From this vast panoramic prospect, Miller begins to move us from perspective to perspective, from time frame to time frame, exploring his new spatial and temporal freedom. His persona has been liberated from material restrictions. He reflects upon geology as apparition, and an entirely new landscape is superimposed upon the view. He imagines a time when all the barren summits were rising out of a warm sea, their shores covered with tropical palms and 'enlivened by fleets of *nautili,* spreading their tiny sails to the wind, and presenting their colours of pearl and azure to the sun' (1835, p. 51). We shift time frames once again and return to the present: 'But, from the pinnacles of the building restored in this way, to at least a pictorial entireness, we must descend to its ruins, and see whether, from its broken sculptures, and its half defaced inscriptions, we cannot trace some faint, imperfect outline of its history' (1835, p. 51). And we find ourselves back along the seashore with Miller, splitting open nodules of limestone and peering at ancient, hieroglyphic forms of extinct fish and tortoise-like creatures of a former creation, rising out of the present in Miller's imagination like a 'wonderful city of the dead, with all its reclining obelisks, and all its sculptured tumuli' (1835, p. 56). Miller thus skilfully positions us before the fossils of his geological empire.

It is possible now to see the complex biographical and intellectual elements that helped to shape Hugh Miller's antiquary persona as of 1835. *Scenes and Legends* is, among other things, an autobiographical memorial to his childhood and the antiquarian rambles with his Uncle Sandy through legend and along the shores and heights of a mystifyingly beautiful childhood locale. The antiquarian, as local historian, produces the memorial to this past, which, like Miller's own memory, threatens to explode and dissipate. In an 1836 letter to his childhood friend, Alexander Finlay, Miller, who had done fine stonework around Inverness some years before, referred to himself as 'a second edition of Old Mortality'—the wandering epitaph cutter of Scott's novel who maintained the memorials of forgotten Cameronians (Bayne 1871, II, p. 101). Miller's antiquarianism is also part of a colourful tradition associated with Scott, Cordiner, and other memorializers of Highland antiquities with whose work Miller would have been familiar. But Miller's antiquary is also a methodologist, adapting his own skills as craftsman to the Cuvierian method of reconstructing wholes from parts. This method is appealing for its epistemological fundamentalism—an important Romantic commitment—that was for Miller the means to intellectual and spiritual independence. Fierce self-striving and self-education are enduring themes of Miller's natural history. Miller resists, at considerable expense, the growing trend of the time toward centrally-transmitted university learning. Miller's voice is also that of populist, producing a market natural history that he intended to be popular and to succeed commercially, as did White's *Selborne,* Chambers's journal and other popular volumes. Finally, and perhaps most significantly, Miller's antiquary is also hermeneutical master of a metaphorical world, superim-

posed through the imagery of Miller's emblematic orientalism upon the materials of natural history—and thus constituting the deep meaning of natural history itself.

THE OLD RED SANDSTONE

Out of Miller's invocation to the muse of antiquity, a mere verbal fragment in the narrative seas of *Scenes and Legends,* arose the epic energy of *The Old Red Sandstone*—an explosion of natural history discourse and one of the nineteenth-century's truly big books about time and life. 'A geological chapter in my little volume of *Scenes and Legends*', Miller had written excitedly to Robert Chambers in 1837, 'has attracted more notice among the learned than all the other chapters put together' (Bayne 1871, II, p. 140). The enthusiasm Miller's geological chapter inspired would, no doubt, have struck a chord in Chambers, who already had run two excerpts from *Scenes and Legends* in *Chambers's Edinburgh Journal,* and who was himself 'in the commencement of a geology fever' in the summer of 1837, when he returned from a trip to Ireland (Second 1989, p. 175). Chambers, who had promoted both Audubon and Miller in *Chambers's Edinburgh Journal* as self-motivated, struggling autodidacts, was no doubt applying their lessons to himself.[12]

In *The Old Red Sandstone,* Miller invoked the voice of the Romantic wanderer in the landscape, reminiscent of Audubon, and made natural history a personal journey across the open landscape:

> I have been an explorer of caves and ravines—a loiterer along sea-shores—a climber among rocks—a labourer in quarries. My profession was a wandering one. I remember passing direct, on one occasion, from the wild western coast of Ross-shire, where the Old Red Sandstone leans at a high angle against the prevailing Quartz Rock of the district, to where, on the southern skirts of Mid-Lothian, the Mountain Limestone rises amid the coal. I have resided one season on a raised beach of the Moray Frith. I have spent the season immediately following amid the ancient granites and contorted schists of the central Highlands
>
> (1841, pp. 13-14).

Working class themes of labour and intellectual quest mix within the psychological framework of Miller's life story, set in the northern Scottish landscape. Autobiography merges with geobiography as Miller brings the vast extent and remarkable contents of the Old Red Sandstone into view.

For sheer stylistic exuberance, *The Old Red Sandstone* is unique among the geological works of its time. Its vision of the fluid, dynamic, transitory nature of geological and organic existence is immensely intensified and made palpable by Miller's continual self-referential presence. Miller recounts his first glimpse of a piece of limestone exposed by a gunpowder blast in a quarry pit. The sample, despite its extreme age, 'was rigid and furrowed', he recalls, 'like a bank of sand that had been left by the tide an hour before. I could trace every bend and curvature, every cross hollow and counter ridge of the corresponding phenomena; for the resemblance was no half resemblance—it was the thing itself' (1841, p. 8). Sudden recognitions of moments frozen in rock, similar to the Wordsworthian 'spot in time', overwhelm Miller with a sense of collapsed time, as geologic epiphany binds him with objects of incalculable age.

As Audubon had wandered through the American wilderness painting its remarkable birds, so Miller wanders through the wilderness of time, verbally sculpting its remarkable fish. Like a disembodied antiquary, Miller gazes upon self-contained worlds, unimaginably ancient, that are strange, beautiful, and sublime.

> Scallops, and gryphites, and ammonites . . . twigs of wood, leaves of plants, cones of an extinct species of pine, bits of charcoal, and the scales of fishes; and, as if to render their pictorial appearance more striking, though the leaves of this interesting volume are of a deep black, most of the impressions are of a chaulky whiteness. I was lost in admiration and astonishment, and found my very imagination paralysed by an assemblage of wonders, that seemed to outrival in the fantastic and extravagant, even its wildest conceptions. I passed on from ledge to ledge, like the traveller of the tale through the city of statues
>
> (1841, pp. 11-12).[13]

Transported backwards through the stream of time, we meet with the imagery of ancient civilizations, dream, and fantasy. These images give Miller's volume a grand, mythopoeic feeling of origination, as they establish the context for Miller's redefinitions of biological form in the unfamiliar shapes of ancient fish. 'Do not be deterred, if you have examined minutely', Louis Agassiz had said to Miller, 'by any dread of being deemed extravagant. The possibilities of existence run so deeply into the extravagant there is scarcely any conception too extraordinary for nature to realize' (1841, p. 56).

Miller recalls the humour of his correspondence over *Pterichthys* with various adepts, including Patrick Duff, Secretary of the Elgin Scientific Society. He is reminded of Sir Walter Scott's antiquary: '. . . we corresponded for several weeks regarding [Miller's drawing of *Pterichthys*], somewhat in the style of Jonathan Oldbuck and his antiquarian friend, who succeeded in settling the meaning of two whole words, in an antique inscription, in little more than two years' (1841, pp. 130-1). Members of the Society, Miller notes, find his drawing of *Pterichthys* bizarre and humorous, 'a fiction of the same class with those embodied in the pictured griffins

and unicorns of mythologic zoology' (1841, p. 131). They *jokingly* dub his drawing *Pterichthys milleri*, 'Miller's winged fish'. Yet, Miller's organisms rise relentlessly like myths from the depths of geological and psychic history, assaulting the conventions of biological form:

> Half my closet walls are covered with the peculiar fossils of the Lower Old Red Sandstone; and certainly a stranger assemblage of forms have rarely been grouped together;—creatures whose very type is lost, fantastic and uncouth, and which puzzle the naturalist to assign them even their class; boat-like animals, furnished with oars and a rudder;—fish plated over, like the tortoise, above and below, with a strong armour of bone, and furnished with but one solitary rudder-like fin; . . . creatures bristling over with thorns; others glistening in an enamelled coat, as if beautifully japanned; . . . The figures on a Chinese vase or an Egyptian obelisk are scarce more unlike what now exists in nature, than the fossils of the Lower Old Red Sandstone
>
> (1841, pp. 33-4).

These 'lost', 'fantastic' forms transform the familiar landscape into a place of vastness, where unsuspected forces have played out strange histories too remote to grasp other than in the language of legend. The reader walks upon a 'platform' that floats in the immensity of time, upon the surface of the sublime.

This is also a world of death. Miller's continual references to 'sepultures', 'tumuli', 'obelisks', and the like invoke an underworld of ancient, silent forms long since expired and embalmed in the geological caverns of the ages. Vast areas of the landscape, stretching between sea and sea, are 'pyramids', inscribed with the hieroglyphic language of the past (1841, pp. 30-3, 136-7). In his dense application of antiquarian imagery to his natural history of the remote past, Miller is constantly reflecting upon the history of life as a history of death. Indeed, the themes of death and extinction track through his entire natural history opus, from the **Poems** through the **Testimony of the Rocks**. In his poem 'On Seeing a Sun-Dial in a Church-Yard', Miller contemplated the irony of a sundial, an instrument of time, presiding over the realm of the dead (1829a, pp. 19-21). In **Scenes and Legends,** he seemed deeply disturbed by the idea of deep time, observing that he stood upon a vast plain raised up to its contemporary level by successive layers of the dead, 'a charnel house, not merely of perished individuals, but of extinct tribes' (1835, p. 55). These observations concerning species death were extended to thoughts of the eighty million people recently killed by cholera (1835, p. 57). The extinction theme continues through The Old Red Sandstone, where Miller contemplates the vast, cataclysmic deaths of ten thousand square miles of ancient fish in 'attitudes of fear, anger, and pain' (1841, p. 232). This sublime vision of stupendous carnage in the temporal house of biology was at once a fact, a powerful source of drama and a morbid constant in Miller's natural history.

Miller's field descriptions of strata and organisms are often sketchy, but the volume steadily gains mass and momentum with accumulating evidence of the Old Red Sandstone—its geographical extent, its structure, and its organisms. The descriptive characterizations of *Osteolepis, Cheiracanthus, Coccosteus, Cephalaspis* and *Pterichthys* draw on the work of Cuvier and Agassiz. 'The ability displayed by Cuvier', Miller observes admiringly, 'in restoring, from a few broken fragments of bone, the skeleton of the entire animal to which the fragments had belonged, astonished the world' (1841, p. 147).

Miller proceeds through a combination of verbal and visual reconstruction to arrange, link by link, the various fossil elements into a plausible whole. This associative process, similar to constructing together the pieces of a puzzle, restores *Pterichthys* in sophisticated visual detail, Miller dwelling on a range of technical issues, including cartilage formation, exoskeletons, mandibles, spinal columns, nervous systems, scales, defense mechanisms (1841, pp. 45-53). Miller gives special attention to the so-called wings, which Agassiz had determined to be weapons of defense that, like the occipital spines of the contemporary river bullhead, are erected at 'moments of danger or alarm' (1841, p. 52). Later in the volume, he recounts Agassiz's reconstruction of a giant lobster, which reminds him of a young girl he had once seen 'arranging the pieces of ivory or mother-of-pearl in an Indian puzzle' (1841, p. 148).

But Miller's ichthyolite structure in **The Old Red Sandstone** is not simply material and functional concept. It is also aesthetical and emblematic vision, as revealed in the dense Greek and Egyptian architectural imagery that colours the formal species characterizations. In reconstructing fossil form, Miller presents the form as the product of process, and he applies the analogy of his own experience as stone worker to the immense labour of world construction. Fossil becomes artefact, and artefact invokes the aesthetic response. *Pterichthys,* in short, becomes paradigm:

> There is unity of character in every scale, plate, and fin—unity such as all men of taste have learned to admire in those three Grecian orders . . . in the masculine Doric, the chaste and graceful Ionic, the exquisitely elegant Corinthian; and yet the unassisted eye fails to discover the finer evidences of this unity: it would seem as if the adorable Architect had wrought it out in secret with reference to the Divine idea alone
>
> (1841, pp. 95-6).

The classical diction of the beautiful, profusely employed throughout **The Old Red Sandstone,** asserts that organic form represents a kind of artistic desire, a yearning for perfection familiar to all artists. Miller observes: There is a feeling which at times grows upon the painter and the statuary, as if the perception and love of the beautiful had been sublimed into a kind of moral sense. Art comes to be pursued for its own sake' (1841, p. 96). Perfection is seen in the detail of organic existence—in the 'glittering enamel' of *Osteolepis,* the 'sculptured' occipital prominences of *Glyptolepis,* and the 'cabinet-like eloquence' of *Cheiracanthus.* Aesthetical desire motivates organic development. In the hidden beauty of the coelacanth, Miller detects the object of his elaborate emblematic imagery—an inexhaustibly inventive Artist of organic development, who has animated an Earth of nearly incalculable age with exquisitely crafted, aesthetically perfect forms (see John Brooke's discussion in Chapter 5 of the present volume).

In viewing organisms in the two lights of function and aesthetic, Miller introduces a profound conflict into traditional natural history. The world of Gilbert White had segregated the content of natural history from the activity of its creator with the simple assumption that the act of creation was miraculous, a production of the Logos that occurred at the beginning of time. This segregation is as much a convenience as a belief, enabling the natural historian to concentrate on physical phenomena in conducting natural history. With Miller's insistence that paleontological objects are artefacts, the project of explaining purpose and function becomes complicated. In Miller's account of ichthyic structure, the material and functional characterizations of his field geology struggle with the aesthetic teleology of his art theory. The resulting tension helps to explain Miller's often puzzling position in regard to organic development and hierarchy. Miller held a partial developmental view that life forms exhibited 'discontinuous progression', a view derived from but not identical to that of Agassiz (Bowler 1976, p. 80). In Miller's own words, 'there is progression in the scale—the arrangement of the classes is consecutive, not parallel. But in this great division there is no such progression.' (Miller 1841, p. 62). Hence, as Bowler points out, it is hard to fix Miller's criteria for what constitutes organic progression. This ambiguity—at least in **The Old Red Sandstone**—stems from Miller's assignment of an aesthetic value to organisms at the level of class. Hierarchy flattens. The ancient ichthyolites in **The Old Red Sandstone** are all aesthetically unique and near-perfect in form. *Pterichthys* is as advanced in point of beauty as the other organisms of its time, or any time. This is the point of the profuse classical aesthetical imagery that attends the species descriptions.

The aesthetic assumptions underlying Miller's views of development are seen even more distinctly in the extremity of his response to the publication of the anonymous *Vestiges of the Natural History of Creation.* He had taken this work as a challenge to **The Old Red Sandstone,** for the *Vestiges* had used his own work as support for development. Chambers's arguments about development had applied hierarchical criteria to Miller's ancient fish and raised the critical issue of progressive sequence (Chambers, 1844, p. 69, 71). In taking up the problem of how to decide hierarchy in ichthyic form, Miller again cast his discussion of natural objects—this time living species—into aesthetic terms by introducing the concept of species 'degradation'. Before embarking, in *The Footprints of the Creator,* on this discussion of degradation, Miller introduced his great coelacanth, *Asterolepis.* The heroic size and finely wrought details of this ancient organism demonstrated, as Ruskin's Grand Ducal Palace would do a few years later in *The Stones of Venice,* a remarkably high level of architectural achievement at an early stage in the history of the form, before slavish and corrupting imitation had overtaken the art—in Miller's case—of fish-construction. This answer—delivered in a remarkable performance of Cuvierian and antiquarian reconstructive method and detail—was meant to overwhelm the vestigian's tentative claim that only the smallest, most poorly developed fish were to be found in the Upper Ludlow Rocks and Lower Old Red Sandstone (Chambers 1844, pp. 70, 202). These claims were probably embarrassing to Miller, editor of a leading religious weekly the *Witness,* since they made plausible use of Miller's own work on Devonian fish to assert a crucial point about the correspondence of embryological development, adult form, and geological record (Chambers 1844, pp. 70-1).

Miller goes on to introduce in his ninth chapter of *The Footprints of the Creator,* ironically titled 'The Progress of Degradation', a principle of decay in organic form (1849, pp. 181-204). Chambers's claim had been that adult Devonian fish exhibit an embryonically early stage in the development of the modern fish dorsal vertebrae and tail (1844, pp. 70-1). In contrast to this embryological argument, Miller's principle of degradation insists that embryonic process is as properly considered an aesthetic corruption of shape and proportion (1849, p. 190). Miller's aesthetic norm was based partly on the neoclassical theory of beauty, formulated by Sir Joshua Reynolds, which emphasized purity and proportion of line (1849, pp. 63-4). Loosely joining this aesthetic principle with Richard Owen's notion of archetypal form as central plan at the level of organic class, Miller held that '[i]n all the higher non-degraded vertebrata we find a certain uniform type of skeleton, consisting of the head, the vertebral column, and four limbs . . .' (1849, p. 183). He spoke of *'monstrosity'* as a principle of deviation from this architectural norm—through *'defect of parts'*, *'redundancy'* of parts, and *'displacement of parts'* (1849, p. 182). Embryological development shows just such processes of degradation. Miller traces this progress of degradation from such minor transformations as the missing hind limbs of *Pterichthys* to the more substantial degradations of the modern order *Malacopterygii* in which 'the hinder legs are brought forward, and stuck on to the base of the previ-

ously misplaced fore limbs. All the four limbs, by a strange monstrosity of displacement, are crowded into the place of the extinguished neck. And such, at the present day, is the prevalent type among fishes'. (p. 186). Miller traces a similar set of design issues in the 'ichthyic tail' (pp. 194-95). These notions of organic erosion are consistent with Buckland's views concerning the periodic ruin and renovation of organic life (1837, I, p. 105).

But Miller offers us no explanation for the remarkable and exciting degradations he is describing. The concept seems loosely allied with Buckland's notion of species decay (1837, I, p. 107) and, more generally, with geological and antiquarian metaphors of erosion. Miller assumes that, as in degraded, derivative art—for example, the slavish imitative contemporary art of his time that copies the architecture of classical Greece—the inferiority will be apparent. Aesthetic judgment is, among other things, a matter of taste. He sounds very like Ruskin on this issue of aesthetic degradation, and one wonders what the two discussed when Ruskin visited Miller to view his fossil collection (Miller 1857, p. 100). In *The Old Red Sandstone,* Miller had scornfully contrasted the superior and thorough classical 'unity' of ancient ichthyolite form with the debased contemporary architectural taste for jumbling Egyptian and Grecian styles (1841, p. 95). In his comment above on the order *Malacopterygii* Miller's underlying idea seems to be that modern ichthyolite form is badly sculpted, its parts having been 'stuck on', 'crowded', 'misplaced', 'extinguished', to use Miller's own verbs. This notion of badly made forms, it should again be noted, is the superior craftsman's position on inferior work. The idea of artistic loss through imitation is also an expression of the doctrine of imagination and originality central to Romantic aesthetic theory (Abrams 1953, pp. 83, 282-3). Although Miller admits that modern organisms may be well adapted to their circumstances and able to thrive biologically, this success has no bearing on their hierarchical location in the scale of their respective class. Thus, at the level of the biological order, hierarchy in organic form becomes purely an aesthetic matter of architectural proportion and elegance, as judged by the 'antiquary of the world' gazing upon the form. To others, however, seeking evidence of progression or simply seeking utilitarian—or merely consistent—explanations, Miller's aesthetic arguments might well have been puzzling and provocative. Among other things, they abandoned the very epistemological principles of Lyellian uniformitarian explanation at the level of local material process to which Miller owed so considerable a debt. To Chambers and Darwin, who read Miller closely, *The Old Red Sandstone* could only have been a provocation—and hardly the last word—to evolutionary speculation.[14] Commenting on Agassiz's demonstrations of the triple correspondence among embryonic stages, adult forms, and geologic record, a correspondence

Miller also described at some length (1841, pp. 241-3), Gould has observed that, despite Agassiz's anti-evolutionist stance, 'Agassiz's view contained an argument that no evolutionist could resist reinterpreting' (1977, p. 68).

Despite the repeated anti-progressionist arguments, ***The Old Red Sandstone*** creates a mesmerizing epic vision of the massive historical transformations of geological and organic form. It is difficult to see Miller's formidable protestations against development as wholly antithetical in spirit. The triple correspondence of geological record, embryological development and adult forms clearly fascinated Miller, who had noted in his autobiographical fragment in *Chambers's* in 1838 that his own early reading of de Maillet's *Telliamed* had 'awakened in me a strong love of theory' (Shortland 1995, p. 252). Miller had again mentioned *Telliamed* and its philosophical 'romance' of transmutation, especially the notion of fish turning into birds, in the third chapter of ***The Old Red Sandstone*** (1841, p. 41). This was the chapter on *Pterichthys milleri,* or Miller's 'winged fish', which members of the Elgin Geological Society had jokingly associated with de Maillet's fantasies. Miller enjoys these fantasies. His insistence that gradation is not progress, his continual use of geology to 'rob' the infidel of his god, progression—not once, but again and again—displays a remarkable imaginative fascination with the problems of progressive theory (1841, pp. 39-41). This discussion, like Samuel Butler's four-volume theoretical rebuttal of Darwin, seems curious, given the realm of discursive possibility.

Miller's efforts to combine a naturalistic view of progression at the level of vertebrate classes—fish, reptile, bird, and mammal—with an aesthetic argument of the hierarchy of form within the individual class, reveals a rather striking epistemological discontinuity at the centre of ***The Old Red Sandstone.*** In Miller's natural history, the Romantic doctrine of natural supernaturalism arrives at an impasse. The growing mass of geological and paleontological detail becomes increasingly difficult to contain within the metaphorical system of aesthetic object and hieroglyphic artefact that Miller has erected. Miller's literary system threatens to collapse, since the imagery he has used to make natural objects into artistically crafted artefacts cannot do the necessary theoretical work of showing how artistic agency intervenes to make organisms like *Pterichthys*. The analogy between natural developmental processes—geological, embryological and morphological—and Miller's own arts of hewing fine stonework breaks down as Miller attempts to apply the analogy literally to increasingly specific material detail. Miller's use of artistic agency, unlike Charles Darwin's use of artificial selection, cannot be identified with a known process that intervenes with organic form, although the two process metaphors are not unlike one another in other respects (see also Young

1985, pp. 98-101; Beer 1983). Epistemological standards well established in the work of Lyell and others, standards upon which Miller's own reputation must ultimately rest in the scientific community, demand continuity of causal explanation at the level of local, material process. In trying to argue that the aesthetic principle is more than the internal subjective response of the beholder, that it is an objective material force shaping organic objects, Miller's natural supernaturalism can only break upon the shores of his own vivid material description.

From the anonymous and mysterious craft that had produced the 'hieroglyphic' remains of the Scottish north—the old Celtic monuments, gothic relics and ancient legends that in ***Scenes and Legends*** are sprinkled across the physical and cultural landscape—Miller extrapolated to the creative forces that must have produced the monumental formations of the Old Red Sandstone. What *contrivance* was to Paley, *artefact* became to Miller: the hinges, lenses and levers of Paley's supernatural mechanic found equivalents in the obelisks, classical columns, and monuments of Miller's divine Artisan. Where Paley's natural theology elevated utility, Miller's natural history elevated art. But, in connecting the materials of geology, paleontology and morphology to the metaphors of world construction and organic development, Miller created a literary system that he could not ultimately force to do his bidding. In ***The Old Red Sandstone,*** Miller gave emblematic significance to the remarkable convergence of the parallel series of embryonic stages, adult forms and geological record, calling it an 'allegory'. 'Is there nothing wonderful in analogies such as these—analogies that point through the embryos of the present time to the womb of Nature, big with all its multitudinous forms of being?' (1841, p. 243). The answer to this question was, of course, vigorously affirmative, but the source of the wonderment was open to interpretation.

LITERARY NATURAL HISTORY

Three of Miller's many innovations as a writer of natural history may be singled out as literary contributions that decisively altered the tradition of natural history, as Miller received it, from Gilbert White and other eighteenth-century and early nineteenth-century natural history writers. Miller's contributions, which may be characterized as the animation of natural history with Romantic idealism, constitute defining elements of modern literary natural history that were taking shape in Miller's time, and to which Miller himself contributed substantially. As David Oldroyd shows in this volume, Miller's natural history was, first and foremost, grounded in a formidable grasp of the material detail of local geology and paleontology of his region. Upon this subject matter, Miller built a superstructure, based on the extended metaphor of the Earth as monument. This metaphor, as we have seen, drew on local antiquarian traditions, with which Miller had become familiar from his early childhood, his work and travel as stonemason and his extensive study of literary culture.

Miller's first contribution to literary natural history was the development of a powerful voice or persona. This persona served to focus the reader in particular ways upon the natural history object. It served, for example, to emphasize the phenomenological experience of witnessing natural locations and objects. We can trace this witnessing aspect of natural history back to Gilbert White, whose voice in the letters from Selborne is full of pleasant pastoral remoteness and natural charm as we tour the region with him. By contrast, Miller's voice, like the voices of Audubon and Thoreau, is much more intense and frankly autobiographical. The personae of these writers, despite their many differences, have become highly self-referential and are themselves among the major subjects of their respective texts. The literary natural historian is a self-conscious presence, a manager of spectacle and metaphor, a figure who places himself prominently in the landscape beside the objects of his or her observations. Miller spends the bulk of his first chapter in **The Old Red Sandstone** positioning himself in the physical, social and intellectual landscape. Thoreau dwells at length on the autobiographical necessity of his enterprise: 'I should not talk so much about myself if there were anybody else who I knew as Well' (Thoreau 1854, p. 1). These voices all promise to use the knowledge of oneself, as well as the knowledge of one's world, in order to capture the experience 'out there'.

For Miller, the ideal persona seemed to have been Wordsworthian, perhaps best approximated in the Romantic figure of Alexander Wilson, who had once passed the way of the ancient Bass Rock in 1789 as a pedlar-poet, before wandering off to the wilds of America. In the American landscape, Wilson composed the *American Ornithology,* which Miller, in his essay on the geology of the Bass Rock, called the 'prose *Excursion*'. Miller thus identified Wilson with Wordsworth himself and with the main character—the pedlar-philosopher—of Wordsworth's *Excursion* (Miller 1873, pp. 311-14). Miller's own persona in the natural history works is also a wandering observer, a working-class stonemason and antiquary who surveys the world and makes artefacts out of natural objects. In many respects, this antiquary-of-the-world persona is the archetypal literary natural historian, a figure who recaptures the content of the natural world for his reader, as an antiquary reconstructs the objects of forgotten history. Whether consciously or not, Miller here tapped into a vigorous and colourful tradition of antiquarian research

and travel that had for generations been practised in the Highlands and elsewhere, a tradition with many connections to the older natural history tradition of White and Pennant.

Miller's second important contribution to literary natural history, and the natural extension of his antiquary persona, is the production of artefacts from the content of natural history. Miller's antiquary converts the natural object into artefact through the use of metaphor, which characterizes the object aesthetically and mythologically. Miller's Devonian fish become aesthetic objects, the occasions of Miller's remarkable descriptive virtuosity. Miller's efforts were self-consciously aimed at fulfilling the Wordsworthian promise in the 1800 Preface to the second edition of the *Lyrical Ballads* that the poet would one day carry the language of sensation 'into the midst of the objects of the science itself' (1932, p. 795). Miller's metaphors link his subject matter of Devonian fish to the world of sensuous experience and to the realm of myth. These strategies were used by other literary naturalists and authors of Miller's time, including Thoreau, whose Walden Pond is the American equivalent of Miller's Old Red Sandstone stratum—a natural geographical locus from which to connect, metaphorically, to the realms of the senses and transcendental experience. Thoreau had read **The Footprints of the Creator** and **The Old Red Sandstone** in 1851, well before the publication of *Walden* in 1854 (Sattelmeyer 1988, p. 237). Thoreau, as Sattelmeyer has noted, protested the way in which Miller and others were converting the natural world into a sepulchre, and vigorously disagreed with Miller's philosophy, to the extent of preferring the developmental program of *Vestiges* over the theology of Agassiz and Miller (Sattelmeyer 1988, pp. 86-9). Still, the structural elements and dynamic of the two writers' natural histories—personae, artifacts, and mythology—are nearly identical.

The third, yet perhaps most important, literary element of Miller's natural history was its use of the materials of natural history as the basis for ontological speculation. Miller's natural history, as do most literary natural histories, leads through artefact to mythology, which in Miller's instance was closest to Carlyle's natural supernaturalism. Miller's strengths, however, proved in many ways to be sources of conflict, for the massive physical system he constructed in **The Old Red Sandstone** was very hard to contain in a philosophical system as abstract and idealistic as that of Carlyle, which dwelled more on mental than material landscapes. Miller's epistemological conflicts were, I think, brought on by his efforts to make his metaphor of aesthetic intervention and decay a literal physical force in organic development—as Darwin was to do some years later more successfully with his metaphor of natural selection. But in all other respects, Miller's work has retained its unparalleled aesthetic and intellectual vigour.

Notes

1. Neither Allen (1976) nor Thomas (1983) examines the role of antiquarian thinking and method in the development of natural history, although there is clearly an old connection between the two traditions.

2. In his *My Schools and Schoolmasters* (Miller 1854, p. 189), Miller again alludes to the problems stated in Wordsworth's 1800 Preface.

3. Miller draws on neo-classical aesthetic theory in some of his later discussions of organic form in *The Footprints of the Creator,* where the aesthetics of vertebral proportion and configuration are under consideration. But he does not share the general neoclassical view of natural form as something to be improved upon; nor does he share the neoclassical aesthetic commitment to the generalized beauty of type and its consequent rejection of the particular. My interpretation differs, in this respect, from Gillispie's view of Miller as an eighteenth-century figure among Victorians (1951, p. 170). For a recent study of Miller as a Victorian natural history writer, see Merrill (1989), which discusses Miller's general nature imagery and compares Miller's with Ruskin's work. More general background studies of the aesthetics of the sublime and of Romanticism are provided in Nicolson (1959) and Abrams (1971). Williams (1990), in a free-ranging study of the underground as cultural metaphor, has applied the metaphor of mining and excavation to the study of the past and its ruins. Gillispie (1951) provides extensive background on the early nineteenth-century cultural response to geology, with a thoughtful section on Miller. Rehbock (1983) examines the philosophical idealism in early nineteenth century natural history with which Miller was loosely associated.

4. Burke, in his *Enquiry* (1757) had identified 'vastness' as the most powerful source of the sublime. Miller makes many references in his work to immense structures and time periods, using the aesthetical diction of the sublime found in Burke and Addison.

5. Another major aesthetic theory of natural history is that of Samuel Taylor Coleridge (Levere 1981). Coleridge, with whose poetry Miller was deeply familiar, exemplified the academic Platonism of the German Academy, to which Miller had little access. Coleridge was mostly interested in the theory of natural philosophy, rather than in any specific field practice of natural history.

6. St Martin's Church, Stuart wrote, 'though one of the best in London, is no more than a very inferior imitation of the Greek Prostyle temple, and will not enter into the slightest degree of comparison with the chaste grandeur, the dignified simplicity, and sublime effect of the Parthenon'. See Stuart and Revett (1787, p. ix).

7. Stuart and Revett's *Antiquities* (1816) contained, in its chapter on 'sculpture of the Parthenon', 34 plates of the Parthenon metopes drawn before the Venetian bombing that destroyed part of the temple. This chapter was published separately by Taylor in 1816 as *The Elgin Marbles from the Temple of Minerva at Athens.*

8. In his extensive visual study of 'deep time', Rudwick examines the origins of visualization of prehistoric scenes, a necessarily imagined scenery. Miller does 'paint' verbal scenes from deep time in several of his works, but his graphic elements mostly reproduce assembled fossil structures, similar to those of Buckland (1837, I, p. 2).

9. Wordsworth travelled to Scotland in 1803, 1814, and 1830, memorializing these trips in *Memorials of a Tour of Scotland,* 1803 (1803); *Memorials of a Tour in Scotland,* 1814 (1814); and *Yarrow Revisited* (1831).

10. An excellent account of the history of 'the Parallel Roads of Glen Roy' issue is given in Tyndall (1901).

11. In the second edition of *Scenes and Legends* (1836), Miller, who had been criticised for introducing paleontological materials into this otherwise colourful local legendry, dropped the antiquary image, as well as much of the paleontological material of Chapter 4 (Bayne 1871, II, p. 140).

12. Audubon's autobiography, which invented a Romantic itinerant model of the natural historian in the wilds, circulated widely in various forms in Edinburgh in the 1830s appearing in the *Ornithological Biography* and in Lauder's edition of *Parrots* (1833). An excerpt from Audubon's autobiography appeared in *Chambers's* in December 1832 (Audubon 1832). Chambers also promoted Miller's work, publishing a piece from Miller's letters on the herring fishing in August 1832. In February of 1834, he published the 'Stanzas on Seeing a Sun-Dial' from Miller's *Poems*; in May of 1835, he ran two different excerpts from Miller's *Scenes and Legends,* praising Miller as a man of 'singular reflective powers'. In May of 1838, he published Miller's 'Gropings of a Working Man in Geology' (Miller 1838), which was the seed of Miller's *The*

Old Red Sandstone. For full details, see the appendix to this volume.

13. The City of Statues is a reference to the tales in the first English translation, by Edward Lane, of the *Thousand and One Nights,* popularly called the *Arabian Nights.* The work first appeared serially in 1838-41. Miller refers to the work by name on page 93.

14. In his discussion of the origins of Chambers's ideas about development, Secord (1989) might well have added the likelihood that *The Old Red Sandstone* was a primary source on development theory for Chambers, who cited Miller's work and knew Miller personally. Prior to Darwin's work, Miller's volume was one of the most robust discussions of progression ever written—knowledgeable, massive, and not altogether hostile to development theory. Chambers, we know, was an avid follower—and promoter—of Miller's career.

References

Abrams, M. H. (1953). *The Mirror and the Lamp: Romantic Theory and The Critical Tradition* (reprint 1958). Norton, New York.

Abrams, M. H. (1971). *Natural Supernaturalism: Tradition and Revolution in Romantic Literature.* Norton, New York.

Allen, D. E. (1976). *The Naturalist in Britain.* Allen Lane, London.

Anderson, G. and Anderson, P. (1834). *Guide to the Highlands and Islands of Scotland, Including Orkney and Zetland.* John Murray, London.

Anderson, R. and Fawzy, I. (ed.) (1987). *Egypt in 1800: Scenes from Napoleon's Description de l'Égypte.* Privately printed, London.

Audubon, J. (1832). 'Sketch of Audubon'. *Chambers's Edinburgh Journal,* 1, 374-5.

Audubon, J. (1967). *The 1826 Journal of John James Audubon,* ed. A. Ford. University of Oklahoma Press, Norman.

Bayne, P. (1871). *The Life and Letters of Hugh Miller,* 2 vols. Gould and Lincoln, Boston.

Beer, G. (1983). *Darwin's Plots: Evolutionary Narrative in Darwin, George Eliot, and Nineteenth-Century Fiction.* Routledge and Kegan Paul, London.

Bowler, P. (1976). *Fossils and Progress: Paleontology and the Idea of Progressive Evolution in the Nineteenth Century.* Science History Publications, New York.

Buckland, W. (1837). *Geology and Mineralogy Considered with Reference to Natural Theology,* 2 vols. Carey, Lea, and Blanchard, Philadelphia.

Burke, E. (1757). *A Philosophical Enquiry into the Origin of our Ideas of the Sublime and Beautiful,* 1990 edn, ed. A. Phillips. Oxford University Press, New York.

Carlyle, T. (1833-4). *Sartor Resartus: the Life and Opinions of Herr Teufelsdröckh,* 1937 edn, ed. C. Harrold. Odyssey Press, New York.

Chambers, R. (1844). *Vestiges of the Natural History of Creation,* reprinted, 1969. Humanities Press, New York.

Cordiner, C. (1780). *Antiquities and Scenery of the North of Scotland, in a Series of Letters to Thomas Pennant.* Anon. published, London.

Cordiner, C. (1795). *Remarkable Ruins and Romantic Prospects of North Britain, with Ancient Monuments, and Singular Subjects of Natural History,* 2 vols. I. and J. Taylor, London.

Davies, G. L. (1969). *The Earth in Decay: a History of British Geomorphology, 1578-1878.* American Elsevier, New York.

Geikie, A. (1871). 'The Scottish School of Geology'. *Nature,* 5, 37-38, 52-55.

Geikie, A. (1905). *Landscape in History and Other Essays.* Macmillan, London.

Gillispie, C. C. (1951). *Genesis and Geology: the Impact of Scientific Discoveries upon Religious Beliefs in the Decades before Darwin,* reprinted 1959. Harper, New York.

Gould, S. J. (1977). *Ontogeny and Phylogeny.* Harvard University Press, Cambridge, Mass.

Gould, S. J. (1987). *Time's Arrow, Time's Cycle: Myth and Metaphor in the Discovery of Geological Time.* Harvard University Press, Cambridge, Mass.

Hutton, J. (1795). *Theory of the Earth, with Proofs and Illustrations,* Vols. 1 and 2, facsimile reprint, 1959. Hafner, New York.

Iversen, E. (1961). *The Myth of Egypt and Its Hieroglyphs in European Tradition.* Gad, Copenhagen.

Jenkyns, R. (1980). *The Victorians and Ancient Greece.* Harvard University Press, Cambridge, Mass.

Lauder, Sir T. D. (ed.) (1833). *Parrots.* The Miscellany of Natural History, Vol. 1. A. and C. Black, Edinburgh.

Lauder, Sir T. D. (ed.) (1834). *The Feline Species.* The Miscellany of Natural History, Vol. 2. Frazer, Edinburgh.

Lauder, Sir T. D. (1873). *The Great Floods of August, 1829, in the Province of Moray and Adjoining Districts* 3rd edn. R. Stewart, Elgin.

Levere, T. (1981). *Poetry Realized in Nature: Samuel Taylor Coleridge and Early Nineteenth-Century Science.* Cambridge University Press, Cambridge.

Lyell, C. (1830-3). *Principles of Geology,* Vols. 1-3, facsimile reprint 1991. University of Chicago Press, Chicago.

Mackenzie, W. M. (1905). *Hugh Miller: a Critical Study.* Hodder and Stoughton, London.

Merrill, L. (1989). *The Romance of Victorian Natural History.* Oxford University Press, New York.

[Miller, H.] (1829a). *Poems, Written in the Leisure Hours of a Journeyman Mason.* R. Carruthers, Inverness.

[Miller, H.] (1829b). *Letters on the Herring Fishing in the Moray Frith.* R. Carruthers, Inverness.

[Miller, H.] (1832). 'The Herring Industry'. *Chambers's Edinburgh Journal,* 29, 231-2.

Miller, H. (1835). *Scenes and Legends of the North of Scotland; or, the Traditional History of Cromarty.* Adam and Charles Black, Edinburgh.

Miller, H. (1838). 'Gropings of a Working Man in Geology', *Chambers's Edinburgh Journal,* 326, 109-10; 330, 137-9.

Miller, H. (1841). *The Old Red Sandstone; or, New Walks in an Old Field.* J. Johnstone, Edinburgh.

Miller, H. (1849). *The Footprints of the Creator; or, the Asterolepis of Stromness.* Gould and Lincoln, Boston.

Miller, H. (1854). *An Autobiography: My School and Schoolmasters; or, the Story of my Education.* Gould and Lincoln, Boston.

Miller, H. (1855). *First Impressions of England and its People.* Gould and Lincoln, Boston. (First published 1847)

Miller, H. (1858) *The Testimony of the Rocks; or, Geology in its Bearings on the Two Theologies, Natural and Revealed,* 1st American edn. Gould and Lincoln, Boston. (First published 1857)

Miller, H. (1873). Geology of the Bass. In *Edinburgh and its Neighbourhood, Geological and Historic; with the Geology of the Bass Rock,* 5th edn. W. Nimmo, Edinburgh. (First published 1864)

Nicolson, M. H. (1959). *Mountain Gloom and Mountain Glory,* reprint 1963. Norton, New York.

Oldroyd, D. (1979). 'Historicism and the Rise of Historical Geology'. *History of Science,* 17, 191-213, 227-57.

Pennant, T. (1774-76). *A Tour of Scotland and Voyage to the Hebrides,* 2 vols. J. Monk, Chester.

Pennant, T. (1796). *The History of the Parishes of Whitefod and Holywell.* B. and J. White, London.

Rehbock, P. (1983). *The Philosophical Naturalists: Themes in Early Nineteenth Century British Biology.* University of Wisconsin Press, Madison.

Rhind, W. (1832). *A Catechism of the Natural History of the Earth.* Oliver and Boyd, Edinburgh.

Rudwick, M. (1976). 'The Emergence of a Visual Language for Geological Science, 1760-1840'. *History of Science,* 14, 149-95.

Rudwick, M. (1979). 'Transposed Concepts from the Human Sciences in the Early Work of Charles Lyell'. In *Images of the Earth: Essays in the History of the Environmental Sciences,* ed. L. J. Jordanova and R. S. Porter, pp. 67-83. British Society for the History of Science, Oxford.

Rudwick, M. (1992). *Scenes from Deep Time: Early Pictorial Representations of the Prehistoric World.* University of Chicago Press, Chicago.

Said, E. (1979). *Orientalism.* Vintage, New York.

Sattelmeyer, R. (1988). *Thoreau's Reading: a Study in Intellectual History, with Bibliographical Catalogue.* Princeton University Press.

Scott, Sir W. (1829). *The Antiquary.* The Waverley Novels, Vol. 5. Cadell, Edinburgh.

Scott, Sir W. (1830). *Old Mortality.* The Waverley Novels, Vol. 10. Cadell, Edinburgh.

Secord, J. (1989). 'Behind the Veil: Robert Chambers and Vestiges'. In *History, Humanity, and Evolution: Essays for John C. Greene,* ed. J. Moore, pp. 165-94. Cambridge University Press, Cambridge.

Sheets-Pyenson, S. (1981). 'War and Peace in Natural History Publishing: The Naturalist's Library, 1833-1843'. *Isis,* 72, 50-72.

Shortland, M. (1994). 'Darkness Visible: Underground Culture in the Golden Age of Geology'. *History of Science,* 32, 1-62.

Shortland, M. (ed.) (1995). *Hugh Miller's Memoir: from Stonemason to Geologist.* Edinburgh University Press, Edinburgh.

Stern, W. T. (1981). *The Natural History Museum at South Kensington: A History of the British Museum (Natural History), 1753-1980.* Heinemann, London.

Stuart, J. and Revett, N. (1787). *The Antiquities of Athens and other Monuments of Greece,* Vol. 2, ed. E. Stuart. John Nichols, London.

Stuart, J. and Revett, N. (1816). *The Antiquities of Athens and Other Monuments of Greece,* Vol. 4, ed. J. Woods. J. Taylor, London.

Thomas, K. (1983). *Man and the Natural World: a History of the Modern Sensibility.* Pantheon, New York.

Thoreau, H. D. (1854). 'Walden; or, Life in the Woods'. In *Walden and Civil Disobedience,* 1966 edn., ed. Owen Thomas. Norton, New York.

Tyndall, J. (1901). 'The Parallel Roads of Glenroy'. In *Fragments of Science,* A Library of Universal Literature, Vol. 5, pp. 218-43. Collier and Son, New York.

White, G. (1876). *The Natural History and Antiquities of Selborne, in the County of Southhampton: with Engravings and an Appendix,* 2nd edn, ed. E. T. Bennett, Rev. J. Hartling. Bickers, London.

Willey, B. (1961). *The Eighteenth-Century Background.* Beacon, New York.

Williams, R. (1990). *Notes on the Underground: an Essay on Technology, Society, and the Imagination.* MIT Press, Cambridge, Mass.

David Alston (essay date 1996)

SOURCE: Alston, David. "The Fallen Meteor: Hugh Miller and Local Tradition." In *Hugh Miller and the Controversies of Victorian Science,* edited by Michael Shortland, pp. 206-29. Oxford: Clarendon Press, 1996.

[*In the following essay, Alston emphasizes Miller's analytical and literary contributions as a folklorist of Scottish legends, myths, and stories.*]

Hugh Miller collected around 350 traditional tales and customs,[1] the bulk of which were published in *Scenes and Legends of the North of Scotland* (1835) and in his autobiographical *My Schools and Schoolmasters* (1854). This number does not include stories from written sources, which he wove together with his own collection into the 'traditional history of Cromarty', the subtitle of *Scenes and Legends.* Traditional stories also form the bulk of *Tales and Sketches* (1863), edited by his wife Lydia after his death, and including his biography of the Cromarty merchant William Forsyth, a work which drew on local memories and tales. Books based on his journeys in Britain in the 1840s and 1850s— *First Impressions of England* (1847) and *The Cruise of the Betsey* (1858)—show continued interest in local traditions, and even his geological and theological writings include a scattering of traditional tales.

Such interest in the stories of the common people was not yet fashionable and Miller briefly, but eloquently, found it necessary to defend his interest in what was revealed in these tales:

> Human nature is not exclusively displayed in the histories of only great countries, or in the actions of only celebrated men; and human nature may be suffered to assert its claim on the attention of the beings who partake of it, even though the specimens exhibited be furnished by the traditions of an obscure village.

> (Miller 1858, p. 9)

Although superstition and custom would continue, it would take new forms; what was passing away was 'the production of centuries' and would not be repeated (Miller 1858, p. 3), so something of the diversity of human nature would be lost, unless such tales were preserved. Miller also made the claim, more cautiously advanced, that the intrinsic quality of some of the tales was such that they could compare with the best of classical mythology (Miller 1858, p. 5).

Miller was preceded in Scotland by only three earlier collectors: Walter Scott, Allan Cunningham and Robert Chambers. Miller was the first collector in the north of Scotland, albeit in a non-Gaelic-speaking area whose cultural links were with the south. Richard Dorson in *British Folklorists* claims that Miller's books 'reveal what the whole literature of folklore rarely divulges, the place that folk tradition occupies *in the life of a town,* and *in the life of a man*'. (Dorson 1968, p. 138, emphasis added) It is a claim which should be treated with caution. The term 'folklore' was coined in 1846, during Miller's lifetime, by William J. Thoms, to describe the beliefs, customs and stories current among the common people and the study of them (Drabble and Stringer 1986, p. 204). Miller did not use the term to describe his own collection; he was, indeed, little concerned with *current* beliefs, customs and stories. He described his material collectively as 'a fallen meteor'—superstitions, customs and tales which had once been fiery and bright, but had now lost their prominence and were curiosities from the past rather than living beliefs. So it is only to a limited extent that we can see the place of these traditions in the life of the town of Cromarty. They throw far more light, and brighter light, on Miller's own life.

MILLER AND CROMARTY: THE TOWN AND HIS SOURCES

It was Miller's interest in local tradition, rather than geology, poetry or church affairs, which first earned him a reputation in his home town. John Barclay, who visited Cromarty in 1833, in an effort to recover some family property from relatives, consulted Miller on the family's history. Barclay described Miller as having published 'a volume of poetry, a history of the herring fishery, and also a history of the antiquities of Cromarty'.[2] Miller was 'quite the lion of that part' and was likely to take an interest in the matter of the Barclay family because it 'jumps with his favourite hobby' (Hill 1978, p. 186).

Cromarty, where Miller lived from his birth until he left for Edinburgh in 1839, had long been recognized as one of the finest and best-sheltered natural harbours in Europe. The portrayal by Miller's biographer, Peter Bayne, of the climate of Cromarty and the Black Isle as 'one of the most bleak and ungenial districts in

Scotland' is peculiarly misleading, for this eastern tip of the Black Isle has a mild climate and is almost completely free from the 'chill fogs' also mentioned by Bayne; nor do gales blow from the North Sea at every season to 'pierce every nook and cranny of the shivering town' (Bayne 1871, I, p. 7). One may suspect that such inaccuracies are features of the image Miller created for himself when in Edinburgh, and a suitably wild place of origin for the bulky, stooped figure, in antiquated shepherd's plaid, which he presented to his public.

In Miller's boyhood Cromarty was a thriving town with a population of over 2,000, but from the 1830s it declined to the point that Miller could describe it as almost 'a second deserted village' (Bayne 1871, II, p. 441). The small estate of Cromarty (consisting of Cromarty Castle, much of the town and surrounding land) had been acquired in 1767 by George Ross, a native of Ross-shire who, having made a fortune in London, devoted himself to the improvement of his property. In consequence, Cromarty enjoyed a remarkable period of growth, becoming a model of what could be achieved with the resources of the area. Ross, with the assistance of a local merchant, William Forsyth, built one of the first factories in Scotland, which employed between 200 and 250 hands within its walls and over 600 outworkers in neighbouring parishes, in the production of handloom-woven hemp cloth for sacking and bagging, using hemp imported principally from St Petersburg. Ross was a local pioneer in many other respects: he introduced lace making, nail and spade manufacture, improved farming practices and introduced large-scale pig rearing; he built a brewery; he obtained government funds for the building of the town's Courthouse and harbour; he financed the construction of a Gaelic chapel for incoming workers; he built Cromarty House on the site of the medieval castle; and he initiated a local fashion for rebuilding, during which most houses in the town were replaced. Visitors remarked on the appearance of the town and its inhabitants: 'the common people are remarkable complaisant and cleanly' (Loch 1778, p. 55); and 'houses are everyday building and neatness and cleanness are studied' (Wight 1781, p. 256). This building boom which continued into the nineteenth century provided steady employment for twenty to thirty local masons and this life, rather than that of a travelling mason, was perhaps what the young Miller had in mind in deciding to apprentice himself to this trade.

By the end of the century, the prominent improver Sir John Sinclair, considered that Inverness was 'the emporium of the Northern Highlands', but, he continued,

> It will have a serious rival in Cromarty . . . which is obviously the best adapted to become the grand depot, the great granary and storehouse of merchandise and trade, in the northern end of the Island of Great Britain; and when the day shall arise (and come it will) that Government will assuredly see the utility and vast importance of a naval establishment at this port, Cromarty will be seen to rise rapidly and become the general mart of the North

> (Sinclair 1795, p. 60).

In 1815 the town grew further with a boom in herring fishing, and by the 1820s it was the eighth largest herring-curing station in Britain. The industries established by George Ross were still for the most part thriving, and the town in which Miller grew up was far grander than the small fishing village it was later to become.

By Miller's day the town had become sufficiently cosmopolitan for a French consular agent to be appointed (probably in the 1820s) and for the Baltic trade to bring regular news from Russia. Cromarty was also something of a frontier town. It had, since its establishment around 1200, been in 'border territory', an outpost of Scots speakers on the edge of the true Highlands. Gaelic was spoken in the neighbouring parishes and by incoming workers in the hemp factory, and in Miller's day the people of Cromarty retained their sense of superiority to the Gaelic-speaking Highlanders. Although he later expressed regret at not speaking Gaelic, Miller championed the townspeople in their opposition to an attempt by the minister of the Gaelic chapel either to have a parish of his own or be appointed joint minister of the existing parish (Miller 1874b, p. 92). The opposition was, at root, based on the perceived inferiority of the Gaelic congregation, mostly workers in the hemp factory. To accede to the request would (as Miller expressed the view of the townspeople) have made the Gaelic-speaking minister into whole minister to half of them or half a minister to all of them.

Miller collected traditions from in and around this town, tales which were on the verge of disappearance. The number of tales collected may suggest that Miller presented a comprehensive account of local lore rather than a personal selection, yet he was aware 'how incalculably numerous must such stories once have been, when the history of one little domicile [i.e. his own house] furnishes so many' (Miller 1858, p. 358). His mother, Harriet Wright, was a principal source and she provided him with the more powerful supernatural tales. Although Miller does not discuss his mother's influence on him, the view of his family, particularly of his wife Lydia, was conveyed in no uncertain terms to Miller's biographer:

> His mother was not remarkable for mental power or strength of character. She had, however, one intellectual faculty in extraordinary vigour, to wit, memory, and she loaded it with knowledge of a peculiarly unprofitable kind. Her belief in fairies, witches, dreams,

presentiments, ghosts was unbounded, and she was restrained by no modern scruples from communicating
her fairy lore, or the faith with which she received it,
to her son

(Bayne 1871, I, p. 15).

Lydia held that almost all the material for *Scenes and
Legends* came from Hugh's mother. She also believed
that Hugh had, as a result of his mother's superstition,
been brought up as a young boy in an atmosphere of
'overpowering terror'—created by the combination of
this superstition with his mother's occupation as a seam-
stress, involving the sewing of shrouds—which 'returned in his last days, stimulating the action of a diseased brain' (Bayne 1871, I, p. 17).

Hugh was much in the company of his mother's brothers, James and Sandy Wright, after his father's death.
The brothers had not married and remained with their
parents, Catherine Rose (who died in 1811) and Robert
Wright (who survived until 1818), and so the young
boy was exposed to the same influences which had provided his mother with her stock of traditional tales.
Catherine Rose was one of three sisters who had been
orphaned at a young age and brought up in the neighbouring parish of Nigg by their grandfather Donald
Roy, a powerful lay leader in the church who was also
regarded as a seer. He was said, for example, to have
known in some supernatural way of Catherine's recovery from a serious illness. Catherine's sister Isobel appears in *Scenes and Legends* as the Gudewife of Minitarf (Miller 1858, pp. 396-407) and the third sister
married a Nigg man, named Munro, who may be the
'elderly relative' who provided Miller with the sequence
of stories which constitute Chapter XXV of the same
book (Miller 1858, p. 358). The three Rose sisters appear to have been brought up in a background which
combined devout religion and a strong belief in the supernatural, a combination for which Miller never lost
respect but which seems to have been alien to his wife's
family and to many of his Edinburgh acquaintances.[3]

Harriet may also have derived some of her lore from
having, as a young girl, spent much time in the company of Ann Feddes, whose daughter (Jean Robertson)
was Miller's father's first wife. Following Jean Robertson's early death Ann Feddes (herself a sailor's widow)
ran a small school, attended by Harriet and an elder sister. As Ann grew old the elder Wright girl moved to
live with her and take care of her and Harriet 'used, as
before, to pass much of her time with her sister and her
old mistress' (Miller 1869, p. 11). Ann Feddes was related to Harriet but was also a cousin of Miller's father,
and through her Harriet had access to the traditions of
her future husband's family.

Miller held that the best traditional tales came from
women. He described women in general as 'more poetical, more timid, more credulous than men' and believed

that when this was coupled with other characteristics
and circumstances, namely 'a judgement not naturally
vigorous, an imagination more than commonly active,
an ignorance of books and of the world, a long cherished belief in the supernatural, a melancholy old age,
and a solitary fireside', then the result was 'that terrible
poetry which revels among skulls, and coffins, and
enchantments' (Miller 1858, p. 7). This description of
'a melancholy old age' does not fit Harriet herself (who
was a young woman when widowed) nor Catherine
Rose (who lived contentedly with her sons), but it corresponds with the 'dreary solitude' of Ann Feddes after
her daughter's death (Miller 1869, p. 11).

We see, then, that the women in Miller's family included a number of powerful story tellers and that their
family traditions extended beyond Cromarty itself to
the neighbouring Highland (Gaelic-speaking) parish of
Nigg and across the Moray Firth to the Lowlands. Thus
the family stories included those of James Mackenzie,
the Episcopalian curate of Nigg, and his twenty children, one of whom (Jenny, who later married Donald
Roy) he once forgot was his own daughter (Miller 1858,
p. 144); a whole clutch of stories of Donald Roy (Miller
1858, pp. 145-152; Miller 1869, p. 32); traditional tales
such as the 'Green Lady of Banff', from his mother's
grandfather who had come from this area (Miller 1858,
p. 366; Miller 1874b, p. 250); and even such detail as
that a pair of ravens had nested on the same spot at
Navity since the boyhood of his great grandfather
(Miller 1874c, p. 296). Miller's oldest story, with a
clearly identified source, was also a family tale, that of
Elspat Hood who reputedly died in 1701 at the age of
120 and could remember a time when the Clach Malloch, a large boulder exposed at low tides, was surrounded by corn fields (IC 25 November 1829).[4]

Despite the obvious influence on him of women storytellers, Miller is more explicit about the influence of his
uncles. From James, who like Miller had a prodigious
memory, he gleaned factual local history and an immense amount of local lore gathered when James travelled as a saddler to surrounding farms. James also encouraged young Hugh in his reading, directing him at
an early age to Blind Harry's *Wallace*. Sandy Wright,
the more intense and serious of the two, provided him
with tales of adventure, stories of life and passion, with
strokes of poetry, and tales of the sea. Sandy's small library included such volumes as *Travels in North
America,* with accounts of the manners and customs of
the Indians, and he also aroused Miller's interest in
natural history.[5] Miller only indirectly revealed James
Wright's own experience of the supernatural, in the tale
of 'The Gudewife of Minitarf'. As a young man, James
had worked as a saddler at Invergordon and while sleeping in the ruined castle he had, in a dream, a vision of
the funeral of his cousin (Isobel Rose's son, John) in
Morayshire—a funeral which he attended a few days

later (Miller 1858, p. 395-407). The honesty and up-rightness of the Wright brothers is stressed by Miller, and it must have been almost impossible for him to doubt the truth of this story.

Stories of a different kind came from the gatherings in the evenings at James's work bench, with local characters such as the eccentric Francie, and here Miller heard many of the local ghost stories. Later, as a journeyman mason, he heard similar tales from the wildly inventive story teller Jock Mo-ghaol in the masons' barrack at Conon. Other story-telling sessions gave him a significant part of his knowledge of his father, who was drowned at sea when Miller was only five years old, through stories told by the mate, Jack Grant and by James Wright, who had greatly admired him (Miller 1869, p. 17).

Miller had to search out many of the other stories he recorded. The body of local tradition—the fallen meteor—had to be unearthed. When Nicholas Dickson visited Cromarty in 1858, little more than a year after Miller's death, a visit inspired by his admiration of Miller's writings, he found that the local fishermen, although they knew the names of places around the coast mentioned by Miller, knew none of the tales associated with them (Dickson 1858, p. 78). Miller had, in fact, drawn many of his tales of the fishing community from George Hossack, who died aged 82 years in the 1820s (IC 13 May 1829). Other old inhabitants were sought out by Miller and, in his own image, cannibalized by him. In this way he received fast-disappearing accounts of Cromarty: of the castle, demolished in 1772 but remembered by an old woman who, as a girl, had been a companion to the last remaining servant (Miller 1858, p. 79); of Meg o' the Shore's grave, which another old woman remembered having seen opened when she was five years old, on which occasion a friend of Meg's removed pins as a keepsake from the linen cap still on Meg's skull (Miller 1858, p. 386). After many inquiries, he discovered the name of the well, simply known as 'the Saint's Well', at Navity from an old man whose father had farmed the place a hundred years before (Miller 1874a, p. 155).[6]

In searching out stories, Miller had an admirable ability to relate to social outcasts, such as the mad woman at Conon and a number of 'idiots', and this coupled with his later position as a respectable member of society provided him with many additional sources. Miller's researches also led him to explore the history of the town in a more conventional manner through local church records and private collections of papers.

However, he had his own place within its society and was not a detached recorder of the affairs of the town. One example is the fact that there is no reference in his writings to the distinctive dialect of the fisher community of Cromarty, and this despite Miller's expressed interest in dialect and his retention of his native pronunciation.[7] There were two distinct dialects of Scots spoken in Cromarty, one by the fisherfolk and the other by the rest of the community. The dialect of the fisherfolk, which was almost identical with the dialect of the fishers of Avoch, also on the Black Isle, was characterized by the dropping and insertion of 'h's, as in Cockney. The *Scottish National Dictionary* (Grant and Murison 1931) in its introductory survey of varieties of Scots claims that this dialect contains some of the oldest forms of Scots. Why did Miller turn a blind eye to it? It may be that the dialect, since it does not reflect what are characteristically seen as the features of Scots, was regarded by him as a degenerate form of language and that he simply ignored it in his descriptions of Cromarty. If so, this is a useful reminder that Miller, far from standing apart from his community, shared its prejudices.

It was perhaps a mark of Miller's success that, despite the oddities of his character and what must have appeared at the time as his peculiar interests, he remained part of and was ultimately honoured by his home town. Miller rose to local fame through his attention to local tradition and history, rather than through an interest in natural history, but he wisely turned his attention away from contemporary customs and from at least some local affairs. Two interesting contrasts are provided by his fellow geologist Robert Dick and the later Cromarty folklorist, Donald A. Mackenzie. Dick, a Thurso baker, was rejected by his own community: his interest in natural history, with the resultant trips into the country at odd hours of the day and night, marked him as an eccentric. Mackenzie, recorded a number of traditional stories and customs of Cromarty early in the twentieth century but, after publishing an article using the fisher dialect, was on occasion pelted with stones by those fisherfolk who thought he was mocking them.[8] Miller trod a fine line, conveying little of contemporary belief and concentrating on past customs and tales.

MILLER AND CROMARTY: THE HISTORY OF THE PEOPLE

The enduring value of Miller's tales of the history of Cromarty, as distinct from his supernatural stories, lies largely in the wealth of local detail and colour, which bring to life the affairs of the town, chiefly in the eighteenth century. They provide little reliable information on the town before 1690 (only six or seven tales refer to events before this) and, indeed, little in detail before the 1730s. Miller heard much of this tradition as a boy and consolidated his knowledge in the 1820s; the timescale here is interesting in illustrating that Cromarty, despite being a long-established burgh, was not a community which transmitted its own history over the centuries.

Miller had remarkably high faith in the reliability of oral testimony:

> There is a habit of minute attention almost peculiar to the common people (in no class, at least, is it more perfect than in the commonest), which leads them to take an almost microscopic survey of every object suited to interest them; and hence their narratives of events which have really occurred are as strikingly faithful in all the minor details as Dutch paintings. Not a trait of character, not a shade of circumstance is permitted to escape
>
> (Miller 1858, p. 4).

Not only did Miller hold such tales to be, in general, historically accurate, but he believed that what was true in such stories could almost invariably be distinguished from false elements.

> Nothing more common than those faithful memories which can record whole conversations, and every attendant circumstance, however minute; nothing less so than that just conception of character and vigour of imagination, which can alone construct a natural dialogue, or depict, with the nice pencil of truth, a scene wholly fictitious. And thus though anyone . . . can mix up falsehoods with the truths related in this way, not one of a million can make them amalgamate. The iron and clay, to use Bacon's illustration, retain their separate natures, as in the feet of the image, and can as easily be distinguished
>
> (Miller 1858, p. 4).

Miller surely claimed too much, perhaps because of his high regard for the Wright brothers' recollections, and on examination it proves that his traditional history conveys some distorted views on the religious history of the parish. Two chief examples are his accounts of Bernard Mackenzie, last Episcopalian incumbent of the parish church, and of the Catholic proprietor of the estate, Captain John Urquhart (Miller 1858, pp. 143-4 and pp. 349-54). Miller described Mackenzie (minister from 1678 until 1690) as 'a quiet, timid sort of man, with little force of character, but with what served his turn equally well, a good deal of cunning' (Miller 1858, p. 143). Such a description is not borne out by the facts. Mackenzie was on occasion prepared to stand up to the Mackenzie lairds, who were his patrons, as when, following a dispute over the payment of grain rents, he vouched for the good character of those who had broken into the laird's storage loft at the castle and removed some of the grain. In 1704, although removed as minister, he was again in the area, championing those who wished to see the restoration of Cromarty's status as a royal burgh and falling foul of the laird by encouraging fishermen to stop making customary payments of fish. Mackenzie emerges from this and other accounts as a forceful man, with popular support and apparent good relations with at least some Presbyterians.

A similar distortion emerges in Miller's account of the dispute in Cromarty in the 1750s over the appointment of a new minister. The Cromarty estate was acquired in 1741 by Captain John Urquhart, a Catholic, who had been out in the Jacobite rising of 1715, subsequently served in the Spanish navy and returned to buy the old family estate. Following the death of the parish minister in 1749, there was a prolonged dispute between Captain John and the elders of the church, over who had the right to appoint a new minister. Miller accurately reports these events but what is missing is an account of the earlier deterioration of relations between Urquhart and the parish, as a result of the bigotry of some of the elders. Moreover, local tradition appears to have forgotten Urquhart's improvements on the estate, with the result that Miller gave the sole credit for the economic development of Cromarty in the 1740s and 1750s to William Forsyth. Much of this was well deserved: Forsyth was an enterprising merchant and a hard-headed business man—but Miller overstated the case for Forsyth whom he credited with first importing coal, developing linen spinning, and first manufacturing kelp. Coal was already imported; it was Urquhart and the local merchant Gilbert Barclay who introduced the linen industry to the area; and Barclay was already shipping kelp in 1746. William Forsyth flourished following, and probably because of, the bankruptcy of Barclay, whom he replaced as agent for the British Linen Company. It is interesting to note that Barclay was an Episcopalian and a supporter of Captain Urquhart, while Forsyth was a Presbyterian.

It appears that the religious revival of the mid-eighteenth century, with the resulting strengthening of Presbyterian attitudes, led not only to a victory for the local elders in church affairs, but to an eclipsing in popular history of the role which had been played by non-Presbyterians in the economic development of the town. This has the strange result that Miller's accounts belittle his own forebear, the Reverent James Mackenzie of Nigg, and obscure the fact that the Feddes family had supported Urquhart's candidate in the patronage dispute.

It is unlikely that Miller's would have deliberately distorted his material but he certainly accepted uncritically, and perhaps credulously, these views of the religious history of the town. This may be explained in terms of Miller's own character. While he could be a fierce, and at times radical, critic of others, he needed a secure base for himself, which was partly provided by his beloved Cromarty. These traditions represented the people of Cromarty as almost wholly united in their Presbyterian and evangelical beliefs (at least from the 1730s) and enabled Miller to perceive himself as the product of a community which, in experiencing evangelical revival and successfully opposing the patronage claims of the laird, had held firmly to those very principles of religious belief and church government which would remain so important to him. Just as he regarded the area around Cromarty as embodying the main truths of his geology and saw the geological world through the rocks of his beloved birthplace, as David Oldroyd shows in his contribution to this book, so Cromarty's ecclesiastical history exemplified values to which he remained attached. And, one may add that, in a similar way, the responsible use of wealth and exercise of power by the eighteenth-century laird, George Ross, and the merchant, William Forsyth (both of whose contributions to Cromarty were recorded by Miller in uncritical and glowing terms), provided enduring models of social responsibility. The traditional history of Cromarty thus encouraged Miller in his tendency to see the world through the microcosm of his native town and, indeed, Mackenzie in his study of Miller suggests that 'in all subjects he had made his mind up before he left Cromarty' (Mackenzie 1905, p. 242).

Stories and the Local Environment

Miller, as we have seen, explicitly stated that most stories were not, when collected, the living beliefs of the community. However, these were the stories of the town (and its environs) in a different and important sense. The tales are, almost without exception, set in a particular place, known to Miller even if not specified in such a way that allows for their identification now (and thus we have, for example, lost the site of St Duthac's chapel). His stories tell of a particular place, at a particular time.

His achievement for his readers is to recreate in his descriptions a landscape in which both the past or the supernatural (often both) are part of the reader's vicarious experience of the natural world. Nor are the stories simply located on the landscape. They penetrate it. Through the Drooping Cave, still to be seen on the shore to the east of Cromarty, lie caverns where ancient warriors sleep (Miller 1858, p. 332); the Fisherman's Widow, in a dream, sees a dead man walking under the sea—perhaps drawing, in the description, on Miller's experiments with diving on the west coast (Miller 1858, p. 179); the spring Sludach rises on one side of the Cromarty Firth, only to dry up and reappear on the other side, mysteriously linked beneath the sea bed (Miller 1858, p. 5); mountains are stones dropped by a giantess (Miller 1858, p. 14); the Guardian Cock protects a house from destruction by meteors from above (Miller 1858, p. 73); the devil is to be met in the depths of the Black Gorge at Evanton (Miller 1858, p. 166).

The power of Miller's story telling mirrors the strength of his popular geological work which conveys to the reader, through a vivid description of the natural world and Miller's own experience, a sense of the geological past. David Oldroyd remarks in this volume that 'Miller's geological writing was as much autobiographical as descriptive of rock types, fossils, geological systems and processes' and, similarly, Miller's folktales are an

important part of his own life history. In retelling the tales, Miller is conveying his own way of experiencing the world in which he grew up.

Why were these tales so important to him? As a boy, despite being a leader of his school fellows, he was often cool and distant, even with his few friends, and lived much in the world of his own imagination. He maintained this coolness in his personal relationships in adult life and was, as Mackenzie puts it, 'shy and strangely reserved, he lived much alone, he had but a few devoted friends and moved in no circle' (Miller 1907, p. xi). From an early age, and perhaps as an alternative to friendship, he enlivened his environment with stories: he was one of the few to spend much of his time on the Gallowhill, above Cromarty, where stories played a large part in his games. Having read *Gulliver's Travels* he recreated his own Lilliputian world on the slopes of Gallowhill and describes how he himself seemed to become a tiny figure (Miller 1874a, p. 174). He re-enacted the stories of Wallace to which his uncle had introduced him, hiding in a cave, pursuing a defeated English army and lifting the siege of Cromarty Castle. His interest in geography, in plans and in historical detail enhanced his stories and imaginative games: the voyages of his toy ships on the horse pond, a quarter of a mile from the town, were as a result more complex than those of his companions and he constructed earth and mud fortifications on a scientific basis (to the amusement of the estate factor, Walter Ross, who had commanded the Loyal Cromarty Volunteers).

Some of his other early reading included descriptions of English landscapes which Miller absorbed in such a way that when he visited England as an adult he already 'knew' some of the places through his boyhood reading of, for example, the eighteenth-century poet and landscaper William Shenstone (to whose works he returned every year until he was nineteen) and the novelist Mary Sherwood. He created his own version of these places in his imagination and seems to have retained much of this, while carrying with him the memory of places he knew at first hand. He found Edinburgh disappointing partly because he had already built, in his mind, a much finer Edinburgh of his own. His imagination gave stories such a vitality that he generally found theatre disappointing. He attended the Theatre Royal in Edinburgh in 1823 only to find that he had already enacted the Shakespearean plays more satisfactorily in his own mind in the settings of Cromarty Hill (Miller 1829).

In his personal relationship with the environment, geology to some extent replaced his interest in traditional history—or became an alternative stimulus to his imagination. He claimed that an important transition took place early in his life. On a visit as a boy of eleven to the Drooping Cave, which he was exploring, alone and by torchlight, in an attempt to retrace the steps of Willie Millar (who, according to local tradition, had encountered sleeping hosts of warriors in caverns far beyond the entrance), Miller realized that the story was false as the cave narrowed and became impassible. But he reflected that he had taken pleasure in the investigation which proved the legend false and had been attracted by the natural phenomena of the cave. He wished things to be both 'marvellous and true' and, although his childhood belief in 'the ghost, and the wraith, and the fairy' had gone, he now knew that his mind would be fed by philosophy and the arts (Miller 1858, p. 339).

This account is part of the material added to *Scenes and Legends* in its second edition of 1850 and its tone establishes Miller more in the role of a recorder of curiosities than a teller of stories. However, it sits uneasily with the account in *My Schools and Schoolmasters* of Miller's exploration of the Drooping Cave with his uncles when he (in this version) saw the caves by torchlight for the first time and was aware of their limited extent. It may be an example of Miller in later life overemphasizing his early scientific interests. Whenever the change took place, Miller did indeed move to a greater interest in geology and in his geological lectures he proposed geology as a form of 'poesy' equal to the old mythology (Miller 1874a, p. 80).

Yet one can also sense the continuing importance of the stories of his native Cromarty. Passing over the ferry from Ardersier and setting out towards Cromarty he entered that 'part of the country where every little locality, and every more striking feature of the landscape, has its associated tradition' (Miller 1874b, p. 294). He had this relationship with no other place. In Edinburgh, his second home, he knew, from his first visit in 1824, of saints' wells at Restalrig and later gleaned one near contemporary story of thieves at Tantallon Castle during a trip to the Bass Rock, but otherwise he lacked the background of tales he enjoyed in Cromarty (Miller 1875, pp. 236, 271).

Miller also had a more conventional appreciation of the picturesque aspects of the countryside and was heartbroken, returning to Cromarty in the late 1840s, to find the hedgerows planted by George Ross in the 1770s pulled out and, in the town, to find the house and garden of Captain Swan (father of his boyhood friend) sadly changed (Bayne 1871, II, p. 442). However, for one to whom the natural environment was so important, it is strange to find that Miller's supernatural tales almost always convey a threatening presence behind the physical world. He delighted, if that is the word, in discovering new monsters haunting lonely glens—such as the one-legged Ludaig who hopped from rock to rock in the bogs near Isle Ornsay, Skye (Miller 1874b, p. 103). On a number of occasions in his later travels he regretted the 'absence' of a ghost: near Evanton 'the

scene lacked but a ghost to make it perfect' (Miller 1874b, p. 337) and there was a similar lack in the burn outside Portsoy (Miller 1874b, p. 264). A hut by the Shin Falls would, 'when the cry of the kelpie mingled with the roar of the flood', have made a 'sublime lodge' (Miller 1869, p. 57).

Miller cites apparitions as the most common form of folktale (a point borne out by his own collection) and again what strikes the reader of these tales is the power and menace of the supernatural figures: the Green Lady crouching by the embers of a fire washing her sickly child in the blood of the baby of the house, now destined to die (Miller 1858, p. 70); the Navity goblin shivering by the hearth, with its dirty cloths pulled down over its knees after destroying the farm's cattle (Miller 1858, p. 71); the half-naked fairy woman of Morial's Den disappearing with a scream on hearing that there is no message of salvation in the Bible for her folk (Miller 1858, p. 72). There is little sense of nature as kindly, few good spirits and little indication of powers of healing. (The ghost of the farmer's wife [Miller 1858, p. 362] who returned to comfort her children, mistreated by their stepmother, is a rare exception.) Whatever Miller's considered theological views, in his collected folklore mankind is pitted against nature.[9]

It may be that Miller, writing with no predisposition to romanticize his subject, is more accurate in the impression he conveys of the tenor of local folktales than later collectors inspired by a romantic view of nature. He was aware of the process by which native tradition might be altered and noted that the Fingalian legends he had heard in the Highlands related the exploits of 'a tribe of gigantic savages' and had little in common with the tales of 'high-minded warriors' passed off by James Macpherson as the work of the bard Ossian.

An indicator of the tenor of native superstition may be found in the one rag well still in use in the Black Isle, known as the 'clootie well' from the cloots [cloths or rags] hung there. The almost universal reaction to this is as an ugly and sinister place and, indeed, it appears from an account published in the 1880s that this well, known then as the Hurdyhill Well, was a site where sickly children were left overnight—allegedly in the hope of a cure but presumably, if the tradition is correct, as a licensed form of child murder by exposure.

Yet, even if Miller is accurately conveying the tenor of local tradition, he did so with considerable input of his own. He undoubtedly focused on these aspects of the tales and the impression of a threatening landscape is enhanced by his deliberate ambiguity towards the supernatural. The general question of the truth of omens, foretelling, even apparitions is seldom addressed, with the result that the impact of the tales on the reader is enhanced.

The Customs of the People

The stories collected by Miller had, at the time they were collected, more of a place in the environment than a function in the community. The supernatural folktales were not stories which mattered any more—though they mattered to Miller. Miller's interest, being avowedly antiquarian, was similarly directed away from contemporary customs and beliefs.

The customs recorded by Miller in his books were, with a few exceptions, extinct or were mere remnants of belief reduced to children's amusements. Fishermen no longer calmed the waves by the motions of their hands, Halloween customs had become children's games and it was children who spat on the carved figure in St Regulus graveyard known as the 'burnt cook' (Miller 1858, pp. 58, 62 and 210). Miller knew, from a fellow workman, of water used as a charm to cure cattle after a belemnite (popularly thought to be a thunderbolt) had been placed in it, but this was in his informant's grandfather's time (Miller 1874b, p. 374; Miller 1873a, p. 41). Some stories reveal older customs and beliefs, but as incidental detail: thus we hear of farmers blessing cattle each morning, of foretelling the future by casting a 'clew' of thread into a darkened kiln-barn, of the herring in the firth leaving when blood was spilt on the water, of the stone 'fairy cradle' used, until 1746, to restore changelings (children stolen by the fairies, who would leave their own sickly offspring in their place) (Miller 1858, pp. 68, 71, 105 and 252). Where customs survived or emerged Miller generally regarded them as trivial or humorous: the masons' customs in the barrack at Conon were little more than horseplay, and fortune-telling with tea leaves, oat stalks or nuts was mere superstition (Miller 1829; Miller 1870, p. 15). The fisherwomen who believed their children had been taken by the fairies after boys of the town moved the children from one house to another were laughed at for their credulity; fishermen who believed in the bad luck brought when anyone asked about their voyage were teased by townboys who would shout 'Men, men! Where are you going?'; and aversion to pigs was a characteristic of Gaelic speakers rather than the townsfolk (Miller 1858, p. 450).

Miller displayed a different attitude in some of his early reporting for the *Inverness Courier.* When he wrote of witchcraft in the neighbouring parish of Resolis (IC 17 February 1830 and 18 August 1830), he mocked, with the same force which later characterized him as editor of the *Witness,* those who had resorted to a local witch, Miss Hay, and to a white wizard in Speyside whose family possessed a bridle once used by the devil to ride a water horse. When superstition lived on and adversely affected the behaviour of the people, Miller had no tolerance of it. He had direct experience of at least one other living superstition in the fishing community, the belief that a wind could be called up by whistling, but in this case he saw no moral harm in the custom (Miller 1858, p. 58).

Miller acted more as an observer (being an outsider) during his stays as a boy with cousins in Sutherland, reporting contemporary customs (although, not speaking Gaelic, he could not understand all he heard). He gleaned some knowledge of folk medicine from his cousin who used herbs to cure cattle of illness and to disenchant bewitched cattle, knew how to make potions to induce love and hate, and told Hugh of how a cow might be given a live fish to swallow in certain cases (Miller 1869, p. 111). In the first edition of *Scenes and Legends,* in a section not carried in the second, Miller described seeing, as a boy, the 'charm of the egg' used for fortune telling in the cottage of his relations in Sutherland, and indicates how he vividly imagined himself in ancient Rome watching a ceremony of augury.

The only other customs which seem to have made a profound impression on Miller were funeral customs: he refers on a number of occasions to the traditional lykewakes at which the corpse was laid out with a plate of salt, candles burning and the furniture draped in white. On his visit to England the only local customs he noted were when he saw a coffin (not, as in Scotland, painted black) being carried to the churchyard by its handles (rather than on the shoulders) (Miller 1870, p. 227).

The absence of customs, charms and rituals in Miller's collection may be accounted for largely by a prudent turning away from recording living beliefs in his own community. Moreover, much ceremony and ritual simply did not appeal to him. There may have been some change in his attitude here or some ambivalence. Although he did not join the Freemasons' lodge in Cromarty, an early contribution to the *Inverness Courier* contains a sympathetic description of an 'impressive' ceremony at the laying of a foundation stone for the new Gardeners' Lodge, as part of which chalices of corn, wine and oil were poured over the stone (IC 21 April 1830). Later in life he was unmoved by ritual in the Church of England which he described as 'common placed by the daily repetition of two centuries' (Miller 1870, p. 23) and he considered, with obvious distaste, that before the Reformation 'pageants and ceremonies . . . constituted the entire religion of the country' (Miller 1873c, p. 28). Yet he was not entirely unmoved by such things. He attended a Roman Catholic Mass and recognized the artistry of the priest—although he regarded it as merely artistry—and in *My Schools and Schoolmasters* he makes a striking comparison between family prayers in the smoke-filled turf house of his Sutherland relations and high mass in the incense-filled cathedral (Miller 1869, p. 48).

Miller was also unresponsive to much symbolism. St Regulus, the graveyard in Cromarty, where he worked and buried his infant daughter, has a fine collection of late seventeenth-century carvings of the emblems of death: skulls, hourglasses, coffins, bells and gravedigger's tools. Miller had a low opinion of their 'heavy grotesque style' and was similarly dismissive of medieval carvings in Manchester Collegiate Church (Miller 1858, p. 210; Miller 1870, p. 38). Gravestones carved by Miller, distinguishable by their scalloped edges, are plain and severe; he seems to have assessed their quality by the workmanship of the lettering and by the sentiments expressed in the inscription.

An explanation can be found in the fact that symbols, ritual and charms are often means of controlling the supernatural by bringing luck, calling up natural or supernatural powers, restoring health or causing harm. In such magic, Miller had no interest. The supernatural world appealed to him as something which, when belief was suspended, was simply there. Its creatures were different, generally frightening, and not within human control. The imaginative world which he created was thus invested with sufficient independence to sustain his relationship with it.

MILLER'S ANALYSIS OF FOLKLORE

Early in *Scenes and Legends* Miller offers an analysis of three classes of tradition. First are traditional and historically truthful stories, with accurate delineation of character, which he associates with male sources. Second are fanciful and imaginative tales, generally of little value other than as humorous stories, although some local tales are of a superior kind within this class. And third are the highest class which combine either historical truth or accurate representation of character with flashes of invention, and these tales Miller associates with women storytellers. Miller's three classes seem to correspond, respectively, with the accurate historical tales and reminiscences of the Wright brothers, the humorous tales and ghost stories heard in gatherings at his uncle's workbench and in the masons' barrack, and the stories told by his mother or gleaned from other women. However, the analysis is not repeated in any other work and seems more a justification for the collection of traditional tales than a tool for study of them. Indeed, Miller's main point seems to be that stories of the third class have a value which compares with, for example, classical myth and legend. Having produced the analysis, Miller gets down to his main business of telling stories.

In his account of the parish of Cromarty for the *Second Statistical Account of Scotland* Miller produced a different analysis, this time of the origins of traditional tales.

> Some belong evidently to a very early period, and seem to have floated into it [i.e. Cromarty] from the Highlands. There are other stories which are peculiar to it as

a remote sea port, inhabited for ages by sailors and fishermen; while a third and more recent class belongs to it as an insulated lowland colony

(Miller 1845, p. 9).

Miller's main contribution to a study of traditional tales is, however, in a number of asides to his main business of telling stories. He is astute in recognizing the role minor superstitions had played within organized religion until what was, for him, the recent past. A few of Miller's examples refer to the seventeenth century when, after the Reformation and the sweeping away of what Miller would have regarded as gross superstition, leading evangelical figures such as Thomas Hogg of Kiltearn were seen as protecting their communities against the Devil, in the tale of the Watchmen of Cullicudden (Miller 1858, p. 167). However, his main examples refer to the evangelical revival of the 1740s and other evidence, particularly from kirk session records, confirms that this marked an important period of change. Before this time local belief in witchcraft was still a sufficiently important issue for Church authorities to act against such practices as counter-charming by cutting the alleged witch's forehead.

The evangelical revival put an end to many beliefs and practices, such as the frequenting of holy wells (at least on Sundays) but incorporated into the new 'enthusiasm' were beliefs that leading figures in the community could work miracles, predict the future, and deal with apparitions of evil spirits or spirits of the dead. The body of tales of Miller's ancestor Donald Roy are of this nature (Miller 1858, pp. 146-52). Donald Roy's gift of rings to his daughters before their marriages, as a reminder of their marriage to Christ is a fascinating example of inventive religious symbolism within a community—and is indeed the one case of such a usage with which Miller seems to have sympathy (Miller 1869, p. 33).

Miller saw the evangelical revival as having done away with dangerous superstition, at least among the most credulous. Superstition remained but it was generally benign. The Cromarty fishers, while they had little acquaintance

> 'with the higher standards of right, had a code of foolish superstitions, which, strange as it may seem, served almost the same end. They respected an oath, in the belief that no-one had ever perjured himself and thriven; regarded the murderer as exposed to the terrible visitations of his victim, and the thief as a person condemned to a down look; reverenced the Bible a protection against witchcraft, and baptism as a charm against the fairies'

(Miller 1829, p. 83).

Miller made some perceptive comments as to the loss of oral tradition, noting the effect of agricultural changes in the 1830s in ending transmission of local lore. The holdings of small tenant farmers were replaced by large farms which relied on a more mobile work force of farm labourers, engaged each year at hiring fairs. Returning to Conon in later life he found, because of these changes, that no one now knew the tales he had heard when working there as a journeyman mason (Miller 1874b, p. 164). In visiting the island of Eigg he noted the lack of long-standing traditions, which he took to be the result of earlier movements of population. He also noted how events, such as the discovery of a skeleton near the Shoremills, might revive a story (in this case, the Guardian Cock) which had lain dormant in the minds of a few old people for over 60 years (Miller 1874b, p. 322).

Miller was interested in parallel myths in primitive peoples, seeing them as the result of the deep psychological roots of myth; and he held that there were remnants of 'the old mythology' in local belief: the legends of Green Ladies, the story of the Guardian Cock and the tale of Morial's Den struck him as such. He held that, in principle, traditional tales might contain very old historical information and presented a sustained analysis of flood traditions in the folklore of various cultures in order to make a theological point in *The Testimony of the Rocks,* but none of the material he collected himself was relevant to this exercise (Miller 1874c, p. 270).

MILLER'S BELIEFS

What did Miller believe about the supernatural elements in the tales he recorded? Of the supernatural tales, a number are presented as having natural explanations: the spectre ships reputedly seen at night on the Mulbuie Common were trees rising above a low-lying sea of mist; some ghostly lights, such as at Castle Craig, may have been from illicit stills (and no doubt the belief in their supernatural origin was encouraged); the apparition at Ferindonald might be attributed to the quantity of drink consumed before it was seen; and the decline in appearances of ghosts might in general be attributed to a change in drinking habits—'tea cam in and ghaists and fairies gaed out' (Miller 1858, pp. 22, 167; Miller 1874b, p. 379). Others stories were transparent and amusing inventions, and Miller gives the opinion that a high proportion of tales might originate with spinners of yarns.

In many other cases Miller's attitude is unclear. He believed that he had experienced an omen of death, through a dream which appears, without identifying Miller, in *Scenes and Legends* as the Apprentice's Dream. While working at Poyntzfield House in 1822 he dreamed that he was in the nearby graveyard of Kirkmichael and saw a large metal bar, like the gnomon of a sundial on the gable end of the church, mysteriously move until the shadow rested at a certain point among the tombs. The sky then grew dark and he fled. Five weeks later he attended a funeral of a relative who was buried at the spot marked by the gnomon (Miller 1858, p. 434).

Miller's own experiences also included the apparition of a disembodied hand, contemporaneous with the drowning of his father, although with no possibility of the disaster being avoided, and he believed that he had seen, as a young boy, the ghost of John Feddes. Such boyhood experiences are recounted in a manner which leaves open to the reader the interpretation that Miller is presenting the events as they appeared to him at the time rather than giving his considered view as an adult, and this is the interpretation of his biographer (Bayne 1871, II, p. 15). But elsewhere Miller makes strong claims for the reliability of early childhood memories, citing the example of a woman who recounted to Miller how she was taken in her nurse's arms to see the burning of a witch at Dornoch in 1722 (Miller 1874c, p. 267; Miller 1869, p. 126). He came close to justifying belief in omens of death in the words of his uncle James (the young saddler in 'The Gudewife of Minitarf') who believed that his foreknowledge (through a dream or vision) of the death of his cousin had led him to see 'that there is indeed an invisible world, and that all the future is known to Him' (Miller 1858, p. 407). Such a view would have allowed Miller to accept as true almost all the stories about his revered great-grandfather Donald Roy.

Miller noted that apparitions of evil spirits were 'the most numerous class of our traditions' (Miller 1858, p. 165). In some cases, as we have seen, he provides a natural explanation, but in general the effective telling of the tale has priority. There is no instance, at least before his final illness, of Miller believing himself to have seen such an apparition, yet he recounts a dream of an attack by 'a frightful female', following a day in which he was soaked and chilled, with startling immediacy, as if it had happened in reality. (Miller 1874b, p. 378)

Other superstitions, including belief in ghosts, Miller held to have an important moral function in the absence of 'a deeper sense of religion . . . than most people entertain' (Miller 1858, p. 357). Ghosts were presumably a reminder of the last things—death, judgement and immortality—and his views on the moral benefits of other superstitions in the fishing community has already been quoted. There is also a strong sense of moral order in many non-supernatural tales, exemplified by the tale of the kindness of Sandy Wright (Miller's great-grandfather) to an orphan, who in later life returned the kindness by preventing Wright from losing his pension as a customhouse boatman.

Yet Miller goes beyond a mere suspension of disbelief and perhaps the most striking feature of his treatment of the supernatural is the absence of any systematic discussion of these questions. An interesting example of his ambiguity is the story of the Eathie fairies, which was sufficiently important to him to warrant a footnote in his geological work *The Old Red Sandstone.* One is tempted to say that he must surely have disbelieved such tales and yet Robert Dick, the Thurso baker and geologist who provided Miller with many specimens, reacted to Miller's death by saying that Miller had always been too taken up with fairies. He related an incident when Miller, with Dick in Buchan, had insisted that the fairies were nipping him, in circumstances which suggest he had merely been bitten by an insect (Smiles 1878, p. 235).

In passing we may note that Miller may himself have been taken in, in the case of the Eathie fairies, by a story originating with a teller of tall tales. Donald Calder, a Cromarty merchant, had, it seems, been passing the ravine of the Eathie Burn when returning from the Fortrose market. He heard a voice calling his name and wandered down into the mist-filled valley. Apparently, a mystery. The voice continued to call but always from some different place. Donald gave up the search after a short time and climbed up from the burn only to find that the whole night had passed. However, contemporary Court records reveal that Donald Calder, merchant in Cromarty, was on one occasion the subject of a paternity suit following his 'connexion' with the widow, Betty Stuart, at the Tain Market. And so a solution to the mystery seems to emerge once we credit Calder with a strong need to account for overnight absences from home.

Such tales—traditional or invented—may have been a 'fallen meteor' for the community in general but they burned brightly enough in Miller's mind and his description of an elderly relative in Nigg might be applied to Miller himself.

> He had . . . a good deal of the sceptic in his composition, and regarded his ghost stories rather as the machinery of domestic poetry than as pieces of real history; but, then, no one could value them more as curious illustrations of human belief, or show less the coldness of infidelity in his mode of telling them
>
> (Miller 1858, p. 359).

MILLER'S ACHIEVEMENT

Miller recognized traditional tales as a suitable subject for serious and analytical study, and his recognition of their value is a credit to his independence of mind. The enduring value of his collection of tales and customs lies in its being predominantly a collection of material from one small area (although, as we have seen, it does not include contemporary customs). The historical material contains much of local interest which would otherwise have been lost or difficult to recover. All the same Miller should not be regarded as an historian: he presents, in his own words, a 'traditional history' which is a view of the history of the community through the eyes of a particular section of the people. Nor, for that matter, is he a systematic folklorist. The stories of *Scenes and Legends* were collected in the late 1820s and early 1830s and primarily articulated his relationship with Cromarty and its neighbourhood. His later collecting in Scotland was limited by time and by the circles in which he then moved, and in his travels in England he did not strike up the relationships which enabled him to hear traditional tales.

Nevertheless, Miller made a contribution to the study of folklore and by providing us with a comprehensive early survey Miller enables us to see the development of folklore in the area. New stories emerge (the Clach Malloch is now said to be cursed because a fisherwoman left her child there while she gathered bait and the child was drowned by the incoming tide), customs are revived (the Saint's Well at Navity, barely used as a rag well in Miller's day, was reportedly decked with rags in 1934), and old stories are transferred to new locations (more than one child has assured me that the Green Lady, who haunted houses in Miller's boyhood, is alive and well and living in the tower of the school building).

Miller also provided us with some analysis of folklore but, despite his analysis, he avoided 'the coldness of infidelity' and remained a storyteller. In doing so he was maintaining a link with his mother, a storyteller who his family, even while deploring her credulity, found had 'a power of enchaining the attention of listeners (which) was quite extraordinary' (Bayne 1871, I, p. 18). One might add that Miller, in turn, delighted in the imaginative vitality of his children, as when one 'saw' the shape of an angel in the head of a fossil describing it as 'the lady in the lobster' (Miller 1859, p. 77).

Miller's cautiously advanced view was that the best of local folktales could equal even the finest parts of 'the old classics' (Miller 1858, p. 5). Although his tales were indeed traditional, Miller rightly noted that 'much depends on the manner in which a story is told' and in the manner of telling they are Miller's creation (Miller 1858, p. 9). Recognizing this may help to explain why Miller stopped creating stories himself; he channelled his creativity, first into the retelling of traditional stories and subsequently into geology and journalism. 'The Boatman's Tale', composed in Edinburgh in 1823 and published in his early volume of poetry, seems to have been his last attempt at an original story[10]—although there are occasional wild flights of fancy in later polemical writings in which Miller exercises once more his story telling art. The effect of these later 'tales' can be bizarre, as in his imaginative fantasy of the two Mr Clerks at Tomnahurich (a 'fairy hill' in Inverness). Clerk, a minister who had changed his views on matters close to Miller's heart, is portrayed stepping out from the thickets of the hill, dressed as a conjuror, whereupon he sets up and brings to life two little human figures made of carrots, cabbages and turnips. Shortly afterwards a landslide sweeps into their midst the 'Mr Clerk of three years ago', dressed in black and 'wriggling . . . like a huge blue-bottle in an old cobweb' (Miller 1873b, p. 346).

The strength of Miller's story telling lies in his capacity for visualization and ability to convey this vision to the reader, characteristics recognized by his early friend and critic William Ross. In the winter of 1820 Ross and Miller would take moonlight walks by Cromarty's Crook Burn where Miller would not only find striking descriptions for the stream (a flash of lightning, a stream of lava, a strip of the Aurora Borealis) but describe trees and stones as the 'fays and spectres by which the place was tenanted', even giving 'a minute detail of the particular expression of their features, and the peculiarities of their attire' (Miller 1829).

In the account of his early life which he wrote for Principal Baird in 1829, Miller described how his thinking relied on clearly conceived images. His image of the solar system was that of 'an orrery of about sixty miles in diameter', the greatest distance which he could see from a mountain top. Miller's mental image was on a vast scale and was conceived in such detail that he could use it as a means of analytic thought:

> I imagine the space . . . to be occupied by an atmosphere like that of the earth, which reflects the light of the sun in the different degrees of excessive brightness, noon-tide-splendour, the fainter shade of evening, and grey twilight obscurity. I perceive that this veil of light is thickest towards its centre; for when my glance rests on its edges I behold the suns of other systems peeping through it. I see Mercury sparkling to the sun with its oceans and rivers of molten glass, and its fountains of liquid gold. I see the ice mountains of Saturn, haar through the twighlight; I behold the earth rolling upon itself from darkness to light, and from light to darkness. . . . I see the pyramid of shade which each of the planets casts from its darkened side into the space behind; and I perceive the stars twinkling through each pyramid, as through the angular doors of a pavilion
>
> (Miller 1829).

Here is the 'poesy' of science which could vie with the 'old mythology' and, as with his folklore, the strength of the account lies in the detail with which it is realized.

This high degree of realism, which gives strength to his geological (and cosmological) writing and description of the natural world, has an added impact in his supernatural tales by Miller's addition of grotesque details, conveyed with this same immediacy. (His vision of geology would seem to lack the dark undertones of the folktales.) The penetrating imagination, which enabled the interpretation of geological data, is applied to the human body in a fascination with death and decay, as in the account from Orkney of a drowned man with his eyes detached from their sockets 'staring from a wreath of seaweed' (Miller 1874b, p. 432). In all this there was no doubt an influence from the death of his father at sea and the consequent imaginings as to the fate of his body.

In collecting and retelling the tales with his power of visualization, his realism and his sense for grotesque detail, Miller's is a literary creation. Miller recognised the unique power of writing to convey experience and in commenting on the effect produced by contemplating monuments of remote antiquity, such as standing stones and cairns, he doubted the ability of a painted image to convey 'that blended feeling of the sublime and solemn' which the writer could evoke (Miller 1873c, p. 344). His description of the natural world, while precise, struck his critic Mackenzie as exhibiting a lack of human interest and a 'certain hardness' (Mackenzie 1905, p. 39). Yet, it is perhaps this quality which gives his supernatural tales their power by creating a sense of a supernatural world independent of the reader's or listener's emotions. One cannot but note that, whatever the cause of Miller's final illness, it manifested itself through this remarkable power for visualization in a nightmare which, in his own words, 'burned' his brain. He was driven to suicide by a tale become too real, too independent—no longer a fallen meteor but a fiery comet.

Notes

1. Of these 350 tales and customs collected by Miller, just over half have a supernatural element. The largest group of supernatural tales is of apparitions: of ghosts (24), beings such as mermaids, the devil, goblins and green ladies (27), fairies (11) and other phenomena (11). A second major group concern supernatural knowledge either of the future or of events as they happen: omens of death (12), prophecies (7) and contemporaneous visions of disasters (5). There are also customs associated with charms, luck and fortune telling (12) and a body of traditional legend and giant lore (13). Accounts of witchcraft (10) reveal some supernatural beliefs, as do some customs (20). The bulk of the non-supernatural tales are, as Miller described them, 'traditional history' from the Black Isle, Easter Ross and Sutherland. Miller's own family background is reflected in the fact that over 30 are tales of fishing and seafaring.

2. This was a series of articles in the *Inverness Courier* (henceforth referred to in text as IC), republished in 1834 as the *Traditional History of Cromarty* and incorporated in *Scenes and Legends of the North of Scotland*.

3. One should note, however, that the tradition of lay evangelism represented by Donald Roy (but without the supernatural trappings) was much admired by Miller's wife, Lydia, as is clear from her novel *Passages in the Life of an English Heiress* (1847). For an account of the novel, see Calder (1993).

4. Although this story appears in *Scenes and Legends,* Miller does not there make it clear that Elspat Hood was his great-great-grandmother.

5. Among books held at Hugh Miller's Cottage. Information supplied by Frieda Gostwick, National Trust for Scotland.

6. Apparently, St Kennat's, although it was noted in the 1760s as being St Bainan's. It is puzzling that Miller in *Scenes and Legends* calls it St Bennet's, even in the first edition of 1835. It may be that Miller had, in *Scenes and Legends,* simply assumed that the well bore the same dedication as the chapel. The discovery of the name 'St Kennat's' apparently interested him because he believed this must have been a saint of the Celtic rather than the Roman church.

7. Mackenzie quotes two examples: 'The buttur kip of affluction' (the bitter cup of affliction) in his introduction to *My Schools and Schoolmasters* (Miller 1907) and 'the exe hed been bussy in the gleds' (the axe had been busy in the glades) (Mackenzie 1905, p. 47).

8. W. M. Mackenzie and his brother, Donald Alexander Mackenzie (both Cromarty men) will be mentioned a number of times in this essay. Their father, Alexander Mackenzie, was noted for his knowledge of local family histories and local affairs, and had met Hugh Miller as a boy, remembering Miller's huge head and the wonderful power of his eyes: Alexander's father, Donald, had been a friend of Miller since boyhood. W. M. Mackenzie was a respected historian, secretary to the Royal Commission in Scotland on Ancient and Historical Monuments and editor of the poems of the medieval Scots poet Dunbar. He was meticulous, with almost an overpowering fear of making a mistake, and his detailed local and family knowledge adds weight to the reliability of his *Hugh Miller: A Critical Study* and to his introduction to and annotation of the 1907 edition of *My Schools and Schoolmasters.* His brother, D. A. Mackenzie, a journalist and folklorist, produced a number of popular collection of myths and legends, studies of folklore, and plays, poems and short stories— but was more 'adventurous' in his beliefs.

D. A. Mackenzie notes a number of sayings and beliefs relating to a figure known as 'Gentle Annie', associated with sudden squalls in the Firth; a forked rowan tree in which fishermen left pebbles before setting out on a voyage; a spitting stone near a rowan, known as the rock tree (boys threw stones at the tree before going rock climbing and turned back if the pebble rebounded from the tree); that curses were delivered by an individual standing or kneeling bare kneed on the Clach Malloch; and of rocks on the Cromarty shore flung by giants (Mackenzie 1935, pp. 100-3, 159-61, 255, 273).

9. A few folk customs from the neighbouring parish of Resolis can be found among the 'hymns and incantations' collected by Carmichael in the late nineteenth century (Carmichael 1992). These are charms for healing and are of a quite different tenor to the customs noted by Miller. However, since there was an influx of Gaelic speakers to this area during the nineteenth century, it is not clear if these traditions were to be found in Miller's day (Carmichael, 1992).

10. In 1837 Miller wrote 'Thomas of Chartres' for Wilson's *Tales of the Borders,* an extended retelling of an episode from Blind Harry's *Wallace,* which had enthralled him as a boy (Miller, 1891). This is perhaps the closest he came to attempting historical fiction and, like his retelling of traditional tales, it is notable for the detail in which Miller visualized the scenes.

References

Bayne, P. (1871). *The Life and Letters of Hugh Miller,* 2 vols. Strahan, Edinburgh.

Calder, A. (1993). 'The Disruption in Fiction'. In *Scotland in the Age of the Disruption,* ed. S.J. Brown and M. Fry, pp. 113-132. Edinburgh University Press, Edinburgh.

Carmichael, A. (1992). *Carmina Gaedelica.* Floris Books, Edinburgh.

Dickson, N. (1858). *Cromarty: Being a Tourist's Visit to the Birthplace of Hugh Miller.* Thomas Murray and Son, Glasgow.

Dorson, R. (1968). *The British Folklorists.* University of Chicago Press, Chicago.

Drabble, M. and Stringer, J. (1990). *The Concise Oxford Companion to English Literature.* Oxford University Press.

Grant, W. and Murison, D. (ed.) (1931). *Scottish National Dictionary,* Vol. 1. Scottish National Dictionary Association, Edinburgh.

Hill, B. (1978). *The Remarkable World of Frances Barkly: 1869-1845.* Gray's Publishing Limited, Sidney, British Columbia.

Loch, D. (1778). *A Tour through most of the Trading Towns and Villages of Scotland.* Edinburgh.

Mackenzie, D. A. (1935). *Scottish Folklore and Folk-life.* Blackie, Glasgow.

Mackenzie, W. M. (1905). *Hugh Miller: A Critical Study.* North Star, Dingwall.

Miller, H. (1829). *Hugh Miller's First Autobiography, to the Very Reverend Principal Baird.* Manuscript in New College Library, Edinburgh.

Miller, H. (1845). 'Parish of Cromarty'. In *A New Statistical Account of Scotland,* William Blackwood and Sons, Edinburgh, 14, 1-18.

Miller, H. (1858). *Scenes and Legends of the North of Scotland, or, the Traditional History of Cromarty.* William P. Nimmo, Edinburgh. (First published 1835)

Miller, H. (1859). *Footprints of the Creator; or, the Asterolepis of Stromness.* William P. Nimmo, Edinburgh. (First published 1849)

Miller, H. (1863). *Tales and Sketches.* William P. Nimmo, Edinburgh.

Miller, H. (1869) *My Schools and Schoolmasters; or, the Story of my Education.* William P. Nimmo, Edinburgh. (First published 1854)

Miller, H. (1870). *First Impressions of England and its People.* William P. Nimmo, Edinburgh. (First published 1847)

Miller, H. (1873a). *The Old Red Sandstone; or, New Walks in an Old Field.* William P. Nimmo, Edinburgh. (First published 1841)

Miller, H. (1873b). *Leading Articles on Various Subjects.* William P. Nimmo, Edinburgh. (First published 1870)

Miller, H. (1873c). *The Headship of Christ, and the Rights of the Christian People.* William P. Nimino, Edinburgh. (First published 1861)

Miller, H. (1874a). *Sketch-book of Popular Geology; being a Series of Lectures Delivered before the Philosophical Institution of Edinburgh.* William P. Nimmo, Edinburgh. (First published 1859)

Miller, H. (1874b). *The Cruise of the Betsey; or, A Summer Ramble among the Fossiliferous Deposits of the Hebrides. With Rambles of a Geologist; or, Ten Thousand Miles over the Fossiliferous Deposits of Scotland.* William P. Nimmo, Edinburgh. (First published 1858)

Miller, H. (1874c). *The Testimony of the Rocks; or, Geology in its Bearing on the two Theologies, Natural and Revealed.* William P. Nimmo, Edinburgh. (First published 1857)

Miller, H. (1875). *Edinburgh and its Neighbourhood, Geological and Historical; With the Geology of the Bass Rock.* William P. Nimmo, Edinburgh. (First published 1864)

Miller, H. (1881). *Essays, Historical and Biographical, Political and Social, Literary and Scientific.* William P. Nimmo, Edinburgh. (First published 1862)

Miller, H. (1891). 'Thomas of Chartres'. In *Wilson's Tales of the Borders* ed. A. Leighton, XVIII, Edinburgh.

Miller, H. (1907) *My Schools and Schoolmasters; or, the Story of my Education* (Introduction and annotations by W. M. Mackenzie), Edinburgh. (First published 1854)

Sinclair, Sir J. (1795). *General View of the Agriculture of the Northern Counties and Islands of Scotland.* London.

Smiles, S. (1878). *Robert Dick, Baker of Thurso, Geologist and Botanist.* Murray, London.

Wight, A. (1781). *Present State of Husbandry in Scotland,* Vol. 3. Edinburgh.

FURTHER READING

Biographies

Bayne, Peter. *The Life and Letters of Hugh Miller.* 2 vols. Boston: Gould and Lincoln, 1871, 928 p.
    Examines Miller's life and writings.

Leask, W. Keith. *Hugh Miller.* Edinburgh: Oliphant, Anderson & Ferrier, 1896, 157 p.
    Comprehensive study of Miller's life and career as a writer and scientist.

Shortland, Michael. "Bonneted Mechanic and Narrative Hero: The Self-Modelling of Hugh Miller." In *Hugh Miller and the Controversies of Victorian Science,* edited by Michael Shortland, pp. 14-75. Oxford: Clarendon Press, 1996.
    Psychological analysis of Miller.

Swiderski, Richard M. "Hugh Miller's Walk: Science, Folklore, and Suicide." *Soundings* 66, no. 2 (summer 1983): 174-88.
    Examines the circumstances surrounding Miller's death.

Criticism

Brooke, John Hedley. "Like Minds: The God of Hugh Miller." In *Hugh Miller and the Controversies of Victorian Science,* edited by Michael Shortland, pp. 171-86. Oxford: Clarendon Press, 1996.
    Emphasizes the aesthetic aspects of Miller's writings on theology.

Gillispie, Charles Coulston. "The Vestiges of Creation." In *Genesis and Geology: A Study in the Relations of Scientific Thought, Natural Theology, and Social Opinion in Great Britain, 1790-1850,* pp. 149-83. Cambridge: Harvard University Press, 1951.

Examination of the early nineteenth-century scientific debate on the progression of organic forms and Miller's contribution to the discourse.

Henry, John. "Palaeontology and Theodicy: Religion, Politics and the *Asterolepis* of Stromness." In *Hugh Miller and the Controversies of Victorian Science,* edited by Michael Shortland, pp. 151-69. Oxford: Clarendon Press, 1996.

Examines Miller's views on theology, science, and history.

Macleod, Donald. "Hugh Miller, the Disruption and the Free Church of Scotland." In *Hugh Miller and the Controversies of Victorian Science,* edited by Michael Shortland, pp. 187-205. Oxford: Clarendon Press, 1996.

Traces Miller's participation, as editor of the Non-Intrusion party's the *Witness,* in the debates revolving around the ideological schism in the Church of Scotland known as the Disruption.

Oldroyd, David R. "The Geologist from Cromarty." In *Hugh Miller and the Controversies of Victorian Science,* edited by Michael Shortland, pp. 76-121. Oxford: Clarendon Press, 1996.

Evaluates Miller's contributions to geology.

Porter, Roy. "Miller's Madness." In *Hugh Miller and the Controversies of Victorian Science,* edited by Michael Shortland, pp. 265-86. Oxford: Clarendon Press, 1996.

Relates Miller's madness as exemplified in his writings on his religious beliefs and nineteenth-century views on mental illness.

Additional coverage of Hugh Miller's life and career is contained in the following sources published by Thomson Gale: *Dictionary of Literary Biography,* **Vol. 190; and** *Literature Resource Center.*

Robert Schumann
1810-1856

German composer and critic.

INTRODUCTION

Schumann composed some of the most original masterpieces of Romantic music. His songs and piano miniatures inhabit an undisputed place in the pantheon of Western music. Schumann's famous struggle with mental illness has also fascinated researchers, including psychiatrists, who endeavor to shed light on the nature of the illness and his ability to create works of genius despite it.

BIOGRAPHICAL INFORMATION

Schumann was born June 8, 1810, in Zwickau, a Saxon town located near present-day Germany's border with the Czech Republic. Official documents do not refer to a middle name, although Schumann's first biographer, Wilhelm Joseph von Wasiliewski, cited it as Alexander. Schumann grew up surrounded by books: his father was a successful bookseller and an author of some repute. After receiving an excellent secondary school education, which enabled him to read the Greek and Latin classics in the original, Schumann went to Leipzig in 1830 to study law. Uninterested in the law, Schumann immersed himself in literature, keeping abreast of all the momentous literary developments in Germany and writing many fragments, poems, and prose pieces which he hoped eventually to develop into great literary works. To his family's consternation, late in 1830 Schumann declared that he wanted to be a musician, and he remained in Leipzig to pursue a musical career. Schumann's future father-in-law, the eminent piano teacher Friedrich Wieck, declared that in his hands Schumann would become a rival to the greatest virtuosos. These hopes were dashed, probably in 1832, when Schumann suffered a mysterious hand injury about which scholars have offered several theories. This event signaled the beginning of Schumann's career as a composer, for it is in the 1830s that he started writing his astonishing piano miniatures. In the meantime, Schumann had made his debut as a music critic. In 1831, in the *Allgemeine musikalische Zeitung*, Schumann reviewed Frederick Chopin's "Là ci darem la mano" variations for piano and orchestra, presciently declaring that the Polish composer was a great genius. Defining his literary work as

a veritable crusade against mediocrity in music, Schumann cofounded the *Neue Zetschrift für Musik,* a journal into which he poured all his efforts, eventually assuming most of the writing and editorial responsibilities. For ten years, Schumann used his journal to champion talented composers, single-handedly establishing what posterity would accept as the canon of Romantic music. In addition, throughout the 1830s and 1840s, he composed his greatest masterpieces, including the *Carnaval,* for piano, and the sublime song-cycle, *Dichterliebe (The Poet's Love)*, based on Heinrich Heine's poems. In 1840—after a fierce legal battle with Wieck, who did not want him as a son-in-law—Schumann married Clara Wieck, an immensely talented pianist on her way to becoming one of Europe's greatest virtuosos. Married life introduced a modicum of stability into Schumann's life, but his mental instability, evidenced by suicidal behavior in late 1833 and early 1834, remained a concern. Furthermore, despite his natural inclination toward smaller musical forms, Schumann constantly forced himself to attempt larger forms such as symphonies and concertos, often feeling despondent and frustrated by the public's lukewarm response. One of these disappointments was the failure of his only opera, *Genoveva* (1843). In 1843, Schumann accepted a teaching post at the newly-founded Leipzig Conservatory, but performed his duties without much enthusiasm. The following year, Schumann resigned from the position and moved his family to Dresden. After he left Leipzig, Schumann started experiencing serious professional difficulties. In 1850, he agreed to become conductor of a civic orchestra and chorus in Düsseldorf. His state of mind steadily deteriorating, Schumann threw himself into the freezing waters of the Rhine in February 1854. After his rescue, he voluntarily entered the asylum at Endenich, near Bonn, where he died in 1856. Hypothetical diagnoses of Schumann's ailments include depression, bipolar disorder, schizophrenia, and syphilis, but none of these have been confirmed. Interestingly, in his 2001 *Schumann,* Eric Frederick Jensen cites evidence suggesting that Schumann's death was not due to his illness, but rather to the barbaric treatment he received at Endenich.

MAJOR WORKS

Among Schumann's numerous critical reviews, scholars generally single out the prophetic "An Opus 2," in which Schumann, upon hearing Chopin's "Là ci darem la mano" variations for piano and orchestra, op. 2, utters the famous "Hats off, gentlemen, a genius!" Much later, in 1853, in another famous piece, "New Paths," Schumann announces the arrival of a new genius, Johannes Brahms. In both cases, Schumann's uncannily accurate assessment was based on slender evidence, the compositions in question being very early works of as yet unknown composers. These reviews exemplify a new style of criticism, inspired by E. T. A Hoffmann but brought to perfection by Schumann. As a critic, Schumann ignored established rules and relied on his intuition. Initially, Schumann's critical writings relied on an elaborate set of literary devices, including dialogues and conversations between imaginary characters. As music historians have pointed out, Schumann worked hard to forge an objective, analytical approach to music despite the immense success of his subjective style. Indeed, as Florestan and Eusebius faded away, Schumann's reviews and essays became a trusted guide to contemporary music. However, as Carl Dahlhaus observed, Schumann formulated his entire approach to music (including a revolutionary philosophy of music) during his early years as a critic. Thus, in "Master Raro's, Florestan's, and Eusebius's Booklet of Thoughts and Poems" (1833), Schumann identified Bach and Beethoven as ideals to be emulated. In linking Bach and Beethoven, Dahlhaus noted that Schumann departed from conventional thinking, which, following stylistic considerations, associated Bach with Handel, and Beethoven with Mozart. In fact, Dahlhaus identified Schumann's insight as the philosophical foundation of an original and epoch-making musical utopia that combined "Bach's contemplative depth and Beethoven's Promethean sublimity."

CRITICAL RECEPTION

Viewed by his contemporaries as a critic in the imaginative and somewhat flamboyant tradition of E. T. A. Hoffmann, Schumann was perceived as a writer driven by his subjective views. This perception was radically revised in the twentieth century, when scholars started examining Schumann's ideas and observations in the larger context of nineteenth-century German culture. Henry Pleasants stated that "it was in his craftsman's appreciation and assessment of craftsmanship that Schumann stands pretty much alone." Often an inspired critic, scholars insisted that Schumann nevertheless strove to attain objectivity. Indeed, not only did Schumann reach his goal of critical objectivity, but he also became a relevant voice in German intellectual life. In his seminal *Schumann as Critic,* Leon Plantinga described Schumann's critical work as truly multi-faceted, one that offered important aesthetical views and an original philosophy of music history. Dahlhaus concurred with this line of thought, even suggesting with other scholars that Schumann's writings established a new paradigm of thinking about music, a paradigm that hardly seems dated in modern times.

PRINCIPAL WORKS

Music and Musicians (nonfiction) n.d.

Die Davidsbündler (prose) 1833; published serially in *Der Komet*

"Master Raro's, Florestan's, and Eusebius's Booklet of Thoughts and Poems" (criticism) 1833

Dichterliebe (songs) 1840

Neue Zeitschrift für Musik [editor and contributor] (journalism) 1834-44

Genoveva (opera) 1843

Gesammelte Schriften über Musik und Musiker. 4 vols. (criticism, aphorism, prose) 1854

Early Letters (letters) 1888

Letters (letters) 1907

On Music and Musicians (nonfiction) 1964

The Musical World of Robert Schumann: A Selection from Schumann's Own Writings (nonfiction) 1965

CRITICISM

Marcel Brion (essay date 1956)

SOURCE: Brion, Marcel. "Chapter 7." In *Schumann and the Romantic Age,* translated by Geoffrey Sainsbury, pp. 148-67. New York: Macmillan, 1956.

[In the following excerpt, Brion defines Schumann's criticism as a work of art.]

It was partly to do justice to the great men of the past, partly to give a helping hand to young musicians scorned by the critics and unnoticed by the public, that Schumann decided to found a musical review. The idea was born in a cloud of pipe and cigar smoke at the *Stammtisch* of the *Kaffeebaum,* where he and his friends were accustomed to meet. This silent meditative man, who liked to sink into himself to listen to the music that was humming in his heart, was also a fighter. It would perhaps be better to say a knight-errant, for he was always ready to take up his lance to tilt at self-satisfied mediocrity and artistic insincerity—in a word at Philistinism. To instruct the ignorant by standing up for all that was great and good and deflating hollow pretensions was for him a sacred duty. It was not in any merely polemical spirit, it was not for the sake of scoring off others, nor was it in order to advance the interests of his friends that he stepped into the arena. To his mother he wrote:

> We are busy planning a new big musical review which Hofmeister will publish. Its programme will be announced next month. . . . A new enterprise always gives rise to a profusion of hopes. . . . There's lots to do, to learn as well as to teach. The difficulties are great but we have plenty of talent to meet them with. I think it will be a great success and of great profit to my intellectual development.

He knew very well how rare good musical reviews were at that period in Germany—or indeed anywhere. Ever since the enthusiastic article he had written two years before for the *Allgemeine Musikalische Zeitung* on Chopin's *"La ci darem" Variations,* op. 2, the editor had made no answer to his offers of collaboration. He was reproached for praising "revolutionary" works, and the tone of his praise—its unrestrained enthusiasm—was considered not quite the thing. To maintain the prestige of criticism, praise should be handed out parsimoniously, patronisingly, and always spiced with a certain amount of salutary fault-finding.

This wretched sterile game, in which all too often the envious sought to redeem their own smallness and avenge their own failures, made Schumann's generous

blood boil. And it was against these censors particularly that Schumann marshalled his battalions, to denounce their ignorance, their insensibility to beauty, their treacherousness, their fear of everything new and benevolence to everything second-rate, their positive ferocity in the presence of genius. Many of them were not even professionals. There were officers like Rellstab, civil servants like Castelli, clergymen like Fink. Let genius judge genius (though it will often hesitate to): for mediocrity to do so, generally in the name of outworn principles and barren laws, was a thing Schumann and his young friends could not stomach. So amongst the stale and rancid reviews of the day—*Iris, Cäcilia,* and the *A.M.Z.*—the *Neue Zeitschrift für Musik* raised its upstart head, ready to do battle with all comers, to herald the "music of the future" and to "spread the morning dew of a new age."

It was on 3rd April, 1834, that the first number appeared, and curiously enough the same year saw the birth of the *Gazette Musicale* in Paris, founded on the same principles and with much the same programme. Nowhere was "modern" music known to the public. How could it be with all the orchestras, the musical reviews, and the publishing houses in the hands of the Philistines? To be known it had to be played, it had to be talked about. The new publication could at least undertake the latter, making known the young musicians whose work looked ahead. It could also clamour for the performance of their works. And it set about the job with joyous ardour and lively pugnacity.

The extent to which Bach, dead less than a century, had been forgotten is proof of the extreme confusion into which German musical opinion had fallen, and the false gods that were being bowed down to. In the preface to the collection of critical essays published in 1853, Schumann paints a gloomy picture of those earlier days.

> The state of musical development was far from satisfactory at that period in Germany. On the stage Rossini still reigned. For the piano, it was Herz and Hünten almost exclusively. Yet, only a few years before, Beethoven, Carl Maria von Weber, and Schubert were living amongst us. Admittedly a new star was rising over the horizon, Mendelssohn, and a Pole called Chopin was much lauded, but it was only later that these artists exerted a lasting influence.

Happily Schumann was not alone. The café to which he went for his evening glass of beer was a rendezvous for other ardent spirits, musicians, poets, painters, who were only too ready to join in the cry: Down with the Philistines!

Passionate discussions went on in the thick clouds of smoke that almost obscured the picturesque paintings which adorned the walls of the *Kaffeebaum.* In the centre of a group of young men, over whom he held sway, would be Friedrich Wieck, his face hard and domineering, delivering trenchant judgments, often with brutal sarcasm. They were not always well received. We know that he sometimes quarrelled with the pianist, Julius Knorr, an old Bohemian, gifted and full of fantasy, who went the round of the taverns of Leipzig looking (and easily finding) an adversary on whom to vent his fierce argumentativeness. Another *habitué* was a painter called Lyser, an extraordinary creature, whom Hoffmann, had he known him, would certainly have made use of in one of his tales. Schumann, who was very fond of him, said: "One could write whole volumes on that young man." For he had put his hand to many trades, having been at one time or another writer, actor, theatrical producer, scene designer, conductor; and on every subject he had opinions of the utmost originality.

The publisher Hofmeister would listen with benevolence to the discussions till he himself was drawn into a long and very learned one with Dr. Reuter. More occasional frequenters of this café in the Fleischergasse were: Wenzel, an odd man who had long vacillated between theology and music before finally choosing the latter; Stegmayer, an eternal lover who played the Eusebius between two rehearsals at the theatre where he conducted the orchestra; Ortlepp, the poet who always managed to find a literary reason for contradicting a musician; Krögen, who only looked up from his newspaper from time to time to put in a scathing remark. Naturally there were others who hovered round the more formidable personalities, gaping at their outrageous views.

Schumann rarely took part in the debates. Generally, he sat to one side, drinking his beer, smoking his cigar and listening less to the argument under way than to his own inner voices. If he did intervene, it would be with passionate conviction: then once again he would relapse into silence, or chat in an undertone with his best friend, Ludwig Schunke, his favourite companion for country walks, the handsome Schunke whose premature death plunged him into despair.

Schumann has himself described the stupefaction caused by Schunke's first appearance at the *Kaffeebaum,* whose *habitués* could only compare him to one of Tilman Riemenschneider's paintings of St. John the Baptist, to the statue of a Roman Emperor recently excavated from the ashes of Pompeii, or to the ardent and majestic young Schiller as sculptured by Thorwaldsen.

> When he introduced himself, saying: "Ludwig Schunke from Stuttgart," I heard an inner voice say: "Here he is, the one for whom we have been waiting." And I could see from his eyes that he was thinking of us much the same.

Naturally the chief topic was music, good music and bad, how to overcome the Philistines entrenched in their mediocrity, and how to turn an indifferent, suspicious, or even hostile public towards the younger composers and their revolutionary work. And the only way was by frontal attack, by creating a review that was more lively and more interesting than any other. First the younger generation must be won over. The others would follow sooner or later.

The *Neue Zeitschrift für Musik* was thus born under the shadow, as it were, of a coffee tree, to champion the work of young composers still unknown and that old one, Bach, whose work had fallen into neglect. Schumann, who had taken the initiative, threw himself into the campaign with that chivalrous ardour which always came to the surface of this silent, meditative young man the moment his ideals were at stake. He was conscious of leading a veritable crusade, of playing his part in a magnificent movement in which romantic music, that is to say, music *par excellence,* would come into its own. Moreover, he saw in the foundation of the review the opportunity of creating a new form of criticism as romantic as the music it was commenting upon. For Schumann had discovered a new language of criticism as new and original as that of his music. No longer was it to confine itself to cold analysis, but to make use of the heart, of the intellect, and of all the senses to reach the inner core of a new work and lay bare its inherent meaning. Instead of contemplating a work externally, the romantic critic would plunge into it, breathe it, commune with it. Instead of a dry, pedantic summary of its points, he would recreate its atmosphere for the reader, kindling in him the same emotions as he had felt himself. Nothing less was needed if the public was to be brought to the point at which it was capable of understanding new work. Feeling, enthusiasm, an ability to project oneself into the music one was listening to—those were the mainsprings of romantic musical criticism, of which there were two great masters, Hoffmann and Schumann.

Ernst Theodor Amadeus Hoffmann had for six years been writing for the *A.M.Z.* edited by Rochlitz, who, it will be remembered, had turned his back on Schumann. Rochlitz had published some of Hoffmann's Tales, in particular the famous Ritter Gluck, one of the finest and most typical products of his genius, also some critical studies, reviews of new works, and essays on Beethoven, Gluck, Méhul, Spohr, and Boieldieu. The essay on Beethoven, included in the first volume of the *Fantasiestücke,* is a perfect example of just that criticism, passionate and subjective, which was Schumann's aim. And in his *Kreisleriana* this is the way in which Hoffmann compares the instrumental music of Hadyn, Mozart, and Beethoven. What dominates in Haydn's, he says:

> . . . is the expression of childlike serenity. His symphonies take us out onto a plain covered as far as the eye can see with cool thickets and populated by a joy-

ous motley crowd of happy people. Boys and girls dance lightly past, and laughing, teasing children hide behind the trees and rose-bushes, throwing flowers at each other. All is love, happiness and eternal youth, as before the Fall. No suffering, no pain; at most a sweet and melancholy aspiration towards that beloved Image floating far away in the brightness of the setting sun, neither approaching nor disappearing; and so long as it is there night does not fall, for it is itself the red glow of evening, lighting up hills and plain.

It is to the abysses of a mysterious kingdom that Mozart leads us. Fear takes hold of us, but it is a fear bereft of torture, rather a portent of the infinite. Love and melancholy sing in the gracious voices of the spirits; night flies away in a purple conflagration; obeying an ineffable call, we rush towards the apparitions floating in the clouds through the eternally whirling spheres and beckoning us to join them (see the *Symphony in E flat* known as the *Swan Song*).

Beethoven's instrumental music also opens up to us the empire of the prodigious and the incommensurable. Brilliant rays strike through the deep night of these realms: gigantic shadows come and go gripping us more and more forcibly, finally crushing us—ourselves but not the anguish and infinite longing in which the jubilant flashes of notes fall and drown. On the bosom of this suffering which absorbs, without destroying them, love, hope, and joy, we expect to burst asunder under the assembled voices of all passions—but we go on living, as ecstatic visionaries.

These last words are characteristic. The romantic listener is an ecstatic visionary, and the critic must express his ecstasy and his vision, rather than discourse scientifically, didactically, on the work that has inspired them. Hoffmann, it may be objected, was really a poet, but he was also a musician and a most severe and exacting one, and for all his poetry, his profession was law. Indeed it is interesting to note that of the three great champions of romantic music, Hoffmann, Wackenroder, and Schumann, two were lawyers, while the third had gone a long way towards becoming one. As advocates they were passionate in defence, virulent in indictment.

In Schumann's view, musical criticism should ideally be a sort of prose poem æsthetically equivalent to the work it was discussing. It should be music in literary garb. This was exactly the same as Goethe's view on the criticism of the plastic arts. His famous essay on the *St. Rochus zu Bingen* is as perfect an example of subjective criticism as the passage of Hoffmann's I have just quoted.

Schumann's first critical article, which had appeared in 1831 (on Chopin's *"La ci darem" Variations*) was nothing else than a cry of ecstasy. "Hats off, Gentlemen! a genius!" he began, and he went on to extol in the most lyrical terms the work of this young Pole, who was then just beginning, but in whom he saw at once all the originality that was later to be accorded him.

It must, however, be stressed that in Schumann's critical work, which fills several volumes, there is a great deal more than passionate outpourings. He discussed at the same time, and in great detail, the quality of the composition, pointing out both its beauties and its weaknesses. Indeed he was as precise and informative on the technical side as he was suggestive and poetical on the other.

Under one of his pseudonyms, Meister Raro he wrote:

> A rosy light is dawning in the sky; whence it cometh I know not; but in any case, O youth, make for the light.

It was to reach out towards the light that was the dominant urge in Schumann and his friends, the will to bring clarity to all that was obscure in the romantic soul. It is a great mistake to imagine, as many do, that German Romantics deliberately cherished obscurity. The exact opposite is the truth: with one accord they demanded of art that it should dissipate the murky clouds within them, liberate them from their anguish, and give them the poise and harmony they longed for. Their plight was often just that—a struggle between their genius and their anguish, a struggle for light. Hölderlin's Greece was simply a version of this ideal light. It had nothing to do with historic Greece. Like Orplid, Mörike's magic island, it remained always a country of the mind, a promised land of the spirit.

Nor were they any more enamoured of their ambiguity. Their inner rifts and conflicts caused them such unutterable suffering that many sought escape—by suicide like Kleist, by fantasy like Hoffmann, by madness like Hölderlin, by resignation like Goethe. Even for Novalis who sang his hymns to the Night, that night was only a road towards the light comparable to the *noche oscura* of the mystics. Far from wallowing in their tribulations, as the French are inclined to accuse them of doing, the German Romantics groped desperately one and all for any sort of inward harmony and health which could be procured without the sacrifice of their essential personalities. Schumann offers us perhaps the best example of this struggle.

With all their exuberant creativeness, the Romantics were excellent critics, lucid and penetrating. Dahms does not overshoot the mark when he maintains that it was they who created musical criticism.

> It had come to be realised that it was impossible to discover the soul of music by arid philosophic speculation or by the use of abstract intellectual faculties. It was through instinct that the Romantics found their way, through character, through feeling, through *Sehnsucht* and passion.

They realised the value of poetic description when commenting on and trying to do justice to a work of art, whether plastic or musical. Rochlitz had already to some extent pointed the way, though timidly, fearing the Philistines. It was left to the genius of Hoffmann and Schumann to give to poetic criticism—make no mistake: poetic not "literary"—its true value both objective and subjective.

Lastly, it was given to the Romantics to recognise and exalt all that was *divine* in genius. At the same time they took the grace which genius endows as the hallmark, not of the Superman (a later invention of Nietzsche's) but of man himself, man enhanced to his highest power, sublimating himself till he takes his place at the right hand of God.

But if Schumann was to interpret by means of poetry the new voice of German music, it was not to be to the exclusion of foreigners, for he paid generous tribute to the Pole, Chopin, the Frenchman, Berlioz, and the Englishmen, Sterndale Bennett and John Field. All the same, his aim was primarily to discover and translate into words the music of his day and of his own country, not from any narrow nationalistic feeling, but from a conviction that the genius of an individual, however personal it might be, belonged none-the-less to a period and a place. Thus he attacked the Italians, the "canaries" as he called them, because of the inner spirit of *bel canto,* which he considered profoundly inimical to the development of German music. He attacked the futile flourishes of Rossini as vigorously as the "empty oratory" of Meyerbeer, and although in his first works he gave way to the prevailing fashion of using French titles, he dreamt of creating a musical terminology emancipated from the Italian language.

It was not merely a part of himself which Schumann devoted to criticism. He plunged into it whole-heartedly and with every side of his character—to be more precise with three sides. For he created three critics, each one himself, but a different self, Florestan, Eusebius, and Raro.

No sooner had the new review shown its vitality and its combativeness than contributors came running from every hand. One of them, Karl Banck, was a song-writer, who had studied church music in Italy, and who was to play not only an important part on the review but also in Schumann's private life. Another, Ludwig Böhner, had been a friend of Hoffmann's. The latter had in fact borrowed many a trait of this "old lion with a thorn in his paw" when creating his character, Johannes Kreisler, that legendary figure in whom so many romantic musicians saw a mirror of themselves, including Brahms, who in his young days sometimes signed himself "Johannes Kreisler, junior." And then there was a young musician who had been *Musikdirektor* at the Magdeburg theatre and had written a curious opera, *Die Feen.* He sent in contributions in which he crossed swords with Rellstab, written with a rough violence

which was quite different to the usual tone of the review. This was Richard Wagner.

The three pseudonyms with which Schumann signed his articles (and sometimes his compositions) were not the only ones to figure in the *Zeitschrift.* In fact there were many others—Jonathan, Juvenalis, Meritis, Fritz Friedrich, Maestro, Serpentinus, Julius, Walt. The Paris correspondent (really Stephen Heller) called himself "Jeanquirit" and the London one (Zuccalmaglio) signed himself "St. Diamond." Moreover, there were references to women whose identity was similarly concealed—Livia (Henriette Graban), Estrella (Ernestine von Fricken), and three, Clara, Chiarina, and Zilai, all of whom were Clara Wieck.

Why all these pseudonyms? To intrigue people. The review was to come out with a bang and take the public by storm. It also pleased the playful, whimsical side of Schumann's character to dabble in a little mystery. Obviously, everyone would try to guess which of the musicians they knew stood behind the mask. Would it be Schunke, Luhe, Lyser, Knorr, Banck or Mendelssohn? They would certainly have had to be clever to guess the three disguises of Robert Schumann, true as each was to one side of his nature.

Sometimes all three would give their verdict in turn upon a single work. Eusebius, always gentle, would be indulgent "even to the weaknesses of the composition." Florestan, quick to prick bubbles, would at once find the right word to show up its emptiness and insipidity. Raro the *Meister,* who had something of Wieck in him, was the stern technician and disciplinarian. Florestan was the personification of poetic fire and impetuousness, Eusebius of dreamy melancholy, Raro of reason and system. Three masks equally true to the person they were masking. The student who ignored one would fail to understand his man.

With curiosity aroused but not satisfied, it soon got around that these mysterious critics were members of a secret society. They were, it was whispered, the *Davidsbündler.* In 1810, Weber had created a somewhat similar society, the *Harmonische Verein,* nor were Hoffmann's *Serapionsbrüder* altogether different, a sort of sect, half real, half fictional. That Schumann's group should have put themselves under the ægis of David was doubly suitable. Were they not marching against the Philistines? And had not David been the musician King, playing, with the house of Israel, on "all manner of instruments" and "leaping and dancing before the Lord"?

A lot has been written about the "riddle" of the *Davidsbund,* in particular by Jansen who has produced a very interesting book on the subject entitled *Die Davidsbündler.* According to Schumann it was purely fictive.

. . . a society that was more than secret, having never existed except in the mind of its founder. . . . To present in turn different points of view on artistic questions it seemed to me not a bad idea to invent artistic personages of opposing characters, of which Florestan and Eusebius are the most striking, with Raro as a sort of hyphen between them.

And he adds, in his preface to the *Gesammelte Schriften*:

This league of the Companions of David runs like a red thread through the pages of the review, humorously interweaving Poetry and Truth.

In the mind of its creator this league was composed of all those, young or old, who were ready to fight to the death the Philistines of music, but was also intended to bring together under a common name the "blood brothers" of all lands and all ages. When it had first appeared in an article on Clara in *Der Komet,* the *Davidsbund* had been just a joke. Gradually it took shape and acquired a deep meaning to its author until it resembled the *Orden* in Hermann Hesse's *Morgenlandfahrt.* In it, actual people, past and present, mingled with fictional characters, weaving a strange tapestry of the real and the imaginary. Of his own pseudonyms, Schumann says:

Florestan and Eusebius represent my double nature, which, as a man, I should dearly like to merge in Raro.

Wandering among the masked figures are others undisguised, Mozart and Berlioz, both doughty *Davidsbündler,* though only honorary members. With all this mystery and disguise, it was only natural that Schumann should put his capricious marionettes of the *Zeitschrift* into a ballet, and this he did in *Carnaval,* **op. 9.** There is a fantastic description of a Roman carnival full of marvels in Hoffmann's *Prinzessin Brambilla* which gives some idea of the inner world which takes the stage in this work of Schumann's, but only a partial one. For *Carnaval,* which is poetry through and through, is a poetry that is beyond the realm of speech, a contact with the supernatural, whether inward or outward, which only music can make.

In this work we see clearer than in the others the duality of the composer. That we have in *Carnaval* a sort of "portrait gallery" of the *Davidsbund* is obvious. We meet Florestan and Eusebius and their doubles of the *commedia dell'arte,* Harlequin and Pierrot. Chiarina evokes Clara Wieck's pianistic talent, Estrella the fresh and simple grace of Ernestine von Fricken. The dancing letters play with the name of her birthplace, Asch. Then there is the **March of the Davidsbündler,** a sturdy declaration of war against the Philistines. That is all we have of the *Davidsbund,* though on the same level is the piece called **Chopin,** a clever pastiche, successfully catching the spirit Schumann greatly admired in that composer's work, which he aptly described as "a can-

non hidden under flowers." The valse too has a documentary value as a period piece. As for the Sphinxes with their slow, heavy notes, full of all that is enigmatic, they are the guardians of the gate of that Fairyland to which we are invited. But here, as in *Papillons,* the titles of the pieces give us the superficial side of the picture: they do not lead us into Schumann's real universe which is truly undefinable and ineffable.

The secret soul of every age is reflected in the mirror of its carnival. The Baroque age regarded it as a screen on which to project in gigantic silhouettes, as in Plato's *Cave,* the dramatic flounderings of its unconscious. The eighteenth century sought to exercise its aching anxieties by submerging them in a joyous masquerade. For the Romantics, heirs alike of the Baroque and the Rococo, the carnival became the prophetic voice of tortured humanity, seeking behind the mask its own essential nature. With its delight in doubles, the carnival is the supreme fête in which the harassed personality alienated or disintegrated, transforms and transfigures itself by the tricks of disguise. It arises from the profound uneasiness by which the Romantic is assailed when he attempts to take stock of himself. The degree to which the mask conceals or, on the contrary, reveals his identity and the mysterious links which bind him to others in a sort of supernatural communion and solidarity is what Hoffmann is showing us in the strange story of the poor actor Giglio, wretched mummer or prince incognito, in the tale of Princess Brambilla; and it is so Schumannesque in character that *Carnaval* could be taken for a musical illustration of it.

Like all Hoffmann's tales this one is imbued with an initiating quality. Here, inspired by Callot's engravings, full of dancing *fanfarons* and gipsy princesses, he has given us one of his most enlightening lessons, and it is precisely in the spirit of these "caprices" that Schumann wrote the solemn and ironical piece called **Reconnaissance** in *Carnaval.* Again, it is to a carnival, sumptuous, voluptuous, yet full of a satanic sadness, that Eichendorff invites the heroes of his *Marmorbild,* one of the most beautiful of all romantic *Märchen,* one of the richest in secret meaning. In this dangerous game with shadows, in this labyrinth of reflections and phantoms, the individual, bereft of all certainty of his own reality, gropes and flounders in his own pursuit.

Schumann was twenty-five when he composed *Carnaval.* Four years later in Vienna he returned to the theme in his *Faschingschwank aus Wien,* **op. 26.** In these two works the diabolic (to which so many Romantics succumbed) was kept at bay by all that was angelic in Schumann's character. The first was originally intended to be dedicated to the girl he was in love with, Ernestine von Fricken, though in the end it was in fact dedicated to Karl Lipinski, the Viennese violinist and conductor. What matters is that it was written by a young man in love, full of fantasy, gay and melancholy by turns, who played with his various masks, taking pleasure in disguising his own inner self, in order to give rein to the superabundance of vitality simmering within him.

The extraordinary resourcefulness displayed, the freshness of the melodies, the joy of the effortless song which ripples with such marvellous happiness through this work, makes it perhaps the most typical of all Schumann's achievements, so much so that, if we had to keep one solitary example of it, we might well choose this as representing him most completely, with all the lights and shadows, in the totality of his character and his genius.

With such a pure effusion, I cannot believe we should take too seriously the titles of these twenty-one pieces, endeavouring to nail them down to precise subjects. It is the musical invention which counts, the spontaneity of the song. The rest matters as little as the picturesque themes from the *Flegeljahre* mattered to *Papillons.* In fact it is safe to say that the music came to him first, and only as it took form was a carnivalesque picture suggested to his mind. If the music could be said to spring from anything it was direct from emotion itself.

The emotions may well have had a contemporary content, for that memorable year 1835 was for him a stirring one. Its three capital events were the creation, more or less imaginary, of the *Davidsbund,* the foundation of the *Neue Zeitschrift* for the promotion of the "music of the future" and the short-lived engagement to Ernestine von Fricken, who, as things turned out, merely paved the way for Schumann's great love—for Clara Wieck.

And, if we must not look for any serious anecdotic value in the titles of *Carnaval,* neither must we give too much importance to the inspiration derived from Ernestine. I know very well that in many of the pieces, a play is made with the notes A, E flat, C and B, which, in the German musical notation gives A, S, C, and H, Asch, which Schumann tells us was a "very musical town," was his fiancée's home, her father having an estate there. She was quite a good musician, with an agreeable voice. Coming to Leipzig in April, 1834, she took lessons with Wieck and lodged in his house. According to contemporary accounts, she was neither very pretty nor even very charming. But Robert had a heart which could not be unoccupied for long, and he was taken by her cool, distant purity. And no sooner was his affection awakened than he found in her calm regular features the grace of a madonna and attributed to her all the merits he wished to find. By dint of love, a decidedly ordinary girl was found to be a marvel. Ernestine responded, and they became secretly engaged, though he prepared his mother for an announcement.

> If fate were now to put the question: which would you choose? I would unhesitatingly answer: her. But that is

a long way off. For the present I brush aside the idea of a closer bond, however inclined I feel towards it.

Of the girl herself, he says that she is:

> . . . of a noble character, pure, childlike, and sensible, very much in love with me, passionately keen on every form of art, and herself extremely musical . . . in a word, just what I should wish my wife to be.

But was Ernestine, who dances through *Carnaval* in the guise of Estrella, really such a "precious stone"? Was her worth "beyond all estimate"? The engagement did not last long. Robert's love did not stand up to the separation when she stayed for a while at Asch with her father. As a matter of fact she was not really his daughter but an illegitimate child he had adopted.

Schumann was the more easily consoled for this disillusionment by being at the same time almost in love with Henriette Voigt, a "soul in A minor" as he called her. A married woman, she played for a time a somewhat similar part in his life to that which Agnes Carus had played—a maternal one. She was loved undoubtedly, but with the love that is given to the inaccessible. Moreover, there was another factor tending to efface Ernestine's memory—his growing feeling, perhaps unknown to himself, for Clara Wieck.

The promptings of his heart were extremely complex, and, just because he felt so keenly, he was little concerned to analyse his feelings. That we can do, however, by comparing the graceful appearance of Estrella (Ernestine) which is marked *con affetto* with, on the other hand, the *appassionata* "*con molta anima*" which ushers Chiarina onto the stage. Estrella could never have been the messenger of sovereign mysteries: she was simply the harbinger who announces the coming of another who was to fill his heart completely. Of that the song of the mage Celionato at the end of *Prinzessin Brambilla* gives the most perfect version.

> In the pure celestial light the pair become conscious of their identity and in faithful union the profound truth of life shines upon the two that have become one.

In *Carnaval* two beings, eternally destined for one another, meet and recognise each other. Schumann's mother guessed the meaning correctly. The hapless Estrella has in the end only to efface herself before the apparition of the ideal woman, whose beauty, intelligence and talent had from the first singled her out to be the perfect companion for Robert. Let there be no doubt about this—it was Clara who really inspired *Carnaval,* dedicated as the work originally was to Ernestine in the blindness of a groping and tender heart, reluctant to wound.

And from now on it was Clara whose presence was to light up the life and work of Robert Schumann. To quote again from *Prinzessin Brambilla*:

Listen! Already they are starting, the sweet strains of the music, and all is hushed to hear them; a brilliant blue glows low on the horizon and from distant streams and forests comes a murmur and a rustling. Open magic country full of a thousand felicities! Open and make desire follow upon desire, as he contemplates his image in the fountains of love! The flood swells. Forward! Plunge into the waves; strike out lustily. Soon the shore will be reached. And supreme delight glitters in cascades of fire.

Leon B. Plantinga (essay date 1967)

SOURCE: Plantinga, Leon B. "Introduction," "Schumann's Style of Criticism," and "Schumann's Aesthetics of Music." In *Schumann as Critic,* pp. ix-xiii; 59-78; 111-34. New Haven: Yale University Press, 1967.

[In the following excerpts, Plantinga examines several facets of Schumann's criticism, with particular emphasis on his style and musical philosophy.]

At the age of twenty, Robert Schumann, thoroughly bored with his law studies at the University of Heidelberg, decided to devote himself to music. This was in the autumn of 1830, and during the next year he plunged wholeheartedly into not one, but three kinds of musical activities: piano playing, composing, and writing music criticism. In the spring of 1832 a hand injury put an end to his ambitions as a pianist; but by that time he had already published his earliest compositions as well as his first essay on music, and the pattern of his life was set for some time to come.

In one of the two musical careers left to Schumann, he seems to have achieved permanent recognition. Though his stock as a composer fluctuates mildly from time to time (less than Mendelssohn's, more than Chopin's) a good bit of his music has long been a stable part of the active repertory. But though Schumann himself once said he preferred writing music to writing about it, during much of his lifetime he was in fact better known and more influential as a critic than as a composer. That this estimate of the relative importance of his two roles has now been reversed is not hard to understand. There are, after all, more people who listen to nineteenth-century music than there are who read nineteenth-century music criticism. Moreover Schumann wrote about a full cross-section of the European musical scene in the earlier nineteenth century—not just the small part of it that is still current in the twentieth. But if this kind of comprehensiveness makes some of Schumann's writings seem a little remote from ordinary contemporary interests, it adds immeasurably to their value as a commentary on nineteenth-century European musical culture as it really was.

Schumann began writing criticism at a time when Germany's musical future looked uncertain. In the second half of the preceding century the German-speaking states had for the first time achieved a certain preeminence in music. Though opera was still borrowed from Italy, the instrumental music of the Mannheim court, of C. P. E. and J. C. Bach, and perhaps most importantly, the symphonies of Joseph Haydn, were largely indigenous—and eminently exportable—products. Beethoven added a powerful impetus to the Germans' pride in their music, but when he died in 1827 there was no one in sight to continue the tradition. Within a decade the most admired composer in the world was Meyerbeer, and the few composers like Spohr, Hummel, and Moscheles who continued to cultivate the large instrumental forms were not of sufficient influence to stem the tide of music, much of it trivial, that flowed from the salons of Paris. Once again the Germans listened, for the most part, to foreign styles of music. It was in response to this state of affairs that Schumann first sharpened his critic's pen.

A music critic in the present day, especially in the United States, is someone who makes judgments, instantaneously arrived at and promptly recorded, on musical performances. A *Rezensent* for a musical journal in Schumann's time acted quite differently: his usual duty was to evaluate not performances but scores. This practice had its beginnings in the semi-popular context of the *Kenner und Liebhaber* journals of the later eighteenth century, and when Schumann arrived on the scene such music criticism still had, usually, a gentle and tolerant tone. Schumann cut sharply from this tradition. Making the most of his pronounced gift for writing, he went about his work with caustic wit and youthful idealism, injecting into music criticism something of the professionalism and severity of standards he saw in contemporary literary criticism. The result is a unique record of the reactions of a first-rate musical mind to a whole decade of European music.

Schumann wrote almost all his criticism in the course of performing his regular duties as editor and writer for the *Neue Zeitschrift für Musik* (cited hereafter as *NZfM*),[1] the journal he helped establish in 1834 and edited from January 1835 until July 1844. He contributed a few scattered articles to other periodicals; his often-mentioned review of Chopin's Variations on *Là ci darem la mano* appeared in the *Allgemeine musikalische Zeitung* (hereafter *AmZ*) of 1831, and in 1833 two essays entitled ***Der Davidsbündler*** were published in a literary journal called *Der Komet*. In addition he wrote a few concert reviews for the *Allgemeine Zeitung* of Leipzig.

In 1853 Schumann himself assembled most of his published prose works, together with a few aphorisms from disparate sources, and arranged them in roughly chronological order for publication. In the spring of 1854, just after he was committed to the asylum at Endenich, they were brought out in four volumes by the Leipzig firm of Wigand under the title **Gesammelte Schriften über Musik und Musiker.**[2] Schumann remained the best editor of his own works until the fourth edition of the **Gesammelte Schriften,** prepared by the dedicated Schumann scholar F. Gustav Jansen, appeared in 1891; Jansen added a number of articles omitted by Schumann and provided some valuable commentary. Martin Kreisig, former director of the *Schumannmuseum* in Zwickau, presided over the fifth and final edition, a model of accuracy and thoroughness. But even this collection lacks several articles and a good many comments, footnotes, and the like that are unquestionably by Schumann. The form and order of the material are the same as in the 1854 edition; things Schumann omitted there are given in footnotes and in a *Nachtrag,* and the true chronological order is shown only in a somewhat abstract table.[3] Whatever the merits of Kreisig's edition, I have felt it was essential to base this study on Schumann's criticism in its original form in the *NZfM.*[4]

In the present day, Schumann the critic has been more used, it seems, than understood. His commentary on music has proved serviceable to countless writers on Schubert, Berlioz, and Mendelssohn; excerpts from his criticism are used in books of various kinds, but much more commonly on record jackets and in program notes. As a result, many people have a faint familiarity with Schumann's writings. Concert-goers recognize "Hats off, gentlemen—a genius!" and "these heavenly lengths," and many of them know that Schumann wrote a long review of the *Symphonie fantastique* and endorsed the young Brahms. In view of this popular currency some of his work enjoys, it is remarkable how little has been written about Schumann's criticism; somehow things he said have become common knowledge without ever having been specialized knowledge.

There may be plausible enough reasons for this. In the first place, musical scholarship is still of rather a tender age, and is only now getting around to investigating the nineteenth century. Music historians have shown a lively interest, as they should, in almost all the composers of the Middle Ages and Renaissance; we know a good deal of music by the contemporaries of Machaut and Landini, and of Josquin and Palestrina. The really obscure composers in Western history are the contemporaries of Beethoven and Schumann. Important musicians like Hummel, Moscheles, Loewe, and Hiller remain obscure, and men like C.-S. Catel, F. W. Grund, and C. G. Reissiger interest almost nobody but lexicographers. Perhaps nineteenth-century music has been last to attract the attention of musical scholars because it is too much with us. Since the nineteenth century, it has—or, rather, *some* of it has—comprised the bulk of the music we hear at concerts (and now on records) and familiarity of this kind, unfortunately, sometimes breeds contempt. In the case of Schumann the field has been left for the most part to generations of simplified and derivative biographies, all based on a few books of substance written long ago.

Though specialized studies in the field are few, I have benefited from a number of publications by people who have worked with Schumann before me, especially the collections of letters edited by Clara Schumann[5] and F. Gustav Jansen.[6] Of the older secondary literature on Schumann, most helpful have been the notes in Kreisig's edition of the **Gesammelte Schriften,** Jansen's *Die Davidsbündler,*[7] and the biography of Frederick Niecks (still probably the best book in English on Schumann).[8] The most extensive research on Schumann of the last forty years is represented by the two books of Wolfgang Boetticher, *Robert Schumann, Einführung in Persönlichkeit und Werk* (Berlin, 1941), and *Robert Schumann in seinen Schriften und Briefen* (Berlin, 1942). These books offer a wealth of previously unpublished documentary matter (copious extracts, particularly, from Schumann's diaries), and one should, I suppose, be grateful for them. But nothing in these wartime publications can be taken on faith; calculated to make both Schumann and Boetticher acceptable to the Nazi regime, they are badly marred by distortions and suppressions. Perhaps it is just as well that murky writing makes the *Einführung*—like many books with this name, it is a gargantuan tome—almost impossible to read. Misinformation in such a form spreads slowly. More recent books on Schumann[9] show little new research, and none of them acknowledges his criticism with more than a respectful nod. The fullest discussion of Schumann's journalistic activities, strangely enough, is in a book about another composer and critic; it is Robert Pessenlehner's *Herrmann Hirschbach, der Kritiker und Künstler.*[10] There have been, from time to time, a few indifferent articles on Schumann's aesthetic views, for example those by Hermann Kretzschmar[11] and Arnold Schmitz,[12] and most recently, a very much better one by Edward A. Lippman.[13]

This book will be about Schumann's work as a critic: the content and style of his writings, and the context within which he operated. Anyone who writes about criticism is potentially two steps removed from the focal point of interest; for what he offers is essentially a commentary upon a commentary. Here I hope to avoid this pitfall by introducing prominently into evidence (especially in the later chapters) the original subject: the music Schumann was writing about. Otherwise it would be impossible in many cases to understand what Schumann is saying, and any sure assessment of his importance as a critic would be out of the question.

· · · · ·

SCHUMANN'S STYLE OF CRITICISM

Until 1830 the young Schumann's interests were about equally divided between literature and music. When in that year he decided to devote himself fully to music, his formal training in the field appears to have been slight—if anything, inferior to his literary education. It consisted almost solely of about eight years' piano study under Johann Gottfried Kuntsch (1775-1855), organist and choir director of the Zwickau Marienkirche, himself an amateur in music, and a man branded by most of the Schumann biographers as decidedly mediocre.[14] Schumann's knowledge of music was otherwise acquired in the homes of amateur musicians where he took part in musical soirées, accompanying vocal music and participating in chamber ensembles. Carl E. Carus (1774-1842),[15] merchant and manufacturer in Bautzen, and later in Zwickau, was the first and perhaps most important patron of the young Schumann's musical career. Upon his death in 1843, Schumann wrote an extended eulogy in the *NZfM*:

> And it was in his house that the names Mozart, Haydn, and Beethoven were spoken of daily with enthusiasm. It was in his house that I first became acquainted with the rarer works of these masters, otherwise never to be heard in a small town, especially their quartets; I was often even permitted to participate at the piano.[16]

In the spring of 1828, Schumann, like many great German musicians before him, enrolled at the University of Leipzig to study law. In his first year there, though law appears to have taken up little of his time, he had no formal studies in music except for a few sporadic piano lessons with Wieck. During this year he submitted some of his compositions to the composer Gottlob Wiedebein (1779-1854), and in a later letter confessed to him, "I have no knowledge of harmony, thorough bass, etc., or counterpoint; I am but a pure, simple disciple of guiding nature, and I merely followed a blind, vain impulse which wanted to shake off all fetters.[17]

This pristine innocence Schumann claimed for himself was surely something of a pose; he was strongly attracted at this time to a naive adulation of nature such as that in Edward Young's "Some are pupils of nature only, nor go further to school." And though during this year in Leipzig, as well as the following one in Heidelberg, his principal contacts with music were through amateur musical circles,[18] in 1830 Schumann was a good enough pianist for Wieck to promise him that, if he applied himself, in three years he would rival Moscheles and Hummel.[19] Schumann's attempts at composing before his return to Leipzig in 1830 were limited for the most part to the improvisation of free fantasias and variations. Yet a few of his early attempts were written down, and some incorporated into later compositions.[20] Between Schumann's return to Leipzig in 1830 and the founding of the *NZfM* in 1834, he studied piano with Wieck, and counterpoint (from July 1831 to April 1832) with Heinrich Dorn—his first sustained professional musical training. Yet by 1834 Schumann had demonstrated his musical proficiency. Some of his best-known compositions date from this period: the *Papil-*

lons op. 2, the "Etudes on Caprices of Paganini" op. 3 and 10, the "Toccata" op. 7, and parts of the *Carnaval* op. 9.

Schumann showed marked literary proclivities from the time of his boyhood in Zwickau. The son of a book dealer and publisher who had literary inclinations himself,[21] Schumann was early immersed in literature ranging from the Greek classics to the writings of Byron and Scott. His school friend, Emil Flechsig, reminisces in his *Erinnerungen* (c. 1875), that "there was abundant opportunity to become acquainted with literature; the entire Schumann house was full of classics."[22] Schumann's linguistic and literary training at the Gymnasium in Zwickau must have been excellent, for if we believe his own report in his **"Materialen zu einem Lebenslauf,"** at the age of fifteen he was making translations from Anacreon, and later from Bion, Theocrites, Homer, Sophocles, Tibullus, Horace and the Latin poetry of the seventeenth-century Polish writer, Matthias Kasmir Sarbiewski. At this time, the report continues, his studies of German literature included the works of Klopstock, Schiller, and Hölderlin, and, especially in 1827, Shakespeare and the novelist who was to exert a formidable influence on his prose style, Jean Paul.[23] Schumann's study of Goethe, as Wörner indicates, did not really begin until about 1830.[24]

In 1825 Schumann and several of his friends, with adolescent exuberance, formed a "German Literary Society" where they discussed literature of various kinds and presented their own poetry for criticism; this society continued to meet until 1828.[25] As a Gymnasium student Schumann was forever composing poetry, essays, aphorisms, and fragments for novels (none of which was ever completed). Jansen pointed out Schumann's remarkable literary precocity in an article in *Die Musik* in 1906.[26] He described there a small manuscript volume from 1823 entitled **"Blätter und Blümchen aus der goldenen Aue,"** in which Schumann had assembled extracts that appealed to him from a great variety of literary sources. He gave a list of Schumann's writings from the years 1826-27, and printed some of them. There are essays entitled **"Ueber die Zufälligkeit und Nichtigkeit des Nachruhms,"**[27] **"Das Leben des Dichters,"** and a few poems. Kreisig adds to the list of youthful essays now in print one on a theme that always interested Schumann, **"Ueber die innige Verwandschaft der Poesie und Tonkunst,"** and one entitled **"Einfluss der Einsamkeit auf die Bildung des Geistes und die Veredelung des Herzens."**[28] Boetticher's two books on Schumann add considerably to our information about his early literary activities; Boetticher cites fragments of projected novels entitled **"Selene"** and **"Juniusabende und Julitage,"** and prints extracts from an attempt at musical aesthetics called **"Die Tonwelt,"** all from 1826-28.[29]

During his years in Zwickau, Schumann's familiarity with books was further nurtured in his family's publishing house. In March 1828, Schumann wrote to Flechsig,

> I am hard at work with Forcellini, correcting, selecting, looking things up, reading through the Grüter inscriptions. The work is interesting; one learns much from it . . . besides, all the distinguished philologists are working on it . . . I have had to ransack the whole library, and have found many unprinted *collectanea* of Gronow, Gräv, Scalliger, Heinsius, Barth, Daum, etc.[30]

The first half of this letter is an extreme example of Schumann's most rapturous, ornate prose—a striking contrast to his exacting, sober work on a major Latin lexicon, and even his description of that work. Schumann was by this time an unabashed admirer of Jean Paul, and often imitated his diffuse, extravagant prose. He did this for a time very consciously—he could turn this kind of writing off and on like a water tap—but his fascination with the rapturous late romantic prose style was a passing phase. Schumann continued to appreciate Jean Paul for the rest of his life; but he stopped imitating him as maturity set in.

Wörner says that Schumann's interests in music and literature interfered with each other, and that his literary activities, in fact, long held him to an amateur level in music.[31] Schumann was painfully aware of this; in December, 1830, after his decision to become a professional musician, Schumann wrote, "If only my talent for music and poetry would converge into a single point, the light would not be so scattered, and I could attempt a great deal."[32] In his career as a music critic, especially the earlier part of it, Schumann was able to reconcile, in more than a superficial sense, his talents for music and literature.

Schumann's earliest journal articles are fantasies in ornate prose that are only incidentally about music. His famous Chopin review in the *AmZ* of 1831 and his *Davidsbündler* articles in *Der Komet* of 1833 are cast as narratives, complete with description of characters, dialogue, and even some action. They look exactly like fragments of novels; the first of the *Davidsbündler* articles (with the subtitle **"Leipziger Musikleben"**) begins:

> A window above me was suddenly thrown open, and behind it, in the half-shadows, I recognized a pointed, angular-nosed Swedish head. And as I was still looking up, something like fragrant falling leaves floated and played about my temples: it was scraps of paper thrown down from above. But at home, as though rooted to the spot, I read (in a paper that held together better) the following:

> Our Italian nights go on. The heaven-storming Florestan has for a time been quieter than usual, and seems to have something on his mind. But then recently Euse-

bius let fall a few words that reawakened the demon in him. After reading a number of *Iris*, he said, namely, "He is just too severe." "What? What did you say, Eusebius?" said Florestan, rising up, "Rellstab is too severe? Is then this damnable German politeness to last for centuries? . . . But the time is coming when we must stand up against this unholy alliance of patronage and perversity, before it engulfs us and makes for no end of trouble. But what do you think, Master Raro?"

> You know Raro's methodical way of speaking—made even stranger because of his Italian accent—how he, fugue-like, sets phrase upon phrase, makes various distinctions, narrows down his material, limits it yet more, finally brings everything together again and seems to say, I agree.[33]

Schumann had no intention that the Chopin review and the *Davidsbündler* articles should remain as isolated essays; both were to have been merely the first installments of extended series, and the *Davidsbündler* articles Schumann specifically intended to expand into a novel. These pieces are clearly examples of the "musical belles-lettres" Schumann mentioned to Mosen in 1833. Schumann apparently intended to give essays like this a prominent place in his journal; he asked Mosen to write a musical *Novelle* for the first issues, and to Franz Otto he suggested "English letters" addressed to an "imaginary person (a sweetheart, a Vult Harnisch or Peter Schoppe)."[34]

As 1834 wore on, the duties of editor and reviewer of instrumental music fell more and more to Schumann. It was already clear from his Chopin review that his novelistic style seemed to him perfectly serviceable for writing music reviews, and he used variations of this style—usually with an element of moderation lacking in 1831—in a good many of his early critiques of piano music in the *NZfM*. The results varied: a review of Hummel's Etudes op. 125 is divided into three parts, each stating a slightly different point of view, and each signed by one of Schumann's imaginary Jean-Paulian characters, Florestan, Eusebius, and Raro (the entire review appears under the heading, **"Die Davidsbündler"**).[35] The gentle Eusebius says,

> The experienced, reflective master writes etudes differently from the young fantast. The former knows intimately the forces with which he must deal, their beginning and end, their means and goals; he lays out his circle of activity about him and never steps over that line. The latter, on the other hand, lays piece on piece, piles up rocks one atop the other, until finally he himself can surmount the herculean structure only at the peril of his life. . . .

> In view of the lightning-fast development of music to the heights of poetic freedom—of this no other art can offer a parallel example—it is inevitable that even the better things can remain current for only about a decade. It is an act of intolerance that many of the younger spirits are ungrateful, forgetting that they are

building a superstructure upon a foundation they have not laid. Every younger generation has committed this act of intolerance, and every future one will too.

Florestan answers:

> Good, kindly Eusebius, you make me laugh. And when you have all turned back your clocks, the sun will still rise as before. However highly I value your tendency to assign everything to its proper place, I think you are really a repressed romantic—but with a certain diffidence about famous names, which time will cure.
>
> Really, my friend, if some had their way, we would soon be back to those golden days when you got your ears boxed for putting your thumb on the black keys. But I won't even go into the falsities of some of your effusions, but instead get to the work itself.
>
> Methods and schools make for rapid progress, to be sure, but such progress is one-sided and trivial. O pedants, what sinners you are! With your Logier-natures you pull the bud forcibly out of its covering. Like falconers you clip the feathers of your students lest they fly too high. You ought to be guides who show the way—without always coming along yourselves! (I'm too embroiled in these ideas to come to the point.) . . .
>
> Who could deny that most of these etudes show an exemplary plan and execution, that each has a distinctive, pure character, and that they were produced with that masterly ease which results from years of application? But that which is necessary to enchant the youth and to make him forget all the difficulties of the work because of its beauties is utterly lacking—imaginative originality . . . I speak of fantasy, the prophetess with covered eyes from whom nothing is hidden, and who in her errors is often most charming of all. But what do you say to this, master?

Master Raro says:

> My young friends, you are both wrong—but especially you Eusebius. A famous name has made one of you captive and the other rebellious. But what does it say in the *Westöstlicher Divan?*
>
> > Als wenn das auf Namen ruhte,
> > Was sich schweigend nur entfaltet
> > Lieb' ich doch das schöne Gute,
> > Wie es sich aus Gott gestaltet.[36]

The second article under the rubric *Die Davidsbündler* is a review of the "Bouquet musical" op. 10, by Schumann's former counterpoint teacher, Heinrich Dorn.[37] This conspicuously disjointed essay begins with a section (signed by Eusebius) in which the various flowers in the bouquet converse, the violet even telling a short story. This device is dropped in the next section where Florestan complains about the French titles. In the final section (unsigned), Schumann gives a short analysis of the music. This style is more consistent and clearly more successful in Schumann's discussion of a series of sonatas by Delphine Hill Handley, Carl Loewe, Wilhelm Taubert, and Ludwig Schunke in the *NZfM* of

1835.[38] Here Schumann writes a review in which the large sections are again represented as speeches by Eusebius, Florestan, and Raro. But within each section there is dialogue and a bit of action. In the course of all this, Schumann actually manages to describe and evaluate the compositions—complete with musical examples.

The more general articles Schumann contributed (in accordance with his original plans) to the early volumes of the *NZfM* were obviously more amenable to his narrative style than were the reviews. In such essays as the **"Fastnachtsrede von Florestan,"** the **"Schwärmbriefe,"** and the **"Monument für Beethoven,"**[39] Schumann writes about the German musical scene in narrative prose that is diffuse, but facile and imaginative. The third of the **"Schwärmbriefe"** includes this remarkable discussion of Beethoven's Seventh Symphony:

> I had to laugh—Florestan began, as he launched into the A-major Symphony—I had to laugh at a dry old actuary who found in it a battle of giants, and in the last movement their final destruction—though he had to pass lightly over the Allegretto because it didn't fit into his plan . . . But most of all my fingers itch to get at those who insist that Beethoven always presented in his symphonies the most exalted sentiments: lofty ideas about God, immortality, and the courses of the stars. While the floral crown of the genius, to be sure, points to the heavens, his roots are planted in his beloved earth.
>
> Now about the symphony itself; this idea is not my own, but taken from an old volume of *Cäcilia* (though there the setting is changed to the parlor of a count, perhaps out of too great a diffidence for Beethoven—which was misguided) . . . it is a most merry wedding. The bride is an angelic child with a rose in her hair, but only one. Unless I am greatly mistaken, in the Introduction the guests gather together, greeting each other with inverted commas, and, unless I am wrong, merry flutes recall that in the entire village, full of maypoles with many-colored ribbons, there reigns joy for the bride Rosa. And unless I am mistaken, the pale mother looks at her with a trembling glance that seems to ask, "Do you know that now we must part?" And Rosa, overcome, throws herself into her arms, drawing after her, with the other hand, that of the bridegroom . . . Now it becomes very still in the village outside (here Florestan came to the Allegretto, taking passages from it here and there); only a butterfly flits past or a cherry blossom falls . . . The organ begins; the sun is high in the sky, and single long, oblique rays play upon the particles of dust throughout the church. The bells ring vigorously—parishioners arrive a few at a time— pews are clapped open and shut—some peasants peer into hymnbooks, others gaze up at the superstructure— the procession draws closer—first choirboys with lighted candles and censers, then friends who often look back at the couple accompanied by the priest— then the parents, friends of the bride, and finally all the young people of the village. And now all is in order and the priest approaches the altar, and speaks first to the bride, and then to the happiest of men. And he ad-

monishes them about the sacred responsibilities and purposes of this union, and bids them find their happiness in profound harmony and love; then he asks for the "I do" that is to last forever; and the bride pronounces it firmly and deliberately—I don't want to continue this picture, and you can do it your own way in the finale. Florestan thus broke off abruptly and tore into the close of the Allegretto; the sound was as if the sacristan was slamming the doors so that the noise reverberated through the whole church.[40]

Schumann's love of aphorism stands in almost paradoxical contrast to his fascination with this kind of discursive prose. During his ten-years' occupation with the *NZfM,* Schuman was continually busy collecting pithy and pertinent quotations from literary sources to be used as mottos. His own aphorisms as well appeared from time to time in the early volumes of the journal.[41] In 1848 he assembled his **"Musikalische Haus- und Lebensregeln,"**[42] and in 1853-54 he gathered together from various of his earlier writings the sets of aphorisms in the *Gesammelte Schriften.* In the first volume of the *NZfM* Schumann printed—in one of the collections of aphorisms—a paragraph in defense of aphorism. This selection is really an extract, only slightly altered, from the second of Schumann's *Davidsbündler* articles, and it shows the undisciplined vehemence of some of Schumann's early writing:

> Why do you turn up your noses with such a superior air at aphorism, you tall Philistines?[43] By God, is the world all a level surface? Doesn't it have Alps, rivers, and all different kinds of people? And is life to be reduced to a system? Isn't it a book put together from single, half torn-up pages, full of children's scrawlings, youthful ideas, overturned epitaphs, and blank, ungovernable fate? I think it is. In fact it might not be uninteresting to portray life with all its concomitants in art,[44] just as Platner and Jacobi[45] have given whole philosophical systems.[46]

Schumann's most fanciful prose stands directly in the tradition of the German literary-musical figures of the early nineteenth century, Jean Paul, E. T. A. Hoffmann, and W. H. Wackenroder. Abert has said that most of the style and content of Schumann's early writing can be attributed to the influence of Jean Paul. The importance of his novels as a model for Schumann's early style is hardly to be doubted; virtually all of Schumann's biographers agree on this point.[47] Boetticher has shown from a diary of 1831 that Schumann also admired and consciously imitated Hoffmann at this time; he was even thinking about writing a "poetic biography" of Hoffmann.[48]

Another important forerunner for Schumann's earlier style, this one from the eighteenth century, is usually overlooked: Christian Daniel Schubart (1739-91). Schubart, who acted out the excesses of the *Sturm und Drang* for most of his adult life, had much in common with the young Schumann: untutored enthusiasm for poetic qualities in music, and a love of rapturous improvisation both in music and prose. Schumann as a boy of thirteen already knew Schubart's *Ideen zu einer Aesthetik der Tonkunst*; Schumann's **"Blätter und Blümchen aus der goldenen Aue,"** compiled in 1823, contains excerpts from this book.[49] Among the articles Schumann wrote for the *Damenkonversationslexikon* in 1834 is one called **"Charakteristik der Tonleitern und Tonarten."**[50] His model for this essay, he tells us, was Schubart; though he disagrees at several points with Schubart's characterization of keys, he finds in it much that is "graceful and poetic."[51] Toward the end of 1838, when Schumann was in Vienna, he borrowed a copy of Schubart's book from Fischhof and read it again.[52] And in March of 1839, mottos from Schubart's *Ideen* began again to appear in the *NZfM.*[53]

It would strike us as peculiar behavior if a present-day critic should write little stories instead of telling us in a straightforward fashion about the things he is reviewing, and Schumann's behavior as a critic certainly seemed peculiar to some of his contemporaries. Fink, for example, sneered in the *AmZ* about the "insufferable followers of Chopin who pursue dreams they aren't dreaming."[54] The special forms of Schumann's fancy—the half-imaginary characters, and the personification of several sides to his own personality—might suggest the aberrations of incipient schizophrenia.[55] But to attribute any substantial part of Schumann's style of music criticism to mental disturbance would be a real error. There is little reason to think that Schumann failed to distinguish between the real world and the imaginary one he peopled with the members of the *Davidsbund.* It was with consciousness and even purposefulness that he indulged his love of anagrams, pseudonyms, and Jean Paulian mystification. He explained all this with perfect lucidity to Zuccamaglio:

> If by any chance you approve of the tone of the *Davidsbündlerbriefe* from Augsburg, Berlin, Dresden, and Munich, I suggest that you adopt it for your own correspondence articles. Indifferent material can thus be presented in an interesting way; the journal gains solidity and colorfulness this way, and the readers will be shown a kindness. Think of the *Davidsbund* merely as a spiritual brotherhood which is now expanding to fairly sizable proportions, also externally, and will, I hope, bear much good fruit. The mystification of this, after all, has an unusual charm for many people; moreover, like everything mysterious, it has a special power.[56]

G. Noren-Herzberg has suggested that Schumann adopted a highly "poetic" style for his journal because literature of all kinds was in great vogue in Germany.[57] Post office clerks read Goethe and accountants tried their hand at sonnets and essays. In such a milieu Schumann's early style of criticism would find a friendly reception. Schumann did not write extravagant and fanciful criticism because he was detached from reality, nor because of any other personal idiosyncrasy. In his work for the journal, as we have seen, he showed a never-failing presence of mind, and his writing for it was no exception. Schumann wrote this way deliberately because he thought this kind of criticism would be effective.

Schumann's early style of music criticism is a highly personal variation of a type that goes back to the music reviews of E. T. A. Hoffmann. Hoffmann's reviews of Beethoven's Fifth Symphony and his Trios op. 70 in the *AmZ* of 1810 and 1813[58] mark the beginning of a new kind of music criticism. Here, language rich in images and figures strains to communicate in words the qualities of music; the result is really the use of one artistic medium to explicate another. In the introduction to his review of Hiller's Etudes op. 15, Schumann offers an eloquent apology for this kind of procedure:

> The editors of this paper have been reproached for emphasizing and extending the poetic side of music at the expense of its scientific side. They have been called young fantasts who have not always been informed that basically not much is known about Ethiopian[59] and other such music, etc. This accusation contains exactly that element by means of which we would hope to distinguish our paper from others. We do not wish to pursue the question of to what degree the cause of art is advanced faster by one manner or the other. We certainly confess, however, that we hold as the highest kind of criticism that which itself leaves an impression similar to the one created by the subject that stimulated it.

A footnote to this passage contains the famous statement,

> In this sense, Jean Paul could possibly contribute more to the understanding of a Beethoven symphony or fantasia through a poetic counterpart (even without talking about the symphony or fantasia alone) than a dozen critics who lean their ladders against the colossus to take his exact measurements.[60]

The style of Hoffmann's reviews and Schumann's early criticism is a natural concomitant of the changing standards for music in the romantic milieu of which both men were so much a part. A critic whose foremost demands have to do with subjective elements—emotion, imagination (in the modern sense), "the characteristic," or Schumann's elusive "poetic"[61]—cuts himself off from established rationalistic ways of talking about his subject. For the romantic music critic it is precisely those qualities he most cherishes that are least susceptible of any kind of conventional discussion. He must find new ways to intimate that which—by his own admission—is inexpressible; it is hardly surprising that the result is something original, subjective, and, in Schumann's sense, poetic. And for Schumann, convinced of a basic similarity of all the arts, but particularly of literature and music,[62] a poetic literary style must have seemed a perfectly appropriate vehicle for conveying his ideas.

In literary criticism there were striking parallels—or more precisely, precedents—for the subjective music criticism Schumann wrote in the early 1830s. They too followed in the train of important changes in standards for the arts in the later eighteenth and earlier nineteenth centuries. The dissolution of the literary principles of the Enlightenment, and their gradual replacement with views of literature associated with romanticism began in Germany in the late 1760s. Lessing, who preferred Shakespeare to Corneille, began to counteract the French neoclassicism so wholeheartedly embraced by the Germans since Gottsched. In the high tide of the *Sturm und Drang,* shortly afterward, all the old rules about the integrity of genre, the unities, the view of art as a product of judgment, the theory of mimesis—all of this was denied. The most important (though hardly the most readable) spokesman for the literary *Sturm und Drang,* this precursor of romanticism more violent in its rejection of established traditions than romanticism itself, was Johann Gottfried Herder.[63] The values he substituted for the neoclassical complex of rules were those we associate with romanticism: an appreciation for history, a "high estimation of the unique, the original, and the irrational . . . [a] conviction of the value of individuality and personality."[64]

René Wellek describes Herder's style of criticism in this way:

> Herder differs from all other critics of the century not only in his radicalism, but also in his method of presentation and argument. In his writings there is a new fervid, shrill, enthusiastic tone, an emotional heightening, a style which uses rhetorical questions, exclamations, passages marked by dashes in wearisome profusion, a style full of metaphors and similes, a composition which often abandons any pretense at argument and chain of reasoning. It is that of a lyrical address, of constant questions, cumulative intensifying adjectives, verbs of motion, of metaphors drawn from the movement of water, light, flame, and the growth of plants and animals.[65]

Wellek also sees in Herder's work:

> the germs of much that is bad in criticism since Herder's time: mere impressionism, the idea of "creative" criticism with its pretensions to duplicating a work of art by another work of art.[66]

"Creative" criticism—criticism which seeks to elucidate a work of art by means of evocative, figurative, impressionistic language—was renewed with the romantic writers. Friedrich Schlegel's attitude toward this kind of criticism, Wellek points out, was favorable but cautious. Schlegel says on one occasion:

> Poetry can only be criticized by poetry. A judgment on art which is not itself a work of art, either in its matter, as presentation of a necessary impression in its genesis, or in its beautiful form and a liberal tone in the spirit of old Roman satire, has no citizens' right in the realm of art.[67]

But on another occasion he is skeptical of any criticism which has no other aim but reproduction of an impression:

> If many mystical lovers of art who consider all criticism dissection and every dissection a destruction of enjoyment were to think consistently, "I'll be damned!" would be the best judgment on the greatest work. There are critics who do not say more, though at much greater length.[68]

Although Schlegel agreed, at least partly, with Herder in his estimation of creative criticism, he differed fundamentally from his predecessor in his love of polemic, and his faith in the possibility and importance of censure. It was out of the acknowledged subjectivity of Herder's judgments that his own tolerant, liberal tone was born. Schlegel, though he absorbed (if indirectly) something of the theory and style of Herder's criticism, was convinced that a critic's judgments can have an objective validity. The possibility of censure in criticism cut loose from the rationalistic moorings of the earlier eighteenth century depends upon such a conviction, and in a very real sense, the justification for it was provided by Kant in his *Critique of Judgment*. In this connection it is easy to appreciate Walter Silz's statement, "One might say that the difference between 'Sturm und Drang' and Romanticism is due chiefly to the appearance of Kant's writings in the interval."[69]

Schumann's impressionistic style of music criticism arose out of the difficulties inherent in talking about anything intangible; in his solution to these difficulties he was by no means alone. In his outlook as a critic Schumann had a good deal more in common with Schlegel than with Herder. Criticism was for him not mere description and appreciation; it entailed serious evaluation. Schumann always had a special talent, in fact, for polemics and censure. He saw the critic's role as a didactic one; he must act not only as an interpreter, but also as a guide.

Like Friedrich Schlegel, Schumann was keenly aware that creative criticism is not by itself sufficient for the fulfillment of the critic's responsibility. From the earliest issues of the *NZfM* Schumann's writings include, too, a radically different type of criticism: an analytic dissection of the composer's craft.[70] Creative criticism was a way of getting at what Schumann would call the poetic qualities of a work of art. But he readily acknowledged his duty as a critic to deal with other aspects of a composition as well—and in any event much of the music he reviewed did not have, in his opinion, anything poetic about it. In his review of Hiller's Etudes, adopting a favorite romantic organic metaphor, Schumann proposes to discuss the "flower, root, and fruit, that is, the poetic, harmonic-melodic, and mechanical "elements" of the music.[71] Vivid contrasts in style within Schumann's criticism result from this variety of elements in music he wanted to talk about: in the *NZfM* of 1834-35 we have conversations between flowers, an account of a dream about a fair, and a painstaking analysis, complete with diagrams, of the form and harmony of the first of Hiller's etudes—an analysis intended to show a "looseness, which even degenerates into a lack of clarity and balance."[72]

The vivid extremes of Schumann's early style are combined in his famous review of Berlioz' *Symphonie fantastique* in the *NZfM* of 1835. This review is generally known only in its reduced (but nevertheless enormous) form in the various editions of the *Gesammelte Schriften*. A large section of the review deleted in the *Gesammelte Schriften* is the introductory installment,[73] an extravagant tribute to Berlioz finishing off with a poem by Franz von Sonnenberg—a "poetic counterpart" to Berlioz' symphony.[74] Here Schumann engages in the most outright kind of creative criticism: he offers to his readers a poem by way of explication of a symphony. In the following analysis of the first movement, he employs diagrams and musical examples, indulging in an almost painful degree of detail. Thus in a single review Schumann touches both extremes of his style as a critic—subjective, metaphorical suggestion, and meticulous, technical dissection.

During his earlier years as a critic Schumann's writings showed signs that he struggled to reconcile the divergent ways in which he wanted to talk about music. Dissatisfied with both the evocative and technical types of reviews by themselves,[75] he adopted something of a middle course and wrote a great many in a mixed style. His review of Mendelssohn's *Melusina* overture, for example, treats the "subject" of the music in richly figurative prose, finishing with an admission that the description falls short of duplicating the evocative qualities of the music. With an abrupt shift in language Schumann then begins to talk about such technical elements as form and orchestration.[76] Schumann still felt confronted with these two possible styles of criticism when he reviewed Berlioz' *Waverly* overture in 1839:

> It would be easy for me to depict the overture either in a poetic fashion by reproducing the various images it evokes in me, or in a dissection of the mechanics of the work. Each method of explaining music has something to recommend it. The first at least escapes the danger of dryness, into which the second, for better or worse, often falls.[77]

The shift in style long remained characteristic of Schumann's more important reviews. But it was often modified to a form in which general observations about the composer and his composition would be couched in a literary style, and specific points about the music dealt with in technical language.[78] It must be remembered that the shift in style, in fact the use of any poetic language at all, was always limited to reviews of music in which Schumann detected poetic qualities. It would have been impossible and pointless for Schumann to lavish his poetic style on every piece of music that crossed his desk. He was in fact very good at adapting his tone and style to the task at hand. If necessary, as we have seen, Schumann could deal with a great stack of mediocre music in a very short space; and in such a situation there is little reason for poetizing.

Schumann's most extravagant literary style disappeared rather quickly from the pages of the *NZfM*. The novelistic type of review was really confined to the years 1834-35, and the *Davidsbündler* names appeared only infrequently after 1836.[79] In his soberer style of the later 1830s and the 1840s Schumann began to use more of the technical language of music theorists. Terms such as "Anlage" and "Ausführung," common in music theory since Sulzer and Koch, begin to appear frequently in his writings of the early 1840s.[80] But the stimulus of a talented new composer such as Hirschbach, Gade, or much later, Brahms, or of a new, exciting composition from Mendelssohn, Chopin, or William Sterndale Bennett never failed to resurrect in Schumann some of his original flair for poetic description.

. . . . .

SCHUMANN'S AESTHETICS OF MUSIC

Philosophers in Schumann's time were very fond of talking about art. The notion of a system of fine arts—distinct from all the other kinds of activities in which people engage—become gradually more articulate in the preceding century in the writings of Abbé Dubos (*Réflexions critiques sur la poésie et la peinture,* 1719), Charles Batteux (*Les Beaux Arts réduits à un même principe,* 1746), and Alexander Baumgarten (*Aesthetica,* 1750).[81] Kant wrote about art somewhat as an afterthought; he felt that his philosophical system, though largely complete after the *Critique of Practical Reason* (1788), still contained a lacuna. This lacuna, he thought, could be filled by developing his ideas about the mental faculty he called "judgment." In his *Critique of Judgment* (1790), Kant characteristically divides this faculty into "determinant" and "reflective" judgment, and then separates the latter into "teleological" and "aesthetical" judgment. Here, finally, in this rather obscure corner of the splendid edifice of Kant's system, he discusses the arts.

The German idealists who followed Kant devoted an ever increasing share of their attention to the arts; the wave of enthusiasm for romantic (i.e. postclassical) art stimulated by Schiller's *Ueber naive und sentimentalische Dichtung* (1795) and the subsequent writings of the Schlegels undoubtedly contributed to this preoccupation with the branch of philosophy now called aesthetics. Schelling, in his *System of Transcendental Idealism* (1800), declared, "the universal organon of

philosophy, and the keystone of its entire arch, is the philosophy of art."[82] Schelling and the other idealists usually thought of the arts as reflections, in one way or another, of things which are very important to idealist philosophers—things they call by such names as "idea," "the absolute," "absolute ego," and "Urselbst."

The German philosophers who discussed art in this period often indulged in classifications of the individual arts and evaluations of their relative importance. In these ratings music came out better and better. Kant's classification divides the field into the arts of speech, the formative arts, and the arts of the "play of sensations"—music belonging to the last of these.[83] In his "Comparison of the respective aesthetical worth of the beautiful arts," Kant places music (with some reservations) second to poetry. One defect music suffers, he says, is "a certain want of urbanity"—it often bothers the neighbors.[84] Less than thirty years later Schopenhauer assigned to music a place of unique importance among the arts. While all the other arts, he tells us, are only indirect portrayals—like the figures on the wall in Plato's cave—of the "Will" (something like an *id* of the universe), music is the *immediate representation* of it.[85]

Such explanations of music attained a wide currency in Schumann's time. Dozens of formidable and sometimes murky books on musical aesthetics appeared in Germany in the 1830s and '40s, most of them strongly influenced by idealistic philosophy and produced by minor writers whose specialties lay somewhere between history, philosophy, and music: for example, Gustav Nauenburg, Gustav Schilling, Ferdinand Hand, Eduard Krüger, August Kahlert, and Amadeus Wendt. Articles on aesthetics appeared in the musical journals (rarely in the *NZfM*), and these journals were occasionally the arenas for lively philosophical debates about music.

In the 1830s Schuman was largely ignorant of what was going on in philosophy. In the dozens of pages in Boetticher's two books devoted to extracts from Schumann's diaries—always rich in records of his reading—there is little evidence that he read philosophy or aesthetics.[86] It is characteristic of Schumann that he read and reread Jean Paul's novels, but apparently ignored his *Vorschule der Aesthetik*. Schumann showed his naiveté about philosophy and philosophers in an interesting way in the extract from his second *Davidsbündler* article reprinted in the *NZfM* under the title **"Das Aphoristische."**[87] Here, when he wants to give an example of some philosophers who have made "complete philosophical systems," he doesn't mention Kant or Hegel, but Ernst Platner and F. H. Jacobi, two distinctly provincial writers, neither of whom left anything that could conceivably be called a complete philosophical system.

Like most practitioners of the arts (but unlike Wagner), Schumann was wary of philosophical explanations of his occupation. In his "motto-book" he cited as the height of the ridiculous a perfectly normal-sounding definition by Christian Weisse: "The idea of beauty is the form of all true being perceived under the pattern of necessity."[88] While his distaste for formal aesthetics was somewhat tempered later on, Schumann always remained aloof from any disputes of a philosophical nature about music;[89] and though he reviewed almost anything else, he never wrote a review of a book on aesthetics.[90]

Several writers have noted that Schumann once began to write an aesthetics of music, but never completed it.[91] They seem to imply that had this work been finished and preserved we should have a systematic exposition of his philosophical views about music. But the evidence these writers rely upon is the nineteen-year-old Schumann's letter to Wieck of November 1829, claiming that he had begun "years ago" to write an aesthetics of music;[92] from what is known about Schumann's adolescent writings one could hardly expect this to be aesthetics in any usual sense of the term. There is in fact a fragmentary document by Schumann, written in 1827 or 1828, that is probably the "aesthetics of music" he mentioned to Wieck. It is called **"Die Tonwelt,"** and it makes some show of describing the effects of music and how they operate. But it really amounts only to a rhapsodic literary effusion similar to many of Schumann's other writings from this period; it may be described as something like the "In praise of music" section from an early medieval treatise as it might have been written by Jean Paul.[93]

The fact is that Schumann paid little attention to aesthetics divorced from artistic practice. Yet some of the ideas of the philosophers reached him indirectly by way of the literary men who absorbed their influence. E. T. A. Hoffmann, for example, one of Schumann's favorite authors, sounded like almost any one of the idealist philosophers when he said of instrumental music that "its sole subject is the infinite."[94] Thus Schumann, quite unintentionally, became interested in some of the questions that occupied the philosophers, and he shared some of their vaguely Platonic views about art. One of the subjects both the philosophers and Schumann discussed, but from quite differing vantage points, was the problem of musical reference.

PROGRAMS AND MUSICAL REFERENCE

Aestheticians of music have for a long time concerned themselves with: (1) whether music refers to anything outside itself (or, simply, whether it *means* anything); and (2) whether it depends for its effect upon association, either by the composer or the listener, with extraneous events, experiences, feelings, and the like.[95] It is often assumed that in the nineteenth century, especially the earlier part of it, most composers and others who thought about these questions believed in musical reference, and that most twentieth-century composers and writers have put away childish things and embraced the "autonomist" position.[96] In other words, most romantics would, roughly speaking, answer "yes" to the questions posed above, and most modern composers and critics would answer "no." But things aren't nearly that simple; for as these answers have changed, the questions, none too clear at the outset, have changed as well.

Onomatopoeic effects, presumably, ought not to be the issue here; not even the most confirmed autonomist would deny that Respighi is able to make his listeners think of the cuckoo bird when he introduces into his music a phonograph recording of its call. Nor would he deny that Strauss can remind his audience of a flock of sheep by a skillful orchestral imitation of their bleating. What he does deny is that the composer *ought* to do these things. So far as onomatopoeic effects are concerned, at least, the question is not "Can a piece of music refer to anything outside itself?" It has become "*Should* a piece of music refer to anything outside itself?" And in answering "no," the twentieth-century critic agrees with most of the major writers on music beginning at least with Vicenzo Galilei.

The real battles between autonomists and referentialists have raged over questions about the relationship between music and the emotions. From the beginning of the seventeenth century, when people began to see in music more similarities to rhetoric than to mathematics, theories about music have allotted a prominent place to the emotions or passions. The most usual and durable explanation of the relationship between music and the emotions has two parts: (1) music expresses or portrays emotions, and (2) its most important effect is to arouse the emotions of the listener. When Hanslick, perhaps the first and certainly the most articulate of the modern autonomists, wrote his famous book in 1854—the same year that Schumann published his *Gesammelte Schriften*—it was still precisely these two propositions, he felt, that had to be refuted. He wrote:

> On one hand it is said that the aim and object of music is to excite emotions, i.e., pleasurable emotions; on the other hand, the emotions are said to be the subject matter which musical works are intended to illustrate.
>
> Both propositions are alike in this, that one is as false as the other.[97]

The first of these statements that Hanslick so vigorously denies—that "the aim and object of music is to excite emotions"—is on the surface a bit puzzling. For can music really have any aim? Aims, objectives, and intentions are the sort of thing, so far as we know, that only people (and perhaps some animals) have. Certainly Hanslick was speaking figuratively—as we did above in calling one chapter of this study "the goals of the journal." What he meant was undoubtedly something like this: "The aim and object a composer has in writing music (or a performer has in performing it) is to excite emotions." But in this case his categorical denial of the proposition is puzzling. Does he really mean to say that no composer or performer aims to excite the emotions of his listeners? Wagner, for one, claimed that he did; and Hanslick was his bitter opponent, not because he thought Wagner was lying (in this instance, at least), but because he thought Wagner's objective (that is, to excite the emotions) was a bad one.

Hanslick's book as a whole reinforces our suspicions that his formulations are more prescriptive than descriptive. He does not deny that music sometimes excites emotions; he admits this on the very next page, and in a later section he gives the improviser permission to do all the things he denied the composer.[98] In any event, as Hanslick would doubtless admit, the way to find out whether or not music excites emotions is to ask those who listen to music; and Hanslick's world was full of people who reported that it did. His point was simply this: that arousing the emotions of the listener ought not to be the primary objective of the composer, and that the kind and intensity of emotion the listener feels is not a stable criterion for judging a musical composition.[99] So again the original question has changed; it is not now "*Is* it the goal of music (or its composer) to excite the emotions?," but more like "*Should* it be the goal of the composer to excite the emotions?"[100]

If an examination of the statements of an arch-autonomist like Hanslick begins to break down the popular notion of a sharp dichotomy between a "romantic" and "modern" view of music, a careful reading of the romantics does so even more. Schumann, like Hanslick, thought a great deal about problems of musical reference, and his thinking was remarkably critical and consistent. He doubted, with Hanslick, that music can portray, as a painting would, a nude reclining on a couch or a group of peasants gathering grain. And he thought that it probably cannot, like a novel, tell a story about a countess who marries an aging duke in order to be near her current lover who is a police official at court. Schumann even agreed with Hanslick that the psychological reactions of people listening to music are not entirely predictable. But he differed with him in the importance he assigned to these psychological reactions and in his interest in discovering their causes and controlling them.

Schumann did not leave us a treatise on the relationship between music and the emotions or on any kind of musical reference because, nonphilosopher that he was, he could never muster up much enthusiasm for these subjects in the abstract. But in the course of performing his duties as a critic he nevertheless discussed them a good deal. Questions about whether or not music refers to events or objects come up most often, as we might expect, in his reviews of program music—that is, instrumental music which the composer provides with specific narratives or evocative titles (like E. Haberbier's piano etude, "Coeur insensé sois calme ou brise-toi"), and which may make use of onomatopoeic effects (like the sound of the head bouncing from the guillotine in Berlioz' *Symphonie fantastique*). Schumann's ideas about programs and musical reference have been subject to such a variety of interpretations that a reexamination of his statements on these subjects seems to be in order.

Aside from musical imitations of the sounds of bouncing heads and the like (which he hardly ever deigned to discuss), Schumann, as I have said, was very skeptical about the ability of music to refer to events, people, or objects in the way that language and pictures do. He never posited a program of any kind as the single possible referent or meaning of a piece of music. In his review of Berlioz' *Waverly Overture* in 1839, in fact, he specifically denied that this was possible, even for the composer:

> Berlioz has now written music to it [Scott's novel]. Some will ask, "to which chapter?, which scene?, for what purpose?, to what end?" For critics always want to know what the composers themselves could not tell them, and critics often hardly understand a tenth part of what they talk about.[101]

Even in 1835, when Schumann was writing his programmatic piano music, he worried about the risks a composer took that the composer's intentions in using programs might be misinterpreted:

> Beethoven was very well aware of the dangers involved with his *Pastoral Symphony*. In the few words with which he prefaced it, "more the expression of emotion than tone-painting," there lies an entire aesthetics for composers. It is ridiculous that a painter should represent him in portraits sitting at a brook, his head resting on his hand, listening to the splashing.[102]

Schumann denied that composers of programmatic music usually have any intention of portraying events, scenes, or characters. In his best-known discussion of programs, that in the review of Berlioz' *Symphonie fantastique,* he wrote: "He surely deceives himself who believes that the composer simply takes up his pen and paper with the sickly intention of expressing, depicting, or painting something or other."[103]

And in his later review of Spohr's programmatic symphony, *Irdisches und Göttliches im Menschenleben,* he declared,

> They [the philosophers] are clearly wrong when they think that a composer working with an idea sits down like a preacher on Saturday afternoon, schematizes his theme according to the usual three points, and works it out in the accepted way—to be sure, they are wrong.[104]

It is clear from Schumann's writings that he seriously doubted that music can denote objects or events or state propositions.[105] A musical composition, in Schumann's opinion, does not *mean* the same thing as its program. If it did, there would seem to be little reason for having both. Yet Schumann thought that the connection between a literary program and the music it accompanies can be an intimate one, and on occasion he found programs and programmatic titles useful. In a review of Julius Schaeffer's *Lieder ohne Worte* he explained, "There are certain mysterious moods of the soul which can be more readily understood by means of these verbal indications from the composer, and we must be thankful for them."[106] And, he said, they can prevent a misinterpretation of the composer's intent; Schumann wrote about Henselt's etude, *Ave Maria,* "Here is an example of how a well-chosen heading can enhance the effect of the music. Without this title most players would rattle it off like a Cramer etude."[107] But a composition should be able, ideally, to achieve its effect independently: "I always say, 'first of all let me hear that you have made beautiful music; after that I will like your program too.'"[108]

The quotation above from the Schaeffer review provides a key to Schumann's ideas about the workings of programs and about the nature of the connection between music and its program. This connection involves a third participant, namely Schumann's "mysterious moods of the soul," which, he tells us, the program can help us to understand. Now it was these moods of the soul (*Seelenzustände*) that Schumann associated with all the best music of his time, not just programmatic music. The program, he felt, could serve as an aid to their clearer apprehension and hence toward a clearer apprehension of an essential part of the music. A program or suggestive title, according to Schumann's notion, acts very much like the poetic descriptions of creative criticism. The Jean Paulian "poetic counterpart" could serve equally well as a descriptive assessment of a composition, or as a program for it; in Schumann's work as a composer and critic, it did both. Thus the music does not denote or portray the program; something like the reverse is true: the program suggests and clarifies certain qualities of the music.

Music and its program are related to each other because both are related to something else, namely certain psychological states, or emotions, or, as Schumann sometimes said, *Stimmungen*. Schumann was never very explicit about the nature of this relationship between the program and the emotions, or—and this is of more immediate concern to us—between music and the emotions. Is it simply that music elicits the emotions of the listener? Or does it express emotion the composer was feeling at the time of composition, or the one the performer feels during performance? Or does it, as language could, communicate the *idea* of an emotion, quite

aside from whether or not any of these people experienced it at any particular time?

Schumann seemed to admit more than one of these possibilities. There can be no doubt that he thought music elicits emotion; his descriptions of his own reactions to music show this plainly enough. But he believed that the listener does more, ideally, than merely react; a full appreciation of music involves receiving and understanding a kind of communication. One of the clearest statements to this effect is in Schumann's article **"The Comic in Music"**:

> less well informed people usually tend to hear in music without text only sorrow or only joy, or that which lies halfway between, melancholy. They are not able to perceive the finer shades of passion, as in one composition, anger and penitence, in another, feelings of satisfaction, comfort, and the like. Because of this it is very hard for them to understand masters like Beethoven and Schubert, who could translate every circumstance of life into the language of tone.[109]

We can gather from this passage (and from a number of others as well) that Schumann thought music is able to *communicate* feelings or psychological states, and in this he was apparently at odds with Hanslick. Schumann surely did not think this would always work— that the reference of music to the emotions was universally valid or necessary, as Boetticher claims. In order to understand it you need to be "well informed"; the whole apparatus of programs, programmatic titles, and poetic critiques in which Schumann indulged, moreover, would have been useless were there no possibility of misunderstanding the emotional message of music.

But we still have not determined whether the communication of which Schumann speaks belongs to the second or to the third of the possibilities suggested above, that is, does music communicate the *idea* of an emotion, or does it express directly the emotions the composer is feeling? The difference between these two possible functions of music amounts to the distinction Susanne Langer draws between a sign and a symbol.[110] A sign, as she uses the word, announces that something is present or that it is occurring. Smoke is a *sign* of fire; a train whistle is a sign that the train is approaching. A symbol conveys the *idea* of something (whether it is present or not); a symbol for fire is simply the word "fire." A symbol for what one feels in a stubbed toe is "pain," while a sign of it might be "ouch."[111]

When Schumann, then, says that a composition communicates anger or penitence, is this the particular anger or penitence of the composer (or of the performer)— i.e. is it a *sign* of someone's psychological state? Or is the music a *symbol* for an abstract anger or penitence? Schumann does not really say. His never-failing interest in such things as form and development of musical materials seems to preclude a view of music as an immediate, exclamatory expression of anyone's feelings. But the composer's ability to communicate any feeling depended, it seems, upon his having experienced it at some time or other; the "circumstances of life" Beethoven and Schubert translated into music were the ones they knew at first hand. The inevitable influence of a composer's experiences, impressions, and temperament upon his music is a dominant theme in Schumann's writings. He explains in a letter to Clara how this works in his own case: "Everything that happens in the world affects me, politics, literature, people; I reflect on all of this in my own way, and then whatever can find release in music seeks its outlet."[112] And in his review of Schubert's Symphony in C, Schumann reflects on the beauties of Vienna, concluding, "it becomes perfectly clear to me how such works could be born precisely in these surroundings."[113]

If music cannot, in Schumann's opinion, induce with any certainty into the mind of the listener a vision of a radiant sunset or thoughts about a heroic woman risking her life to save her husband, it *can* communicate the kind of feelings which attend such things—provided that the listener is properly perceptive and properly conditioned. Feeling in a broad sense (or "conditions of the soul" or *Stimmungen*), then, lies at the center of Schumann's theories about musical significance. They become part of the composer's experience simply as a result of his own environment and his own impressions. They are communicated in music to the receptive listener, who, the composer hopes, will understand them and at least to some extent experience them himself. The literary program is meant to reinforce this communication by suggesting to the listener ideas, events, or narratives with which he might associate such feelings. It is an alternate route to the same goal.

Perhaps this interpretation of Schumann's ideas will help to explain his seemingly inconsistent statements about program music. For sometimes he favors programs and at other times not; sometimes he wants to substitute different programs and titles for the ones composers have given their music, or he provides more than one program for the same piece; sometimes, as in the case of the **Papillons,** he associates a single program with pieces composed independently and at various times, and always stoutly insists that the programs and titles, even of his most programmatic music, are applied ex post facto.

Schumann's apparent inconsistency about the value he sets upon programs is now easier to understand. If the music itself is communicative, a program, ideally, should not be necessary. Several times Schumann said that it would be "a good test of the composer's success" if his listeners knew nothing of his programs or titles.[114] And he reproved Berlioz and Spohr for habitu-

ally providing their music with programs or programmatic titles, though he never had any serious quarrel with either their music or their programs per se.[115] In Schumann's opinion, attaching a program to a piece of music was something like telling a joke and then explaining the punchline.

If the music itself were not communicative, Schumann insists, attaching a program or evocative title to it would be as futile as writing a poetic critique of it. This is true of the etude by Haberbier mentioned above, "Coeur insensé sois calme ou brise-toi." Such a heartbreaking title, he says, can do nothing for this pedestrian music.[116]

Schumann was sometimes willing to accept more than one program for the same composition; in his review of the Schubert C-major Symphony he implies that the suitability of a program or poetic counterpart may depend upon the sensibilities of the listener:

> I will not attempt to provide the symphony with a foil, for the different generations choose very different words and pictures to apply to music. And the youth of eighteen often hears in a piece of music an event of worldwide importance, while the grown man sees only a local happening, and the musician thought of neither the one nor the other.[117]

The possibility of fitting more than one program to a composition with satisfactory results is consistent with Schumann's view of the program as a supplement or accessory. Just as a single piece of music could be subject to various poetic descriptions—and often was by the contrasting personalities of Florestan and Eusebius in Schumann's early criticism—so its message could be suggested by more than one program.

But in many cases, Schumann seems to say, the composer describes in his program the very events, experiences, or impressions that aroused in him the feelings he wishes to communicate in his composition. Schumann apparently thought Berlioz did this in his *Symphonie fantastique.*[118] But even such a program has no special claims to authenticity. Schumann, in fact, wanted to forget Berlioz' program and make his own: "In the beginning the program spoiled all my enjoyment and all my freedom of outlook. But as this receded more and more into the background and my own imagination became creative, I found all this and much more. . . ."[119] But this is not to say that program-making was an arbitrary and entirely subjective matter. Not just any one would do; Schumann often quarreled with the names composers gave their music (Johann Kittl was a habitual offender in this respect) and the programs they associated with it. Though more than one poetic counterpart to a piece of music was possible, finding a really appropriate one, Schumann thought, was a difficult and exacting task.

The ideas about musical reference emerging from Schumann's writings also cast some light on the seemingly erratic treatment of programmatic elements in his own music.[120] The individual movements of the *Phantasie* op. 17, for example, were originally to have borne the names *Ruinen, Trophaeen,* and *Palmen;* Schumann later changed these to *Ruine, Siegesbogen und Sternbild,* and *Dichtungen,*[121] and finally eliminated them altogether. The Intermezzo from the *Faschingsschwank aus Wien,* as we have seen, was to have been included in a set of pieces with quite different programmatic connotations, the *Nachtstücke*—which itself Schumann first intended to call *Leichenphantasie.*[122] This kind of indecision bolsters Schumann's claim that he did not compose to illustrate preexistent literary schemes, but that, as he said, programs and titles occurred to him only after he had composed the music.[123] This is perfectly consistent with Schumann's view of the program as a supplement to a composition, not a subject of it.

In the case of one of Schumann's compositions, the *Papillons,* he certainly seems to say that he composed the music with a preexistent literary scheme in mind, namely the last chapter of Jean Paul's *Flegeljahre.* When copies of the *Papillons* were sent to various journals for review in 1832, Schumann, fearful that the reviewers would not know what to make of it, sent a few words of explanation to each of four editors, Rellstab, Fink, Castelli, and Gottfried Weber. These explanations are substantially similar; this one is from his letter to Rellstab:

> Less for the editor of *Iris* than for the poet and spiritual kin of Jean Paul, I shall allow myself a few words about the origins of the *Papillons;* for the thread that binds them together is barely visible. You will remember the last scene of the *Flegeljahre*—masked ball—Walt—Vult—masks—Wina—Vult's dancing—the exchange of masks—confessions—anger—disclosures—hurrying away—closing scene and then the departing brother.—I turned the last page over again and again; for the end seemed to me but a new beginning—and almost without knowing it I was at the piano, and thus arose one *Papillon* after another. May you find in these origins an apology for the whole, which in its particulars often needs one![124]

And in a letter to his family in Zwickau he says,

> and tell them all to read, as soon as possible, the final scene of Jean Paul's *Flegeljahre,* and that the *Papillons* are in fact meant as a translation into tone of this masked ball. And then ask them if the *Papillons* accurately reflect, perhaps, something of Wina's angelic love, Walt's poetic nature, and Vult's lightning-sharp spirit.[125]

Boetticher has found some marginal notes in Schumann's own copy of the *Flegeljahre* (now in the Robert Schumann-Haus, Zwickau) which seem to make the connection between the *Papillons* and Jean Paul's novel even more explicit. Schumann marked specific passages in the last chapter of the *Flegeljahre* with numbers designating the individual *Papillons.*[126] Thus the *Papillon* no. 1, for example, is linked with this passage:

> As he stepped out of the little room, he asked God that he might be happy when he returned to it; he felt like a hero who, thirsty for fame, goes forth into his first battle.[127]

So Schumann's own testimony apparently indicates that in this case a literary program (though one unmentioned in the published music) preceded and in some sense gave rise to the composition. Schumann seems to be afraid, furthermore, that the music will not be intelligible without this program, and he even speaks of his music as a "translation into tone." Boetticher's discovery, moreover, shows very detailed connections between program and music; these would tend to strengthen his position that Schumann was trying in his *Papillons* to communicate directly the events of Jean Paul's story. All of this apparently contradicts Schumann's statements that he always made connections with programs after the music was finished, and his professed belief that programs are but extrinsic aids—that music communicates states of the soul, not events.

Now when Schumann insisted that he always chose his titles, mottos, and programs ex post facto, he surely did not mean to say that a single piece of literature could never serve both as the impetus for a composition and as its program. The factors which influenced a composer in the making of a piece of music often became part of its program, as in the case, Schumann said, of Berlioz' *Symphonie fantastique.* His point is simply that the whole question of programs and titles had to be settled after the music was finished, and, as in the case of the *Symphonie fantastique* again, even things which influenced the composer have no inviolable claim to validity as programmatic aids for his music.

Thus if Schumann in fact composed the *Papillons* under the spell of the *Flegeljahre* and then recommended that novel to various people as a program for it, this was not inconsistent with his assertions that he applied programs ex post facto. But it is very doubtful that this is even what happened. For whatever Schumann told the editors, he wrote thus to Henrietta Voigt about the *Papillons:*

> I must also mention that I added the text to the music, not the reverse—for that would seem to me a silly beginning. Only the last, which by strange coincidence formed an answer to the first,[128] was aroused by Jean Paul.[129]

If we must make a choice as to which we are to believe, Schumann's statement to the editors, or to Henrietta Voigt, surely it has to be the latter. Schumann felt that the editors would require a plausible explanation for the novel form of the **Papillons,** while he could be much more frank with an intimate friend. The history of the **Papillons** throws even more suspicion on Schumann's report to Rellstab and the others that he read Jean Paul and then immediately composed these pieces. For they existed previously as independent waltzes and polonaises, and were composed intermittently over a long period of time.[130]

Boetticher treats the marginal notes in the *Flegeljahre* as final authority on what Schumann meant to communicate in composing the **Papillons.**[131] But we do not know what Schumann intended by these markings, nor even when they were made. It is perfectly plausible that he wrote these notations (his letter to Henrietta Voigt clearly suggests this) after the **Papillons** were complete, just as he suddenly discovered in his **In der Nacht** from the **Fantasiestücke,** long after it was finished, a certain kinship with the legend of Hero and Leander.[132] The notes in the *Flegeljahre* certainly do not justify Boetticher's opinion that Schumann intended in his **Papillons** to depict the specific events and characters of Jean Paul's novel.

Schumann's literary style is often highly figurative and sometimes it is more notable for its grace than for its precision. Yet it will pay us to read his statements about the **Papillons** and their program attentively. The letter to his family cited above comes closest, seemingly, to positing an immediate connection between the **Papillons** and events in the *Flegeljahre.* But even here Schumann does not say that the **Papillons** portrays Wina, Walt, or Vult, or anything they did, but "something of Wina's angelic love, Walt's poetic nature, and Vult's lightning-sharp spirit"—in short, it communicates states of the soul. And when Schumann speaks of his music as "a translation into tone," he specifies what it is that is translated: the masked ball. A ball is precisely the sort of thing that music can imitate through onomatopoeia, for the most noticeable sound at a ball is, of course, music. And the **Papillons,** like the music for a ball, consists simply of a series of dances.[133]

For Schumann the literary program was an aid to comprehension, a means for getting at an elusive and fragile content which is already present in the music—a content that any number of conventional performance directions or any straightforward, literal description would be helpless to communicate. Schumann's programmatic piano compositions, like his essays in creative criticism, were largely confined to the 1830s. As time passed, Schumann apparently became convinced that if the music itself is really communicative, there is no need for either of them.

INSPIRATION AND CRAFTSMANSHIP

If music communicates feeling, as Schumann says it does, it would seem perfectly reasonable to ask *"How?"*

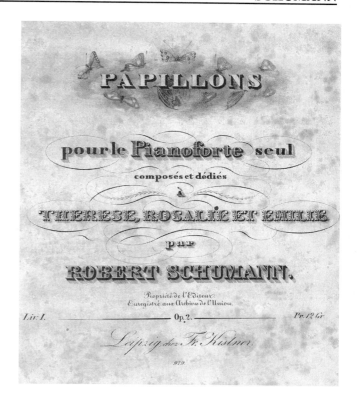

Title page for Schumann's piano composition Papillons.

We know that language employs symbols with fairly well fixed referents, so that a person speaking or writing these symbols can communicate information of many kinds (including information about feelings). Whatever the claims of Schering, Boetticher, and others, music lacks a repertory of defined symbols; thus if music communicates anything, it must do so in some other way. The question, then, is "How?" This problem has been written about a good deal, especially by philosophers. Susanne Langer, for example, whose ideas about musical significance are in some respects very much like Schumann's, argues that music can symbolize and communicate "general forms of feeling," or "the morphology of feeling."[134] It can do this, she says, because music fulfills various requirements (which she enumerates) for a nonverbal language. Among these is that it shows a "logical form" similar to that of its referent; the motions of waxing and waning and of tension and relaxation, which serve to define its "logical form," are characteristic of both music and our feelings. In fact, Langer continues, "Because the forms of human feeling are much more congruent with musical forms than with the forms of language, music can *reveal* the nature of feelings with a detail and truth that language cannot approach."[135]

The principal clause of this last sentence might have been uttered by Schumann or almost any of the romantics. But Schumann would not have been interested in the explanatory dependent clause. Schumann's "mysterious states of the soul" are mysterious because they are inaccessible to any ordinary linguistic description. The workings by which music conveys them, too, are mysterious, and Schumann was not particularly eager to explore these mysteries. Music that is genuinely expressive, Schumann believed, is at least partly a gift of inspiration, and he sometimes showed a real reticence about inquiring too closely into the nature of that gift.

There was of course nothing new in Schumann's belief that inspiration—nonrational and inexplicable—plays a role in musical invention. Even the most formal descriptions of the process of musical composition in the late eighteenth century emphasized the importance of inspiration. In his book on composition, Heinrich Christoph Koch, for example, makes use of J. G. Sulzer's term *Anlage* ("laying out," or initial conception) and explains to his readers "the manner in which such an *Anlage* arises in the soul of the composer." Before this can happen at all, he says, the composer must be in "a special state of inspiration."[136] This special state of inspiration—sometimes indistinguishable from a kind of feverish emotional excitement—is further emphasized as a factor in musical creation by the earlier romantic writers on music, Wackenroder, Tieck, and Jean Paul.

Schumann too was convinced of its importance, and at times he seems to embrace the peculiarly romantic doctrine of the infallibility of initial inspiration. In a review of Cherubini's second string quartet, he says he suspects that the composition is really a reworking of an unsuccessful symphony. "I am averse to all such transformations," he writes, "for they seem to me like a sin against the divine first inspiration."[137] And in his review of F. W. Grund's sonata for piano, op. 27, Schumann speculates that the second of the two movements was written much later than the first, and that the composer was unable to recapture the original mood of the piece:

> For the stimulation of the composer's imagination is such a delicate matter, that once the track is lost, or time intervenes, it is only by a happy coincidence that in a later rare moment it can be recovered. For this reason, a work discontinued and laid aside is seldom completed; it would be preferable for the composer to begin a new one, and give himself over completely to its *Stimmung*.[138]

Schumann included in his *Gesammelte Schriften* an aphorism to the same effect—one which shows that Schumann, like many of his predecessors, tended to identify inspiration with the strong emotions accompanying artistic creation: "The first conception is always the most natural and the best. Reason errs, but never feeling."[139]

During his ten-year stint as critic, Schumann's descriptions of the process of composition changed somewhat in emphasis. He became more and more impressed with the importance of the rational processes of the craft—of systematic development of themes, of revision and refining. In the 1840s Schumann began to find *Ausführung* ("working out") fully as necessary as *Erfindung* ("invention").[140] Expressions foreign to his early vocabulary, such as *Reinheit des Satzes* ("purity of phrasing") and *Geschicklichkeit der Anordnung* ("skill in ordering"),[141] began to show up in his reviews, and in 1843 he even recommended to his readers one of the most rationalistic of all books on composition, Mattheson's *Kern melodischer Wissenschaft*.[142]

But this change was one only of emphasis. For Schumann had a healthy respect—as any active composer must—for the ordinary operations of musical craftsmanship from the time he first became a critic. In one of his early critical essays, a review of sonata by Wilhelm Taubert, Schumann (in the person of Raro) praises Taubert's *Fortführung* and *Ausbauung* (approximately "carrying out" and "finishing off") as well as his *Anlagung*.[143] A major proportion of Schumann's attention in both the Hiller and Berlioz reviews of 1835 is addressed to technical matters such as form, harmony, and phrase structure—the sort of things that are hardly the free gift of inspiration. And even when inspiration is dispensing her bounties, a good deal is left to the discretion of the composer; in another review from 1835, Schumann speculates rather accurately about Beethoven's method of composition:

> In his *Pastoral Symphony* Beethoven sings simple themes such as any child-like mind could invent. Yet surely he did not merely write down everything presented by the initial inspiration, but made his choices from among many possibilities.[144]

In their explanations of how art is made, the early romantics in Germany, as heirs of both Herder and Kant, wavered in their allegiances between the inexplicable visitations of *furor poeticus* and the controlled operations of reason and craftsmanship. Both as theorists and practitioners, they often longed for an ideal balance between craftsmanship and inspiration, between reason and feeling. Wackenroder writes in his *Wesen der Tonkunst*:

> But when beneficent nature brings together the unlike artistic sensibilities, when the feelings of the listener burn more brightly in the heart of the learned master artist, and he forges his profound science in these flames, there will result a work of indescribable value. In it feeling and science will be bound together inseparably, like the stone and coloring of an enamel.[145]

Schumann offers some explanation of how both inspiration and craftsmanship can affect the outcome of a composition in his review of a concerto by E. H. Schornstein:

> But in general we might wish for more sifting, selection, and refinement. The first plan for the whole, to be sure, is always the most successful. Yet details must of-

ten be molded and polished; in this way talent gains for itself recognition, and for its product, permanence. And in this way, too, interest is maintained—an interest not inherent in the first conception of the whole. In this we include elegance of passagework, the charm of accompaniments to cantabile melodies, color in the middle voices, the elaboration and fashioning of the themes, the juxtaposition and combination of various ideas.[146]

Here Schumann describes the learned procedures of musical craftsmanship as a second stage in the process of composition. Inspiration provides not a finished product, but only an outline. The detail—figuration, accompaniments, and even developmental procedures—must all be worked out later. So the two kinds of processes Schumann says are involved in composing music turn out to be not contradictory, but complementary. Schumann explains the origins of music much as Wordsworth explains the origins of poetry; it results from a powerful emotion (or inspiration) recollected—and improved upon—in tranquillity. But there always remained a duality in the qualities Schumann appreciated in music and the ways in which he thought these qualities came about. In 1841 (in a review of a set of piano pieces by A. H. Sponholtz) Schumann mused about the difficulty of enjoying the "freedom of genius," and still constructing pieces with a good form,[147] and in one of his last reviews for the *NZfM,* he asserted that a composition must have two quite different kinds of excellence: purity of form, orderliness, and, on the other hand, "richness of invention, freshness, originality."[148]

In the quotations above from the Schornstein and Sponholtz reviews, Schumann seems to associate the two kinds of operations involved in composing music, the rational and nonrational ones, with "talent" and "genius" respectively. This association is rather consistent in his writings as a whole. Kant had defined genius as the "innate mental disposition (*ingenium*) through which nature gives the rule to art," and he explained its operation this way:

> It cannot describe or indicate scientifically how it brings about its products, but it gives the rule just as nature does. Hence the author of a product for which he is indebted to his genius does not know himself how he has come by his ideas; and he has not the power to devise the like at pleasure or in accordance with a plan, and to communicate it to others in precepts that will enable them to produce similar products.[149]

In Schumann's time genius was still regarded as a quality—like inspiration—whose operation could be neither understood nor explained; genius was a kind of direct pipeline from a higher reality, and the value and authority of its products were unassailable. Schumann himself usually understood the term in this way.[150] Talent, the faculty responsible for the details and final form of the art work, deals with procedures that can be learned, and is itself susceptible to training and development. As Schumann said, "Talent labors, but genius creates."[151]

Schumann did not explore very far the implications of his ideas about inspiration and craftsmanship and their correlation to genius and talent. He never said, for example, whether inspiration entailed genius, or genius entailed either inspiration or talent. His statements about these matters are not systematic, but sketchy and suggestive. They are like the first *Entwurf* given by inspiration; they have not been submitted to the rational processes of development and working out of detail. This is because Schumann's expressions of his aesthetic views were always to some extent by-products of his criticism. He was always interested, first of all, in discussing music, and in particular, specific musical compositions. In the following chapters we shall see what he had to say about them.

Notes

1. Published in Leipzig by C. H. F. Hartmann (1834), J. A. Barth (1835-37), and Robert Friese (1837-51). In 1834 the journal appeared under the title *Neue Leipziger Zeitschrift für musik,* but for the sake of convenience this first *Jahrgang* will also be called "*NZfM.*"

2. Hereafter *GS* 1854.

3. Robert Schumann, *Gesammelte Schriften über Musik und Musiker,* ed. Martin Kreisig (Leipzig, 1914, hereafter cited as *GSK*), xxxiv-xxxv.

4. There are now three anthologies of Schumann's writings translated into English. The earliest one, Fanny Raymond Ritter's two-volume work of the late 1870s, by far the most extensive of the three, is shot through with errors. A much smaller selection prepared by Konrad Wolf and Paul Rosenfeld (Pantheon, 1946; now in a McGraw-Hill paperback), though rather dependent upon Mrs. Ritter for its translations, is more accurate. The most recent collection, that of Henry Pleasants, is so heavily edited as to be misleading. Henry Pleasants, ed., *The Musical World of Robert Schumann. A Selection from Schumann's Own Writings* (New York, 1965). See my review in *Journal of the American Musicological Society, 17* (1965), 417-19. Quite aside from any deficiencies of these translations, they are all based on one or another edition of the *Gesammelte Schriften,* not the *NZfM;* for all quotations from Schumann in this book, therefore, I have made new translations.

5. Clara Schumann, ed., *Jugendbriefe von Robert Schumann* (Leipzig, 1885).

6. F. Gustav Jansen, ed., *Robert Schumanns Briefe, neue Folge* (Leipzig, 1904), hereafter cited as *Briefe.*

7. F. Gustav Jansen, *Die Davidsbündler. Aus Robert Schumanns Sturm- und Drangperiode* (Leipzig, 1883).

8. Frederick Niecks, *Robert Schumann,* ed. Christina Niecks (London and Toronto, 1925).

9. The most satisfactory of these is Karl H. Wörner's *Robert Schumann* (Zürich, 1949), a concise and accurate "life and works."

10. Düren-Rhld., 1932.

11. "Robert Schumann als Aesthetiker," *Jahrbuch der musikalischen Bibliothek Peters, 13* (1906), 50-73.

12. "Die aesthetischen Anschauungen Robert Schumanns in ihren Beziehungen zur romantischen Literatur," *Zeitschrift für Musikwissenschaft, 3* (1920), 111-18; also "Anfänge der Aesthetik Robert Schumanns," *Zeitschrift für Musikwissenschaft, 2* (1920), 535-39.

13. "Theory and Practice in Schumann's Aesthetics," *Journal of the American Musicological Society, 17* (1964), 310-45.

14. See W. J. von Wasielewski, *Robert Schumann,* trans. A. L. Alger (Boston, 1871), p. 17, where Kuntsch is described as provincial and amateurish; also K. Wörner, *Schumann,* p. 27, and Rehberg, *Schumann,* pp. 19-20. Jansen, in the footnotes to the *Briefe,* p. 528, offers some defense of Kuntsch's competence. Schumann was always respectful toward Kuntsch (See *Jugendbriefe,* p. 186), and Clara reported in later years to Frederick Niecks that "my husband thought a great deal of him. He certainly was not distinguished enough to be my husband's teacher." Frederick Niecks, *Robert Schumann* (London, 1925), p. 32.

15. See Niecks, pp. 35-36.

16. *NZfM, 18* (1843), 27.

17. *Briefe,* p. 7.

18. In Heidelberg, Schumann was exposed to many performances of Baroque music at the home of A. F. J. Thibaut, jurist, amateur musician and author of *Ueber Reinheit der Tonkunst* (Heidelberg, 1825; 2d ed., 1826). This work was furiously attacked for its amateurish reactionism by Hans Georg Nägeli in his *Der Streit zwischen der alten und der neuen Musik* (Breslau, 1826). Mendelssohn as a youth of 18 years describes his favorable impressions of Thibaut (and especially of his library) in a letter from Heidelberg in 1827. Yet he remarks, "It is strange; the man does not know much about music, even his historical knowledge of it is limited, his judgments are mostly purely instinctive." Felix Mendelssohn, *Letters,* ed. Seldon Goth (New York, 1945), *1,* 34. Schumann always remembered Thibaut with respect. *Ueber Reinheit der Tonkunst* provided a large number of the mot-tos heading individual issues of the *NZfM,* and one of Schumann's "Musikalische Haus- und Lebensregeln," written about 1848, reads, "Thibaut's *Ueber Reinheit der Tonkunst* is a fine book. Read it often when you are older." *GSK,* 2, 167.

19. See Niecks, pp. 93-94.

20. Many passages of the four-hand polonaises (1828) published by Geiringer (Universal edition, 1933), for example, reappear in the *Papillons,* op. 2. See Geiringer's explanation of the relationship of the compositions in "Ein unbekanntes Klavierwerk von Robert Schumann," *Die Musik, 25, Bd.* 2 (1932), 725-26.

21. August Schumann was well known as the translator of the works of Sir Walter Scott. Wörner, pp. 12 ff.

22. Quoted in Boetticher, ed., *Schriften,* p. 8.

23. Cited in Boetticher, *Einführung,* p. 225. Boetticher's transcription of Schumann's entries appears to be in error at some points. I have taken "Anacova" to mean Anacreon, "Titull" I interpret as Tibull, and "Sarbiesky" as Sarbiewsky. Schumann's report of his own linguistic prowess seems almost too good to be true. Even the best Gymnasium education would hardly equip him to unscramble the Doric dialect of Bion.

24. Wörner, p. 11.

25. See the description in Niecks, pp. 41-42.

26. F. Gustav Jansen, "Aus Robert Schumanns Schulzeit." *Die Musik, 5* (1906), *Bd.* 4, pp. 83-99.

27. Kreisig (*GSK,* 2, 449) points out a similarity of part of this essay to some of the commentary in an encyclopedic series called *Bildnisse berühmter Männer aller Zeit,* a publication of August Schumann with which Robert had recently assisted.

28. *GSK,* 2, 173-75, and 186-90.

29. Boetticher, ed., *Schriften,* pp. 9-10, 24-28, and *Einführung,* pp. 114-15 and 623. Perhaps it was an indication of Schumann's maturing tastes that in 1833 he ridiculed the idea of naming his musical journal "Tonwelt."

30. *Jugendbriefe,* pp. 16-17. The work with whose publication Schumann assisted was correctly identified by Niecks (p. 42) as Forcellini's *Totius Latinitatis Lexikon* (first edition, Padua, 1771). More precisely, it was the four-volume German version of the third edition of this work that Schumann's brother published (the original third edition appeared in Padua in 1827).

31. Wörner, p. 26.

32. *Jugendbriefe*, p. 136.

33. *GSK*, 2, 260-61.

34. *Briefe*, p. 45 and *Jugendbriefe*, p. 223.

35. *NZfM, 1* (1834), 73-75. In *GS* 1854 and succeeding editions of the *Gesammelte Schriften,* this heading was changed to "Aus den kritischen Büchern der Davidsbündler." In a footnote to this review in the *NZfM,* Schumann promises a later explanation of the *Davidsbund.* A "clarification" in a later issue (*NZfM, 1* [1834], 152.) merely says:

> "There are many rumors afoot about the fraternity whose name appears below. Since, unfortunately, we must still withhold the reasons for concealing our identity, we will ask Herr Schumann (should he be known to any of the editors) to represent us, should the occasion arise, under his own name."
>
> —THE DAVIDSBÜNDLER

> "I shall do so with pleasure."
>
> —ROBERT SCHUMANN

The most lucid and concise discussion of the nature of the *Davidsbund* and its members, Florestan, Eusebius, and Raro, is in Kreisig's footnotes to his edition of the *Gesammelte Schriften* (*GSK*, 2, 367-69).

36. *NZfM, 1* (1834), 73-75. See Appendix I, 24.

37. *NZfM, 1* (1834), 97-99.

38. *NZfM, 2* (1835), 125-27, 133-34, and 145-46.

39. *NZfM, 2* (1835), 116-17; *3* (1835), 126-27, 147, 151-52, 182-83; and *4* (1836), 211-13.

40. *NZfM, 3* (1835), 152.

41. See, for example, the series under the heading "Grobes und Feines" in *NZfM, 1* (1834), 147-48, and 150-51.

42. The "Musikalische Haus- und Lebensregeln," according to Kreisig (*GSK, 2,* 448), were originally to have been inserted between individual numbers of the *Jugendalbum,* op. 68, composed in 1848. Instead they were first published in an "Extrabeilage" of the *NZfM* in 1850, and they appeared together as an appendix to the second edition of the *Jugendalbum* in 1851.

43. An allusion, apparently, to Goliath.

44. The original version of this passage in the *Davidsbündler* article (*GSK, 2,* 268) makes more sense: it has "Aphorismen" instead of "der Kunst."

45. Schumann refers to the German philosophers Ernst Platner (1744-1818), and Friedrich Heinrich Jacobi (1743-1819).

46. *NZfM, 1* (1834), 151. See Appendix I, 26.

47. Except Niecks (pp. 122-23) who tends to dismiss Jean Paul's influence as negligible. He is undoubtedly right in limiting it almost exclusively to Schumann's earlier years.

48. Boetticher, *Einführung*, p. 144, n. 90, and p. 319.

49. Jansen, "Aus Robert Schumanns Schulzeit," *Die Musik, 5* (1906), *Bd.* 4, p. 85.

50. *Damenkonversationslexikon, 2,* 332-33. Schumann incorporated this essay, with certain changes, into the *NZfM* in 1835 (*NZfM, 2,* 43-44), and Kreisig has reprinted both versions (*GSK, 1,* 105-06, and *2,* 207-08).

51. Schubart's essay on the keys is in his *Ideen zu einer Aesthetik der Tonkunst* (Vienna, 1806), pp. 377-82.

52. See *Briefe,* p. 145, and Erich Schenk, "Halbjahr der Erwartung," in H. J. Moser and E. Rebling, eds., *Robert Schumann, aus Anlass seines 100. Todestages* (Leipzig, 1956), p. 21. The page reference to the *Briefe* in Schenk's citation is in error.

53. *NZfM, 10* (1839), 77, 157, and 185.

54. *AmZ, 40* (1838), 668.

55. There is little reasonably scientific information on Schumann's illness. P. J. Möbius considered the problem in an entire book, *Ueber Robert Schumann's Krankheit* (Halle, 1906). A more recent study is Gerhard Granzow's "Florestan und Eusebius, zur Psychologie Robert Schumanns," *Die Musik, 20* (1928) *Bd.* 2, pp. 660-63. Despite Boetticher's infatuation with a movement in German psychology called Charakterologie (a study of personality which became contaminated with strong implications of racism), his discussion of Schumann's illness (*Einführung,* pp. 161 ff., and 167 ff.), appears to be sensible. There is general agreement that Schumann's affliction would now be diagnosed as schizophrenia.

56. *Briefe,* p. 70.

57. G. Noren-Herzberg, "Robert Schumann als Musikschriftsteller," *Die Musik, 5* (1906), *Bd.* 4, p. 104.

58. *AmZ, 12* (1810), 630-42, and 652-59; *15* (1813), 141-54. See the later condensed version of these reviews in Strunk, ed., *Source Readings,* pp. 775-81.

59. In the *Gesammelte Schriften,* Schumann changed this to "griechischer . . . Musik." *GSK, 1,* 44.

60. *NZfM, 2* (1835), 42.

61. In his *Einführung,* p. 106, n. 5, Boetticher has assembled a series of early statements to show what

Schumann meant by "poetic." Schumann almost always used this word in an analogical sense, that is, not to distinguish poetry from prose, but to distinguish works of art which were original and imaginative from those which were not. The term "poetry," in German literary criticism as well, no longer referred only to a general category of literary composition; it described any literary creation rich in imagery and emotional connotations. Thus Novalis said, "The novel must be poetry through and through." See R. Wellek, *A History of Modern Criticism* (New Haven, 1955), *2,* 85. Schumann referred in a similar vein to his journal as "the defender of the rights of poetry." *Jugendbriefe,* p. 222.

62. A typical statement is this: "We believe that the painter can learn from a Beethoven symphony, just as the musician, for his part, can learn from a work of art by Goethe." *NZfM, 1* (1834), 36.

63. Wellek (*1,* 176-81) considers none of the other writers associated with the *Sturm und Drang,* Lenz, Bürger, Stolberg, Gerstenberg, or even Hamann an important critic. Herder played a vital role as a forerunner of the literary theories of both the German classicists and romantics. The romantics themselves tended not to recognize this in Herder, but to extract from Goethe and Schiller ideas they could have gotten firsthand from Herder.

64. Walter Silz, *Early German Romanticism. Its Founders and Heinrich von Kleist* (Cambridge, Mass., 1929), p. 6.

65. Wellek, *1,* 182.

66. Wellek, *1,* 184.

67. Wellek, *2,* 10.

68. Ibid. Though Schlegel shows vacillation on this point, his earlier writings are as a whole conspicuously coherent and perceptive. It is inconceivable that an impartial reader of his works should, like Irving Babbitt, repeat Nietzsche's senseless aspersion that "no one had a more intimate knowledge of all the bypaths to chaos." *Rousseau and Romanticism* (Cleveland, 1962), p. 85.

69. Silz, *Early German Romanticism,* pp. 6-7.

70. Almost all writers on Schumann have ignored this side to Schumann's criticism. See, for example, the description by H. Kretzschmar in "Robert Schumann als Aesthetiker," *Peters Jahrbuch, 13* (1906), 47-73.

71. *NZfM, 2* (1835), 43.

72. *NZfM, 2* (1835), 56.

73. *NZfM, 3* (1835), 1-2. Schumann also deleted in his *Gesammelte Schriften* the first two paragraphs of the second installment (*3,* 33). The first installment is signed "Florestan." The opening paragraphs of the second offer the pretense of having been written by a different author and question the adequacy of the "psychological method" of the first installment.

74. *NZfM, 3* (1835), 2. The opening lines of the poem are:

> Du bist!—und bist das glühend ersehnte Herz,
> Durch stumme Mitternächte so heiss ersehnt
>
>   * * *
>
> Du bist's, die einst süsschauernd am Busen mir
> In langem Tiefverstummen, in bebenden
> Gebrochnen Ach's, verwirrt, mit holdem
> Jungfraunerröthen in's Herz mir lispelt:
> "Ich bin das Ach, das ewig die Brust dir eng
> Zusammenkrampft' und wieder zum Weltraum hob."

75. Schumann's comment in the Berlioz review about the inadequacy of "psychological criticism" is one of his few explicit statements to this effect. His doubts about the efficacy of "technical" criticism, however, he reiterated frequently. A most explicit discussion of this subject also appears in the review of Berlioz' symphony (*NZfM, 3* [1835], 37). A review that analyzes the form and harmony of a piece of music, Schumann maintains (quite sensibly), is of no use whatever to those completely unfamiliar with the music. An analysis, when addressed to readers who do know the music, can be useful if the reviewer has some special point to make about the form or harmony of the piece (as in the case of the Berlioz symphony to demonstrate that the first movement has a clear and rather traditional form). Schumann had no use for the aimless, matter-of-course analysis that was habitual in the longer reviews of the *AmZ.*

76. *NZfM, 4* (1836), 6-7.

77. *NZfM, 10* (1839), 187. See Appendix I, 28. C. M. von Weber discusses the possibilities open to the critic in a similar fashion in his review of E. T. A. Hoffmann's opera *Undine.* See Strunk, ed., *Source Readings,* p. 802.

78. A good example of this style in Schumann's later writing is his review of the *Marienlieder* of his erstwhile *Mitarbeiter,* Carl Banck. *NZfM, 17* (1842), 10-12.

79. Of the principal names representing Schumann, "Raro" was the first to be dropped, in 1836. "Eusebius" appeared sporadically until 1839, and "Florestan" made one final appearance in 1842. A Paris correspondent (Stephen Heller?) persisted in

signing his contributions "Dblr" until 1843. See *NZfM, 18* (1843), 146. In 1837 Schumann was disinclined to protract the half-imaginary existence of the *Davidsbund,* and wished to form in its place a real musical society. See *Briefe,* p. 87.

80. See *NZfM, 18* (1843), 14, 31; *21* (1844), 58.

81. For Baumgarten, "aesthetics" was a science of sensation or perception in general (from αἰσθητικός, capable of perceiving). He discusses, among other things, telescopes and thermometers as aids to perception. It was only somewhat later, especially after Hegel's *Vorlesungen über die Aesthetik,* that the word came to mean specifically "the science of the perception of the beautiful in art."

82. Quoted in B. Bosanquet, *A History of Aesthetic* (New York, 1957), p. 321.

83. I. Kant, *Critique of Judgment,* trans. Bernard (New York, 1951), pp. 164-69.

84. *Critique of Judgment,* pp. 172-74. Kant adds in a footnote, "Those who recommend the singing of spiritual songs at family prayers do not consider that they inflict a great hardship upon the public by such noisy (and therefore in general pharisaical) devotions, for they force the neighbors either to sing with them or to abandon their meditations."

85. A. Schopenhauer, *Die Welt als Wille und Vorstellung,* ed. Deussen (Munich, 1924), *1,* pp. 303 ff.

86. Boetticher was very much bent upon showing that "Schumann is to be included among the philosophers of art of his time" (*Einführung,* p. 340) and musters all the evidence he can to prove that Schumann was abreast of current events in philosophy. His evidence is thoroughly unconvincing; he is reduced, for example, to making a great deal of Schumann's casual acquaintance with the "psychophysicist" and amateur philosopher Gustav Theodore Fechner (Friedrich Wieck's brother-in-law). Ibid., pp. 337-38.

87. *NZfM, 1* (1834), 151. Quoted above, p. 69.

88. Quoted in Boetticher, ed., *Schriften,* p. 58.

89. Schumann's closest brush with such a controversy was in his article known as "Das Komische in der Musik." *NZfM, 1* (1834), 10. This is the title appearing over the article in all the editions of the *Gesammelte Schriften;* consequently almost all writers on Schumann have taken it to be an autonomous essay. The title of the article in the *NZfM* is "Ueber den Aufsatz: das Komische in der Musik von C. Stein im 60. Hft. der Cäcilia." In this article in the *Caecilia* (60 [1833], 221-66), Gustav

Keferstein (who wrote in several of the musical journals under the pseudonym K. Stein, or C. Stein) refutes an article in an earlier volume of the *Caecilia* (*51*) by one Stephan Schütze, who claimed that music cannot be comic. Keferstein gives a lengthy, systematic exposition of his position and provides a number of musical examples to show that music often is comic. Schumann's article, which consists almost entirely of musical examples, was meant only as a supplement to the examples given by Keferstein.

The fight about "the comic" went on and on—in the *Caecilia,* the *Iris,* and the *AmZ* (See the description of the controversy in Julius Knorr's *Journalschau* article on the *Caecilia, NZfM, 1* (1834), 190-91). Schumann never paid any more attention to it in print.

90. Schumann once wrote to Ferdinand Hand that he had been reading the review copy of his *Aesthetik der Tonkunst. Briefe,* p. 230. Nevertheless, Schumann would not undertake the review of the book himself, but, after it had been on his desk "for a year and a day," asked August Kahlert to take care of it. *Briefe,* p. 216. Kahlert's review appears in the *NZfM, 17* (1842), 75-77 and 85-86.

91. See H. Kretzschmar, "Robert Schumann als Aesthetiker" *Peters Jahrbuch, 13* (1906), p. 50, and the recent article by Edward A. Lippman, "Theory and Practice in Schumann's Aesthetics," *Journal of the American Musicological Society, 17* (1964), 310.

92. *Jugendbriefe,* p. 83.

93. Parts of it are printed in Boetticher, *Einführung,* pp. 114-15.

94. Strunk, ed., *Source Readings,* p. 775.

95. I shall use the term "musical reference" somewhat broadly, admittedly, to cover the subjects of both these questions.

96. See Leonard B. Meyer's review of Donald M. Ferguson, *Music as Metaphor* in *Journal of the American Musicological Society, 15* (1962), 234.

97. E. Hanslick, *The Beautiful in Music,* trans. G. Cohen (New York, 1957), p. 9.

98. Ibid., pp. 76 ff.

99. In his enthusiasm for making this point Hanslick tends to overstate his opponents' views. "Beauty in music," he says, "is still as much as ever viewed only in connection with its subjective impressions, and books, critiques, and conversations continually remind us that the emotions are the only aes-

thetic foundations of music, and that they alone are warranted in defining its scope" (*The Beautiful in Music*, p. 9). Which critics could these be who view music "only in connection with its subjective impression," and who regard the emotions as the "only aesthetic foundations of music"? Schumann, clearly, was not one of them. The late baroque music theorists probably believed more implicitly than anybody else in a connection between music and the emotions (although their term "passion," deriving largely from Descartes' *Les Passions de l'âme,* was a somewhat broader one than our "emotion"). Yet these theorists were also concerned, as their composition books show, with a host of other considerations: correct harmony, facile melody, and the like. When Heinichen shows how to extract the proper passions from an "unfruitful" text and illustrate them in music, it is assumed that the illustrations will take all these other considerations into account. See J. D. Heinichen, *Der General-Bass in der Composition* (Dresden, 1728), pp. 31 ff.

100. Stravinsky, the most determined autonomist of all (in his writing, that is—many of his compositions are of types that presuppose close association with stories, events, and scenes), also gives us more preferences than postulates. For if his dicta about the independence of music are taken as descriptions of fact (see his *Autobiography,* New York, 1936, p. 53), he would seem to be condemning the romantics (and Berlioz in particular) for doing what he claims is impossible. See also his *Poetics of Music* (New York, 1936), pp. 74 and 130.

101. *NZfM, 10* (1839), 187.

102. *NZfM, 2* (1835), 65.

103. *NZfM 3* (1835), 50.

104. *NZfM, 18* (1843), 140.

105. In saying this I believe (though I cannot be sure) that I am contradicting Boetticher. He repeats throughout his *Einführung* that genuine German romantic music is always referential; the kind of reference involved is "symbolism" (See pp. 66-83). And because Schumann was a genuine German romantic, he used symbolism in his music and insisted that everyone else do so. Boetticher tries to show this, typically, by stating what he claims is Schumann's position, and then by way of demonstration, quoting something irrelevant from Schumann's writings (see especially p. 323). Though it is very difficult to discern what Boetticher means by "symbols," it is clear that he considers their significance to be universally valid; the connection between a musical symbol (he gives a schematic list of them on pp. 84-86) and

its referent, he states, is a "necessary" one. But why this should be true he explains in language I cannot understand (and shall not attempt to translate): "Der äussere und innere Teilsinn erreicht niemals den Hochstgrad der Verschmelzung, die Erkenntnisnotwendigkeit muss aus einer Spannung zwischen Symbolträger und -gehalt hervorgehen." *Einführung,* p. 68.

106. *NZfM, 15* (1841), 33.

107. *NZfM, 10* (1839), 74. And in his review of Moscheles' Etudes op. 95 (which bear titles such as "Das Bacchanal" and "Volksfestscenen"), Schumann wrote, "The use of such headings for musical compositions, which have become common again recently, is now and then criticized. It is said 'a good piece of music has no need of such indications.' Certainly not, but neither does it become less valuable because of them, and they are the surest means by which a composer can guard against gross misunderstandings of the character of a composition." *NZfM, 8* (1838), 201.

108. *NZfM, 18* (1843), 140.

109. *NZfM, 1* (1834), 10.

110. Susanne Langer, *Philosophy in a New Key* (New York, 1951), pp. 54 ff. Philosophers and literary critics often do not mean the same thing by "symbol." Philosophers speak of "conventional symbols." The symbols of logic provide examples; there is nothing about the figure $\supset$ which makes it more suitable than any other to denote negation. But in literary criticism (this has been true at least since the time of Goethe) symbols are thought to have some kind of intrinsic affinity with their referents. The bull, for example, has long been a symbol for passion and virility, and most people would agree that it is more appropriate for this than would be, say, a butterfly.

111. In the preface to the second edition of her book Miss Langer suggests the substitution of "signal" for "sign." Whichever term is used, there remain, I believe, certain loose ends to this distinction as she presents it. The utterances: "The train is approaching," and "I am in pain" would function, apparently, just as the train-whistle and the exclamation "ouch." But these statements certainly do not appear to be signs (or signals) as she thinks of them; both, for one thing, make use of symbols ("train" and "pain").

112. *Jugendbriefe,* p. 282.

113. *NZfM, 12* (1840), 82. Schumann was convinced that a composer's geographical location had an important effect on his music. On several occasions he printed his audacious aphorism, "Tell me

where you live, and I will tell you how you compose." *NZfM, 4* (1836), 198, and *5* (1836), 128.

114. *NZfM, 2* (1835), 65, 202.

115. *NZfM, 2* (1835), 65; *18* (1843), 140; and *20* (1844), 11.

116. *NZfM, 16* (1842), 103.

117. *NZfM, 12* (1840), 82. See Appendix I, 49.

118. He says, "In any case, the five principal headings would have sufficed; oral tradition would have passed on the other details of these events quickly enough. The interest stimulated in the person of the composer, who himself lived through this symphony, would assure that." *NZfM, 3* (1835), 50. See Appendix I, 50.

Barzun has shown convincingly enough that Berlioz' program for the *Symphonie fantastique* is not autobiographical; it was synthesized from various literary sources. Jacques Barzun, *Berlioz and the Romantic Century* (Boston, 1950), *1,* 157 ff.

119. *NZfM, 3* (1835), p. 50.

120. Mr. Lippman's article on this subject (*Journal of the American Musicological Society,* 17 [1964], 310-45) is thorough and thoughtful. But it does not take sufficient note, I think, of Schumann's profound skepticism about the ability of music to depict events, objects, or people.

121. *Jugendbriefe,* p. 281.

122. Ibid., p. 301.

123. In 1837 Schumann wrote to Moscheles about the *Carnaval,* "I hardly need assure you that the arrangement of the individual numbers as well as the headings came about only after the composition of the music." *Briefe,* p. 92. And later he wrote to his admirer Simonin de Sire, "The titles of all my compositions occur to me only after I have finished composing the music." Ibid., p. 148. Boetticher (*Einführung,* p. 332) collects a series of Schumann's statements to this effect, but chooses not to believe them.

124. *Jugendbriefe,* pp. 167-68.

125. Ibid., p. 166.

126. *Einführung,* pp. 331-32, and 611-13. Boetticher provides for each of the *Papillons,* in parallel columns, the passage Schumann marked in Jean Paul, his own description of the music (this is in some places seriously inaccurate; the *Papillon* no. 5, for example, is in B-flat major, not G minor), and the later explanations of the *Papillons* given by Julius Knorr.

127. From Boetticher, *Einführung,* p. 611. The remainder of these passages are given in accurate translation in Lippman, pp. 315-16.

128. Lippman, p. 320, has a good explanation for this passage.

129. *Briefe,* p. 54.

130. See Wolfgang Gertler, *Robert Schumann in seinen frühen Klavierwerken* (Leipzig, 1931), pp. 4 ff. Some of the polonaises incorporated into the *Papillons* have been published by Geiringer in a Universal edition; Geiringer discusses them in "Ein unbekanntes Klavierwerk von Robert Schumann," *Die Musik,* 25 (1932), Bd. 2, pp. 725-26.

131. Several of these passages seem disturbingly unconvincing as counterparts to the music. The scherzando, leaping, harmonically spicy middle section to the *Papillon* no. 4 refers, Boetticher tells us, to "a simple nun with a half mask and a fragrant bunch of auriculas." Boetticher attempts to mitigate this incongruity by describing the music as "stepwise and pianissimo"—neither of which it is. *Einführung,* p. 611.

132. *Jugendbriefe,* pp. 286-87

133. A number of these pieces (e.g. nos. 1, 2, 6, 10) even have the introductory section which announces the next dance of the ball. This collection of dances reflects the importance in Schumann's early musical experience of amateur music-making; many of them clearly show the influence of the style of four-hand piano music in vogue at the time.

134. Langer, p. 202.

135. Langer, p. 199. In Miss Langer's opinion, then, music is a symbol for the emotions, but not a "conventional symbol"; for its significance is not based on either general agreement or a stated definition, but on a natural similarity to its referent. But why this similarity—i.e. that both music and the emotions wax and wane, etc.—should be called a similarity of *logical form* is not clear.

136. Heinrich Christoph Koch, *Versuch einer Anleitung zur Composition* (Leipzig, 1787), 2, 70.

137. *NZfM, 9* (1838), 79.

138. *NZfM, 11* (1840), 186. See Appendix I, 51.

139. *GSK, 1,* 25.

140. See the review of C. G. Likl's *Elegies. NZfM, 19* (1843), 121.

141. See *NZfM, 19* (1843), 158.

142. *NZfM, 19* (1843), 124. Schumann prints some short excerpts from the book with this comment: "This book (which appeared 107 years ago and is now out of print) contains a good deal that is practical, substantial, and still valid today."

143. *NZfM, 2* (1835), 133.

144. *NZfM, 3* (1835), 158. See Appendix I, 52.

145. W. H. Wackenroder, *Werke und Briefe* (Jena, 1910), *1,* 185-86.

146. *NZfM, 4* (1834), 71-72. See Appendix I, 53.

147. *NZfM, 15* (1841), 17.

148. *NZfM, 19* (1843), 158.

149. *Critique of Judgment,* p. 151.

150. In some of his early letters and diaries Schumann used the word in its earlier sense, to mean a kind of personal attendant spirit.

151. *GSK, 1,* 25. See also the comparison between genius and talent in *GSK, 1,* 21.

Bibliography

Abert, Hermann J., *Robert Schumann,* Berlin, Schlesische Verlagsanstalt, 1920.

Abraham, Gerald, "Modern Research on Schumann," *Proceedings of the Royal Musical Association, 75* (1949), 65-75.

————, ed., *Schumann, a Symposium,* London, Oxford University Press, 1952.

Allgemeine musikalische Zeitung, ed. F. Rochlitz (1798-1819), G. W. Fink (1827-41), C. F. Becker (1842), Moritz Hauptmann (1843), J. C. Lobe (1846-48), Leipzig, Breitkopf und Härtel, 1798-1848.

Allgemeiner musikalischer Anzeiger, ed. J. F. Castelli, Wien, Haslinger, 1829-41.

Athenaeum, ed. A. W. Schlegel and F. Schlegel, 1798-1800, Facsim, Stuttgart, Cotta, 1960.

Auden, W. H, ed., *Nineteenth-Century British Minor Poets,* New York, Delacorte Press, 1966.

Babbitt, Irving, *Rousseau and Romanticism,* Cleveland and New York, The World Publishing Co, 1962.

Baldensperger, Fernand, "'Romantique' et ses analogues et ses équivalents: tableau synoptique de 1650 à 1810," *Harvard Studies and Notes in Philology and Literature, 19* (1937), 13-105.

Bate, Walter, J, *From Classic to Romantic, Premises of Taste in Eighteenth-century England,* Cambridge, Mass., Harvard University Press, 1946.

Becker, Carl Ferdinand, *Systematisch-chronologische Darstellung der musikalischen Literatur,* Leipzig, R. Friese, 1836.

————, *Die Tonkünstler des neunzehnten Jahrunderts,* Leipzig, Kossling, 1849.

Becker [Constantine], Julius, *Der Neuromantiker,* Leipzig, J. J. Weber, 1840.

Bigenwald, Martha, *Die Anfänge der Leipziger Allgemeinen musikalischen Zeitung,* Diss. Freiburg, 1938.

Bobeth, Johannes, *Die Zeitschriften der Romantik,* Leipzig, Haessel Verlag, 1911.

Boetticher, Wolfgang, "Neue Materialien zu Robert Schumanns Wiener Bekanntenkreis," *Studien zur Musikwissenschaft, 25* (1962), 39-55.

————, "Robert Schumann an seine königliche Majestät," *Die Musik, 33* (1940) i, 58-65.

————, *Robert Schumann, Einführung in Persönlichkeit und Werk,* Berlin, Bernhard Hahnfeld, 1941.

————, "Robert Schumann in seinen Beziehungen zu Johannes Brahms," *Die Musik, 29* (1837), ii, 548-54.

————, ed., *Robert Schumann in seinen Schriften und Briefen,* Berlin, Bernhard Hahnfeld, 1942.

Bosanquet, Bernard, *A History of Aesthetic,* New York, Meridian Books, 1957.

Boucourechliev, André, *Schumann,* trans. A. Boyars, New York, Grove Press, 1959.

Bray, René, *Chronologie du romantisme (1804-1830),* Paris, Boivin, 1932.

Brocklehurst, J. Brian, "The Studies of J. B. Cramer and his Predecessors," *Music and Letters, 39* (1958), 256-61.

Brown, Maurice J. E., *Schubert, a Critical Biography,* London, Macmillan, 1958.

Caecilia, ed. Gottfried Weber, Mainz, Schott, 1824-39.

Cannon, Beekman C., *Johann Mattheson, Spectator in Music,* New Haven, Yale University Press, 1947.

Chantavoine, Jean, *L'Ére romantique: le romantisme dans la musique européenne,* Paris, A. Michel, 1955.

Chopin, Frederick, *Selected Correspondence of Fryderyk Chopin,* London and Toronto, Heinemann, 1962.

Critica musica, ed. Johann Mattheson, Hamburg, 1722-25.

Critischer Musikus, ed. J. A. Scheibe, Leipzig, Breitkopf, 1745.

Dadelsen, Georg von, "Robert Schumann und die Musik Bachs," *Archiv für Musikwissenschaft, 14* (1957), 46-59.

Dahms, Walter, *Schumann,* Stuttgart, Deutsche Verlags-Anstalt, 1925.

Damenkonversationslexikon, ed. H. Herlsssohn, Leipzig, 1833-34.

Deutsch, Otto Erich, *Schubert, A Documentary Biography,* trans. Eric Blom, London, J. M. Dent and Sons, 1946.

———, *Schubert, Thematic Catalog of All his Works,* London, J. M. Dent and Sons, 1951.

Dieters, Hermann, Review of Robert Schumann, *Gesammelte Schriften,* iv. Auflage, ed. G. Jansen, *Vierteljahrschrift für Musikwissenschaft, 9* (1893), 355-63.

Dolinski, K., *Die Anfänge der musikalischen Fachpresse in Deutschland,* Berlin, Hermann Schmidt, 1940.

Dörffel, Alfred, *Geschichte der Gewandhausconcerte zu Leipzig,* Leipzig, 1884.

Ehinger, Hans, *Friedrich Rochlitz als Musikschriftsteller,* Leipzig, Breitkopf und Härtel, 1929.

Ehmann, Wilhelm, "Der Thibaut-Behaghel-Kreis. Ein Beitrag zur Geschichte der musikalischen Restauration im 19. Jahrhundert," *Archiv für Musikforschung, 4* (1939), 21-67.

Einstein, Alfred, *Music in the Romantic Era,* New York, W. W. Norton, 1947.

———, *Schubert, A Musical Portrait,* New York, Oxford University Press, 1951.

Erler, Hermann, "Ein ungedruckter Canon für vier Männerstimmen und sechs ungedruckte musikalische Haus- und Lebensregeln Robert Schumanns," *Die Musik, 5* (1906), iv, 107-09.

Faller, Max, *Johann Friedrich Reichardt und die Anfänge der musikalischen Journalistik,* Kassel, Barenreiter, 1929.

Feldmann, Fritz, "Zur Frage des 'Liederjahres' bei Robert Schumann," *Archiv für Musikwissenschaft, 9* (1952), 246-69.

Fétis, F.-J., *Biographie universelle des musiciens et bibliographie générale de la musique,* 2d ed., Paris, 1875-83.

Flechsig, Emil, "Erinnerungen an Robert Schumann," *Neue Zeitschrift für Musik, 117* (1956), 392-96.

Freystatter, W., *Die musikalischen Zeitschriften seit ihrer Entstehung his zur Gegenwart,* München, Theodor Riedel, 1884.

Geiringer, Karl, "Ein unbekanntes Klavierwerk von Robert Schumann," *Die Musik, 25* (1933), ii, 721-26.

Granzow, Gerhard, "Florestan und Eusebius. Zur Psychologie Robert Schumanns," *Die Musik, 20* (1928), ii, 660-63.

Harrison, Frank Ll., Mantle Hood, and Claude V. Palisca, *Musicology,* Englewood Cliffs, N. J., Prentice-Hall, 1963.

Haym, R., *Die romantische Schule,* Berlin, R. Gaertner, 1870.

Hegel, G. W. F., *Selections,* ed. J. Loewenberg, New York, Charles Scribner's Sons, 1957.

Heinichen, Johann David, *Der General-bass in der Composition,* Dresden, 1728.

Hempel, Gunter, "Leipzig," *Die Musik in Geschichte und Gegenwart, 8,* 540-69.

Herder, Johann Gottfried von, *Kritische Wälder, 3, 4* in *Sämmtliche Werke,* ed. B. Suphan, Berlin, Weidmann, 1877-1913.

Hernreid, R., "Four Unpublished Compositions by Robert Schumann," *Musical Quarterly, 28* (1942), 50-62.

Hofmeister, Adolph, ed., *C. F. Whistling's Handbuch der musikalischen Literatur,* 3d ed., Leipzig, Hofmeister, 1844.

Homeyer, H., *Grundbegriffe der Musikanschauung Robert Schumanns,* Diss. Münster, 1956.

Hopkinson, Cecil, *A Bibliography of the Musical and Literary Works of Hector Berlioz, 1803-1869,* Edinburgh, Edinburgh Bibliographical Society, 1951.

Iris im Gebiete der Tonkunst, ed. H. F. Ludwig Rellstab, Berlin, Trautwein, 1830-41.

Jansen, F. Gustav, "Aus Robert Schumanns Schulzeit," *Die Musik, 5* (1906), iv, 83-99.

———, *Die Davidsbündler, Aus Robert Schumanns Sturm- und Drangperiode,* Leipzig, Breitkopf und Härtel, 1883.

———, "Ein unbekannter Brief von Robert Schumann," *Die Musik, 5* (1906), iv, 110-12.

Kamieński, Lucian, *Die Oratorien von Johann Adolf Hasse,* Leipzig, Breitkopf und Härtel, 1912.

Kant, Immanuel, *Critique of Judgment,* trans. J. H. Bernard, New York, Hafner, 1951.

Kerst, Friedrich, "Carl Maria von Weber als Schriftsteller," *Die Musik, 5* (1906), iii, 324-30.

Kimmich, Anne, *Kritische Auseinandersetzungen mit dem Begriff "Neuromantik" in der Literaturgeschichtsschreibung,* Diss. Tübingen, 1936.

Kirchner, Joachim, *Das deutsche Zeitschriftenwesen, seine Geschichte und seine Probleme,* 2d ed., Wiesbaden, O. Harrassowitz, 1958-62.

———, *Die Grundlagen des deutschen Zeitschriftenwesens,* Leipzig, Karl W. Hiersemann, 1928-31.

Koch, Heinrich Christoph, *Versuch einer Anleitung zur Composition,* Leipzig, A. F. Böhme, 1782-93.

Kretzschmar, H., "Robert Schumann als Aesthetiker," *Jahrbuch der Musikbibliothek Peters, 13* (1906), 49-73.

Kristeller, Paul O., "The Modern System of the Fine Arts: A Study in the History of Aesthetics," *Journal of the History of Ideas, 12* (1951), 496-527.

Kritische Briefe über die Tonkunst, ed. F. W. Marpurg, Berlin, 1759-63.

Krome, F., *Die Anfänge des musikalischen Journalismus in Deutschland,* Leipzig, Pöschel und Trepte, 1896.

Langer, Susanne K., *Philosophy in a New Key. A Study in the Symbolism of Reason, Rite, and Art,* New York, The New American Library, 1959.

Leichentritt, Hugo, "Schumann als Schriftsteller," *Signale für die musikalische Welt, 68* (1910), xxiii, 912-15.

Lippman, Edward A., "Schumann," *Die Musik in Geschichte und Gegenwart, 12,* 272-325.

———, "Theory and Practice in Schumann's Aesthetics," *Journal of the American Musicological Society, 17* (1964), 310-45.

Liszt, Franz, *Gesammelte Schriften,* ed. L. Ramann, Leipzig, Breitkopf und Härtel, 1880-83.

Loesser, Arthur, *Men, Women, and Pianos, A Social History,* New York, Simon and Schuster, 1954.

Loewenberg, A., *Annals of Opera,* 2d ed. Geneva, Societas bibliographica, 1955.

Lovejoy, Arthur O., *Essays in the History of Ideas,* Baltimore, Johns Hopkins University Press, 1948.

Marpurg, F. W., *Historisch-kritische Beiträge zur Aufnahme der Musik,* Berlin, F. W. Birnstiel, 1759-63.

Martin, U., "Ein unbekanntes Schumann-Autograph," *Musikforschung, 12* (1959), 405-15.

Mendelssohn, Felix, *Letters,* ed. G. Seldon-Goth, New York, Pantheon, 1945.

Meyer, Leonard, Review of Donald N. Ferguson, *Music as Metaphor, Journal of the American Musicological Society, 15* (1962), 234-36.

Mizler, Lorenz, *Neu-eröffnete musikalische Bibliothek,* Leipzig, 1739-54.

Mizwa, Stephen P., ed., *Frederick Chopin, 1810-1849,* New York, Macmillan, 1949.

Möbius, P. J., *Über R. Schumanns Krankheit,* Halle, 1906.

Moser, H. J., and E. Rebling, eds., *Robert Schumann, aus Anlass seines 100. Todestages,* Leipzig, Breitkopf und Härtel, 1956.

Müller, Wilhelm Christian, *Aesthetisch-historische Einleitung in die Wissenschaft der Tonkunst,* Leipzig, Breitkopf und Härtel, 1830.

Musical World, The, London, J. A. Novello, 1836-50.

Nägeli, Hans Georg, *Der Streit zwischen der alten und der neuen Musik,* Breslau, Förster, 1826.

Neue Leipziger Zeitschrift für Musik, ed. Julius Knorr, Leipzig, C. F. H. Hartmann, 1834.

Neue Zeitschrift für Musik, ed. Robert Schumann (1835-44), Oswald Lorenz (1844), Franz Brendel (1845-68). Leipzig, J. A. Barth, 1835-37, R. Friese, 1837-51.

Niecks, Frederick, *Frederick Chopin, as a Man and Musician,* 3d ed., London, Novello and Company, c. 1902.

———, *Robert Schumann,* ed. C. Niecks, London, J. M. Dent and Sons, 1925.

Noren-Herzberg, G., "Robert Schumann als Musikschriftsteller," *Die Musik, 5* (1906), iv, 100-06.

Pessenlehner, Robert, *Hermann Hirschbach, der Kritiker und Künstler,* Düren-Rhld., 1932.

Phöbus. Ein Journal für die Kunst, ed. Heinrich v. Kleist and Adam H. Müller, Dresden, C. G. Gärtner, 1808.

Preussner, Eberhard, *Die bürgerliche Musikkultur, ein Beitrag zur deutschen Musikgeschichte des 18. Jahrhunderts,* Hamburg, Hanseat, 1935.

Proelss, Johannes, *Das junge Deutschland,* Stuttgart, Cotta, 1892.

Redlich, Hans, "Schumann Discoveries," *Monthly Musical Record, 80* (1950), 143-47, 182-84, 261-65; *81* (1951), 14-16.

Rehberg, Paula and Walter, *Robert Schumann, sein Leben und Werk,* Zürich and Stuttgart, Artemis Verlag, 1954.

Revue et Gazette musicale de Paris, Paris, Schlesinger, 1835-80.

Revue musicale, ed. J. F. Fétis, Paris, 1827-35.

Richter, Jean Paul Friedrich, *Vorschule der Aesthetik, Sämmtliche Werke, 18, 19,* Berlin, G. Reimer, 1826-38.

Schenk, Erich, "Robert Schumann und Peter Lindpaintner in Wien," *Festschrift für Joseph Schmidt-Görg,* ed. D. Weise, Bonn, Beethovenhaus, 1957, pp. 267-82.

Schering, Arnold, "Aus der Geschichte der musikalischen Kritik in Deutschland," *Jahrbuch der Musikbibliothek Peters, 35* (1928), 9-23.

———, "Kritik des romantischen Musikbegriffs," *Jahrbuch der Musikbibliothek Peters, 44* (1937), 9-28.

———, "Künstler, Kenner, und Liebhaber der Musik im Zeitalter Haydns und Goethes," *Jahrbuch der Musikbibliothek Peters, 38* (1931), 9-23.

Schilling, Gustav, ed., *Encyclopädie der gesammeten musikalischen Wissenschaften oder Universal-Lexikon der Tonkunst,* Stuttgart, Franz Heinrich Köhler, 1840-42.

Schmieder, Wolfgang, *Thematisch-systematisches Verzeichniss der musikalischen Werke von Johann Sebastian Bach,* Leipzig, Breitkopf und Härtel, 1950.

Schmitz, Arnold, "Die aesthetischen Anschauungen Robert Schumanns in ihren Beziehungen zur romantischen Literatur," *Zeitschrift für Musikwissenschaft, 3* (1920), 111-18.

———, "Anfänge der Aesthetik Robert Schumanns," *Zeitschrift für Musikwissenschaft,* 2 (1920), 535-39.

Schnapp, Friedrich, *Heinrich Heine und Robert Schumann,* Hamburg and Berlin, Hoffmann und Campe, c. 1924.

Schneider, Max, "Verzeichnis der bis zum Jahre 1851 gedruckten (und geschrieben in Handel gewesenen) Werke von Johann Sebastian Bach," *Bach-Jahrbuch,* 1906, pp. 84-113.

Schubart, Christian Daniel, *Ideen zu einer Aesthetik der Tonkunst,* Wein, J. V. Degen, 1806.

Schuberth, J., *Thematisches Verzeichniss sämmtlicher im Druck erschienenen Werke Robert Schumanns,* 4th ed., Leipzig and New York, J. Schuberth, 1868.

Schünemann, G., "Jean Pauls Gedanken zur Musik," *Zeitschrift für Musikwissenschaft,* 16 (1934), 385-404, 459-81.

Schumann, Eugenie, *Robert Schumann, ein Lebensbild meines Vaters,* Leipzig, Koehler und Amelang, 1931.

Schumann, Robert, *Early Letters,* trans. May Herbert, London, George Bell and Sons, 1888.

———, *Gesammelte Schriften über Musik und Musiker,* Leipzig, Georg Wigand, 1854.

———, *Gesammelte Schriften über Musik und Musiker,* ed. F. Gustav Jansen, Leipzig, Breitkopf und Härtel, 1891.

———, *Gesammelte Schriften über Musik und Musiker,* ed. M. Kreisig, Leipzig, Breitkopf und Härtel, 1914.

———, *Jugendbriefe von Robert Schumann,* Leipzig, Breitkopf und Härtel, 1885.

———, *Music and Musicians, Essays and Criticisms,* trans. Fanny Raymond Ritter, London, William Reeves, n.d.

———, *The Musical World of Robert Schumann. A Selection from Schumann's Own Writings,* ed. Henry Pleasants, New York, St. Martin's Press, 1965.

———, *On Music and Musicians,* trans. Paul Rosenfeld, ed. Konrad Wolff, New York, Pantheon, 1946.

———, *Robert Schumanns Briefe, neue Folge,* ed. F. Gustav Jansen, Leipzig, Breitkopf und Härtel, 1904.

Silz, Walter, *Early German Romanticism, Its Founders and Heinrich von Kleist,* Cambridge, Mass., Harvard University Press, 1929.

Spitta, Philipp, "Ueber Robert Schumanns Schriften," *Musikgeschichtliche Aufsätze,* Berlin, Paetel, 1894, pp. 383-401.

Stege, Fritz, *Bilder aus deutscher Musikkritik,* Regensburg, Bosse, 1936.

Stravinsky, Igor, *An Autobiography,* New York, W. W. Norton, 1962.

———, *Poetics of Music in the Form of Six Lessons,* New York, Vintage Books, 1956.

Strunk, Oliver, ed., *Source Readings in Music History,* New York, W. W. Norton, 1950.

Sulzer, J. G., ed., *Allgemeine Theorie der schönen Kunste,* Biel, Heilmann, 1777.

Thibaut, A. F. J., *Ueber Reinheit der Tonkunst,* Heidelberg, J. C. B. Mohr, 1825, 2d ed., 1826.

Tiersot, Julien, "Schumann et Berlioz," *Revue musicale, 16* (1935), 409-22.

Ullmann, Richard, and Helene Gotthard, *Geschichte des Begriffes "Romantisch" in Deutschland,* Berlin, Emil Ebering, 1927.

Van der Straeten, E., "Mendelssohns und Schumanns Beziehung zu J. H. Lübeck und Johann J. H. Verhulst," *Die Musik,* 3 (1903), i, 8-20, 94-102.

Wackenroder, W. H., *Werke und Briefe,* ed. Friedrich von der Leyen, Jena, Eugen Diederichs, 1910.

Wasielewski, W. von, *Life of Robert Schumann,* trans, A. L. Alger, Boston, Oliver Ditson, 1871.

Wehl, Feodor, *Das junge Deutschland,* Hamburg, J. F. Richter, 1886.

Wellek, René, *A History of Modern Criticism: 1750-1950, 1, 2,* New Haven, Yale University Press, 1955.

———, *Concepts of Criticism,* ed. Stephen G. Nichols, Jr., New Haven, Yale University Press, 1963.

———, "Periods and Movements in Literary History," *English Institutes Annual,* 1940, pp. 73-93.

Werner, Eric, *Mendelssohn, A New Image of the Composer and his Age,* trans. Dika Newlin, New York, The Free Press of Glencoe, 1963.

Wieck, Maria, *Aus dem Kreise Wieck-Schumann,* Dresden und Leipzig, E. Pierson, 1912.

Wöchentliche Nachrichten und Anmerkungen die Musik betreffend. Ed. J. A. Hiller, Leipzig, 1766-70.

Wolff, V. E., *Lieder Robert Schumanns in ersten und späteren Fassungen,* Berlin, 1913.

Wörner, Karl H., *Robert Schumann,* Zürich, Atlantis, 1949.

Wustmann, Gustav, "Zur Entstehungsgeschichte der Schumannischen Zeitschrift für Musik," *Zeitschrift der Internationalen Musikgesellschaft,* 8 (1907), 396-403.

Zoff, Otto, *Great Composers through the Eyes of their Contemporaries,* New York, E. P. Dutton, 1951.

Leon Botstein (essay date 1994)

SOURCE: Botstein, Leon. "History, Rhetoric, and the Self: Robert Schumann and Music-Making in German-Speaking Europe, 1800-1860." In *Schumann and His World,* edited by R. Larry Todd, pp. 3-46. Princeton: Princeton University Press, 1994.

[*In the following essay, Botstein places Schumann's literary and musical work in the context of nineteenth-century German culture and thought.*]

INTRODUCTION: RESCUING THE HISTORICAL SCHUMANN

"I often wonder whether my cultural ideal is a new one, i.e. contemporary, or whether it derives from Schumann's time." This thought, jotted down by Ludwig Wittgenstein in 1929, identifies how the work of Robert Schumann has come to be thought of as emblematic of a past discontinuous with our own.[1] Schumann's music is understood to represent a critique of the twentieth-century present. An idealized and vanished culture whose qualities we wish we retained reappears to us in the music.

Wittgenstein's observation was a species of early twentieth-century nostalgia for a preindustrial world of *Hausmusik* (obliterated by a late nineteenth century that Wittgenstein found uncongenial)—for a civilized *Biedermeier,* bourgeois, domestic life of culture readily associated with Schumann, particularly with his piano and vocal music. The interconnection between the literary and musical in much of Schumann's music, particularly the keyboard works, evoked a moment in the past when art and ideas mattered to the individual.

No composer in the European tradition, in fact, was so actively engaged in the public arena with literature and, indirectly, aesthetic philosophy.[2] Felix Mendelssohn, who worked to further Schumann's career as a composer and who stood as godfather to Schumann's offspring, never freed himself from the doubt—owing to Schumann's considerable reputation and achievement as a critic—that in some fundamental manner Schumann was, as a composer, a remarkable amateur.

Wittgenstein's implicit understanding of Schumann as somehow at odds with a twentieth-century cultural ideal mirrors a distinctly modernist enthusiasm for Schu-

mann. Theodor Adorno identified Schumann rather than Richard Wagner as a forerunner of Alban Berg. In Adorno's view, Schumann's music was not manipulative. It did not employ a surface of lyricism or a clear pattern of tonal structure and resolution intended to lull the listener into a false sense of security. Schumann's music was not, therefore, an example of how music was consumed successfully to induce in the listener the arrogant inner sense of authentic aesthetic judgment. It resisted the use of the musical experience to falsify or camouflage the painful contradictions of existence.[3] The epigrammatic character of the early Schumann was therefore not the only point of comparison that Adorno had in mind. In 1941 Adorno orchestrated selections from the *Album für die Jugend,* **Op. 68,** in order to underscore the modernist essence beneath the surface of Schumann's most accessible music.[4]

The fascination with Schumann from the perspective of a critique of modernity is observed best, however, in Roland Barthes' view of Schumann. Barthes used Schumann to suggest a debasement in the evolution of our connection to music. The matter was not entirely left the prisoner of a musical text. When one played and listened to Schumann, one realized how faulty modern habits of listening had become.

Schumann, for Barthes, was "truly the musician of solitary intimacy, of the amorous and imprisoned soul that *speaks to itself* . . . ; loving Schumann, doing so in a certain fashion against the age . . . can only be a responsible way of loving."[5] Playing Schumann could reaffirm the sensual and spiritual sense of oneself; a respite from contemporary psychic alienation could be discovered.

Although it may be methodologically self-deceptive, one needs to set aside carefully this legacy of modernist and postmodern enthusiasm for Schumann and try to reconstruct the historical Schumann. In what sense was he typical of a culture? As early as December 1846, Eduard Hanslick, in one of his first published essays, sought to explain why Schumann would never be popular. He noted that his works were "too interior and strange . . . too deep, too simple, too sharp, and too dry . . . I believe Schumann is not for the majority but for individuals."[6]

Indeed, the most well-remembered aspect of Schumann's life was his strangeness. The story of his attempted suicide, mental illness, and hospitalization, not to speak of his carefully documented romantic life, has been the object of uninterrupted popular and scholarly fascination from the time of his death to the present.[7] Schumann's reputation as psychologically deviant has played into historical generalizations about the nineteenth century, particularly with respect to the image and role of art and the artist in society.

The idea that this manic-depressive and pathologically laconic musician can stand as a symbol of creativity per se continues to be argued.[8] In the later nineteenth century Schumann exemplified the ideal type of the genuine artist as necessarily abnormal (one thinks of Thomas Mann's views on this issue). In 1905 Wilhelm Dilthey, in an essay on Hölderlin, noted: "Feeling and fantasy proceed unregulated on their eccentric path. Who does not think immediately of Robert Schumann and Friedrich Nietzsche."[9] Great art and thought ("feeling and fantasy") needed to be "out of season."

Schumann and his music have become synonymous with the aesthetics of authenticity. Both the realization of self-critical individuality and the costs of that ambition can be found in the case of Schumann. His life story and his music vindicate the struggle to protect the intimate power of art against the brutal facts of modernity. Intimacy and autonomy seem to have been systematically suppressed and nearly obliterated by the world after 1848. Counted among the enemies of the aesthetic values realized in Schumann have been industrialization and the politics of the modern nation-state, capitalist commerce in the arts—the exploitation of sentimentality—and the musical aesthetics of Wagner and late romanticism.

In order to reconstruct the historical Schumann, one needs to respond to the challenge most recently put forward by Anthony Newcomb about whether there was *one* Schumann, so to speak, or several different incarnations of Schumann engineered by the composer himself. Newcomb alleges that the habitual reliance on Schumann's critical writings, which date from only one period of his life, as the key to the entire range of his music has resulted in a distorted view.[10]

Scholars frequently have noted apparent contradictions in Schumann's ideas and wide disparities in the quality of his music.[11] Some have argued that these were the result of his fleeting self-conscious imitations of Jean Paul's own *Doppelgänger* literary technique. Schumann's extreme mood shifts and outbursts of short-lived enthusiasm are used to explain inconsistencies. Newcomb suggests, however, that the shifts in Schumann's career are fundamental.

The claim that one must not consider the life and work of Schumann as a whole was first put forth by Richard Wagner. Wagner argued that there was an early Schumann marked by a distinct and promising originality and a late Schumann whose talent was trivialized and destroyed by the Jewish influence of Mendelssohn. Schumann's unexceptional but persistent anti-Semitism aside—evident in his not entirely admirable relationship to Mendelssohn[12]—the Wagnerian view has had a permanent echo in the conventional devaluation of the late music of Schumann.[13]

Recent scholarship, for example, has nearly unanimously indicated a preference for the first editions of the early piano music. The mature Schumann had severe doubts about his early piano compositions. Not unlike many other composers, he was critical of his early work. When the opportunity came to bring out new editions, he reheard his work and made changes. The rejection of these emendations has been implicitly tied to the judgment that the new music he was writing when he re-edited the early work is inferior.[14]

The claim of this essay is that there was indeed just "one" Schumann. His work presents the historian with a uniquely coherent subject. By implication, therefore, neither the late work nor the later editions deserve diminished respect. Furthermore, late Schumann is not inconsistent with the composer's earlier achievements and ideas. The phases in his career, his approach to the acts of music making—to playing, listening, and writing music—as well as his construction of the role of music in personal and social life were indelibly and coherently shaped by the intellectual and social foundations of his early years.

Perhaps Schumann was representative, in Wittgenstein's sense, of a cultural ideal precisely because he was, of all composers of his generation, the least professional. His career was even less the consequence of the heritage of guildlike patterns in musical training characteristic of the eighteenth and earlier centuries than Richard Wagner's. Schumann's approach to music was distinctly from the outside.[15]

In Schumann's childhood home the practice of music was a component in a conception of the cultivated individual characteristic of a segment of society ascendant in the early 1800s. In contrast to Bach, Mozart, Beethoven, and Brahms, Schumann's turn to music as a career was not the result of any family pattern. Unlike the case of Mendelssohn, it was not the result of stunning precocity. Schumann was perhaps the first in a line of great musicians whose prominent, affluent middle-class family, despite the prestige it placed on musical culture, fought the turn to music as a profession.

In Schumann the extramusical was transposed, self-consciously, into the musical. This did not prevent subsequent generations, particularly Hanslick, from recasting Schumann's music and aesthetics into an ideology of so-called absolute music. In contrast, the least sophisticated and nearly vulgar current in late nineteenth-century bourgeois culture remained, rather, closer to Schumann's ambitions. His vocal and keyboard music served as models for salon music during the later nineteenth century. The emotional relationship to music exploited by the mass-produced, sentimental piano works that made up the popular domestic repertoire around the turn of the century was an authentic extension of a compositional intent characteristic of Schumann's work. Salon music adopted his strategies in the reciprocal association between music, emotion, images, and ideas.[16]

Four dimensions of the composer's life and world merit reconsideration in the search for the historical Schumann: first, his relationship to the work of Jean Paul and Wolfgang Menzel and to early nineteenth-century constructs of reading and writing; second, the philosophical discourse that Schumann encountered as a young man regarding the place of aesthetics within systematic accounts of knowledge and experience; third, his relationship to his own historical age in terms of past and future; and fourth, his interest in art history and early nineteenth-century painting.

JEAN PAUL AND WOLFGANG MENZEL

No fact is more often repeated in the literature on Robert Schumann than his profound admiration for Jean Paul Richter. Schumann asserted that he learned more from Jean Paul about counterpoint than from anyone else. Hermann Kretzschmar placed Jean Paul at the center of Schumann's aesthetics.[17] Newcomb has alleged, however, that by the 1840s Schumann had drifted away from Jean Paul. Public taste had already abandoned his novels. It was Jean Paul's posthumous fate that most of the more than sixty volumes of his collected works were ultimately forgotten, even though his reputation during his lifetime and for decades thereafter rivaled that of Goethe and Schiller.

Robert Schumann's diaries cast doubt on Newcomb's assertion. Throughout the late 1840s and 1850s Schumann noted his persistent rereading of Jean Paul. The last references are in the spring, summer, and fall of 1853, when Schumann reported that he (and Clara) read *Flegeljahre, Die unsichtbare Loge, Hesperus, Siebenkäs,* and *Titan.*[18]

What were the consequences of this lifelong fascination and admiration for Jean Paul? In one of the most famous prose passages in Jean Paul's work, "Das Kampaner Tal," in the subsection called "Suffering without Consolation," Jean Paul writes:

> Human suffering is also substantively different from the suffering of animals. The animal feels wounds somewhat the way we do in our sleep. The animal, however, does not see those wounds, and its pain is a fleeting moment and not more. It is not enlarged threefold and made more intense by expectation, memory, and consciousness. And therefore tears appear in our eyes alone.[19]

Within the human soul lies the capacity to transform mundane existence into the spiritual confrontation with the ecstasy of sorrow and joy. In contrast to Goethe and Schiller, Jean Paul saw his task as a writer to evoke in readers a sense of the profound and the beautiful within the ordinary and frequently dismal surroundings of life. However, by comparison with the realism of the later nineteenth century, Jean Paul was not politically didactic. The intent of the systematic philosophy and theology of Jean Paul's father's generation—together with its idealization of universal categories such as humanity, truth, and beauty—remained.

The truth of those ideas had to be discovered in life by the individual. Jean Paul set aside the mid-eighteenth-century philosophic traditions about the proper forms and subjects of art. His turn to the ephemeral and modest facts of daily life reflected a closer affinity to Herder, and his experiments with forms of fiction vindicated Friedrich Schlegel's comparison of him to Friedrich Schleiermacher. For Jean Paul, the power of subjective imagination and feeling was stronger than the self-conscious act of abstract reasoning. If a synthesis of art and life was achieved in fiction to which the reader responded in the act of reading, the surface of the work need not necessarily conform to formalist conventions that had been validated by classical and neoclassical-classical aesthetic theory. This point was not lost on the young Schumann. Reading Jean Paul induced an inner transformation that the reader could transfer from the book to his own everyday surroundings. A synthesis of art and life emerged from the book that altered the reader's sense of his own capacities.

As Dilthey pointed out, what was unusual about Jean Paul was that in his prose there were no memorable descriptions, and there was a striking absence of the evidently artful poetic use of language.[20] One of the reasons later generations abandoned Jean Paul was that in the language and narrative there was little surface evidence of artistry and no text of representation sufficiently compelling to hold the attention of later nineteenth-century readers in search of an evidently literary aesthetic achievement.

Jean Paul's long-winded and rambling prose works were designed to render the act of reading the temporal equivalent of philosophical and emotional contemplation. The use of extended imagination by the reader was indispensable; characters and events were never fully realized. With respect to Jean Paul the conceit that the text is defined or becomes complete only in the act of reading, therefore, does not derive from the imposition of modern criticism. That idea was integral to authorial intention.

For Schumann, the reading of Jean Paul successfully induced what might be considered a sympathetic experience. The reader—in this case Schumann—felt parallels to what the protagonists in the novels felt as they responded to events; even to Jean Paul's philosophical interventions into the text. Schumann, as reader, sensed the experience of the act of writing. This was achieved by subordinating descriptions of events and objects, which remained opaque. The process of subjective reaction to the world was at the center. Schumann's *Papillons,* **Op. 2**—the work he himself linked most closely to Jean Paul—reveals fragmentary, descriptive, and evocative musical references to recognizable external experience, which are organized into a loose musical narrative that communicates the inner reaction of the composer. In the many transitions within each piece the player's own expressive response is given room.

At stake was a sympathetic vibration—in terms of the expressive reactions to life—with the characters and the author. The key to Jean Paul can be expressed in the German word *Ausdruck,* which, as Arnfried Edler has pointed out, played a central role in Schumann's musical aesthetics.[21] Jean Paul and Beethoven were frequently compared in the early nineteenth century. This seemed appropriate, particularly for Schumann, since Beethoven's ambitions regarding the playing and hearing of music paralleled Jean Paul's ideas about writing and reading. In his notations concerning the "Pastoral" Symphony, Beethoven distinguished between description and illustration, and the expressive realization through music of the impact of nature, people, and events—items of real experience.

Jean Paul helped to shape Schumann's views about the functions of improvisation and the playing and hearing of worked-out musical texts. The use of the interrupted phrase, distorted repetition, self-quotation, sudden modulations and shifts in pulse, fragmentary echoes, and clearly undramatic endings in the early piano music speak to Schumann's ideal of how the author could best stimulate the creative fantasy of the player and listener. The musical text re-created the relationship of the reader and the book as constructed by Jean Paul.

In a letter to Friedrich Wieck, describing a performance of Schubert's four-hand Rondo in A major, D. 951, published in 1828, Schumann wrote:

> Schubert remains my "one and only" Schubert just as Jean Paul remains my "one and only." They share everything in common. When I play Schubert it is as if I were reading a novel of Jean Paul's turned into music. . . . Can you compare it to anything that has the same eerie, quiet, compact, and lyrical madness [*Wahnsinn*] and the same unified, profound, graceful, and ethereal melancholy that wafts over the absolutely true whole? I can visualize Schubert clearly: in his room, pacing back and forth, wringing his hands full of despair; how it resonates in music in his soul. . . . I remember having played this Rondo for the first time at a soiree at Probst's. At the end, players and listeners looked at each other for a long time and did not know what they sensed or what Schubert intended. As far as I know they never talked about it. . . . Apart from Schubert, there is no music that is so psychologically

remarkable in the sequence of ideas, their interrelationships and in the seemingly logical transitions. How few, like Schubert, have been able to impress one single individuality onto such a diversity of tonal images. How few have written so much for themselves and their own heart. What the diary is to others, in which their momentary emotions and so forth are recorded, so to Schubert was music paper, to which he entrusted all his moods. His thoroughly musical soul wrote notes where others used words. This is my humble opinion.[22]

Dilthey, writing in the late nineteenth century, reversed the historical sequence and termed Jean Paul Richter a musical writer. Too often modern commentators have focused only on Jean Paul's overt celebration of the power of music—his aesthetic theories and the response of musicians to his embrace of the musical experience—and not enough on the fact that Jean Paul himself was inspired by his encounter with music.[23] He employed musical terms to delineate discrete sections of his prose. Jean Paul's use of words and formal structure inspired techniques that, owing largely to Schumann's influence, composers emulated in structuring rhythm, melody, and harmony within the musical time of a composition. Through Jean Paul, reading became the nineteenth-century model for the shift in musical culture from playing to listening.

Included in a popular book entitled *Original Musical Anecdotes and Miscellany for the Elevation of the Music-Loving Public as Well as for the Pleasurable Entertainment of Every Man,* edited by C. F. Müller and published in 1836, was Jean Paul's allegory about how the pagan gods gave humanity a "better language" by which to feel "unending desire . . . the language of the heart." That language, of course, was music. Jean Paul's father was an organist. Writing, for Jean Paul, aspired to the status of music.[24]

Jean Paul's metaphor of music as language stayed with Schumann to the very end of his career. The use of music in *Manfred* and Schumann's allegiance to the melodrama are explicable by the tripartite consequences of Jean Paul's idea. First, music can speak together with words, as in song and opera, at a level extending the meaning of words. But poetry has a power on its own, as does music in its instrumental form. Therefore, it was in third type, in the melodrama, that the reader-listener, the observer, was placed in the most elevated position. The audience was left to integrate the events and levels of meaning to create the unified aesthetic experience.

The key was Jean Paul's idea that "music was, in itself . . . a recollection of the beautiful, in what lived and died on earth."[25] In *Manfred,* the music evoked the past both for the characters of the drama and for the listeners. The poetry defined the present moment. Neither medium was subordinated; each was left to exert its unique power to fire the imagination of the individual.

The inner imagination and the intensity of feeling generated by poetry and music could create a bittersweet but redeeming reflection on the beauty contained in the ugly. In 1827 Schumann quoted in his diary Jean Paul's observation that when "life becomes darkened by great suffering" the individual can respond with the expectation of sunrise. Likewise, at sunrise one recognizes the inevitability of twilight and therefore of youth and death.[26]

The confrontation of how time reverses the contradictory experience of the moment demanded humor, irony, and an appreciation for the ugly and bizarre as opposed to a refined exclusive concentration on the harmonious, the symmetrical, the profound, and the beautiful. The reversals encountered in life mirrored Jean Paul's concentration on dualities in life. "The human being has a heavy double role on earth," he wrote.[27] The flight of fantasy and the emotional journey induced by reading and playing music required not only lyricism, resolution, and regularity but dissonance, harshness, accentuated asymmetry, and the reversal of expectation, because these qualities were analogous to the harsh contrasts in life. The work of art exploited these dualities in order to create a transcendent imaginative self.

In Jean Paul's novel *Die unsichtbare Loge* (which Schumann read), the young Gustav is described as never having heard music ("the poetry of the air"). After hearing a French horn ("the flute of desire"), Gustav (the name Schumann used in his notes for a novel entitled **Selene**) experiences his first tears of joy.[28] Art creates the interior emotional space of the individual by manipulating the consciousness of expectation and memory. The result of art, however, is a real experience in life—manifested by tears—of which the individual may not otherwise be capable.

In the short autobiographical fragment written at the end of his career, Jean Paul relates, with a typical tinge of irony, one of the most seminal experiences of his childhood:

> My soul (perhaps just like my father's) was entirely open to music . . . I devoted hours banging out my fantasies on an old out-of-tune piano whose tuner and regulator was the weather; these fantasies were no doubt freer and more daring than any other in all of Europe, just because I didn't know a single note or any hand position . . .[29]

This is reminiscent of Schumann's descriptions of his own passionate fantasizing at the piano, particularly early in his life. Even the untrained but aspiring individual could sense the intensity of musical fantasy and creation. The keyboard was the musical mirror of ordinary language. The power of music, in Jean Paul's view, could be emancipated from the monopoly of systematic learning, theory, and professionalism. Schumann's later derision of virtuosity and mere technical proficiency and his lifelong effort to write for amateurs and children derived from his encounter with Jean Paul's construct of how accessible the transformative act of music making in one's private space could be.

For Jean Paul, twilight and sunrise were the decisive metaphors for the human being's relationship to nature. These changes in the day—the essence of nature's logic—were matched by the power of music to achieve, in the duration of time, the reconciliation between the painful experience of temporality, and faith in God and immortality. Music was the language of the heart because it could parallel the sorrow (twilight) and desire (sunrise) that emerged in the conduct of everyday life.

Jean Paul and Schumann recognized that playing and hearing instrumental music paralleled the time-bound nature of events and the internal emotional reactions to those events. Tears came to the player and listener because conscious anticipation of desire carried with it the awareness and fear of loss, just as the suffering of loss reminded one of desire. Jean Paul's coherence of opposites was completed by the reader-player. The direct and fragmentary character—as well as the mix of sustained lyricism with displaced harsh interjections—evident in early Schumann parallels the comparable shifts Schumann experienced in reading Jean Paul's writings.

Among Jean Paul's most celebrated ideas was his focus on the jest (*Witz*) as a primary aesthetic form. The jest mirrored the event in time, replete with its emotional residue and reflection of the duality within nature and life. The jest revealed the irrationality of daily life and the individual's resentment of that irrationality. Disguised similarities were unmasked. The rational and unexceptional, therefore, masked the grotesque and bizarre. Likewise, the eccentric, the ironic, and the unusual overtly camouflaged the reasonable, the ordinary, and the decorous.[30]

Jean Paul's affection in his novels for contrasting twins and interrelated dualities was part of his aesthetic translation of a systematic philosophical and theological effort at universally valid explanations and descriptions. Through the act of writing fiction as a profession, Jean Paul reshaped the systematic philosophical agenda of his father's generation. The ambitions of Leibnitz and Kant could be mediated by the encounter with the work of art. Jean Paul was central to the flowering of romantic writing out of the "self-satisfaction" and "self-absorption" of German philosophy.[31] As a locus for the recognition of philosophical truth, the jest was itself a provocative irony that communicated the contingent limitations (body) and the infinite and free essence of human existence (soul).

The individual's capacity for aesthetic perception and fantasy and its translation into ideas required the assertion of the freedom of each human being's soul. The role of the aesthetic, whether in poetry or in music, was to inspire the reader, the observer (in the case of painting), the draftsman, the player, the listener, the writer—all these incarnations of the subjective self—to recognize the interior freedom of the individual. The psychic and emotionally plausible resolution of the terrifying truth about life's tenuous and finite dimensions could be found in the "anticipation of a better future." Remote and abstract claims regarding the immortality of the soul were replaced by the unseen and nearly infinite possibilities conjured up by the imagination in its contact with art.[32]

Hegel gave Jean Paul's version of the specific power of the musical experience—particularly of instrumental music—a coherent philosophical form:[33]

> music . . . lies too near the essence of that formal freedom of the inner life to be denied the right of turning more or less above the content. . . . Recollection of the theme adopted is at the same time the artist's inner collection of himself, i.e. an inner conviction that he is the artist . . . and yet the free exercise of imagination in this way is expressly to be distinguished from a perfectly finished piece of music. . . . In the free exercise of imagination, liberation from restriction is an end in itself so that the artist can display . . . freedom to interweave familiar melodies and passages into what he is producing at present, to give them a new aspect, to transform them by nuances of various kinds.[34]

Jean Paul came out of a fundamentally theological intellectual milieu. The Protestant theology that framed his outlook took as a premise the essential depravity of the human being. Mortality was justified. By virtue of human consciousness, the pain associated with mortality was itself evidence of some residue of immortality and freedom from a predetermined death. The individual, therefore, was left to search for the underlying truth—the unity of spiritual immortality and inevitable finitude. These ideas help to explain Schumann's attraction to Byron's *Manfred*. Schumann's decision to leave long stretches of Byron's text free of a musical setting may have been in part because the long soliloquies by Manfred constitute an intense distillation of thoughts and sentiments with which the mature Schumann was intimately familiar through his encounter with Jean Paul.[35]

Jean Paul's ambitions as a writer masked a secularization of theology. Through reading and the engagement with art the willing individual could find access to the inner experience (however fleeting) of the power of divine grace. The achievement of philosophical conviction and theological belief in the systematic sense practiced by the academics of the mid-eighteenth century was a tortuous accomplishment of abstract reasoning. The aesthetic surrogate peddled by Jean Paul, as the evidence of the young Schumann's manic vacillations in mood when reading Jean Paul, was far less stable.

Jean Paul's aesthetic route to the recognition of inner freedom and the immortality of the individual soul demanded constant reaffirmation, because its source, as Jean Paul knew, was temporal and emotional. The transference to reflection demanded the constant engagement with reading and playing, the wholesale integration of the aesthetic experience into everyday life.

For Jean Paul the key element remained language, the instrument of abstract thought. Although ordinary language could connect exterior experience to interior experience, its limitations, vis-à-vis music, demanded testing. Philosophical language and stylized aesthetic formal procedures were too distant from life. The virtues of rational philosophic discourse—clear and distinct ideas and impeccable logic—could not suffice.

In his autobiographical fragment Jean Paul described how as a child he sought to construct a new language by creating a new alphabet. He wanted to become a "writer of secrets" and a "player of hide-and-seek with himself."[36] This playful creation of an individualistic language, comprehensible only to oneself, that generates exclusive secrets and games in the interior soul, described Jean Paul's sense of what the writer must do for himself and his readers.

This illuminates Robert Schumann's vision of the composer. The short musical text, like the jest, possesses carefully constructed secrets. The player-reader engages the hide-and-seek search for meaning. Aesthetic appreciation demands the capacity to decode the secret languages of others, to discover hidden treasures, and to appropriate the findings into one's own everyday existence. The reader becomes the young Jean Paul, improvising and creating, by interpretation, a new personal alphabet.

Pain and sorrow become ennobled and rendered tolerable, if not desirable. The confrontation with the sources of sorrow and suffering is welcome as the occasion for the self-affirming task and game of unraveling the hidden. Irony, satire, and humor are the most honest means by which the aesthetic transfiguration of pain can be accomplished, not only because they acknowledge contradiction but because they test the capacity for imagination and fantasy. The location of foreground and background material in Schumann's keyboard and vocal music can be seen as structural devices that organize (metaphorically speaking) the relationships among single events, the surroundings of the world, individual protagonists, and the writer, which the reader unravels in a unique fashion.

Not unlike many of his contemporaries, Jean Paul was a polymath. His belief in the ultimate reconcilability of contradiction, in the symbiosis between the bizarre and the refined, led him to an insatiable curiosity. Everything, including natural philosophy (science), religion, and art, was integral to a unified physical and spiritual universe. Through art the individual could mirror in himself unity within diversity. That emotional and intellectual achievement reinforced the sense of the self. Like the stars, the individual was at once part of a system and yet distinct and self-contained. Surface originality revealed universality.

Dilthey was right: Jean Paul's prose appears episodic to the modern reader. Small units of narrative are punctuated by direct addresses to the reader. Characters speak to one another as the reader observes stories being told to someone else. Books appear within books, as do letters. Writing becomes its own character in the novel, and seemingly tangential texts appear. No doubt much of this was the result of Jean Paul's imitation of known eighteenth-century models, particularly Laurence Sterne. But the effect on Robert Schumann and his generation was profound. Books themselves became protagonists. The reader encountered readers within the book he was reading. The reading self became the metaphor for an underlying spiritual idealism.

Jean Paul's prose was a version of the *Bildungsroman*; the act of reading inspired, as it did in Schumann, the individual's own novel of self-creation.[37] The remembrance of emotional experience through the work of art helped to generate an internal sense of coherence. Music, therefore, had to be written in relationship to the capacity to recall it, even in fragments. Rereading—returning to the text—had its analogue in memory and rehearing.

Stendhal, another author with strong affinities to music, described in *The Red and the Black* the power of books during the first half of the nineteenth century to shape the course of life of an individual. Jean Paul flattered the self-confidence and sense of self-importance of the explosively growing number of civil servants, merchants, and professionals who, not unlike Schumann's father, made up the reading public at the end of the eighteenth century and beginning of the nineteenth. Like the romances of Walter Scott, Jean Paul's prose gave the reader the sense of his own creative powers of imagination and inner enthusiasm. The marriage of unpretentious and ordinary material with a never-ending stream of allusions to the whole encyclopedia of knowledge through a prose that did not draw attention to itself in a sequence of anecdotes and small stories and events, each of which was a mirror of the short form model—the jest—was a unique triumph of the age.

Jean Paul's stature was confirmed decisively for Schumann's generation by Wolfgang Menzel (1798-1873). In the summer of 1828 Schumann remarked in his diary, "Menzel has penetrated more deeply than anyone else into our character. . . ." A few days later he re-

turned to his reading of Menzel.[38] The book in question, *Die deutsche Literatur,* had been published earlier that year and created a great sensation. A second edition came out in 1836. Menzel's tract earned a long and admiring view from Heinrich Heine.

Menzel took the contrast between Jean Paul and Goethe and made it the basis of a coherent analysis of the relationship between German literature and politics. *Die deutsche Literatur,* written in an almost Jean Paul-like style, was marked by irony, humor, and self-consciously outrageous claims, the most famous of which was that "Goethe was no genius, only a great talent."[39] Menzel divided the politics of the age into the "servile" and the liberal. Freedom, and therefore what in the 1820s was regarded as political liberalism, was the only legitimate foundation for art and culture.

Menzel used his analysis of Goethe's limitations to outline an aesthetics that could serve as a political symbol of a new generation. Jean Paul marked the emancipation of art from the politics of servility. Menzel spoke directly to his fellow German readers, including Schumann, about what it meant to make reading and aesthetics a central part of life without succumbing to fake sentimentality.

Art was conceived no longer as an abstract idea but rather as a social fact central to the possibilities of a new and vital political and communal life. Not the solitary reader but a nation of readers who embraced the transformative intervention of the aesthetic into everyday life became the focus. The first half of Menzel's tract outlined the social significance of the production of literary output, the reading public, book publishers, the influence of schools and school reform, and the university.[40]

Germany was at a crossroads. Either it gave way to foreign influence, commerce, outmoded traditions of schooling, and superficiality or it built carefully upon the achievement of the early romantic movement in German literature to create language and writing befitting the unique German character and its historical role. For Menzel there were dangers lurking on all sides. At one extreme was irrelevant aesthetic formalism; on the other, cheap and ephemeral but fashionable and destructive popular literature.[41]

Literary work had emerged as the decisive public medium for Menzel. He identified for the eighteen-year-old Schumann the extended community—a public—that was poised to play a significant role in history. The young Schumann recognized that community, for it described a world he had seen in his father's milieu in Zwickau.

Menzel, whose *en passant* observations on music corresponded closely to Schumann's, provided Schumann with an ideological framework. Bach was given a central place, as was the work of Schumann's teacher Anton Friedrich Justus Thibaut. The context, once again, was the cultural crisis, the need to generate a new German spirit and taste in music. Menzel deplored the dominance in writing about music of the "false spontaneity of the romantics, the excessive desire for conclusions and the high-minded rhetoric of the philosophers, and even the frivolity of humorists and masters of irony."[42]

Following Jean Paul's literary transformation of the tradition of systematic philosophy, Menzel filled his text with material from the widest range of subjects. In his attack on an older generation's conception of schooling, philosophy, literature, and art and its role in society, Menzel, like Jean Paul, turned to the jest as an essential aesthetic unit. As aspects of literature, humor and sarcasm were species of realism that undercut the high-minded, theoretical, abstract claims of neoclassical art and Kantian idealism.

Menzel's forte was not only satire; his prose communicated energy and enthusiasm. His directness, simplicity, and candor celebrated the vital power of youth and its response, through literature, to the distinct social and natural character of Germany. His description of the German university and the aristocratic sensibilities of the reading public of the past was devastating.

The language and strategy of Schumann's music criticism, particularly his attack on old-fashioned pedantry and contemporary philistinism—his explicit political ideal of a public emancipated from superficiality—were inspired by Menzel. The result was Jean Paul's prose strategy (the use of characters, e.g., Eusebius, Florestan, Raro, and the creation of an internal dialogue with differing points of view), filled with Menzel's tone and ideas. Schumann's use of the word *philistine* may have derived from Menzel's furious attack on popular poetry that created a veneer of formal beautification and therefore falsification. Menzel decried its popularity among readers.[43]

Menzel's satirical critique of the heritage of abstract academic philosophy was motivated by the realization that in order to create new cultural ideology, writing had to engage politics, religion, history, and science in a new manner. Given the explosion in the reading public, the danger, of course, was that in the rage for books and the expanding market the opportunity for corrupt influences to dominate was equally great. In a line typical of Menzel, the evil of censorship was characterized in terms not of the loss—what censorship suppressed—but of what it encouraged.[44]

Menzel's outspoken admiration for Jean Paul as a forerunner reinforced the idea that the new generation of readers and writers could be freed from seemingly tran-

shistorical and transnational normative claims about beauty and the heavy hand of classical models. As Heine put it, Menzel dismissed the idea of art of the age of Goethe. New ideas for a new age heralding "nature and youth" were forcing back the "troops" of "art and antiquity." The memorable moment in Menzel's manifesto, the wholesale attack on Goethe (without question in 1828 the leading figure in German-speaking Europe), was too much for Heine, who, unlike Schumann, recognized that underneath Menzel's brilliance, insight, and wit lurked something uncivilized and disturbing.[45]

Indeed, Menzel's own advocacy of his generation's unique credo was short-lived. He went on to betray the radicals of 1830 during the reaction and was later pilloried by Ludwig Börne, Heine, and D. F. Strauss. Menzel's vision of the political potential of the new aesthetics later led him to embrace a rabid nationalism and to wage a moralistic campaign against his former allies. As early as 1828, unlike Heine and others in the "Young Germany" movement, Menzel professed a seemingly uncritical admiration for the pietistic movement in Protestantism, which, in part, anticipated a subsequent sharp turn in his views.[46]

What remained with Schumann (who, for example, was unsympathetic to the *Burschenschaften* movement that influenced the nationalism Menzel later endorsed) was Menzel's framing of the historical role of the artist in society in political and generational terms. Reading Menzel confirmed the social significance of a career as a creative artist. Menzel's cultural nationalism circa 1828 underwent little change in Schumann, whose nationalism, although pronounced, never evolved into the more aggressive and modern form he would encounter in Dresden in the 1840s. The narrow realm of aesthetics as politics (the creation of a like-minded public) remained Schumann's arena.

Menzel offered Schumann a way to bypass legitimately the strenuous effort of writing and studying systematic philosophy. Unlike Jean Paul, who wrote his own aesthetic tract, Menzel provided Schumann an example of the legitimacy of journalism, intellectually and politically. His book vindicated the idea that criticism could and would be taken seriously, even when it dealt with religion and philosophy. It elevated criticism as creative work. As Schumann wrote in his diary, "Censure elevates those with great character; the petty individual is undone. Praise has the opposite effect."[47]

As the legendary eccentric and impoverished vagabond of the previous generation who finally settled down to an idyllic domestic life, Jean Paul served as a personal model for the young Schumann. Menzel offered the professional example. The significance of the social station from which Schumann came becomes evident in his identification with Menzel, whose explicit assignment of a cultural role to Schumann's social class rang true. Menzel's observation—that there was perhaps too much silly talking about music and too little listening—may have functioned as a challenge.

Schumann's father, despite his success and relative fame as a bookseller and publisher (Heine mentioned him as the publisher of Walter Scott[48]), did not mask the fact that he did not complete formal university training. In terms of the social hierarchy of intellect of the mid-eighteenth century, the elder Schumann was an aspirant and a parvenu. The ethos of Schumann's household, apart from its love of books, was tinged with a sharp sense of practicality. Literacy clearly afforded avenues by which one might earn a decent living. The achievement of a proper standard of living and the domestic comfort necessary for the pursuit of culture were central to Schumann and never, in theory, in conflict with artistic integrity.

In terms of the late eighteenth-century debate on the quality and influence of books, the goal was to produce works that edified the public and were, like classical texts, worthy not only of initial reading but of rereading. The emulation in the world of music by critics and musicians of Schumann's generation of the widespread late eighteenth-and early nineteenth-century debate over the influence of ephemeral literature (to be read and then forgotten) as opposed to books of lasting value has been overlooked. Consider Schumann's active part in defining the right "classical" models for composers and the music public; his references to classicism in form; the use of quotation in his music; his crusade against ephemeral music; and his ambition to create new music that could function as classical texts did, as works to which the individual could return profitably over and over again.[49]

Schumann's father not only dealt in the commerce of publishing but wrote and edited others' work. Just as the activities of performing, composing, publishing, and commercial trade in instruments (e.g., Clementi, Diabelli, Kalkbrenner, and Pleyel) were inextricably linked in the careers of musicians in the early nineteenth century, so too were book publishing and selling, journalism, and the writing of fiction. Menzel's chapter "The Commerce of Literature" confirms the extent to which the generations of the early nineteenth century were aware of the social, economic, and political significance of the expanded reading public.[50]

In accounts of the early nineteenth century the term *Bildungsbürgertum* is often used without a specific context. Menzel calculated that between 1814 and 1835, one hundred thousand books were published in Germany.[51] That growth catapulted men like Schumann's father—those without academic careers—into a position of unanticipated success. One of the reasons Robert Schumann was always more at home in Leipzig as opposed to Düsseldorf or Dresden was that Leipzig, which had become the center of the printing industry, contained more citizens like the elder Schumann than any other city of comparable size. The allegation that the Leipzig public was more sophisticated than its counterparts elsewhere was not unfounded. Self-made men of business who established their careers in the wake of the growth of literacy at the end of the eighteenth century mixed freely with an older commercial elite and the academic community of Leipzig's university.[52]

Schumann easily could feel comfortable in Leipzig. Owing to the commercial opportunities that stemmed from expanded literacy, the city became a magnet for writers, journalists, and free-lance intellectuals of all kinds. It was not dominated by an aristocracy of birth. In his legendary *Konversations-Lexikon,* the great Viennese satirist Moritz Saphir (with whom the Schumanns became acquainted in Vienna and who then wrote a penetrating but unflattering critique of Clara Schumann's playing that earned their lifelong enmity)[53] printed the following description:

> Leipzig is made up of fifty thousand writers, among whom there are only a few inhabitants. The streets are to a large extent paved with square novellas. The sidewalks are made of very wide prose romances on which pedestrians walk comfortably. The trees in Leipzig sprout leaves of opinion. . . . The citizens of Leipzig wear waterproof pants in order to protect themselves from damp translations.[54]

The Leipzig of the 1830s and 1840s was the beneficiary of a marked social transformation in the access to schooling, which began during the second half of the eighteenth century. The association between the acquisition of culture and political liberalism heralded by Menzel was more than theoretical. The school reforms of the previous century gave individuals the means to construct notions of personal and political autonomy. By the early nineteenth century approximately 20 percent of all pupils in German municipal schools had completed pre-university schooling, the *Abitur.* Of that group, a third came from the lower middle class. For the very lowest strata, particularly in rural areas, schooling was severely limited. Ten percent of all *Abiturienten* came from petit-bourgeois families, 35 percent from artisans and tradespeople, and 25 percent from middle-level civil servants.[55]

The marked explosion in advanced schooling was felt by the German university system after 1815. In 1800 there were approximately six thousand university students in Germany; by 1830 there were sixteen thousand. In the 1820s approximately 0.5 percent of the urban population was studying at a university. Robert Schumann had good reason to think of himself as a member of a new generation determined to make its own way and imagine a role for himself. Among the tasks was the effort to free culture from the nearly exclusive domination by an aristocracy and by men of letters committed to an aesthetic ideology linked to absolutism, no matter how enlightened by eighteenth-century ideas.[56]

It is ironic that around 1830 the turn away from cultural currents of the late eighteenth century in part was the result of pedagogical reforms based on Enlightenment ideas regarding the humanism and power of reason as an instrument of progress. A philosophical psychology that was egalitarian with respect to an individual's susceptibility to the cultivation of reason through schooling spurred entirely new pedagogical strategies. Menzel devoted a considerable portion of his book to the consequences of the new pedagogy. Jean Paul, for example, was an advocate of pedagogical reforms along the lines of Rousseau and Pestalozzi (who, as Schumann knew, also placed great emphasis on the role of music in education). The notion of the reader implicit in Jean Paul's writings and the link between art and life led to an emphasis in schooling on freedom and the development of the individual. The burden in pre-university schooling was shifted from a theologically based scheme of indoctrination (*Erziehung*) to the cultivation of the self-directed intellectual faculties of each individual. This pedagogical theory fit neatly with the notion that each individual was capable of developing the capacity for creation and criticism. The cultivation of ambition and self-conscious individualism was the pedagogical ideology of Schumann's years in school.[57]

Napoleon was the single most powerful symbol in German-speaking Europe during Schumann's youth. His portrait hung in Schumann's student rooms, alongside those of his father and Jean Paul.[58] Schumann was born just four years after the seminal event in German history, Napoleon's defeat of Prussia at Jena in 1806. The attitude of Schumann's generation toward Napoleon was ambivalent. On the one hand Napoleon was a symbol of the emancipation of career and achievement from birth and aristocracy. But at the same time he was viewed in terms of Fichte's challenge to his countrymen in 1808 and the cultural patriotism of Friedrich Jähns's *Berlinische Gesellschaft für deutsche Sprache.*

In Schumann's generation the definition of national character and the concomitant rediscovery of a distinct cultural past and mission were at the center of literary, philosophical, and cultural debate. Schumann's and Menzel's cultural nationalism of the late 1820s was radical—in opposition to the post-1815 restoration. Napoleonic ambitions were internalized and directed through cultural achievement. The complementary coherence between an individual's ambition to gain public prominence as a musician and man of letters and a gen-

erational politics in which culture served as an instrument of national identity was central to Schumann's intellectual development. The achievement of greatness in the image of Jean Paul was therefore a distinctly German task. The challenge was to find a way to reach the new public in a manner that did not debase culture and lull the reader-player-listener—through his or her newfound skills—into political and cultural indifference. Friedrich Schlegel, in his lectures on the history of literature, given first in Vienna during the winter of 1812, articulated eloquently the larger context in which both Menzel and the young Robert Schumann explicitly defined their ambitions:

> In Germany, owing to the special character of the nation, the spirit of the age was mirrored not in bloody revolution but in the tangled conflicts of metaphysical philosophy. The rebirth of fantasy has become evident in many countries through the revival of past traditions and through romantic poetry. No nation in Europe, however, can compete with the extent and profundity with which Germans have developed the love of fantasy. These nations have had their moment in history. It is only fitting that we should now have our own.[59]

"THE VERY IMAGE OF LIFE . . .": SCHUMANN AND THE RHETORIC OF AESTHETIC DISCOURSE

Few writers were so much at the center of turn-of-the-century aesthetic debates as Friedrich Schlegel.[60] Menzel, who was decidedly ambivalent about Schlegel, singled him out for "his enormous influence." The evidence of Schumann's direct relationship to Schlegel, however, is thin. Although Schumann was familiar with Schlegel's poetry, neither the diaries nor the letters indicate that he read Schlegel's philosophic and critical writings to any extent. Nothing approximating Schumann's relationship to Jean Paul or E. T. A. Hoffmann can be located. The importance of Schlegel in the discussion of Schumann, therefore, rests on the extent to which Schlegel's ideas shaped the rhetoric of aesthetics of the early nineteenth century.[61]

John Daverio ties Schlegel's prominence as the master of the philosophically loaded aphorism to a set of aphorisms Schumann published in the *Neue Zeitschrift für Musik* in 1834. Schumann made the following claim: "To be sure, it might not be without interest to sketch out the very image of life in art, just as Platner and Jacobi have similarly done in entire philosophical systems."[62]

The reference to Platner and Jacobi is most revealing. Platner (1744-1818) was a professor of medicine and philosophy in Leipzig whose *Philosophische Aphorismen,* published in various editions from 1776-1800, was widely read. He was the one academic who exerted a profound influence on Jean Paul. Platner's critique of Kant led him to a position of profound skepticism. Little else was left of philosophy but the "way of thinking of the individual," the perspective of the subject.[63]

Friedrich Heinrich Jacobi (1743-1819) was a contemporary of Goethe and Herder who also attempted a critique of Kant's epistemology. He generated a comprehensive philosophy based on Spinoza and the limits of rational atheism. Jacobi was convinced that Kant had not succeeded in dispensing with the need to assume a basic naive faith in the reality of external phenomena. Rationalism demanded a leap of faith, which in turn was based on feeling. Jacobi's synthesis of religious and aesthetic sensualism with empiricism gave his work a close affinity to Jean Paul.

Schumann referred to Jacobi admiringly and extensively during the 1820s. Jacobi went farther than Jean Paul in the critique of rational philosophy. Feeling was prior to reason and therefore the source of aesthetic recognition. The sentiments an individual felt in his "beautiful soul" took precedence. Despite the absence of a Kantian or Hegelian thoroughness, Jacobi's emotionalism resulted in a comprehensive outlook. The individual without a conventional religious faith (e.g., Schumann) could find truth and the divine—precisely through a transformative emotional contact with the real world. This became the task of art.[64]

Jacobi's example encouraged Schumann in the idea that by making and criticizing art a comprehensive, overarching approach, merging feeling and reason, could be developed. The task of the artist in creative work and journalism was the construction of "the very image of life" in a manner directly understood as an alternative to the philosophical systems of an earlier generation. Aesthetics became the common ground between a rational empirical epistemology and emotion. Jean Paul had taken the first step by linking art with real life. Jacobi had substituted the experience of feeling and faith as the source of a comprehensive *Weltanschauung*.

Schumann believed that the aesthetic experience through the nonliterary medium closest to the emotional experience—music—could realize this project. In this sense Schumann's aesthetics confirm Hegel's description of the role of music in romanticism. Music, by being the "language of the heart," was the language of the consciousness of time and nature. Therefore it was capable of generating a true image of life. Schumann took from Jacobi the idea that emotion possessed an ontological priority as the root of a unified approach to ethics and knowledge. Schumann's perspective can be compared with that of Schleiermacher's, in which the priority of feeling and the emphasis on the aesthetic led to a conception of individuality that implied the necessity to create a religious community of like-minded individuals not dissimilar to Schumann's own organizing efforts in this regard.[65]

Friedrich Schlegel's rhetoric and ideas most clearly illuminate the path traveled by Schumann's generation, from Kant to Jacobi, and from Jean Paul and Menzel to Hegel. The preponderance of fragments in Schlegel's work was the result of his desire to reclaim philosophy for the arena of poetics. Schlegel, like Schumann, sought to innovate in formal terms. The fragment, like the jest, despite its outward appearance, could encompass the comprehensive. The fragment and aphorism were aesthetic alternative to the philosophical argument.

In certain fragments Schlegel included diagrams describing the unified scope of aesthetic expression. By visualizing the disparate arenas of aesthetic activity, the individual's aesthetic experience could be understood to encompass the spiritual geography of the whole world. In a fragment written during the first decade of the nineteenth century, Schlegel untangled the strands by which the individual "grasped the divine." He pursued Jacobi's and Jean Paul's project. Using the vocabulary and traditions he associated with Schelling, Fichte, Schleiermacher, and Schiller, Schlegel divided the aesthetic realm into four modes of apperception, which he placed visually in a configuration comparable to a compass. On the northern point was *Anschauung*—a visually based form of knowing that was the essence of drama. Its opposite on the southern point was *Ahnung*—a suggestive mix of foreboding and resentment that exemplified lyric poetry.[66] On the west was *Erklärung*—explanation (including representation and description) in language. This was the realm of the novel. On the east was *Erinnerung*, the realm of the epic.[67]

For Schlegel, language in drama was connected to the pictorial, and lyricism to the play element. The language of the epic was linked to song and therefore to music. The rhetoric of explanation of the novel was associated with myth and legend. Instrumental music emerged from the merger of language and music in the epic. In the *Athenaeum* fragment quoted on p. 28, Schlegel defended how the rhetoric of instrumental music displayed its historically contingent dependence on language. The relevance to Schumann's conception of musical form and its apperception lies in the idea that the logic and meaning of instrumental music were tied to the epic as the proper linguistic analogue.

Schlegel argued that an "infinitely progressive aesthetic" in the age of Christianity called for a return to the ancient combination of music and language: the merger of song and legend. Modernity demanded the integration of the epic and the novel. The modern forms were the romance, the *Novelle*, and the legend, all terms crucial to Schumann's musical compositions, including the notion from the manuscript of the *Fantasy, Op. 17, Erzählend in Legendenton*. These exemplify Schlegel's synthesis of song and legend.[68] In modern times, the epic's dependency on memory and its role in collective consciousness had to be expanded through the novel and the art of explanation. Music uniquely achieved that. It could express remembrance and ideas within a community.

Schumann's search for the "very image of life" paralleled Schlegel's effort to identify, for the poetic and the aesthetic, an explanatory, rational function within a social and historical framework. In all Schumann's music the conscious merger of three elements—narrative, emotional expressiveness, and the evocative (in the sense of memory, including the historical citation and imitation)—was accomplished with a keen ear to the response of players-listeners.

The function of music, therefore, becomes more than an emotional solitary experience. Its capacity for linguistic logic in the philosophical, epistemological sense permits music to assume a public function. Jean Paul observed that music possessed a kind of language of both apperception and recollection. That aspect renders music capable of assuming a public function akin to the kind advocated by Menzel for literature.

In 1823 Schlegel pursued this line of thought further and created another map of parallel opposites. Poetry and philosophy were linked, further underscoring the idea that aesthetics and epistemology were inextricable in the modern age. In these 1823 fragments Schlegel returned to the theme of music as a dimension of the epic. Painting was ultimately "theological" and lyric poetry symbolic, particularly in its use of "allegories" and "hieroglyphics." "Music in its magical impact and psychological character is most related to the epic," Schlegel wrote.[69] The epic functioned through the use of myth. A work of music was therefore a narrative suffused with a nearly irrational link to the imagined past, replete with a contemporary collective aura and significance.

The mark of the aesthetic in the contemporary age of the 1820s was, for Schlegel, the overriding presence of the phantasmagoric, which was a synthesis of reason and fantasy. The rational (the explanatory function) was contained in formal procedures—in the case of Schumann's music, in sonata form, variation form, and counterpoint. The phantasmagoric emerged from the free interplay of fantasy in harmony, melody, and asymmetrical rhythm, which worked in contrast to the expectations of form. As if to parallel the distinction between the unconscious and the conscious, the epic and therefore each piece of music—in the spirit of Jean Paul's twins—had two levels of compositional intentionality in the text.

Unlike Menzel, Schlegel identified both Goethe and Jean Paul as having contributed to the achievement of this modern sensibility. In his musings about aesthetics

Schlegel anticipated Schumann's embrace of both classical and romantic ideas in his observation that Schiller and Fichte were admirable writers of reason, even though Jean Paul and Schleiermacher had created the "dynamic rhetoric" of the age. For Schlegel that rhetoric was "encyclopedic," connected to a theology of feeling and experience. In modern life, the experience of music in the single work of art held the possibility of offering a comprehensive synthesis of life and experience superceding other forms of discourse: "The poetic is the original condition of humanity and also its final state. All oriental philosophy is poetic. . . . Only through the poetic can a human being expand his existence into the existence of humanity. Only in the poetic do all means serve one end. The jest is the path of return to the poetic."[70]

Rhetoric of this sort not only defined Robert Schumann's journey from literature to law, then to virtuoso performer, and finally to critic and composer (with intermittent phases of thinking of his father's business). The university years and the encounter with philosophical discourse in Leipzig and Heidelberg also strengthened the conclusion that a career in the arts was a humanistic and philosophic endeavor with moral overtones. Schlegel's musing also hints at a coherent compositional agenda. The musical epigram from Schumann's early work shares the ambition of ***Genoveva*** and the symphony: the coherent reflection and penetration of life through the formal structure and content of the single work of art brought forward to the public.

This ethical and epistemological framework helps to explain the severity of Schumann's critical judgments and his obsession with the formation of a public community of like-minded individuals. A crucial dimension of the ambition to render the arts (in Schumann's case, criticism and composing) something greater than mere entertainment—into a rival of the conduct of philosophy in the German university—was based on faith in music as a language more precisely in terms of explanation, not merely as Jean Paul's "language of the heart." In a well-known fragment, Schlegel put the matter succinctly. The pursuit of music was part of a larger political and cultural project tied to ordinary language discourse:

> Many people find it strange and ridiculous when musicians talk about the ideas in their compositions; and it often happens that one perceives they have more ideas in their music than they do about it. But whoever has a feeling for the wonderful affinity of all the arts and sciences will at least not consider the matter from the dull viewpoint of a so-called naturalness that maintains music is supposed to be only the language of the senses. Rather, he will consider a certain tendency of pure instrumental music toward philosophy as something not impossible in itself. Doesn't pure instrumental music have to create its own text? And aren't the themes in it

developed, reaffirmed, varied, and contrasted in the same way as the subject of meditation in a philosophical succession of ideas?[71]

The parallelism between music and "the philosophical succession of ideas" demanded formal procedures dependent on rational notions of argument. Schumann's attention to counterpoint and sonata form and to classical models from Bach to Beethoven reflects the consequences of these philosophical premises. The public had to be educated to respond to music not only in the sense of Jean Paul or Jacobi but in Schlegel's terms. The ability to interpret through hearing and playing meant the capacity to generate a complementary discourse of ideas. *Audsruck,* then, for Schumann was more than expression of an emotional response or the flight of fantasy inspired by sound. The power of music was located in its logical function as the expression of thought.

One of Schlegel's many influential contributions was his role in placing the question of history at the center. An intensely self-conscious historical anxiety characterized Schumann and his contemporaries. The shift from the epistemological to the aesthetic was framed as a part of a larger historical process. The character and political function of art changed in history, Schlegel argued, initially in the transition from paganism to Christianity, and then within the evolution of Christendom.

Hegel continued this line of argument, claiming that the aesthetic experience, with its emphasis on subjectivity, had become in contemporary culture a historical phenomenon whose meaning could be unraveled only by a dialectic not entirely divorced from Jean Paul's *Doppelgänger* strategy of reconciling contradiction into unity. Lecturing in the 1820s, Hegel observed that in the aesthetics of romanticism "the fundamental character of the romantic is the musical."[72]

Schlegel's assertion—that "the poetry and romanticism of the north was an *Aeolsharfe* through which the storm of reality streams as melodies that culminate in a frenzy of sounds"—confirmed Hegel's more systematic argument that the true subject matter of the romantic movement was absolute interiorness, a form of spiritual subjectivity that the musical generated best. Hegel's historical characterization helps to illuminate Schumann's intense concern that his generation discharge its noble historical and moral obligation by generalizing the capacity for spiritual subjectivity.

Hegel located the sense of autonomy and freedom generated by the engagement with romantic art, particularly music, in the capacity of the individual to abandon aesthetic formalism. The recognition of an impersonal aesthetic ideal in objects of art was replaced by subjectivity. Therefore overt appearances, even of ugliness and

emptiness, were given scope. The creator and receptor played (as in a game) at aesthetic transformation and punctured the surface illusions of empirical observation. The real, then, could be understood in a new way. Romantic art, therefore, did more than create a new formalism. Music, for the historic moment, revealed a reality that was otherwise hidden.

Music was the quintessential contemporary aesthetic vehicle of the everyday supplanting literature. Schumann's shift from literature to music during his university years found resonance in these ideas of aesthetic evolution in history. Music demanded a reconsideration of realism. The self and the subjective experience through music stripped away the masks of language and image. Philistinism and superficiality were crimes because, for both the individual and the age, they were lies analogous to surface realism; corruptions of the free capacity of the individual to penetrate the surface of existence.

The nineteenth-century historian Karl Lamprecht used the Hegelian premise as the justification for describing the early nineteenth century as the age of subjectivity. An explicit democratization in the embrace of spiritual autonomy of the self had taken place. From the point of view of musical life, the most significant consequence of Hegel and Lamprecht's characterizations was the prestige granted all art, criticism, and the process of critical reflection by the educated individual.[73] Reading alone at home or aloud with friends, Jean Paul's fantasizing at the piano, learning to draw, looking at art, and the concert experience were converted into public icons of freedom and a sea of change in history.[74] Subjectivity became a social reality. The act of criticism, therefore, gained new status. The critic did what every reader needed to do. The critic was the teacher of the reader in that he was, in Schlegel's terms, the secondary author. Each reading added to the text and enlarged the public capacity of any work of art to fulfill its historical, philosophical, and moral function. The same could be true for music.[75]

It was not surprising that during the first decades of the nineteenth century the drive to acquire musical culture followed rapidly on the heels of the spread of literacy. The making of music in the sense of Jean Paul's and Schumann's hours of "reveries" at the piano (*Schwärmerei*) became a popular image of the autonomy of the self. The public acts of playing and active listening underscored the conceit of the individual that through one's own subjectivity one became part of a community and a historical moment.

Music's new philosophical underpinnings only underscored the social prestige of music. The generation of Schumann's parents and Schumann himself knew very well that in the eighteenth century, music had been largely the province of an aristocracy, the nobility, and an elite upper strata of civil servants and merchants. The musical achievements of Frederick the Great and Louis Ferdinand were not distant memories.[76] The philosophical rhetoric of romantic writers and philosophers only added to music's aura as a dimension of aristocratic manners.

The enormous role that the aristocracy and royalty continued to play in the patronage of music was not lost on Schumann's contemporaries. It created a natural and understandable ambivalence with regard to the contradictions inherent in the pursuit of a musical career that was, at best, in transition from one form of exclusive patronage to the nineteenth-century mixed system of expanding commerce and patronage.

In rewriting the role of Beethoven, Mozart, Bach, and Palestrina in the creation of the present state of art, Schumann, unlike Wagner, skirted the task of interpreting the consequence of the economic and political conditions under which these figures from the past worked. Schumann's ambivalence toward the audience of the nonaristocratic public in Düsseldorf, Dresden, and Leipzig and his embarrassing enthusiasm for Metternich were part of his contradictory relationship to the realities of daily musical life, past and present. He hoped that in his generation there would be a new wave of connoisseurs that could replace, in economic terms, the lost aristocracy from the past.

The spread of musical culture between the years 1813 and 1840 was remarkable because it reflected both an aesthetic ideology specific to a new middle class conscious of its historical and political moment and the desire to imitate habits of life associated with an elite noble culture. This is no better revealed than in the public announcement issued in 1836 to the subscribers of the Gewandhaus concerts. Mendelssohn's appointment was designed to elevate taste. The concert became a forum for both bourgeois *Bildung* and aristocratic *Erziehung,* particularly in terms of civility.[77]

The historical specter against which Schumann fought was the possibility that the spread of musical culture and the removal of aristocratic privilege would result in the opposite of a utopia of freedom and culture, that it might debase the power of music. It was incumbent on the composer and the critic to reconcile novelty and originality with an indisputable respect and admiration for historical models. And this forced Schumann as a composer to confront the issue of history and his generation's conception of the relationship of past, present, and future.

CULTURAL POLITICS AND THE CRITIQUE OF THE PRESENT, 1815-1848

Schumann and his generation, despite the rhetoric of philosophers, were profoundly ambivalent about the moment in time in which they lived.[78] The enthusiasm

for reveries at the keyboard, particularly at twilight, were internalized personal expressions of a widespread desire to escape the present moment. Once again Jean Paul helped to set the tone. "Memory and hope . . . childhood and the beyond fill his spirit," wrote Dilthey, obliterating the "knife point of the present."[79]

The use of art to escape present pain—through the evocations (no matter how fantastic) of both remembrances and dreams—fit precisely Schumann's careful description of his life in letters and diaries, not only before he began to train with Friedrich Wieck but during the years of separation from Clara. His art responded to a malaise that coexisted with his generation's sense of its historical mission and the general enthusiasm for art and culture.

The popularity of the fairy tale, the dream, and the romance—all self-conscious distortions of reality that trigger hope and expectation—mirrored the mix of nostalgia and cultural criticism inherent in music and literature of the *Vormärz.* Schumann's engagement with music for children and the fairy tale was part of a cultural obsession with childhood as the moment of vanished hope and the source of memory. In the act of playing music for children, adults could idealize a childhood they had lost or never had, with all its inherent unrealized possibilities and suggestions of innocence. The most characteristic and successful example of Schumann's engagement with these tendencies was his selection of the German translation of Thomas Moore's poetry and its use in **Das Paradies und die Peri.** The amalgam of naive religiosity, orientalism, and fairy tale-like simplicity helped to make this not only one of Schumann's greatest works but also his most significant public triumph.

"If writing is a form of prophecy," Jean Paul wrote, "so romantic writing is the anticipation of a greater future."[80] The critique of contemporary existence in the decades before 1848 triggered two dominant ideologies, both of which influenced Schumann: utopianism and historicism. Utopianism, with which Schumann flirted actively only in a restricted sense (in the creation of the *Davidsbund*), exaggerated the failings of the day by distorting the capacities for change. It paralleled an aesthetic experience familiar to Schumann: the flight of the imagination into the infinite.

The lure of utopianism and the aura attached to shattered utopian dreams can be understood, in terms of Schumann, through the example of Nikolaus Lenau, with whom Schumann was often compared in the nineteenth century. A few years after Schumann's death, Eduard Bernsdorf wrote, "They both had the same heavily laden seriousness, and a natural bent toward hypercritical contemplativeness . . . , and a certain coldness and reserve of expression with at the same time much warmth and energy in feeling; . . . they were possessed by restless, truly artistic drive that sought to realize aims in ever higher and more idealistic spheres."[81]

Lenau was devastated by the political reaction after the Revolution of 1830. In 1832 he went to America—his generation's symbol of all future possibilities (with which Clara and Robert also flirted and to which one charter member of the *Davidsbund* emigrated)—only to experience disappointment once again. Lenau's expectations were not dissimilar to those embodied by the utopian colony of New Harmony on the Wabash, founded by German Protestants seeking to re-create the ideals of primitive Christianity. The Lenau poems that Schumann set in 1850 were written in the years immediately following the poet's return. Two of the poems, "Kommen und Scheiden" and "Der schwere Abend," exemplify Lenau's sensibilities.[82] Schumann understood the facts of Lenau's life and work. The sense of failure in terms of the individual's engagement in a political project of extreme expectations, when transposed into the language of love poetry, deepened the rhetoric of desire, pain, and loss.

The reverse side of utopianism was the search for a way out of the present by means of the past. On the eve of the Revolutions of 1848 Joseph Eichendorff put it this way: "Romanticism was no mere literary movement. It undertook, far more, an inner regeneration of collective life."[83] Eichendorff credited the romantic movement with a rediscovery and construction of a cultural past that could serve the future. The revival of J. S. Bach was part of this phenomenon. As Schumann explained to Clara in 1841, "And it really is very necessary for an artist to be able to give an account of the entire history of his art."[84] History was essential to art because in the recognition of the past within art of the present day, the "inner "source of Eichendorff's collective regeneration could be found. The historical imagery, so to speak, within an individual artist's craft was central to the aesthetic and political project of the present. Bach's achievement formed the centerpiece of the "account" of the past because of its public and collective power and significance. Schumann's advocacy of Palestrina fit into the same pattern.[85]

The premium on historical memory and the link to a program of regeneration influenced Schumann's approach to the longer musical forms with which he worked in the early 1840s. In the late 1830s the process of listening to larger-scale musical forces deployed over a longer time period—in the symphony, for example, or the extended melodrama, the opera, or oratorio—had become a plausible arena for cultural politics.

An expanding community of listeners and participants in the world of choral music could encounter music in the concert hall on a temporal scale sufficient to make listening analogous to engaging a sustained account of history. Unlike the smaller piano work or the song, the large forms of oratorio and symphony were similar to narratives of history—a collective past—in terms of scale and complexity. The music was also modeled on forms that derived from the great ages gone by, yet the realization was novel and defied traditional habits of expectation in the listener.

Originality was integrated into the historical. The use of thematic reminiscence and linkages between movements paralleled the notion of how the past must return in the continuous process of life to assert itself into the future. Desire, rendered musical, became historical in the symphony. It became the vehicle for Eichendorff's project. A corrupt and faded present can be brought alive as the spiritual essence of the past is cast into a new future form. The four symphonies can be viewed structurally as Schumann's emulation of the romantic project of reclaiming history on behalf of the future.[86]

It is in this context that Schumann's relationship to Beethoven can be understood. A mixture of envy and nostalgia shaped Schumann's approach to Beethoven, who was the equivalent of Napoleon in musical culture. The generation of 1810 realized they had just missed the great classical age in their art. That sense of loss was tempered by the realization that therefore the process of regeneration in music was more hopeful than in the other arts.

In no piece of music is this complex of ideas more evident than in the *Fantasy,* **Op. 17.** Written in the late 1830s, it was put into its final form, appropriately enough, for the dedication ceremony for the 1845 Bonn Beethoven monument (which the Schumanns did not attend). Schumann's desire to present this work at the Bonn ceremony fit perfectly, as he knew, into the composition's own history, which was spurred by the plans, announced in 1836, to erect the Beethoven monument.

The original title bore the three words "ruins, trophies, palms." The references are all about the present's conception of the past within its midst. The ruin is the surviving remnant of greatness as realized in architecture (e.g., Rome). The trophy is the symbol of the great deed in the past, a symbol that partook of a classical as well as pagan mythological character. The palm is nature's expression of warmth and the sun—the "other" place evocative for Germans of both the historical Italy and the fantastic, utopian, and natural New World.[87]

GERMAN ROMANTIC PAINTING AND THE MUSIC OF ROBERT SCHUMANN

Robert Schumann's lifelong interest in painting and sculpture was not exceptional. As both Jean Paul and Schlegel made clear, the visual was an integral part of the aesthetic experience. Karl Wörner, in a nearly inadvertent manner, compared one Schumann work to the paintings of the Nazarene group.[88] Schumann came of age in an era dominated in the visual arts by German painters who had gone to Italy.[89]

What drove Johann Overbeck and other Nazarenes and their successor German-Roman painters to Italy was not merely the neoclassical sensibilities we associate with the work of the architect Karl Friedrich Schinkel. Rather, the admiration for the pagan classical model became intertwined with the desire to reclaim the essential spirit of Christianity. This quest for spiritual regeneration seemed realizable only in that mix of "palms" and "ruins" found in Italy. It was the land of memories and the historical landscape of faith and hope.

The fascination with Italy also had literary and musical roots. Goethe's Italian sojourn of the 1780s had become a model for the requisite pilgrimage to the South, which every aspiring German intellectual writer and artist undertook, including Schumann. Present musical taste in the late 1820s was dominated by Rossini, and the past had more than its share of Italian masters.

In 1829, in a diary entry on the difference between universal geniuses and ideal human beings, Schumann placed Mozart, Shakespeare, and Michelangelo in the former group and Schiller, Handel, and Raphael into the latter.[90] Schumann's engagement with Raphael would be lifelong. As if to deny his own psychic nature, Schumann's ambitions were more to emulate the "ideal human being." In the universal genius, art entirely overpowered mundane life, as in the case of Michelangelo, Shakespeare, and Mozart. Following Jean Paul, Schumann sought a more intimate integration of mundane life and art.

During Schumann's trip to Italy in 1829 he filled his diary with detailed descriptions of art and architecture. One of the most interesting and revealing entries was his painstaking copying of what must have been a leftover newspaper clipping from 1825, which was from the *Elegante Zeitung* and referred to a set of parallels made by "Carpani." Carpani created two lists, one of composers and one of painters, and placed them side by side according to the most exact parallels. The curious matter, of course, was the historical asymmetry. Eighteenth-century composers were deemed the equivalents of Renaissance masters. Haydn was paired with Tintoretto, Cimarosa was compared to Paolo Veronese, Mozart to G. Romano, Gluck to Caravaggio, Piccini to Titian, Handel to Michelangelo, and Pergolesi to Raphael.[91]

During his trip to Vienna in 1838 Schumann evidently spent a fair amount of time in museums. In a diary entry from November 1838 he responded to looking at the originals by Raphael, Titian, Rubens, and others with these words: "I was overcome with happiness at the memories of the engravings at which I looked so often in my childhood."[92] For Schumann, the experience of seeing was comparable, in terms of *Bildung,* to that of reading and, more important, to that of hearing music. Nowhere was this more evident than in the diary entry of 16 October 1837. Schumann described the following sequence of events. First he noted his revision of his essay on piano variations, then he remarked with delight at the landscape painting of K. F. Lessing and at paintings depicting Cinderella, an Italian maiden, Friedrich Barbarossa, and a Roman figure bent in prayer. Immediately thereafter Schumann noted that he began to read *Siebenkäs* by Jean Paul.[93]

The icons of art history that carried the aura of a brilliant past continued to serve their double function as inspirations for the artwork of the future and as occasions for interior self-recognition. Schumann's museumgoing was at once an affirmation and a spur to his creative work. During the somewhat ill-fated trip to Russia in 1844 he once again described his many sojourns to look at art. For him the work of Benvenuto Cellini stood out along with the architecture of Moscow. Among the most memorable events was his visit to the Winter Palace, the Hermitage, in St. Petersburg.

Of all the many diary entries from the 1844 trip, it was Schumann's contempt for the artificial ruins—the fake modern reconstruction of the ravages of history—that he saw in Tsarskoe Selo that is most revealing. Neither slavish imitation of the past nor the even more philistine affectation to create an artificial item from the past deserved respect.[94] Regeneration was not accomplished by either neoclassicism or the affectation of a historical patina but rather by the evocation of the past in new forms.

Schumann's youthful education in art and his lifelong attachment to contemplating the great art of the past, particularly that from the Renaissance, led him to be interested in painters and sculptors of his own generation. In Copenhagen in the 1840s he visited the Thorvaldsen Museum. Unlike Mendelssohn, Schumann did not take to Thorwaldsen's neoclassic, restrained, and somewhat cold formalism. He marveled, however, at Peter Cornelius's frescoes in Schinkel's buildings in Berlin.[95]

Indeed, Schumann's search for a like-minded community led him to his own generation of German romantic and historical painters who lived and worked in Leipzig, Dresden, and, most of all, Düsseldorf. The painter Schumann seems most to have favored was Eduard Bendemann, with whom he was quite friendly and through whom he developed a new and strong admiration for the North German heritage, particularly the work of Albrecht Dürer.[96] Schumann's interest during the 1840s in a Germanic historical past, mostly medieval in character, was not merely the function of changes in the political culture of the mid- and late 1840s. Rather, Schumann's interests were influenced in part by his contact with contemporary painters who remained in the North. Alfred Rethel, Karl Friedrich Lessing, Julius Hübner, Ludwig Richter, J. W. Schirmer, and Karl Sohn are among the most significant painters with whom Schumann came into contact.

As with music, Schumann's evaluation of his contemporaries was persistently mediated by his references to and experiences with an idealized painterly past. In 1851 in Antwerp and Brussels, Schumann marveled at Rubens and van Dyk. At the same time he reacted with enthusiasm at the narrative canvases of Bendemann and Hübner.[97] In March 1852 Schumann made one of his last references on art by noting his visit to a collection of etchings by Raphael on display in Leipzig.[98] As with the novels of Jean Paul, Schumann returned repeatedly to the passions of his youth.

Robert Schumann had closer contact with two schools of German painters, the Düsseldorf School and the Dresden School. The most significant Düsseldorf painters with whom he was familiar included Bendemann, Hübner, Theodor Mintrop, Lessing, and Schirmer. In Dresden the most significant figures to Schumann were Richter, Johann Christian Dahl, and Ernst Rietschel. Bendemann bridged both schools, since during Schumann's lifetime he was in Dresden and subsequently in Düsseldorf. What is significant in Schumann's engagement with Lessing, Schirmer, Rietschel, and Rethel is these painters' enthusiasm for the large narrative and landscape canvas,[99] an enthusiasm that might bear on the development of Schumann's career. Schumann's attraction not only to the iconography and surface of the painting of his time but to the act of seeing and interacting with the large-scale canvas betrays an ambition that can help to provide a key to his development as a composer and to the consistency of his aesthetic concerns.

Scholars have sought explanations for Schumann's transition as a composer from the short piano form to the longer form and from the song finally to the symphony, oratorio, and opera. One key to Schumann's evolution is psychological and has to do with his growing confidence, given his unsystematic training and autodidactic route to composition. Another hypothesis is based on his relationship to Mendelssohn, which vacillated between adulation and envy. There is also the thesis that Schumann wanted greater public recognition, which led him to compose music that would enhance his reputation. The more simplified and accessible late style is said to reflect Schumann's awareness of particular domestic markets of the midcentury. Biographical events also have been cited, such as the impact of Men-delssohn's death in 1847. Did Schumann seek to assume a role as Mendelssohn's successor in writing music, under the banner of Mendelssohn's conception of aesthetic education, which called for a more neoclassical and transparent music?[100]

A further possibility lies in the notion that Schumann followed a very self-conscious dynamic strategy derived from Jean Paul. He invented himself along lines he had discovered in Jean Paul's prose as an adolescent. For example, Jean Paul's continuing dialectic between short and long forms and between the joke and the novel was emulated directly. Schumann's search later in life for a style that was narrative but also self-referential in formal terms conformed as well to the pattern of Jean Paul's own career. Like Schumann, Jean Paul began with an attraction to the grotesque and bizarre and ended his career in a celebration of idyllic domestic bliss. Indeed, like Flaubert's Emma Bovary or Stendhal's Julien Sorel, Schumann led his life in imitation of what he read in books. The sustained courtship of Clara, the flirtation with public romantic martyrdom, the diaries, the marriage diaries, and the correspondence, as well as the sequence of aesthetic projects in his career, can be tied to close models in Jean Paul's life and work.

But yet another key may lie in Schumann's interest in painting. Rethel, about whom Schumann had mixed views, was immensely impressive in the small form, the miniature. One thinks of the *Märchenerzählungen,* **Op. 132,** and the *Märchenbilder,* **Op. 113,** in relationship to Rethel's *Monatsbilder.* Rethel's and Richter's historicism was more self-consciously German, linked to Dürer where the refined line evoked a quality used by Schumann with regularity as a sign of approbation: *volkstümlich.* Richter's painting *Der Brautzug* is a case in point.[101]

The Düsseldorf School painters followed the direction described by Eichendorff. Likewise, in the work of the Dresden painters spiritual regeneration took the form of the rediscovery of an indigenous German past, ranging from landscape to myth and to historical memory. Their narrative painting would reach a large audience. Bendemann's and Lessing's work may have inspired Schumann to undertake the musical equivalent of their richly colored, spacious, scenic and narrative depictions. The evocation of the residues of the past and expectations transmitted to the viewer located in the present that were visible in the landscape canvases of romantic painting can be compared to Schumann's larger-scale works.

The works of the late 1840s and early 1850s—*Manfred* and *Der Rose Pilgerfahrt*—are cases in point. The Düsseldorf painter Theodor Mintrop designed the title page of *Der Rose Pilgerfahrt.* These works and the "Rhenish" Symphony have their analogues in Lessing's *Fels-und Waldlandschaft mit dem Mutter-Gottes Bild* or the other version of this painting, *Die tausendjährige Eiche*.[102] Orchestral colors have their equivalents in Lessing's use of light and dark and color.[103] ***Das Paradies und die Peri*** constitutes the first massive work by Schumann that can be compared with the paintings and frescoes of his immediate contemporaries.[104]

Schumann's response to paintings such as *Die trauernden Juden* by Bendemann might be compared to the interior intensity associated with the reactions he sought to evoke in music. In that canvas Bendemann made the inner journey of the viewer the subject. In this sense, the late songs might be linked to Bendemann's work. The character of Schumann's late **"Violin Sonata in D minor," Op. 121,** and the last section of *Faust* are reminiscent of the scale, coloration, and sweep of the canvases of Schirmer, just as the later, more bizarre and fragmentary work of late Schumann can be related to the smaller Rethel etchings.

In subject matter and execution, the emphasis in these paintings on the interior concentration of the human subjects on the canvas and the enormous disparity of scale between the figures and the natural environment helped the viewer to respond to the psychic power of nature and its mediation through art. The iconography was a Jean Paul-like mix of surface realism and fantasy. The Düsseldorf School painters eschewed the monumentality of the Munich School of historical painters. Nevertheless, evident in the paintings with which Schumann was most familiar and that he most admired was a constant reference either to the past or to the flight from the moment—toward legend, myth, and, periodically, Christianity.

HISTORY AND PERFORMANCE PRACTICE: THE CASE OF SCHUMANN

Robert Schumann's vacillation between the spiritual and aesthetic predicament of the individual (Jean Paul) and the aesthetic education of the public (Menzel) was lifelong. The various forms it took in Schumann's music speak to an evolution in strategy and a desire to accommodate the changes in the historical moment that occurred between 1830 and 1850. The engagement with history and painting in Schumann's later years helps to illuminate the sources of the strikingly simple style and formal fastidiousness of much of the choral and piano music of the later years, including the children's music. One thinks first of the Op. 60 B A C H fugues from 1845, piano works such as Opp. 85, 124, and 126, and the last secular choral pieces.

This self-conscious identification with a national movement of cultural regeneration, however, grew directly out of Schumann's encounter with Menzel in 1828. The concern for the standard of public taste that Schumann exhibited as a critic in the late 1830s reemerged in his musical work a decade later as he sought to emulate the public role of Mendelssohn after the latter's death.

As a young man, Robert Schumann began to imagine himself and create his world through the act of reading. With remarkable discipline he lived out an approach to the world that was characteristic of the reigning ideas and influences of his generation. It is necessary for late twentieth-century observers to note that Schumann wrote music with the full expectation that it would function for the listener the way reading functioned. The shared literary and linguistic foundation behind Schumann's sense of musical time and form are fundamental.

What this suggests may be nothing short of radical, particularly for the modern interpreter. As Schumann's own revisions of his earlier music imply, the act of making music resembles rereading. Rereading is never a replica of a past event. What is perceived and recalled has as much to do with the life history and place of the reader as it does with the printed text. Playing involves the creation of new meanings and experiences.

If printed music is, then, like a poetic or prose text, the conceit of faithful representation of past practices—including the category of authorial intention—as understood by late twentieth-century performance practice may be irrelevant. Only if that conceit inspires one to tears can it serve as a surrogate for imaginative interpretive transformation.

The twentieth century's notions of authenticity and the musical text demand redefinition if Schumann is the subject. Perhaps playing Schumann according to performance practices of his day requires that the player take striking liberties including improvisation, alteration, amplification, and addition to create the intensity of memory, expectation, and consciousness in the audience. Or perhaps Schumann should be set aside in favor of a living composer inspired directly by him (e.g., Adorno's advocacy of Berg).

The speculative historical reconstruction of the cultural world around Schumann suggests than when scholars and performers consider the musical canon written after the death of Beethoven, the imposition of seemingly objective notions of textual reading and interpretation not only are ahistorical but may cut directly against the meaning and role that music making and listening possessed in the historical era in which the works were written. It is ironic that our obsession with the sophisticated, self-critical historical methods designed to rescue the music of the past allegedly obscured by falsifying subsequent traditions, in the case of Schumann and his contemporaries, might compel us to abandon the historical critical enterprise as we now know it. The making of "correct" editions, re-creating old instruments, utilizing forgotten techniques, and wiping out traces of older reinterpretations may be, historically speaking, a travesty. Schumann's additions to the texts of his beloved Bach, his close emulations of Bach, and his early and late appropriations of Paganini are the alternative models of what we might do to Schumann, all in the name of history.

Exploring Schumann as history, then, reminds us of how performance strategies need to be evaluated in terms illuminated by extramusical historical categories, including reading and the viewing of art. The consequences of this approach need to be considered if we wish to conjure up among our fellow citizens the spirit as well as the personal and public significance that history teaches us actually marked music making and listening in Schumann's world.

Notes

1. Ludwig Wittgenstein, *Culture and Value,* trans. Peter Winch (Chicago, 1980), p. 2.

2. See, for example, the work of John Daverio; and Anthony Newcomb's article "Schumann and Late Eighteenth-Century Narrative Strategies," *19th-Century Music* 11 (1987): 164-74.

3. Theodor W. Adorno, "Berg: Der Meister des kleinsten Übergangs," in *Musikalische Monographien* (Frankfurt, 1986), p. 330; see also Max Paddison, *Adorno's Aesthetics of Music* (Cambridge, 1993), pp. 242-45.

4. See Theodor W. Adorno, *Kompositionen,* ed. Heinz-Klaus Metzger and Reiner Riehn (Munich, 1980), vol. 2, pp. 73-113.

5. Roland Barthes, "Loving Schumann" and "Rasch," in *The Responsibility of Forms,* trans. Richard Howard (Berkeley and Los Angeles, 1991), particularly pp. 293, 298. In his recent book, in an analysis of F. Khnopff's 1883 painting *En écoutant du Schumann,* Richard Leppert extends Barthes' analysis to probe how Schumann came to be heard and how that hearing was represented in art at the end of the nineteenth century. Leppert's brilliant excursus assumes that the hand of the player in the painting is male and that the process of music making and hearing has been disembodied, making it "anti-conversational." This analysis is relevant only insofar as to assert that Leppert's reading of the painting and Schumann may be genuine twentieth-century impositions that bear little resemblance to the experience of hearing and listening that either Schumann or enthusiasts (even Khnopff) circa 1883 of his music had. See Richard Leppert, *The Sight of Sound: Music Representation and the History of the Body* (Berkeley and Los Angeles, 1994), pp. 230-33.

6. Eduard Hanslick, *Sämtliche Schriften,* vol. 1: *Aufsätze und Reszensionen, 1844-1848,* ed. Dietmar Strauss (Vienna, 1993), p. 106.

7. Two recent studies are Peter Ostwald, *The Inner Voices of a Musical Genius* (Boston, 1985); and Udo Rauchfleisch, *Robert Schumann: Leben und Werk* (Stuttgart, 1990).

8. Kay Jamison, *Touched with Fire: Manic-Depressive Illness and the Artistic Temperament* (New York, 1993), pp. 144-46, 201-7.

9. Wilhelm Dilthey, *Das Erlebnis und die Dichtung* (Göttingen, 1905; reprint, 1985), p. 315.

10. Anthony Newcomb, "Schumann and the Marketplace: From Butterflies to *Hausmusik,*" in *Nineteenth-Century Piano Music,* ed. R. Larry Todd (New York, 1990), pp. 258-315, esp. p. 271.

11. Hans Gál, *Schumann's Orchestral Music* (London, 1979), p. 7.

12. English-language readers can find two choice examples of Schumann's anti-Semitism in his marriage diaries. Schumann writes disparagingly of Mendelssohn's indelible Jewish characteristics and of how the "Jewish physiognomy" of E. Marxsen (Brahms's teacher) disgusted Clara and Robert. In *The Marriage Diaries of Robert and Clara Schumann,* ed. Gerd Nauhaus, trans. Peter Ostwald (Boston, 1994), pp. 31, 132.

13. Richard Wagner, "Judaism in Music," in *Richard Wagner's Prose Works,* trans. W. A. Ellis (New York, 1966), vol. 3, p. 117. See the precise echo of this view in, of all places, the ideas of Richard Strauss's father, Franz. Cited in R. Larry Todd, "Strauss before Liszt and Wagner: Some Observations," in Bryan Gilliam, ed., *Richard Strauss: New Perspectives* (Durham, N.C., 1992), p. 33.

14. See Newcomb, "Schumann and the Marketplace"; and Linda Correll Roesner, "The Sources for Schumann's *Davidsbündlertänze,* Op. 6: Composition, Textual Problems, and the Role of the Composer as Editor," in *Mendelssohn and Schumann: Essays on Their Music and Its Context,* ed. R. Larry Todd and Jon W. Finson (Durham, N.C., 1984), pp. 53-70.

15. See Jörg-Peter Mittmann, "Musikerberuf und bürgerliches Bildungsideal," in *Bildungsbürgertum im 19. Jahrhundert,* vol. 2: *Bildungsgüter und Bildungswissen,* ed. Reinhart Koselleck (Stuttgart, 1990), pp. 237-58.

16. See Andreas Ballstädt and Tobias Willmaier, *Salonmusik: Zur Geschichte und Funktion einer bürgerlichen Musikpraxis* (Stuttgart, 1989), pp. 52-53, 88-94, 255-57, 315-50, 385; also Carl Dahlhaus, *Klassische und romantische Musikästhetik* (Laaber, 1988), p. 171.

17. Hermann Kretzschmar, "Robert Schumann als Aesthetiker" (1906), in *Gesammelte Aufsätze aus den Jahrbüchern der Musikbibliothek Peters* (Leipzig, 1911; reprint, 1973) p. 297.

18. Robert Schumann, *Tagebücher, Band III: Haushaltbücher,* ed. Gerd Nauhaus (Leipzig, 1982), pp. 629-38.

19. Gerhard Stenzel, ed. *Die deutschen Romantiker* (Salzburg, n.d.), vol. 2, p. 394.

20. Wilhelm Dilthey, "Klopstock, Schiller, Jean Paul," in *Von deutscher Dichung und Musik: Aus den Studien zur Geschichte des deutschen Geistes* (Leipzig and Berlin, 1933), pp. 436-37.

21. Arnfried Edler, *Robert Schumann und seine Zeit* (Laaber, 1982), pp. 90-101, 212-22.

22. Clara Schumann, *Jugendbriefe von Robert Schumann* (Leipzig, 1886), pp. 82-83.

23. This is true not only of Oliver Strunk's extract in his classic 1950 collection of readings but also of Kretzschmar's essay.

24. C. F. Müller, *Musikalische Original-Anekdoten* (Erfurt, 1836), pp. 365-66. An English version can be found in Thomas A. Brown, *The Aesthetics of Robert Schumann* (New York, 1968), p. 16.

25. Quoted in Kretzschmar, "Robert Schumann als Aesthetiker," p. 301.

26. Schumann, *Tagebücher, Band I: 1827-1838,* ed. Georg Eismann (Leipzig, 1971), p. 36.

27. Quoted in Dilthey, "Klopstock, Schiller, Jean Paul," p. 442.

28. *Jean Pauls Sämtliche Werke: Historisch-kritische Ausgabe,* ed. Eduard Berend (Weimar, 1927; reprint, 1975), vol. 2, p. 51.

29. *Jean Paul's Werke,* ed. Wolgang Hecht (Berlin, 1987), vol. 1, p. 26.

30. Jean Paul, *Die Vorschule der Aesthetik,* in *Jean Pauls Sämtliche Werke,* vol. 11, pp. 89-93, 153-61. The *Witz* figured as well in Schlegel and in secondary figures of Schumann's generation such as Arnold Ruge (who later would play an important role in German politics), whose *Neue Vorschule der Aesthetik* (Halle, 1837) was derivative of Jean Paul.

31. G. G. Gervinus, *Geschichte des neunzehnten Jahrhunderts,* vol. 8, part 1 (Leipzig, 1866), p. 75.

32. Ibid., p. 77.

33. The tie between Hegel and Jean Paul, and ultimately Schumann, is not speculative. Hegel knew Jean Paul and Thibaut and spent time at Heidelberg with both of them at Thibaut's soirees. See

Adolf Nowak, *Hegels Musikaesthetik* (Regensburg, 1970), p. 20.

34. Hegel, *Aesthetics,* trans. T. M. Knox (Oxford, 1975), vol. 2, p. 897.

35. Robert Schumann, *Manfred: Dramatisches Gedicht,* Op. 115 (Leipzig, 1853), piano score, pp. 1, 3, 5, 6.

36. Jean Paul, "Selberlebenbeschreibung," in *Jean Paul's Werke,* vol. 1, p. 25.

37. Dilthey, "Klopstock, Schiller, Jean Paul," p. 450.

38. Schumann, *Tagebücher, Band I: 1827-1838,* pp. 109, 115-16.

39. Heinrich Heine, *Sämtliche Schriften* (Munich, 1976), vol. 1, pp. 444-56, esp. p. 454.

40. Wolfgang Menzel, *Die deutsche Literatur,* 2d ed. (Stuttgart, 1836), part 1, pp. 42-48.

41. Ibid., pp. 3-41.

42. Ibid., part 3, p. 174.

43. Ibid., part 4, pp. 5f.

44. Ibid., part 1, p. 103.

45. Heine, *Sämtliche Schriften,* vol. 1, p. 455.

46. Ibid., p. 451.

47. Schumann, *Tagebücher, Band I: 1827-1838,* p 101; on the role of criticism see Walter Benjamin's "Der Begriff der Kunstkritik in der deutschen Romantik," in *Gesammelte Schriften* (Frankfurt, 1980), vol. 1, part 1, pp. 62-72.

48. Heine, *Sämtliche Schriften,* vol. 2, p. 34.

49. See Martha Woodmansee, *The Author, Art, and the Market: Rereading the History of Aesthetics* (New York, 1994), pp. 22-33, 87; on Schumann's criticism see the classic book by Leon B. Plantinga, *Schumann as Critic* (New Haven, 1967).

50. Menzel, *Die deutsche Literatur,* part 1, pp. 24-32, 86-116.

51. Ibid., p. 32.

52. See Hans Joachim Köhler, *Robert Schumann: Sein Leben und Wirken in den Leipziger Jahren* (Leipzig, 1986), pp. 7-18.

53. Eva Weissweiler, *Clara Schumann: Eine Biographie* (Hamburg, 1990), pp. 93-95.

54. *M. G. Saphir's Konversations-Lexikon* (Berlin, n.d.), pp. 259-60.

55. Hans Erich Bödeker, "Die 'gebildeten Stände' im 18. und frühen 19. Jahrhundert: Zugehörigkeit und Abgrenzungen, Mentalitäten und Handlungspotentiale," in *Bildungsbürgertum im 19. Jahrhundert,*

vol. 4: *Politischer Einfluss und gesellschaftliche Formation,* ed. Jürgen Kocka (Stuttgart, 1989), pp. 26-30.

56. See Wolfgang Hardtwig, "Auf dem Weg zum Bildungsbürgertum: die Lebensführungsart der jugendlichen Bildungschicht, 1750-1819," in *Politischer Bildungsbürgertum im 19. Jahrhundert,* vol. 3: *Lebensführung und ständische Vergesellschaftung,* ed. M. Rainer Lepsius (Stuttgart, 1992), pp. 35-41.

57. Karl Lamprecht, *Deutsche Geschichte* (Freiburg im Breisgau, 1905), vol. 1, part 3, pp. 297-302.

58. K. H. Wörner, *Robert Schumann* (Munich, 1987), p. 13.

59. Friedrich Schlegel, *Kritische Schriften und Fragmente,* ed. Ernst Behler and Hans Eichner (Paderborn, 1988), vol. 4, pp. 233-34.

60. See Gerald N. Izenberg, *Impossible Individuality: Romanticism, Revolution, and the Origins of Modern Selfhood, 1787-1802* (Princeton, 1992), pp. 54-138.

61. See, for example, Dahlhaus's references to Schlegel in *Klassische und Romantische Musikästhetik.* See the discussion of the origin of the motto for the *Fantasy,* Op. 17, which comes from Schlegel's "Die Gebüsche," in Nicholas Marston, *Schumann: "Fantasie," Op. 17* (Cambridge, 1992), pp. 21-22.

62. John Daverio, *Nineteenth-Century Music and the German Romantic Ideology* (New York, 1993), pp. 11-14, 55.

63. Frederick C. Beiser, *The Fate of Reason: German Philosophy from Kant to Fichte* (Cambridge, Mass., 1987), pp. 214-17.

64. See Schumann, *Tagebücher, Band I: 1827-1838,* pp. 109-16, 200-202. See also the discussion complementary to this point, in Norbert Nagler's "Der konfliktuöse Kompromiss zwischen Gefühl und Vernunft im Frühwerk Schumanns," in *Robert Schumann: Text und Kritik,* ed. Klaus Metzger and R. Riehn (Munich, 1981), vol. 1, pp. 221-80.

65. W. H. Bruford, *The German Tradition of Self-Cultivation: "Bildung" from Humboldt to Thomas Mann* (Cambridge, 1975), pp. 82-87.

66. Schlegel's idea of *Ahnung* calls for careful examination in terms of Schumann's approach to musical settings of lyric poetry.

67. Schlegel, *Kritische Schriften und Fragmente,* vol. 6, p. 44.

68. The derivation of the title "Novelettes" from Clara Novello's name does not undermine the obvious double meaning: the reference to the short novel form. See Edler, *Robert Schumann und seine Zeit,* p. 133.

69. Schlegel, *Kritische Schriften und Fragmente,* vol. 6, p. 54.

70. Ibid., vol. 5, p. 256.

71. Friedrich Schlegel, *Philosophical Fragments,* trans. Peter Firchow (Minneapolis, 1991), p. 92.

72. Hegel, *Aesthetics,* vol. 2, pp. 888-98.

73. Lamprecht, *Deutsche Geschichte,* pp. 3-93.

74. One forgets that musical gatherings such as the Schubertiade had their literary counterparts in reading aloud. Consider, for example, the drawing by L. Pietsch entitled *An Evening with Ludwig Tieck.*

75. Benjamin, "Der Begriff der Kunstkritik," p. 68.

76. See Carl Dahlhaus, "Der deutsche Bildungsbürgertum und die Musik," in *Bildungsgüter und Bildungswissen,* ed. Reinhart Koselleck, pp. 220-36; and Bödeker, "Die 'gebildeten Staende,'" in *Politischer Einfluss und gesellschaftliche Formation,* ed. Jürgen Kocka, pp. 33-41.

77. Alfred Dörfel, *Die Geschichte der Gewandhauskonzerte zu Leipzig: 1781-1881* (Leipzig, 1884; reprint, 1980), pp. 87-88.

78. See Werner Busch, "Die fehlende Gegenwart," in *Bildungsgüter und Bildungswissen,* ed. Reinhart Koselleck, pp. 286-316.

79. Dilthey, "Klopstock, Schiller, Jean Paul," p. 446.

80. Jean Paul, *Jean Pauls Sämtliche Werke,* vol. 11, part 1, p. 77.

81. Eduard Bernsdorf et al., *Neues Universal-Lexikon der Tonkunst* (Dresden, 1856-61), vol. 3, p. 536.

82. These are part of Op. 90 and were taken from a set entitled *Liebesklänge* in *Nikolaus Lenaus Sämtliche Werke,* ed. E. Castle (Leipzig, n.d.), vol. 1, p. 177. See Josef Haslinger, "Nikolaus Lenau," in *Österreichische Porträts,* ed. Jochen Jung (Salzburg, 1985), vol. 1, pp. 207-31.

83. Quoted in *Die deutschen Romantiker,* p. 258.

84. *The Marriage Diaries of Robert and Clara Schumann,* p. 98.

85. See Dahlhaus, "Zur Entstehung der romantischen Bach Deutung," in *Klassische und romantische Musikaesthetik,* pp. 121-39.

86. See Peter Gülke, "Zur Rheinischen Sinfonie," in Metzger and Riehn, *Robert Schumann: Text und Kritik,* vol. 2, pp. 237-53.

87. Marston, *Schumann: "Fantasie," Op. 17,* pp. 1-10; and Daverio, *Nineteenth-Century Music and the German Romantic Ideology,* pp. 42-47. The reference to "palm" is, of course, intimately con-

nected with the Christian symbolism of Palm Sunday and Easter. The pagan celebration of nature and life in springtime merges with the Christian notion of redemption and resurrection. Schumann's use of the palm is therefore not only characteristic but ideally matched to the notion of the ruin and the trophy.

88. Schumann knew the last of the Nazarene painters, Wilhelm Schadow, who was director of the fine arts academy in Düsseldorf. See Schumann, *Tagebücher, Band III: Haushaltbücher,* pp. 578, 589.

89. Wörner, *Robert Schumann,* p. 135; see also Theodore Ziolkowski, *German Romanticism and Its Institutions* (Princeton, 1990), pp. 337-55.

90. Schumann, *Tagebücher, Band I: 1827-1838,* p. 230.

91. Ibid., p. 281.

92. Ibid., *Band II: 1836-1854,* ed. Gerd Nauhaus (Leipzig, 1987), p. 81.

93. Ibid., p. 39.

94. Ibid., pp. 262-370.

95. Ibid., pp. 223 and 417.

96. Ibid., p. 398.

97. Ibid., pp. 428-29.

98. Ibid., p. 432.

99. In the *Tagebücher, Band III: Haushaltbücher, Teil I: 1837-1847* and *Teil II: 1847-1856,* see the many references to Schumann's contact with these painters—for example, pp. 453-55, 473, 495, 509, 543, 545, 547, and 638.

100. It is ironic that despite Schumann's numerous expressions of admiration and his sorrow at Mendelssohn's death, at the end of his life Mendelssohn was quite bitter about their relationship. Writing to his friend Karl Klingemann a few months before his death, Mendelssohn confided that Schumann acted in quite a "two-faced" manner and had engaged in some "ugly" behavior, decidedly cooling his enthusiasm for further dealings. See the letter dated 31 January 1847 in *Felix Mendelssohns Briefwechsel mit Karl Klingemann* (Essen, 1909), p. 320; also Leon B. Plantinga, "Schumann's Critical Reaction to Mendelssohn," in *Mendelssohn and Schumann: Essays on Their Music and Its Context,* ed. R. Larry Todd and Jon W. Finson, pp. 11-20.

101. Too frequently only Richter's etching *Hausmusik* is discussed because of its direct relationship to Opp. 68 and 79. Ludwig Richter was responsible for the illustrations on the title page of the first edition of the *Album für die Jugend,* Op. 68. See pp. 184ff. in this volume.

102. For information on and reproductions of the painters and painters discussed here, see Anton Springer, *Handbuch der Kunstgeschichte,* ed. Max Osborn (Leipzig, 1912), vol. 5, pp. 35-61; Friedrich Haack, *Die Kunst des 19. Jahrhunderts* (Esslingen, 1913), pp. 146-70; and Christoph Heilmann, *Die Kunst der Deutsch-Römer* (Munich, 1987), pp. 317-23.

103. See Reinhard Kapp, "Das Orchester Schumanns," in Metzger and Riehn, *Robert Schumann: Text und Kritik,* vol. 2, pp. 191-236.

104. The painterly dimension of the "Rhenish" Symphony was not lost on contemporaries; see Ernst Lichtenhahn, "Sinfonie als Dichtung: Zum geschichtlichen Ort von Schumanns 'Rhenischer,'" in *Schumanns Werke: Text und Interpretation,* ed. Akio Mayeda and Klaus Wolfgang Niemöller (Mainz, 1987), especially pp. 18-21.

John Daverio (essay date 1997)

SOURCE: Daverio, John. "Music Criticism in a New Key." *Robert Schumann: Herald of a "New Poetic Age,"* pp. 105-30. New York: Oxford University Press, 1997.

[*In the following excerpt, Daverio demonstrates how Schumann's criticism reflects his passionate desire to unite music and language.*]

A BARRIER AGAINST CONVENTION

In March 1833 Schumann arrived in Leipzig after a four-month stay in Zwickau and nearby Schneeberg, the home of his brother Carl and sister-in-law Rosalie. As noted in the previous chapter, the first movement of his G-minor Symphony was performed at both locations: in Zwickau on 18 November 1832 and in Schneeberg in mid-February of the following year. On returning to Leipzig, Schumann took an apartment with Carl Günther, a law student, in Franz Riedel's Garten, an establishment on the outskirts of the city. He continued to work on his G-minor Symphony (certainly on the last movement, and perhaps also on the second and third as well), the first movement of which was rendered, but only with limited success, at Clara's "grand concert" of 29 April at the Gewandhaus. But at about the same time, which Schumann described as the beginning of his "richest and most active period," his thoughts turned to a project that would have tremendous consequences not only for his own career but also for the future course of music journalism: the founding of a new journal for music.[1]

Unfortunately, a thorough account of the initial stages of Schumann's "richest" phase is hampered by the suspension of his diary for much of the four-year period between March 1833 and October 1837.[2] Never again would he go for so long without maintaining some record of his daily activities. Hence, for documentary information on the composer's fortunes (and misfortunes) during the mid-1830s, we must rely largely on letters and on the lapidary notices written in Vienna while he was "filled with melancholy" on the evening of 28 November 1838.[3]

Schumann's abandonment of his diary may be linked to his recent decision to pursue a full-time career as composer, and indeed, shortly after returning to Leipzig in March 1833 he embarked on a variety of compositional projects that no doubt absorbed much of his time and energy. In addition to his attempts to complete the G-minor Symphony, which according to an entry in his *Kompositions-Verzeichnis* occupied him until May, Schumann finished a second volume of Paganini transcriptions (*VI Etudes de Concert* after Paganini's Caprices, op. 10) between April and July, and drafted the *Impromptus, op. 5,* in the remarkably short space of five days in late May.[4] There is a good chance that many of the other works that were either begun (the **"Piano Sonata in F# minor,"** op. 11; the **"Piano Sonata in G minor," op. 22**; the **"Variations"** on Schubert's *Sehnsuchtswalzer*) or completed (the second version of the *Etuden* or *Exercises* on the Allegretto theme from Beethoven's Seventh Symphony, the final revisions of the Toccata) in 1833 likewise date from the spring and early summer of that year; but as we shall see, it is unlikely that Schumann did much composing from July through early December.[5] If this is the case, it would mean that following on his only partially successful attempt to establish his credentials as a symphonist, Schumann undertook a systematic exploration of the keyboard genres. As a group, the works of 1833, both projected and realized, constitute a veritable compendium of forms and styles: Schumann's interest in cultivating the larger forms is exemplified by his preliminary work on the F#-minor and G-minor sonatas; his conflation of variation and character piece by the variations (in free form) on themes of Beethoven and Schubert, and by the *Impromptus*; his fusion of virtuoso style and pedagogical intent by the Paganini transcriptions. Thus Schumann's turn to the keyboard as a vehicle for his creativity in mid-1833, and his almost total concentration on keyboard music for the remainder of the decade, can be interpreted from two points of view. On the one hand, it allowed him to shore up his compositional skills in the wake of his frustrated attempt at symphonic composition. On the other hand, the piano works of the 1830s comprise more than an episode, a stepping stone on the path toward the symphonies and chamber music of the 1840s;[6] ranging from the slightest of miniatures to the grandest of designs, they attest to the love of system that characterizes Schumann's creativity from the first to the last.

Probably the most fascinating of the compositions of mid-1833 are those in variation forms. We have already discussed the *Etuden/Exercises* in the context of Schumann's reception of Beethoven in the spring of 1832. The Variations on the *Sehnsuchtswalzer* in turn demonstrate a continued engagement with the musical idol of Schumann's youth: Franz Schubert. In **"Der Psychometer"** (1834), an extraordinary essay about a machine capable of responding to critical questions, Schumann divided waltzes into three categories: head-waltzes, foot-waltzes, and heart-waltzes. The third type "comprises [dances] in the visionary keys of D♭ and A♭, and its fathers appear to be the *Sehnsuchtswalzer,* evening flowers, twilight shapes, and memories of long-gone youth and a thousand loves."[7] Mistakenly attributed to Beethoven when it was published in 1826, the *Sehnsuchtswalzer* ("Yearning Waltz") combines Schubert's so-called *Trauerwalzer* in A♭ ("Sorrowful Waltz"; No. 2 of the *36 Originaltänze für Klavier,* op. 9/D. 365) and the second of three *Deutsche* for piano, D. 972. A sketch for the composition now in the Stiftung Preussischer Kulturbesitz in Berlin vividly demonstrates Schumann's rethinking of the variation form. Anxious to overcome the sectional nature of the traditional design, he links several of the variations with transitional ritornelli. Furthermore, the titles of the sketch as a whole, *Scenes musicales sur un thême connu,* and the draft for the fourth movement, Intermezzo, indicate that Schumann was nudging the variation in the direction of the character piece.[8] Thus it is hardly surprising that although these variations were never published, the opening two-dozen measures or so of the introductory movement to the set found their way into the *Préambule* of *Carnaval.*

In the *Impromptus sur une Romance de Clara Wieck,* composed between 26 and 30 May 1833, Schumann more fully realized his novel conception of the variation idea. In one of several autobiographical sketches, he even suggested that the work "might be seen as a new form of variation,"[9] a reference, perhaps, to the grounding of the *Impromptus* in not one, but two themes: the bass theme, a product of Schumann's contrapuntal study in the preceding years and the point of departure for an extended fugato in the unfinished finale of the G-minor Symphony, announced unadorned at the outset of the piece; and the slightly altered version of the melody from Clara's *Romance variée,* op. 3, with which the bass theme is combined immediately thereafter[10] (Example 3.1). But in a sense, Schumann's recourse to a kind of "double theme" is not so new after all. He would have found ample precedent for the technique in Beethoven's *Fünfzehn Variationen mit einer Fuge* for piano, op. 35, the so-called "Eroica" Variations of 1802. Even the outward designs of these pieces are similar: both begin with the bass theme alone (followed, in Beethoven's case, with three contrapuntal variations), proceed with the introduction of the melodic theme and an extended series of variations, and close with an impressive fugal finale.[11] Still, the more obviously Bachian pedigree of Schumann's variations

Example 3.1. **Impromptus,** op. 5 (first version): mm. 1-32.

distinguishes them from Beethoven's. As he wrote in the autobiographical sketch mentioned above, the ***Impromptus*** were conceived "as a result of the stimulation" afforded by a steady exposure to Bach's music in the early 1830s. This assertion is further supported by a diary entry of 29 May 1832, where Schumann maintains that the falling-fifth motive C-F-G-C, the opening gesture of the ***Impromptus*** bass theme, came to him after sightreading several of Bach's fugues with Clara.[12] Moreover, the spirit of Bach extends past the character of the bass theme and the contrapuntal gamesmanship

of the finale to encompass the body of the variations themselves, witness the subtle use of invertible counterpoint in No. 3, and the treatment of Clara's theme as a migrating cantus firmus in Nos. 4 and 8.

Yet the chief novelty of the variation form as rethought in the ***Impromptus*** probably lies elsewhere, in the subsumption of the allusions to Beethoven and Bach under an overriding poetic idea. The work, after all, is the first in a long and impressive series of "Clara" pieces, musical lyrics of personal experience intimately bound up with the young woman destined to play a crucial role in Schumann's life. Schumann summons up Clara's theme (in the second half of No. 1), elaborates it (Nos. 2-4), gradually converts it into a dreamy recollection (a process culminating in No. 11), effaces it (for the bulk of the Finale), and only at the last moment restores it as a fleeting reminiscence in the closing measures of the piece. The composition, in other words, turns on the transformation of Clara's melody into a memory.[13] Though Schumann draws on time-honored (Beethovenian), even archaic (Bachian) techniques, he places them within the eminently modern context of the cycle of character pieces. Thus the *Impromptus* certainly count as a musical realization of what we will soon encounter as the historical imperative of Schumann's criticism: the invocation of the past as an inspirational source for a "new poetic age."

After completing the *Impromptus,* Schumann both continued with works-in-progress (the second volume of Paganini transcriptions) and moved on to newer projects (the F#-minor Sonata), but the events of summer 1833 brought his composing to a standstill. During July and August, he suffered from an attack of malarial fever, his recovery no doubt slowed by heavy and persistent drinking (the Vienna précis of 1838 refers to "champagne nights" before the onset of malaria and to a "dissolute life" shortly thereafter).[14] Then on 2 August his brother Julius (who, together with Eduard, had continued to manage the family book business in Zwickau) died at the age of twenty-eight from tuberculosis. But the death in mid-October of his favorite sister-in-law, Rosalie, a victim of the same disease from which Schumann was slowly recovering, took him over the edge. His first major neurotic spell, again as described in the Vienna précis, was characterized by the onslaught of anxiety and depression:

> The night of 17-18 October [1833]—the most frightful of my life—
> Rosalie's death just before
> At this point, a crucial segment of my life begins.
> The tortures of the most dreadful melancholy from October until December—
> I was seized by an *idée fixe*: the fear of going mad.[15]

Of the various accounts of Schumann's illness, the closest in time to the episode itself is a letter to his mother of 27 November. According to this document, the psychological symptoms detailed above were accompanied by a number of physical disturbances as well: "I felt like hardly more than a statue, without cold or warmth. . . . Violent congestion of the blood, unspeakable fear, loss of breath, [and] momentary loss of consciousness alternate rapidly, although now less so than in past days. If you had any inkling of this numbing of the spirit through melancholy, then you would forgive me for not writing." While Schumann noted some im-

provement in his condition at this time, he remained so "shy and timid" that he was afraid to fall asleep without someone else in his room (in September he had moved to a fifth-floor apartment at Burgstrasse 21, located near the center of town), and shared lodgings with his former roommate, the "fundamentally good-hearted" Günther; nor did he have the courage to travel alone to Zwickau, "for fear that *something might happen to me.*" He adds a heartrending plea: "My mother, really love me! Because I'm often close to madness when I think of Julius and Rosalie. . . ."[16] A letter to Clara written a little over four years later sheds further light on the causes and nature of Schumann's disturbance. There he attributes the "gloom" that enveloped him in the latter half of 1833 not only to the deaths of his brother and sister-in-law, but also to the "disappointments experienced by every artist when things don't go as swiftly as he had imagined," to the realization, in other words, that the road to fame and fortune as a composer would be an arduous one. Indeed, the less than enthusiastic reception of the first movement of his G-minor Symphony would have fed into Schumann's recognition of this fact. Horrified by the thought that he might be losing his senses—"the most dreadful of heaven's punishments"—and fearful that this thought might lead him "to lay a hand" on his life, Schumann sought medical advice. His doctor, however, failed to acknowledge the seriousness of his patient's complaint, ascribing it to adolescent malaise and little more: "Find yourself a woman," Schumann was told, "she'll cure you in a flash."[17]

Although Schumann's bout with mental illness was triggered by the deaths of two of his closest relatives, it occurred at the culmination of a period marked by physical and emotional decline. Debilitated by malarial fever and over-indulgence in alcohol, and dejected by his failure to launch a brilliant career as composer, Schumann easily lapsed into a condition whose psychological symptoms comprised intense depression, fear of madness, generalized panic, and suicidal thoughts, and whose physical consequences involved inflammation ("congestion of the blood"), shortness of breath, and numbness in the limbs.[18] The first of three more-or-less evenly spaced and progressively worsening episodes (the others flared up in 1844 and 1854) Schumann's near breakdown in the autumn of 1833 should have set off a warning bell. Tragically, few were willing to listen, nor were those who did competent to act.

As Schumann indicated to his mother in November 1833, his "return to life came about only gradually, through hard work."[19] Much of this hard work centered around the "musikalische Zeitschrift" ("musical journal") that he listed in his diary under "Plans" as early as 8 March of the same year.[20] By late June, a group of like-minded individuals had clustered around Schumann, its members including the theologian and pianist Julius Knorr, Ernst Ferdinand Wenzel (then a philosophy student and fellow pupil of Wieck's), the deaf painter, journalist, and composer Johann Peter Lyser, the music critics Ernst August Ortlepp and Gustav Bergen, Schumann's old friend Willibald von der Lühe, the philosopher Johann Amadeus Wendt, and Ludwig Ferdinand Stolle, a writer for Karl Georg Herlosssohn's *Der Komet.*[21] During the early part of the summer, the group met at Friedrich Hofmeister's music shop, but by late in the year, it assembled for informal, weekly meetings at the Kaffeebaum, a pub owned and operated by Andreas Poppe, where Schumann was a regular customer. Gustav Jansen provides a colorful picture of Schumann's direction of the proceedings: "When he sat at his usual place at the head of the table, with the indispensable cigar in his mouth, he never had to ask for a fresh glass of beer; he had arranged that it would be brought to him without even a nod, as soon as the innkeeper or waiter noticed that his glass was empty."[22] United in their displeasure over the current musical scene that was dominated by the frivolous strains of Italian opera in the theatre, and by the facile but vapid stunts of virtuoso pianists such as Herz and Hünten in the concert hall and salon, Schumann and his friends determined to publish a journal whose "tone and coloring . . . would be more varied than that of similar enterprises." Above all, it was their highminded intention "to erect a barrier against convention," but, as Schumann wrote to his mother on 28 June 1833, the venture would also provide him with the "definite social standing" for which he, as an artist with an "undefined position," had long craved.[23] (The establishment of the journal in 1834 allowed Schumann to describe himself as a *Musikgelehrter* [musical scholar] on the new passport he acquired at that time).[24] Thus from the start, Schumann's career as a journalist was marked by a blend of idealism and practicality.

There can be little doubt that the preparatory work for the founding of the journal—and the moderation of his alcohol consumption—set Schumann on the path to recovery from the neurotic episode of late October and November 1833; immediately after sketching out the events of his traumatic autumn in the Vienna précis, he added: "Sobriety. Journalistic activities. The idea of the Davidsbündler further developed."[25] Moreover, Schumann associated his decisive "return to life" with one individual more than any other. The last entry for 1833 in the précis reads: "Then in December, *Ludwig Schunke,* like a star."[26] Soon this extraordinarily gifted young pianist became his most treasured companion. Schumann's description of his newly found confidant in a letter to his mother dated 19 March 1834 brims over with superlatives: "[Schunke] is a splendid fellow and friend, who always takes hearty pleasure in striving for and accomplishing the most beautiful and the best. A patch of blue often brings more pleasure than an entirely clear sky; I could do without all my friends for

the sake of this one."[27] At about the same time, the pair decided to share an apartment, Schunke perhaps participating in the "frequently dissolute life style" into which Schumann again slipped in the spring of 1834.[28] Within months, however, the young artist was gravely ill; and although his doctor gave him "only one more winter to live," he didn't manage to survive for even that brief a period. Schunke died on 7 December 1834 at the age of twenty-four, a victim of tuberculosis.[29]

While Schumann's friendship with Schunke was cut painfully short, it was not without artistic consequences for both young men. Schunke's *Variations concertantes* on Schubert's *Trauerwalzer,* for example, were probably inspired by Schumann's variations on the *Sehnsuchtswalzer* (both works, incidentally, were dedicated to Henriette Voigt, the wife of a prominent Leipzig merchant, an excellent pianist, and a warm supporter of Schumann since late in 1833). In acknowledgment of his friend's superior gifts as a piano virtuoso, Schumann dedicated his Toccata in its final form to Schunke. The latter, in turn, dedicated his Sonata in G Minor, op. 3, whose first movement, like the Toccata, aims to mediate technical display and contrapuntal textures, to "son ami R. Schumann." Schumann closed this circle of homages with a review (actually more of a poetically colored eulogy) of the composition, culminating in the following account of Schunke's rendition of his sonata:

> Ludwig sat more or less in front of the piano, as if transported there by a cloud; without knowing quite how, we were drawn into the stream of this work, unknown to any of us—I still see everything before me, the fading light, the walls silent, as if listening, friends gathered round, hardly daring to breathe, Florestan's pale face, the Master [Raro] deep in thought, and Ludwig in the center, who like a sorcerer held us in a magical ring.

After Schunke had finished, Florestan offered words of high praise: "You are a master of your art, especially when you play. Verily, the Davidsbündler would be proud to count such an artist as yourself among their number."[30]

When Schumann wrote this piece in 1835, the Davidsbund, his band of crusaders against philistinism in contemporary musical life, was still relatively new to the reading public. The group made its official debut in ***Der Davidsbündler,*** an article published in three installments in *Der Komet* between 7 December 1833 and 12 January 1834, during just the period, that is, that Schunke entered Schumann's life "like a star."[31] A fanciful blend of imaginative prose, critical commentary, and aphorisms attributed to Florestan, Eusebius, Raro, and other members of the Davidsbund (Hofmeister and Bergen), ***Der Davidsbündler*** brought together a cast of characters and a constellation of ideas about the nature of writing on art that had occupied Schumann for some time. To review what we have already detailed in Chapter 2: on 8 June 1831, his twenty-first birthday, Schumann decided to give his friends "more beautiful and fitting names"; a week later, many of these same friends appeared as characters in *Die Wunderkinder,* the projected "musical novel" in which Schumann intended to thematize the complex interplay of art and life; on 1 July of the same year, Florestan the Improviser, one of the protagonists in *Die Wunderkinder,* was joined by Eusebius; in a fragmentary tale possibly dating from the same time (like the later essay, titled *Der Davidsbündler*), Schumann and some of his "friends" from the 8 June diary entry took up the same theme broached in *Die Wunderkinder*: the need for the creative genius to recognize the fine line between ideality and reality; on 7 December, Florestan and Eusebius appeared in print for the first time as the two principal critical voices in Schumann's review of Chopin's Opus 2; and by May of the following year, *Die Wunderkinder* had been rechristened as *Florestan.*[32] To be sure, some of these strands appear to trail off into nothingness; Schumann's "musical novel," for instance, never materialized. But in the essay for *Der Komet* published in late 1833 and early 1834, personal confession, a poetic reshaping of reality, and critical awareness found a meeting point in the Davidsbündler idea.

By the mid-1830s, the notion of an artist-band primed to ward off philistinism was hardly new. As early as 1800, Friedrich Schlegel exhorted his colleagues to follow the example of the "medieval merchants" and "unite in a Hansa to defend themselves."[33] Similarly, at the heart of E. T. A. Hoffmann's "serapiontic" principle was a brotherhood of poetic individuals firm in their opposition to a world dominated by shallow tastes (it is probably no accident that Schumann had read Hoffmann's *Die Bergwerke zu Falun,* one of the tales in his *Serapionsbrüder,* less than a month before hitting upon the idea for *Die Wunderkinder*).[34] Nor were precedents lacking for actual artist associations united by this principle: witness the intellectual fraternity/sorority comprised of the Schlegel brothers and their wives, Novalis, and Schleiermacher, all of them contributors to the *Athenäum,* the short-lived journal (1798) whose contents represent the ideological core of early Romanticism; or, to cite a more specifically musical example, Carl Maria von Weber's Harmonische Verein, the statutes for which include the provision that "since the world is inundated with so many bad works, often upheld only by authorities and by wretched criticism, we are obliged to expose them and warn about them."[35] Groups such as the Ludlamshöhle in Vienna (founded 1817) and the satirically oriented and fancifully named Tunnel über der Spree in Berlin (founded 1827) counted both musicians and literati among their members and met regularly to discuss the latest happenings in the world of art. Clearly the *Litterarischer Verein* of Schumann's teenage years in Zwickau belongs to the same

tradition. In Leipzig's Tunnel über der Pleisse, which met weekly and often sponsored literary and musical entertainments, Schumann would have found a direct model for his Davidsbund. Interestingly enough, several of the members of the Leipzig Tunnel—Wieck, Lühe, Lyser—became collaborators on or contributors to Schumann's *Neue Zeitschrift für Musik.*[36]

In all of these artist associations, we encounter precedents for the features that characterized Schumann's Davidsbund: the use of pseudonyms (Weber's Harmonische Verein, the Ludlamshöhle, the Leipzig Tunnel), the production of humorous essays or feuilletons (the Berlin Tunnel), the organization around a journal (the *Athenäum* group). Yet there is at least one important respect in which Schumann's Davidsbund differs from other comparable groups. If Hoffmann's Serapionsbrüder was a sheer product of the author's imagination, and if the Berlin and Leipzig Tunnels were firmly rooted in reality, then the Davidsbund came about at the juncture of *both* imagination and reality. It was this feature that Schumann had in mind when, in the Introduction to his collected writings (1854), he described the group as "more than a secret society." The Davidsbund, he went on to explain, "runs like a red thread through [my] journal, uniting poetry and truth ["Dichtung und Wahrheit"] in a humorous manner."[37] The group was not only the mouthpiece through which Schumann and his colleagues expressed their opinions on the state of the contemporary musical scene, it was, in addition, the central theme, the "red thread," around which their journalistic undertaking was organized. Moreover, Schumann's allusion to Goethe's autobiography, *Dichtung und Wahrheit,* points to the higher truth born of poetic expression toward which he and his associates aspired. The path to their goal led through fact and fantasy, realism and idealism, the poetry of an imagined utopia and the prose of everyday life. These oppositional pairs commingle at every level in the pages of the *Neue Zeitschrift.* Consider even the names of the "members" of the Davidsbund as they appear in the journal. Some are pseudonyms for actual individuals ("Walt"—the pianist Louis Rakemann; "Serpentinus"—the song composer and critic Carl Banck; "Fritz Friedrich"—J. P. Lyser; "Chiara," "Chiarina," or "Zilia"—Clara Wieck; "Juvenalis"—Willibald von der Lühe; "Sara"—Sophie Kaskel, a pianist and student of Adolph Henselt; "F. Meritis"—Mendelssohn; "Jeanquirit"—Stephen Heller; "St. Diamond"—Anton von Zuccalmaglio; and, of course, "Florestan-Eusebius-Raro" for Schumann's double nature and its synthesis into a single being);[38] others, in contrast, are at least partly fictional ("Hector," "Ambrosia," "Beda").[39] The procedure of assigning such pseudonyms stems directly from Schumann's decision, on his twenty-first birthday, to give his friends "more beautiful and more fitting names"; Lühe and Clara already appear at that point as "Rentmeister Juvenal" and "Cilia," respectively.[40] Thus through the medium of the Davidsbund, Schumann found a means of transforming this confessional practice into a critical one, of converting "poetry" into "truth."

Soon after the members of Schumann's band made their public debut in Herlosssohn's *Komet,* preparations for the appearance of the *Neue Zeitschrift* went into high gear. On 19 March 1834, Schumann announced confidently to his mother: "Apart from the advantages for my intellectual development, I believe a great success is in store." The contract establishing the journal was drafted exactly a week later. Titled the *Neue Leipziger Zeitschrift für Musik,* and thus emphasizing its origination in a city known throughout the German lands as a center for liberal thought,[41] the journal was slated to appear twice weekly. Its editorial board, in whose hands the contract vested chief control, was comprised of Knorr, Schumann, Schunke, and Wieck, while Christian Hartmann, a local book-dealer, served as publisher.[42] In addition, the document included stipulations for the payment of the editors (10 thalers for the first 500 copies sold), the annual subscription price (2 thalers), an honorarium for Julius Knorr, who at first acted as editor-in-chief (25 thalers quarterly), weekly meetings of the editorial staff, and the nullification of the contract if, after a year, 500 subscribers could not be found.[43]

On 3 April 1834, a little over a year after Schumann first seriously considered launching a musical journal, the first issue of the *Neue Zeitschrift* appeared. Its prospectus, printed as the lead item in the issue, promised much: "theoretical and practical articles," "belletristic pieces" (short tales on musical subjects), "critiques of the imaginative products of the present," "miscellanies" (passages on musical subjects culled from the writings of figures such as Goethe, Jean Paul, Heine, and Novalis), accounts of musical life by correspondents in the chief European musical centers, and a chronicle devoted to announcements of significant musical events. As time would tell, Schumann's journal by and large lived up to this promise. So too did it live up to its title as a fundamentally "new" journal for music. Not only did its independence from an established music-publishing firm (unlike the *Allgemeine musikalische Zeitung,* the *Berliner Allgemeine Musikzeitung, Cäcilia,* and *Iris,* the journalistic arms of Breitkopf und Härtel, Schlesinger, Schott, and Trautwein, respectively) ensure an impartial critique of the musical scene, it aimed at and often achieved an all-encompassing view of that scene. With representatives in Paris, London, Vienna, Berlin, St. Petersburg, and Naples (not to mention a healthy interest in the musical goings-on in Poland, Hungary, Belgium, and even the United States and South America), the journal provided a breadth of coverage unparalleled by any of its competitors. As Schumann wrote in the 1834 prospectus: "Whoever wants to investigate the artist should visit him in his workshop. It also seemed necessary to create a medium that would stimulate him to have an effect, beyond that of his direct sphere of influence, through the printed word."[44] Universal in content and scope, the *Neue Zeitschrift* did indeed provide just such a medium.

By Schumann's account, the project got off to an auspicious start; on 2 July he boasted to his mother that 300 of the requisite 500 subscribers had been found. But the same letter likewise makes clear that within months of the journal's founding, Schumann was shouldering most of the editorial responsibilities. "*I must dedicate my whole energy to the journal,*" he stated emphatically, "one can't depend on the others. Wieck is always on tour, Knorr is ill, [and] Schunke doesn't handle a pen very well."[45] What's more, strife had already broken out among the ranks; in a probable reference to late spring 1834, the Vienna précis alludes to "arguments with Wieck and the other editors." Further disagreements, coupled with Schunke's death in December, led to the "complete dissolution of the entire circle" by the end of the year.[46] The files of Heinrich Conrad Schleinitz, a lawyer retained by Hartmann late in 1834, help us to fill in some of the gaps regarding the near collapse of the venture. Hartmann took advantage of a dispute with Knorr (who wanted to print an infamatory declaration against Wieck in spite of the publisher's objections) to stage a kind of palace coup. Hoping to make the *Neue Zeitschrift* into a more conventional publication and thereby increase sales, Hartmann sought out legal counsel in an attempt to gain editorial control over the journal. His plans were foiled, however, by Schumann's return to Leipzig in mid-December from a more than month-long stay in Zwickau and nearby Asch. By the day before Christmas, Schumann had negotiated a new contract (which he may have drafted himself), thereby acquiring sole ownership of the journal for 350 thalers payable to Hartmann. Within a week, he found a new publisher, the book-dealer Wilhelm Ambrosius Barth.[47] Alluding to his resolution of the crisis in the 1854 Introduction to his collected writings, Schumann spoke of the takeover of the journal by "the visionary of the group, who up to then had spent less of his time with books than in a dreamy reverie at the piano."[48] Yet Schumann's actions in December 1834 demonstrate that this visionary could be a shrewd businessman when the need arose, and also that he well knew how to put his spotty legal training to good use when the survival of his journal was at stake. Not surprisingly, the reorganization of the journal's directorship further exacerbated the already strained relations among some of the Davidsbündler. A particularly unpleasant episode ensued with Knorr, who threatened to take legal action over the payment of 25 thalers owed him for his (less than efficiently executed) editorial work in the last quarter of 1834. But on 20 July 1835, the day before he was scheduled to appear in court, Schumann settled the matter through Schleinitz.[49]

The first issue of the newly constituted journal appeared on 2 January 1835. While Schumann was certainly interested in preserving an image of continuity for his readers, subtle changes in focus indicate his equally strong desire both to broaden and to sharpen the original intent of the undertaking. Previously titled the *Neue Leipziger Zeitschrift für Musik,* the journal was henceforth issued simply as the *Neue Zeitschrift für Musik,* the elimination of *Leipziger* probably geared to ward off suspicions of parochialism. In the same spirit, Schumann added two cities, Prague and Weimar, to the list of centers whose musical activities would be regularly covered and struck the clause from the April 1834 prospectus concerning the journal's "special emphasis on reviews of piano compositions." And as we will see, Schumann's New Year's editorial for the January 1835 issue brought into relief the philosophical underpinnings of the Davidsbund's critical program.

While Schumann's activities in 1834 were dominated by his work for the *Neue Zeitschrift,* the same year brought important developments in his personal life. The founding of the journal in April roughly coincides with his meeting Ernestine von Fricken, a young woman from Asch (a village on the Bavarian-Bohemian border) whom the Wiecks had met after one of Clara's performances in Plauen, and who came to Leipzig for piano lessons with Wieck beginning on 21 April 1834. (Although Schumann did not know it at the time, she was the illegitimate daughter of Captain I. F. von Fricken, who adopted her only on 12 December 1834). According to the Vienna précis, Schumann's relationship with Ernestine intensified so rapidly over the course of the summer that by September they were engaged; visits to her hometown followed in October and December.[50]

Little wonder, then, given his all-consuming efforts on behalf of the *Neue Zeitschrift* and the complications in his private life, that Schumann's compositional productivity slackened considerably in 1834. A set of piano variations on Chopin's Nocturne, op. 15 no. 3 (preserved, in a fair copy, through the middle of the fifth variation) occupied him late in the year, but was never seen through to publication.[51] Intermittent work on the F#-minor Sonata is likewise a possibility. The remainder of what little composing Schumann did manage was associated with Ernestine (the dedicatee of the Allegro, op. 8) and her father. While in Zwickau in December, he began on **Carnaval,** its celebrated three- and four-note "themes," or "Sphinxes," as Schumann called them, derived from the letters ASCH. At the same time, he set to work on the **Etudes Symphoniques,** an extended cycle of variations on a theme by Captain von Fricken.[52] But in the months before, the writerly side of Schumann's creativity surely had the upper hand.

HISTORY, POETRY, AND MUSIC CRITICISM

Writing in 1838, Schumann called the year 1834 "the most important in my life."[53] No doubt its importance was closely linked with the founding of the *Neue Zeitschrift,* the refinement of the Davidsbündler idea, and the cultivation of a brand of music criticism quite unlike that encountered in any of the other journals of the day. The designation of Schumann's writings, in the title of this chapter, as music criticism "in a new key" is justified by two features in particular. In the first place, although Schumann's knowledge of the facts of music history was quite limited, especially before 1840, he had already as a young law student in Heidelberg evolved a philosophy of history, a systematic framework for the evaluation of temporally discrete cultural phenomena.[54] This historical outlook pervades his writings at practically every turn. Second, Schumann was keenly aware of an obvious problem posed by the concept of music criticism itself, namely, its employment of a verbal medium to describe and evaluate tonal events. His highly idiosyncratic, but always engaging "poetic" criticism emerged as a response to this dilemma.

Nowhere did Schumann articulate his philosophy of music history more clearly than in his New Year's editorial for the 2 January 1835 issue of the *Neue Zeitschrift,* the lead essay in the first issue of the journal to appear under his sole editorship:

> In the short period of our activity, we have acquired a good deal of experience. Our fundamental attitude was established at the outset. It is simple, and runs as follows: to acknowledge the past and its creations, and to draw attention to the fact that new artistic beauties can only be strengthened by such a pure source; next, to oppose the recent past as an inartistic period, which has only a notable increase in mechanical dexterity to show for itself; and finally, to prepare for and facilitate the advent of a fresh, poetic future.[55]

According to this scheme, the past is a nurturing source for the present; the present a site of imperfection; and the future a poetic age toward which the imperfect present should aspire. Past, present, and future are not so much discrete categories as they are mutually interdependent phases in a teleological sequence. Schumann's care in designating these phases underscores the point. He does not refer to the past as *Vergangenheit,* a term implying definitive closure, finality, even death, but rather as *die alte Zeit* (the bygone age), thus implying that the past should continue to inform the present. It is rather the present, or at least those aspects of the musical present concerned with "mechanical dexterity" and little more, that Schumann designates as *die letzte Vergangenheit* (the recent past). Born under the star of death, the "inartistic" products of those who cater to the fad for empty virtuosity are doomed to oblivion. And to highlight the parallels between past and future, Schumann altered "junge, dichterische Zukunft" (fresh, poetic age) to read "neue, poetische Zeit" (new, poetic age) in the 1854 collected edition of his writings.[56] Only the past ("die alte Zeit") and the future are "ages," *Zeiten,* while the present is continually consumed by the fleeting moment.[57]

We may thus think of Schumann's view of music history as a "triadic" one. On 16 August 1828, he writes: "Love the past, act in the present, and fear the future. In this way a beautiful harmony, a powerful triad comes into being." Speaking through Eusebius in the **Denk- und Dichtbüchlein** of 1834, he takes the notion of temporal succession as harmonic construct a step further, and emphasizes the transitional function of the present: "Triad=[historical] epochs. The [interval of a] third, as present, mediates the past and future."[58] In this, Schumann's philosophy of history discloses an affinity with the outlook of the Jena Romantics in general and Friedrich Schlegel in particular. For Schlegel, too, criticism must be firmly grounded in a historical framework. And Schlegel's ideas, like Schumann's, derive their unity from the tripartition of this framework, which comprises a body of revered, "classical" texts, a critique of contemporary conditions, and a "redemptive" phase in the future.[59]

Schumann's tripartite scheme allowed him to view music history not as an undifferentiated continuum, but far more as a series of interlocking periods. Though he hardly subscribed to a rigid opposition of "classic" and "romantic" phases—much less to the crass notion that romanticism represented a reaction against classicism—he did, for instance, situate Beethoven's Ninth Symphony at the "turning point from a classical to a romantic period" in a letter of 18 August 1834 to Anton Töpken.[60] By the end of the decade, he had both refined and expanded his periodization of music history. Based largely on his reading of Wilhelm Christian Müller's *Ästhetisch-historische Einleitung in die Wissenschaft der Tonkunst* (Leipzig, 1830), Schumann's **Chronologischer Geschichte der Musik** (**Chronological History of Music**) includes twenty pages of tables and brief descriptions of the highlights in the development of musical genres, instruments, notation, and aesthetics. In a summary of the chief events in music history from 1200 B.C. (!) to the present, Schumann divides this three-thousand-year span into ten periods (*Zeiträume),* each of the later phases an outgrowth of its predecessor. While the art of counterpoint entered a crisis phase in the fifteenth century, given the "overly artificial" approach of figures such as Ockeghem (Schumann writes "Ockenheim"), it attained a new and less mannered significance in the sixteenth century with Willaert and Lassus. Schumann in turn designates his seventh period, 1700-1750, as an era of "melodic counterpoint," its chief proponents including Porpora, Telemann, and of course, J. S. Bach. Then from 1775 to 1800 comes the "period of universality," the age of Haydn and Mozart, characterized by the "development of melody and melodic harmony," and the "unity of art, imagination, and thoughtful congeniality." Finally, the tenth period (1800 to the present) marks the "summit of musical art" in figures such as Beethoven and Schubert, whose works represent the fulfillment of the aspirations of previous ages.[61] Music history is thus construed not only as a succession of great men, but also as the logical progression of stylistic trends embodied in their works.

At the same time, music-historical progress, for Schumann, was not a purely continuous phenomenon. Its potential leaps and reversals come into play in his view of the relationship between Bach and the talented representatives of Schumann's own generation. "The profound combinatorial power, the poetry and the humor of modern music," he wrote to Gustav Keferestein on 31 January 1840, "have their origin mainly in Bach: Mendelssohn, [William Sterndale] Bennett, Chopin, Hiller, the whole of the so-called romantic school (of course I have the Germans in mind) are much closer than Mozart was to the music of Bach; indeed they all know his work thoroughly. I too make my daily confession to his lofty one, and strive to purify and strengthen myself through him."[62] Just as Schumann and his colleagues drew liberally on Bach's example, the latter's achievements were viewed as premonitions of the present and future. This mode of thought would allow Schumann to make the startling assertion that "most of Bach's fugues are character pieces of the highest kind; some of them are truly poetic creations, each of which requires its own expression, its own lights and shades."[63] As indicated in the letter to Keferstein, Mozart stands fundamentally apart from this line of influence. In an 1834 review of Hummel's *Studien,* op. 125, Schumann also maintained: "Cheerfulness, repose, grace, the characteristics of the artworks of antiquity, are also those of Mozart's school. Just as the Greeks gave their thundering Zeus a cheerful expression, so too does Mozart restrain his lightning bolts."[64] Hence Mozart's music partakes of the dialectical synthesis of opposites that Schumann, in a diary entry of 7 July 1831, associated with classical art and which he defined as: "the ingenious in the guise of the folk-like, the unfathomable in the guise of thrifty affluence, infinity of content in a beautifully rounded form, boundlessness in graceful limitation, the ponderous in the guise of the facile, darkness in luminous clarity, the corporeal inspirited, the real ennobled through the ideal."[65] In Schumann's estimation, then, the most promising trends in the musical present derive their inspiration less from the immediately preceding "period of universality" than from the blend of melody and counterpoint that dominates the music of the first half of the eighteenth century.

Schumann was similarly convinced that portions of Beethoven's output, like Bach's, would make their most profound impact only gradually. This was especially so of the late quartets, works "for whose greatness no words can be found," and which appeared to Schumann, "next to some of the choruses . . . of J. S. Bach, to represent the extreme limits that human art and imagination have yet reached."[66] Among his contemporaries, Schumann saw Hermann Hirschbach as one of the few who had seriously confronted this difficult music. Reviewing Hirschbach's *Lebensbilder in einem Cyklus von Quartetten,* op. 1, in 1842, Schumann asserted: "Beethoven's last quartets serve him as the starting point for a new poetic era."[67] True, Hirschbach's quartets have long since disappeared from the standard repertory, but the general thrust of Schumann's remarks on the reception of Beethoven's late quartets has been borne out by the passage of time: as sources of compositional inspiration, these works skipped not one but several generations.

Of course, Schumann's judgments of the artworks of the past frequently misfired. Domenico Scarlatti's keyboard sonatas, he wrote, occupied an important place in the repertory, but "how clumsy their form, how undeveloped their melody, how limited their modulation!"[68] And as for Haydn: "One can no longer learn anything new from him; he is like a familiar friend of the house who is always greeted with pleasure and respect, but is of no further interest for the present day."[69] But on the whole, Schumann's flexible view of music history as a process marked by continuities and discontinuities should strike us as remarkably prescient.

Just as intriguing as his conception of the relationships between past and future is Schumann's diagnosis of the present. No historicist, he remained firmly committed to the here-and-now and its special problems. He emphasized this stance in an aphorism from one of the 1834 issues of the *Neue Zeitschrift*: "*critics should engage themselves with the recent activity of the young creative spirits,* rather than dawdle over past love affairs. Fashionable withdrawal into the past or pedantic clinging to antiquated customs or dreaming about youthful infatuations is of no use. Time marches on, and we must march with it."[70]

On more than one occasion, Schumann appeared to contradict himself in evaluating the central term in his triadic historical scheme. In the 1835 New Year's editorial, for instance, he brands the present as an age of decline, but in the *Chronologischer Geschichte* drafted several years later, he designates it as the "summit of musical art." Yet Schumann had not made an abrupt volte-face in the intervening years. The apparent contradiction is far more a result of his recognition of the complexities and contradictions in current musical life. Indeed, the present as Schumann saw it was not characterized by a single, overriding trend, but by three distinct forces, each corresponding to one of the phases in his tripartition of historical time as a whole. The present thus reflects, in microcosm, the entire span of music history. (Just as Schumann's musical output enfolds smaller systems within larger ones, so too does his philosophy of history.) Schumann accords this view a decidedly political slant in **"Der Psychometer"** (1834), where he suggests that his contemporaries can be placed into three "parties": "classicists," "justemilieuists," and "romantics."[71] He elaborates on this division in a review of Johann Kalliwoda's overtures:

> The present is characterized by its political parties. Like their political counterparts, musical parties can be divided into liberal, middle-of-the-road, and reactionary, or romantic, modern, and classic. On the right sit the old-timers, the contrapuntists, the anti-chromaticists, on the left the young newcomers, the Phrygian hotheads, those who scorn formal strictures, the impudent geniuses, among whom the Beethovenians are most conspicious. In the juste-milieu, old and young commingle. This group is responsible for most of the products of the age, the creations of the moment, brought forth here only to be destroyed.[72]

Both "classicists" and "juste-milieuists" belong to what Schumann called *die letzte Vergangenheit,* the recent, but moribund past. (The **Chronologischer Geschichte** implicitly locates composers such as Czerny, Bellini, and F. W. Pixis in this category).[73] Only the romantics, those capable of transforming past practice into something fundamentally new, will at once survive the present and point the way toward the "new poetic age." To be sure, Schumann was circumspect in his employment of the term "romantic," probably because it was often used by his opponents (for example, Gottfried Fink, the editor of the rival *Allgemeine musikalische Zeitung*) as a term of derision for the very principles that the *Neue Zeitschrift* sought to promote.[74] Although by 1837 Schumann claimed to be "heartily sick of the word 'romantic'," he nonetheless found in it an apt designation for the younger generation of composers—Bennett, Chopin, Stephen Heller, Adolf Henselt, Ferdinand Hiller, Mendelssohn, Schunke, Wilhelm Taubert—who, like himself, combined an abiding respect for tradition with an equal commitment to the cause of musical progress.[75]

Given the flooding of the market with compositions of negligible worth, Schumann the critic was principally interested in the works of genuinely talented composers. Responding in the 1835 New Year's editorial to those who found his journal's editorial policy exclusionary, Schumann asserted that there were many items "that simply don't exist so far as criticism is concerned," and even proposed "stereotypical," prefabricated reviews for pieces by one of the three "archenemies" of art: the "untalented," the "cheap talents," and the "prolific scribblers."[76] Simply put, only art could supply an appropriate object for Schumann's criticism. This is the sense behind Florestan's exhortation for his cohorts to root out mediocrity in the cultural life of the present: "Assembled Davidsbündler, youths and men alike, prepare to slay the Philistines, musical and otherwise."[77] Yet it is important to bear in mind that he hardly viewed the artistic products of even the most gifted of his contemporaries—the young romantics—as embodiments of perfection: they lay claim to neither the impeccable craftmanship of Bach nor the Olympian grace of Mozart. When asked to evaluate E. Güntz's recently published set of *Tänze* for piano, the psychometer offers a mixed review: "Does he show outstanding talent?"—"I think so"; "Has he founded a school?"—"no"; "Should he have withheld his work?"—"certainly"; "To which party does he belong?"—"romantic." The fantastic machine goes on to say: "[Güntz] feels deeply, but for the most part incorrectly—in spite of isolated flashes of moonlight, he fumbles in the dark; while now and again he seizes a flower, he also grasps at straw . . . his aim is well-meaning, though like unpracticed marksmen, he fires with his eyes closed." But still—and here we come to the crucial point—the psychometer would prefer to deal with a "scattershot, poetic hobgoblin" such as this than with "a dozen dim-eyed, pointy-nosed pedants."[78] Long forgotten today, Güntz is nonetheless representative of the ambivalent status of the "romantic school" as a whole: their works are imperfect but hold out much promise for the "new poetic age" to come. Even those compositions that "distinguish themselves through only one tiny felicitous trait," Schumann wrote in his 1835 editorial, would be considered for review.[79] In this too, Schumann's critical attitude bears comparison with that of the Jena Romantics. As Friedrich Schlegel maintained in an essay entitled "On the Limits of the Beautiful" (1794): "Our failings themselves are our hopes, for they arise from the supremacy of the understanding, whose perfection, while slow to come, knows no bounds."[80]

Schumann recognized both the positive and negative aspects of the music of his day, but the truly radical quality of his criticism lies in its willingness to acknowledge that even the latter offered a measure of hope for the future. For example, we may consider his reactions to three of the most prominent characteristics of the recent compositional scene: the surfeit of light, even "trivial" music, the tendency toward fragmentation, and the demise of the classical forms.

The waltzes of Johann Strauss (Senior) might not attain the same heights as a Bach fugue, but it is still important for a young composer to know them, for, as Schumann maintained, Strauss may well be the most representative figure of his time. Schumann further prized Strauss's dances for their naturalness, their lack of affectation, their easy-going grace and charm, qualities

toward which compositions in the more serious genres should aim. In an 1837 review of Mendelssohn's Preludes and Fugues for Piano, op. 35, he expressed this thought in extreme terms: "the best fugue will always be the one that the public mistakes for a Strauss waltz, in other words, where the artistic roots are concealed like those of a flower, so that we only perceive the blossom."[81] And just as fugues should strive for the elegance of waltzes, so too can the waltz and other dances, when infused with wit and irony, serve as the basis for the poetic character piece. Schumann's own *Papillons* and *Intermezzi* readily come to mind.

Schumann's ambivalent attitude toward the present—as an imperfect but perfectible age—is most apparent in his writings on the musical miniature. Speaking through his Florestan persona in 1834, he chides the philistines for "turning up their noses" at aphorisms, musical and otherwise, since after all, "isn't life itself patched together from half-torn pages?" But in the same year he cautions the pianist and composer Joseph Kessler against "seeking refuge in the miniature." Interestingly enough, Schumann's skepticism regarding the musical fragment intensified over the course of the 1830s, precisely when he was composing some of the most enduring keyboard miniatures of all time. In 1839 he exhorts Henselt to turn away from the smaller forms and toward the "higher genres" such as the sonata and concerto, but then, in an 1842 critique of Ludwig Berger's songs, returns to his earlier position: "One should not undervalue such short pieces. A certain breadth of foundation and a commodious structure . . . may elicit praise for an endeavor. But there are tone-poets who can say in minutes what others need hours to express."[82] As we will see in the following chapter, the dichotomy in Schumann's thinking on the fragment is reflected in the dialectic between smaller and larger forms played out in his own compositions of the 1830s.

The sorry state of the "classical" forms during the same period provided another cause for Schumann's anxiety as critic. The "most brilliant period of the variation," he feared, was drawing to a close; younger composers treated the sonata as a variety of academic exercise, while older composers avoided the genre altogether; the concerto was in serious danger of becoming obsolete; and composers of symphonies were, for the most part, content to write pale imitations of Beethoven.[83] But there was a positive side to this tale of decline, for Schumann recognized that while the older forms were on the wane, newer ones were emerging to take their place: the variation was giving way to the more freely conceived capriccio; the sonata to the fantasy and ballade; the three-movement concerto to a composite, one-movement form; and the traditional symphony to more rhapsodic conceptions, such as Berlioz's *Symphonie fantastique*.[84] Moreover, the alternation of decay and rebirth was a perfectly natural process. The sonata, Schumann noted in 1839, "has practically run out its life course, but this is indeed in the order of things, for rather than repeat the same forms for centuries, we should be intent on creating new ones instead."[85] The positive light in which Schumann casts the negative moments embedded in the music of his day underscores the teleological thrust of his thinking. As he put it in an aphorism from the *Denk- und Dichtbüchlein* (1833/34), "criticism should rush ahead of the sinking present and at the same time fight it off from the vantage-point of the future."[86] The critic who wages this battle is also a historian, "a prophet facing backward" in Friedrich Schlegel's suggestive formulation.[87]

In addition to its deep engagement with history, Schumann's criticism is notable for a poetic quality quite unlike that in any earlier writings on music. But what may first strike us as florid excess is in fact a solution to an acute problem: that of forging a specifically romantic music criticism. Like the Jena Romantics, Schumann displayed an antipathy toward the normative approach to criticism as often practiced in the eighteenth century. According to the early nineteenth-century view, the critic was neither a judge nor a dispenser of rigid, formal laws, but rather a kind of poet. As Friedrich Schlegel maintained, "the true critic is an author to the second power."[88] Insofar as "poetry can only be criticized by way of poetry," the critic ensures the continued growth of the literary canon itself.[89] Through criticism the romantic dreamer, who turns out to be not so dreamy after all, finds a means of putting his or her reflections to productive use. According to Novalis's even more radical presentation of the same conceit, the critic provides not just a complement but an actual completion of the literary artwork.[90] Untiring in his efforts to make musical journalism into an intellectually respectable enterprise, Schumann shared in these views. But at the same time, he recognized the obvious discrepancy between musical and verbal discourse. The principal objects of his attention were not literary texts but musical works whose "criticism" by way of other musical works was possible only in a metaphoric sense. Hence his crusade against philistinism takes up the tone, style, and even the form of early romantic literary-philosophical criticism, but derives its content from the musical phenomena under consideration. The result is the inimitably "poetic" criticism with which Schumann made his mark as a writer on music.

Two features more than any others account for the poetic quality of Schumann's criticism: its attempt to evoke the spirit of the musical work that called it forth and its reliance on a fanciful perspectival technique. In his articulation of the critical ideal in an 1835 review of Hiller's *Etudes*, op. 15, Schumann wrote: "we recognize the highest criticism as that which leaves an impression similar to the one evoked by the motivating original." On this view, the critic neither replicates, de-

scribes, nor passes judgment on the artwork, but rather responds to it with a "poetic counterpart" *(poetische Gegenstück),* that is, with another artwork in its own right.[91] In 1828, Schumann had done just this in the closing portion of the **"Tonwelt"** essay, a prose poem titled **"Beethoven,"** its high-flown language intended to call up the feelings inspired by the composer's music: "All my desires and cravings were quelled—a deep stillness, a great waveless ocean! Formless spirit shadows in clear white garments like distant sails pressed toward their homeland."[92] In Schumann's writings of the 1830s, Eusebius is largely responsible for effusions of this sort, though Florestan too can rise to poetic heights. On one occasion, Raro even praises him for offering, instead of a judgment, an "image" *(Bild),* a metaphoric account "through which understanding is more easily attained than through technical-artistic expressions that remain incomprehensible to the musically uneducated."[93] Serving a similar purpose is Florestan's recounting of a "scenario" for Beethoven's Seventh Symphony he had read in *Cäcilia,* where the work is said to recall the "merriest of peasant weddings."[94]

Yet the critic must be more than a crafter of images, since metaphors, suggestive though they may be, function as only one means toward understanding. To accommodate other approaches, Schumann developed a wide array of perspectival techniques. In the Introduction to the 1854 collected edition of his writings, he provides a succinct rationale for the strategy: "In order to express different points of view on artistic matters, it seemed appropriate to invent contrasting artist-characters, of whom *Florestan* and *Eusebius* were the most important, with Master *Raro* occupying a mediating position between them."[95] Therefore Florestan and Eusebius, who constitute the flipsides of the double nature that Schumann hoped to resolve through a character like Raro, function as spokesmen for the diverse voices competing for attention within the critic himself.

We can observe the technique at work in an 1834 review of Dorn's *Bouquet musical,* op. 10, a set of three character pieces for piano, each named after a flower: the narcissus, the violet, and the hyacinth. Eusebius begins by relating a conversation among the flowers on which he has eavesdropped, their speeches taking the form of Jean-Paulian polymeters: "What then did the hyacinth say?—She said 'My life was as beautiful as my end, because the most beautiful Lord loved and destroyed me.' But from the ashes sprang a flower that might console you."[96] Eusebius is endowed with the power to comprehend the secret language of the flowers; like the poet, he transmits the mysterious utterances of Nature in a form understandable to ordinary mortals. Yet his poetic language likewise makes a significant critical point. Since the "ashes" emerging from the flower are an emblem for the musical composition itself, he suggests that the artwork arises from a mysterious transformation of the natural object that inspired it. Then Florestan continues in a more prosaic vein, gently chiding Dorn for "placing such German flowers into French pots" (that is, giving his pieces French titles), and commenting, not without irony, on the implications of descriptive titles for the possible content of the pieces: "Perhaps the flower is as fragrant for the deaf as the tone is sonorous for the blind. The language translated here is so congenial and finely differentiated that there can be no thought of 'tone-painting.'"[97] In this way, Schumann illuminates the object of his critical attention from different but complementary angles. The ideal critic, he implies, must be both poet and pragmatist, dreamer and realist, Florestan and Eusebius.

Furthermore, if music critics are to arrive at informed conclusions about the artworks under consideration, they must possess a deep understanding of the workings of a composition and also of the relationships among compositions. "In music everything depends on the contextual position of the whole," Schumann asserted in an 1835 review of Joseph Kessler's works, "and this applies to [the relations between] the small and large scale, to the isolated artwork as much as to the artist's entire output."[98] In order to effect the shuttling back and forth from part to whole associated with the hermeneutic method, critics must also be analysts, even if they don't flaunt their skills for a reading public who may not have much knowledge of or interest in the nuts and bolts of musical composition (recall Raro's words of praise for Florestan's avoidance of "technical-artistic expressions").[99] While in the nineteenth century detailed analyses were mainly the province of learned theoretical tracts, such as Gottfried Weber's *Versuch einer geordneten Theorie der Tonsetzkunst* (1832), a work Schumann knew well,[100] Schumann's interest in the "contextual position" of parts within wholes implies that, for him, analysis too had a place in critical discourse. Indeed, in his review of Dorn's *Bouquet musical,* he follows Eusebius's poetic reading and Florestan's ironic rejoinder with an analytical account of the first piece in the set by "Rohr," who illustrates his comments on thematic relationships and unusual harmonies with musical examples.[101]

Even in his 1831 review of Chopin's Variations on "Là ci darem la mano," often viewed as the example par excellence of Schumann's emulation of Jean Paul's quirky prose style, music-analytical issues play a significant role. His "musico-aesthetic Opus 1 of 'epoch-making' importance"[102] aims in part to present Chopin as an individual who nonetheless belongs to a tradition embracing both Beethoven and Schubert. Hence intermingled with Florestan's account of the Variations as a wordless drama are observations touching on musical structure (the connection, or rather lack of connection, between the slow introduction and the rest of the work) and the affective logic of the overall tonal plan (which moves

from B♭ major to the parallel minor for Variation 5 and back to major for the Finale).[103]

But nowhere in Schumann's writings does analysis play such an extensive part as in his review of Berlioz's *Symphonie fantastique.* Published over six installments of the 1835 volume of the *Neue Zeitschrift,*[104] the review, by far Schumann's longest, falls into two parts: a "psychological" reading signed "Florestan" and a close analysis signed "R. Schumann." The former is a quasi-programmatic interpretation of the symphony as a reflection of the artist's life and his stormy relationship with his beloved, the latter, a consideration of form, "compositional fabric," the "specific idea" represented in the work, and "spirit." As in the Dorn review, though on a larger scale, the various perspectives complement one another. To take one example, Schumann's critique of Berlioz's program in the analytical portion of the essay resonates with Florestan's opening comments. In his discussion of the "specific idea" embodied in the *Symphonie fantastique,* Schumann argues that, on the one hand, programs are detrimental to the unfettered exercise of the listener's imagination while, on the other, people tend to worry too much about the capacity of music to represent thoughts and events: what counts is the intrinsic merit of the music. The second portion of the review, in other words, might be read as a gloss on the first, which, interestingly enough, Schumann omitted from the collected edition of his writings.

While the structure of the review, its bipartition into subjective/psychological and objective/analytical sections, recalls the similar division in E. T. A. Hoffmann's well-known account of Beethoven's Fifth Symphony,[105] Schumann's approach in the analytical portion recalls the strategies of the Jena Romantics. Just as Friedrich Schlegel, in his seminal critique of Goethe's *Wilhelm Meisters Lehrjahre,* had argued that the rhapsodic design of the novel was tempered by an artfully crafted web of topical relationships, so too does Schumann aim to demonstrate that the "formlessness" of the first movement of Berlioz's work is only an "apparent formlessness." While Berlioz seems to depart radically from the "older model" for opening movements, he merely reversed the order of themes in the reprise to produce a symmetrical and perfectly satisfying arch form.[106] Similarly, in the portion of his analysis devoted to "compositional fabric" (harmony, melody, continuity, workmanship, style), Schumann counters Fétis's disparaging appraisal of Berlioz's melodic and harmonic manner with a penetrating commentary on the work's harmonic freshness, syntactic freedom, and the logic of its thematic invention.[107] Thus, Schumann puts his analysis at the service of a higher goal: an argument for the grounding of Berlioz's work in a system of thoughtfully conceived musical relationships.[108]

The review culminates with a striking passage on the "spirit" that rules over form, matter (or "fabric"), and idea in Berlioz's *Symphonie fantastique*. Here Schumann synthesizes the psychological and analytical approaches developed thusfar, bringing them both together under the banner of his philosophy of history. The determination of the presence or lack of spirit in a musical composition is clearly a subjective activity, but given his objective look at the inner workings of Berlioz's symphony, Schumann is confident in asserting that it is indeed imbued with this quality. The work certainly has its flaws (Schumann reserves his harshest judgment for what he views as lapses of taste in the finale's representation of the witches' sabbath), but these flaws may well be inextricably linked to an age "that tolerates a burlesque of the *Dies irae*."[109] On Schumann's view, burlesque, parody, and irony are very much a part of the texture of the present; moreover, all of these categories have been given poetic expression in the writings of Heine, Byron, and Hugo. To deny them to contemporary poets and composers would be tantamount to setting ourselves against the times—a futile and foolish exercise. As an artist living in an imperfect but perfectible age, Berlioz should not be too harshly criticized for what he has failed to do but rather praised for what he promises to accomplish in the future, in the "new poetic age" toward which Schumann looked forward.[110]

As we will see, Schumann eventually came to view his journalistic undertakings as a noisome drain on his time and energy. Just under a decade after assuming full editorial control of the *Neue Zeitschrift,* he sold his share in the journal to Franz Brendel, ostensibly to pursue his compositional projects undistracted. But in the mid-1830s, Schumann's work as critic answered to a real need: it provided him with a means of mediating a longstanding inner struggle between his dual inclination toward music and poetry, thus serving as yet another manifestation of his attempt to approach all creative activity as a form of literature. Moreover, there is a fascinating give-and-take between Schumann the critic and Schumann the composer throughout the middle and later 1830s. Often his comments on the triumphs and failings of other artists amount to veiled critiques of his own compositional endeavors. And if much of Schumann's criticism reads like "poetry", so too can much of his music be interpreted as a kind of critique in sound, a point to which we will return in the following chapter.

Notes

1. *TB* [Schumann, R., *Tagebücher*] 1, pp. 417, 419.

2. Entries in what Schumann called a "kleines Tagebuch" cover the period 28 July 1836 to 28 October 1837; see *TB* 2, pp. 22-42.

3. *TB* 1, pp. 419-23.

4. See [Schumann, R.,] *Briefe, Neue Folge*, p. 537.

5. The case for a period of heated compositional activity in the first half of 1833 is further strengthened by the Vienna précis, where Schumann notes that immediately after drafting the *Impromptus* [26-30 May], he set to work on the F#-minor Sonata, and "more or less finished [it] up to the last part." See *TB* 1, p. 419.

6. This is one of the central arguments of Kapp's *Studien zum Spätwerk*; see, e.g., pp. 9, 32-34, 41, 57-58, 61-62.

7. *GS* [Schumann, R., *Gesammelte Schriften* . . .] 1, p. 63.

8. For a discussion of the Berlin sketch and transcriptions of the *Intermezzo* and several of the *Ritornelli,* see Boetticher, *Schumanns Klavierwerke* 1, pp. 87-90. A presumably later sketch, once part of a private collection in Munich, but now lost, also bears the title *Scenes musicales*; see Boetticher, *Schumanns Klavierwerke* 1, pp. 85-86.

9. Schumann, *Selbstbiographische Notizen,* ed. Schoppe.

10. For an excellent summary of the genesis of Schumann's themes, see Becker, "New Look," pp. 570-77. As Becker points out, the opening of Clara's theme bears an uncanny resemblance to a four-measure sketch drafted by Schumann on 30 September 1830 while en route from Paderborn to Detmold (see *TB* 1, p. 321). Since Clara's composition probably dates from 1831 (and since even if it dates from 1830, Schumann, who was in Heidelberg at the time, would not have seen it), Becker convincingly argues that after resettling in Leipzig in October 1830 Schumann may have shared his sketch with Clara, who then elaborated it as the theme of her *Romance*. As Becker also notes, "Clara's" theme was destined for a long history. When Clara and Brahms wrote variations on the fourth piece in Schumann's *Bunte Blätter,* op. 99—Clara's Variations, op. 20 (1853) were dedicated "to HIM," that is, Robert, while the manuscript of Brahms's Opus 9 (1854) refers to Variations on a "theme by HIM" and "dedicated to HER"—they both alluded to the theme of Clara's youthful *Romance* (see mm. 201-6 of Clara's Variations, and Variation 10, mm. 30-31, of Brahms's). Clara's theme, in other words, had evolved into an emblem for shared artistic ideals among the members of Schumann's circle.

11. The resemblance between Schumann's and Beethoven's variations was not lost on Liszt. See the comments on the *Impromptus* in his 1837 review of Schumann's Opp. 5, 11, and 14 for the *Gazette musicale,* reproduced in Wasielewski, *Schumann,* p. 521.

12. See *Selbstbiographische Notizen,* ed. Schoppe; and *TB* 1, p. 400. On Schumann's debt to Bach in

the *Impromptus,* see also Rosen, *Romantic Generation,* pp. 664-668. As Rosen points out, Schumann draws upon (but transforms) the tradition of the fugal gigue in the finale of the work.

13. To be sure, Schumann's revision of the *Impromptus,* published in 1850, in which he excised the rhapsodic No. 11 altogether and made the concluding references to Clara's theme more explicit, undercuts this interpretation. For a thorough account of the differences, great and small, between the two versions of the work, see Becker, "A Study of Robert Schumann's *Impromptus,*" and "A New Look," pp. 583-85. Becker makes a good case for the affective "imbalance" of the revision. In my view as well, the later version lacks the poetry of the original.

14. *TB* 1, p. 419.

15. *Ibid.*

16. [Schumann, R.,] *Jugendbriefe,* pp. 227-28. The last quotation, omitted from the *Jugendbriefe,* is cited from Ostwald, *Schumann: Inner Voices,* p. 103.

17. Litzmann, *Clara Schumann* 1, pp. 84-85. This letter, when considered along with Schumann's reference to his move from a fifth-floor to a ground-floor apartment, strengthens the conjecture that he may have contemplated suicide by flinging himself out of his apartment window on the "most frightful evening" of 17 October 1833; see *TB* 1, p. 419. Wasielewski notes, however, that while some individuals supported the claim, others denied it. See Wasielewski, *Schumann,* p. 11.

As we have already seen (Introduction, pp. 5-7), there is little evidence to support Ostwald's claim that "homosexual panic" hastened the onset of Schumann's illness. True, a group of "attractive young men," many of them eventual collaborators on his journal, had begun to gather around him, and to be sure, "revelry as well as rivalry" prevailed in that circle, but the composer's supposed "desire for intimacy with men" was probably more of a cultural than a sexual phenomenon. Cf. Ostwald, *Schumann: Inner Voices,* pp. 102-4.

18. These together with related symptoms (depression, anxiety, fear of death, physical weakness, trembling in the limbs, insomnia) would recur with greater intensity about a decade later. But the effects of the breakdown that Schumann suffered following his return from a Russian tour with Clara in 1844 would persist for almost three years. See *TB* 2, p. 396; Litzmann, *Clara Schumann* 2, p. 76; and Wasielewski, *Schumann,* p. 352.

19. *Jugendbriefe,* p. 227.

20. *TB* 1, p. 417.

21. See Schumann's letter to his mother of 28 June 1833, in *Jugendbriefe,* p. 209; and *TB* 1, p. 419.

22. Jansen, *Davidsbündler,* p. 53. See also *TB* 1, p. 420; and Schumann's Introduction to the collected editions of his writings (1854), in *GS* 1, p. 1.

23. *Jugendbriefe,* pp. 209ff. Likewise, Schumann was not indifferent to the possible material benefits of the enterprise. See the letter of 19 March 1834 to his mother (*Jugendbriefe,* p. 233): "Apart from honor and fame, I can also expect some profit [from the journal], so that you can really rest easier about my getting along in the future."

24. See Marc Andreae's Preface to Schumann, *Sinfonie G-moll für Orchester* (Frankfurt, London, New York: Litolff's Verlag/Peters, 1972).

25. *TB* 1, p. 419.

26. *Ibid.*

27. *Jugendbriefe,* p. 232.

28. *TB* 1, p. 420.

29. See Schumann's letter of 25 August 1834 to Henriette Voigt, in *Briefe, Neue Folge,* p. 55; and *TB* 1, p. 420.

30. *NZfM* [*Neue Zeitschrift für Musik*] 2 (1835), p. 146.

31. A somewhat abridged version of the article appears in *GS* 2, pp. 260-72.

32. See *TB* 1, pp. 339, 342-44, 379, 382; and Schoppe, "Schumanns frühe Texte," p. 13.

33. Schlegel, *Kritische Friedrich Schlegel Ausgabe* (cited hereafter as *KFSA*) 2, p. 271.

34. See the entry for 6 June 1831, in *TB* 1, p. 337.

35. Warrack, *Weber,* p. 104.

36. The leading lights of Leipzig's cultural elite belonged to the Tunnel über der Pleisse; other members whom Schumann knew well included the music dealer and publisher Friedrich Hofmeister, Karl Herlosssohn, and Heinrich Dorn. Although Schumann never joined the group, he did attend some of the functions it sponsored. A diary entry for January 1837, for example, reads: "Masked ball at the Tunnell" (*TB* 2, p. 31). For an excellent summary of the activities of the Ludlamshöhle, the Tunnel über der Spree, and the Tunnel über der Pleisse, along with an account of their relationship to Schumann's Davidsbund, see, Appel, "Schumanns Davidsbund," pp. 1-15.

37. *GS* 1, p. 2.

38. Letter of 14 September 1836 to Dorn, in *Briefe, Neue Folge*, p. 77.

39. There are some differences of opinion over the identities of the individuals masked by these Davidsbündler names. "Knif," for instance, may refer to Gottfried Fink, the editor of the rival *Allgemeine musikalische Zeitung* ("Knif" = "Fink" in reverse); or to Julius Knorr, who also appears in the *Neue Zeitschrift* simply as "Julius." Jansen (*Davidsbündler*, p. 31) held to the first view, Kreisig (*GS* 2, p. 460, note 520) to the second.

40. Entry for 8 June 1831, in *TB* 1, p. 339.

41. As Appel points out, Leipzig enjoyed a relatively loose enforcement of the censorship laws in the period after the enactment of the Carlsbad Decrees (1819); see "Schumanns Davidsbund," pp. 17-18.

42. In the months leading up to the founding of the journal, the makeup of the editorial committee underwent several changes. Schumann included Ortlepp, Wieck, and two unnamed music teachers among the journal's "directors" in a letter to his mother of 28 June 1833 (*Jugendbriefe*, p. 210); a week before the March 1834 contract was drawn up, he listed Ferdinand Stegmeyer (who, according to the final arrangements, was retained as a tie-breaker should the four editors fail to reach a concensus), Knorr, Schunke, Wieck, and himself as editors; see *Jugendbriefe*, p. 233, and Kross, "Aus der Frühgeschichte," p. 432.

43. The contract is reproduced in Kross, "Aus der Frühgeschichte," pp. 429-32.

44. *GS* 2, p. 273.

45. *Jugendbriefe*, p. 242.

46. *TB* 1, p. 420.

47. For a detailed account of the entire affair and a transcription of the 24 December 1834 contract, see Kross, "Aus der Frühgeschichte," pp. 426-29, 433-38.

48. *GS* 1, p. 1.

49. Kross, "Aus der Frühgeschichte," p. 445.

50. *TB* 1, pp. 420, 473 (notes 447, 448).

51. See Boetticher, *Schumanns Klavierwerke* 2, p. 47.

52. See Eismann, *Quellenwerk* 1, p. 124; and *TB* 1, pp. 420-21.

53. *TB* 1, p. 419.

54. See Plantinga, *Schumann as Critic*, pp. 82-85. Before the founding of the *Neue Zeitschrift* in 1834, Schumann is known to have studied two books dealing with music history: C. F. D. Schubart's *Ideen zu einer Aesthetik der Tonkunst* (1806), and Thibaut's *Über Reinheit der Tonkunst* (1825/26), both of them highly unreliable on matters of historical fact. Only around 1840, and perhaps under the influence of C. F. Becker, who reviewed publications on historical themes for the *Neue Zeitschrift*, did Schumann make a serious effort to improve his knowledge in this area. After selling the journal in 1844, he continued along the same course; among the entries in the *Lektürebüchlein* for 1847 are Forkel's biography of Bach, Mattheson's biography of Handel, and Kiesewetter's *Geschichte der Europaeisch-Abenalaendischen oder unsrer heutigen Musik* (1834/1846); see Nauhaus, "Schumanns *Lektürebüchlein*," pp. 71, 83. As Boetticher has pointed out, Schumann also read Baini's biography of Palestrina during this period; see *Schumann: Einführung*, pp. 291-292.

55. *NZfM* 2 (1835), p. 3.

56. *GS* 1, p. 60.

57. As early as May 1828 Schumann expressed the same conceit in even more starkly existential terms: "The past is the angel of destruction of the present, and every moment a victim of suicide, for a single beautiful moment kills not only itself but also millions of its future sisters." See *TB* 1, p. 89; and Mayeda, "Schumanns Gegenwart," p. 18.

58. *TB* 1, p. 110; and *GS* 1, p. 23.

59. See Szondi, "Friedrich Schlegel and Romantic Irony," pp. 57-59. For discussions of the points of contact between Schumann's thinking and Schlegel's, see Botstein, "History, Rhetoric," pp. 23-29; Dahlhaus, *Analysis*, p. 16; Dahlhaus, *Klassische und Romantische*, p. 260; and my *Nineteenth-Century Music*, p. 12. Other precedents for Schumann's philosophy of history include Heine's faith in a future informed by the spirit of progress (as articulated in *Zur Geschichte der Neueren Schönen Literatur in Deutschland* [1833]) and Jean Paul's conviction that the past and future can only be experienced poetically, as "memory" and "hope" (see "Über die Realität des Ideals" from *Titan*, in [Paul, Jean,] *Jean Paul Werke* 3, p. 221). For further commentary on the relationships among Schumann, Heine, and Jean Paul, see Knepler, *Musikgeschichte*, p. 774; and Mayeda, "Schumann's Gegenwart," p. 13.

60. *Briefe, Neue Folge*, p. 52.

61. For excerpts from Schumann's *Chronologische Geschichte*, see Boetticher, *Schumann: Einführung*, pp. 291-92.

62. *Briefe, Neue Folge*, pp. 177-78. Schumann's reference to the "profound combinatorial power" of

Bach's music resonates with the critical categories of Jena Romanticism. For Friedrich Schlegel, the combinatorial power *par excellence* is *Witz* (wit), the faculty that allows us to discern similarities between apparently dissimilar entities. See, e.g., *Athenäum* Fragment 220 (*KFSA* 2, p. 200), *Ideen* Fragment 123 (*KFSA* 2, p. 268), *Philosophische Fragmente, Zweite Epoche II*, no. 729 (*KFSA* 18, p. 381), and especially the commentary on the literary fragment in *Lessings Gedanken und Meinungen* (*KFSA* 3, p. 83).

63. 1838 review of Czerny's edition of the *WTC*, in *GS* 1, p. 354.

64. *GS* 1, p. 9.

65. *TB* 1, p. 348.

66. *Leipziger Musikleben 1837/38*, in *GS* 1, p. 380.

67. *GS* 2, p. 74.

68. 1839 review in *GS* 1, p. 401.

69. 1841 review of the 13th through 16th subscription concerts of the Leipzig Gewandhaus Orchestra, in *GS* 2, p. 54. By the following year, Schumann had somewhat tempered this position. In a review of recently composed string quartets, he noted that while Hirschbach took Beethoven as his model, "many fruit-laden trees still stand in the gardens of Mozart and Haydn." *GS* 2, p. 75.

70. *NZfM* 1 (1834), p. 78.

71. *NZfM* 1 (1834), p. 62.

72. *NZfM* 1 (1834), p. 38. For further discussion of Schumann's politicization of the current musical scene, see Dahlhaus, *Nineteenth-Century Music*, 247-48; Dahlhaus, *Klassische und Romantische*, p. 261; and Knepler, *Musikgeschichte*, p. 773.

73. Boetticher, *Schumann: Einführung*, p. 292.

74. See Plantinga, *Schumann as Critic*, pp. 102-3.

75. Review of Heller's *Drei Impromptus*, op. 7, in *NZfM* 7 (1837), p. 70. Cf. also Schumann's 1839 New Year's editorial, *NZfM* 10 (1839), p. 1; and his letter to Keferstein of 31 January 1840, in *Briefe, Neue Folge*, pp. 177-78. As Plantinga further points out, Schumann and his confrères were often dubbed "*neo*romantics," a term emphasizing their position as restorers of tradition, by contemporary writers; see *Schumann as Critic*, p. 107.

76. *NZfM* 2 (1835), p. 3.

77. *Fastnachtsrede von Florestan*, in *NZfM* 2 (1835), p. 116.

78. *NZfM* 1 (1834), p. 63.

79. *Ibid.*, p. 4.

80. Schlegel, *KFSA* 1, p. 35.

81. *GS* 1, p. 252. See also "Etüden für das Pianoforte" (1839), *GS* 1, p. 76.

82. See *NZfM* 1 (1834), p. 151; *NZfM* 1 (1834), pp. 113-14; *NZfM* 10 (1839), p. 74; and *NZfM* 16 (1842), p. 174.

83. *NZfM* 5 (1836), p. 63; *NZfM* 10 (1839), p. 134; *NZfM* 10 (1839), p. 6; *NZfM* 11 (1839), p. 1.

84. *NZfM* 5 (1836), p. 63; *NZfM* 15 (1841), p. 141; *NZfM* 4 (1836); p. 163; *NZfM* 3 (1835), p. 33.

85. "Sonaten für Clavier," *NZfM* 10 (1839), p. 134.

86. *GS* 1, p. 30.

87. *Athenäum* Fragment 80, *KFSA* 2, p. 176.

88. *Philosophische Fragmente, Erste Epoche, II*, no. 927, *KFSA* 18, p. 106.

89. See *Kritische Fragmente* 117, *KFSA* 2, p. 183; and "Vom Wesen der Kritik" (1804), in *KFSA* 3, p. 55.

90. See Benjamin, *Begriff der Kunstkritik*, pp. 60-63.

91. *GS* 1, p. 44.

92. Otto, *Schumann als Jean-Paul Leser*, p. 75.

93. "Der Davidsbündler," *GS* 2, p. 263.

94. "An Chiara" (1835), *GS* 1, pp. 121-22.

95. *GS* 1, p. 2.

96. *Ibid.*, p. 13.

97. *Ibid.*, p. 14.

98. *Ibid.*, pp. 52-53.

99. For a discussion of the points of contact between hermeneutics and Schumann's critical strategies, see Bent, *Music Analysis* 2, pp. 122-23.

100. See the entry for 31 May 1831, in *TB* 1, p. 335.

101. *GS* 2, pp. 210-11.

102. Dahlhaus, *Nineteenth-Century Music*, p. 54.

103. The "first kiss," which Florestan locates in Variation 5, occurs in G♭ major, not B♭ major as he says. See *GS* 1, pp. 6-7.

104. *NZfM* 3 (1835), pp. 1-2, 33-35, 37-38, 41-51. For translations, see Cone, *Berlioz*, pp. 220-248; and Bent, *Music Analysis* 2, pp. 166-94.

105. Hoffmann's review, first published in 1810 in the *AmZ*, begins with a florid account of Beethoven's ability to awaken "just that infinite longing which is the essence of romanticism" and proceeds with

a demonstration of the thematic unity of the Fifth Symphony, supported by numerous musical examples. See Hoffmann, *Schriften* 5, pp. 34-51. Three years later, Hoffmann combined material from this review with another on Beethoven's piano trios, op. 70; the newly titled essay, "Beethovens Instrumentalmusik," was published in the *Zeitung für die elegante Welt.* The essay also appeared in the *Kreisleriana* section of the *Fantasiestücke in Callot's Manier* (1814-1815).

106. Cf. *NZfM* 3 (1835), p. 37; and the gloss on Schumann's analysis in Cone, *Berlioz,* pp. 250-261.

107. Though Fétis is not mentioned by name, Schumann published his 1 February 1835 review *(Revue musicale)* in the 19 and 23 June 1835 issues of the *Neue Zeitschrift* and thus knew it well. See Bent, *Music Analysis,* vol. 2, pp. 162-63.

108. As Bent also points out, it is remarkable that Schumann should have come to such insightful conclusions working from Liszt's piano transcription of the score alone. See Bent, *Music Analysis,* vol. 2, p. 161.

109. *NZfM* 3 (1835), pp. 50-51.

110. Berlioz was much heartened by Schumann's review. In a letter of 28 December 1836, he expressed his wish for a meeting with Schumann; this, however, did not take place until February 1843 (Boetticher, ed., *Briefe und Gedichte,* pp. 35ff. and 232ff.) As time went on, Schumann grew more uncertain of Berlioz's ability to make good on this promise. In an 1839 review of the *Waverley* Overture, he wrote: "If one traces the derivation of isolated thematic ideas, they often seem conventional, even trivial in themselves. But the whole exerts an irresistible charm on me, in spite of its assault on a German ear unused to such things. Berlioz reveals himself differently in all of his works and charts out new territory in each: it's difficult to know whether he should be called a genius or a musical adventurer." (*NZfM* 10 [1839], p. 187). Four years later, Schumann's reaction to Berlioz's music had cooled further: "At present, I confess, I would certainly be harsher with much of his work. The years make one more severe, and the unlovely things I found in Berlioz's earlier music . . . have not become more beautiful in the interim. But I also maintain that a divine spark resides in this musician." (*NZfM* 19 [1843], pp. 177-78).

Works Cited

Appel, Bernhard R. "Schumanns Davidsbund: Geistes- und sozialgeschichtliche Voraussetzungen einer romantischer Idee." *Archiv für Musikwissenschaft* 38 (1981): 1-23.

Becker, Claudia Stevens. "A New Look at Schumann's Impromptus." *Musical Quarterly* 67 (1981): 568-86.

———. "A Study of Robert Schumann's *Impromptus,* Op. 5: Its Sources and a Critical Analysis of its Revisions." D.M.A. diss., Boston University, 1977.

Benjamin, Walter, *Der Begriff der Kunstkritik in der deutschen Romantik.* 1919-20. Frankfurt: Suhrkamp, 1973.

Bent, Ian. *Music Analysis in the Nineteenth Century. Vol. 2, Hermeneutic Approaches.* Cambridge: Cambridge University Press, 1994.

Boetticher, Wolfgang. *Robert Schumann: Einführung in Persönlichkeit und Werk.* Berlin: Hahnefeld, 1941.

———. *Robert Schumanns Klavierwerke—Neue biographische und textkritische Untersuchungen, Teil I, Opus 1-6.* Wilhelmshaven: Heinrichshofen's Verlag, 1976.

———, ed. *Briefe und Gedichte aus dem Album Robert und Clara Schumanns.* Leipzig: VEB Deutscher Verlag für Musik, 1979.

Botstein, Leon. "History, Rhetoric, and the Self: Robert Schumann and Music Making in German-Speaking Europe, 1800-1860." In *Schumann and His World,* ed. R. Larry Todd. Princeton: Princeton University Press, 1994.

Cone, Edward T. *Berlioz: Fantastic Symphony* (Norton Critical Score). New York: Norton, 1971.

Dahlhaus, Carl. *Analysis and Value Judgment,* trans. Siegmund Levarie. New York: Pendragon, 1983.

———. *Klassische und Romantische Musikästhetik.* Laaber: Laaber Verlag, 1988.

———. *Nineteenth-Century Music,* trans. J. Bradford Robinson. Berkeley: University of California Press, 1979.

Daverio, John. *Nineteenth-Century Music and the German Romantic Ideology.* New York: Schirmer Books, 1993.

Eismann, Georg. *Robert Schumann: Ein Quellenwerk über sein Leben und Schaffen,* 2 vols. Leipzig: Breitkopf & Härtel, 1956.

Goethe, Johann Wolfgang von. *Wilhelm Meister's Apprenticeship,* ed. and trans. Eric A. Blackall. Vol. 9 of *Goethe's Collected Works.* New York: Suhrkamp, 1989.

Hoffmann, E. T. A. *Schriften zur Musik.* Munich: Winkler, 1977.

Jansen, Gustav. *Die Davidsbündler: Aus Robert Schumanns Sturm- und Drangperiode.* Leipzig: Breitkopf & Härtel, 1883.

Kapp, Reinhard. *Studien zum Spätwerk Robert Schumanns.* Tutzing: Schneider, 1984.

Knepler, Georg. "Robert Schumann." In *Musikgeschichte des 19. Jahrhunderts,* vol. 2. Berlin: Henschel Verlag, 1961.

Kross, Siegfried. "Aus der Frühgeschichte von Robert Schumanns Neuer Zeitschrift für Musik." *Musikforschung* 34 (1981): 423-45.

Litzmann, Berthold. *Clara Schumann: Ein Künstlerleben,* 2 vols. Leipzig: Breitkopf & Härtel, 1902 and 1905.

Mayeda, Akio. "Schumanns Gegenwart." In *Robert Schumann: Ein romantisches Erbe.* Mainz: Schott, 1984.

Nauhaus, Gerd. "Schumanns *Lektürebüchlein.*" In *Robert Schumann und die Dichter,* ed. Appel and Hermstrüwer. Düsseldorf: Droste Verlag, 1991.

Ostwald, Peter. *Schumann: The Inner Voices of a Musical Genius.* Boston: Northeastern University Press, 1985.

Otto, Frauke. *Robert Schumann als Jean Paul-Leser.* Frankfurt am Main: Herchen Verlag, 1984.

Paul, Jean. *Jean Paul Werke,* ed. Norbert Miller, 6 vols. Munich: Carl Hanser Verlag, 1960-63.

Plantinga, Leon. *Schumann as Critic.* New Haven: Yale University Press, 1967.

Rosen, Charles. *The Romantic Generation.* Cambridge: Harvard University Press, 1995.

Schlegel, Friedrich. *Kritische Friedrich Schlegel Ausgabe,* ed. Ernst Behler, Jean-Jacques Anstett, and Hans Eichner, 35 vols. Munich, Paderborn, Vienna: Schöningh, 1958-.

Schoppe, Martin. "Robert Schumanns frühe Texte und Schriften." *Robert-Schumann-Tage 1985,* ed. Günther Müller. Wissenschaftliche Arbeitstagung zu Fragen der Schumann-Forschung in Zwickau, 1985.

Schumann, Robert. *Briefe, Neue Folge,* 2d ed., ed. Gustav Jansen. Leipzig: Breitkopf & Härtel, 1904.

———. *Jugendbriefe,* 2nd ed., ed. Clara Schumann. Leipzig: Breitkopf & Härtel, 1886.

———. *Selbstbiographische Notizen—Faksimile,* ed. Martin Schoppe. Robert-Schumann-Gesellschaft [n.d.].

———. *Tagebücher, Band I: 1827-1838,* ed. Georg Eisman. Leipzig: VEB Deutscher Verlag für Musik, 1971.

———. *Tagebücher, Band II: 1836-1854,* ed. Gerd Nauhaus. Leipzig: VEB Deutscher Verlag für Musik, 1987.

Szondi, Peter. "Friedrich Schlegel and Romantic Irony, with Some Remarks on Tieck's Comedies." In *On Textual Understanding and Other Essays,* tr. Harvey Mendelssohn. Minneapolis: University of Minnesota Press, 1986.

Thibaut, Anton Friedrich. *Ueber Reinheit der Tonkunst,* 7th ed. Freiburg and Leipzig: Mohr, 1893.

Warrack, John. *Carl Maria von Weber,* 2d ed. Cambridge: Cambridge University Press, 1976.

Wasielewski, Wilhelm Joseph von. *Robert Schumann: Eine Biographie,* enlarged ed. Leipzig: Breitkopf & Härtel, 1906.

Weber, Gottfried. *Versuch einer geordneten Theorie der Tonkunst.* Mainz, 1817-21.

Eric Frederick Jensen (essay date 2001)

SOURCE: Jensen, Eric Frederick. "Schumann and Literature." In *Schumann,* pp. 39-57. New York: Oxford University Press, 2001.

[*In the following excerpt, Jensen explains how Schumann's literary erudition informed his critical style.*]

> The greatest pleasure in life is that of reading, while we are young.
>
> —Hazlitt, "Whether Genius is Conscious of Its Powers"

For much of the nineteenth century, the interest of composers not just in music but in all the arts was truly extraordinary. An interrelationship among the arts was commonly recognized. "The well-educated musician," wrote Schumann, "can study a Madonna by Raphael, the painter a symphony by Mozart, with equal benefit. Yet more: in sculpture the actor becomes a silent statue while he brings the sculptor's work to life—the painter transforms a poem into an image, the musician sets a painting to music."[1] Coupled with a broad interest in the arts was a preoccupation with the "extramusical" properties of music itself. It was a literary age, and program music flourished. That may, to a certain extent, help explain the interest many composers had in literature. Not a few were distinguished writers themselves: Berlioz as critic, essayist, and autobiographer; Liszt as critic and essayist; Wagner as dramatist, essayist, and theoretician; and Weber as critic and author of an unfinished novel.

Yet Schumann's passion for writing and his enthusiasm for literature set him distinctly apart. Until he was twenty, he was considering writing as a career. His diary and letters confirm his intentions and reveal a deliberately cultivated literary style. What makes Schumann's literary interests particularly intriguing is the close association in his mind of word with music. While still a student at the Lyceum in Zwickau, Schumann wrote an essay: **"On the Intimate Relationship between Poetry and Music."** Although a juvenile effort with little original thought, it indicates where his sympathies lay. In his diary for 1828, he wrote: "Tones are words, but on a higher level. . . . Music is the higher power of poetry; angels must speak in tones, spirits in words of poetry. . . . Every composer is a poet, only at a higher level."[2] It probably appeared natural to Schumann to associate composers with writers. "When I hear music by Beethoven," he noted, "it is as if someone were reading to me a work of Jean Paul. Schubert reminds me of Novalis."[3] Distinct similarities did not serve as the basis of Schumann's reactions; the resemblance between Schubert and Novalis, for example, is hardly striking. It was because of his enthusiasm for particular authors and composers that he was eager to couple them. This linking of poets and composers, however, was subject to change: "When I play Schubert," he wrote to Wieck on 6 November 1829, "it is as if I were reading a novel by Jean Paul."[4]

During the 1820s, music and poetry (word and tone) were interwoven for Schumann. It was a concept that, to a certain degree, he retained for years: one of the titles considered for the **Fantasie op. 17** (1836) was *Dichtungen (Poems)*. Believing himself gifted both as a writer and composer, the confusion and frustration he experienced in determining a choice of career could only have been compounded by the intimate association he perceived between the two arts. "If only my talents for poetry and music were concentrated in but *one* point," he confided to his mother.[5] It reveals much about Schumann that, in eventually choosing music as a career, in his own mind he was selecting an art that he believed to be more elevated—"at a higher level"—than poetry.

Schumann's love of the arts, and of literature in particular, owed much to his father, particularly August Schumann's work as a writer. Although he was a part-time writer, August Schumann was astonishingly prolific. It is possible to assign to him the authorship of nine substantial works of fiction—well over four thousand pages—between 1793 and 1800. Publications after 1800 are more difficult to trace, but at least three other novels appeared. His writings are representative of the popular literature of the day, for which there was a growing demand in the latter decades of the eighteenth and early nineteenth centuries. Preferred settings were the Middle Ages, or exotic locales such as India; there were inevitable struggles between good and evil, with often colorful villains and, working behind the scenes, secret societies reminiscent of freemasonry. With their fantastical settings and fanciful themes, novels of this type provided inspiration to writers such as Tieck, Arnim, Hoffmann, and Jean Paul.

There are no references in Schumann's diary and published correspondence to his father's work. Of the leading writers of popular literature—such as Christian August Vulpius, Christiane Benedicte Naubert, Heinrich Zschokke, or Carl Friedrich Grosse—mention is made only of Zschokke. But it is inconceivable that Schumann was unfamiliar with this more popular literature, including the work of his father. Insatiable reader that he was, he would have encountered popular literature at an early age, probably during adolescence. That may explain why his diary is silent on the matter: he did not begin keeping a diary until 1827, at which time his interests were directed toward more "serious" literature. That he was familiar with the popular literature of the day is best seen both in the style and content of his own writings, and by his admiration for Jean Paul—of all contemporary German writers perhaps the one most strongly indebted to popular literary styles.

Schumann's first efforts as a writer were poems. He began creating them in his early teens, and included examples in the two anthologies he assembled, *Blätter und Blümchen aus der goldenen Aue* (*Leaves and Little Flowers from the Golden Meadow*) (1823) and the *Allerley* (*Miscellany*) (1825-28). Yet another collection, *Einzelgedichte* (*Detached Poems*), primarily 1825-30, contained additional poetry, "polymeters" (poetic aphorisms in the style of Jean Paul), and notes about composers. "'**Melancholy at Evening**' was a poem where I first felt myself to be a poet," Schumann confided to his diary in 1828, "and tears came from my eyes as I wrote it."[6] Schumann's poetry from the time, however, is surprisingly stiff and conventional.

Although he continued to write poetry sporadically during his life—including the ballad **"The Bell of Ivan Veliky"** in 1844 during a visit to Moscow—he wrote far more prose. His early prose attempts are also derivative, and owe much to Jean Paul. The diary for August 1828 contains fragments from *Juniusabende und Julitage,* which he enthusiastically described as "my first work, my truest, and my most beautiful."[7] That autumn, excerpts from *Selene* as well as ideas for its content appear in the diary.[8] Both works are in the style of Jean Paul (who also wrote a *Selena*), and they bring to mind *The Invisible Lodge,* a work that itself is much indebted to the popular literature of the day. Schumann worked on *Selene* in November 1828 and had some unusual ideas for it: both Jean Paul and Prince Louis Ferdinand were to appear as characters.

Drama interested Schumann as well. He wrote "robber plays" (a popular genre of the time, owing much to the success of Schiller's *Die Räuber (The Robbers)*, and he acted in them. There are also references in Schumann's diary to the creation of two tragedies, one based on the life of Coriolanus and another on the political struggles of the Montalti family in fourteenth-century Genoa. As late as June 1831, he completed the first scene of a pro-jected drama based on the story of Abelard and Heloise.

In the 1830s, much of Schumann's writing was music criticism, especially for his own paper, the *Neue Zeitschrift für Musik* (*New Journal for Music*). But he still managed to find time to write fiction, although his attempts remained unpublished and incomplete. In 1831, he began work on a tale, **"The Philistine and the Rascal King"**; its title brings to mind fairy tales by Hoffmann or Eichendorff. Of particular interest is an eight-page fragment for a novel Schumann began at about the same time: ***Die Davidsbund*** (***The League of David***). This appears to be the same work referred to in his diary as **"Wunderkinder,"** whose characters were to include Paganini, Hummel, Wieck, and Clara, among others.

In many ways, Schumann's writing was a natural outgrowth of what he read. His passion for reading—no doubt encouraged by his father—began early. Over the years his diary, household books, and a special "reading notebook" attest to the breadth of his reading. It is truly astonishing. His knowledge of European literature was comprehensive and included not just poetry, drama, and fiction, but history and biography. Of foreign literature, nearly all was read in German translation. Although in school and on his own he studied Latin, Greek, French, Italian, and English, Schumann's grasp of foreign languages was limited.

From his study in school, Schumann acquired the expected familiarity with Roman and Greek classics, particularly Aeschylus, Euripides, and Sophocles; in 1825 he tried his hand at translating Anacreon, Homer, and Horace. Among European writers, Schumann read Calderón, Dante, Petrarch, Cellini, Pellico, Alfieri, Racine, Rousseau, Ponsard, Hugo, Sand, and Sue—although contemporary French writing tended to disturb him with what he perceived as its cheap sensationalism. Like his father, he was fond of English writers, Byron in particular. Other English writers with whom he was familiar include Goldsmith, Fielding, Burns, Shelley, Moore, Macaulay, Scott, and Bulwer-Lytton. American literature does not seem to have interested him greatly; he read *Uncle Tom's Cabin* and *Bracebridge Hall*, but Cooper—an author extremely popular in Europe at the time—is surprisingly absent.

Contemporary German writers held the greatest attraction for Schumann. References to the works of Immermann, Grillparzer, Goethe, Humboldt, Friedrich and August Wilhelm von Schlegel, Schiller, Tieck, Hauff, Arnim, Brentano, Geibel, Mörike, Uhland, Novalis, Platen, and Chamisso, as well as lesser-known writers, such as Hölty, Droste-Hülshoff, Ernst Schulze, Heinse, Seume, Herwegh, and Gutzkow, are found in Schumann's diary and household books. Frequently what he read influenced his musical direction. His fondness for the poetry of Justinus Kerner inspired his first songs (and in 1840 also served as the basis for the ***Zwölf Gedichte*** op. 35). In fact much of Schumann's reading of German poetry was with an eye toward its suitability for setting to music.

Friedrich Rückert was an early favorite, reverently described by Schumann as a "beloved poet, a great musician in words and thoughts."[9] Schumann set more than four dozen of Rückert's poems to music. His translations from Hariri (Rückert was an orientalist) served as inspiration for the collection of Schumann's four-hand piano pieces, ***Bilder aus dem Osten*** (***Pictures from the East***) op. 66; poems from his *Liebesfrühling* (***The Springtime of Love***) were selected and set to music by Schumann and his wife as a poetic and symbolic statement shortly after their marriage in 1840 (published as **op. 37**). A copy of the songs was sent to Rückert, who responded with a poem that delighted Schumann.

Of the many poets whose work he set to music, Rückert may have been Schumann's favorite. But because of the popularity of Schumann's ***Liederkreis*** **op. 24** and ***Dichterliebe*** (***A Poet's Love***) **op. 48,** the poetry of Heinrich Heine is probably most closely associated with him. When Schumann and Heine met in Munich in May 1828—their only meeting—Schumann had not set any of Heine's poetry and had yet to make music his career. In May 1840—the year in which Schumann wrote most of his lieder—he wrote to Heine in Paris (where Heine had moved), enclosing several of his settings of Heine's poetry. Schumann was hoping not only for a favorable reaction from Heine but to draw closer to him. But Heine never responded, and Schumann was offended. Although he continued to read Heine's new works, he was disgusted by Heine's *Romanzero*—probably by what he perceived as the excessively personal and often depreciative nature of the poetry in the collection.

Also closely associated with Schumann is the poetry of Josef von Eichendorff. Schumann's setting of selected poems by Eichendorff in the ***Liederkreis*** **op. 39** is one of remarkable sensitivity. Schumann described it as his "most Romantic" song cycle, a reference not to any love interest within the poetry, but to the emotional and dramatic intensity of many of the texts.[10] He always seemed eager to meet those poets whose writings he admired, curious to determine the association between the artist and his work (the two, Schumann felt, were closely related). He met Eichendorff on several occasions in January 1847. Eichendorff was twenty-two years older than Schumann, recently retired, and with musical interests (he played the violin). But although he professed "delight" with Schumann's settings of his poems, no intimacy resulted.

Schumann's meeting with Hans Christian Andersen—another writer he greatly admired—was more engaging, and it was one they both remembered fondly. Andersen's reputation today is that of a writer of fairy tales. During the nineteenth century, he was greatly esteemed not just for his tales but for his novels, travelogues, and poetry. Schumann seems to have read everything by Andersen he could get his hands on, invariably with great enjoyment. By nature, Andersen was open and kindly. He was fond of music, and counted among his friends several composers. In 1842 Schumann dedicated and sent to Andersen a copy of his *Fünf Lieder op. 40* (which included in German translation four settings of Andersen's poetry). Andersen was an inveterate traveler (he never owned a home of his own), and in 1844, while traveling through Germany, made a point of visiting Schumann in Leipzig. A memorable evening resulted with performances of Schumann's Andersen songs as well as readings by the poet. Schumann later wrote to Andersen describing the experience as "unforgettable" (14 April 1845), a response shared by Andersen in his autobiography.

Just as Schumann was naturally drawn while reading poetry to thoughts of a musical setting, his reading of dramas (and fiction in general) often led to thoughts about the work's suitability as a basis for opera. He completed but one opera, *Genoveva,* based on dramas dealing with the Genoveva legend by Tieck and Friedrich Hebbel. The more psychological setting of Hebbel particularly appealed to him. At first, unsure of how to proceed, he wrote to Hebbel anxious for him to collaborate on the libretto. Hebbel was three years younger than Schumann. Like Schumann, he had studied at the University of Heidelberg and had been befriended by Thibaut. But Hebbel's career had been one of constant struggle. *Genoveva* was completed in March 1841, but not published until 1843 and not performed until six years later.

Schumann's diary reveals his great admiration for him and his work. Unfortunately, Hebbel did not respond in a similar manner. His knowledge of music was limited, and conservative (Mozart was his favorite composer). When they met, he found Schumann to be quiet and excessively introverted. There was no collaboration. They kept in touch, however, and in 1853 when Schumann dedicated and presented to Hebbel his setting of Hebbel's *Nachtlied,* he responded with gratitude and dedicated to Schumann his play *Michael Angelo,* sending him the manuscript of it.

What appeared to be of particular attraction to Schumann was the distinctive individuality of Hebbel's thought, often pervaded with a dark pessimism and somber melancholy (a reflection perhaps of the extreme poverty and depressing circumstances of much of Hebbel's life). Not long after the completion of *Genoveva* in 1848, Schumann turned again to Hebbel's work for the piano pieces, *Waldszenen* (*Forest Scenes*) *op. 82.*

For one of the pieces in the set, **"Cursed Place,"** Schumann set the mood by prefacing it with a short poem by Hebbel. It is a gruesome text, describing flowers "pale as death," with a single, dark red flower among them, its color the result of having been nourished on human blood.

Those characteristics that attracted Schumann to the work of Hebbel were traits that he found intriguing in literature in general. He was intrigued by works of marked originality, and fascinated by those that contained elements of the bizarre and unusual. That was particularly true of Schumann's youthful interests. In 1828, during his first year of university study at Leipzig, he discovered the controversial plays of Christian Dietrich Grabbe. Although an admirer of Grabbe's skill as a writer, Heine dryly noted in his work "a lack of good taste, a cynicism, and a wildness that surpass the maddest and most abominable things conceived by the human mind"—precisely those traits that Schumann probably found of interest.[11]

Schumann's curiosity about Grabbe extended both to his life and work. The diary includes references to Grabbe's *Marie und Nannette; Comedy, Satire, Irony, and Deep Meaning; Marius und Sulla; Herzog Theodor von Gothland* (all read in 1828); and *Hannibal* (read in 1846). *Gothland* made an unusually strong impression on Schumann, so much so that nearly an entire page in his diary was devoted to thoughts about the work. He discussed at length the plot, and concluded it was a "tragedy without parallel, unique. . . . It often brings to mind those bizarre traits of Heine's Lieder, that burning sarcasm, that *great* despair."[12] Schumann's fascination with Grabbe led him in November 1828 to write to Gisbert Rosen—who lived in Detmold, where Grabbe was then residing—to ask for information about him. Grabbe's life was in many ways a counterpart to the "wildness" noted by Heine in his writings. After Grabbe's death in 1836, Schumann read with interest Karl Immermann's recollections of the dramatist.

Similar eccentricity—in life, work, or a combination of the two—attracted Schumann to three other writers: Friedrich Hölderlin, Heinrich von Kleist, and Nikolaus Lenau. Hölderlin's popularity as a poet was broadened by both the intensity of his writing and the sensationalized circumstances of his mental illness. Schumann knew Hölderlin's work well; as a mark of his esteem, several excerpts from Hölderlin's writings were used as the mottos Schumann placed at the head of each issue of the *Neue Zeitschrift für Musik.* He knew as well of his madness and, according to Emil Flechsig, in the 1820s "spoke about it with fear and awe."[13] Although Hölderlin had been diagnosed as being incurably insane in 1807, Schumann's interest in him was no doubt stimulated by the fact that a collected edition of Hölderlin's poems had only recently appeared in print for the first time (1826).

Kleist, too, was a tragic figure. He belonged to a distinguished Prussian military family, and his suicide in 1811 (at age thirty-four) had created scandal not just in literary circles but in the upper society of which he had been a part. His writing is unsettling, with characters seeming to be always at the mercy of the whims and caprices of fate. Schumann described Kleist's stories as "monstrous, but nonetheless very interesting," and considered one of them ("Michael Kohlhaas," a remarkable tale of justice gone awry) as the basis for a possible opera libretto.[14] For Kleist's play, *Kätchen von Heilbronn,* perhaps his most idyllic and conventional work, Schumann contemplated writing an overture.

Like Hölderlin and Kleist, Nikolaus Lenau suffered from depression and mental instability. The last six years of his life were spent in an asylum. Lenau's poetry is often pervaded by profound melancholy, a trait that seemed to have particular appeal to Schumann. In 1838, through a mutual friend, Schumann attempted to obtain some verse from Lenau for the *Neue Zeitschrift für Musik.* No new poetry by Lenau appeared in the journal, but perhaps he never received Schumann's invitation. It is unlikely that he would have turned down the opportunity: his interest in music—particularly that of Beethoven—was considerable.

Later that year when visiting Vienna (where Lenau resided), Schumann wanted very much to meet him, but was shy about doing so. "I saw Lenau in a cafe, but did not speak to him," he noted in his diary.[15] When Schumann was later presented to Lenau, he seemed pleased to detect "a melancholy, very gentle and captivating look about his mouth and eyes."[16] Shortly after Lenau's death in 1850, Schumann offered as a tribute his **op. 90**: setting of six of Lenau's poems with a brief requiem added, all published with an unusually elaborate cover including depictions of a cross and funereal wreath.

Of the many German writers who interested Schumann, it was E. T. A. Hoffmann and Jean Paul Richter who had the most profound effect upon his work. Once again, it was the distinctive nature of their writing—both in style and content—that appear to have prompted his initial attraction. The first extended reference to Hoffmann in Schumann's diary occurs in 1831, but at that point he had been familiar with Hoffmann's writings for a number of years, having previously noted resemblances between Hoffmann's work and Schubert's. His reading of Hoffmann found him in a strange frame of mind. 5 June 1831: "In the evening read that damned E. T. A. Hoffmann. Klein Zaches [one of Hoffmann's tales] and an ugly, loathsome idea as basis. . . . Concept for a poetical biography of Hoffmann. . . . One can scarcely breathe while reading Hoffmann. . . . Reading Hoffmann unceasingly. New worlds. The Mines at Falun [another Hoffmann tale]. Opera text which greatly inspires me."[17]

Hoffmann and Schumann had much in common. Both were gifted in literature and music. Like Schumann, Hoffmann had been obliged to study law. After completing his law study, attempts to make his living as a writer, composer, and conductor were unsuccessful, and influential friends secured for him a position as a judge. Although he never achieved comparable recognition for his music, Hoffmann was a composer of considerable skill. It is worth noting that Schumann thought enough of it to examine in manuscript the score for his opera, *Aurora* (1812).

As a composer, Hoffmann's indebtedness to the music of others (particularly Mozart) is unmistakable. His short stories and novels, on the other hand, are strikingly original: highly imaginative, visionary, and often grotesque (which helps explain Schumann's reference to "an ugly, loathsome idea" in "Klein Zaches"). In his use of the *Märchen*—the cultivated, German version of a fairy tale for adults—Hoffmann was particularly adept, and created a world with a constant and dizzying shift between fantasy and reality.

Hoffmann's most famous literary creation was the eccentric musician Johannes Kreisler—gifted, temperamental, and at odds with the prosaic life of his time, a personality not unlike that of Hoffmann himself. Kreisler appears in two major works by Hoffmann: *Kreisleriana* (a collection of essays and tales), and *Kater Murr,* a novel left unfinished at Hoffmann's death in 1822. Schumann, like a number of nineteenth-century musicians, was particularly fond of Kreisler, in many ways the Romantic musician *par excellence.* In an unusual indication of his regard for the work, excerpts from *Kreisleriana* were published in the *Neue Zeitschrift für Musik* in 1834 and 1836.

Inspired by Hoffmann's work, Schumann published his own ***Kreisleriana*** for piano (subtitled ***Fantasies***) in 1838 as **op. 16**. It is likely as well that Hoffmann's first published work—a collection of tales entitled *Fantasiestücke in Callots Manier (Fantasy Pieces in the Manner of Callot)*—led to Schumann's title for his **op. 12**: ***Fantasiestücke.***[18] The *Nachtstücke* (***Night Pieces***) **op. 23** may similarly have been inspired by Hoffmann's collection of stories, *Nachtstücke*—although in this instance the word was not unique to Hoffmann. In the 1830s, Hoffmann consistently provided Schumann with a source of inspiration that led him to designate compositions as musical counterparts to Hoffmann's work. One senses as well that they were intended as homage to a writer whom he regarded with unusual affection.

Despite the measure of pride Hoffmann derived from the singularity of his work, he willingly acknowledged the influence of one contemporary author: Jean Paul Richter. "Your works," he wrote to Jean Paul, "have inspired my innermost being and influenced my development."[19] It was a sentiment with which Schumann would have concurred. In Schumann's eyes, no writer had so great an influence on his own life and work.

Johann Paul Friedrich Richter—Jean Paul was his pen name—was born in 1763, the son of a clergyman (who was, incidentally, a talented musician). Like August Schumann, from an early age he showed a great love for literature, becoming a voracious and not always discriminating reader. At the age of fifteen, he began keeping a series of notebooks filled with arcane material he had encountered in books, excerpts from which invariably later found their way into his own writing—often as amusing, erudite, and generally irrelevant footnotes to the text.

In 1781, Jean Paul entered the University of Leipzig as a student of theology. But he had little money, did not enjoy his course of study, and devoted much of his time to reading on his own. He remained for only one semester. Determined to become a writer, he published anonymously his first book, *Greenland Lawsuits,* in 1783. It attracted little attention, and it wasn't until ten years later with the appearance of *The Invisible Lodge* that he began to make a name for himself. Widespread fame followed with *Hesperus* (1795), *Siebenkäs* (*Flower, Fruit, and Thorn Pieces*) (1797), and *Titan* (1803). A year after the publication of *Titan,* Jean Paul settled in the small town of Bayreuth, where, despite the rather peculiar nature of his writings, he led by all accounts a solidly middle-class existence. One of the major attractions Bayreuth held for him was the superior quality of its local beer. Before his death in 1825, two additional novels appeared (both unfinished): *Flegeljahre* (*Walt and Vult*) (1805) and *The Comet* (1822).

Today, Jean Paul is all but forgotten. During his life, and for about a half century after his death, he was a writer of enormous popularity. His fame extended well beyond Germany. To a great extent, the extreme sentimentality and emotional excess of his writings were a major attraction. But his unique prose style—tangled, prolix, and discursive—had many admirers. Thomas Carlyle, Jean Paul's most vocal partisan in England, characterized it as "a perfect Indian jungle . . . nothing on all sides but darkness, dissonance, confusion worse confounded. Then the style of the whole corresponds, in perplexity and extravagance, with that of the parts. . . . That his manner of writing is singular, nay in fact a wild, complicated Arabesque, no one can deny."[20]

Within Jean Paul's novels—each typically nearly a thousand pages in length—scenes of sentiment and emotion of an astonishing extravagance are commonplace. The beauties of nature are a frequent subject, one in which Jean Paul gives free rein to exuberant, at times

incomprehensible, descriptions teeming with fanciful metaphor. Jean Paul had studied piano as a youth, and was particularly fond of music. It plays an important role in his novels, frequently as a means of transporting his characters beyond themselves:

> Clotilda without any hesitating vanity consented to sing. But for Sebastian, in whom all tones came in contact with naked, quivering feelers, and who could work himself into sadness at the very songs of the herdsmen in the fields—this, on such an evening, was too much for his heart; under cover of the general musical attentiveness, he had to steal out of the door. . . .
>
> But here, under the great night-heaven, amidst higher drops, his own can fall unseen. What a night! Here a splendor overwhelms him, which links night and sky and earth all together; magic Nature rushes with streams into his heart, and forcibly enlarges it. Overhead, Luna fills the floating cloud-fleeces with liquid silver, and the soaked silver-wool quivers down-ward, and glittering pearls trickle over smooth foliage, and are caught in blossoms, and the heavenly field pearls and glimmers. [. . .] He glowed through his whole being, and night-clouds must cool it. His finger-tips hung down, lightly folded in one another. Clotilda's tones dropped now like molten silver-points on his bosom, now they flowed like stray echoes from distant groves into this still garden [. . .] But it seemed to him as if his bosom would burst, as if he should be blest could he at this moment embrace beloved persons, and crush in the closeness of that embrace in blissful frenzy his bosom and his heart. It was to him as if he should be over-blessed, could he now before some being, before a mere shadow of the mind, pour out all his blood, his life, his being. It was to him as if he must scream into the midst of Clotilda's tones, and fold his arms around a rock, only to stifle the painful yearning.[21]

The passion and sentiment displayed in Jean Paul's novels often appear alongside sinister and foreboding elements, including violence and extravagant eroticism. In *Titan,* for example, the villainous Roquairol assumes the identity of his best friend, Albano, in order to seduce Albano's fiancée. Roquairol then publicly reveals his act during the presentation of a play that he has written, at the conclusion of which he kills himself on stage—the audience casually dismissing it all as an entertaining part of the drama itself. What contributes to the distinctiveness of Jean Paul's style—Carlyle's "perfect Indian jungle"—is the unpredictable association of macabre, often frightening occurrences with scenes of overweening sentiment and sublime emotion.

As an additional means of disorienting the reader, there is Jean Paul's singular sense of humor. He was a great admirer of Laurence Sterne, in whose whimsy and caprice he discovered a kindred spirit. The first chapter of *Titan*—called, incidentally, a "Jubilee" by Richter (chapters as such rarely exist in his works)—is fifty-six pages in length. It is followed by what should have preceded it: a thirteen-page "Introductory Program to *Ti-*

tan." It is this juxtaposition of humor, sentiment, and the bizarre, and the abrupt and unpredictable movement between them that makes his work so disconcerting. Coupled with Jean Paul's numerous asides and footnotes, a dualistic structure often results: the plot itself, and the author's digressions, comments, and reaction to it.

Schumann's enthusiasm for Jean Paul first became apparent in the summer of 1827. (Here again, the influence of his father is evident. Jean Paul had been one of August Schumann's favorite writers.) In his diary, his literary attempts, and in his letters, he imitated the style of Jean Paul, emphasizing the excessive sentimentality and emotional extravagance characteristic of him. The following example—found in both his diary and in a letter to Flechsig—is a typical tirade à la Jean Paul, and representative of Schumann at his most sentimental:

> Oh friend! Were I a smile, I would want to hover about her eyes; were I joy, I would skip lightly through her pulses; Yes!—were I a tear, I would weep with her; and if she then smiled once again, gladly would I die on her eyelash, and gladly—yes, gladly—be no more.[22]

Schumann's source of inspiration—in this instance he surpassed his mentor—can be traced to a passage in one of his favorite novels by Jean Paul, *Flegeljahre*:

> Were I a star . . . I would shine upon thee; were I a rose, I would bloom for thee; were I a sound, I would press into thy heart; were I love, the happiest love, I would dwell therein.[23]

Throughout 1828 and 1829, Schumann avidly read Jean Paul. He was a sensitive and impressionable reader, and his diary documented the often potent effect his reading had on him. 18 January 1829: "Bedtime reading: Jean Paul's Gianozzo [*Comic Appendix to Titan*] and his life and death—poor sleep." 25 January 1829: "Bedtime reading: Diocha from Nikolaus Marggraf [*The Comet*] by Jean Paul—voluptuous sleep."[24] Schumann's reaction to *Siebenkäs* bordered on frenzy: "Siebenkäs is frightful, but I would like to read it a thousand times more. . . . [After reading it] I sat completely enraptured among the trees and I heard a nightingale. But I didn't cry—and I struck out with my hands and feet, because I felt so happy. But on the way home I felt as if I had taken leave of my senses. I was in my right mind, but I still thought I was not. I was actually crazy."[25] "If the entire world were to read Jean Paul," Schumann concluded, "it would become a better place, but unhappier. He has often nearly driven me mad, but the rainbow of peace and of the human spirit always hovers gently above all tears, and one's heart is marvelously exalted and gently transfigured" (5 June 1828).

At times, Schumann felt and acted as if he were living in a novel by Jean Paul. In his diary he wrote: "[Moritz Semmel] said again how much he would like to die. He

was beside himself, and it was a scene from Jean Paul."[26] When during his visit to the Rhine in 1828, Schumann closed his eyes at the approach of the river in order to enjoy all at once the magnificent spectacle, he was imitating the character Albano in *Titan* who acted similarly when about to behold the beauty of Isola Bella. And when in 1829 Schumann visited Italy, the sight of Isola Bella was inextricably interwoven with thoughts of *Titan*. "Gran albergo al lago—bliss—Albano!," he wrote in his diary.[27]

Over the years Schumann's devotion to Jean Paul remained strong. Selections from his writings were published in the *Neue Zeitschrift für Musik,* and excerpts frequently appeared as mottos for individual issues. His exceptional interest in Jean Paul attracted attention. In 1839, the composer Stephen Heller, also a devoted admirer of Jean Paul, enthusiastically wrote to Schumann: "Your compositions are Jean Paulish Fruit, Bloom, and Thorn pieces, and Siebenkäs, Schoppe-Leibgerber (Euseb-Florestan), Lenette, Pelzstiefel, etc. are found note for note in them. And because I love Jean Paul so deeply, I love you as well."[28]

To his fiancée, Schumann wrote expressing his delight that she was reading *Flegeljahre*. But he warned her that on first reading all might not be clear to her: "It is in its way like the Bible" (20 March 1838). Within six weeks of their marriage, Schumann was reading Jean Paul's *Life of Fibel* with her so that "for the first time she could better understand" Jean Paul.[29] It was as if Schumann felt everyone should be familiar with Jean Paul, and was genuinely astonished when he learned that was not the case. Emilie Steffen, a friend of the family in the 1840s and a piano student of his wife, recalled that "one day Schumann asked her if she were studying Shakespeare and Jean Paul diligently, and whether she knew *Coriolanus* and *Siebenkäs*. On receiving a negative answer, he looked at her with such surprise and at the same time so kindly that she at once began to read, and was grateful to him ever after."[30]

Although Schumann's affection for the work of Jean Paul remained constant, over the years his admiration for another author whom he had discovered during his youth—William Shakespeare—grew. By the 1850s, as maturity supplanted the enthusiasm of his youth, Shakespeare became his favorite author. Schumann's admiration for Shakespeare coincided with a rediscovery and reevaluation of Shakespeare's work during the first half of the nineteenth century.

The interest of German Romanticism in Shakespeare did much not only to broaden his international reputation but to place him on a pedestal as possibly the greatest of all writers. During the eighteenth century, Shakespeare had been perceived as at times tasteless and a bit of a barbarian. But it was precisely his emotional "excess" and profusion of lively action that appealed to nineteenth-century audiences. In Germany, the criticism and translations of Tieck and August Wilhelm von Schlegel did much to promote Shakespeare's popularity. For the first time, his works became available in uncut and truly poetic translations.

Schumann read Shakespeare throughout his life, singling out for praise his universality. But Shakespeare's skill at character development probably provided a major source for Schumann's attraction. The first mention of Shakespeare in Schumann's diary is of *Hamlet.* On 25 October 1828, Schumann saw the play, prompting a reading of it two days later. The melancholy figure of Hamlet was one with particular appeal in the nineteenth century, and in 1831 and 1832 Schumann considered an opera on the subject, writing sketches for a "Sinfonia per il Hamlet."[31]

Schumann's knowledge of Shakespeare's plays was extensive. In 1831, he compiled (for reasons unknown) a listing of the female characters in his dramas. Nine years later, while in negotiation to receive an honorary doctorate from the University of Jena, Schumann, as an indication of his accomplishments, offered to send to the university a study of Shakespeare and music. He received the degree shortly thereafter, and, except for a four-page sketch, the study was not written. But it was an idea that Schumann returned to later in the year, when in October he marked passages in Shakespeare's works intending to use them as the basis for an article on Shakespeare and music, probably for the *Zeitschrift.*

The direct influence of Shakespeare on his own compositions was not inconsiderable. Schumann intended as a motto for the third Intermezzo (**Rasch und wild**) of the **Novelletten op. 21** (1838) the opening lines from *Macbeth*: "When shall we three meet again? / In thunder, lightning, or in rain?". And he set to music the concluding song of the clown in *Twelfth Night.* During his extensive search for a suitable subject for an opera, Schumann considered *The Tempest* and *Romeo and Juliet* (in 1846 and 1850, respectively). Toward the end of his career, inspired by Shakespeare's *Julius Caesar,* he wrote a concert overture on the subject.

But probably the most intriguing of Shakespeare's influences on Schumann is for a work never, as far as is known, even begun. On 4 July 1832, Schumann noted in his diary: "Why are there no operas without texts; that would quite certainly be dramatic. There is much for you in Shakespeare."[32] Later in the month (or possibly in August), there is the cryptic entry: "The opera without a text."[33] It was an idea he returned to in December of that year in a letter to the music critic, Ludwig Rellstab. But what Schumann meant remains unclear. Could he have had in mind a programmatic, instrumental composition? Or would singers have been

involved? And, most interesting, how had this idea been developed by Schumann from his reading of Shakespeare?

Beginning in April 1852 Schumann commenced a concentrated and systematic rereading of Shakespeare's plays. The study took one year, a time when he composed little and seemed particularly interested in literary pursuits; during this same period he put together in book form his music criticism. Schumann's reading of Shakespeare was part of a larger project that was to occupy him intermittently until his death. It necessitated rereading many of his favorite books, including a great deal of Jean Paul in the summer and autumn of 1853. What Schumann had in mind was an anthology of writings from celebrated authors from antiquity to the present, an anthology devoted solely to excerpts from their work that dealt with music. It was to be called **Dichtergarten** (**A Poet's Garden**). The possibility of finding a publisher for the work was not great. Schumann had recently experienced considerable difficulty in finding a publisher for his collected music criticism, for which there would surely have been a broader market than for a specialized, literary anthology. Yet, he worked extensively on the project, completing nearly three hundred pages in manuscript. It was a labor of love, and the final testament not just of Schumann's passion for literature but of his long-abiding interest in the relationship between word and music.

Notes

1. "Aus Meister Raros, Florestans und Eusebius' Denk-und Dichtbüchlein," (c. 1833) in *GS* [*Gesammelte Schriften*] I, p. 26.

2. *Tgb* [*Tagebücher*] I, pp. 96, 41.

3. *Ibid.*, p. 97.

4. *JgBr* [*Jugendbriefe*], p. 82.

5. Letter of 15 December 1830 in *JS* [*Der junge Schumann*], p. 213.

6. May 1828 in *Tgb I*, p. 76.

7. 29 July 1828 in *Ibid.,* p. 98. Nineteen pages of the work survive.

8. Only about six pages of this work (much of it strongly autobiographical in nature) are extant.

9. Review published in 1840 of H. Esser's *Lieder* op. 6 in *GS I*, p. 496.

10. Letter to Clara Wieck of 22 May 1840 in Wolfgang Boetticher, *Robert Schumann in seinen Schriften und Briefen* (Berlin, 1942), p. 340.

11. Quoted in Alfred Bergmann, ed., *Grabbe in Berichten seiner Zeitgenossen* (Stuttgart, 1968), p. 24.

12. Entry for 31 October 1828 in *Tgb I*, p. 129.

13. Emil Flechsig, "Erinnerungen an Robert Schumann," *Neue Zeitschrift für Musik* CXVII (1956), p. 396. From 1828 to 1835 Schumann kept a book of literary extracts suitable for mottos (including those by Hölderlin); it was nearly 250 pages in length.

14. 27 and 30 August 1852 in *Tgb II*, p. 436.

15. Entry of October 1838 in *Ibid.*, p. 74.

16. Entry of December 1838 in *Ibid.*, p. 83.

17. Entries of 5 and 6 June 1831 in *Tgb I*, pp. 336, 337.

18. The bizarre creations of the artist Jacques Callot (c.1592-1635)—particularly those in his *Caprici di diverse figure* (1617)—enjoyed renewed popularity during the nineteenth century.

19. Letter of 30 January 1822 in Johanna C. Sahlin, ed. & trans., *Selected Letters of E. T. A. Hoffmann* (Chicago, 1977), p. 321.

20. *The Works of Thomas Carlyle* (New York, 1897), XIV, p. 13. Carlyle's essay on Jean Paul (from which this quotation is taken) was originally published in the *Edinburgh Review* in 1827.

21. Jean Paul, *Hesperus*, 2 vols., trans. Charles T. Brooks (Boston, 1865), I, pp. 118-120. I have used, whenever possible, nineteenth-century translations of Jean Paul, because these capture—with unusual success—his often convoluted imagery and syntax.

22. *Tgb I*, p. 69 and letter of July 1827 to Flechsig in *JS*, p. 109.

23. Jean Paul, *Walt and Vult, or The Twins*, 2 vols. (Boston, 1846), II, p. 32.

24. *Tgb I*, pp. 168, 170.

25. Entry of 29 May 1828 in *Ibid.*, p. 83.

26. July 1828 in *Ibid.*, p. 93.

27. 7 September 1829 in *Ibid.*, p. 255.

28. Letter of 18 September 1839 in Stephen Heller, *Briefe an Robert Schumann*, ed. Ursula Kersten (Frankfurt, 1988), p. 142. Siebenkäs, Schoppe, Leibgeber (not "Leibgerber"), Lenette, and Pelzstiefel are all characters in *Flower, Fruit, and Thorn Pieces*. Heller later wrote a work for solo piano inspired by Jean Paul's novel (published as op. 82, and usually referred to by the French title, *Nuits blanches*).

29. Entry for 25-31 October 1840 in *Tgb II*, p. 118.

30. Frederick Niecks, *Robert Schumann* (London, 1925), p. 250.

31. Although the work was never completed, thematic material was later incorporated into Schumann's Symphony in G minor.

32. *Tgb I*, p. 411.

33. *Ibid.*, p. 412.

Select Bibliography

THEMATIC CATALOGUE AND LISTING OF FIRST EDITIONS

Hofmann, Kurt. *Die Erstdrucke der Werke von Robert Schumann.* Tutzing: Hans Schneider, 1979.

Hofmann, Kurt and Keil, Siegmar. *Robert Schumann: Thematisches Verzeichnis samtlichen im Druck erschienen musikalischen Werke.* 5th ed. Hamburg: Schuberth, 1982.

CORRESPONDENCE, DIARIES, AND WRITINGS BY SCHUMANN

Erler, Hermann. *Robert Schumann's Leben: Aus seinen Briefen geschildert.* 2 vols. Berlin: Ries & Erler, 1887.

Holde, Artur. "Suppressed Passages in the Brahms-Joachim Correspondence Published for the First Time," *The Musical Quarterly* XLV (1959), pp. 312-24.

Jansen, F. Gustav. "Briefwechsel zwischen Robert Franz und Robert Schumann," *Die Musik* VIII (1908/09), pp. 280-91; 346-59.

Kross, Siegfried, ed. *Briefe und Notizen Robert und Clara Schumanns.* 2nd ed. Bonn: Bouvier Verlag, 1982.

Schumann, Clara and Schumann, Robert. *Briefwechsel: Kritische Gesamtausgabe,* ed. Eva Weissweiler. 2 vols. Frankfurt am Main: Stroemfeld/Roter Stern, 1984-.

Schumann, Clara and Schumann, Robert. *The Complete Correspondence of Clara and Robert Schumann,* ed. Eva Weissweiler. Trans. Hildegard Fritscht and Ronald L. Crawford. 2 vols. New York: Lang, 1994-.

Schumann, Clara and Schumann, Robert. *The Marriage Diaries,* trans. P. Ostwald. Boston: Northeastern University Press, 1993.

Schumann, Robert. *Briefe. Neue Folge,* ed. F. Gustav Jansen. Leipzig: Breitkopf und Härtel, 1904.

Schumann, Robert. *Briefe und Gedichte aus dem Album Robert und Clara Schumanns,* ed. Wolfgang Boetticher. Leipzig: VEB Deutscher Verlag für Musik, 1981.

Schumann, Robert. *Gesammelte Schriften über Musik und Musiker,* ed. Martin Kreisig. 2 vols. Leipzig: Breitkopf & Härtel, 1914.

Schumann, Robert. *Haushaltbücher, 1837-1856,* ed. Gerd Nauhaus. 2 vols. Leipzig: VEB Deutscher Verlag für Musik, 1982.

Schumann, Robert. *Jugendbriefe,* ed. Clara Schumann. Leipzig: Breitkopf & Härtel, 1886.

Schumann, Robert. *Der junge Schumann: Dichtungen und Briefe,* ed. Alfred Schumann. Leipzig: Insel-Verlag, 1917.

Schumann, Robert. *Letters,* ed. Karl Storck. Trans. H. Bryant. New York: Blom, 1971 (reprint of 1907 edition).

Schumann, Robert. *Manuskripte—Briefe—Schumanniana—Katalog Nr. 188.* Tutzing: Musikantiquariat Hans Schneider, 1974.

Schumann, Robert. *The Musical World of Robert Schumann: A Selection from Schumann's Own Writings,* ed. and trans. Henry Pleasants. London: Gollancz, 1965.

Schumann, Robert. *Tagebücher: 1827-1838,* ed. Georg Eismann. Leipzig: VEB Deutscher Verlag für Musik, 1971.

Schumann, Robert. *Tagebücher: 1836-1854,* ed. Gerd Nauhaus. Leipzig: VEB Deutscher Verlag für Musik, 1987.

BOOKS

Abraham, Gerald, ed. *Schumann: A Symposium.* London: Oxford University Press, 1952.

Bischoff, Bodo. *Monument für Beethoven: Die Entwicklung der Beethoven-Rezeption Robert Schumanns.* Cologne: Verlag Dohr, 1994.

Boetticher, Wolfgang. *Robert Schumanns Klavierwerke: Teil I: Opp. 1-6; Teil II: Opp. 7-13.* 2 vols. Wilhelmshaven: Heinrichshofen's Verlag, 1976, 1984.

Brion, Marcel. *Schumann and the Romantic Age.* Trans. G. Sainsbury. London: Collins, 1956.

Daverio, John. *Robert Schumann: Herald of a "New Poetic Age."* New York: Oxford University Press, 1997.

Eismann, Georg. *Robert Schumann: Ein Quellenwerk über sein Leben und Schaffen.* 2 vols. Leipzig: Breitkopf & Härtel, 1956.

Finson, Jon. *Robert Schumann and the Study of Orchestral Composition: The Genesis of the First Symphony op. 38.* Oxford: Clarendon Press, 1989.

Finson, Jon W. and Todd, R. Larry, eds. *Mendelssohn and Schumann: Essays on Their Music and Its Context.* Durham, NC: Duke University Press, 1984.

Fischer-Dieskau, Dietrich. *Robert Schumann—Words and Music: The Vocal Compositions.* Portland: Amadeus Press, 1988.

Hallmark, Rufus. *The Genesis of Schumann's Dichterliebe.* Ann Arbor: UMI Press, 1976.

Jansen, F. Gustav. *Die Davidsbündler.* Leipzig: Breitkopf & Härtel, 1883.

Kapp, Reinhard. *Studien zum Spätwerk Robert Schumanns.* Tutzing: Hans Schneider, 1984.

Kast, Paul, ed. *Schumanns rheinische Jahre.* Düsseldorf: Droste, 1981.

Litzmann, Berthold. *Clara Schumann—Ein Künstlerleben: Nach Tagebüchern und Briefen.* 3 vols. Hildesheim: Georg Olms, 1971 (reprint of 1908 edition).

Marston, Nicholas. *Schumann: Fantasie Op. 17.* Cambridge, UK: Cambridge University Press, 1992.

Mayeda, Akio. *Robert Schumanns Weg zur Symphonie.* Zürich: Atlantis, 1992.

Niecks, Frederick. *Robert Schumann.* London: J. M. Dent, 1925.

Ostwald, Peter. *Schumann: The Inner Voices of a Musical Genius.* Boston: Northeastern University Press, 1985.

Ozawa, Kazuko. *Quellenstudien zu Robert Schumanns Lieder nach Adelbert von Chamisso.* Frankfurt: Peter Lang, 1989.

Reich, Nancy B. *Clara Schumann: The Artist and the Woman.* Ithaca, NY: Cornell University Press, 1985.

Sams, Eric. *The Songs of Robert Schumann.* 3rd edition. Bloomington, IN: Indiana University Press, 1993.

Schumann, Eugenie. *The Memoirs of Eugenie Schumann.* New York: Dial, 1927.

Schumann, Eugenie. *Robert Schumann: Ein Lebensbild meines Vaters.* Leipzig: Koehler & Amelang, 1931.

Taylor, Ronald. *Robert Schumann: His Life and Work.* New York: Universe Books, 1982.

Todd, R. Larry, ed. *Schumann and His World.* Princeton, NJ: Princeton University Press, 1994.

Walker, Alan, ed. *Robert Schumann: The Man and His Music.* London: Barrie & Jenkins, 1972.

Wasielewski, Wilhelm Joseph von. *Robert Schumann: Eine Biographie.* 4th ed. Leipzig: Breitkopf & Härtel, 1906.

ARTICLES

Abert, Hermann. "Robert Schumann's 'Genoveva'," *Zeitschrift der Internationalen Musikgesellschaft* XI (1910), pp. 277-89.

Abraham, Gerald. "Schumann's Op. II and III," in *Slavonic and Romantic Music.* London: Faber and Faber, 1968, pp. 261-66.

Dadelson, Georg von. "Robert Schumann und die Musik Bachs," *Archiv für Musikwissenschaft* XIV (1957), pp. 46-59.

Deutsch, Otto Erich. "The Discovery of Schubert's Great C-major Symphony: A Story in Fifteen Letters," *The Musical Quarterly* XXXVIII (1952), pp. 528-32.

Draheim, Joachim. "Schumann und Shakespeare," *Neue Zeitschrift für Musik* CXLI (1981), pp. 237-44.

Dusella, Reinhold. "Symphonisches in den Skizzenbüchern Schumanns," in Kross, Siegfried, ed. *Probleme der symphonischen Tradition im 19. Jahrhundert*. Tutzing: Hans Schneider, 1990, pp. 203-24.

Eismann, Georg. "Zu Robert Schumanns letzten Kompositionen," *Beiträge zur Musikwissenschaft* XXVIII (1968), pp. 151-157.

Finson, Jon. "Schumann, Popularity, and the *Overtüre, Scherzo, und Finale*, Opus 52," *The Musical Quarterly* LXIX (1983), pp. 1-26.

Finson, Jon W. "Schumann's Mature Style and the *Album of Songs for the Young*," *The Journal of Musicology* VIII (1990), pp. 227-50.

Fiske, Roger. "A Schumann Mystery," *The Musical Times* CV (1964), pp. 574-78.

Gülke, Peter. "Zu Robert Schumanns 'Rheinischer Sinfonie'," *Beiträge zur Musikwissenschaft* XXI (1974), pp. 123-35.

Hallmark, Rufus. "The Rückert Lieder of Robert and Clara Schumann," *19th-Century Music* XIV (1990-91), pp. 3-30.

Jensen, Eric Frederick. "Explicating Jean Paul: Robert Schumann's Program for *Papillons*, Op. 2," *19th-Century Music* XXII (1998-99), pp. 127-44.

Jensen, Eric Frederick. "A New Manuscript of Robert Schumann's *Waldszenen* Op. 82," *The Journal of Musicology* VII (1989), pp. 69-89.

Jensen, Eric Frederick. "Norbert Burgmüller and Robert Schumann," *The Musical Quarterly* LXXIV (1990), pp. 550-65.

Jensen, Eric Frederick. "Schumann at Endenich," *The Musical Times* CXXXIX (1998, March and April), pp. 10-19; 14-24.

Jensen, Eric Frederick. "Schumann, Hummel, and 'The Clarity of a Well-Planned Composition,' *Studia Musicologica* XL (1999), pp. 59-70.

Kross, Siegfried. "Aus der Frühgeschichte von Robert Schumanns *Neue Zeitschrift für Musik*," *Die Musikforschung* XXXIV (1981), pp. 423-45.

Laux, Karl. "'Dresden ist doch gar zu schön'—Schumann in der sächsischen Hauptstadt—Eine Ehrenrettung," in Moser, Hans Joachim and Rebling, Eberhard, eds. *Robert Schumann: Aus Anlass seines 100 Todestages*. Leipzig: VEB Verlag, 1956, pp. 25-42.

Lester, Joel. "Robert Schumann and Sonata Forms," *19th-Century Music* XVIII (1994-95), pp. 189-210.

Lippman, Edward A. "Theory and Practice in Schumann's Aesthetics," *Journal of the American Musicological Society* XVII (1964), pp. 310-45.

Mintz, Donald. "Schumann as an Interpreter of Goethe's *Faust*," *Journal of the American Musicological Society* XIV (1961), pp. 235-56.

Myers, Rollo H. "Finding a Lost Schumann Concerto," in Aprahamian, Felix, ed. *Essays on Music: An Anthology from 'The Listener'*. London: Cassell, 1967, pp. 223-27.

Nauhaus, Gerd. "*Der Rose Pilgerfahrt* op. 112: Schumanns Abschied von Oratorium," in Appel, Bernhard R., ed. *Schumann in Düsseldorf: Werke-Texte-Interpretationen*. Mainz: Schott, 1993, pp. 179-99.

Newcomb, Anthony. "Once More 'Between Absolute and Program Music': Schumann's Second Symphony," *Nineteenth-Century Music* VII (1983-84), pp. 233-50.

Roe, Stephen. "The Autograph Manuscript of Schumann's *Piano Concerto*," *The Musical Times* CXXXI (1990), pp. 77-79.

Roesner, Linda Correll. "Schumann's 'Parallel' Forms," *19th-Century Music* XIV (1990-91), pp. 265-78.

Roesner, Linda Correll. "Schumann's Revisions in the First Movement of the Piano Sonata in G Minor, Op. 22," *Nineteenth-Century Music* I (1977-78), pp. 97-109.

Roesner, Linda Correll. "Tonal Strategy and Poetic Content in Schumann's C-major Symphony, Op. 61," in Kross, Siegfried, ed. *Probleme der symphonischen Tradition im 19. Jahrhundert*. Tutzing: Hans Schneider, 1990, pp. 295-306.

Sams, Eric. "Politics, Literature, and People in Schumann's Op. 136," *The Musical Times* CIX (1968), pp. 25-27.

Sams, Eric. "Schumann and Faust," *The Musical Times* CXIII (1972), pp. 543-46.

Schnapp, Friedrich. "Robert Schumann and Heinrich Heine," *The Musical Quarterly* XI (1925), pp. 599-616.

Schoppe, Martin. "Schumanns frühe Texte und Schriften," in Mayeda, Akio and Niemöller, Klaus Wolfgang, eds. *Schumanns Werke: Text und Interpretationen*. Mainz: Schott, 1987, pp. 7-15.

Shitomirski, Daniel. "Schumann in Russland," in *Sammelbände der Robert-Schumann-Gesellschaft*, Vol. I. Leipzig: VEB Deutscher Verlag für Musik, 1961, pp. 19-47.

Siegel, Linda. "A Second Look at Schumann's *Genoveva*," *The Music Review* XXXVI (1975), pp. 17-43.

Sietz, Reinhold. "Zur Textgestaltung von Robert Schumanns 'Genoveva'," *Die Musikforschung* XXIII (1970), pp. 395-410.

Temperley, Nicholas. "Schumann and Sterndale Bennett," *19th-Century Music* XII (1988-89), pp. 207-20.

Truscott, Harold. "The Evolution of Schumann's Last Period," *The Chesterian* XXXI (1957), pp. 76-84, 103-111.

Turchin, Barbara. "Schumann's Conversion to Vocal Music: A Reconsideration," *The Musical Quarterly* LXVII (1981), pp. 392-404.

Wendt, Matthias. "Zu Robert Schumanns Skizzenbüchern," in Mayeda, Akio and Niemöller, Klaus Wolfgang, eds. *Schumanns Werke: Text und Interpretationen.* Mainz: Schott, 1987, pp. 101-14.

FURTHER READING

Biographies

Jensen, Erick Frederick. "Schumann at Endenich." *The Musical Times* CXXXIX (March-April, 1998): 14-24.
  Sheds light on Schumann's time as an inmate at Endenich, suggesting that his condition was aggravated by unenlightened medical practices.

Ostwald, Peter F. *Schumann: The Inner Voices of a Musical Genius.* Boston: Northeastern University Press, 1985, 373 p.
  Discusses Schumann's mental ailments, with an emphasis on manic depression as a possible diagnosis.

Criticism

Dahlhaus, Carl. *The Idea of Absolute Music.* Chicago and London: University of Chicago Press, 1989, 176 p.
  Discusses the philosophical and cultural foundations of thinking about music in nineteenth-century Germany, with particular reference to Schumann's originality as a writer and thinker.

Lippman, Edward A. "Theory and Practice in Schumann's Aesthetics." *Journal of the American Musicological Society* XVII (1964): 310-45.
  Discerns original aesthetical ideas in Schumann's criticism.

Plantinga, Leon. *Romantic Music: A History of Musical Style in Nineteenth-Century Europe.* New York and London: Norton, 1984, 523 p.
  Discusses Schumann's music and writings in the context of nineteenth-century European music.

———. "Schumann's Critical Reaction to Mendelssohn." In *Mendelssohn and Schumann: Essays on Their Music and Its Context,* edited by Jon W. Finson and R. Larry Todd, pp. 11-19. Durham: Duke University Press, 1984.
  Analyzes Schumann's critical assessment of Mendelssohn, arguing that Schumann was the only contemporary critic to form an objective view of Mendelssohn's music.

Pleasants, Henry. "Schumann the Critic." In *Robert Schumann: The Man and His Music,* edited by Alan Walker, pp. 179-187. New York: Harper & Row, 1974.
  Praises Schumann's criticism as an extraordinary blend of intuitive writing and meticulous analysis.

Additional coverage of Schumann's life and career is contained in the following source published by Thomson Gale: *Literature Resource Center.*

The Cenci

Percy Bysshe Shelley

The following entry presents criticism of Shelley's play *The Cenci* (1819). For information on Shelley's complete career, see *NCLC,* Volumes 18 and 93.

INTRODUCTION

Philosophically complex and controversial in its subject matter, *The Cenci* conveys Shelley's Romantic ideas on patriarchal authority, religion, and morality. Written in blank verse as a five-act tragedy, the play relates the infamous true story of Beatrice Cenci, who was executed for the murder of her father, Count Cenci, in sixteenth-century Italy. Although generally considered a closet drama, *The Cenci* was written with the explicit intent of being staged. Shelley believed that by avoiding political didacticism, incorporating Gothic motifs, and reducing the purely poetic elements of his style in *The Cenci,* he could communicate more broadly the themes he was developing for his less-accessible lyrical drama, *Prometheus Unbound* (1820). However, Shelley miscalculated the critical response to such taboo subjects as incest and parricide in the play; *The Cenci* was never performed during the poet's lifetime, receiving its first staging in 1866 when the Shelley Society presented it privately with amateur actors. It was not publicly presented in England until 1922, upon the centenary of Shelley's death. Although it remains a rarely performed work, *The Cenci* continues to generate considerable critical interest and debate, with scholars remarking on the play's structural merits, historical origins, literary influences, characters, and its thematic relation to Shelley's oeuvre.

PLOT AND MAJOR CHARACTERS

The lurid story of a young woman put to death for the assassination of her tyrannical father was a well-known Roman legend, passed down through oral tradition and documented in the *Annali d'Italia,* a twelve-volume chronicle of Italian history written by Ludovico Antonio Muratori in 1749. Shelley was initially inspired to dramatize the tale after viewing Guido Reni's portrait of Beatrice Cenci, a painting that captivated Shelley's poetic imagination and that of many nineteenth-century writers. Shelley drew upon volume ten of Muratori's

manuscript for his story line, translating "The Relation of the Death of the Family of the Cenci" into English in 1818, and altering it to suit Romantic sensibilities and English audience expectations. The expository scenes of Shelley's play establish Count Cenci as an embodiment of evil, revealing that he has sent two of his sons to Salamanca in the hope that they might starve. The Count's virtuous daughter, Beatrice, and Orsino, a prelate in love with Beatrice, discuss petitioning the Pope to relieve the Cenci family from the Count's vicious reign. However, Orsino withholds the petition, revealing himself to be disingenuous, lustful for Beatrice, and greedy. Upon news that Cenci's sons have been violently killed in Salamanca, the Count holds a feast in celebration of their deaths, commanding his guests to revel with him. During the feast, Beatrice pleads with the guests to protect her family from her sadistic father, but the guests refuse, in fear of Cenci's brutality. In Act II, Cenci torments Beatrice and her stepmother, Lucretia, and announces his plan to imprison them in his castle in Petrella. A servant returns Beatrice's petition to the Pope, unopened, and Beatrice and Lucretia despair over the last hope of salvation from the Count. Orsino encourages Cenci's son, Giacomo, upset over Cenci's appropriation of Giacomo's wife's dowry, to murder Cenci. In Act III, Beatrice unveils to Lucretia that the Count has committed an unnameable act against her and expresses feelings of spiritual and physical contamination, implying Cenci's incestuous rape of his daughter. Orsino and Lucretia agree with Beatrice's suggestion that the Count must die. After the first attempt at parricide fails, Orsino conspires with Beatrice, Lucretia, Giacomo, and Cenci's youngest son, Bernardo, in a second assassination plot. Orsino proposes that two of Cenci's ill-treated servants, Marzio and Olimpio, carry out the murderous task. In Act IV, Olimpio and Marzio enter Cenci's bedchamber to conduct the murder, but hesitate to kill the sleeping Count and return to the conspirators with the deed undone. Threatening to kill Cenci herself, Beatrice shames the servants into action, and Olimpio and Marzio strangle the Count. Shortly thereafter, a papal legate arrives with a murder charge and execution order against Cenci. Upon finding the Count's dead body, the legate arrests the conspirators, with the exception of Orsino, who escapes in disguise. The suspects are taken to trial in Rome in Act V. Marzio is tortured and confesses to the murder, implicating Cenci's family members. Despite learning that Lucretia and Giacomo have also confessed, Beatrice refuses to do so, steadfastly insisting on her innocence. At the trial, all of the conspirators are found guilty and sentenced to death, except for young Bernardo, who is permitted to serve a prison sentence. Bernardo attempts a last-minute appeal to the Pope to have mercy on his family. The play concludes with Beatrice walking stoically to her death.

MAJOR THEMES

The Cenci addresses themes which reflect Shelley's Romantic ideals, and which are prevalent in his other literary works. Critics have drawn parallels between the play's chief thematic concerns and those of *Prometheus Unbound*, which Shelley was in the process of writing when he began work on *The Cenci*. Specifically, scholars have highlighted the conflicts of good versus evil and humanity versus tyranny in the play, noting Shelley's preoccupation with the dynamics of evil and mankind's ability to resist the power of cruelty. Central to this theme is the notion that Beatrice could have endured Cenci's wickedness through her own volition. In choosing to seek revenge, however, Shelley's heroine employs evil for her own ends, taking on the characteristics of her tyrannical father. As Shelley articulated in his Preface to *The Cenci,* Beatrice exercises poor moral judgment in her decision to combat evil through evil

means rather than through forbearance and non-violent resistance. A related theme in the play is that moral fortitude cannot be tarnished by the actions of others, only by one's own actions and ethical choices. Thus, the destruction of Beatrice's innocence is not a consequence of her father's brutal treatment, but rather a result of her acquiescence to the desire to retaliate with violence. Critics have examined Beatrice as a tragic figure representing humanity suffering at the hands of unjust authority, underscoring another thematic current in *The Cenci*. Throughout the play, commentators have found evidence of Shelley's radical, anti-authoritarian ideals. Citing the poet's use of such taboo subjects as incest and parricide, critics have characterized *The Cenci* as an implicit attack on every form of patriarchal authority, be it political, religious, or familial. Additionally, Shelley's views on religion contribute to a central theme in *The Cenci*. Through the play's religious undertones, Shelley revealed his views on the ecclesiastical hierarchy, presenting Orsino—a clergyman—as hypocritical and avaricious, and highlighting the venality of the Roman Catholic Church in its dealings with Count Cenci. Critics have also interpreted Shelley's portrayal of Cenci as a Catholic as a critique of the Church, noting that although the Count was identified as an atheist in Shelley's source material, he was characterized as wicked, yet deeply religious, in the play. To underscore the distinction between religion and morality, Shelley's characters call upon God to justify their unethical choices, employing religious language and symbols as they commit acts of brutality and vengeance.

CRITICAL RECEPTION

Upon its publication in 1819, *The Cenci* elicited an emotionally charged critical response. An anonymous reviewer writing for the *Literary Gazette* in 1820 deemed the play "noxious," "odious," and "abominable," and accused Shelley of rampant plagiarism. In contrast, Alfred and H. Buxton Forman hailed *The Cenci* a "tragic masterpiece," placing Shelley in the company of Sophocles, Euripides, and Shakespeare. Furthermore, Leigh Hunt, to whom the play is dedicated, effused over Shelley's "great sweetness of nature, and enthusiasm for good. . . ." Despite the attention afforded the play, the purportedly immoral subject matter prevented *The Cenci* from reaching the stage for forty-five years. Critics have long debated the play's suitability for production, labeling it a "non-acting" play replete with structural defects. Commentators have complained that the play and its monologues are exceedingly long and lacking in consistent plot progression. They have also pointed out inconsistencies in the characterization of Beatrice and have noted an abrupt change in thematic direction after Cenci's death. However, scholar Charles L. Adams has refuted these arguments, analyzing the author's structural intentions and defending the play's merits. Moreover, as critic Roger Blood has observed, recent discourse on *The Cenci* has moved beyond issues of structure to explore thematic topics. In addition to the play's moral and religious themes, critics have focused on character studies, horror motifs such as vampirism, and the role of politics in the work. Scholars have also discussed the play in relation to the Shakespearean tragedies, such as *Macbeth,* as well as Shelley's other works, including his epic poem *Laon and Cythna* (1818), which shares with *The Cenci* controversial themes of incest and attacks on religion. As testament to the enduring quality of *The Cenci,* critics have remarked that Shelley's Romantic depiction of Beatrice inspired numerous writers, artists, and filmmakers to retell her story, including authors Stendhal, Alberto Moravia, Francesco Guerrazzi, and Giovanni Battista Niccolini; painters Charles Robert Leslie and Francesco Hayez; and Expressionist film director Mario Caserini.

PRINCIPAL WORKS

Original Poetry by Victor and Cazire [as Victor; with Elizabeth Shelley] (poetry) 1810

Posthumous Fragments of Margaret Nicholsen, Being Poems Found amongst the Papers of That Noted Female Who Attempted the Life of the King in 1786 [with Thomas Jefferson Hogg] (poetry) 1810

Zastrozzi: A Romance (novel) 1810

The Necessity of Atheism (essay) 1811

St. Irvyne; or, The Rosicrucian: A Romance, by a Gentleman of the University of Oxford (novel) 1811

An Address to the Irish People (essay) 1812

A Declaration of Rights (essay) 1812

Queen Mab: A Philosophical Poem, with Notes (poem) 1813

A Refutation of Deism, in a Dialogue (dialogue) 1814

Alastor; or, The Spirit of Solitude, and Other Poems (poetry) 1816

An Address to the People on the Death of Princess Charlotte [as The Hermit of Marlow] (essay) 1817

Hymn to Intellectual Beauty (poem) 1817

A Proposal for Putting Reform to the Vote Throughout the Kingdom [as The Hermit of Marlow] (essay) 1817

Laon and Cythna; or, The Revolution of the Golden City: A Vision of the Nineteenth Century (poetry) 1818; revised as *The Revolt of Islam; A Poem, in Twelve Cantos*

The Cenci: A Tragedy in Five Acts (verse play) 1819

Rosalind and Helen: A Modern Eclogue, with Other Poems (poetry) 1819

Prometheus Unbound: A Lyrical Drama in Four Acts, with Other Poems (drama and poetry) 1820

Adonais: An Elegy on the Death of John Keats (poetry) 1821

Epipsychidion (poetry) 1821

Hellas (verse drama) 1822

Julian and Maddalo (poetry) 1824

Posthumous Poems of Percy Bysshe Shelley (poetry and verse drama) 1824

The Triumph of Life (unfinished poetry) 1824

The Witch of Atlas (poem) 1824

The Masque of Anarchy (poetry) 1832

A Defence of Poetry (essay) 1840

Essays, Letters from Abroad, Translations, and Fragments by Percy Bysshe Shelley. 2 vols. (essays, letters, translations, and prose) 1840

The Works of Percy Bysshe Shelley (poetry, verse drama, and essays) 1847

*The Complete Poetical Works of Percy Bysshe Shelley. 4 vols. (poetry and verse drama) 1892

Notebooks of Percy Bysshe Shelley. 3 vols. (prose) 1911

The Letters of Percy Bysshe Shelley. 2 vols. (letters) 1914

The Complete Works of Percy Bysshe Shelley. 10 vols. (poetry, verse drama, essays, and translations) 1926-30

The Letters of Percy Bysshe Shelley. 2 vols. (letters) 1964

*Includes Shelley's translation "The Relation of the Death of the Family of the Cenci," written in 1818.

CRITICISM

The Literary Gazette, and Journal of Belles Lettres, Arts, Sciences (review date 1 April 1820)

SOURCE: "Unsigned Review, *The Literary Gazette, and Journal of Belles Lettres, Arts, Sciences.*" In *Shelley: The Critical Heritage,* edited by James E. Barcus, pp. 164-68. London: Routledge & Kegan Paul, 1975.

[*In the following excerpt, originally published in 1820, the critic condemns* The Cenci, *describing the play as "the production of a fiend, and calculated for the entertainment of devils in hell."*]

Of all the abominations which intellectual perversion, and poetical atheism, have produced in our times, this tragedy appears to us to be the most abominable. We have much doubted whether we ought to notice it; but, as watchmen place a light over the common sewer which has been opened in a way dangerous to passengers, so have we concluded it to be our duty to set up a beacon on this noisome and noxious publication. We have heard of Mr. Shelley's genius; and were it exercised upon any subject not utterly revolting to human nature, we might acknowledge it. But there are topics so disgusting . . . and this is one of them; there are themes so vile . . . as this is; there are descriptions so abhorrent to mankind . . . and this drama is full of them; there are crimes so beastly and demoniac . . . in which *The Cenci* riots and luxuriates, that no feelings can be excited by their obtrusion but those of detestation at the choice, and horror at the elaboration. We protest most solemnly, that when we reached the last page of this play, our minds were so impressed with its odious and infernal character, that we could not believe it to be written by a mortal being for the gratification of his fellow-creatures on this earth: it seemed to be the production of a fiend, and calculated for the entertainment of devils in hell.

That monsters of wickedness have been seen in the world, is too true; but not to speak of the diseased appetite which would delight to revel in their deeds, we will affirm that depravity so damnable as that of Count Cenci, in the minute portraiture of which Mr. S. takes so much pains, and guilt so atrocious as that which he paints in every one of his dramatic personages, never had either individual or aggregate existence. No; the whole design, and every part of it, is a libel upon humanity; the conception of a brain not only distempered, but familiar with infamous images, and accursed contemplations. What adds to the shocking effect is the perpetual use of the sacred name of God, and incessant appeals to the Saviour of the universe. The foul mixture of religion and blasphemy, and the dreadful association of virtuous principles with incest, parricide, and every deadly sin, form a picture which, 'Too look upon we dare not.'

Having said, and unwillingly said, this much on a composition which we cannot view without inexpressible dislike, it will not be expected from us to go into particulars farther than is merely sufficient to enforce our warning. If we quote a passage of poetic power, it must be to bring tenfold condemnation on the head of the author—for awful is the responsibility where the head condemns the heart, and the gift of talent is so great, as to remind us of Satanic knowledge and lusts, and of 'archangel fallen.'

The story, we are told, in a preface where the writer classes himself with Shakespeare and Sophocles, although two centuries old, cannot be 'mentioned in Italian society without awakening a deep and breathless interest.' We have no high opinion of the morality of Italy; but we can well believe, that even in that country, such a story must, if hinted at, be repressed by general indignation, which Mr. Shelley may, if he pleases, call breathless interest. It is indeed, as he himself confesses, 'Eminently fearful and monstrous; any thing like a dry exhibition of it upon the stage would be insupportable' (Preface, p. ix). And yet he presumes to think that that of which even a dry exhibition upon the stage could not

be endured, may be relished when arrayed in all the most forcible colouring which his pencil can supply, in all the minute details of his graphic art, in all the congenial embellishments of his inflamed imagination. Wretched delusion! and worthy of the person who ventures to tell us that, 'Religion in Italy is not, *as in Protestant countries,* a cloak to be worn on particular days; or a passport which those who do not wish to be railed at carry with them to exhibit; or a gloomy passion for penetrating the impenetrable mysteries of our being, which terrifies its possessor at the darkness of the abyss to which it has conducted him:' worthy of the person who, treating of dramatic imagery, blasphemously and senselessly says, that 'imagination is as the immortal God, which should assume flesh for the redemption of mortal passion.'

The characters are Count Cenci, an old grey haired man, a horrible fiendish incarnation, who invites an illustrious company to a jubilee entertainment on the occasion of the violent death of two of his sons; who delights in nothing but the wretchedness of all the human race, and causes all the misery in his power; who, out of sheer malignity, forcibly destroys the innocency of his only daughter; and is, in short, such a miracle of atrocity, as only this author, we think, could have conceived. Lucretia, the second wife of the Count, a most virtuous and amiable lady, who joins in a plot to murder her husband; Giacomo, his son, who because his parent has cheated him of his wife's dowry, plots his assassination; Beatrice the daughter, a pattern of beauty, integrity, grace, and sensibility, who takes the lead in all the schemes to murder her father; Orsino, a prelate, sworn of course to celibacy, and in love with Beatrice, who enters with gusto into the conspiracy, for the sound reason, that the fair one will not dare to refuse to marry an accomplice in such a transaction; Cardinal Camillo, a vacillating demi-profligate; two bravos, who strangle the Count in his sleep; executioners, torturers, and other delectable under-parts. The action consists simply of the rout in honour of the loss of two children, of the incest, of the murderous plot, of its commission, and of its punishment by the torture and execution of the wife, son, and daughter. This is the dish of carrion, seasoned with sulphur as spice, which Mr. Shelley serves up to his friend Mr. Leigh Hunt, with a dedication, by way of grace, in which he eulogizes his 'gentle, tolerant, brave, honourable, innocent, simple, pure,' &c. &c. &c. disposition. What food for a humane, sypathizing creature, like Mr. Hunt! if, indeed, his tender-heartedness be not of a peculiar kind, prone to feast on 'gruel thick and slab,' which 'like a hell-broth boils and bubbles.'[1]

We will now transcribe a portion of the entertainment scene, to show how far the writer out herods Herod, and outrages possibility in his personation of villany, by making Count Cenci a character which transforms a Richard III. an Iago, a Sir Giles Overreach, comparatively into angels of light.

[quotes Act I, Scene iii, lines 1-99]

This single example, which is far from being the most obnoxious, unnatural, and infernal in the play, would fully justify the reprobation we have pronounced. Mr. Shelley, nor no man, can pretend that any good effect can be produced by the delineation of such diabolism; the bare suggestions are a heinous offence; and whoever may be the author of such a piece, we will assert, that Beelzebub alone is fit to be the prompter. The obscenity too becomes more refinedly vicious when Beatrice, whose 'crimes and miseries,' forsooth, are as 'the mask and the mantle in which *circumstances clothed her* for her impersonation on the scenes of world'² is brought prominently forward. But we cannot dwell on this. We pass to a quotation which will prove that Mr. Shelley is capable of powerful writing: the description of sylvan scenery would be grand, and Salvator-like, were it not put into the mouth of a child pointing out the site for the murder of the author of her being, 'unfit to live, but more unfit to die.'

[quotes Act III, Scene i, lines 245-74]

It will readily be felt by our readers why we do not multiply our extracts. In truth there are very few passages which will bear transplanting to a page emulous of being read in decent and social life. The lamentable obliquity of the writer's mind pervades every sentiment, and 'corruption mining all within,' renders his florid tints and imitations of beauty only the more loathsome. Are loveliness and wisdom incompatible? Mr. Shelley makes one say of Beatrice, that

> Men wondered how such loveliness and wisdom
> Did not destroy each other!

Cenci's imprecation on his daughter, though an imitation of Lear, and one of a multitude of direct plagiarisms, is absolutely too shocking for perusal; and the dying infidelity of that paragon of parricides, is all we dare to venture to lay before the public.

> Whatever comes, my heart shall sink no more.
> And yet, I know not why, your words strike chill:
> How tedious, false and cold seem all things. I
> Have met with much injustice in this world;
> No difference has been made by God or man,
> Or any power moulding my wretched lot,
> 'Twixt good or evil as regarded me.
> I am cut off from the only world I know,
> From light, and life, and love, in youth's sweet prime.
> You do well telling me to trust in God,
> I hope I do trust in him. In whom else
> Can any trust? And yet my heart is cold.

We now most gladly take leave of this work; and sincerely hope, that should we continue our literary pursuits for fifty years, we shall never need again to look into one so stamped with pollution, impiousness, and infamy.

Notes

1. We are led to this remark by having accidentally read in one of Mr. Hunt's late political essays, an ardent prayer that Buonaparte might be released from St. Helena, were it only to fight another Waterloo against Wellington, on *more equal terms.* A strange wish for a Briton, and stranger still for a pseudo philanthropist, whether arising from a desire to have his countrymen defeated, or a slaughter productive of so much woe and desolation repeated. (Reviewer's footnote)

2. Preface, p. xiii, and a sentence, which, if not nonsense, is a most pernicious sophistry. There is some foundation for the story, as the Cenci family were devoured by a terrible catastrophe; and a picture of the daughter by Guido, is still in the Colonna Palace. (Reviewer's footnote)

Leigh Hunt (review date 26 July 1820)

SOURCE: Hunt, Leigh. "Leigh Hunt, Review, *The Indicator.*" In *Shelley: The Critical Heritage*, edited by James E. Barcus, pp. 200-06. London: Routledge & Kegan Paul, 1975.

[*In the following excerpt, originally published in 1820, Hunt lauds Shelley's use of imagination, details his characterization, and compares the author to classical dramatists.*]

'The highest moral purpose aimed at in the highest species of the drama, is the teaching the human heart, through its sympathies and antipathies, the knowledge of itself; in proportion to the possession of which knowledge, every human being is wise, just, sincere, tolerant, and kind. If dogmas can do more, it is well: but a drama is no fit place for the enforcement of them. Undoubtedly, no person can be truly dishonoured by the act of another; and the fit return to make to the most enormous injuries is kindness and forbearance, and a resolution to convert the injurer from his dark passions by love and peace. Revenge, retaliation, atonement, are pernicious mistakes. If Beatrice had thought in this manner, she would have been wiser and better; but she would never have been a tragic character: the few whom such an exposition would have interested, could never have been sufficiently interested for a domestic purpose, from the want of finding sympathy in their interest among the mass who surround them. It is in the restless and anatomizing casuistry with which men seek the justification of Beatrice, yet feel that she has done what needs justification; it is in the superstitious horror with which they contemplate alike her wrongs and revenge; that the dramatic character of what she did and suffered, consists.'

Thus speaks Mr. Shelley, in the Preface to his tragedy of *The Cenci,*—a preface beautiful for the majestic sweetness of its diction, and still more lovely for the sentiments that flow forth with it. There is no living author, who writes a preface like Mr. Shelley. The intense interest which he takes in his subject, the consciousness he has upon him nevertheless of the interests of the surrounding world, and the natural dignity with which a poet and philosopher, sure of his own motives, presents himself to the chance of being doubted by those whom he would benefit, casts about it an inexpressible air of amiableness and power. To be able to read such a preface, and differ with it, is not easy; but to be able to read it, and then go and abuse the author's intentions, shews a deplorable habit of being in the wrong.

Mr. Shelley says that he has 'endeavoured as nearly as possible to represent the characters as they really were, and has sought to avoid the error of making them actuated by his own conceptions of right or wrong, false or true, thus under a thin veil converting names and actions of the sixteenth century into cold impersonations of his own mind.' He has done so. He has only added so much poetry and imagination as is requisite to refresh the spirit, when a story so appalling is told at such length as to become a book. Accordingly, such of our readers as are acquainted with our last week's narrative of the Cenci and not with Mr. Shelley's tragedy, or with the tragedy and not with the narrative, will find in either account that they are well acquainted with the characters of the other. It is the same with the incidents, except that the legal proceedings are represented as briefer, and Beatrice is visited with a temporary madness; but this the author had a right to suppose, in probability as well as poetry. The curtain falls on the parties as they go forth to execution,—an ending which would hardly have done well on the stage, though for different reasons, any more than the nature of the main story. But through the medium of perusal, it has a very good as well as novel effect. The execution seems a supererogation, compared with it. The patience, that has followed upon the excess of the sorrow, has put the tragedy of it at rest. 'The bitterness of death is past,' as Lord Russell said when he had taken leave of his wife.

We omitted to mention last week, that the greatest crime of which Cenci had been guilty, in the opinion of the author of the Manuscript, was atheism. The reader will smile to see so foolish and depraved a man thus put on a level with Spinoza, Giordano Bruno, and other spirits of undoubted genius and integrity, who have been ac-

cused of the same opinion. But the same word means very different things to those who look into it; and it does here, though the author of the MS. might not know it. The atheism of men like Spinoza is nothing but a vivid sense of the universe about them, trying to distinguish the mystery of its opinions from the ordinary, and as they think pernicious anthropomorphism, in which our egotism envelopes it. But the atheism of such men as Cenci is the only real atheism; that is to say, it is the only real disbelief in any great and good thing, physical or moral. For the same reason, there is more atheism, to all intents and purposes of virtuous and useful belief, in some bad religions however devout, than in some supposed absences of religion: for the god they propose to themselves does not rise above the level of the world they live in, except in power like a Roman Emperor; so that there is nothing to them really outside of this world, at last. The god, for instance, of the Mussulman, is nothing but a sublimated Grand Signior; and so much the worse, as men generally are, in proportion to his power. One act of kindness, one impulse of universal benevolence, as recommended by the true spirit of Jesus, is more grand and godlike than all the degrading ideas of the Supreme Being, which fear and slavery have tried to build up to heaven. It is a greater going out of ourselves; a higher and wider resemblance to the all-embracing placidity of the universe. The Catholic author of the MS. says that Cenci was an atheist, though he built a chapel in his garden. The chapel, he tells us, was only to bury his family in. Mr. Shelley on the other hand, can suppose Cenci to have been a Catholic, well enough, considering the nature and tendency of the Catholic faith. In fact, he might have been either. He might equally have been the man he was, in those times, and under all the circumstances of his power and impunity. The vices of his atheism and the vices of his superstition would, in a spirit of his temper and education, have alike been the result of a pernicious system of religious faith, which rendered the Divine Being gross enough to be disbelieved by any one, and imitated and bribed by the wicked. Neither his scepticism nor his devotion would have run into charity. He wanted knowledge to make the first do so, and temper and privation to make the second. But perhaps the most likely thing is, that he thought as little about religion as most men of the world do at all times;—that he despised and availed himself of it in the mercenary person of the Pope, scarcely thought of it but at such times, and would only have believed in it out of fear at his last hour. Be this however as it might, still the habitual instinct of his conduct is justly traceable to the prevailing feeling respecting religion, especially as it appears that he 'established masses for the peace of his soul.' Mr. Shelley, in a striking part of his preface, informs us that even in our own times 'religion co-exists, as it were, in the mind of an Italian Catholic, with a faith in that, of which all men have the most certain knowledge. It is adoration, faith, submission, penitence, blind admiration; not a rule for moral conduct. It has no necessary connexion with any one virtue. The most atrocious villain may be rigidly devout; and without any shock to established faith, confess himself to be so. Religion pervades intensely the whole frame of society, and is according to the temper of the mind which it inhabits, a passion, a persuasion, an excuse; never a check.' We shall only add to this, that such religions in furnishing men with excuse and absolution, do but behave with something like decent kindness; for they are bound to do what they can for the vices they produce. And we may say it with gravity too. Forgiveness will make its way somehow every where, and it is lucky that it will do so. But it would be luckier, if systems made less to forgive.

The character of Beatrice is admirably managed by our author. She is what the MS. describes her, with the addition of all the living grace and presence which the re-creativeness of poetry can give her. We see the maddened loveliness of her nature walking among us, and make way with an aweful sympathy. It is thought by some, that she ought not to deny her guilt as she does;—that she ought not, at any rate, to deny the deed, whatever she may think of the guilt. But this, in our opinion, is one of the author's happiest subtleties. She is naturally so abhorrent from guilt,—she feels it to have been so impossible a thing to have killed a FATHER, truly so called, that what with her horror of the deed and of the infamy attending it, she would almost persuade herself as well as others, that no such thing had actually taken place,—that it was a notion, a horrid dream, a thing to be gratuitously cancelled from people's minds, a necessity which they were all to agree had existed but was not to be spoken of, a crime which to punish was to proclaim and make real,—any thing, in short, but that a daughter had killed her father. It is a lie told, as it were, for the sake of nature, to save it the shame of a greater contradiction. If any feeling less great and spiritual, any dread of a pettier pain, appears at last to be suffered by the author to mingle with it, a little common frailty and inconsistency only renders the character more human, and may be allowed a young creature about to be cut off in the bloom of life, who shews such an agonized wish that virtue should survive guilt and despair. She does not sacrifice the man who is put to the torture. He was apprehended without her being able to help it, would have committed her by his confession, and would have died at all events. She only reproaches him for including a daughter in the confession of his guilt; and the man, be it observed, appears to have had a light let into his mind to this effect, for her behaviour made him retract his accusations, and filled him so with a pity above his self-interest, that he chose rather to die in torture than repeat them. It is a remarkable instance of the respect with which Beatrice was regarded in Rome, in spite of the catastrophe into which she had been maddened, that Guido painted her portrait from the life, while she was in prison. He could not have done this, as a common artist might take the likeness of a common criminal, to satisfy vulgar curiosity. Her family was of too great rank and importance, and retained them too much in its reverses. He must have waited on her by permission, and accompanied the sitting with all those attentions which artists on such occasions are accustomed to pay to the great and beautiful. Perhaps he was intimate with her, for he was a painter in great request. In order to complete our accounts respecting her, as well as to indulge ourselves in copying out a beautiful piece of writing, we will give Mr. Shelley's description of this portrait, and masterly summary of her character.

[quotes Shelley's description of the portrait of Beatrice in the Colonna Palace]

The beauties of a dramatic poem, of all others, are best appreciated by a survey of the whole work itself, and of the manner in which it is composed and hangs together. We shall content ourselves therefore, in this place, with pointing out some detached beauties; and we will begin, as in the grounds of an old castle, with an account of a rocky chasm on the road to Petrella.

[quotes Act III, Scene i, lines 238-65]

With what a generous and dignified sincerity does Beatrice shew at once her own character and that of the prelate her lover.

[quotes Act I, Scene ii, lines 14-29]

The following is one of the gravest and grandest lines we ever read. It is the sum total of completeness. Orsino says, while he is meditating Cenci's murder, and its consequences,

> I see, as from a tower, the end of all.

The terrible imaginations which Beatrice pours forth during her frenzy, are only to be read in connexion with the outrage that produced them. Yet take the following, where the excess of the agony is softened to us by the wild and striking excuse which it brings for the guilt.

> What hideous thought was that I had even now?
> 'Tis gone; and yet its burthen remains still
> O'er these dull eyes—upon this weary heart.
> O, world! O, life! O, day! O, misery!

LUCR.

> What ails thee, my poor child? She answers not:
> Her spirit apprehends the sense of pain,
> But not its cause: suffering has dried away
> The source from which it sprung.

BEATR.

(Franticly). Like Parricide,
Misery has killed its father.

When she recovers, she 'approaches solemnly' Orsino, who comes in, and announces to him with an aweful obscurity, the wrong she has endured. Observe the last line.

Welcome, friend!
I have to tell you, that since last we met,
I have endured a wrong so great and strange
That neither life nor death can give me rest.
Ask me not what it is, for there are deeds
Which have no form, sufferings which have no
  tongue.

ORS.

And what is he that has thus injured you?

BEATR.

The man they call my father; a dread name.

The line of exclamations in the previous extract is in the taste of the Greek dramatists; from whom Mr. Shelley, who is a scholar, has caught also his happy feeling for compounds, such as 'the all-communicating air,' the 'mercy-winged lightning,' 'sin-chastising dreams,' 'wind-walking pestilence,' the 'palace-walking devil, gold,' &c. Gold, in another place, is finely called 'the old man's sword.'

Cenci's angry description of the glare of day is very striking.

The all-beholding sun yet shines: I hear
A busy stir of men about the streets;
I see the bright sky through the window panes:
It is a garish, broad, and peering day;
Loud, light, suspicious, full of eyes and ears,
And every little corner, nook, and hole
Is penetrated with the insolent light.
Come darkness!

The following is edifying:—

The eldest son of a rich nobleman
Is heir to all his incapacities;
He has wide wants, and narrow powers.

We are aware of no passage in the modern or ancient drama, in which the effect of bodily torture is expressed in a more brief, comprehensive, imaginative manner, than in an observation made by a judge to one of the assassins. The pleasure belonging to the original image renders it intensely painful.

MARZIO.

My God! I did not kill him; I know nothing:

Olimpio sold the robe to me, from which
You would infer my guilt.

2d Judge.

Away with him!

1st Judge.

Dare you, with lips yet white from the rack's kiss,
Speak false?

Beatrice's thoughts upon what she might and might not find in the other world are very terrible; but we prefer concluding our extracts with the close of the play, which is deliciously patient and affectionate. How triumphant is the gentleness of virtue in its most mortal defeats!

[quotes Act V, Scene iv, lines 137-65]

Mr. Shelley, in this work, reminds us of some of the most strenuous and daring of our old dramatists, not by any means as an imitator, though he has studied them, but as a bold, elemental imagination, and a framer of 'mighty lines.' He possesses also however, what those to whom we more particularly allude did not possess, great sweetness of nature, and enthusiasm for good; and his style is, as it ought to be, the offspring of this high mixture. It disproves the adage of the Latin poet. Majesty and Love do sit on one throne in the lofty buildings of his poetry; and they will be found there, at a late and we trust a happier day, on a seat immortal as themselves.

Alfred Forman and H. Buxton Forman (essay date 24 April 1886)

SOURCE: Forman, Alfred, and H. Buxton Forman. Introduction to *The Cenci: A Tragedy in Five Acts,* pp. v-xii. New York: Phaeton Press, 1970.

[*In the following essay, originally published in 1886, Forman and Forman delineate elements of horror and poetry in* The Cenci, *labeling Shelley the "chief tragic poet since Shakespeare."*]

When Milton gave to the world in 1671 his dramatic poem *Samson Agonistes,* he set before it a short discourse "Of that sort of Dramatic Poem which is call'd Tragedy." The discourse opens thus:—

"Tragedy, as it was antiently compos'd, hath been ever held the gravest, moralest, and most profitable of all other Poems: therefore said by *Aristotle* to be of power by raising pity and fear, or terror, to purge the mind of those and such like passions, that is to temper and reduce them to just measure with a kind of delight stirred up by reading or seeing those passions well imitated."

Of the emotions to which man is subject, pity and terror are the most urgent and tense and the most completely concentrated to a single point of time. Unlike the appetites hunger and desire, to which they bear a certain analogy in respect of urgency, tension and concentration, the emotions pity and terror have a large share of unselfishness; for pity is mainly unselfish, though closely knit up with the consideration of what one would himself feel in the circumstances of the person pitied; and terror, though primarily selfish, is largely called into play by circumstances affecting other persons and not the person assailed by the emotion. Thus these two emotions which it is the gift of tragic poetry to raise and purify are not only extreme in their urgency, tension, and concentration, but eminently purifiable by exaltation of the unselfish element and elimination of the selfish.

The high tension on the moral chords of our nature produced by pity and terror is not readily obtainable by other emotions; and, as the strings of a musical instrument must be tense in a high degree before the player can evolve with their assistance those vibrations which constitute the basis of music, so the moral nature of man and woman must be as it were strung up, before the highest effects of art can be evoked from it. Hence the test of a great tragedy is not only the measure of its power to awaken pity and terror, but also, and chiefly, its success in purifying those emotions of all that is base or unpleasant and leaving the whole moral and intellectual nature in a state of complete and *vibrant* equilibrium.

It is almost needless to say that tragedies answering satisfactorily this severe test are of extreme rarity. Among dramas of the nineteenth century one looks in vain for an acted tragedy fulfilling the conditions; and the unacted drama yields but one example,—that tragedy which Shelley wrote for the stage and greatly wished to have upon the stage, but which has been reserved during sixty-seven years for a Society of his special adherents to get acted.

But we must go further than this; for tragedies, in the full specific sense, are so few in the whole world's literary history that the small number of companions for Shelley's work must be sought in almost as many ages and literatures. We cannot find several tragedies answering fully to the test even in the sumptuous collection of great works left us by Shakespeare. We cannot find several in ancient literature, or several in French classic literature, or even one in modern literature of the rest of Europe. But, let it be clearly understood, this is no question of relative greatness alone, simply one of greatness combined with the true tragic quality, the exaltation and purification of pity and terror. In this regard we must exclude from the competition the stately name of Æschylus, and the high names of Calderon, Alfieri,

Goethe, Hugo, Wagner. The material introduction of the supernatural deducts largely from the essentially tragic character of the Oresteian Trilogy, as from *Macbeth* and the *Ring des Nibelungen*: *Hamlet* lacks for the intense appeal to pity and terror that concentration to a single point which we find in the few typical tragedies: *Othello* is comparatively domestic and un-ideal: Hugo stirs up rather than purifies pity and terror; and in the Wagnerian lyrical drama there is the further differentiating element of music.

Companionship for *The Cenci* must be sought in the *Œdipus Tyrannus* of Sophocles, in the *Medea* of Euripides, in Shakespeare's *King Lear,* and in the masterpiece of French classic drama, *Phèdre.*

It does not follow that a claim is set up for these five tragedies to rank as the greatest of all dramatic works. No question arises as to the relative importance of these and of the *Oresteia, Macbeth, Hamlet, Othello, Athalie, Faust, Les Burgraves,* or the *Nibelungen* Tetralogy. But, as pure tragedy, none of these latter will stand comparison with any one of the former: that is to say, the catharsis of pity and terror is not so complete in them.

Mythology and inner significance themselves deduct from the urgency and concentration of the appeal to pity and terror; and the supernatural and musical elements are comparatively cheap methods, so to speak, of helping to bring the intellectual and moral nature into a state of vibrant equilibrium. The purification of pity and terror, without any adventitious aid, but by simple concentration of human interest, is the dramatist's most difficult task;—not necessarily his highest task; but its superlative difficulty suffices to account for the rarity of pure tragedy.

For genuine tragedy of idea, conception, and laying out, there is little in English literature, outside Shakespeare's work, to compare with Otway's *Venice Preserved* and *The Orphan*; but Otway was poor as a poet and weak as a delineator of character: hence his work does not come seriously into the present comparison. Nevertheless it is noteworthy that *The Orphan,* as horrible in subject as it could well be, held the stage in the early part of this century in the hands of that Miss O'Neil to whom a squeamish Covent Garden manager could not even venture to submit *The Cenci.*

Now the extreme horror of the main subject of *The Cenci* is precisely what it has in common with its few great compeers in addition to the splendour of poetic treatment, without which there can be no such thing as tragedy properly so called. For just as in *The Cenci,* in *Phèdre,* in *King Lear,* in *Medea,* in *Œdipus Tyrannus,* the poetical style of each dramatist is at its highest level, so in each of those works we find a subject more terrible than elsewhere in the works of Shelley, of Racine, of Shakespeare, of Euripides, of Sophocles. In every one of those tragic masterpieces of the world the heart is pierced and the spirit is appalled by crimes violating the most sacred ties of nature.

It is not as dealing with real events that the tragic masterpiece of Shelley has a supreme value to the world. It is purely as an ideal work that it is of so rare a price. Antiquarian research was in its infancy when Shelley became saturated with the subject of his tragedy; and at that time, beyond the alleged outrage and the murder and execution, the real merits of the Cenci family history were but vaguely known. The documents from which he drew for his conception are the portrait of Beatrice prefixed to this volume and the **"Relation of the Death of the Family of the Cenci,"** of which a translation is appended. It is of no consequence whatever in judging of this tragic work whether the portrait represents Beatrice and was painted by Guido or not; and it is equally inessential whether the **"Relation"** [**"of the Death of the Family of the Cenci,"**] is true or untrue. That portrait and that narrative supplied the material; and Sophocles and Shakespeare supplied the bulk of what was not individual in the conception and treatment. The form is Shakespearean; and so very often is the language. The general sense of an awful impending doom is Sophoclean. But it was from Shelley's own deep heart that the transfiguring forces welled up to make a great tragic character of the Beatrice whose history we have in the **"Relation"** and whose bodily semblance we find in the picture.

The sense of that perfect human loveliness in which the Italian girl presented herself to Shelley, living within the shadow of a nameless crime, under the menacing and ever-encroaching power of a demoniac father, stirred the ardent sympathies of Shelley, his resentment against tyranny and "victorious wrong," from their very foundations. And while on the one hand the realized spectacle of that tender and lovely girlhood, pitted against the most abandoned of criminals, evokes pity from every heart where pity is not dead, on the other hand the austere dignity and unflinching courage with which, in her despair of release or relief, this gentle creature assumes in her turn the part of a criminal, and reasons of parricide as of a high duty, stirs up horror from its lowest depths.

But it is not the complicity of Beatrice alone in her father's murder that appeals to our sense of the terrible. The picture is in truth one of a series of horrors growing, as it were naturally, out of a prodigious defection from nature's rule. The spectacle of an old man, consumed with hatred of his wife, children, retainers, and indeed all who come within the scope of his dread personality, is horrible in a high degree. The terror of this picture, however, derives half its force from the mild and humane character of the wife, son, and daughter, who are transformed by the power of Count Cenci's own egregious wickedness into instruments of his death. The overpowering criminality of the one is such as to beget in the others not so much hate as fear of what may yet come to pass; and that fear becomes an imperious need which gives its victims no rest until they have accomplished their unnatural end. The expiation of the whole series of crimes by the mere death of all the principals is unimpressive compared with the surrounding and motive circumstances of guilt and tyranny, endurance and eventual resistance, despair and sudden revenge. The final horror concentrates in the innocent young brother, who sees every member of his family swept away by a devastating wave of crime.

The intolerable nature of the worst offence of Count Cenci has been urged as a reason for keeping this great tragedy off the stage. But it should not be forgotten that the same reason has been found wholly insufficient to prevent the performance of other tragedies, or even to keep from the glare of the footlights works radically unsuited for stage representation by reason of their structure. Let it be remembered that Byron's *Manfred,* one of the least actable of dramas, has been publicly performed, notwithstanding the crime which overshadows the hero's life, and which leaves the poem open to the same censure as *The Cenci.* It is remarkable that this should be the case with what is certainly one of Byron's best works, and the most poetical at all events of his dramas. In *Manfred* we are not left in any real doubt that the crime was actually committed. In *The Cenci,* the atmosphere is that of abominable outrage and impending crime against the heroine, by whom, at the close, we are assured that, "tho' wrapt in a strange cloud of crime and shame," she "lived ever holy and unstained."

An ungenerous prejudice against Shelley, and the general debasement of our national drama, have combined to prevent the performance of this masterpiece, in which, notwithstanding the horror of the subject, there is positively not an offensive word. Great and grave authorities have from the first treated *The Cenci* with the profound respect which it merits. To name Landor and Browning among those who acknowledge loyally this "noble tragedy" and "superb achievement" should suffice to make it certain that, when the time comes for a public performance of *The Cenci* to be seriously mooted, such performance will take place without let or hindrance. Our "faith is large in time"; and the time is well-nigh ripe for this consummation of Shelley's wish, this payment of the world's due, this act of simple justice to the fame of England and England's chief lyric poet, for whom we claim, in virtue of the tragedy now about to be acted for the first time, the prouder title of chief tragic poet since Shakespeare.

Kenneth N. Cameron and Horst Frenz (essay date December 1945)

SOURCE: Cameron, Kenneth N., and Horst Frenz. "The Stage History of Shelley's *The Cenci*.¹" *PMLA* 60, no. 4 (December 1945): 1080-1105.

[*In the following essay, Cameron and Frenz summarize the critical response to various performances of* The Cenci *across Europe and the United States, highlighting the complications involved in staging the play and reappraising Shelley's talents as a dramatist.*]

Although some of Shelley's Victorian critics—notably Forman[2]—believed *The Cenci* to be an acting play, it now seems to have become a settled dictum of Shelley scholarship that it is a closet drama. Woodberry in his edition of the play[3] and Bates in his study of it both conclude that it is unsuitable for stage production, Bates summarizing his views as follows:

> From all these facts it should be sufficiently clear what answer must be given to the question, how far is *The Cenci* an acting drama? As a whole it is not an acting drama at all. A play, one of whose acts fails to advance the plot in the least, ten of whose scenes are purely conversational and without action, and four-fifths of whose speeches are of impossible length, is surely not to be called an acting drama.[4]

Such, too, is the view of Shelley's most recent biographer, Professor Newman I. White:

> So much has been loosely written about *The Cenci* as one of the great English tragedies and about Shelley as potentially a great writer of stage plays that it has seemed well to set the matter straight. *The Cenci* can hardly be called a tragedy at all, in anything like the traditional meaning of the word. In spite of an intelligent and clever use of the materials, it is obviously defective in structure, when considered as a play for the stage.[5]

Standing in rather sharp contrast to this position is the fact that *The Cenci* has had a long and varied stage history. How long and how varied has not generally been recognized. Professor White lists three productions: London, 1886; Prague, 1922; London, 1922.[6] Professor Arthur C. Hicks in his excellent article on the 1940 Bellingham, Washington, production, in which he himself played the role of Count Cenci, lists two more: London, 1926 and New York, 1926.[7] To these we are able to add the following: Paris, 1891; Coburg, 1919; Moscow, 1919-20; Leeds, 1923; Frankfurt am Main, 1924. And in addition to these, we might note that plays on the Cenci theme have been acted in Italy (Nicollini's adaptation from Shelley) and France (Custine's in 1834 and a "thriller" version in 1935).

So far there has been no real attempt to trace this stage history. Professor White simply lists the three productions and Professor Hicks gives short excerpts from only three reviews of the 1922 performance. It is our purpose in this paper to present a brief account of each of these eleven productions, country by country, giving, where available, the reactions of audience, critic and producer. We make no claim to completeness in view of the chaotic state of stage bibliography and the present difficulties in searching the European field, but it seems likely that these eleven represent the main body of Cenci productions. Certainly, sufficient material is now available to make possible at least a first attempt at a task obviously long overdue.

ENGLAND

When the Shelley Society was founded in March, 1886, one of its main objects was to stage *The Cenci*.[8] Permission for a public performance being refused by the Lord Chamberlain the society decided on a private showing to be attended only by members and friends. This performance—a matinee—was put on at the Grand Theatre, Islington on May 7, 1886, Miss Alma Murray (Mrs. Alfred Forman) playing the part of Beatrice, and Hermann Vezin that of the count. This production is of unusual importance in the stage history of the play for two reasons. Although not the first production of a play on the Cenci theme—the Niccolini adaption of Shelley had been previously played in Italy and the Custine drama in France—it was the first actual production of Shelley's play as a whole. (Miss Murray in 1885 acted the final scene for the Wagner Society.)[9] Secondly, it was the reception of this production by the critics which established, more than any other single factor, the still prevalent dictum that *The Cenci* is a closet drama.

A study of the reviews of the production (as assiduously collected by the Shelley Society)[10] leads to three conclusions: the audience was enthusiastic about the play, the leaders of the Shelley Society—who included most of the great names in nineteenth century Shelley scholarship—were enthusiastic about it, the critics almost unanimously condemned it as an non-acting play.

Of all these, clearly the most important in deciding the stage merits of the play is the audience reaction. If a play goes over with an audience, it is an acting play, all comments of the critics notwithstanding. In this case, however, such reaction must be accepted with some reserve as the audience was a select one, an audience of distinctly literary interests. (It included Browning, Meredith, and Lowell.)[11] But that the play pleased this audience, there can be no doubt (and it is reasonably certain that an indubitably closet drama—*The Borderers, Otho The Great*—would not have pleased them). *The Saturday Review* commented:

> Was the result then proportionate to the exertions and hopes of the experimenters? To judge from the conduct of the audience there can be no doubt on the subject. The applause was loud and continuous. In the lobbies the comments were enthusiastic.[12]

Lloyd's Weekly London Newspaper: "It was a performance which deeply impressed the audience from the first, and finally roused them to a perfect tumult of applause."[13] *The Hornsey and Finsbury Park Journal*: "The building was packed from floor to ceiling, every eye was riveted upon the actor, and the audience was spellbound by the powerful performance."[14]

In contrast to this is the general agreement of the critics that the play, in spite of some good scenes—Cenci's curse (iv. i. 115 ff.) and the final scene were praised—was not suited for stage presentation. "Its place in English literature," said *The Times* "remains what it was; but the Shelley Society may, if they are so disposed, claim to have effectually demolished its pretensions as a play."[15] *The Daily Telegraph* was equally caustic: "Four long hours of a lovely May afternoon were yesterday occupied by the Shelley Society in laboriously proving the worthlessness of *The Cenci* for all practical stage purposes."[16] And these comments, although rather more acidous than the average, are not untypical. *The Cenci*, the Victorian dramatic critics agreed, had better remain in the closet.

The reasons for this condemnation, when analysed, are seen to fall into two categories: moral and structural. That the theme of the play was revolting, horrible and immoral was generally agreed. *The Times* found it "blood-curdling, horrible, revolting even."[17] *The Morning Post* lamented that "no flash of genial humour, no gleam of innocent gaiety" relieved its "Stygian darkness";[18] the *Scotsman*:

> The play of *The Cenci*, as readers know, turns on an incident so terrible, so revolting, and so utterly obscene as hardly to bear telling, and while willing to accord the utmost liberty to dramatic art, it seems a thousand pities it should ever have been presented in public.[19]

Lloyd's Weekly London Newspaper commented that the "fearful speeches" of Count Cenci made "strong men writhe in anguish," and hoped that a play full of such "unnatural horrors," would ever remain "forbidden."[20] *The Daily Telegraph* was worried about the possible effects of "the atrocious and bloodthirsty utterances of Cenci" and the "self-communings," of Beatrice upon the ladies in the audience, "many of them young."[21] And the only American comment we have come across reiterates the same position:

> . . . the realism with which she portrayed the outraged daughter only served to make the performance, as a whole, more offensive, and is the talk of the town today. But, although Browning stood up waving his handkerchief at the close all the critics condemned the Shelley Society in severe terms for such a revolting and unnecessary spectacle.[22]

As to the structural defects, they may most conveniently be presented in the following excerpts from, respectively, *The Saturday Review* and *The Liverpool Courier*:

There is no forming or following up of a plot or story. For three long acts the situation never varies. In one scene after another we have the violence of Francesco, the terrors of Beatrice, and the abject cowardice of the other members of the family. It remains doubtful when the inexpiable wrong is committed and whether it is repeated. There is an absolutely superfluous scene in the house of Giacomo. There is so much doubting and talking before the great act of wild justice is done that the splendid climax which might have been obtained by making the punishment follow instantly on the outrage is lost. Francesco's crime is not kept back and led up to, as it assuredly would have been by a born dramatist, but is thrown before the audience with both hands in the very first scenes. The denial of her deed by Beatrice when in prison is wholly out of keeping with the exaltation of rage and sense of wrong by which it is inspired. To be consistent, she should have avowed the act, but denied its criminal character. As it is, she falls below herself, and no reason is given for the fall. *The Cenci* leaves us with the impression not of an action advancing through a climax to a catastrophe, but of a succession of scenes.[23]

It is now made clear that, quite apart from the horror of its theme, *The Cenci* is unfitted for the stage. It is, to begin with, by far too long. It takes just four hours (with the inevitable "waits") to enact. Begun at half-past seven, it would detain the audience till half-past eleven, and that in itself is fatal. It is stuffed full of long speeches which no ordinary assemblage of playgoers would tolerate; and, what is more to the purpose, no amount of "cutting" would render the drama really dramatic. And in prolonging the play after the death of Cenci the poet made a double mistake. He caused the action to drag, and he made Beatrice become a bore, if not worse. She is tedious, and, unhappily, she is unsympathetic. Her clinging to life is unheroic, and her endeavour to prove that she is innocent of the crime she prompted is specious and a failure.[24]

The structural defects are, thus, found to be six in number: the play is too long; the speeches are too long; the action lacks variety; the action lacks movement; the play declines after the murder of Cenci; the scenes which announce, first, the threats, and, second, the action, of Beatrice's father are confused; Beatrice's denial of her guilt withdraws audience sympathy from her.

The charges are of especial interest as, along with that of the unsuitability of the subject, they are similar to much of the subsequent judgements of Shelley scholars. Woodberry repeats them, one by one;[25] Bates, although charitably disposed to the merits of the play as a whole and granting acting power to some of the scenes, was clearly influenced by them;[26] Peck follows their general tenets.[27] White finds that the play "lacks consistent progression," that "in actual presentation" it seems to fall apart "with the death of Count Cenci," that Beatrice's denial of her guilt is a dramatic flaw, that it is "essentially melodrama rather than tragedy," that one so "totally devoid of experience behind the footlights" as was Shelley could not be expected to produce "good theatre"; but he denies the unsuitability of the subject *per se* for dramatic treatment.[28]

Although this production derives significance from the fact of being the first and having so distinguished an audience, a much more important production was that by Sybil Thorndike at the New Theatre, London in 1922. This was a regular, professional stage production, put on in a leading London theatre, going through four performances, and viewed by a representative section of the present century London theatre-going public and critics. It is clear that such a production gives a more solid basis for judging the stage qualities of the play than that of 1886, which was restricted to one amateur (even though competent) performance, presented as an experimental venture before a select audience and subjected to criticism by men who, however much they may have wished to be fair, were nevertheless influenced by the moral prejudices of their age.

Before giving a representative cross section of the views of the best known of the 1922 critics, let us first note that in 1922, as in 1886, the audience was enthralled by the play:

> Although the performance lasted three solid hours, with only one short break, the audience listened with rapt attention from start to finish, and, exhausted as it must have been by the effort required to grasp Shelley's magnificent imagery, it would not leave until everybody had been called again and again, and Miss Thorndike, looking positively worn out after playing the long trying part of Beatrice, had come forward to make a speech.[29]

One of the most enthusiastic reviews was that by James Agate. The review appeared first in *The Saturday Review*[30] and was later reprinted (with some additional remarks on Sybil Thorndike) as an essay in his book *At Half-Past Eight*.

> When I entered the theatre my recollection of the play was of the haziest. Before the end of the first scene I realized that I was not to feel pity for the man, nor terror at his example, who was the prey of unlawful passion. Cenci proclaimed himself outside all lusts save that of cruelty, a case not for the artist, but the alienist. It seemed, for an act or so, that the thing was not quite worth while, that it hardly needed a Shelley to put together this tale of injury, vengeance, and the law's insensible machinery. So far the theatre remained the theatre. One could admire Miss Thorndike's admirably collected beginning and her cresscendo of nerves. One had time to admire the colour and grouping of the scenes. Cenci dispatched, a new spirit at once disengaged itself. The motive changed from incest to parricide, and what I have called the second story of spiritual significance became apparent in Miss Thorndike's idealized figure of injury and the justiciary's identification of her deed of murder with that of rebellion against the paternal authority of the Church. One felt that if Beatrice had been the chief figure in a non-metaphysical

tragedy she would have trumpeted her guilt and proclaimed it innocence. Here she was, however, equivocating like a Greek and lying like a Trojan, fighting authority with its own weapons. Subtle as any casuist, and since to her this killing was no murder, she swore roundly that she had no hand in it. More than ever was Miss Thorndike the play here. First she had been an individual victim, then a symbol of maiden virtue rudely strumpeted, and now she rose to the embodiment of a pure philosophic idea—the idea of Rebellion.[31]

Another enthusiastic response was that of Marrice Baring in *The New Statesman*:

> The drama had not proceeded far before one realized that **The Cenci** was more than a great piece of literature. The Banquet Scene at the end of Act I was drama, and drama which would be recognised as such in any time, in any place, and before any audience—(why were the guests dressed as Christmas-crackers in the style of the Russian Ballet?)—and the impression of drama increased as the play proceeded.
>
> The arrangements for the murder of Cenci (how beautifully Miss Thorndike spoke the Chasm speech!), the murder itself, the ironic arrival of the Papal authorities for the arrest of Cenci when it is too late, and then the unforgettable scenes of the trial and the prison. I would like to protest with all my strength against the introduction of the tortured Marzio's screams at the beginning of the trial. There is no sanction in the text for any such thing, and even as a Grand Guignol thrill they miss their effect, since there is no preparation for them. They are merely an ugly blot. As the play drew to a close, its greatness, and the greatness of Shelley as a poet and as a dramatic poet, seemed to be revealed to us with a great sweep as of opening wings. When Beatrice in the prison says to Lucretia:
>
> Your eyes look pale, hollow and overworn,
> With heaviness of watching and slow grief
> Come, I will sing you some low, sleepy tune,
> Not cheerful, nor yet sad; some dull old thing,
> Some outworn and unused monotony,
> Such as our country gossips sit and spin,
> Till they almost forget they live.
>
> As these beautiful and simple words were spoken in their situation, so dramatically right, so scenically effective, one felt that it was true that Shelley has been so far the only meet successor of the Elizabethan dramatists.[32]

And still another comes from the pen of W. J. Turner in *The Spectator*:

> Well, now that we have seen **The Cenci** on the stage what are we to think of it? I can say at once that I did not find it a moment too long. When one considers the extraordinary difficulty of the theme and the entire absence of any relief from its pitch of sustained gloom and suffering it must be reckoned a marvel of dramatic construction. It holds our attention from the first moment to the last. It might be thought that after the murder of Count Cenci the interest would flag, but, on the contrary, it deepens. In fact, the last Act of the play is

the most moving of all. It is what it should be, the culmination of the tragedy, the moment when its meaning flowers with a complete and extraordinary beauty.[33]

And Mr. Horace Shipp, critic for *The English Review* is lyrical in his praise:

> In our minds was a memory of that afternoon of 1919 when Lewis Casson and Sybil Thorndike revealed to us the potency of Euripides, and showed that *The Trojan Women* was as relevant to our day as it was to the time when the master of Greek drama gave it as a message to his own generation. Now again we stand indebted to their lofty conception of the theatre for the revival of Shelley's masterpiece, the flashing might of its message, the "purging by pity and terror" of its tragic theme. . . . The first public performance of *The Cenci* and its reception is an event of no small importance in the theatre. Poetic drama proved its potency; aesthetically, socially, intellectually it achieved its ends.[34]

One of the most discriminating reviews was that of St. John Ervine in *The Observer*.[35] Although he feels that Count Cenci is too monstrous to be credible and that Beatrice's lying "diminishes her nobility," he believes that the play has true dramatic greatness, and agrees with his fellow critics on the superiority of the last two acts to the first three. So great an interest did the play arouse in Ervine that some eleven years later he read a paper before the Royal Society of Literature arguing that Shelley was a real stage dramatist.[36]

In this paper—the most significant treatment of Shelley's dramatic work by a leading theatrical critic—Ervine flatly declares:

> *The Cenci* was written for the theatre and is, in all respects, a stage play. Dowden does not regard it as an actable piece, but there is scarcely any proof that Dowden knew what is actable and what is not.[37]

This view of *The Cenci* as a stage play Ervine supports by a series of examples of which the following are representative:

> Shelley, as I have hinted earlier in this paper, knew the tricks of the theatre trade by instinct. A common and exceedingly effective device in drama is that which I shall call the trick of suspended intensity. By this I mean the trick of making the audience think that a character of immense importance is about to enter the scene, and instead, causing a subordinate character to appear. Then, when his entrance is not expected, the important character comes in. There are two examples of this trick in *The Cenci*. At the beginning of the second act, Beatrice, now undisguisedly in fear of her father, thinks she hears him approaching:
>
> > "Did he pass this way? Have you seen him, brother?
> > Ah, no! that is his step upon the stairs:
> > 'Tis nearer now; his hand is on the door;
> > Mother, if I to thee have ever been
> > A duteous child, now save me! Thou, great God,
> > Whose image upon earth a father is,
> > Dost Thou indeed abandon me? He comes;
> > The door is opening now; I see his face;
> > He frowns on others, but he smiles on me,
> > Even as he did after the feast last night."
>
> But the incomer is not Count Cenci: he is Orsino's servant. Then follows a fairly long passage in which Beatrice's terror of her father's appearance is forgotten by the audience. It closes in a little scene of affectionate approaches between Beatrice and her brother, Bernardo, and their step-mother, Lucretia, who, deeply moved by their love of her, murmurs, "My dear, dear children!" and as she does so, the door suddenly opens and Count Cenci comes in. That is drama. Shelley, who had seldom been in a theatre and had read no books on how plays should be written, chiefly because no one in those days was fool enough to suppose that playwriting can be taught and, therefore, manuals on how to be a successful author were not published, knew this device by intuition. His knowledge, thus acquired, proved him to be a born dramatist. He used the device again in the third act as effectively as he had used it in the second. Beatrice conspires with her step-mother and Orsino to have her father murdered. While they are conspiring together a footstep is heard, and each is convinced that the Count is approaching:
>
> > "That step we hear approach must never pass
> > The bridge of which we spoke,"
>
> Beatrice whispers to Orsino. But it is Giacomo, the Count's elder surviving son, not the Count himself who enters. The Count, indeed, does not appear in this scene, which opens abruptly with Beatrice staggering in and speaking wildly. She has just been outraged by her father. Shelley had to write this scene under great disability. The play is about incest, but the temper of England then was not tolerant of works in which this theme is treated, nor, indeed, is it tolerant of them now. He had, therefore, to write his play with, so to speak, his theme in his cheek: to let his heroine be violated by her unnatural parent without telling anyone in the theatre that she has been violated. The task was difficult, and Shelley cannot be said to have accomplished it successfully, but he managed with singular dexterity to obtain the horror of the revelation without making the revelation. It is hardly possible to write an effective play by dodging the drama, but Shelley almost performs the feat. His theme demands a terrific scene between Beatrice and her father, but the law forbade him to supply it. The scene in which Cenci is murdered is as grand and awful as that in which Duncan of Scotland is murdered by Macbeth. Shelley, indeed, uses an effect in this scene not unlike the knocking on the gate in Shakespeare's play after Duncan is dead. The murderers have been rewarded by Beatrice and hurried away, and as they leave a horn is heard:
>
> > "Hark, 'tis the castle horn; my God! it sounds
> > Like the last trump"
>
> Lucretia cries, but Beatrice, un-humanly calm now, says only, "Some tedious guest is coming," and bids her step-mother "retire to counterfeit deep rest."[38]

One other leading dramatic critic who was enthusiastic over the 1922 production was Charles Morgan. Morgan, although present at the production did not review it at the time, but in 1935 he engaged in an interesting controversy with Philip Carr in the columns of *The New York Times* on the stage merits of the play. Morgan, like Ervine, asserted that it was eminently suited for stage production: "rich with splendors, vigorous and subtle in action, various and determined in character-drawing, and yet full of gentleness and music." "How the theatre was held! I can remember now over an interval of perhaps ten years the tension of that performance and the agony of Beatrice's farewell before she was led out to torture and execution."[39]

This chorus of praise was not unanimous. There were still a few critics who agreed with their predecessors of 1886 that the play itself was unsuited for stage production or that the subject was too objectionable for presentation. Thus Mr. Ivor Brown in the *Theatre Magazine* remarks that "its passion and splendor are spread thin over three hours of acting," and goes to comment:

> But it is more a poem than a play, because the essence of all past Drama is conflict and here the conflict is between Pure Innocence and Vilest Guilt. There's nothing to be said for the tyrannical, incestuous Cenci; there's everything to be said for Beatrice, his blameless victim. Great drama occurs when the fine shades of right and wrong are evenly distributed between two parties or between two parts of a single personality. Shelley, flaying Count Cenci, flays a dead horse.[40]

The critic for *The Graphic* considers that while the drama is "great literature," it "belongs essentially to the study and not to the stage";[41] while *The Illustrated London News* reviewer writes:

> The removal of the Censor's ban corresponds with the general feeling that the policy of taboo in connection with such a work of art is absurd; but the monstrous nature of the theme of *The Cenci,* a father's unspeakable crime, is certainly a handicap to illusion. Under the test of stage presentation this theme is found hardly so much to outrage as to paralyse a modern audience's feelings; not until Count Cenci himself is removed from the action can playgoers respond to the rhetorical and emotional appeal of the tragedy. There is more rhetoric than action; little sense of climax, and far too much indulgence in anti-climax.[42]

This unfavorable opinion, however, was a minority voice, and the sum total of critical judgement was favorable.[43] This judgement, it is clear, contradicts on almost every point the views of the critics of 1886. There is still a disapproval of Beatrice's denial of her guilt and St. John Ervine reiterates the feeling of one of the earlier reviewers that the scene in which Beatrice announced her injury is confused.[44] But for the best twentieth century critics there is no feeling of the unsuitability of the subject for presentation; only a very few echoed the old charge of immorality or horribleness. Nor is there any feeling that the play is structurally un-

suited for the stage; that its action is slow and lacking in variety. On the contrary there is almost unanimous agreement on the true theatrical qualities of the play and the intensity of its movement.

It is interesting, too, to note the scenes which are praised. Instead of the emphasis on Cenci's curse—which was probably due to Vezin's proficiency in the declamatory style of acting then fashionable—the critics now select such scenes as the banquet scene, the trial scene, the murder, the arrival of the papal nuncio as outstanding. The final scene, with its power of simple pathos, was praised on both occasions. Most striking of all, however, is the complete reversal of the old idea that the play declined after the death of Cenci. Almost every reviewer of the 1922 production was struck by exactly the opposite phenomenon: it is only with the death of Cenci that the play begins to rise to its full strength.

A few months after the production at the New Theatre, *The Cenci* was put on at the Industrial Theatre at Leeds—January 15 and 16, 1923—by an amateur cast and before a mainly working class audience.[45] The only two reviews we have been able to obtain are not very enlightening: the *Yorkshire Post* found the play "repellant in the extreme to the Christian type of mind," but offered little concrete comment;[46] the undergraduate periodical of the University of Leeds, *The Gryphon,* found it too blood-and-thundery.[47] We have, however, through the kindness of Professor Bruce Dickins of the University of Leeds obtained a most interesting letter from the producer, Mr. James R. Gregson (at present with the British Broadcasting Corporation), from which we excerpt the following as most revealing:

> We played a whole torture scene in the semi-darkness until the poor wretch was screaming in agony and fainted. Then the act-drop was raised on what to the audience was a surprising scene—no sign of the tortured man or his tormentors, but the three clerics calmly discussing the case. Then the wounded, broken wretch was brought in and the action sent on. The full effect of this was apparent later in the scene when one of the judges looking with pity on Beatrice said, "Yet she must be tortured,"—we had several faints in the audience at this point at each performance. Which brings me to the most oustanding fact about this play—its terrific power. It is a badly constructed play—its most effective lines are re-writings of passages from Shakespeare and other Elizabethan dramatists—over and over again one strikes an idea "borrowed" from older dramatists; but the play has power, not only over an audience but the players. We found it impossible to rehearse in cold blood—even in the first rehearsals when we plotted the mechanics of movement and grouping, it was impossible to meander or gabble through the lines—before long we were acting with as much intensity as at a performance. One of my players said, "The play's possessed—it grabs hold of you!" Its effect upon even hardened playgoers was amazing—one critic of

many years' experience came round after, looking drawn and ill. He told me afterwards that it was days before he was free of its lingering power to flood him with temporary sickness—"Worse than anything in Grand Guignol" he said. "The worst belly-scourer I've struck!" But the construction is faulty to a degree, and we had some difficulty in designing exits and entrances which built up a scene rather than let it down.[48]

The play may not have appealed to the *Yorkshire Post,* but it seems, as ever, to have exerted a powerful influence over the audience and cast.

In March, 1926, Miss Sybil Thorndike, encouraged by the success of her 1922 production, revived *The Cenci,* this time at the Empire Theatre. Few of the critics who had reviewed the play in 1922 apparently rereviewed it, with the exception of Ivor Brown who had not liked it the first time and liked it even less this time.[49] Miss Clemence Dane, the well known dramatic author and novelist, made a preliminary speech on the play in which she referred to it as one of the world's great tragedies, and this high praise irked some reviewers. R. J., in *The Spectator* waxed sarcastic both on Miss Dane's speech and on the play itself, condemning Cenci as a mere "typical figure of the horror tragedies," whose "lunatic frenzies may be found in Tourneur, Kyd, Ford and Webster," and considering as "odious" the scene in which Beatrice tries to overawe Marzio.[50] Another reviewer, in contrast, although also annoyed by Miss Dane's speech, hails this latter scene: "Her stand for justice and the wonderful scene in which the tortured assassin Marzio, is moved by her eyes and that impassioned outburst to recant all that he confessed on the wheel are magnificent." He concludes that "the total effect of a performance of *The Cenci* is ennobling."[51]

There have been many attempts to translate Shelley's *The Cenci* into German. Among the most noteworthy translators are Felix Adolphi (1837), Julius Seybt (1844), Adolph Strodtmann (1867), Georg-Hellmuth Neuendorff (1907), and Alfred Wolfenstein (1924).[52] The last three have made very definite statements that they believe strongly not only in the poetic value of *The Cenci* but also in its adaptability to the stage. Strodtmann was convinced that *The Cenci* would be a successful stage play and, in order to induce some theatre producer to produce it, even prepared a special acting version as we can gather from the following statement attached to his translation: "Das Recht zur Aufführung der Cenei nach dieser Uebersetzung ist zuvor von dem Unterzeichneten zu erwerben. Eine gekürzte Bearbeitung für die Bühne steht den Herren Theaterdirektoren auf Wunsch zu Gebote."[53] In a discussion of a number of dramas in various countries which make use of the Cenci-theme Neuendorff expresses his hope that people will see that Shelley's

drama possesses "neben seinem poetischen Werte auch eine eminente Bühnenfähigkeit," and claims that "Szenen, wie das Bankett I 3, die erschütternde Verfluchung Beatricens IV 1, die Kerkerszenen im 5ten Aufzuge müssen von überwältigender Wirkung sein." Neuendorff concludes his article by saying: "vielleicht erleben wir in nicht allzuferner Zeit sogar eine Aufführung der Shelleyschen *Cenci.* Damit würde ein Wunsch, der immer aufs neue geäussert worden ist, ein Lieblingsgedanke Shelleys selbst, erfüllt sein!"[54]

Twelve years later Neuendorff's plea—and certainly he must have hoped that his own version would find its way to the stage—materialized and *The Cenci* was presented for the first time in Germany. All we have been able to ascertain about this production is that it took place in the Coburg Landestheater in November of 1919 under the direction of Anton Ludwig who evidently was also responsible for its adaptation.[55]

In 1924, the poet and dramatist Alfred Wolfenstein[56] published his translation of the play, a translation which a literary critic in the *Archiv für das Studium der Neueren Sprachen und Literaturen* referred to as follows: "Die Uebersetzung hat Schwung und Wohlklang. Auf Blankvers ist oft verzichtet, um in kurzen Versen und rhythmischer Prosa die Musik des Originals treuer wiederzugeben."[57] Since this version has been used for the most significant German production of *The Cenci,* it might be well to discuss briefly Wolfenstein's conception of Shelley's drama and the changes he made in it.

Wolfenstein gave his special interpretation of the play in an article in *Die Szene,* namely that the incest theme is but part of a larger theme—that of a struggle for human freedom. He felt that the modernized drama had to show even more clearly than the original had done "die über-individuelle Bedrängung der von allen Angriffen umstellten Frau" and "die Tyrannei der Herrschenden, in der die väterliche Notzucht nur eine unter vielen Ausbeutungen der Guten durch die Bösen bedeutet." To the German poet Beatrice represents all suffering humanity. Count Cenci is more than merely a sensualist. Passion, it is true, drives him beyond all human bounds; not, however, for purely sensual reasons, but for the enjoyment of a more complete and sadistic domination—as Wolfenstein calls it, "Imperialismus eines Liebesverbrechen, begangen an einer Menschenfreundin."[58]

To bring out this motif and to dramatize a play which he considers fundamentally lyrical but containing a powerful element of "dramatischen Schwung"—Wolfenstein rearranged a few scenes, and occasionally made additions and omissions pursuing a fairly consistent policy of breaking up the longer speeches. He transformed the language from 5-foot iambics to a "rhythmisch freiere, zugleich dialogisch schärfer gebundene Versprosa."[59] The dramatic critic of *Die Schöne Litera-*

tur finds that Wolfenstein has made some skilful changes and that he has produced a language which is closer to the modern manner of speech, but finds the poetic value of the German play extremely uneven:

> Der Bearbeiter hat den lyrisch weiten Schwung, das breit ausladende Barock des Shelleyschen Textes zusammengefasst und einige Szenen recht geschickt gekürzt und umgestellt. Dafür wurde freilich der meerwogengleiche Rhythmus der Jambenverse zugunsten eines nervösen Wechsels zerstückelt. Es stolpert, jetzt, was vorher strömte. Zugegeben sei, dass dies der modernen Sprechweise, die Verse ja gern durch 'sinngemässe' oder 'ausdrucksvolle' Pausen zerhackt, gemässer ist. Der dichterische Gehalt der Uebersetzung ist äusserst ungleichmässig: neben gut gelungenen Partien stehen prosaische Dinge von unverständlicher Hässlichkeit.[60]

Bernhard Diebold, the dramatic critic of the *Frankfurter Zeitung,* writes along similar lines:

> Aber ganz Shelley ist diese Fassung nicht mehr. Die Elegie, das Getragene und Fliessende der Sprache, das luftig Undeutliche der Objekte, die "Zerschwebung" . . . ist deutlich, konturiert und "gradezu" geworden.[61]

He calls Wolfenstein's language beautiful and refined, but, at the same time, he thinks it is a language of communication and not, like Shelley's, one of imagination. Commenting on the dramatis personae in **The Cenci** Bernhard Diebold claims that in Wolfenstein's hands their behavior has become more cunning than in the original: "Sie sind aus ihrem Renaissance—Typus aufgeweckt zu raffinierterem Gehaben."[62] Francesco and the judge appear more sadistic in their inordinate desire; Orsino, on the other hand, has assumed the characteristics more of a problematic lover than a loathsome intriguer:

> Der Anstifter und Agent des Verbrechens, Orsino, ist— nicht zum Vorteil der theatralischen Schlagkraft—aus einem widerlichen Intriganten zum problematischen Liebhaber geworden; was er zwar auch bei Shelley ist, jedoch mit materiell dramatischer Hauptfunktion. Es wäre Wolfenstein zu raten, diesen Orsino jeder lyrischen Atmosphäre zu entreissen und ihn durchaus in Shelleys Sinn als Treiber der Handlung stärker auszunutzen.[63]

It is interesting to note that Diebold expresses his preference for Shelley's interpretation of Orsino as instigator of the action and regrets that Wolfenstein has made less use of him as a dramatic force.

The production of Alfred Wolfenstein's version of **The Cenci** took place on October 23, 1924, in the Schauspielhaus in Frankfurt am Main under the direction of Fritz Buch.[64] According to the critic of the *Frankfurter Zeitung* the production was carried out with gravity and restraint; he praises the magnificent scenery and calls the banquet scene the highlight of the play: "Der Spiel-

leiter F. B. Buch legte weniger auf laute Dynamik als auf schwere Stimmung an. Sein Höhepunkt, der jedes Lob verdient: die grausige Bankettszene."[65] According to the critic of *Die Schöne Literatur* the production revealed a firmly defined dramatic pattern; the speeches were well thought through, and the whole tone of the performance was balanced, but occasionally an attempt to make things too explicit led to some unnaturalness:

> Aber so klar auch der Grundriss erfasst war, so sinn- und ausdrucksvoll der Raum gestaltet, die Rede durchdacht, der Klang gewogen war, so führte doch ein stellenweise gefühltes Ueber-deutlich-machen-wollen zu Unnatur und peinlicher Stilisierung. Wie zu grosse Bewusstheit den Lebensvorgang nicht mehr dirigiert— sondern zerstückelt, so ertötete sie auch hier den brutalen Schwung, ohne den eine solche Tragödie nicht leben kann. So kam es, dass an manchen Stellen das Tragische zum Quälenden, das Feurige zum Erstarrten, das Monumentale zur Stilisierung wurde.[66]

Ferdinand Hart as Count Cenci is said to have portrayed a smooth and lascivious vampire:

> Dieser Francesco Cenci, der sich unter anderen Regieauspizien die Seele aus den Lungen gebrüllt hätte, wurde in Ferdinand Harts mit ungewöhnlichem Instinkt erfasster Zeichnung zu einem leisen, geilen, qualligen Vampyr; einem unheimlichen Tier mit offenem Maul und lächelnder Genugtuung im Bösen.[67]

Of Fritta Brod as Beatrice Werner Deubel says that she "zu sehr im Dekorativen stecken blieb,"[68] while Diebold stressed her elegiac qualities: ". . . diese Künstlerin dient *nolens volens* stets der Elegie. Sie ist nie Plastik, sondern Relief. Die Töne bleiben gemässigt, die Gebärden in der linear bestimmten Fläche. Ihre Wirkung ist Schönheit."[69] He concludes his critique by the following comments on the secondary roles:

> Herr Schneider (etwas unentschieden als Orsino) und Gerr Odemar (mit der vorzüglichen Charakterleistung des in hysterische Verzweiflung gehetzten Bruders Giacomo) hätten ihre Rollen tauschen sollen. Denn die wichtigere Partie des Intriguenführers Orsino verlangte auch den sichereren Schauspieler. Alexander Engels stellte mit schöner Würde den Vertreter des geschäftstüchtigen Papstes vor; peinliche Aufgabe für einen so aufrechten Mann. Herr Ettel gab dem Richter sein vollgerüttelt Mass an Gemeinheit. Ben Spanier starb als Bandit Olimpio einen schönen Tod für den Adelsruhm der Familie Cenci, den ihm Shelley und sein Bearbeiter etwas gar zu anspruchsvoll zur weiteren Ertragung seiner Folter nahelegten. Aber in diesem schlechten—schlichten Bravo sollte nach Wolfenstein der einzige Mann in Beatricens erotischem Dunstkreis verherrlicht werden, der sie mit Leib und Seele nicht verriet. Mit dieser idealen Betonung hat der Verarbeiter—wie an anderen Stellen—den eindeutigeren Renaissance character kompliziert und verweichlicht.[70]

That the performance was enthusiastically greeted by the audience is clear from Diebold's final remark: "Aber die moderne Retouche wird ein modernes Publikum gewinnen. Der starke Beifall bewies es."[71] Unfortunately, we are unable to find out how often the tragedy was performed at the Schauspielhaus in Frankfurt,[72] but we may assume that the performance described above was not the only one. A few days before his death, Albert Steinrück[73] voiced his intention to present *The Cenci* on the radio, and since Wolfenstein is our informant for this statement,[74] Steinrück may very well have intended to use Wolfenstein's version.

Without a doubt, in Germany as in England, it was the incest theme that prevented Shelley's drama from being produced on the stage of the nineteenth century. After the World War, however, similar themes were presented in the German playhouses and encountered no objections from critics and theatre-goers. Professor Liptzin informs us that in the spring of 1922, for instance, "Fritz von Unruh's drama *Ein Geschlecht,* was successfully staged at Leipzig, and failed to arouse any indignation, even though the theme of incest, which was one of the essential themes of the play, was there treated with even less reserve than was done in Schelley's tragedy."[75] It is not surprising in view of this general interest in such themes that an expressionistic writer like Wolfenstein was attracted to Shelley's *The Cenci* and produced a translation which found its way to a successful presentation on the stage.

FRANCE AND ITALY

Although a version of the Cenci story—apparently owing nothing to Shelley—by Adolphe de Custine was played in Paris as early as 1833,[76] Shelley's play was not produced until 1891,—at the Théâtre d'Art in Paris, with Lugné-Poe directing. This French production was thus the second production of the play in point of time, following the London 1886 version by five years.

The Théâtre d'Art, founded by the poet Paul Fort in 1890 with the help of a group of young enthusiasts, some of them students at the Conservatory, was apparently intended mainly for the production of plays of unusual or literary interest. It received the patronage of such distinguished men of letters as Stéphane Mallarmé, Paul Verlaine and Emile Verhaeren and had Paul Gauguin as one of its program illustrators.[77] In addition to *The Cenci,* Fort also produced Marlowe's *Dr. Faustus,* Ford's *'Tis Pity She's a Whore* and Paul Verlaine's *Les Uns et Les Autres.*[78]

The only review of the performance of *The Cenci* so far uncovered—although others must surely exist—is one in the *Mercure de France* by Alfred Vallette. Vallette, unfortunately, spends most of his time criticizing the translation (by Felix Rabbe) but he finally gets around to some critical comments on the play itself:

La tentative du Théâtre d'Art n'en est pas moins intéressante, et M. Paul Fort a quelque mérite a l'avoir osée, car il y fallait du courage. Monter en *quatorze* tableaux—pour la donner intégrale, sans tripatouillage aucun—une œuvre réputée injouable et que, même tripatouillé, refuseraient les théâtres à subvention, c'est en effet pour une jeune entreprise, nécessairement pauvre encore de moyens, un immense effort, et même un tour de force. Evidemment, il y eut des *gaffes* de mise en scène et l'interprétation ne fut point, parfaite, mais—on l'a dit ailleurs—qu'est-ce que cela devant le résultat obtenu? Au total, il est indéniable qu'ait réussi cette périlleuse aventure de dégager, *suffisante,* l'impression incluse en son drame par l'un des plus difficiles à bien entendre.[79]

Vallette praises the acting of Mlle. Cammée as Beatrice and that of M. Prad as the count. The audience, he informs us, was "hilare et bavarde," but enchanted into periodic silences by the acting of M. Prad and Mlle. Cammée.[80] Some two months later he added to these comments the following interesting observation: "Le Théâtre d'Art, definitivement sorti de ses langes le soir des *Cenci,* s'affirme l'entreprise dramatique la plus originale de ce temps."[81]

From this account it is clear that this 1891 production was not a regular theatrical performance but an experimental venture put on before a group of Parisian intelligentia. As such it seems to have had a moderate success. And as Professor Henri Peyre intimates one could hardly expect more from one performance in a "théâtre d'avantgarde."[82]

Shelley's play was not, however, so far as we have been able to ascertain again played in France, but in 1935 a rather interesting production of a Cenci drama was given at the Folies-Wagram by M. Antonin Artaud, a dramatist interested in applying certain surrealist techniques to the theatre. Artaud founded a "Théâtre de la Cruauté,"[83] with the avowed intention of making the flesh of his intellectual clientele creep by various psychological and histrionic excesses. And such apparently was his object with *The Cenci.* He exaggerated the sadistic and pathological elements of the play to a point of violence and depended largely upon this artificial heightening of tension for his effect. How much he owed to Shelley's play we do not know as we have not been able to secure a copy of Artaud's work. Pierre Jean Jouve, however, writing in *La Nouvelle Revue Française* has the following to say on the subject:

Le texte d'Antonin Artaud descend plus directement de la tragédie de Shelley que de la "chronique" de Stendhal; plutôt que la minutie sanglante et le sauvage caractère italien du fait-divers de Rome en 1599, il offre ces lourdes résonnances, ces draperies de sentiment et ces poses baroques que les Romantiques furent les derniers à oser employer. Il faut signaler d'abord le sérieux, le registre grave de l'action, "l'état théâtral" qui règne de la première parole à la dernière. Ce théâtre n'est pas fait pour plaire: Artaud joue constamment contre la salle, et gagne. La tension la plus âpre ne cesse pas de troubler le spectateur et parfois de le blesser. Tout au plus pourrait—on reprocher au drama-turge de demeurer sur le paroxysme, comme si l'histoire des Cenci était saisie dans le coeur d'une unique scène de rage. Si d'autre part Artaud avait "activé" certains actes fondamentaux de Cenci et de Béatrice, manifes-tant une totale cruauté, il aurait peut-être évité plus sûrement l'excès de matière verbale.[84]

Jouve's comments on Artaud's treatment of Count Cenci gives a further impression of Artaud's extreme methods:

> Le Cenci d'Artaud est un *furieux coupable,* moins éro-tique que destructeur, démoniaque, trop au clair sur lui-même et pas assez "bestial somptueux" pour être vrai-ment une créature de la Renaissance; mais ce furieux, blasphémateur de Dieu et athée dans la manière de Sade, dont l'orgueil à faire le mal et l'esprit revendica-teur sont indéniablement sous le signe de la *paranoia,* contient assez de douleur sanglotante et de défi pour nous attacher à sa torture.[85]

For all these devices of exaggeration, however, the play was not a success. The critics seem to have unanimously waxed sarcastic about it. The comment of the critic for *La Revue de Paris* may be taken as typical:

> Dans ces décors bizarres, où flottent des réminiscences de Chirico, sous ces éclairages heurtés, sommaires, vulgaires, au milieu de ces ronflements, battements et sifflements auxquels M. Roger Desormières donne le nom de "musique," parmi ces cris d'amateur dechaîné, comme en pousse M. Artaud, et sous les rafales d'accent russe qui caratérisent la diction de la princi-pale interprète, o Shelley, o Stendhal, que restait-il de vous?[86]

The part of Beatrice was taken by a Russian lady, Mme. Iya Abdy, the beauty of whose body seems to have aroused some enthusiasm among the Parisian reviewers but whose histrionic talents they agree to have been something less than zero (and hardly aided by a thick Russian accent).[87]

In regard to Italy we have not been able to find any record of a performance of Shelley's **The Cenci**. A cor-respondent writing in *Notes and Queries* in 1873, how-ever, had the following to say:

> A tragedy called *Beatrice Cenci* has been performed at the Goldoni, in Florence, and at the theatres in Pisa, Pavia, Bologna, and in many other places. It is, *in part,* a translation from Shelley's play, but some of the re-volting truths have been suppressed, and Beatrice is represented as the victim of cruelty and religious big-otry.[88]

This *Beatrice Cenci* was probably that by the well-known Italian playwright G. B. Niccolini written be-tween 1838 and 1844.[89] Niccolini, himself, referred to this work as an "imitation" of Shelley's play but Pro-fessor Newman I. White in an article in 1922 showed that it was more of a translation than an imitation, acts I

and V and the first half of II following Shelley "speech for speech and often line for line."[90] The Cenci story it-self has, of course, long become an Italian classic tale and has even been circulated in pamphlet form in the Italian sections of American cities.[91]

RUSSIA AND CZECHOSLOVAKIA

Professor H. W. L. Dana in his *Handbook on Soviet Drama* lists a performance of Shelley's **The Cenci** in Moscow. On writing to Mr. Dana for further informa-tion we received the following reply:

> The performance of Shelley's **The Cenci,** to which I referred in my *Handbook on Soviet Drama,* was one at the Korsch Theatre in Moscow during the season of 1919-1920, the second season after the Russian Revo-lution of November, 1917. It was called *Beatrice Cenci.* This title was transliterated as Беатрцсц Чеичц which seems to me quite phonetically correct for the Italian pronunciation of the name, as is the author's name Щеггц for Shelley. Transliterating them back into En-glish, letter by letter, they would be "Beatriche Chen-chi" and "Shelli." In that same theatre during that same season, they acted Shakespeare's *Midsummer Night's Dream* and also a play by the French Romantic poet Alfred de Musset. In the Moscow Art Theatre during that same 1919-1920 season they acted Byron's *Cain.* I mention these other plays in Moscow at that time as an indication of the vogue for the Romantic movement there then. . . . **The Cenci** ran at the Korsch for just that one season, 26 performances at scattered intervals but with an excellent attendance of 26,880 spectators. No doubt there have been other performances, but I do not happen to know of them.[92]

This, in spite of other efforts, is all the information we have been able to gather on this production. It is, how-ever, clear that this is the most extensive production of the play ever given and it is of especial interest as indi-cating the interest of the Russians for a great revolu-tionary poet. (Some of Byron's plays, we note, were also played in Moscow in these years.)

The Czechoslovakian production of **The Cenci** seems to have been of some consequence. This production was put on by the Capek brothers in the Municipal Theatre in Prague in 1922, the year of the Shelley cen-tenary celebrations.[93] The special feature of the produc-tion was the staging which relied for its effects on a se-ries of colored cubes. The following description of these effects is from the London *Graphic* for December 9, 1922:

> In ten of the fifteen scenes of this play appear one or two or three porphyry pillars. They are as high as the stage used, are set on a wide, low platform, are dull dappled red, and are built of cubes laid one upon an-other, a small one between a large one and a large one. They act as a sort of architectural *leit-motif* in the play, appearing now here, now there, sometimes single, sometimes grouped, and always functioning impor-

tantly. For example, in the scene in which Beatrice begins to fear greatly half the stage is a sharply lit screen of red cubes, the other half is a yawning black entrance, and one of the porphyry pillars stands between. The same device is used when "The beautiful blue heaven is flecked with blood, and the sunshine on the floor is black!" except that this time the screen is a veined mass of blue and bloody colours. Once two of the pillars make the doorway through which the murderers pass into Count Cenci's chamber. Twice a stream like a strip of wall with a picture on it is placed between them, and the result is a room. For the banquet scene all three pillars—placed far apart—are used, and in the trial scene the three are put close together and form one huge block of cubes back of the judgment set.[94]

Accompanying this article in *The Graphic* is a series of illustrations showing the depositions of these cubes and pillars.

UNITED STATES

Apparently the first American theatrical critic to take an interest in **The Cenci** as a possible stage play was Robert Edmond Jones.[95] In the *Theatre Arts Magazine* for February, 1917, he presented pictures of clay modellings of stage settings for the play,[96] and in *The Theatre Arts Monthly* for June, 1924, he presented a series of drawings for other settings (of a modernistic type) on which he wrote as follows:

The six drawings reproduced here were made in Italy in the summer of 1912 out of over-mastering desire to present this great drama in a form as simple and as direct as itself—or rather, to allow it to create its own form in the theatre. It seemed to me then, as it seems to me now, that most theatrical productions are really explanations of the original dramas, elaborations, never the dramas themselves. One must somehow come closer, one must find some nearer approach to the dramatist's vision. External form and inner vision must somehow be focussed, be fused into a new entity—the vision itself be made manifest by its own light. In this production as planned there are no indications either of time or place. There is no theatre proscenium, no setting, no background. The action takes place on a raised platform set in the center of the auditorium, surrounded by spectators on all four sides. The figures move in an intense white radiance against unlighted space. In their movements and their groupings the essential idea of each scene perpetually crystallizes and re-crystallizes. For example, the first scene: a throne; Count Cenci, smiling, immune; a ring of guards with spears pointing outward, shifting ever so slightly in the direction of the Cardinal as he approaches. Nothing more. Only this abstract visual presentation of impregnable evil, evoked directly from the dialogue, from the moving visual image latent in Shelley's word. Or the prison scene: no prison bars, no bolts or locks. Grave figures in heavy armor kneel closely about the white figure of Beatrice as she sings. Or the last scene of all: the ring of encircling spears pressing closer and closer till they become a spire pointing upward.

These drawings can be no more than the barest hint of actual production. The only adequate record of a theatrical idea is the memory, however evanescent, of its performance in a theatre. Today, after nine years of sustained work on Broadway, it still seems almost impossible to discover and develop the ideally selfless and limpid talents through which alone a production such as this can come to life. It is the hope that such talents may be developed in the American theatre that these designs are now offered to the readers of *Theatre Arts*.

To present **The Cenci** adequately would be to live greatly: for to move among these gigantic dreams and passions is to draw one step nearer to Shelley's own vision of the invisible soul of the world.[97]

The drawings and comments are interesting as exemplifying, once more, the attraction which Shelley's play seems to exercise over so many fine theatrical minds, actors, critics, producers, designers.

In spite of this interest by Jones, however, **The Cenci** was not to receive its American premiere until two years later. In June, 1926, it was produced in New York by a talented amateur group known as the Lenox Hill Players, who have been among the pioneers in the little theatre movement.[98] This performance does not appear to have been reviewed either very widely or very intelligently but the reviewers seem generally to have agreed that it was a worth-while production. One critic praises the banquet scene, the murder and the trial scene, and concludes that "Altogether it is a most creditable, courageous, and interesting production."[99] Another reviewer declared that all who thought of the play as a "closet drama" were in for a surprise.[100] F. J. G., in the *Telegram* wrote:

It is impossible to come away from their performance without realizing that this great drama—redolent as it is of the romance and violence of the Renaissance—loses half of its power by being read and not seen.[101]

In addition to these reviews we have received a letter from Benjamin DeCasseres, who in 1926 was dramatic critic for *Arts and Decoration*. He attended the performance of **The Cenci** and informs us that there were about 150 persons in the audience, and that "it was a very good performance—impressive and dramatic."[102]

The next (and last) American production of Shelley's **The Cenci** was that at The Civic Playhouse, Bellingham, Washington, March 6, 7, 8, 9, 1940 by the Bellingham Theatre Guild. This production, directed by Mr. R. Milton Clarke, has been written up in a most interesting article by Professor Arthur C. Hicks, who acted the part of Count Cenci. Professor Hicks begins his article with a vigorous denunciation of the idea that **The Cenci** is not an acting play and tells of his own efforts to get it produced.[103] Finally when production was decided upon it was agreed "to follow Shelley's text with a minimum of alteration or cutting:"[104]

The major excision was Beatrice's long description in Act Three of the overhanging rock near the Castle of Petrella, which seriously interferes with the flow of the action. One line from Count Cenci's part and another from Orsino's were deleted for special reasons, and a few minor textual changes were necessary in adapting the four scenes of Act Four to one setting.[105]

Professor Hicks then gives a detailed account of the audience reaction scene by scene, noting in general, enthralled and ever-increasing attention:

> Everyone in the audience has a catch in his throat as the play ends. For what seems like a long interval there is a breathless silence throughout the auditorium. Then the applause breaks out, and for the first time in years a Guild production is honored by three curtain calls. It is nearly midnight, but no one is in a hurry to leave. Shelley has held them in a spell for three and one-half hours, and as they go out the spell remains. One young man remarks as he reaches the street, "Now I know what Aristotle meant by *catharsis.*"[106]

As to the monetary and attendance records:

> The play was so well received that the business manager and the director decided on a fifth performance for the following Tuesday. The total attendance was 667, which compared favorably with the total of 661 for *Abie's Irish Rose,* 668 for *Accent on Youth,* and 651 for *Ah, Wilderness!* The cash revenue taken in at the box office from the general public, that is, those who were not Guild members or holders of season tickets, was higher than that for any other production of the year.[107]

Professor Hicks concludes:

> With a group of amateurs, on a small stage, with limited technical and financial resources, before average American audiences unaccustomed to poetic drama, the Guild presented **The Cenci** with a success that few if any other Guild productions have attained. I can find only one explanation for this success, namely, that **The Cenci** is a great acting drama, one of the best of its kind.[108]

A review from the *Bellingham Herald* for March 7, 1940, supports Mr. Hicks' enthusiastic estimate by referring to the opening night of **The Cenci** as "the greatest artistic triumph ever achieved by the Bellingham Theatre Guild."

Although it cannot be claimed that **The Cenci** has yet established itself as part of the main body of popular literary drama along with, for instance, *Phèdre* or *Antigone,* nevertheless, as the preceding account of productions has indicated, there is sufficient evidence to show that it is a genuine acting drama. Why, one may well ask, has the misconception that it is a closet drama so long persisted? There are, in our opinion, several reasons for this. In the first place, **The Cenci** was refused production in its own day because of the incest theme, and a play which begins without a stage history is likely to continue without one. In the second place, the popular concept of Shelley as an "ineffectual angel" doubtless influenced producers and others in the notion that he could not produce anything so "practical" as a genuine stage play. And, in the third place, as we have indicated, the adverse comments of the 1886 critics—dictated largely by moral prejudice—influenced later scholars and critics. In the present century, however, as audiences are becoming more liberal in their acceptance of challenging themes, there seems no reason why **The Cenci** should not take its recognized place as one of the classics of the stage.

As a result of this new approach to **The Cenci** Shelley is seen to be an even more versatile writer than we had realized. Not only can he produce realistic political tracts, such as **A Philosophical View of Reform,** and complex metaphysical-social lyrical drama such as **Prometheus Unbound** but he can also produce a great acting play.

Notes

1. In the long task of collecting material on this subject from many scattered sources we have received especially valuable assistance from the following scholars and would like both to acknowledge their help and give them our sincere thanks: Dr. George Freedley and Dr. Franz Rapp, New York Public Library; Dr. Kurt Pinthus, Library of Congress; Professor H. W. L. Dana, Harvard University; Professor Henri Peyre, Yale University; Professor Bruce Dickins, University of Leeds; and Mr. Benjamin DeCasseres.

2. Cf. the Introduction to the edition of *The Cenci,* published for the Shelley Society in 1886, pp. IV-XII.

3. George Edward Woodberry (ed.), The Cenci, *by Percy Bysshe Shelley,* The Belles Lettres Series (Boston, 1909), p. XXI.

4. Earnest Sutherland Bates, *A Study of Shelley's Drama* The Cenci (New York: Columbia University Press, 1908), p. 60.

5. Newman I. White, *Shelley* (New York: Alfred A. Knopf, 1940), II, 141.

6. *Ibid.,* p. 575.

7. "An American Performance of *The Cenci,*" *Stanford Studies in Language and Literature* (Stanford University, 1941), p. 287. Professor Hicks—we note as we go to print—recapitulates this material in the preface to the recent valuable acting edition of *The Cenci* (A Stage Version of Shelley's Cenci. By Arthur C. Hicks and R. Milton Clarke. Caldwell, Idaho: Caxton Printers, 1945).

8. The society, however, had several other objects in view and besides bringing out editions of Shel-

ley's works put on a performance of *Hellas.* For a discussion of these objects see the controversy between Professor Newman I. White and Professor Walter E. Peck in *MLN* [*Modern Language Notes*]: XXXVII (1922), 411-415; XXXVIII (1923), 159-163; XXXIX (1924), 18-21; XXXIX (1924), 312-314.

9. Newman I. White, "Shelley's Debt to Alma Murray," *MLN,* XXXVII (1922), 411-415.

10. *The Shelley Society's Note-Book,* Part I, pp. 12-13.

11. *Ibid.,* p. 62.

12. *Ibid.,* p. 65.

13. *Ibid.,* p. 76.

14. *Ibid.,* p. 77.

15. *Ibid.,* p. 54.

16. *Ibid.,* p. 55.

17. *Ibid.,* p. 54.

18. *Ibid.,* p. 56.

19. *Ibid.,* p. 59.

20. *Ibid.,* pp. 75-76.

21. *Ibid.,* p. 55.

22. *The World* (New York), May 9, 1886.

23. *The Shelley Society's Note-Book,* Part I, p. 66.

24. *Ibid.,* p. 60. In partial contrast to these general critical condemnations we might note the following comments by Oscar Wilde in the *Dramatic Review* of May 15, 1886, reprinted in *The Complete Works of Oscar Wilde,* XII (New York: Wm. H. Wise, 1927), pp. 346-349: "The production of *The Cenci* last week at the Grand Theatre, Islington, may be said to have been an era in the literary history of this country, and the Shelley Society deserves the highest praise and warmest thanks of all for having given us an opportunity of seeing Shelley's play under the conditions he himself desired for it . . . no one has more clearly understood than Shelley the mission of the dramatist and the meaning of the drama."

25. Woodberry, *op. cit.,* pp. XV-XXI.

26. Bates, *op. cit.,* pp. 48, 63, 91-95.

27. Walter Edwin Peck, *Shelley, His Life and Work* (New York, 1927), II, 122-123. On page 123 Professor Peck has the following curious footnote: "The performance of the play by Alma Murray, for the Shelley Society, in 1866, and its later representation by John Barrymore, in London (1921) have sufficiently established this," (i. e. that the play is a closet drama only). 1866 is evidently a slip for 1886 but the reference to the Barrymore production is more puzzling. A diligent search of the bibliographies and journals for 1921 fails to reveal any evidence for the existence of such a production. It is, however, mentioned also in M. Renzulli, *La Poesie di Shelley* (Rome, 1932), p. 192. How the rumor of such a production started we do not know; at any rate it seems to have no foundation in fact.

28. White, *Shelley,* II, 140-142.

29. *The Graphic,* CVI (November 18, 1922), 724.

30. "Scandal About Count Cenci" in *The Saturday Review,* CXXXIV (November 25, 1922), 785.

31. New York, 1923, pp. 187-188.

32. XX (November 18, 1922), 204.

33. CXXIX (November 18, 1922), 727. Turner's statements in the *London Mercury* of December, 1922, 201, are also very illuminating: "Turning to *The Cenci,* I find a similar absence of comprehension on the part of many critics who will insist on going to an author's work with their own idea of what he should have done and measuring it as it approaches or departs from that idea. To call a play undramatic which deals with the single unattractive theme of incest and has no relief whatever from the profoundest gloom and misery—no subordinate episodes, no humour, no sentiment, no fiery Marlowesque hyperbole; to call such a play undramatic which, lasting three hours with only one interval yet holds the audience spellbound, as if enchanted; this is, I maintain, simply to make a mockery of language. A play is undramatic when it fails to hold the attention of an audience in a theatre. That is the sole criterion of what is or what is not dramatic."

34. XXXV (December, 1922), 523-525.

35. November 19, 1922.

36. "Shelley as a Dramatist," *Essays by Divers Hands, Transactions of the Royal Society of Literature of the United Kingdom* (London: Oxford University Press, 1936), new series, XV, 77-106.

37. *Ibid.,* p. 90.

38. *Ibid.,* pp. 96-98.

39. August 18, 1935.

40. XXXVII (April, 1923), 58.

41. CVI (November 18, 1922), 724. See also D. L. M. in *The Nation and The Athenaeum,* XXXII (November 18, 1922), 296, 298.

42. CLXI (November 25, 1922), 876.

43. Professor Allardyce Nicoll's opinion may be summarized in this one sentence from his *A History of Early Nineteenth Century Drama 1800-1850* (1930), p. 197: "*The Cenci* is perhaps the most beautiful thing given to us by the poetic dramatists, but it shares the same defects and weaknesses which are so patent in the other plays of the time."

44. *Op. cit.,* pp. 97-98.

45. In *Theatre Arts Monthly,* XVI (September, 1932), 756-757, Mr. J. R. Gregson writes: "But it is to Leeds that we must look for the most original and vital theatrical phenomenon in Yorkshire. . . . Meanwhile W. B. Dow began a most interesting and promising experiment with his Industrial Theatre. Its second season's programme, all the work of numerous amateur groups, included no less than nine Shakespearean plays, Ibsen's *Peer Gynt* and *A Doll's House,* Shelley's *The Cenci* and plays by Shaw, Maeterlinck, Strindberg, Tchekov, Galsworthy, not to mention the lesser-known fry, and two operas and a pantomime."

46. January 17, 1923.

47. December, 1922, and January, 1923.

48. Dated April 22, 1943. The reviews from the *Yorkshire Post* and *The Gryphon* we have also received through the courtesy of Professor Dickins.

49. *The Saturday Review,* CXLI (March 13, 1926), 333-334.

50. CXXXVI (March 20, 1926), 523-524.

51. From *The Era* (London), March 17, 1926.

52. *Die Cenci.* Drama in fünf Akten. In neuer deutscher Bearbeitung von Alfred Wolfenstein (Berlin: Paul Cassirer, 1924).

53. Solomon Liptzin, *Shelley in Germany* (New York: Columbia University Press, 1924), p. 69.

54. *Bühne und Welt,* XVII (Berlin, 1907), 488-490.

55. Herbert Huscher in *Anglia Beiblatt,* XXXVI (1925), 52. Dr. Franz Rapp writes in a letter of June 11, 1943: "I have the impression that the Intendant Anton Ludwig is identical with the translator of the play. He was the head of the Coburg Landestheater during that year only. In 1921 he was Direktor of the Stadttheater at Aachen; after 1923 he is listed as Dramaturg and Oberspielleiter at different private opera houses in Vienna. In 1939 he had been again at Aachen for several years as an Oberspielleiter and Dramaturg der Oper. The adaptation in question evidently has not been published."

56. Alfred Wolfenstein was a protagonist of expressionism. He was the author of such collections of poems as *Die gottlosen Jahre* (1931), *Die Freundschaft* (1917), *Menschlicher Kämpfer.* Among his plays are *Mörder und Träumer* (1923), *Der Narr der Insel* (1925), *Bäume in den Himmel* (1926), *Sturm auf den Tod* (1926), *Die Nacht unter dem Beil* (1928). He translated Shelley and Verlaine.

57. CLXXXIV (1925), 306.

58. *Die Szene,* XIX (Berlin, 1929), 324-325.

59. *Ibid.*

60. Werner Deubel, *Die Schöne Literatur,* XXV (December 15, 1924), 492-493.

61. *Frankfurter Zeitung,* October 24, 1924.

62. *Ibid.*

63. *Ibid.*

64. Fritz Buch was Oberspielleiter at the Schauspielhaus in Frankfurt am Main from 1924 to 1933.

65. *Frankfurter Zeitung,* October 24, 1924.

66. XXV (December 15, 1924), 492.

67. *Frankfurter Zeitung,* October 24, 1924.

68. *Die Schöne Literatur,* XXV, 493.

69. *Frankfurter Zeitung,* October 24, 1924.

70. *Ibid.*

71. *Ibid.*

72. According to Dr. Rapp, "there is no possibility to find out in this Library how often *The Cenci* has been performed at Frankfurt in the season 1924-25. One would get it from *Der Deutsche Bühnenspielplan,* a periodical which listed every production in Germany, or from the local *Almanach* published by the prompter of the theatre. The Library of Congress has a copy of the *Deutsche Bühnenspielplan*; but I understand from the Union List of Serials that v. 28 and v. 29 which could answer your question are missing there too."

73. Albert Steinrück (1872-1929) was an actor in various German playhouses. From 1909 to 1920 he was connected with the Hof- und Nationaltheater in Munich as an actor, director, and finally as the Schauspieldirektor. After this time he lived in Berlin, acting at many theatres there, and gave guest performances throughout Germany and in the films.

74. *Die Szene,* XIX, 325.

75. Liptzin, *op. cit.,* p. 70, note.

76. Henri Peyre, *Shelley et La France* (Le Caire, 1935), p. 215. In the *Histoire Générale Illustrée Du Théâtre* (Paris, 1934), V, 312, is to be found a

picture of Mme. Allan Dorval in the role of Beatrice Cenci. The legend reads: "Mme. Allan Dorval, rôle de Beatrice Cenci. Pour l'unique représentation de la Porte-Saint-Martin, le 21 mai 1833. Texte d'As de Custine, d'après Shelley. Gravé d'après Jozen, par E. Rouargue. (Galerie Théât., pl. 24)."

77. Antoine, *Le Théâtre* (Paris, 1932), I, 252. Cf. Henri Peyre, *op. cit.,* pp. 376-377, and Charles Morice in *Mercure de France* (March, 1893), 249-251.

78. Anna Irene Miller, *The Independent Theatre in Europe* (New York, 1931), p. 75.

79. March, 1891, 181-182.

80. *Ibid.,* 182.

81. *Mercure de France* (May, 1891), 300.

82. Peyre, *op. cit.,* p. 377.

83. Pierre Jean Jouve, "Les Cenci D'Antonin Artaud" in *La Nouvelle Revue Francaise* (June, 1935), 911. See also Gaston Rageot's remarks in *Revue bleue,* LXXIII (May 18, 1935), 353.

84. P. 912. Philip Carr in a letter to *The New York Times,* June 16, 1935, considered Artaud's version an adaptation from Shelley's *The Cenci.* He admits, however, some fundamental changes: "The author of this version, Monsieur Artaud, who also plays the principal male part in it, has set himself to accentuate rather than to modify the horrible nature of the subject. His avowed aim is to create a 'théâtre cruel,' and in order to produce the desired effect he spares nothing in the way of rancous cries and piercing shrieks, despairing gestures, violent movement, strident 'noises off' and strange and cacophonous musical accompaniment, made more overpowering still by mechanical 'loud speakers'." Charles Morgan on August 18 gave the following answer to Carr's contention, evidently based upon his visit to the Folies-Wagram, that Shelley's play is not a dramatic piece: "Mr. Carr was seemingly unfortunate in the Parisian production that was the occasion of his letter. I can well believe that translated into French and inadequately played, *The Cenci* might be a shambles. What would he have said of *Macbeth* as a stage-play if he had been asked to criticize it on the basis of that French performance which contained the following immortal line: 'Monsieur Macbeth! Monsieur Macbeth! Méfiez-vous de Monsieur Macduff'!"

85. *Ibid.,* pp. 912-913.

86. XLII, 3 (May-June, 1935), 479-480.

87. For instance, R. de B. in *Illustration,* CXCI (May 18, 1935), 96.

88. Stephen Jackson in *N&Q,* [*Notes and Queries*], 4th series, XII (December 20, 1873), 504.

89. Nicollini's was the best known of these works and the only one, so far as we can ascertain, that directly follows Shelley. However, we find record of at least three plays with the title of *Beatrice Cenci*: a drama written by G. Carbone in 1853; a drama by Alcide Oliari in the *Rivista Contemporanea* of 1855; a tragedy by Luciano Calvo in 1872. For the date of the composition of Nicollini's play see the article by Professor White referred to in the following footnote.

90. Newman I. White, "An Italian 'Imitation' of Shelley's *The Cenci,*" PMLA [*Publications of the Modern Language Association*], XXXVII (1922), 683-690. See also Maria Lusia Giartosio de Courten, *Percy Bysshe Shelley e l'Italia* (Milan, 1923), p. 215 ff. Corrado Ricci in the second volume of *Beatrice Cenci* (Milan, 1923), lists the following four Italian translations of Shelley's play: Ettore Sanfelice (Verona, 1892), Adolfo DeBosis in *Il Convito* (1898), Gualtiero Guatteri (1912), Francesco Pagliara in *Il nuovo Convito* (1919).

91. Clarence Stratton, "The Cenci Story in Literature and Fact," *Publications of the University of Pennsylvania,* XIV, *Studies in English Drama* (1917), p. 130.

92. Letter of June 29, 1943.

93. For a short period (1921-22) Karel Capek held the position of literary manager at the Muncipal Theater in Prague. The translator of Shelley's *The Cenci* was Otokar Fischer, known for his many translations of classical drama from different languages, like Goethe's *Faust,* Shakespeare's *Macbeth,* Lope de Vega's *Fuente ovejuna.*

94. CVI (December 9, 1922), 878.

95. It is interesting to note that Professor Ashley H. Thorndike who discussed *The Cenci* in *Tragedy* (1908), pp. 353-355, claimed that "though faulty in the details of dramatic art, *The Cenci* is, for a first tragedy, without an equal in its mastery of the great essentials of tragic poetry."

96. I, 74. See also the description of Jones's "production" of *The Cenci* in *Theatre Arts Magazine* (February, 1917), I, 61, and (July, 1920), IV, 184-185.

97. VIII, 408-409.

98. "If there were no other organization of the sort but the Lenox Hill Players, and if there were no other little theatre but the Lenox, and if it had never done anything but produce *The Cenci,* no further argument would be needed to demonstrate

the importance of the little theatre movement, which has spread to this country from the Abbey Theatre in Dublin."—*Telegram* (New York), June, 1926. The Lenox Hill Players came into existence around 1917 at the Lenox Hill Settlement on the upper east side. In 1924, the group became affiliated with the Community Church. Then they moved to West 14th Street and finally rented the Cherry Lane Theatre. For *The Cenci* the Lenox Hill Players had the services of Vladimir Nelidoff, formerly director of the Imperial Theatre of Moscow.

99. *Stage* (London), June 24, 1926.

100. *American* (New York), May 20, 1926.

101. June, 1926.

102. Letter of June 14, 1942.

103. Hicks, "An American Performance of *The Cenci*," *op. cit.,* pp. 287-290.

104. *Ibid.,* p. 290.

105. *Ibid.*

106. *Ibid.,* p. 310.

107. *Ibid.,* p. 311.

108. *Ibid.*

Joan Rees (essay date 1961)

SOURCE: Rees, Joan. "Shelley's Orsino: Evil in *The Cenci.*" *Keats-Shelley Memorial Bulletin,* no. 12 (1961): 3-6.

[*In the following essay, Rees investigates the role of Orsino as a minor character and emblem for evil in Shelley's play.*]

Shelley's treatment of his minor characters in *The Cenci*—all the dramatis personæ, that is, except Beatrice and Cenci himself—has never been found very satisfactory, and the general judgment as far as it concerns their dramatic effectiveness cannot be disputed. Nevertheless, the ideas behind Orsino, at least, are worth some attention and they have not been fully brought out by any commentator. Swinburne thought Orsino's rôle potentially interesting (*Essays and Studies,* London 1911, p. 221) but considered that Shelley had failed to make use of his opportunities. The portrait of Orsino could have been developed, he thought, into a subtle study of a curly-haired young priest, playing on villainy as on a lute, a Caponsacchi choosing self-indulgence and damnation instead of misery and redemption. But, he concludes, the hand was wanting for such a picture.

He was right to the extent that Shelley was no collector of psychological curios in the Browning manner, but, all the same, he has missed the point.

Cenci and Orsino are the two principal agents of evil in the play. The religious background is supposed to be Roman Catholic but it is perfectly plain that it is in fact nothing of the sort. Fatherhood is another name for cruelty and oppression whether it is an attribute of God, Cenci or the Pope. These three are the unholy but supremely powerful trilogy, in league together, supporting each other, perverting or destroying all good impulses which might dispute their sway. When Cenci prays to God he is always answered, Beatrice never. But she rebels against the power of evil and her rebellion threatens to be dangerous. Therefore she must be crushed and in such a way, if possible, as 'To poison and corrupt her soul' (IV, i, 45) for her goodness, as it is, is capable of abashing even Cenci. The most effective way of drawing the sting of her goodness is to corrupt it and this Cenci attempts to do by sexual violation. Yet though it is Cenci who performs the rape, it is Orsino who delivers Beatrice up into Cenci's power and puts not only her body but also her soul in danger of defilement. He suppresses her petition to the Pope and so cuts off her last channel of escape, and after the outrage he encourages her to murder Cenci, thus offering her up as a sacrifice to embattled authority. What is the significance of Orsino's part?

He has two soliloquies which explain his motives and attitudes precisely. In the first (II, ii, 104-61), he plots to work Giacomo up to the point of murdering Cenci and calculates that the family will then fall into his power and he can take Beatrice as his mistress. He has every confidence in the success of this plan because:

> Some unbeheld divinity doth ever,
> When dread events are near, stir up men's minds
> To black suggestions; and he prospers best,
> Not who becomes the instrument of ill,
> But who can flatter the dark spirit, that makes
> Its empire and its prey of other hearts
> Till it become his slave . . . as I will do.

In other words Orsino, though the story requires him to be a priest of the Roman church, acknowledges no Christian god but a 'dark spirit' whose evil suggestions he intends to use in order to bring others under his domination. By the time of the second soliloquy (V, i, 74-104), the whole plan has miscarried. Orsino betrays Giacomo to the guards, makes his own escape and reviews briefly what has happened:

> I thought to act a solemn comedy
> Upon the painted scene of this new world,
> And to attain my own peculiar ends
> By some such plot of mingled good and ill
> As other weave; but there arose a power

> Which grasped and snapped the threads of my device
> And turned it to a net of ruin. . . .

The dark spirit has proved more powerful than he thought. Orsino's confidence that he could 'flatter' it and manipulate it to his own service has been gravely misplaced. He himself was all the time but a tool of the black god who has used him to knit up a 'net of ruin' in which he has been enmeshed as well as Beatrice and all her family.

Orsino's part makes clear much of what lies behind the whole play. Cenci and Beatrice face each other as the chief antagonists, the two poles of human activity as Shelley sees it. Cenci is Jupiter, or his alter ego, the power which reigns and crushes the good under foot. Beatrice is no Titan like Prometheus but a young girl, for in the world as it is evil is full grown but good as yet weak and uncertain of its rôle. Cenci acts consciously as the agent of the evil power, in complete confidence of his god's care of him. Beatrice has been brought up also to believe in God, a god of justice and mercy, but her god does not exist. He is only a lie, one of the many imposed on the good in order to persuade them to acquiesce in suffering and to delude them in their struggles to resist evil—as Beatrice is deluded when she commits murder and descends to brazen lies, denying the noblest qualities of her nature in the faith that she has divine sanction for what she does. In fact, in her planning of the murder she is responding to the evil suggestions of the dark spirit. 'I pray thee God', she begs, 'Let me not be bewildered while I judge' (III, i, 126-7) but the irony of this is patent for her appeal to the deity produces only:

> . . . an undistinguishable mist
> Of thoughts, which rise, like shadow after shadow,
> Darkening each other. . . .

> (170-2)

The whole of this scene bears out Orsino's account of the operations of his 'dark spirit' who when dread events are near stirs up men's minds to black suggestions and Orsino throughout, with his insinuations and promptings, is doing what he planned, 'flattering' the dark spirit, abetting its work in the minds of others so that, as he believes, his own ends may be served.

In the end Beatrice knows that she has been deceived. In a terrible speech when Camillo brings the final death sentence, she suspects at last that God and Cenci are not opposed, as she had always believed, but one (V, iv, 47-74). Disillusioned, however, she is not crushed, but once more superb. She relies at last on nothing but self-control and the fellowship of human love and, strong in these, asserts her ultimate freedom from poison and corruption in spite of the concerted attack of the forces of evil. In the murder and the trial scenes she has de-

nied the human virtues of compassion and honesty in the name of a god who was really a devil and who tempted her to destroy her own virtue, but she has drawn back in time, cast violence and fear behind her, and regained her strength.

In *Prometheus Unbound* the Fury taunts Prometheus with the weakness of goodness in the world:

> . . . In each human heart terror survives
> The ravin it has gorged: the loftiest fear
> All that they would disdain to think were true:
> Hypocrisy and custom make their minds
> The fanes of many a worship, now outworn.
> They dare not devise good for man's estate,
> And yet they know not that they do not dare.
> The good want power, but to weep barren tears.
> The powerful goodness want: worse need for them.
> The wise want love; and those who love want wisdom;
> And all best things are thus confused to ill.
> Many are strong and rich, and would be just,
> But live among their suffering fellow-men
> As if none felt: they know not what they do.

> (I, 618-31)

The minor characters of *The Cenci* exemplify these various kinds of impotence in the conflict with evil: Camillo who thanks his god he does not believe Cenci's own account of his villainies, the guests at the banquet, Lucretia with her platitudinous piety, the priests with their hypocrisy, the whole society which allows Beatrice to suffer without lifting a finger to help her. Orsino alone does not quite come into any of the categories described by the Fury for he is neither one of the good but weak nor is he a powerful man rejoicing in his own wickedness. He is ambitious and he covets power but he wants the additional luxury of believing that he has not violated too many moral scruples in attaining it. 'I'll do as little mischief as I can', he promises himself (II, ii, 118-9), but this palterer, who faced with the choice between good and evil tries to play with both for the gratification of his own mean desires, is a traitor more dangerous to the struggling champion of good than the avowed oppressor. By Orsino and his like the cause of humanity striving to throw off the tyranny of evil is betrayed from within. He has a clearer intellectual recognition of the issues involved in the struggle than anyone else in the play and he deliberately chooses to reduce them to a calculation of selfish advantage.

The Cenci is not a wholly successful play in spite of its dramatic and poetic power and could never be so because Shelley quite failed to recognize how far his own 'peculiar feelings and opinions' had entered into what was meant to be a more or less accurate rendering of a sixteenth century Italian story. Orsino is a key figure in the movement of unacknowledged ideas just below the surface and it is one aspect of Shelley's failure that he is dramatically so insignificant.

Paul Smith (essay date winter 1964)

SOURCE: Smith, Paul. "Restless Casuistry: Shelley's Composition of *The Cenci.*" *Keats-Shelley Journal* 13 (winter 1964): 77-85.

[*In the following essay, Smith explores Shelley's alteration of his source material to emphasize moral and ethical concerns in* The Cenci.]

Sometime during the late summer or early fall of 1819, Shelley set about to write a preface to the play he had just finished, *The Cenci.* He wrote hurriedly, leaving sentences incomplete, sketching out the paragraphs as they occurred to him, paying little attention to continuity. He mentioned the Italian manuscript, the Guido painting, the interest the story had awakened in the social circles of Rome, and the moral implications he saw in the story of the Cenci family. He wrote:

> It is in the restless casuistry with which we seek her justification, (*who*) with which we feel that she has done an unnatural deed, but urged to it by one (*far*) more unnatural, (*with which we think one*) in which consists the dramatic character of (*her*) what she did & suffered—[1]

He left the sentence here, but he was not finished with it. He revised it later, and it appeared in the preface to the 1819 Italian edition of the play in this form:

> It is in the restless and anatomizing casuistry with which men seek the justification of Beatrice, yet feel that she has done what needs justification; it is in the superstitious horror with which they contemplate alike her wrongs and their revenge; that the dramatic character of what she did and suffered, consists.[2]

Between the rough draft and the printed preface there is the process of projection, definition, and analytic comment; the first person (we) becomes the third (men, they), feeling becomes superstitious horror, and the essential idea has been underlined and extended. The poet has moved away from his subject as the tragedy is consigned to the public. But there is still the singular image: *the restless and anatomizing casuistry.* It remains as a metaphor for the habit of mind of the Cencis: Francesco's "captious fancy" that perverts any remnant of morality in the patriarchal ethical system, Giacomo's agony of mind as he awaits the news of his father's death, and Beatrice's cold logic, discovered at the edge of madness, that leads her to a denial of her father's existence and inevitably to parricide. It was, as Orsino knew,

> a trick of this same family
> To analyse their own and other minds.
> Such self-anatomy shall teach the will
> Dangerous secrets: for it tempts our powers,
> Knowing what must be thought, and may be done
>
> (II. ii. 108-112)[3]

Of all the changes that have been worked on the Cenci legend (most of them to the family's dishonor) this inference of a ruling passion for analysis is Shelley's peculiar contribution. It was derived, not from the story, but from Shelley's own perplexity before the ethical enigma the legend evokes. After Shelley had read the lurid account in the *Varii successi curiosi,*[4] there began in his mind another sort of casuistry, and the record of this is **The Cenci.**

Shelley's remarks on the legend and his play are scattered throughout his letters from May, 1819 to January, 1822, and in his remarks there are several preoccupations. He thought of the play as something quite different from anything he had written; he speaks of a new style, something for the multitudes, something that was to bring him popularity.[5] He was convinced of the inherent drama in the legend. He was caught up in a fascination for the theme of incest and parricide and the moral dilemma that tortured Beatrice, and at the same time he was aware of the objections to a public presentation of the subject.

> My principal doubt, as to whether it would succeed as an acting play, hangs entirely on the question as to whether such a thing as incest in this shape, however treated, would be admitted on the stage. I think, however, it will form no objection: considering, first, that the facts are a matter of history; and, secondly, the peculiar delicacy with which I have treated it.[6]

Here, as elsewhere in the letters, is that sort of pathetic innocence in the idea that references to what he thought was reality would justify the choice of his subject. He felt that he could attract the "curious" and allay the fears of the fastidious by printing a translation of the manuscript source, and thereby asserting its "sad reality."[7] At one time he intended to annex a translation of the manuscript source to the 1819 edition, for there are these canceled introductory lines in the rough draft of the preface:

> The Story upon which the "Family of the Cenci" is written is perhaps fearful domestic tragedy which was ever acted on the scene of real life. The annexed.[8]

The story had the authenticating dust of history about it; there was evidence, old manuscripts, the Guido painting *La Turbantina,* the conversations of Italian society; and Shelley brought to all this the interest, the wish to be among the *cognoscenti,* the readiness to judge and abstract a moral, all the characteristics of a tourist on the grand tour. But more than this, there is in the preface the feeling of a sense of relief that follows accomplishment, when the enigmatic, inconclusive material of history is given some kind of meaning and order in art.

Shelley's work on this material can be followed in three documents: **"The Relation of the Death of the Family of the Cenci,"**[9] translated from the Italian manuscript by Shelley in the latter part of May, 1818; the **"Memorandum about the Cenci Case"**[10] in the Notebooks, written sometime between May 25, 1818, and May 14, 1819, probably after April 22, 1819, when he saw the Guido painting; and the play *The Cenci,* written between May 14 and August 8, 1819.

The **"Relation"** [**"of the Death of the Family of the Cenci"**] is an incredible combination of contradictions, lachrymose sentiments, and relentless condemnations, all with a pervading and rather prurient insistence upon sanguinary details that in one instance required an editorial ellipsis and a reference to the Italian text for the "curious." Shelley made an outline of this in his **"Memorandum"** [**"about the Cenci Case"**], taking details from the first 13 of the **"Relation"**'s 26 paragraphs. Here the creative process had already begun. He rejected the improbable: in the **"Relation"** it is stated that Francesco built the Chapel of St. Thomas expressly "to bury there all his children, whom he cruelly hated."[11] In the **"Memorandum"** Shelley wrote only, "He built a chapel in the court of his palace to St. Thomas, where he meant to be buried."[12] (That the chapel was built long before Francesco's time is some indication of the legendary details that have collected about the Cenci story. By rejecting the parts of the legend that were unfit for the nineteenth-century theater, Shelley inadvertently came closer to history.) The sordid and the abnormal are similarly rejected. Shelley was thrown into a state of indecision when he came to note the perversions Francesco forced Beatrice to witness: he canceled one word, obliterated another, and finally struck upon "He tempts Beatrice."[13] When he read that Francesco, with all the resourcefulness of Boccaccio's Fra Alberto, tried to convince Beatrice of the "enormous heresy, that children born of the commerce of a father and his daughter were all saints, and that the saints who obtained the highest places in Paradise had been thus born,"[14] Shelley noted in a delicate understatement, "He thinks by mild means to bring her to his will."[15] Mild means for Francesco were hardly mild enough for the patrons of the London theater.

As he wrote the **"Memorandum,"** Shelley was working out the plot of his play and developing the personalities of his characters. The mention of Francesco's joy at the deaths of Cristofero and Rocco in the **"Relation"** suggested the feast scene, and he wrote, "Cenci says that now he will die content, & gives a feast on the occasion."[16] That the part Beatrice was to play was beginning to form in his mind is evident in five parallel passages:

Beatrice is transformed from an active to a more passive participant in the crime. All the minor preparation and plotting is transferred to Giacomo, Lucretia, and Guerra, who was later to become Orsino.

RELATION (pp. 450–452)	MEMORANDUM (pp. 85–86)
1) Beatrice let fall some words [to Guerra] which plainly indicated that . . . [they] . . . contemplated the murder	1) She consults with him & her mother & they resolve to kill him
2) Beatrice communicated the design to her eldest brother, Giacomo	2) Guerra gains Giacomo his eldest son to the murder
3) Giacomo . . . resolved to commit the murder of Francesco to two of his vassals . . . Marzio and Olimpio were called to the castle; and Beatrice . . [and Lucretia] . . . conversed with them	3) Beatrice *(pers)* [for persuades] finds Marzio & Olimpio
4) They dexterously mixed opium with a drink of Francesco	4) *(They)* She [Lucretia] gives him opium
5) . . . his daughter herself led the two assassins into the apartment	5) Beatrice & her Mother wait while the murderers go in to kill Cenci

There are three notes in the **"Memorandum"** to "see MSS." referring to bits of dialogue and the details of the murder. Shelley probably intended to work on the play with the **"Relation"** and the **"Memorandum"** before him, one providing the details, the other the outline and major revisions.

The figure of Orsino was beginning to emerge as he wrote the **"Memorandum."** What is to some the inordinate amount of attention Shelley gave to the prelate was required by the dramatic character of Beatrice. She was at once an embodiment of guilt and innocence. In order to re-create this ambiguity, she must be seen at one remove from the details of the crime. And Orsino is the only person in a position to perform that function. His love for Beatrice was enough of a motive, but even that is carefully qualified to cast no reflection upon the purity of the heroine. Nothing is said of Orsino in the printed preface, but in the rough draft there are three references that were ultimately canceled:

(. . . *The story is much the same in the tragedy as in the manuscript except that in the latter (sic) the action is hurried more hurried, & that Orsino—whose real name was Guerra—plays a more conspicuous part.*)

(*She had a lover also who appears by the story to b*)

A young prelate (*of the*) in love with (*Beatrice acted according to the*) Beatrice assists them in their design, & so soon as their deed is discovered abandons them (—*If he had pos[s]essed anything like virtue or courage*)[17]

The last of these passages leaves little doubt as to Shelley's opinion of Orsino, but it provokes some speculation on the canceled phrase, *acted according to the.* Shelley's interest in the motive of Orsino suggests another reason for the rather long part he has in the play. Orsino acted according to the dictates of his ambition, his love for Beatrice, and, most significantly, of the

Church. Ambition and selfish love lead him to assist the parricides. He deserts them just as the Church deserts them. It is he who withholds the petition from the Pope. It is in him that we see an emblem of the corrupt ecclesiastical hierarchy, indifferent to suffering in its determined veneration for the patriarchal order. Orsino's behavior is the *modus vivendi* required in this degenerate period of history.

Now the ***Letters*** [***The Letters of Percy Bysshe Shelley***] and the ***Notebooks*** [***Notebooks of Percy Bysshe Shelley***] reveal Shelley's three major concerns: first, to underscore what was for him the profoundly moving reality of the events of the legend; second, to objectify the story and the play itself by shifting his own attention from the events themselves to a consideration of the moral environment that created them; and third, to revise the story in order to lift the character of Beatrice out of the realm of petty circumstances to the level of something like theoretical ethics. No matter what the impulse for this revision was, its effect is a partial justification of the heroine. Not that this was Shelley's intention; in the preface he condemns Italian society for its "passionate exculpation" of Beatrice, and in the rough draft he wrote:

> —they [Italian society] appeared to me, even to think (*too*) with too much lenity [Here watch the poet search for the correct phrase, unsatisfied until he strikes upon the important word *alternative*.] (*of the monstrous action unnatural action dreadful alternative of the action which*) of the dreadful side of the alternative chosen by the heroine of the tale.[18]

Shelley was at once attracted to and repelled by the story: he was attracted to its reality, to the tearful, imploring portrait of Beatrice, to a partial justification of her crime; he was repelled by the sordidness of the tale, by the image of a golden-haired parricide, by the very idea of justification. Shelley, like Orsino, had an ambitious interest in Beatrice. To follow this similarity to the end is to arrive at another implication in Orsino's lines,

> even I,
> Since Beatrice unveiled me to myself,
> And made me shrink from what I cannot shun,
> Shew a poor figure to my own esteem,
> To which I grow half reconciled.
>
> (II, ii, 114-118.)

The final revisions and additions to the original material outline the rather complicated creative process that was involved in the writing of this play. Shelley compressed a series of events during three years of history, reported to have occurred in a year's time in the "**Relation,**"[19] into a play that seems to cover the occurrences of only two or three weeks. Francesco's three arrests for sodomy become three arrests for murder. His feast in celebration of the deaths of his two sons and the curse

upon his daughter are amplifications of ideas suggested in the "**Relation.**" These changes, like those in the murder scene, were begun in the "**Memorandum**" and are in some way relevant to the problems of dramaturgy: compression, credibility, motivation, character delineation.

Among all the changes there are two of compelling interest, the character Giacomo and the scene of the arrest. In the "**Relation**" Giacomo is sent to Salamanca with Cristofero and Rocco, Beatrice confides in him after his return, he conceives the plan to enlist Marzio and Olimpio, is arrested, tortured and confesses, and after the execution of Lucretia and Beatrice he is killed with a hammer and quartered. In the "**Memorandum**" Shelley notes his study at Salamanca, his inclusion in the plot by Guerra (Orsino), with whose help Giacomo conceives the Marzio-Olimpio plan, his arrest and confession. But at one point in the "**Memorandum**" there are these lines containing a curious parenthesis:

> They hire murderers for 10000 crowns to waylay him in the road to Petrella a place in the Regno di Napoli (something about Giacomo) Cenci goes there a few days before & escapes.[20]

The parenthesis is in a sentence that refers to the ninth paragraph of the "**Relation,**" where, curiously, there is no mention of Giacomo, nor is there any mention of him until the eleventh paragraph a page and a half later. It must refer then to the two previous paragraphs, particularly the passage:

> This latter [Giacomo] was easily drawn into consent, since he was utterly disgusted with his father, who illtreated him, and refused to allow him sufficient support for his wife and children.[21]

Now Shelley's method in the "**Memorandum**" was to copy the salient details of the story, making references to the manuscript for dialogue and intricate details, following the sequence of the "**Relation,**" exactly *except* for this one remark, *something about Giacomo.* In the act of outlining the first attempt at parricide, one that *failed*, Shelley was reminded of a passage he had, perhaps deliberately, overlooked. In the play the position corresponding to the parenthesis in the "**Memorandum**" is taken up by Act III, ii, in which Giacomo is at first tortured by feelings of guilt and then incited to resolution by Orsino, a dramatic representation of the heart of the play.

From the one reference in the "**Relation**" Shelley created nearly 160 lines of Act II, ii, over 100 lines of Act III, i, some 90 lines of Act III, ii, and parts of Act V, i, the equivalent of three scenes, 400 lines, one-sixth of the play. Yet none of these scenes advances the action any more than to establish the hiring of the assassins. The details in the "**Memorandum**" that enclose the parenthesis figure in the play at Act II, i, 233, and end at Act III, ii, 34, but *something about Giacomo* extends from two scenes before this to its last mention four scenes later. There is nothing more than the indefinite word *something,* but what it represented seems to have haunted the poet and demanded expression.

This is not to deny the dramatic function of Giacomo and Orsino; it is evident that the "psychological 'malady of thought' is noted as a family trait by Orsino and reflected in Giacomo, the Count's son, whose dramatic character lies only in its expression."[22] But remembering the restless casuistry that was for Shelley the essence of the play, Giacomo's part assumes another dimension. The crimes against him in part justify the murder, yet at the same time he is the only one of the children directly involved who feels a profound guilt. Like Orsino he is involved and he condemns, unlike Orsino he is punished. It is conceivable that his dramatic function could have been assumed by Bernardo or Beatrice or Orsino, singly or in combination. But Giacomo's position had for Shelley certain indispensable features that those of the younger brother and sister lacked: he was the eldest, he was married, he was a father, he was in debt, he was, according to the **"Relation,"** "not more than twenty-eight years of age when he died."[23] Shelley was twenty-seven four days before he completed the play. Parts of this play were more real to Shelley than any sixteenth-century legend.[24]

However much the poet denies in the preface any imposed moral in the drama, his intense interest in the ethical meaning of the play could not be wholly restrained from suggesting a possible solution of the moral dilemma. The scene which replaces the rather involved account of the arrest, was created almost entirely from Shelley's imagination without reference to the **"Relation."** And within this scene there is the gratuitous reference to the warrant for Cenci's instant death (Act IV, iv, 28). Beatrice clutches at this as an irrefutable justification of the murder, but to Shelley it was the ultimate condemnation.

> Undoubtedly, [he wrote in the preface] no person can be truly dishonoured by the act of another; and the fit return to make to the most enormous injuries is kindness and forbearance, and a resolution to convert the injurer from his dark passions by peace and love. Revenge, retaliation, atonement, are pernicious mistakes. If Beatrice had thought in this manner she would have been wiser and better; but she would never have been a tragic character.[25]

If this was to be the moral intention of the play, we can be rather grateful that Shelley did not dwell too long on the subject. That the warrant for Cenci's death is only reported as the passing remark of one of the Legate's followers and is never stated by Savella suggests that Shelley, too, was averse to laboring the point. It is left

as a moral paradox shifting between condemnation and justification. Though Shelley implied that Beatrice should have endured and resolved to convert her father, he perhaps was aware of the highly questionable outcome of this attempt. In all probability Beatrice would have been reduced to increasing the population of the highest of the saintly ranks.

The paradox remains; it rests in the characters of Orsino and Giacomo and in the revisions Shelley worked on the legend. But Shelley had thought too long, had written too much, to leave the problem after the last act. His questioning efforts demanded some answer, and he wrote the preface. He was to the last the most restless casuist of them all.

Notes

1. "The Rough Draft of the Preface," *Notebooks of Percy Bysshe Shelley,* ed. H. Buxton Forman, 3 vols. (Boston, 1911), II, 91-2.—Hereafter cited as *Notebooks.* The passages italicized and in parentheses are those canceled or intended to be canceled by Shelley. They appear in footnotes in this edition.

2. "Preface" to *The Cenci, The Works of Percy Bysshe Shelley,* ed. H. Buxton Forman, 8 vols. (London, 1880), II, 12.—Hereafter cited as *Preface.*

3. All references to the text of the play are from the edition and volume cited in note 2 above.

4. Shelley read the account of the Cenci family in the spring of 1818 in "one of those numerous manuscript collections of horrors entitled 'Varii successi curiosi' ('Divers Curious Occurrences'), which were collected in the seventeenth and eighteenth centuries. . . ." F. Marion Crawford, "Beatrice Cenci . . . ," *The Century Magazine,* LIII (January, 1908), 456. There is a similar account, presumably taken from one of the *Varii successi curiosi,* in *Narrazione della morte di Giacomo e Beatrice Cenci . . . 11 Settembre, 1599,* (London, 1821) in the Harvard College Library.

5. See *The Letters of Percy Bysshe Shelley,* ed. Roger Ingpen, 2 vols. (London, 1914), II, 690-1, 697-8, 713, 715, 766, 809, 850.—Hereafter cited as *Letters.*

6. *Letters,* II, 698 (To Thomas Love Peacock, July, 1819).

7. See *Letters,* II, 690, 697-8, 720.

8. *Notebooks,* II, 87.

9. Reprinted in *The Complete Poetical Works of Percy Bysshe Shelley,* ed. George Edward Woodberry, 4 vols. (Boston, 1892), II, 447-463.—Hereafter cited as "Relation."

10. *Notebooks,* II, 85-7.

11. "Relation," 448.

12. *Notebooks,* II, 85.

13. *Notebooks,* II, 85.

14. "Relation," 449-450.

15. *Notebooks,* II, 85.

16. *Notebooks,* II, 85.

17. *Notebooks,* II, 94, 96, 97.

18. *Notebooks,* II, 89.

19. The earliest events mentioned in the play are the deaths of Rocco in 1596 and Cristofano (Cristofero in the "Relation") in the following year. These are mentioned together without any reference to a date in the "Relation." Shelley assumed the deaths happened on the same day and gives a date, December 27, presumably 1598. The play opens then in the middle or latter part of January, 1599, allowing time for the news of the deaths to come from Salamanca. The move to Petrella in the first week of September, 1598, the death of Francesco on the 9th, the arrest of the Cencis in January, 1599, all these historical events occur in compressed and rearranged sequence in the first four acts. Acts I and II cover two consecutive days in mid-January, Acts III and IV, three consecutive days (Tuesday, Wednesday, Thursday) about one week later. After the murder the "Relation" fails to mention any date until that of the execution, May 11, 1599, and this is an error for September 11, 1599, made obvious by references to the passage of at least seven months following the arrest. Act V covers events in this period making them seem to occur within a week's time.

20. *Notebooks,* II, 85.

21. "Relation," 451.

22. George Edward Woodberry, ed., Introduction to *The Cenci,* (Boston, 1909), p. xvi.

23. "Relation," 462.

24. For a discussion of the psychological origins of the play see Otto Rank, *Das Inzest-Motiv in Dichtung und Sage,* (Leipsig, 1912), esp. pp. 402-404.

25. *Preface,* 12.

Charles L. Adams (essay date summer 1965)

SOURCE: Adams, Charles L. "The Structure of *The Cenci.*" *Drama Survey* 4, no. 2 (summer 1965): 139-48.

[*In the following essay, Adams defends Shelley against charges that* The Cenci *is structurally defective and argues that understanding Orsino's role in the first two acts is vital to an appreciation of the play.*]

In the conclusion of their article "The Stage History of Shelley's *The Cenci,*" Kenneth Cameron and Horst Frenz summarize their findings (". . . there is sufficient evidence to show that it is a genuine acting drama.") and ask the question, "Why . . . has the misconception that it is a closet drama so long persisted?"[1] An important reason for this "misconception" concerns the structure of the play. Critics have long maintained that the play is structurally defective. Theatre-goers, on the other hand (as pointed out by Cameron and Frenz), have apparently not felt this deficiency. I would like to present a possible explanation of this contradiction.

It is interesting to note that specific structural objections were raised by only *one* of the critics who reviewed the play following its publication.[2] Rather, as Cameron and Frenz have pointed out, structural objections seem to derive from the reactions of the critics to the 1886 performance—a performance by amateurs for a select audience. Subsequent favorable opinion by critics who attended professional performances does not seem to have affected Shelley scholars.[3]

Briefly, the major objections to the structure are as follows: (1) Both the play itself and the individual speeches are too long. (2) Beatrice's denial of her guilt is inconsistent with her character and her function in the play. (3) Much of the play (mostly scenes involving Orsino) fails to advance the action in any way. (4) The focus of interest changes sharply with the death of Count Cenci.

I believe we can discard the first objection immediately. The proper length of a play and the proper length of individual speeches are highly relative distinctions. Only an audience can determine what is "too long" for it. The Cameron and Frenz stage history points out that audiences do not seem to feel this defect.[4] Perhaps, too, more recent audiences are more tolerant in this respect. (We might note that four-hour motion pictures have ceased to be unusual.)

The second objection, too, can be disposed of quickly. Leigh Hunt's explanation of Beatrice's denial of her guilt—that it was "a lie told . . . for the sake of nature, to save it the shame of a greater contradiction" and that "a little frailty and inconsistency . . . may be allowed a young creature about to be cut off in the bloom of life, who shows such an agonized wish that virtue should survive guilt and despair"—seems sufficient to indicate the motivation and the proper interpretation of her actions. Beatrice *did not* think she was guilty—she considered her actions justified. As Shelley points out, this is what makes her a tragic figure.[5] Ellsworth Barnard, in the 1944 Odyssey Press edition, points out too that "Shelley feels, despite his sympathy for his heroine, that she has done wrong; that, as he says, she has done what 'needs justification.'"[6] The problem is perhaps one of ethics, but it is not one of dramatic structure.

The remaining objections to the play's structure, how-ever, are more serious and ought to be considered in detail. Perhaps the best statement of these defects is found in Newman Ivey White's biography of Shelley:

> Structurally the play is far less suitable to the theatre than Shelley supposed. It lacks consistent progression, and in one important detail it lacks unity. All three scenes of Act I barely fall short of being pure character scenes. They do little more than set the stage for action that is to follow. In the second act the first scene brings us no closer to the accomplishment of Cenci's design, while the second scene, in which Giacomo and Orsino are both shown to be thinking of Cenci's murder, has only the slightest bearing on the murder as later executed under the direction of Beatrice. Thus Shelley consumes two whole acts with interesting characterization and background, but with practically no progress in the action. In the third act Count Cenci has accomplished his crime and Beatrice reaches her resolution to kill him. The first plan for Count Cenci's murder miscarries and new murderers are engaged. The fourth act opens with Cenci's wife, Lucretia, vainly trying to change his course of persecutions, and succeeding only in eliciting an intense prayer to God for the utter destruction of his daughter. . . . Thereafter the act moves swiftly through three scenes in which the murderers approach Cenci's couch, recoil, and are induced by Beatrice's reproaches and determination to complete the deed. One of the murderers is soon arrested with an incriminating note, and the arrest of Beatrice and Lucretia follows. . . . The fifth act, after wasting the first scene, proceeds rapidly and impressively through three scenes describing the trial, the conviction, and the preparations for the execution. . . . In actual presentation it was found that the play seemed to fall apart with the death of Count Cenci. His character had so dominated the first part of the play that the substitution of judges and Pope as Beatrice's antagonists seemed almost to begin a new play. . . . *The Cenci* can hardly be called a tragedy at all, in anything like the traditional meaning of the word. In spite of an intelligent and clever use of the materials, it is obviously defective in structure, when considered as a play for the stage.[7]

White's evaluation, and his assumptions, are in general those of both earlier and subsequent commentaries upon the play. In 1908 Ernest Sutherland Bates observed: "A play, one of whose acts fails to advance the plot in the least . . . is surely not to be called an acting drama."[8] George Woodberry (1909) observed that the action lagged in some places and was not advanced in others and that with the death of Count Cenci the theme changed "so much as to become almost a new play."[9] Walter E. Peck (1927) is in general accord with these views,[10] and Barnard (1944) observes that Shelley allows the action to drag while relatively unimportant characters (Giacomo and Orsino) reveal themselves, and that Beatrice and Cenci are so much the focus of interest that with Cenci's death the reader "almost feels that he is beginning a new play."[11]

It is possible that all of these scholars are following the early critics of the play, and it is possible, too, that each has observed these deficiencies because of his own interpretation of the play. In any case, their judgments are compatible, if not identical. These critics seem to share, too, the same set of underlying assumptions. Let us examine these assumptions in relation to the so-called "structural defects." (1) First of all, the objection to Acts I and II (that they fail to advance the action) is based on the assumption that the first and second act of a play must advance the action of that play. (2) The objections to "wasted scenes" given to Orsino are based on the assumption that he is a minor character and that he does little to advance the central theme of Beatrice versus Cenci. (3) The objection that the theme of the play changes with the death of Count Cenci is based on the assumption that the central theme is one of antagonist (Count Cenci) versus protagonist (Beatrice) and that the high point of this theme is reached with Cenci's death.[12] It is important to notice that the first of these assumptions involves a rather questionable value-judgment, that there is one "proper" way in which a play should be built, and that, in the case of the second and third assumptions, the meaning of the play is known *before* the structure is examined. With regard to the latter point, it is significant that it seems to have been the usual practice (e. g., with Bates, Woodberry, and White) to comment first upon the theme of the play and then to criticize the structure for not being compatible with that theme. Is it not more logical to examine the play itself, assuming that Shelley created the various parts and arranged them in a certain way in order to communicate a certain meaning? to assume when we begin reading that the number, size, and arrangement of the parts is *not* defective and then to see what message that structure imparts?

Before doing that, however, let us look more closely at the "structural defects." Is there any real basis for considering as automatically defective first and second acts that "fail to advance the action of the play"? I think not. Many dramatists have withheld the "start of the action" through two acts of background and characterization. Shakespeare, for example, apparently deliberately made this change from earlier versions when creating *Hamlet,* and also sought this "delayed action" effect in *Romeo and Juliet* and in other plays.[13]

The question then arises, if these acts are not automatically defective—that is, if they are not "wasted" but instead function according to the author's intentions—what do they do? If they were never intended to advance the action (since they obviously do not), what do they do? Let us look at the play itself. Briefly, this is what happens:[14]

> I. i. Introduction of Cenci with Camillo; characterization of Cenci; illustration of his thoroughly evil nature;

suggestion of the situation which will lead to the conflict: ". . . then, as to Beatrice—" (ln. 136).

I. ii. Introduction and characterization of Beatrice and Orsino; Orsino urges her to petition the Pope and reveals his plan to hold back the petition. Beatrice revealed as pure, noble, trusting. Orsino revealed as hypocritical and false: "A friendless girl / who clings to me, as to her only hope: / I were a fool, not less than if a panther / were panic-stricken by the antelope's eye, / if she escape me" (ln. 87-91).

I. iii. The feast celebrating the death of Cenci's sons; Cenci and Beatrice brought together and their relationship illustrated; Beatrice's appeal to the guests and its failure.

II. i. Lucretia and Beatrice speak, revealing Beatrice's increased fear of Cenci; Cenci enters and taunts Beatrice; she leaves; Cenci taunts Lucretia and tells of his plan to remove them to Petrella. Lucretia exits; Cenci soliloquizes, "Would that it were done!" (ln. 193).

II. ii. Giacomo and Camillo discuss Giacomo's hopeless case. Orsino enters, Camillo exits, and Orsino encourages Giacomo: "A father who is all a tyrant seems, / were the profaner for his sacred name" (ln. 80-81). Giacomo exits, and Orsino calls, "Be your thoughts better or more bold" (ln. 104). Act II closes with Orsino's long soliloquy: "Now what harm / if Cenci should be murdered? Yet, if murdered, / wherefore by me?" (ln. 120-122). "I see, as from a tower, the end of all" (ln. 147). "He prospers best, / not who becomes the instrument of ill, / but who can flatter the dark spirit, that makes / its empire and its prey of other hearts / till it becomes his slave—as I will do". (ln. 157-161)

Many critics have criticized Shelley for giving Orsino too many scenes, too many lines. Isn't it more logical simply to accept these scenes and lines as Shelley has presented them to us, waiting for the total meaning to develop, than to assume that somehow Shelley has erred, having one of his minor characters "competing" with the major characters, speaking lines that don't really belong in the play? Orsino is, more than other characters in the play, Shelley's creation. It would be well to study that creation closely.

We should notice in particular the changes Shelley made from Orsino's historical counterpart. White has pointed out that in the original narrative from which Shelley drew his material, the character of Orsino appeared to be motivated only by sympathy and friendship and that Shelley converted him into "a sly false friend actuated by avarice and lust."[15] Bates has observed how Shelley altered this character from its counterpart in the manuscript source, making hypocrisy and treachery Orsino's chief characteristics, and also notes that Orsino's insinuations, which strengthen the half-formed plans of Giacomo and Beatrice, are not to be found in the source, that Orsino's passion for Beatrice is of Shelley's invention, and that there is no suggestion in the original that Orsino betrayed Beatrice as well as Count Cenci.[16] And

Bates notes, as a structural defect, the fact that while Count Cenci has six soliloquies in the play, Orsino, "a minor character," has four.[17] I think that it is necessary to account for the changes Shelley made with some reason other than that advanced by Bates, that Shelley altered the character in accordance with his "general attitude toward the clergy."[18] And we cannot assume that Orsino is a minor character when, in these first acts, he is presented to us as a major character.

The problem here is to see Orsino as he actually is presented to us. Sara Ruth Watson has pointed out the similarity between Orsino and Iago, noting that:

Of all Shakespearean villains, Iago is the only consistent Machiavellian, whose medium of evil is the manipulation of other men's minds. He never works directly to bring about a desired end—except at the last, when he is desperate. Such a villain, too, is Orsino, a psychologist with a criminal mind. Just as Iago gradually bends the natural proclivities of his victims to his own advantage, so Orsino realizes that he can manage the thoughts and emotions of all the Cencis. . . . He . . . plants in the minds of Giacomo and Beatrice the justifiability of parricide, but he also manages to extricate himself from the responsibility of action.[19]

The description which Miss Watson gives of Orsino is accurate. But it is not a description of a character who "serves the play only in minor ways." We must remember that it is not Count Cenci but Orsino who causes the deaths of Beatrice, Lucretia, Giacomo, Olimpio, Marzio, and Cenci himself.[20] We should remember, too, as early as the second scene of Act I, Beatrice's lines when she and Orsino are first presented to us and the relationship between them is first established:

You have a sly, equivocating vein
That suits me not. Ah, wretched that I am!
Where shall I turn? Even now you look on me
As you were not my friend, and as if you
Discovered that I thought so, with false smiles
Making my true suspicion seem your wrong.

(11. 28-33)

If we accept the first two acts of the play as they are presented to us, if we assume that the construction is intentional and that the function of the opening acts is to present those characters, speaking those lines, which it does present, and if we follow the first two acts themselves and regard Orsino as a major character that Shelley has created for us, rather than following the long chain of commentaries and regarding Orsino as a minor character inadvertently inflated to dimensions that damage the total play, we find that we are being told a story in which the central theme is *not* that of protagonist versus antagonist, Beatrice versus Cenci, and thus arrive at the final objection to the play's structure—that the play seems to fall apart after the central theme of Beatrice versus Cenci reaches its climax in Cenci's death.

Let us return to the play itself. We should notice among other things that, in the first scene of Act III, the first plan for Cenci's murder is prompted by Orsino's suggestion, "Should the offender live?" (ln. 172). In the next scene, after the first plan has failed, Orsino encourages Giacomo and proposes the second plan. In Act IV the murder is accomplished. Act V, scene i, which has been called "wasted," should be examined in detail.

> V. i. Orsino and Giacomo have learned of the arrest of Beatrice and Lucretia. Giacomo accuses Orsino: ". . . hadst thou / never with hints and questions made me look / upon the monster of my thought, until / it grew familiar to desire. . . ." (ln. 21-24). Orsino proposes flight. Giacomo prefers to stay: "Rather expire in tortures, as I may. / What! will you cast by self-accusing flight / assured conviction upon Beatrice?" (ln. 39-41). Giacomo's realization of Orsino's true nature: "Thou art a lie! Traitor and murderer! / Coward and slave!" (ln. 53-54). Orsino's betrayal of Giacomo; his exit lines: ". . . such was my contrivance / that I might rid me both of him and them. / I thought to act a solemn comedy . . . / and to attain my own peculiar ends. . . . / But there arose a Power / which grasped and snapped the threads of my device / and turned it to a net of ruin . . ." (ln. 75-83). ". . . where shall I / find the disguise to hide me from myself, / as now I skulk from every other eye?". (ln. 102-104)

We ought to note, too, Beatrice's lines in Act V, scene ii, "Who stands here / as my accuser?" (ln. 172-173) and "Here is Orsino's name; / Where is Orsino? Let his eye meet mine" (ln. 175-176).[21]

Instead of being the story of Beatrice versus Count Cenci, this is the story of Beatrice versus evil—or, if you wish, versus tyranny, a typical Shelley theme.[22] It is the story of a girl who, faced with gigantic evil, is encouraged by a man working for personal gain to fight back with evil.[23] But Beatrice, unable to see into the hearts of men, was unaware of the machinations of Orsino, unaware that the evil at work was much more complex than she suspected, just as she was unaware that a papal decree would render the murder unnecessary. Beatrice does not murder Cenci; Marzio does. She does not plan the murder; Orsino does. But she does desire passionately that the murder be committed, and therein lies her tragedy. Shelley had recently pointed out in *Prometheus Unbound* that evil exists because of man's acceptance of it. Barnard has characterized Jupiter in *Prometheus Unbound* as being the sum of evil, including unjust laws and false religion, with unknown origin, existing because man permits it to exist.[24] Such a character, exactly, is Count Cenci. Yet he is the evil which a kind of providential order takes care of, or would have taken care of, had the murder not already been accomplished. But with the encouragement of Orsino (who states that he uses evil consciously for his own purposes), Beatrice, Lucretia, Giacomo, Marzio and Olimpio undertake to employ evil for *their* own

purposes. Shelley seems to be saying that isolated, total evil can be combated, or at least endured, without damage to the individual, for we can at least know what we are fighting. But the other evil, as represented by Orsino, the "human evil" as opposed to the "inhuman," constitutes as much of a threat: The tragedy in *The Cenci* lies not in the nature of Count Cenci, but in that part of the other characters which individually justifies to them the use of evil for their own ends.

And is not much of this the philosophy behind *Prometheus* [*Unbound*]? Beatrice appeals in Act I to her father's guests, but they abandon her to Cenci, not because they disbelieve her story or are not moved by her pleas, but because they fear Cenci and feel inadequate to combat him. Is this not the role of Mercury in *Prometheus*? Is not Beatrice lost because of her reaction to unspeakable persecution, just as Prometheus is saved because of his opposite reaction? And is not Orsino the hypocrite mentioned repeatedly in *Prometheus,* who, "with firm sneer, trod out in his own heart / the sparks of love and hope till there remained / those bitter ashes, a soul self-consumed, / and the wretch crept a vampire among men, / infecting all with his own hideous ill. . . ."?[25] And compare, in Act V, scene iv, Beatrice's reference to her father's spirit, "Even though dead, / does not his spirit live in all that breathe, / and work for me and mine still the same ruin, / scorn, pain, and despair?" (ln. 69-72) with Demogorgon's "He reigns." Perhaps, having finished three acts of *Prometheus,* Shelley wished to express his ideas in a more direct form and in a medium which would present them to the general public.[26] My suggestion that the themes of *Prometheus* and *The Cenci* are similar is certainly not original. Dr. White, without pointing out the structural implications of his observations, has noted that the evil of *Prometheus Unbound* is a perversion of ideas originally good and that *The Cenci* presents an historical example of such perversion, Beatrice being the victim of both social and religious corruption. White comments, "It would be hard to name two other poems in English in which the power and the subtlety of evil are more poignantly realized."[27] With reference to *The Cenci,* I would like to add: the *power* of Count Cenci, the *subtlety* of Orsino. It is the combination of these two s in *The Cenci* which illustrates the theme of *Prometheus.*

Undoubtedly it is the nature of Cenci's crime which has focused attention on him and on his role in the play for so many years. And the initial shock which the early reviewers seem to have felt when reading of Cenci's crime seems to have had much influence on later criticism. But as Bates has observed, Shelley himself deemphasized the details of the crime almost to obscurity. Bates' conclusion that this obscurity "emphasizes them all the more" is a highly subjective one.[28] Perhaps an additional reason for Cameron and Frenz's conclusion that modern audiences do not seem to have found the play "structurally defective" is that modern audiences are less likely to feel this shock. Perhaps they are able to see Count Cenci without letting him obscure their view of the other characters and of the larger theme.

Further implications of the structural unity of *The Cenci* I will leave to other investigators. One point, however, does seem clear: While existing criticism insists that the play is structurally defective, primarily because Shelley wasted scenes in "overdeveloping" the character of Orsino and thus marred the central theme of the conflict between Beatrice and Cenci, careful study of the play itself reveals *The Cenci* to be structurally effective in presenting an Iago-like Orsino to initiate action, control pace, and represent a separate kind of evil, in order to present a larger theme parallel to that of *Prometheus Unbound.*

Notes

1. Kenneth Cameron and Horst Frenz, "The Stage History of Shelley's *The Cenci*," *PMLA* [*Publications of the Modern Language Association*], LX (1945), 1080-1105. See also Bert O. States, Jr., "Addendum: The Stage History of Shelley's *The Cenci*," *PMLA,* LXXII (1957), 633-644, for additional stage history and an attempt to arrive at another conclusion. For a criticism of this addendum and for Mr. States' reply see *PMLA,* LXXV (Mar. 1960), 147-149. I believe my paper answers many of the questions which Mr. States raises.

2. These reviews are available in N. I. White's *The Unextinguished Hearth* (Durham, North Carolina, 1938), pp. 167-216. Twelve notices are reprinted, two of them by the same person (Leigh Hunt).

3. Cameron and Frenz, pp. 1084-1085, 1090.

4. *Ibid.,* p. 1087.

5. White, *The Unextinguished Hearth,* p. 200.

6. *Shelley: Selected Poems, Essays, and Letters,* edited by Ellsworth Barnard (New York, 1944), footnote on p. 197.

7. Newman Ivey White, *Shelley* (New York, 1940), II, pp. 140-141.

8. Ernest Sutherland Bates, *A Study of Shelley's Drama* The Cenci (New York, 1908), p. 60.

9. *The Cenci,* ed. George Woodberry ("Belles Lettres Series," Boston, 1909), pp. xviii and xx.

10. Walter E. Peck, *Shelley, His Life and Work* (Boston, 1927), Vol. II, pp. 122-123.

11. Barnard, *Shelley,* footnotes on pp. 253 and 248. This phrase, "almost to begin a new play," which seems to have become something of a critical heirloom, was apparently originally Woodberry's in the 1909 edition. But the source of the objection seems to have been, partly at least, in the way in which Shelley's contemporaries approached drama. White has pointed out (*Shelley,* II. 141), "This theatrical flaw is far more perceptible to the spectator than to the reader [The Cameron and Frenz study shows the opposite, Who *does* see the flaw?], but it had been perceived from the first by managers who considered staging the play." White relates how Mr. Samuel Phelps, wishing to produce the play for Sadler's Wells, consulted with Mr. Jonas Levy, who in turn consulted Mr. R. H. Horne. It was the opinion of Levy and Horne that "from an acting point of view, its interest terminated with the death of Francesco Cenci. . . ." (*Notebook of the Shelley Society,* 1888, I. I. 187). White does not observe, however (and I think it is worth noting), that the *Notebook of the Shelley Society* continues (speaking of Mr. Levy), "as in his opinion *The Merchant of Venice,* from an acting point of view, came to an end with the exit of Shylock." The *Notebook* also adds that after Mr. Levy had *seen* the Shelley Society production of *The Cenci,* "He could only say that a great many he knew who went to scoff remained to pray . . ." and that he had "sat it out, with feelings of the utmost satisfaction, to the end." (*Notebook of the Shelley Society,* 1888, I. I. 187).

12. It is interesting that the one review following the publication of *The Cenci* which *did* raise objections to the structure of the play also shared this assumption. The reviewer wrote, "The technical structure of the piece is faulty as its subject matter is blamable. The first two acts serve only to explain the relative situation of the parties, and do not in the least promote the action of the play; the fifth, containing the judicial proceedings at Rome, is a mere excrescence. The whole plot, therefore, is comprised in the incestuous outrage and in the subsequent assassination of the perpetrator; the former enormity occurs in the interval between the second act and the third; the latter in the fourth act. The play has, properly speaking, no plot except in the third and fourth acts. But the incurable radical defects of the original conception of this drama render a minute examination of its structure superfluous." (*The Unextinguished Hearth,* White, pp. 213-214).

13. See T. W. Baldwin, *William Shakespere's Five-Act Structure,* (Urbana, Illinois, 1947), pp. 747-748. Prof. Baldwin discusses the use of this delayed-action pattern in Shakespeare's plays and its use in the plays of Terence. While it is quite possible that Shelley derived this structural pattern from his close study of Shakespeare, my point here is

simply that the pattern itself does not automatically constitute a defect.

14. My analysis of these acts might appear to some to be weighted in favor of Orsino, but I have endeavored to follow the text quite closely. Most summaries of the play either ignore the role of Orsino or minimize it greatly. (See, for example, that of N. I. White previously quoted. Woodberry [*The Cenci*, p. xix] says that "on the play itself, as a chain of action, Orsino has little concrete influence," and comments that he serves the play only in a minor way, is of slight use to the plot, and that nothing depends upon him except the hiring of the assassins.) It is interesting to note that in this respect my summary is quite similar to that of the reviewer for *The Theatrical Inquisitor and Monthly Mirror* (April, 1820, 16:205-218), who seems to have fully understood the function of Orsino in the play and who gave the play one of its few favorable reviews. See White's *The Unextinguished Hearth*, pp. 176-181.

15. White, *Shelley*, II, p. 143.

16. Bates, p. 68.

17. Bates, p. 53.

18. Bates, p. 68.

19. Sara Ruth Watson, "Shelley and Shakespeare: An Addendum. A Comparison of *Othello* and *The Cenci*," *PMLA*, LV (1940), pp. 611-614.

20. We have already observed how Shelley literally created the character of Orsino, but perhaps there was a suggestion for Shelley's character in the manuscript source. The manuscript reads: ". . . Monsignore Guerra [Shelley's Orsino] not only showed approbation of their design, but also promised to cooperate with them in their undertaking. *Thus stimulated,* Beatrice communicated the design to her eldest brother. . . ." (Italics mine. Manuscript available in appendix to Woodberry's edition, p. 134.)

21. There is a fine echo here of Orsino's exit line "as now I skulk from every other eye," and also of his lines at the end of Act I, scene ii, "I were a fool, not less than if a panther were panic-stricken by the antelope's eye, if she escape me." I suspect that most readers forget that had Beatrice been freed at the trial, she would still, in all likelihood, have had Orsino to cope with. The eye image brings to mind, too, Marzio facing Beatrice: The panther *was* panic-stricken. While it is not a specific reference, it is worthwhile to notice, too, Beatrice's song, in the next scene. "False friend, wilt thou smile or weep / when my life is laid asleep / . . . There is a snake in thy smile, my

dear; / and bitter poison within thy tear" (ln. 130-131, 136-137). To the best of my knowledge, no one has attempted to show the relation between this lyric and the plot structure. It seems almost unthinkable that the poet who had just finished the structure of three acts of *Prometheus* would add a lyrical element for the sake of convention or decoration. Can we not surmise that the lyric is structurally functional, and that the reference is to Orsino?

22. *The Notebook of the Shelley Society,* 1888, contains the following comment on the original production of the play: "Mr. Buxton Forman said he must certainly defend Shelley from the charge of making the play drag toward the end. Neither he nor the rest of the audience had found such to be the case, the third act being the pivot and in no sense the climax, and Beatrice throughout being the supremely important character" (p. 184).

23. "Revenge, retaliation, atonement, are pernicious mistakes. If Beatrice had thought in this manner she would have been wiser and better; but she would never have been a tragic character." (Shelley, Preface to *The Cenci*)

24. Barnard, *Shelley,* p. 87.

25. Shelley, *Prometheus Unbound,* III, iv, 144-148.

26. White has observed, "It is indeed remarkable that a poem practically every line of which is immediately clear to the average reader should have been written between the acts of *Prometheus Unbound.*" (Shelley, II, p. 142).

27. White, *Shelley,* II, pp. 142, 143.

28. Bates, p. 58.

Justin G. Turner (essay date February 1972)

SOURCE: Turner, Justin G. "*The Cenci*: Shelley vs. the Truth." *American Book Collector* 22, no. 5 (February 1972): 5-9.

[*In the following essay, Turner examines the veracity of Shelley's source material for* The Cenci *and contends that Shelley would have found little interest in Beatrice as a tragic heroine had he known the truth behind the Cenci legend.*]

All Italy was stirred by the most sensational criminal case in its history, the Cenci murder. After the execution of the family in 1599, rumors reached England of the wicked father who had poisoned his wife, killed his son, and ravished his daughter. Many years later, historians were to ascertain that these three crimes were the only ones of which Francesco Cenci was accused but of which he was not guilty. However, Elizabethan England was not interested in historical accuracy. Englishmen were enthusiastic about good stories, and Philip Massinger found in this Cenci story, material for a great tragedy, although in his play he changed the family name from Cenci to Malefort.

The dramatic late sixteenth century tragedy, *The Cenci,* written by Percy Bysshe Shelley, when he was twenty-six years old, is relatively little known outside of Shelley circles. Its inspiration was a factual patricide which shocked Italy in the late 1500's and has remained to this day a controversial discussion piece among literary critics, authors and Shelley enthusiasts.

Shelley had first asked Mary Godwin to attempt to write the tragedy, but she felt that she was far too young to have any chance of succeeding. *The Cenci* was the only one of Shelley's poems about which he consulted Mary constantly while it was in progress. This work was written rapidly between March 14 and August 8, 1819. Shelley was fearful that he had insufficient talent to write such a tragedy, that he would be unable to formulate the plot of this story, that he was defective of imagination, and that he was too fond of the theatrical and ideal to succeed as a tragedian. Formerly he had thought of writing a tragedy concerning Charles I, but he set this aside when an Italian manuscript of *The Cenci* was placed before him in 1819. His imagination was thereafter strongly excited and he proceeded swiftly, after being urged on by the intense sympathy with the suffering of the human beings whose passions he revived and gifted with poetic language.

In her note on *The Cenci,* Mary stated that Shelley wished it to be acted. *The Cenci* story has fascinated writers for more than three centuries. Its appeal does not suffer from retelling. This play, which has had more than thirty stagings, is not one of Shelley's better-known works but because of the circumstances surrounding its writing, it remains perhaps the most disputatious of all his works. Many of these stagings have been termed by such critics as George Bernard Shaw, St. John Ervine, and Oscar Wilde as well as by general audiences, to be surprisingly dramatic and lively.

Dramatically, *The Cenci* is a powerful and moving piece of writing. Swinburne hailed it as the greatest blank verse tragedy since the writings of Shakespeare. The beauty of its blank verse is a great achievement. This work was dedicated to Leigh Hunt who reviewed it in *The Indicator* of July 19 and 20 and praised it highly. Reviews of *The Cenci* continued in many publications throughout 1821 although *The Lonsdale Magazine* and *The Provincial Repository,* also *Blackwood's Edinburgh Magazine,* acknowledged Shelley's genius, they condemned his principles. *The Cenci* was the only

work of Shelley's which passed into an authorized second edition during his lifetime. The production of George Bernard Shaw's *Ghosts,* which was banned by the Lord Chamberlain of England because, like Shelley's *Cenci* which he also banned, it has a hint of incest in it.

Today we should consider the source material from which Shelley borrowed so extensively as being highly slanted, but Shelley had no way of realizing this when he utilized *The Cenci* story. In his time, communication between England and the mid-Continent was, at best, hazy. The poet was thus unaware of the partisan nature of his research.

From his early youth, Shelley had championed the cause of all oppressed humanity, which had been the subject of most of his poems. It is quite justifiably claimed that Shelley never would have written *The Cenci* had he known the actual truth about the internecine affair. In any event, Shelley's interpretation remains one of the more absorbing stories within the fact-crime vs. fiction genre as are the details of the crime itself.

The amoral father, Francesco Cenci, certainly deserved the fate meted out to him, and one loses no sympathy for Beatrice as she initiates and insists upon her father's death at the hands of her more or less willing co-conspirators.

Francesco had committed many crimes and in his third trial for sodomy he had been found guilty and sentenced to pay a fine of 100,000 scudi. He was a cruel and vicious person but because of his connections and his ability to pay money to the Roman hierarchy and to transfer some of his holdings to them, he was not obliged to serve time for his criminal acts.

When Francesco, gross, vulgar and rich, moved Beatrice and his plump, naive wife, Lucretia, from their palace in Rome and locked them up inside the lonely castle La Petrella on the Naples road, it is understandable that rebellion, frustration, and loneliness would prompt Beatrice into an affair with the handsome Olimpio, the castellan at La Petrella.

While shut up at the castle at La Petrella she and her stepmother were placed under heavy guard and denied the privilege of leaving their rooms. When their clothing was sent to him so that he could verify the necessity for its replacement, he refused to renew their outworn dress.

A few months after her first secret rendezvous, Beatrice discovered she had been made pregnant by Olimpio and this fact merely compounded her decision toward the murder of her father. She persuaded the unhappy Lucretia and one of her brothers, Giacomo, to aid in the plot. The affectionate and powerful Olimpio wavered a number of times but he finally consented.

The end result was a messy job of murder performed by rank amateurs. The perpetrators might never have been found out and executed excepting for the suspicious whisperings of neighbors and of others who knew the truth of Beatrice's being with child. These whisperings snowballed to such an extent and turned to such open accusations, they compelled Pope Clement VIII to take action. Justice in the Italy of that era could not be served in a murder trial unless the accused confessed. However, the confessions were forced, if necessary, by means of excruciating torture and self-accusation had little to do with the validity of the murder.

Beatrice and her brother, Giacomo Cenci, who confessed, perished under the chopping block, as did her mother, Lucretia. Olimpio, who had become conscience-stricken, had been murdered previously, otherwise he too would have perished in a like manner. These, then, are the basic facts. But let us examine how Shelley utilized them.

Shelley, in writing *The Cenci* as he had so often done before, chose a subject with which his convictions and sympathies were in accord and he developed it so that it became an argument for the rectitude of his principles regarding humanitarian ideals. His main source of "research" was the large body of tales that came to be known as *The Relacioni*. This was entirely sympathetic to Beatrice since the complete facts of the trial had not been made public during the writing of the tales. Thus Shelley colored his chief protagonist, Beatrice, and her motivation. A social propagandist, Shelley quickly seized upon and magnified the injustices set forth in *The Relacioni,* which Beatrice and her co-conspirators suffered at the hands of Count Cenci.

Later, Senator Corrado Ricci's scholarly two volumes entitled *Beatrice Cenci,* (on which this writer has constantly relied) was to set the record straight, as opposed to *The Relacioni.* But at the time of Shelley's composition, he utilized a romanticized legend which favored Beatrice and her associates, and so forged his play as to form a medium of expression for his own principles: his love of decency, his hatred of tyranny and cruelty.

The poet envisioned Beatrice Cenci as his ideal woman whose struggles represented the noble effort of downtrodden humanity to triumph over evil. Had Shelley been aware of the harsh facts that Ricci, and still later, more modern research have made known concerning the true history of the Cenci, it is indeed doubtful that he would have given the story a second thought. There was little beauty of soul, innocence or nobility of reli-

gious faith in the original members of the evil Cenci family. He hardly would have used their "tragedy" as a basis for any of his writings.

Shelley's Count Francesco Cenci remains basically consistent with the real Francesco,—a vulgar, cruel, lewd boy and man. The Cenci sons—Giacomo, Christofor and Rocco—in fact were of the same mold as their father, involved in numerous lawsuits with him, but lacking his strong will and fearlessness. In a will which was never notarized, the Count accused both Giacomo and Christofor of having plotted against his life, honor and property. Rocco, after a number of attacks upon peaceful citizens, was killed in a duel by Amilcare Orsino, an adversary whom the Cenci son vastly underrated.

Bernardo, the younger son, has his own place in the Shelleyan and the historical versions of the tale. For the most part, history presents Bernardo as having no trace of the characteristic family violence, cruelty or lust. The fact of his lack of family traits, of course, might very well be attributed to the reason attested to by a number of witnesses, namely that Bernardo was a half-wit.

Lucretia was what we today would call an insignificant nonentity. In direct contrast to Lucretia, Beatrice Cenci had inherited much of her father's nature and personality, including his strong and forceful manner. It was she who determined and decided upon her father's murder. It was Beatrice who urged Olimpio and Marzio, the hired assassins, to renew their resolve when they weakened. She it was who swept aside Lucretia's protests. After the crime Beatrice was calm and collected, when she expressed contempt for Lucretia's fearful regrets at the trial and she flung at the weeping woman the ejaculation—"blockhead!" Beatrice persisted in her denial of knowledge of the murder even when confronted with the weight of overwhelming evidence, much of it rendered by the members of her own less-spirited family. When she did confess, she shrewdly attempted to cast the onus of guilt on the dead Olimpio, her paramour.

Shelley eagerly clasped to his romantic bosom the charge of Beatrice's defense that her father, Francesco, who had been previously fined for sodomy, attempted to force sexual relations upon her. The accusation, unfounded and without the slightest element of proof, fired the imagination and sympathy of the public and, needless to say, of the English poet who accepted the charge. In his dramatic play Shelley has the Count commit incest.

Monsignore Mario Guerra who was well connected in Rome is given much more prominence in the Shelleyan version than in the actual case. Though closely connected with the Cenci family and undoubtedly having knowledge of the intended murder, he had very little to do with it. Nowhere in the historical record is there evidence of any feeling of affection between Guerra and Beatrice. True, he killed Olimpio—but that can be attributed more to his friendship for certain members of the Cenci family.

The facts of the actual murder show that after an abortive attempt to do away with the father by poison, the co-assassins Olimpio and Marzio were willing to forget the whole thing but Beatrice persisted. Early the next morning Olimpio and Marzio attacked the Count in his sleep, Olimpio beating him about the head with a hammer, and Marzio beating his legs to prevent Francesco from rising. Lucretia remained in an anteroom while the murder was executed. Beatrice went to the window to open it to afford the killers better light.

The family explained that Francesco had fallen to his death from a rickety balcony, a fact which was too easily disproved. Marzio fled into the hills and Olimpio went into the village. Not until a year later did an official investigation take place by Rome and then Marzio was taken into custody. He died in jail after confessing his part in the crime. Giacomo, Bernardo, Lucretia and Beatrice were brought to trial for their various parts in the plot. Only Bernardo was permitted to live—to serve in prison and in the galleys. At the time of their deaths, the father, Francesco, was forty-nine years of age and Beatrice was twenty-two.

Shelley's *The Cenci* differs considerably from the established facts. Dramatic unity and dramatic liberty are necessary ingredients of the writer's craft. But, as has been pointed out, drama was not the reason that motivated the poet to pen this play. The chief reason was that he seized upon, almost selfishly it would appear and certainly hurriedly, what he believed to be a factual account as a vehicle for an expression of his own nature and to give voice to his principles.

In his play, Beatrice is a glorious creature endowed with the greatest physical and spiritual beauty. She is,—

". . . that most perfect coinage of God's love that ever came sorrowing upon the earth."

Amilcare Orsino, who loves and desires Beatrice, also recognizes her unusual intellect. Shelley, in short, portrays Beatrice not as a young woman who willingly, perhaps even eagerly gave herself to a man out of wedlock, not as the daughter who triggered the murder of her father, but as a girl striving to attain justice. Rocco is described by Shelley as being killed at Mass when the church walls collapsed. Christofor's death is presented as being caused by a jealous man in error.

In Act III of the Shelleyan play, it is established that Francesco has ravished his daughter; her outraged innocence and defiled purity motivate her decision for vengeance. Both Orsino and Lucretia agree with Beatrice that the wealthy Count must die, and Orsino proposes two outlaws to do the deed. Orsino, Giacomo and Marzio are given sympathetic reasons for becoming involved in the murder.

In Act IV of *The Cenci,* Francesco works himself into such an emotional pitch at the thought of going to Beatrice's bed that he determines upon an hour's rest. At this point a first attempt upon the Count's life is made by Olimpio and Marzio who later abruptly return to declare that they cannot kill "an old and sleeping man."

At this juncture Shelley's Beatrice reacts more like the factual Beatrice. Angered, she snatches a dagger from one of the two would-be assassins and vows to kill her father herself, and afterwards to kill Olimpio and Marzio. Cowed, the two men exit to hasten to Francesco's chamber. Shortly after they reappear to tell Beatrice and Lucretia that they had strangled Francesco and thus completed their murderous task: adding that they had strangled Cenci to eliminate blood, and cast his body into the garden beneath the balcony to make it appear that he had fallen to his death.

The fact of the matter, of course, is that there was so much blood spilled that Beatrice and Lucretia never did fully succeed in hiding what had occurred. Also, they were careless about the bloodied bed sheets, coverlet and Francesco's clothing—physical evidence that helped to bring them to trial, and, together with their confessions, to convict them.

In *The Cenci* the Count's body was discovered almost immediately by a papal legate and his men who had come for Francesco to answer to charges of murder brought against him by the papacy. When the premises were searched, the body was found; the women and Bernardo were arrested and taken to Rome where the fifth and last act of the Shelley play takes place.

In Ricci's factual two-volume report, Beatrice gave instructions for the body of her father to be buried at once, which was done. Neither Beatrice nor Lucretia attended the burial service, however—a fact that aroused comment, and, in some quarters, grave suspicion. Then, as one author puts it in a discussion of the facts vs. Shelley—Sir Lionel Cust in The Cenci—*A Study in Murder*—"It is not difficult to get a body put underground, but it is impossible to silence gossip. . . ." Still more serious were the discoveries made later of the blood-stained bed clothes, in which the murder had taken place.

Shelley has the tried assassin Marzio confess when tortured. In the second scene of Act V Beatrice makes a stirring appeal to Cardinal Camillo that the word of Marzio wrung from him by torture should not be used against them.

When in the third scene, Beatrice is told that Giacomo and Lucretia have also confessed, Shelley once again comes closer to fact as Beatrice denounces her mother and her brother for their weakness. Poor Giacomo, already tortured with redhot pincers, had his head smashed with an iron hammer, his throat slit, and his body quartered. Beatrice's lover, Olimpio, who had actually assisted in murdering Francesco, with the help of Marzio, had been murdered some time previously. In the play Beatrice who is convicted without a confession, and while a crowd of Romans looked on, she laid her head on the chopping block and a single stroke of the executioner's axe, disposed of her. Did Shelley not know that at that time Italian law in a murder trial demanded a confession, no matter how strong the circumstantial evidence, before the accused could be found guilty? Whether the confessions were true confessions or obtained partly because of the pain inflicted by torture, was immaterial. The law states that confessions must be obtained; it did not specify as to *how* that confession should be obtained.

In the last scene of the Shelley drama, Bernardo appeals personally to the Pope, but is refused. Beatrice and Lucretia arrange each other's clothing and hair and they are ready to go to their deaths.

While the difference to be found in the play as opposed to fact can be laid primarily to the partisan manuscript which fell into Shelley's hands, the poet created—as would any writer—incidents and characterizations of his own interpretation. Also, Shelley, the intensely idealistic poet, when romanticism was at its apex, compressed the year's murder events concerning the Cenci into a period of a few days.

Sympathy is created for the Shelleyan Beatrice in a number of ways. When Orsino wishes to marry her, she informs him that it will always be her duty to remain at home where she may by her presence share in the sufferings which afflict Lucretia and Bernardo, and thus help them.

And when Francesco commits his outrage upon her, she experiences an inescapable pollution of body and spirit that she will never be able to eradicate. She sees the act too, as a stain on the honor of God. She prays to God to direct her and becomes imbued with the necessity to be the avenger of this horror befallen her:

> ". . . something must be done
>
> something which shall make the thing that I have suffered but a shadow in the dread lightning which avenges it."

She believes that she is acting as God's agent in the patricide she undertakes. Beatrice then, is an embodiment of that Shelleyan world where human beings strive ever to achieve and waste no time in vain regret for that which is past; she is an individual person held under tyranny—one of the oppressed among mankind—possessing an inner spirit that compels her to act according to the dictates of her conscience.

During the course of the play, Shelley never mentions Count Cenci's worst crime. Everyone knew that it must be incest but it was never mentioned in words, the nearest allusion to it being that portion of Cenci's beginning, "that if she have a child. . . ." Shelley enlarges upon Count Cenci's evil personality by involving him in a premeditated incestuous act with his daughter. Shelley had to be very careful in preparing *The Cenci* for publication because he bore in mind that his publishers first refused to publish his *Revolt of Islam* as they feared that its publication would convict them of condoning incest as well as the more ordinary conventions. However, Shelley met his publishers' demands by cancelling the title page and substituting twenty-six pages of new text in order to have *The Revolt of Islam* published. In the banquet scene in the play, Cenci calls upon his guests to join him in his exultation over the deaths of two of his sons. Each fresh crime adds to his satisfaction, spurring him on to new and darker deeds. He feels himself to be—

> ". . . like a fiend appointed to chastise the offenses of some unremembered world."

His appointment he fully believes comes from an omnipotent God.

In Francesco Cenci we perceive once again much of that which in reverse made up Shelley's character. The Count represents for Shelley those forces of evil against which the poet spent his life fighting: namely power, malice, and avarice. As the climax of his career of evil, Shelley has Francesco become obsessed with the desire to destroy his daughter's soul. This he hopes to achieve not only by his incestuous act but by so brainwashing her as to cause her to consent to a repetition of the incest.

In his concept of the factual Count Cenci, Shelley omitted the vulgarity and obscenity found in his source material. He changes Francesco from a creature of low vices and of average intellect to a being animated by one all-consuming vice and directed by a very superior intelligence.

The minor characters of the play most definitely represent Shelley's philosophy of life, of his tripartite division of the world into tyrants, heroes and slaves. Lucretia remains what she was in real life—a timid, submissive woman of her times. Shelley's Giacomo is made even more irresolute and wavering than the one who died on the block. Orsino, sly and villainous, is used to further increase sympathy for Beatrice. The Pope is so depicted as to illustrate the type of papal representative which Shelley personally scorned.

A true and unbiased account of the Cenci and their associates would not have enlisted the sensitive Shelley's interest. Their sordid lives would never have appealed to his sympathy. Beatrice's crime would have repulsed rather than attracted the poet-playwright. With great singleness of purpose, however, *The Relacioni* prompted Shelley to devote himself almost entirely to Beatrice and Francesco. The other characters and indeed the incidents of the plot were drawn lightly and solely to bring into relief the great struggle in the minds and emotions of father and daughter.

Francesco and Beatrice are not real in the sense of being common, every day man and woman, but they are real in the higher sense which Shelley wished to project; they are the living concepts of an idealist's view. The one represents the injustice and cold, formal cruelty of man pitted against the other, the exponent of the ever-desirous, ever-struggling innermost soul of humanity. The result of their battle is the necessary victory which Shelley felt must ultimately come to the forces of virtue. It was natural for Shelley, the exemplification of universal love and brotherhood, to portray Beatrice as a virtuous young woman.

Harry White (essay date spring 1978)

SOURCE: White, Harry. "Beatrice Cenci and Shelley's Avenger." *Essays in Literature* 5, no. 1 (spring 1978): 27-38.

[*In the following essay, White explains that Shelley's changes to his source material downplay themes of tyrannical power and rebellion in favor of notions of retribution and atonement.*]

A significant number of readers are not entirely convinced that the murder in *The Cenci* can be construed as an act of vengeance. Aware of Shelley's explicit condemnation of "revenge, retaliation, atonement," they will nevertheless insist that "there is no evidence that she [Beatrice] seeks revenge. . . . [S]he is not thinking in such terms. For her it is a deed that is as yet unexpiated and that asks atonement"[1] (this despite Shelley's association of revenge and atonement). Tending to regard the murder as an "act of rebellion,"[2] they prefer to describe Beatrice as a "public benefactor," one who resorts to bloodshed to extirpate "social and domestic evil"[3] (this despite the fact that no lasting public benefit or social reform results from her deed). Newman I. White even goes so far as to suggest that Shelley "can scarcely tolerate his own notion of revenge as part of

her character. Her real motive for the murder is self-protection. . . ."[4] On the contrary, I think we will be able to see that revenge was the very part Shelley wrote into the figure of Beatrice Cenci when refashioning her character for his drama. In fact I propose to show that all the major changes Shelley made in the Cenci story work toward the end of underplaying the theme of tyranny and rebellion evident in his manuscript source and replacing it with the significantly different issue of revenge and atonement. Just why Shelley made such changes will be a final consideration.

It seems to me that the wide range of critical opinion regarding Beatrice's justification is to a great degree the result of unintentional ambiguities introduced into the play by those changes Shelley made in the Cenci story. Specifically, the difficulty with the play is that the murder is rationalized by its perpetrators as an act of revenge and atonement, but it is executed upon a stage originally set for a drama of tyranny and possible revolt. As a result, the play presents its readers with two Beatrices, the rebel and the avenger. However, I believe we may see that the characterization of Beatrice as killing in self-defense or in revolt against tyranny can only be based upon a knowledge of Shelley's manuscript source or the character of Beatrice as she is represented in the opening two acts of the play. Beyond these there is little or no reason for regarding the heroine of Shelley's tragedy as anything but a woman destroyed by a religious compulsion to seek revenge and atonement.

It is noteworthy first of all that nowhere in his preface to the play does Shelley specifically condemn violence undertaken with the end of either rebellion or self-defense. Shelley does of course bring up the subject of rebellion, but not with reference to the heroine of his play. He notes in the first paragraph that Beatrice "after long and vain attempts to escape from what she considered a perpetual contamination of both body and mind, at length plotted with her mother-in-law and brother to murder their common tyrant" ("Preface," p. 275).[5] But we must recognize that at this point Shelley is relating the Cenci legend and speaking of Beatrice as she appeared to him largely through the manuscript, **"Relation of the Death of the Family of the Cenci."** There we are similarly informed that at "length, these unhappy women, finding themselves without hope of relief, driven by desperation, resolved to plan his death."[6] The manuscript speaks simply of their "hope of relief" while Shelley insists upon Beatrice's desire to escape from "perpetual contamination." This novel emphasis upon contamination is our first hint at a shift away from the theme of self-defense toward that of pollution and atonement, and it should be kept in mind for upcoming discussion. In any case, Shelley does accept and present the explanation given in the manuscript that Beatrice of story and legend killed to escape oppression.

However, he does not begin to discuss the heroine of his drama until the fourth paragraph of the Preface, the pivotal significance of which is apparent from its opening sentence: "This *story* of the Cenci is indeed eminently fearful and monstrous: anything like a dry exhibition of it on the *stage* would be insupportable" (p. 276, italics added). Turning from the story itself to consider under what conditions it might be successfully transferred to the stage, Shelley explains in this paragraph how and why he transformed Beatrice, not into the "wiser and better" person he might have wished her to be, but into a tragic character who mistakenly believes that a "person can be truly dishonoured by the act of another" ("Preface," p. 276) and is thereby driven to seek revenge and atonement. Privately, Shelley confessed that **The Cenci** was "written for the multitude" and "calculated to produce a very popular effect. . . ."[7] It is in fact modeled after a genre of proven popularity, the revenge tragedy; and its heroine, Shelley admits, was created to appeal to a mass audience that would have no interest in a wise and good protagonist:

> Revenge, retaliation, atonement, are pernicious mistakes. If Beatrice had thought in this manner she would have been wiser and better; but she would never been a tragic character: the few whom such an exhibition would have interested, could never have been sufficiently interested for a dramatic purpose, from the want of finding sympathy in their interest among the mass who surround them. It is in the restless and anatomizing casuistry with which men seek the justification of Beatrice, yet feel that she has done what needs justification; it is in the superstitious horror with which they contemplate alike her wrongs and their revenge, that the dramatic character of what she did and suffered, consists.
>
> ("Preface," pp. 276-77)

This passage, which is often taken to allow in some way for a justification of Beatrice, is actually only an explanation of why an unenlightened, mass audience would seek her justification in the first place. For Shelley begins by stating unequivocally that her action is unjustifiable—a pernicious mistake. (The specific condemnation is of violence employed for the purpose of revenge and atonement; to repeat, there is nothing in the Preface which states that violent rebellion is unjustifiable!) But he anticipates that the masses for whom he has written will seek, by resorting to "casuistry," to justify the very motives he had condemned. The difficulty they will face is not having to justify revenge, which they find morally acceptable, but defending revenge enacted against one's own father. Violence of this sort is what will strike them with "superstitious horror." For certainly Shelley would never use the adjective "superstitious" to describe anyone's abhorrence of revenge—or oppression for that matter. But "superstitious horror" could appropriately describe the reaction of an audience aroused by scenes of incestuous rape and parricide. Thus Beatrice "has done what needs

justification" only because the multitude believe that revenge is justified in her case, but they cannot reconcile their superstitions concerning the need for revenge and atonement of the crime of incestuous rape with their equally superstitious horror at the prospect of violence directed against one's father. A draft of this passage states the precise nature of their dilemma more clearly. It reads, Beatrice "has done an unnatural deed, but urged to it by one more unnatural. . . ."[8]

From the Preface we may therefore conclude that Shelley understood the murder to be in retaliation for the "one," singular crime of forced incest. He never applies the escape-from-tyranny interpretation to the heroine of his drama, nor does he raise the issue of honor and revenge when discussing her prototype. We may thus further conclude that Shelley understood these two women to be motivated by entirely different ends. Of course in Shelley's version it is Cenci's tyranny which ultimately drives Beatrice to murder; however, when she does have her father killed, it is not with the aim of eliminating tyranny, as we shall soon see. If we seek a rebel Beatrice, the Preface, for one, indicates that we might better look for her not in the play but in the legend from which it was adapted.

Yet Shelley was not totally successful in making the motive for the murder revenge instead of rebellion or self-defense. The changes he wished to make were introduced into the play too late and too abruptly. The revenge motif is not sufficiently foreshadowed and indeed runs contrary to the direction established in the play's exposition. It is the problem these changes create that we should now consider.

The woman we discover in Act I is modeled after the legendary figure of Beatrice, and if anything, represents a more idealized portrait. Her predicament is also the same. She and her family are hopelessly seeking relief from Cenci's endless persecution, and their plight is conveniently summarized in Beatrice's plea for help:

BEATRICE.

> I do entreat you, go not, noble guests;
> What, although tyranny and impious hate
> Stand sheltered by a father's hoary hair?
>
> . . . . .
> Shall we therefore find
> No refuge in this merciless wide world?
> O think what deep wrongs must have blotted out
> First love, then reverence in a child's prone mind,
> Till it thus vanquished shame and fear! O think!
> I have borne much, and kissed the sacred hand
> Which crushed us to the earth, and thought its stroke
> Was perhaps some paternal chastisement!
> Have excused much, doubted; and when no doubt
> Remained, have sought by patience, love, and tears
> To soften him, and when this could not be
> I have knelt down through the long sleepless nights

And lifted up to God, the Father of all,
Passionate prayers: and when these were not heard
I still have borne,—until I meet you here,
Princes and kinsmen, at this hideous feast
Given at my brothers' deaths. Two yet remain,
His wife remains and I, who if ye save not,
Ye may soon share such merriment again
As fathers make over their children's graves.

(I. iii. 99-125)

The situation as Beatrice represents it is quite clear: She has borne "deep wrongs" (keep in mind her reference at this time to a plurality of wrongs); and unless she and her family can be rescued from Cenci's "tyranny," he will most likely destroy them. But Cenci successfully intimidates those who would come to their aid; and shortly afterward, Beatrice learns that her petition to the Pope has not been answered (II. ii. 24-25). Thus the first act of Shelley's drama depicts the same inescapable conditions that in the story had originally driven Beatrice to murder. At this point there can be no doubt in the reader's mind that the problem is relief from oppression and escape from inevitable death. Except for a remark by Cenci on the enjoyment of "revenge" (I. i. 77-91), which has more to do with sadism that retribution, there is no mention of honor, revenge, or atonement.

But it is at this crucial point in the development of the action that Shelley forces the play to shift direction. The circumstances compelling Beatrice to actively resist her father's persecution reach a crisis with the Pope's refusal to come to her aid. This rejection originally stood as the turning point, the tragic climax of a story exposing the ineptitude and expediency of the Papacy. For prior to the rejection of her petition, Beatrice had not been represented as a thoroughly desperate woman; but almost immediately thereafter, the manuscript relates how she and Lucretia, "finding themselves without hope of relief . . . resolved to plan his death" (**"Relation"** [**"of the Death of the Family of the Cenci"**], p. 160). Now there can be no doubt that Shelley understood the significance of the moment, since he has Lucretia acknowledge that the unopened petition means their "last hope has failed" (II. i. 28). However, Shelley deliberately altered the sequence of events at the very moment of crisis because he sought to cast an entirely different light upon the murder. Instead of dramatizing a possible outcome of this crisis, he circumvented the problem by making certain alterations. The rape of Beatrice, which had originally compelled her to petition the Pope, does not occur in Shelley's version until after her petition is returned. So instead of the original sequence: persecution including *rape*, petition, its rejection, murder plot; we have: persecution, petition, its rejection, *rape*, murder plot. The entire second act of the play serves to divorce two events directly related in the manuscript, the collapse of all hope for re-

lief (II. i. 28) and the first thought of murder (III. i. 117-26). In Shelley's version the thought of murdering Cenci occurs well after their last hope of relief has failed, but immediately after Beatrice is raped; and for this reason, the murder plot comes to be thought of as an act of vengeance and atonement and not justifiable tyrannicide.

The effect these interpolations have upon the development of the plot is that although the action climaxes naturally and inevitably enough at the beginning of Act II, it climaxes too early and for the wrong reasons. Thus the function of the second act is largely one of re-organization, and this is what accounts for the sluggish and inconsequential nature of the action throughout it. The purpose of Act II, as I see it, is to bridge the gap between the significant action of the first act, culminating in Act II with the petition's return, and the significantly different action of the third, beginning with the rape of Beatrice. As a result, the dramatic structure is so drastically altered that there are in effect two climaxes within one tragedy, the Pope's (and the banquet guest's) non-intervention and the rape of Beatrice. Consequently, there have been two generally plausible explanations for the murder of Cenci: self-defense and revenge.

However, the plot changes Shelley made render the first climax and much of the action of the first act inconsequential. At the exact moment when Cenci's death seems the only means by which his family may be relieved of endless torment, the action is suddenly redirected toward a future crisis:

SERVANT.

> My master bids me say, the Holy Father
> Has sent back your petition thus unopened.
> . . . . .

LUCRETIA.

> *So, daughter our last hope has failed; Ah me!*
> *How pale you look*; you tremble, and you stand
> Wrapped in some fixed and fearful meditation,
> As if one thought were over strong for you:
> Your eyes have a chill glare; O, dearest child!
> Are you gone mad? . . .
> . . . . .
>
> You talked of something that your father did
> After that dreadful feast? Could it be worse
> Than when he smiled, and cried, "My sons are dead!"
> . . . . .
>
> Until this hour thus have you ever stood
> Between us and your father's moody wrath
> Like a protecting presence: your firm mind
> Has been our only refuge and defence:
> What can have thus subdued it? . . .
> . . . . .

BEATRICE

> (*speaking very slowly with a forced calmness*).
> It was one word, Mother, one little word;
> One look, one smile. (*Wildly*) Oh! He has trampled me
> Under his feet, and made the blood stream down
> My pallid cheeks. And he has given us all
> Ditch-water, and the fever-stricken flesh
> Of buffaloes, and bade us eat or starve,
> And we have eaten.—He has made me look
> On my beloved Bernardo, when rust
> Of heavy chains has gangrened his sweet limbs,
> And I have never yet despaired—but now!
> What could I say?   [*Recovering herself*]
>   Ah, no! 'tis nothing new.
>
>   (II. i. 24-73, my italics)

No sooner has Lucretia acknowledged that their "last hope has failed"—indicating presumably that in the history of Cenci's persecution of them the moment of mortal crisis has arrived—than with the very next words she manages to turn the scene and the drama completely about: "Ah me! / How pale you look. . . ." Now one might assume that the sudden change in Beatrice's appearance, her radically different behavior, reveals shock at the terrible news they have just received. That this is not the case is as clear an indication as any that Shelley is deliberately turning away from the line of action already established. In fact, he has Beatrice insist that her strange behavior has nothing to do with any of Cenci's previous crimes. This one will be worse than all of them taken together.

Beatrice's words seem to anticipate problems arising from the changes which the play is undergoing as she speaks. At this very moment Shelley is beginning to translate the rape which had originally stood at this place in the story for the ultimate act of tyranny into what will be, when it occurs, the act that initiates Beatrice's revenge and serves as its primary motive. In other words, the scene marks the beginning of a second exposition within the play; and it does so by attempting at the same time to all but discount the continued relevance of the first beyond this turning point. Dismissing all of Cenci's former outrages as nothing compared with what he now conceives, Beatrice's words do indeed anticipate the introduction of something "new": the theme of contamination and atonement. In fact they indicate a breakdown in the continuity of the action and even go so far as to encourage the audience to accept a discontinuity of development: We must somehow largely discount what we have learned of Cenci's tyranny in preparation for understanding the now delayed murder plot as growing not directly out of the context of Cenci's previous crimes so much as about to result from a single outrage yet to be enacted. And as anticipated, the rape will have the effect of so overwhelming

Beatrice with superstitious horror that she will regard it, not as the worst instance of Cenci's tyranny, but as an extraordinarily monstrous act which calls for immediate and forceful action, as did none of his numerous other crimes.

But while Beatrice's hysterical response is psychologically plausible and in keeping with other changes Shelley made in the story, there is reason to question whether it is dramatically suitable, whether it is not similar to those other changes in that it also runs counter to the major thrust of the action up to the second act. We should note that Beatrice originally regarded the rape—more fittingly I believe—as an indication of how impossible it would be "to continue to live in so miserable a manner . . ." ("**Relation**," p. 160). Her response to an outrage, the details of which Mary found "unfit for publication" ("**Relation**," p. 160n.), was simply to send "a well-written supplication to the Pope, imploring him to . . . [withdraw] her from the violence and cruelty of her father" ("**Relation**," p. 160). Even after she is violated, there is no mention of contamination or revenge; and her continued composure is in marked contrast to the hysteria Shelley wrote into his character:

BEATRICE.

>   My God!
> The beautiful blue heaven is flecked with blood!
> The sunshine on the floor is black! The air
> Is changed to vapours such as the dead breathe
> In charnal pits! Pah! I am choked! There creeps
> A clinging, black, contaminating mist
> About me . . . 'tis substantial, heavy, thick,
> I cannot pluck it from me, for it glues
> My fingers and my limbs to one another,
> And eats into my sinews, and dissolves
> My flesh to a pollution, poisoning
> The subtle, pure, and inmost spirit of life!
> My God! I never knew what the mad felt
> Before; for I am mad beyond all doubt!
>
>   (III. i. 12-25)

The "mad" Beatrice is obviously Shelley's own creation, an addition to the legend. It is she who dissociates the rape from Cenci's other now purely tyrannical acts to comprehend it anew under the influence of honor codes and religious superstition, believing that in this instance she has been "dishonoured by the act of another." For the compulsion to revenge is dictated by the understanding that though innocent of having committed a dishonorable act one may yet be guilty of having suffered it. Guilt is objective, without regard to an individual's intent or active involvement in the crime. Thus, in such matters, responsibility for righting the wrong readily falls upon the victim of the crime, who remains guilty so long as he or she allows his or her dishonor to persist unavenged and unatoned for. As Shelley knew, revenge is an act of atonement on the part of the *victim* of a crime who, as in Beatrice's case, seeks retaliation as the only means of ridding herself of dishonor and cleansing away the polluting and contaminating effects of the offending act.

The above words, the very first Beatrice utters after being raped, reveal that although still an unwilling victim, Beatrice no longer thinks of herself as an innocent one, but as a woman infected with a moral contamination for which she must make amends. That is why she insists that this "wrong . . . is such / As asks atonement . . ." (III. i. 213-15). Her immediate concern after the rape is to expiate *her* guilt and *her* dishonor, and thus she first considers taking her own life, not that of her father:

> O blood, which art my father's blood,
> Circling through these contaminated veins,
> If thou, poured forth on the polluted earth,
> Could wash away the crime, and punishment
> By which I suffer . . . no, that cannot be!
> Many may doubt there was a God above
> Who sees and permits evil, and so die:
> That faith no agony shall obscure in me.

(III. i. 95-102)

Beatrice conceives of death, whether hers or her father's, largely as a cleansing act of atonement which has as its primary aim to rid the world of the pollution caused by the particular crime of incestuous rape. To rid the world of Cenci's evil power remains a consideration secondary both to the need for atonement and to a sense of justice that is almost totally theological and metaphysical in character, rather than moral and political in its concerns. Stuart Curran is certainly correct when he says that Beatrice struggles "not to save herself, but the moral universe."[9] To rectify the moral order is frequently the justification for revenge. However, it needs to be emphasized that such an aim reveals not a larger, less self-centered purpose, but outright religious fanaticism on Beatrice's part. We must not forget that from the first Shelley insisted that "there is neither good nor evil in the universe" and that belief in a moral universe was the cornerstone of fraudulent religious doctrines which opposed humanitarian concerns.[10] Under the influence of such doctrines, Beatrice sacrifices human life to maintain this abstract notion of a moral universe, imitating by her deed the traditional practice of the Church which will soon sacrifice her, as it has others, to the same principle of a moral universe.

That Cenci is murdered almost exclusively for religious and not social-political reasons is apparent furthermore from the fact that Beatrice never does publicize the real reason for the murder, even though she had formerly spoken out against Cenci's "tyranny and impious hate." Were oppression the matter, she might have reiterated in her defense any number of already revealed crimes. Her problem is that the one crime that explains and justifies the murder is unmentionable. To make known the "crime of . . . [her] destroyer," would, she knows, ef-

fectively ruin her "unpolluted fame" (III. i. 152-66). Beatrice's silence reveals how troubled she is by a problem central to the whole question of honor and revenge, not to mention practical considerations regarding the status of a raped woman in sixteenth century Italy. Calderon, whom Shelley was reading at the time he wrote *The Cenci,* dealt with the dilemma that the act of revenge must somehow keep secret the fact of one's dishonor or contamination (see especially *A Secreto Agravio, Secreta Venganza*); and not incidentally, Mary felt the need for silence regarding certain details of the manuscript she edited.

We should take note of Beatrice's silence to counter any notions that she is rebellious, and we might compare her silence with the typical wordiness of rebel figures Shelley did create: Ahasuerus (in *Queen Mab*), Prometheus, Laon and Cythna (also a rape victim) never lack for words, eager as they are to publicize at length the reasons for their actions so as to enlighten and convert to the cause of public benefit and social reform. Their humanitarian sense of justice is altogether different from Beatrice's fanaticism. In the final analysis we find Beatrice capable of withstanding acts of inhumanity involving the worst kinds of mental torture and physical abuse. The sight of Bernardo gangrenous in chains or the news of her brothers' deaths does not disturb her as does the horror she feels at the mere hint of incestuous rape (see II. i. 24-73, quoted above). Human compassion does not have the force of religious superstition, and so Beatrice is roused to violent action only when she feels an offence has been committed not against other men, but against God:

BEATRICE.

> Ay, death . . .
> The punishment of crime. I pray thee, God,
> Let me not be bewildered while I judge.
> If I must live day after day, and keep
> These limbs, the unworthy temple of Thy spirit,
> As a foul den from which what Thou abhorrest
> May mock Thee, unavenged . . . it shall not be!

(III. i. 125-31)

"Keep thy body as a temple for the holy spirit," said Paul. Cenci has violated the temple and sinned unpardonably against the holy spirit. His other acts were merely crimes against humanity; the rape is a sacrilege. That is why Beatrice and her co-conspirators, all "Catholics deeply tinged with religion" ("Preface," p. 277), do not think of the rape as the last and most vicious in a long series of tyrannical abuses, but as an outrage that in and of itself demands retaliation. In their defense, they do not allude to the history of Cenci's oppression, basically ignoring what has been planted in the reader's mind by the opening acts of the play. In plotting his death these characters do not now refer, as Beatrice did in Act I, to "tyranny" and "deep wrongs," but allude to the single act of rape as sufficient motive and justification for murdering Cenci: Beatrice must avenge "The thing that I have suffered . . ." (III. i. 88). Orsino speaks of Cenci's "late outrage to Beatrice . . . [which] makes remorse dishonour, and leaves her / Only one duty, how she may avenge . . ." (III. i. 198-201); and after the murder is accomplished, Giacomo says that Beatrice has avenged "a nameless wrong / As turns black parricide to piety . . ." (V. i. 44-45). When arrested, Beatrice significantly criticizes "human laws," not for permitting injustice, but for barring "all access to retribution," claiming that Heaven has permitted her "the redress of an unwonted crime" (IV. iv. 116-21); and she refers during her trial to her father's singular "wrong" (V. ii. 130). Admittedly Beatrice does speak of her "wrongs [which] could not be told" (V. ii. 141); but the plural is puzzling here, since there is truly only one wrong that cannot be told. However, Mary did edit out details of sexual abuse when she published the manuscript story, and it seems that originally Beatrice might have been violated on more than on occasion. We should also note here that the Preface does speak of Beatrice's "wrongs and their revenge" (p. 277), although, as we have seen, a draft of this passage, states that her unnatural act was motivated by "*one* more unnatural" (italics added).

Two conclusions appear certain. One is that we find uncertainty as to the extent to which the murder may have been motivated by a single outrage or by the totality of Cenci's tyranny. And secondly, this confusion results from the changes Shelley made in the story, all of which serve to downplay the rebellious and defensive nature of Beatrice's actions, tending to represent the murder, instead, as an act of vengeance. Nevertheless, this is not to say that we can find no meaningful relationship between the need for self-protection, evident in the opening acts, and the compulsion to revenge that later overwhelms Beatrice—only that the transition is poorly plotted. What *The Cenci* attempts to show is how a decent woman's hope for change and desire for the protection of self and others can readily degenerate within an unenlightened society into the wish for revenge. As Shelley noted in his **"Essay on the Punishment of Death,"**

> the passion of revenge is originally nothing more than an habitual perception of the ideas of the sufferings of the person who inflicts an injury, as connected as they are in a savage state, or in such portions of society as are yet undisciplined to civilization, with the security that the injury will not be repeated in future. This feeling, engrafted upon superstition and confirmed by habit, at last loses sight of the only object for which it may be supposed to have been implanted and becomes a passion and a duty to be pursued and fulfilled, even to the destruction of those ends to which it originally tended.[11]

In her passion Beatrice seeks "something which shall make / The thing . . . [she has] suffered but a shadow / In the dread lightning which avenges it . . . *destroying / The consequence of what it cannot cure*" (III. i. 87-91, my italics). And Orsino, we recall, finds that Cenci's outrage "makes remorse dishonour" and leaves Beatrice "[o]nly one *duty,* how she may avenge" (III. i. 198-201, italics added). Revenge is symptomatic of hopelessness regarding the possibility of security and/or reform. Not only does it not seek as its object any change in individuals or society, but it appears to be a duty precisely when the situation seems incurable.

In both the play and the manuscript, Beatrice turns to violence out of a sense of hopelessness, but in the play it is clearly despair over the possibility of reform. The first mention of despair occurs when Beatrice alludes darkly to some monstrous deed her father has hinted at: "I have never yet despaired," she says, "—but now!" (II. i. 72). After the rape she comes to see her father as "a spirit of deep hell" in "human form" (IV. ii. 7-8), a reprobate totally beyond redemption and therefore deserving the punishment of death. Punishment is not an inducement to reform (its only possible justification); rather, Beatrice seeks the ultimate punishment because she despairs of Cenci ever changing.

But despair and the use of violence are of a different sort in the original story. Beatrice and Lucretia, we recall, turn to violence, finding "themselves without hope of relief." Here then, in the original manuscript, is where we may look to find the means-and-ends issue so often discussed with reference to the play itself. Here is where Beatrice, after all other means have failed, turns to violence for the purpose of protecting herself and the remaining members of her family from Cenci's tyranny. But this transition from passively suffering to actively resisting evil never occurs in Shelley's version of the story. His heroine, unlike her prototype, is so dehumanized by tyrannical abuse and vicious notions, that she, a once innocent victim, comes to return evil for evil, employing violent means to evil ends. That is what the Preface quite appropriately criticizes Beatrice for doing, but appropriately so only because of the changes Shelley made in the plot.

Thus while acknowledging Shelley's tragic depiction of the destructive effects an unenlightened civilization can have upon a decent individual, I cannot help being curious about what does *not* occur in the play and wondering if the issue of revenge is not something of a red herring. It seems to me that the play avoids facing up to the consequences of Shelley's position regarding forbearance. For one entire act we see how forbearance of evil fails to reform either the individual or the political situation—how even the pleas of innocent victims cannot encourage the aid of good men. But Beatrice is not shown to forbear evil to the point where she voluntarily succumbs to it, allowing herself and her family to be destroyed. On the other hand, at the very moment when active resistance appears a viable alternative to the forbearance of torture, destruction, and the general persistence of tyrannical evil (i. e., the point at which her petition is returned unopened), active resistance is no longer at issue, but revenge and atonement will be. Since revenge is not resistance, but retaliation, Beatrice does not have to be condemned for actively resisting violence. In other words, Shelley avoided putting himself in the position of having to say what most mistakenly believe the Preface does say: that a decent woman was morally wrong for taking the life of a vicious tyrant to save her own and those of other innocent victims.

As a result of certain very deliberate changes in the story, the play dramatizes the evils of vengeance and not the difficulties inherent in Shelley's notions of forbearance, forgiveness, and passive resistance. It never puts his moral idealism dramatically to the test, and one has to suspect that Shelley was aware of how politically impractical his idealism was when confronting life's "sad reality." My concern is that he never openly admits to its possible weaknesses or drawbacks. Rather, he insists upon a moral imperative in prefatory remarks that implies that it would be wrong to employ evil means to worthy ends—while all along he had created a drama in which the problem is that evil means are employed for evil ends. Indeed, the latter is what the Preface does in fact rather conveniently condemn. Of course, we do not have to know much about Shelley, the revolutionary age in which he wrote, the moral-political issue of peaceful reform versus violent revolution that has troubled his and other men's consciences, to know that the real question was and is not whether one can justify violence for *evil* ends. The problem Shelley had to face—he had it before him in the manuscript version—was whether violence is justified in fighting political oppression. It was a problem which, in **The Cenci** at least, he never truly faced up to.

Notes

1. Melvin R. Watson, "Shelley and Tragedy: The Case of Beatrice Cenci," *Keats-Shelley Journal,* 7 (1958), 15-16.

2. Robert Whitman, "Beatrice's 'Pernicious Mistake' in *The Cenci,*" PMLA [*Publications of the Modern Language Association*], 74 (1959), 252-53.

3. Carlos Baker, *Shelley's Major Poetry* (Princeton, N. J.: Princeton Univ. Press, 1948), pp. 141-42.

4. *Shelley* (New York: Knopf, 1940), II, 139.

5. All quotations from *The Cenci* and its prefatory material are taken from *Shelley: Poetical Works,* ed. Thomas Hutchinson, rev. G. M. Matthews

(London: Oxford Univ. Press, 1970), and hereafter citations will be given parenthetically in the text.

6. "Relation of the Death of the Family of the Cenci," in *The Complete Works of Percy Bysshe Shelley,* ed., Roger Ingpen (New York: Gordian Press, 1965), II, 160. Hereafter noted parenthetically in the text, using the short title, "Relation," and the page number of this volume.

7. *The Letters of Percy Bysshe Shelley,* ed. Frederick L. Jones (Oxford: The Claredon Press, 1964), II, 116-17. See also pp. 127 and 174 where Shelley again expresses the opinion that he has compromised to reach a mass audience.

8. *Note Books of Percy Bysshe Shelley,* ed. H. Buxton Forman (New York: Phaeton Press, 1968), II, 91-92.

9. *Shelley's* Cenci (Princeton, N. J.: Princeton Univ. Press, 1970), p. 96.

10. "Notes on Queen Mab," *Shelley: Poetical Works,* p. 812.

11. *Shelley's Prose,* ed. David Lee Clark (Albuquerque: Univ. of New Mexico Press, 1966), p. 157. The further relevance of the "Essay on the Punishment of Death" may be gauged by an earlier statement: "It is sufficiently clear that revenge, retaliation, atonement, expiation are rules and motives so far from deserving a place in any enlightened system of political life that they are the chief sources of a prodigious class of miseries in the domestic circles of society" (p. 155).

James D. Wilson (essay date July 1978)

SOURCE: Wilson, James D. "Beatrice Cenci and Shelley's Vision of Moral Responsibility." *Ariel* 9, no. 3 (July 1978): 75-89.

[*In the following essay, Wilson alleges that* The Cenci *is not a tragedy, despite Shelley's claim in the Preface.*]

The supposed moral disintegration of Beatrice after she is violated by her father has become the central source of dismay among scholars who analyze Shelley's gothic drama, **The Cenci** (1820). Despite Shelley's prefatory attempt to elevate his heroine to angelical stature, labelling Beatrice "a most gentle and amiable being . . . one of those rare persons in whom energy and gentleness dwell together without destroying one another . . . ,"[1] scholars insist that after the rape in Act III Beatrice becomes a calculating demon whose actions and insensitivities rival the atrocities of her sadistic father. Bertrand Evans links her to Lady Macbeth, while Robert Whitman insists that despite her pathetic and hopeless plight, Beatrice commits a "pernicious mistake" in becoming a self-appointed executor of God's will and is consequently driven by a "fanatical need for self-justification after the murder of the Count. . . ."[2] Earl Wasserman argues that in shifting the responsibility for her parricide to God, Beatrice echoes her father's abdication of culpability and approaches the depths of his iniquity; and according to Carlos Baker ". . . the tragic flaw in Beatrice . . . was the crack in the armor of her righteousness"; the transformation of Shelley's heroine, from a ". . . devout, chaste, dutiful, forgiving, and altruistic . . ." angel in Act I to an "ignoble liar" in Act V who denies her part in the Count's murder though she knows such denial results in the torture of her accomplices, displays the ". . . inevitable corruption of human saintliness."[3] Those few scholars who come to Beatrice's defence do so on the grounds that her father morally deserves the fate which she devises for him. Newman I. White argues that "her real motive for the murder is self-protection and an almost religious mission to rid her family and the world of a dangerous monster. It is only by a narrow margin that she escapes the dramatic fault of being a flawless character."[4] Stuart Curran labels Beatrice a "good angel," "a mythic figure of the Italian consciousness, a symbol of the human spirit in revolt against all that is unjust and oppressive."[5]

The fundamental cause of the scholarly dilemma concerning Beatrice is that in her actions she violates principles dramatically portrayed in *Prometheus Unbound,* which Shelley wrote simultaneously with *The Cenci.* Prometheus demonstrates that moral liberation is achieved only by renouncing the principles of hatred and revenge embodied in Jupiter and passively submitting oneself to the spirit of love which forms the core of our being.[6] Man is, Shelley writes in **"Ode to Liberty,"** ". . . a willing slave; / He has enthroned the oppression and the oppressor" (11. 244-245). Central to Shelley's ethical thought, according to Mary Shelley, is the conviction "that evil is not inherent in the system of the creation, but an accident that might be expelled. . . . Shelley believed that mankind had only to will that there should be no evil, and there would be none" (p. 271). With the Reign of Terror in the background, Shelley saw that in meeting tyranny and cruelty with their own weapons the oppressed became indistinguishable from the oppressor. Hence Shelley wrote in his preface to *The Cenci*: "Undoubtedly . . . the fit return to make to the most enormous injuries is kindness and forbearance, and a resolution to convert the injurer from his dark passions by peace and love. Revenge, retaliation, atonement, are pernicious mistakes" (p. 276).

But in *Prometheus Unbound* Shelley, by his own admission, portrays an ideal world; in *The Cenci* he turns to the problem of evil in the real world. In the dedication to Leigh Hunt he says: "Those writings which I have hitherto published, have been little else than visions which impersonate my own apprehensions of the beautiful and the just . . . they are dreams of what ought to be, or may be. The drama which I now present to you is a sad reality" (pp. 274-75). Though ideally one—like Christ—opposes hatred and tyranny with love and forgiveness, in the real world such response is rendered ineffectual when confronted with evil on the scale of the Count, or of the *Ancien Regime.*

A large segment of Shelley's poetry is governed by a Manichean vision of the world in which evil and good are polar opposites having substantial existence. The Woman—". . . fair as one flower adorning / An icy wilderness" (I, 11. 264-65)—encountered by the poet in *The Revolt of Islam* informs him that "Two Powers o'er mortal things dominion hold / Ruling the world with a divided lot, / Immortal, all-pervading, manifold, / Twin Genii, equal Gods—when life and thought / Sprang forth, they burst the womb of inessential Nought" (I, 347-351). In his essay, **"On the Devil, and Devils,"** Shelley grants the Manichean vision considerable validity: "The Manichean philosophy respecting the origin and government of the world, if not true, is at least an hypothesis conformable to the experience of actual facts."[7] An incident from the poet's youth, reported by Dowden, suggests that Shelley had long been fascinated by demonology, and believed in the existence of a supernatural force of darkness:

> One day Mr. Bethell, suspecting from strange noises overhead that his pupil was engaged in nefarious scientific pursuits, suddenly appeared in Shelley's room; to his consternation he found the culprit apparently half enveloped in a blue flame. "What on earth are you doing, Shelley?" "Please sir," came the answer in the quietest tone, "I am raising the devil."[8]

The fortunate irony of evil—in Shelley's Manichean view of the world—is that it contains the seeds of its own destruction; the tyrant by his own example provides the oppressed with tools which they eventually turn back upon him. He is a devil who is exorcised by his own nature reflected in the oppressed masses who imitate his actions. If, as in the Reign of Terror, the oppressed continue to wear the mask of their fallen tyrant, then no revolution has been effected, no demon exorcised. But if, as in the case of Beatrice Cenci, the masses can return to a state of love and benevolence, they can assume the nature Shelley claims to be inherent in man. Then a revolution has indeed occurred and the mass is vindicated; in the final analysis they were only a catalyst by means of which evil destroyed itself by its own nature. This is the sense in which "mankind had only to will that there should be no evil, and there would be none."

For the most part Shelley presents the violent war between the forces of light and the forces of darkness as an inevitable natural occurrence, similar to ". . . the rushing of a wind that sweeps / Earth and the ocean" (***The Revolt of Islam,*** I, 145-46). In language and imagery foreshadowing the later **"Ode to the West Wind,"** Shelley in ***The Revolt of Islam*** tells of "the irresistible storm" which "had cloven / That fearful darkness, the blue sky was seen / Fretted with many a fair cloud interwoven / Most delicately . . ." (I, 154-58); eventually ". . . the vast clouds fled, / Countless and swift as leaves on autumn's tempest shed." Such a process is always violent and frequently filled with bloodshed:

> Such is this conflict—when mankind doth strive
>   With its oppressors in a strife of blood,
> Or when free thoughts, like lightnings, are alive,
>   And in each bosom of the multitude
> Justice and truth with Custom's hydra brood
> Wage silent war; when Priests and Kings dissemble
>   In smiles or frowns their fierce disquietude,
> When round pure hearts a host of hopes assemble,
> The Snake and Eagle meet—the world's foundations
>   tremble!

(I, 415-23)

Though he theoretically abhors violence and bloodshed, Shelley can thus greet the violent revolutionary activity sweeping Europe during the period 1776-1822 as signalling the approach of the millennium.[9] David Perkins has called attention to the political overtones in Shelley's **"Ode to the West Wind"**—published in 1820 with ***Prometheus Unbound***—overtones which clarify Shelley's attitude toward revolutionary activity. In **"Ode to the West Wind,"** Perkins writes, "Shelley allies himself with a numinous violence which in creating a new golden age brings death and destruction into the old world."[10] "Destroyer and preserver," the West Wind is an "unseen presence" who "didst waken from his summer dreams / The blue Mediterranean." The "blue Mediterranean" calls to mind Greece and Italy, centers of old regimes holding men in subjection; its "old palaces and towers" quiver "within the wave's intenser day," and its "sapless foliage . . . suddenly grow gray with fear, / And tremble and despoil themselves" (pp. 577-78)—the characteristic response, as Perkins points out, of tyrants to the violent revolution. A militant and powerful force, "the wind symbolizes the destruction and regeneration which are twin aspects of any sudden revolution."[11]

Most of Shelley's poetry presents man as passive to momentary visitations of a transcendent realm which inform his vision and propel him on an unrealizable quest to bring his mortal self in harmony with the ideal. Perkins writes: "For social revolution and utopian order will result from the descent of numinous force into human life, and, in this context as in others, man is passive to the sudden visitations of transcendence."[12] In the vision or dream of the ideal, mortal man loses his identity and is possessed by the spirit of intellectual beauty. Visited while asleep by a "veiled maid" whose "voice was like the voice of his own soul," Alastor surrenders

his own melancholy nature to fold "his frame in her dissolving arms" (11. 187). In **"Epipsychidion"** the poet seeks "All that is insupportable in thee / Of light, and love, and immortality" which he locates in his angelic sister-soul. "Veiling beneath that radiant form of Woman"; possessing a "glory of . . . being" which "stains the dead, blank, cold air with a warm shade / Of unentangled intermixture, made / By love, of light and motion . . ." the sister lures the poet to surrender his nature, a process Shelley depicts in erotic language:

>   . . . and our lips
> With other eloquence than words, eclipse
> The soul that burns between them, and the wells
> Which boil under our being's inmost cells,
> The fountains of our deepest life, shall be
> Confused in Passion's golden purity,
> As mountain-springs under the morning sun.
> We shall become the same, we shall be one
> Spirit within two frames. . . .

(11. 566-574)

The incestuous union of the poet with his sister-soul in **"Epipsychidion"** is prototypical of the process by which man becomes infused with the nature of divinity. Significantly, however, in ***The Cenci*** this process is reversed. The innocent, angelic Beatrice is "visited" by the embodiment of absolute evil, and through the incestuous union loses her own nature to assume the tyrannical aspect of her father. The key to understanding ***The Cenci*** lies in the extent to which we hold Beatrice responsible for her actions. If we accept her own account of the ordeal, then we must realize that she merely served as a catalyst by means of which the Count unconsciously effected his perverse will to self-destruction, an impulse revealed in his desire to destroy all his possessions at his death and to blot out all his heirs; the destruction of Beatrice, the Count reveals, ". . . shall soon extinguish all / For me" (II, ii, 188-89). The central symbol suggesting the validity of Beatrice's defense is the act of incest, occurring at the structural heart of the play.[13] Incest is richly appropriate for Shelley's drama not just because it is ". . . like many other *incorrect* things a very poetical circumstance. It may be the excess of love or of hate."[14] Nor is it employed primarily, as Wasserman suggests, because it epitomizes the extremity to which tyranny can manifest itself, ". . . the radical expression of sadism inherent in every form of oppression."[15] Rather the incestuous act serves as the symbolic and literal moment at which the Count's demonism is implanted in the daughter. At this moment Beatrice becomes an unwilling vessel for the spirit of absolute evil. Subsequently possessed by the devil, she can only let the spirit exorcise itself by destroying its progenitor.

Shelley presents a Manichean vision in which the Count and Beatrice clearly embody the poles of evil and goodness. The Count is worse than "Hell's most abandoned fiend" (I, i, 117); he envisions himself as "a fiend appointed to chastise / The offences of some unremembered world" (IV, i, 161-62); his abode, Giacomo informs Orsino, ". . . was hell / And to that hell will I return no more . . ." (III, i, 330-31); the act of parricide, Beatrice tells her stepmother, "Will but dislodge a spirit of deep hell / Out of a human form" (IV, ii, 7-8). Asserting that, ". . . I love / The sight of agony, and the sense of joy, / When this shall be another's, and that mine. / And I have no remorse and little fear, / Which are, I think, the checks of other men" (I, i, 81-85), Shelley's Count is an "unnatural man," a sadist whose malignity transcends human motivation. Beatrice on the other hand is angelic. Lucretia, her stepmother, praises her as the force of goodness keeping the powers of darkness in check: "Until this hour thus you have ever stood / Between us and your father's moody wrath / Like a protecting presence; your firm mind / Has been our only refuge and defence" (II, i, 46-49). The Count labels her "a fallen angel" after her violation; Giacomo says that Beatrice "Stands like God's angel ministered upon / By fiends" (V, i, 44-45). Camillo thinks that "her sweet looks . . . might kill the fiend within" the Count (I, i, 44-45). Recognizing in Beatrice a "bright loveliness" which "Was kindled to illumine this dark world," (IV, i, 121-22), the Count looses "this devil / Which sprung from me as from a hell" (IV, i, 119-120) in an attempt to destroy the soul of his natural enemy "Whose sight infects and poisons" him (IV, i, 119).

The means chosen by the Count to effect the destruction of Beatrice's soul is incest. As in *Prometheus Unbound* the central act of the drama is sexual, only in *The Cenci* the protagonist is infused with and transformed by a demon wholly different from the power of love manifested in Asia. Stuart Curran has called attention to the pattern of imagery in *The Cenci* which adumbrates the polar dichotomy drawn by Shelley in his portrayal of the Count and Beatrice.[16] The father is linked imagistically to blood and darkness; he is described as "dark and bloody" (II, i, 55), a man who in his youth was "dark and fiery" (I, i, 49). Beatrice on the other hand is characterized in images of light and vision; she is a "bright form" who possesses an "awe-inspiring gaze, / Whose beams anatomize [Orsino] nerve by nerve / And lay [him] bare" (I, ii, 83-86). Through the incestuous rape the Count hopes to blot out the light of Beatrice's soul and wrap her in a ". . . bewildering mist / Of horror" (II, i, 184-85): ". . . if there be a sun in heaven / She shall not dare to look upon its beams; / Nor feel its warmth . . ." (II, i, 185-87).

And indeed the Count is successful. Immediately after the rape, after he has introduced the demon into Beatrice, she stands transformed—possessed by an alien spirit that clouds her vision. Act III opens as Beatrice staggers into Lucretia's room after the rape: "My eyes are full of blood; just wipe them for me . . . / I see but

indistinctly" (III, i, 3-4). She is obsessed with an image—blood—previously applied to her father, exclaiming, "The beautiful blue heaven is flecked with blood!" (III, i, 13). Curran contends that Shelley uses blood as "a euphemism for her father's semen."[17] This is appropriate, for Beatrice describes the incestuous act in highly sexual language, indicating that she had been invaded and enveloped by a demon:

> . . . There creeps
> A clinging, black, contaminating mist
> About me . . . 'tis substantial, heavy, thick,
> I cannot pluck it from me, for it glues
> My fingers and my limbs to one another,
> And eats into my sinews, and dissolves
> My flesh to a pollution, poisoning
> The subtle, pure, and inmost spirit of life!
>
> (III, i, 16-23)

Possessed by an alien force—her "eyes shoot forth / A wandering and strange spirit" (III, i, 81-82)—Beatrice hopes that she might be a catalyst through which the demonic blood effects its own demise: ". . . O blood, which art my father's blood, / Circling through these contaminated veins, / If thou, poured forth on the polluted earth, / Could wash away the crime, and punishment / By which I suffer . . ." (III, i, 95-99).

Her body a "foul den" (III, i, 130), Beatrice maintains a firm belief that as God's agent she can exorcise the demon possessing her; the agent driving her to parricide, she tells Savella, was "Not hate, 'twas more than hate" (IV, iv, 103). Her father's death ". . . will be / But as a change of sin-chastising dreams, / A dark continuance of the Hell within him, / Which God extinguish" (IV, ii, 32-35); hence ". . . it is a high and holy deed." Harassed by a superhuman force, Beatrice cannot depend on the existing institutional framework to free her: ". . . In this mortal world / There is no vindication and no law / Which can adjudge and execute the doom / Of that through which I suffer" (III, i, 134-37). Rather she must allow her father's own demon—"a dark continuance of the Hell within him"—to circle through her passive veins in accomplishing its self-destruction. Once the demonic spirit has run its course and the tyrant is destroyed, Beatrice is free. Immediately she is conscious of a change within her; she is purified:

> . . . Even whilst
> That doubt is passing through your mind, the world
> Is conscious of a change. Darkness and Hell
> Have swallowed up the vapour they sent forth
> To blacken the sweet light of life. My breath
> Comes, methinks, lighter, and the jellied blood
> Runs freely through my veins. . . .
>
> (IV, iii, 38-44)

In the next line Beatrice learns that her father—the demon—is dead. And her regeneration is complete: "I am as universal as the light; / Free as the earth-surrounding air; as firm / As the world's centre . . ." (IV, iv, 48-50).

We can now, I trust, understand Beatrice's protestations of innocence as the drama moves toward its conclusion. She is indeed innocent, as she in no way encouraged the demon to enter her body, and she can hardly be held responsible for the process by which the demon is exorcised. To admit her guilt would be to admit no difference between the forces of darkness and the forces of light. She will "overbear" accusations of her guilt "with such guiltless pride, / As murderers cannot feign" (IV, iv, 45-46). The implication here is that Beatrice realizes that she is no murderer. ". . . 'Tis most false," Beatrice exclaims, "That I am guilty of foul parricide, / Although I must rejoice, for justest cause, / That other hands have sent my father's soul / To ask the mercy he denied to me" (IV, iv, 145-49). Protected by her innocence, she is willing to go with Lucretia to face trial in Rome, for ". . . There as here / Our innocence is as an armed heel / To trample accusation. God is there / As here, and with His shadow ever clothes / The innocent, the injured and the weak; / And such are we" (IV, iv, 158-63). Beatrice has no reason to deceive anyone in these scenes; in the presence of only the sympathetic Lucretia, she has no cause to act the Lady Macbeth critics have accused her of becoming.

Once on trial in Rome, Beatrice is so persuasive in her denial of guilt that she even convinces the men who carried out her orders; Marzio dies a martyr to Beatrice, utterly transformed by her goodness and purity: ". . . As soon as we / Had bound him on the wheel, he smiled on us, / As one baffles a deep adversary; / And holding his breath, died" (V, ii, 180-83). Beatrice's defence, and a convincing one, is that she is not to be held responsible for her actions:

> . . . I, alas!
> Have lived but on this earth a few sad years,
> And so my lot was ordered, that a father
> First turned the moments of awakening life
> To drops, each poisoning youth's sweet hope; and then
> Stabbed with one blow my everlasting soul;
> And my untainted fame; and even that peace
> Which sleeps within the core of the heart's heart;
> But the wound was not mortal; so my hate
> Became the only worship I could lift
> To our great father, who in pity and love,
> Armed thee, as thou dost say, to cut him off.

> (V, ii, 118-129)

Steadfastly convinced of her innocence, Beatrice does not become an "ignoble liar" to save her life, as Baker asserts; indeed she is willing to die, to be tortured, rather than utter what she knows is untrue—that she is responsible for the crime:

> Brother, lie down with me upon the rack
> And let us each be silent as a corpse,
> It will be as soft as any grave.

> 'Tis but the falsehood it can wring from fear
> Makes the rack cruel.

> (V, iii, 47-52)

The Cenci is a tragedy not of character—as most critics read it—but of the cosmos. Carlos Baker asserts that "if Shelley were really to write a tragedy, it was unthinkable to invent a denouement in which Beatrice succeeded in converting the injurer 'from his dark passions' by the exercise of peace and love;" and he goes on to suggest that the tragedy is the breaking of the heroine's character, her willingness to cast off "the armor of her righteousness" to assume "the cloak of a murderess."[18] But this, I argue, Beatrice never does.

The scholarly tendency to read *The Cenci* as a tragedy of character receives support from Shelley's prefatory assertion that "the fit return to make to the most enormous injuries is kindness and forbearance, and a resolution to convert the injurer from his dark passions by peace and love." Had Beatrice acted according to this principle, however, "she would never have been a tragic character." Shelley clearly implies that Beatrice is a tragic heroine because her character breaks; consequently she commits "pernicious mistakes." But Shelley seems to protest too much. The extended preface with its insistence on Beatrice's tragic fall camouflages the drama's weakness as a portrayal of character disintegration. Shelley wanted to write a tragedy but in fact did not; hence he attempts to remedy his failure with a didactic preface. If Shelley's drama portrayed what the author in his preface claims it does, the reader might rightly expect more soul-searching on Beatrice's part, more awareness of the two opposing courses of action, and more evidence of conscious choice. Such elements are essential to tragedy: Claudius in *Hamlet* becomes tragic as we see him agonizing at prayer, aware of two courses of action and consciously forgoing repentance in favour of his love for his queen and crown; Hamlet's tragedy is heightened by his agonizing awareness of his inability—by nature—to pursue the course of action he knows he should follow without delay; Melville's Ahab achieves tragic stature in *Moby-Dick* during quiet moments on ship when he is tempted to forgo revenge and turn back in his quest for the white whale, only to realize that he is too "far gone on the dark side of this earth." As if aware of this element of tragedy, Shelley in the preface asserts that Beatrice, "after long and vain attempts to escape [her] contamination," plots "with her mother-in-law and brother to murder their common tyrant." But unfortunately the facts of the play belie Shelley's claim of "long and vain attempts"; Beatrice clearly knows her course of action immediately after the rape, ridiculing Orsino's suggestion that she "endure" with the assertion, "All must be suddenly resolved and done" (II, i, 169). In [the] last analysis Beatrice is not tragic; she seems too often the victim of forces over which she has no control. Furthermore, her actions claim too strong a hold on the reader's sympathies to render Shelley's moralizing about her "pernicious mistakes" very plausible. Hamlet may err in delaying his revenge; Claudius clearly chooses wrongly in preferring Gertrude and his crown to repentance; Ahab should have turned back from his fatal quest. But should Beatrice have allowed her father to continue his ruthless and demonic tyranny without opposition? Beatrice—and the dilemma facing her—are simply not sufficiently complex to qualify *The Cenci* as a tragedy of character.

The real tragedy of *The Cenci* is similar to that in *Alastor* or the **"Epipsychidion"**—that all too acute awareness that mortality obliterates the few glimpses we have of the good and the beautiful. Though the demon has been exorcised, Beatrice painfully discovers that the world has not been transformed; the spirit of tyranny embodied in her father persists in the figures of the Pope and the judge presiding over her trial.[19] For a brief moment this leads Beatrice to despair. When Lucretia tells Beatrice to "Trust in God's sweet love," the heroine mourns in despair that the "sweet love" seems nowhere evident in the mortal world:

> How tedious, false and cold seem all things. I
> Have met with much injustice in this world;
> No difference has been made by God or man,
> Or any power moulding my wretched lot,
> 'Twixt good and evil, as regarded me.
> I am cut off from the only world I know,
> From light, and life, and love, in youth's sweet prime.
> You do well telling me to trust in God,
> I hope I do trust in Him. In whom else
> Can any trust? And yet my heart is cold.
>
> (V, vi, 80-89)

But such despair is momentary; Beatrice realizes the tragic fact that the kingdom of light is not of this earth: ". . . No, Mother, we must die: / Since such is the reward of innocent lives; / Such the alleviation of worst wrongs. / And whilst our murderers live, and hard, cold men, / Smiling and slow, walk through a world of tears / To death as to life's sleep; 'twere just the grave / Were some strange joy for us" (V, iv, 109-115). Beatrice, the ". . . perfect mirror of pure innocence," realizes and becomes reconciled to the fact that only in an immortal realm can she find rest from the demon which pursues her: ". . . my Lord, / We are quite ready. Well, 'tis very well" (V, iv, 164-165).

"Well, 'tis very well"—Beatrice's last words are hardly those of a nihilist, as some—like Curran—portray her.[20] Rather she resembles Edgar in *King Lear,* who after witnessing the inexplicable demise of innocence in a world out-of-joint can nevertheless assert that "The gods are just" (V, iii, 170). Likewise, Beatrice knows that "Ill must come of ill" (I, iii, 151). Matured by her experience, Beatrice comes to the tragic awareness of "sad reality"; the ideal portrayed by Shelley in *Prometheus Unbound* is attainable only in a realm radically different from the mortal world we inhabit.

Notes

1. "Preface" to *The Cenci* in Shelley's *Poetical Works,* ed. Thomas Hutchinson, rev. G. M. Matthews (London: Oxford Univ. Press, 1970), pp. 275, 278. All subsequent references to Shelley's works are to this edition, unless noted otherwise.

2. Evans, *Gothic Drama from Walpole to Shelley* (Berkeley: Univ. of California Press, 1947), pp. 230-31; Whitman, "Beatrice's 'Pernicious Mistake' in *The Cenci,*" PMLA [*Publications of the Modern Language Association*], 74 (1959), 249-53.

3. Wasserman, *Shelley: A Critical Reading* (Baltimore: Johns Hopkins Univ. Press, 1971), pp. 81-89; Baker, *Shelley's Major Poetry: The Fabric of a Vision* (Princeton, N. J.: Princeton Univ. Press, 1948), pp. 147-8.

4. Newman I. White, *Shelley* (New York: Knopf, 1940), II, 139.

5. *Shelley's* Cenci: *Scorpions Ringed with Fire* (Princeton, N. J.: Princeton Univ. Press, 1970), vi-xii. For Curran, Beatrice "is another Shelleyan 'Spirit that strove / for truth, and like the Preacher found it not'" (p. 130).

6. Wasserman, pp. 257-61.

7. *The Complete Works of Percy Bysshe Shelley,* eds. Roger Ingpen and Walter Peck (New York: Scribner's, 1965), VII, 87.

8. *The Life of Percy Bysshe Shelley* (Philadelphia: J. B. Lippincott, 1887), I, 30.

9. See Carl Woodring, *Politics in English Romantic Poetry* (Cambridge, Mass.: Harvard Univ. Press, 1970), pp. 317-19.

10. *The Quest for Permanence: The Symbolism of Wordsworth, Shelley and Keats* (Cambridge, Mass.: Harvard Univ. Press, 1959), p. 166.

11. *Quest for Permanence,* p. 165.

12. *Quest for Permanence,* p. 163.

13. Curran points out that Shelley clearly wanted to highlight the incestuous rape of Beatrice. In adapting his source material for the play Shelley carefully deleted the Count's three convictions for sodomy so as not to offend the delicate sympathies of potential theatregoers. But he took an "originally questionable incest" and made it the crux of the tragedy (p. 43).

14. Letter to Maria Gisborne, 16 Nov. 1819 (*The Letters of Percy Bysshe Shelley,* ed. F. L. Jones, London: Oxford Univ. Press, 1964, II, 154).

15. *Shelley: A Critical Reading,* p. 85. Peter Thorslev argues that the Count's incestuous rape symbolizes his attempt to recapture his fleeting youth ("Incest as Romantic Symbol," *Comparative Literature Studies,* 11, 1965, 47).

16. *Shelley's* Cenci, pp. 106-07.

17. *Shelley's* Cenci, p. 116. Curran demonstrates too that Shelley "draws on the physiological symptoms of syphilis for imagery" in describing the rape and its aftermath (p. 92).

18. *Shelley's Major Poetry,* p. 142; pp. 147-48.

19. Curran, p. 43.

20. *Shelley's* Cenci, p. 90.

James B. Twitchell (essay date 1979)

SOURCE: Twitchell, James B. "Shelley's Use of Vampirism in *The Cenci*." *Tennessee Studies in Literature* 24 (1979): 120-33.

[*In the following essay, Twitchell studies Shelley's use of the vampire myth in the imagery of* The Cenci.]

The Cenci is certainly one of the most philosophically intricate works Shelley ever wrote. It is intricate in that Shelley set for himself the complex task of reconstructing historical events in a form that demands sequential as well as imaginative cohesion, and it is philosophical in that he deals with the problem of casuistry, the use of evil means for good ends.[1] It is a drama that shows through a fiction the real workings of evil: how evil is generated, how it is transferred, and how it can destroy and be destroyed. While one could say the same thing about *The Cenci*'s companion piece, *Prometheus Unbound,* there is an important difference. *Prometheus Unbound* is a work, as Shelley himself said, of "pure idealism," while *The Cenci* is one of "sad reality." In artistic terms, this means that while in *Prometheus Unbound* Shelley can resolve casuistical problems by fiat (which he does by having Prometheus forgive Jupiter prior to the action of the drama), in *The Cenci* he must "work them out" through action and imagery within the play. In *The Cenci* there can be no apocalyptic resolution, no Act IV where cosmic harmonies are struck, no Spirits of the Mind floating out to millennial levels; instead, only the sad irresolution of Actuality.

Shelley must have realized in late April 1819, when he set *Prometheus Unbound* down at the end of Act III, that the writing of *The Cenci* would demand a significant change, not only in action, but in imagery as well. For he wrote in the "Preface"

> I have avoided with great care in writing this play the introduction of what is commonly called mere poetry, and I imagine there will scarcely be found a detached simile or a single isolated description, unless Beatrice's description of the chasm appointed for her father's murder should be judged to be of that nature.
>
> In a dramatic composition the imagery and the passion should interpenetrate one another, the former being reserved simply for the full development and illustration of the latter. Imagination is as the immortal God which should assume flesh for the redemption of mortal passion. It is thus that the most remote and the most familiar imagery may alike be fit for the dramatic purposes when employed in the illustration of strong feeling, which raises what is low, and levels to the apprehension that which is lofty, casting over all the shadow of its own greatness.[2]

He continues, asserting that in such a drama "we must use the familiar language of men" so that the widest possible audience will be reached. For if art can move this audience to "true sympathy," lasting social reform may be achieved.

This paper will attempt an explanation of how imagery and passion do indeed "interpenetrate one another" in *The Cenci* through the specific example of an image as familiar in our day as it was in Shelley's—the vampire. The image of the vampire had artistic currency in the early nineteenth century, first as a translation of German Gothicism and then as an independent English literary type that culminated in Bram Stoker's *Dracula* (1897). Before Shelley, Southey had used the vampire superstition in *Thalaba the Destroyer* (Bk. 8), Coleridge had used it in *Christabel* as had Keats in *Lamia,* but the real development of the myth occurred as the result of a serendipitous meeting in 1816 on the shores of Lake Geneva. There, during a rainy summer evening, Shelley, Mary Shelley, Byron, and Dr. John Polidori (Byron's traveling physician) each pledged to write a ghost story. We remember Mary Shelley's contribution, for her *Frankenstein* is still very much a part of our popular culture, but we may forget that here also the other Romantic monster, the vampire, saw the light of day. Byron produced a "Fragment" of a vampire novel (usually published after *Mazeppa* in collected works) that he showed John Polidori. Polidori, ever mindful of Byron's fame, substantially rewrote the story and published it under Byron's name in the April 1819 issue of Colburn's *New Monthly Magazine.* It was a stunning success—Goethe claimed it was the best thing Byron had ever written!—and was soon reprinted and translated almost into tatters. It provided the first real popular audience for vampire fiction and to Shelley, as we have seen in the "Preface" to *The Cenci,* this familiarity between audience and imagery was essential.[3]

Stuart Curran in *Shelley's* Cenci: *Scorpions Ringed with Fire* has already discussed how specific clusters of images reveal a depth of meaning barely suggested by the surface plot. Professor Curran contends that this figurative language is an essential organizing principle of drama by which the poet is able to disclose the subtlest nuances of thought. And given the nature of *The Cenci,* where moral ambiguity constantly attends upon the destruction of conventional values and one character after another is compelled toward solipsism, the structural demands on this essential organizing principle are extraordinary, necessitating the creation of intricate metaphorical patterns.[4]

And Curran points to aggregations of images around such subjects as commerce, hunting, darkness, bestiality, and imprisonment to show how this organizing principle operates. But he overlooks an important image cluster that I believe more than any other illustrates his point that when the movement of the work is not toward resolution but ambiguity, there is a special need for intricate metaphorical patterns. The major theme of the play is the dynamics of evil, and the vampire as both solipsist and casuist is a ghoulishly apt mythologem of the centripetal and centrifugal forces of disorder. For the vampire is both a festering center of evil and a contaminating carrier, an ambiguous destroyer of others and preserver of himself.

Finding an image for evil as a human process seems to have been in Shelley's mind at the end of Act III of *Prometheus Unbound.* For some sixty lines before he leaves man "pinnacled dim in the intense inane," Shelley has the Spirit of the Hour explain to Asia what the world looks like devoid of evil. The Spirit reports that everything looks the same except that thrones are kingless, prisons are empty, and altars are unattended. There is no more "hate, disdain, or fear"; evil, "the wretch crept a vampire among men, / Infecting all with his own hideous ill," (III. iv. 147-48) has been cast out. Shelley's use of the image of the vampire serves here, as in *The Cenci,* to reinforce his conviction that evil is a perverse human process, that it is communicable, like an infectious disease, and that if properly destroyed, the forces of Good will automatically be asserted. The questions become: what is the vampire of Evil, how do we inoculate ourselves against him, and how do we properly dispose of him? In part *The Cenci* is Shelley's answer, but to understand it we need first to examine the mythic vampire.

Basically the vampire is the devil incarnate in a sinner's body. For any number of reasons (excommunication, burial without rites, suicide, improper tithing, attack from a vampire) the devil will possess the body before the soul can depart.[5] Then for an eternity, unless properly destroyed, the fiend will wreak havoc, primarily on those people who were closest to the sinner before demonic possession. This point, although lost in our twentieth-century retelling of the mythology, was a most important part of the Romantic version as seen, for example, in Byron's highly successful *Giaour* (first edition, 1813; fourteenth edition, 1815). Here is the Giaour curse, which seems an obvious influence on a number of different aspects of *The Cenci* as well:

But first on earth, as Vampire sent,
Thy corpse shall from its tomb be rent
Then ghastly haunt thy native place,
And suck the blood of all thy race;
There from thy daughter, sister, wife,
At midnight drain the stream of life;
Yet loathe the banquet, which perforce
Must feed thy livid living corpse,
Thy victims, ere they yet expire,
Shall know the demon for their sire;
As cursing thee, thou cursing them,
Thy flowers are withered on the stem.
But one that for thy crime must fall,
The youngest, best beloved of all,
Shall bless thee with a father's name—
That word shall wrap thy heart in flame!
Yet thou must end thy task and mark
Her cheek's last tinge—her eye's last spark.
And the last glassy glance must view
Which freezes o'er its lifeless blue;
Then with unhallowed hand shall tear
The tresses of her yellow hair,
Of which, in life a lock when shorn
Affection's fondest pledge was worn—
But now is borne away by thee
Memorial to thine agony!
Yet with thine own best blood shall drip
Thy gnashing tooth, and haggard lip;
Then stalking to thy sullen grave
Go—and with Ghouls and Afrits rave,
Till these in horror shrink away
From spectre more accursed than they.

(755-86)

In the curse we are told that the vampire must first attack those he loves most, and that these victims are the females of his own family. Shelley has spared us the "gnashing tooth, and haggard lip," but the Cenci's victims are, as we shall see, first his wife and then his children, especially Beatrice, "The youngest and best beloved of all." The vampire's course of action is singularly horrible because he is initially hesitant about destroying his loved ones, but of course he cannot help himself. He is "possessed." Even more complicated is the fact that the loved one must make some initial advance in his direction—she must initiate the rapprochement. Once this initial move has been made, however, the vampire, through the hypnotic powers of his eye, mesmerizes the victim who, once "enthralled," cannot later recall what has happened, other than that it was exciting and sexually traumatic. It is only after the vampire's destruction that she will remember.

The actual encounter is both erotic and awful. For the vampire partially drains the life fluid, through a long, sensuous kiss on the victim's neck. She turns pale as he strengthens. But he does not kill her, at least not yet. She can still escape by protecting herself with religious icons, garlic, or various other talismans that differ depending on the cultural milieu. But if she hesitates too long, he will return again and again, until she becomes so enervated that she quite literally shrivels up and dies a seemingly physical death. However, this is a deception, for in reality she passes into the world of the "walking dead," becoming a second-generation vampire (technically a "lamia") now on the prowl for virginal male victims of her own.

Actually much of this vampire lore is still part of our culture, although the medium has changed from print to celluloid. Any schoolboy can tell you that vampires prefer to work at night, especially around midnight, that they travel in mist and cause storms, that they can be killed only with a stake through the heart, and of course that they depend on the elixir of blood. But what we have forgotten is that in an historical sense the vampire is a product of the very religion he abhors—Roman Catholicism. To be sure the vampire myth antedates Christianity, but it was revived by the Roman Catholic Church in the Middle Ages to shepherd the unconvinced, the unconfirmed and the apostate back into the church.[6] Excommunication, burial in an unsanctified ground, suicide, and a refusal of the sacraments were all invitations to the devil to enter the sinner's body. The myth still thrives in south central Europe where it was belligerently used for generations as a wedge against encroaching Greek orthodoxy.[7] Conveniently the superstitions had more than a political use in the Middle Ages; they also bolstered the newest and most uneasy sacrament—the eucharist. This was the most abstract of the sacraments, depending on the metaphorical understanding of Christ's words:

> Whoso eateth my flesh, and drinketh my blood, hath eternal life, and I will raise him up at the last day. For my flesh is meat indeed, and my blood is drink indeed. He that eateth my flesh, and drinketh my blood, dwelleth in me, and I in him. As the living Father hath sent me, and I live by the Father: so he that eateth me, even he shall live by me.
>
> (St. John, VI. 53-57)

Was it not equally sensible that this transubstantiation process could be reversed by the devil, who would celebrate a diabolical eucharist by drinking the blood of the sinner?

I would not contend that Count Cenci is an actual practicing vampire, but only that Shelley is evoking the image cluster with all its horrible connotations to show how evil is generated, transferred and destroyed. The most obvious use of the metaphor is in Act I, where Cenci twice celebrates a perverse eucharist. Here he is, first celebrating the deaths of his sons:

> (*Filling a bowl of wine, and lifting it up*) Oh, thou
>   bright wine whose purple splendour leaps
> And bubbles gaily in this golden bowl
> Under the lamplight, as my spirits do,
> To hear the death of my accursed sons!
> Could I believe thou wert their mingled blood,

> Then would I taste thee like a sacrament,
> And pledge with thee the mighty Devil in Hell,
> Who, if a father's curses, as men say,
> Climb with swift wings after their children's souls,
> And drag them from the very throne of Heaven,
> Now triumphs in my triumph—But thou art
> Superfluous; I have drunken deep of joy,
> And I will taste no other wine to-night.
>
> (I. iii. 76-89)

Although Cenci claims he will drink no more—that he is sated with evil for awhile—this is not to be. For later that evening, after Beatrice has initiated a confrontation at the party, he again returns to the communion wine:

> (*Exeunt all but Cenci and Beatrice.*)
>   My brain is swimming round;
> Give me a bowl of wine!   (*To Beatrice.*)
>   Thou painted viper!
> Beast that thou art! Fair and yet terrible!
> I know a charm shall make thee meek and tame,
> Now get thee from my sight!   (*Exit Beatrice.*)
>   Here, Andrea.
> Fill up this goblet with Greek wine. I said
> I would not drink this evening; but I must;
> For, strange to say, I feel my spirits fail
> With thinking what I have decreed to do.
>   (*Drinking the wine.*)
> Be thou the resolution of quick youth
> Within my veins, and manhood's purpose stern,
> And age's firm, cold, subtle villainy;
> As if thou wert indeed my children's blood
> Which I did thirst to drink! The charm works well;
> It must be done; it shall be done, I swear!
>
> (I. iii. 163-78)

A number of important motifs are developed here in addition to the recurring image of wine as blood. First, the Count is not all-powerful; his "spirits" fail; and although he is revived by the metaphorical blood, we get a definite sense of hesitation, almost as if part of him were unwilling. He repeats this hesitancy: ". . . I bear a darker deadlier gloom / Than the earth's shade, or interlunar air, / Or constellations quenched in murkiest cloud, In which I walk secure and unbeheld / Towards my purpose.—Would that it were done!" (II. ii. 189-93). But he is powerless to stop, for the Count is truly a man possessed, as everyone, including himself, understands. Cardinal Camillo recognizes that Cenci harbors a "fiend within" (I. i. 45); his wife Lucretia can "see the devil . . . that lives in him" (II. i. 45); Beatrice realizes that only his death will ". . . dislodge a spirit of deep hell / Out of a human form" (IV. ii. 7-8); and ironically even Cenci himself is aware that "I do not feel as if I were a man, / But like a fiend appointed to chastise / The offenses of some unremembered world" (IV. ii. 160-63).

Another important motif, introduced in the Count's communion speech, is that he knows a "charm" to make Beatrice "meek and tame" (I. iii. 167). What that charm is we are never told—perhaps it is an ironic reference to his incestuous plans; perhaps it is also the trance the vampire uses to subdue his victim and make her receptive to evil. The two possibilities are by no means mutually exclusive; rather, they are complimentary and overlapping. The spell, whatever it is, seems to be transferred through Cenci's eye, and is so powerful that when Beatrice attempts to recount what has happened, she can only mumble, "He said, he looked, he did . . ." (II. i. 76). The evil eye is an important element of the play, for after Beatrice has been attacked, Lucretia notices that her daughter's eyes ". . . shoot forth / A wandering and strange spirit" (III. i. 81-2). And by the end of the play, when Beatrice is cornered by both Camillo (the Church) and the Judge (the State); she attempts to use this new-found power to force her henchmen to remain quiet: "Fix thine eyes on mine," she demands of Marzio; but he cannot meet her gaze (V. ii. 82). His "brain swims round," he cannot speak (V. ii. 88), but when Beatrice attempts to use her power to influence the judge and Camillo (both of whom are already in the service of different devils), she is thwarted by their implacability.

The last motif introduced in Cenci's eucharist speech is that his heinous activity will take place later at night. Cenci is a creature of the night, not just because Gothic monsters prefer midnight work, but specifically because as a vampire—even a figurative vampire—he is positively photophobic. The daytime for him is "—garish broad and peering . . . / Loud, light, suspicious, full of eyes and ears, / And every little corner, nook and hole / Is penetrated with the insolent light. / Come darkness!" (II. ii. 176-81). Little wonder then that he demands that Beatrice "attend me in her chamber / This evening: . . . at midnight and alone" (I. i. 145-46).

Their awful nocturnal conjunction is reminiscent of that part of the Giaour curse where the vampire must

> . . . ghastly haunt thy native place,
> And suck the blood of all thy race;
> There from thy daughter, sister, wife,
> At midnight drain the stream of life;
> Yet loathe the banquet, which perforce
> Must feed thy livid living corpse,
> Thy victims, ere they yet expire,
> Shall know the demon for their sire.
>
> (757-64)

And now, with the overlapping of the incest motif, the central horror is increased. For as Count Cenci is draining goodness, he is not leaving behind an empty husk, but rather impregnating a neutralized life with evil. This Manichean transformation occurs before us as Beatrice, once goodness personified, is undone and then reconstituted as evil when she accepts the "pernicious error" of allowing the ends to justify the means. For when she decides to destroy her father she destroys her self, in a sense becoming the person she hates. At the end she is indeed her father's "wretched progeny."

The image that links these processes of transformation, vampiric and incestual, is the image of fluid, or more specifically, the two fluids central to each process—blood and semen. Much of the blood imagery in the play is hymeneal, showing the trauma that innocence suffers when actually impregnated with evil. But often the images of blood are used to show, not how blood results from rupture, but rather how it has been drained from the characters by Cenci. Although all the characters in the Cenci family have been psychologically bled of the energy of goodness, Beatrice is most obviously described as pale and wan, especially after her encounter with her father (III. ii. 351). But the same pallid condition is also true of her brother Bernardo (II. i. 123) and her mother Lucretia (II. i. 41-42). They are now only shells of their former selves, but the Count has not seen fit—as will his literary descendant, Count Dracula—to make all his victims actively participate in evil. Only Beatrice will finally execute his will.

The image of blood is more than a metaphor of energy exchange; it also symbolizes initiation into Cenci's demonic world. Paradoxically, although Beatrice is unable to recount what has happened between her and her father, her actual organs of perception are colored with the satanic stain: "My eyes," she says, "are full of blood; just wipe them for me . . . / I see but indistinctly . . ." (III. i. 2-3). And she continues:

> My God!
> The beautiful blue heaven is flecked with blood!
> The sunshine on the floor is black! The air
> Is changed to vapours such as the dead breathe
> In charnel pits! Pah! I am choked! There creeps
> A clinging, black, contaminating mist
> About me. . . .
>
> (III. i. 12-18)

Here Beatrice's transformation is literally occurring before not only her eyes but our own as well.[8] Just as the vampire rises in mist from his "charnel pit," so evil clouds the inner world and alters "reality." The *modus operandi* of both external vampire and internal corruption is synchronized. This process is further developed when Cenci claims that Beatrice may well carry his child, an organic division of his demonic energy. He hopes his evil seed will develop into "a hideous likeness of herself, that as / From a distorting mirror, she may see / Her image mixed with what she abhors . . ." (IV. i. 146-48). Here again the incest and vampire motifs are dovetailed, for part of the superstition is that a vampire can cause hideous offspring if he even so much as looks at a fertile female.[9] The Cenci is the incubus, the living nightmare, visiting evil and chaos on the unprotected and unwary. He quite literally incubates evil by contact with those he visits. The residue of this evil, the image of this potentiality for disorder, is represented by the other important fluid in the play—semen.

The relationship between blood and semen is a close one as they are both life-giving or life-supporting fluids. Ernest Jones, the Freudian psychologist, contended that "in the unconscious mind blood is commonly an equivalent for semen," and Anthony Masters elaborates:

> There existed in vampire belief a very strong love motive which involved the vampire in having intercourse with a living woman. This belief probably grew up via the occasional erotic stimulant of blood-letting in intercourse, the breaking of virginity, and, on a more mystic level, the medieval succuba, an erotic demon who preyed upon and destroyed man's virility.[10]

Shelley depends on the blood/semen linkage to express almost subliminally not only the transfer of evil, but its organic development as well.

Shelley is concerned not only with the clash of good and evil but with the consequences of this clash as well. The moral bind Beatrice faces is that once having been corrupted, having become literally a carrier of evil, what can she do to escape? She recognizes that evil has her "enthralled," and cries out:

> O blood, which art my father's blood,
> Circling through these contaminated veins,
> If thou, poured forth on the polluted earth,
> Could wash away the crime, and punishment
> By which I suffer . . . no, that cannot be!
>
> (III. i. 95-99)

Death, her own death, would seem to be the answer. In fact, Lucretia even tells her that "death alone can make us free" (III. i. 78), but Beatrice knows otherwise. For suicide is no palliative—it is, after all, one of the sins that created the vampire to begin with. Her religion (for she, like Cenci, is devoutly religious—he to the letter, she to the spirit) has forbidden this escape:

> Self-murder . . . no, that might be no escape
> For Thy decree yawns like a Hell between
> Our will and it. . . .
>
> (III. i. 132-34)

> I thought to die; but a religious awe
> Restrains me, and the dread lest death itself
> Might be no refuge from the consciousness
> Of what is yet unexplained.
>
> (III. i. 148-51)

And here, as far as Shelley is concerned, she makes her mistake. For she will "expiate" the crime, she will assume the role Cenci has claimed for himself—as a "scourge," a redresser of wrongs. She will become the

solipsist, the casuist, the Lady Macbeth. She decides to destroy not herself, but him, and in doing so ironically makes herself party to the same horrible processes that Cenci has initiated. She now faces the central problem of the play: how to develop the means to accomplish what all will agree is a noble end.

The problem of disposing of vampires is a complicated one. In nineteenth-century fiction it was usually a priest who destroyed the demon by driving an apple, maple, hawthorn, or blackthorn stake through the fiend's heart; in twentieth-century cinema it is usually a doctor (chances are, a hematologist) who destroys the villain. In the folk tale it was the task of the vampire's child (usually a son) who, perhaps because he is a blood descendant, intuitively knew the father's weaknesses. The Dhampire, by a complicated ritual, exorcises the parental demon, allows the soul to escape, and then destroys the now-neutralized husk of a body.[11] Shelley understandably does not emphasize this aspect, for again it would have made actual what he wanted metamorphical; but Cenci's death is nonetheless peculiar. Beatrice takes control, orchestrating the henchmen, who first refuse to kill the sleeping Cenci but then are exhorted to finish the heinous task. They throttle the Count and then heave the body over the parapet, where it is later found hanging (impaled?) on the branches of a tree (IV. iv. 73-76). Shelley thus only implies a death by staking.[12] As soon as Cenci is killed the spell on Beatrice seems broken; she feels that "My breath / Comes methinks, lighter, and the jellied blood / Runs freely through my veins" (IV. iii. 42-44). She is confident: "The spirit which doth reign within these limbs / Seems strangely undisturbed. I could even sleep / Fearless and calm: all ill is surely past" (IV. iii. 64-65).

But all ill is not passed. Her very act proves that Cenci has succeeded in corrupting her. In death he has achieved what he wanted in life, spiritual domination. The instant Beatrice acts as God's ministering angel she is tainted with the pride of her father, and in a fallen and scurvy world she will have to pay the price of initiation. Shelley has so devised her plight that there can be no reprieve for evil regardless of intention. The ends simply cannot justify the means. She has met evil head-on, and now there is no escaping its consequences. Suicide is ruled out (that would only lead to an eternity of suffering); exile is denied (witness the fate of her brothers); remaining to redress wrongs by patience will not work (she has the example of Lucretia)—she cannot go, she cannot stay. And so at the end, battling like a cornered animal, she reverts to the same methods her father used: she employs the powers of evil and subterfuge.

This must have been a most difficult philosophical problem for Shelley to resolve. How much simpler to make her tragic, nobly accepting an unfair fate. But Shelley wants no martyr. He has gone to considerable pains to show us a Beatrice contaminated with evil. He has so fitted the vampire motif into both the artistic and philosophic structure of his work that ultimately we will not be able to understand the one without the other. Finally, once we understand how the vampire of Evil works, we will be forced into disagreeing with those characters in the play who insist on seeing Beatrice as a force of pure Good. For what Giacomo, Bernardo, and Lucretia (all of whom are effusive in their praise of Beatrice) cannot see is that violence met with violence can only lead to violence. Evil can vamp the good, forcing it to resort to the very evil means it despises.[13]

Perhaps Orsino, with Iago-like insight, understands Beatrice best when he soliloquizes: "'Tis a trick of this same family / To analyse their own and other minds. / Such self-anatomy shall teach the will / Dangerous secrets . . .'" (II. ii. 108-11). For early on Beatrice has analysed herself and found only Innocence. She is then attacked by Evil, and for the rest of the play her primary concern is to return to that lost innocence, that prelapsarian world. She, like Blake's Thel, has seen the ugliness of the fallen world and wants to return to Har. But too late. Instead of trying to live with sin, she must destroy it. "It is sufficiently clear," Shelley wrote elsewhere, "that revenge, retaliation, atonement, expiation are rules and motives, so far from deserving a place in any system of political life, that they are the chief sources of a prodigious class of miseries in the domestic circles of society."[14] It is Orsino who is able to apply this to the world of Realpolitik: "he prospers best, Not who becomes the instrument of ill, / But who can flatter the dark spirit, that makes / Its empire and its prey of other hearts / Till it become his slave . . ." (II. ii. 157-61). Whereas Orsino seeks to use this knowledge for his own aggrandizement, it is also possible, as Shelley attempted to show in *Prometheus Unbound,* to use this wisdom for the good.

Passive resistance would then seem the only alternative. And Shelley, at least at this time in his life, seriously promulgated it as the proper response to evil.

> And if then the tyrants dare
> Let them ride among you there,
> Slash, and stab, and maim, and hew,—
> What they like, that let them do.
> With folded arms and steady eyes,
> And little fear, and less surprise,
> Look upon them as they slay
> Till their rage has died away.

(Mask of Anarchy, 340-47)

However, Beatrice is not one who can stand by "with folded arms and steady eyes" and wait until evil has run its course. Like the Assassins in Shelley's unfinished novel, she is so convinced of her own innocence, so sure she can set things right, that she accepts any

means for the "restitution" of justice. In so doing, she is consumed by the very thing she wishes to destroy. For again as Shelley wrote, "men, having been injured, desire to injure in return. This is falsely called a universal law of human nature; it is a law from which many are exempt and all in proportion to their virtue and cultivation."[15]

But Shelley's use of the vampire myth makes the exception to this "universal law" not just a matter of "virtue and cultivation," but one of almost superhuman fortitude as well. For once one has succumbed even unconsciously to evil, once Beatrice did indeed go to the Cenci "at midnight and alone," her fate was cast to the powers of darkness. She did not meet evil passively; rather, she allowed herself to be drawn in against it, and in so doing made herself party to it. It is here in this confrontation that the vampire myth resolves some of the ambiguity; for in being so intractable to evil, Beatrice has made herself easy prey. Admittedly if she did not act, Cenci might attack her again as he has planned. But if she had passively resisted, there is the possibility that Cenci would have withered away. For Cenci realizes that he pushes best against people who shove back. He understands that "'tis her stubborn will / Which by its own consent shall stoop as low / As that which drags it down" (IV. i. 10-12). Evil does not want to destroy good. Cenci as vampire makes this clear: "I rarely kill the body, which preserves, / Like a strong prison, the soul within my power . . ." (I. i. 114-15). But Beatrice, flawed by evil and impatient to restore Innocence, cannot withstand the onslaught of experience. Having been attacked, she will retaliate and this action constitutes for Shelley her "pernicious mistake."[16]

Notes

1. For the best explanation of philosophical problems in *The Cenci* see Earl Wasserman, *Shelley: A Critical Reading* (Baltimore: Johns Hopkins Univ. Press, 1971), pp. 84-130.

2. "Preface to *The Cenci," The Complete Works of Percy Bysshe Shelley* (Julian edition), ed. Roger Ingpen and Walter E. Peck (New York: Gordian, 1965), II, 72.

3. That Shelley was fascinated with vampire lore has already been well-established. We have been told by Medwin that as a young man Shelley translated Bürger's "Lenore," which he (as Dowden continues the story) often enjoyed reciting, "working up the horror to such a heighth of fearful interest" that the guests fully expected to be visited by the Prussian vampire (Thomas Medwin, *The Life of Percy Bysshe Shelley* [1847; rev. ed., London: Oxford Univ. Press, 1913], I, 62; and Edward Dowden, *The Life of Percy Bysshe Shelley* [1886; 7th impression, London: Routledge and Kegan

Paul, 1954], II, 123). A later biographer, Charles Middleton, even went so far as to assert that Bürger's poem first kindled the Gothic flame that especially flared up in Shelley's early poems and adolescent novels (Charles Middleton, *Shelley and His Writings* [London: T. C. Newby, 1858], I, 47). But there was such general interest in translating the vampire-horror from German literature to English (witness the astonishing success of Goethe's "The Bride of Corinth," a poem translated again and again) that Shelley was probably reacting more to literary fashion than to any specific work.

4. Stuart Curran, *Shelley's* Cenci: *Scorpions Ringed with Fire* (Princeton: Princeton Univ. Press, 1970), p. 100.

5. The best books on vampires are: Montague Summers, *The Vampire: His Kith and Kin* (London: Routledge and Kegan Paul, 1928); Anthony Masters *The Natural History of the Vampire* (London: Mayflower Books, 1972); Raymond McNally and Radu Florescu, *In Search of Dracula* (New York: Popular Library, 1972); Leonard Wolf, *A Dream of Dracula* (New York: Popular Library, 1972); Nancy Garden, *Vampires* (New York: Lippincott, 1973); Gabriel Ronay, *The Truth about Dracula* (New York: Stein and Day, 1974); and Basil Cooper, *The Vampire in Legend, Fact and Art* (Secaucus, N. J.: Citadel Press, 1974).

6. For more on this, see Masters, *The Natural History of the Vampire,* ch. IV, "The Vampire in Christianity"; and Wolf, *A Dream of Dracula,* ch. IV, "Vampires and the Taste of Blood."

7. The best explanation of the political and religious use of the vampire myth in the Balkan countries is in McNally and Florescu, *In Search of Dracula,* chs. 3-7.

8. Stuart Curran believes that the imagery here is drawn from the physiological symptoms of syphilis, see *Shelley's* Cenci, p. 92. If this is true it serves to strengthen the theme of the infectious nature of evil.

9. The relationship between the vampire and the fertile woman is discussed in Masters, pp. 91-92.

10. Ernest Jones, "On the Nightmare of Bloodsucking," from *On the Nightmare* (New York: Liveright, 1971), pp. 116-25), is still the best psychological interpretation of the vampire superstition. See also Masters, p. 45.

11. The role of the Dhampire is discussed in Masters, pp. 44, 143; and Garden, pp. 67-70.

12. In this context it is interesting that later when Beatrice has a vision of her own burial it is "under the obscure, cold, rotting, wormy ground! / To be nailed down into a narrow place" (V. iv. 50-51). Is she to be staked into the earth like a lamia?

13. This misunderstanding of Beatrice has continued until recently outside the play as well, with those critics who interpret her almost as an archetype of purity. So she has been variously labelled "an ennobling vision of maidenly purity," "a harrassed maiden," and "a feminine ideal," with the emphasis always on her ethical virginity (E. S. Bates, *A Study of Shelley's Drama* The Cenci [New York: Columbia Univ. Press, 1908], p. 80; Bertrand Evans, *Gothic Drama from Walpole to Shelley* [Berkeley: Univ. of California Press, 1947], p. 231; and John Symonds, *Shelley* [New York: Macmillan, 1902], pp. 127-28). But this is quite literally denied in the play—she is not pure; she is not a maiden; she is not ideal. Just as erroneous, however, is the interpretation of her as pathetic victim, a personification of "oppression and female suffering" (Neville Rogers, *Shelley at Work* [Oxford: Clarendon, 1956], p. 202; or Newman Ivey White, *Shelley* [New York: Knopf, 1940], II, 140). In either case, to assume she is goodness unfairly victimized or an object of masculine oppression denies her the very humanity that makes her actions benevolently mistaken.

14. *On the Punishment of Death,* Julian edition, VI, 185.

15. *Philosophical View of Reform,* Julian edition, VII, 55.

16. Shelley expressed his own feelings about Beatrice's action in the "Preface" to *The Cenci*: "Undoubtedly no person can be truly dishonoured by the act of another; and the fit return to make to the most enormous injuries is kindness and forbearance, and a resolution to convert the injurer from his dark passions by peace and love. Revenge, retaliation, atonement, are pernicious mistakes."

John F. Schell (essay date 1981)

SOURCE: Schell, John F. "Shelley's *The Cenci*: Corruption and the Calculating Faculty." *University of Mississippi Studies in English* n. s. 2 (1981): 1-14.

[In the following essay, Schell evaluates Shelley's suggestion that reason is inadequate compared to imagination in The Cenci.*]*

Shelley believed drama to have a greater potential for influencing man's moral improvement than any other art form. In *A Defense of Poetry* he notes: "the connexion of scenic exhibitions with the improvement or corruption of the manners of men, has been universally recognized,"[1] and he then remarks that "the connexion of poetry and social good is more observable in the drama than in any other form" (p. 492). In light of such statements, one would expect to find an unequivocal social message in the one drama that Shelley wrote for a mass audience. But the failure of critics to agree on an interpretation of *The Cenci* proves that this is not the case. Some commentators read the play as pure allegory, and others find it to be unrelieved realism; it has been construed to be either politically or philosophically motivated; even the theme of the play has been variously identified as religious, epistemological, historical, or moral. It is not surprising, therefore, that the character of the drama's protagonist, Beatrice Cenci, remains in dispute.

Understanding Beatrice is certainly crucial to any interpretation of *The Cenci.* An early commentator, Mary Shelley, helped establish a critical tradition when she interpreted Beatrice as an ideal figure: "The character of Beatrice, proceeding from vehement struggle to horror, to deadly resolution, and lastly to the elevated dignity of calm suffering joined to passionate tenderness and pathos, is touched with hues so vivid and so beautiful, that the poet seems to have read intimately the secrets of the noble heart imagined in the lovely countenance of the unfortunate girl."[2] To this ennobled picture, Leigh Hunt added a rationalization for her crime of parricide: "The reader refuses to think that a daughter has slain a *father,*" Hunt observes, "precisely because a dreadful sense of what a father ought not to have done has driven her to it. . . ."[3] Subsequent critics have arrived at similar conclusions. John Flagg writes that "Shelley conceives of her as a morally superior being," and in a recent essay, Erika Gottlieb claims that Beatrice's "behaviour requires our recognition of her allegorical function as a personification of Innocence, or of man's potential for purity, perfection, and immortality."[4] A lesser critic is even persuaded to hazard a most un-Shelleyan thought, praising the "inversion of moral values implied by this most right of all murders."[5]

Many critics, however, can not attribute to Shelley the defense of murder. Rather, they discover in Beatrice's crime the flaw that defines her tragic essence. This flaw is sometimes described as a desire for revenge, a "crack in the armour of her righteousness," her "failure to persevere in 'passive resistance,'" "hybris," or "her tragic faith in a God who sanctions and even enjoins revenge and murder."[6] By this reasoning, her crime is the means for her transformation into a tragic heroine deserving our sympathy, not our contempt. In recent years, a reaction against this idolization of Beatrice has begun thanks to the careful readings of the drama by James Rieger, Donald Reiman, and Earl Wasserman.[7] A more negative construction of her character is taking shape. Examples of this are Walter Evert's suggestion that the tragedy of

the drama might be the demise of Beatrice's moral nature and Ronald Lemoncelli's idea that "Cenci . . . simultaneously *reveals* Beatrice's evil and *creates* an evil Beatrice. . . ."[8]

There apparently is no resolution to this Babel of interpretations. Yet an accurate assessment of Beatrice's character is necessary if we are to decipher the lessons for the human heart that Shelley claims are inherent in drama of the highest species. Since the play, alone, offers no indisputable reading of Beatrice's character, there remain two options: to be contented with the existing uncertainty (professional suicide for a critic!), or to go outside the drama for help. The second task has been tried by several critics who have read *The Cenci* and *Prometheus Unbound* as companion pieces. Unfortunately, an even better heuristic method has been largely (and surprisingly) ignored—less than nineteen months after completing *The Cenci,* Shelley set down his aesthetic principles in *A Defence of Poetry.* Shelley's *Defence [of Poetry]*, with its lengthy analysis of the dramatic genre, might clarify (or at least help to explain) the play.

Shelley's theoretical statement was written to refute Peacock's assertion in "The Four Ages of Poetry" that verse is irrelevant to an advanced society. Peacock argues that reason, not poetry, is modern man's need. Shelley avoids attacking Peacock's premise of utility and posits that poetry is *more* utilitarian than reason. He opens his defense by discriminating between two classes of mental action, "reason and imagination." According to Shelley's analysis, the imagination is the synthetic agent, reason the analytical: "Reason is to Imagination as the instrument to the agent, as the body to the spirit, as the shadow to the substance" (p. 480). Although the two are not opposites, they are not quite complementary, either. Imagination is clearly preferable. When he then states that the "expression of the imagination" is poetry, he has established the prestige of poetry relative to the like productions of reason. The remainder of the *Defence* is the working out of this duality. Shelley declares that "the great instrument of moral good is the imagination; and poetry administers to the effect by acting upon the cause" (p. 488). Having arrived at this conclusion, it is impossible for Shelley to "resign the civic crown to reasoners and mechanists" or to agree that "reason is more useful" (p. 500). "Poetry differs from logic," Shelley asserts. "Poetry is not like reasoning, a power to be exerted according to the determination of the will" (p. 503). Instead, the "calculating faculty" (a frequent synonym for reason in the *Defence*) is both the product of poetry and dependent upon it: "Poetry is indeed something divine. It is at once the centre and circumference of knowledge; it is that which comprehends all science, and that to which all science must be referred" (p. 503).

Shelley applies this distinction between the imagination and reason to the dramatic genre as well. He identifies two types of drama, the poetic and the non-poetic, and it is this discussion which sheds light upon his own dramatic practice. Poetic drama he defines in imaginative terms: "The drama, so long as it continues to express poetry, is as a prismatic and many-sided mirror, which collects the brightest rays of human nature and divides and reproduces them from the simplicity of these elementary forms, and touches them with majesty and beauty . . ." (p. 491). Non-poetic drama, on the other hand, is corrupt, "cold," and obscene. It need not induce immorality; it is enough that the drama itself lacks imagination: "the corruption which has been imputed to the drama as an effect, begins, when the poetry employed in its constitution, ends" (p. 490). The poetic drama is splendid with poetry; in the "unimaginative" drama, "the calculating principle pervades all forms of dramatic exhibition, and poetry ceases to be expressed upon them" (p. 491).

The two types of drama Shelley identifies in his *Defence* find reflection in the two dramas he composed in 1819, *Prometheus Unbound* and *The Cenci.* There can be little disagreement that *Prometheus Unbound* is a drama imbued with imagination. In his preface to the lyrical drama, he observes that the mind of the poet who composes such a work is "the mirror of all that is lovely in the visible universe." He expands this image in terms that echo his discussion of poetic drama in his *Defence*: "A Poet, is the combined product of such internal powers as modify the nature of others, and of such external influences as excite and sustain these powers. . . . Every man's mind . . . is the mirror upon which all forms are reflected, and in which they compose one form" (p. 135).

Furthermore, Shelley states that *Prometheus Unbound* is not a "*reasoned* system" (emphasis added) or a "didactic work," and thus he anticipates his comment in *A Defence* that "in periods of the decay of social life, the drama . . . becomes a weak attempt to teach certain doctrines . . ." (p. 491). It is as if Shelley had formed his thoughts concerning drama in his *Defence* with one eye upon the "Preface" to his mythic masterpiece. Although his lyrical drama is suffused with poetry and operates on the imaginative level, Shelley himself declared that *The Cenci* was a "composition of totally different character."[9]

Shelley is not alone in comparing the two dramas. Donald Reiman and Earl Wasserman anchor much of their explication of *The Cenci* upon *Prometheus Unbound.* Though both critics compare and contrast the two plays, neither views the dramas as antipodal. Nor do they connect Shelley's practice and his theory in *A Defence of Poetry,* a connection that might produce valuable results. If *Prometheus Unbound* represents

imaginative drama as defined in *A Defence, The Cenci* may be its unimaginative counterpart. This popular drama would then be Shelley's attempt to dramatize the consequences of faith in reason, to portray the error of trusting in the calculating faculty, and to demonstrate— through the example of Beatrice—the corrupting power of failed imagination upon virtue. And support for such an hypothesis may be found in *The Cenci.*

Before attempting such a reading, one qualification is needed. Shelley's discussion of "unimaginative" drama in *A Defence* occurs within his historical survey of corrupt dramatists and corrupt times. Because much of his discussion refers to existing works, he never specifically states that a poet might purposely compose a work that reflects an "unimaginative" world for a moral end. Simultaneously, he fails to preclude such a possibility. While his focus is upon corrupt drama as the product of corruption, his theories concerning reason and imagination may be applied to *The Cenci* without suggesting that Shelley is a corrupt artist.[10] At the beginning of his historical survey of drama, in fact, Shelley notes: "the presence or absence of poetry in its most perfect and universal form has been found to be connected with good and evil conduct and habit" (p. 490). This principle pertains, whether within the dramatic world of *The Cenci* or the historical world of Shelley's study. In *The Cenci,* Shelley creates a world whose inhabitants are divorced from imagination and proud of their calculating facility; they embody Shelley's theoretical speculation concerning reason, corruption, and obscenity. Having established such a world, Shelley studies the inevitable results, and the corruption that occurs remains within the dramatic framework for the edification of the audience.

From the opening scene, Count Cenci appears to be a man of the most subtle analyzing ability. Conversing with Camillo, the Pope's representative, the Count brags about his ability to discern human motivation, and he reminds the legate: "you gave out that you have half reformed me, / Therefore strong vanity will keep you silent / If fear should not; both will, I do not doubt" (I. i. 74-76). Likewise, Cenci comprehends his own personality and discloses that "I am what your theologians call / Hardened" (I. i. 93-94). The Cenci we see on stage is fully aware of his strengths and weaknesses. He admits that in youth he "was happier," but also realizes that there is little he can do but go on. He understands that his own pride compels him to "act the thing thought" (I. i. 97), although old age makes that compulsion increasingly difficult to carry out. He also couples his self-knowledge with his insight into the motivation of others when he states: "I have no remorse and little fear, / Which are, I think, the checks of other men" (I. i. 84-85).

This penchant for self-anatomizing that characterizes Cenci is complemented by a calculating nature; both depend upon reason for their existence. During the drama, consequently, we witness Cenci plotting and intriguing. He is driven to action and surrounds himself with conspiracies. Never is he without a scheme. When his ultimate strategy is confounded by Beatrice, he is both prophetic and perceptive as he states: "'tis her stubborn will / Which by its own consent shall stoop as low / As that which drags it down" (IV. i. 10-12). The lengthy speech that follows, where Cenci first threatens his absent daughter and then curses her, is a model of reason, deranged. Cenci initiates his harangue with faulty inductive logic that permits him to posit a special relationship to God. From this semi-divine position, he hopes his daughter might "Die in despair, blaspheming" (IV. i. 50). As his anger mounts, he comes to see himself as a divine "scourge" charged with the punishment of Beatrice. And by the close of his speech, Cenci casuistically fuses the temporal "father" and the spiritual "father." He assumes the authority of God, and "like a fiend" calls curses upon Beatrice.

Cenci's reliance upon his own mental ability does not bring him happiness; one of the ironies of the drama is that this same mental agility discloses to him his failure. At one point in the planning of his revenge, Cenci laments: "'Tis an awful thing / To touch such mischief as I now conceive" (II. i. 124-125). Alone on stage, he admits to himself his weakness: "I said / I would not drink this evening; but I must" (I. iii. 169-170). Fortified with alcohol, he vows his revenge upon Beatrice, but hesitates: "I feel my spirits fail / With thinking what I have decreed to do" (I. iii. 171-172). He drinks more wine, clouds his reason, and then says: "the charm works well." But before his resolution again fails, he vows to himself, "It must be done; it shall be done, I swear" (I. iii. 178). With characteristic insight, Cenci comes to realize that he is the victim of his own pride and compulsion. As forthright as he is discerning, just prior to his own murder, Cenci, addressing Beatrice, calls her "my bane and my disease, / Whose sight infects and poisons me" (IV. i. 118-119). In Kenneth Neill Cameron's words, Count Cenci is "no stock villain."[11]

Giacomo (Cenci's weak but well-intentioned son), acting as a foil to his father, helps to illustrate the Count's weakness. When goaded by Orsino to revenge against Cenci, Giacomo demurs and remarks that the mind is a fallible instrument. He says to Orsino: "Ask me not what I think; the unwilling brain / Feigns often what it would not" (II. ii. 82-83). Rather than chance the mind's trickery, rather than court the possibility of being compelled to act upon what is thought, Giacomo relies upon his heart. He spurns Orsino and says: "My heart denies itself / To *think* what you demand" (emphasis added; II. ii. 86-87). Unfortunately for the entire Cenci family, his father knows no such deference.

As the play progresses, Count Cenci is seen to be a man trapped by his own intellect and scornful of his feelings. For him, the will takes precedence over all else. He is dimly aware of the compulsive, self-destructive nature of his own personality, yet pride in his own mental ability drives him on. Early in the play, Orsino (with unusual sensitivity) reflects on Cenci's character:

> 'tis a trick of this same family
> To analyse their own and other minds.
> Such self-anatomy shall teach the will
> Dangerous secrets: for it tempts our powers,
> Knowing what must be thought, and may be done,
> Into the depth of darkest purposes:
> So Cenci fell into the pit.
>
> (II. ii. 108-114)

The calculating principle, the analytical power, tempts pride and will. This leads to corruption.

Orsino's indictment includes the entire Cenci family; he charges them all with the potential for pride, willfulness, and a misplaced trust in their intellectual prowess. Reasonably, we may infer from Orsino's statement the fall of any person who participates in this family "trick," including Beatrice. This does not mean that Beatrice must be a corrupt figure either at the beginning of the drama or its end. But the possibility exists. Furthermore, if (as some critics recognize) Count Cenci contaminates Beatrice during the drama, she may just as easily have been corrupted by him prior to the play's opening. Beatrice's corruption at the start of the drama must remain a moot question. What is certain is that, from the beginning of the play, she (like Count Cenci) analyzes her own and other minds, she is proud and willful, and she excels at oratory. From the first, indeed, Shelley is careful to parallel the two protagonists. The play opens with Cenci negotiating his freedom from a priest whom he controls; in the subsequent scene, Beatrice does the same with a priest whom she controls. When the two first meet on stage, the clash of their personalities implies a similarity that is borne out by later events. At the Count's heinous banquet, for instance, Beatrice is a match for her father's arrogance when she commands him: "Retire thou, impious man! Aye hide thyself / Where never eye can look upon thee more" (I. iii. 146-147). As the play proceeds, the virtuous Beatrice comes to resemble her father more and more, until they both blaspheme, assume the prerogatives of God, and die in despair. In fact, the *innocent* Beatrice is little more than a memory within the play. On stage, her actions are selfish and her speeches are models of dissemblance. Even her own frequent references to her goodness become suspect when, a murderess before the Pope's court, she tries to conceal her guilt by touting that same reputation for virtue. When *The Cenci* draws to a close, qualities that *A Defence of Poetry* attributed to "unimaginative" and "corrupt" characters are equally applicable to Count Cenci and Beatrice. Both are "cold, cruel, and sensual"; the two are "insensible and selfish"; they are motivated by "lust, fear, avarice, cruelty, and fraud." In his "Preface" to the drama, Shelley faults Beatrice when he says: "Undoubtedly, no person can be truly dishonoured by the act of another, and the fit return to make to the most enormous injuries is kindness and forbearance, and a resolution to convert the injurer from his dark passions by peace and love. Revenge, retaliation, atonement, are pernicious mistakes" (p. 240).

The Beatrice who is her father's daughter begins to appear from her first words. She commands the priest, Orsino: "Pervert not the truth" (I. iii. 1). The remainder of her speech, ironically, is a rhetorical stratagem designed to effect exactly the twisting of truth that she warns against. To gain his sympathy while maintaining her own independence, she introduces amatory diction, and when Orsino responds in kind, she retorts: "speak to me not of love" (I. ii. 14). Exemplifying that Cenci knack for analyzing other minds, she remarks that Orsino's "equivocating vein" does not please her. By this tactic, she subtly encourages a greater commitment by him to disprove the charge. Lest he be offended and abandon her, though, she immediately blames the criticism upon her "misery." In this way, she manages to turn an insult into the means for increasing his sympathy for her plight. Throughout this speech, Beatrice presents herself as a weak and vulnerable girl, easy game for the aggressive Orsino. But she seduces the would-be seducer and ensnares Orsino in the net he has woven for her. When she swears to him a "cold fidelity," her true nature appears. And after she leaves him, Orsino is justifiably troubled and ponders aloud: "I fear / Her subtle mind, her awe-inspiring gaze, / Whose beams anatomize me nerve by nerve / And lay me bare, and make me blush to see / My hidden thoughts" (I. ii. 83-87). No sooner has he expressed these doubts than he recants, proving the power of Beatrice's rhetoric. He chooses to accept her construction of reality and to deny his intuition: "Ah, no! A friendless girl / Who clings to me, as to her only hope" (I. ii. 87-88).

The next scene offers Beatrice another chance to display her deliberative oratorical skills. While her presence before the assembled guests is occasioned by the death of her brothers, she is not overcome with grief. She seizes, instead, upon the opportunity to argue her case against her father. Her opening appeal establishes the affected tone of the total performance: "I do entreat you, go not, noble guests . . ." (I. iii. 99). This obsequiousness is followed by a condemnation of her father that advances her own innocence at the same time. In a brilliant maneuver, she asks her audience: "Oh, think what deep wrongs must have blotted out / First love, then reverence in a child's prone mind / Till it thus vanquish shame and fear" (I. iii. 108-110). Throughout this scene, her hortatory skills are on full display, and near the close of her appearance, she again flatters her audience and says: "Father, never dream / That thou mayest

overbear this company" (II. i. 149-150). But this time her insincerity is apparent to everyone because Count Cenci's control of those assembled is well-known. Southerland Bates recognizes the falseness of Beatrice's speeches to the banquet guests, and he terms them "unnatural and artificial."[12] While Bates charges Shelley with a stylistic slip, the remaining speeches of Beatrice will indicate that this artificiality is fully appropriate to her character.

Beatrice's mad speech that follows is spoken "wildly" and "frantically," yet it is a masterpiece of dissimulation. Never was madness so designing. Indeed, her suffering is so great that she can not bear to speak its cause, and so the audience must conclude the worst that it might imagine.[13] As her performance continues, her self-pity becomes too much for even her patient stepmother to bear, and Lucretia finally scolds: "Hide not in proud impenetrable grief / Thy sufferings from my fear" (III. i. 105-106). But Beatrice chooses not to hear. Instead, in the midst of her ravings—while she can not recognize herself or Lucretia, she claims—she utters the word "parricide." Accidental or cunningly planned, once the idea is in her mind, Beatrice (like her father) is compelled to act the thing, thought. After Orsino appears and is also moved by her grief, Beatrice begins her revenge. Having gained sympathy for her plight, she now seeks collaborators for her plot. This "friendless girl" whom Orsino purportedly manipulates, tells him: "put off, as garments overworn, / Forbearance and respect . . . / And all the fit restraints of daily life . . ." (III. i. 208-212). With these words, she enlists the aid of family and friends to accomplish her personal retribution against her father.

By the close of this third act, Beatrice has come to usurp divine prerogatives. She refers to her revenge as a "holier plea" and an "atonement." Then she proves that her revenge is not one of passion, but a crime of calculated premeditation; she says: "I have talked with my heart, / And have unravelled my entangled will, / And have at length determined what is right" (III. i. 219-221). Next she commands her confederates to be "brief and bold." The identification between herself and her father becomes more complete, however, when she uses the same words that the Count had used to describe himself, and she tells the conspirators to "put off . . . remorse and fear" (III. i. 208-209).

Just as the opening scenes parallel the two protagonists, so do the closing scenes in which they both appear. In the Count's last scene, he controls the action but is deterred by first Lucretia and then Beatrice. He calls Lucretia a "Vile palterer" and then speaks his famous imprecations against his daughter. Following these curses, Cenci contemplates revenge and becomes excited by the thought. He notes that "My blood is running up and down my veins" (IV. i. 163), yet he says he will sleep a "deep and calm" rest, undisturbed by conscience, before he commits his ultimate retribution. In the subsequent scene, Beatrice similarly controls the action as she directs the parricide she has planned. When the hired assassins first lose their nerve, she refers to them as "Base palterers" and goes on to curse them and her father. She proposes to murder Cenci herself and is excited by the prospect: "the jellied blood / Runs freely through my veins" (IV. iii. 43-44). After a short delay, the assassins return and report that the Count is dead, and Beatrice, undisturbed by conscience, remarks that "I could even sleep / Fearless and calm" (IV. iii. 64-65).

Beatrice's murder of Cenci eliminates one source of evil only to create another. Her corruption now supplants her father's, and her hubris rivals his when she announces: "I am as universal as the light; / Free as the earth-surrounding air; as firm / As the world's centre. Consequence, to me, / Is as the wind which strikes the solid rock / But shakes it not" (IV. iv. 48-52). With the arrival of the papal legate and the possibility of the murder's detection, Beatrice advises Lucretia: "Be bold," and then counsels her how to proceed: "We can blind / Suspicion with such cheap astonishment / Or overbear it with such guiltless pride . . ." (IV. iv. 43-45). This radical dissociation of sensibility recommended by Beatrice is precisely the antithesis of poetry as defined by Shelley in *A Defence of Poetry*. There he explains that language and thought are harmoniously synthesized when the imagination is at work, but when language is divorced from thought, only malignancy and obscenity result.[14] From this point forward, Beatrice's speeches reflect this dissociation of sensibility. They are models of rhetorical dissimulation, twisted truth, specious reasoning, and blatant lies that equal the cunning stratagems of Iago or Dryden's Achitophel. She manipulates ethos, logos, and pathos to persuade the tribunal of her innocence. Perjuring herself, she says: "Hear me, great God! I swear, most innocent" (V. ii. 152). Then she tricks Camillo into condemning himself, provokes the death of Marzio, and even berates her mother and brother by calling them "ignoble hearts." In the midst of all these self-serving ploys, Beatrice unwittingly describes her own situation when she warns her judges: "Worse than a bloody hand is a hard heart" (V. ii. 133). And she has, undoubtedly, become hard-hearted and resourceful. So adroit is she at feigning innocence and wielding spurious logic, indeed, that she almost eludes conviction. Only the more human weakness of her confederates gives her away, and they confess their part in the scheme. Good Giacomo then urges Beatrice: "For pity's sake say thou are guilty now" (V. iii. 54), to which Lucretia adds, "Speak the truth." Beatrice, nevertheless, remains unmoved.

By the close of the drama, the relationship between Beatrice and Count Cenci is remarkably similar to the relationship between God and Satan that Shelley described in his essay **"On the Devil and Devils,"** probably written in the same year. Cenci's actions seem to be analogous to those Shelley attributes to God, and Beatrice's actions to those of Satan: "He [God] turned his [Satan's] good to evil, and, by virtue of his [God's] omnipotence, inspired him [Satan] with such impulses as, in spite of his better nature, irresistibly determined him to act what he most abhorred and to be a minister to those designs and schemes of which he was the chief and the original victim."[15] That Shelley conceived of Beatrice as an equivalent to Satan finds corroboration in two of his prefaces. In the forward to **Prometheus Unbound,** he warns that "the character of Satan engenders in the mind a pernicious casuistry" (p. 133), in the "Preface" to **The Cenci,** he applies the same words to describe the reaction of men to Beatrice: "It is in the restless and anatomizing casuistry with which men seek the justification of Beatrice" (p. 240). Although Cenci instigates the evil, Beatrice falls into the pit because she is unable to *imagine* an alternative.

Beatrice's final identification with Satan helps to explain the one revision Shelley made to the original Cenci manuscript source that did not "increase the ideal, and diminish the horror of the events" (p. 239). The historical account of the Cenci family tragedy ends on an uncompromisingly high moral note. It records how Beatrice repented her crime before her execution: "Lucretia . . . with gentle exhortations induced her daughter-in-law to enter the chapel with her." Together, the account goes on to relate, they spent their last days "reciting psalms and litanies and other prayers, with so much fervour that it will appear that they were assisted by the peculiar grace of God."[16] But Shelley's version contains no such penitence. Beatrice, instead, dies fulfilling the Count's final curse, that "Beatrice shall . . . Die in despair, blaspheming" (IV. i. 49-50). Therefore, when Lucretia anticipates Paradise and entreats her daughter-in-law to "trust in God's sweet love, / The tender promises of Christ" (V. iv. 25-26), Beatrice retorts: "your words strike chill: / How tedious, false and cold seem all things" (V. iv. 80-81).

The Satanic identification of Beatrice is one explanation for her failure to repent her parricide. But there is another explanation which more fully substantiates the thesis of *this* analysis. Beatrice, from this point of view, is unable to attain salvation because such a response depends upon faith, and faith is an imaginative act unavailable to such an unimaginative character. At the close of the drama, therefore, it is fitting that Beatrice views the world in starkly realistic terms. She laments: "So young to go / Under the obscure, rotting, wormy ground" (V. iv. 49-50). When she considers man, it is not his spiritual essence that comes to mind, but "cold, cruel, and formal man" (V. iv. 108). Beatrice is captive to her senses; faith is beyond her ability. And when faced with death, she perceives it only in terms of the material world and exclaims: "How fearful! to be nothing" (V. iv. 55). Worse than death is "hope," she concludes, and denies herself an imaginative escape. Her final observation concerning death proves her failure to accept the possibility of an afterlife and her ultimate despair: "rock me to the sleep from which none wake" (V. iv. 115-118). Beatrice admits "my heart is cold"; she then dispassionately binds back her hair for the beheading. Even at the final moment, she is preoccupied with material rather than spiritual concerns.

The critical disagreement over Beatrice's true identity, though important, is overshadowed by a more disconcerting problem: Why does Shelley permit such confusion to occur when he repeatedly notes that drama is supposed to instruct the human heart? One possibility is that the potential for misinterpretation is intentional and exists to advance the play's instruction. In short, Shelley hopes that the reader will first try to justify Beatrice's actions, realize the error of his logic, and transfer his trust, instead, to his more reliable emotional responses. Should the reader fail to reevaluate his first, reasoned response, Shelley adds a warning in the "Preface" about the "anatomizing" casuistry of those readers who would defend the actions of Beatrice. The final interpretation of *The Cenci,* therefore, depends upon the same duality of reason and imagination as that which controls the play's plot and characters. Just as within the dramatic situation, the participants are duped by their reason and consequently destroyed, likewise a reader will also be duped if he acquiesces to Beatrice's faulty logic or the self-serving observations of her confederates. Reason is fallible; only the heart rings true. Parricide and despair are not exculpatory. The wholesale destruction of a family is beyond defense.

In his recent study *The Unacknowledged Legislator,* P. M. S. Dawson calls attention to this participatory drama and notes: "*The Cenci* poses the story of Beatrice as a problem, and impels the audience to an examination of their own reactions to work out its solution, rather than imposing authorial design."[17] In his "Preface" to the play, Shelley implies much the same thing when he observes that "the highest moral purpose" of drama is the "teaching of the human heart, through its own sympathies and antipathies, the knowledge of itself . . ." (p. 240). The larger world of *The Cenci* includes its audience, and only when the reader realizes that he is rationalizing that which is beyond rationalization is the dramatic experience completed. It is this action which Shelley refers to in *A Defence of Poetry* when he writes that "tragedies . . . are as mirrors in which the spectator beholds himself" (p. 490). The reader undergoes a similar deception by his calculating faculty as does Beatrice. On the stage and in the audience, by example and through experience, Shelley teaches the error of faith in reason.

Notes

1. *Shelley's Poetry and Prose,* ed. Donald H. Reiman and Sharon B. Powers (New York, 1977), p. 491. All future references to Shelley's poetry and prose are from this source unless noted otherwise.

2. "Notes" to *The Poetical Works of Percy Bysshe Shelley,* ed. Mary Shelley (Philadelphia, 1839), p. 182.

3. *Lord Byron and Some of His Contemporaries,* 2nd ed. (London, 1828), p. 368.

4. Flagg, "Shelley and Aristotle: Elements of the Poetics in Shelley's Theory of Poetry," *SIR [Studies in Romanticism]* 9 (1970), 66; Gottlieb, "Cosmic Allegory in *The Cenci,*" *Aligarh Journal of English Studies,* 3 (1978), 32.

5. Leslie G. Burgevin, *The Mount Holyoke (Mass.) News,* quoted in Bert O. States, "Addendum: The Stage History of Shelley's *The Cenci,*" *PMLA [Publications of the Modern Language Association],* 72 (1957), 638.

6. Newman Ivey White, *Shelley* (New York, 1940), 2:139; Carlos Baker, *Shelley's Major Poetry: The Fabric of a Vision* (Princeton, 1948), p. 148; Floyd Stovall, *Desire and Restraint in Shelley* (Durham, 1931), p. 250; Melvin Watson, "Shelley and Tragedy: The Case of Beatrice Cenci," *KSJ [Keats-Shelley Journal],* 7 (1958), 14; Robert F. Whitman, "Beatrice's 'Pernicious Mistake' in *The Cenci,*" *PMLA,* 74 (1959), 253.

7. Rieger, *The Mutiny Within: The Heresies of Percy Bysshe Shelley* (New York, 1967); Reiman, *Percy Bysshe Shelley* (New York, 1969); Wasserman, *Shelley: A Critical Reading* (Baltimore, Md., 1971).

8. Evert, "Coadjutors of Evil: A Romantic and Modern Theory of Evil," *Romantic and Modern: Revaluations of Literary Tradition,* ed. George Bornstein (Pittsburgh, 1977), p. 41; Lemoncelli, "Cenci as Corrupt Dramatic Poet," *ELN [English Language Notes],* 16 (1978), 112.

9. *The Letters of Percy Bysshe Shelley,* ed. Frederick L. Jones (Oxford [England], 1964), 2:219.

10. Lemoncelli, in his excellent article, uses the discussion of drama in *A Defence of Poetry* to establish Count Cenci as a possible analogue of the corrupt poet figure.

11. *Shelley: The Golden Years* (Cambridge, Mass., 1974), p. 409.

12. *A Study of Shelley's Drama* The Cenci (New York, 1908), p. 88.

13. So successful is Beatrice in hiding the cause of her grief that some critics doubt she was ravished.

Milton Wilson in *Shelley's Later Poetry* (New York, 1959), for instance, suggests that Shelley "has left it ambiguous whether the Count's plot was successful or not" (p. 85).

14. See *A Defence of Poetry,* passim.

15. *Shelley's Prose or The Trumpet of a Prophecy,* ed. David Lee Clark (Alburquerque, 1954), p. 270.

16. "Relation of the Death of the Family of the Cenci," Appendix, *Shelley's Works in Verse and Prose,* ed. Harry Buxton Forman (London 1876-1880), 2:401.

17. (Oxford, [England], 1980), p. 216.

D. Harrington-Lueker (essay date 1983)

SOURCE: Harrington-Lueker, D. "Imagination versus Introspection: *The Cenci* and *Macbeth*." *Keats-Shelley Journal* 32 (1983): 172-89.

[*In the following essay, Harrington-Lueker compares* The Cenci *and* Macbeth *and contends that Shelley borrowed Shakespearean themes to heighten audience understanding of his play.*]

As the Preface to *The Cenci* (1819) indicates, the story of the Cenci family immediately impressed Shelley with its dramatic and, more precisely, its tragic possibilities. Yet, as his letters show, the playwright conceived of a popular drama—a tragedy written with the English theater-going public in mind. So, despite the inherent power and passion of his source, Shelley realized that he would have to make certain significant adaptations if his conception were to be realized. Minimizing the horror of the act of incest was only one of the poet's concerns. His foremost task was to make the infamous Italian tale, so foreign to the English tradition, familiar to the sympathies of his audience:

> Nothing remained as I imagined, but to clothe it [the Cenci story] to the apprehensions of my countrymen in such language and action as would bring it home to their hearts. The deepest and the sublimest tragic compositions, *King Lear* and the two plays in which the tale of Oedipus is told, were stories which already existed in tradition, as matters of popular belief and interest, before Shakespeare and Sophocles made them familiar to the sympathy of all succeeding generations of mankind.[1]

"To clothe it to the apprehensions of my countrymen"—this detail provides the basis for an alternative interpretation of the numerous Shakespearean allusions in *The Cenci.* While Shelley's "appropriations" from Shakespeare have been variously noted and meticulously catalogued, the borrowings have been dismissed by modern critics as unconscious plagiarisms of little import for the artistic integrity of the piece.[2] Such a dismissal is myopic. If Shelley were concerned with adapting his story to the apprehensions of his countrymen, he would have no more likely tradition from which to draw than the works of Shakespeare. And if he wished to explore the issue of the morality of the imagination (an issue central to *The Cenci*), he could not have made a more appropriate choice than to allude to that drama in which the Macbeths battle with a moral imagination of their own. Far from unconsciously plagiarizing material from *Macbeth,* Shelley uses the allusions to set up not only thematic similarities but also important differences between the two plays, differences that can shed light on the troublesome vision *The Cenci* has been taken to represent.

To note at length the possible allusions to *Macbeth* is merely to repeat the work of earlier scholars; however, some of Shelley's more significant borrowings do need to be rehearsed. For example, a number of speeches in *The Cenci* echo those in *Macbeth.* In the first act of the drama Count Cenci contemplates his plan to violate his daughter and apostrophizes,

> O, thou most silent air, that shalt not hear
> What now I think! Thou, pavement, which I tread
> Towards her chamber,—let your echoes talk
> Of my imperious step scorning surprise,
> But not of my intent!
>
> (I. i. 140-144)

Before committing a similarly heinous crime (killing Duncan), Macbeth ruminates:

> Thou sure and firm-set earth,
> Hear not my steps, which way they walk, for fear
> The very stones prate of my whereabout,
> And take the present horror from the time,
> Which now suits with it.[3]
>
> (*Macbeth,* II. i. 56-60)

The address to the pavement is a thin disguise for Macbeth's address to the "firm-set earth"; in addition, though Count Cenci scornfully dares the steps to sound and Macbeth counsels them to be silent, the inversion does not alter the essential idea conveyed in the Shakespearean passage. Both men are apprehensive that their designs may be betrayed to their unsuspecting victims.

In another passage, Beatrice chastises her mother for fearing that the murder of Count Cenci will be discovered and attributed to them:

> The deed is done,
> And what may follow now regards not me.
> I am as universal as the light;
> Free as the earth-surrounding air; as firm
> As the world's centre. Consequence, to me,

Is as the wind which strikes the solid rock
But shakes it not.

(IV. iv. 46-52)

The blunt assertion of fact parallels Macbeth's announcement to his wife ("I have done the deed"); the extended natural metaphor that expresses Beatrice's imperviousness parallels Macbeth's description of his desire to be free of consequences:

But let the frame of things disjoint, both worlds suffer,
Ere we will eat our meal in fear, and sleep
In the affliction of these terrible dreams
That shake us nightly.

(III. ii. 16-19)

To such parallels a number of more subtle verbal echoes may be added. Speaking of his incestuous designs upon Beatrice, the Count asserts, "It must be done; it shall be done, I swear!" (I. iii. 178); Macbeth repeats throughout the play some variant form of "I go, and it is done" (II. i. 62). Orsino is dismayed that fear may enter between his wish and the effecting of it (II. ii. 129-132); Lady Macbeth uses the same formula to express her view on the potentially paralyzing power of remorse (I. v. 43-47). Both Macbeth and the Count use the image of a man wading in a river to suggest irreversible involvement in a course of action they have undertaken (*Cenci,* II. i. 123-128; *Macbeth,* III. iv. 135-137). Further, the papal legate Savella murmurs "Strange thoughts beget strange deeds" in response to Beatrice's curious denial of culpability (IV. iv. 139); the doctor in the final act of *Macbeth* observes, regarding Lady Macbeth's betrayal of culpability (her sleepwalking), "Unnatural deeds / Do breed unnatural troubles" (V. i. 71-72).

Shelley also includes a number of situations and entire scenes that recall *Macbeth.* It is a critical commonplace to cite the correspondences between Duncan's murder and Cenci's: how Cenci's murderers (like Lady Macbeth) balk at killing a sleeping old man, or how noises and staccato dialogue follow the murders in both plays. While in some cases Shelley is indeed following his manuscript, simple fidelity cannot in turn account for his deviations from his source.[4] From the detail that the Count rejoiced upon hearing of his sons' deaths, Shelley constructs a banquet scene not unlike Banquo's feast, particularly in its concluding lines. The Count dismisses his guests with the words

My friends, I do lament this insane girl [Beatrice]
Has spoilt the mirth of our festivity.
Good night, farewell; I will not make you longer
Spectators of our dull domestic quarrels.

(I. iii. 160-163)

The sentiment of the passage recalls Lady Macbeth's request that her guests excuse Macbeth's behavior:

Think of this, good peers,
But as a thing of custom. 'Tis no other;
Only it spoils the pleasure of the time.

(III. iv. 95-97)

Further, Shelley uses the untimely arrival of the papal legate Savella not only for irony but also as an excuse to include more Shakespearean materials not accounted for in the Cenci manuscript. Beatrice and Lucretia (like Lady Macbeth and her husband) can now resolve to go to bed and feign sleep (*Cenci,* IV. iii. 61; *Macbeth,* II. ii. 62-65). Lucretia can moan, "Would that he might yet live!" (IV. iv. 26) with regard to the Count, while Macbeth wishes that Duncan might still be awakened (II. ii. 71). And throughout these scenes, as Carlos Baker points out, Beatrice does resemble Lady Macbeth, unwavering in purpose and, when standing trial, "more willfully callous to all accepted moral codes" than the Shakespearean model herself.[5]

The allusions thus operate like a leitmotif throughout the first four acts of the drama as a speech, an image, a character, or a situation suggests a Shakespearean context. Admittedly, Shelley's debt is amorphous, more impressive in its cumulative effect than in the import of any single allusion. Admittedly, too, the moral universes that can be extrapolated from the dramas are hardly identical. Though a Jacobean drama, *Macbeth* is firmly rooted in the Elizabethan world view where paternal authority—father, king, god—is a social mainstay, a principle whereby the universe is given order and meaning. To break the bonds of authority is to send the universe into chaotic throes of discord until, as the drama progresses, the wrong is finally and inexorably righted and the evil expelled. In *The Cenci,* this guarantee of a meaningful and ordered universe is lacking. It is a critical commonplace to cite the poet's attitude toward paternalism and to note that he viewed the force of social convention as pernicious. It is even more commonplace to note that in *The Cenci* the demoniacal trinity of fathers—God, Pope, and Cenci—conspire to perpetuate a universe infused with the power of evil. For Beatrice, there is no Great Chain of Being with its attendant ordering impulse, and tragedy, in the obverse of *Macbeth,* thus ensues.

But to ignore or dismiss the allusions because Shelley's universe is uninformed by the metaphysical or even the metaphorical sanction of the Great Chain of Being is to overlook what Shelley could hope to gain by their inclusion. Chronologically, *The Cenci* was written as an entr'acte to *Prometheus Unbound,* the lyrical drama in which the poet presented his case for the genesis, growth, and eradication of evil. But if he wished to treat the same problem in *The Cenci,* he could not depend on his audience—a popular audience—being familiar with his "beautiful idealisms" or even with the dynamics of evil he had presented in that work. In *Macbeth,* however, he could find a congenial vehicle for his "sad reality."[6]

The themes that could have animated the poet's mind as he began composition—or that would animate an audience's mind as it experienced the play—are apparent. For example, in a passage not normally listed among the allusions to *Macbeth,* Count Cenci invokes the darkness in a characteristically histrionic speech:

> Come darkness! Yet, what is the day to me?
> And wherefore should I wish for night, who do
> A deed which shall confound both night and day?
> . . . I bear a darker deadlier gloom
> Than the earth's shade, or interlunar air
> Or constellations quenched in murkiest cloud,
> In which I walk secure and unbeheld
> Towards my purpose.
>
> (II. i. 181-183, 189-193)

Referring to his incestuous designs upon his daughter (the catalyst for the dramatic action), the Count recalls Lady Macbeth as she invokes the devil's emissaries to possess her. In so doing, he announces themes that mark both dramas. In both dramas the diabolical pervades, upturning the world in a tumultuous display of force. The shared subject is the perversion of man's will, for the oxymoronic "Fair is foul, and foul is fair" figures alike in both *Macbeth* and *The Cenci.* For the Weird Sisters—the objectification of spiritual evil—substitute Count Cenci; for the corruption of the best—Bellona's bridegroom—substitute the corruption of the purest, Beatrice Cenci. For like Macbeth, Beatrice does fall, does fail. As the Preface indicates, as *Prometheus Unbound* leads us to believe, as the value of forbearance in *The Masque of Anarchy* confirms, Beatrice is to be considered as profoundly wrong as she is profoundly tragic. However strongly the enlocking circumstances may weigh upon her, Beatrice's involvement in them (in contrast to her early detachment) is of her own making, as the complexities the Macbeths come to face have been theirs. Frank Kermode writes that *Macbeth* is a play preoccupied with the fears and tensions of darkness;[7] having witnessed the Count's black mass, the tangled depths of Petrella, and the conversion of Beatrice culminating in her callous abandonment of Marzio, the reader of *The Cenci* would recognize this kinship.

More specifically, too, in *Macbeth* Shelley's protean imagination could have found the outlines of a psychology of evil that would complement his own. The pattern to Shelley's borrowings in fact suggests such a fairly well-defined debt, for most of the allusions to *Macbeth* involve the dynamics of the will: how thoughts become deeds, how the unconscious becomes conscious, what happens when one commits oneself to a course of action. But if Shelley exploits that particularly Jacobean

theme—the study of the will in extreme circumstances and, more particularly, of how evil comes to direct that will—he does so with his own metaphysics in mind. As Earl Wasserman points out, Shelley's metaphysics involves an evil that is a persistent and pressing potentiality, made actual if man's will is in some measure weak or misguided. Yet, however strong, the ultimate cause of this evil lies outside the human mind.[8] Mary Shelley wrote that Shelley believed that man "had only to will that there should be no evil, and there would be none,"[9] and, while her estimate has served as ammunition for those who would charge Shelley with philosophical callowness, she is nonetheless in part correct. Conceived as autonomous and transcendent, evil can be willed away in the sense that it is not inherent in man as Judeo-Christian teleology would have it; it can enter the universe only insofar as man permits it to enter. Essentially, the vision is borne out in *The Cenci.* The Count—more the objectification of evil than a character in his own right—opposes Beatrice, the patient, resolute, and pacific young woman who is capable of opposing evil even amidst the physical and psychological turmoil of the Cenci palace. His aim: "to poison and corrupt her soul," to force the girl to allow evil to enter and control her mind, as it once entered and enthralled his.

Such a bald statement of Shelley's metaphysics risks misrepresenting the complexities of the artist's vision—a complexity that is the earmark of *The Cenci* where the force of evil is so potent that casuistry must often enter into our understanding of the heroine's character. However, the explanation so stated does succinctly express the essential components to Shelley's vision of evil: the transcendent nature of evil and its unceasing pressure on the individual. And, again, he could find in *Macbeth* a paradigm for his vision—even in its extremity. Opening the play, the witches chant the perversion of man's will to come ("Fair is foul, and foul is fair"), and their sudden appearance is as suddenly followed by a tale of apocalyptic turmoil—the messenger's tale of the bloody battle the witches had merely termed the "hurly burly." Nature and supernature are in turmoil; thane betrays king, breaking a bond that cements both society and the universe. And the witches stand at the opening of the scene, bearing the weight of all this unnatural discord and serving to symbolize that dominant spiritual evil which operates in man's universe—an interpretation the Romantics popularized over their Enlightenment predecessors. Like the source of evil in Shelley's Manichean universe, the witches exist as an independent and autonomous symbol for consummate evil—not as fantastical superstitions nor as figments of Macbeth's own mind. They wait, as the Count waits, for that susceptible individual who will allow his mind to be invaded and his will to be corrupted.

The two dramas, then, share a number of thematic pre-occupations, and a reading of the play is enriched by realizing where and why the parallels might exist. But Shelley is not content with enriching his drama with the themes of another—even if in doing so he could channel his audience's attention from the incestuous act to the central theme of the dynamics of the will. Rather, Shelley seems finally to have constructed this nimbus of similarities in order to exploit the differences between the two dramas and their attendant visions of evil, differences that suggest finally a solution for the problem of an ever-pressing evil.

Again, the pattern of Shelley's borrowings is telling. For example, both Shelley and Shakespeare use the metaphor of sleep as healer. In an oft-cited parallel to Macbeth's apostrophe to conscience (II. ii. 32-37), the Count observes:

> Conscience! Oh, thou most insolent of lies!
> They say that sleep, that healing dew of Heaven,
> Steeps not in balm the foldings of the brain
> Which thinks thee an impostor. I will go,
> First to belie thee with an hour of rest,
> Which will be deep and calm, I feel.
>
> (IV. i. 177-182)

Yet while this concept is expressed in both dramas, in one play such sleep is a forfeited (though desired) state while in the other it is mocked. The guilt-stricken Macbeth senses immediately and with remorse that the healing properties of sleep have been denied him by his murder of Duncan. To the extent that sleep symbolizes the peaceful conscience, Macbeth is conscience-stricken. On the other hand, Count Cenci, a hardened man (to use his own terms), feels no stirrings of guilt; though the deed he contemplates (incest) is dire, he will have no trouble sleeping.

In capsule form this particular allusion suggests the underlying difference between the two dramas that Shelley wishes to exploit. Throughout *Macbeth,* one notes, there is no indissoluble link between evil thoughts and evil actions. Macbeth's prolonged indecision indicates that in this moral universe options are available; evil does not have to be realized once it is recognized. After Malcolm has been named heir apparent to the Scottish throne (thus thwarting Macbeth's ambitions), Macbeth deliberates:

> The Prince of Cumberland! that is a step
> On which I must fall down, or else o'erleap,
> For in my way it lies. Stars, hide your fires,
> Let not light see my black and deep desires;
> The eye wink at the hand; yet let that be
> Which the eye fears, when it is done, to see.
>
> (I. iv. 48-53)

Macbeth's ambition impels him to the kingship; his humanity recoils from the desires providing the basis for the action. And, though Lady Macbeth browbeats her husband with the query, "Art thou afeard / To be the same in thine own act and valor / As thou art in desire?" (I. vii. 39-41), her husband would answer affirmatively even until the murder of Duncan is accomplished. Macbeth's two prolonged soliloquies ("If it were done, when 't is done" [I. vii. 1-23] and "Is this a dagger" [II. i. 33-61]) are but dramatizations of his indecision. There is time enough for a hundred decisions and revisions for the Macbeths, and if evil is consciously recognized, it is also subconsciously recoiled from. Witness the mind's dagger, the appearance of Banquo's ghost, the spot that will not wash away.

In *The Cenci,* however, what can be thought *must* be done. As the Count himself says to Camillo:

> Any design my captious fancy makes
> The picture of its wish, and it forms none
> But such as men like you would start to know,
> Is as my natural food and rest debarr
> Until it be accomplished.
>
> (I. i. 87-91)

Age has hindered this facility (I. i. 96-102); the Count uses wine now to stir him to his resolve (I. iii. 169-170) and revels in God's powers to transform his thoughts to realities (I. iii. 21-34). But the lapses are ones of physical capacity and not of psychological intent. Further, Beatrice, an initiate to evil, acts as the young Count perhaps did. "All must be suddenly resolved and done," she murmurs before going into a trance (III. i. 169); "We must be brief and bold . . . Be cautious . . . but prompt," she announces when her resolution has been made (III. i. 227-232). "The act seals all" (IV. iii. 6). For the Count and Beatrice, there are no regrets. No conscience mocks their sleep. They feel no compunction.

What allows Beatrice and the Count to act without a thought of remorse while the Macbeths, even until the end of the drama, must battle with their consciences against ambition? Again, the difference is telling, particularly in its implications for the metaphysics of evil Shelley develops in *The Cenci.* When informed of his elevation to the title of Thane of Cawdor, Macbeth ruminates:

> This supernatural soliciting
> Cannot be ill; cannot be good. If ill,
> Why hath it given me earnest of success,
> Commencing in a truth? I am Thane of Cawdor.
> If good, why do I yield to that suggestion
> Whose horrid image doth unfix my hair
> And make my seated heart knock at my ribs,
> Against the use of nature? Present fears
> Are less than horrible imaginings:
> My thought, whose murther yet is but fantastical,
> Shakes so my single state of man that function
> Is smother'd in surmise, and nothing is
> But what is not.
>
> (I. iii. 130-142)

Macbeth realizes that he could become king only by some violent and unnatural alteration of the existing political system, and the thought of assassination takes shape in his mind. For the first time in the play evil has been allowed to enter the human psyche, and Macbeth's convoluted and difficult final lines indicate the danger of allowing this to happen. Thought and surmise, in this instance, become tremendous and tangible realities, capable of evoking fear and, more important, of paralyzing the mind's powers. Fixed on itself, on its own operations, the will is unable to resist the influence of evil.

The lesson was not lost on Shelley, nor did he wish it to be lost on his audience, for it is such a prolonged and paralyzing process of introspection, or what Milton Wilson has termed the "centripetal pressures of ingrown soul,"[10] that at last damns its practitioners in *The Cenci*. Orsino, the Iago-like Machiavel, succinctly outlines the process when he speaks of the Cencis' predisposition to self-anatomy:

> It fortunately serves my close designs
> That 'tis a trick of this same family
> To analyse their own and other minds.
> Such self-anatomy shall teach the will
> Dangerous secrets: for it tempts our powers
> Knowing what must be thought, and may be done,
> Into the depth of darkest purposes.

(II. ii. 107-113)

To scrutinize one's own mind with the Cencis' depth and persistence is to become transfixed, paralyzed with an evil that seemingly cannot be recoiled from or challenged. It is, to use Wasserman's terms, to inform the conscious mind of what it ought not know and thereby to lead to self-contempt "by luring one to reconcile himself with these thoughts and hence to carry them out."[11] And compounded with the Catholic heritage that the participants in Shelley's drama share—a heritage that emphasizes the innate depravity of man by espousing the doctrine of original sin—such introspection can only damn its practitioners.

Orsino's analysis implicates more than this weak-willed Machiavel and the Count, however; despite more recent efforts to absolve Beatrice, she too is implicated in this introspective web, startled into self-anatomy by her father's heinous act. As Milton Wilson observes, "It is this family characteristic [i. e., their bent toward self-anatomy] that Cenci decides to make use of in order to degrade her. . . . By his act of incest Cenci will force Beatrice to turn her stern gaze inward. . . . Cenci tries to make the unwilling Beatrice follow his own development."[12] Indeed, contemplating the various trials to which he could subject his daughter, the Count definitively concludes: "No, 'tis her stubborn will / Which by its own consent shall stoop as low / As that which drags it down" (IV. i. 10-12).

That such introspection rather than the enormity of the crime is responsible for Beatrice's wild behavior and her resolve for revenge is difficult to substantiate: the encounter between the two antagonists takes place off-stage, and one is provided only with a glimpse of its immediate effects. Yet given the Count's intent ("To poison and corrupt her soul" [IV. i. 45]), given Beatrice's reaction (her wild madness with its emphasis on visual perception as an analogue for self-anatomy [III. i. 1-3; II. i. 4-5]), and given that Shelley purposely has Beatrice commune apart from the others before arriving at her decision to pursue revenge (III. i. 167-204), one may conclude that the Count's brutal act has only succeeded too well. "Undoubtedly, no person can be truly dishonoured by the act of another," Shelley writes in his Preface (p. 276); but the incestuous rape is so heinous, so psychologically as well as physically fouling, that it challenges Beatrice's integrity. The challenge causes her to look within herself, and what she finds is not integrity but the potential for depravity. Here transfixed, as with Macbeth's murder when yet fantastical, she decides on revenge, and evil is returned for evil in an ironic twist on her own triumphant words to her father: "But ill must come of ill" (I. iii. 151). The chain of evil remains unbroken, and, as the drama progresses, Beatrice exhibits to greater degrees the characteristic tyrannies and hypocrisies of her father. In her development the reader at last realizes that the Cencis' is a world made black by the process of introspection.

Yet, clued by the allusions to *Macbeth*, the audience learns what the characters of *The Cenci* could not: that though it may be potential, evil is not the necessity their introspection compels them to accept. As has been noted, the differences between the two psychologies outlined above is that in *Macbeth*, once the potentiality for evil is made conscious, it is nonetheless warred against by another unconscious force. Though Shakespeare did not so term it, the unconscious force may appropriately be termed the moral imagination. As the early acts of the drama show, Macbeth's imagination is one of his more salutary moral attributes: it informs him of consequences, allows him to see alternatives, and, in effect, hinders him from realizing his evil intent. Macbeth's most "imaginative" speeches (notably the two soliloquies of the early acts, which are marked by an abundance of imagery and metaphor) are those in which he is most indecisive concerning the murder of Duncan. Imagination is Macbeth's moral reflex, and it is only when he denies the imaginative faculty (witness in the later acts his ability to conceive only literally, particularly with regard to the witches' final three prophecies) that he becomes a beast, an animal, an automaton of self-perpetuating evil.

Lady Macbeth, on the other hand, is more literal-minded and prosaic in the first acts, and this state of mind corresponds to her ability to assert continuously (though in variant forms), "Glamis thou art, and Cawdor, and shalt be / What thou art promis'd" (I. iv. 15-16), as if potentiality and reality were identical. Yet, as the play concludes, as she fitfully tries to wash the spot from her hand and envisions the murkiness of Hell, Lady Macbeth finally exhibits the same moral reflex that her husband had once possessed but lost. Where in the initial acts she can conceive only of the literal, now, even as she sleepwalks, she is imaginative, able to see consequences and to sense the enormity of her actions. Indeed, in her cries (the paradigm for the conscience-stricken), she exhibits that retrospective display of remorse which could have prevented thought from becoming deed (v. i. 35-52).

This moral imagination of the Macbeths contrasts radically with the Cencis' compulsion toward introspection. And to the extent that the former force can combat the human potentiality for evil, it offers the audience a substitute moral sphere for the Cencis' world in which, transfixed with evil, nothing blocks the conscious will from becoming tangible reality.

The action in the fifth act, however problematical, bears out this intention. Indeed, an awareness of the allusions finally allows the audience to perceive the playwright's "signal" that his tragic heroine has been redeemed or has at least been able to free herself of the transfixing hold of evil, for the redemption can be traced to the appearance of imagination in the hardened Cenci daughter. Throughout most of the final act, Beatrice is complacent and awesomely self-satisfied. *She* has not committed parricide; *her* God is just and vengeful of wrongs. Psychologically, her security is comparable to that which Macbeth derives from his literal interpretation of the witches' final prophecies. None of woman born can harm Macbeth; "The God who knew my wrong, and made / Our speedy act the angel of His wrath" protects Beatrice and her co-conspirators (v. iii. 113-114).

Yet when her conviction of God's protection and justice is shattered by the news of her death sentence, Beatrice begins a series of speeches marked by imagery and a predominance of metaphor—much as Macbeth's expressions of indecision were marked:

> O
> My God! Can it be possible I have
> To die so suddenly? So young to go
> Under the obscure, cold, rotting, wormy ground!
> To be nailed down into a narrow place;
> To see no more sweet sunshine; hear no more
> Blithe voice of living thing; muse not again
> Upon familiar thoughts, sad, yet thus lost—
> How fearful! to be nothing! Or to be . . .
> What? Oh, where am I? Let me not go mad!
> Sweet Heaven, forgive weak thoughts! If there should
>   be

> No God, no Heaven, no Earth in the void world;
> The wide, gray, lampless, deep, unpeopled world!
> If all things then should be . . . my father's spirit,
> His eye, his voice, his touch surrounding me;
> The atmosphere and breath of my dead life!
> If sometimes, as a shape more like himself,
> Even the form which tortured me on earth,
> Masked in grey hairs and wrinkles, he should come
> And wind me in his hellish arms, and fix
> His eyes on mine, and drag me down, down, down!
> For was he not alone omnipotent
> On Earth, and ever present? Even though dead,
> Does not his spirit live in all that breathe,
> And work for me and mine still the same ruin,
> Scorn, pain, despair?

> (v. iv. 47-72)

Often cited by critics as Beatrice's final wisdom, the speech is one of the few occasions in which a character in *The Cenci* rises above the prosaic levels of speech Shelley had designed for his audience. In his Preface Shelley had come to the defense of familiar imagery and the "familiar language of men," contending that in both the writer could readily find the power to stir men's sympathies (pp. 277-278). By and large, *The Cenci* bears out this contention, as well as his observation that "I have avoided with great care in writing this play the introduction of what is commonly called mere poetry, and I imagine there will scarcely be found a detached simile or a single isolated description" (p. 277). While Beatrice's speech in this instance is indeed dramatically motivated (rather than "detached"), it also contrasts radically with her usually prosaic speeches.

"Imagination is as the immortal God which should assume flesh for the redemption of mortal passion," Shelley announces in his Preface (p. 277). While in context the sentence refers to technique and not theme, it is nonetheless revealing, for in the passage quoted above the paralyzing hold of introspection is loosened, and, in a self-revealing desperation akin to that of Macbeth's "Tomorrow and tomorrow and tomorrow" speech, Beatrice shows a resurgence of imagination, a force that animates and expands her world beyond the literal confines to which she had in her complacency sunk. On only one occasion prior to the fifth act had Beatrice's speech become notably imagistic—her description of the ravine on the way to the castle of Petrella where "a mighty rock . . . leans [over] the dread abyss" (III. i. 247, 254-255). In this speech, however, the choice of imagery is governed by the centripetal powers of introspection as the description of the pass reflects Beatrice's diseased state of mind; the abyss that Beatrice describes is the abyss of her own mind so recently turned upon itself by the Count's heinous crime. With the exception of the final few lines, the speech's movement is one of increasing descent, as if the speaker is plunging mentally into a labyrinthine world comprehensible not by the senses (which gradually fail) but by the mind's eye. In this descent into a world sealed in darkness "By the dark ivy's twine" (III. i. 264) the mind is active, transforming the obscured external world into a vivid, if terrifying, mental landscape. The dark entanglement of the speaker's own mind—so recently resolved to murder, so recently compelled to introspection—overshadows the boulder's objective existence. Perched precariously on a ledge midway between the road and the bottommost reaches of the abyss, it becomes a paradigm for Beatrice's own state. Prior to the incestuous act, Beatrice is the one who has sustained herself "with terror and with toil / Over a gulph" (III. i. 249-250), returning the Count's pressure with a practiced and stoic patience, and she is the one who now agonizingly inclines into the dread abyss of Orsino's darkest purposes. She is the one who fears the fall, yet resolves, as the speech itself indicates, on a world of darkness.

To this imagery one can readily contrast that of the speech cited earlier. For all its despair, the images suggest an outward rather than an inward movement as Beatrice's mind moves from the narrow confines of the grave to an expansive vision of an entire universe. No longer is her speech literal; no longer is she self-righteous. And as she follows one "poetic" speech with another, the self-righteous hypocrite and tyrant disappears. In her stead is a woman who can now conceive of a world without God, a world animated not by justice—as she has narrowly conceived it—but by scorn and despair (v. iv. 48-75). In her stead is a woman whose speeches are vivified with an abundance of natural imagery (v. iv. 96-107). Finally, as this growing release of imaginative powers builds, in her stead is a Beatrice who recognizes that her father's act did not stain her honor. As she counsels Bernardo,

> One thing more, my child:
> For thine own sake be constant to the love
> Thou bearest us; and to the faith that I,
> Though wrapped in a strange cloud of crime and
>   shame,
> Lived ever holy and unstained.

> (v. iv. 145-149)

Read as a reference to the parricide, the lines are evidence that Beatrice remains unwavering in her self-righteousness—a conclusion that accounts for much of the ambiguity often ascribed to Shelley's vision. But read as a reference to the effect of her father's incestuous act, the lines are evidence that Beatrice realizes what Shelley contends in the Preface: "Undoubtedly, no person can be truly dishonoured by the act of another" (p. 276). This is the wisdom to which the imaginative release finally builds. The release that began with a recognition of despair ends with the insight that might have made melioration possible or at least would have saved Beatrice the violent mental upheaval she has undergone. And to mark the change this newfound faculty

has brought about on the once hardened Beatrice, one notes that, for the first time since the earliest portions of the play, Beatrice initiates acts of simple human kindness. In the bleak world of *The Cenci,* this hope alone remains; and if such hope remains an ineffectual glimmer amidst the stifling forces of tyranny and psychological abuse, it is perhaps the final measure of Shelley's sad reality.

Thus, by alluding to *Macbeth,* by allowing his audience to both compare and contrast the worlds of the Macbeths and the Cencis, Shelley in effect anticipates a view of human morality that he explicitly develops in *A Defence of Poetry* (1821):

> The great secret of morals is love; or a going out of our own nature, and an identification of ourselves with the beautiful which exists in thought, action, or person, not our own. A man to be greatly good, must imagine intensely and comprehensively; he must put himself in the place of another and of many others; the pains and pleasures of his species must become his own. The great instrument of moral good is the imagination; and poetry administers to the effect by acting upon the cause.[13]

"Going out of ourselves"—if not to the beautiful at least in this case so as to break the paralyzing hold of introspection. Such is the knowledge of the human heart Shelley wishes to be the effect of tragedy; such indeed is the knowledge that *The Cenci* provides, replete with its allusions to *Macbeth.* Rather than being classified as unconscious plagiarisms, the borrowings from *Macbeth* are integral to an understanding of *The Cenci,* for Shelley has indeed purposely and skillfully clothed his drama in trappings that his "countrymen" could appreciate.

Notes

1. Preface to *The Cenci,* in *Shelley: Poetical Works,* ed. Thomas Hutchinson; rev. G. M. Matthews (London: Oxford University Press, 1970), p. 276. Subsequent references are to this edition.

2. For the critics' reactions to Shelley's appropriations, see *Shakespeare Society Papers,* 1, No. 13 (1884), 52-54; "Some Notes on *Othello,*" *Cornhill Magazine,* 18 (1868), 419-440, *Edinburgh Review,* 133 (1871), 440-448; E. S. Bates, *A Study of Shelley's Drama,* The Cenci (New York: Columbia University Press, 1908), pp. 54-55; David Lee Clark, "Shelley and Shakespeare," *PMLA* [*Publications of the Modern Language Association*], 54 (1939), 261-287; Sarah Ruth Watson, "Shelley and Shakespeare: An Addendum," *PMLA,* 55 (1940), 611-614; Frederick L. Jones, "Shelley and Shakespeare: A Supplement," *PMLA,* 59 (1944), 591-596; Beach Langston, "Shelley's Use of Shakespeare," *Huntington Library Quarterly,* 12

(1949), 163-190; Stuart Curran, *Shelley's* Cenci: *Scorpions Ringed with Fire* (Princeton: Princeton University Press, 1970), pp. 37-39. Finally, departing from the tradition of either cataloguing or dismissing the allusions in *The Cenci,* Paul Cantor argues for the thematic significance of the allusions to *King Lear* and *Macbeth* in his article "'A Distorting Mirror': Shelley's *The Cenci* and Shakespeare's Tragedy," in *Shakespeare: Aspects of Influence,* ed. G. Blakemore Evans, Harvard English Studies, No. 7 (Cambridge, Mass.: Harvard University Press, 1976), pp. 91-108. Cantor argues that Shelley was deeply dissatisfied with Shakespeare's view of authority and rebellion, so dissatisfied that he purposely misquotes both plays. Lear becomes the repellent figure of authority; Macbeth, a more attractive rebel. I shall argue for a more orthodox interpretation of Macbeth on Shelley's part.

3. *Macbeth* is quoted from *The Riverside Shakespeare,* ed. G. Blakemore Evans, et al. (Boston: Houghton Mifflin, 1974).

4. See "The Relation of the Death of the Family of the Cenci" in *The Complete Works of Percy Bysshe Shelley,* eds. Roger Ingpen and Walter E. Peck (London: Ernest Benn; New York: Charles Scribner's, 1926-30), II, 159-166. Curran (*Scorpions,* pp. 37-39) argues that Shelley is not so much borrowing from Shakespeare as faithfully following the details he found in his source.

5. Carlos Baker, *Shelley's Major Poetry: The Fabric of a Vision* (Princeton: Princeton University Press, 1948), p. 150.

6. My interpretation runs counter to the direction the most recent criticism of the play has taken. In *Scorpions Ringed with Fire* and (with some revision) in *Shelley's* Annus Mirabilis, Stuart Curran emphasizes the extremity of Beatrice's position—beyond the bounds of normal moral recourse—in order to argue that Beatrice is an existential heroine, confronting a world in which evil is the only force; she is "impelled by her fate into a no-man's land where both action and nonaction are evil and where objective ethical standards dissolve into the absurd" (*Scorpions,* p. 141). Beatrice's revenge—and its attendant callousness and hypocrisy—ceases to be blameworthy; the young woman becomes instead an existential rebel, asserting the integrity of her own moral position in the face of a hostile and otherwise meaningless universe. See also *Scorpions,* pp. 129-164, and *Shelley's* Annus Mirabilis: *The Maturing of an Epic Vision* (San Marino, Calif.: Huntington Library, 1975), esp. pp. 120-136. In part Curran's studies are the culmination of an approach to the play that in recent years has empha-

sized the increasing complexity and ambiguity of Shelley's vision of evil. See Earl Wasserman, *Shelley: A Critical Reading* (Baltimore: Johns Hopkins University Press, 1971), pp. 84-130; James Rieger, "Shelley's Paterin Beatrice," *Studies in Romanticism,* 4 (1965), 169-184. But while Wasserman and Rieger emphasize the extremity of Beatrice's position, they do not depart from the school of criticism that faults Beatrice for her acceptance of the same punitive theology that conspires to make her world, to use Rieger's term, a "syphilitic chancre." Curran, however, overturns this mainstream critical position. Curran's argument cannot be dealt with at any length or with any specificity in this study. As Curran himself admits, the unorthodox interpretation is gained by isolating *The Cenci* from the rest of Shelley's canon; my argument, on the contrary, is constructed on the assumption that Shelley's Preface and his *Prometheus Unbound* should be used as aids in clarifying the ambiguities in the text. Though somewhat more "moralistic," the approach is consonant with (though not identical to) the mainstream interpretation of the play. See also Robert O. Whitman, "Beatrice's Pernicious Mistake in *The Cenci,*" *PMLA,* 74 (1959), 249-253; Milton Wilson, *Shelley's Later Poetry: A Study of his Prophetic Imagination* (New York: Columbia University Press, 1959).

7. *The Riverside Shakespeare,* p. 1307.

8. *Shelley: A Critical Reading,* pp. 84-94.

9. Notes to *Prometheus Unbound,* in Hutchinson-Matthews, p. 271.

10. *Shelley's Later Poetry,* p. 78.

11. *Shelley: A Critical Reading,* p. 111.

12. *Shelley's Later Poetry,* p. 84.

13. *A Defence of Poetry,* in Ingpen and Peck, VII, 118.

Jean Hall (essay date fall 1984)

SOURCE: Hall, Jean. "The Socialized Imagination: Shelley's *The Cenci* and *Prometheus Unbound.*" *Studies in Romanticism* 23, no. 3 (fall 1984): 339-50.

[*In the following essay, Hall analyzes the relationship between* The Cenci *and* Prometheus Unbound, *specifically focusing on themes of imagination and social reality in the works.*]

The Cenci was written during an interlude between Shelley's creation of the first three acts of ***Prometheus Unbound*** and the last. Obviously these plays stand in opposition to each other: the poet describes ***Prometheus***

Unbound as a "Lyrical Drama" employing imagery drawn from "the operations of the human mind" and designed to encourage "beautiful idealisms of moral excellence"; on the other hand, *The Cenci* is a tragedy featuring imagery adapted to "the illustration of strong feeling" and depicting "sad reality."[1] *Prometheus Unbound* appears to be the drama of the human imagination and its poetries, whereas *The Cenci* charts the course of social actuality. I shall argue that Shelley creates this opposition not to suggest exclusive possibilities, but instead, to imply continuities and relationships.[2]

For this poet, the link between social behavior and the imagination tends to be dramatic. This is suggested by the passage in *A Defence of Poetry* where he discusses the Athenian tragedies as examples of reflexive audience response. These plays "are as mirrors in which the spectator beholds himself, under a thin disguise of circumstance." Such a view relates the individual and the social by making the dramatic performance a "mirror" of the beholding self, the public world a reflex of personal consciousness. Shelley adds that these dramatic mirrorings are cognitive, because "Neither the eye nor the mind can see itself, unless reflected upon that which it resembles." To see oneself projected as a world is a transformation that allows for recognitions otherwise impossible. As the poet remarks, drama teaches its beholders "self-knowledge and self-respect" (pp. 490-91). This claim is repeated in the Preface to *The Cenci*, where Shelley describes his purpose as "the teaching the human heart, through its sympathies and antipathies the knowledge of itself" (p. 240).

These remarks suggest that self-knowledge arises from a position of simultaneous identification and distance, a vantage point provided by dramatic transactions. When Shelley's Athenian audience beholds tragedies, they see a vision that is the same as themselves and yet different; for if they identify with the world of the drama they also recognize that it exceeds them. It portrays themselves, but "stript of all but that ideal perfection and energy which every one feels to be the internal type of all that he loves, admires, and would become" (p. 490). In the *Defence [of Poetry]*, tragedy becomes an idealizing agent because it depicts a world related to but larger than the audience, thereby creating recognitions that open the possibility of personal growth. The audience does not become the ideal, which remains different from themselves, but they are moved toward it. Their imaginations are "enlarged by a sympathy with pains and passions so mighty, that they distend in their conception the capacity of that by which they are conceived" (p. 490).

This imaginative process described in *A Defence of Poetry* is enacted in *Prometheus Unbound* Act I, where Prometheus recognizes and changes himself through dramatic visions. The most important of these is his dialogue with the Phantasm of Jupiter, which he indicates in an attempt to avoid self-recognition. Prometheus wants to recall his curse but also to disassociate himself from it; so he chooses the Phantasm of Jupiter, a presence as far removed from himself as possible, to repeat his words. As he instructs the Earth, "Mother, let not aught / Of that which may be evil, pass again / My lips, or those of aught resembling me" (I. 218-20). But in this confrontation with Jupiter, Prometheus discovers that if he is different from the tyrant, he is also the same. The Phantasm is "a frail and empty phantom" which yet appears as a "Tremendous Image"—a huge surface without an interior. The words spoken by this image belong to Prometheus, who witnesses his own part being acted by another. The Phantasm becomes a surface reflecting Prometheus, a poetic mirror that allows him to see and hear himself in a way not otherwise possible. He discovers that when he spoke his curse he took on the form of Jupiter, for these "gestures proud and cold, / And looks of firm defiance, and calm hate" are appropriate to the delivery of Prometheus' own words. Like Shelley's Athenian audiences, Prometheus gains self-knowledge from this performance. The image of Jupiter simultaneously establishes relationship and distance, allowing Prometheus both to see what he was and to grow beyond his past self.[3]

In *The Cenci,* the vision of identity and difference experienced by Prometheus is heightened into a tragic vision of identity and alienation. In Beatrice, Shelley creates a character who simultaneously compels audience sympathy and antipathy. The audience response sought by Shelley is a "restless and anatomizing casuistry with which men seek the justification of Beatrice, yet feel that she has done what needs justification" (p. 240). As the character that the audience most loves, Beatrice also becomes the character who most urgently requires justification. In Beatrice, Shelley creates a mirror image of the audience's best self, a figure who corresponds not to Prometheus but to Asia in *Prometheus Unbound*. Like Asia, she is the Life of Life, the object of the audience's desire and an idealized reflection of itself. Her brother Bernardo calls her "That perfect mirror of pure innocence / Wherein I gazed, and grew happy and good" (V. iv. 130-31). But if Beatrice is the ideal with whom we identify, at the same time she is also a murderess—and more than a murderess, a parricide.

In her aspect of perfect goodness Beatrice resembles not only Asia, but also Coleridge's Christabel.[4] The subject of both *The Cenci* and "Christabel" is the contamination of the ideal, the inability of pure goodness to resist evil. And in both works, the invasion of evil becomes obscurely sexual. Christabel is possessed by Geraldine because she sleeps a night in her arms, and Beatrice is mastered by her father because of a deed she cannot name, but which Shelley implies is incestuous rape. As a result of these invasions Beatrice and Christabel lose the power of speech. But where Christabel becomes a passive reflection of Geraldine, able to produce only a serpentine "hiss" when she tries to explain her condition to her father, Beatrice is speechless not because her tongue is locked but because she herself cannot comprehend her condition. As she says, "there are deeds / Which have no form, sufferings which have no tongue" (III. i. 141-42). The evil done to her is so alien from herself that she cannot name it, cannot bring it into any relationship with her own identity. For Prometheus the interplay of identity and difference leads to dramatic recognition and personal growth, but Beatrice's violation produces the opposite result of self-alienation. As she says to her stepmother, "What are the words which you would have me to speak? / I who can feign no image in my mind / Of that which has transformed me" (III. i. 107-9). Where Prometheus can call up the image of Jupiter, Beatrice is alienated not only from speech but from imagery. Her desire is not to see and learn, but to remain blind, to suppress. By refusing to recognize evil, she hopes to deny its existence. If Prometheus' response to his condition creates integration, Beatrice's promotes divisions.[5]

And Shelley compels the audience of *The Cenci* to follow Beatrice's pattern. He works to produce a "restless and anatomizing casuistry," a conflict between sympathizing with Beatrice and judging her. Where *Prometheus Unbound* evolves toward growth and fusion, *The Cenci* forces its audience to maintain a split response. Simultaneously we identify with Beatrice's goodness and sympathize with her private sensibility, but are alienated from her father's murder and therefore compelled as social beings to judge her. *The Cenci* deliberately works to split the personal from the social, the pure imagination from actuality.[6]

To compare Beatrice and Asia illuminates the nature of this split response. In the Life of Life lyric Asia appears clothed in a kind of radiant dimness, an "atmosphere divinest" which "Shrouds thee where so'er thou shinest." Her voice "folds" her "From the sight . . . / And all feel, yet see thee never" (II. v. 62-64). She appears as a poetic and eroticized presence, a being at the same time revealed but protected in shining obscurity. In *Prometheus Unbound* the image of desire manages to be at once private and public. But in *The Cenci,* the radiant dimness of Asia's presence is converted to Beatrice's fear of being stripped naked. She refuses to grant voice and imagery to her rape, because her private response cannot be embodied in public forms. To tell of the crime would be to "lay all bare / So that my unpolluted fame should be / With vilest gossips a stale mouthed story; / A mock, a bye-word, an astonishment" (III. i. 157-60). The public word becomes an indecent exposure, and so the safeguard of Beatrice's private experience must be suppression. To tell her story would

be to play into her father's hands, for his antisocial desire is to achieve eminence through his heroic perversions. He says, "I will drag her, step by step, / Through infamies unheard of among men: / She shall stand shelterless in the broad noon / Of public scorn, for acts blazoned abroad." Cenci wants his legacy to be "nothing but my name, / Which shall be an inheritance to strip / Its wearer bare as infamy" (IV. i. 80-83, 60-62). The only alternative to nakedness becomes secrecy, the body suppressed. As Cenci remarks of his victims, "I rarely kill the body which preserves, / Like a strong prison, the soul within my power" (I. i. 114-15). Where Asia's body becomes a poetic image, the Life of Life that blends private and public response, Beatrice's entrapped body symbolizes her divided existence.

But Beatrice's suppression conceals the truth not only from society, but from herself as well. This is because words and images are simultaneously public and private: they tell stories to the world, but they also clarify one's inner experience. Shelley takes this view in *Prometheus Unbound,* where the god "gave man Speech, and speech created thought, / Which is the measure of the Universe" (II. iv. 72-73). Here the word clarifies thoughts, the area of innerness; and in turn, thought makes the world coherent.[7] But in opting for speechlessness and internal incoherence, Beatrice also renders her public actions obscure. Just as she refuses to name the crime, she also declines to name its redress. She will only say that "something must be done . . . something which shall make / The thing I have suffered but a shadow / In the dread lightning which avenges it" (III. i. 86-89). Her family is left to infer her meaning, and so it is they who name the murder of Cenci and carry it out.[8] Herself unreflective, she forces her family into a course of arbitrary action. The murder in *The Cenci* therefore corresponds to Prometheus' unreflective curse, which he cannot remember at the beginning of Act I because he delivered it "eyeless in hate" (I. 9).

In *The Cenci* Beatrice tries to cope with evil by refusing to recognize it, denying it a word and an image. But the ironic consequence is that she also fails to recognize herself. Her development is the opposite of Prometheus', and actually is a kind of regression into the arbitrary. Her split responses display this kind of arbitrariness and rigidity, and so do her formal beliefs. She justifies her actions through an appeal to God, who she believes could not have sanctioned her violation. In invoking the authority of the heavenly against the earthly father, she believes she is affirming a transcendent world of justice against the earthly world of tyranny. In fact, what she is doing is appealing to an unknown outside herself. The reflexiveness achieved by Beatrice is not dramatic but ironic, for by blindly appealing to absolute authority she repeats her own father's arbitrariness. Parricide becomes the reflection, not the remedy, of incest.

In his Preface to *The Cenci* Shelley suggests that Beatrice's thinking is culture-bound, reflecting not only the mind of her father but also the mores of sixteenth-century Rome. In this arbitrary society the law is bought for gold and religion is superstition: "It is adoration, faith, submission, penitence, blind admiration; not a rule for moral conduct" (p. 241). The historical particularity of this society is stressed throughout *The Cenci,* but in *Prometheus Unbound* historical references are generalized. When the Furies torture Prometheus with visions of a failed religious reformer and a failed revolution, Shelley takes care not to identify these as visions of Christ and the French Revolution. In a sense they indeed are not, for as the Furies make clear, their visions mirror Prometheus' own fears—"from our victim's destined agony / The shade which is our form invests us round, / Else are we shapeless as our Mother Night" (I. 470-72). And indeed, the historical failures imaged by the Furies turn out to recapitulate Prometheus' own failure—he championed mankind but then surrendered the world to tyranny by his curse on Jupiter. *Prometheus Unbound* suggests that history is the reflexive vision of its own audience, and that this vision can be mastered by poetic distancing. By seeing his fears mirrored in the form of historical theater Prometheus can recognize and overcome them. The procedures of *Prometheus Unbound* Act I suggest that poetry simultaneously distances us from history and relates us to it, for by recognizing our own assumptions we become free to change them. In contrast, Beatrice remains a victim of her own culture because she stays so close to it that she cannot see what it has made of her.[9]

And here *The Cenci* implies an immense irony, for Beatrice believes herself to be an absolute idealist, a pure agent of God uncontaminated by her own society. But at the same time she sees herself as transcending history, the audience of *The Cenci* realizes that she is largely an historical expression. Just as her acts of suppression mirror her father's, expressing the impulses of an arbitrary society, her relation to her ex-lover Orsino dramatizes a complementary aspect of this cultural arbitrariness. Where Cenci represses people, Orsino draws them out—but this seeming difference collapses into ironic identity when we recognize that both characters behave as they do for tyrannical ends. Cenci hopes to master other people by his acts, but so does Orsino. His procedure becomes a parody of the dramatic interchange between Prometheus and the Phantasm of Jupiter, for he draws out the speech of his confidants not to help them achieve self-knowledge, but to entrap them.[10]

Orsino's relationship with Beatrice's brother Giacomo makes this clear. Orsino feigns friendship, letting Giacomo use him as a mirror which yields visions of self-abasement. He urges his victims to "Fear not to speak your thought," because he knows what will come forth are "such phantasies / As the tongue dares not fashion into words, / Which have no words, / their horror makes them dim / To the mind's eye" (II. ii. 74, 84-87). By enabling the mind's eye to see what it fears, Orsino helps Giacomo to legitimize his secret wish for his father's death. Orsino's manipulations bring obscure desires out into clarity, but what is seen is distorted. As Giacomo says to Orsino after the family is ruined: "O, had I never / Found in thy smooth and ready countenance / The mirror of my darkest thoughts; hadst thou / Never with hints and questions made me look / Upon the monster of my thought, until it grew familiar to desire" (V. i. 19-24).

In effect, where Cenci practices an active tyranny, Orsino tyrannizes through a calculating passivity. When the Cenci family attempts to cope with Beatrice's nameless distress in Act III, Orsino waits until they have given the word to Cenci's murder, and then quickly offers to supply the assassins. As he muses, "Now what harm / If Cenci should be murdered?—Yet, if murdered, / Wherefore by me? And what if I could take / The profit, yet omit the sin and peril / In such an action?" (II. ii. 120-24). By becoming a willing tool Orsino hopes to convert passivity into risk-free activity: the family will bear the moral responsibility for Cenci's murder, but Orsino will reap the benefit, for he will know the secret of their guilt and use it to control them. When he achieves this position Orsino will no longer need to draw out the speech of others; for in possessing their secret he will have the repressive power of a Cenci. The lover will replace the father as family tyrant.

Orsino is a crucial figure in *The Cenci,* for his calculating passivity becomes a conscious version of Beatrice's self-alienated behavior.[11] In refusing to see or give a name to her rape, she too draws out her concerned family's speech, which emerges as interpretation of her obscure intimations. And so it is her stepmother Lucretia who must give the name to Cenci's murder. By Beatrice's refusal to contaminate herself she shifts the moral responsibility to those around her; her idealism becomes unconsciously manipulative, and she turns into an unwitting reflection of Orsino even as she is a reflection of her father. Indeed, in a sense she is even worse than Cenci and Orsino, for where evil clearly can be expected of them Beatrice is the finest flower of her culture, the only hope of *The Cenci.* Her failure signals the death of all hope, for only the idealist herself can murder idealism.

In *Prometheus Unbound* Asia becomes the Life of Life, the object of poetic desire that draws forth the expression of a transformed world. *The Cenci* reverses this to show Beatrice as the center of the Cenci's plot, the inarticulate and obscure object of desire who draws forth the actualization of the family doom. Considered together, the two plays form a commentary on the uses of idealism. Shelley is aware that his reflexive, theatrical view of poetic language harbors manipulative implications. As we have seen, his remarks on the Athenian tragedies in the *Defence* suggest that plays are fictions that mirror the audience, drawing them out into a performance of themselves that results in self-knowledge. But this view implies that self-knowledge is a product of poetic manipulation. It follows that poetry can be easily corrupted—that it can be used to produce self-deception rather than self-knowledge. Therefore the safeguard of poetry, in *Prometheus Unbound* and the *Defence,* becomes its public character. Shelley values the drama because it is a public performance, a community endeavor that creates not secret knowledge of the isolated self but a socialized imagination. Poetry remains an idealizing force only insofar as it is open to all. It is properly the creative voice of its culture, not the voice of one individual.

And so the last Act of *Prometheus Unbound* becomes the song of the socialized imagination, the fusion of public and private concerns in a dance of world-creating harmony. But Shelley created this vision only after writing out the end of *The Cenci,* which carries Beatrice's split response forward to a tragic, world-destroying conclusion. Act v of *The Cenci* is comparable not to the ending of *Prometheus Unbound* but to its beginning; the final alienation of Beatrice and her world corresponds to the initial fallen condition of the Promethean universe. But this inversion of the creative process in *The Cenci* does not necessarily imply that Shelley wrote the play as a counsel to abandon all hope. On the contrary—the case of Prometheus' dialogue with the Phantasm of Jupiter suggests that a split response may be extremely effective in promoting self-knowledge.

The last Act of *The Cenci* splits the audience away from identification with Beatrice by making us witness her trial. In one stroke this gives us distance from Beatrice and also from the society that judges her: the secret and arbitrary proceeding within the play is opened up by the public vision of Shelley's drama. This allows poetry to truly become a form of legislation, as Shelley argues it is in *A Defence of Poetry,* where poets become "the unacknowledged legislators of the World" (p. 508). For if Beatrice and her judges remain blind to themselves, the audience of *The Cenci* achieves the proper distance for comprehension. Not only do we see the self-deceptions that suppression and arbitrary behavior create in this play's characters—we also become aware that we too could dupe ourselves by allowing our best selves to become the justification for our unacknowledged dark acts.[12]

Beatrice herself feels that she is alien to her society, an uncontaminated idealist misunderstood in a corrupted world. But where she perceives absolute difference, the audience of *The Cenci* must concede a considerable element of identity. As soon as her father is murdered, her disturbed and incoherent responses are replaced by an imperturbable calm—a stillness that she regards as a sign of her transcendence. But the trial reveals her to be the ironic reflection of the Pope, who is also calm in his embodiment of the inflexible law of church and state. If he is impervious, "as calm and keen as the engine / Which tortures," a "marble form, / A rite, a law, a custom: not a man" (v. iv. 2-5), Beatrice too is not to be swayed. As she says, "Consequence to me, / Is as the wind which strikes the solid rock / But shakes it not" (IV. iv. 50-52).

To be arbitrary is to deny the validity of relationships and consequences—to say the self can exist as an absolute untouched by the world.[13] Unwittingly Beatrice extends this false transcendence into a manipulation of language when she claims that "I am more innocent of parricide / Than is a child born fatherless" (IV. iv. 112-13). By denying the father she also denies parricide, for if she has no father, then she cannot have murdered him. But if this arbitrary use of language is plausible to Beatrice herself, it cannot convince the audience of *The Cenci.* We see that Beatrice's usage undermines public language, conferring exclusive and unstable meanings on the word. From the perspective of her acknowledged self and the higher truth she embodies, we indeed do sympathize with the view that the innocent has a right to isolate herself from contamination—but at the same time, we cannot avoid recognizing that her unacknowledged self has drawn her family into murder. The Pope's law and Beatrice's word both designate narrow and arbitrary public areas of clarity which become social facades that screen forbidden activity. The state pays homage to its law while allowing individuals secretly to buy it with gold, and Beatrice upholds her innocence while allowing her own unconscious obscurities to engender a dreadful action. Ironically, her final condemnation of humanity, "Cruel, cold, formal man; righteous in words, / In deeds a Cain" (v. iv. 109-10) could apply to herself as well as to the Pope. *The Cenci* ends in the destruction of poetry and society, but in anatomizing this catastrophe the play manages to imply that an authentic poetry would have to be relational and public.

Thinking through the issues presented by *The Cenci* must have helped Shelley to create Act IV of *Prometheus Unbound.* There he celebrates the socialized rather than the isolated imagination, which becomes the legislator of the world because it continually reshapes human obscurities into comprehensible public forms. To create the world is to bring it to light, to make it transparent and penetrable to social view. The Spirits of the Human Mind in Act IV of *Prometheus Unbound* are freed "from the mind / Of human kind / Which was late so dusk and obscene and blind" (IV. 93-95), and this release from obscurity is accompanied by an expressive rapture. As the Earth sings, "The joy, the triumph, the delight, the madness, / The boundless, overflowing, bursting gladness, / The vaporous exultation not to be confined!" (IV. 319-21). Where Beatrice and the Pope preserve themselves through a deadly calm, the spirits of **Prometheus Unbound** experience an irrepressible excitement that leads them into eroticized modes of relationship. The Earth and the Moon wheel together in a dance of love, interpenetrating and fully knowing each other. The world's body becomes sexual and public, repealing the body as prison and the secrecy of incest that grounds **The Cenci**. This sexual dance, which is also the gravitational interrelation of a planetary system, becomes a relational model for a self-regulating human society. Man, "who was a many-sided mirror / Which could distort to many a shape of error," renders up his absolute individuality and privacy to join the unfolding relational expression of a poetic society. He becomes "one harmonious Soul of many a soul / Whose nature is its own divine controul / Where all things flow to all. . . . Heaven, hast thou secrets? Man unveils me, I have none" (IV. 382-83; 400-402, 423).

Although **The Cenci** and **Prometheus Unbound** come to opposite endings, by no means do they support opposing conclusions about the nature of imagination or man's fate. If the former play appears to anatomize "sad reality" while the latter celebrates the pure imagination, in fact both dramas suggest that poetry is a dramatic transaction which features identifying and alienating potentials. When poetry is used aright, it removes us from ourselves only to finally create more coherent relations; for by achieving poetic distance, we are able to see ourselves and make ourselves anew. But when distance is asserted in order to avoid perception and recognition, as in the case of Beatrice, then relationship is replaced by alienation, and creation is subordinated to arbitrariness. This double potential holds not only in the case of individuals but of cultures; just as it is possible for the individual to be self-alienated or creative, so it is possible for a society to be culture-bound or innovative. Imagination and actuality are not intrinsically separate categories for Shelley—they certainly may become alienated, but it is within our power to bring them into relationship.

Notes

1. See the Prefaces to *Prometheus Unbound* and *The Cenci*, pp. 132-36 and 238-42 of *Shelley's Poetry and Prose*, eds. Donald H. Reiman and Sharon B. Powers (New York: W. W. Norton & Company, 1977). Subsequent references to Shelley's poetry and prose are to this edition.

2. The clearest case for *The Cenci* and *Prometheus Unbound* as embodying exclusive possibilities has been made by Stuart Curran in *Shelley's* Cenci: *Scorpions Ringed with Fire* (Princeton: Princeton U. Press, 1970) and again, in "The Rule of Ahri-

man" in his *Shelley's* Annus Mirabilis: *The Maturing of an Epic Vision* (San Marino, CA: Huntington Library, 1975), pp. 119-36. James Rieger's study of *The Cenci*, "The Paterin Beatrice," in his *The Mutiny Within: The Heresies of Percy Bysshe Shelley* (New York: George Braziller, 1967), accords with Curran's view that *The Cenci* embodies a universe of evil, but Rieger sees this not as an absolute opposition to *Prometheus Unbound* but as "a pyrrhonistic exercise in aid of the affirmation celebrated by Shelley's lyrical drama. In *The Cenci* the whole creation is a syphilitic chancre and the god of this world (Shelley argues from design) a witty degenerate" (p. 112).

3. Milton Wilson was the first to suggest that the Phantasm of Jupiter is a self-projection of Prometheus. See *Shelley's Later Poetry: A Study of His Prophetic Imagination* (New York: Columbia U. Press, 1959), pp. 63-64. Earl R. Wasserman concurs in *Shelley: A Critical Reading* (Baltimore: The Johns Hopkins U. Press, 1971), pp. 258-61. Also see "Dark Mirrors: *Prometheus Unbound,*" in Lloyd Abbey's *Destroyer and Preserver: Shelley's Poetic Skepticism* (Lincoln and London: U. of Nebraska Press, 1979).

4. For an intelligent comparison of Christabel and Beatrice, see Terry Otten's "Christabel, Beatrice, and the Encounter With Evil," *Bucknell Review*, vol. xvii, no. 2 (May 1969), 19-31.

5. Two approaches to Beatrice as a divided character deserve special mention. The first is Joseph W. Donohue Jr.'s "*The Cenci*: The Drama of Radical Innocence" in his *Dramatic Character in the English Romantic Age* (Princeton: Princeton U. Press, 1970). Donohue suggests that romantic dramatists tended to think of character transcendentally. For them, "the radically innocent character of Romantic drama lives in a guileless world out of time," a pure existence that is momentarily disrupted by historical contingency; the character "ironically must render up his innocence in a 'dramatic' world where time and circumstance enchain a once free, joyous spirit" (p. 162).

The other noteworthy discussion of Beatrice as a divided character is Michael Worton's "Speech and Silence in *The Cenci*," in *Essays on Shelley*, ed. Miriam Allott (Totowa, NJ: Barnes & Noble Books, 1982). Worton analyzes Beatrice's condition as a phenomenon of repression. He suggests that where Count Cenci deliberately suppresses both his own words and the free speech of his family for his own tyrannical ends, Beatrice suppresses the words that would communicate Cenci's violation of her because "The verbal formulation of the nature of the crime, far from having a beneficial therapeutic effect, would demand an intellectual structuring of her emotions which remain uncodifiable" (p. 108).

6. For an excellent account of how Shelley compels his audience to experience a split response to *The Cenci,* see pp. 187-96 of Michael Henry Scrivener's *Radical Shelley: The Philosophical Anarchism and Utopian Thought of Percy Bysshe Shelley* (Princeton: Princeton U. Press, 1982). Scrivener is concerned with the social dimensions of Shelley's art, and sees the dilemmas of the play as devices that promote social awareness.

7. For an account of how thought and word are related in *Prometheus Unbound* see Susan Hawk Brisman, "'Unsaying His High Language': The Problem of Voice in *Prometheus Unbound,*" *SiR* [*Studies in Romanticism*] 16, no. 1 (Winter 1977), 51-86. Brisman argues for a conception of language in *Prometheus Unbound* in which existence is a function of expression. Her analysis is focussed on Milton and sublime language, whereas my discussion of the relationship of thought and word in *Prometheus Unbound* concerns lyrical language. See *"Prometheus Unbound,"* in my *The Transforming Image: A Study of Shelley's Major Poetry* (Urbana: U. of Illinois Press, 1980). Michael Worton's discussion of verbal repression in *The Cenci* (see footnote 5) gains resonance when it is read in connection with these two accounts of the evolution of poetic expression in *Prometheus Unbound.*

8. See Paul Smith's essay, "Restless Casuistry: Shelley's Composition of *The Cenci,*" *KSJ* [*Keats-Shelley Journal*], vol. xiii (Winter 1964), 77-85. Smith compares Shelley's source for *The Cenci,* "The Relation of the Death of the Family of the Cenci," with the notes he took on this account and the drama he finally wrote. In *The Cenci* "Beatrice is transformed from an active to a more passive participant in the crime. All the minor preparation and plotting is transferred to Giacomo, Lucretia, and Guerra, who was later to become Orsino" (p. 81). For another account of Shelley's adaptation of his source, see Stuart Curran's *Scorpions Ringed With Fire,* pp. 39-46. Curran remarks that "Beatrice, who bore an illegitimate child presumably by the Castellan of Petrella, Olimpio, was hardly the pure and heroic figure canonized by the Shelley Society" (p. 42).

9. For an account of *The Cenci* which relates it to the temptations offered by the Furies in *Prometheus Unbound,* see "The Temptations of Prometheus" in Milton Wilson's *Shelley's Later Poetry: A Study of His Prophetic Imagination* (New York: Columbia U. Press, 1959). Wilson discusses the connection between self-love and self-contempt, and the imagery of mirroring in *The Cenci,* concluding that "*The Cenci* is a strangely disquieting vision of evil, in which the characters peer into themselves and greet the depths which they discover with various degrees of horror, fascination, and acceptance. The play can be regarded both as a defense of the idea of natural depravity and as an attack on it, or at least on our tendency to justify our shortcomings by making them seem inevitable and universal" (pp. 90-91).

For another account of how *The Cenci* accords with *Prometheus Unbound* in promoting self-knowledge while dissecting introspective self-anatomy, see Earl R. Wasserman's "Sad Reality and Self-Knowledge: *The Cenci,*" in his *Shelley: A Critical Reading* (Baltimore: The Johns Hopkins U. Press, 1971). Wasserman suggests that "As judges presiding over Beatrice's case we are to be baffled, for Shelley consistently conceived of tragedy not as a case to be tried but as a mirror in which we are made unwittingly to see and understand ourselves . . ." (p. 120).

For another comparison of the possibilities of reflexive perception as enacted in *The Cenci* and *Prometheus Unbound,* see pp. 71-81 of my *The Transforming Image.*

10. Wasserman is excellent on this point. He argues that "With the psychoanalyst's goading questions and leading hints . . . Orsino at length guides Beatrice into verbalizing her undistinguishable mist of thoughts and so into anatomizing her inner responses to her father's deeds. . . . Since, according to Shelley, the mind cannot see itself except as reflected by another, our mirror image may give us self-knowledge—the self-knowledge the audience is to gain by seeing its own reflection in Beatrice—or, like the verbalizing of our subconscious, it may make us viciously aware of what should remain suppressed" (*Shelley: A Critical Reading,* p. 114).

11. Just as Shelley converted the historical Beatrice's relatively active role in Cenci's murder to passive participation (see footnote 8), he also changed the historical Guerra of his source, "The Relation of the Death of the Family of the Cenci," into the Orsino of *The Cenci,* whose role in the crime becomes greatly expanded. Charles L. Adams speculates on the artistic reason for this change in "The Structure of *The Cenci,*" *Drama Survey* vol. 4, no. 2 (Summer 1965), 139-48.

12. In his study of verbal repression in *The Cenci* (see footnote 5) Michael Worton calls attention to what he calls the "world external to that of the text" in *The Cenci,* aligning Shelley's drama with the theories of Antonin Artaud as an exercise in "funda-

mental modernity" (p. 105). And indeed, Artaud did choose *The Cenci* for the first production of his projected theater of cruelty. For an account of Artaud's production, see Curran's *Scorpions Ringed With Fire*, pp. 237-46. I believe that a reading of Artaud's critical views in their English translation, *The Theater and Its Double*, trans. Mary Caroline Richards (New York: Grove Press, Inc., 1958), will suggest that Artaud's and Shelley's aims are quite opposite: where Artaud intends to abolish aesthetic distance in order to release audience participation, Shelley works to set up a distancing that will allow for proper comprehension. Shelley does not try to abolish the word and textuality; rather, he aims to redeem language.

13. I am reading Act v as Shelley's critique of a false transcendence, which I would remind the reader, disputes the transcendentalist interpretation of Beatrice's character argued for by Donohue (see footnote 5).

Barbara Groseclose (essay date fall 1985)

SOURCE: Groseclose, Barbara. "The Incest Motif in Shelley's *The Cenci*." *Comparative Drama* 19, no. 3 (fall 1985): 222-39.

[*In the following essay, Groseclose discusses how parent-child incest functions as a metaphor for tyranny in* The Cenci.]

Mary Shelley admired her husband's 1819 play, *The Cenci,* because it was, she felt, the most direct of his works.[1] The author himself, apparently both pleased and abashed that the writing of the drama consumed scarcely two months, implied a similar simplicity when he told E. J. Trelawny that in *The Cenci* he had expended considerably less effort on poetic language and "metaphysics" than was his wont.[2] One scarcely wishes to contradict the two persons most intimately connected with the work, but a survey of the critical literature suggests that the drama is among the poet's densest, richest, and most ambiguous creations.[3] Explored from every viewpoint—i. e., from its theatricality to its philosophy—*The Cenci* has yielded itself to interpretation in a most rewarding manner, though its paradoxes stubbornly remain. One feature, Shelley's decision to include incest among Count Cenci's crimes, has been regarded as a self-explanatory action; since Cenci's violation of his daughter provides the controlling symbol of the play, it establishes the rationale for its inclusion (and its rejection). But incest was not, in fact, an aspect of the original story. I should like to offer some analyses which will attempt to delineate the reasons which might have led Shelley to draw upon the incest motif and to sketch out some of the consequences for later treatments of the Cenci's history.

I

At the turn of the eighteenth century, there were few Italophiles who did not fall under the spell of Beatrice Cenci, for emotions were easily stirred by the pathos of her sorrowful life and her equally soulful "portrait" by Guido Reni. Today accepted neither as a portrait of Beatrice nor as the hand of Reni, the painting in Shelley's day rivalled Raphael's *Transfiguration* as the most famous picture in Rome.[4] The image satisfied the early Romantic propensity for mournfulness, an attribute believed to endow mere physical beauty with spiritual distinction. Certainly Shelley succumbed to the painting's charms in just these terms:

> There is a fixed and pale composure upon her features. . . . Her head is bound with folds of white drapery from which the yellow strings of her golden hair escape, and fall about her neck. The moulding of her face is exquisitely delicate; the eyebrows are distinct and arched; the lips have that permanent meaning of imagination and sensibility which suffering has not repressed. . . . Her forehead is large and clear; her eyes, which we are told were remarkable for their vivacity, are swollen with weeping and lustreless, but beautifully tender and serene. . . .[5]

Beatrice won the hearts of viewers, however, neither because of the canvas' superbly delineated features nor because of the ascription to Guido Reni (to which was added the piquant notion that he had taken the likeness the night before her execution).[6] She was also the protagonist of a tale abundant with Gothic horrors. Shrewd Nathaniel Hawthorne remarked, "I wish . . . it were possible to see the picture without knowing anything of its subject or history; for no doubt, we bring all our knowledge of the Cenci tragedy to the interpretation of it."[7] Indeed legend, which had encrusted history and tied the painting to its fancies, had rendered the painting less portrait than icon. It is impossible now to ascertain the details of the case beyond the fact that a young Roman named Beatrice Cenci was beheaded by the Church in 1599 for parricide; the defenders and detractors of Beatrice have between them impugned whatever evidence existed.[8] Shelley and Hawthorne knew the story through the heavily embellished manuscript accounts in wide circulation at the time. Shelley was, I think, being ingenious when he declared that his manuscript source, **"The Relation of the Death of the Family of the Cenci,"** had been suppressed, since he knew (and counted on) how widely the story had spread. An extensive transcription of the Cenci episode, apparently drawn from the manuscript accounts, had been published in Volume X of Ludovico Antonio Muratori's *Annali d'Italia* (1749), a very public document.[9] In any case, Shelley seemed truly to believe in the accuracy and authenticity of the **"Relation"** [**"of the Death of the Family of the Cenci"**], purportedly taken from the "Cenci Palace Archives," that Mary Shelley copied in

1818 at Leghorn. Upon arriving in Rome the following spring and discovering that "the story of the Cenci was . . . not to be mentioned in Italian society without awakening a deep and breathless interest," Shelley settled on the **"Relation"** as a source for the tragedy he had long planned to write.[10] He candidly acknowledged that the narrative's two-hundred-year notoriety in Rome assured its future popularity as much as it recommended its dramatic potency.

Briefly, the events described in the manuscript were these: Count Francesco Cenci, a wealthy and dissolute Roman nobleman, ensured the wellbeing of his soul by paying huge sums to Pope Clement VIII Aldobrandino in return for the dismissal of sexual offenses and other serious crimes, including the assassination of two of his sons. Debauched himself, he continually sought to corrupt his younger daughter Beatrice, and eventually he imprisoned her and her step-mother Lucretia in Castle Petrella, near Naples. The two women, who determined to kill Cenci, received aid from Monsignor Guerra, Beatrice's would-be suitor, and Giacomo and Bernardo, the Count's eldest and youngest sons. The actual perpetrators were Marzio and Olimpio, Cenci's disaffected servants, who murdered their employer at Beatrice's instigation—indeed, at her insistence—by driving a nail through his eye and another through his neck. Shortly thereafter, Olimpio was killed in an unrelated incident. Marzio, however, was arrested and tortured, whereupon he confessed, implicating all the others. Monsignor Guerra escaped from Rome in disguise; Beatrice and her family were imprisoned, tried by the Church, and executed (with the exception of the youth Bernardo) on the eleventh day of May 1599. The beheaded Beatrice was buried in San Pietro in Montorio. A description of *la bella Parricida,* as she was called, accompanied the manuscript account:

> Beatrice was rather tall, of a fair complexion; and she had a dimple on each cheek, which, especially when she smiled, added a grace to her lovely countenance that transported every one who beheld her. Her hair appeared like threads of gold; and . . . the splendid ringlets dazzled the eyes of the spectator. Her eyes were of a deep blue, pleasing, and full of fire. To all these beauties she added, both in words and actions, a spirit and a majestic vivacity that captivated every one. She was twenty years of age when she died.[11]

The holograph in Mary Shelley's hand of an English translation of the **"Relation"** and the translation Shelley sent to Thomas Love Peacock are comparable to other extant versions with respect to the broad outlines of the story.[12] The play differs from the source in that Shelley altered several details, but variations were abundant and his departures are not singular. What *is* unusual is that he introduced the act of incest; all versions, including the one from which Shelley worked, mention Francesco Cenci's attempts to seduce his

daughter but no consummation. The memorandum Shelley prepared from the manuscript account as outline for his drama is even more vague, stating only that Francesco "tempts" Beatrice, and then, astonishingly, Shelley adds, "He thinks by mild means to bring her to his will."[13] The "mild means" listed in his source include in addition to debauching of maidservants and prostitutes whom Cenci placed in his wife's bed and with whom he cavorted in front of Beatrice, his attempts to convince his daughter that "children born of the commerce of a father and daughter [are] all Saints. . . ." When Mary Shelley first copied the translation, she omitted Francesco's efforts to seduce Beatrice and explained: "the details here are too horrible and unfit for publication." Kenneth Neill Cameron has supposed that her omission and attendant remark referred to the rape, but this is not the case.[14] Although not mentioned in the **"Relation,"** the loss of her honor was the extenuating motivation attributed to Beatrice during her trial by the renowned defense attorney, Prospero Farinaccio, whose argument was rejected by the adjudicating Roman Catholic prelates as unproven.[15] Muratori alludes to Farinaccio's defense, but there is no evidence Shelley had read the *Annali.*

In any event, Shelley willfully altered his source in order to make the attempted rape actual. It is possible that he simply augmented the **"Relation"** by drawing upon rumors current in Roman folklore, but how does one determine what was or was not the gossip about the Cencis in Shelley's day or earlier? The only testimony I can offer is that, immediately after her death and for several years following, a large crowd traced the route of her funeral cortege from the Piazza Castel Sant'Angelo to San Pietro in Montorio as though in honor of a martyr or someone unjustly punished.[16] If rumor of her rape still existed, therefore, Shelley was responsible for changing heresy to "fact." If no such rumors persisted and Farinaccio's defense was forgotten or discredited by 1819, then Shelley—far from drawing on "facts [which] are a matter of history" to rationalize "whether such a thing as incest in this shape . . . would be admitted on the stage"—manufactured history.[17]

Dramaturgically the decision was a necessity. No less than Beatrice's attorney, Shelley needed to link serious provocation with the magnitude of the crime. The absence of the rape/incest incident would render the Count a one-dimensional figure of insensible wickedness, Beatrice merely wayward, and the parricide trivial. So Cenci's violation of his daughter, occurring offstage between Acts II and III, is the event that controls the play structurally and histrionically. The first two acts belong to Count Cenci, who initially overwhelms the other characters through the sheer force of his malignancy: "All men delight in sensual luxury; / All men enjoy revenge, and most exult / Over the tortures they can never feel, / Flattering their secret peace with other's pain. /

But I delight in nothing else. I love / The sight of agony . . ." (I. i. 77-82). Shelley steadily constructs a portrait of jaded sensuality, of rage at the incapacitating encroachment of age, and of malicious wielding of power which will culminate in the enactment of a "deed . . . whose horror might make sharp a duller appetite than [Cenci's]" (I. i. 100-02). In contrast, Beatrice presents a mild impression in the drama's first half. Her personality is that of a submissive child made melancholy and pathetic by a "home of misery," while she weakly bears her share of suffering along with her stepmother and younger brother. The midpoint of the play, the opening of Act III, changes all of this. Thereafter Beatrice becomes the dominant character, and the Count is reduced in Act IV to a spite-filled shell of a man whose enmity is no match for Beatrice's steely determination to avenge herself. Finally, in the last act, after she has been arrested for murder, Beatrice resumes a pathetic demeanor, but now her suffering is balanced by a nobility and dignity that the frightened girl-child of the first acts could never achieve.

II

In his fine article on incest in Romantic literature, Peter Thorslev discusses the "symptomatic" (i. e., biographical) and symbolic uses of the theme.[18] He shrugs off allegations that Shelley's neurotically suppressed desire for his sister erupts in certain poems and concentrates instead on the undeniably stronger case for the symbolic role of incest in *The Cenci*. I am prepared to support Thorslev's argument, but there is a biographical factor he does not mention that has a bearing on the play itself. When Shelley was writing *The Cenci*, he was amorously involved with Claire Claremont, his wife's half-sister. How far sexually this attachment progressed we do not know, and Shelley's (and Claire's) biographers agree only that in all likelihood their union was physical.[19] *Leviticus* 18. 18, in a list of incestuous practices, specifically denounces intercourse between a man and his sister-in-law; the prohibition is yet included in the canons of the Anglican Church. If he knew it, Shelley would scarcely take such an injunction seriously. He would, in fact, probably welcome the opportunity to reject once again the conventions governing moral conduct—conventions which he felt were paltry. I do not know if Mary Shelley would have concurred. Certainly she tried valiantly to adapt herself to Shelley's rigorous, yet free-wheeling personal code, though in regard to his repeated affairs she never wholly succeeded. References to her coldness (in Shelley's own poetry as well as his contemporaries' assessments), her querulousness, and her bitterness gain in frequency around the times Claire formed their spasmodic *menáge à trois*. In light of this, it is interesting that Mary herself wrote about incest soon after *The Cenci* was completed and at a time when Claire was still a member of the household.[20]

In *Mathilda,* a feeble novella unpublished until 1959, Mary Shelley bravely if not well treats the subject of father-daughter incest. The story is straightforward. The parents of Mathilda enjoy a true love match that tragically ends when the mother dies shortly after giving birth. Stunned by grief, Mathilda's father entrusts the infant to the care of an aunt and is absent for sixteen years. After father and daughter eventually meet, they share a few idyllic months before the father commits suicide as a consequence of falling in love with his daughter. Mathilda, in turn, isolates herself from society and gradually, in spite of a friendship with a young poet (Shelley?), wastes away. Written during a time of severe personal tragedy for Mary, the novella is neither tough-minded nor psychologically acute but rather sentimental and wistful.[21] The language is overwrought and the plot minimal.

In *Mathilda* Mary wrote of events closely, almost embarrassingly, associated with her own life. The young girl's mother dies giving birth; her father first rejects her, then is overwhelmed by love for her—a sad fantasy in the face of the similarity of events with Mary's own life, for William Godwin remained cold to his daughter. It is not easy to determine what Mary comprehended by the autobiographical nature of her novella. Nevertheless, one is tempted to assign the credibility of her treatment of incest not only to innocent wish-fulfillment on her part—i. e., simply that her father would love her—but also to a personal apprehension of the circumstances in which illicit passion within a family group and the unhappiness thereby induced might develop.

Prior to *The Cenci,* Shelley's personal response to incest had not been so sensitive. Amongst friends, he had not been averse to making jocular, indulgent references to brother-sister love, and he had, of course, treated sibling incest very positively in the *Revolt of Islam* (1817).[22] As in the earlier poem, however, he seemed at pains to dissociate himself from the action portrayed in *The Cenci*. "My chief endeavor," Shelley wrote Thomas Medwin, "was to produce a delineation of passions which I had never participated in. . . ." Later he told Trelawny that "In writing *The Cenci* my object was to see how I could succeed in describing passions I had never felt. . . ." In reference to either the incest or the murder, the interesting aspect of these statements is that he felt it necessary to make them. Was Shelley here anticipating the calumny his already tainted reputation and the scandalous play would together elicit? Did he fear a revival of the "league of incest" story?[23] Was he, and this seems most likely, combatting the gossip which at the very time not only linked him to Claire Claremont but also provided them with issue, the baby Elena Shelley?

III

Whether one adds a biographical element to Shelley's choice of (or use of) incest as a theme in *The Cenci*, its symbolic role is paramount and multifarious. The philosophical base—the existence and power of evil—has been admirably explicated; without minimizing this reading, I would like to take up the notion that the metaphorical sense of the play might also be political.[24]

There is little difficulty in discerning the political ramifications of Shelley's depiction of Francesco Cenci. The character's impressive quality as Shelley portrays him is not so much the depth of his depravity (which alone would be merely grotesque) but the acuity of his perceptions *about* his depravity. He recognizes whence it originates, the hypocrisies that sustain it, and the voraciousness of its easily-jaded appetite. The social order of his time and place being structured on absolute rather than discriminating power, Cenci is the domestic agent of a patriarchal despotism ruling Church and State. As oppression seeps inevitably into the exercise of absolute power, the fictions which shroud its actions must be carefully maintained. Thus an autocratic Pope such as Clement VIII Aldobrandino may rely on the derivation of the authority of the "Holy Father" from God the Father and, at the same time, refuse to discipline Cenci, who is also a father: "[The Pope] holds it of most dangerous example / In aught to weaken the paternal power, / Being, as 'twere, the shadow of his own" (II. ii. 54-56). Cenci scoffs at these shams by ripping the façade of mercy from the Papal dispensations he has received: "No doubt Pope Clement, / and his most charitable nephews, pray / . . . that I long enjoy / Strength, wealth, and pride, and lust, and length of days / Wherein to enact the deeds which are the stewards / Of the revenue" (I. i. 26-33). Mocking the line of authority, he ironically and caustically pleads that to accomplish his iniquitous designs "the world's Father / Must grant a parent's prayer against his child" (IV. i. 106-07). Cenci will not hide from what he is, for he has "no remorse and little fear, / Which are . . . the checks of other Men" (I. i. 84-85). Finally, he comprehends the quickly-sated desire for domination that is the driving force of corrupted power (I. i. 96-109) and unflinchingly discerns that to debase his victim spiritually is ultimately more devastating than any form of physical injury. "I rarely kill the body, which preserves, / Like a strong prison, the soul within my power," he gloats (I. i. 114-15). Thus does Cenci plot incest, an appropriate act to demonstrate his cognizance of the ineluctable degeneracy that corrupted power breeds.

With the character of Beatrice, Shelley approaches the situation from the non-aggressor's point of view. In Acts I and II he carefully presents Beatrice as an innocent, and then, with unforgettable imagery, describes her contamination as the transference of an infection by rape. Her innocence allows misfortune because it is ignorance; she is easy prey for her father, the representative of a duplicitous social order, because she believes the premises of the authority by which her world is controlled. And endowed not with one father but three, she is too fragile to withstand the seemingly contradictory demands of so cumbersome a patrimony.[25] Poignantly, she cries out her bewilderment to "God, whose image on earth a Father is" (II. i. 16-17) and conflates the familial and religious patriarchies she must obey: "What if we / . . . were his own flesh, / His children and his wife, whom he is bound / To love and shelter? / . . . / I have borne much, and kissed the sacred hand / Which crushed us to earth, and thought its stroke / Was perhaps some paternal chastisement!" (I. iii. 103-06, 111-13). When the incest has been committed, Beatrice instantly perceives her physical violation as a spiritual defilement. Flesh is dissolved "to a pollution, poisoning / The subtle pure, and inmost spirit of life!" she moans (III. i. 22-23), and decries the blood "which [is] my father's blood, / Circling through these contaminated veins . . ." (III. i. 95-96). The polluted blood now coursing through her veins will be purged by blood-letting.

Shelley knew that Francesco Cenci's evil had a specific political name: tyranny. Cenci's incestuous behavior is no wanton deed of lust. It is a deliberate attempt by a despot to compel Beatrice's submission to her place in the autocratic order. "I will drag her, step by step, / Through infamies unheard of among men," resolves Francesco (IV. viii. 80-81), until "she shall become . . . to her own conscious self / All she appears to others / . . . A rebel to her father and her God" (IV. i. 85-90). Of their union a monstrosity will be born: "May it be a hideous likeness of herself . . . turning her mother's love to misery" (IV. i. 144-51). What is born of the unnatural coupling *is* an abnormal thing: parricide. More important than the forceful subversion of Beatrice's independent spirit that the act of incest represents is its result, since the murder, too, may be comprehended as a political act. When Beatrice lashes out, it is against the "power moulding my wretched lot," the entire hierarchy of fathers to whom she is subject. It is, in a word, insurrection.

In other words, if parent-child incest is a symbol of tyrannical oppression, then the parricide must represent the possibility of eliminating tyranny through violence. Although Shelley was always a persuasive and powerful spokesman for non-violent reform, he had gradually begun to conclude that, on occasion, armed resistance might be necessary. "No man," he wrote in 1812, "has a right to disturb the public peace by personally resisting the execution of a law, however bad."[26] He seemed to reiterate this position in 1819 in his **"Philosophical**

Essay on the Nature of Reform": "if the tyrants command their troops to fire upon [the assembled people] or cut them down unless they disperse, [their leader] will exhort them peaceably to risk the danger, and to expect without resistance the onset of the cavalry, and wait with folded arms the event of the fire of the artillery."[27] Shortly after the Peterloo Massacre occurred on 16 August 1819, Shelley had dashed off a poetic solution in **"The Mask of Anarchy"**:

> And if the tyrants dare
> Let them ride among you there,
> Slash, and stab, and maim, and hew,—
> What they like, that let them do.
>
> With folded arms and steady eyes,
> And little fear, and less surprise,
> Look upon them as they slay
> Till their rage has died away.

(*Works* [*The Complete Poetical Works of Percy Bysshe Shelley*], II, 338-39)

The discriminating ear will pick up a subtle threat running through the verses in various paraphrases like an implacable *basso continuo*: "Ye are many, they are few." Similarly a reluctant but clear-eyed Shelley had added to his essay: "The last resort of resistance is undoubtedly insurrection. The right of insurrection is derived from the employment of armed force to counteract the will of the nation."[28]

If he admitted violence could be countenanced, although only as a last resort and after passive resistance had failed, then Shelley's quasi-Biblical declaration in his preface to *The Cenci* is stunningly fatuous: "No person can be truly dishonored by the act of another, and the fit return to make the most enormous injuries is kindness and forbearance, and a resolution to convert the injurer from his dark passions by peace and love" (*Works*, II, 200). Did he truly mean that Beatrice should respond to her father with "kindness and forbearance" after he had raped her? In fact, her behavior in the first two acts embodies just that passivity he advocated, and its consequence is to enrage Cenci more and ultimately to drive him to his horrific act. On the one hand demonstrating the failure of passive resistance, the poet implies that Beatrice is nevertheless guilty twice over— for the parricide and, later, for lying about her role in the murder. She is a criminal then, or would be, if Shelley's admiration for her were not everywhere evident, particularly in the nobility of her demeanor and the beauty of the lines which she speaks as she faces death.

Perhaps the confusion arises from the desire, manifested in choosing to make incest the crux of his plot, to create neither criminal nor heroine but a special kind of political victim. To support this hypothesis, one must add to the **"Relation"** as source for *The Cenci* another essay, Shelley's **"An Address to the People on the**

Death of the Princess Charlotte" (1817). The demise of Liberty was his theme, its symbol the passing of the Princess, but its cause the execution of the leaders of the so-called Derbyshire Insurrection. Three workers, Jeremiah Brandreth, Isaac Ludlam, and William Turner, had been incited by a government-employed *provocateur* to march on Nottingham, where they were arrested. The government's tactic in exciting the workers to disobedience was to demoralize their opposition by a swift, brutal punishment: "On the 7th November, Brandreth, Turner, and Ludlam ascended the scaffold. We feel for Brandreth the less, because it seems he killed a man. But recollect who instigated him to the proceedings which led to murder."[29] Drawing on newspaper accounts, Shelley describes the execution scene: "These men were shut up in a horrible dungeon, for many months, with the fear of a hideous death and of everlasting hell thrust before their eyes. . . . What these sufferers felt shall not be said. But what must have been the long and various agony of their kindred may be inferred from Edward Turner, who, when he saw his brother dragged along the hurdle, shrieked horribly and fell into a fit, and was carried away like a corpse by two men. . . . Brandreth was calm and evidently believed the consequences of our errors were limited by that barrier [death]. Ludlam and Turner were full of fears, lest God should plunge them in everlasting fire."[30] It seems to me that Shelley, reading the **"Relation"** scarcely a year later, might have been struck by the similarity of Bernardo's collapse upon the execution of his family members, the anxiety of Lucretia and Giacomo as they faced the ax, and Beatrice's serenity in the same situation. More important, Beatrice's rape by her father and execution by the Church—the conflation of the two as her dual patrimony stressed throughout the play—parallels the provocation and retribution of the Derbyshire episode.

In other words, the statement "No person can be truly dishonored" was not sanctimony but warning, motivated by genuine alarm. Shelley could have anticipated how very inflammable Beatrice's example might be, especially to the smouldering anti-clerical factions in Italy and the anti-monarchical parties in England. Embracing these causes himself, he foresaw how readily such dissatisfaction could be exploited by the very agents of victimization and how the noblest, most justifiable rebellion might be defeated thereby. The oppressed must beware meeting violence with violence, lest, in succumbing to vengeance, they become pawns of power— lest they become, like Beatrice, victims.

IV

An international array of writers, Hawthorne, Guerrazzi, Niccolini, Landor, Stendhal, and the Marquis de Custine among them, employed the Cenci story as subject or symbol, many in ways that directly or indirectly acknowledge Shelley's precedent.[31] Less well-known to-day, however, is the popularity the image of Beatrice accrued in the visual arts. Her story, its Gothic horror and melancholy easily magnified in the quest for emotionally-charged themes, became a staple of Romantic iconography for the Italian School particularly. In my opinion, the quantity and kind of attention the image of Beatrice Cenci received in the visual arts is attributable to the incest motif in Shelley's drama.

There are basically two types of depictions: copies of the so-called Guido Reni portrait and representations of the events associated with her unhappy life and, especially, her death. Within the first group may be found the numberless engravings and canvases that were almost omnipresent in the Roman art market for nearly a century, all hyperbolically touted as duplicates taken directly from the original. In many ways, the most important of these reproductions is an engraving made to accompany Johann Kaspar Lavater's *Physiognomische Fragmente* (4 vols.; 1775-78) because the inscription gives the first identification of a previously unnamed head of a young girl in the Colonna collection as Beatrice and the artist as Guido Reni.[32] The ascription to Guido was not immediately accepted, for to *cognoscenti* of the Bolognese master the attribution seemed somewhat far-fetched. Claiming the appealingly mournful portrait to be of Beatrice, however, was instantly successful, and in 1786 Luigi Cunego became the first of a veritable host of graphic artists to publish "una stampa reppresentatante il rittrato della famosa nobil Donzella Beatrice Cenci Roman, che lascio la Testa supra un palco nel' anno 1599."[33] Perhaps it was Cunego's engraving that Shelley carried with him in Rome, although by the turn of the century several other artists were competing for the patronage the prints enjoyed.

For wealthy or more devoted admirers of the portrait, copies in oil were executed with equal frequency. Readers familiar with Hilda and Miriam, the protagonists of Hawthorne's *Marble Faun,* will not be surprised to learn that women artists, at that time frequently forced into the role of copyist, produced versions of the Cenci canvas (e. g., the copy by Augusta H. Saint-Gaudens). Established American painters such as Thomas Sully, Cephas Thompson, and Elihu Vedder also produced duplicates. Moreover, the tourist trade in copies of the painting apparently could provide a regular occupation: Bonfiglio's *Guide*—giving the studio address and thematic specialty of foreign and native painters in Rome for the convenience of prospective buyers—recognized two men solely for their Beatrice reproductions.[34] So plentiful did the patrons become that access to the original had to be curtailed; copies were then made from copies, a circumstance that accounts for the broad range of verisimilitude one finds in the portraits.

Of the second type of imagery associated with Beatrice—episodes taken from her life—favorite topics were

her trial and punishment. Only a handful of these works are currently known, even to specialists in the field, and then mostly by means of photographs. Still, some generalizations may be made, for the depictions are characteristically Romantic. For example, a propensity for fabricating biographies of the Old Masters, oftentimes with emphasis on the painter's love life, led to imaginative reconstructions of a painter's relationship with his model. Raphael's portrait of *La Fornarina* (c. 1516, Borghese Gallery, Rome), a baker's daughter presumed to be his mistress, was the basis of J. A. D. Ingres' several versions of the two embracing in the studio. Likewise, embedded in the legend that Guido took his likeness of Beatrice the night before her execution is implied the warmth of his appreciation for his beautiful sitter. Since the sitter's approaching death was also an issue, the erotic quotient is heightened by horror. It is probably no coincidence that Guido's alleged *Beatrice,* when it went to the Barberini collection at mid-century, hung in the gallery next to Raphael's *Fornarina.*

At least two paintings are directly drawn from Shelley's play. Francesco Hayez's *Il Cenci e la Figlia* (c. 1845; whereabouts unknown) illustrates the evil Count attacking his daughter in her bed, and Charles Robert Leslie's *Scene from Shelley's* The Cenci (1853) visualizes the ranting Francesco and his terrorized family. However, almost all contemporary references to representations of Beatrice, even the portrait copies, assume a relationship to Shelley's drama and frequently use quotations therefrom to bolster their emotional impact. An example that well illustrates this sympathetic association is the observation of American art critic Henry Tuckerman: "I paused long before two famous original paintings—Raphael's Fornarina and Guido's portrait of Beatrice Cenci. The one from the perfection displayed in its execution, the other from the melancholy history of its subject, are highly attractive."[35] He appends, without further explanation, the passage from **The Cenci** that begins with Beatrice's moan, "I am cut off from the only world I know. . . ."

All of the depictions of Beatrice fall within the larger genre of paintings devoted to heroines who prefer death to sexual violation. Lucretia, wife of Tarquin, for instance, who stabs herself after being raped by her husband's political rival, and Virginia, whose father stabs her to save her from a lustful ruler, were popular topics of Italian history painters. Beatrice was compared with these "Roman women of the heroic time, whose firmness she recalled while she surpassed their charms."[36] One difference—unremarked, as far as I can determine, at the time—is that Beatrice dies dishonored. She is resurrected as a heroine only after her death.

After the publication of Shelley's play, therefore, the number and variety of images of Beatrice dramatically increase. The trade in copies of Guido's portrait becomes virtually a mania after 1819; tellingly, this is accompanied by a noticeable mutation of sweet to sensual in Beatrice's physiognomy. In fact, all representations reveal to a greater or lesser degree a preoccupation with sexuality, a concern I believe to be inculcated by the incest motif in **The Cenci**. Does this situation mean that the great seriousness with which the poet approached the story and the tragedy he discerned therein was trivialized? In part, the answer is yes. His philosophical and political subtleties were easily overshadowed by the sensationalism of his plot and outweighed by the pathos of his characterizations. Nevertheless, in the sentimentalized visual treatment of Beatrice are potent iconographic implications which in particular manifest themselves in the comparison with Lucretia and Virginia. The deaths of Lucretia and Virginia brought about uprisings that drove out corrupt governments, since the sexual aggressor in each case had been a tyrant whose lasciviousness was the final outrage to his aggrieved subjects. As the intermittent political turmoil steadily worsened throughout the nineteenth century and nationalistic fervor concomitantly grew, Beatrice came to be regarded as a *potential* Lucretia or Virginia, the connection of Roman liberty with a sexually victimized yet heroic woman now assuming a prophetic note. An indication of the Italian public's attitude toward Beatrice was a proposal in 1872 to erect to her honor a monument inscribed with the following verse:

> Not cruel death,
> Not the ravished flower of youth,
> Not the denial of love's bliss, . . .
> These wrongs did not so grieve me as that my honorable name
> Was for long years defiled.
> Roman sisters
> Now that you are free so to do,
> Give again a sepulchre to my ashes
> And honor to my memory,
> So will you do service
> To eternal justice
> To the fatherland
> To me
> And to yourselves likewise.[37]

In Shelley's play the act of incest as a symbol constitutes a variation on the classic theme of Saturn devouring his children, an attempt to retain power by a monstrous act. The politically rebellious found tempting parallels between their own situation and Cenci's oppression by physical force. Did not their antagonists (the Papacy, the French, the Austrians, various Italian petty princes, depending on one's persuasion) make invidious use of their traditionally paternalistic relationship with the Italian people? The visually acute were quick to act on Shelley's example in transforming Beatrice from an historical figure to a politically-charged emblem. As a result, her pictorial import recalls that of Joan of Arc, whose story was also revived by artists and writers of the nineteenth century, especially when France had need of a symbol of nationalism and unity. Joan of Arc's execution for witchcraft in 1431 is literally rendered a martyrdom by her sanctification nearly five centuries later. Beatrice, whom Shelley conceived as a victim, became a secular martyr.

Notes

1. See Mary Shelley's notes to *The Cenci*, published in *The Complete Poetical Works of Percy Bysshe Shelley,* ed. George Edward Woodbury (Boston: Houghton Mifflin, 1948), II, 441-42. All references to *The Cenci* are to this edition.

2. Ibid., II, 469.

3. The most comprehensive account is Stuart Curran, *Shelley's* Cenci: *Scorpions Ringed with Fire* (Princeton: Princeton Univ. Press, 1970). See also E. S. Bates, *A Study of Shelley's Drama* The Cenci (New York: Columbia Univ. Press, 1908), and the chapter devoted to *The Cenci* in Kenneth Neill Cameron, *Shelley, the Golden Years* (Cambridge: Harvard Univ. Press, 1974).

4. See Barbara Groseclose, "A Portrait Not by Guido Reni of a Girl Who Is Not Beatrice Cenci," *Studies in Eighteenth Century Culture,* 11 (1981), 107-32.

5. *Works,* II, 202-03.

6. Shelley repeats this story in his Preface (*Works,* II, 202).

7. *Passages from the French and Italian Notebooks,* ed. Randall Stewart (New Haven: Yale Univ. Press, 1932), pp. 39-90.

8. See, for example, Carlo Tito Dalbono, *Storia de Beatrice Cenci e di suoi tempi con documenti inediti* (Naples: G. Nobili, 1864); Antonio Bertolotti, *Francesco Cenci e la Sua Famiglia,* 2nd ed. (Florence: Gazzetta d'Italia, 1879); Ilario Rinieri, *Beatrice Cenci* (Siena: Typ. Pontificia S. Bernardino, 1909); and Corrado Ricci, *Beatrice Cenci,* trans. Morris Bishop and Henry Logan Stuart (New York: Boni and Liveright, 1925), 2 vols.

9. *Works,* II, 1989-99. I should take the opportunity to correct here my error in "A Portrait Not by Guido Reni of a Girl Who Is Not Beatrice Cenci," as I state that the manuscript accounts were probably based on Muratori's 1749 *Annali d'Italia.* At the time I was writing, I was unaware of Truman Guy Steffen's article (see below, footnote 12) which dates extant manuscripts by watermarks; two (in the Strunk collection, Univ. of Texas) are seventeenth-century.

10. *Works,* II, 199.

11. *Works,* II, 462. The translator is not named.

12. Truman Guy Steffen, "Seven Accounts of the Cenci and Shelley's Drama," *Studies in English Literature 1500-1900,* 9 (1967), 601-18, surveys and dates seven extant manuscripts.

13. Paul Smith, "Restless Casuistry: Shelley's Composition of *The Cenci,*" *Keats-Shelley Journal,* 13 (1964), 80.

14. Cameron, p. 399; see also Steffen, p. 603.

15. Dalbono, Bertolotti, Rinieri, and Ricci all examine this issue; see also George Bowyer, *A Dissertation on the Statutes of the Cities of Italy; and a Translation of the Pleading of Prospero Farinaccio in Defense of Beatrice Cenci and her Relatives* (London: Richards, 1838), pp. 73ff.

16. Interestingly, as Smith notes (p. 82), Shelley "[condemned] Italian society for its passionate exculpation" of Beatrice although his own revisions of the story (Smith does not refer specifically to the rape) had the effect of partially justifying her action.

17. Letter to Peacock, July 1819, quoted in *Works,* II, 445.

18. Peter Thorslev, "Incest as Romantic Symbol," *Comparative Literature Studies,* 2 (1965), 41-58.

19. Cameron, p. 264, writes that Mary's "jealousy must have been directed with special force against Claire, for Shelley and Claire had either had an affair or came close to having one in 1815, following which Claire was ejected from the household amid 'a turmoil of passion and hatred.' In 1817 the 'Constantia' poems reveal a passionate interest in Claire and contain derogatory comments on Mary." An even-handed though inconclusive account is given in Richard Holmes, *Shelley the Pursuit* (New York: E. P. Dutton, 1975), pp. 468-74; however, Holmes adds on an appendix (pp. 482-84) that indicates his bewilderment on the subject. See also *The Journal of Claire Claremont,* ed. Marion Kingston Stocking (Cambridge: Harvard Univ. Press, 1968), p. 97.

20. Elizabeth Nitchie, "Mary Shelley's *Mathilda,*" *Studies in Philology,* extra ser., No. 3 (1959), p. 25, dates the work to the latter part of 1819.

21. In mourning for their daughter Clara, who died in Venice on 24 September 1818, a scant five months after the publication of *Frankenstein,* the Shelleys arrived in Rome on 20 November, residing there for much of the following year. On 7 June 1819, their son William Shelley died, the severity and propinquity of the two tragedies inducing in Mary a depression severe enough to alienate the couple briefly. See Carlos Baker, *Shelley's Major Poetry: The Fabric of a Vision* (Princeton: Princeton Univ. Press; 1948), pp. 287-91.

22. Laon and Cythna became, in *The Revolt of Islam,* childhood sweethearts rather than siblings, as Shelley's publisher resisted the incest motif. See especially Thorslev, pp. 50-52.

23. Cf. Cameron, p. 29: "When English society heard of this visit [in 1816] of Shelley, Mary, and Claire to Byron, a story spread (perhaps begun by Southey) of a 'league of incest' at Geneva." The term "incest" was presumably used because it was assumed that Shelley and Byron both were conducting affairs with the (half-) sisters. Cameron believes that Shelley's disclaimer of a personal knowledge of incest in the Preface to *Laon and Cythna* is the consequence of his knowledge of the Geneva rumors; see p. 621. See also Holmes, p. 543, on Samuel Taylor Coleridge's review of *The Revolt of Islam* in the *Quarterly* for April 1819. Coleridge made much of Shelley's "penchant for incest" and delved into his relationships with Harriet, Mary, and Claire.

24. Cf Curran, pp. 209-19, on the mounting of *The Cenci* by the Korsch Theater of Moscow in 1919-20; "The play was chosen and presented . . . for its political and social message. The raw denunciation of a corrupt ruling class . . . ends in Shelley's play without hope for release, except insofar as the individual human being is willing to stand in unheroic martyrdom rather than succumb to an unnatural and inhuman system. Russian revolutionaries . . . would find in Beatrice Cenci not Shelley's image of despair, but a heroic symbol of their struggle." Of interest for the light it may throw on Shelley's political perceptions, though the examination is of metaphysics, is James Rieger, "Shelley's Paterin Beatrice," *Studies in Romanticism,* 4 (1965), 169-84.

25. Cf. Rieger, p. 173: "The tragedy's great developmental irony is Beatrice's growing awareness . . . that Cenci, Clement, and Almighty God form a triple *entente.* Her father, *il Papa,* and *Pater Omnipotens* constitute a tacit hierarchy."

26. "A Declaration of Rights," in *Shelley's Prose or the Trumpet of a Prophecy,* ed. Daniel Lee Clark (Albuquerque: Univ. of New Mexico Press, 1954), p. 70.

27. Ibid., p. 257.

28. Ibid., p. 259.

29. Ibid., p. 168.

30. Ibid., p. 165.

31. Francesco Guerrazzi, *Beatrice Cenci, Storia del Secolo XVI* (Pisa: Typ. Vannuccini, 1854), comes closest to the political thrust of Shelley's drama, though his novel is mostly an anti-clerical diatribe

designed to muster public support for his own views. To my mind, Hawthorne's use of the Guido portrait of Beatrice as a symbol of "unconscious sin" in *The Marble Faun* (Boston: Ticknor and Field, 1860) most effectively parallels the spiritual complexities Shelley revealed. Louise K. Barnett, "American Novelists and the 'Portrait of Beatrice Cenci'," *New England Quarterly*, 53 (1980), 168-83, suggests the incest motif in Melville's *Pierre* is related to the author's knowledge of the Beatrice legend.

32. See also Charlotte Steinbrucker, *Lavaters Physiognomische Fragmente in Verhaltnis zur Bildenen Kunst* (Berlin: W. Bonngräbner, 1915), p. 51.

33. *Giornale delle Belle Arti per l'Anno MDCCLXXXVI*, No. 8 (February), p. 63.

34. See F. Saverio Bonfigli, *The Artistical Directory, or a Guide to the Studios in Rome with Much Supplementary Information* (Rome: Typ. legale, 1858).

35. *Italian Sketchbook* (Boston: Light and Stearns, 1837), p. 42.

36. Francis Alphonse Wey, *Rome* (London: Chapman and Hall, 1872), p. 61.

37. See Ricci, p. 272. The verses are said to have been composed by Francesco Guerrazzi.

Stuart M. Sperry (essay date fall 1986)

SOURCE: Sperry, Stuart M. "The Ethical Politics of Shelley's *The Cenci*." *Studies in Romanticism* 25, no. 3 (fall 1986): 411-27.

[*In the following essay, Sperry considers the moral dilemma inherent in Beatrice's decision to seek violent revenge.*]

I

Politics begins in the family, as Shelley well knew and as the title of **The Cenci** reminds us. Begun in Rome in May of 1819, the drama has intellectual and emotional roots that extend far back into the poet's career. As early as May 1811, we find him carrying on an argument with his friend, Thomas Jefferson Hogg, as to the reconcilability of law with private judgment and of politics with morality. Hogg's assertion, "that it is a duty to comply with the established laws of yr. country," is one the poet flatly denies. "Have you forgotten it," Shelley begins his letter, flaunting the aristocratic blazon of *noblesse oblige,* "have you forgotten that 'laws were not made for men of honor'—? Your memory may fail, it is human," he goes on, in his en-

gaging way of running roughshod over his opponent. However the arguments he adduces mount up tellingly as he proceeds. First there is the universal relativity of law, the fact that, as Byron might later discover, what was "a crime in England" was "praiseworthy at Algiers." More interesting are those cases where one can perceive conflicting obligations, where it is necessary to draw a "distinction between two different kind of duties, to *both* of which it is requisite that virtue should adapt itself." Then, just to add a further complication, he adds: "What constitutes real virtue[:] motive or consequence?" This whole range of reasoning brings him before the end of his letter to a consideration of Sophocles' Antigone, the heroine who stands as the clearest archetype to the character who was to become his own Beatrice Cenci. "But is the *Antigone* immoral"? he exclaims to Hogg. "Did she wrong when she acted in direct in noble [sic] violation of the laws of a prejudiced society"? Then, gathering fresh impetus from the force of the Sophoclean example to resume his high-handed ways, he brushes Hogg aside with amusing irony: "You will I know have the candor to acknowledge that yr. premise will not stand & I now *most perfectly* agree with you that political affairs are quite distinct from morality, that they cannot be united."[1]

The gordian knot of issues thus neatly severed by the precocious teenaged controversialist was, of course, to return to haunt him throughout his career. The youthful Shelley could hope to keep the bright realm of ethical absolutes protected from the tainted arena of worldly politics. Still was it not necessary to understand, perhaps even compromise with, the one in order to carry out the eternal dictates of the other? Moreover Shelley found his reasoning, though always acute, less decisive against the arguments of older and more experienced thinkers like Robert Southey and William Godwin. Already he has come round to a more complicated view of the problem in writing to Elizabeth Hitchener early the next year:

> Southey says Expediency ought to [be] made the ground of politics but not of morals. I urged that the most fatal error that ever happened in the world was the seperation of political and ethical science, that the former ought to be entirely regulated by the latter, as whatever was a right criterion of action for an individual must be so for a society which was but an assemblage of individuals, 'that politics were morals more comprehensively enforced.'—Southey did not think the reasoning conclusive.

"He has," Shelley went on to complain, "a very happy knack when truth goes against him of saying, 'Ah! when you are as old as I am you will think with me'—this talent he employed in the above instance" (**Letters [of Percy Bysshe Shelley]** I: 223).

The justification for tempering ethical ideals with expediency in order to achieve practical results was again an issue that surfaced almost from the start of Shelley's personal acquaintance with William Godwin. It is clearly Godwin whom Shelley has in mind in writing again to Elizabeth Hitchener the next month:

> The persons with whom I have got acquainted, approve of my principles, & think the truths of the equality of man, the necessity of a reform and the probability of a revolution undeniable. But they differ from the mode of my enforcing these principles, & hold *expediency* to be necessary in politics in as much as it is employed in its utmost latitude by the enemies of innovation:—I hope to convince them of the contrary of this. To expect that evil will produce good, or falsehood generate truth is almost as rational as to conceive of a patriot king or a sincere Lord of the Bedchamber.
>
> (*Letters* I: 263)

How was it possible to act in the spirit of moderation and compromise, the need for which Southey and Godwin were continuously urging, and preserve the integrity of one's ideals? Shelley's brief intervention in the politics of the Irish question provided no conclusive test, for the poet succeeded in speaking his mind forthrightly only to withdraw from the scene in deference to Godwin's increasingly agitated protests that the counsels he was urging would prove disastrous. The conflict between commitment to ethical idealism and the seeming demands of political reality remained a potential plaguespot in the back of his conscience throughout his early years. As he wrote to Elizabeth Hitchener toward the end of 1811, "what conflict of a frank mind is more terrible than the balance between two opposing importances of morality—this is surely the only wretchedness to which a mind who only acknowledges virtue it's [sic] master can feel" (*Letters* I: 149).

Now this moral problem, the potential opposition between an uncompromising idealism and a practical expediency, is the very issue that, realized dramatically within a deeply moving human situation, he returned some years later to reconsider in *The Cenci*. The fundamental issue upon which the drama turns, to put it simply, is: was Beatrice wrong in planning the murder of her father, Count Franceso Cenci; or was she rather justified in following, like Antigone, the dictates of her conscience and in adopting violent means to relieve both her family and herself from the toils of an insupportable tyranny? The dilemma is one Shelley deliberately prepares for his audience from the outset when he declares in his "Preface" to the play:

> Undoubtedly, no person can be truly dishonoured by the act of another; and the fit return to make to the most enormous injuries is kindness and forbearance, and a resolution to convert the injurer from his dark passions by peace and love. Revenge, retaliation, atonement, are pernicious mistakes. If Beatrice had thought in this manner she would have been wiser and better; but she would never have been a tragic character.[2]

The passage underlines the terms of an inflexible moral imperative, one Beatrice violates in carrying out the murder of her father. What, however, of the practical reality of her situation, the terror disguised within the brief, unobtrusive phrase, "the most enormous injuries"? The threat of incestuous rape which her father first holds over her and then, we are led to believe, actually carries out during the course of the play is simply too terrible for her to endure. The violation, as Shelley movingly presents it, is not simply physical but psychological, one she has no means of defending herself against and that deprives her of all necessary self-possession, driving her to the point of madness. Isolated by the political corruption of the society, church, and state that surrounds her, Beatrice seems to have no other course than to adopt the violent means of her persecutors. Shelley deliberately centers his drama around an ethical problem, a fact in no way diminished by his disclaimer in the "Preface" that "I have endeavoured as nearly as possible to represent the characters as they probably were, and have sought to avoid the error of making them actuated by my own conceptions of right or wrong, false or true" (240), a statement that bears most on the issue of dramatic probability. Clearly he was drawn to Beatrice Cenci not simply by the Guido Reni portrait and the legendary account of her character and fortitude but by the moral problematics of her situation. James D. Wilson is right when he argues that "The key to understanding *The Cenci* lies in the extent to which we hold Beatrice responsible for her actions,"[3] even if the answer to that question is hardly the whole of Shelley's play. The "Preface" sets forth an ideal of human forbearance; yet as the play proceeds and forces us not simply to observe but both sympathize and judge, we ask ourselves, is there no limit to what Beatrice must endure?

Despite the fact that *The Cenci* crystallizes, as we have seen, political and ethical problems of such long standing in Shelley's thought, it is a remarkable fact that there exists today no consensus as to how we are to interpret his drama with regard to the issues it raises. The older view, the groundwork for which was laid in Carlos Baker's pioneering study of the poet's development,[4] is best expressed in a well-balanced and trenchant essay of Robert F. Whitman. "If Beatrice is admirable," Whitman writes, "it is in spite of, not because of, her act of rebellion. By taking what she thought to be the law of God into her own hands, she acted as a brave and desperate human being—but she was wrong."[5] Shelley's drama lends itself to a more contemporary reading, however, and Beatrice emerges from Stuart Curran's later, full-length study of the play as an existential heroine. Faced with the necessity of acting within an illogical universe so corrupt as to be morally absurd, Beatrice has no recourse but to attempt to establish an existential order of her own, and there is neither justification nor point in condemning her in terms of simple ethical platitudes.[6] The two précis I have provided hardly do justice to the detailed and rea-

THE CENCI

A TRAGEDY

IN FIVE ACTS

BY

PERCY BYSSHE SHELLEY

SECOND EDITION

LONDON
C AND J OLLIER VERE STREET BOND STREET
1821

Title page for the 1821 edition of Shelley's The Cenci.

soned arguments they summarize. The differing viewpoints indicate, however, the extent of disagreement over the essential outlook of the play and how it invites or requires us to assess its heroine and her dilemma. The two extremes of reasoning also define a spectrum of opinion within which any number of other judgments arrange themselves, some inclining toward one pole, some toward the other.

The questions I have touched on are the more material for the reason that they involve the whole logic of Shelley's career and the relationship *The Cenci* bears to *Prometheus Unbound* between the third and fourth acts of which the former play was written. In shifting from the style of Greek tragedy to that of Jacobean revenge drama, Shelley was also moving, partly with his wife Mary's urging, from the esoteric to the exoteric mode with the hope of writing a play that might actually be produced on the London stage and win him popular acclaim and financial reward. But there are also overtones of something like a principle of psychological compensation involved in the remarkable transition. Having celebrated the triumph of love and the millennium in

the rarefied atmosphere of *Prometheus Unbound* and its "beautiful idealisms of moral excellence" ("Preface" 135), he was now impelled to depict a far darker scene, what he described in his letter dedicating *The Cenci* to Leigh Hunt as the "sad reality" (237) reflected in the despairing plight of a virtuous heroine pressed beyond the limits of human endurance. If, by bringing him back down to earth, *The Cenci* served Shelley as an emotional counterirritant, does it, however, also represent a reweighting of moral emphasis? Given his dedication throughout his career to the principle of love, it is hardly likely, for that matter hardly decent, to suppose that, having dramatized the victory of the godlike Prometheus, he should now want to draw down the deprecation of an audience upon a human and fallible heroine for her "error." If the play teaches, it does so in a way that transcends any such kind of simple moral demonstration. Viewing the extraordinary pattern of similitude in dissimilitude that links *Prometheus Unbound* and *The Cenci,* Earl R. Wasserman, the most distinguished modern commentator on the two works, is quick to warn that "it would be misleading to read them merely as exactly opposite sides of the same moral coin";[7] but the uneasy juxtaposition of his "merely" and "exactly" may leave one without much confidence as to the proper balance to strike between them. In moving from *Prometheus Unbound* to *The Cenci,* Shelley was shifting his perspective from the immutable and ideal to the temporal and actual as he does throughout so much of his work, like *The Revolt of Islam,* where the seeming defeat of Laon and Cythna in the world of mortality is framed by the eternal Temple of the Spirit from which the lovers depart and where they are triumphantly reunited at the end. The two perspectives are quite different, but there is no necessity to assume any kind of incompatibility between them. Beyond this easy, partly familiar correlation, however, what most strikes one, despite the curious pattern of analogies that link the two plays, is the total difference in their emotional dynamics, centered, perhaps, in their quite different notions of catharsis. If in *The Cenci* Shelley employs certain Promethean themes, he does so in an entirely different way and with a quite different effect than in the earlier composition.

The special problems *The Cenci* still raises might seem to justify one more full-length critical reading of the drama. Some works of literature lend themselves to explication, however, in terms of a single crux of such importance that it crystallizes in itself the vital interpretive problems; and *The Cenci* is a play of this kind. The crux I refer to is the most obvious and dramatic piece of irony in the play: the arrival of the Pope's legate, Savella, with a warrant for Cenci's arrest and instant execution only moments after Beatrice and her hirelings have carried out the Count's murder near the end of Act IV. The timing of Savella's totally unexpected and seemingly fortuitous appearance is so striking as to assume, beyond any other element in the play, the aura of deliberate dramatic contrivance. The sense of irony the legate's entry generates is so powerful that, given what we know of Shelley's craftsmanship, it is hard not to sense that the poet saw the effect as somehow vital to the significance of his play. But just how are we to interpret the irony? It is significant that critics of the play, differing on so much else, have found themselves in sharpest disagreement on this single issue. For some older commentators, the irony served to underline Beatrice's error in adopting violent means to do away with her father by showing that, had she only waited, the course of justice would have been taken out of her hands.[8] For others, quite to the contrary, Savella's arrival is the culminating absurdity in a cruel and illogical world where the only course open to Beatrice is to seek to impose a moral order of her own and where she is punished for bringing about the very end that society itself has at last belatedly ordained.[9] The two analyses are closely similar in their perception of the irony but diametrically opposed in the conclusions they draw from it. Even Earl Wasserman largely begs the question when he warns that "the reader falls into a moral trap" if he interprets Savella's arrival as "an intentional cosmic irony"; for, he goes on, "To think, as many readers have thought, that this is cosmic irony is to assume that the Count's crimes *should* have been entrusted to the law, an assumption that contradicts the ethics upon which the drama is built."[10] Assuming the reader avoids the moral trap Wasserman describes, however, how does the episode influence us? If Savella's arrival is not an instance of cosmic irony, what kind of irony is it and what are its effect and purpose?

Savella's unexpected arrival and the questions it raises crystallize the ethical problem Shelley sought to treat in *The Cenci*. To see this fully it is necessary to trace some of the major tensions of the play back to the psychological roots it shares with *Prometheus Unbound*. As critics have partly observed, there is a train of Promethean imagery that runs throughout *The Cenci*, while the struggle of wills between Jupiter and Prometheus in certain ways resembles that between Count Cenci and his daughter. Beyond this, however, there is a deeper logic underlying the two plays, one that finds its source in Shelley's peculiar fascination with the Promethean situation and the major ironies investing it. We know that Prometheus from the start possesses, in his knowledge of Zeus's fatal marriage to Thetis and the offspring destined to depose the tyrant, the secret that is the key to Zeus's tenure and the safety of his reign. Zeus's intent, therefore, is not merely to punish Prometheus for his theft of the fire but to crush him, to break his will, to force him to reveal the secret that will render the monarch eternally secure. Prometheus's role, correspondingly, is to defy the ty-

rant's power, to endure, and to persevere until the arrival of the inevitable hour that is destined to liberate him and to bring his assailant's downfall.

Now this particular relationship between the two antagonists sets up a tension that is the essence of the Promethean situation and that Shelley was quick to grasp. For in one way the hero has Zeus already in his power; in one sense his victory is assured. All that is required of him is the perseverance necessary to hold out until the arrival of the promised hour hidden, in Shelley's phrase, in that "far goal of Time" (*Prometheus Unbound* III. iii. 174). Indeed, his failure is virtually unthinkable since the survival of mankind and of human hope depends upon him. All he needs is patience, primarily in the older sense of the word: the ability to suffer, to endure. Granted this, he cannot fail.

Yet look at his position from the opposite perspective: how long must Prometheus, how long can he, endure? Whether one contemplates the horrors of the eagle and the pain of avian dismemberment or the more sophisticated psychological tortures of historical awareness that Shelley, in his adaptation of the myth, obliges his hero to undergo, how is it possible for Prometheus to hold on? All these agonies are, moreover, subservient to a crueller aspect of his position: the fact that while the *end* of his travail is determined, its *extent* is by no means fixed. Aeschylus's hero declares that the term of his suffering is ten thousand years; and later he tells Io that he will be rescued by offspring (that is to say Hercules) from the thirteenth generation of her descendants. For Shelley's hero, however, there is not even this kind of distant fixity, as Mercury's tormenting questioning reveals: "Once more answer me: / Thou knowest not the period of Jove's power?" To Prometheus's resolute rejoinder, "I know but this, that it must come," Mercury goes on: "Alas! / Thou canst not count thy years to come of pain?" (I. 411-14). The taunting questions prepare the way for a truly frightening train of speculation that takes us to the heart of the peculiar terror of the Promethean situation:

MERCURY.

                                       Yet pause, and plunge
Into Eternity, where recorded time,
Even all that we imagine, age on age,
Seems but a point, and the reluctant mind
Flags wearily in its unending flight
Till it sink, dizzy, blind, lost, shelterless;
Perchance it has not numbered the slow years
Which thou must spend in torture, unreprieved?

                                       (I. 416-23)

Mercury's argument employs the logic of the asymptote in which time and eternity, though theoretically distinct, come to appear for all practical purposes indistinguishable. Of what use to Prometheus is the promise of an end to his ordeal if he has not the means of envisioning it, of foreseeing its actual place in the future as the way of measuring the diminishing time that divides him from it?

Shelley's grasp of the Promethean situation derives from his understanding of the particular dynamics of its terror. The imagination of the reader or spectator is violently propelled back and forth between two opposing poles of speculation. Given the perpetuation of the *status quo*, Prometheus's continued endurance, his ultimate triumph, however distant, is preordained and assured, so that any surrender must seem to us virtually unthinkable, especially since all human hope depends upon his victory. Yet this movement of mind is immediately countered by another rush of the imagination when we suddenly realize the immensity of time and suffering that must, at least potentially, elapse before the arrival of the promised end, a burden that defeats our own ability even to imagine, not to say endure, it. How can Prometheus fail to triumph? How can he possibly hold out against the terrible sufferings that beset him? The paradox that so forcibly grips our minds is driven home by another even more terrifying chain of speculation. Let us suppose that, after centuries of defiance, Prometheus's endurance finally breaks so that he yields to Jupiter the fatal secret only to discover that his promised deliverance was immediately at hand—a day, an hour, perhaps even only a minute beyond the point of his capitulation. What an intimidating hypothesis, one that thrusts itself on us even while we reject it as intolerable! Yet the contingency is the very one Shelley dramatizes at the turning point of *The Cenci* with the arrival of Savella.

Prometheus Unbound portrays the advent of the millennium through the triumph of a hero of godlike capacities as an ideal vision of what is potentially achievable if only in the reaches of futurity. In *The Cenci* Shelley was moved to trace, by way of contrary reaction, the undoing of a virtuous but intensely human heroine who, representing the Promethean ideal, was to fail, partly on account of the overwhelming force of oppression and partly through the vulnerability of her human nature, a drama producing that keen sense of loss we customarily associate with great tragedy and which *Prometheus* [*Unbound*] necessarily lacks. It is almost as if Shelley, having depicted the victory of Prometheus, now felt himself drawn to the mortal Io, the maiden whom the hero comforts in the latter part of Aeschylus's play but whom he is unable to save from the terror of Hera's dreadful persecution.[11] In the visionary and triumphant drama the possibility of heroic failure, if never inconceivable, is deliberately suppressed. What, however, of those human souls less fortified, less determined than Prometheus who might fail where he was destined to succeed? How, as a matter of practical eth-

ics, were they to be seen and ultimately judged? In thinking about the two plays and their common relationship to the myth, it is important to recognize how much Shelley, while introducing the subtler psychological torments of Mercury, deliberately eschewed in his *Prometheus* the primitive violence that characterizes the primeval legend. The point emerges with some clarity if we compare Shelley's play with the work of his contemporary, the painter Henry Fuseli, whose treatment of the bound Prometheus has that nightmare quality characteristic of the artist at his best.[12] The bird—eagle or vulture—is lurking and obscene, nor do we require the insights of depth psychology to sense, as the bird forces open the god's thigh with its talons, how much Fuseli has taken the liver as an obvious euphemism in a way that goes straight to the roots of the male ego. In Shelley's *Prometheus* this aspect of the hero's ordeal is never treated. In *The Cenci* the genital threat is not merely explicit but overpowering. It is Beatrice's ability to endure everything except sexual violation that explains her collapse.

To understand how much *The Cenci,* and in particular the Savella episode, is grounded in the Prometheus myth is not of itself to resolve the controversies that, as we have seen, surround the episode's significance or, for that matter, the interpretation of the drama. As we find her at the outset of the play, Beatrice Cenci is a maiden of exceptional fortitude and courage, defiant before the threats of her father and a tower of support to her beleaguered mother and younger brother. She is, in fact, a kind of feminine counterpart to Prometheus transposed to a domestic situation that is no less terrifying for the absolute power and fiendish tyranny exercised by her father. Just as Jupiter is intent to break Prometheus's will, so Cenci is intent to break his daughter's; only he knows by intuition and exults in the sure weapon of his success. For Count Cenci possesses one notable advantage over Jupiter: a father's insight into the nature of his daughter. Cenci knows she cannot withstand the ordeal of being sexually forced. If Beatrice Cenci possesses a tragic flaw, it is her virginity or, more exactly, her idealization of her virginity, as the center of her moral life and nature. It is the element essential to her sense of her own integrity as a human being. Shelley brings to his study of Beatrice's anguish a sympathy and psychological insight that quite transcend the few celebrated but meretricious treatments in the fiction of the earlier century. It was, indeed, his hope that the genuine seriousness of his moral purpose and the delicacy of his handling would palliate the drama's more sensational aspects and permit its presentation at Covent Garden, a hope that was disappointed when the subject was found objectionable and his play rejected.

I have said that Beatrice's tragic flaw is her idealization of her own virginity, a statement that implies an element of moral condemnation. But how else are we to take the major ethical declaration of the "Preface" to the play, which, as we have seen, Shelley himself applies specifically to his heroine, that "Revenge, retaliation, atonement, are pernicious mistakes"? From the outset of the drama Shelley succeeds in engaging our sympathies strongly in the plight of his heroine. At the opening of the third act she staggers wildly on stage towards her mother having been violated for the first time by her father:

> How comes this hair undone?
> Its wandering string must be what blind me so,
> And yet I tied it fast.—O, horrible!
> The pavement sinks under my feet! The walls
> Spin round! . . .
> . . . My God!
> The beautiful blue heaven is flecked with blood!
>
> (III. i. 6-10, 12-13)

By the fifth act, when the persecution of her father, condoned and extended by the authorities of state and church, has run its full course, the figure of violation recurs, but now as an image of desolation and terror enveloping the universe:

> If there should be
> No God, no Heaven, no Earth in the void world;
> The wide, grey, lampless, deep, unpeopled world!
> If all things then should be . . . my father's spirit,
> His eye, his voice, his *touch* surrounding me;
> The atmosphere and breath of my dead life!
>
> (v. iv. 57-62; my emphasis)

For all this Shelley's drama never lets us forget, as Beatrice becomes gradually drawn into the conspiracy to murder her father, the precepts of forbearance and non-violence dramatized in *Prometheus* and reaffirmed in the "Preface" to *The Cenci*, a standard by which she must be ultimately judged. As a part of the conspirators' first unsuccessful attempt to destroy the Count on his way to the Castle of Petrella, Beatrice describes the huge rock which she suggests can be rolled down to crush him as he passes through a ravine beneath:

> . . . there is a mighty rock,
> Which has, from unimaginable years,
> Sustained itself with terror and with toil
> Over a gulph, and with the agony
> With which it clings seems slowly coming down;
> Even as a wretched soul hour after hour,
> Clings to the mass of life; yet clinging, leans;
> And leaning, makes more dark the dread abyss
> In which it fears to fall: beneath this crag
> Huge as despair, as if in weariness,
> The melancholy mountain yawns.
>
> (III. i. 247-57)

The stone never descends, for Count Cenci passes by the intended spot an hour too soon. Ironically the lines describe Beatrice herself as a kind of failing Prometheus, slowly giving way to the insupportable weight of her miseries as they drag her down into despair.

Borrowing a device of the Elizabethan history play, Shelley partly reverses the balance of our sympathies in the latter portion of his drama. We see the Count on his deathbed, in appearance like the gracious Duncan:

> an old and sleeping man;
> His thin grey hair, his stern and reverent brow,
> His veined hands crossed on his heaving breast,
> And the calm innocent sleep—
>
> (IV. iii. 9-12)

whom even the hired assassins Olimpio and Marzio, at first dare not molest. Throughout the play, we may admire Beatrice's strength of character; but we are also appalled, near the end, as we watch her brazenly lie to her judges and mercilessly browbeat the pain-crippled Marzio into retracting his confession so that he dies upon the rack. In entertaining the malign suggestions of her treacherous lover, Orsino, in joining the ranks of the conspirators and first condoning the murder of her father, then urging the murder of her father, she in fact adopts the violence and absolutism of his ways. Nor can we escape the irony that in the end she becomes her father's child in a way she was not at the outset of the play. He triumphs not by despoiling her of her virginity but by corrupting her deeper integrity, by inducing her to believe that she can escape injuries that appear to her intolerably monstrous only by assuming his power and spirit, by becoming one with the very being she detests. The fact that at the last she is unwilling or unable to see the way she has been in fact perverted only makes the essence of her tragedy the more compelling.

II

It remains to examine the peculiar nature of the catharsis *The Cenci* produces and its means for doing so. Shelley's drama of divided sympathies achieves its power of ethical realization by the way it succeeds in placing the reader or spectator directly on the horns of that dilemma at the heart of the Promethean situation, the situation best crystallized in *The Cenci* by the arrival of Savella. Like Earl Wasserman, I find the central statement on the moral problem of the play in the part of the "Preface" where Shelley writes:

> It is in the restless and anatomizing casuistry with which men seek the justification of Beatrice, yet feel that she has done what needs justification; it is in the superstitious horror with which they contemplate alike her wrongs and their revenge; that the dramatic character of what she did and suffered, consists.
>
> (240)

The statement is difficult and condensed, and the psychological process, the movement of imagination to which it refers, demands elucidation. Let us consider the conflicting and alternative judgments the passage contemplates: on the one hand murder, parricide; the most heinous of crimes; the betrayal of one's begetter to whom, as the source of our being, honor and obedience are naturally due. Yet weigh against this our revulsion at incestuous rape, a violation, moreover, that is deliberately meditated as the culminating cruelty against an innocent child who merits love and not dishonor. Caught up in the emotional dialectics of the predicament, the imagination of the reader is propelled back and forth between two sets of ethical imperatives in the effort to establish some preponderance between them, in the attempt, that is, to justify the one enormity by the other, only to find the task impossible. The effort of mind is both "superstitious" and "pernicious" not only because, driven by some of the deepest guilts and fears of the human psyche, it is profoundly irrational in origin but because at the same time it seeks a carefully reasoned resolution of the "either/or" kind to the human dilemma confronting it.

Paradoxically, it is precisely out of this struggle of the imagination, erring though it may be, that the play's catharsis—ethical and profoundly emotional—arises. Here again I turn to Wasserman who in his analysis of the drama has shown how Shelley deliberately draws the reader into a situation that excites "pernicious casuistry" but does so with an artifice the poet elsewhere describes as "sublime casuistry" and for a deliberate moral end.[13] That aim, as Wasserman goes on to declare, is self-knowledge, the knowledge of ourselves, the highest kind of knowledge tragedy can impart. Yet Wasserman's discussion of such realization as it arises in and through our understanding of Beatrice's example seems curiously judicial and impassive. Thus he argues that the play brings us to an understanding that "Inherent purity of character can coexist with moral error; and, since sublime casuistry reveals that error cannot be reconciled with the purity, that purity is unaltered by the error." What follows for Wasserman is our realization that Beatrice's "moral nature has not been corrupted by her acts; she has been 'thwarted'—turned aside—from it, but it persists." Moreover "we misread," he goes on to add, "if we believe it a sign of her corruption that after the crime she can say, 'The spirit which doth reign within these limbs / Seems strangely undisturbed' (IV. iii. 63-64)."[14]

Through his grasp of Shelley's skeptical methodology, Wasserman has, I think, seen more deeply into the play than any other critic, and his discussion is one to which I am considerably indebted. Yet his scholastic determination to preserve a purity of ethical distinction has led him to neglect the emotional dynamics of the work and the crucial role they play in determining the drama's effect and meaning. From the time when we first see her bravely defy her father's tyranny to the end when, with different feelings, we watch her excoriate her judges and prepare herself for execution seemingly in complete conviction of her own innocence, we are deeply involved in and moved by Beatrice. The moral and emotional catharsis of the play proceeds out of this sympathetic identification and, as we have seen, from our struggle to reconcile our inescapable recognition of the way she has usurped her father's violence with our abhorrence of the forces driving her to it as her only means of deliverance. Such is the power of the dilemma in which Shelley places the spectator, so traumatic our predicament, that its effect is ultimately to force us to see the necessity of moving beyond a conventional standard of ethical judgment, based on counterpoise and calculation, to one that is more difficult and complex but also necessary and humane. It is to urge the transcendence of the moral imperative of love. As Shelley wrote in his review of Godwin's novel, *Mandeville,* comparing it to *Caleb Williams,* "there is no character like Falkland, whom the author, with that sublime casui[s]try which is the parent of toleration and forbearance, persuades us personally to love, while his actions must forever remain the theme of our astonishment and abhorrence."[15]

In her next to last speech in the play Beatrice turns to her younger brother, Bernardo, to exclaim:

> One thing more, my child,
> For thine own sake be constant to the love
> Thou bearest us; and to the faith that I,
> Though wrapped in a strange cloud of crime and shame,
> Lived ever holy and unstained.
>
> (v. iv. 145-49)

As we hear these parting words pronounced in such a solemn and authoritative way, a number of conflicting thoughts run through us. Is Beatrice mad? Is she simply self-deceived? Is she, rather, clinging to the pretense of innocence necessary to sustain her to the end of her ordeal? Or is she speaking the literal truth? These questions, which are not easy to separate one from another, force themselves upon us and demand some kind of resolution. Beatrice, we know, *has* erred. She has committed an act of retaliation. She has been guilty, in the terms Shelley himself sets out in the "Preface," of a "pernicious mistake." Yet this line of reasoning is not, by itself, adequate to our understanding of her plight. The full sense of her tragedy lies, I think, in our recognition of the fact that she has been so wrenched by her injuries that, whether we consider her mad or sane, she has lost the ability to judge of her own situation. It is as if the searing pain of her violation has cauterized her other faculties, leaving her oblivious to everything but the burning sense of her injuries and the trauma of her father's touch. This deeper wound to her psychological and moral equilibrium is perhaps the worst that can befall a character on the stage, a condition that traditional approaches to the ethics of tragedy are reluctant to admit. In arraigning Beatrice before her judges, in forcing us to adjudicate between her lies and their hypocrisy, Shelley places us in an intolerable situation. It is a strategy deliberately contrived to compel us to recognize the bankruptcy of conventional kinds of ethical discrimination, to force upon us the necessity of ascending to a higher level of moral awareness. It is to invite, indeed require, us to condemn Beatrice's actions unblinkingly and to love her (an act incorporating but transcending mere forgiveness) simultaneously. Shelley's reasoning, needless to say, will strike many of his critics as ethical relativism of a sort both sentimental and dangerous. Nevertheless I have no doubt that he regarded the moral recognition of his play truer to the underlying spirit of Christianity than the sacrilegious politics of false piety and self-interest he everywhere exposes. One might add that in the way it both manipulates and educates the emotions of its viewers, his drama makes its point with a characteristic ferocity of logic.

Throughout *The Cenci* Shelley maintains a delicate balance between commitment to unchanging ethical principles and a recognition of the way our judgment is actually shaped and formed by the human drama that unfolds before us on the stage. His play suggests both permanent ideals of conduct and the way those ideals can appear to alter under the pressure of human circumstance. In her speech just before the one last cited, at a point where hopes have been raised by Bernardo's last-minute appeal to the Pope, Beatrice exclaims:

> O, trample out that thought! Worse than despair,
> Worse than the bitterness of death, is hope:
> It is the only ill which can find place
> Upon the giddy, sharp and narrow hour
> Tottering beneath us.

> (v. iv. 97-101)

The still possible arrival of some new Savella, this time with a warrant for release, together with Beatrice's allusion to the fateful hour confronting them, put us in mind once again of the Promethean situation. Her speech makes clear that what we are beholding is something more terrible, even, than a failed Prometheus. What we are witnessing is a radical perversion, at least in Beatrice's mind, of the principle of hope, the extinction of the vital Promethean spark essential to mankind's redemption. In Shelley's ethics hope is necessarily the cardinal virtue (except in so far as it is subsumed within the greater power of love). Hope alone can provide the resolution necessary to await the promised hour when the tide of evil ultimately must reverse itself—the expectation that gives man the courage to last out the term of his ordeal. Brutalized by anguish and repeated disappointment, however, Beatrice has come to see hope as not simply fruitless but as its very opposite, "the only ill," "worse than despair." If it serves only to draw out endlessly the period of human suffering, hope is an unpardonable self-deception. In the way

she steels herself against the temptation to yield once again to the most instinctive of all human impulses, we sense the dreadful change that has overcome her. It is this more awful kind of capitulation, or derangement, that Shelley asks us to judge and understand in *The Cenci.*

If, as I have argued, the important moral issues Shelley raises in his play cannot be finally settled in terms of abstract principles alone but are shaped and informed by the drama of the play itself and the way it determines our attitude toward Beatrice, then the ending of the final act and the way, in particular, in which she goes to her death emerge as crucial. One can recall Mary Shelley's judgment that "The Fifth Act is a masterpiece. It is the finest thing [Shelley] ever wrote, and may claim proud comparison not only with any contemporary, but preceding, poet. The varying feelings of Beatrice are expressed with passionate, heart-reaching eloquence."[16] It is above all Beatrice's final speech, the last in the play, delivered before she steps forth to execution, that best substantiates Mary Shelley's judgment and that marks a high point of Shelley's dramatic genius. We live in a day of modern directorial practice, the art of lending old plays new emphasis. Change and reinterpretation are no doubt essential. Nevertheless it is disconcerting to imagine how quickly one could destroy through misemphasis the delicate balance of sympathy and ironic awareness Beatrice creates in us in the brief speech in which she bids the Cardinal Camillo and her mother a final farewell:

> Give yourself no unnecessary pain,
> My dear Lord Cardinal. Here, Mother, tie
> My girdle for me, and bind up this hair
> In any simple knot; aye, that does well.
> And yours I see is coming down. How often
> Have we done this for one another; now
> We shall not do it any more. My Lord,
> We are quite ready. Well, 'tis very well.

> (v. iv. 158-65)

Our attention is caught by the imagery of knotting and untying and of Beatrice's hair, the metaphor Shelley uses throughout with great delicacy for his heroine's virginity, on which, as we have seen, the construction of her character depends. The scene moves us with its domesticity and quiet pathos: mother and daughter providing for each other the common services they will never again exchange. At the same time we are struck by the muted sarcasm of her words to Camillo, "Give yourself no unnecessary pain, / My dear Lord Cardinal," and her tone of domination toward Lucretia, "Here, Mother." In her self-assurance the woman is summed up in all her strength of character and all her weakness as she moves together with her parent toward her death with her insistent "Well, 'tis very well." For we know it is *not* well. The tragedy of Beatrice Cenci is not her physical undoing but the violation of her spirit and her mind. It lies in an ultimate failure of will and endurance that is the more compelling for the reason that we are made to comprehend it so completely. If in **Prometheus Unbound** Shelley left us a model of heroic resolution to admire, he gave us in Beatrice a heroine whose failure must move us to compassion and love.

Notes

1. *The Letters of Percy Bysshe Shelley,* ed. Frederick L. Jones (Oxford: Clarendon, 1964) I: 80-82. The edition is hereafter cited as *Letters* in the text.

2. *Shelley's Poetry and Prose,* ed. Donald H. Reiman and Sharon B. Powers (New York: Norton, 1977) 240. Citations of Shelley's work are to this edition.

3. "Beatrice Cenci and Shelley's Vision of Moral Responsibility," *Ariel* 9 (1978): 80.

4. *Shelley's Major Poetry: The Fabric of a Vision* (Princeton: Princeton UP, 1948) 138-53.

5. "Beatrice's 'Pernicious Mistake' in *The Cenci,*" *PMLA* [*Publications of the Modern Language Association*] 74 (1959): 253.

6. See Curran's chapter, "The Tragic Resolution" in his *Shelley's* Cenci: *Scorpions Ringed with Fire* (Princeton: Princeton UP, 1970) 129-54.

7. *Shelley: A Critical Reading* (Baltimore and London: Johns Hopkins UP, 1971) 101.

8. For the clearest statement of this viewpoint, see Whitman 253.

9. See Curran 141-42.

10. Wasserman 93.

11. Stuart Curran has perceptively pointed out a number of resemblances between Shelley's Beatrice and Aeschylus's Io in *Shelley's* Annus Mirabilis: *The Maturing of an Epic Vision* (San Marino: Huntington Library, 1975) 130-33.

12. There are an oil painting and a pen and ink drawing that are closely related. See Paola Viotto, *L'Opera Completa di Füssli* (Milano: Rizzoli Editore, 1977) nos. 20, 20[1], page 88.

13. See Wasserman 118-20.

14. Wasserman 119, 125.

15. *Shelley's Prose; or, The Trumpet of a Prophecy,* ed. David Lee Clark (Albuquerque: U of New Mexico P, 1954) 309. The passage is cited by Wasserman 119.

16. "Note on *The Cenci,* by Mrs. Shelley," *The Complete Poetical Works of Percy Bysshe Shelley,* ed. Thomas Hutchinson (London: Oxford UP, 1945) 337.

Laurence S. Lockridge (essay date spring 1988)

SOURCE: Lockridge, Laurence S. "Justice in *The Cenci.*" *Wordsworth Circle* 19, no. 2 (spring 1988): 95-8.

[*In the following essay, Lockridge addresses Shelley's belief in non-violent resistance to cruelty and oppression.*]

Questions of moral psychology, freedom, and justice are explored by Shelley in his five act play, **The Cenci** (1819), his dramatization of Count Cenci's murderous hatred of his children, his incest with his daughter Beatrice, her plotting with her stepmother Lucretia and brother Bernardo to have the Count murdered by two hired assassins, and their subsequent arrest, torture, and execution by order of Pope Clement VIII in 1599. The play is a severe testing of a principle Shelley urges elsewhere: of returning hate with love or of resisting injustice non-violently. Here he draws our sympathies to a heroine who violates this principle. He portrays the extreme circumstances that appear to compel Beatrice to retaliation, and yet he does not in his Preface excuse her. The play is a good example of how, in Ricoeur's phrase, the "ethical laboratory" of literature permits writers to experiment with values, to revise preconceptions, even to contradict themselves.

To pose most precisely the questions raised by Beatrice's predicament, we can first turn to Shelley's ethical writings elsewhere. In the fragmentary **"Essay on Marriage"** we find him arguing, with Godwin, for a universal act utilitarianism: "To consider whether any particular action of any human being is really right or wrong we must estimate that action by a standard strictly universal. We must consider the degree of substantial advantage which the greatest number of the worthiest beings are intended to derive from that action" (**Shelley's Prose,** ed. D. L. Clark, p. 215). The principle of utility is generated by "benevolence," our wish to "seek the happiness of others," he writes in **Speculations on Morals** (1817, 1821), in accordance with a hedonistic concept of value—that is "called good which produces pleasure; that is called evil which produces pain" (p. 187).

Like Godwin and Hazlitt, Shelley thinks that the principle of benevolence or utility is insufficient: one could within its terms promote the pleasure of the majority and yet wreak pain and indignity on some minority group. Hence he adds that "there is a sentiment in the human mind that regulates benevolence in its application as a principle of action. This is the sense of justice. It is through this principle that men are impelled to distribute any means of pleasure which benevolence may suggest the communication of to others, in equal portions among an equal number of applicants" (p. 190). He draws an example of ten men shipwrecked on a desert island who must distribute subsistence equally.

There are therefore three principles of human action to keep in mind: benevolence, which impels to beneficent acts and which Shelley calls the principle of utility; distributive justice, which "regulates benevolence" by spreading its effects equally; and retributive punishment, which he considers intrinsically wrong—"The distinction between justice and mercy was first imagined in the courts of tyrants" (p. 203). In *The Cenci* he fashions a conflict between the claims of benevolence and the claims of retributive punishment in a historical situation where the possibility of distributive justice is nil.

Benevolence is said to have been part of Beatrice Cenci's basic nature. Her brother Giacomo speaks of Beatrice,

> Who in the gentleness of thy sweet youth
> Hast never trodden on a worm, or bruised
> A living flower, but thou has pitied it
> With needless tears!

> (III, i, 365-69)

In his Preface, Shelley describes her as "one of those rare persons in whom energy and gentleness dwell together without destroying one another," and he emphasizes her "patience," "imagination," and "sensibility." What causes her to plot her murderous father's death? and what would Shelley have her do otherwise? To this latter question, he provides a direct answer in his Preface, but its implementation is, to say the least, difficult to conceive:

> Undoubtedly, no person can be truly dishonoured by the act of another; and the fit return to make to the most enormous injuries is kindness and forbearance, and a resolution to convert the injurer from his dark passions by peace and love. Revenge, retaliation, atonement, are pernicious mistakes. If Beatrice had thought in this manner she would have been wiser and better; but she would never have been a tragic character. . . .

We might recall Julian's assurance to Maddalo that "Much may be conquered, much may be endured / Of what degrades and crushes us. We know / That we have power over ourselves to do / And suffer—what, we know not till we try, / But something nobler than to live and die—."

But Count Cenci, who rejoices publicly over the deaths of two of his sons, is degrading and crushing in the extreme. Perversely analogous to Necessity, he is an external power that literally becomes internal. Nature in the form of the West Wind enters and heightens the self in its freedom and power. But Count Cenci enters his daughter incestuously and corrupts her nature, depriving her of all power, freedom, and identity, in an extreme Blakean "hindering." In all this he appears to have God on his side: his prayers for the deaths of his

sons are swiftly answered, one of them dying when a church falls on top of him. Shelley never suggests that the Count is capable of redemption, that he *could* warm to his daughter's love or refrain from raping her. He lacks the potential shame that Shelley credits to British soldiers, who could be won over by passive resistance in the populace. Significantly, Beatrice has in the past futilely "sought by patience, love and tears / To soften him . . ." (I, ii, 115-16). What is Shelley implying that Beatrice ought to do or not do beyond this? Earl Wasserman writes that she "should have defeated the tyrant with patient, stoic endurance and pity." But does not "should" imply "could"? And she has already tried this tactic.

Rather than create a character as a blunt ideological tool in the resolution of such a question, Shelley has given Beatrice a complex characterization that shows how psychological dislocation infects ethical perception and will. Much of the play dwells on her response to the incest and on her vocalized decision-making. She weighs committing the patricide like a well-intentioned moralist, but comes to the wrong conclusion from the standpoint of the playwright who writes the Preface. "I have prayed / To God, and I have talked with my own heart, / And have unravelled my entangled will, / And have at length determined what is right" (III, i, 218-21). Shelley has said in his Preface that no human being can be dishonored by the act of another. Beatrice's response to incestuous rape, however, is one of a profound sense of contamination, so profound that her mental imagery compounds incest with necrophilia, herself the corpse. She complains of "a clinging, black, contaminating mist / About me . . . 'tis substantial, heavy, thick, / I cannot pluck it from me, for it glues / My flesh to a pollution, poisoning / The subtle, pure, and inmost spirit of life!" (III, i, 17-23). She is not "mad" but "dead," her limbs putrefied. A good actor playing Count Cenci can convince any audience that her response is not overblown.

Is hers not the special case limiting the general rule that one should respond to hate with love? Does not the play's logic insist that circumstances can so collude as to make retributive punishment both necessary and to that degree right? To the claims of retributive punishment are added those of self-defense—the Count is eager to repeat the rape. "What have I done? / Am I not innocent?" she cries, and most of us agree.

But following the rape she begins to speak in a way that reveals her own moral contamination. She has absorbed her oppressor's poison. To her stepmother Lucretia she says:

>   Aye, something must be done;
> What, yet I know not . . . something which shall make
> The thing that I have suffered but a shadow

In the dread lightning which avenges it;
Brief, rapid, irreversible, destroying
The consequence of what it cannot cure.
Some such thing is to be endured or done:
When I know what, I shall be still and calm,
And never any thing will move me more.

(III, i, 86-94)

Throughout the play, she stops short of naming the deed, whether patricide or incest. Terming the incest "expressionless," she can "feign no image in my mind / Of that which has transformed me" (III, i, 108-09); "there are deeds / Which have no form, sufferings which have no tongue" (III, i, 141-42). She asks her stepmother not to "speak" a simple matter of fact—that Lucretia is indeed Lucretia—for if this were true, then the world would be real, and it would follow "that the other [the incest] too / Must be a truth, a firm enduring truth, / Linked with each lasting circumstance of life, / Never to change, never to pass away" (III, i, 59-63).

These speeches imply her deep evasiveness about the nature of "deeds." The incest and the patricide do and do not exist in fact. Beatrice's unhinging has its psychological component in the breaking of an incest taboo, compounded with the horror of rape. It also has a more conceptual component in her assuming false alternatives as to the nature of the act: either that the incest has somehow never taken place, or that it has become for all time part of her essence.

In this error we find the key to the Beatrice who is horrendously injured, the Beatrice who orders the murder of the Count, and the Beatrice who unheroically denies that she has participated in the murder plot. In not naming the incest, she tries to lend it an unreality, but the attempt results only in a psychically dislocating dread, the deed taking on the overpowering indefiniteness of dark sublimity. In saying that "something must be done" without naming the deed of patricide, she betrays the same kind of evasion.

The signal phrase here is "destroying / The consequence of what it cannot cure." Unlike Blake's Oothoon, she regards the sexual contamination as incurable, yet in retaliation she will contradictorily attempt to deny the consequence that has already seized upon her. Later speeches bear out that she wishes to contain the event almost mathematically. Revenge or "atonement" implies an equivalency that would result in erasure, leaving her "calm and still." When Lucretia fears the consequences of the murder, Beatrice replies: "O fear not / What may be done, but what is left undone: / The act seals all" (IV, iii, 5-7). Thus she would bracket the patricide, regard it as a self-sealing act without consequence, the incest and the patricide cancelling one another out. After the Count is dead, she says to Lucretia:

The deed is done,
And what may follow now regards not me,

I am as universal as the light;
Free as the earth-surrounding air; as firm
As the world's centre. Consequence, to me,
Is as the wind which strikes the solid rock
But shakes it not.

(IV, iv, 46-52)

She errs: acts do have consequences and there is no such thing as complete erasure of the past. Retributive punishment, instead of balancing and cancelling, is inefficient; it compounds the original crime, and makes the avenger vulnerable to the powers she challenges.

Her subsequent unheroic denial in court of patricide is a continuation of the effort to cancel both incest and patricide. It is not out of cunning that she self-righteously forces Marzio, the assassin she hired, to lie about her involvement, even though this sends Marzio back to the torture chamber and to his death. She has almost convinced herself, through these evasions, of her own non-involvement. There is a split in her consciousness between being and doing—her being disclaims the doing as a desperate means of protecting what remains of her ego. Perhaps Shelley has Coleridge's play *Remorse* (1812; revision of *Osorio,* 1797) in mind, for **The Cenci** is written as if in qualifying refinement of Coleridge's conviction that acts necessarily stick to us because of conscience, no matter what our tactics of evasion or repression. Only Count Cenci's son, Giacomo, feels the stylized remorse of Jacobean tragedy (V, i, 2-4). Beatrice feels no remorse, but not because she defiantly knows retaliation to have been just. Rather, she has dissociated herself mentally from the act. To confess the patricide would be to admit to herself, as Coleridge puts it, the "abiding *presentness*" of both the patricide and, worse, the incestuous rape that provoked it. Thus, she voices explicitly the doubleness, not duplicity, that has been characteristic of her throughout. When the judge asks if she is guilty of her father's death, she refuses to decide. Her father's death

. . . is or is not what men call a crime
Which either I have done, or have not done.

(V, iii, 84-85)

How, then, do we see the role of Beatrice in relation to Shelleyan ethics? She demonstrates in the first place that her natural benevolence is not enough to soften tyrants or even to prevent its own conversion into hate. Her own heart becomes "cold," just as Count Cenci's is "hardened." Some other virtue or power is necessary, as complement of benevolence. We must ask whether there *is* any personal virtue or power she might have practiced that would have prevented her victimization.

I think the answer is no. She is wholly coerced into moral compromise despite her many strengths. Shelley acknowledges that there are victims in the world.

Wasserman has argued that she does have the prior choice of whether to permit the motive of revenge to enter her will, and is therefore culpable. Once she has freely given admission to the motive, she becomes part of a causal chain of evil; motive is to act as cause is to effect, as the Count is to Beatrice. Humans always have the choice as to whether they will break the causal chain of evil and deny it entrance into their own will. (*Shelley: A Critical Reading* [1971], pp. 101-15.) Wasserman's reading has the strength of making the play consistent with the Preface, where Shelley says that no person can be truly dishonored by the act of another and that Beatrice has erred in taking revenge. But this is one instance, in my view, where we should trust the play, not the playwright. Beatrice's prior power of choice is in no way dramatized or alluded to. What we do know is that she *has* attempted by love and patience to convert the Count prior to the rape. The revenge motive is indeed *implanted* against her will by her father's act of rape; about this she has no choice. Shelley has used the strongest possible images of violation and contamination to make vivid the fact of evil having been forced upon her from without. Like Christabel, Beatrice becomes evil without having been culpable. His statement in the Preface that no person can be dishonored by another's act must be regarded as a wishful misreading of his own play. *The Cenci* portrays a world so evil that it can tragically infect the innocent. Shelley is more cogent when he says Beatrice is "violently thwarted from her nature by the necessity of circumstance and opinion." Evil is a power that overrides the question of culpability. Ours is a world so evil that retributive punishment can seem attractive to the most hardened pacifist.

If the moral force of an individual—here, Beatrice's benevolence—is insufficient to extreme situations, the other tactic, retributive punishment, proves self-defeating for reasons beyond the self-corruption of the agent. The Count is part of a larger network of depravity and power, a network so canny it is prepared to dispense with him when his grotesquerie endangers it. Shelley is not indulging a cheap irony when he has it disclosed that the Count was to be executed by the church anyway. This turn of events in no way exonerates the church from its collusion with power; it simply reaffirms its commitment to power at whatever cost. The moral force of an individual, working as an assassin seeking retribution, does not stamp out evil in the state and, as it turns out, only makes Beatrice more vulnerable to the powers that be. Shelley has written a play in which no act totally right can be undertaken by the heroine; only the "wild justice" of revenge is available to her.

Since neither benevolence nor retributive punishment redresses tyranny, how can hope persist? The covert answer is a reordering of power within the state that would make Count Cencis and corrupt cardinals unthinkable. This reordering would be under the dictates of distributive justice. Beatrice and the rest of us could be free only in a state free of the authoritarian collusion with which *The Cenci* begins. The Count's parental tyranny is a figure of tyranny in general; to redress it would require a socio-political, not domestic, solution. At this point, however, Shelley's vacillation between a revolutionary and a reformist politics makes itself felt. He wants the ends of revolution, but unlike Blake he cannot stomach violent means. Beatrice's act of assassination proves futile, but what means are available? To be sure, none in late-Renaissance Rome. Shelley is writing in a post-revolutionary period that does have paradigms for collective action against tyranny. He proposes a reformist program for England in *A Philosophical View of Reform*; America, France, Spain, Italy, and Greece set forth the revolutionary posture, whether successful or abortive. It would have been anachronistic, however, to suggest these options in *The Cenci*. What Shelley says of the persecuted Tasso applies well to Beatrice: "Tasso's situation was widely different from that of any persecuted being of the present day, for from the depth of dungeons public opinion might now at length be awakened to an echo that would startle the oppressor. But then there was no hope" (*Letters* [*of Percy Bysshe Shelley*] II, 47).

The Cenci implies that authority can truly dishonor the innocent and powerless, and that there may be, at certain times in history, no salvation for individuals. Salvation must come through a larger socio-political movement seeking distributive justice. Short of this, individuals can only band together for local and temporary retaliation. Beatrice has been forced, for all her inherent benevolence, into the role of an assassin; a truly revolutionary role is unavailable to her. *The Cenci* has demonstrated that the moral life of individuals must in extreme circumstances be supplemented by a larger politics. The Poet in *The Triumph of Life* laments that "God made irreconcilable / Good and the means of good"—a lament suitable to a moment in the historical continuum but not with reference to the larger dialectics of history. The complete vindication of Shelleyan ethics can only come by way of historical accommodation, and the historical moment for it is necessarily closer now than it was in Beatrice's day.

The Cenci, then, is a dark play, a tragedy, but this is not to say that it represents a "negative" view of humankind in contradistinction to the "positive" of *Prometheus Unbound*. Rather, it is an analytic of human action that explores the limits of benevolence and personal ethics, and the dangers of a wildly just resistance. Within its historical setting the "dark spirit" is certainly in control, but Shelley is not legislating nihilism here. The principle of human action only implied in the play—distributive justice—can be engaged now, if it could not have been in late Renaissance Rome. He gives the tyrannies of church and state the worst possible face, as if to say to his audience that they must be resisted now in England and elsewhere.

Note

Abridged from a discussion of *The Cenci* in *The Ethics of Romanticism,* forthcoming from Cambridge University Press in 1989. Editions cited: *The Cenci* in *Shelley's Poetry and Prose,* ed. Donald H. Reiman and Sharon Powers (1977); *Shelley's Prose,* ed. David Lee Clark (1954, rev. 1966); and *The Letters of Percy Bysshe Shelley,* 2 vols., ed. Frederick L. Jones (1964).

Alan M. Weinberg (essay date April 1990)

SOURCE: Weinberg, Alan M. "Religion and Patriarchy in Shelley's *The Cenci.*" *Unisa English Studies* 28, no. 1 (April 1990): 5-13.

[*In the following essay, Weinberg assesses the role of religion as it relates to the characters and themes in* The Cenci.]

In writing **The Cenci,** Shelley was scrupulous in his attention to historical detail. The reason for this is explained in a comment he made in his 'Dedication' of the play to Leigh Hunt. Speaking of the poems he had already published, Shelley says they are 'dreams of what ought to be, or may be'. By contrast,

> [t]he drama which I now present to you is a sad reality. I lay aside the presumptuous attitude of an instructor, and am content to paint, with such colours as my own heart furnishes, that which has been.
>
> (Reiman and Powers 1977: 237)

Shelley was committing himself to 'actuality': he wanted the sad facts of history, not his personally held beliefs, to dictate his sense of reality to him. By keeping intact all the major incidents of his source (**"The Relation of the Death of the Family of the Cenci"**), Shelley allowed the ambiguities present in the legend to reappear in the play, thus taking up the challenge to give them their due, rather than omitting them to suit his personal whim.[1] In *Julian and Maddalo* Shelley adopts a similar approach, for the Madman's 'story' and actual experience of madness were 'dreadful realities' which put to the test the optimistic theories of Julian, Shelley's surrogate. Even in **"Lines written among the Euganean Hills,"** it is the live setting, eloquently manifesting the Italian past, which, to a large extent, shapes the response of the speaker.[2] One detects, in these literary works, a new phase in Shelley's development as a poet, a willingness to give more scope to the 'realities' of culture, setting and history than he had hitherto prac-

tised in England.[3] The story of the Cenci family was a 'sad reality', particularly as it was co-involved with the radical decline in personal and political liberty that marked the period of the Counter-Reformation. Shelley could sense the truth of this 'reality' when visiting the Cenci palace, which is situated close to the Jewish ghetto.[4] In the 'Preface' to the play, Shelley describes the palace as sombre and menacing, almost as if it belonged to some region of Dante's *Inferno*. It is a 'vast and gloomy pile of feudal architecture' which remains 'in the same state as during the dreadful scenes which are the subject of this tragedy' (242).

The historical element in the play is strengthened by the inclusion of religious issues. It must be remembered that with the waning of the High Renaissance from 1527 onwards, Italy underwent, in the period of the Counter-Reformation, a time of great religious ferment and despotic government. In the Vatican, the ruling Popes aligned themselves with conquering Spain, and in their attempt to restore the Papacy to credibility after a period of extreme laxity, severely imposed the notorious system of the Inquisition. Expressing his contempt for tyranny, Symonds writes that

> . . . the Papacy at this period committed itself to a policy of immoral, retrograde, and cowardly repression of the most generous of human impulses under the pressure of selfish terror [while] the Spaniards abandoned themselves to a dark fiend of religious fanaticism . . . were merciless in their conquests and unintelligent in their administration of subjugated provinces [and among other defects] cultivated barren pride and self-conceit in social life.
>
> (1935: II, 544)

It is in this period of religious and political suppression, which was nevertheless historically bound to the Renaissance, that Cenci rose to power. Though, in the play, Cenci is merely a family despot, his rule within that domain is almost unbounded, since he cynically exploits the religious hypocrisy of the time, which had become even more flagrant than during the hey-day of Renaissance 'libertinism'. It is important to observe that in the **"Relation"** [**"of the Death of the Family of the Cenci"**] Cenci is presented as an immoral atheist, the stock figure of depravity. Shelley's Cenci is, on the other hand, a Catholic whose religious faith, in his eyes, is in no way compromised by the atrocities he commits. Stuart Curran (1970: 43) suggests that the change to a religious Cenci was a concession made to English taste, since the audience of the time would not tolerate the horrors of atheism on the stage. While Curran appreciates the manner in which Shelley capitalises on this alteration to his source, adding that, to an English audience, a Catholic was probably no more acceptable than an Atheist, he omits to mention a more basic reason for the change: namely, that in Italy—as Shelley states in the 'Preface'—'[t]he most atrocious villain may be rigidly devout, and without any shock to established faith, confess himself to be so' (241).[5] Shelley was in fact applying the rule of Aristotelian probability to his protagonist: though the historical Cenci might have been an atheist, Shelley's experience of Italy had taught him that, more likely than not, Cenci was a religious man, and that the **"Relation"** may have wished to cover up Cenci's Catholicism. Though implicitly critical of Papal leniency towards Cenci and severity towards his family, the **"Relation"** is not anti-clerical: the characters are all, at the last, repentant of their crimes, and their execution, by order of the Pope, is considered to be the work of Divine Justice. Thus the Church is absolved from any guilt attaching to the death sentence or even to the torture which preceded it. As regards Cenci's religion, Shelley has adjusted his source to achieve greater historicity. This is a technique which may well have been derived from Shakespeare, whose treatment of legendary figures seems to penetrate deeper layers of historical fact. Having stated his aim of representing his characters 'as they probably were', Shelley adds, pointedly:

> and [I have] sought to avoid the error of making them actuated by my own conceptions of right or wrong, false or true, thus under a thin veil converting names and actions of the sixteenth century into cold impersonations of my own mind. They are represented as Catholics, and as Catholics deeply tinged with religion.
>
> (240)

The neglect, by critics, of the religious dimension in the play[6] can be attributed to the fact that, in modern tragedy, this aspect tends to be very broadly generalised. However, Shelley was impressed by the Athenian practice of employing 'religious institutions' in their attempt to represent 'the highest idealisms of passion and power' (*A Defence of Poetry*, 489).[7] In the case of *The Cenci*, Shelley not only strove to elevate his drama on classical lines, but knew that the downfall of the Cenci family could not be divorced from the religious issues of the time. His pervasive concern with the tyranny of religious belief and its link with superstition—a concern which expressed a Lucretian habit of mind—was well served by the 'facts' of the legend. (The projected, but never completed, *Charles I* probes similar issues.) Religion could not be regarded as a secondary issue in Italy. Shelley observes in the 'Preface' to *The Cenci* that, in Catholic Italy, religion is 'interwoven with the whole fabric of life' (241). Consequently, in the play, it is a fundamental aspect of Cenci's and Beatrice's experience. They refer to God, in speech after speech, while their strong faith motivates them to action. In Italy, religion is 'never a check', Shelley continues, referring obliquely to its restraining influence in Protestant countries; rather it is a 'passion, a persuasion, an excuse, a refuge' (241). The religious feelings of the characters commonly justify personal feelings. As far as Cenci is concerned, his hatred for his children has the sanction of divine will. God is an omniscient father demanding obedience and sanctioning the authority of all fathers over their children.[8] As his children, and Beatrice in particular, commit the grave sin of filial disobedience, he has no hesitation in calling on God to aid him in his curses. As he puts it,

> The world's Father
> Must grant a parent's prayer against his child
> Be he who asks even what men call me.
>
> (IV. i. 106-8)

His terrible curse in Act IV invites God to rain down horrible afflictions on Beatrice. She is his 'bane and [his] disease' (i. 118) and all her good uses must be turned to ill.

In his desperate mood, and with the weight of accusation against him, Cenci none the less regards himself as a scourge:

> I do not feel as if I were a man,
> But like a fiend appointed to chastise
> The offences of some unremembered world.
>
> (IV. i. 160-2)

He will relinquish his soul and his humanity, but he will not relinquish his faith in God. This shows how far he is prepared to go in order to justify his acts in the name of religion, and Shelley makes the further point that even the most depraved person believes he is in the right. Cenci sees himself as serving God's will in chastising others whose offence is, like Adam and Eve's or like Beatrice's, their disobedience of authority. He transmits his vengeful feelings to God who works hand in hand with the devil.[9]

Cenci refutes the generally held belief that a man of religion is necessarily a man of conscience. His heart 'beating with an expectation / Of horrid joy' (IV. i. 166-7) as he prepares to demolish Beatrice's 'stubborn will' (10), Cenci takes an hour of rest which, he feels, will be 'deep and calm' (182). In his opinion, conscience is an impostor, 'thou most insolent of lies!' (177). There can be no doubting the satanic nature of Cenci's mind: his own obedience to God is a complete distortion of the Christian ethic of love, charity, mercy. His God is a vengeful fiend. Yet the genuineness of his religious feelings is not in dispute: his commitment is real. His conviction is sanctioned by the fact that Catholicism has, indeed, subjected the devil to God's will and accommodated the vindictive principle to an omnipotent deity. If it be thought that Shelley has overstepped the bounds of probability in his depiction of Cenci's religious zeal, then one might recall that the Reformation drew its strength from the gross corruption of religious practices in the Catholic world. Symonds

comments that '[i]n Italy . . . religion survived as superstition even among the most depraved' and that 'the
crimes of the Church had produced a schism between
this superstition and morality' (1935: I, 233). Shelley
shows that religion and morality, as practised in Italy,
have no necessary connection with each other. Catholicism is 'adoration, faith, submission, penitence, blind
admiration; not a rule for moral conduct' ('Preface',
241).[10] At the same time, Shelley is far from condoning
Protestant alternatives. Protestantism has not succeeded
in disabusing itself either of the paternalism or the retributive character of its predecessor.[11] Shelley suggests
that religion leads inevitably to superstition, idolatry
and self-justification when it insists on the creed of obedience, a creed which makes it a vengeful oppressor of
the free human spirit. Roman Catholicism was not an
aberration from normal religious observance. Rather, it
served as a glaring example to men, that an 'undoubt-
ing persuasion of the truth of the popular religion' may
and does exist side by side with 'a cool and determined
perseverance in enormous guilt' (240). Earl Wasserman
comments that, in *The Cenci,* 'Catholicism is merely
the artificial apotheosis of unrestrained human conduct. . . . It is descriptive of actual human conduct in
fictitious theological terms and thus permissive' (1971:
90).

The distorting effects of religion are also revealed in
Beatrice's tragic conflict. In the early stages of the play,
while maintaining a Promethean attitude of forbearance
towards Cenci, Beatrice holds on to her view that the
God of Catholic worship is both merciful and just towards the oppressed. God, in her eyes, could not possibly condone the cruelty of her father, in spite of the fact
that her 'passionate prayers' through the 'long and
sleepless nights' have not been answered (I. iii. 119,
117). After she has been violated by Cenci, Beatrice is
so humiliated and undergoes such anguish at the feeling
of being stained for life, that she places herself under
God's protection. She believes, with Paul, that the violation of her body has made it the 'unworthy temple of
[God's] spirit' (III. i. 129).[12] She sees herself, therefore,
as an innocent victim who, paradoxically, will be redeemed from the corruption she endures, when God
takes the life of her tyrannical father. Though she plans
his murder and is even prepared ultimately to kill him
with her own hands, she insists on the belief that she is
but the instrument of God's will. Hers is a 'high and
holy deed' (IV. ii. 35) and she tells the murderer Marzio,
'Thou wert a weapon in the hand of God / To a just
use' (IV. iii. 54). Beatrice rids herself of a father whose
intention was to corrupt her soul; but, ironically, in
sensing her corruption, and seeking to regain the purity
of her soul, she adopts intrinsically the same attitude to
God as Cenci does. Foregoing individual choice, she allows her father's God of Vengeance to take the upper

hand over her God of Mercy. In this manner, Beatrice
unwittingly perpetuates the licence with which the
Church invokes the powers of a punitive deity.

Like Cenci, Beatrice perseveres in her actions, persuaded that God is on her side. Her religious self-
justification is called into question throughout the second half of the play. On each occasion the weakness of
her standpoint is underlined by dramatic irony. In the
first instance, she is subtly prompted to kill her father
by Orsino who, despite his priesthood, believes in 'flatter[ing] the dark spirit' (II. ii. 159). An obsessive passion for Beatrice allows him to exploit her ruthlessly.
He aims to win her love and her dowry by first making
her dependent upon his favour (it is he who handles
and secretly withholds her petition to the Pope), and
then by using her to get Cenci out of the way. In a soliloquy in II. ii. he lets it be known that 'while Cenci
lives / His daughter's dowry were a secret grave / If a
priest win her' (126-8). In the incest scene, he takes advantage of Beatrice's traumatic state: he foments her incipient feelings of revenge by knowingly exploiting the
weakness in the Cenci family for 'self-anatomy': that
process which, as he says,

> tempts our powers,
> Knowing what must be thought, and may be done,
> Into the depth of darkest purposes.
>
>   (II. ii. 111-13).[13]

Orsino's suggestion that Cenci will destroy her power
of resistance if she lets him live, causes Beatrice to retire in thought. She returns, having fatefully 'determined what is right' (III. i. 221). Orsino cleverly justifies Beatrice's thoughts when he tells Lucretia that 'high
Providence commits . . . their own wrongs / Into the
hands of men' (181-3), adding that Beatrice has 'Only
one duty, how she may avenge' (201). When he manipulates Giacomo to make him party to the parricide,
it becomes clear that Orsino, rather than God or even
Beatrice, is the controlling agent of the revenge plot.
The comparison of Orsino with Iago is just, as far as it
goes. The characters are alike in their concern with
'realpolitik'—as Arline Thorn has suggested (1973:
223). Each, playing on the weaknesses of others for his
own gain, believes that he remains untouched by the
corruption he causes. But while conceding the parallel
between Iago's manipulation of Othello and Orsino's
exploitation of the plight of Beatrice and Giacomo (a
parallel which suggests the 'self-interested malignity' of
both villains), P. Jay Delmar points out that, unlike
Iago, 'Orsino is not merely initiating . . . evil; in his
lust for the sexual control of Beatrice, which is equivalent to the Pope's lust for political power, he is really
reflecting his superior's evil qualities and thus the evil
qualities of his society at large' (1977: 39). In representing the less elevated ranks of the clergy, Orsino acts
as an 'emblem of the corrupt ecclesiastical hierarchy'

(Smith 1964: 81), and his sanctioning of vengeance shows the ease with which religious ideas are exploited by the Church for expedient ends.

Giacomo (whose inconstant wavering between 'remorse' and 'vengeance' is the most notable thing about him), falls into the same trap as Beatrice when, influenced by Orsino's guile, and hearing of Cenci's outrage against her, he fatuously exclaims,

> There is a higher reason for the act [of revenge]
> Than mine, there is a holier judge than me,
> A more unblamed avenger.
>
> (III. i. 363-5)

Giacomo uses the language of religion to bolster his sister's cause, which he would like to regard as just. The irony of Orsino's role is further suggested when, later, he is not brought to trial and makes his escape—albeit with a heavy conscience—by betraying Giacomo. Beatrice, on the other hand, at the expense of acute suffering, pays the full penalty for her actions.

Beatrice's religious standpoint is again in question when she actively and consciously uses the murderers, Marzio and Olympio, to kill Cenci. She considers them to be worthless characters but insists that, in killing him, they will be carrying out God's will. Like Cenci, she convinces herself that the devil can do the work of God. Ironically, the murderers actually turn out to be more humanly sensitive than expected, as they are unable to kill Cenci at first.[14] Beatrice regards this as a weakness in them. As men hardened to crime, they must stamp out their compassion and misgivings, and see that the act they are required to perform is a deed where 'mercy insults heaven' (IV. iii. 30). She even taunts them by threatening to do their work for them. Repeated echoes in IV. iii. of Lady Macbeth and the murder of Duncan make it clear that, in resorting to parricide, Beatrice has become a heartless murderess. In the trial scene she forces Marzio to deny the truth of her involvement, insisting on her total innocence and on the fact that God's 'hand at length did rescue her' (V. ii. 142). She then allows him to be tortured to death in order to protect her innocence. Although one recoils from Beatrice in this scene, it is, ironically, her religious faith which strengthens her resolve and relieves her of the burden of guilt. She never wavers in her conviction of having done the right thing: in this respect, her behaviour in Acts IV and V is consistent throughout.[15]

A further example of dramatic irony occurs when Savella arrives to announce the arrest of Count Cenci on 'charges of the gravest import' (IV. iv. 12). The placing of this announcement directly after the murder, and the consternation Savella's commission causes in Lucretia, suggest the folly of taking the law into one's own hands. Beatrice receives the news as an earthly confirmation of God's will:

> Both Earth and Heaven, consenting arbiters
> Acquit our deed.
>
> (IV. iv. 23-4)

Lucretia, notwithstanding her own unquestioning faith in God, counters with the view that

> All was prepared by unforbidden means
> Which we must pay so dearly having done.
>
> (29-30)

Events, if left to themselves, might well have made the whole business of murder superfluous. Yet neither Beatrice nor Lucretia realises that the process of law, which both respect, is entirely arbitrary and corrupt. Given the venality of the Church towards Cenci (established in the opening scene of the play) there is little doubt that the eventual arrest of Cenci would not have been made solely for reasons of justice. Thus the law loses its 'unforbidden' aspect: to act within the law and to act, as Beatrice has done, outside it, are equally indefensible positions. Again, the above allusion to the Macbeths implies culpability on the part of Beatrice as well as the existence of a just standard; but, whereas justice ultimately triumphs over the forces of disorder in *Macbeth* (the Macbeths pay dearly for what they do), there is no such prospect in store for Beatrice: she is neither vindicated by God nor judged fairly by an impartial system of law. Beatrice simply plays into the hands of those who unscrupulously wield power.

In spite of her situation, Beatrice persists in asserting the wisdom of what she has done. While her freedom of conscience is admirable when she advises Lucretia to

> Be faithful to thyself,
> And fear no other witness but thy fear[,]
>
> (IV. iv. 40-1)

her attitude requires that they resort to gross deception in order to avoid arrest:

> we can blind
> Suspicion with such cheap astonishment,
> Or overbear it with such guiltless pride,
> As murderers cannot feign.
>
> (43-6)

Beatrice bluntly refuses to be called a murderer (however 'just') and claims the right to deceive on religious grounds of 'innocence'. Given the extreme circumstances in which she is placed, and the nature of the society into which she is born, it is, perhaps, inevitable that Beatrice should regard herself as innocent of the crime. It is in the nature of oppression that it strip the victim of any sense of culpability or responsibility for his actions. This is an idea which recurs frequently in Shelley's writings. Beatrice, however, goes one step further, turning her innocence into a divine decree, which doubly reinforces the conviction. She then proceeds to act as if she were a completely free agent:

> The deed is done,
> And what may follow now regards not me.
> I am as universal as the light;
> Free as the earth-surrounding air; as firm
> As the world's centre. Consequence, to me,
> Is as the wind which strikes the solid rock
> But shakes it not.
>
> (46-52)

These are noble words, asserting the Romantic idea that man can liberate himself from the tyrannising forces of society, and thus achieve moral autonomy. The release from Cenci has indeed freed Beatrice from oppression and fear; but it has done so only temporarily. Beatrice cannot be regarded as existentially 'free', for she has, by her act of vengeance, forfeited her 'real' freedom. A religious fanaticism possesses her, and nothing shows this up more clearly than her failure to perceive the irony of her situation. She loses sight of all that exists outside her own righteous and uncompromising self.[16]

* * *

The high-handed, self-justifying strain in Beatrice does not, on the whole, alienate the audience because, firstly, it is wrought out of the most trying circumstances imaginable; secondly, it is an attempt to preserve her autonomy and her belief in a just universe; and thirdly, it expresses an impressive strength of purpose. Yet, even though confidence in her innocence is the only defence available to her for the maintenance of her sanity, it must still be recognised that her self-righteous conviction reflects the principle of authoritarianism upon [which] the structure of sixteenth-century Italian society was based.

Supreme at the head of the hierarchy and ruling omnipotent, God the father is constantly invoked: he is everyone's protector in time of need or trouble, irrespective of 'right' or 'wrong'—the projected principle, as it were, of self-preservation. The Pope, God's regent on earth, and 'father' designate of the Catholic Church, represents the authoritative will of God: in so doing he assumes absolute powers. His position is constitutionally one of 'blameless neutrality' (II. ii. 40), a phrase which suggests that, in the eyes of the Catholic hierarchy, he can do no wrong. He is above the law and, in fact, proclaims the will of God. To this end, he takes refuge behind the 'law' of the Church. He, therefore, threatens Cenci with damnation if the latter continues to act like a tyrant, but Cenci is, in reality, filling the coffers of the Papacy, and is only too aware of it. In continuing to let Cenci go free, the Papacy becomes accomplice to the crimes he commits and the sufferings

he imposes. As a father, Cenci merely confirms the pattern of unquestioned authority invested in him by the structure of society. He has, in fact, even greater freedom to act out his impulses than the clergy, which must, as a rule, maintain an image of sanctity. Consequently, Cenci is blatantly open about his crimes—and to this degree is, as Curran points out, 'honest' (1970: 72)—whereas the Church, in its pursuit of secular power, is more underhand and circumspect. Cenci's acts are certainly diabolical, yet they are less insidious than those of the Papacy, which institutionally holds the keys of Justice and Salvation, and at the same time feeds like a parasite on the evil of others.[17] This point, made right at the beginning of the play, prevents the audience from reacting to Cenci as if he were merely an isolated instance of depravity. In the opening dialogue with Camillo, Cenci sees through the Pope's charade of an offer of clemency:

> Respited me from Hell!—so may the Devil
> Respite their souls from Heaven.
>
> (I. i. 26-7)

He recognises the religious hypocrisy and bigotry of the Church, but his insight does not prevent him from behaving as he does. He knows that his 'authority' has divine and religious sanction and he does not fail to take advantage of it.

In killing Cenci, Beatrice would seem to be actively rebelling against the society that invests such power in her father. This might in fact be the case on a symbolic or unconscious level. But Beatrice, generally speaking, takes her society for granted. She does not question the power base upon which it is established. She accepts the fatherhood of God (I. iii. 118; II. i. 16-17) and the authority of the Church, as Wasserman points out (1971: 88-9). It is only because her father grossly abuses his powers that she is forced to disobey him. Her response to Cenci is also not self-consciously intellectual but deeply personal. The murder is an act of self-preservation: she has no wish to reform society or to set the world an example of heroism or emancipation. In effect, her unbending faith in God's protection and her continued hope for clemency from the Pope uphold the paternalistic structure of Italian society: in removing her father, she has only removed the immediate cause of oppression. Beatrice is trapped by her society. She believes that God will save her through the law, and that she is the instrument of His will. But the power of God in her society is invested in Cenci and in the hands of the Pope, who sentences her to death on the grounds that

> Parricide grows so rife
> That soon, for some just cause no doubt, the young
> Will strangle us all, dozing in our chairs.

Authority, and power, and hoary hair
Are grown crimes capital.

                                                    (V. iv. 20-4)

The Pope cannot allow Beatrice to threaten his (or
God's) authority, and the whole fabric of society from
which it draws its sustenance. Murder is, apparently, a
less serious offence to the Papacy than is the undermining of parental power. Inevitably, it is the government
of the Church and the complicity of Italian society
which decide Beatrice's fate.

Defeated even by her God at the last, and facing immi-
nent death, Beatrice breaks free of the Catholic dominion and its patriarchal hierarchy, acquiring an independent, disillusioned attitude towards life. Enjoined by
Lucretia, in the final scene of the play, to

            Trust in God's sweet love,
    The tender promises of Christ: ere night
    Think we shall be in Paradise,

                                                    (V. iv. 75-7)

Beatrice, in reply, shows clearly enough the change she
has undergone:

                            I
    Have met with much injustice in this world;
    No difference has been made by God or man,
    Or any power moulding my wretched lot,
    'Twixt good or evil, as regarded me.
    I am cut off from the only world I know,
    From light, and life, and love, in youth's sweet prime.
    You do well telling me to trust in God,
    I hope I do trust in him. In whom else
    Can any trust? And yet my heart is cold.

                                                    (V. iv. 80-9)

The directness and simplicity of her thoughts reveal
that—however painfully—she has made a breakthrough
in self-knowledge. Her trials have shattered her dependence on any absolute law or power, and refined away
illusions she has harboured of the justness and compassion of 'God or man'. Left 'cold' by the world, she yet
acknowledges the beauty of life which Cenci has denied her.[18] At the same time, Beatrice retains her belief
in her innocence right to the end, claiming that death 'is
the reward of innocent lives' (110). This belief gives
her the nobility of a Greek heroine who accepts her fate
from a position of strength. She is like the Niobe in the
Uffizi gallery, in whom Shelley saw 'a tender and serene despair'; or like the Minerva in the same gallery
who, as the emblem of Wisdom, pleads 'earnestly with
Power', but knows she must plead in vain (Clark 1966:
353, 349). Even more to the point is the portrait of Beatrice in which 'despair . . . is lightened by the patience
of gentleness' ('Preface', 242). Beatrice is 'sad and
stricken down in spirit' (242), the figure of grief, but
not overwhelmed by grief.[19] She can advise her brother

Bernardo to 'Err not in harsh despair, / But tears and
patience' (V. iv. 144-5). Her language is eloquent, subdued and dignified. If a measure of righteous conviction
underlies her sceptical vision, it is also true, as Wasserman suggests, that Beatrice is 'innocent in some fundamental sense, even though she herself is incapable of
understanding the reason as she searches about for
justification' (1971: 124). A crucial moment occurs in
her farewell speech to Bernardo, just as the guards are
ready to take her off to execution. Looking back on her
life, Beatrice claims that she was 'wrapped in a strange
cloud of crime and shame', yet 'Lived ever holy and
unstained' (V. iv. 148-9). These sentiments coincide
with the view put forward by Shelley in the 'Preface'
that

> [t]he crimes and miseries in which [Beatrice] was an
> actor and a sufferer are as the mask and the mantle in
> which circumstances clothed her for her impersonation
> on the scene of the world.

                                                    (242)[20]

Shelley is saying that her essential being (her 'soul of
goodness') has remained untouched by all that she has
done, and it is this assumption on the part of Beatrice
which must be set against her earlier conviction that she
had been debased by Cenci. That the soul is, in fact, inviolable dispels the impression that evil is the only
'reality' in the Cencian world,[21] an impression which,
ironically, Cenci has himself supported, thereby
strengthening the dreaded engine of Catholic oppression. In affirming her innocence, Beatrice actually subverts orthodox Catholic virtue and saintliness. Yet,
tempted as he must have been to idealise Beatrice, Shelley does not mitigate the tragedy of her experience: she
dies the victim of an unjust world, and of her own faith
that it would vindicate her. In this manner, Shelley
heightens the tragedy—which is Aristotelian in so far as
the discovery or 'anagnorisis' is contingent upon the
heroine's 'fall'—and remains faithful to the Beatrice of
legend.

Notes

1. 'That Shelley made only minor alterations suggests that, aside from finding the limitations congenial to his needs, he also believed his primary
   duty to be the dramatisation of the myth with its
   many ambiguities intact. But by compressing the
   events into a manageable sequence, the poet accentuates these ambiguities' (Curran 1970: 45-6).
   It is also clear that Shelley was training himself to
   give full weight to the story. Hitherto he had, according to Mary, 'shown no inclination for, nor
   given any specimen of his powers in framing and
   supporting the interest of a story'. Yet he rightly
   'believed that one of the first requisites [for writing drama] was the capacity of forming and
   following-up a story or plot' ('Note on the Cenci',
   Hutchinson 1983: 335, 334).

2. In his comment on *Euganean Hills,* Karl Kroeber (1974: 321-4; 334-9) shows that the poet's concern to combine history and vision is characteristic of Romantic art.

3. Although Shelley's maturity as a poet is often said to coincide with his exile in Italy, it is not usually recognised how formative Italy was in the shaping of that maturity. Italy had become a reliable index of the 'nature of things'.

4. Its present location is marked by 'piazza Cenci' and the street name along the Tiber, 'Lungotevere dei Cenci'. The sight, in St Peter's Square, of three hundred labouring convicts, heavily ironed and under the watch of armed soldiers, was dramatic confirmation of the loss of personal liberty in Italy. '[M]oral degradation contrasted with the glory of nature & the arts' was, in Shelley's opinion, 'the emblem of Italy' (Jones 1964: II, 93, 94).

5. Shelley's idea finds support in the religious 'comedies' of Calderón. For parallels between *The Cenci* and the plays *El Purgatorio de San Patricio* and *La Devoción de la Cruz,* the two 'ideal dramas' (Jones 1964: II, 153) Shelley was reading in July 1819, see Webb (1976: 212). The 'Calderónian cult' was apparently 'sparked by Italians in Germany' (Hernández-Araico 1987: 481).

6. Critics who devote their attention to the play's socio-political 'reality' are James Rieger (1965: 169-84); Harry White (1978: 27-38); and Eugene Hammond (1981: 25-32); while Earl Wasserman contributes many valuable insights to this topic (1971: 84-128). Commentaries on *The Cenci* tend, in general, to focus on the characters of Beatrice and Cenci, the moral dilemma which Beatrice faces, the tragic element and the stageworthiness of the play. Curran's monograph (1970) exemplifies each of these approaches. Bates argues that Shelley's changes to the original 'take away all possibility of regarding the play as a careful study of Italian life in the sixteenth century, or as any contribution to our historical knowledge' (1908: 34). He excuses Shelley on the grounds that the poet was writing 'not a history but a tragedy' (33).

7. Shelley follows the example of Calderón whose 'dramatization of religion' is for him and the Schlegels 'comparable to the ancients' use of mythology in drama', Hernández-Araico (1987: 482). But while praising Calderón for attempting 'to fulfil some of the high conditions of dramatic representation neglected by Shakespeare; such as the establishing a relation between the drama and religion', Shelley adds, in *A Defence of Poetry,* that Calderón compromises the scope of his drama by substituting 'the rigidly-defined and ever-repeated idealisms of a distorted superstition for the living impersonations of the truth of human passion' (490). Thus, in *The Cenci,* Shelley subverts Calderón's religious confidence since he 'disdains the Spaniard's adherence to dogma' (482) and aligns religion, for the most part, with tyranny.

8. It is on similar grounds that the Pope rejects Camillo's appeal for clemency towards the Cenci children:

> CAMILLO:
>
> He holds it of most dangerous example
> In aught to weaken the paternal power,
> Being, as 'twere, the shadow of his own.
>
> (II. ii. 54-6)

9. This religious conception reflects the poet's satirical view that in the Christian dispensation '[t]he dirty work is done by the Devil' (*On the Devil and Devils*: Clark 1966: 269).

10. The severance of morality from religion during the Renaissance is excellently documented by Symonds. See *The Age of Despots,* Ch. VIII: 'The Church and Morality' (1935: I, 225-49).

11. Commenting on religious practice in the seventeenth century, Shelley says that it 'subsisted under all its forms, even where it had been separated from those things especially considered as abuses by the multitude, in the shape of intolerant and oppressive hierarchies' (*A Philosophical View of Reform,* Clark 1966: 232).

12. '[K]now ye not that your body is the temple of the Holy Ghost which is in you, which ye have of God, and ye are not your own? For ye are bought with a price: therefore glorify God in your body, and in your spirit, which are God's' (I Corinthians 6: 19, 20). So restrictive are the mores of Catholic society regarding the chastity of women, that Beatrice cannot utter the dreaded word 'incest' at any stage; nor does she openly plead her innocence in the palace of Justice on the grounds of incest.

13. For a full discussion of 'self-anatomy' and its role in the play, see Wasserman (1971: 101-26). He identifies 'self-anatomy' with the heroine's 'hamartia', her justification of revenge on the grounds that 'circumstances alter cases'. His interpretation (which I support) runs counter to the one proposed by Curran that 'there is no tragic "flaw" in Shelley's play: the tragedy is that good is helpless to combat evil' (1970: 259). More recently, Stuart Sperry identifies Beatrice's hamartia with her 'idealization of her virginity, as the center of her moral life and nature. It is the element essential to her sense of her own integrity as a human being' (1986: 420).

14. Shelley has been charged here with plagiarising *Macbeth,* but, in point of fact—as Curran is keen to show (1970: 41)—he is following his source closely: 'Soon after[,] the assassins entered, and told the ladies that pity had held them back, and that they could not overcome their repugnance to kill in cold blood a poor sleeping old man' ("Relation," Ingpen and Peck 1965: II, 161). Shelley exploits the parallel with *Macbeth* in order to promote that process of 'restless casuistry' which compels the audience to question Beatrice's actions, even as it desires to justify them.

15. In *The Cenci* Shelley shows how the oppressor and the oppressed justify violence: both end up employing the same tactics, as is tragically—and for the Romantic poets—disconcertingly demonstrated in the French Revolution.

16. Harry White is one of the few critics to have highlighted the fanatical strain in Beatrice. His view, for this reason, deserves quoting. Agreeing with Stuart Curran that 'Beatrice struggles "not to save herself but her moral universe"', White adds: 'To rectify the moral order is frequently the justification for revenge. However, it needs to be emphasized that such an aim reveals not a larger, less self-centred purpose, but outright religious fanaticism on Beatrice's part.' Like Wasserman, White claims that 'Beatrice sacrifices human life to maintain this abstract notion of a moral universe, imitating by her deed the traditional practice of the Church which will soon sacrifice her, as it has others, to the same principle of a moral universe' (1978: 33-4).

17. As a functionary of the Church, Orsino, it has been claimed, is 'a traitor more dangerous to the struggling champion of good than the avowed oppressor'. He is a 'palterer, who faced with the choice between good and evil tries to play with both for the gratification of his own mean desires' (Rees 1961: 6). It is also significant that in the aftermath of murder, Cenci's tyranny is replaced by that of the Pope, a silent Patriarch who never appears as a character, but whose influence over the action is all the more insidious for that reason.

18. One recalls the last line of *Julian and Maddalo* in which Julian's disillusioned reference to the 'cold world' contrasts with his admiration for Maddalo's daughter.

19. This union of intense suffering and graceful bearing, what Joseph Donohue calls 'pathetic tragic character' (1968: 53), again finds expression in Shelley's poem "On the Medusa of Leonardo da Vinci in the Florentine Gallery," written in the autumn of 1819. Cf. ll. 14-16:

'Tis the melodious hue of beauty thrown

Athwart the darkness and the glare of pain,
Which humanize and harmonize the strain.

(Hutchinson 1983: 582)

It is no coincidence that the three works of art which elicited the deepest response from Shelley at this time were the 'Niobe', the 'Minerva' and the 'Medusa': these are all representations in the Uffizi of female Greek mythological figures, whose nobility enables them to withstand acute distress. There seems little doubt that in the closing moments of *The Cenci,* Shelley attempted to approximate the tragic intensity of Greek and Italian art.

20. Cf. 'The beauty of the internal nature cannot be so far concealed by its accidental vesture, but that the spirit of its form shall communicate itself to the very disguise, and indicate the shape it hides from the manner in which it is worn' (*A Defence of Poetry,* 487).

21. It is this view that Curran (1970) argues in what is, to date, the most thorough (if contentious) reading of the play.

Bibliography

Bates, Ernest Sutherland. 1908. *A Study of Shelley's Drama* The Cenci. Columbia University Studies in English, Series II, vol. III, no. 1. New York: Columbia University Press.

Clark, David Lee, ed. 1966. *Shelley's Prose or the Trumpet of a Prophecy.* Albuquerque: The University of New Mexico Press (1st pub. 1954).

Curran, Stuart. 1970. *Shelley's* Cenci: *Scorpions Ringed with Fire.* Princeton, New Jersey: Princeton University Press.

Delmar, P. Jay. 1977. 'Evil and Character in Shelley's *The Cenci*'. *Massachusetts Studies in English,* VI (1 & 2): 37-48.

Donohue, Joseph W. Jr. 1968. 'Shelley's Beatrice and the Romantic Concept of Tragic Character'. *Keats-Shelley Journal,* XVII: 53-73.

Hammond, Eugene R. 1981. 'Beatrice's Three Fathers: Successive Betrayal in Shelley's *The Cenci*'. *Essays in Literature,* VIII (I): 25-32 (Spring).

Ingpen, Roger and Peck, Walter E[dwin], eds. 1965. *The Complete Works of Percy Bysshe Shelley* (Julian Edition), vol. 2. London: Ernest Benn, rpt. of 1926-30 edn.

Hernández-Araico, Susana. 1987. 'The Schlegels, Shelley and Calderon'. *Neophilologus,* LXXI (4): 481-8 (October).

Hutchinson, Thomas, ed. 1983. *Shelley: Poetical Works.* Oxford: Oxford University Press.

Jones, Frederick L. 1964. *The Letters of Percy Bysshe Shelley.* 2 vols. Oxford: Clarendon Press.

Kroeber, Karl. 1974. 'Experience as History: Shelley's Venice, Turner's Carthage'. *Journal of English Literary History,* XLI (3): 321-39 (Fall).

Rees, Joan. 1961. 'Shelley's Orsino: Evil in *The Cenci*'. *Keats-Shelley Memorial Bulletin,* XII: 3-6.

Reiman, D. H. and Powers, Sharon, B., eds. 1977. *Shelley's Poetry and Prose* (Norton Critical Edition). New York: W. W. Norton. All references to the play, the 'Preface' to the play, and to *A Defence of Poetry* are to this edition.

Rieger, James. 1965. 'Shelley's Paterin Beatrice'. *Studies in Romanticism,* IV (3): 169-84 (Spring).

Smith, Paul. 1964. 'Restless Casuistry: Shelley's Composition of *The Cenci*'. *Keats-Shelley Journal,* XIII: 77-85.

Sperry, Stuart M. 1986. 'The Ethical Politics of Shelley's *The Cenci*'. *Studies in Romanticism,* XXV (3): 411-27 (Fall).

Symonds, J[ohn] A[ddington]. 1935. *Renaissance in Italy* (The Modern Library). 2 vols. New York: Bennet A. Cerf, Donald S. Klopfer (1st pub. 1875, 1886).

Thorn, Arline R. 1973. 'Shelley's *The Cenci* as Tragedy'. *Costerus: Essays in English and American Language and Literature,* IX: 219-28.

Wasserman, Earl. 1971. *Shelley: A Critical Reading.* Baltimore: Johns Hopkins Press.

Webb, Timothy. 1976. *The Violet in the Crucible: Shelley and Translation.* Oxford: Clarendon Press.

White, Harry. 1978. 'Beatrice Cenci and Shelley's Avenger'. *Essays in Literature,* V (1): 27-38 (Spring).

Daniel Davy (essay date fall 1990)

SOURCE: Davy, Daniel. "The Harmony of the Horrorscape: A Perspective on *The Cenci*." *Journal of Dramatic Theory and Criticism* 5, no. 1 (fall 1990): 95-113.

[*In the following essay, Davy explores elements of Gothic darkness and mystery in* The Cenci.]

Most of the body of criticism devoted to Shelley's **The Cenci** approaches it as tragedy, and, moreover, as tragedy which is essentially in the Aristotelian mold.[1] Beatrice, the obvious protagonist in the play, goaded by countless outrages at the hands of her father Count Cenci, finally retaliates in kind by murdering her tor-

mentor, and is consequently destroyed. Her capacity to participate in the Count's basic "action" (the pervasive evil which he embodies and represents—killing, blood lust, etc.) constitutes her *hamartia*; the actual murder of the Count constitutes the *peripety* of the play's action which then leads on to Beatrice's fall.[2] The Count, a lurid and sensational figure, is usually relegated to a relatively minor role. Indeed, it is the very size and nature of the "evil" which he represents in the play which results in a downgrading of his significance, for Count Cenci is a figure of truly spectacular malignancy:

> All men enjoy revenge; and most exult
> Over the tortures they can never feel—
> Flattering their secret peace with others' pain.
> But I delight in nothing else. I love
> The sight of agony, and the sense of joy,
> When this shall be another's, and that mine.
> And I have no remorse and little fear. . . .
>   yet, till I killed a foe,
> And heard his groans, and heard his children's groans,
> Knew I not what delight was else on earth,
> Which now delights me little. I the father
> Look on such pangs as terror ill conceals,
> The dry fixed eyeball; the pale quivering lip,
> Which tell me that the spirit weeps within
> Tears bitterer than the bloody sweat of Christ.
>
>   (I. i. 78-84,106-113)

And referring to his daughter, Beatrice:

> Might I not drag her by the golden hair?
> Stamp on her? Keep her sleepless till her brain
> Be overworn? Tame her with chains and famine?. . . .
> No, tis her stubborn will,
> Which, by its own consent, shall stoop as low
> As that which drags it down. . . .
> Beatrice shall, if there be skill in hate,
> Die in despair, blaspheming. . . .
> What sufferings? I will drag her, step by step,
> Through infamies unheard of among men. . . .
> Her corpse shall be abandoned to the hounds;
> Her name shall be the terror of the earth;
> Her spirit shall approach the throne of God
> Plague-spotted with my curses. I will make
> Body and soul a monstrous lump of ruin.
>
>   (IV. i. 6-12,49-50,80-81,91-95)

Carlos Baker comments on "the sneaking suspicion that Count Cenci is far too evil to be credible," and a considerable amount of the criticism devoted to the play follows a similar strategy of devaluation.[3] This approach to the play thus tends to regard the Count as performing an essentially abstract dramatic function within the structure of the action—he catalyzes and activates a hitherto dormant aspect of Beatrice's character which then leads her to destruction. The Count's *own* character—spectacular, lurid and "(in)credible" as it is, is regarded as of only marginal significance. Such a reading of the play, while no doubt yielding valuable insights in a number of areas, nevertheless seems to me to run a clear risk of essentially overlooking the very source of the play's expressive power. As an alternative approach, I would suggest that we should look at the Count and his world not from the vantage point of the *clarity* of our own highly rationalized perspective (in which the Count might well appear as a kind of cartoon figure), but from the *obscurity* of the world of nineteenth century "dark romanticism," a world which **The Cenci** preeminently embodies. To what degree is the "dark" or "gothic" ambience of the play relevant to an interpretation of its content?

The principal definition—or certainly connotation—for "darkness" in this context is of course "evil"—a role very amply embodied by Count Cenci. That the Count is "evil" is indisputable; what does, however, seem to me open to question is the idea that the obvious villainy of the Count's *actions* exhausts the potentiality of the notion of "darkness" as applied to this character. For the "dark deeds" of Count Cenci represent only the objective aspect of his malignancy; of greater significance—in the context here of the play's "romantic" side—is his persistent and inexorable influence over the subjective sphere, his command over the forces of *imagination* at work throughout the totality of the play's world.[4]

A wonderful explanation, or rather, a kind of metaphor, for exactly what I mean here can be found in an essay by Ann Radcliffe, one of the most prominent of the "gothic" novelists of the early nineteenth century. The essay is structured as a fictional dialogue between two travellers in the English countryside, Messrs. "S" and "W." The discussion turns to the witches of *Macbeth,* and to the then common practice of attempting to "naturalize" these figures in stage presentation. Mr. S is in favor of such an interpretation, but Mr. W dissents:

> I, now, have sometimes considered, that it was quite suitable to make Scotch witches on the stage, appear like Scotch women. You must recollect that, in the superstition concerning witches, they lived familiarly upon the earth, mortal sorcerers, and were not always known from mere old women; consequently they must have appeared in the dress of the country where they happened to live, or they would have been more than suspected of witchcraft, which we find was not always the case."
>
> "You are speaking of old women, and not of witches," said W, laughing. . . . "I am speaking of *the only real witch—the witch of the poet;* and all our notions and feelings connected with terror accord with his. The wild attire, the look *not of this earth,* are essential traits of supernatural agents, working evil in the darkness of mystery."

(1st emphasis mine; 2nd emphasis Radcliffe)[5]

Radcliffe's phrase "poet's witch" seems to me very suggestive indeed. For the notion of "poet's witch" mates the creativity and potency associated with the idea of *imagination* with the sinister potentiality inherent in the condition of *darkness*; why, we must ask, the "working of *evil* in the darkness of (this) mystery" if not an avowal of that primordial dread necessarily aroused in the presence of the utterly unknown? Gothic "darkness" here establishes hegemony, not over its traditional terrain of windswept moors and bats in the night, but over and within the *mind* itself—its interiority, its mystery, its potentially unknowable status. An unknown but, paradoxically, not an *alien* presence. Mrs. Radcliffe continues:

> Whenever the poet's witch condescends, according to the vulgar notion, to mingle mere ordinary mischief with her malignity, and to become familiar, she is ludicrous, *and loses her power over the imagination.* . . . In nothing has Shakspeare (sic) been more successful than in this . . . that of selecting circumstances of manners and appearance for his supernatural beings, *which, though wild and remote, in the highest degree, from common apprehension, never shock the understanding by incompatibility with themselves.* . . .

(147) (my emphasis)

The eldritch imagery of the gothic world holds its "power over the imagination" by virtue of linking the extraordinary with the somehow familiar, and it is precisely this shadowy recognition of the "alien within" which can stimulate the darkest corners of existential dread.

An intriguing echo of Radcliffe's "witch of the poet" can be found in our own time in the psychoanalytical theories of Jacques Lacan. Lacan, who is himself regarded as a maverick revisionist by orthodox Freudians, asserts in his turn that the various functions associated with the Freudian "unconscious" have become overly and falsely systematized by contemporary "Freudians"; the "unconscious" has been reduced to a closed system of causalities, rendered into a finite and altogether *knowable* phenomenon. In contrast to such a view, Lacan urges a return to the Freud who is himself a "revisionist," the man whose analyses could render meaningful the mystery of the dream, but who foundered before "the navel of the dream," whose deductive powers located—at or near the very center of the psyche—an "infernal opening" which he perceived as ultimately impenetrable.[6] At this primordial and critical locus of the psyche, Lacan himself finds an "ultimately unknown centre," and a "cause . . . that, in the last resort, is unanalysable" (23, 21).

And yet however impenetrable this psychic center may appear from without, or if regarded and scrutinized "objectively," subjectively one is nevertheless "at home" (Lacan 36) within its mysterious depths, which are not, for all of that, any the less mysterious for the self who lives there. The "poet" creates, but can nevertheless find his "creation" at least partially inexplicable. It is this capacity for being both "known" and "unknown," "there" and "not there" as it were, which Lacan finally designates as "neither being nor non-my empbeing, but the 'unrealized.'" (30)

It is in my view precisely at this nexus of the psyche, the realm of the "poet's witch" or, as Lacan elsewhere puts it, this "zone of shades," that the drama of *The Cenci* occurs. Here is an arena which is at once a source of power and at the same time an area of acute vulnerability, both notions comprehended in Lacan's term "unrealized": the creative source of any particular "realization" associated with the concept of *imagination* on the one hand, and the notion of impenetrability and mystery—"the look not of this earth"—associated with the condition of psychic *darkness* on the other.

This dark and potent center of the psyche, in its "unrealized" status, remains but a sleeping enigma, a wholly dormant potentiality. "Reality," Lacan tells us, "is in abeyance there, awaiting attention." (56) What kind of attention? Within itself, as a still and sheltered interiority, the self maintains its autonomy; its dark, unpotentiated center carries no sinister implications. But, returning now to our play, what might be the implications or ultimate consequences if such a subject not only found itself within a world which is *itself* wholly "dark," but was also subjected to the incessant and malevolent "attentions" of an agency who functions as both the dominant center of that objective world, as well as its spiritual personification? In order to discover how such dark potentialities might disclose themselves as a dramatic action, we must now turn our attention to a close examination of the play.

"Darkness" and "mystery" are not only generalities which can be applied to the overall ambience of *The Cenci,* but also function as essential ingredients of the "precipitating crisis" of the play, the rape of Beatrice which occurs between Acts two and three. It is significant that the word "rape" is never used in the play, nor is the specific act even euphemistically referred to. The fact that we do not know *what really happened* in this dark interval is to some degree an observance of contemporary sensibilities, but it is also an essential strategy of the play. Given the overall ambience of *The Cenci* and the specific obscurity of the interval between Acts two and three, the labeling of the Count's attack unequivocally as "rape" seems to me potentially misleading. What do we mean by this term? The word has taken on a host of "clinical" connotations; our empathy and sense of outrage with reference to this crime has grown so acute that we have come to associate the word with its only potential remedy—healing, therapy. The aim of our contemporary therapies is to *illuminate,* to provide as comprehensive an understanding as possible so that the hurtful effects of this act can be assimilated and hopefully neutralized. Our use of the concept of

"rape," therefore, tends toward the *finite*—it renders it *known.* But the Count's attack on Beatrice, I would suggest, is something more than the latest and greatest of the long series of crimes he has already perpetrated upon her—crimes which have failed in their objective of breaking his daughter's spirit, which remains, as it were, *in the light.* I would suggest that "darkness" is a fundamental constituent of the Count's deed, that his crime was deliberately designed to disallow the possibility of present or future illumination. Beatrice is violated, but she *does not know* exactly what has occurred. And yet, uncannily, she does.

The Count's intention was first revealed at the close of Act I, following the tumult generated by the Count's celebration of the death of his sons, and Beatrice's desperate and failed attempt to enlist support from among the hastily departing guests. Only the Count and his daughter remain on stage, but Beatrice is soon to follow the departed guests, lashed off the stage by the following invective:

> Thou painted viper!
> Beast that thou art! Fair and yet terrible!
> I know a charm shall make thee meek and tame,
> Now get thee from my sight!
> (*Exit* BEATRICE)
>
> (I. iii. 165-168)

It is clear what the term "charm" refers to; what is somewhat strange is the Count's assumption that even this enormity will indeed "tame" his daughter. Is this act, hideous to be sure, of a fundamentally different nature than the abominations already inflicted? Beatrice has been "tortured . . . from her forgotten years": dragged by the hair through the halls of the palace, "trampled" so that the "blood stream(s)" down "pallid cheeks," fed a diet of "ditch water" and "fever-stricken buffaloe," cast naked with "scaly reptiles" into dungeons, forced to witness her gangrene infested brother rotting in his chains, and has been the object of numerous other atrocities only hinted at in the text. As yet "untamed" by this treatment, why the certitude that even this new and probably greatest outrage will do the trick?

But there is a still greater anomaly here. Beatrice's exit is immediately followed by these lines from the Count:

> Here Andrea,
> Fill up this goblet with Greek wine. I said
> I would not drink this evening; but I must;
> For, strange to say, I feel my spirits fail
> With thinking what I have decreed to do.—
>
> (I. iii. 168-172)

"Strange to say," indeed, rather extraordinary! If the Count really imagines that her rape will "tame" Beatrice, then his sense of the psychological and spiritual agony this crime will cause her to suffer must be very great indeed. Why, then, the "failing spirits" from the man who "exults over torture," "loves the sight of agony," and who "delights in nothing else"? The feeling expressed here is totally atypical, and if we turn from the Count's own reaction to his intended deed to his anticipation of his daughter's reaction, we find additional peculiarities.

The Count makes but a single additional appearance on stage before the rape occurs, entering the action about midway during Act II, scene i. The scene closes with Count Cenci once again alone on stage, voicing the following meditation:

> Come darkness! Yet, what is the day to me?
> And wherefore should I wish for night, who do
> A deed which shall confound both night and day?
> 'Tis she shall grope through a bewildering mist
> Of horror: if there be a sun in heaven
> She shall not dare to look upon its beams:
> Nor feel its warmth. Let her then wish for night;
> The act I think shall soon extinguish all
> For me: I bear a darker deadlier gloom
> Than the earth's shade, or interlunar air,
> Or constellations quenched in murkiest cloud,
> In which I walk secure and unbeheld
> Towards my purpose.—Would that it were done!
> *(Exit.)*
>
> (II. i. 181-93)

Is there not something more here than the Count's anticipation of the intense and natural revulsion he believes his daughter will suffer? The Count invokes darkness, claiming to bear a "darker deadlier gloom than the earth's shade . . .", and so forth. There is nothing surprising in this. But note his assertions with reference to Beatrice. She "shall not dare to look upon (the) sun in heaven," and will "wish for night," just as he does. He anticipates, does he not, not only the natural horror of Beatrice at her victimization, but also *her participation,* at least to some degree, *in his own spiritual condition.* On what grounds does the Count assume that Beatrice, in response to being so vilely treated as an *object,* will begin to participate in the *subjectivity* of her tormentor? The victim and the victimizer would seem to be at opposite psychological poles; for the victim to begin to participate in the *identity* of the victimizer would appear to be a reversal of the natural order of things.[7] And yet is it not just this "natural order" which is so comprehensively violated within the world of the play? The Count's baleful eye falls on all he surveys, but he reserves for his daughter Beatrice, where "natural" affections should be at their peak, the purest culture of his venom. Indeed, the Count's intention here is doubly criminal; he plans not rape alone, but incestuous rape. Does this second aspect of the Count's crime carry any additional implications?

The prohibition against incest is ultimately based, not upon elements which may be only indigenous to indi-

vidual cultures, but upon the biological imperative of preserving the genetic integrity of the race. To violate this taboo is to threaten, over the long term, the very life of the race. The sexual act is of course fundamentally expressive of life itself; incestuous sexuality introduces a paradoxical element of eventual "death" in the very act of life creation. No such paradox exists, however, in Shelley's midnight landscape; the profound antagonism which this world exhibits toward our own "natural" moral order is perfectly expressed in Count Cenci's intended violation of his own daughter.

And yet consideration of this aspect of the Count's deed does not fully explain the anomalies discussed above. Let us shift our attention from the aberrations of rape and incest to the more general context of the sexual act itself. A world which is ultimately perceived to be governed by beneficent spiritual forces carries, as its earthly corollary, the proposition that "sex equals life." But what does sex equal in the world of *The Cenci,* a world whose spiritual order is governed by something quite different? And specifically, what is the *life* to issue from the Count's paternity, who bears a "darker, deadlier gloom than the earth's shade," and who will presumably *transmit* this essence in the moment of climax? And is it not conceivable that *transmission of spiritual essence* is the very purpose of the act, the essential constituent of the "charm" that will "tame"? There are two additional elements in the text which bear upon this point.

Near the beginning of the play, in response to the Count's itemization of his delight in atrocities, the Pope's emissary Camillo queries: "Art thou not most miserable?" The Count replies:

> Why, miserable?—
> No.—I am what your theologians call
> Hardened;—which they must be in impudence,
> So to revile a man's peculiar taste.
> True, I was happier than I am, *while yet*
> *Manhood remained* to act the thing I thought;
> While lust was sweeter than revenge; and now invention palls:—Ay, we
>   must all grow old—
>
> (my emphasis) (I. i. 92-99)

The Count's remark here is the only explicit reference to the sexual act in the play, a reference which clearly establishes that his natural ability to engage in sexual activity is a thing of the past. Nevertheless, he obviously succeeds in his act, and his certainty that he will succeed is never in question. In the absence of lost "manhood," what agency or power does the Count call upon in order to "walk secure and unbeheld toward (his) purpose"?

The knowledge that Beatrice has been violated is gradually revealed in Act III, scene i during her impassioned and hysterical outbursts which continue throughout the scene. Toward the end of the scene Beatrice exits with Lucretia; shortly thereafter her brother Giacomo enters, and is informed by Orsino of this latest outrage. Beatrice then returns, and by her response to Giacomo's first line reveals her understanding that Giacomo now "knows" what has occurred:

GIACOMO:

> My sister, my lost sister!

BEATRICE:

> Lost indeed!
> I see Orsino has talked with you, and
> That you conjecture things too horrible
> To speak, yet far less than the truth.

> (III. i. 381-384)

To be raped by one's own father is certainly to be on the receiving end of an act "too horrible to speak," but even this enormity is "far less than the truth." What truth? What secret lies within that "darker gloom (than) constellations quenched in murkiest cloud"?

I would suggest that we consider the possibility that this act, this "charm," conjured from the very depths of the Count's being, and administered no doubt exactly during "that very witching time of night, when churchyards yawn, and hell itself breathes out contagion to this world," was conceived and designed as the expression of the very essence of that being: death. "Death," not conceived as the natural end of life, its "defeat" as it were, but as the spiritual condition of life itself, of the Count, and of the world in which he dwells.[8] The Count's sexual potency is, in turn, both derived from and *transmitted* on this spiritual plane; the climax of the act discharges the germ seed, the death seed, of the Count's inner being, which, like the sexual seed, knows and seeks its receptors. Count Cenci, as the quintessential being of the world in which he dwells, has achieved a quintessential expression of the nature of this world in a "sexual" act which expresses death rather than life, and which penetrates not the vulnerable body alone, but the infinitely more vulnerable and intimate sphere of the inner self, the womb of the spirit.

Such an interpretation of the Count's assault on his daughter would explain many of the anomalies previously discussed, and yet also raises as many questions as it answers. Does additional evidence exist which might give credence to such an argument? What are the implications of such an impregnation? What are the consequences from the gestation to follow? And what hardly imaginable and prodigious "birth" might we eventually anticipate?

Beatrice bursts into Act III, scene i in a near hysterical condition, which is not surprising given the nature of the event that has just transpired. Many of the specific images she employs to express her horror are, however, of considerable interest. The first of these functions as a kind of "topic sentence" for much that is to come, and is followed by an interchange with Lucretia and a subsequent long speech which reveal, not only acute psychological distress, but also a far deeper disturbance, an *alteration of the functioning of consciousness itself*:

BEATRICE:

> (*She enters staggering and speaking wildly*):
> Reach me that
> handkerchief!—*My brain is hurt*;
> My eyes are full of blood; just wipe them for me
> . . .
> I see but indistinctly . . .

LUCRETIA:

> My sweet child,
> You have no wound; 'tis only a cold dew
> That starts from your dear brow . . . Alas! Alas!
> What has befallen?

BEATRICE:

> . . . . O, horrible!
> The pavement sinks under my feet! The walls
> Spin round! I see a woman weeping there,
> And standing calm and motionless, whilst I
> Slide giddily as the world reels . . . My God!
> The beautiful blue heaven is flecked with blood!
> The sunshine on the floor is black! The air
> Is changed to vapours such as the dead breathe
> In charnel pits! Pah! I am choked! *There creeps*
> *A clinging, black, contaminating mist*
> *About me . . .* 'tis substantial, heavy, thick,
> I cannot pluck it from me, for it glues
> My fingers and my limbs to one another,
> And eats into my sinews, and dissolves
> My flesh to a pollution, *poisoning*
> *The subtle, pure, and inmost spirit of life!*

> (my emphasis) (III. i. 1-23)

At this point Beatrice becomes aware of her altered state, and attempts to make sense of it by assuming that she has become mad, but she quickly drops this idea and arrives at that terminus which explains so much in this play, and which will increasingly dominate and grow within the consciousness of Beatrice herself from this point forward:

> My God! I never knew what the mad felt
> Before: for I am mad beyond all doubt!
> (*More wildly*) No, *I am dead!*

> (my emphasis) (24-26)

There is a grim logic connecting the sequence of images we have seen thus far in Beatrice's outburst, from "my brain is hurt," through a series of images expressing perceptual derangement, to a "conclusion" that arrives at the apparently bizarre notion that she is "dead" yet clearly not dead, at least in any obvious way. The significance of this progression will become clearer if we examine a similar speech which occurs somewhat later on in the scene. Beatrice finally responds to Lucretia's persistent efforts to obtain a clear explanation of what has occurred:

> What are the words which you would have me speak?
> I, who can feign no image in my mind
> Of that which has transformed me: I, whose thought
> Is like a ghost shrouded and folded up
> In its own formless horror: of all words,
> That minister to mortal intercourse,
> Which wouldst thou hear? For there is none to tell
> My misery: if another ever knew
> Aught like to it, she died as I will die,
> And left it, as I must, without a name.
> Death! Death!
>
> (III. i. 107-117)

Here we see a progression of thought which establishes a relationship markedly similar to the earlier speech, from a "premise" of "transformation," to the strange "conclusion" of the reiterated exclamation "Death!" In this case, however, the relationship is linked by a phrase which offers a significant clue into the specific nature of Beatrice's malaise: "I, whose thought / Is like a ghost, shrouded and folded up . . ." Her "death" occurs on the level of "thought"—consciousness—but takes a "ghost" like form, an apt metaphor for the condition of death in life implied in the earlier speech. But the note of finality sounded by the above is misleading, for the speech does not end in "death," but goes on to inquire into the nature and condition of whatever reality might lie beyond: "Death! Death! Our law and our religion call thee / A punishment and a reward . . . Oh, which / Have I deserved?" The above lines express in abstract, capsule form the fundamental moral conflict implicit throughout the play, with "law," "religion," and "reward" on the one side, and "death" and "punishment" on the other. Beatrice's psychological crisis is analogous to a sudden drop in barometric pressure; the resultant near vacuum polarizes the value-content of consciousness into the two extremes of good or evil, white or black; no gray area remains. As the play has progressed it has become abundantly clear that it is Beatrice who exemplifies the forces of "good" or "light," and the Count who embodies the power of "evil" or "darkness," etc. It is therefore somewhat astonishing that Beatrice should conclude her outburst with "Oh, which have I deserved?" Would not this despairing conclusion indicate that Beatrice has lost her moral "ground" in the values she formerly embodied, and stands, now, she knows not where? And let us now recall the Count's enigmatic prophecy in Act II, that Beatrice will come to avoid the "sun," and "wish for night." Beatrice seems to have indeed lost her moorings in the "light," and although not yet "wishing" for darkness, she is perhaps halfway there—pregnant, as she is, with death.

Beatrice's confusion over her own identity and values is acute, but only temporary. She quickly determines upon a course of action, and it is notable that the forbearance which has always characterized her response in the past to great adversity is now contemptuously dismissed. What is to be done? Orsino: "You will endure it then?" Beatrice: "Endure?—Orsino, it seems your counsel is small profit." No, ". . . something must be done . . . something which shall make / The thing that I have suffered but a shadow / In the dread lightning which avenges it." This "something" very quickly evolves into the plot to murder the Count, a deed, only hinted at by the others, which is first openly articulated by Beatrice herself. This plot, and the murder that follows from it, would appear to present a significant problem for my own thesis in this essay. I have suggested that the Count's assault on his daughter was designed to result in her spiritual destruction, and yet we find that the direct consequence of this act is the Count's own death. Given such an outcome, could we not accurately say that the Count is akin to a would be modern "terrorist" who, fatally miscarrying in the preparation of his bomb, roasts in his own fire?

Although it may appear that his plan results in ultimate failure, it is nevertheless true that the Count does succeed in commanding Beatrice's full attention in a new and unique way. "Turning the other cheek" in response to evil is, in a sense, a refusal to acknowledge it; it is a denial of the potency, or indeed of the very reality of evil. It is a strategy in response to evil conceived independently of the direct influence of evil. Beatrice's new posture of violent retaliation, however, is directly attributable to the actions and *will* of Count Cenci.

The stage is therefore apparently set for a direct clash of wills as Act IV begins. The Count has avoided the first attempt on his life while en route to the Castle of Petrella, and a second plan is immediately devised. Beatrice is not, however, the only character who appears to be planning something. The following interchange between the Count and Lucretia occurs early in Act IV:

CENCI:

> For Beatrice worse terrors are in store
> To bend her to my will.

LUCRETIA:

> Oh! to what will?
> What cruel sufferings more than she has known
> Canst thou inflict?

CENCI:

> . . . . .
>
> What sufferings? I will drag her, step by step,
> Through infamies unheard of among men:
> She shall stand shelterless in the broad noon

Of public scorn, for acts blazoned abroad,
One among which shall be . . . What? Canst thou
        guess?

        (IV. i. 75-84)

Lucretia's point would appear to be well taken. What more, indeed, can the Count inflict upon his daughter that he has not already attempted? The general critical view is that the Count now intends additional sexual assaults upon Beatrice, an interpretation which seems to be reinforced by a speech later in the scene which occurs during a brief interval when the Count is alone on stage:

CENCI:

    I do not feel as if I were a man,
    But like a fiend appointed to chastise
    The offences of some unremembered world.
    My blood is running up and down my veins;
    A fearful pleasure makes it prick and tingle:
    I feel a giddy sickness of strange awe;
    My heart is beating with an expectation
    Of horrid joy.

        (IV. i. 160-167)

There can be little doubt that the Count is anticipating *something* here, and the imagery and intensity of expression of the above speech strongly suggests some climactic and terminal event. And yet it is this very sense of some impending enormity that makes the speech appear disproportionate to an expression of anticipation of a second rape attempt. The Count has already tasted of this forbidden fruit; surely it is only the first violation that is capable of evoking, in both the victim and the victimizer, that unique sense of horror which would give legitimacy to the above expression. An additional objection is raised by my own thesis in this essay. I have suggested that the Count's attack on Beatrice was carried out in order to impregnate his daughter with his own spiritual essence. The seed has been sown, and, as I have tried to show, taken root and grown in his daughter's mind and spirit. If this is indeed the case, additional assaults are unnecessary and redundant. The Count need now only wait for his original deed to come to fruition, and indeed, "waiting" seems an accurate description of the Count's basic activity throughout the scene. What decisive action does the Count take following the above speech? He goes to sleep!

    It must be late; mine eyes grow weary dim
    With unaccustomed heaviness of sleep.
    Conscience! Oh, thou most insolent of lies!
    They say that sleep, that healing dew of Heaven,
    Steeps not in balm the foldings of the brain
    Which thinks thee an imposter. I will go
    First to belie thee with an hour of rest,
    Which will be deep and calm, I feel . . .

        (IV. i. 175-182)

He sleeps; he waits, but for what? The Count's last action in the play seems a purely passive one—he retires to sleep and is then murdered in his bedchamber by Marzio and Olimpio. There is, however, a slight delay in carrying out the killing. The murderers fail in their first attempt, unaccountably getting "cold feet" at the very bedside of the sleeping Count. They return to Beatrice with the deed undone, she urges them on again, and they immediately return and carry out the murder. This very brief delay seems inconsequential, and we must wonder at its dramatic function. The Count is murdered in the second attempt almost immediately after the failure of the first attempt. Why not simply dispatch him the first time and thereby tighten the dramatic structure of the play? Perhaps an answer is to be found in Beatrice's response to the initial failure:

        Miserable slaves!
    Where, if ye dare not kill a sleeping man,
    Found ye the boldness to return to me
    With such a deed undone? Base palterers!
    Cowards and traitors! . . .
    Why do I talk? (*Snatching a dagger from one of them
        and raising it.*)
            Hadst thou a tongue to say,
    'She murdered her own father!'—I must do it!
    But never dream ye shall outlive him long!

        (IV. iii. 22-33)

If we compare the scathing and vituperative language employed by Beatrice here to many of the Count's characteristic earlier speeches, we will find little to distinguish between them. And let us examine Marzio's explanation for his failure to kill the Count the first time:

        And now my knife
    Touched the loose wrinkled throat, when the old man
    Stirred in his sleep, and said, 'God! hear, O, hear
    A father's curse! What, art Thou not our Father?'
    And then he laughed. I knew it was the ghost
    Of my dead father speaking through his lips,
    And could not kill him.

        (IV. iii. 16-22)

Let us consider the possibility that the Count is consciously manipulating this moment with the objective of bringing about Beatrice's raging response, which serves as a final "quickening" of her inner transformation. And let us now consider the Count's concluding statement in his first speech in Act IV:

        No, 'tis her stubborn will
    Which by its own consent shall stoop as low
    As that which drags it down.

        (IV. i. 10-12)

What must Beatrice do in order to "stoop as low" as Count Cenci, and whose "will" are we talking about here? And let us also consider the implications of another earlier remark of the Count, an enigmatic taunt

spoken in response to Lucretia's pathetic effort to persuade the Count to desist in his persecution of Beatrice,
as he is old and will soon die and come to judgement:
"My death may be / Rapid, her destiny outspeeds it"
(IV. i. 27-28). And let us, finally, also consider the implications of the Count's last words in the play, spoken
immediately after his announced intention to seek sleep,
"deep and calm . . . and then . . ."

> O, multitudinous Hell, the fiends will shake
> Thine arches with the laughter of their joy!
> There shall be lamentation heard in Heaven
> As o'er an angel fallen; and upon Earth
> All good shall droop and sicken, and ill things
> Shall with a spirit of unnatural life
> Stir and be quickened . . . even as I am now.
>
> (IV. i. 183-189)

What is Count Cenci's plan? What is his *will*? To put
the question in his own words, "Canst thou guess?"

John Murphy refers to the Count as an embodiment of
"perfect evil,"[9] a characterization which would be difficult to dispute. The Count's evil is indeed so great, so
"perfect," as to appear transcendent—as I have argued,
the Count and his world exist in a sphere beyond our
own natural order, while at the same time remaining ee-
rily and darkly connected to it. It is the very perfection
of the Count's evil, the purity of his *will to darkness,*
which leads us now to the conclusion that his design
throughout has been leading consciously to this moment—to play the role of *murder victim* under the
bloody hands of his daughter, Beatrice. Such an act reverses the moral relationship between killer and victim
while at the same time keeping it intact. Suicide, homi-
cide—the Count's final embrace with his daughter establishes a perfect union of moral and spiritual darkness, an intimacy far greater than the obscure act of
incest which generated and preceded it. Let us recall
the Count's strange irresolution at the end of Act I when
he first determined upon this course of action ("For
strange to say, I feel my spirits fail / With thinking
what I have decreed to do."). Even Count Cenci hesitates before plunging into the ultimate darkness, but
only momentarily; for let us also recall his cold and
confident assertion in the following scene, "The act I
think shall soon extinguish all / For me. . . ." And yet
even following this climactic moment the Count's
charm continues to work.

If the murder of the Count seems to pose a problem for
my own thesis, the "trial" which follows it poses a
problem for those who regard Beatrice as a tragic figure
in the traditional or Aristotelian sense outlined earlier.
Her passionate assertions of innocence seem suspiciously near an effort to evade moral responsibility for
her actions; if so construed, her character becomes
tainted with expediency, a potentially disastrous defla-

tion of her stature as a tragic figure. Critics have attempted to deflect such an interpretation by attributing
to Beatrice the sincere conviction that she has sustained
or affirmed a moral purity by killing the Count, in ridding the world of his evil.

In considering this issue, we take up again the larger
problem of Beatrice's role and significance in the play.
If Beatrice is to maintain her stature as a tragic heroine,
we must accept her genuine conviction of innocence;
or, a weaker alternative, we may simply excuse her
weakness at this point because of the enormity of that
with which she must contend.

But suppose we consider a third alternative: what if we
were to interpret her tremendous emphasis on her innocence as incipient hysteria? What if the "no, no, no!" of
her passionate denials were functioning as a psychological *displacement* of a "no, no, no" directed at something else? And what if that "something else" was Beatrice's appalled realization that her *conscious* mind and
spirit were giving way, were in the initial stages of intimate penetration by the black, reptilian vapor of the
spirit of Count Cenci, what then?

In her essay cited earlier, Anne Radcliffe spoke of the
sense of uncanny familiarity with which we dimly perceive the apparitions of darkness. Such an awareness
creates and sustains a deep and unbreakable tension
along a shadowy continuum of knowing and not knowing, or "unknowing." With reference to this dynamic,
Radcliffe makes an interesting distinction between the
esthetic functions of "terror" and "horror":

> They must be men of very cold imaginations . . . with
> whom certainty is more terrible than surmise. Terror
> and horror are so far opposite, that the first expands the
> soul, and awakens the faculties to a high degree of life;
> the other contracts, freezes, and nearly annihilates them
> . . . where lies the great difference between terror and
> horror, but in the uncertainty and obscurity, that ac-
> company the first, respecting the dreaded evil? . . .
> Obscurity leaves something for the mind to exagger-
> ate.[10]

In the case of Beatrice, indices of the summit of the
state of terror can be observed in the climactic spasms
of wild rage which constitute a final reaction against
this force as an *object,* the *other,* in this case of course
Count Cenci. Within as well as without there is still division, for the swollen incubus of the Count's progeny
has heretofore exerted its pressure only indirectly, *un*-
consciously. With the murder of the Count, however,
the birth struggle has begun, and the darkness within
now threatens and demands entry into the light, into the
lengthening shadows of the conscious mind. The tragedy of Beatrice has reached critical mass.

The final scene of the play finds Beatrice and her remaining family imprisoned in the dungeons of the
Church. The trial and its histrionics are over, Giacomo

and Lucretia have confessed, the Pope has denied their final appeal, and their fate is certain. It is over. It is the moment of tragic stillness before the very end; the energies of conflict have played themselves out, and the dramatic gives way to the lyric. It is the time for introspection, the time, finally, *to know who you are.* But in the case of Beatrice, do we witness the birth of this tragic self, a "realized higher beauty" as one critic puts it,[11] or the birth of something quite different?

BEATRICE:

> (*wildly*)   Oh
> My God! Can it be possible I have
> To die so suddenly? So young to go
> Under the obscure, cold, rotting, wormy ground!
> To be nailed down into a narrow place;
> To see no more sweet sunshine; hear no more
> Blithe voice of living thing; must not again
> Upon familiar thoughts, sad, yet thus lost—
> How fearful! To be nothing! Or to be . . .
> What? Oh, where am I? Let me not go mad!
> Sweet Heaven, forgive weak thoughts! If there
>   should be /
> No God, no Heaven, no Earth in the void world;
> The wide, gray, lampless, deep, unpeopled world!
> If all things then should be . . . my father's spirit,
> His eye, his voice, his touch surrounding me;
> The atmosphere and breath of my dead life!
> If sometimes, as a shape more like himself,
> Even the form which tortured me on earth,
> Masked in gray hairs and wrinkles, he should come
> And wind me in his hellish arms, and fix
> His eyes on mine, and drag me down, down, down!
> For was he not alone omnipotent
> On Earth, and ever present? Even though dead,
> Does not his spirit live in all that breathe,
> And work for me and mine still the same ruin,
> Scorn, pain, despair? Who ever yet returned
> To teach the laws of Death's untrodden realm?
> Unjust perhaps as those which drive us now,
> Oh, whither, whither?[12]

(V. iv. 47-75)

Othello "turns out the light" of his temporal existence, but in doing so climbs onto a previously unattained and higher plateau of spiritual self knowledge; he illuminates and realizes his identity and destiny. I would argue that the tragedy of *The Cenci* takes Beatrice in an opposite direction; she attains not the realized self, but, in Lacan's words, the unrealized; she does not ascend, but rather descends—"down, down, down"—into the toxic mist of a terminally darkening imagination, the "unconscious" considered as a purely sinister potential.

In the preceding pages I have tried to show that *The Cenci* can be interpreted as something more than a traditional Aristotelian tragedy which has been trimmed and dressed in the clothing of "dark" romanticism. As I have argued, *The Cenci* is a tragedy which incorporates this ethos in fundamental ways, a play which explores the deepest and darkest instincts of the gothic sensibil-

ity. It is a meditation on the night, a tragedy of oblivion which gives form and life to absence within the presence of self. Count Cenci is a monster beyond the monstrous, a force which drives the mind from pity and fear to terror and horror and finally beyond, transcending the relativity of his own category in the scale of good and evil. The Count's ability to compel and fascinate the imagination is derived from what is ultimately his transcendental status—he commands the imagination because he *becomes* the imagination; he becomes, not the God of the night, but simply, the God.

Notes

1. Although the play carries no specific label, Shelley referred to it on more than one occasion as "my tragedy" in his correspondence [Percy Bysshe Shelley, *Complete Works,* 10 vols., ed. Roger Ingpen and Walter E. Peck (New York: Gordian, 1965) vol. 10: 61, 165], and also referred to Beatrice as a "tragic character" in the preface to the play: Percy Bysshe Shelley, *The Cenci,* ed. Roland A. Duerksen (Indianapolis: Bobbs-Merrill, 1970) 7. All subsequent references to the play will refer to this edition and will be included in parentheses after each quotation.

2. The really significant notion here is the idea of *hamartia,* which many critics take up as an essential ingredient in an interpretation of the play as a *tragedy of character*: ". . . [A]lthough Cenci himself may have failed to contaminate her, his act causes her to contaminate herself. She murders Cenci and by her 'pernicious mistake' (Shelley's translation of *hamartia*) becomes a tragic character." Milton Wilson, *Shelley's Later Poetry: A Study of His Prophetic Imagination* (New York: Columbia UP, 1957) 87.

   "But he was not now seeking to prove an ethical point—he was writing a tragedy. The tragic flaw in Beatrice, in Shelley's mind, was the crack in the armor of her righteousness." Carlos Baker, *Shelley's Major Poetry: The Fabric Of A Vision* (Princeton: Princeton UP, 1948) 148.

   "Since we know that she is a tragic character . . . the heroine must have a tragic flaw, which, of course, always grows out of pride. With Beatrice, the flaw (lies) . . . in her failure to understand what true innocence is." John V. Murphy, *The Dark Angel: Gothic Elements in Shelley's Works* (Cranbury, N. J.: Associated University Presses, 1975) 172.

3. Baker 147. Both Robert Whitman and D. Harrington-Lueker conceive the Count, not as a living dramatic character, but as more or less an abstraction symbolizing evil—a "symbol of tyranny" as Whitman puts it, and "more the objecti-

fication of evil than a character in his own right . . ." in Harrington-Lueker's terms. Robert Whitman, "Beatrice's 'Pernicious Mistake' in *The Cenci,*" PMLA [*Publications of the Modern Language Association*] 74:3 (June, 1959): 250; D. Harrington-Lueker, "Imagination vs. Introspection: *The Cenci* and *Macbeth,*" *Keats-Shelley Journal* 32 (1983): 179. Charles Adams echoes this evaluation: "Barnard has characterized Jupiter in *Prometheus Unbound* as being the sum of evil, including unjust laws and false religion. . . . Such a character, exactly, is Count Cenci. . . . Instead of being the story of Beatrice versus Count Cenci, this is the story of Beatrice versus evil—or, if you wish, versus tyranny, a typical Shelley theme." Charles L. Adams, "The Structure of *The Cenci,*" *Drama Survey* 4:2 (1965): 145.

4. It is notable that, even on the level of its apparent "objectivity," the "world" of *The Cenci* bears a striking resemblance to the mind of the Count. Consider, for example, the relatively petty but nevertheless sinister machinations of Orsino (which function as a kind of sub-set to the more spectacular activities of the Count), the corruption of the Church (which operates as both the temporal and spiritual authority governing the play's world), and even the operation of metaphysical "fate" (exemplified by the fact that the family is almost immediately arrested for the Count's murder by the very authorities who were en route to arrest the Count for his crimes). This "objective" reflection of the inner, spiritual condition of Count Cenci carries, as I will argue, a very far reaching significance.

5. Anne Radcliffe, "On the Supernatural in Poetry," *New Monthly Magazine* VII (1826): 146-47.

6. Quoted in Jacques Lacan, *The Four Fundamental Concepts of Psycho-Analysis,* ed. Jacques-Alain Miller, trans. Alan Sheridan (1973; New York: Norton, 1981) 23, 30. The phrase "infernal opening" is Lacan's summary of Freud.

7. I am not referring to sado-masochism here, a known, "natural" syndrome, but to a case in which a victim of sadism, who is neither sadist nor masochist, begins to participate in that state of consciousness which gives rise to sadistic activity.

8. The closest approximation of this condition in our own world is found in someone suffering from cancer, a disease which paradoxically violates the ground of its own existence, thereby creating a condition of "indwelling agony" as its natural state of being.

9. Murphy 173.

10. Radcliffe 149-150.

11. Benjamin P. Kurtz argues that Beatrice experiences a genuine, indeed an elevated, Aristotelian *catharsis* at play's end, that she is "purified in suffering," and that "the death of Beatrice becomes tragic in the full sense of the term: not meanly painful, but nobly and necessarily . . . painful, because of the very constitution of things. . . . Death has been subdued to a moral struggle that culminates in a realized higher beauty: the beauty of a tragic magnanimity." *The Pursuit of Death: A Study of Shelley's Poetry* (New York: Oxford UP, 1933) 192, 200-201.

12. Although in her next speech, in response to Lucretia's entreaty to "Trust in God's sweet love," (75) Beatrice immediately disclaims the above— "Tis past! / Whatever comes my heart shall sink no more" (77-78)—these words are in turn followed by, "And yet, I know not why, your words strike chill" (79), and the speech concludes with, "You do well telling me to trust in God, / I hope I do trust in Him. In whom else / Can any trust? And yet my heart is cold." (87-89) Cold comfort indeed is the God of *The Cenci*; rather than the light and warmth of divinity, the repeated emphasis on spiritual "chill, cold," etc. seems far more suggestive of the growing encroachment of Radcliffe's "horror"—that which "contracts, freezes, and nearly annihilates" the "faculties" of mind and spirit.

Suzanne Ferriss (essay date 1991)

SOURCE: Ferriss, Suzanne. "Reflection in a 'Many-Sided Mirror': Shelley's *The Cenci* through the Post-Revolutionary Prism." *Nineteenth-Century Contexts* 15, no. 2 (1991): 161-70.

[*In the following essay, Ferriss interprets* The Cenci *as Shelley's comment on the French Revolution and its aftermath.*]

Following his visit to Versailles in September 1816, Shelley proclaimed the French Revolution "the master theme of the epoch in which we live" (**Letters** [*of Percy Bysshe Shelley*] I: 504), recommending it to Byron as "a theme involving pictures of all that is best qualified to interest and to instruct mankind" (**Letters** I: 508). Shelley himself took up the "theme": its influence can be seen not only in overtly political compositions such as his own **Declaration of Rights** and "tyrannicidal version of the Marseillaise" (McNiece 35-6), and in his early poetic works (**Queen Mab,** the now lost **Hubert Cauvin,** and **Laon and Cythna**), but also in his later works, most notably **Prometheus Unbound.** As Earl Wasserman has claimed, the French Revolution "was inevitably and persistently Shelley's assumed frame of reference" (96).

Although Shelleyan commentators have been aware of the revolutionary references in *Prometheus Unbound,* most have denied that events in France serve as the backdrop for his drama *The Cenci,* even though this tragedy was written in 1819 during the hiatus between the composition of the third and fourth acts of *Prometheus Unbound.*[1] *The Cenci* serves as a coda to the idealized image of revolutionary potential presented in *Prometheus Unbound.* The French Revolution remains an undercurrent in *The Cenci,* but without any idealization of revolutionary action, political or otherwise. His tragedy offers a comprehensive critique of the poet's endeavor to effect revolution, whether in the political arena or in the human mind; as such *The Cenci* may more properly be called a post-revolutionary work, not simply by date of its composition but because it endorses revolutionary ideals while exhibiting a profound skepticism that these ideals may be incarnated in revolutionary action—political or poetic.[2]

Shelley depicts tyranny as linguistic oppression and uncovers this same "rhetoric of tyranny" in the language of the post-revolutionary figure.[3] He focuses on a series of documents and speeches to present the corruption of revolutionary action and rhetoric in the language of Beatrice Cenci. In this way, *The Cenci* seeks to foster in its audience a higher level of moral awareness and a recognition that, through the agency of poetry, moral change can and must precede political change. Yet, simultaneously, the tragedy calls into question the poet's ability to realize this ideal revolution. Shelley pictures the tyrant as a poet, specifically a dramatic poet, and thus extends his post-revolutionary critique to the characterization of the poet as "unacknowledged legislator" offered contemporaneously in his political tract, *A Philosophical View of Reform* (1819), and subsequently in his own poetic manifesto, *A Defence of Poetry* (1821).

Two of Shelley's comments on the purpose of drama provide a key to the complex allusive method he employs in *The Cenci.* In his Preface he argues, "There must also be nothing attempted to make the exhibition subservient to what is vulgarly termed a moral purpose. The highest moral purpose aimed at in the highest species of drama, is the teaching of the human heart, through its sympathies and antipathies, the knowledge of itself" (240). He elaborates on the character of this knowledge in a later work that crystallizes many of the suggestions made in his Preface to *The Cenci* and in the drama itself. In *A Defence of Poetry,* Shelley claims, "In drama of the highest order there is little food for censure or hatred; it teaches rather self-knowledge and self-respect. Neither the eye nor the mind can see itself, unless reflected upon that which it resembles" (491). Not only does the play erect such a mirror through the character of Beatrice, but its very relationship to the French Revolution enacts this principle. The drama is understood by reflection "upon that which it resembles," the Revolution. This is not to say that *The Cenci* directly mirrors the events of 1789 and following, for the dramatic mirror is "prismatic and many-sided"; it "collects the brightest rays of human nature and divides and reproduces them with majesty and beauty, and multiplies all that it reflects, and endows it with the power of propagating its Eke wherever it may fall" (491). *The Cenci*'s relationship to the Revolution, then, takes shape not simply as imitation, as direct correspondence, but as a collection of echoes and reversals, "sympathies and antipathies."

Thus, in Count Cenci, we glimpse traces of an anarchic, revolutionary figure (Curran 75). Dismissive of external dictates, he follows only his own desires: "I please my senses as I list" (I. i. 69). His is a corrupted fulfillment of the Revolutionary credo of personal liberty, one made horrific by the emendation: "And [I] vindicate that right with force or guile" (I. i. 69-70). His vow to employ "force" to "vindicate that right" echoes the actions of the Revolutionary figures of the Terror, who employed violent means in defiance of all law to uphold perverted revolutionary ideals. Shelley complicates his image of Cenci as a corrupt revolutionary, as a post-revolutionary, in depicting Cenci's force as only partly physical. Cenci seeks to impose psychic torture, rather than merely physical terror, on those who prevent him from pleasing his senses as he "lists."

In the Count's incestuous assault on Beatrice, then, Shelley offers a palpable image of psychic domination. As a particularly shocking subversion of moral authority, incest is allied with revolutionary action, though not sympathetically, as in Shelley's earlier work, *Laon and Cythna* (1817). Significantly, the incestuous assault which provokes Beatrice's radical act of revenge is silenced in the drama (Worton 107-109). Though never overtly mentioned, the radically oppressive act of Cenci's incestuous assault does reveal itself in his discourse. The Count's voiced *threat* to violate Beatrice is enough to unhinge her: to Lucretia's question, "What did your father do or say to you?" (II. i. 59), Beatrice replies, "It was one word, Mother, one little word; / One look, one smile" (II. i. 63-4). The oppressive effects of Cenci's verbal threat recall his earlier claim that, like the king, he wields the *lettre de cache*: after learning of the accidental deaths of his two sons, he warns the remaining members of his family, "Beware! For my revenge / Is as the sealed commission of a king / That lulls, and none dare name the murderer" (I. iii. 96-8). Through this obvious reference to the "sealed letter" which served as a warrant for arbitrary arrest and imprisonment prior to the Revolution, Shelley overlays Cenci's rebellion with the political tyranny of eighteenth-century monarchist France. In his portrait of Cenci he conflates the rebel and the monarch, presenting the revolutionary figure as the tyrannical agent of the Terror, yoking violence to the arbitrary and manipulative uses of language. Cenci and others of his ilk employ a "rhetoric of tyranny" (*Queen Mab* V. 121). In Julia Kristeva's terms, they enforce the law of the symbolic, the structuring and ordering principle of language that represses all heterogeneity and disruption under the cover of ideology.

Ironically, though, Cenci purports to undertake a revolution in *words*. As Curran has argued, "the Count is an artist, conscious of his every effect" (73). Paradoxically, however, his creation is his tyranny: Cenci speaks of his revenge as an "invention" (I. i. 99), as a product of his "fancy."[4] Shelley pictures the Count as a *literary* creator: the events depicted in Shelley's drama appear as Cenci's invention. He is a "corrupt dramatic poet," according to Ronald Lemoncelli, plotting his family's ruin. Even Beatrice's parricide fulfills Cenci's vision: "she shall die unshriven and unforgiven, / A rebel to her father and her God" (IV. i. 89-90). In this way, Shelley's portrait of Cenci as a decidedly literary creator, and more specifically, as a dramatic poet, has profound implications for the idea that poets are "the unacknowledged legislators of the world" (*A Philosophical View of Reform* 20, *A Defence of Poetry* 508).

In fact, Shelley's portrait of the Count as a corrupted literary artist as well as a failed revolutionary undermines his own comments about the revolutionary role of the poet in *A Philosophical View of Reform* and *A Defence of Poetry*. Cenci's boast that his fancy produces radically unfamiliar visions, images other men "would start to know" (I. i. 89), appears gruesomely ironic when compared to Shelley's comment on the ethical potential of poetry in his *Defence [of Poetry]*, for there he argues that "the great instrument of moral good is the imagination" (488). Poetry, as "the expression of the imagination" (480), especially "strengthens that faculty which is the organ of the moral nature of man" (488). But Cenci can imagine what the decorous poet finds "unspeakable": his unnatural creation of the dual acts of incest and parricide undermines this idealized image of poetry as Elysian visions.

Initially, Beatrice serves as a counter to the Count's dual corruption of the revolutionary impulse as her early discursive productions function as a response to his perversion of poetic legislation. Beatrice's public plea for aid against her father's oppression appears as an attempt to appropriate speech and to silence her father; hers is an ideal revolutionary subversion of his linguistic tyranny. Her speech to the guests at the "celebratory" banquet is "revolutionary" in the Kristevan sense: her language bears traces of the *semiotic*, the rhythmic, pulsional pressures that disrupt the symbolic, transgressing simultaneously linguistic and socio-political order.[5] Immediately after Cenci has enforced the socio-symbolic law in threatening to employ the *lettre de cachet*, Beatrice pleads,

I do entreat you, go not, noble guests;
What although tyranny, and impious hate
Stand sheltered by a father's hoary hair?
What, if 'tis he who clothed us in these limbs
Who tortures them, and triumphs? What, if we,
The desolate and the dead, were his own flesh,
His children and his wife, whom he is bound
To love and shelter? Shall we therefore find
No refuge in this merciless wide world?

(I. iii. 99-107)

Her repeated questions establish an incantatory rhythm that grows increasingly insistent in response to the perceived pressures of Cenci's threat. The repetitive structure of Beatrice's questions, "What . . ." and "What, if . . . ," further underscores the movement of her remarks from statement of fact to supposition. Her revelations of Cenci's domestic violence take the form not of direct accusation but of speculation: "What, if we . . . were his own flesh, / His children and his wife?" In this near absurd contradiction of fact, Beatrice at once reveals Cenci's horrific designs and veils her charge under the cloak of fiction.

She makes a similarly subversive assault against her father's oppression in asking the guests for empathy, to envision the events that have provoked her outburst: "Oh, think what deep wrongs must have blotted out / First love, then reverence in a child's prone mind / Till it thus vanquish shame and fear! O, think!" (I. iii. 108-110). Her insistent repetition of the imperative, "O, think!" builds to an insupportable crescendo as she begs for release at once from the physical and linguistic tyranny imposed by her father.

But Beatrice's semiotic effusions go unheeded. For the men she exhorts for help are simply more representatives of paternal tyranny, and they are equally ruled by the law of the symbolic. From the perspective of the symbolic her language appears the product of a "wild girl" (I. iii. 132), an "insane girl" (I. iii. 160). Beatrice herself reveals the cause of her plea's ineffectuality, in asking, "is it that I sue not in some form / Of scrupulous law, that ye deny my suit?" (I. iii. 135-36). As a subversive assault on the law of the symbolic (of the father), Beatrice's "suit" remains unacknowledged and uncomprehended.

In the final moments of her speech, however, Beatrice retreats from her subversive stance and launches a direct attack upon her father in language that bears no traces of the semiotic. Beatrice issues a series of commands to Cenci: "Retire thou, impious man! Aye hide thyself" (I. iii. 146), "Frown not on me!" (I. iii. 151), "Cover thy face from every living eye" (I. iii. 154), "Seek out some dark and silent corner" (I. iii. 157), "Bow thy white head before offended God" (I. iii. 157). This string of imperatives, borrowed at once from the language of religious exorcism and political propaganda, bears traces of force and represents a subversion of her earlier revolutionary stance—in both political and poetic terms. Her recourse to the terms of the symbolic, the language of Cenci, marks a retreat from the semiotic and from its potential to disrupt symbolic law. Beatrice rejects the revolutionary possibility of poetic language to confront the tyranny enforced by symbolic law and in so doing appears as a failed artist. She appropriates the speech of linguistic tyranny and joins Cenci in corrupting the revolutionary impulse.

Beatrice's parricidal designs represent a further retreat from the revolutionary stance upheld in her banquet speech. Not only does she betray the revolutionary potential of poetic language; she disavows it entirely. As the revolutionary impulse is transferred from language to physical action it is perverted. Her parricide marks a descent into physical violence, an embodiment of the implied violence contained in her verbal threats against Cenci. Contrary to Barbara Groseclose's assertion that "if parent-child incest is symbolic of tyrannical oppression, then the parricide must represent the possibility of eliminating tyranny through violence" (230), Beatrice's act is a corruption of the revolutionary impulse, for it, too, is a tyrannical instance of oppressive force. Her attempts to veil her parricide in discourse invoking patriarchal authority, including God's, only compounds its violence. She claims that Marzio, the assassin she hires, commits "a high and holy deed" (IV. ii. 35), acting as "a weapon in the hand of God / To a just use" (IV. iii. 34-5). Like her father, Beatrice employs language as a defensive and repressive structure to defend herself against the charge of parricide. Ironically, *Beatrice,* not Cenci, now appears to wield the *leure de cachet.* Her subversion of the law has made her as tyrannical as her father. She unwittingly, and inevitably, becomes a reflection of her father.

Beatrice's violent act further subverts the revolutionary potential of her banquet speech and casts her as a failed poetic, no less than political, revolutionary. In *A Philosophical View of Reform,* Shelley pictures poets and philosophers as "mirrors of gigantic shadows which futurity casts upon the present" (7:20). And in his *Defence,* he argues, "poetry is a mirror which makes beautiful that which is distorted," unlike prose, which as "the story of particular facts is as a mirror which obscures and distorts that which should be beautiful" (485). In *The Cenci,* however, the only mirror pictured distorts: Cenci envisions the child of his incestuous coupling with Beatrice as "a hideous likeness of herself," as an image seen from "a distorting mirror" (IV. i. 146-47). Beatrice's tragedy is that she unwittingly becomes the image of her father. She assumes his art and his artfulness, similarly perverting the revolutionary possibility of poetic language. Ironically, this places Shelley's tragedy at odds with his own definition of the drama:

The drama . . . is as a prismatic and many-sided mirror, which collects the brightest rays of human nature and divides and reproduces them from the simplicity of these elementary forms, and touches them with majesty and beauty, and multiplies all that it reflects, and endows it with the power of propagating its like wherever it may fall.

(491)

The propagation of "like" pictured in *The Cenci* as the Count's creation contradicts this image of the proper role of drama and, by extension, Shelley's vision of poetry's revolutionary function.

This is not to say that Shelley completely denigrates the potential of poetry to effect change, but that he complicates the issue in his graphic presentation of the poet's difficulties in the figures of Cenci and Beatrice. Just as Beatrice becomes an unwitting reflection [of] her father, and revolutionary action a distorted image of tyrannical oppression, so the "aesthetic revolution" risks mirroring linguistic tyranny. Shelley's portraits of literary creation in *The Cenci* underscore the dangerous possibility that actions, filtered through the prism of a discredited, post-revolutionary language, may become distorted. More generally still, Shelley's invention of a series of misdirected documents—Beatrice's petition, Orsino's letter, the Pope's arrest warrant—highlights the potential of words, including those of the poet, to mislead. If "the spirit of poetry must incarnate itself in the letter" (Dawson 257), then the poet's expression is itself subject to distortion.

Through the example of Beatrice, Shelley questions the possibility of *any* revolutionary action following the disillusioning example of France. He passes both poetic creation and political revolution through the post-revolutionary prism of his drama, *The Cenci.* Beatrice's parricide, combined with her use of the same "rhetoric of tyranny" that had been her father's tool of oppression, subverts the revolutionary potential held forth by her banquet speech. As a result, within the drama, she unwittingly becomes a reflection of the tyrannous forces she sought to overthrow and, in the larger context of Shelley's time, of the French Revolution itself as it inevitably descended into the renewed despotism of the Terror. In Beatrice's arbitrary use of violence and, above all, in the discourse she employs to justify and veil this act, *The Cenci* casts doubt on the possibility that the revolutionary ideals betrayed in France by the Terror and Napoleon's rise to power may be recaptured either politically or poetically. The revolutionary potential of both political action and poetic production bear the brunt of Shelley's skepticism in this radical questioning of the legislator's potential to effect positive change, whether functioning as the people's recognized political representative or their "unacknowledged" advocate, the poet.

Notes

1. Only P. M. S. Dawson and Rolf P. Lessinich have recognized *The Cenci* as a response to revolutionary possibility, yet neither examines the play in detail to support such claims and both view the drama as simply a rejection of "violent revolution."

2. As Hoagwood argues, Shelley "repeatedly links the social and political environment with such intellectual products as poetry, philosophy, and religion" (*Skepticism and Ideology* 82-83). He further cites the poet's own citation of lines from *The Cenci* in a letter discussing the Manchester massacre as evidence that "his poetic work and his political interests and activities condition and reflect one another" (164). Curran further notes that, in *The Cenci*, Shelley has "translated into drama the poetics of the Romantic revolution" (99).

3. Worton notes the "linguistic preoccupation" (106) of the drama and McWhir gives similar attention to representations of language in the play. My approach focuses more specifically on documents and speeches as evidence of Shelley's preoccupation with revolution—both in France and in Romantic poetry. At the heart of the tragedy's "preoccupation" with language is Shelley's questioning of the poet's ability to enact revolution in and through poetry.

4. Gold notes Cenci's "aesthetic tyranny" (59) but overlooks the decidedly *dramatic* character of Cenci's aesthetics. McWhir does argue that Cenci acts as "the playwright of a drama in which he is also an actor" (153) and Lemoncelli that Cenci is a corrupt dramatic poet and that he resembles the description of this specific type of poet in the *Defence*. But both downplay the implications of this insight for Shelley's own creation in *The Cenci*.

5. Kristeva envisions the semiotic not only as a disruptive force within language, transgressing the law of the symbolic, but as a political disruption. She identifies semiotic mobility with revolutionary practice: "poetry confronts *order* at its most fundamental level: the logic of language and the principle of the State" (80).

Works Cited

Curran, Stuart. *Shelley's* The Cenci*: Scorpions Ringed with Fire*. Princeton, NJ: Princeton UP, 1970

Dawson, P. M. S. *The Unacknowledged Legislator: Shelley and Politics*. Oxford: Clarendon Press, 1980.

Gold, Elise M. "*King Lear* and Aesthetic Tyranny in Shelley's *The Cenci, Swellfoot the Tyrant* and *The Witch of Atlas*." *English Language Notes* 24 (Sept 1986): 58-70.

Groseclose, Barbara. "The Incest Motif in Shelley's *The Cenci*." *Comparative Drama* 19 (1985): 222-236.

Hoagwood, Terence Allan. *Skepticism and Ideology: Shelley's Political Prose and its Philosophical Context from Bacon to Marx*. Iowa City: University of Iowa Press, 1988.

Kristeva, Julia. *Revolution in Poetic Language*. Trans. Margaret Waller. New York: Columbia, 1984.

Lemoncelli, Ronald L. "Cenci as Corrupt Dramatic Poet." *English Language Notes* 16 (December 1978): 103-17.

Lessenich, Rolf P. "Godwin and Shelley: Rhetoric versus Revolution." *Studia Neophilologica* 47 (1975): 40-52.

McNiece, Gerald. *Shelley and the Revolutionary Idea*. Cambridge: Harvard University Press, 1969.

McWhir, Anne. "The Light and the Knife: Ab/Using Language in *The Cenci*." *Keats-Shelley Journal* 38 (1989): 145-161.

Shelley, Percy Bysshe. *The Cenci. Shelley's Poetry and Prose*. Ed. Donald H. Reiman and Sharon B. Powers. New York: Norton, 1977. 236-300.

———. *A Defence of Poetry. Shelley's Poetry and Prose*. Ed. Donald H. Reiman and Sharon B. Powers. New York: Norton, 1977. 478-508.

———. *The Letters of Percy Bysshe Shelley*. Ed. Frederick L. Jones. Oxford: Clarendon Press, 1964. 2 vols.

———. *A Philosophical View of Reform. The Complete Works of Percy Bysshe Shelley*. Ed. Roger Ingpen and Walter E. Peck. New York: Gordian Press, 1965. 7:3-55.

———. *Queen Mab. Shelley's Poetry and Prose*. Ed. Donald H. Reiman and Sharon B. Powers, New York: Norton, 1977. 42.

Wasserman, Earl R. *Shelley: A Critical Reading*. Baltimore: Johns Hopkins University Press, 1971.

Worton, Michael. "Speech and Silence in *The Cenci*." *Essays on Shelley*. Ed. Miriam Allott. Totowa, NJ: Barnes and Nobles, 1982. 105-124.

Roger Blood (essay date fall 1994)

SOURCE: Blood, Roger. "Allegory and Dramatic Representation in *The Cenci*." *Studies in Romanticism* 33, no. 3 (fall 1994): 355-89.

[*In the following essay, Blood comments on* The Cenci*'s critical reception and considers theoretical interpretations of the play.*]

To judge from the work of Shelley's recent critics, *The Cenci* has now taken its place securely in the canon of Shelley's work. The ambivalence concerning its aesthetic stature and lingering doubts about its suitability for performance have been set aside in favor of thematic considerations—rape, incest, murder, deceit, and the abuse of power—more in line with our contemporary tastes. None of the questions which formerly inhibited the canonization of *The Cenci* have been resolved: its stage history has remained short enough to document,[1] and the battles over its aesthetic stature have been abandoned rather than won. *The Cenci*'s theatrical and theoretical potential has as consequence yet to be realized, and the critical reception of Shelley's solitary stage play remains a history that is largely yet to happen. In the meantime, *The Cenci* has begun to respond productively to a criticism oriented towards textual rather than dramatic models of representation,[2] and this change of emphasis has, perhaps ironically, permitted a more direct access to the political and institutional issues that abound in Shelley's play. The "question of the text" has permitted interpreters to skip the act of aesthetic judgment entirely, as an unproductive distraction, or even an actual hindrance to the progress of interpretation. As a result, the canonization of *The Cenci* has occurred as a critical and interpretative phenomenon isolated from its aesthetic legitimation. The ready alignment of social and political concerns with textual models has given *The Cenci* a critical stature as a *text* it never received as a poem or a play. The somewhat apologetic tone that once predominated among all critics of *The Cenci* has now been replaced by a relish on the part of critics which is not necessarily a compliment to Shelley's achievement. *The Cenci,* almost alone among Shelley's major poems, provides an opportunity to dodge the complications of his "ideal" mode, and to connect the aesthetic work of this radical poet directly with the concerns of his political prose and with our own political problems. Our belated discovery of *The Cenci* has, in effect, reversed the act of aesthetic judgment it appeared to elide: the advent of a text-oriented criticism, far from being neutral or unconcerned with aesthetic questions, has legitimated a somewhat indelicate thematic content precisely because its aesthetic appeal is in question.

Whether the debate over the canonical stature of *The Cenci* is simply in temporary abeyance for a critical generation which finds all such acts of judgment doubtful, or whether the canonization of *The Cenci* is being performed, as is so often the case with literary works, by default in a critical development ostensibly concerned with other matters, may in the end matter very little. Our current critical discourse deliberately neglects the explicit formulation of aesthetic questions, and in the case of *The Cenci,* this avoidance can only come with a sigh of relief, as those questions have long proven difficult to resolve. Now that the canonicity of *The Cenci* is generally assumed, one may ask what role the question of the aesthetic played, and continues to play, in the critical reception of the play before *The Cenci*'s awkward acceptance foreclosed the question. For as the recent critical enthusiasm for the play makes only too clear, the repression of explicit aesthetic considerations has only displaced them. The moral and dramatic constraints that once inhibited the acceptance of the play now frequently serve as the grounds of critical interest, and this reversal extends the complications of the aesthetic throughout the interpretative discourse while avoiding the explicit formulation of the issues involved. Whether *The Cenci* belongs in the canon is no longer debated, but the crucial function of the aesthetic in establishing the link between the literary text and its psychological and historical implications has continued unchanged.

The attractiveness of *The Cenci* to social and political analysis is a case in point. The appeal of the drama's simpler mode of representation has been noted by all critics of *The Cenci* since Mary Shelley,[3] and it appeals once again precisely because it permits an escape from those "aestheticizing" tendencies that make the political analysis of his other work so difficult. Shelley himself remarked, in a letter to Peacock in July 1819,[4] that *The Cenci* was written "without any of the peculiar feelings and opinions which characterize my other compositions," and that "the facts [of the case were] a matter of history." Shelley insisted repeatedly in his letters, in his "Dedication" of the play to Leigh Hunt, and (at least as reported by Trelawney[5]), in his conversation, on the absolute impersonality of *The Cenci,* and its distance from the personal tone of his other work. The substitution of a dramatic for a lyrical or narrative mode, of an historical for a mythopoeic discourse, distinguishes *The Cenci,* as a "sad reality," in Shelley's words, from the "visions" of his other poetry, which he considered, in a wording curiously self-conscious of his own allegorizing tendencies, to "impersonate my own visions of the beautiful and the just."[6] The substance of *The Cenci,* in both character and action, are instead, he wrote to Byron, "a matter-of-fact" (May 26, 1820 in Jones 198), not a product of his own invention.

The continuity of *The Cenci* with his other work was not, by this change alone, put into doubt, and Newman Ivey White's summation has remained essentially unchallenged: "In *The Cenci* [Shelley] gave objective, dramatic representation to what he was otherwise presenting as abstract theory."[7] The "otherwise" here, however, for White as for other critics, is *Prometheus Unbound,* and White is therefore stating what has become an obligatory *topos* of Shelley criticism: the articulation of the theoretical question posed by the drama's representational mode as the necessity to read Shelley's two plays as interpretations of each other. The "abstract theory" is thus not (say) any of Shelley's prose tracts, and certainly not *A Defence of Poetry,* but the explicitly figural and mythopoeic mode of *Prometheus Unbound.* The question of abstraction is contained entirely *within* Shelley's poetic corpus, and not in its contrast to his prosaic work, and this question has, indeed, long defined the interpretive challenge posed by his verse. Likewise, the "objectivity" that White refers to has little to do with the historical facticity of the events represented, but concerns instead their representation in the mode of the drama. The objectivity of *The Cenci* that White, and many others, have emphasized in specific contrast to *Prometheus Unbound,* is not the distinction of fact from fiction, but of the drama from the lyric. *Prometheus Unbound* is a "lyrical drama," as Shelley understood, precisely because it cannot be staged, since the characters and events it portrays are not available to our eyes and ears, and this decisive break with the phenomenal continuities of perception and experience is the crucial question which must be resolved if the representational mode of *Prometheus* [*Unbound*] is to be understood.

The objectivity of *The Cenci* by contrast resides not merely in the representation *of* human action (where Mary thought Shelley's true talent lay), but in its representability (as Peacock noted[8]) *by* human subjects, as actors who speak and perform on stage. The "objectivity" of the drama that Shelley and his critics have found so attractive is founded on the reduction in the dramatic text of all representation to what is spoken and acted by individual subjects. The "objectivity" of the drama, that is, turns out paradoxically to be a purely "subjective" structure, as the representation of the subject by the text is in turn represented on stage by other *subjects.* In the stage realization of a play, the representation of the subject by the text is reversed as the text is represented by the subject, and this reversal establishes the curious circularity of all dramatic representation. The dramatic subject is therefore both *what* represents, and what *is* represented, and the representation of the subject in the drama thus always resolves into the specularity of self-representation. It turns out that the theoretical crux of the dramatic mode is condensed in the traditional aesthetic question of the play's stageability, and the success of a performance coincides with the effective disappearance of the text from view in the continuity of perception between unmediated subjects. The objectivity of the drama as a genre results not from its rather questionable fidelity to the facts of history, but from the continuity of the drama's representational mode with the nontextual phenomenality of perception and experience.

The challenge presented by the drama therefore goes far beyond the traditional question of dramatic illusion. The question posed by the drama is not merely its ability to deceive—which would not distinguish it from any other fictional mode—but that it deceives while allowing sight and hearing to continue unhindered. As in any other fiction, what is represented on stage may or may not be false, but even what is farthest from the truth on stage is still *perceived.* The critical repression of aesthetic questions in the realm of the drama, that is, has only served to articulate the theoretical crux of the concept of the aesthetic itself, by raising the question of the relation between the aesthetic, as an act of judgment (which articulates the distinctions that establish the canon) and the aesthetic as *aesthesis,* the act of perception. And the question of perception, and the objectivity founded in perception, as we have seen, directly confronts the mediating role of the subject in dramatic representation. The question of *The Cenci*'s dramatic objectivity, it turns out, far from escaping the complications of the aesthetic, has permitted the concept of the aesthetic itself to be articulated, by revealing the link between perception, the act of judgment, and the specularity of the subject. The unresolved questions surrounding *The Cenci*'s canonical stature may remain as a latent and unarticulated component of our critical discourse, but they are bound to be played out nevertheless as the theoretical challenge posed by its dramatic mode.

In this respect, the recent critical enthusiasm for *The Cenci,* which dodges aesthetic questions, reconnects with the issues raised by the long history of the play's critical rejection, which were always expressed in primarily aesthetic terms. For the text of *The Cenci,* instead of disappearing into the aesthetics of perception, has long called awkward attention to itself. The formal problems that dominated critical discussion of *The Cenci* for over a century, and that have now fallen somewhat into abeyance, uniformly indicate a disruption of the process whereby the literary text is realized in the phenomenality of performance, preventing the act of dramatic representation from disappearing into the aesthetics of experience. One is too often reminded of the mechanics of the stage, as if the strings in a puppet theater were suddenly to become visible. Ernest Bate's remarks of 1904 still state the consensus on the problems of performance: "A play, one of whose acts fails to advance the plot in the least, ten of whose scenes are purely conversational and without action, and four-fifths of whose speeches are of impossible length, is surely not to be called an acting drama" (quoted in Curran 262). Desmond King-Hele adds, in a similar vein, that after dithering in Act II, "the scene changes are too frequent, the speeches are over-long, there are more soliloquies than in Hamlet"[9] and so on. The play is alternately too slow, and then too fast: Savella's arrival with the warrant for Cenci's arrest in Act IV is too abrupt for the irony to be missed, and Beatrice's change of heart, after lingering indecision, can only appear too sudden to be judicious. It is easy enough to blame, as many of Shelley's critics do, his lack of stage experience for the disruptions of the play, but such formal and aesthetic problems, by inhibiting the interpretation, serve to articulate the otherwise self-effacing representational processes present in the text. The unevenness of the temporal progress in the dramatic exposition puts into question not only the veracity of representation (its believability), but the suitability of the representation for dramatic stage presentation. The failure of the plot is a failure to represent, and the failure to represent is in turn a failure to produce appropriate effects on cue, and these failures make the mechanics of the plot only too apparent.

With the disruption of the temporal pattern, *The Cenci* descends into "character scenes," where time is marked while the plot is not advanced, but the frequently noted emphasis on character is deceptive. The uncertain exposition of the plot also inhibits the fundamental exhibition of character, and as a result, the interpretation of the characters in the play has remained problematic. Instead of appearing as historical *givens,* facts beyond question, they have seemed to Shelley's critics to be unnatural, awkward on stage because not quite like reality. "The reader," Harold Bloom has written, "is asked to accept as human characters whose states of mind are too radically and intensely pure to be altogether human,"[10] whereas White considered Count Cenci especially to be "too monstrous to be credible" (139). The monstrosity of the Count is read equally as grotesquely obsessed, or fundamentally unmotivated: Earl Wasserman has resolved the problem in the suggestive formulation of the Count as the "uncaused cause,"[11] leaving this beast to occupy a position in the structure of the play analogous to the temporal and interpretive paradoxes involved in any representation of divinity. As subjects, the characters of *The Cenci* are questionable representations because they are both without sufficient cause *and* are too given to easy rationale. Such absoluteness of character interferes with the transitions of the exposition: characters in *The Cenci* may hesitate or break, but they do not develop. The apparent changes in character therefore either lack substance, as the Count's moments of doubt come to nothing, or Orsino's false resolution in Act I excuses what it does not understand, or, alternatively, the transitions of the plot take the subject "out of character," as Beatrice betrays herself (or her character type) by her acts rather than advancing in understanding or maturity. The transition from mimesis to narration, the return from what is represented in the drama to the intelligibility of understanding, and the reversal of plot as action to plot as causal explanation, have all been interrupted, and the consequent failure of the development inhibits the interpretability of the resulting characters.

This complication inevitably crystallizes in the critical reception as the lack of consensus on the character of Beatrice as the main interpretative problem of the play.

In the formal tradition of literary analysis, determining the sense of the plot has depended largely on understanding it as an exposition of character, just as the interpretation of character is in large part the attempt to define the consistency between various actions. The necessity of this transition is condensed in Henry James's remark, "What is character but the determination of incident? What is incident but the illustration of character?"[12] The primary burden in the interpretation of tragedy thus becomes to demonstrate the destruction of the subject as a necessary consequence of its own character, and thus to interpret the violence of the plot as an act of self-destruction, the inevitable realization of the self-contradiction of the subject as an act on stage and as an event in history. The nature of such a contradiction in the character of Beatrice has proven difficult to define, and there is not even unanimity over whether such a flaw exists. White attributes Beatrice's "tragic flaw" to a motivation for revenge, but this seems somewhat amiss, and even he feels the need to qualify the motivation for her actions as "self-protection" (139). Self-protective they may be, but self-protection leaves Beatrice too passive, merely reactive to events rather than an agent in her own right, and we are thus in little position to identify her acts as her own, or to hold her responsible for her own death. The essential passivity of the central agent of *The Cenci* leads White to suggest that the play belongs to melodrama rather than to tragedy, thus resolving the interpretation of character by a change of genre. Harold Bloom has offered a similar resolution, but redefines the central problem. Beatrice's actions are for him "the falling away from imaginative conduct on the part of a heroically imaginative individual . . . Beatrice is tragic because she does not meet [the] high standard" set implicitly by "'**The Mask of Anarchy**' of a nonviolent resistance to evil" (Bloom xxx). Bloom's formulation aligns suggestively with Shelley's own remarks in the "Preface" that if Beatrice had recognized that "revenge, retaliation, atonement, are pernicious mistakes" she "would have been wiser and better; but she would never have been a tragic character" (240). But Bloom breaks with Shelley in seeing Beatrice's actions as a contradiction of her consistent character, rather than a realization of a contradictory subject, and in this separation of the subject from its own actions Bloom is led to consider *The Cenci* as an implicit revision of the tragic tradition. The question of the consistency of Beatrice's character will in fact be decisive, but Bloom preserves the attractiveness of her character, in effect, by cutting her out of the play in which she is so hopelessly compromised.

Stuart Curran has similarly defended Beatrice by denying the presence of such a traditional, Aristotelean contradiction of character: "There is no tragic 'flaw' in Shelley's play: the tragedy is that good is helpless to combat evil" (259). The tragedy is now in the nature of things, the sheer "wickedness" of society. The denial of the flaw of character in the subject, that is, displaces the contradiction into the collective subject of a society hopelessly at odds with itself. Curran's interpretation therefore dovetails with his later reconsideration, in *Shelley's* Annus Mirabilis, that "if Beatrice has a tragic flaw, it is implicitly her Christianity."[13] The subject of *The Cenci* is therefore Christianity itself, whose contradictions are realized explicitly when it is put into practice as a social and judicial institution. The Christian context also requires such a reconsideration of character in the reading of Earl Wasserman. "Shelley's tragedy," he insists, "is not rooted in the flaw of character, [since] all human constitutions are flawed" but Wasserman nevertheless considers the interpretation of Beatrice thwarted by "the impossibility of ignoring or explaining away either Beatrice's faults or her noble character" (117, 121). She is for Wasserman both undeniably good and what she does is inexcusably wrong; her acts therefore do not realize a flaw of character but break with a character that remains consistent. Critics alternate between a conviction that her acts reveal an inconsistency that puts the interpretation of her character into doubt, or she is so pure and consistent of character that her acts cannot be deciphered because they are so thoroughly at odds with what we know about her. The translation of character into action, of subject into plot, has been interrupted, producing the distinctive pattern of irresolution in the critical reception. But the inconsistency which all critics sense, in precisely the way Shelley predicted, in the "anatomizing casuistry with which [they] seek the justification of Beatrice, yet feel that she has done what needs justification" (240) is not merely the result of a discrepancy between character and action, nor between different, contrasting tendencies within her character, but the absolute self-contradiction, the literal counter-statement of her public deceit, which mars her self-representation and self-justification after the murder. The question of the relation of her character to her acts, of the subject to the action, cannot be resolved because her own self-interpretation is so clearly egregious. The problem of interpreting Beatrice is posed less by the murder of the Count than by her deceit in her own defense, her inability to explain and to defend her actions, which means to represent her own deeds to herself and to understand what she has done. The question of the *hamartia* as a judgment of character cannot be determined because the *anagnorisis,* the moment of self-recognition, has misfired. The crux of the play, therefore, is not contained entirely within the traditional problem in tragedy of the relation of character to action, but resides in the quandary of the loss, rather than a growth, of self-consciousness on the part of the central character. It is easy enough (at least in literature) to rationalize murder (and especially murder of the self) as consistent with character, but the elision of consciousness, the utter lack of self-knowledge Beatrice reveals, is incomprehensible. The destruction of another subject, or even one's self, is entirely understandable, but the loss of one's own subjectivity cannot be represented.

The cumulative result of such formal considerations is that the aesthetic effect is ambiguous. The mechanical conventions of the stage, and of the manipulation of facts for dramatic effect are too obvious, and point to the contingencies of its representational mode, while the self-deception of the central character dissipates the tragic focus. Detached from the development of character, the plot of *The Cenci* is left to be both too random and brutal—going beyond the rather routine murder and mutilation of conventional tragedy—*and* inadequately active. The action of *The Cenci* is insufficient to fill up the plot but is still excessive enough to consume the agents, while the causal, and hence explanatory, function of the plot is abridged, reversed into irony, or left incomplete. The doubts about *The Cenci*'s generic definition, or its suitability for the stage, restate the questions posed by the history of interpretation, as the recurrent difficulty critics have found in making the representation of character align with the structure of the plot. What these persistent formal problems indicate, that is, is that the syntheses involved in any aesthetic process, of the subject of representation with its effect, of perception with knowledge, and of understanding with experience, is being undone, and that with the loss of structural concision in the drama the focus of critical interpretation is bound to be dissipated. The formal complications inevitably interrupt the transition from the descriptive poetics of the text to the aesthetic questions of effect, and this extends to include its place in literary history, leaving critical defenses of the play with the burden of explaining why *The Cenci* has failed to impose itself on the stage and in the canon. The text refuses to disappear into the unproblematic phenomenality of experience, or to take its place in the historical development of the drama, which has largely proceeded without it.

The hesitant and critical reception of *The Cenci* is frequently reflected back into the play itself, revealing a negative and even destructive component to the assessment of quality. Even the most positive critics concede that it is not a "well-made" play in the traditional (i. e., Aristotelean) sense, while the biographer White bluntly distinguishes *The Cenci*'s claim to be "great literature" from its failure as a tragedy (141). As one among many, Carlos Baker sums up the *The Cenci*'s stage history with the practical conclusion that "it would undoubtedly require cutting, transposition of scenes, and . . . other editorial tinkering, particularly among the supporting characters."[14] The unresolved questions of aesthetic judgment, that is, not only inhibit the interpretation and historical realization of the play, they turn the text against itself. The formal complications that surface in *The Cenci*'s stage history and in its critical reception not only articulate conflicting interpretations of the work, they also reveal a conflict between the meaning of the text and the very text that produces it. The text of *The Cenci* generates an aesthetic imperative at odds with its own formal integrity, an imperative for the actual destruction of the text in editorial excision and alteration. The aesthetic judgment restores the phenomenality of the text, its persuasiveness as a representation and its suitability for performance, by putting into question its mode of existence as a text. The act of aesthetic judgment resolves the problems of interpretation with violence, as if any text could be made to tell the truth if one only crossed out enough words.

Such textual mutilation is of course commonplace in the tradition of the drama, and the reversal that turns the aesthetic judgment of *The Cenci* against its own text only brings the play closer to a recurrent necessity in the drama for a textual self-immolation from which not even the greatest plays are immune. The representational mode of the drama is unprecedently self-negating, producing a compulsive self-erasure as the text turns back on itself, as one statement or act literally puts into question the necessity or existence of other acts and expressions. The specularity of dramatic representation, so readily figured as mirror and reflection, doubling and repetition, in fact contains a negative moment which is exposed by the contingencies of its stage realization. It is this very commonplace mutilation of the dramatic text that would be unthinkable in the lyric or the epic, a generic compulsion to be consistent and effective, even at the expense of its own textual existence. The drama, the literary mode that necessarily predominates in all discussions of the aesthetic, as presenting the closest approximation to an assimilation of the language of literature to the perception and sensation of *aesthesis,* is also the place where the incompatibility between the aesthetic and language is most explicitly revealed. The editorial activity of a stage director is an inevitable correlative of a self-critical structure within the drama's representational mode, and reveals the duplicity involved in the dramatic illusion of the subject representing itself, speaking in its own voice and character, and acting at its own initiative, to our perception and observation. The aesthetic negation of the text at the hands of the stage director is a necessary consequence of a contradiction at the heart of the drama, which founds the objectivity of the mode in the representation of the subject.

It is this self-immolation of the dramatic text that reveals the theoretical specificity of the drama, establishes what is at stake in the drama's mode of representation, and prefigures the complications that will predominate in the interpretation of the genre. The most successful and comprehensive attempts to reconsider *The Cenci* have thus always begun by reversing the implications involved in the act of aesthetic judgment, reversing the formal complications into an historical and theoretical potential. The negative judgment is turned into a self-critical awareness, and this permits the text to be reinterpreted as a critique of the genre and the tradition which had provided its definition. The disparities of the development can be reconsidered, as Curran has remarked perceptively, as a break with the centrality of action in the conception of plot, producing a "play in which mere action is never as important as its psychological ramifications" (*Shelley's* Cenci 270). In this "structure of non-action" the inadequacy of the plot becomes a precursor of the modern psychological drama of O'Neill or Pinter, where the very presence of action in the drama is no longer taken for granted. Reconsideration of the function of action allows the narrative history of the drama to be reconstructed, and *The Cenci* is reread as one of literature's missed opportunities, where the tension between the traditional structure of the five-act play and the progressive social content first becomes apparent. The same reversal allows the generic uncertainty of *The Cenci* which so many critics have discussed to be reconsidered in Jerrold Hogle's interpretation as revealing the reflexive structure of generic self-commentary, *The Cenci* now being considered to be "so comprehensive . . . that it is almost a meta-tragedy in relation to the tradition," and which therefore reveals "the foundations of tragedy" (Hogle 148, 149 [see note 2]). The historical failure of *The Cenci* to establish itself on stage, and the aesthetic judgments that questioned its viability as a tragedy, are no longer explicitly considered, but the formal complications they articulated return with a reversal of valorization, as *The Cenci* is promoted into a critique of tragedy itself.

The repression of the unresolved aesthetic judgment, however, only re-establishes the specularity of the drama. Whether as the critique of plot which reduces the drama, as Curran puts it, to "the realm of the psyche" (*Shelley's* Cenci 276), or as mimetic subjects whose subjectivity is checked, in Hogle's construal, by other subjects, the critical moment of the drama always occurs as a *subject* of representation. The critique of representation is itself represented, and represented as the experience of a *subject,* and this circularity restores the representational function of the dramatic subject by the same gesture that challenges it. The critique of the drama is always a *self*-critique, a critique of the subject *by* the subject, and is therefore always represented effectively by the very subject that it supposedly put into question. This critique of the subject always represents the subject to itself, reversing the loss of the subject (in death) into the subject's own self-understanding. However the subject is critiqued or questioned, reflected or divided, as long as the critique of the subject is itself the subject of representation, as in the classical *anagno-*

risis of the tragic subject who understands himself by stating his own condemnation, the specularity of the drama cannot be questioned.

In the specularity of the drama the critique of the subject, therefore, is identical to the process of self-legitimation, a reversal by which the fiction of a representation becomes the representation of a truth. By representing itself (to itself), the representation of the subject removes in effect the distinction between *what* is represented, and what *represents*. Since the subject of the drama does both, it provides its own mediation, and so is both the start and the finish of any representation or interpretation. The representational circularity revealed by the dramatization of the subject is inherent in the subject as a grammatical structure in advance of any psychological or social considerations. The issues that surface in the reception of *The Cenci,* in the suspended development of character and the unevenness of the action, or in the relation between the aesthetic judgment of the play and the narration of its historical place in the development of the drama, are all questions that concern the representational structure of the subject because they are all dependent upon mediation, and in particular, on the grammatical structure of its own language to mediate the drama's phenomenal realization on stage. The formality of the aesthetic consists in this mediation, the process by which consideration of the mode or the medium of representation underwrites the subject by changing it.

Aesthetic judgment is traditionally considered subjective, in the sense of being personal and individual, but it is "subjective" in this more important sense as well, which is the antithesis of individuality. Aesthetic judgment is subjective because it represents, as the subject of a judgment, a process of mediation, establishing the link between the formal integrity of the work of art and its claims to provide understanding, or between the veracity of its representation and its persuasive effect on an audience or reader. The mediation of the aesthetic is the synthesis of distinct judgments into one as the categorical judgment of quality, from which, once it is established, all others might be inferred. The canonicity of the work of art is not simply an expression of artistic value, but the judgment that provides, as we saw in Stuart Curran's suggestive reconstruction, the terms and the narrative which allow for our understanding of its place in the history of literature and the development of a genre. It is, likewise, as a demonstration of *The Cenci*'s aesthetic viability that Wasserman defends Shelley's success in analyzing his audience, or that Hogle affirms the mimetic construction of social identity in Shelley's play. The substance of the play, the truthfulness of its representation, is determined by an (often implicit or repressed) act of aesthetic judgment, which, in each case, provides the mediation between the literary form and a non-literary application. The mediation

of the aesthetic reverses the analysis of the internal integrity of the work of art (which always turns out to mean its self-interpretation, its "dramatization" of its own process of representation) as a formal structure (however negatively, or discontinuously this structure is conceived) into the grounds for an external synthesis of that work with other discourses. The psychology of modern man is analyzed in the breakdown of plot, and the political consequences of conformity are revealed by the mimetic patterns of dramatic dialogue. The aesthetic is the conceptual reversal that permits history to be studied through a fiction and self-understanding to be sought in a book.

However gregarious the range of discourses the aesthetic offers to unite, as indicated by the steadily increasing variety of issues which *The Cenci* is found to concern, the process of canonization relentlessly performed by aesthetic judgment is always powerfully reductive in its discovery that a single text can relate to so many different topics. The synthesis of judgments in the aesthetic is the reversal of the specificity of the text—what is unique to itself—into general subject matters which can be applied to any text, no matter what its explicit content. The canonization of *The Cenci* discovers in the play the same psychological, social and political applicability we habitually read in Euripides or Proust. What is lost in this process of canonization is the theoretical potential lodged in its specificity, the play's challenge to the habitual mechanics and duplicities of literary representation, which had been articulated indirectly in the criticism as long as *The Cenci*'s aesthetic stature was still in contention. The critical resistance to the assumption of the formal integrity of the play, or its pragmatic effectiveness on stage, permitted the modality and veracity of its representation to be questioned. The critical rejection which Shelley's play suffered for so long was not merely an aesthetic and moral revulsion, but a critique of its claims to represent, and a refutation of the understanding it implicitly claims to perform. Once *The Cenci*'s place in the canon is no longer explicitly in doubt, the specularity of the subject guarantees that the analysis of its representational structure will be foreclosed. The power of the aesthetic is only multiplied by its repression, and once the aesthetic is repressed, the self-confirming specularity of the subject cannot be challenged. The fundamental question of whether the play has understood what it attempts to represent, the criteria of any historical or philosophical discourse, is reversed in the act of aesthetic judgment into the unavoidable assumption that the play *performs* an understanding simply because it *has* represented. A literary fiction claims more truth than any mere fact could ever hope to embody, and the indirection and mediation of the aesthetic is reversed into an understanding that is more direct and immediate than representation itself ever achieves. The representational claims of literary texts are tautological because the aesthetic judgment that underwrites their claims to understanding is founded in the self-mediation, self-representation, and self-interpretation of the specular subject.

The drama, and interpretative models drawn on the drama, therefore predominate in all discussions of the aesthetic from Aristotle onward because the representational mode of the drama articulates, in the specularity of the subject, the circularity of aesthetic judgment. To the extent that literature is conceived as aesthetic, all other genres will be assimilated to the phenomenality and specularity of the drama, and the analysis of the language of literature will be formal, in the tradition of Aristotle, in assuming both the phenomenal perceptibility, as a medium and as a mediation, of language, and the subsequent disappearance, in the aesthetics of perception, of what is not in fact available to the senses. The theoretical question posed by the drama as a genre is therefore the relation between a phenomenalized model of linguistic meaning, which understands signification in words as if it were, or were the substitute for, the perception of the senses, and the conceptual reversal that turns all representation into self-understanding. The aesthetic is subjective because it reverses the representation of any object whatsoever into the self-representation of the subject, and therefore prefigures the relapse of the study of literature into psychology. What makes the aesthetic as such so difficult to analyze is the fact that this return to and generalization of the subject coincides, precisely on the pattern of dramatic representation, with the presumed objectivity involved in the phenomenal specification of time and place, perception and effect. The phenomenality of the aesthetic, its claims to ground thought and judgment in the facts of perception and sensation, to "think," as it were, with the objectivity of things rather than with ideas (the very illusion that accounts for its permanent ideological attractiveness across the entire political spectrum), is in fact identical to its absolute generalization of the subject. The paradox of the aesthetic, and the claim that must be put into question if the aesthetic is to be analyzed, is that the "objectivity" of literary discourse is established by the specularity of the subject being both what represents and what it is that is represented, both the content and the medium of the act of representation.

It is this very process of mediation that the formal objections to *The Cenci* address. The complications that have been implicitly raised by the aesthetic judgments against the play—the question of the transition between the language of the text and the phenomenality of the stage, the problematic relation between character and action, and the duplicity of the dramatic representation of and by the subject—all concern the function and reliability of mediation in the process of literary representation. The critical resistance to the canonization of *The Cenci* is thus also necessarily a resistance to the conceptual claims involved in any *aesthesis*, a resistance to

the consequences of assuming that signification performs a representation, and that perception is identical to understanding. The rejection of *aesthesis* is the critique of such mediation, the critique of the specular, representational structure of the subject. In none of these critical issues is the necessity for the presence or the representational *function* of the subject in question, but each puts into question what the subject represents, undercuts the specificity of its reference. The generalization of the subject in any *aesthesis,* it turns out, distinguishes between the subject, as the content or meaning of the play, and the subjects who are represented as characters, a distinction that the specularity of the dramatic mode eliminates. The negative component in the specularity of the subject, which destroys the subject who understands, now resurfaces as a disruption of the aesthetic synthesis. The crux of the critical challenge to the aesthetic canonization of *The Cenci* is the distinction between what is represented in the play and what the play means, the distinction that articulates the alternate meanings of the concept of the "subject." For the generalization of the subject matter of the play, the discovery that follows on its canonization and is a corollary to it, and which finds that *The Cenci* has so much to say about the psychology of modern man, or the oppression of women, or the abuse of authority, or the duplicities of convention in our social lives, achieves this range of applicability by negating the specificity of the actual subjects of the characters who perform the representation. The subject of the play is no longer historically given, but mediated, represented only indirectly by the characters. Whatever *The Cenci* is taken to be "about," whatever it is taken to "mean," it is not the Count, Beatrice, a debased papacy, a few petty murders, and the like. A purely literal reading of the play, as representing *just* the private debauchery and political machinations of a Roman noble family in the Papal States of 1599, is so difficult as to be in fact impossible, and would certainly put into question Shelley's authority as witness to such events. The specularity of the drama, which represents any content as the *experience* of a subject, does so only at the expense of an absolute generalization of its subject, in the contrasting sense, and therefore entails an erasure of its historical specificity. The exemplarity of the aesthetic reverses the act of representation: instead of the text representing long dead events, the play appropriates an historical incident for the representation of other, more general, subjects, which, due to their generality, cannot be represented as such. What the play means, how it is to be understood, is now up for grabs, and is no longer given by the identification of what it presumably represents.

Once the inevitable distinction between meaning and representation has surfaced, the substitution of a meaning different from what is represented not only becomes possible, it becomes an imperative. A literal representation is unreadable; only the attribution of meanings other than what is literally represented permits the text to be interpreted. An explicit *allegoresis,* a turning away from representation, is the condition of interpretation. The actual referents of the text—the place and time, the individuality of character—are negated, and this negation permits something else to be represented in their stead which is not actually referred to in the text at all. The literality of Renaissance Rome is readily reconstrued in time and place to Regency England, or a murder and an abusive papacy is presently reinterpreted as an allegory of the French Revolution.[15] The temporal and geographical relocatability reveals the failure of such historical specificities to be determinate in the production of the meaning. *The Cenci* is understood as a critique of patriarchy, of political complicity, the corruption of authority, the self-legitimating structure of social institutions, or the self-immolating tendencies of violent revolution; in each case, the conceptual connection with social and political analysis is established through the explicit indirection of allegory, the negation and reconstrual of what is given in the representation, and in each case, the analysis that results is inevitably psychological, as an analysis of the subject, revealing a fault in our human nature, or displaying the discontinuity of the subject at war with itself.

Shelley himself, in the *Defence of Poetry,* as in the "Preface" to *The Cenci,* gives this loss of the specificities of representation its most traditional, and most conceptually radical, formulation. "The tragedies of the Athenian poets" Shelley writes, "are as mirrors in which the spectator beholds *himself*" and what he learns is consequently "*self-knowledge*" (490-91; my emphasis). Regardless of its apparent subject, the final subject of *The Cenci* is bound to be, as Wasserman affirms, ourselves. The play is read proleptically to represent an audience and a readership who come, historically, after it, and this reversal undermines our own historical specificity, our ability to differentiate ourselves from the patterns of the past, or to be determined by the conditions and imperatives of our own time rather than to repeat predictably the models of a literary genre. The specularity of the drama erases the identity of its audience: the play represents us because it represents anyone, without limit or discretion, including those who aren't like us at all. Which is to say that the final extension of the specular subject reveals that this subject does not in fact represent at all: the specularity which reflects the audience back to itself is absolutely general, without determination of time or place, distinction of person or individuation of character. The absolute generality of the subject produced by this *aesthesis* likewise erases the text entirely: Rome and the papacy, the Cencis and their actions literally disappear from the considerations of interpretation. When the text represents *us,* it has been reduced to a tool for our own self-analysis, a process which is anything but representational. As a result, the function of representation in the drama, and the media-

tion it performs in the course of understanding, is in doubt. The formal objections to *The Cenci*'s canonization, the challenge they present to the assumptions of *aesthesis,* served to articulate the modulation of the concept of the subject in the course of interpretation, and the representational reversals and self-erasures that accompany the generalization of the subject in any act of aesthetic judgment. The aesthetic structure of exemplification, which allows the monuments of the canon to serve as the objects of political and social analysis, and the presumed ground for historical investigation, turns out to be allegorical, a reversal that puts into question all the representational claims of the text. The self-erasure of the specular subject, the disappearance of the text into our own self-analysis, reveals the linguistic structure that simultaneously grounds aesthetic over-representation and articulates the critique of representation proper.

Allegory puts into question the mediation, the synthesis, performed by *aesthesis,* the act of aesthetic judgment in all its senses. Allegory remains utterly representational, but the failure of the component parts of the process to synthesize leaves the meaning of the text never to coincide with, or be identical to what is represented. The subject of the text can never coincide with the subjects it represents. Far from eliminating representation, the allegory restores it, establishing the representational claims of the text for historical and political purposes precisely by negating the specificities of its own representation. The aesthetic text consequentially preempts precisely those critical questions which would permit its representational veracity to be examined. The sheer facticity of the original event, the accuracy of its reproduction in the literary representation, or even whether such events existed in the first place—the irreducible questions of historical fact, what is established because it has occurred as an event in the past—are now entirely beside the point. It becomes impossible, or irrelevant, in the interpretation of the play to ask precisely those *historical* questions which would, in effect, challenge the exemplarity implicit in the play's representation. What is the authority of Shelley's source? (Questionable.) How typical was the situation of the Cenci family? (Not very.) How innocent was the historical Beatrice? (Not so clear.) None of these historical questions are considered relevant to the interpretation of the play precisely because the meaning of the play is not founded in representation, but what is represented in the play has been appropriated and manipulated on behalf of the meaning. The allegorical process which puts into question the mediation of the text only makes the text *im*mediate, self-justifying in a way that no historical document, beholden to the banality of facts independent of their representation, could ever hope to be. The allegorical structure of the aesthetic text, which, as we have seen, makes the conceptual moments of self-criticism and self-justification identical, grounds the text in the full philosophical sense of the term, by eliding the mediation that qualifies representation and that would therefore permit actual conceptualization to occur.

The grounding of the aesthetic text, the establishment of its claim to mean, thus takes place at the expense of its own representational content. The allegorical moment which creates the illusion of immediacy is the same linguistic structure which accounts for the indirection that proliferates throughout the aesthetic. This recurrent pattern represents one subject by referring to another, analyzes one's own time by representing the past, and claims a moral justification for the representation of depravity. The indirection of the aesthetic, which renounces reference and intention, reestablishes such representational claims for the text beyond what could ever be provided by facts or perception, evidence or experience. The epistemological question appropriate to any representation, did he get it right? is displaced into the interpretive puzzle (and representational tautology) of: do *we* understand ourselves? The representation of the world literally disappears as we discover in the world only the reflection of ourselves, and the constraint placed upon representation by the object itself is lost as the representation is explicitly manipulated into an allegory in the subject's self-analysis. Yet it is just this specularity, the self-analyzing/self-confirming alliance between the aesthetics of perception and the allegorical structure of language that the formal complications posed by the debates surrounding *The Cenci* put into question. The theoretical question posed by *The Cenci* is whether the aesthetic, as both the act of judgment and the phenomenality of representation, can be validated, and grounded as a form of understanding, by the critical structure of self-analysis. *The Cenci* is a critique of the function of self-understanding in any representation—a critique, that is, of the attempt to establish representational authority and veracity through an examination of the self, and therefore to judge the subject of a representation entirely by its specular dramatization in the subject's analysis of itself.

The questions raised in the critical reception concerning *The Cenci*'s formal integrity inevitably expose the allegorical pattern of aesthetic representation, and define the theoretical challenge presented by the play. The *allegoresis* involved in any interpretation whatsoever as the modulation of meaning—the determination of what the text is about, what the representation means—restores the representational claims and function of the text by putting its actual referents into question. The formal complications, however, challenge explicitly the mediation performed by the representation, and explicitly put into question the syntheses of understanding: what the subject represents, what the transitions of the plot reveal, whether the effect corresponds with the meaning, and the like. In however indirect a manner,

the debate surrounding *The Cenci*'s aesthetic stature reveals a conflict between the mediation provided by the dramatic mode of representation and the allegorical modulation of meaning in the interpretations to which it has given rise. The burden of interpreting *The Cenci* is therefore the articulation of the representational form of the drama as a genre with the complications and indirections of the allegorical mode.

Despite the distractions of a subplot, some deflection of responsibility, confusion of agency, and corruption of motive, the plot of *The Cenci* is quite simple. After years of torturing his family, the old Count Cenci, in search of the ultimate in depravity, violates his daughter, who has been steadfast both in resistance to his evil and in loyalty to the other suffering members of her family. Her spirit broken, she conspires with the others to hire some thugs who do the Count in while asleep. They are caught in the act by a papal legate, who, as it happens, is under orders to dispatch the Count himself. Instead, he arrests the conspirators, and they are tried by a papal court. Beatrice asserts her innocence, the others confess, all are put to death. An endless torment culminates in a final act of abuse, which produces in reaction a corresponding resolve, and a single, violent response is met with a single concluding judgment. The formal concision of the plot allows the reversals to be clear and effective: the criminal becomes the victim of those he abuses, while his victims commit a crime worthy of him. A paragon of goodness is reduced to a murderess and a liar, and a debauched papal curacy by trying the murders can shine forth as defender of truth and justice. The neatness of such reversals results from the singularity of the acts that produce them: however long her suffering, *one* act pushes Beatrice over the brink, and however established her character, *one* contrary act of her own in turn destroys her. The "dramatic capital," as one critic has put it (Baker 145), of the single, decisive act cannot be denied, yet this very singularity also leaves it at odds with the plot. Briefly put, the action is so concise that little is left to fill up the remaining acts, leaving the play with the "plot of non-action" diagnosed by Curran.[16] The endurance of Beatrice is largely a matter of narrative reconstruction, but the passivity of the central character is nevertheless present enough on stage to interfere with the action of the plot. The delay, or rather, the principled resistance to action on the part of Beatrice exposes the mechanics of the plot even more than the suspicious clarity of contrast in the reversals. Her independence as a character, of course, is founded in her rock-like fortitude, her resistance to evil. Beatrice resists acting where action itself would be, as she is only too well aware, simply re-acting, and thus resists having her actions predetermined as a response within a preestablished plot line which she is not free to write on her own. Such fortitude is however starkly at odds with dramatic representation: not only is it boring on stage, since it is successful only as long as *nothing* happens, but it literally leaves the audience with nothing to see. Even Shelley's famous depiction of her resistance in the Banquet scene that closes Act I displays less the qualities established by the narrative depiction of her character by her mother or her brother than the difficulty she experiences in maintaining that stance, as her challenge to her father there resembles more the Charge of the Light Brigade in the futility of melodramatic overactivity than a passive turning of the other cheek. Such resistance would be precisely the absence of action, the refusal to take initiative, and would leave the subject without an action to represent it, or to reveal its nature. No action on the part of a character means nothing in fact is represented by the character we perceive, and we are left with nothing to understand. Unless the transition from character to action takes place, the connection between subject and predicate in the act of judgment cannot be made. Understanding may be a form of representation, but what is represented must *change* (by acting) or it cannot be understood. The transition from the representation of character into narrative understanding (from mimesis into diegesis) takes place only by the mediation of action. Characters who do not act evacuate their representation, just as minor characters remain stick figures regardless of how frequently they appear.

Having been so long delayed, the action, when it comes, is "sudden and complete."[17] "All must be suddenly resolved and done" (III. i. 169), says Beatrice at the moment of her resolution, and as an agent, she is as good as her word. The reversal—her conversion from passivity to action, from good to evil—is accomplished with a single decision. The process is so complete that the crucial mediation is cut short: the quandaries of doubt, the see-saw of argument, even the tactical selection of means are all rapidly run through in a single scene at the beginning of Act III. The transition into action, the defining act of character, occurs abruptly, eliding the temporal and narrative component of change. The transition is thus reduced to the merest sequence, the absolute contrast between meekest passivity and murderous activity, without gradation, nuance, or intermediary stages. We are left with the starkest polarization, the conceptual contrasts between action and passivity, goodness and evil which articulate the antitheses of the act of judgment. The change of character in Beatrice's resolution occurs as an explicit judgment, in the choice that Aristotle felt revealed character.

Beatrice's decision may be an act, but the acts it produces in *The Cenci* are all left to be somewhat "after the fact." The abruptness of her decision is not only isolated from the gradual transitions of a narrative development, or from the extended deductions of a more considered process of reflection, but has effectively cut off the change, the reversal, as a decision from the events and actions to which it gives rise. The murder of the Count, Beatrice's primary action, is a consequence of the change in her character that occurs as her resolution to act, and of her descent into the very evil she had long resisted. The moment of decision precedes the murder and makes it possible. Yet Beatrice's change of heart is in fact paradigmatic for all the events in the play. Action in *The Cenci* follows on explicit decisions of the characters, but the consequences of those actions are never chosen by the agents. The Count's rape of his daughter merely puts into effect, with unforeseen consequences, a well constructed scheme of deliberate abuse, just as the trial in Act V is, as the judges frankly admit ("His Holiness / Enjoined us to pursue this monstrous crime / By the severest forms of law; nay even / To stretch the point against the criminals" [V. ii. 71-74]), merely an effort to make the facts fit the verdict the Pope has already determined. The facts, of course, prove only too ready to oblige. Each of the characters is caught in the traps each has set for others, save the Pope, who contrives an abuse of justice at the very moment when the truth, for once, is on his side. The transition into action, that is, gains its conclusiveness by losing its initiative; action in *The Cenci* may be a direct consequence of decisions of the characters, but the acts they then perform are not theirs to control. With the loss of such control, the consequences for the subject, in both the narrative and ethical senses, increase enormously. Beatrice, at the moment of her arrest, seeks to forestall the fatal consequences of her own actions by insisting to the papal legate, Savella, that "if you arrest me / You are the judge and executioner" not just of her life, but "Of that which is the life of life: the breath / Of accusation kills an innocent name" (IV. i. 140-44). The ethical burden increases precisely at the point where the consequences of one's own actions cannot be delimited, where one loses the ability to say, as Cenci had, that "this shall be another's, and that mine" (I. ii. 83). The more decisive the resolution, the less cooperative the action, and the plot begins to take on an agency that can no longer be attributed to the deeds of the characters. The action becomes a recognizable plot-line that leaves little to happen that one cannot, literally, see coming.

However preordained and predictable the direction of events, when the causality of the plot is not controlled by the subjects who act it, the meaning of those events is lost to those who participate in them. The characters fail to foresee the results of their deeds or to interpret their consequences; whatever their intention or initiative, in each case "there arose," as the corrupt prelate Orsino regrets, "a Power / Which graspt and snapped the threads of my device / And turned it to a net of ruin" (V. i. 83-85). The proleptic and metaleptic structure of thought to action, the power of the subject to represent itself in what has been and what will be, has been interrupted, leaving the present moment inscrutable to those involved, without clear narrative history or discernible direction. Beatrice's decision to act does indeed change her, but instead of permitting her subsequent actions to represent her character, and to make it understandable, her choice confounds that process, and makes her an enigma. The interpretation of Beatrice is suspended, as Shelley himself declared, by an unresolvable contradiction, the simultaneous presence of conflicting qualities. Beatrice becomes simultaneously an example of moral good, of heroic resistance to evil, and a counterexample, who falls off from the high demands of ethical behavior by repeating the violence and self-exculpation of true depravity. Whatever her history, her action succeeds in legitimating the legal judgment against her, and in justifying the acts of a court so corrupt that it is incapable of establishing its own legitimacy. For however debased the machinery of papal justice, and no matter what may be said in amelioration of her, the act that she committed is not in doubt. Yet even as the court's judgment represents the truth, it does not understand what it represents, and the judges are no further along in understanding the meaning of, or the reasons behind, the plot they have accurately reconstructed at the end of their investigation than they were at the beginning.

The act of judgment separates from understanding in the same way that the synthesis of Beatrice's character is blocked by the act that would represent her. The lack of mediation in the transition from judgment into action makes Beatrice's resolution, like the corresponding decisions of other characters, into an act itself, but cuts that act off from the subject who performs it. The subject becomes uninterpretable, to itself as to others, by the contrary predicates that appear in its representation, of goodness and evil, or of activity and passivity. The alignment and correlation between individual subjects and the predicates attributed to them are lost, not merely because the distinction between the various attributes fails to distinguish between the characters (good intentions and foul sin both being generally available to all comers), but because the representation of the subjects confounds the distinction between the predicates. Count Cenci would seem to make a fair case for the purity of his character, as absolutely evil, but this is precisely the reason critics find him unbelievable, which is to say, that the representation of his subject is being hindered by being too clearly just a personification of abstract evil—being too clearly, that is, just the allegory of an identifiable quality. The Count is too good at being bad, too passively resigned to his own monstrous activity to be understood as human. The intensification of the focus, the sheer recognizability of the distinguishing quality, for the Count as for Beatrice, does not eliminate the contrasting quality, but paralyzes the interpretation of the relation between them in the process of representation. The representation of Beatrice through her action contradicts her character, whereas the character of the Count prevents his actions from being viable as a repre-

sentation. The interpretation of the characters of *The Cenci* is inhibited by a process of representation which makes them simultaneously too identifiable as dramatic allegories and too contradictory to be understandable.

With this contradiction in the representation of character, the dominance and function of the subject in the text has been put into question. Not only is the interpretation of character no longer the principal burden of understanding, but the subjects of the characters no longer *perform* the representation. Just as the plot takes on an agency of its own, leaving the predicates of action to behave as if they were subject-agents in their own right, the articulation of the predicates no longer correlates with the representation and comprehension of individual subjects. The text of *The Cenci* seems incapable of stating any proposition without stating its contradiction somewhere else, or restating it quite literally in circumstances that reverse or negate its meaning. The process can occur within a single subject, with all the potential for irony that such a subjective dialectic provides, as when the Count, in his sleep, repeats his curse of Beatrice at the point of having his own throat cut (IV. iii.). Or the restatement can function as a reversal of position between characters, as when the Count's pride at being a "scourge" in the hand of God, "a fiend appointed to chastise / The offences of some unremembered world" (IV. iv. 63; 161-62) provides Beatrice unknowingly with the words with which to commend her hired hoodlums: "Thou wert a weapon in the hand of God / To a just use" (IV. iv. 54-55). The Count's early explanation of his character to the Cardinal Camillo, "I am what your theologians call hardened" (I. i. 93-94), is likewise echoed by his son Giacomo as he stiffens his determination under the rain-machine and the thunder-sheet to murder his father: "Why should we quail / When Cenci's life, that light by which ill spirits / See the worst deeds they prompt, shall sink for ever? / No, I am hardened" (III. ii. 43-46). The counterstatement may have no direct relation to any subject, as when Lucretia, hearing the horn announce the arrival of the papal legate, declares "it sounds / Like the last trump" (IV. iv. 57-58); her metaphor of the Last Judgment will be proven literal by the turn of events, true in more ways than one, and thus ironic in a mode that requires no repetition. The reversal of a statement may simply not discriminate among characters, and thus advance no definition of any subject, as in the modulation of a recurrent figure. Dreams, for example, show no prejudice in *The Cenci,* and are partisan to no prognosis or strategy: Lucretia fakes the report of a dream to her husband the Count (IV. i. 31 ff.), hoping to induce him to repent before his impending murder, rather than urging him to relent in his crimes, but the strategy backfires, and the Count resolves instead to speed up his assault on his daughter lest he die before its accomplishment. Lucretia, appalled, confesses her lie, which leads Cenci moments later to disregard the report of an actual vision by Beatrice. Cenci dies in the course of a dream (IV. iii), and Beatrice belittles the significance of his death, which will be, she claims, "But as a change of sin-chastising dreams, / A continuance of the Hell within him" (IV. iii. 32-33).

Such frequent passage in and out of dreams leaves the significance of death itself ambiguous; not only is its distinction from life less than certain, but Beatrice, confronting death, dreams both of Paradise (v. iii. 10), and of being pursued by the ghost of her father through all eternity (v. iv. 60 ff). The pattern of reversals, the compulsive counterstatement of the allegorical text, neither corresponds to, nor contradicts, the representation of character, because the pattern of statement and counter-statement simply does not recognize the distinctions between, nor the synthesis within, any individual subject. Like the plot that acts as an impersonal agency, such reversals act and react, without being themselves agents of their own. The reversals relentlessly articulate the consequences that turn on and entrap the subjects, regardless of the judgments they perform, as the divisions between self and other, active and passive, innocent and guilty in any act of judgment are confounded by a process which respects no distinction of subjects. The actions of a character become as inscrutable, and as deceptive, to that character as the actions of anyone else. Each of the characters of *The Cenci,* criminals, victims, conspirators or judges, to the extent that each acts, loses control of his or her actions, is surprised and perplexed by the results and is left uncomprehending in front of a self each had once assumed he or she understood. The priority of the subject, the assumption of any privilege or advantage in the representation of the subject to self-understanding or self-evidence, has been lost.

Action in *The Cenci* not only turns against the characters, as the subjects are destroyed by their own acts—the standard substance of Classical tragedy—but, much more crucially, the action leaves the subjects utterly unenlightened after the event. Action as such becomes entirely problematic, as what is not comprehended by the subject who performs it, either proleptically in advance or on reflection afterwards, in its attempt to represent and to understand itself. The unease which has been so often felt about *The Cenci*'s generic definition as a tragedy in fact results less from the play's slipping into other, less appropriate modes, like melodrama or the grotesque, or from the descent of the tragic mode itself into anachronism, than from the refusal of the play to reverse the reversals of the plot back into the representational form of self-understanding, and thus to make the self-destruction of the subject the grounds for the subject's insight into itself. In remarkable fidelity to the Classical genre, the crux of *The Cenci* is not the reversal (or *peripeteia*) but the *anagnorisis,* the scene of recognition, where the agent discovers his own complicity with evil events, and achieves insight into himself by

recognizing his inability to control his own actions, and therefore understands himself through expressing his own condemnation. It is this *anagnorisis* that fails to crystallize in *The Cenci,* and Shelley's most perceptive critics, like Wasserman, have responded to this uncertainty by insisting on reconstructing the scene of recognition. The reconstruction, closely following Shelley's own comments, displaces the emphasis on the moment of self-revelation into the *catharsis,* the *effect* of the play on the audience. Self-knowledge is restored in the audience by abandoning it in the play, and this reversal shifts the *anagnorisis* from a purely poetic structure of self-check and self-confirmation within a representation to the aesthetics of an audience's experience, where the contradictions within the representation are resolved in the way that they compel the subject of the audience to confront itself. The explicit abandonment of the *anagnorisis,* that is, underwrites greatly increased claims for the *aesthesis,* the phenomenality of perception and experience, of fear, pity, and emotion, as what can alone generate true understanding, but restores knowledge as self-understanding only by abandoning what is represented in the text. "We are the ultimate objectives of *The Cenci,*" writes Wasserman, "and it is our own character that is ultimately under scrutiny, as though *we* were *both* the actors and the audience. To paraphrase Shelley's account of the function of the maniac in *Julian and Maddalo,* Beatrice's tortured expressions of her moral dualism are a sufficient commentary on the text of every heart in the audience—and *that is the text we are actually reading*" (122; my emphases). Wasserman's reinscription of the *anagnorisis* reveals the paradigmatic structure hidden within the specularity of self-representation, as an understanding of the subject is achieved by literally changing what is represented, negating the specificities of the subjects represented in favor of a representation of the "subject" proper, as the truth "of every heart."

Within the poetics of the play, the failure of the *anagnorisis* is a failure of retrospection, a failure to connect past actions with the present subject. Self-consciousness may be caught in an eternal present, but it is the reflection on past events that alone gives meaning to the representation of the subject, by inferring a causality to the endless, differentiated sequence of events, and a direction to distinct and distant actions. The explanatory power of reflection is its narrative reconstruction, which reconnects a series of actions with a subject by rereading the past as the plot of one's own character. The tragic *anagnorisis* is the paradigmatic reflexive moment in the text, the textual expression of the text's own interpretation of itself, in which the text is represented and interpreted by a subject by being narrated as that subject's own history. The knowledge produced by the scene of recognition is not so much new, as a reinterpretation of what was already known, the literal recognition of the subject which identifies the subject by reinterpreting the subject's own deeds. The explicit connection of the subject with past action equates the subject with a string of predicates which permits the subject to be understood by being articulated in a judgment. In the Classical scene of recognition, such as in the tragedy of Oedipus, the subject connects himself with his own actions by stating his own condemnation; the understanding of the self, the connection between the subject and the predicates that define it, is itself expressed by stating those actions as the *negation* of the subject, as the act which destroys the subject. The scene of recognition, the reflexive moment of the text, is the moment when the subject states its own negation, and founds its intelligibility, to itself as to others, in this self-negation. The subject of representation (of mimesis) is understood by articulating its narrative history (its diegesis), while the diegetic exposition of the text is in turn understood by being represented as a mimesis, as a subject of representation. The reflexive moment of the text establishes the intertranslatability, the seamless assimilability, of mimesis and diegesis, as well as representation and understanding, by establishing the explicit connection between the grammatical subject and predicate in any proposition or judgment. What is troubling about the reflexivity of *anagnorisis,* and what defines the theoretical content and specificity of the tragic genre, is that this reflexivity of the subject, which permits the modulation from representation through self-representation to understanding, and which founds the phenomenal and aesthetic claims of the dramatic mode, is established *not* as an identification of what we see with what we understand, of subject with predicate, but by an explicit negation, the loss of self and subject as the price of understanding.

The plot reversal in tragedy turns the acts of the subject against itself, and the subject is destroyed by performing its own negation. None of this self-immolation upsets the economy of representation: the *anagnorisis* serves to restore the relation between understanding and events by establishing the transition of the subject of representation into the predicates of action as causal, explanatory narrative. The relation of the subject to its own predicates may be antithetical, the character may do itself in, but such an antithesis is not only comprehensible, it serves to give tragedy the greatest formal integration of any literary mode of representation. It is no mere coincidence of literary history that the formal analysis of literature is historically founded in the *Poetics* of Aristotle not just in the drama, but in tragedy. The formality of such analysis consists entirely in the consideration of the language of literature as a medium of representation, and the specification of the distinctive qualities of such language in the course of such an analysis performs a dialectical mediation, serving to increase the meaning, and the representational claims, of the text by negating the specificities of its literal representation. (It should be recalled, more often than it is,

that the formal analysis of literature was invented by a logician, and that the proper commentary on the *Poetics* is not *De Anima* but the *Prior Analytics.*) In no other genre will the formal analysis be so productive, and the pursuit of such formal analysis in the novel or the lyric inevitably entails the imposition onto them of the deceptive phenomenal and aesthetic imperatives of the dramatic mode. The mediation that permits the transition from representation to understanding in the reflexive moment, as the pattern of *anagnorisis* makes evident, is *always* phenomenal, as a perception or sensation, and *always* negative, as the pity and fear, the pain and the horror that translate experience into self-awareness. The *anagnorisis* induces self-understanding in the subject by destroying it as a phenomenal object; the dramatic character demonstrates (that is, etymologically, proves logically by showing phenomenally) his insight into himself by dying. The specularity of the subject, the crux of the drama, is established by destroying the very subject that it represents.

It is precisely this *anagnorisis* that does not take place, is not represented, in *The Cenci.* The characters judge, and the characters act, but the action of the characters does not produce judgment. Beatrice, who understood herself perfectly well, loses what she knew by acting. The act itself produces blindness: the act, as the translation of the subject into the predicates of action, is still negative, but the destruction of the subject induces no self-understanding. Not only does she fail to comprehend the chain of events in which she is caught, but what she does induces oblivion, erasing self-consciousness as effectively as death erases the mind. However brutal it may be, action in *The Cenci* is no longer the realization of character, the recuperation of violence in the specularity of representation. Action in *The Cenci* undoes character, compromises the subject and confounds its representation. The specification of the predicates, instead of permitting the representation and judgment of the subject, now render the subject uninterpretable. As a result, no *locus* can be found in the play which establishes Beatrice's moment of recognition. Even her violation induces madness (III. i.), the opposite of insight, and the now crucial event in her own self-determination resists articulation, "for there are deeds / Which have no form, sufferings which have no tongue" (III. i. 141-42), and therefore "her wrongs could not be told, not thought" (v. ii. 141), and are bound to remain "expressionless" (III. i. 214). The act of judgment that asserts her resolution to act, to take initiative in her own defense, speaks of freedom and determination ("And I have unravelled my entangled will, / And have at length determined what is right" [III. i. 220-21]), but is indeed the moment both when she is ensnared in a plot not her own and when she is in her actions quite explicitly wrong. When caught in the act of murder by the inopportune arrival of the papal legate Savella, she denies her deeds with outright sophistry ("My Lord, / I am more innocent of parricide / Than is a child born fatherless" [IV. iv. 111-12]) and blatant wishful thinking ("Mother, / What is done wisely, is done well. Be bold / As thou art just" [IV. iv. 34-36]). In her attempts at defense, she compulsively renarrates her actions to herself, to her fellow conspirators, and to her accusers in search of a causal narrative that will legitimate her by removing her own responsibility for her deeds, by making her own actions merely passive consequences of the actions of others. Beatrice seeks legitimation in the renunciation of her own initiative, and deliberately refuses to admit her own complicity at the very moment, ironically, when her independence has most been lost, and when her own actions have already in fact been reduced to mere reactions to the deeds of others.

Just as Beatrice can no longer explain herself by narrating her own history, critics can no longer judge her by synthesizing her hopelessly contradictory predicates into a coherent character. Opinions abound, since the temptation she presents for self-righteousness is unlimited, but the possibility of a critical consensus has been lost long ago. Beatrice's duplicity, however it may be explained away, has greater consequences than private deceit or the desperate strategies of self-respect and survival. By *renarrating* her acts, Beatrice establishes her own interpretation of what has happened only by distinguishing what has been represented in the drama from the narrative explanation she gives it. By refusing the *anagnorisis,* the explicit *mea culpa,* Beatrice disarticulates the mimesis of representation from the diegesis of narrative explanation: the facts no longer support the spin she gives to them. She may be innocent in her own eyes, but she can now only be guilty to all others. In the absence of the reflexive moment of the text, the mimesis of representation no longer synthesizes with the diegesis of the narrative, and the character of the subject no longer correlates with the deeds that represent it.

As a consequence, the act of judgment and the possibility of interpretation has been suspended. The loss of the specularity of the subject, as the loss of the subject's own understanding of itself, isolates the subject as a grammatical structure from the predicate in the propositional form of judgment itself. The separation of the subject from the predicate in *The Cenci* rediscovers Hegel's definition of allegory, *die Trennung von Subjekt und Prädikat* as the conceptual distinction of the subject as a grammatical structure from the interpretative modulations it makes possible.[18] The inevitable return of allegory describes concisely the challenge presented by Shelley's text to the act of interpretation. The characters of *The Cenci* cannot be understood by the actions they perform, nor are the actions of the play identifiable with the characters who perform them. Action itself has separated from the agency of the subjects, and the plot line takes on a force of its own, the explicit *allegoresis* of *Atropos,* the Greek goddess of Fate: the relentless, ineluctable, destructive power of a plot accountable, and attributable, to no one. "Who" or "what" acts is beyond the determination of the subjects, who become mere objects, passive victims incapable of influencing the course of events or interpreting the results. The course of the plot no longer serves as the development of character, each of whom remains rather static, "true to character," as it were, revealing the formulaic types they have such difficulty escaping. The characters become identifiable as *types* at precisely the moment when they do not understand themselves: the isolation of subject from plot, character from agency, marks an absolute check on the psychological interest of the play, whose representational imperatives can no longer be understood in terms of a subject at all.

The complication presented by the text of *The Cenci* can therefore be understood as neither psychological in origin nor merely pragmatic in its consequences. The challenge of Shelley's play goes all the way to the fundamental linguistic structure of the act of logical judgment. With the dissolution of the reflexive moment of the text in the failure of the *anagnorisis,* the transition between subject and predicate in the representational process of the text can no longer be an *inference.* Given such subjects, their deeds remain as unpredictable as the consequences of those deeds will be overdetermined, and with such a sequence of events, any subject would serve equally well as a victim of the plot. With the loss of inference, the relation between the subject and predicate, which permits any deed to be performed or any judgment to be articulated, must be *predicated* as the explicit act of a subject, with the degree of irreducible arbitrariness that always accompanies whatever can be attributed to the election and initiative of a subject. Just as the reversals of the plot take place as explicit decisions rather than as acts, the interpretations of those acts by the subjects themselves remain incapable of representing at all accurately the facts of the matter. The elision of the process of mediation that had been articulated by the aesthetic challenges to *The Cenci* turns out to be founded in an elision of the logical structure of inference. The critical challenge to the specularity of self-representation has vacated the representational claims of the dramatic subject, and this critique of the subject exposes in turn the linguistic structure of predication, as what in the act of judgment cannot be inferred from a representation or a deed. The phenomenality of the drama, the quality that permits the text to be represented on stage, and words to be realized as characters, corresponds exactly with the reduction, so obvious in the text of any drama, of all statements in the text to explicit predications, spoken by individual characters. The reduction of the text in the representational mode of the drama to the phenomenality of the subject only serves to expose the linguistic structure that is present in any predication, any act of judgment whatsoever. What was being refused in the aesthetic resistance to *The Cenci* is the relentless exposition of the linguistic structure which links the grammatical structure of the subject with the phenomenality of representation, and that therefore establishes the connection between the *aesthesis* of perception and the cognition of understanding. In both affirmation of, and in explicit contradiction to, the tragic genre which provides its definition, *The Cenci* moves beyond the rather commonplace destruction of the tragic subject to the articulation of the explicitly linguistic form of judgment itself, and explores the potential for a degree of verbal depravity and self-deceit that exceeds the violence of rape and murder.

However horrible death may be, the prospect of death to Beatrice immediately conjures up another fate far worse. When her sentence is reported by the Cardinal Camillo near the end of Act v, Beatrice descends into panic. The fear of death, of burial ("To be nailed down into a narrow place; / To see no more sweet sunshine . . ." [v. iv. 50-51]) is soon overtaken by the fear that accompanies loss of faith: "If there should be / No God, no heaven, no earth, in the void world; / The wide, grey lampless, deep, unpeopled world! / If all things then should be . . ." But that fear of absolute oblivion is soon overtaken in turn by the prospect that the escape from horror that annihilation might provide may not be available:

> my father's spirit
> His eye, his voice, his touch surrounding me;
> The atmosphere and breath of my dead life!
> If sometimes, as a shape more like himself,
> Even the form which tortured me on earth,
> Masked in grey hairs and wrinkles, he should come
> And wind me in his hellish arms, and fix
> His eyes on mine, and drag me down, down, down!
> For was he not alone omnipotent
> On Earth, and ever present? Even though dead,
> Does not his spirit live in all that breathe,
> And work for me and mine still the same ruin,
> Scorn, pain, despair? Who ever yet returned
> To teach the laws of death's untrodden realm?
> Unjust perhaps as those which drive us now,
> O, whither, whither?

(v. iv. 60-74)

The fear of death is little to the fear of being pursued through eternity by the father who tormented her on earth. Likewise, the ultimate evil that the Count contrives for his daughter is not death, nor rape, nor even the physical torture and mutilation for which he has shown a marked proclivity ("The dry fixed eyeball; the pale quivering lip . . . I rarely kill the body which preserves, / Like a strong prison, the soul with the breath of fear / For hourly pain" [i. i. 111; 114-17]). What the Count seeks is *consent*, Beatrice's agreement to his incestuous advances until "her stubborn will / Which by its own consent shall stoop as low / As that which drags

it down" (iv. i. 10-12). It is not enough that the tragic subject is the agent of its own destruction, nor even that the tragic subject must articulate its own condemnation by accepting guilt for an action done (as it were) "in all innocence." Cenci's aim is to break the economy of guilt and remorse, the recuperation of sin by self-judgment which permits expiation, and to compel an innocent Beatrice to seek the damnation from which no remorse or repentance can provide escape. The Count, that is, seeks to make his own acts superfluous to the accomplishment of his low ends; he seeks to make his evil, like Fate, selfless and self-perpetuating, and to make Beatrice knowingly to blame beforehand for the doom she would bring upon herself. No room is left for reflection, and any *anagnorisis* is preempted by having the guilty fully conscious of the evil of his deeds. The doom he seeks for her in foreclosing remorse is the loss of her ability to judge herself, and hence to cut her off from the specularity of *anagnorisis,* and the possibility of representing her acts herself and understanding what she represents. The impossibility of remorse is the impossibility of being the "subject" of one's own reflection, and hence entails the loss of any direction, intent, or design. The loss of the subject is the loss of judgment, of consciousness, of all that pertains to the "subjectivity" of the subject, leaving the subject, or what remains of it, the hapless victim of actions which can no longer be attributable to it.

By destroying the possibility of reflection, the inferential relationship between representation and judgment is totally undermined, so that the act of judgment neither can be performed nor made to accord with the specularity of self-interpretation. The verbal form of judgment does not synthesize with the phenomenal processes of representation, leaving the understanding completely at sea. Judgment has been reduced to defamation and deceit, perverting the subject by preventing any representation of it. The purely verbal form of depravity that the Count has hit upon makes the actual murder of his victim superfluous (he drops even suggesting new forms of violence, and henceforth resorts more to curses than to dirty deeds), as even the death of the subject cannot restore a reputation that was never founded on representation.

In the final act, the scene of the trial, all reputation is set aside, both of the murdered Count and his beatific, murderess daughter. The Court seeks not truth, but confession; representation of the facts is abandoned in the effort to force the characters to represent themselves, and thus to reconstruct the specularity of the subject that had been lost with the failure of the *anagnorisis.* The pure verbality of confession removes the judges' need to infer an understanding from the representations they are offered, or to interpret the evidence they are presented. The judges seek not the grounds for judgment, but seek to make their own interpretation unnecessary, by forcing the criminals to interpret themselves. Their own judgment against the condemned is rendered redundant, relieving them of all responsibility, when the subject is forced to confess, to express his own negation. Marzio, with a little assistance from the rack, confesses, and the First Judge comments: "This sounds as bad as truth" (v. ii. 19). No plea of innocence can be accepted as such, but confession of sin cannot be denied: the negative is self-confirming. Once again, the self-representation of the specular subject is true only as self-condemnation, the act of denouncing oneself. Self-negation proves the presence of guilt (if not exactly crime) even when the facts may contradict it, which is why a guilty plea removes the necessity of a trial. The Court, by compelling confession, seeks to assert its own authority by making itself superfluous to the articulation of judgment, just as the Count sought to make his own action unnecessary to the accomplishment of his ends. As in the scene of *anagnorisis,* the ultimate in evidence, the conclusive proof, is self-condemnation. The confession obviates the necessity, and the responsibilities, of judgment by making the representation self-evident. Confession as self-evidence rediscovers the self-positing structure that is the tautological form of truth, but in fact is true only because it states its own negation.

In the well established tradition of dramatic reflexivity, the text of *The Cenci* stages the scene of judgment as the trial of its characters. Instead of staging, like *Hamlet* or *A Midsummer Night's Dream,* a play within a play, *The Cenci* stages the criticism of the play within the play itself. The trial inscribes the activity of the audience by performing its own judgment against the characters, inscribing the consequences of interpretation, and thus exposing the freedom such interpretation takes with literary figures who can never speak in their own defense. The trial does this in the most literal way possible, by killing them off and claiming the justification to do so. The Classical foresight of the gods, which stacked the deck against the human agents, has been reversed, and the hindsight of the interpreter has been incorporated into the course of the plot itself. No judgment could be less appropriate as a representation of the play, even as that judgment succeeds in getting at the truth of the murder and judging the criminals correctly. However correct the Court's judgment may be, staging the act of judgment as a scene in a play which is itself so often condemned only calls that judgment into question. Staging the act of judgment judges the judgment, distinguishing the legal correctness of its verdict from the understanding it claims to perform. No insight is gained into character, no rationale for the murder is educed, no motives established or considered, no aggravating circumstances are introduced: the act of judgment that the Court has performed for it is isolated

from all its inferences, what could be drawn or inferred from it, or what could support or explain it. The judgment of the Court represents the crime only because it performs no understanding of what it represents, while as an act it exposes to condemnation the duplicity of the judges, who are reduced to stooges in a mechanism they neither influence nor comprehend, and it reveals the depravity of a justice that even when dealing with confessed criminals is no better than the whim of a debauched papacy. Judges and criminals are identical in this trial in their loss of self-reflection, the utter loss of their ability, even as they judge others and excuse themselves, to connect their actions with their understanding. The judges are no more the agents of their own judgments than the criminals they condemn understand the acts they have committed.

The specularity of the subject, as the self-confirming judgment of the subject against itself, founds the representational mode of the drama in the reflexive moment of the *anagnorisis,* but once this specularity is itself dramatized as the scene of confession and judgment in the play, the specularity ends in the suspension of judgment. The judgment fails not because it is "wrong," but because it fails to differentiate, because it cannot distinguish criminals from judges, excuse from explanation, abuse from legitimacy. Judgment fails because the attribution of predicates no longer differentiates among the subjects to be judged, and the judgments apply equally and indifferently to all. The mediation of the subject, the key to any aesthetics, has been reversed into the absolute generality of a subject indifferent to its predicates. Judges are confounded with criminals in the same generality that, as Wasserman remarks, has cast us back on our own reflection, oblivious to a play whose self-judgment has preempted our own critical activity. The "subject" of the play has extended to include us (as its ultimate grammatical referent), but only by removing all specificity, all judgment, and all "subjectivity" from the subject it now represents. *We* become the allegorical subject of *The Cenci,* and *The Cenci* is read as an allegory of ourselves, but we are no longer, as Shelley insists, the subject of a judgment, either ethical or aesthetic. It is no longer *we* who judge or are judged, nor is it *we* who understand, or are understood. The specularity of the drama has become all-inclusive but has become evacuated of all content.

Allegory returns after the specular reversals of the subject as the reassertion of the absolute generality of the subject, as its capacity to represent with utter indifference to distinctions within what it represents. The absolute generality of the subject is the subject reduced to its pure grammaticality, its grammatical function conceived as such, a function uncontrolled by the specificity of its referents. The grammatical subject is the subject distinguished from any predicate, which is to say, a subject about which no judgments can be made. "In the drama of the highest order," writes Shelley in the *Defence [of Poetry]*, "there is little food for censure or hatred: what we learn is self-knowledge and self-respect" (491). The "self-knowledge" of the drama is a knowledge of the subject as a purely grammatical construct, without the differentiation of selves, and without the specification of predicates. The "self-respect" it teaches is thus the absolute equanimity, the absolute distance that comes with the loss of all individual identity. The referent of *The Cenci* includes us only because we are not who we think we are. The specularity of *The Cenci*, which has been so clearly articulated by the critics precisely because its aesthetic effect could not be assumed, is more radical than its critics have been willing to admit, and performs a critique of its own dramatic mode so thorough that it made *Prometheus Unbound* possible. What *The Cenci* teaches is that we lose our identities when we see ourselves in a play, that we lose our agency when we undertake to act in history, and that we lose our powers of judgment when we locate the grounds for judgment in our understanding of ourselves.

Notes

1. Stuart Curran, *Shelley's* Cenci: *Scorpions Ringed with Fire* (Princeton: Princeton UP, 1970) 183-256.

2. Foremost among many others, see William Ulmer, *Shelleyan Eros: The Rhetoric of Romantic Love* (Princeton: Princeton UP, 1990), and Jerrold Hogle, *Shelley's Process: Radical Transference and the Development of His Major Works* (New York: Oxford UP, 1988).

3. See her brief critical commentary included in her edition of 1839.

4. F. L. Jones, ed. *The Letters of Percy Bysshe Shelley,* Volume II: *Shelley in Italy* (Oxford: Clarendon, 1964) 102.

5. "In answer to my questions, Shelley said, 'In writing the *Cenci* my object was to see how well I could succeed in describing passions I have never felt, and to tell the most dreadful story in pure and refined language.'" Edward Trelawney, *The Last Days of Shelley and Byron [The Recollections]*, ed. by J. E. Morpurgo (Garden City, New York: Anchor Books, 1960) 61.

6. Donald Reiman and Sharon Powers, eds. *Shelley's Poetry and Prose* (New York: Norton, 1977) 237. All subsequent quotes from *The Cenci,* its Dedication and Preface, as well as quotations from the *Defence of Poetry,* are to this edition and will be cited in the text.

7. Newman Ivey White, *Shelley* (New York: Alfred A. Knopf, 1940) 2: 143.

8. "He only once descended into the arena of reality, and that was with the tragedy of the *Cenci.* This is unquestionably a work of great dramatic power . . . But he could not clip his wings to the littleness of the acting drama . . . If the gorgeous scenery of his poetry could have been *peopled* from actual life, if the deep thoughts and strong feelings which he was so capable of expressing, had been *accommodated to characters* such as have been and may be, however exceptional in the greatness of passion, he would have added his own name to those of the masters of the art" (my emphasis; *Memoirs of Percy Bysshe Shelley,* in Howard Mills, ed., *Thomas Love Peacock: Memoirs of Shelley and other Essays and Reviews* [London: Rupert Hart-Davis, 1970] 73). Peacock's hesitations directly affirm the aesthetic potential invested in the dramatic subject, and the comparative uniqueness of *The Cenci*'s representational mode in Shelley's work.

9. Desmond King-Hele, *Shelley, His Thought and Work* (Rutherford, N. J.: Fairleigh Dickinson UP, 1984) 127.

10. "Introduction" to Harold Bloom, ed., *The Selected Poetry and Prose of Shelley* (New York: New American Library, 1966) xxix.

11. Earl Wasserman, *Shelley: A Critical Reading* (Baltimore: Johns Hopkins UP, 1971) 87.

12. James E. Miller, Jr., ed., *Theory of Fiction: Henry James* (Lincoln: U of Nebraska P, 1972) 37.

13. Stuart Curran, *Shelley's* Annus Mirabilis. *The Maturing of an Epic Vision* (San Marino, CA: The Huntington Library, 1975) 135.

14. Carlos Baker, *Shelley's Major Poetry* (Princeton: Princeton UP, 1948) 152.

15. Cf. Ronald Paulson, *Representations of Revolution 1789-1820* (New Haven: Yale UP, 1983) 281.

16. *Shelley's* Cenci 266. Curran compares the lack of action to *Hamlet,* and infers a shift from dramatic to psychological interest.

17. Baker's phrase (148); Baker is discussing Beatrice's "conversion," her resolution to commit a deed previously unthinkable to her. Curran contests the concision of her resolution, writing that "a transformation such as Beatrice's cannot occur in an instantaneous resolve" and perceives it as being somewhat more drawn out (*Shelley's* Cenci 269), but agrees in essence with the extremity of the change.

18. See G. W. F. Hegel, *Vorlesungen über die Ästhetik* (Frankfurt: Suhrkamp Verlag, 1970) Bd. I, S. 512.

Ginger Strand and Sara Zimmerman (essay date winter 1996)

SOURCE: Strand, Ginger, and Sara Zimmerman. "Finding an Audience: Beatrice Cenci, Percy Shelley, and the Stage." *European Romantic Review* 6, no. 2 (winter 1996): 246-68.

[*In the following essay, Strand and Zimmerman concentrate on the moral problem associated with Beatrice's role as a heroine.*]

> ". . . in spite of all that has been said to the contrary, Beatrice Cenci is really none other than Percy Bysshe Shelley himself in petticoats . . ."[1]

The action of *The Cenci* revolves around two violent events, both of which take place off stage. Count Cenci's rape of his daughter Beatrice leads to the second brutal incident, his murder at the hands of assassins she has hired. Critics of *The Cenci* have typically read the play as the story of a heroine who, unable to suffer in silence, takes matters too firmly into her own hands and thus falls from the elevated position of virtuous daughter persecuted by tyrannical father to that of tyrant herself.[2] This reading focuses on what Stuart Sperry calls the play's "ethical problem," (414) that is, the apparent moral dilemma with which the audience is faced: by having her father murdered, Beatrice Cenci seems to have lost the moral high-ground she needs in order to be our heroine.[3] According to this reading, her "tragic fall" occurs when she assumes for herself the arbitrary authority that her father had wielded and for which she—and we—easily condemn him. In the first half of the play, her obvious victimization contrasts starkly with his abusiveness, but when, in Act III, Beatrice Cenci hires assassins to kill her father and then allows them to take the fall as she steadfastly asserts her own innocence, we are put into an awkward situation. Can an audience continue to sympathize with a daughter who commits parricide without remorse? How do we interpret her sustained denial of her guilt? We saw her arrange Cenci's murder, and we know that she knows that others are being tortured for confessions, and yet she continues to insist that she is "more innocent of parricide / Than is a child born fatherless" (4. 4. 112-13).

The play is often read as a continuation of Shelley's sustained investigation of how to rebel against despotism without becoming degraded in the process, an issue which he had just been treating in the three acts of *Prometheus Unbound* completed before beginning *The Cenci*. According to this account, whereas *Prometheus Unbound* represents a joyous apocalypse that follows the hero's act of forgiveness and rejection of counter-violence, *The Cenci*'s heroine takes the opposite course, resorting to her father's own means of domination—murder and coercion. Prometheus wins rejuvenation for himself and for his world; Beatrice Cenci loses the fight against both tyranny and the temptation to tyrannize. Earl Wasserman makes an argument foundational to this account of the play, claiming that both the Count and Beatrice Cenci, along with several other characters in the play, "repeatedly claim that in carrying out their monstrous deeds they are merely agents of God's will . . . thereby fabricating a sanction for any evil they care to perform and releasing themselves from moral responsibility" (90).

Shelley seems to lend credence to this reading of Beatrice Cenci's actions in the Preface, when he states, "Undoubtedly no person can be truly dishonoured by the act of another; and the fit return to make to the most enormous injuries is kindness and forbearance, and a resolution to convert the injurer from his dark passions by peace and love." He goes on to concede that "revenge, retaliation, atonement, are pernicious mistakes" (*Cenci* 240).[4] Moving beyond *The Cenci*'s Preface to other writing, Shelley's statements about reform clearly indicate his disapproval of methods like those Beatrice Cenci uses to effect change. Reading *The Cenci* against Shelley's essays on reform—as Marjean Purinton does—casts the play all too perfectly as a straightforward demonstration of how not to go about social transformation.[5] But read as a play—a literary experiment for Shelley—keeping in mind both the emotional force commanded by the stage and the playwright's attraction to self-dramatization, *The Cenci* looks very different indeed. Even the Preface needs to be viewed in its context: rather than a simple statement of intent, it was written as a kind of program note for what Shelley thought would be a very public event—the presentation of a piece for the stage.

"Revenge, retaliation, atonement, are pernicious mistakes." Pernicious mistakes? Even as Shelley offers a prefatory line of argument which helps to convict his heroine, his tone reflects a certain defensiveness which indicates a subtext; as James Wilson suggests, the poet "seems to protest too much" (85). Shelley's comments seem to anticipate objections to his heroine's actions, a reasonable anticipation given a choice of subject matter that would certainly be objectionable to the Examiner of Plays. But Shelley had additional reasons for presenting his play to the public carefully—motivations both personal and more broadly political. His proleptic defense of Beatrice Cenci may be read as a strategy to protect himself, heralding an analogy between playwright and heroine which will have further implications in what follows. Shelley's comments in the Preface must be read within the context of his situation at the time of composition.

To rehearse well-known circumstances, Shelley wrote the play and its Preface in Italy, an exile imposed upon himself in 1819 after a series of personal and professional setbacks. He sent his play back into a world which he and Mary Wollstonecraft Shelley had left after his own poor health encouraged a move to a warmer climate, a motivation strengthened by the pressure of mounting financial debts and his failure to find an appreciative audience for his writings. In addition, Percy and Mary had suffered the sharp disappointment of a recent Chancery court decision denying him custody of his two children by Harriet Westbrook Shelley after her suicide. The fact that he had lost the custody battle partly because of his political writings is significant. Lord Eldon, the Lord Chancellor, ruled in March 1817 against Shelley partly on the basis of evidence of his unsound political and personal pronouncements in **Queen Mab,** the **Letter to Lord Ellenborough,** and several personal letters that he had written after his separation from Harriet Shelley. Shelley wrote **The Cenci** immediately following the experience of having his own words used against him in a legal forum. The parallels with Beatrice Cenci's own failed attempt to use words to make her case to a judge in a courtroom must have seemed disturbingly familiar—and provocative. The prospect of reaching a sympathetic audience with a popular play was presumably tempting to Shelley. After hearing in Italy that in "people reprobate the subject of my tragedy," he observed to Leigh Hunt with rather plaintive exasperation, "I wrote this thing partly to please those whom my other writings displeased" (**LPBS** [**Letters of Percy Bysshe Shelley**] 2:200).[6] Shelley had hopes that **The Cenci** might help him to win not only compensation for his sense of personal wrongs; it might also provide him with a vehicle for speaking to various political crises then reaching a revolutionary boil in 1819 England.

It seems clear that in writing the play, Shelley sought to address not only the "sad reality" of Beatrice Cenci's history, but also the "sad realities" of his day. Critics have noted that **The Cenci** is an integral part of his exploration at this time of the potential for language and action to supplement one another in envisioning real political change.[7] He wrote **"The Mask of Anarchy"** for the planned volume of political poems in September 1819, the same month in which he had 250 copies of **The Cenci** printed in Italy. **"The Mask of Anarchy"** advocates for the workers of England exactly what Beatrice Cenci seeks and fails to find: an audience that can render her language politically effective. The speechless but eloquent gesture of the workers' passive resistance in the poem is transformed into "words" which "shall then become / Like oppression's thundered doom / Ringing thro' each heart and brain, / Heard again— again—again." In early September, Shelley wrote to Charles Ollier shortly after learning about the Peterloo

Massacre, the August 1819 event which inspired **"The Mask of Anarchy,"** proclaiming that "the torrent of my indignation has not yet done boiling in my veins." Significantly, Shelley borrows Beatrice Cenci's words to express a desire for action, writing that "'Something must be done . . . What, yet I know not'" (**LPBS** 2:117).[8] Shelley's identification with Beatrice Cenci's desperation to take action seems pointed.

His Preface, then, had to perform a crucial function: to introduce a work containing volatile material—both on the surface level, in its narrative of incestuous rape and patricide, and on a more implicit political level as an account of resistance to tyranny. Terence Hoagwood's theory of romantic drama provides a paradigm for understanding how Shelley attempted to address contemporary political concerns indirectly. Hoagwood suggests that in an era of strict censorship, playwrights often handled themes of tyranny and rebellion by removing the scene of these events temporally and geographically, and that in fact that "this displacement of revolutionary sociopolitical content is the central fact about Romantic drama" (51).[9] Read within this context, Shelley's disclaimers about Beatrice Cenci's actions seem more proleptic defense of his play than definitive gloss on her character.

Another reason for declining to take the playwright's words condemning Beatrice Cenci's actions at face value is found in the body of the work itself. The argument that the play is a kind of cautionary tale against responding to oppression in kind suggests that Beatrice Cenci ends up becoming as diabolical as her father. But within the world of the play this claim is insupportable on a fundamental level: the Count's vicious acts are possible only because, in the course of a career of intimidation and retribution, he has made himself untouchable. Impervious to the interventions of both church and state, he is an omnipotent presence whose power is based on his ability to control public discourse by determining who will and who will not speak in important public forums. The significance of this power in the play is foregrounded in the banquet scene in Act I, in which Cenci displays his capacity to control public discourse by announcing his two sons' deaths as cause for celebration. Before the announcement, Beatrice Cenci's stepmother, Lucretia, expresses her disbelief that her husband could stage a scene so reckless. After the Count has spoken, Beatrice Cenci seizes the occasion— and tries to steal the scene—by pleading for protection for her family from this tyrant. She begins her plea, "I do entreat you, go not, noble guests" (1. 3. 99). But Cenci regains control by threatening his guests, suggesting that they "think of their own daughters—or perhaps / Of their own throats," (1. 3. 130-31) thus demonstrating Beatrice Cenci's vulnerability and inability to protect her family. In this scene Cenci makes clear his control over public forums in which his daughter's complaints could be heard. For Beatrice Cenci, as for all other characters in the play (except for the Pope, who never appears on stage) this kind of power is unavailable.

The play demonstrates that the use of words to disrupt tyranny is dependent upon the speaker's ability to command a forum. What Beatrice Cenci learns, and finally acts upon, is central to the play: for language to assume the efficacy of action it must reach an audience. Although she fails to save her own life or her stepmother's, her final pleas to the judge enable her to announce her family's victimization in a public forum and to win sympathy from her listeners. This victory comes too late to stop the progress toward their executions, but she succeeds in gaining a position from which to announce her father's crimes, an act that no one else in the play accomplishes. Within the context of the play, Beatrice Cenci begins in a position of helplessness against her father's machinations, despite her determination to resist them. By the end of the play, she has gained a platform from which to convince others of her father's villainy. A focus on the need to gain a stage from which to make her words effective provides the play's strongest link between its heroine's story and Shelley's decision to tell it. Concentration on Beatrice Cenci's moral culpability has served to exclude the parallels between the two. As a consequence, a broader issue has been elided: why her story attracted Shelley so strongly and why he decided to write it for the stage. We believe that Shelley was interested in Beatrice Cenci's story not primarily because of an ethical dilemma she faced, but rather because she managed to do what he thus far had been unable to accomplish: find a forum for a narrative about tyranny. She finds one not only in the play itself, but also in Rome, where for generations she had been a popular hero. She thus becomes a model for Shelley, rather than a negative example of how to respond to oppression. Critics have tended to consider Beatrice Cenci implicitly as a rejected "other" self, one exorcised by her tragic fall, but we view the relationship between playwright and heroine as closer to that of identification.

We are not suggesting that the situations of Shelley and his heroine are consistently analogous. Rather, our argument is that concern with the play's overall moral import has overshadowed the complexity of Shelley's treatment of his heroine. Our aim is to identify and emphasize what Shelley may have seen in Beatrice Cenci and her story in order to help explain his attraction to her, which has been well-documented but rarely weighs into critical assessments of her actions. The Victorian critic who provides our epigraph expresses our point most pithily: Shelley's identification with his heroine is significant for understanding the play. Rather than representing the abject—qualities Shelley rejected in his grappling with the problem of tyranny—as most critics

have implicitly or explicitly contended, Beatrice Cenci embodies something more positive—and hence more useful—for Shelley. What he found in Beatrice Cenci and her story was a theatricality which had moved him and which he felt might move others.

Shelley encountered Beatrice Cenci's story in an environment more conducive to pitying than to condemning her. Kenneth Neill Cameron reports that in Italy, "as the story grew, it acquired political significance as a heroic struggle against feudal and papal tyranny." Moreover, "the source that Shelley used for his play was one of the seventeenth or eighteenth century 'relazioni,' which treated the story in sensational style as a struggle against inhuman oppression." In these "relazioni," "Count Cenci was represented as a monster of wickedness and Beatrice as a martyr" (399).[10] This reading—the cultural narrative by which Shelley first encountered the story—stops short of the final step in most readings of the play, which suggest that Beatrice Cenci becomes as wicked as her father by resorting to murder. In these sources, Beatrice Cenci is represented as a martyr, an historical interpretation which shifts emphasis away from moral culpability to what Shelley calls, if not in the classical then in the everyday sense, a "tragedy."

Mary Shelley tells us that Percy was strongly affected by seeing a painting erroneously reputed to be Beatrice Cenci's portrait by Guido Reni. Mary recalls that Percy's "imagination became strongly excited, and he urged the subject to me as one fitted for a tragedy." She reports, "I entreated him to write it instead; and he began and proceeded swiftly, urged on by intense sympathy with the sufferings of the human beings whose passions, so long cold in the tomb, he revived, and gifted with poetic language" (*Collected Works* 2:156). According to Mary Shelley, Percy's first response, the one that motivated him to write the play, was "intense sympathy" with Beatrice Cenci. His own account of the portrait in the play's preface is worth including in its entirety because it demonstrates his attitude toward his heroine:

> There is a fixed and pale composure upon the features: she seems sad and stricken down in spirit, yet the despair thus expressed is lightened by the patience of gentleness. Her head is bound with folds of white drapery from which the yellow strings of her golden hair escape, and fall about her neck. The moulding of her face is exquisitely delicate; the eye brows are distinct and arched: the lips have that permanent meaning of imagination and sensibility which suffering has not repressed and which it seems as if death scarcely could extinguish. Her forehead is large and clear; her eyes, which we are told were remarkable for their vivacity, are swollen with weeping and lustreless, but beautifully tender and serene. In the whole mien there is a simplicity and dignity which united with her exquisite loveliness and deep sorrow are inexpressibly pathetic.

(*Cenci* 242)

The qualities he emphasizes are somewhat unexpected given the story that the play proceeds to tell. He attributes to her nothing of the murderous desperation, the hard-hearted betrayal of Marzio, or the stubborn insistence of innocence on which critical arguments often dwell. Instead what Shelley sees is "the patience of gentleness," delicacy, lips that suggest "imagination and sensibility," eyes "beautifully tender and serene," and finally a "simplicity and dignity" combined with a look of "deep sorrow." He summarizes the effect of the portrait as "inexpressibly pathetic." It is important to realize that Shelley believes that the portrait was taken "during her confinement in prison"—that is, after the murder, not before, when she was "innocent." Her appeal outlasts her actions for Shelley. The play rehearses a history of brutality and complicated motivations, but he seems to have been drawn to Beatrice Cenci not in horrid fascination nor in moral repugnance but rather in sympathy.

David Marshall has discussed at length the eighteenth- and nineteenth-century concern with sympathy and fellow-feeling, a concern taken up by both moral philosophy and aesthetics. As Marshall demonstrates, the possibilities—and dangers—of sympathy were inextricably linked with issues of theatricality. Acts of sympathy depend, as Adam Smith argues in *The Theory of Moral Sentiments,* not only upon the sympathizer's capacity for fellow-feeling, but also upon the sympathized-with's ability to represent himself or herself as a readable text, tableau, or spectacle (5). What Shelley learns from Beatrice Cenci is that she must present herself as a sympathetic figure to a responsive audience in order to gain some measure of control over her situation. We are suggesting that what she offers is not only, or even primarily, a negative lesson—that revenge corrupts the perpetrator—but rather that a person who had committed moral transgressions, and even a crime, could still win sympathetic listeners. In the wake of Harriet Shelley's suicide, which inspired speculations both in and out of the courtroom about the possibility of Shelley's culpable negligence, this lesson must have been powerfully attractive.

What Shelley finds in Beatrice Cenci is a person circumscribed by events and by an inability to find a forum in which to be heard. By the end of her story, she finds both an audience within the play—in the courtroom—and then another, posthumously, in Italian society, both of which respond sympathetically to her plight. Her example provides an important lesson for Shelley: that failure to find responsive listeners is not the result of the inadequacy of language but rather of the difficulty of gaining a forum in which to speak. The play has inspired critical analyses about the failures of language, but what it dramatizes is that a social context is needed in order for language to be rendered effectual.[11] From the opening banquet scene to the final courtroom

scene, *The Cenci* may be read as a series of struggles between Beatrice Cenci and her father for public forums which are, in effect, stages. A focus on the performative helps explains Shelley's choice of genre for telling the story: Shelley puts into action what he learns from Beatrice Cenci by staging a play.

Critics have noted that language and the capacity to speak are foregrounded in the plot.[12] Cenci coerces people into complicity by commanding or threatening them; more importantly, he is able to determine who may speak and who will not be heard. His daughter is the player whom he is unable to silence. As Lucretia reminds her, at a point of her near collapse when she has begun to comprehend her father's plans for her: "Until this hour thus you have ever stood / Between us and your father's moody wrath / Like a protecting presence: your firm mind / Has been our only refuge and defence" (2. 1. 46-49). Cenci's effort to silence his daughter and her struggle to control her own words and to find listeners for them are at the center of the play, a claim supported by Shelley's source. The manuscript of the **"Relation of the Death of the Family of the Cenci,"** derived from Lodovico Antonio Muratori's account in his *Annali d'Italia* reports that, even after the confessions of her co-conspirators, "the Signora Beatrice, being young, lively, and strong, neither with good nor ill treatment, with menaces, nor fear of torture, would allow a single word to pass her lips which might inculpate her; and even, by her lively eloquence, confused the judges who examined her" (**Collected Works** 2:162).

The Count temporarily silences his daughter by raping her, an extremely resourceful ploy on his part, since he knows that shame and the lack of socially-sanctioned speech will prevent her telling what has happened to her. As he warns his daughter after her failed appeal to the guests at the banquet, "I know a charm shall make thee meek and tame" (1. 3. 167). Cenci's plot against her includes the hope that the rape will succeed in degrading her language itself. In subduing Beatrice Cenci, her father intends to turn her ability to silence others against her. He tells her:

> Never again, I think, with fearless eye,
> And brow superior, and unaltered cheek,
> And that lip made for tenderness or scorn,
> Shalt thou strike dumb the meanest of mankind;
> Me least of all.
>
>   (2. 1. 116-20)

But as the Count implicitly recognizes, Beatrice Cenci also knows a "charm" that will silence him: she uses gesture—her "brow superior" and "unaltered cheek"—rather than language. Her performative skills—the statuesque bodily presence of the nineteenth-century actress—will help her to create what no one else in the play has been able to: a public forum in which her speech will be heard. Beatrice Cenci pays for the murder with her life, a simple equation that makes clear the lesson that crime does not pay. But her martyrdom has broader implications for a playwright seeking his own audience.

Beatrice Cenci wins her stage inadvertently, when her murder plot fails. But her choice of action over speech is made when she decides to plot her father's demise. Her first attempt involves staging an ambush of her father's carriage on his trip to the Castle Petrella, where he intends to sequester and torture his family. Like the murder itself, the ambush represents a reversal of Cenci's own diabolic intentions toward his daughter. Critics have noted that the murder strongly resembles the murder of Duncan in *Macbeth*.[13] Shelley emphasizes the theatricality of the story by foregrounding her role as an actor—and even as a kind of playwright—within the play. Beatrice Cenci's final performance in the courtroom is the last in a succession of scenes she stages after forsaking speech for performance after the rape. Recognizing that her words will be ineffectual as long as her father controls the public forums in which they could be heard, she resorts to action, a path which leads her to another forum—a courtroom in which she is finally heard, although too late to save her own life.

In writing his only completed work intended for the stage, Shelley follows her example by using performative strategies to reach unwilling or indifferent listeners. Stephen Behrendt's reading of the play supports this claim. He suggests that "In composing a play specifically intended for the stage, Shelley was attempting to enter into a significantly different relationship with an audience based not on the solitary and tranquil act of reading but on the social and more subjective act of witnessing live theater" (*Shelley and His Audiences* 145).[14] The audience Beatrice Cenci engages must have been attractively broad to Shelley: she reaches both characters in the play who are initially resistant to her cause and an audience of successive generations who continued to respond to her legend. In the nineteenth-century Rome in which the Shelley's acquired the manuscript, Beatrice Cenci cut a popular figure. Shelley recalls, "On my arrival at Rome, I found that the story of the Cenci was a subject not to be mentioned in Italian society without awakening a deep and breathless interest" (*Cenci* 239). In Beatrice Cenci, Shelley found an historical figure who—temporarily—reversed the interrogative purposes of the courtroom and made it her stage. Her attempts to gain this forum—and her success as character if not as defendant—must have been appealing to Shelley in the wake of the Chancery court decision.

For Beatrice Cenci, the possibility of simply describing her oppression would jeopardize her position further, a circumstance which her father shrewdly anticipated. To name her plight would mean to accept her own public shame. Enactment provided a way for her to represent her story in a different way. Critics who have read the play as an ethical dilemma to be resolved have insisted that Beatrice Cenci's tragic flaw is in thinking that she was "dishonored" when she was raped—that her virtue is now tarnished and cannot be restored. These critics have charged Beatrice Cenci with taking matters into her own hands unnecessarily—since surely there can be no shame in being victimized. We want to suggest that, on the contrary, Beatrice Cenci—like Shelley—knows that her "honor" is irreparably damaged when she was incestuously raped—"honor" is a social term. She understands that she will never be the same in her community's eyes. Beatrice Cenci herself draws our attention to the fact that her place in society has been taken away from her: "Oh, what am I?" she asks, "What name, what place, what memory shall be mine?" (3. 1. 74-75). Beatrice Cenci, recognizing that she has in fact experienced a fall—a social fall—begins to plan her actions outside the laws of the social order that could only have seen her as a fallen woman. As Julie Carlson puts it, the play suggests "the radical contingency of female innocence as their honor is passed from mouth to mouth of men" (*Theatre* [*In the Theatre of Romanticism*] 191).

Beatrice Cenci knows that she cannot simply tell her story for another reason: because even a narration of what had happened would not precipitate her father's punishment—we are told that he has managed to escape justice for past transgressions, including murder, by bribing the Pope. Furthermore, there is no socially-sanctioned language in which she could represent her experience, even to her stepmother: "What are the words which you would have me speak?" (3. 1. 107) she asks rhetorically. After the rape, in a fit of near madness, she tries to articulate what has happened but stops short each time: "worse have been conceived" she says, "than ever there was found a heart to do." "But," she continues, "never fancy imaged such a deed / As . . ." (3. 1. 53-56). We get a dash here at the unspeakable act. She asks Lucretia:

> . . . of all words,
> That minister to mortal intercourse,
> Which wouldst thou hear? For there is none to tell
> My misery; if another ever knew
> Aught like to it, she died as I will die,
> And left it, as I must, without a name.

(3. 1. 111-16)

This passage conveys a key point in the play: Beatrice Cenci's speechlessness comes not from the fact that there is no language to describe what has happened, but rather that there is no language which "ministers to mortal intercourse." In other words, there is no language that society will listen to sympathetically. When

Orsino asks her why she doesn't simply publicly say what happened, she tells him:

> If this were done, which never shall be done,
> Think of the offender's gold, his dreaded hate,
> And the strange horror of the accuser's tale,
> Baffling belief, and overpowering speech;
> Scarce whispered, unimaginable, wrapt
> In hideous hints . . . Oh, most assured redress!
>
> (3. 1. 161-66)

Her father's ability to buy forgiveness—the "offender's gold"—and his propensity to punish her for speaking—"his dreaded hate"—are mentioned, but rhetorically outweighed by the four lines describing the "strange horror of the accuser's tale." Should she speak out, Beatrice Cenci knows that her tale would be "strange" and "horrifying" in the effect it must have on a society so entirely unprepared to deal with the "sad reality" of incestuous rape.

When Beatrice Cenci stages her father's murder, she inadvertently accomplishes what she could not have managed otherwise: she moves the discussion of her father's criminal acts into a public realm. By this point in the play, Beatrice Cenci's lack of a sympathetic audience has already been demonstrated. At the banquet scene, in Act I, she attempts to take advantage of a public gathering to make a plea for her safety and that of her mother and surviving brothers. But even after hearing the Count rejoice in his sons' deaths, the company ignores her eloquent entreaty. It's not that they don't understand her, but rather that this audience refuses to be engaged by her. "Dare no one look on me" she asks,

> None answer? Can one tyrant overbear
> The sense of many best and wisest men?
> Or is it that I sue not in some form
> Of scrupulous law, that ye deny my suit?
>
> (1. 3. 132-36)

Beatrice Cenci wonders here why her words aren't finding an audience, speculating that the lack of a socially-sanctioned frame for her words makes speaking pointless. Only then does she choose action over speech. We are not suggesting that she commits the crime in order to win a courtroom audience. She takes pains to see that the crime would not be discovered. But events move on despite her, as they have throughout the play, only now she gains what she had failed to find before: a stage from which to speak, if only briefly. Furthermore, her action moves the struggle from the private domain of her father's castle—from the domestic space in which the rape occurs and where her father has absolute control—to a public realm where she has a better, although still limited, chance of being heard. Beatrice Cenci explicitly comments that even the most repressive public space—a prison—is better for her than the privatized world of the Castle Petrella—"thou knowest / This cell

seems like a kind of Paradise / After our father's presence" (5. 3. 10-12).

In committing a crime which prompts a trial, Beatrice Cenci steps onto a stage and gains a forum in which her family's story is made public but her "dishonour" is never articulated. By steadfastly stating her innocence to her audience, she induces Marzio to retract the confession that he has made off-stage. She forces him to look at her and to say again on her stage that she is guilty; he can't. He in turn resorts to action, now that his own words have worked against him: he holds his breath until he dies, thereby refusing to be coerced into a second verbal confession. Julie Carlson observes that Beatrice Cenci is a "commanding actress" (*Theatre* 192); no one who listens to her in the courtroom can deny the effect of her words. Camillo, having decided earlier that she is guilty, now appears before the Pope and pleads for her life and Lucretia's. The Pope is unmoved: he has not been present to hear her defense, and so is able, unlike those who have listened, to turn a deaf ear to her pleas. He orders the execution, never having intended to listen to Beatrice Cenci's words. Camillo tells how in response to pleas for clemency for Beatrice and Lucretia, the Pope

> . . . frowned, as if to frown had been the trick
> Of his machinery, on the advocates
> Presenting the defences, which he tore
> And threw behind. . . .
>
> (5. 4. 6-9)

The Pope's authority is precedented upon limiting the circulation of language. Camillo explains:

> He turned to me then, looking deprecation,
> And said these three words, coldly: "They must die."
>
> (5. 4. 13-14)

Like Cenci, the Pope does not need great eloquence: his powers of speech are such that they require very few words to effect action against his enemies. But those powers of speech are based upon his ability to control language—both his and others. His last words to Camillo are:

> "Here is their sentence; never see me more
> Till, to the letter, it be all fulfilled."
>
> (5. 4. 26-27)

The presentation of the Pope's brief "sentence," concurrent with his denial of Camillos pleas, reminds us of Cenci's own assertion to his guests:

> Enjoy yourselves.—Beware! For my revenge
> Is as the sealed commission of a king
> That kills, and none dare name the murderer.
>
> (1. 3. 96-98)

Cenci, too, must lay claim to language in a delimited state: a "sealed commission" which allows no response and no intervention.

In the world of the play, both the Count and the Pope have managed to consolidate their power by retaining strict control over how language is deployed, both by issuing "sealed" decrees—in which language equals action—and by capitalizing on the fact that there is no audience in the play capable of hearing Beatrice Cenci and responding adequately to what she says. She herself understands her complete lack of such an audience when she refers to the "strange horror of the accuser's tale." By writing a play for the stage, Shelley highlights the suggestion that a person's words are only effective if there is an audience to be moved by them. The one force capable of pardoning Beatrice Cenci—the Pope—is willfully absent at her performance. Her tragedy, ultimately, is not the tragedy of being unable to speak—it is the tragedy of being forced to speak only within a society which simply turns a deaf ear to her words. Camillo says about Bernardo, who has just rushed out of the prison to make his last-minute appeal to the Pope, that he might as well "pray / To the deaf sea" (5. 4. 42-43). Camillo, after having made his own entreaty, reports, "The Pope is stern; not to be moved or bent" (5. 4. 1). The play demonstrates that if you have an audience, you don't need very many words—you need one or three. Cenci has managed to terrorize his daughter almost to the point of madness with only "one little word" (2. 1. 63) which we never hear, and the Pope, upon rejecting the prisoners' requests for clemency, says simply, "'They must die,'" (5. 4. 14) and they are escorted offstage to their executions. Shelley here stages not the failure of language, but its dependence on engagement between speaker and audience.

The Cenci represents a complex effort on Shelley's part to win a broad audience. In writing the play, his only completed work for the stage, Shelley follows his heroine's example by using performative strategies to reach unwilling or indifferent listeners. His hopes that the play might be a popular success were founded on his sense that it represented a departure from his usual methods in terms of subject matter, language and genre.[15] Letters show that Shelley made these decisions self-consciously, and with the end of reaching a mass audience in view. In August 1819 he wrote to Leigh Hunt "on the eve of completing another work, totally different from anything you might conjecture that I should write; of a more popular kind; and, if anything of mine could deserve attention, of higher claims" (*LPBS* 2:108). In an April 1820 letter he promised Thomas Jefferson Hogg, "You will see that it is studiously written in a style very different from any other compositions" (*LPBS* 2:186). In September 1819 he informed Charles Ollier, one of his publishers, that he was about to send a transcript of *Prometheus Unbound* along with "another work, calculated to produce a very popular effect & totally in a different style from anything I have yet composed" (*LPBS* 2:116-17). In March 1820 he informed Ollier that he estimated "the *Prometheus [Unbound]* cannot sell beyond twenty copies," and instructed them "specially to pet him and feed him with fine ink and good paper" for an audience he describes as "select" in the play's Preface. In contrast, he had *The Cenci* printed more cheaply in Leghorn and then again in London, anticipating to his publisher that "*Cenci* is written for the multitude, and ought to sell well" (*LPBS* 2:174).

His efforts to produce a popular work took several forms. In the Preface, he tells us that he has intentionally kept the language of the play simple, having "avoided with great care in writing this play the introduction of what is commonly called mere poetry" even to the point of writing "carelessly; that is, without an over-fastidious and learned choice of words" (*Cenci* 241). In a letter he describes the kind of language he had used as "chaste" (*LPBS* 2:189). and he tells Keats that the play was "studiously composed in a different style" (*LPBS* 2:221). These reiterations underscore how intent Shelley was on adopting a Wordsworthian "familiar language," a gesture he made, he tells us, "in order to move men to true sympathy" (*Cenci* 241). This effort was not lost on contemporary reviewers. Shelley's decision to simplify his language for a theater audience also enabled him to reach some critics who were antagonistic to his writing style. A predominantly negative response in the *British Review* begins with a backhanded compliment: "*The Cenci* is the best, because it is by far the most intelligible, of Mr. Shelley's works" (380). And John Scott, who begins his review in *London Magazine* with a diatribe against writers who seek "gratification in conjuring up, or presenting, the image or idea of something abhorrent to feelings of the general standard," praises the play's language. He observes that Shelley "preserves throughout a vigorous, clear, manly turn of expression" and that "his language, as he travels through the most exaggerated incidents, retains its correctness and simplicity" (546-47).

Shelley also made a conscious decision to handle a new kind of subject in the play: historical fact rather than what he refers to in the Dedication as "visions which impersonate my own apprehensions of the beautiful and the just" (*Cenci* 237). He announces that *The Cenci,* instead of "dreams of what ought to be, or may be," represents "a sad reality" (*Cenci* 237). Writing in July 1819 to Thomas Love Peacock, whom he hoped would arrange for the play's production at the Theatre Royal in Covent Garden, Shelley makes it clear that this new, "real" subject matter was chosen for its popular appeal, "having attending [*for* attended] simply to the impartial development of such characters as it is probable the persons represented really were, together with the greatest degree of popular effect to be produced by such a development" (*LPBS* 2:102). The material itself, Shelley hoped, would generate a broad appeal for a diverse and popular audience.

In the Preface he recalls having discovered in Rome that "all ranks of people knew the outlines of this history, and participated in the overwhelming interest which it seems to have the magic of exciting in the human heart" (*Cenci* 239). Beatrice Cenci's audience, encompassing "all ranks of people," is one that he sought as a writer and that he courted assiduously in writing *The Cenci*. Shelley was impressed that whenever Beatrice Cenci's story was rehearsed "the feelings of the company never failed to incline to a romantic pity for the wrongs, and a passionate exculpation of the horrible deed to which they urged her, who has been mingled two centuries with the common dust" (*Cenci* 239). She had won sympathy despite her rebellious actions, becoming a heroine in her struggle against her family's "common tyrant" (*Cenci* 238) as Shelley refers to Cenci in the Preface.

His choices of style and subject comprise an effort to make the play ready for the London stage, an ambition for which he was prepared to sacrifice authorial credit during its premiere. In the July letter, Shelley asks Peacock to insure his anonymity, deeming it "essential, deeply essential to it's [sic] success" (*LPBS* 2:102), probably because the poet felt that his name might incite reviewers. Writing to Amelia Curran in September, Mary Shelley undoubtedly reflects her husband's feelings: "it is still *a deep secret* & only one person, Peacock who presents it, knows anything about it in England—with S.'s public & private enemies it would certainly fall if known to be his—his sister in law alone would hire enough people to damn it" (*LMWS* [*The Letters of Mary Wollstonecraft Shelley*] 1:106). Nonetheless, Percy Shelley confesses to Peacock in the July letter that he is hopeful that the play will be a vehicle for gaining not only public recognition, but also a measure of empowerment: "After it had been acted & successfully (could I hope such a thing), I would own it if I pleased, & use the celebrity it might acquire to my own purposes" (*LPBS* 2:102). Although Shelley does not elaborate on these "purposes," we can only assume that they might have encompassed both the recuperation of his personal reputation and broader political goals. Shelley's efforts to employ a simpler idiom, a popular subject, and a sense of historical immediacy are founded on *The Cenci*'s central departure from what Keats called "habitual self"—its theatricality.

Shelley's own sense that *The Cenci* was different from anything he had written before is based on its theatricality, and Mary Shelley concurs in her note to the play, claiming that "There is nothing that is not purely dramatic throughout" (*Collected Works* 2:158). Although Shelley hedged his bets by having the 250 copies of *The Cenci* printed in Leghorn in advance, in case the play was rejected by Covent Garden's manager, Thomas Harris, his intention was that the play was to be performed. Writing to Charles Ollier, he explains that *The Cenci* was "expressly written for theatrical exhibition" and maintains, "*I* believe it singularly fitted for the stage" (*LPBS* 2:178). In the July letter to Peacock, he announces, "I have written a tragedy on the subject of a story well known in Italy, & in my conception eminently dramatic." He assures Peacock that he has "taken some pains to make my play fit for representation." At the same time he seemed confident of his success in this new forum, going on to assert that "as a composition it is certainly not inferior to any of the modern plays that have been acted, with the exception of Remorse," and "that the interest of its plot is incredibly greater & more real, and that there is nothing beyond what the multitude are contented to believe that they can understand, either in imagery opinion or sentiment" (*LPBS* 2:102). His fixation on reaching a "multitude" reverberates throughout his letters on the subject and is reflected in these efforts to make his play accessible and palatable to a general audience.

Clearly Shelley had a stage production in mind, and not just any kind of production. The stage that he sought would insert him into a mainstream public world. The Theatre Royal at Covent Garden, one of London's two licensed theaters at the time, had been rebuilt after its complete destruction by fire in 1808. Seating 2,800 people in the pit, galleries and boxes, the new theater hosted audiences that included people of all ranks and classes. One critic describes a nineteenth-century theater audience as "the upper-class Sir Mulberry Hawk and his friends, Pendennis and David Copperfield, sometimes Lord Byron and Sir Walter Scott; tallow-chandlers, lawyers' clerks, Charles Lamb's relatives, to speak of the middle class; and all that extraordinary congeries of street-peddlers and coalheavers and dog-stealers and prostitutes and the whole world of low-life that we read of in Mayhew" (Davies 23). Theater historians agree that the evidence from ticket prices, theater capacities and contemporary accounts all point to the changing nature of London audiences between 1792 and 1812 (Booth, et al. 7-9). In designing his play specifically for Covent Garden, Shelley sought a forum which was not only popular, but increasingly open to members of all classes.

The poet would have [been] familiar with this forum, having attended the theater and opera frequently in 1818, often with Peacock or Marianne and Leigh Hunt, in the weeks that he and Mary Shelley resided in London before leaving for the Continent. It was at this time that he was struck with the acting skills of the leading man and lady he envisioned for *The Cenci*. Mary Shelley's journal notes that Peacock joined the Shelleys in attending the new play, *Fazio,* by the Revd. Henry Hart Milman, at Covent Garden on February 16, 1818. Eliza O'Neill starred in the play. Shelley appears to have been taken with her performance enough to want to see the play again: Mary Shelley's entry for March 5 of that year reports having seen *The Libertine,* a new play by Isaac Pocock which was playing at Covent Garden on a double bill with *Fazio* that night (*Journals* [*The Journals of Mary Shelley*] 1:193 ff.). During these weeks Shelley saw Kean as well, starring at Drury Lane in a gothic musical called *The Bride of Abydos,* written by William Dimond and based on Byron's poem. The Shelleys also attended the opera many times, and saw what Mary describes as "a new comedy damned," *The Castle of Glendower* by Samuel William Ryley at Drury Lane (*Journals* 1:196).

Shelley was quite familiar, then, with what was selling on the London stages, and his tastes were by no means exclusive. Kean and O'Neill were all the rage among critics and audiences alike. Again, it is clear that Shelley envisioned *The Cenci* as a play which would please popular audiences and lend to its author mainstream celebrity. Shelley's comparison of *The Cenci* to Coleridge's *Remorse,* which played successfully at Drury Lane in 1813, is telling as well. Both dramas are thought to diverge from Romantic poets' tendency to write "closet dramas," and both do so mainly by utilizing a widely-recognizable set of conventions popular at the time: the conventions of the gothic drama. *The Cenci*'s irredeemably evil tyrant, his pathetic heroine-victim, and her self-divided suitor reflect one of gothic drama's standard groupings of stock characters. Shelley engages a host of gothic devices in the play as well: the medieval setting, the gloomy castle, the intercepted letter, the constant appeals to heaven, the Inquisition, and the dungeon scene—even the drugged drink Lucretia gives Cenci on the night of his murder is typical gothic fare. And Beatrice Cenci's lengthy and grim description of the intended forest location for her father's murder indulges in the gothic tradition in which "castles were always ruinous, forests set in deep gloom, and the seashore lashed by storm-driven waves" (Ranger 10). Given his use of the contemporary stage's most scintillating attractions, it's easy to understand Shelley's conviction that *The Cenci* would prove popular, and his subsequent frustration when it could not be performed.

In writing *The Cenci* as a gothic drama, however, Shelley was seeking more than box office draw. The over-the-top turbulence and sensation of gothic drama can be seen as a means of portraying the real-life sense of struggle and breakdown which characterized late eighteenth- and early nineteenth-century England, while avoiding the overt political commentary which would have alarmed the Examiner of Plays. The good versus evil nature of the gothic plot conveniently encapsulates moral dilemmas which were very often analogous to current political ones. Furthermore, the highly conventionalized nature of the gothic plot allowed Shelley to write a form of drama which in and of itself became a commentary on the necessity of having an engaged and sympathetic audience. The gothic drama was a form of theater in which "the audience was an integral part of the performance of the play" (Ranger 104). Awaiting its cues to laugh, weep, or recoil in horror, the nineteenth-century audience provided the response that guaranteed the success or failure of any play. The attention and sympathies of an audience are crucial for a play's performance more overtly than they are for the success of any other literary form; in a genre form such as the gothic, the play's effect depends entirely upon its reception by an audience. The playwright's desire for the rapt attentions and hearty response of such an audience reflects, for Shelley, the poet's desire for the understanding and complicity of an engaged readership. Historical displacement has often been used by writers to protect polemical references to contemporary events, a strategy which, as Hoagwood demonstrates, Romantic playwrights often employed. But drama supplements this protective distancing with another quality: the sense of immediacy that staged events can convey. Shelley indicates an awareness of this capacity by choosing, for his first attempt at staging a play, a heroine who embodies theatricality's potential for urgency in order to reach an audience.

Recalling Marshall's claim that winning an audience's sympathy depends upon effective self-presentation, in seems clear why Percy Shelley would turn to Beatrice Cenci to help him with this task. He stages his own difficulty in eliciting the sympathy of an audience by presenting us with an historical figure who overcame similar obstacles to win listeners and with whom he shares a past publicly marked by acts of rebellion and blame. Returning, in closing, to the Preface, we see Shelley cautiously negotiating his identification with his heroine. He assumes, in effect, the position of his own reader in acknowledging his reluctance to sympathize with Beatrice Cenci when he concedes that "Revenge, retaliation, atonement, are pernicious mistakes" (*Cenci* 240). When he goes on to defend her, then, it is seemingly in spite of his own hesitation—a reluctance he could assume he shared with readers facing his own story. His identification with her may be read as a tacit acknowledgment that winning an audience required an act of sympathy. In the Preface, we see him making the sympathetic gesture toward Beatrice Cenci that he desired from his own audience.

Notes

1. The critic for *Fraser's Magazine* advises Shelley to "leave philosophy and politics, which he does not understand, and shriekings and cursings, which

are unfit for any civilized and self-respecting man." His caricature of a feminized Shelley as shrill and politically aggressive emphasizes the misogyny implicit in the most extreme critical castigations of Beatrice Cenci as a vengeful woman. The critic attempts to distance this instance of Shelley's harpy-like behavior from the "perfect" writer that he is "when he will be himself—Shelley the scholar and the gentleman and the singer" (574). For our purposes, however, this parodic depiction of Shelley in petticoats represents a telling identification on a critic's part of playwright with heroine. Stuart Curran cites Charles Kingsley as the likely author (*Shelley's Cenci* 23).

2. Perhaps the most important exception is Stuart Curran's full, subtle study of the play (*Shelley's Cenci*). Curran defends Beatrice Cenci by claiming that she is a kind of existential heroine because she realizes that there are no absolute standards of good and evil in the "sad reality" in which tyrants often have their way. Curran suggests that by acting on this understanding in the only way that her circumstances allow, Beatrice Cenci reflects the poet's own skepticism about any idealistic hope for rejuvenation, a parallel between the two that is useful to our argument, although our terms of comparison between Shelley and Beatrice Cenci differ from Curran's. Other critics have complicated the "moral dilemma" as well. Marjean Purinton agrees with the traditional reading in asserting that "Beatrice, unlike [*Prometheus Unbound*'s] Asia, dons the cloak of patriarchal tyranny rather than the vestments of matriarchal freedom" (104), but argues that readers should not fall into the trap of judging Beatrice Cenci, for "if we ascribe evaluative labels to Beatrice's behavior as good or evil, vice or virtue, however, we risk falling into the trap of dichotomies that privilege one over the other—the very authority/submission hierarchy that *The Cenci* questions and depicts as false" (105). James Wilson defends her by making her the "unwilling vessel" for her father's "evil," and thereby the "catalyst by means of which the Count unconsciously effected his perverse will to self-destruction" (80-81). While his argument is useful in relocating the source of "evil" firmly with the Count, our treatment of Beatrice Cenci focuses on her as an active agent. Newman Ivey White also comes to her defence by arguing that "her real motive for the murder is self-protection and an almost religious mission to rid her family and the world of a dangerous monster." He, too, finds Shelley "sympathetic" with his heroine (2:139).

In her reading of the play in the context of Romantic antitheatricalism, Julie Carlson makes an important argument for "Beatrice's inseparability from theatre" (*Theatre* 187). Like us, she is troubled by critiques of the play that focus on its heroine's flaws, pointing to "the inadequacy of moral interpretations of her character" (*Theatre* 187-88). But while she makes a case crucial to our argument for Shelley's sympathy with his heroine, Carlson maintains that he ultimately reacts against his own portrait of a strong woman acting out violent rebellion.

3. Sperry claims that "the fundamental issue upon which the drama turns, to put it simply, is: was Beatrice wrong in planning the murder of her father, Count Franceso Cenci; or was she rather justified in following, like Antigone, the dictates of her conscience and in adopting violent means to relieve both her family and herself from the toils of an insupportable tyranny?" (413).

4. All references to *The Cenci* are from *Shelley's Poetry and Prose,* eds. Donald H. Reiman and Sharon B. Powers. All references to Mary Shelley's "Note on the Cenci" are from *The Complete Works of Percy Bysshe Shelley,* ed. Roger Ingpen and Walter E. Peck, Vol. 2.

5. Citing Shelley's essay, "A Philosophical View of Reform," begun in 1819, Barbara Groseclose points out that Shelley did rethink his position against violent rebellion: "he had gradually begun to conclude that, on occasion, armed resistance might be necessary" (230). Groseclose makes an interesting argument relevent to ours, that Shelley makes incest "the crux of his plot" in order to make Beatrice Cenci "a special kind of political victim." She differs from us, however, in arguing that his aim was to make her "neither criminal nor heroine" (231-32).

6. References to Mary's letters are from *The Letters of Mary Wollstonecraft Shelley,* ed. Betty T. Bennett, Vol. 1 (hereafter *LMWS*).

7. For broader explorations of this point, see Steven Goldsmith, *Unbuilding Jerusalem,* and Stephen C. Behrendt, "Beatrice Cenci and the Tragic Myth of History."

8. Beatrice Cenci's lines read: "Ay, something must be done; / What, yet I know not . . . something which shall make / The thing that I have suffered but a shadow / In the dread lighting which avenges it" (3. 1. 86-89). Purinton also notes this congruence.

9. Julie Carlson makes an argument that supplements Hoagwood's: "A critical focus on theater," she claims, "helps restore the complexity and political seriousness of romantic poetics" ("Impositions of Form" 151).

10. Curran reports that when Shelley encountered the story in Italy, it was "commonly reproduced as a veiled attack against the Italian aristocracy and the Papacy" (*Shelley's* Cenci 40).

11. See Michael Worton, "Speech and Silence in *The Cenci.*"

12. Steven Goldsmith finds "the ability to control access to speech, the ability to assert one's power by diminishing the linguistic capacities of others" to be central to the play. But he maintains the standard critical line on Beatrice Cenci's actions, concluding that after the rape "she speaks in a new voice that distinctly resembles her father's" (236-37, 238).

13. Curran outlines the play's literary debts in great detail in *Shelley's* Cenci.

14. Behrendt also argues that Shelley's attempt to reach a mainstream audience in *The Cenci* reveals the political message behind the play. Behrendt's reading of the play, however, and of Beatrice Cenci in particular, differs from ours in that he holds that *The Cenci* represents an effort subtly to introduce political ideas to his audience, rather than to dramatize exactly the problem of reaching that audience.

15. Behrendt suggests that with *The Cenci,* Shelley "determined to take an entirely new approach to language and style in an attempt to increase the play's accessibility for the theatergoer" (*Shelley and His Audiences* 145).

Works Cited

Anon. rev. of *The Cenci. British Review* 17 (June 1821): 380-89.

Anon. [Kingsley, Charles?]. "Thoughts on Shelley and Byron." *Fraser's Magazine* 48 (November 1853): 568-76.

Behrendt, Stephen C. "Beatrice Cenci and the Tragic Myth of History." *History & Myth: Essays on English Romantic Literature.* Ed. Behrendt. Detroit: Wayne State U P, 1990. 214-34.

———. *Shelley and His Audiences.* Lincoln: U of Nebraska P, 1989.

Booth, Michael and Richard Southern, Frederick and Lise-Lone Marker, and Robertson Davies. *The Revels History of Drama in English.* Vol. 6. London: Methuen, 1975.

Cameron, Kenneth Neill. *Shelley: The Golden Years.* Cambridge: Harvard U P, 1974.

Carlson, Julie A. "Impositions of Form: Romantic Antitheatricalism and the Case Against Particular Women."

ELH [*Journal of English Literary History*] 60 (Spring 1993): 149-79.

———. *In the Theatre of Romanticism.* Cambridge: Cambridge U P, 1994.

Curran, Stuart. *Shelley's* Cenci*: Scorpions Ringed With Fire.* Princeton: Princeton U P, 1970.

Davies, Robertson. *The Mirror of Nature.* Toronto: U of Toronto P, 1983.

Goldsmith, Steven. *Unbuilding Jerusalem: Apocalypse and Romantic Representation.* Ithaca: Cornell U P, 1993.

Groseclose, Barbara. "The Incest Motif in Shelley's *The Cenci.*" *Comparative Drama* 19 (Fall 1985): 222-39.

Hoagwood, Terence Allan. "Prolegomenon for a Theory of Romantic Drama." *The Wordsworth Circle* 23 (Spring 1992): 49-64.

Marshall, David. *The Surprising Effects of Sympathy: Marivaux, Diderot, Rousseau, and Mary Shelley.* Chicago: U of Chicago P, 1988.

Purinton, Marjean D. *Romantic Ideology Unmasked: The Mentally Constructed Tyrannies in Dramas of William Wordsworth, Lord Byron, Percy Shelley, and Joanna Baillie.* Newark: U of Delaware P, 1994.

Ranger, Paul. *'Terror and Pity Reigned in Every Breast': Gothic Drama in the London Patent Theatres, 1750-1820.* London: The Society for Theatre Research, 1991.

Scott, John. Rev. of *The Cenci. London Magazine* 1 (May 1820): 546-55.

Shelley, Mary Wollstonecraft. *The Journals of Mary Shelley.* Ed. Paula R. Feldman and Diana Scott-Kilvert. Vol. 1. Oxford: Clarendon P, 1987.

———. *The Letters of Mary Wollstonecraft Shelley.* Ed. Betty T. Bennett. Vol. 1. Baltimore: Johns Hopkins U P, 1980.

Shelley, Percy Bysshe. *The Complete Works of Percy Bysshe Shelley.* Ed. Roger Ingpen and Walter E. Peck. Vol 2. New York: Gordian P, 1965.

———. *The Letters of Percy Bysshe Shelley.* Ed. Frederick L. Jones. Vol. 2. Oxford: Clarendon P, 1964.

———. *Shelley's Poetry and Prose.* Ed. Donald H. Reiman and Sharon B. Powers. New York: Norton, 1977.

Sperry, Stuart M. "The Ethical Politics of Shelley's *The Cenci.*" *Studies in Romanticism* 25 (Fall 1986): 411-27.

Wasserman, Earl. *Shelley: A Critical Reading.* Baltimore: Johns Hopkins U P, 1971.

White, Newman Ivey. *Shelley.* Vol. 2. London: Secker & Warburg, 1947.

Wilson, James D. "Beatrice Cenci and Shelley's Vision of Moral Responsibility." *Ariel* 9 (July 1978): 75-89.

Worton, Michael. "Speech and Silence in *The Cenci*." *Essays on Shelley.* Ed. Miriam Allott. Liverpool: Liverpool U P, 1982. 105-24.

Stephen Cheeke (essay date 1998)

SOURCE: Cheeke, Stephen. "Shelley's *The Cenci*: Economies of a 'Familiar' Language." *Keats-Shelley Journal* 47 (1998): 142-60.

[*In the following essay, Cheeke asserts that Shelley's play is "deeply insecure about its theater, its audience, its style and its language."*]

Shelley's composition of **The Cenci** in the late spring and summer of 1819 was an experiment in the rigorous economies of an unfamiliar genre.[1] Writing to Peacock in late July announcing the new work, Shelley stresses the "pains" he has taken to make the play "fit for representation" on the London stage.[2] The play itself thematizes some of the pain of representation, and there is perhaps from our own perspective the attendant pain of knowing that Shelley's high hopes for a popular theatrical success, desires which permeate the work, were unrealized. The problematic preface to the play invokes the folk-lore nature of the Cenci myth in Italy as a kind of guarantee that a drama based upon that myth is predestined to success. The story was "a subject not to be mentioned in Italian society without awakening a deep and breathless interest. . . . All ranks of people knew the outlines of this history, and participated in the overwhelming interest which it seems to have the magic of exciting in the human heart. I had a copy of Guido's picture of Beatrice which is preserved in the Colonna Palace, and my servant instantly recognized it as the portrait of La Cenci."[3] The "human heart" is the focus and measure of an experience common to all—here it seems the human heart listens as the theater-goer listens, excited, rapt, with "breathless" interest.[4] Shelley's theater of the heart is linked to the portrait of a young lady (supposed to be Beatrice Cenci, supposed to be by Guido Reni), and, as many critics have noted, the pathos Shelley found compelling in the Reni portrait is exactly that which he had found so powerful in the performances of the actress Eliza O'Neill, for whom, to a certain extent, the part of Beatrice was written.[5] But the Reni portrait also seems important to Shelley the playwright in ways which intersect with the broader relationship of Romantic drama and portrait painting, and which reveal the generic economies at the heart of the play.

Michael S. Wilson has written of the "analogy of painting" at work within the theatre of the late eighteenth and early nineteenth century.[6] Stage representations are operating at an allusive level, Wilson argues, to evoke paintings, in particular well-known history paintings, for an audience literate in art history. This allusiveness in turn influences and is influenced by portraits of famous actors and actresses (often in the "historical" roles of Shakespeare), whilst also drawing from the popular acting manuals which offered sketches of certain "expressive norms" themselves taken from classic painting. The correspondence and exchange between classic painting (particularly portraiture), and the acting styles of the early nineteenth century theatre is given extra focus in **The Cenci** by the "fame" of the Reni portrait. Shelley's servant, himself prefiguring Shelley's anticipated "popular" audience, instantly recognizes the painting of "La Cenci"; the overwhelming pathos of the portrait causes "breathless" interest among all classes. This breathless interest is itself an anticipated prefiguring of the heart-stopping excitement of Eliza O'Neill in the role of Beatrice. Indeed her performance might itself be literally heart-stopping and breathless, drawing as it would upon the so-called "hits" which were central to the acting styles of the day, in which the action would be arrested for a moment as O'Neill would present her motionless study of a certain passion.[7] This breathlessness is therefore also associated with certain silent moments in the performance, when the actress, like the portrait, is frozen in an expression of pathos. Shelley, who uses the painting analogy to characterize his own compositional methods in the preface to the play, in some sense "sees" the play in the Reni portrait: O'Neill's economy of gesture in the framed studies of pathos and the breathless interest of a popular audience, are analogous with the economies of language employed in composition and the breathless dramatic moments in which Beatrice will be constrained *not* to name the crime she has suffered. These crucially silent and static instances of representation, however, also summon that which is *not* represented, that which Shelley has taken pains to keep offstage, and which is heart-stopping in its horror. Silence in **The Cenci,** as has often been noted, is a particularly powerful and fraught silence, one both sought and resisted by Beatrice, whose gravest anxiety is that she herself will be economized into a silently speaking portaiture, forever 'La Cenci' of the infamous story.[8]

But silent auditoriums can be equally heart-stopping for a playwright. The play's preface assumes an audience composed of all ranks of society within the London theaters, an audience both more democratic and yet at the same time more discerning than the contemporary London theater-going public, at precisely the historical moment when such a notion of democratic representation and popular "taste" in the theaters is being fiercely (if covertly) contested. The "universal" theater of the human heart, in which Shelley hopes his play might find a home, is also of course a political hope, and involved in Shelley's anxiety about writing "down" to his audience is the concomitant anxiety about radical political en-franchisement or reform. The popular audience is also a tribunal sitting in judgment and reaching a verdict, and in having to endure this other form of heart-stopping theater Shelley and Beatrice are again cross-fated.[9] Moreover, in addition to the fact that Shelley asked Peacock to submit the play anonymously and to pre-serve the author's incognito,[10] the preface emphasizes the pains Shelley had taken to avoid sounding like him-self: "in order to move men to a true sympathy we must use the familiar language of men . . . But it must be the real language of men in general and not that of any particular class to whose society the writer happens to belong." Along with the perhaps unexpected Wordswor-thian alignment here, there go darker shades to the word "familiar." It is the language of "family" and the viola-tion of the "familiar" which will be at the center of the tragedy. The "familiar language" of *The Cenci,* un-heightened by literary color, unadorned by "learned" or "over-fastidious" diction (as the preface assures us) and studiously unpoetic, is the language spoken by the fam-ily members who constitute the main protagonists of the work. What lies outside this "familiar language," what this shared language fails or refuses or is con-strained *not* to give voice to, is centrally related to the compositional economies of the generic experiment.[11]

Shelley was aware of the risk he had taken in choosing to write a play about an incestuous rape. Critical read-ings of *The Cenci* have tended to subsume the horror of rape in the encompassing horror of incest, eliding the double nature of Beatrice's violation. As a literary sub-ject or, as Shelley put it, a "poetical circumstance,"[12] in-cest has a long and venerable tradition, as does rape, whereas incestuous rape does not. Byron, voicing an opinion most likely shared by Shelley's close friends, declared in 1821 that the story of Beatrice's life was "essentially undramatic."[13] Shelley had not simply seen it differently, but oppositely. The "historical" Beatrice is invested in theatrical metaphor for Shelley; moreover, he links what he calls the "ideal . . . horror" of her sufferings to the kind of stylistic and modal economies (a "peculiar delicacy," as it is described to Peacock) im-posed as playwright. The not-naming of Cenci's crime is thus not simply one of the problems faced in writing for the London stage, nor simply a revealing aspect of Beatrice's "character," but everything to do with this play.[14] Although critical attention invariably notices the unnameable within the play, it very rarely notices that the play is itself in some sense circumscribed *within* the unnameable and that this non-voicing or economizing is operating at every level of Shelley's dramatic experi-ment.[15]

Shelley's chief endeavour in *The Cenci,* he told Med-win in 1820, had been to "produce a delineation of the passions which I had never participated in, in chaste language, and according to the rules of enlightened art."[16] The play puts pressure on chaste language (particularly in its guise as the "familiar") until it threat-ens to become unchaste in the mouth of Count Cenci, but more importantly in the language spoken by Beat-rice. The Count, as has frequently been noted, is a mas-ter of the "familiar language of men," whilst at the same time that language is an alien one for a man who has no faith in the systems of meaning and morality en-coded within it. In this he has been described as a "cor-rupt dramatic poet," an artist, a vampire.[17] But it is im-portant to remember that Count Cenci speaks the economized language of Shelley's play, a language in which "mere Poetry" is absent, from which Shelley has all but erased the "detached simile" and the "isolated description." Cenci speaks in euphemisms and evasions, hints and suggestions; he is adept at a salacious kind of aposiopesis, and has a fondness for the *double entendre* in which chaste language becomes unchaste, in which meaning is simultaneously concentrated and expanded.

Central to Beatrice's suffering is that she too must speak an equivocal language, one in which words betray (or are betrayed to) unchaste meanings. Early on in the play she appeals to the guests at her father's banquet (or anti-mass) to understand what is happening to her: "I have borne much, and kissed the sacred hand / Which crushed us to the earth, and thought its stroke / Was perhaps some paternal chastisement!" (I. 3. 111-16). The word "stroke" might be vicious blow or loving ca-ress, though the loving caress may now be even more of a threat to Beatrice than the violent blow. The chaste image of a daughter kissing her father's hand is vio-lated in the uninvited play of that single word. And it is a single word, what Beatrice calls the "one little word" which would name Cenci's crime (is that word "rape" or "incest"?), which cannot be spoken on stage, but which an audience is repeatedly invited to articulate for itself in the silences and gaps the play breeds, in the frozen moments of a "familiar" dramaturgy that aims to reproduce the pathos of the Reni portrait. *The Cenci* la-bors this non-naming, moves towards an excess of non-representation, or a conspicuousness-in-absence which may perhaps place it in an uneasy relationship to those theories of Romantic drama that suggest violent spec-tacle was taken off the Romantic stage as part of a con-trolling or limiting process.[18] The opposite threatens to be the case with the non-spectacle of *The Cenci*; even as Shelley struggles to accommodate the rigorous economies of the popular drama, nevertheless the un-nameable is everywhere, the off-stage violence is cen-tral and the taboo word starkly legible.

Moreover, it was part of Shelley's design to make the fact that Beatrice is doomed to this taboo-association a tangible part of her suffering. She fears becoming a bye-word for incestuous rape, her identity reduced to the most economized of verbal units or the most frozen of portraits. In a play in which the naming (or not naming) of a central action becomes so significant, the currency and value of her own name and the possibility of it becoming synonymous with other things, preys upon her mind. Moreover, the play is as acutely sensitive to the potency of the articulated word as it is to that of silence. Vocalization of an act (whether it be of incest, or parricide) is somehow felt to be akin to committing the act itself. It is as if the economies imposed upon language have become so acute that deed occurs almost spontaneously with utterance, closing down the realm of what we might call discourse in which words and deeds preserve a distance from one another. The horror of saying the unsayable is not, then, merely a question of delicacy, or tact, but a powerful epistemological anxiety about naming. In **The Cenci** to *name* is somehow to admit the presence of the act itself (a fact acutely noted in Leigh Hunt's reviews of the play). This in turn of course means that the holy (private) site of Romantic imagination is violated in the play, shown to be vulnerable to invasion,[19] not least of all through the inability to control the process by which thought becomes articulated by words which immediately become deeds. If language is economized and pared down to the "familiar," does this mean that it sheds its holy powers of de-familiarization? Does this itself constitute a kind of violation?[20]

When Beatrice staggers onto the stage at the beginning of act III she is unable to say what has happened to her. Instead she says, "Like Parricide . . ." (III. 1. 36). Her sentence is incomplete. Whatever it is that has occurred to her is simply "Like Parricide." This is only the second time the word "parricide" has been spoken in the play (the first is by Cenci himself) and it is the closest Beatrice is able to come to naming what she has suffered: like parricide, incest is a taboo; the enormity of her injury has moved her to economized expression, indeed for a moment the phrase "Like Parricide" seems to spell out that one little word; it is one of the play's few (and in this case *necessary*) "detached similes." In fact it is both simile and synonym, and something more, an invisible sign, the word itself on the page of the imagination, the portrait made visible. At this key moment the audience can of course be in no doubt as to what has happened to her, and no doubt too as to what she will do to avenge her wrong.[21] She has spoken directly, disturbingly, of an incestuous rape.

But of course the deed remains unnameable, and "like parricide" both is and is not "incest." Already, however, imprisoned within the simile, Beatrice is able to speak of herself as a figure in a story:

> Do you know
> I thought I was that wretched Beatrice
> Men speak of, whom her father. . . .
> . . . pens up naked in damp cells
> Where scaly reptiles crawl, and starves her there,

> Till she will eat strange flesh.

> (III. 1. 42-48)

The sexual undertones in this are unmistakable; the fearful sense of being imprisoned within the act of sexual violation, an act further reduced by the fact that it exists *within* a story men tell of a woman named Beatrice. This doom will come to obsess Beatrice. But there is also a hint of another taboo here, that of filial cannibalism ("Till she will eat strange flesh"), which, in the context of imprisonment, recalls the Ugolino episode of the *Inferno*. Medwin's translation of this passage Shelley would correct with an interesting revision of the appeal Ugolino's son makes to his father: "tu ne vestisti / queste misere carni, e tu le spoglia" ("you who dressed us in this miserable flesh, you strip us of it"). Shelley translated the imperative "spoglia" as "despoil": "'twas you who clad / Our bodies in these weeds of wretchedness; / Despoil them."[22] Shelley's "despoil" makes overt the sexual undertones in the act of cannibalism, the way the chaste is brutally forced to be unchaste; in other words cannibalism is clothed in the metaphor of incestuous rape, just as in **The Cenci** incestuous rape takes a metaphor of filial cannibalism ("Till she will eat strange flesh"). The horror of each taboo is compounded by the figure of another, just as Beatrice reaches for the verbal simile "Like parricide" to describe what she has suffered, at once both a means of representing *and* screening her injuries in the "familiar" language. For Shelley, the potency of the taboo seemed to stimulate vocal contagion or proliferation through the similes and metaphors of other taboos: incest is like parricide, is like cannibalism. The impossibility of naming Cenci's crime on stage gives this metaphorical disease or replication further point, in that it becomes a means of saying in several different ways what you cannot say in one way. The bare economy of style, the real language of men in general, is mined for riches to compensate for its own taboo-dependent limitations; it is an economy bound to produce this silent surplus or supplement. Beatrice's sufferings are "like" other sufferings which *can* be named. What more can she do to make her audience comprehend?

> What are the words which you would have me speak?
> I, who can feign no image in my mind
> Of that which has transformed me. I, whose thought
> Is like a ghost shrouded and folded up
> In its own formless horror. Of all words,
> That minister to mortal intercourse,
> Which wouldst thou hear? For there is none to tell
> My misery: if another ever knew
> Aught like to it, she died as I will die,
> And left it, as I must, without a name.

> (III. 1. 106-115)

Beatrice's refusal (or inability) to name the deed has, quite rightly, received much critical attention. The compulsion to conceal an injury as part of the psychology of revenge;[23] the impossibility of "replaying" the violation on the body through the language of pain;[24] the internalization of the "moralistic strictures of bourgeois proprieties";[25] the assumption of "false alternatives as to the nature of the act."[26] Beatrice is sometimes characterized as strong in silence, sometimes as allowing the rape to distort her vision.[27] Her refusal to name is so compelling from this moment onwards in the play that readers tend to interpret her silence in exhaustive terms of "character": why does Beatrice refuse to speak? Why is she unable to speak? Certainly, such questions are central. But Beatrice's character is also caught up in a broader vocal matrix that should be recognized. Her pathetic question: "What are the words which you would have me speak?" initiates a new phase of not-speaking by the play itself. Beatrice cannot name because Shelley cannot name. Where does this take us?

She is now suggesting that there is no word for what she has suffered, no adequate word, and no way of telling what has happened to her. Her pain—she suggests—is in some way superior, greater, than a mere name, a little word. It must be left unnamed *not* because she is unable to contemplate what has occurred, but because no name can do it justice. At this moment in the play Shelley asks his audience to move towards an understanding of the way in which the power of this one word or phrase is not commensurate with the suffering inflicted by the deed itself. We are expected for the first time in the play to perceive the hollowness and poverty of a "familiar" chaste language when pressed so close by the agency of the unchaste. Paradoxically, however, Beatrice seems to gain strength through this poverty; she seems to grow *into* this style, *gaining* articulation in the economies and non-poeticisms of the play's language. It is a refuge for her to depict her own sufferings as "unnameable." And it is to her advantage, now, that the taboo association of parricide only works to deny the existence of the act itself.

The pattern of broken taboo / nameless crime / atonement is of course the Sophoclean one of *Oedipus Tyrannus,* the influence of which, particularly in the sense of linguistic economies, has been undervalued in criticism of *The Cenci.* The prolonged hesitation in revealing Cenci's crime is, in one sense, a re-working of the protracted disclosure of Oedipus' past, the terrible hesitation on the brink of the final anagnorisis. When the truth is finally revealed (the first part of that truth is that Oedipus has committed incest with Jocasta), the Sophoclean chorus repeatedly describes his crime in verbal quibbles, with the paradox that Oedipus can be divided into both father and son ("When the same bosom enfolded the son and father" [line 1218], "Time . . . has found you and judged that marriage-mockery, bridegroom son" [line 1221].). Oedipus, like Beatrice, fears that his name will become a bye-word: "Husband of mother is my name" [line 1363].[28] A peculiar involution

occurs when the breaking of a taboo is voiced: the act of incest seems itself to breed a chaotic set of verbal paradoxes which defeat vocalization, which obstruct and trouble the normal relations of words. Although verbal paradox is more central to the whole of Sophoclean (and classical Greek) drama than it was to Shelley's purposes, nevertheless, the sexual horror which breeds the verbal pun, bearing too a distinctly Jacobean flavor, colors Beatrice's language from this point on. The pun is the most economical of verbal phenomena: word-play and equivocation a kind of antithesis to "detached simile" and "isolated description." Cenci's daughter has become his wife; Beatrice's father has become her husband; there is no single word for their new relation, only self-engendered paradox and quibble, or namelessness in the economy of a familiar language.

Two-thirds of the way through the play critical readings reach a crossroads. Worrying over the remarks Shelley made in the preface about Beatrice's "pernicious mistake" and the audience's "restless casuistry," readings tend to follow one of three paths: either that Beatrice now degenerates into evil, forfeits "sympathy" and is "wrong" to murder her father; that Beatrice makes a mistake in committing parricide but the circumstances are so mitigating that this error is heavily qualified; or that Beatrice is "wrong" to do so, but at the same time she has no choice. Almost everyone who has written about *The Cenci* has made something of the fact that Beatrice seems in some ways to come to resemble Count Cenci.[29] Often these Beatrice-centric readings seem to transport us to an odd interpretive realm where it is suddenly as if we are talking about someone we know in real life called Beatrice Cenci, someone whose psychology/personality can be endlessly (fascinatingly) "anatomized," someone who makes us angry or censorious for not making the right choices or behaving in a different way. In other words, Beatrice becomes detheatricalized, removed from her defining context within the stage play *The Cenci.* This is in one sense proof of the power of Shelley's play. But it can also obscure the picture. Leaving Beatrice aside for the moment, is it possible to understand Beatrice?

This later Beatrice is the textual site of deep equivocation about the familiar language of men (the gender distinction darkens as the play continues); she masters what might be called the radical language economy of the play, a kind of skepticism (unShelleyan in terms of its *consequences* here), a creed which has protected her father in his depravity and which emerges as the most destructive element in the drama. This radical economy empties men's words of meaning, robs them of their relation to shared ethical values, and so enables the journey from word to deed to be made with a consequent lightness of conscience. Shelley reveals that the origins of such a breakdown in the ethical consensus of a shared language lie in the impossibility, for Beatrice, of naming what has occurred to her, with the subsequent impossibility of having men believe in her sufferings. The word "parricide" loses all meaning and terror for her, just as the word "incest" (or "rape," or the single word that would mean both) is inadequate to describe what she has suffered.

She orchestrates the murder of her father through the radical economies of this familiar language. "Conscience," she assures the hired killers, is an "equivocation" that "sleeps over / A thousand daily acts disgracing men" (IV. 2. 28-29). Equivocation, word-play, puns. Beatrice breaks off in the middle of a sentence and asks herself the simple question, "Why do I talk?" (IV. 2. 31). Why does she speak with these men? Why does she speak at all? "I am more innocent of parricide / Than is a child born fatherless . . ." (IV. 4. 111-13). Again and again the familiar language is pared down to a play on words. She is taken to Rome for judgment.

Giacomo, Beatrice's brother, begins to suffer remorse at the beginning of the act v, but he is the exception. *The Cenci* does not move towards a general re-securing of the "awful voice" of our ruling conscience as we see in the two other major dramatic efforts of this period: *Remorse* and *The Borderers*. Both Coleridge and Wordsworth portray their villains as capable of talking away the matter of conscience through skeptical reasoning similar to that spoken by Cenci and his daughter (Ordanio in *Remorse* and Oswald in *The Borderers*). But conscience re-asserts itself in both plays, and, interestingly, is perceived in terms of a familiar inner voice—"The substance of my being" Coleridge's Teresa calls it, whilst in the third act of Wordsworth's play Herbert describes hearing "a voice / Such as by Cherith on Elijah called; / It said, 'I will be with thee.'"[30] This guiding, imperative voice re-affirms a common (familiar) language of ethical values which had seemed to be casuistically undermined by the plays' villains. But the familiar language of Shelley's play has become deeply equivocal, and "right" and "wrong" not so easily reaccommodated. Even Giacomo exculpates Beatrice in his rationalization of what he feels to be heavy crimes. She "Stands like God's angel ministered upon / By fiends; avenging such a nameless wrong / As turns black parricide to piety . . ." (v. 1. 42-44). Her wrong threatens in a sense to transform the meaning of the word "parricide," to question its meaning in the common language (again threatening the word with the economy of double meaning); it is able to do this since it is without a name, more than that, "incestuous rape" is *beyond* a name. So parricide becomes piety, with the irony that this would literally be the case if Beatrice *had* been God's avenging angel exercising His will. Instead she is "ministered upon / By fiends." Giacomo sees her in terms restricted by the simile (again the simile is an index of enforced resourcefulness in the familiar language): she is "*like* God's angel," but she is *not*

God's angel. Casting Beatrice into simile (she is *like* an innocent, though not innocent) is a fragile though necessary equivocation by which the characters sustain themselves as they face death.

If Beatrice is to survive, she must now convince her prosecutors to participate in this radical economy of language. Parricide must be seen to be an equivocation, a mere word. Camillo at least is persuaded by Beatrice's words and pronounces her "as pure as speechless infancy" (v. 2. 69), as innocent in other words as a child before she has found a voice (in-fans: another pun). But Beatrice has *lost* a voice; her suffering has made her speechless, her injury is unnamed; she speaks a familiar language which is without meaning, and is consequently only *like* an infant in the sense that she is voice-less. Is this purity? Well, yes in that it is savagely economized, "sincere," unadorned (we can talk of pure evil, or pure madness, or perhaps in this case pure theatricality). Beatrice's final speeches have baffled critics who search for a clear distinction between Beatrice's actions and her "acting" (can she possibly believe in what she is saying?) This is where it is most helpful to read her as a textual site in which the familiar language of men is put under intense pressure and scrutiny. Beatrice reveals that the theatrical space is one in which the familiar language cannot simply exist unchallenged but must be *claimed*, it must be *played* for. This public space is one of terrifying freedom, an imaginative space vulnerable to invasion and colonization where that which *is* represented is likely to be penetrated by that which is *not*. The familiar, in other words, suddenly seems de-familiarized, uncertain, equivocal. This climaxes in the superbly dramatic moment when Beatrice asks Marzio the simple and yet by now infinitely complicated question:

> Am I, or am I not
> A parricide?
>
> (v. 2. 156-57)

Marzio of course answers that she is not. He is taken back to the rack but does not yield. He smiles at his torturers "As one who baffles a deep adversary" (v. 2. 182), and he dies.

Beatrice's ability to baffle her adversaries as well as her critics is considerable. She rejects all versions of her story other than her own, whilst at the same time dreads becoming "a mockery and a byeword" (v. 3. 33), having her name become synonymous with the injuries she has suffered. Whereas she has erased the word "parricide", she fears the ineradicable association of incestuous rape: the possibility that she herself may become inscribed in the familiar language as a word with double meaning, framed in a famous portrait. This infamy that she dreads so much she pictures partly in terms of the theater:

so that our hair should sweep
The footsteps of the vain and senseless crowd,
Who, that they make our calamity
Their worship and their spectacle, will leave
The churches and the theatres as void
As their own hearts?

(v. 3. 35-40)

Shelley had probably read accounts of the intensely ritualistic and theatrical public execution of Beatrice, and exploited the terror of such *ritual* (it is both *church* and *theater* which are left "void"), to blur distinctions between his audience and the people of Beatrice's Rome. The theaters would be empty in Rome as the crowds gathered to gape at the players in this horrifying drama, making Beatrice's "calamity" their "spectacle." A popular success would ensure that the theaters in London would not be "void," though audiences are implicitly warned here against inappropriate responses to Beatrice's suffering, the obvious temptation to indulge morbid interest in the unmentionable horrors of the Cenci story. In fact there is more than a warning here; there is fear of popular "effect." The image of Beatrice's hair sweeping the "footsteps of the vain and senseless crowd" is one in which she has, in effect, been seized by her audience; a terrifying reversal in which she is forced to descend to their feet (lines which would have particular power delivered from a stage), sacrificed to the consuming appetites of the spectacle-seeking (always French-Revolutionary) mob. Behind this is anxiety about the familiar becoming the over-familiar, liberty-taking, the murderous, the popular becoming the non-discriminating, the applause of Covent Garden becoming the sentence of death for Shelley.

There is anxiety too that the familiar language of men may be so powerfully bound up in the institutions of church and state that the public stage of theater is itself an instrument of hegemony. Once again the heart is located as the center of a correct response and a true understanding. Indeed Beatrice's metaphor pictures the heart itself as a kind of theater, an ideal stage, left empty as the people are drawn out to witness the notorious spectacle of her death. Beatrice's dread is a dread of the wrong kind of fame. In the ideal theater of the heart her sufferings would find a true audience, an audience turned away from spectacle to contemplate Beatrice, as Shelley's preface had implied. Beatrice, however, is condemned to exist in the theater of Rome, and so condemned to act out her part to the "wrong" audience and to the "wrong" responses. Finally, she declines to say any more: "Say what ye will. I shall deny no more" (v. 3. 78-86). This is an absolute economy, a complete withdrawal from participation in the familiar language.[31] At the same time it is a confession.

The intense theatrical (and textual) self-reflexivity of Beatrice's last speeches as she internalizes and thematizes the reception of *The Cenci* on a popular London stage, reveal perhaps more clearly than anywhere else Shelley's own equivocation over his generic experiment. The play is deeply insecure about its theater, its audience, its style and its language. This insecurity is not disguised in the play; *The Cenci* "represents" its own unrestrained desires for (and anxieties about) popular success, and everywhere images its own compositional cruxes. The economies of style and language Shelley draws attention to in his preface test the capacity of a chaste and familiar language to withstand the pressures of the unchaste. A dramaturgy of arrested and frozen moments in which familiar passions are represented on stage can also create (like Reni's portrait, like Beatrice's name) a space or gap which is soon inhabited by the unfamiliar and *non*-represented. The language of *The Cenci*'s contemporary reviewers (of whom there were many) reveals their sense of a certain kind of knowledge beyond-the-familiar being opened up, of the veil being lifted from the objects of taboo, of Shelley's rigorous economy merely breeding hidden and unwanted surpluses. We find the reviews frequently reaching for parallels with *Genesis* and the gaining of the knowledge of death.[32] In June 1821 *The British Review and London Critical Journal* comments that such works as *The Cenci* "teach nothing; and, if they did, knowledge must not be bought at too high a price. There is knowledge which is death and pollution."[33] This refusal to partake of the fruit of the Tree of Knowledge had been the reaction of *The Edinburgh Monthly Review* for May 1820, which proclaimed that, "In an evil hour does the pleasure of exhibiting might, first tempt the hand of genius to draw the veil from things that ought for ever to remain concealed."[34] Consciously or unconsciously remembering Milton's "O Eve, in evil hour thou didst give ear" (*Paradise Lost.* IX. 1067), here Shelley is Satan the tempter *and* Eve the tempted, *and* responsible for the Fall. The phrase "draws the veil" in turn anticipates (albeit with a very different emphasis) Shelley's famous description of poetry in the *Defence of Poetry* as that which "strips the veil of familiarity from the world." Life-giving and/or death-bringing, Shelley's *The Cenci* certainly reveals anxiety about a process of defamiliarization (and the theatrical representation of this process) circumscribed by corrupt social and political institutions. For Beatrice this spells death and pollution.

Notes

1. Donald H. Reiman and Sharon B. Powers, *Shelley's Poetry and Prose* (New York: Norton, 1977), cite May 1819 as the beginning of composition. Paul Smith argues for composition dates between 14 May and 8 August 1819: "'Restless Casuistry': Shelley's composition of *The Cenci*," *Keats-Shelley Journal*, 13 (1964), 79.

2. *The Letters of Percy Bysshe Shelley,* ed. Frederick L. Jones, 2 vols. (Oxford: Clarendon Press, 1964), II, 102 (hereafter cited as *Letters*).

3. All quotations from *The Cenci* are from *Shelley's Poetry and Prose,* ed. Donald H. Reiman and Sharon B. Powers (New York: Norton, 1977).

4. The conscious heart will play a central role in *The Cenci.* The play is dedicated to Leigh Hunt, the person for whom Shelley's "heart'" was most consistently significant. See Timothy Webb, "Religion of the Heart: Leigh Hunt's Unpublished Tribute to Shelley," *Keats-Shelley Review,* 7 (1992), 1-61.

5. See Joseph W. Donohue, *Dramatic Character in the English Romantic Age* (Princeton: Princeton University Press, 1970); see especially pp. 164-66 for a discussion of the Guido Reni portrait and Eliza O'Neill's acting style. See also Stuart Curran, *Shelley's* Cenci: *Scorpions Ringed With Fire* (Princeton: Princeton University Press, 1970), pp. xi-xii; and Barbara Groseclose, "The Incest Motif in Shelley's *The Cenci,*" *Comparative Drama,* 19 (Autumn 1985), 222-39.

6. Michael S. Wilson, "Ut Pictura Trageodia: An Extrinsic Approach to British Neoclassic and Romantic Theatre," in *Theatre Research International,* 12. 3 (1987), 201-220: ". . . the art of painting was the greatest determinant of the sensibilities that the educated audiences of this period brought to their theatre" (203). "As the analogy encouraged knowledgeable patrons to view stage representations of poetic drama as history paintings, the aesthetic norms and ideology of history painting increasingly constituted for that audience a powerful metatext that endorsed specific aspects and qualities of the performance as if they were inherent in the poetic text" (206). For discussion of the acting manuals and the link with Joanna Baillie's 1798 *Plays on the Passions* see Curran, pp. 173-75. See also Martin Meisel, *Realizations: Narrative, Pictorial, and Theatrical Arts in Nineteenth-Century England* (Princeton: Princeton University Press, 1983), especially chapter 3, "Speaking Pictures: The Drama."

7. Michael S. Wilson "That the rupture of narrative continuity entailed by such extended pictorial effects was an accepted convention certainly implies the degree to which audience perceptions had been shaped by the static, spatial medium of painting" (212). Joseph W. Donohue is less positive about this interaction: "The crux of the situation, it may be suggested, is that the notion *ut pictura poesis,* while an important agent of imaginative creation in Romantic lyric and narrative verse, became an ultimately devitalizing one for Romantic drama. . . . The moment 'frozen' out of time and set down as a kind of speaking sculpture ultimately and inevitably succumbed to the influence of the 'Laocoon' theory of passion imprisoned, with its stultifying implication of process uneventuating in action" (p. 185). In the letter to Peacock quoted above, Shelley anticipated the effect of seeing O'Neill act the role of Beatrice: "God forbid that I shd. see her play it—it wd. tear my nerves to pieces" (*Letters,* II, 102). The specific sense of breathlessness was itself part of the repertoire of grief as promulgated in the acting manuals. Meisel quotes from the anonymous *Thespian Preceptor* (London, 1810): "Grief, sudden and violent, expresses itself by beating the head or forehead, tearing the hair, and catching the breath, as if choking" (Meisel, p. 5).

8. See Michael Warton, "Speech and Silence in *The Cenci,*" in *Essays on Shelley,* ed. Miriam Allott (Liverpool: Liverpool University Press, 1982), 105-24, which argues that "the fundamental modernity of *The Cenci* lies in its analysis of the efficacy of language" (105).

9. For the link between the agitation for dramatic and for electoral reform see Clive Barker, "A Theatre for the People," in *Nineteenth Century British Theatre,* ed. K. Richards and P. Thomson (London: Methuen, 1971), pp. 3-24; Robert J. Goldstein, "Political Censorship of the Theatre in Nineteenth Century Europe," in *Theatre Research International,* 12. 3 (1987), 220-41; Dewey Ganzel, "Patent Wrongs and Patent Theaters: Drama and the Law in the early Nineteenth Century," *PMLA* [*Publications of the Modern Language Association*] 76. 4. 1 (September, 1961), 384-96. The ambiguities involved are summarized by Julie Carlson: "Writing in the wake of the Terror, poets compose 'bad' drama as part of their legislation of 'good' politics. The interiority, sluggishness, and inactivity of romantic plays counter an impetuous, sensationalist, and Gallicized English public. Crucial to national reform, these poets contend, is an anatomizing of mind that is meant to be enacted for and imitated by theatre audiences. Indispensable to the health of that public mind is a theatre reform that places imagination centre stage"; *In the Theatre of Romanticism: Coleridge, Nationalism, Women* (Cambridge: Cambridge University Press, 1994), p. (14). See also Gillian Russell, *The Theatres of War: Performance, Politics and Society 1793-1815* (Oxford: Clarendon Press, 1995); Marc Baer, *Theatre and Disorder in Late Georgian London* (Oxford: Clarendon Press, 1992); Paula R. Backsheider, *Spectacular Politics: Theatrical Power and Mass Culture in Early Modern England* (Baltimore: Johns Hopkins University Press, 1993). For Shelley-as-Beatrice see, for example, William Ulmer, *Shelleyan Eros: The Rheto-*

ric of Romantic Love (Princeton: Princeton University Press, 1990): "The contradictions embroiling Beatrice have precise correlatives in Shelley's own efforts to address a public sitting in judgement" (p. 124).

10. Shelley requested that Charles Ollier should not even open the boxes containing copies of The Cenci until directions arrived for its publication. Stephen C. Behrendt argues that Shelley's desire for an anonymous success with The Cenci involves a desire for revenge upon his reviewers; see chapter 5 of Shelley and His Audiences (Lincoln: University of Nebraska Press, 1989).

11. My use of the word "economy," and of the notion of the "economies of language," is meant to be richly and broadly suggestive in a theoretical sense: much has been written about different kinds of linguistic or conceptual economies across a range of fields in the last thirty years. In this sense what I have to say about The Cenci will perhaps have acquired its central emphasis from the Derridean critique of Saussure's notion of language as an economy of relations, and most particularly Derrida's sense of this economy being imbalanced towards infinite supplementarity (Shelley's "familiar language" is disrupted in the play by the failure of its "economy" to exclude the meanings it is designed to exclude). See especially Jacques Derrida, "Linguistics and Grammatology," in Of Grammatology, trans. Gayatri Chakravorty Spivak (Baltimore and London: Johns Hopkins University Press, 1974). My reading also inevitably raises Foucaultian spectres, particularly in its sense that the economies of discourse organize and in some sense control or determine ethical consensus: see, for example, Michel Foucault, The Order of Things: An Archaeology of the Human Sciences, trans. anon. (London: Tavistock Publications, 1970); the argument also has obvious connections with post-Freudian examinations of the ways in which "chaste" language comes to be haunted by the "unchaste" (see n 21 below).

12. Shelley, Letters, II, 154.

13. Byron's letter of 26 April 1821, in Shelley, Letters, II, 284. Shelley told Byron in May 1821 that he was aware of the "unfitness of the subject, now it is written." (Letters, II, 290.)

14. I am arguing that there is much greater significance to the not-naming than, for example, Stuart Curran suggests: "Probably only an inexperienced and radically optimistic playwright would attempt to form an entire play around an event that could not be named on stage. . . . Shelley deserves credit for attempting to turn an almost unworkable disadvantage into positive gain" (pp. 90-91).

15. One exception is William Ulmer, who describes the mirroring between the playwright and Beatrice: "The play's prospective relation to spectators, or readers, is proleptically figured in the play itself, metadramatically incorporated in scenes of mirroring in which one character will seek to reshape the values and actions of another" (Shelleyan Eros, p. 112). Elsewhere Ulmer observes that "The play thematizes its own errant reception . . ." (p. 115).

16. Shelley, Letters, II, 189. The inability to say the "unchaste" word has a similarly dominating effect in Mary Shelley's Mathilda, also written at the Villa Valosano during the summer of 1819, and taking as its theme a father's incestuous desire (unconsummated) for his daughter. In Mary Shelley's novella Mathilda's father threatens to reveal the nature of his passion: "'Now, beware! Be silent! . . . One word I might speak and then you would be implicated in my destruction; yet that word is hovering on my lips. Oh! There is a fearful chasm; but I adjure you to beware!'" Mathilda's response is resolute: "'I will not be put off thus: do you think I can live thus fearfully from day to day—the sword in my bosom yet kept from its mortal wound by a hair—a word!—I demand that dreadful word; though it be as a flash of lightning to destroy me, speak it.'" Mary Shelley, Mathilda, ed. Elizabeth Nitchie (Chapel Hill: University of North Carolina Press, 1959), pp. 29-30.

17. Ronald L. Lemoncelli, "Cenci as Corrupt Dramatic Poet," English Language Notes, 16. 2 (1978), 103-117. According to Lemoncelli, Cenci is "the poet of misguided imagination . . . the corrupt dramatic poet that Shelley condemns in the Defence" (104). For Cenci as artist see Stuart Curran: "the Count is an artist, conscious of his every effect, careful of the placement of accents on this canvas over which he is master, relishing each bold and dramatic stroke" (p. 73). For Cenci the vampire, see James B. Twitchell, "Shelley's Use of Vampirism in The Cenci," Tennessee Studies in Literature, 24 (1979), 120-33.

18. Steven Bruhm argues that Coleridge, Byron and Shelley all wished "to move the excess of spectacle off-stage and make the real site of theater a more internalized, mental, pedagogical one . . . the Romantic theater banished from the stage the image of violence because it sought to relegate it to the imagination, where it could be formed and controlled within the solitary imagination." Gothic Bodies: The Politics of Pain in Romantic Fiction (Philadelphia: University of Pennsylvania Press, 1994), p. 62.

19. As Steven Bruhm has argued: "Shelley makes problematic the holy space of the secret as the po-

tential site of barbarism and cruelty" (p. 87), and "makes spectacle an internal phenomenon: he depicts it as a product of the active sensitive imagination" (p. 89).

20. This would offer a reversal of the famous defamiliarizing/ravishing metaphor in the *Defence of Poetry*: "[Poetry] strips the veil of familiarity from the world, and lays bare the naked and sleeping beauty which is the spirit of its forms." I return to this point below.

21. "She invents a simile—parricide—that immediately generates a second process," says Alan Richardson, in *A Mental Theater: Poetic Drama and Consciousness in the Romantic Age* (Pennsylvania: Pennsylvania State University Press, 1988), p. 113. Psychoanalytic theory of course makes much of the encounter between the "chaste" aspects of a socially "familiar" language and the silent or repressed element of the "unchaste," or that which language resists. See, for example, Julia Kristeva's account of "The Semiotic and the Symbolic" in *Revolution in Poetic Language,* trans. Margaret Waller (New York: Columbia University Press, 1974). For the sense of the feminine as the non-voiced, or the "non-knowledge" of a masculine master narrative, see Alice A. Jardine, *Gynesis: Configurations of Woman and Modernity* (Ithaca: Cornell University Press, 1985); for the effect a masculine "economy of discourse" has upon the political exploitation of women see, for example, Luce Irigaray's chapter "The Power of Discourse" in *This Sex Which Is Not One,* trans. Catherine Porter (Ithaca: Cornell University Press, 1985).

22. *The Complete Works of Percy Bysshe Shelley,* ed. Roger Ingpen and Walter E. Peck, 10 vols. (New York: Scribner's, 1930), IV, 296.

23. Harry White, "Beatrice Cenci and Shelley's Avenger," *Essays in Literature,* 5. 1 (Spring 1978), 34.

24. See Steven Bruhm, p. 90.

25. See William Ulmer, p. 127.

26. Laurence Lockridge, "Justice in *The Cenci,*" *The Wordsworth Circle,* 19. 2 (Spring 1988), 95-98 (97).

27. Stuart M. Sperry, in *Shelley's Major Verse: The Narrative and Dramatic Poetry* (Cambridge: Harvard University Press, 1988), p. 135, writes: "If Beatrice Cenci possesses a tragic flaw, it is her virginity or, more exactly, her idealization of her virginity as the center of her moral nature." Julie Carlson responds: "Those critics who see a 'tragic flaw' in Beatrice's idealization of virginity fail to admit that the flaw is in a 'world' that anchors

women's moral life in their virginity" (p. 191). Jerold Hogle, like Sperry, presents the rape as impairing Beatrice's judgment: "Beatrice objectif[ies] it as the undeniable dishonor that interpretation need not automatically make it." *Shelley's Process: Radical Transference and the Development of his Major Works* (Oxford: Oxford University Press, 1988), p. 156.

28. All quotations from *Oedipus Tyrannus* are from *Sophocles: The Theban Plays,* trans. E. F. Watling (Harmondsworth: Penguin, 1947).

29. For evil in *The Cenci* see Joan Rees, "Shelley's Orsino: Evil in *The Cenci,*" *Keats-Shelley Memorial Bulletin,* 12 (1966), 3-6; for variations on the theme of Beatrice's own evil or "wrong" see Lockridge, 95-98; Sperry, pp. 127-41; James D. Wilson, "Beatrice Cenci and Shelley's Vision of Moral Responsibility," *Ariel,* 9 (1978), 75-89; Robert F. Whitman, "Beatrice's 'Pernicious Mistake' in *The Cenci,*" *PMLA,* 74 (1959), 249-53; Milton Wilson, *Shelley's Later Poetry: A Study of His Prophetic Imagination* (New York: Columbia University Press, 1959), pp. 78-101; Ulmer, pp. 109-30. For Beatrice's having no choice see Lockridge, p. 98; Paul A. Cantor, "'A Distorting Mirror': Shelley's *The Cenci* and Shakespearean Tragedy," in *Shakespeare: Aspects of Influence,* ed. G. B. Evans (Cambridge: Harvard University Press, 1976), 91-108; Curran, pp. 129-54. For Beatrice as a "religious fanatic" see White, p. 34; as a radical innocent see Donohue, pp. 162-81; as a poet see J. N. Cox, *In the Shadows of Romance: Romantic Tragic Drama in Germany, England and France* (Athens, Ohio: Ohio University Press, 1987). On Beatrice becoming her father, see, for example, Lemoncelli, 112-15; R. Paulson, *Representations of Revolution* (New Haven: Yale University Press, 1983); Hogle, pp. 153-56; Richardson, p. 118; J. F. Schell, "Shelley's *The Cenci*: Corruption and the Calculating Faculty," *University of Mississippi Studies in English Series,* 2. 2 (1981), 1-14.

30. Wordsworth, *The Borderers,* in *The Poetical Works of William Wordsworth,* ed. E. de Selincourt, 5 vols. (Oxford: Oxford University Press, 1940-1949), I. Coleridge, *Remorse,* in *The Complete Poetical Works of Samuel Taylor Coleridge,* ed. E. H. Coleridge, 2 vols. (Oxford: Oxford University Press, 1912), II. For *The Cenci* as written against *Remorse* see Carlson, p. 193.

31. This refusal to disclose is reminiscent of the act of reticence which closes Shelley's *Julian and Maddalo,* a poem also engaged with notions of a "familiar language" and the limits of such a language when pressured by forces alien to it (in this case the disruptive power of the maniac's soliloquy).

See, for example, Shelley Wall, "Baffled Narrative in *Julian and Maddalo*" in *New Romanticisms: Theory and Critical Practice* (Toronto: University of Toronto Press, 1994), 52-68.

32. Curran, p. 10, bewails the "peculiar lack of awareness that kept these writers from realizing that Adam's curse was itself Shelley's tragic subject, as necessary to comprehend as it was unavoidable."

33. *The Romantics Reviewed: Contemporary Reviews of British Romantic Writers,* ed. Donald H. Reiman (New York: Garland Publishing, 1972), part C, I, 253.

34. *The Romantics Reviewed,* part C, I, 347.

Margot Harrison (essay date summer 2000)

SOURCE: Harrison, Margot. "No Way for a Victim to Act?: Beatrice Cenci and the Dilemma of Romantic Performance." *Studies in Romanticism* 39, no. 2 (summer 2000): 187-211.

[*In the following essay, Harrison contrasts Shelley's opinions on romantic drama espoused in his Preface to* The Cenci *with those implicit in the play itself.*]

Two problems have historically preoccupied readers of *The Cenci.* First of all: what does this verse-play have to do with the theatre? If only by default, Shelley's drama occupies the liminal space between closet and stage. Shelley indisputably "wished *The Cenci* to be acted," picked out his lead actors, and even asked a friend to "procure . . . its presentation at Covent Garden."[1] The play's subject made such a performance impossible. Yet, while the moral strictures against a play about incest had expired by 1886, the aesthetic judgment of *The Cenci* as "undramatic" (first voiced by Byron) has lasted considerably longer. Until recently, critics tended to view the dramatic form and stage destination of the play as contingencies to be overlooked in favor of its "poetic" aspects and/or its political subtexts, on the assumption that *The Cenci* makes poor theatre. This assumption derives in part, as Stuart Curran notes, from critical stereotypes of Shelley as an inward-turning poet who coveted the power of a stage performance while lacking a pragmatic grasp of the medium.[2]

But the traditional judgment against *The Cenci* as theatre is also deeply grounded in the text itself, and here we approach the second critical problem. At first glance, "unspeakable" incest aside, *The Cenci* seems to serve up just the sort of Gothic/melodramatic duel which pleased early nineteenth-century spectators. But the problem with this duel as melodrama or tragedy is that

its sole survivor is finally neither heroic, nor even "sympathetic." Critics agree that Beatrice Cenci turns readers and spectators against her in the fifth act, where, under arrest for the murder of the father who raped her, she undertakes to save herself by lying about her role in the crime. Not content with having "a higher truth" on her side in court, Beatrice denies the petty facts of her story as well. "I know thee! How? where? when?" (to her hired assassin).[3] Worse still, perhaps, Beatrice fails to make the audience a party to her deceit. Unlike many a romantic antihero, she does not expose and deplore her own hypocrisy in soliloquy. Joseph Donohue observes that even jaded modern spectators of *The Cenci* are repelled by this breach of trust[4]—one which seems to implicate the author as well as his creation. (In the Preface, Shelley condemns the parricide but makes no mention of Beatrice's cover-up performance.)

Critics have expressed their own discomfort with Beatrice by charging Shelley with the aesthetic error of "inconsistency." Roger Blood pinpoints this reaction, even as he suggests that the supposed "inconsistency" between various moments in Beatrice's performance merely externalizes the deceit which is the basis of theatre. "[T]he inconsistency [in Beatrice] which all critics sense . . . is not merely the result of a discrepancy between character and action . . . but the absolute self-contradiction, the literal counter-statement of her public deceit, which mars her self-representation and self-justification after the murder."[5] Julie Carlson is more explicit about why Beatrice bothers readers and viewers who want a tragic victim-heroine. "The trial scene allows her to finally appear as what and who she 'is': a commanding actress."[6] In short, and strangely enough, Shelley's heroine proves her own unfitness for the stage by acting.

Yet, is this (anti-)climax of *The Cenci* "inconsistent" with its beginnings? On the contrary, I contend that Beatrice's performance of "public deceit" is merely the most off-putting of the play's densely layered theatrical metaphors. From Cenci's declaration that his crimes are "a public matter" (I. i. 71), to Beatrice's prediction that "the vain and senseless crowd, / . . . that they may make our calamity / Their worship and their spectacle, will leave / The churches and the theatres as void / As their own hearts . . ." (v. iii. 36-40), *The Cenci* is a text which seems to refuse to let us forget that it was intended for the stage, and what such an intention entails.

In recent years, increased attention to this metadramatic imagery has led critics to read the play no longer as an accidental failure *as* theatre, but as a deliberate dramatization of the necessary failure *of* theatre. For readers like Blood, Carlson and Andrea Henderson, *The Cenci* is a self-referential drama where Shelley incarnates the object of his inextricable fascination and repulsion—the stage—in the person of an actress-heroine (Carlson), or a playwright-villain (Henderson),[7] or a whole cast of characters as allegorically depthless as marionettes (Blood). These interpreters search for the "key" to Beatrice's mysterious duplicity in Shelley's own shiftiness; they suggest that we read Shelley's decision to write for the theatre as itself a double-edged performance. But they do not explore the implications of Shelley's possible self-identification with the actor.

In order to gain a more precise sense of what Beatrice Cenci's "acting" meant to Shelley (and to Beatrice herself), I suggest that we read *The Cenci* with reference to a proto-romantic late eighteenth-century debate about performance. The "classicist" position in this debate is summed up in Denis Diderot's trenchant opposition of a new breed of *sensible* actors, who genuinely feel (or try to feel) the emotions they represent, to those who practice learned, traditional techniques of mimicry.[8] Not only is there no middle ground between these two modes of performance, Diderot insists, but great actors do not, cannot feel. They master the audience because they master themselves, and Diderot ascribes this mastery to their lack of "character": an interiority so impoverished that, paradoxically, it becomes "universal." "[T]hey are fit to play all characters because they have none."[9] Such a thesis took direct aim at the ideals of the "Age of Sensibility." Rousseau set the pattern for romantic "performance theory" by making his autobiographies read like one long refutation of Diderot's claim that real affect is less compelling than its polished simulacrum. He stresses the genuineness of his most dramatic self-transformations: "I acted nothing: I became in fact what I appeared to be."[10] Thus, Diderot's opposition of feeling to acting survived in romanticism with its values reversed. What typically fascinated romantic writers in great actors was not the virtuosity of deceit, but the havoc of spontaneity. Ambivalent about the very notion of performance, romantic actor-characters carefully script their roles, only to end up falling out of character.

An example well known to Shelley was the hero of Godwin's *Caleb Williams,* who tellingly sums up his life as "a theatre of calamity."[11] On repeated occasions, the falsely accused Caleb addresses an "audience" in an effort to clear his name. But, as long as he merely details his persecution by his former master, his eloquence serves to condemn him. His efforts to perform his way out of the realities of "domestic despotism," using rhetoric learned from his oppressor, are futile. At length, Caleb's luck turns when the sight of a decrepit Falkland startles him out of his plan of formal accusation. Abandoning the rhetoric of the courtroom, he describes and performs his conflicted feelings (sympathy with Falkland and reluctance to accuse him). The result is a triumph that evokes contemporary descriptions of "sublime" acting. "Every one that heard me was petrified

with astonishment. Every one that heard me was melted into tears" (334). Even Falkland is unable to resist the tide of "sympathy" generated by a heartfelt performance: "'Williams,' said he, 'you have conquered!'" (335). The greatest *coup de théâtre,* it seems, is an accidental one, for Caleb disclaims all calculation, indeed virtually all agency in his "conquest": "my heart was pierced, and I was *compelled* to give vent to its anguish" (334; my emphasis).

We shall see that Shelley's Beatrice makes the word "compel" work for her in an altogether more "compelling" way. Yet, though Beatrice never expresses "sympathy" with her rapist, critics have tended to read her performance in the courtroom in much the same way Caleb's performance has been read: as a case of the internalization of oppression. Where Falkland compels his servant to sympathize with him, thereby perpetuating his own aristocratic privilege, Cenci forces his daughter to kill him, thereby perpetuating his "unnatural" violence. Thus, *The Cenci* (like *Caleb Williams*) poses a limit-case which invites us to ask hard, specific questions about the application of romantic ideals of spontaneous performance. How do oppressed people "act" when they take action? Is it possible for them to "conquer" by speaking from the heart? Or must they perform within the bounds of the roles prescribed by their local circumstances, even in the act of revolution? If so, do they approach these conventional performances critically? Or do they mistake them for self-expression? Are they sometimes, like Diderot's great actors, so opaque that we cannot even decide whether they *have* "conquered" their oppressors? Throughout *The Cenci,* as I will show, Shelley calls Godwin's model of the sincere "conquering" performance into question.

But this questioning begins outside the play's text, in its very writing. In a remark reported by Trelawney, Shelley raised the possibility that he approached the task of writing a drama in much the same way in which Diderot's masterful, unfeeling actor approaches his role. "In writing the *Cenci* my object was to see how well I could succeed in describing *passions I have never felt,* and to tell the most dreadful story in pure and refined language."[12] This quotation puts an unexpected spin on another remark, a reaction to Kean's *Hamlet* (transcribed into Mary Shelley's journal) which is often cited as evidence of Shelley's "antipathy" to the theatre. What bothers Shelley (as it bothered Hazlitt and Lamb) is Kean's inability to put off his own actorishness in order to play an inner-directed Hamlet. "The inefficacy of acting to encourage or maintain the delusion. The loathsome sight of men of [sic] personating characters which do not and cannot belong to them."[13] By contrast, the introspective poet believed himself equal to representing the violent passions of the (as we shall see) highly theatrical Cenci family. Whereas Kean had failed as a Diderotian actor, unable to "delude" Shelley into forgetting that the character of Hamlet was not his, Shelley would succeed in feigning passions which he had "never felt." Moreover, he would do so in order to write Kean a great role—Count Cenci—which *could* "belong to him."[14] (Mary Shelley notes that Shelley was "very unwilling that any one but Kean should play" Cenci.[15]) The apparent reversal in Shelley's attitude toward Kean between his viewing of *Hamlet* and his writing of **The Cenci** might thus perhaps be read as a ripple in the poet's ongoing rivalry with the star actor.

The play's Preface is pervaded with this same intense awareness of the difference between the technical demands of poetic expression and those of dramatic concealment. Shelley indulges the former impulse in his lengthy rendering of the Guido Reni portrait of Beatrice, which condenses the plot of the play into a static, pregnant image of her interiority. The portrait, Shelley suggests, transcends theatre and reveals the limits of dramatic artifice. But it thus also gives the actor-dramatist an occasion to plan the strategy he will deploy within those limits. In contemplating the artist's "just representation" of Beatrice, we become aware that "[t]he crimes and miseries in which she was an actor and a sufferer are as *the mask and the mantle in which circumstances clothed her for her impersonation on the scene of the world*."[16] It is not an exaggeration to say that this statement contains the germ of the theatrical self-consciousness which pervades **The Cenci**. By figuring the protagonist of his play as an actress, Shelley affirms the ease with which it will be possible for an actress to incarnate her, and hence (once again) the necessary destination of the play for the stage. At the same time, by describing Beatrice's acting as passive and "circumstantial" ("an actor and *sufferer* . . . circumstances clothed her . . ."), he opposes it to the evidence in the portrait of what even the most successful drama cannot represent: the "simple and profound" inwardness which escapes outward circumstances and vicissitudes, but not the artist's eye (278). Thus, if the Preface serves to define the play's Beatrice Cenci as an actress, it also cautions us against believing that Beatrice's acting bears any relation to her "true" character. Furthermore, Shelley's yoking of "actor and sufferer" reminds us that Beatrice Cenci is exhibited to our judgment only because her father raped her, and suggests that such theatrical exhibition may constitute a second and parallel violation.

By thus representing Beatrice as double (visual representation and dramatic character), the Preface exposes the doubleness or duplicity of its author, who turns to the second Beatrice even as he expresses his preference for the first; who uses the play to exploit the very dramatic violence which he uses the Preface to condemn. (I will return to the issue of Shelley's doubleness at the end of this essay.) But, in emphasizing and indicting drama's *difference* from poetry or portraiture, the Pref-

ace does not merely function as a disclaimer. On the contrary, it serves as an opportunity for Shelley to take his distance from a popular model of romantic drama, today often called "mental theatre." The turn-of-the-century theorist of this model, Joanna Baillie, argued that the most effective psychological drama is essentially monodrama, in which the supporting characters serve as static allegorical personifications of the forces at war within a central "great impassioned character."[17] Hence Baillie advised playwrights against dramatic conflict precipitated by "outward circumstances," on the grounds that the dilemmas of complex characters should be direct emanations of their inner lives (15). Against this view of the drama, Shelley reminds us that Beatrice Cenci would never have appeared "onstage" or before the public eye had her inner life *not* been subjugated to "circumstances" ("circumstances clothed her for her impersonation on the scene of the world"). Indeed, the predominance of chance and circumstance in Beatrice's story—the sheer bad luck of having an "unnatural" father, of dispatching him at the wrong moment, of having her actions judged by another "father" (the Pope)—throws doubt upon her status as the "great impassioned character" of her drama. (Only the portrait, which is *outside* the drama, attests to this status.) From the beginning, this uncertainty disrupts the impulses of readers and spectators to "sympathize" with Beatrice. But it is only when this sympathy reaches a low ebb, as I shall show, that the links between the audience's alienation, the author's self-alienation (impersonating characters which "do not belong to him"), and the story's historical otherness come to light.

For historical difference takes a central place among the "circumstances" which serve to make **The Cenci** a highly dubious example of "mental theatre." We shall see that, even as Shelley frames his dramatic conflict in terms of "oppressor and oppressed" (v. iii. 75) which echoes the Radical rhetoric of his own time, he never loses sight of the other scene where his characters find themselves (Rome, 1599). Within this scene, the most determining "circumstance" in Beatrice Cenci's life is, of course, the accident of birth. The structure of the feudal patriarchal family mimics (or parodies) that of the romantic monodrama, for its father is figured as both the incarnation of the whole and the "author" of its separate parts, "the form that moulded mine" (Giacomo, III. ii. 20). Religion sanctifies the allegory. Count Cenci, a father who experiences paternity as unbearable self-division, justifies incest as an attempt to resubjugate a "part" which has come loose and turned against him, appealing to God to rid him of "this most specious mass of flesh, / Which thou hast made my daughter; this my blood; / *This particle of my divided being*, / Or rather, this my bane and my disease" (IV. i. 115-18; my emphasis). This patriarchal allegory pulls incessantly against the romantic psychodrama, with Beatrice at its center, which Shelley has superimposed upon it. In the Preface, Shelley asks us to judge Beatrice as a free moral agent (what is often called a "bourgeois subject"), yet reading the drama we find that Beatrice lacks much of the vocabulary she needs to define and defend herself this way. Sometimes it even appears, contrary to what Shelley insists in the Preface, that there is no one behind the "mask and mantle" of victimhood. Called upon to defend her, family members can describe Beatrice *before* her violation only in terms of a "purity" which lacks characteristics: "the one thing innocent and pure / In this black guilty world" (v. iii. 101-2); "That perfect mirror of pure innocence" (v. iv. 130).

Too often, I believe, readers of the play have assented in this view of Beatrice as a non-actor in her own drama. Because Shelley seems in the Preface to equate Beatrice's strength with her innocence, and her innocence with passivity, some of the play's most astute critics foreclose the issue of her struggle with her father. As a self-reflecting portrait-subject, they point out, Beatrice loses this struggle as soon as she enters it. By taking action, and still more by "acting," she merely impersonates Cenci, reaffirming her subjection to the paternal body which violated her. And indeed, certain passages in the play suggest that dramatic stardom is a fate inflicted upon Beatrice from without. Moments after her rape, she envisions herself transformed into "that wretched Beatrice / Men speak of . . ."; her experience into a dramatic fiction ("This woful story / So did I *overact* in my sick dreams . . .") (III. i. 43-44, 48-49; my emphasis). Using this and similar evidence, Alan Richardson has traced "Beatrice's transition from Cenci's victim to his double . . . as [her] consciousness becomes the self-estranged image of her father's."[18] Henderson suggests that Beatrice's rape irretrievably "bifurcate[s]" her character, relieving her of consciousness altogether as she compulsively repeats Cenci's actions (115).

Certainly, the Count's ability to personify "circumstances" (both dramatic and historical) prompts us to ask, like Beatrice herself near the end of the play, "was he not alone omnipotent / On Earth, and ever present?" (v. iv. 78-79). But I will demonstrate that, if Cenci figures the authorial force which puts Beatrice onstage, once there she does anything but yield this stage to him. Staging Baillie's one-character-drama as a problem, Shelley depicts Beatrice not simply as a figure of pathos (inward-turning reaction to Cenci's action) but as one side in an interminable struggle for control of the "stage," literal and metaphorical, of the drama. A sense of this struggle is crucial to our understanding of those scenes in which Beatrice perjures herself and foregoes the audience's sympathy. I will approach the problem of Beatrice's courtroom performance, first, by showing that both father and daughter place their conflict in a theatrical frame of reference, and second, by

asking just how deep that frame is. How self-conscious are their performances? How close do they—and we—come to insight into the history and meaning of dramatic violence?

The conflict between Cenci and Beatrice pivots upon oppositions which structure much of the play's imagery: visibility and invisibility, form and formlessness, light and dark. Such are the basic ingredients of theatrical incarnation, for Shelley has realized Lamb's suggestion that, in the theatre, literary characters all become actor-orators.[19] Count Cenci is introduced to us as the star actor whose exhibitionistic "perversity" drags his family onstage. His vices are "a public matter," "the deeds / Which you scarce hide from men's revolted eyes" (I. i. 13-14; 71). Beatrice is introduced as a spectator and witness to these deeds, yet her eyes are not merely "revolted." Rather, as Orsino explains, she has a tendency to look back, wielding an "awe-inspiring gaze, / Whose beams anatomize me nerve by nerve / And lay me bare . . ." (I. ii. 85-87). The spectatorial gaze which performs these acts of "anatomy" and exposure is a spectacle in its own right ("awe-inspiring"), and hence poses a challenge to the onstage performer. Beatrice leaves no doubt about this challenge in the banquet-scene, where Cenci stages his pleasure in the deaths of his two older sons as a spectacle for aristocratic Rome. Ordered to her room after she has protested, she in turn orders her father off the stage:

> Retire thou, impious man! Ay, hide thyself
> Where never eye can look upon thee more!
>   . . . . .
>
> Cover thy face from every living eye,
> And start if thou but hear a human step:
> Seek out some dark and silent corner. . . .
>
> (I. iii. 146-47, 154-56)

Refusing to obey these words, Cenci nonetheless shows that he understands their import, and that of the "awe-inspiring gaze" which backs them. "[Y]esternight you dared to look / With disobedient insolence upon me . . ." (II. i. 106-7). Cenci thus plans the rape of his daughter not solely as an offense against her moral purity, but also as a defense against her rival performance. With "one look, one smile," he declares his intent to (as Carlson puts it) "give her stage-fright" (192). "Never again, I think, with fearless eye, / . . . / Shalt thou strike dumb the meanest of mankind" (II. i. 64; 116; 119).

Here the play's theatrical allegory expands beyond the simple dualism of actor and spectator. In recognizing his daughter as a threat to him, Cenci unearths Diderot's distinction between self-exhibition and great acting: between merely being seen onstage and mastering all that is seen there. By ordering him to "hide thyself" from the "avenging looks" of his victims (I. iii. 153), Beatrice introduces her father to the potential terrors of exposure. But she also suggests to him that the power to induce this terror in *others* (with words or gaze) brings with it a mastery of visibility and invisibility which overarches their opposition, and hence the whole theatrical situation. Terrifying unwilled visibility, therefore, is the fate which the Count wishes upon Beatrice, as he plots to replace the public spectacle of his crimes with that of her degradation. "She shall stand shelterless in the broad noon / Of public scorn, for acts blazoned abroad . . ." (IV. i. 82-83). Cenci's curse is twofold. On the one hand, it can be fulfilled only by Beatrice's eventual transformation from "sufferer" into "actor" of the vengeance which "the crowd" will make "their worship and their spectacle" (V. iii. 38). On the other, it must ensure that she cannot enact this vengeance on her own initiative, as she did her protests in the banquet-hall. Cenci's plan is not simply to force his daughter onstage, but to transform her from a masterful actress into a "sincere" actress who cannot distinguish inside from outside, being from seeming. "She shall become . . . / . . . / . . . to her own conscious self / All she appears to others . . ." (IV. i. 85; 87-88). And indeed, the moments after the rape find Beatrice, by her own admission, blinded by the "clinging, black, contaminating mist" of genuine self-delusion (III. i. 17). The rape has rendered her visibility so unbearable that to act *is* to suffer, and vice versa.

As Carlson points out, Cenci is aided in his staging of his daughter not only by the mythos of paternity, but also by the sexual ideology which defines women's honor/chastity (and hence their identity) as a mere costume, "alienable with or without their consent" (190). Once her "innocence" has been removed, Beatrice can at best only impersonate herself; at worst, she impersonates her father. Is this second scenario indeed what ensues in the last acts of the play, as critics like Richardson and Henderson argue? Before addressing this question, I want to stress the fact that the foregoing reading prevents us from automatically interpreting signs of Beatrice's "acting" as signs of Cenci's acting through her. The rape does not pull her onstage and transform her into an actress, though it does dictate a role (avenger). It is in light of her theatrical history that we must read her behavior once she recovers from her initial madness.[20] In Act III, Beatrice once again wields a power of the "gaze" with which she strives to master others' sight and seeing; to "make / The thing that I have suffered but a shadow / In the dread lightning which avenges it" (I. 88-89). Accordingly, she attempts to "awe" Cenci with a "vision" of his death (IV. i. 71-72). Later, in order to realize that vision without implicating herself, she casts Olimpio and Marzio as assassins and costumes Marzio in the mantle which "shining bright / . . . / Betrayed them [the assassins] to our notice" (IV. iv. 84; 86). Finally, when Marzio refuses to ac-

cept full responsibility for the murder, she stages him as guilty for the judges ("I prithee mark / His countenance . . ." [v. ii. 82-83]) and intimidates him, once again, with the power of her gaze ("He shrinks from her regard like autumn's leaf" [v. ii. 113]).

By expanding her efforts in the last two acts of the play from merely acting to authoring and staging, Beatrice clearly mounts her own claim to centrality in her family's drama in opposition to her father's. But is this claim nonetheless merely an impersonation of Cenci's? Are the tactics which Beatrice adds to her repertoire in these acts—strong-arm manipulation of supporting players, downright duplicity—those of a "character which cannot belong to her"? For the play's critics, these questions pivot around that of Beatrice's "self-consciousness," that very tormenting "consciousness" that Cenci wished upon his daughter ("to her own conscious self / All she appears to others"). Perhaps no question has aroused more disagreement than that of what is beneath the mask Beatrice presents to the courtroom. Richardson claims that Beatrice's post-rape consciousness is divided or "self-estranged" in the "image of her father's" (112). Henderson would have it that Beatrice is "bifurcated" between her father's influence and her inner purity (115). Carlson argues that Beatrice is actually "undivided" in her consciousness of doing right (187), while Blood says that her act of murder "eras[es] self-consciousness as effectively as death erases the mind" (382). Such a case might seem to confirm Diderot's lesson about the folly of trying to look for the "subject" behind a great performance.

But this folly is inside as well as outside the play, for, prior to her arrival in the courtroom, Beatrice herself several times poses the question of her performative authenticity. Nor is she alone in this questioning, since Shelley characterizes the Cenci not merely by their drive to upstage each other but also, as Orsino points out, by their tendency to "self-anatomy." ("'[T]is a trick of this same family / To analyse their own and other minds" [II. ii. 108-10].) Just as we strive to link the performative effects of the Cenci to internal motives, so both father and daughter work self-consciously to connect their actions to a truth that exceeds the limits of their actor's universe, "this keen-judging world, this two-edged lie, / Which seems, but is not" (IV. iv. 115-16). But their truth is not our truth. For Shelley's Cenci "are represented as Catholics, and as Catholics deeply tinged with religion" (Preface 277). Because the articles of Catholic faith are visible represented, writes Shelley, that faith "is interwoven with the whole fabric of life" and of rhetoric. When the characters of *The Cenci* approach the world as if it were a stage ("the painted scene of this new world" [v. i. 78]), their faith backs them by defining their world as an allegorical shadow-play of the next. Lacking a legacy of Puritan antitheatricalism, they act upon a performance theory which is inseparable from Christian allegory. Thus, while critics (and Shelley in the Preface) worry the question of whether Beatrice regains her moral and mental integrity after the rape, Beatrice herself poses the question of her justification in quite a different way. Christianity provides an unimpeachable script for the drama of her vengeance, in which the Count is the mere impersonator of a father, and his assassin the embodiment of divine will. "What thou hast said persuades me that our act [the murder] / Will but dislodge a spirit of deep hell / Out of a human form" (IV. ii. 6-8). "Thou wert a weapon in the hand of God / To a just use" (to Marzio, IV. iii. 54-55). And Beatrice is not alone in justifying her actions allegorically. "The world's Father / Must grant a parent's prayer against his child" (Cenci, IV. i. 106-7). "I could see / The devil was rebuked that lives in him" (Lucretia, II. i. 44-45). As the very notion of embodiment or incarnation belongs to the ancient sacral function of the theatre, so to impose a particular role upon others is invariably, in this play, to justify one's staging as part of the divine spectacle.

In this sense, the self-conscious theatricality of the Cenci family is deeply un-romantic, and rejects the Preface's attempts to moralize and "internalize" it as an anachronism. Sacred allegory is a script which leaves no room for *sensibilité* or even for individuality. It is, in Walter Benjamin's phrase, not simply a "convention of expression" (for individuals to appropriate) but an "expression of convention": divine, infallible performance acting through the individual.[21] This is the allegory whose despotic arbitrariness Coleridge rejected in favor of the unifying, conciliating symbol. It is an allegory which, Cenci reasons, "must" uphold a father's authority in the name of God the father—"Be he who asks even what men call me" (IV. i. 108). And yet, to reason about what convention "must" express is already to begin to humanize and motivate allegory as if it were a romantic symbol. This is precisely what the Count and Beatrice, betraying their hybrid origins in 1599 and 1819, proceed to do. Each appeals to God to define his or her staging as symbolic/essential, the other's as merely allegorical/conventional; each claims to constitute a *necessary* link between the human and the divine. For Beatrice, this means relying upon the script of the New Testament to confirm the identity of her suffering "innocence" with divine moral law. At first, naive, she simply denies the reality of her father's challenge to this law ("Had it been true, there is a God in Heaven, / He would not live to boast of such a boon" [I. iii. 52-53]). But, when God fails to smite the Count, Beatrice begins describing her own interiority as the only possible solution of continuity between the will of "God in Heaven" and real events. "I have prayed / To God, and I have talked with my own heart, / And have unravelled my entangled will, / And have at length determined what is right" (III. i. 218-21). Her (initial) defense of the murder rests upon her claim to a pure, Christ-like

"heart" through which she communicates with a "will" beyond her own. Cenci, meanwhile, while invoking the truth of "the word of God" against Beatrice (I. iii. 55), defines this truth as the Old Testament law of the father. If Beatrice has the conventional interpretation of Christian dogma ("what is right") on her side, he has the conventional dispensation of Christian authority.

But the Count also, and repeatedly, has events on his side. The Pope "holds it of most dangerous example / In aught to weaken the paternal power, / Being, as 'twere, the shadow of his own" (II. ii. 54-56). The ironclad historical "circumstances" of feudal patriarchal society, together with other circumstances which we might call coincidences, combine to give Cenci less of a stake in romantic models of subjectivity than his daughter. While Beatrice searches for truth within herself ("my entangled will"), Cenci gradually recognizes and affirms the impossibility of locating truth anywhere in the dramatic representation which is (as the Preface has told us) a "mask and mantle." He rejects interiority and other standards of truth in favor of the empirical evidence of a divine performance which seems invariably to "favor" him. "'Tis plain I have been favored from above, / For when I cursed my sons they died" (IV. i. 39-40). In ordering him to "confess himself," then, Beatrice misinterprets her father's faith (IV. i. 34). In a world where absolution can be bought from the Pope, "repentance" is not to be found in the buyer's conscience, but in the same expression of convention where Cenci found his "favor." For a performance of contrition, he awaits his cue: "Repentance is an easy moment's work / And more depends on God than me" (IV. i. 42).

In this depiction of Cenci presuming upon the will of his creator, we glimpse, perhaps, Shelley's doubts about the prospect of giving Kean his words to speak. But Cenci, unlike many a star actor, is content with a free interpretation of his "author"'s word. Still a man of 1599, he does not view the death of God as a necessary consequence of the revelation that Christianity is a Nietzschean master-morality and God's universe an incarnation of power, not truth. Instead, Cenci merely embraces the performative function which subjugates him to the play's author, in an "insight" which momentarily pushes the bounds of Christian allegory toward the "real" confines of stage or text. "My soul, which is a scourge, will I resign / Into the hands of him who wielded it; / Be it for its own punishment or theirs, / He will not ask it of me . . . / . . . / Until its hate be all inflicted" (IV. i. 63-66, 68). By reducing the motive of his acts to his antagonistic or scourge-function in the play ("*its* hate"), Cenci repudiates the interiority already so deeply compromised by the allegory of paternity which defined it as a "divided being."

Just as Cenci's growing awareness of his own performative function produces a quasi-blasphemous rhetoric, targeting the conventions which enable that performance, so Beatrice's late moment of theodicy seems to result from a *prise de conscience* of theatre. But, as I have already shown, one can only say "seems." For, while every reader of the play may agree that what Beatrice does in the courtroom is "acting," there is no consensus on whether or to what degree the actress herself is complicit in the performance. Does Beatrice form a conscious decision to deny her role in the murder to the authorities; to confess to the "desire" and the "interest," but not to the deed? (IV. iv. 67-70; 132). Or does she believe in the literal truth of her assertions? Because Shelley does not stage Beatrice's decision to feign—if decision there is—in a soliloquy like Cenci's, he places a blank spot at the center of the play's fifth act. Like Diderot's great actor, Beatrice resists unmasking, in some quarters raising the suspicion that she has ceased to have an inner life at all.[22] All that is certain is that she fails to confess, and hence to take one of the tragic/heroic stances which a confession might have justified in the audience's eyes. Insisting upon her factual innocence, Beatrice loses her opportunity to persuade her judges that the truth of this innocence is "a higher truth" than that of facts (v. ii. 164): an allegorical truth of divine justification. (Marzio has to make this claim for her.) Nor does Beatrice opt for the humanist martyrdom of Shelley's Prometheus: her conduct demonstrates her unwillingness "[t]o suffer woes which Hope thinks infinite; / To forgive wrongs darker than death or night."[23] Rather than embracing (and thereby "transcending") the inevitability of her earthly suffering, Beatrice places herself in the awkward position of proving her repeated claims to embody the "truth of things" (IV. iv. 182) by lying. It might appear that she is less interested in being a heroine than in beating the rap.

But what is behind this appearance? Carlson envisions Beatrice as a sort of living contradiction to Diderot, whose power as an actress derives directly from her inner conviction that she is not one. "[W]hat enables the power of her performance, particularly in the trial scene, is that her conscious self entertains no doubts about the 'truth' of her performance" (193). "Undivided" and unremorseful, as Carlson portrays her, Beatrice has lost the power to distinguish between the allegorical truth of her innocence and the literal truth of her guilt: she earnestly believes that God "shaped" the assassins for her father's destruction. But I feel that, in the absence of more evidence, to give such credence to Beatrice is to make the assumption persuasively refuted by Diderot: that a good performance *must* be in earnest. Moreover, far from acting complacent or "undivided" in the courtroom, Beatrice herself speaks a highly self-conscious rhetoric of difference and division. Specifically, she dwells upon the dilemma of an "appearance" severed from its "truth." "[T]he breath / Of accusation kills an innocent name, / And leaves for lame acquittal the poor life / *Which is a mask without it*" (IV. iv. 142-45; my

emphasis). Beatrice betrays her knowledge of stagecraft in this suggestion that the "innocence" of a life inheres as much in its external, alienable "name" (reputation) as in the hidden truth to which that name corresponds. Once the inner consciousness of innocence is severed from its outer appearance, to retain the former alone is to live a life which is a mask; to practice unending petty duplicity (as she herself does at this moment). Yet, to submit to appearances and confess is to come no closer to the truth, for guilt is another mask: "O white innocence, / That thou shouldst wear the mask of guilt to hide / Thine awful and serenest countenance . . ." (v. iii. 24-26).

This last formulation is telling, for where Beatrice might have said that innocence is passively obscured or eclipsed by an appearance of guilt, she chooses an image—wearing a mask—which suggests that innocence conceals *itself*. If innocence itself is such a perverse performer, then there can be no shame in the mask of innocence which Beatrice knowingly consents to wear. And there is evidence that she does so knowingly. Her instructions to her stepmother after the discovery of the murder suggest an acting-lesson:

> . . . 'Tis like a truant child
> To fear that others know what thou hast done,
> Even from thine own strong consciousness, and thus
> Write on unsteady eyes and altered cheeks
> All thou wouldst hide. Be faithful to thyself,
> And fear no other witness but thy fear.
> For if, as cannot be, some circumstance
> Should rise in accusation, we can blind
> Suspicion with such cheap astonishment,
> Or overbear it with such guiltless pride,
> *As murderers cannot feign*. . . .

> (IV. iv. 36-46; my emphasis)

Like Rousseau's autobiographical anecdotes, this passage demonstrates just how difficult it is in practice for an accomplished performer to "entertain no doubts about the 'truth' of her performance." On the one hand, Beatrice simply exhorts Lucretia to appear as she is. On the other, she asks her specifically to appear as that which "cannot be feigned," and thereby all but acknowledges that feigning is in order. As long as nothing "rises in accusation," Beatrice suggests, innocence can remain "faithful to [it]self" in an inexpressive self-closure. But an innocence forced actively to display itself is indistinguishable from a "feigned" innocence, if not to its spectators then still to its actor's "strong consciousness." For this consciousness also cuts the other way: it is a consciousness of allegorical (divine) justification and a consciousness of factual guilt. Even as Beatrice tells Lucretia that she will *seem* more effectively because she *is*, she recognizes, like Diderot, the irrelevance and perhaps even the danger of this doubling of artifice by authenticity. To add seeming to being, to *pose as what one is* is to deliver either a weak performance or a strong self-travesty. For one only *needs* to "pose" as what one is not—or so one's audience is apt to assume.

In short, by betraying the fact that she is "anxious as to the reception [her story] experience[s]," Beatrice casts doubt upon her own belief in that story. This description comes from the manuscript ending of *Caleb Williams,* where Falkland uses it as a damning critique of Caleb's public accusations against him (342). In Godwin's published version of that ending, Caleb "conquers" all such objections with the sheer force of his performance. Because Beatrice fails to do the same, a contrast between the performance strategies of the two characters may help us to pinpoint her "mistake." Caleb ultimately solves the problem of performance anxiety by telling Falkland's story instead of his own. Rather than confronting Falkland, he confronts and accuses himself, describing himself as "compelled" by remorse to confess to the (purely metaphorical) "murder" of his oppressor. Beatrice, who has really committed such a murder, resists this compulsion to confess. Indeed, she resists the compulsion to tell a story at all: she offers no plausible alternative version of events and (despite her plan) shows no "cheap astonishment" at the accusation. Instead of elaborating a lie, she uses a variety of tactics to "compel" her accusers to swallow the flat denials she offers. (In this she also differs from a hypocrite like Orsino, who "weaves" a tapestry of deceit.)

But Beatrice's differences from Caleb do not, in themselves, explain her "failure" as a performer. For, as part of an unabashedly performative strategy, her "strong consciousness" works to her advantage. The flimsiness of appearances and evidence is her explicit rationale for refusing to submit herself to judgment. Rather than encouraging her viewers to forget that she is performing (as did Caleb), Beatrice heightens their consciousness of rhetoric with repeated references to "show" and appearance. Addressing Marzio, who knows perfectly well that she is guilty, she demands that he judge or "discriminate" *as she dictates* between appearances of guilt and innocence which, because they are both mere appearances, are always subject to confusion:

BEATRICE:

> . . . Think
> What 'tis to blot with infamy and blood
> All that which *shows like innocence,* and is,
> Hear me, great God! I swear, most innocent,
> So that the world lose all discrimination
> Between the sly, fierce, wild regard of guilt,
> And that which now *compels thee* to reply
> To what I ask: Am I, or am I not
> A parricide?

MARZIO:

> Thou art not!

> (v. ii. 149-58; my emphases)

At first, Beatrice's substitution of "all that which *shows* like innocence" for "innocence" may sound like an involuntary confession. But, in fact, the effect of the word "shows" is to unsettle Marzio's certainty that he knows the truth of events, by reminding him that the truth of earthly appearances can only be recognized and averred by "great God." Until it is, Beatrice's interpretation of her "innocence" is as good as Marzio's—better, in fact, for it is backed by the strength of the performative "that which now compels thee." In a fallen world where appearances obscure truth, Beatrice's innocence *must* "show" itself as a performative, a demand that compels assent and obliterates contradiction: "Our innocence is as an armèd heel / To trample accusation . . ." (IV. iv. 159-60).

It is this naked performativity of Beatrice's rhetoric, this preference for "trampling" her audience over persuading it, which has turned real audiences and readers against her. While the violence of the murder was funneled at Cenci, that of its cover-up seems to target us. Beatrice's most "conquering" rhetoric is addressed to the assassin Marzio: a character who, like the audience, knows that she is lying, and who alone can exonerate her. Hence we feel our own "judgment" attacked by this speech which is shaped not to convince but to "compel." For Marzio, "that which now compels thee to reply" is simply Beatrice's success in inducing a "keener pang" (v. ii. 164) than all the physical tortures to which the court has yet subjected him. (He acknowledges her felicitous performance with a performative: "*I here declare* those whom I did accuse / Are innocent" [158-59; my emphasis].)

Beatrice has more trouble, as we have seen, conquering the reader. Does it follow that her performance in the courtroom is a fatal lapse out of "character" which can only be attributed to a self-deception, or to her father's "pollution" of her will? On the contrary, I argue that the (post-)romantic reader's perception of Beatrice's performance as an ethical failure (and not simply a practical one) merely measures her distance from romantic ideals of action and acting. For Beatrice's is a rhetoric shaped by and for "outward circumstances," those same circumstances of birth and history from which Shelley refuses throughout to emancipate her inner life. Among these circumstances is the fact that she appears not before a court regulated by written conventions for establishing a truthful narrative, but before one which defines truth as any performance of confession compelled from the accused under torture ("Let tortures strain the truth till it be white . . ." [v. ii. 169]). Precisely because it is pure theatre ("a wicked farce" [v. ii. 38]), this is a court which the accused cannot "convince," but must seize and dominate with her own performance. Hence the irrelevance of factual truth to Beatrice in forming her defense.

But this self-consciousness is not the only aspect of Beatrice's rhetoric which is already "anachronistic" in 1819. For hers is not a genre of performance accessible to a Marzio or a Caleb Williams or even a Rousseau, as it revolves around the display of an aristocratic name with "compulsions" of its own. The "innocent name" which Beatrice asks the court to preserve is not hers alone: it is Cenci. To accuse her of parricide is to pit oneself against ancient hereditary power, as she reminds Savella ("stain not a noble house / With vague surmises of rejected crime" [IV. iv. 150-51]), then Marzio ("Think . . . what it is to slay / The reverence living in the minds of men / Towards our ancient house, and stainless fame" [v. ii. 144-46]), and finally the other Cenci, whose confessions have proved them unworthy of their name ("For some brief spasms of pain . . . / . . . / Are centuries of high splendour laid in dust?" [v. iii. 28; 30]). Here is another sort of "expression of convention." For Shelley's model in scripting his heroine's aristocratic performance, we may perhaps look again to *Caleb Williams,* although not to its hero. When Falkland defends himself publicly against the charge of murdering Tyrrel, he uses strikingly similar tactics to Beatrice, ceaselessly redirecting his audience's attention from the facts of the crime to the still greater crime of accusing him. "It is not in the power of your decision to restore to me my unblemished reputation, to obliterate the disgrace I have suffered, or to prevent it from being remembered that I have been brought to examination upon a charge of murder" (105). His assertion of "innocence" rests not upon a plausible narrative, but upon the reiterated invocation of his "honor" and "reputation": proofs not subject to verification. "Great God! what sort of character is that which must be supported by witnesses?" But these are precisely the proofs which compel Falkland's judges to *self*-accusation and full acquittal; to the self-reproach "How unfeeling to oblige him to defend himself from such an imputation? [sic]" (106-7). Such is the guilt of "oppressed" toward "oppressor" which Beatrice inspires in Marzio, finally compelling her vassal (or her "slave" [v. ii. 95]) to condemn himself for the crime of casting aspersions upon "that fine piece of nature" (167). The parallels do not end here. Both characters are corrupted when they murder the perpetrator of a physical assault upon their "honor."[24] Like Beatrice, Falkland is prompt to let subalterns suffer the penalty for his crime, and like her he nonetheless inspires his inferiors to "sympathetic feeling" through the sheer force of his performance (107).[25]

Unlike Falkland, Beatrice fails to acquit herself. But the comparison should help us to understand that this failure has no causal link to the "pernicious [ethical] mistakes" which Shelley attributes to Beatrice in the Preface (276). Beatrice's failure to move the Pope to clemency is of a different order from her inability to move the drama's reader or viewer to sympathy. The former results not from a personal flaw, but from the built-in, circumstantial limits of the role she has chosen to play. For the noble "name" that she invokes in her defense is the same as the name of the man she has murdered: the name which confirms a daughter's identity with—and subjection to—her father. Beatrice's death thus inscribes the selfsame lesson that Falkland (inadvertently) taught Caleb: namely, that the tactics of aristocratic performance cannot be adapted to serve revolutionary ends. Beatrice does not explicitly identify herself as a rebel against authority.[26] Indeed, we have seen that much of her courtroom rhetoric is reactionary, pivoting around her Cenci honor (just as her allegorical self-justification invokes God the father). Yet, whatever her intentions, her crime is only readable as an act of revolution. The broader revolution foreshadowed in every parricide is the Pope's rationale for putting Beatrice to death. "Parricide grows so rife / That soon, for some just cause, no doubt, the young / Will strangle us all, dozing in our chairs. / Authority, and power, and hoary hair / Are grown crimes capital" (v. iv. 20-24).

Beatrice thus appears before us as a hybrid, anomalous figure among romantic actor-characters. On the one hand, because she is self-evidently an aristocrat giving an aristocratic performance of power, she fails to win the reader's sympathy for her violent "revolutionary" action. On the other, and for precisely the same reason—because she abjures the bourgeois/romantic performance of self-exposure—Beatrice is placed in the unique position (for a revolutionary character) of never having to disown that action. At one point in Act v, Beatrice momentarily seems to renounce performance: she refuses to say anything more in support of her cause, and withdraws her earlier claims to be innocent. Yet, in so doing, she does not submit herself to judgment so much as perform the irrelevance—and hence the revocation—of any standard by which she might be judged:

> Or wilt thou rather tax high-judging God
> That he permitted such an act as that
> Which I have suffered, and which He beheld;
> Made it unutterable, and took from it
> All refuge, all revenge, all consequence,
> But that which thou hast called my father's death?
> Which is or is not what men call a crime,
> Which either I have done, or have not done;
> Say what ye will. I shall deny no more.
> If ye desire it thus, thus let it be,
> And so an end of all. Now do your will. . . .
>
> (v. iii. 78-88)

Through her apparently total renunciation of agency, Beatrice returns into herself. At the same instant, she reserves her inward-turning passivity as a means of revolutionary action. By describing her worldly role as a mere function of discourse ("Which is or is not what men call a crime"), she unmasks the world of "oppressor and oppressed" as nothing more; unmasks it, in other words, as theatre. Addressed at once to her interrogator and to the capricious public of Regency theatre, which *desires* the representation of crimes like parricide so as to be able both to savor and to "judge" them, the utterance "If ye desire it thus, thus let it be" speaks the performative injustice of judgment, and performs the refusal of self-justification.

This metadramatic moment is the closest that Beatrice ever comes to unmasking herself. "She is convicted, but has not confessed" (v. iii. 90). By refusing to abjure her power as that of a mere "scourge" (as her father did) she forfeits the sympathy vouchsafed to characters who open their minds—full or empty—to the public. Yet it might be argued that Beatrice thereby keeps her audience's attention focused on imbalances of power which are more material (and hence more remediable) than that between the Godlike author of a drama and its actor. The result is an implicit critique of the mode of "conquering" romantic acting that Godwin promoted. Can a display of honest feeling conquer entrenched power? Beatrice's performance tells us how she answers this question, and it is an answer with echoes in Shelley's contemporary work. Even in *Prometheus Unbound,* tyranny is "conquered" not directly by Love/ Asia but by the dark protean figure of Demogorgon, who, like Beatrice, takes upon himself the burden of incarnating revolutionary violence.

But, if Shelley does indeed use *The Cenci* to make such a critique of "romantic performance," how is it related to his statements in the Preface, and to the "duplicity" we detected there? Dramatic writing, Shelley speculated, demands a mortification and travesty of the poet's being; a submission to the vulgar material details ("flesh") of a direct, disguising mimesis (277). Yet, might this self-travesty not effectively double as the ruse of a poet who has no intention of offering to his audience what he says that he is offering? Might he refuse to lift the "mask and mantle" of circumstances which cover his heroine, simply because this heroine is also his rival?[27] Carlson suggests that Beatrice nearly gets the better of her creator: Shelley "seeks to deny sympathy to female commanding genius," but cannot stop his actress-heroine from "stag[ing] a *coup de théâtre* for female honor" (198-99). By this reading, Shelley's ruse consists of extending sympathy to Beatrice in the Preface (where she appears as a static portrait) only to withdraw it in the drama (where she acts). We cannot affirm the performance of Beatrice (i. e. read her as a feminist heroine) without confronting and removing a reactionary "mask and mantle" of Shelley's own choosing.

With all due respect to Carlson's critique of the misogynist underpinnings of "mental theatre," I would like to suggest that Shelley's ruse consists of more than simply pushing Beatrice into the closet. For a critique of the (male) author's authority is already, to some ex-

tent, at work in the play. For the model of Carlson's version of Shelley's ruse and its failure, we need look no further than Orsino, the character in the play who most self-consciously strives to combine the functions of author and actor. Overshadowed by the more spectacular Beatrice/Cenci conflict, the conflict between Beatrice and Orsino is no less significant, for what is at stake is precisely what is at stake in the drama as a whole: the allocation of Beatrice's performative energies. While never doubting that these energies exceed him ("her awe-inspiring gaze" ([I. ii. 84]), Orsino hopes to harness them, by means of deceit, to the fulfillment of his personal desires: "I think to win thee at an easier rate" (I. ii. 67). Accordingly, while Cenci can imagine himself at best as a performative "scourge," Orsino aspires to the position of the author who wields it. If he is the designated actor/hypocrite of *The Cenci,* modelling Beatrice's evolution into a conscious deceiver ("I thought to act a solemn comedy / Upon the painted scene of this new world" [v. ii. 77-78]), Orsino also appears persistently and tellingly in connection with texts. He is the chosen conveyer of Beatrice's petition to the Pope; later, the author of an incriminating note which is assumed to "speak" more truly than human witnesses ("Their language [of 'these lines'] is at least sincere" [IV. iv. 89]). Finally, he confides to us that he is the author of "some such plot of mingled good and ill / As others weave" (v. ii. 80-81). To author the "plot" of one's own drama, Orsino suggests, is to place oneself in a site of mastery to which no mere actor in that drama can aspire. "I see, as from a tower, the end of all: / . . . / I have such foresight as assures success" (II. ii. 147; 154). He banks on the assumption that the text is finally the most effective because the least verifiable of performances, as Beatrice herself suggests in her reaction to his note's testimony against her: "Where is Orsino? Let his eye meet mine. / What means this scrawl? Alas! ye know not what, / And therefore on the chance that it may be / Some evil, will ye kill us?" (v. ii. 176-79).

But Orsino's bid to be both author and actor, at once to "see the end" of the drama and to effect that end from within, results in a crippling division of his strength. As an actor, he is largely ineffective. (He accomplishes nothing on his own beyond disposing of the petition and influencing the weak Giacomo; although he tries to influence Beatrice as well, Shelley makes it clear that she arrives at her resolution independently of him [III. i].) As the author of a "scrawl," by contrast, Orsino succeeds in revealing the murder-plot and precipitating the action of the fourth and fifth acts. But he does so inadvertently: the note was not intended to have the effect of exposing the crime to which it alludes. Rather, it is a text which works against its author, in league with the "Power / Which grasped and snapped the threads of my device / And turned it to a net of ruin" (v. i. 81-83). Like Shelley with his reputed "contempt" for the audience (Donohue 181), Orsino aims his deceptions cannily at "the misdeeming crowd / Which judges by what seems" (v. i. 87-88). But in so doing, he is foiled by his own over-subtlety, i. e. a deception from within. He authors a text which, by describing the crime in which he is implicated with euphemistic vagueness ("the atonement of what my nature sickens to conjecture" [IV. iv. 91]), clearly conveys its enormity. The note conceals nothing, but only occults the murder enough to dramatize it, instantly furnishing the Pope's investigator with a likely motive.

What renders Orsino's acts and text so ineffective, or (at the worst) so counter-effective? For the answer, we need perhaps look no further than what Carlson provocatively calls "the tedium of male ambivalence": the divided, struggling or remorseful consciousness at the center of so many romantic "mental dramas" (211). As we have seen, neither Beatrice nor her father is sufficiently independent of "outward circumstances" to embody this model of an over-full interiority. But Orsino, who is neither a scourge nor a scourge's victim, has the leisure to agonize over his own doubleness. Like almost all "romantic actors," Orsino cannot keep himself out of his acting, however he may strive for a cold-blooded mastery of appearances. "Oh fair Beatrice! / Would that I loved thee not . . ." (II. ii. 128-29). Hence he is divided not merely without, between external mask and internal motive, but also within, where the truth of his emotions clashes with his desire to exaggerate and exploit them by feigning. This division lays him open to Giacomo's accusation of *constitutive* falsity: "Thou art no liar? No, / Thou art a lie!" (v. i. 52-53). While Beatrice speaks her piece and dies, Orsino is left mulling over the impact of this word "lie":

> Shall I be the slave
> Of . . . what? A word? which those of this false world
> Employ against each other, not themselves;
> As men wear daggers not for self-offence.
> But if I am mistaken, where shall I
> Find the disguise to hide me from myself,
> As now I skulk from every other eye?
>
> (v. i. 98-104)

Beatrice, we remember, freed her words to perform and "compel" by deciding that only an absent God could make language refer to the true state of affairs. Speaking more like an atheist of 1819, Orsino worries about the power of a word to stick to him. He recognizes that, in "this false world," words like "lie" are "daggers not for self-offence," performing more effectively than they refer. But his own propensity to self-reflection and "self-offence"—the compulsive internal repetition of Giacomo's insult—nonetheless frightens him more than the possibility of offenses or exposures by others. Having a "full" interiority, he can be his own scourge ("where shall I / Find the disguise to hide me from myself . . ."). While Beatrice realizes herself in martyrdom to a purely performative universe, then, Orsino is left in

the ignominious position of soliciting "this false world" as an escape from his intolerable inner life. Like Caleb Williams at the end of that novel, he is compelled to self-negation because he cannot *believe* in the performative tactics which he nonetheless exploits.

Such is the situation of a poet who writes a play intended for a stage and an actor which repel him with their "falsity." But, just as Orsino's "tedious ambivalence" is marginal to the action of *The Cenci,* so I believe I have shown that Shelley's authorial performance is not encompassed by his own version of this particular self-deception. The satire of an overweening "author" in *The Cenci* works against its author's antitheatricalism, as it highlights the efficacy of actor-characters who are *not* divided against themselves. But Shelley goes a little beyond this satire, by reviving modes of acting to which the whole romantic dilemma of imitation and authenticity is foreign. For Beatrice, acting is a means of self-preservation, not self-transformation. Post-Rousseau, we are used to seeing acting as a constant dazzling play of true expression and deceit, self-display and self-concealment. *The Cenci* returns us to a time when nothing could be more distinct than the performance that displays and the performance that conceals: when the former tactic was clearly reserved for the "oppressor" (the self-staging aristocrat) and the latter for the "oppressed" (the hypocrite or sycophant). The Cenci family practices a self-display which has as yet no pathological connotation of "exhibitionism": only the urge to "hide oneself" is ignoble (hence the efforts of both father and daughter to instill this stage-fright in the other). Like Falkland, Beatrice both displays and conceals herself in the courtroom, but this strategy is a pragmatic response to her anomalous "circumstances" as an aristocrat who is also a subaltern (a woman). Her self-conscious, attention-getting, "compelling" rhetoric is designed (like Falkland's) to blind her spectators to the simple fact that she is guilty. Trusting to the traditional distinction between social performance (which makes no truth-claims for itself) and active deception (which does), she plays one against the other, and need not involuntarily betray herself. By contrast, the romantic subject tends to fall into compulsive confession (or "self-offence"), because he or she is convinced, like Rousseau, that speech that is not expressive must be a lie. The atavism of Beatrice's performance consists in her un-"anatomized" assumption that power makes the truth of the subject—at best, God's power; at worst, her father's. She stands as a warning, to those who might seek to escape "this false world" by turning inward, that the actor's profession will endure as long as the realities of oppressor and oppressed do.

Notes

1. "Note on *The Cenci,* by Mrs. Shelley," *Poetical Works of Percy Bysshe Shelley,* ed. Thomas Hutchinson (London: Oxford UP, 1970) 336-37.

2. Stuart Curran, *Shelley's* Cenci: *Scorpions Ringed with Fire* (Princeton, NJ: Princeton UP, 1970) 177.

3. Percy Bysshe Shelley, *The Cenci,* in *Poetical Works* v. ii. line 23. Hereafter cited parenthetically in the text.

4. Joseph W. Donohue, Jr., *Dramatic Character in the English Romantic Age* (Princeton, NJ: Princeton UP, 1970) 177. Hereafter cited parenthetically in the text.

5. Roger Blood, "Allegory and Dramatic Representation in *The Cenci,*" *SiR* [*Studies in Romanticism*] 33. 3 (1994): 362. Hereafter cited parenthetically in the text.

6. Julie Carlson, *In the Theatre of Romanticism: Coleridge, Nationalism, Women* (Cambridge: Cambridge UP, 1994) 192. Hereafter cited parenthetically in the text.

7. Andrea K. Henderson, *Romantic Identities: Varieties of Subjectivity, 1771-1830* (Cambridge: Cambridge UP, 1996) 102-4. Hereafter cited parenthetically in the text.

8. Denis Diderot, "Paradoxe sur le comédien," *Oeuvres esthétiques,* ed. Paul Vernière (Paris: Garnier, 1959) 299-381.

9. Denis Diderot, "The Paradox of Acting," trans. William Archer, *The Paradox of Acting and Masks or Faces?* (New York: Hill and Wang, 1957) 48. For a powerful modern reading which links Diderot's characterless great actor to the Aristotelian notion of mimesis as production (not reproduction), see Philippe Lacoue-Labarthe, "Diderot: Paradox and Mimesis," *Typography: Mimesis, Philosophy, Politics,* ed. Christopher Fynsk (Cambridge, MA: Harvard UP, 1989) 249-66.

10. "Je ne jouai rien: je devins en effet tel que je parus." Jean-Jacques Rousseau, *Les Confessions,* vol. 2 (Paris: Hachette, 1956) Book IX: 105. My translation.

11. William Godwin, *Caleb Williams, or Things as They Are* (New York: Penguin, 1988 [1794]) 5. Hereafter cited parenthetically in the text.

12. Edward Trelawney, *The Last Days of Shelley and Byron* [*The Recollections*], ed. J. E. Morpurgo (Garden City, NY: Anchor Books, 1960) 61. Quoted in Blood 357. My emphasis.

13. *The Journals of Mary Shelley 1814-44,* ed. Paula R. Feldman and Diana Scott-Kilvert, vol. I (Oxford: Clarendon, 1987) 35 (13 October 1814). (The passage is in Shelley's hand.)

14. Curran suggests that, in writing the character of Cenci, Shelley showed that he "understood the potential of Kean's mannerisms," and particularly of Kean's talent for "savage and explosive violence" (169). Henderson agrees that "the loathsomeness of [Kean's] palpably artificial acting would perfectly suit the impersonation of the deliberately theatrical Count" (104).

15. "Note on *The Cenci*" 337.

16. Percy Bysshe Shelley, "Preface to *The Cenci,*" *Poetical Works* 278. My emphasis. Hereafter cited parenthetically as Preface in the text.

17. Joanna Baillie, "Introductory Discourse" to *Plays on the Passions* [1798], *Dramatic and Poetical Works,* 2nd ed. (London: Longman, Brown, Green and Longmans, 1851) 15. Hereafter cited parenthetically in the text.

18. Alan Richardson, *A Mental Theater: Poetic Drama and Consciousness in the Romantic Age* (University Park, PA: Penn State UP, 1988) 112. Hereafter cited parenthetically in the text.

19. Charles Lamb, "On the Tragedies of Shakespeare, Considered with Reference to their Fitness for Stage Representation," *English Romantic Writers,* ed. David Perkins (New York: Harcourt Brace Jovanovich, 1967) 571-72.

20. And there are strong whiffs of "consciousness" even in the mad scene. True to the "self-anatomizing" tendency of her family, Beatrice interrupts her ranting to classify it: "My God! I never knew what the mad felt / Before; for I am mad beyond all doubt!" (III. i. 24-25).

21. Walter Benjamin, *Ursprung des deutschen Trauerspiels, Gesammelte Schriften,* ed. Rolf Tiedemann and Hermann Schweppenhaüser, vol. 1, part 1 (Frankfurt am Main: Suhrkamp, 1974) 351.

22. This is the argument of Blood's compelling essay: in the courtroom, Beatrice exposes her allegorical emptiness.

23. *Prometheus Unbound, A Lyrical Drama,* in *Selected Poetry and Prose of Shelley,* ed. Carlos Baker (New York: Random House, 1951) IV. 570-71.

24. I am mindful, of course, of the difference between "male honor" and "female honor" (chastity): the former supposedly inherent in the subject and the latter (as Carlson points out) alienable from the outside. But Falkland's concept of knightly honor is too archaic to recognize this distinction. Like chastity, it is persistently physical, and hence alienable: "There is a mysterious sort of divinity annexed to the person of a true knight that makes any species of brute violence committed upon it indelible and immortal" (101). Falkland reacts to

Tyrrel's assault as if it were an intimate violation: "He wished for annihilation. . . . Horror, detestation, revenge, inexpressible longing to shake off the evil, and a persuasion that in this case all effort was powerless, filled his soul even to bursting" (100). The more salient difference, then, is that Falkland's honor already struck most of Godwin's readers as an archaism, while the ideology of female chastity had a strong purchase on the minds of Shelley and his readers.

25. A force to which Shelley was not immune. In a review of Godwin's *Mandeville,* he expresses his fascination with Falkland, "whom the author, with that sublime casuistry which is the parent of tolerance and forbearance, persuades us personally to love, whilst his actions must for ever remain the theme of our astonishment and abhorrence" ("On Godwin's *Mandeville," The Complete Works of Percy Bysshe Shelley,* ed. Roger Ingpen and Walter E. Peck, vol. 6 [New York: Gordian P, 1965] 220). The word "casuistry" links this appreciation of Falkland to *The Cenci,* in whose Preface Shelley speaks of "the restless and anatomizing casuistry with which men seek the justification of Beatrice . . ." (276).

26. With occasional exceptions, most notably her defiance of the Judge *after* her conviction: "My pangs are of the mind . . . / . . . / To see . . . / . . . / . . . what a tyrant thou art, / And what slaves these; and what a world we make, / The oppressor and the oppressed . . ." (v. iii. 65, 68, 73-75).

27. We might recall a parallel use of the phrase "mask and mantle" in *A Defence of Poetry,* where it is authors and not characters who are masked. Because it reflects the historical "circumstances" that limit genius, suggests Shelley, the Christian ideology of Dante and Milton is "merely the mask and mantle in which these great poets walk through eternity enveloped and disguised" (*English Romantic Writers,* ed. David Perkins [New York: Harcourt Brace Jovanovich, 1967] 1081).

FURTHER READING

Criticism

Baker, Carlos. "The Human Heart: The Conversation-Poems of 1818-1819." In *Shelley's Major Poetry: The Fabric of a Vision,* pp. 119-53. Princeton, N. J.: Princeton University Press, 1948.

   Analyzes the work as a dialogue-poem in which Shelley discusses his views of morality.

Barcus, James E., ed. *Shelley: The Critical Heritage.* London: Routledge & Kegan Paul, 1975, 432 p.

   Collection of contemporary reviews of Shelley's work including several on *The Cenci.*

Bates, Ernest Sutherland. *A Study of Shelley's Drama The Cenci.* New York: The Columbia University Press, 1908, 103 p.

   Includes sections on composition, criticism, and productions of *The Cenci.*

Brigham, Linda C. "Count Cenci's Abysmal Credit." *Texas Studies in Literature and Language* 38, nos. 3/4 (fall/winter 1996): 340-58.

   Explores corruption during the Restriction Period of 1797 through 1821 and its impact on Count Cenci's career.

Brophy, Robert J. "'Tamar,' *The Cenci,* and Incest." *American Literature* 42, no. 2 (May 1970): 241-44.

   Describes parallels between *The Cenci* and Robinson Jeffers's verse narrative "Tamar."

Cameron, Kenneth Neill. "Shelley as Dramatist." In *Shelley: The Golden Years,* pp. 394-421. Cambridge, Mass.: Harvard University Press, 1974.

   Discusses the structure of the play including specific acts and scenes.

Cantor, Paul A. "'A Distorting Mirror': Shelley's *The Cenci* and Shakespearean Tragedy." In *Shakespeare: Aspects of Influence,* edited by G. B. Evans, pp. 91-108. Cambridge, Mass.: Harvard University Press, 1976.

   Examines Shelley's borrowings from Shakespeare and notes that the two authors had fundamentally different understandings of tragedy.

Cave, Richard Allen. "Romantic Drama in Performance." In *The Romantic Theatre: An International Symposium,* edited by Richard Allen Cave, pp. 79-104. Buckinghamshire, England: Colin Smythe, 1986.

   Presents challenges in writing and performing *The Cenci.*

Clark, David Lee. "Shelley and Shakespeare." *PMLA* 54, no. 1 (March 1939): 261-87.

   Probes the extent of Shelley's knowledge of Shakespeare and his indebtedness to him.

Clarke, George Elliott. "Racing Shelley, or Reading *The Cenci* as a Gothic Slave Narrative." *European Romantic Review* 11, no. 2 (spring 2000): 168-85.

   Finds parallels between *The Cenci* and slave narratives.

Curran, Stuart. *Shelley's Cenci: Scorpions Ringed with Fire.* Princeton, N. J.: Princeton University Press, 1970, 298 p.

Includes sections on characterization, imagery, structure, and resolution.

Curran, Stuart. "Shelleyan Drama." In *The Romantic Theatre: An International Symposium,* edited by Richard Allen Cave, pp. 61-78. Buckinghamshire, England: Colin Smythe, 1986.
 Posits that Shelley's approach to drama was self-reflexive and cautionary.

Donohue, Joseph W., Jr. "Shelley's Beatrice and the Romantic Concept of Tragic Character." *Keats-Shelley Journal* 17 (1968): 53-73.
 Underscores the influence of actress Eliza O'Neill and *La Cenci,* a portrait by Guido Reni.

————. "*The Cenci*: The Drama of Radical Innocence." In *Dramatic Character in the English Romantic Age,* pp. 157-86. Princeton, N. J.: Princeton University Press, 1970.
 Discusses the nature of closet drama and provides a character analysis of Beatrice.

Ferriss, Suzanne. "Percy Bysshe Shelley's *The Cenci* and the Rhetoric of Tyranny." In *British Romantic Drama: Historical and Critical Essays,* edited by Terence Allan Hoagwood and Daniel P. Watkins, pp. 208-28. Cranbury, N. J.: Associated University Presses, 1998.
 Asserts that the play questions whether revolutionary ideals will take hold in Regency England.

Finn, Mary E. "The Ethics and Aesthetics of Shelley's *The Cenci.*" *Studies in Romanticism* 35, no. 2 (summer 1996): 177-97.
 Interprets the play as the means by which Shelley animated Reni's portrait of Beatrice.

Forman, Elsa. "Beatrice Cenci and Alma Murray." *Keats-Shelley Memorial Bulletin,* no. 5 (1953): 5-10.
 Describes the reception of *The Cenci*'s first performance in 1886.

Gates, Eunice Joiner. "Shelley and Calderon." *Philological Quarterly* 16, no. 4 (1937): 49-58.
 Examines the influence of Pedro Calderón de la Barca on Shelley's drama.

Hammond, Eugene R. "Beatrice's Three Fathers: Successive Betrayal in Shelley's *The Cenci.*" *Essays in Literature* 8, no. 1 (spring 1981): 25-32.
 Contends that the play is an indictment of biological fathers, religious fathers, and God the Father.

Hogle, Jerrold E. "The Key to All Tyrannies: From *Laon and Cythna* to *The Cenci*." In *Shelley's Process: Radical Transference and the Development of His Major Works,* pp. 87-166. New York: Oxford University Press, 1988.

Argues that the play questions whether one's life is determined by personal choices or cultural pressures.

Johnson, Betty Freeman. "Shelley's *The Cenci* and *Mrs. Warren's Profession.*" *The Shaw Review* 15, no. 1 (January 1972): 26-34.
 Explores George Bernard Shaw's relationship to *The Cenci.*

Kurtz, Benjamin P. "The Burden of Life and the Moral Victory." In *The Pursuit of Death: A Study of Shelley's Poetry,* pp. 143-213. New York: Oxford University Press, 1933.
 Contends that the play's tragic quality is emphasized by the dual nature of death as punishment and reward.

Langston, Beach. "Shelley's Use of Shakespeare." *The Huntington Library Quarterly,* no. 2 (February 1949): 163-90.
 Finds parallels between the poetry of Shakespeare and Shelley.

Miller, Sara Mason. "Irony in Shelley's *The Cenci.*" *Studies in English* 9 (1968): 23-35.
 Notes the lack of dramatic irony in *The Cenci.*

Milne, Fred L. "Shelley's *The Cenci*: The Ice Motif and the Ninth Circle of Dante's Hell." *Tennessee Studies in Literature* 22 (1977): 117-32.
 Analyzes Dante's influence on Shelley's writing.

Murphy, John V. "The Gothic Sensibility in *The Cenci.*" In *The Dark Angel: Gothic Elements in Shelley's Works,* pp. 152-85. Lewisburg, Pa.: Bucknell University Press, 1975.
 Explains why Shelley was drawn to the Gothic tradition.

O'Neill, Michael. "*The Cenci*: Language and the Suspected Self." In *The Human Mind's Imaginings: Conflict and Achievement in Shelley's Poetry,* pp. 73-91. Oxford: Clarendon Press, 1989.
 Details Shelley's concern with the dependency on audience awareness of language.

Peterfreund, Stuart. "Seduced by Metonymy: Figuration and Authority in *The Cenci.*" In *The New Shelley: Later Twentieth-Century Views,* edited by G. Kim Blank, pp. 184-203. Hampshire, England: Macmillan Academic and Professional Ltd, 1991.
 Defines the change in Beatrice's speech from metonymical to metaphorical.

Richardson, Donna. "The *Hamartia* of Imagination in Shelley's *Cenci.*" *Keats-Shelley Journal* 44 (1995): 216-39.
 Argues that Beatrice's defense is specious.

Scrivener, Michael Henry. "*Prometheus Unbound* in Context (1818-1820)." In *Radical Shelley: The Philosophical Anarchism and Utopian Thought of Percy Bysshe Shelley,* pp. 140-246. Princeton, N. J.: Princeton University Press, 1982.

Provides sketches of the principal characters in terms of their naiveté or self-consciousness.

Steffan, Truman Guy. "Seven Accounts of the Cenci and Shelley's Drama." *Studies in English Literature 1500-1900* 9, no. 4 (autumn 1969): 601-18.

Examines variations in Shelley's source material and discusses the significance of the author's alterations.

Steyaert, Kris. "A 'Massive Dramatic Plum Pudding': The Politics of Reception in the Early Antwerp Performance of Shelley's *The Cenci*. . . ." *Keats-Shelley Journal* 50 (2001): 14-26.

Discusses Dutch criticism of the published work and the stage production by the Royal Dutch Theater in 1929.

Svaglic, Martin J. "Shelley and *King Lear.*" In *Nineteenth-Century Literary Perspectives: Essays in Honor of Lionel Stevenson,* edited by Clyde de L. Ry-

als, pp. 49-63. Durham, N. C.: Duke University Press, 1974.

Comments on Shelley's appreciation of Shakespeare's *King Lear* and its impact on *The Cenci.*

White, Robert L. "'Rappaccini's Daughter,' *The Cenci,* and the Cenci Legend." *Studi Americani,* no. 14 (1968): 63-86.

Provides evidence that Nathaniel Hawthorne was influenced by the Cenci legend and Shelley's telling of it.

Worton, Michael. "Speech and Silence in *The Cenci.*" In *Essays on Shelley,* edited by Miriam Allott, pp. 105-24. Liverpool: Liverpool University Press, 1982.

Presents Shelley's thoughts on the relationship between words, events, and language in the play.

Yost, George. "Shelley's Cooperative Dramatic Overthrows." In *All the World: Drama Past and Present, Volume II: The University of Florida Department of Classics Comparative Drama Conference Papers,* edited by Karelisa V. Hartigan, pp. 125-35. Washington, D. C.: University Press of America, 1982.

Exposes Shelley's critique of father figures in *The Cenci* and *Prometheus Unbound.*

Frank J. Webb
1828?-1894?

American novelist.

INTRODUCTION

Webb was a nineteenth-century African-American novelist whose literary reputation rests on his single novel, *The Garies and Their Friends* (1857). The second earliest novel to be written by an African American, Webb's work traces the lives and misfortunes of two middle-class black families—one of mixed and the other of pure ethnicity—in antebellum Philadelphia. Although most critics have recognized that *The Garies and Their Friends* is a largely mediocre example of the popular nineteenth-century melodramatic novel, they have also pointed out that the work is the first to address a number of key themes and issues that would occupy the black literature movement in the late nineteenth- and early twentieth-centuries. These "firsts" include the sober depiction of racism and segregation in the free North; a graphic account of a racially charged mob riot; the benign portrayal of blacks as middle-class social climbers; and an implicit condemnation of mulattos who cross the color barrier.

BIOGRAPHICAL INFORMATION

Little is known about Webb's life and career. Biographical details are scant and often contradictory given that a number of Frank Webbs flourished at the same time as the author. Nevertheless, literary historians have been able to reconstruct a basic—albeit sometimes hypothetical—outline of Webb's life though his works, contemporary accounts, and government statistical records. Scholars generally believe that Webb was born in Philadelphia in 1828. This date is based on the corroboration of census data and on the fact that Harriet Beecher Stowe describes Webb as "a colored young man, born and reared in the city of Philadelphia" in her preface to his 1857 novel. Although nothing is known about his family or formal education, one census record indicates that he worked as a "designer," leading historians to speculate that he was either a printer or a tailor. More details become known in 1845, when Webb married a mulatto named Mary. In succeeding years, Mary Webb achieved minor fame for her public dramatic readings of Shakespeare and other major poets. Indeed, Stowe

adapted a portion of *Uncle Tom's Cabin* for her use in public readings. Mary made her debut as a dramatic reader in 1855, probably to support her family, given that Webb's business had failed the previous year. In 1856, the Webbs traveled to London where Mary had been engaged to perform her dramatic readings. While there, they became acquainted with members of some of the highest social circles in England. Scholars have speculated that Webb utilized this period of unemployment to write his novel. Indeed, *The Garies and Their Friends* was first published in London by G. Routledge & Co. Around this time, Mary contracted consumption and, after a brief stay in the south of France, the Webbs moved to Jamaica, perhaps assuming that the warmer climate would alleviate Mary's suffering. Once the Webbs settled in Jamaica in 1858, he secured employment as a postmaster in Kingston. Later that year, Mary died.

Contemporary records indicate that Webb remained in Jamaica for several years after Mary's death. During this time, he married a Jamaican native named Mary Rodgers and started a second family. Webb departed from Jamaica in 1869, leaving his family behind while he attempted to reestablish himself in the United States. In the early 1870s, while residing in Washington, D.C., he worked briefly for the Freedman's Bureau before becoming affiliated with *The New Era*. Webb serialized two novellas—*Two Wolves and a Lamb* and *Marvin Hayle*—in the black national periodical in 1870. By 1872 Webb had left Washington and settled in Galveston, Texas. Scholars have been puzzled about why the author made such a drastic move after rekindling his writing career for *The New Era*. This puzzle is complicated by the fact that the details about Webb's life again become murky after his move to Texas. Records indicate that he may have served as the editor of a short-lived radical newspaper before gaining more secure employment in the Galveston post office. Unverified contemporary accounts further suggest that Webb became a teacher and perhaps even a principal after 1880. These accounts also posit that Webb died in Galveston in 1894.

MAJOR WORK

Although it was written at a time when there was intense international scrutiny on the institution of slavery in the American South, *The Garies and Their Friends* does not explicitly deal with this controversial issue; rather, the novel focuses on the lives of free blacks in the North who try to improve their social and economic standing in the face of malevolent, omnipresent racism. Despite the gravity of his subject matter, Webb wrote *The Garies and Their Friends* in the popular literary tradition of the sentimental novel. This genre features such elements as highly melodramatic episodes, one-dimensional characters, and far-fetched coincidences that bind the narrative together. Many critics have pointed out that the limitations of this literary device have obscured the profundity of Webb's literary style and his treatment of complex themes. Indeed, some commentators have suggested that Webb's writing is stylistically similar to Charles Dickens's in its compelling depiction of the urban milieu and the conditions of the working class. Further, some have compared Webb to Horatio Alger for his shrewd insights into the phenomenon of social climbing through the development of astute business skills. Still others have suggested that Webb's perceptive portrayal of children in his novel anticipates Mark Twain's creation of Tom Sawyer and Huckleberry Finn. Webb's pioneering treatment of significant ethnic themes also establishes *The Garies and Their Friends* as perhaps the earliest foray into social realism in the African-American literary tradition. The work is an exposé on the hypocrisy of white values in the North where the fervent advocacy of the abolition of slavery is undermined by virulent bigotry and segregation in their own cities. The novel is also a realistic examination of the complex psychology of blacks who try to assimilate white values and culture through social integration versus those who assimilate through miscegenation and crossing the color barrier by "passing as white." The two prominent families in Webb's novel—the Garies and the Ellises—represent the dichotomy of this psychology. Despite enduring hardship, the ethnically pure Ellises achieve social status and economic prosperity while preserving and cherishing their black ethnicity and culture. By contrast, the racially mixed Garies who attempt to assimilate ethnically with the white majority suffer brutally at the hands of a white mob and become destitute victims of racism from all of the social classes.

CRITICAL RECEPTION

Despite Webb's pioneering treatment of racism and black social mobility in *The Garies and Their Friends,* the novel has remained in obscurity—even in the field of African-American literature. Critics have asserted that while the novel's artificial romantic convention is partly to blame for its neglect, they have also suggested that Webb's discussion of racism was perhaps too blunt for nineteenth-century audiences. Indeed, the work did

not begin to receive serious critical attention until it was published as a reprint in 1969. In his introduction to that edition, Arthur P. Davis was the first modern critic to identify *The Garies and Their Friends* as a ground-breaking examination of the black experience in the antebellum northern United States. Commenting on the novel's surprisingly ambivalent attitude toward slavery, Davis has suggested that Webb might have intended the work to be a "goodwill" book which promises social and economic progress for blacks who demonstrate pride and perseverance in the face of white oppression. R. F. Bogardus has analyzed the implications of this struggle in depth, concluding that Webb pioneered the device of black social realism in his novel. According to Bogardus, Webb's elucidation of such key themes as ethnic pride, ubiquitous racism, miscegenation, and black militancy anticipates many of the crucial issues which will receive fuller analysis in African-American works of the late nineteenth- and early twentieth-centuries. Robert S. Levine has been more skeptical of Webb's influence, arguing that the author presents a questionable moral vision by pragmatically advocating the assimilation of white values and mores so that blacks can attain the American dream. In two studies published in 1997 and 1999, Robert Reid-Pharr has posited that Webb elucidated the concept of "black domesticity" in *The Garies and Their Friends,* which represents "an ideological orientation that emphasizes the family and family life as the wellspring of black economic, political, and social development." According to the critic, Webb maintains that black identity, security, and social improvement all depend on close-knit familial and community relations; by contrast, interracialism and miscegenation are acts which corrupt and weaken this social bond. Reid-Pharr has concluded that Webb ultimately challenges the ideological conception that miscegenation is a viable avenue for racial assimilation and modernization in American society. In addition, Anna Engle has analyzed the connection between ethnic and class status in *The Garies and Their Friends,* noting how Irish immigrants are subjected to many of the same racial prejudice as blacks. Ultimately, Engle has asserted, Webb registers optimism for both ethnic groups in his portrayal of the working-class Irish and the middle-class blacks as active participants in social mobility.

PRINCIPAL WORKS

The Garies and Their Friends (novel) 1857

Marvin Hayle (novella) 1870; published serially in *New Era*

Two Wolves and a Lamb (novella) 1870; published serially in *New Era*

CRITICISM

Harriet B. Stowe (essay date 1857)

SOURCE: Stowe, Harriet B. Preface to *The Garies and Their Friends.* 1857. Reprint, pp. v-vi. New York: AMS Press, 1971.

[*In the following preface to the 1857 edition of Webb's* The Garies and Their Friends, *Stowe characterizes the work as a "simple and truthfully-told story" of the plight of free blacks, emancipated slaves, and fugitive slaves in antebellum Philadelphia.*]

The book which now appears before the public may be of interest in relation to a question which the late agitation of the subject of slavery has raised in many thoughtful minds; viz.—Are the race at present held as slaves capable of freedom, self-government, and progress?

The author is a coloured young man, born and reared in the city of Philadelphia.

This city, standing as it does on the frontier between free and slave territory, has accumulated naturally a large population of the mixed and African race.

Being one of the nearest free cities of any considerable size to the slave territory, it has naturally been a resort of escaping fugitives, or of emancipated slaves.

In this city they form a large class—have increased in numbers, wealth, and standing—they constitute a peculiar society of their own, presenting many social peculiarities worthy of interest and attention.

The representations of their positions as to wealth and education are reliable, the incidents related are mostly true ones, woven together by a slight web of fiction.

The scenes of the mob describe incidents of a peculiar stage of excitement, which existed in the city of Philadelphia years ago, when the first agitation of the slavery question developed an intense form of opposition to the free coloured people.

Southern influence at that time stimulated scenes of mob violence in several Northern cities where the discussion was attempted. By prompt, undaunted resistance, however, this spirit was subdued, and the right of free inquiry established; so that discussion of the question, so far from being dangerous in Free States, is now begun to be allowed in the Slave States; and there are some subjects the mere discussion of which is a half-victory.

The author takes pleasure in recommending this simple and truthfully-told story to the attention and interest of the friends of progress and humanity in England.

Arthur P. Davis (essay date September 1969)

SOURCE: Davis, Arthur P. "*The Garies and Their Friends*: A Neglected Pioneer Novel."[1] *CLA Journal* 13, no. 1 (September 1969): 27-34.

[*In the following essay, Davis emphasizes the significance of Webb's* The Garies and Their Friends *while also elaborating on its shortcomings and the reasons for its neglect.*]

Most students of Negro American literature know *The Garies and Their Friends,* by Frank J. Webb, only from what they have read in Loggins, Bone, and Gloster; and there is not much to be found in these works. Loggins gives the book two and one-half pages; Bone, one; and Gloster, a half page.[2] Moreover, few scholars have been able to read the novel because it is a rare book. There is a copy at Howard University, another at the British Museum, but none in the Library of Congress. There must be at least a few others extant, but obviously not many. And yet, *The Garies and Their Friends* was the *second* novel by an American Negro. The first, William Wells Brown's *Clotel,* was published in London in 1853; Webb's book appeared four years later, 1857, also in London. Why do we know one work so much better than the other?

It is true that *Clotel* is a more sensational story, but *The Garies* is by no means tame; it has plenty of action, and it tells us almost as much about the life of free Negroes in the North as Brown does about slave life in the South. Also, *The Garies* is a better written novel than *Clotel.* Neither, of course, is a masterpiece, but Webb's work technically is superior to that of Brown. In addition, *The Garies* may be credited with several significant "firsts." It is the first work of fiction to describe the lives and problems of free Northern Negroes; the first to *treat with any appreciable depth* the "mixed marriage,"[3] the first to emphasize the middle class slant characteristic of Negro novels down to the 1940's; the first to include a lynch mob in a free state; the first to treat ironically (as Chesnutt would do later) the vagaries of the "color line"; and the first to make "passing for white" a major theme in a novel (as James Weldon Johnson, Nella Larsen, Jessie Fauset, and other New Negro writers would do). In short, this novel anticipates much that appears in later Negro fiction. It is a pioneer work in every sense of the word. Why then has it been so neglected?

Perhaps one reason for the neglect is that we know so little about the author, Frank J. Webb. He doesn't appear in the usual biographical sources like William

Wells Brown's *The Black Man: His Antecedents, His Genius, and His Achievements* (1863) or William J. Simmons' *Men of Mark* (1887). Practically all that we have learned about Webb comes from one source—the prefatory material for **The Garies** written by Harriet Beecher Stowe. Mrs. Stowe had promised a preface to the novel but because of some domestic difficulty did not get it to London at the agreed time. In order not to delay publication, Lord Brougham, the famous English statesman and abolitionist, supplied a prefatory note with material taken from a letter Mrs. Stowe had written to an English friend. Mrs. Stowe's Preface, however, arrived just before publication, and the publishers wisely decided to use both contributions. As a result, we get a generous comment from the author of *Uncle Tom's Cabin*.

Mrs. Stowe tells us that "the author is a coloured young man, born and reared in the city of Philadelphia." Describing Philadelphia as a "frontier" between "free and slave territory," she states that it has "accumulated naturally a population of the mixed and African race." (She means, of course, light and dark-skinned Negroes.) She adds that this "large class" of Negroes constitutes in the Brotherly love City "a peculiar society of their own." Concerning the novel itself, Mrs. Stowe states that "the incidents related are mostly true ones, woven together by a slight web of fiction." From the Stowe letter used by Lord Brougham, we learn that most of the characters in the work are "faithfully drawn from real life and are quite fresh." We learn also that she thought "highly" of **The Garies and Their Friends,** that it had "worth in itself," and that it showed what *free people of colour* do attain, and what they can do in spite of all social obstacles."

There is one additional biographical fact which comes from the work. The novel is dedicated to Lady Noel Byron by her "grateful Friend, The Author." Evidently Webb knew Lady Byron; he probably knew Lord Brougham also. But when and under what circumstances did he meet such persons? Since he was "born and reared" in Philadelphia, he didn't have to go abroad for protection as the ex-slaves Brown and Douglass were forced to do. Why, then, did he go to London? How long did he stay in Europe? Unfortunately, we can't answer these questions.

It is always dangerous to draw biographical data from an author's work; but having so little else to go on in this case, we are inclined to grasp at straws. In 1870, Webb printed in the *New Era* (A Colored American National Journal) published in Washington, D. C., two serialized novelettes, **"Two Wolves and a Lamb"** and **"Marvin Hayle."**[4] The plots need not concern us here, but both stories deal with "high society" life in London, Paris, and Cannes. The characters are sophisticated members of an international set who talk of books, art,

museums, watering-places, gourmet restaurants, and all of the other things that rich and leisured people discuss. One gathers from reading these novelettes that the author had a better than superficial acquaintance with London and Paris, that he was fairly well-read, and that he appreciated so-called "cultural" things and experiences. Hugh Gloster suggests that Webb may have been white.[5] I can understand Dr. Gloster's doubts, but I don't share them. I am convinced, not only by Mrs. Stowe's statement, but also by many small "inner group" attitudes in the novel, that Webb was a Negro—a Negro who was probably fed up with the "Problem" and sought his escape through travel and through writing romantic, high society stories. He was doing in his way what Jean Toomer did after publishing *Cane*.

The plot of **The Garies and Their Friends** concerns the fortunes of two families, one all-Negro, the other "mixed"—the Garies and the Ellises. Mr. Garie, a Southern plantation owner, has a lovely mulatto common-law wife and two beautiful children. Because he couldn't marry a Negro in the South and because his children could, therefore, become slaves if he were to die, Mr. Garie moved his family to Philadelphia. When it is discovered that Mrs. Garie is colored, their troubles start. Garie is lynched by a mob; his pregnant wife dies from shock and terror. The Gary girl stays with Negroes and finally marries the Ellis boy. Clarence the son, reared as white, falls in love, hopelessly in love, with a white girl whom he can't marry after his identity is discovered. The most tragic of tragic mulattoes, he comes back to his people to die the death of a miserable and defeated man. On the other hand, the dark-skinned Ellis family, after several setbacks and a major disaster also caused by the mob—the Ellis family finds comfort and a happiness of sorts in the successful marriages of the three children. The villain of the plot is a "poor white" shyster who was related to Mr. Garie.

The novel tells us a great deal about the lives of free Negroes in a Northern city. We learn about their constant problem with segregated transportation, with their lack of police protection, with their dislike of the antagonistic immigrant Irish, and their difficulties in becoming apprentices even when highly qualified. We are taken into their clean, decorous, and well-run homes, and we attend their correct teas and reading circles. Above all else, we note their efforts to be like the best white people in speech, manner, morality, and business pursuits, especially the latter.

To these Negroes, as to their models the white middle class, money was all-important. The strongest character in the book, Mr. Walters, a black man well on his way to becoming a millionaire, is a dramatic example of the power of money even in a Negro's hands. When a white hotel refuses to serve him, he buys the place and discharges the manager. Because he is wealthy, he can manhandle a crooked white lawyer and get away with it. Walters has the typical American belief in business. On one occasion he advises Mrs. Ellis not to put her son Charlie in service, but to start him off, as whites do their children, by giving him something to sell—like matches. "The boy," he tells her, "that learns to sell matches soon learns to sell other things; . . . he becomes a small trader, then a merchant, then a millionaire" (the fulfillment of the American Dream). Even the poor white villain in the novel recognizes this power of money to make things easier for a Negro. "If I was black," Slippery George said, "living in a country like this, I'd sacrifice conscience and everything else to the acquisition of wealth."

The free Negroes delineated here had pride, but it tended to be more of a class than a race pride. They boasted that they were more literate than the "poor whites," that they took care of their own poor and helped the poor in the other group. They were smugly pleased and proud when whites visiting their homes expressed surprise at the elegance and refinement found. They were inclined to look down on newcomers like the Irish.

But these black Philadelphians would not have understood the present day Black Power position. They were not proud of being black. To them white was right. They not only wanted to be *like* whites; some wanted to *be* white. Though he was a handsome, dark-skinned man, though he had money, Mr. Walters flatly admits that he often wished he were white because in this country Caucasians have an "incalculable advantage." Moreover, he believes that those Negroes who claimed they didn't want to be white were either "liars" or "fools." In another scene, Esther Ellis expresses the same view. Her brother Charlie had just been denied a job because of his color, and she tries to console him. "Charlie, my dear boy," she says, "I'd give my life if it would change your complexion—if it would make you white." Considering the Negro's position at the time—slave in the South and barely a third-class citizen in the North—this attitude is understandable. Mr. Walters, Esther, and their kind didn't have "white fever"; they were simply black realists.

But these Negroes could also hate "whitey" on occasion. After finding out that the mob had crippled their father for life, Caddy Ellis hysterically tells her brother: "Oh, Charlie! What those white devils will have to answer for! When I think how much injury they have done us, I hate them! . . . and I believe God hates them as much as I do!" The reader may feel that she has in mind only those whites who had done the harm, but at another time she says bluntly and unequivocally, "I hate them all." We note that she uses the phrase "white devils." In his *Appeal*, David Walker also calls the whites devils. He, too, felt that God hated whites who oppressed Negroes.

One of the inconsistencies in *The Garies*, or rather one of the inconsistencies in the character of Mr. Walters is his attitude on "passing." Although admitting, as we have seen, that he often wanted to be white, he was bitterly opposed to having Clarence Garie reared as white after the loss of the boy's parents. His impassioned analysis of the unhappiness and agony the "passer" suffers because of insecurity impresses me as coming from a very deep conviction not only on the part of the character, but also on the part of the author. Webb's delineation of Clarence is one of the strongest condemnations of passing in Negro literature. He makes Clarence a weak, lovesick, and at times a thoroughly despicable person; and we somehow feel that the author enjoys what he is doing, that he gets a kind of personal satisfaction out of destroying his own creation. We wonder if Clarence is one of those characters described by Harriet Beecher Stowe as "faithfully drawn from real life." The subject is intriguing.

Equally as intriguing is the author's attitude towards the South. In at least two instances he implies or suggests that the South in certain racial matters was more understanding than the North. Except for the slavery threat which hung over their children, the Garies led a happier life, or at least a more peaceful life in Georgia than in Philadelphia. They certainly had no fear of mob violence in the South. To take another case: Webb shows young Charlie Ellis answering an advertisement which had been placed by a firm owned by two men—one a Yankee, the other a Southerner. Both partners were impressed by the boy's competence, and the Southerner wanted to hire Charlie as an apprentice on the spot. But the Yankee flatly refused. The Southerner was shocked. I don't understand you folks up here, he said in effect; you pay taxes to "educate niggers for these jobs" and then won't take them, whereas in New Orleans—. "Ah," the Northerner interrupted, "but New Orleans is a different place; such a thing never occurred in Philadelphia." Writing in 1857, Webb certainly couldn't be suggesting seriously that the South was a better place for the free Negro than the North. In all probability, he made the ironical comparison to point out the North's hypocrisy.

Actually Webb is not a strong protest writer. *The Garies* has a tendency to be a "goodwill book." Like Booker T. Washington in *Up from slavery*, Webb balances the good and the bad white folks so that they neutralize each other. Slippery George is almost a comic book type villain, bad through and through; but his daughter, Lizzie, is an angelic character who urges the dying father to return the money he swindled from the Garie children. Webb depicts a vicious riot scene in which Mr. Ellis is crippled for life, physically and mentally, but he offsets this evil through the kindness of Mr. and Mrs. Burrell, who sound like white patrons of the Urban League. In order to compensate for opportunities denied to Negroes through prejudice, they decide to "make a want" in their business. One also notes that Webb's allusions to abolition are all timid and ambivalent; and more significantly, that there is nowhere in the book a frontal attack on slavery. The one plantation scene, when the Garies leave the South, could have been written by Thomas Nelson Page. Another curious thing is the absence of real anti-slavery persons that Webb could have woven into his plot or at least into the conversation of his characters. From the national scene he could have taken, among others, David Walker, Douglass, and Garrison; from the local scene, Robert Purvis, James Forten, and Bishop Allen, all well-known Philadelphians and strong civil right fighters. Was he opposed to the radical approach taken by these leaders? Was he really interested in the anti-slavery fight? We don't know; we do know, however, that the work is not the kind of protest novel that one would expect from an intelligent free Negro in 1857. Perhaps its mildness accounts in some measure for its unpopularity.

With its highly contrived plot, its sharp contrasts of right and wrong, its purple patches, its tear-jerking scenes, its deathbed repentances and near-reconciliations, and its happy endings in marriage for the good characters, *The Garies and Their Friends* is typical nineteen century melodrama, a form which Bone thinks is "a natural vehicle for racial protest."[6] Webb also attempted to instill a bit of humor in the work, but he was not too successful. His major comic figure, Kinch, unlike the comic characters in Brown's works, is a Dickens type rather than a blackface minstrel type. Webb's best example of racial humor is a variant of the "fooling Cap'n Charlie" (the white man) kind. In this case, Negro bellmen in a Philadelphia hotel, all of them members of an Underground Railroad Vigilance Committee, raise funds for their work by "Uncle Tomming" for Southern white guests. They pulled a boner and received a tongue-lashing for their efforts when they put on their act for Mr. Winston, a Negro who was "passing" at the time. The Negro characters in the volume are more convincing on the whole than the white, who tend to be stereotypes. The titular characters, Mr. and Mrs. Garie, somehow never come fully alive. Webb is more successful with Mr. Walters; and whether by accident or design (I am not quite certain), he created a truly complex and fascinating character (and symbol) in Clarence, the tragic mulatto.

In spite of its several shortcomings, *The Garies and Their Friends* is an exciting and significant novel. Because of its pioneer position and because it foreshadows later important developments in Negro American fiction, it should be much better known.

Notes

1. This article is an *enlarged* and slightly *altered* version of the introduction written by the author

for the recently issued Arno Press reprint of *The Garies and Their Friends.*

2. Vernon Loggins, *The Negro Author* (New York: Columbia University Press, 1931), pp. 249-251, 309, 439; Robert Bone, *The Negro Novel in America,* rev. ed. (New Haven: Yale University Press, 1965), p. 31; Hugh M. Gloster, *Negro Voices in American Fiction* (Chapel Hill: University of North Carolina Press, 1948), p. 27, 260.

3. William Wells Brown, of course, has mixed marriages but he doesn't make them central to the action of his novel.

4. These novelettes appear in Vol. I, nos. 1-4; 10-15 (Jan.-Feb.; Mar.-April, 1870) in the *New Era.*

5. Gloster, p. 260.

6. Bone, p. 24.

James H. DeVries (essay date December 1973)

SOURCE: DeVries, James H. "The Tradition of the Sentimental Novel in *The Garies and Their Friends.*" *CLA Journal* 17, no. 2 (December 1973): 241-49.

[*In the following essay, DeVries argues that Webb's examination of Northern racism in* The Garies and Their Friends *is thematically incompatible with the conventions of the sentimental novel.*]

First published in London in 1857, Frank J. Webb's *The Garies and Their Friends* is the second novel written by a black American and the first to consider the problems of free blacks in a Northern city. This pre-Civil War novel generally ignores the evils of slavery and instead focuses on the malevolence of Northern racism. In her "Preface" to *The Garies* Harriet Beecher Stowe recommends ". . . this simple and truthfully-told story to the attention and interest of the friends of progress and humanity in England." This indicates that Webb probably wrote the novel for a readership similar to that of numerous novels protesting the degradation of the working class during England's industrial revolution. Preceding Webb's novel there were numerous English protest novels utilizing the well-established conventions of the sentimental novel such as Mrs. Trollope's *Michael Armstrong, The Factory Boy* (1840), Mrs. Touna's *Helen Fleetwood* (1844), Disraeli's *Sybil* (1845), and Dickens' *David Copperfield* (1850), *Bleak House* (1853), and *Hard Times* (1854).

We accept the use of the sentimental novel to communicate the degradation of working-class whites in Nineteenth-Century England, but according to Jean Fagan Yellin, we are inclined to see the sentimental novel as a poor "vehicle" for communicating the "black experience."[1] This may not have been the main reason for *The Garies'* lack of popularity at the time of its original publication. It is worth noting that William Wells Brown's *Clotel* (London, 1853), the first black American novel, improved in popularity in America as its subject matter and style became increasingly sentimental. The first edition of *Clotel* frontally assaults slavery in an uneven style of narrative prose, poetry, and energetic polemic. This *Clotel* combines the conventions of the sentimental novel with militant protest, biting sarcasm, and stark realism. It is easy for us today to identify with the first edition's realism and irony and to understand the more forceful aspect of its message.

But later, more sentimental editions were the most popular at the time of their original publication. *Clotel* went through two new editions before the Civil War ended and one after the war, and it was revised and retitled each time. With each revision the North was further exonerated of racism (the third edition was sold to Union soldiers, evidently to help improve their morale), and the novelist adopted more and more of the conventions of the sentimental novel. We may tentatively assume, then, that the subject of *The Garies*—Northern racism—was the primary cause of its lack of popularity rather than the use of the conventions of the sentimental novel.

Conversely, one might also assume that the sentimental novel technique enhanced rather than decreased reader interest. Although there are no indications that *The Garies* was ever serialized, some chapters form episodes which leave the reader in suspense until the next chapter. As in most melodramas, the climactic events are elaborately foreshadowed in earlier ones. Furthermore, *The Garies* has its share of melodramatic scenes such as the death of Mrs. Garie as the result of childbirth and exposure to the cold, and the destruction of Mr. Ellis' self-respect when his hands are maimed in the riot. The novel has numerous sentimental partings and reconciliations, and its share of death-bed repentances. Toward the end of the story all the good people, with one exception, are properly rewarded with marriage and good fortune while the villain is suitably punished. The entire plot encourages comparison of the relatively fortunate all-black family, the Ellises, with the ill-fated Garie family, composed of a white Southerner and his mulatto wife and children.

The plot is not necessarily a recapitulation of actual events but may have been constructed to expound upon particular moral issues. As Myron Brightfield indicates, any Victorian who desired factual accounts of social problems could consult other sources.[2] The readers of *The Garies* were reading mainly for pleasure although many probably had philanthropic inclinations. These readers probably needed to be informed in bold outlines

of the nature of American racism, and since the readers were already trained to understand and vicariously experience such melodrama, it would be the appropriate vehicle. Also, this melodrama anticipates and accentuates the tragedies of the "good" characters in order to evoke reader sympathy.

Yet there is a tendency for us now to perceive melodrama as reducing moral issues to a simple-minded dichotomy of "good" and "bad" characters. Arthur P. Davis, the only critic to evaluate *The Garies* in some detail, lists its melodramatic characteristics as among the faults of the novel.[3] As Davis observes, *The Garies* does have its share of over-simplified moralization, but actually the melodramatic caricatures communicate complex observations about white racism. In fact, Webb does not construct the characters' personalities strictly according to whether they are prejudiced against blacks. Thus, we find compassionate bigots and inconsiderate abolitionists. Like Dickens, Mrs. Gaskell, and other sentimental writers, Webb believes that good heartedness is the most important, though not the only, ingredient necessary to correct the ills of society. Mrs. Bird befriends Charlie Ellis because her own son had died tragically. Similarly, Mr. Burrell, another color-blind white, later hires Charlie as an apprentice because his wife encourages him to see Charlie as their own son. "I was trying to imagine, Burrell, how I should feel if you, I, and baby were coloured; I was trying to place myself in such a situation. Now we know that our boy, if he is honest and upright—is blest with great talent or genius—may aspire to any station in society that he wishes to obtain."[4] In both the case of Mrs. Bird and the Burrells, filial love binds the black and white in the common goal of raising the next generation.

Webb is not implying that affection is all that is needed. Wrong attitudes, lack of knowledge, and the evil intentions of others often counter the goodheartedness. Mr. Garie's Uncle John, a white Southern gentleman, plays the role of the indulgent uncle by giving the Garie children toys and making them stuff themselves at dinner. Yet one of Uncle John's arguments for the Garies' remaining on the plantation contradicts his own personal feelings about Emily and his niece and nephew: "As long as you live here in Georgia you can sustain your present connection with impunity, and if you should ever want to break it off, you could do so by sending her and the children away . . ." (100). In terms of Southern values, Uncle John is presenting the only reasonable solution—to remain in Georgia. His learned attitude that black people are little more than animals overrides his avuncular affection.

North of the Mason-Dixon line, well-intentioned and good-hearted whites are often forced to conform to the prejudice of others. Miss Jordan's anti-abolitionism does not stifle her natural affection for the Garie children, but her affection for the Garie children does them little good. Since Miss Jordan is not particularly strong-willed or financially secure, she must succumb to the influential Mrs. Stevens' demands to dismiss the Garie children. Economic pressure also forces Mr. Blatchford, an abolitionist printer faced with a contractual deadline, not to hire Charlie Ellis when his white employees refuse to work with a black man.

Other Northern whites of good will fail because they do not realize the impact of racial bigotry. Mr. Balch underestimates the pressures that Clarence Garie will be subjected to by passing. Mr. Garie, however, is the prime example of the white man who is unable to comprehend the malevolence of racism. Though he is the victim of the riots, ideologically he is a Southern gentleman:

> He was a Southerner in almost all his feelings, and had never a scruple respecting the ownership of slaves. But now the fact that he was the master as well as father of his children, and that whilst he resided where he did it was out of his power to manumit them; that in the event of his death they may be seized and sold by his heirs whoever they might be, sent a thrill of horror through him. He had known all this before, but it had never stood out in such bold relief until now [that Emily was again pregnant]
>
> (56).

At the opening of the novel we see his compassion and respect for his wife and children and his kindness to his slaves. He is shocked by the degeneracy of some whites who applied for the job of overseer and relieved when he found a sympathetic and just man for the position. His slaves actually have tears in their eyes when he leaves.

Making Garie a slaveholder strengthens rather than weakens the point that is made by his persecution and death in the North. If he had any tendency toward abolitionism, one could see his death as a logical outcome of the prejudices of other white Philadelphians. Garie is neither philanthropic nor morally righteous; he does not have the purity of the crusader. His death later in the story cannot be martyrdom for the cause of abolitionism.

It is because Garie is not an idealist and because he is a man with strong familial ties that his portrait is compelling—especially to the white reader. He is not to me, as he is to Davis, a character which "somehow never seem[s] to come fully alive."[5] It may be Mr. Garie's rigidity, his failure to respond to the prejudice about him, which Davis finds uninteresting.

Mr. Garie's ignorance is tragic. He is warned by Mr. Winston and by Uncle John of the disadvantages of living in the North with his mulatto wife. He himself intellectually realizes that it may be dangerous for him and his family. Emotionally he is exempt from pain: it is as if he believes he has a protective armor about him because he is white.

In his last moments his first response is to close his eyes; to respond with disbelief. He is so naive as to assume that the commotion outside his window was made by firemen. When they come so close that he can understand their cries, he responds with incredulity, "It's a mob—and that word Amalgamationist—can it be pointed at me? It hardly seems possible; and yet I have a fear that there is something wrong" (221). Moments before his death he cannot believe that someone would wish to harm him simply because he has a black wife. He is still a Southern gentleman who expects no one to judge what he does because he is white.

The deadly serious story of Mr. Garie, a Southern aristocrat, is contrasted by the extended comic portrait of Mrs. Thomas, a Northern aristocrat. Mrs. Thomas vainly tries to cover her age with a wig and powder, and her stomach rebels against the French food she serves to impress her society guests. During the day when no guests are expected, she dresses in a dirty, ragged dressing gown. Between her parties she spends her time managing her servants and spying to catch them in idleness.

The most compelling white character of *The Garies* is Mr. George Stevens, alias Slippery George, the villain of the story. Involved in crooked law practices that no one else would dare to execute, Slippery George is both literally and figuratively a Philadelphia lawyer.

With an almost Dickensian eye for caricature through physical detail, Webb gives a full physical description of Stevens before he enters into the action of the story. He is above "middle height, with rounded shoulders, and long, thin, arms, finished off by disagreeable-looking hands" (124). His head is bald on top with tufts of reddish-gray hair which stick up on the sides like horns. His face reveals the most about his personality: "His baldness might have given an air of benevolence to his face, but for the shaggy eyebrows that overshadowed his cunning-looking grey eyes. His cheekbones were high, and the cadaverous skin was so tightly drawn across them, as to give it a very parchment-like appearance. Around his thin compressed lips there was a continual nervous twitching, that added greatly to the sinister aspect of his face" (124). His physical weakness suggests that he has perverted his natural affection for people; the nervous twitching foreshadows his madness at the end of the story; the cadaverous skin symbolizes that he is dead inside; and, of course, the "horns" represent his demonic nature. In line with sentimental portraiture, Stevens has at least one good quality—his love for his family.

He also has one monomania, his unreasoning hatred of blacks. His contempt for black people is what mainly motivates his revenge against Mr. Garie when he discovers that his next-door neighbor is married to a black woman. Rather than openly oppose Mr. Garie, Slippery George organizes a riot of Irish immigrants in order to murder Mr. Garie in addition to harassing blacks and destroying some of their homes.

The general riot is planned with the hope that the residents of the black neighborhood and the surrounding area will sell their homes at a reduced price. Stevens hopes to resell them at their usual valuation at a later date, after things have quieted down. *The Garies* emphasizes the economic motives of white conspiracies against blacks long before black militancy condemned exploitation in the ghetto.

The Irish themselves are left strangely in the background of the story, indicating, perhaps, that Webb wanted them to be the victims of circumstance. Stevens forces a murderer, McCloskey, to actually lead the Irish so that he himself is not directly involved. He holds this murderer in his power by threatening to reveal incriminating evidence. When McCloskey cannot bring himself to kill Mr. Garie, the diabolical Stevens takes the gun from McCloskey and kills his neighbor point blank. Shortly after Garie's murder, Stevens discovers he is remotely related to Garie, and hence qualifies for his inheritance.

The caricature of Slippery George Stevens represents the clandestine aspects of Northern racism. While in the South the conflict between the races is overt; Northern racism is a conspiracy. Those with the political power or the chicanery of Slippery George can manipulate the prejudice of the working class against black people to further their own ends.

Davis makes a statement which ignores the impact of Stevens' actions: "Webb, like Booker T. Washington in *Up From Slavery,* balances the good and the bad white folks so that they neutralize each other. He depicts a vicious riot scene in which Mr. Ellis is crippled for life mentally and physically, but he offsets this evil through the kindness of Mr. and Mrs. Burrell."[6] The kindness of the Burrell's—a job for Charlie Ellis—will not repay a man crippled for life. Davis does not mention the other effects of the riot: the deaths of the Garies, the pain and sorrow, and the people left homeless. If Webb had presented a balance between good and bad whites, the effects of prejudice would be canceled out. Obviously they are not.

What Webb does do is give a catalogue of white types: the Southerner, the Northern aristocrat, the genuinely philanthropic individuals, the white man limited by his own blindness about racism, the white man pressured

by economic conditions. These pictures, unrealistic "stereotypes" though they may be, do provide an insight into how Webb, one black man, may have perceived white people.

Davis correctly asserts that the blacks in the novel have assimilated white values of success. Their way of life is so similar to that of whites that it is difficult to realize that one is reading about black people.

The domesticity of the Ellises entails a sentimental caricature of the family members. We see Mrs. Ellis, the typical worrying mother; Esther, the oldest daughter, practical and assuming much of the responsibility; and Caddy, a comic paragon of domestic tidiness. Above all, there is Charlie Ellis, a black Tom Sawyer whose mischief is both delightful and exasperating, and whose precocious intelligence and initiative make him a perfect Afro Horatio Alger. Charlie has his own Huckleberry-like friend, Kinch DeYounge. They participate in childhood fantasies such as marking a certain board fence with skull and crossbones to tell the other that he has already gone to school. Kinch, like the later Huck, aids Charlie in his mischievous rebellion against his parents.

Though the larger portion of the novel is concerned with the Ellises, the most imposing black of the novel is Mr. Walters, the black millionaire. According to Davis, the black people in *The Garies* try to emulate the white man not only by striving for economic success but also by imitating the white man's life style and moral code: "To Mr. Walters, white was right; and though he was a very handsome black man, he admits that he often wished to be white because in America the whites had an 'incalculable advantage.'"[7] However, Mr. Walters makes this confession to Mr. Balch, who is white, in order to make his argument against Clarence's passing more persuasive: "'Often I have heard men of colour say they would not be white if they could—had no desire to change their complexions: I've written some down fools; others, liars. Why,' continued he, with a *sneering expression of countenance* [italics mine], 'it is everything to be white . . .'" (275). Possibly he is sneering because he realizes that he cannot be white; probably he is expressing his disgust about white supremacy. This latter interpretation is more consistent with the sarcasm that follows: "one feels that [white is right] at every turn in our boasted free country, where all men are upon an equality" (275).

The description of the Ellises' everyday life, our visits at the teas, their interests in libraries and museums, Caddy's constant strife about tidiness, Charles' precocious knowledge of Chaucer—and many other such details may be Webb's efforts to convince his white audience of the desire of Philadelphia blacks to "better themselves." Webb evidently felt that a description of their black culture would only point out the differences between the Philadelphia blacks and the English working class and thus undermine his use of the sentimental novel techniques. We can conclude that the picture of the Ellises and Mr. Walters is valid for some blacks of Philadelphia, for Mrs. Stowe calls **The Garies** a "truthfully-told story." That **The Garies** is a representative picture of Philadelphia blacks though, is doubtful. Even the language used seems to be tailored for the white audience. Only Aunt Rachel, the irascible but servile cook in Mrs. Thomas' household, speaks black dialect. All the others speak a stilted, rather pompous, Victorian prose. In short, most blacks in the novel bear the trappings of white culture. Whether this was done to enable the white readers to easily identify with the blacks or whether the blacks of that city had not yet developed a strong racial identity is impossible to discover.

Notes

1. Jean Fagan Yellin, "Preface" to William Wells Brown's *Clotel, or, The President's Daughter* (New York: Arno Press, Inc., 1969), p. vi.

2. Myron F. Brightfield, "Introduction" in Mrs. Gaskell's *Mary Barton* (New York: Norton and Company, 1958), p. v.

3. Arthur P. Davis, "New Preface" in Frank J. Webb's *The Garies and Their Friends* (New York: Arno Press, Inc., 1969), pp. xii-xiii. Robert A. Bone's *The Negro Novel in American* (New Haven: Yale University Press, 1958) and Hugh M. Gloster's *Negro Voices in American Fiction* (Chapel Hill: University of North Carolina Press, 1948) provide very short critiques of *The Garies*.

4. Frank J. Webb, *The Garies and Their Friends* (1857; rpt. New York: Arno Press, Inc., 1969), p. 302. Subsequent references to this edition will appear in the text.

Webb uses a number of devices similar to Dickens which attack social evils not necessarily related to racism. A device which both Dickens and Webb frequently use is giving characters names which suggest their noticeable attributes. Dr. Blackly refuses to marry the white Mr. Garie to his black common-law wife (136). A Southern lawyer, evidently often a prosecution lawyer or counsel to reclaim run-away slaves, is named Mr. Ketchum. The black Aunt Comfort attends the sick (246), while Lord Cutanrun had to do just that to get out of an embarrassing situation (75). Topically related to Dickens' writing is Webb's disdain for the people who join philanthropic organizations but who do not realize that charity begins at home. For instance, Mrs. Stevens hires "a little servant" for philanthropic reasons but later persecutes her next-door neighbors because their family is part black and part white (154). In *Bleak House* Dickens devotes several chapters to Mrs. Jellyby, who lets her children go in rags while she campaigns for missions in Africa. Furthermore, Webb's comments about the calloused hospital attendant who knew the patients only by number resembles Dickens' hostility toward unfeeling bureaucratic functionaries. Furthermore, like Dickens, Webb focuses on the legal profession for his most vituperative satire. For instance, in Dickens' works we see Jaggers of *Great Expectations* and Tulkinghorn of *Bleak House*.

5. Davis, p. xiii.

6. Davis, p. xi.

7. Davis, pp. ix-x.

R. F. Bogardus (essay date summer 1974)

SOURCE: Bogardus, R. F. "Frank J. Webb's *The Garies and Their Friends*: An Early Black Novelist's Venture Into Realism." *Studies in Black Literature* 5, no. 2 (summer 1974): 15-20.

[*In the following essay, Bogardus maintains that Webb's* The Garies and Their Friends *transcends popular nineteenth-century melodramatic literary conventions to become a sophisticated literary exercise in social realism.*]

In *The Negro Novel in America*, Robert A. Bone asserts that the black American writer remained tied to romanticism until the 1920's.[1] That view is largely true and, as such, only partly misleading. But Bone's opinion that Frank J. Webb's **The Garies and Their Friends**[2] is exclusively a Negro shopkeeper's melodrama is not merely misleading, it is wrongheaded.[3] On the contrary, a sensitive reading of Webb's novel within the context of nineteenth century American literature proves it to be far more than that: it is a transitional work which broke with a corrupted romantic tradition and sought to become realism. Instead of failing to equal—in Bone's words—"the incipient social realism of Howells,"[4] Webb anticipated that movement. Though his novel is often burdened by pretentious language, conventional values and aspirations, and a somewhat mechanical plot, it transcends popular melodrama and becomes an early and partly successful attempt at literary realism. And it is in this accomplishment that the literary importance of the novel lies.

Let me again caution the reader that Webb's realism is only incipient. He was, after all, partly a child of a nineteenth century romantic tradition that often degenerated into melodramas and genteel romances. These vulgarizations constituted a literature of the fantasized hopes and dreams of a growing middle class society.[5] The conventional ideas, the moral and economic values, and the emotional attitudes of that world were portrayed—never challenging the audience to question this ethical system or disturbing their belief in its rightness. This system was personified through shallow characterization and stock, but usually ridiculous, plot situations—containing unbelievable, though predictable, heroes, heroines, and villains. Usually, these unlikely facts were shrouded by over-emotional presentation, abundant action, and pretentious language. Thereby, common reality was avoided, and the audience was both affirmed and inspired.

Realism, however, is a very different thing. If melodrama and genteel romance are a literature of middle class fantasy and convention, realism is the literature of actuality and questioning. American realism evolved slowly, of course, its elements being present in such early works as Whitman's *Leaves of Grass* (1855) and DeForest's *Miss Ravenal's Conversion* (1867). And mostly, it grew out of the bitterness and upheaval of the post-Civil War world, for the Gilded Age could not be ignored by pragmatic intellectuals and artists. "American writers," Jay Martin tells us, "were thus committed during this period to the absorption of the new conditions of culture into a systematized consciousness. They were obliged not to experiment for the sake merely of a delight in aesthetic advance, but in order to make a literature that could truly reflect the actualities by which they and their fellows lived."[6] Thus, realism evolved into a literature that observed life firsthand, presenting reality as it was, cutting to the core of its truths. Unlike melodrama and genteel romance, it strove to be critical of the dominant conventions and values of its day—often earning it a hostile audience. And it did these things with as little authorial intrusion as possible, letting the characters and events reveal their truths.

The plot of **The Garies and Their Friends** revolves around two families, the Garies and the Ellises. The Ellises are a black Philadelphia family, striving to enter the middle class. The Garies are a mixed couple: Clarence is a white southern aristocrat, and Emily is a lovely mulatto, whom Clarence owns and lives with on his Georgia plantation. They have two white-looking children. Subsequently, Clarence moves his family to Philadelphia, so that Emily and the children may be freed. The Ellises and Mr. Walters help the Garies find accommodations and become their friends. But instead of the good life promised by migration to the North, Clarence and Emily meet brutal deaths at the hands of white rioters. The riot has been contrived by Mr. Stevens, the Garies' neighbor, and some business associates who hope to profit on the real estate they plan to buy cheaply from riot-frightened blacks. When Stevens learns that

Clarence is his first cousin, he also directs the riot leaders to attack the Garie home, having the Garies killed in order to be the sole heir to the Garie fortune.

After the riot, the lives of the Ellises, Mr. Walters, and the Garie children are traced. Emily Garie remains with the Ellises, and eventually marries Charlie Ellis. Little Clary, however, is sent off to New England to be raised as a white by a kind spinster. In Philadelphia, particular attention is given to Charlie Ellis, who pursues his education and seeks an apprenticeship in printing. After being rebuffed many times because of his race, Charlie finally secures a position and succeeds. But things do not work out well for Clary, who has grown up "passing" as a white gentleman. While engaged to a New York socialite, he is exposed as being "A COLOURED MAN,"[7] whereupon he is immediately rejected by his fiancee and her family. Eventually, he dies of consumption (and a broken heart)—but reconciled with his sister. In the meantime, Stevens has been exposed and dies, and the stolen inheritance is returned to its rightful heirs.

Clearly, the plot is melodramatically creaky. Many of the coincidences are preposterous. And when examining certain details, we find the novel's melodramatic devices even balder than the plot implies. The riot conspiracy, for instance, is too smoothly created and executed, and we wince when it is uncovered in advance by Walters. Moreover, the descriptive language is often too ponderous, and authorial intrusions interfere with the novel's continuity. And, though the dialogue is often accurately recorded, it, too, occasionally rings false. Finally, as Bone argues,[8] Webb's characterization is often flat. Some characters are little more than embarrassingly one-dimensional stereotypes. Good ones are described as having attractive physical characteristics while evil ones are pictured as unattractive. And many whites, particularly, are unconvincing.

If what I have so far discussed is all there is to Webb's book, I have little to argue about with the critics. But there is a more compelling reason why I believe the novel partially succeeds in becoming a realist work. **The Garies and Their Friends** not only succeeds in bringing some reality to the dialogue but, more importantly, it subjects the conventions and values of its day to a disparagingly critical scrutiny and utilizes certain characters to illustrate the complex psychology of the black mind. In doing these things, Webb proves to possess far shrewder insights regarding the complexity of his society and fellow human beings than has been recognized. For in addition to openly dealing with miscegenation, the author lays open the North's prejudices at a time when most criticism was being directed towards the South. Webb exposes its bigotry and segregation, lampoons white genteels social climbing, probes and questions the "white is right" attitude of both blacks and whites, sees through "the plantation myth" South, comprehends the destructive psychology implicit in "passing," and introduces the first black militant into literature. And though he does seem to applaud the seeking of economic success, his acceptance of this middle class convention is not so worshipful as it is pragmatic.

The North has always tended to think itself superior to the South regarding racial matters. Of course, this has been a mendacious self-conceit. Race hatred and segregation have always existed among all levels of northern society—from the most genteel to the lowest classes. Webb understood this and his novel holds the North up to critical examination. We see the conscious bigotry of Mrs. Bird's white servant: "'What on earth can induce you to want to eat with a nigger?'" (p. 141). And it is expressed by the middle class, socialclimbing Mrs. Stevens: "'ever since Mr. Stevens purchased our house we have been tormented with the suspicion that Walters would put a family of niggers in this; and if there is one thing in this world I detest more than another, it is coloured people, I think'" (p. 129). But Webb does not stop with conscious racism. He shows us the more unconscious variety, making us fully aware that it is just as vicious and destructive as the other kind. When the genteel Mrs. Thomas urges Mrs. Ellis to permit Charlie to become a servant, Mrs. Ellis responds that her husband wishes Charlie to complete school. So Mrs. Thomas admonishes her:

> "Nonsense, nonsense, Ellen! If I were you, I wouldn't hear of it. There won't be a particle of good result to the child from such acquirements. It isn't as though he was a white child. What use can Latin or Greek be to a coloured boy? None in the world—he'll have to be a common mechanic, or, perhaps, a servant, or barber, or something of that kind, and then what use would all this fine education be to him? Take my advice, Ellen, and don't have him taught things that will make him feel above the situation he, in all probability, will have to fill."
>
> (p. 25)

These attitudes are made concrete by Webb's depiction of how blacks of his day were discriminated against and segregated in almost every facet of public and private existence. And in doing so, he again attacks and exposes all levels of white society. The Garies, for instance, seek to marry when they arrive in Philadelphia, but they are confronted by the racism of a prominent white minister who refuses to marry them. Later, as if to bring the poor Garies full circle, Clarence's white lawyer is told by the Walters that the dead Mr. and Mrs. Garie will not be allowed a burial in a white cemetery. After the lawyer registers amazement, Walters ironically comments, "'why should you be astonished at such treatment of the dead, when you see how they conduct themselves towards the living?'" (p. 233).

The ugliness of segregation is given deeper dimension by showing what happens when its dictates are challenged. To illustrate this, Webb creates a particularly nasty scene. On a train, in which Mrs. Bird (a gentle, white patroness) and Charlie Ellis are riding, the conductor orders Charlie to ride in another car. When Mrs. Bird responds that Charlie has been sick and cannot go, the conductor retorts: "'I don't care whether he's sick or well—he can't ride in here. We don't allow niggers to ride in this car. . . .'" (p. 110). Mrs. Bird refuses to give in, and the crowd gets meaner: "'Why don't you hustle the old thing out,' remarked a bystander . . .' she is some crack-brained abolitionist. Making so much fuss about a little nigger! Let her go into the nigger car—she'll be more at home there'" (p. 111). Mrs. Bird finally agrees to go and upon entering the car, finds it wretched: "'I would not force a dog to ride in such a filthy place'" (p. 112). Nevertheless, she stays.

An even uglier example of the brutality of racism is provided by the riot scene. Though it is instigated for private economic gain by Stevens, he finds it fairly easy to provoke because of the bigotry of the working class Irish participants. Recognizing reality, Webb plausibly works into the plot the anti-black hostility of this class—itself close to the bottom and uncertain in status. And the major riot is made believable by previous sporadic clashes between whites and blacks. After the riot plan is discovered, Walters tries to get the authorities to act against it—but to no avail, for the authorities have persistently overlooked the incidents from the beginning, thereby tacitly condoning them. When the riot breaks out, its viciousness is fully exposed. The rioters use clubs, stones, and guns; they beat up men and women, ransack homes, and set fires. It is in the riot that Mr. Ellis is beaten and disabled for life by a gang of whites who catch him while he is trying to warn the Garies of the danger.

Webb's attack on white values and behavior is as broad as it is blunt, excluding no one—not the white clergy, the genteel middle class, or the authorities. Even the abolitionists are not spared. When Charlie is given an apprenticeship by a leading Abolitionist, Mr. Blatchford, the employees refuse to work with him because he is black. In order to save his business from ruin—which a walkout would have caused—Blatchford sacrifices his principles and lets Charlie go.

Webb's attitude towards the racial situation, though, is more complex than some of these examples may at first glance suggest. For while he attacks the racism of the genteel classes, he recognizes that a Mrs. Bird can and does exist. While an Abolitionist caves in at the moment of truth, Webb illustrates exactly how hated they are and, by implication, how courageous they must be. And finally, even though the Ellis and Walters families are said to live happily ever after, Webb is not naive about the future of the free black in America. When Mrs. Ellis says "'I do hope I shall live to see the time when we shall be treated as civilized creatures,'" Walters replies, sardonically, "'I suppose we shall be so treated when the Millennium comes . . . not before I'm afraid'" (p. 64).

Clearly, Webb knew that blacks lived in a world where white values dominated. He portrays blacks who find themselves in the schizophrenic situation of being brutalized and rejected by the white world at the same time they are expected—and expect themselves—to aspire to assimilation into it. The cruelest example of this dilemma is the decision to have Clary "pass for white." Walters opposes this, for he knows Clary will always "'live in constant fear of exposure; this dread will embitter every enjoyment, and make him the most miserable of men'" (p. 275). And yet Walters, himself, cannot deny—albeit ironically—the advantage of being white: "'I admit . . . that in our land of liberty it is of incalculable advantage to be white . . . and no one is more painfully aware of it than I'" (p. 275). So, he acquiesces, and Clary grows up white. Of course, Walters is right. Not only is Clary plagued by the predicted fear of discovery, but he consciously degrades himself doubly. His fiancee's family, he says, "'seem to have the deepest contempt for coloured people; they are constantly making them a subject of bitter jests . . . and . . . I, miserable, contemptible, falsehearted knave . . . I join them in their heartless jests, and wonder all the while my mother does not rise from her grave and *curse* me as I speak'" (p. 325). It is a tragic situation indeed. Clary is incapable of restoring his integrity by proudly revealing his ancestry, while the fear of discovery and burden of guilt over his self-denial destroy him.

This ambivalence is illustrated elsewhere through the use of irony. When Mrs. Thomas makes her condescending offer to take on Charlie as a servant, Mrs. Ellis deferentially listens. Yet while she accepts the white world's wishes for her son, he does not. Through Charlie's behavior, Webb makes this clear. Charlie succeeds in forcing Mrs. Thomas to send him home—very much at the expense of her, and the genteel white world's, dignity. Webb's Charlie does everything wrong, usually with purpose and humor. For instance, after Mrs. Thomas instructs Charlie to tell visitors that she is not at home—a practice she thinks fashionable—he admits an English lord into the parlor. Mrs. Thomas turns around with a bowl of dirty water in her hands. Thinking the lord is a servant, she orders, "'Here, take this'" (p. 75). But when she looks up and sees the lord, she drops the pan on him and the carpet and rushes from the room embarrassed and angry. Another time, Mrs. Thomas is described at one of her dinner parties as being a ludicrous snob. Indeed, her comeuppance occurs at one of these pompous affairs. While serving, Charlie succeeds in knocking off her wig. To her extreme embarrassment

and the muffled amusement of her guests, she restores the wig backwards on her gray stubbled head. Mortified, she storms out of the room, accompanied by the unconstrained laughter of the guests. Charlie has triumphed, and he goes home.

Though Webb mocks the genteel white social world, Bone accuses him of possessing a shopkeeper's soul because of his supposed approval of the white middle class success ethic.[9] Walters is seen particularly to embody this ethic, but other characters are not exempted from its taint. Mr. Ellis does strive to earn modest respectability for his family, and Charlie secures a position in which he believes he can succeed. But this point of view oversimplifies Walters in particular, and the position of the mid-nineteenth century northern black middle class in general. Arthur P. Davis suggests—correctly, I think—that success-seeking was a more pragmatic proposition for the black than for the white.[10] Certainly this is true in Webb's novel when contrasted with works by Horatio Alger. In Alger's books, business success is put forth as a moral duty which one has to fulfill in order to become a good man. Thus, success is elevated to the level of morality and, finally, mythologized. But Webb does not worship success.

To begin with, it is interesting to note that almost all the businessmen in the novel are ruthless—even Walters, at times. They are also greedy: Recall the unprincipled creation of the riot in order to secure real estate profits.[11] Alger's successful businessmen are never portrayed in these ways. And as for Walters, specifically, he cannot be dismissed simply by quoting his advice on starting a boy towards wealth by having him sell matches. Success is not so much Walters' concern as is comfortable survival in a hostile world. He knows that money is power, one of the few powers available to the black man in America: "'Time after time, when scraping, toiling, saving, I have asked myself. To what purpose is it all?—perhaps that in the future white men may point at and call me, sneeringly, "a nigger millionaire," or condescend to borrow money of me. Ah! often, when some negro-baiting white man has been forced to ask a loan at my hands, I've thought of Shylock and his pound of flesh and ceased to wonder at him'" (pp. 276-277). Even the villainous Stevens, in a reflective moment, recognizes this: "'I tell you, Jule, if I was a black . . . living in a country like this, I'd sacrifice conscience and everything to the acquisition of wealth'" (p. 127). Here, somewhat ironically, Webb points out that money is sensed to be power by white minds as well as black, because white Mr. Stevens sacrifices just those things in order to get money. And they are right in their comprehension of evolving America—an America whose character would not become clear until the Gilded Age. Walters' money, while it does not shield him entirely, gives him more power over his life than most blacks then or later possess.

The Garies and Their Friends contains an aspect of black experience that has seldom been treated by history or literature until recent years. And this aspect adds a dimension to Walters' character which not only renders him more complex but examines a layer of black psychology that was usually ignored. This is the presence of the black militant theme, here introduced into the black novel for the first time.[12]

Though more ingredients are necessary, black militance can exist only when anti-white attitudes are clearly expressed by the author. In Webb's novel, they are present—not only in the criticism of white society but in the explicit attitudes expressed by some of the characters. Mrs. Ellis, for example, says to Mrs. Garie, Mr. Garie "'must love you, Emily, for not one white in a thousand would make such a sacrifice [i.e. marriage] for a coloured woman . . . It's real good in him, I declare, and I shall begin to have some faith in white folks after all'" (p. 135). Besides portraying this open hostility, Webb makes it clear that blacks are "'Not so aisily bate out—they fight like sevin divils. One o' 'em, night before last, split Mikey Dolan's head clane open, and it's a small chance of his life he's got to comfort himself wid'" (p. 176).

But the most explicitly militant and hostile ingredient of the novel is Walters, who takes no abuse from whites without attempting retaliation. Webb describes Walters as being "of jet-black complexion, and smooth glossy skin. His head was covered with a quantity of woolly hair" (pp. 121-122)—a description asserting black pride and stature. And Webb quickly gives us another clue that reveals Walters' forcefulness:

> As [Garie] was leaving the room, he stopped before the picture which had so engaged his attention, when Mr. Walters entered.
>
> "So you, too, are attracted by that picture," said Mr. Walters with a smile. "All white men look at it with interest. A black man in the uniform of a general officer is something so unusual that they cannot pass it with a glance.
>
> . . . . .
>
> "That is Toussaint l'Ouverture . . . and I have every reason to believe it to be a correct likeness. . . . That, "continued Mr. Walters, "looks like a man of intelligence. It is entirely different from any likeness I ever saw of him. The portraits generally represent him as a monkey-faced person, with a handkerchief about his head."
>
> "This," said Mr. Garie, "gives me an idea of the man that accords with his actions."
>
> (pp. 122-123)

This foreshadowing of Walters' militancy is borne out when the riot occurs. Walter's house is one of the targets of the rioters, and when he learns this, he first seeks protection of the authorities. After they refuse, he unhesitatingly turns his house into a fortress, inviting others to take shelter there and fight if necessary. Webb describes the preparations: "Mrs. Ellis and Esther . . . stood at the door of the drawing room surveying the preparations for defence that the appearance of the room so abundantly indicated. Guns were stacked in the corner, a number of pistols lay on the mantelpiece, and a pile of cartridges was heaped up beside a small keg of powder that stood up on the table opposite the fireplace" (p. 204). After Esther Ellis has unleashed her anger at the whites—"'I felt as though I could have strangled them'"—Walters admiringly looks at her and says "'You are a brave one, after my own heart'" (p. 205). Then he teaches her how to load guns—against the remonstrances of Mrs. Ellis.

Shortly after this, Walters sums up the militant's position: "'We look belligerent enough, I should think . . . I have asked protection of the law, and it is too weak, or indifferent, to give it; so I have no alternative but to protect myself'" (p. 208). When they see the fires of the riot in the distance, he urges "'we must defend ourselves fully and energetically'" (p. 211). As the attack on the house begins, Walters commands just as his hero, Toussaint, might have: "'When we do fire, let it be to some purpose—let us make sure that some one is hit'" (p. 213). The battle rages, with the surprised rioters getting the worst of it. First, stones are showered down upon them, and when they resort to guns, bullets are returned—causing many injuries. The rioters respond by trying to knock the door down, but they are bathed in scalding hot water poured on them from an upper window. The temper of the defenders is one of courageous seriousness coupled with exhilaration, and the house and its inhabitants are saved. Through his forceful leadership, Walters has earned a place alongside other prominent black militants.

It is clear that black literature is distinct from white literature in that blacks have had unique cultural and historical experiences. But while, as Bone correctly asserts, "the Negro novelist must achieve universality through a sensitive interpretation of his own culture," he has an added burden, because he has "two cultures to interpret."[13] And "if his art cuts deep enough, he will find the Negro world to be liberating rather than confining."[14] Certainly, in Webb's case, that world has been liberating, for I believe that it is precisely because Webb was a black man, experiencing the realities of black existence in "free," white, pre-Civil War Philadelphia, that his book goes beyond mere romantic melodrama. His culture and its clash with white society could not have been honestly confined to genteel romance. On the contrary, it insisted on a kind of realism, and *The Garies and Their Friends* has partially succeeded in achieving that in spite of its weaknesses.

Notes

1. *The Negro Novel in America,* rev. ed. (New Haven: Yale Univ. Press, 1965), p. 28. See Darwin T. Turner, *"The Negro Novel in America*: In Rebuttal," *CLA Journal,* 10 (December 1966), 122-134, for a general critique of Bone's conclusions about nineteenth century black writing.

2. (1857); rpt. New York: Arno Press, 1969).

3. Bone, *The Negro Novel,* p. 31. On p. 15, Bone attributes "the soul of a shopkeeper" to Webb and other early black writers. Unfortunately, Webb's book has been given little critical attention by Bone and other critics. And they mostly lack insight regarding Webb's book. Sterling Brown, in *The Negro in American Fiction* (Port Washington, N.Y.: Kennikat Press, Inc., 1937), briefly dismisses the book as "badly overwritten" (p. 40). Hugh M. Gloster, in *Negro Voices in American Fiction* (Chapel Hill, N.C. North Carolina Press, 1948), meagerly sketches the plot, suggests that the theme is about the tragic mulatto, and ends with the short comment that the book "is unlike most other early fiction by Negroes in that it analyzes the effects of race prejudice above the Mason-Dixon line" (p. 27). Bone, too, dismisses the book as a melodrama. Only Arthur P. Davis, in his preface to Webb, *The Garies,* pp. v-xiii, urges that the book deserves to be read "for its intrinsic worth" (p. vi), but even he consigns the book to the nineteenth century melodramatic genre. To give perspective to the fact that there is truth to this criticism, it is well to recall that, Richard Chase argues, in *The American Novel and Its Tradition* (Garden City, N.Y.: Anchor-Doubleday, 1957), romance is very much a part of the American tradition in literature, being found in authors as spacially and temporally disparate as Hawthorne, Henry James, and Faulkner.

4. *The Negro Novel,* p. 21.

5. For a discussion of melodrama as used by the black novelist, see Bone, *The Negro Novel,* pp. 23-28.

6. *Harvests of Change: American Literature, 1865-1914* (Englewood Cliffs, N.J.: Prentice-Hall, 1967), pp. 11-12. The notion that realism arose as a critical response to the Gilded Age is also well developed in chapter one in Alfred Kazin, *On Native Grounds: An Interpretation of Modern American Prose Literature* (New York: Harcourt, Brace & Co., 1942).

7. Webb, *The Garies,* p. 351. Page references to the novel are from this edition and will be hereafter cited parenthetically.

8. *The Negro Novel,* pp. 25-26.

9. Bone, *The Negro Novel,* p. 31.

10. "Preface," in Webb, *The Garies,* p. x.

11. Should this appear to be just another example of melodrama to some readers, let me remind them that "robber barons" were often just as imaginative and coldly exploitative in their business ventures as Stevens. See Matthew Josephson, *The Robber Barons: The Great American Capitalists* (1934; rpt. New York: Harcourt-Harvest, 1962).

12. See Charles D. Peavy, "The Black Revolutionary Novel: 1899-1969," *Studies in the Novel,* 3 (Summer 1971), 180-189, where it is asserted with much truth that Sutton Griggs' *Imperium in Imperio* (1899) "is the first black revolutionary novel" (p. 180).

13. Bone, *The Negro Novel,* p. 2

14. Bone, *The Negro Novel,* p. 3.

Phillip S. Lapsansky (essay date 1991)

SOURCE: Lapsansky, Phillip S. "Afro-Americana: Frank J. Webb and His Friends." In *The Annual Report of the Library Company of Philadelphia for the Year 1990,* pp 27-43. Philadelphia: Library Company of Philadelphia, 1991.

[*In the following excerpt, Lapsansky discusses how Webb's personal life and experiences affected the portrayal of Philadelphia in* The Garies and Their Friends.]

For nearly two decades Frank J. Webb's novel ***The Garies and Their Friends*** (London and New York, 1857) has eluded us. When we narrowly missed buying a copy three years ago, we alerted international dealer and collector circles of our interest. This year a British dealer finally offered us one. This is the second novel by an African-American writer, which in itself makes the work of extreme interest to us. But, even more interesting, Frank Webb was a Philadelphian, a product of this city's black middle class, and his novel is set in Philadelphia, in the racially tumultuous period of the late 1830s to the early 1850s. Though the book has all the elements of a typical sentimental potboiler of the period, it is in fact an important narrative of black life in antebellum Philadelphia. Webb drew exclusively upon his own experiences and those of the determined, self-educated, and steady-working Philadelphia blacks among whom he was raised.

Though the book was well received in England, in its time it had no American career, even though the publisher, G. Routledge & Co., as the imprint indicates, had a distribution network here. After diligent though hardly complete digging, we have yet to find an American review of the work, and no mention of it even in antislavery newspapers. The black intellectual and educator Charlotte Forten of Philadelphia knew the Webbs and writes in her diary of socializing with them in 1858. Ms. Forten also diligently reported on her reading in her diary. She makes no mention of Webb's book. Robert Adger and William Carl Bolivar, local 19th-century black bibliophiles who collected Afro-Americana, both published catalogues of their collection; neither owned the novel.

Webb's novel has suffered from 133 years of political incorrectness—ignored, probably disliked, in his time; and misunderstood in ours. Though published with impeccable antislavery credentials—prefaces by Harriet Beecher Stowe and the British antislavery leader Henry Brougham, and dedicated to Lady Byron—most antislavery Americans of the time were not prepared to confront the issues of northern racism and colorphobia raised in the novel. The book, however, does appear to have had a sub rosa career among black readers. In 1870 Webb's two novellas, *Two Wolves and a Lamb* and *Marvin Hayle,* were serialized in Frederick Douglass' newspaper *The New Era,* where he was introduced as "Author of '*The Garies,*'" an indication of prior knowledge of the work by Douglass' primarily black readers.

In our time the book has been equally bemusing. Arthur P. Davis, who wrote an introduction to the 1969 Arno Press reprint—effectively the first American edition—seems to have expected—and preferred—a strong antislavery work. "The work, in short, is not the kind of protest novel that one would expect from a free Negro in 1857. Perhaps its mildness [toward slavery] accounts in some measure for its lack of popularity." Critic James H. DeVries confuses Webb's black characters' acceptance of American middle class values with a lack of black identity and culture. "In short, most blacks in the novel bear the trappings of white culture. Whether this was done to enable the white readers to easily identify with the blacks or whether the blacks of that city had not yet developed a strong racial identity is impossible to discover."

The Garies and Their Friends is not an antislavery novel, rather it is an anti-racist work, and the first American novel to deal with race relations and colorphobia in the urban north. It is also the first novel written from the point of view of northern free blacks, and the first to explore the role of color and complexion and crossing the color line—a theme much worked by later black writers. And the more we learn of Frank Webb the more we agree with Stowe's remark that "the incidents related are mostly true ones, woven together by a slight web of fiction." If this fictionalized study of race relations by the son of the free black urban middle class

was offensive to his contemporaries and lacking acceptable racial consciousness to us today, that, we submit, is not Webb's problem. The dilemma itself underscores the importance of a book which highlights the discomforting issues of race and class pulsating through American life and thought. The critics also ignore the fact that Webb's novel celebrates the supportive and nurturing role of the black extended family and community.

The novel follows the fortunes of two families as they confront the virulent and violent racial climate of Philadelphia. The Garies of the title refers to Mr. Garie, a Georgia planter and slaveowner who lives in comfortable near-feudal self-sufficiency with Emily, his mulatto slave mistress, and their two children, Clarence and little Emily. Mr. Garie is a warm-hearted, loving, ingenuous man who sincerely regards himself as husband and father to his slave family, though he knows Georgia law will never recognize their union nor permit the emancipation of his wife and children. Living as he does a comfortable day at a time, he is stunned when Emily implores him to consider relocating the family to Europe or to a free state so they can legally live as man and wife and free her and the children from the threat of slavery. She is pregnant with their third child, and does not want it to be born a slave. "He was a Southerner in almost all his feelings, and had never had a scruple respecting the ownership of slaves. But now the fact that he was the master as well as the father of his children, and that whilst he resided where he did it was out of his power to manumit them; that in the event of his death they might be seized and sold by his heirs, whoever they might be, sent a thrill of horror through him. He had known all this before, but it had never stood out in such bold relief until now." Mr. Garie agrees to find a manager for the plantation and settle the family in Philadelphia.

He selects this city after a visit from George Winston, a very light skinned former slave from New Orleans. Originally from the Savannah region, and a friend of Emily's from childhood, Winston was sold to a New Orleans businessman as a child, raised and educated by this kindly master, and finally freed and taken into his former master's business. Winston routinely travels north on business and is light skinned enough to pass for white when it is to his advantage to do so. He too is looking to settle outside the South, and tells Garie and Emily of the bustling black community of Philadelphia with its schools and religious, social, and cultural organizations, where Emily can find company and friends.

George Winston's role is brief, but central. He articulates the dilemma of an educated light skinned black in America. ". . . amongst the whites, he could not form either social or business connections, should his identity with the African race be discovered; and whilst, on the other hand, he would have found sufficiently refined associations amongst the people of colour to satisfy his social wants, he felt that he could not bear the isolation and contumely to which they were subjected. He, therefore, decided on leaving the United States, and on going to some country where, if he must struggle for success in life, he might do it without the additional embarrassments that would be thrown in his way in his native land, solely because he belonged to an oppressed race." While most blacks rejected the program of African resettlement of the American Colonization Society, many were supporters of black controlled emigration movements, most targeting Central America or the Caribbean region, where people of color were a majority. Many leaders of black Philadelphia supported Haitian emigration in the 1820s, and later supporters of such movements among the Philadelphia black intelligentsia included the artist Robert Douglass, Jr. and the mathemetician and educator Robert Campbell, both probably known to Webb. And, shortly after the publication of his book, Frank Webb, in March of 1858, left to settle in Jamaica, where he had obtained a position as postmaster.

In Philadelphia we meet the Ellis family, possibly modeled on Webb's family, at the least a composite of characteristics of black Philadelphians known to him. Charles Ellis is a self-employed carpenter who owns his own home in a small side street in either the southern section of the city or the immediately adjacent Moyamensing area, where blacks and white workers lived cheek by jowl in uncomfortable and often hostile proximity. His wife Ellen occasionally works in service to a rich white family. They have three children—Esther, Caddy, and a young son Charlie, about ten when we meet him, who might possibly be the young Frank Webb.

The other central black character in Philadelphia is Mr. Walters, a black capitalist and property owner described by Mr. Ellis: "He is as black as a man can conveniently be. He is very wealthy; some say that he is worth half a million of dollars. He owns, to my certain knowledge, one hundred brick houses." Walters is modeled on several wealthy black community leaders who would have been known to Webb, such as James Forten, Joseph Cassey, and Robert Purvis, all with extensive property holdings in the city.

The villain of the piece is a creation George Lippard would have envied. George Stevens, known as Slippery George, is a corrupt and unscrupulous Philadelphia lawyer, politically connected to some of the more violent street gangs (mainly Irish) and fire companies, over whom he exercises considerable control. His practice consists mainly of using forgery and perjury to free his frequently arrested clients, supplemented by a variety of

very shady business dealings. As repulsive physically as he is morally, and a thoroughgoing racist, he is destined to become the Garies' new neighbor and Mr. Garie's assassin.

In a grand convergence of sentimental literary conventions, all the principal players either know each other or discover a relationship. George Winston knows Charles Ellis from his Georgia boyhood. Mr. Walters is a friend of the Ellises, is introduced to Winston, and thus becomes Mr. Garie's business agent in Philadelphia and procures him a house. Ellen Ellis remembers Emily as a child back in Georgia, and the Ellis women agree to help set up the new Garie household. And George Stevens will discover he is a long lost relative of Mr. Garie and heir to his fortune.

In Philadelphia the newly settled Garies and the long established Ellises confront racism in a variety of forms, from petty to homicidal. The Garies have moved from a region where their relationship was generally tolerated to one where they have become hated "amalgamationists." They have trouble finding a minister to marry them. When Mrs. Garie's race becomes known to their neighbor Stevens, he and his wife organize other parents to drive the Garie children out of their school. After Mr. and Mrs. Garie are killed in George Stevens' race riot, they are laid to rest in a black cemetery, since Emily cannot be interred with whites.

The Ellis family—the main focus is on young Charlie—struggle to avoid living down to expectations. The children are well schooled—in Webb's time there were public schools for blacks and about a dozen private, mostly black-run schools—and active members of black literary and educational societies. Mrs. Ellis' employer, the rich and socially prominent Mrs. Thomas, urges Ellen to forget about Charlie's education and put him into domestic service. "It isn't as though he was a white child. What use can Latin or Greek be to a coloured boy? None in the world—he'll have to be a common mechanic, or, perhaps, a servant, or barber, or something of that kind, and then what use would all his fine education be to him? Take my advice, Ellen, and don't have him taught things that will make him feel above the situation he, in all probability, will have to fill." A few years later Charlie, who is artistically inclined, tries to find an apprenticeship in the printing trade as a commercial designer, but finds white workers refuse to allow it. He is finally hired by Mr. Burrell who, visiting a shop, witnesses the rejection of Charlie. For him, as for a few other whites in the novel, this witness to racism is an epiphanous event that shows its petty and mean spirited consequences, and, rather than sink into such a slough, Mr. Burrell finds a position for Charlie in his shop. Interestingly, Frank Webb was, for about three years, a commercial designer.

The dramatic high point of the novel centers around a racial attack on the black community. George Stevens has, for a while, been hatching a scheme to start a race riot to terrorize the black community, drive many away, and acquire the abandoned properties at a fraction of their value. When, through a series of incidents, he discovers his distant kinship to Garie, he includes the Garie house on his list of targets and plans to have his white working class minions, headed by his henchman McCloskey, murder Garie. Stevens' plot unfolded pretty much as planned, as his working class and street gang cronies attack and loot black homes, assault the occupants, and drive them out. In the attack on the Garies' home, McCloskey loses his nerve and Stevens is obliged to shoot Garie himself. Emily and their unborn child also die in the assault.

Stevens, however, made one fateful error. He lost his copy of the list of specific targets in a black-run used clothing store where he went to outfit himself for the occasion. The black proprietor passed the list on to Mr. Walters, also one of Stevens' targets. Walters, a man of action, acts. Several of the targeted families are warned and able to flee or prepare a defense. The Ellis family, who live in the heart of the district occupied by the rioters, are brought to Walters' home. Walters summons the mayor to demand action to stop the impending attack. The mayor refused to act, as Philadelphia officials had in actual race riots. Faced with official indifference, Walters and the Ellis family organize their defense. They are well armed, and Esther Ellis at her insistence quickly learns the art of loading pistols. Caddie and Charlie Ellis, with Charlie's friend Kinch, like defenders of a medieval castle, prepare a vat of boiling water heavily laced with cayenne pepper. The combination of pistols and pepperpot successfully repels the attack on Walters' house, but not all escape unharmed. Charles Ellis, attempting to sneak through the mob to warn the Garies, was spotted, chased, cornered by a gang, and thrown from a three-story building. He was left physically and psychologically crippled.

The depiction of the mob is a product of fact and fiction. Webb was old enough to be aware of the riots of 1842 and certainly 1849. The 1842 riots in particular involved a white working class attack on black homes that destroyed many and led to the abandonment of even more. An 1847 report on the condition of the black community attributed a less-than-anticipated population growth to many blacks' abandoning their homes in the area of the 1842 riots. Both episodes, particularly the 1849 riot, featured armed black resistance. And, in these and earlier anti-black riots, officials blamed the victims and made excuses for white violence against blacks. Webb had probably also read such George Lippard novellas as *The Life and Adventures of Charles Anderson Chester, The Killers,* and *The Bank Director's Son,* published here in 1850 and '51, in which the 1849 riots

were depicted as quickly "gotten up" at will by white street gangs and their leaders. While this may seem contrived, it may also express the view of part of the black community. The several major riots involving serious loss of property and lives were notable, and lesser episodes were frequent. Blacks living in the crowded sections of South Philadelphia and Moyamensing lived in expectation of unexpected violence. Also, the view that these riots were part of a scheme to drive blacks from their homes and cheaply acquire their property may well have been a widespread opinion among Philadelphia blacks.

Following the Garies' deaths, Mr. Walters and the Garies' white lawyer Mr. Balch make fateful arrangements for the Garie children. Though Garie's money goes to Stevens, Walters' possession of Stevens' hit list for the riots is incriminating enough to oblige Stevens to settle a large sum in trust for the children. Emily, the younger, is placed in the care of Mr. Walters and the Ellis family. Clarence is sent to Sudbury, Pennsylvania, to live with a white family and attend a private boys school, admonished never to reveal his black ancestry. Walters is apprehensive about this arrangement to oblige Clarence to live out his life as white, and utters his prophetic fears: "There's no doubt, my dear sir, but that I fully appreciate the advantage of being white. Yet, with all I have endured, and yet endure from day to day, I esteem myself happy in comparison with that man, who, mingling in the society of whites, is at the same time aware that he has African blood in his veins, and is liable at any moment to be ignominiously hurled from his position by the discovery of his origin. He is never safe. I have known instances where parties have gone on for years and years undetected; but some untoward circumstance brings them out at last, and down they fall for ever."

And such is the fate of Clarence who, several years later as a young adult, is living comfortably in New York society and engaged to the daughter of a prominent businessman. He is "exposed," ironically, by George Stevens' son, who remembers him. Cast out by white society, and unable to bring himself to accept the rigid restraints imposed on black society, Clarence literally languishes to death—victim of a fatal plot device. His sister, by contrast, marries Charlie Ellis and settles happily into the warm embrace of the Ellis family and the black community.

Little is known about Frank Webb, or his equally fascinating wife Mary, and we owe sincere thanks to our friends Dorothy Sterling, Dorothy Porter Wesley, and Professors Allan Austin and Jean Fagan Yellin for generously sharing their information on the Webbs. Harriet Beecher Stowe's introduction to *The Garies* briefly describes Frank as "a coloured young man, born and reared in the city of Philadelphia." Frank was born around 1828; the 1850 census lists him as 21 years old. Perhaps he was the son of an earlier Frank Webb, active in the 'teens and 1820s as an elder of the First African Presbyterian Church, and a colleague of Absalom Jones and others in the Augustinian Society, a black interdenominational organization which promoted formal and classical education for the rising black clergy. The elder Webb is listed in city directories as a China packer living on Relief Alley, a small South Philadelphia back street similar to the location of the Ellis family. City directories for 1851 through 1854 list Frank J. Webb as a designer, or commercial artist in the printing trade, the same occupation Charlie Ellis finally secures.

In the novel we find the Ellis family active in black community educational affairs such as literary societies and lyceums. Webb's obvious literacy suggests his family was also active in such groups as the Philadelphia Library Company of Colored People, the Rush Library Company and Debating Society, the Desmosthenian Institute, the Minerva Literary Association, the Edgeworth Literary Association, and the Gilbert Lyceum, all black literary and educational organizations active during Frank's youth. We do know that in 1854 Frank gave a public lecture on "The Martial Capacity of Blacks" for a later-formed literary and debating society, the Banneker Institute, composed of some of black Philadelphia's brightest young men who became leading community figures in the later 19th century.

Around 1845 Frank married his beautiful and talented wife Mary. According to a biographical account by Frank, she was the daughter of a fugitive slave and "a Spanish gentleman of wealth." This interracial affair may have inspired the creation of the Garie family, though Webb would have been aware of several black families settled in Philadelphia by white father-masters. Born in Bedford, Massachusetts, in 1828, Mary enjoyed comfortable circumstances and a good education, provided first by her father's wealth and later by her mother's hard work. When Frank's business failed Mary cultivated her elocutionary talents with an eye towards a career giving dramatic readings. Mary had previously met Harriet Beecher Stowe, who dramatised portions of *Uncle Tom's Cabin* for Mary's readings. Debuting in Philadelphia in April of 1855, she was a success. She toured New York and New England later in 1855, and in 1856, armed with letters of introduction from Stowe, Frank and Mary were off to England, Mary to continue her successful dramatic presentations, and Frank to finish and publish his novel.

While Frank may have been working on his novel for some time, he probably wrote the bulk of it during his enforced leisure after his business failed. Chapter 4 provides a clue. George Winston, passing as a white southerner at a Philadelphia hotel, is hustled by the black staff who are members of the Vigilance Committee, the local black underground railroad organization. It was their practice to pose as former slaves and sham a longing for the old plantation to pry loose a few dollars from visiting southerners. While Frank may have been aware of the black hotel workers' involvement in the underground railroad, their role received extensive—and probably unwanted—publicity in a slave rescue episode from Bloodgood's Hotel in July of 1855.

Stowe's introduction gave the Webbs entree to the wealthy and aristocratic British antislavery establishment. *The Illustrated London News* for August 2, 1856 gives a glowing review of Mary's reading at the home of the Duchess of Sutherland. An illustration of Mary at the podium accompanying the article shows her a strikingly beautiful woman. "Her color is a rich olive," the reviewer notes, "and her features are remarkably delicate and expressive."

Stowe, travelling in England with her sister Mary Beecher Perkins, met the Webbs frequently. "Harriet and I went to lunch with Mr. & Mrs. Webb—who are very nicely established in Portman Place," Mary Perkins wrote her husband in August of 1856. "She is engaged to read in London for a long time—it is very successful—Mr. Webb has written a story & we hope it will take." "Mr. and Mrs. Webb were here in high feather," she again wrote in the summer of 1857, "intimate with dukes & duchesses & lords & ladies without number. It would have made a southerner gnash his teeth to see the attentions she rec'd."

Mary Webb was apparently somewhat frail and became sick in the fall of 1857. The Webbs spent most of the winter in southern France and returned to Philadelphia briefly in March of 1858, en route to Kingston, Jamaica, where Frank had secured a position as postmaster. "Bade Mr. and Mrs Webb farewell," Charlotte Forten wrote in her diary on March 26, "They sail on Sunday." And they sailed, at least for now, into obscurity. Mary, we have been told, died within a couple of years. In 1870 Webb's two novellas appeared in *The New Era*. In 1890 and 1896, two articles appeared in the *A. M. E. Christian Review* by one Frank J. Webb, Jr. We trust the several scholars currently interested in Frank Webb will eventually flesh out his story. We need a new edition of *The Garies* that centers the novel in the life and experiences of its author and recognizes it as an important black narrative.

Though this is our 1990 report, we are preparing it in 1991. It is Spring. In Philadelphia we have just concluded a fractious primary election marked by intense racial polarization. Nationally, the news is filled with controversy on quotas, minority rights, affirmative action, and reverse discrimination. On university campuses arguments rage over the theory and practice of diversity. Suddenly Frank Webb's novel seems depressingly current.

Robert S. Levine (essay date 1994)

SOURCE: Levine, Robert S. "Disturbing Boundaries: Temperance, Black Elevation, and Violence in Frank J. Webb's *The Garies and Their Friends.*" *Prospects: An Annual of American Cultural Studies* 19 (1994): 349-74.

[*In the following essay, Levine considers* The Garies and Their Friends *in the context of the black temperance movement in Philadelphia during the 1830s and 1840s. Further, the critic documents the hypocritical—and even violent—white response to blacks' attempts to improve themselves and assimilate into the white culture.*]

At the inaugural 1837 meeting of the American Moral Reform Society, one of Philadelphia's many African American reform groups, William Whipper called for blacks to commit themselves to total abstinence and "temperance in all things." The group itself offered a resolution that subsumed a number of social desires and reforms under the rubric of temperance: "*Resolved,* That the successful promotion of all the principles of the Moral Reform Society, viz.: Education, Temperance, Economy, and Universal Love, depends greatly upon the practical prosecution of the Temperance Reform." But of course temperance could only go so far, and at times those blacks most committed to temperance—whether conceived narrowly in terms of drinking, or more broadly in terms of a Franklinian commitment to economy and industry—seemed to lose sight of the limits of the black temperance movement in a racist culture. At the same 1837 meeting of the American Moral Reform Society, James Forten, Jr., addressed this issue head on. While endorsing temperance as a worthy social program of black elevation, he pointed to the central reality of the black experience in America: "that the arm of oppression is laid bare to crush us; that prejudice, like the never satiated tiger, selects us as its prey; that we have felt the withering blight of tyranny sweeping from before us, in its destructive course, our homes and our property." But despite these obstacles, Forten advised, blacks should not give up the struggle to improve their lot and, as temperate and productive citizens, "to set an example to the rising generation." As he rhetorically put it in his concluding remarks: "What . . . would the cause of learning and our country have lost, if a Franklin, a Rittenhouse, a Rush, could have been made to quail before the frowning brow of persecution?"[1]

Emphasizing industry, frugality, and self-restraint, temperance, arguably the most influential reform movement of the antebellum period, was championed by a number of free blacks as a self-help program promising to bring about the social and economic elevation of the African American community.[2] Adopting what historian Gary Nash terms "the gospel of moral improvement,"[3] Whipper and other leaders of Philadelphia's black middle class were at the forefront of this movement. Perhaps it was for this reason that it was in early national and antebellum Philadelphia, more than in any other urban center, that African Americans managed to create a relatively cohesive community. Attracted by the city's Enlightenment and antislavery ideals, and by the existence of a number of highly visible and prospering blacks, fugitive and freed slaves from the South flocked to Philadelphia, helping to make it, with a population of 15,000 African Americans by 1830, the largest black community in the antebellum North. As Emma Jones Lapsansky notes, this community, compared with others, "was economically well off," to the extent that "a survey published in 1845 listed six Afro-Americans among the city's several dozen wealthiest people."[4] While the successes of these six people, and even of the less spectacularly successful black middle class, should not blind us to the reality that the majority of Philadelphia's black citizenry remained relatively poor, the important fact remains that Philadelphia's African Americans had succeeded in developing numerous autonomous institutions—Bethel and many other black churches; schools; reading societies; moral reform groups; Masonic fraternities; temperance organizations—that centrally contributed to their ability to survive and prosper in a city that by no means had transcended the racist beliefs and practices of the time.

With their insistence on the importance of blacks trying to achieve middle-class status, or, we could say, middle-class American identity, through the adoption of temperance ideals of self-help, Philadelphia's black reformers sought to break down or, at the very least, disturb the boundaries erected by whites to thwart black elevation. But as the litany of white names in Forten's listing suggests, the promotion of temperance could be taken as a surrendering to the Protestant-capitalist norms of the white community, a destructive abandoning of African traditions and values. We might therefore ask the following questions: In their apparent embrace of the economic and behavioral values of the dominant white culture, in their pursuit of material goods and comforts through the promotion of temperance and self-help, did not Philadelphia's black middle and upper classes risk cutting themselves off from their less economically successful brothers and sisters? Moreover, though temperance was promoted by many African Americans as a mode of antislavery action—show Northern and Southern whites that blacks are capable of leading temperate and productive lives, and slavery, lacking for legitimation, will disappear—did not such a strong commitment to the middle-class values of the white community threaten to diminish the interest of materially well-off blacks in the plight of the slaves? In short, were Philadelphia's black reformers disturbing or, unwittingly, firming up boundaries—between, say, free blacks and enslaved blacks, wealthy blacks and poor blacks, rich and poor, blacks and whites? Nowhere are these questions addressed more honestly and powerfully than in Frank J. Webb's grossly underrated *The Garies and Their Friends* (1857), a historical novel that represents the situation of Philadelphia's hardworking and temperate blacks of the middling and upper classes from the late 1830s to the 1850s.

Let me say at the outset of what will be an extended contextual reading of *Garies,* the second novel to be published by an African American, that I find Webb's novel to be deeply sympathetic in its portrayal of the contradictions and vulnerabilities of black middle-class life in Philadelphia, and often more realistic in its portrayals, and bracingly so, than sentimental or melodramatic, as some critics have complained.[5] Though there are annoying lapses (and blind spots) in the book's moral vision, the novel, I will be arguing, values black pride over shame, community over the individual, integrity and freedom over money.[6] To be sure, in his celebratory narrative of blacks' efforts to elevate themselves within capitalist culture, Webb can appear to be complicitous in promoting the very values that have contributed to the blacks' subordination. But as Brook Thomas observes on minorities' appropriations of such progressive narratives, "when previously excluded groups employ narratives of progressive emergence, they are not necessarily ironically inverting them," in large part because the act of claiming rights of access to these narratives is, in and of itself, given the differing "temporal logic" of the oppressed group's situation, politically subversive.[7] In *Garies,* I will be arguing, Webb challenges hierarchical and racialist models of exclusion by depicting blacks pragmatically making use of the master's tools in order to assert their claims to equal rights and opportunities in America.

In this respect, the novel must be viewed as an intervention in a key debate among blacks of the 1850s: whether or not to emigrate from America. From the point of view of Martin Delany, James Holly, and many others, the passage of the Fugitive Slave Law and the Kansas-Nebraska Bill made a mockery of the temperance values and ideals of "race-blind" groups such as the American Moral Reform Society, revealing that blacks, because of the color of their skin, will forever be an exploited, subordinate group in America.[8] In 1854 Delany successfully sponsored a black emigration convention, which called for emigration to Central and South America and the Caribbean, and shortly thereafter Holly began to develop his own plans to lead blacks to Haiti. Frederick Douglass, of course, remained the principal black spokesperson for the anti-emigrationist position, maintaining throughout the 1850s that blacks had a moral right and responsibility to remain in America. In an 1855 column, "Colored People of Pennsylvania," he suggested that the example of Pennsylvania's "thrifty, enterprizing and industrious" blacks, who "plant more stakes, instead of digging up those already planted," called into question all emigrationist (and colonizationist) projects.[9] Here and elsewhere, Douglass, an exponent of temperance reform during the 1840s and 1850s, celebrates the heroic, oppositional, and reformative nature of black economic activity in America; a shared sense of the heroism and urgency of working toward black elevation in America informs Webb's representations of Philadelphia's temperate black capitalists.

Garies' blacks, it should be noted at the outset, are not portrayed as temperance reformers: There are no scenes of inebriated blacks giving up the bottle, no discussions of temperance. In Webb's novel, it is the whites, not the blacks, who are in dire need of temperance reform, as the blacks generally are presented as industrious bourgeois capitalists. For this reason, perhaps, *Garies,* the second novel to be published by an African American writer, has not been much admired by the few critics who have read it. In his magisterial *A History of Afro-American Literature,* Blyden Jackson condemns Webb for perniciously preaching a gospel of self-help and money-making that is naive and selfish: "His plot declares that Negroes need, above all, in America to get rich."[10] Even admirers of the novel have been troubled by what they take as Webb's uncritical adoption of Franklinian ideals of industry and temperance as a panacea for the black population. Though Addison Gayle, Jr., views the novel, in formal terms, as "the finest production by a black writer between 1853 and 1900," he remains distressed by its informing ideology. *Garies,* he declares, is at bottom "nothing so much as the *Poor Richard's Almanack* of the black middle class," a novel that regards hopes for preserving a sense of black heritage and racial unity in the United States "to be little more than the romantic hopes of foolish men."[11]

Webb's putative lack of racial unity and commitment to his black heritage has been adduced, by some commentators, not only from his novel, but from what little we know of his biography. Harriet Beecher Stowe, in her preface to *Garies,* refers to Webb as "a coloured young man, born and reared in the city of Philadelphia."[12] The book, Webb's only novel, is dedicated to Lady Noel Byron and includes, in addition to Stowe's preface, another preface by the well-known abolitionist Lord Brougham. Given the novel's London publication, and the somewhat glamorous circle of white reformers associated with it, one might be tempted to posit that Webb, in entering the rarefied world of upper-class British reformism, had lost a sense of connectedness with America's free and enslaved blacks.

From this perspective, to turn now to Webb's novel, I suspect that some readers would be immediately alienated by the opening chapter, which has the Stowe-like ironically understated title "In which the Reader is introduced to a Family of peculiar Construction."[13] The family, the Garies of Savannah, is "constructed" of Mr. Garie, a slaveholder, his mistress Emily, a mulatto and former slave, and their two children, Clary and Emily, who look white to the eye. An abundance of food predominates: baskets are heaped with a variety of cakes and fruits, doused in syrups, sugar, and brandy. Perhaps Webb is criticizing the luxury that the slave plantation makes available to the owner and his family. Yet social criticism on the part of the narrator seems lacking. Garie is presented as a kindhearted patriarch whose act of purchasing Emily for two thousand dollars served both of their interests. As the narrator remarks, "[A]s time developed the goodness of her heart, and her mind enlarged through the instructions he assiduously gave her, he found the connection that might have been productive of many evils, had proved a boon" (p. 2). The implication here is that Emily would not have "developed" had she remained within the plantation's slave community.

A similar denial of the value of black community comes across in the account in the same chapter of Emily's cousin George Winston, who had recently "passed" as a white among high society in the North. The "offspring of a mulatto field-hand by her master" (p. 8)—the end product of white patriarchal violation, a fact that seems obliterated from his consciousness—Winston as a boy had been separated from his mother and purchased by a kindly cotton broker of New Orleans. Like Emily, George is "improved" by his master. After being taught to read and write, the grateful Winston is given a job at the brokerage house and the opportunity to rise within it. While he had once refused a picayune, because, as he put it, "If it won't buy mammy, I don't want it" (p. 9), he now eagerly embraces the capitalistic world of the enslavers. Industrious and temperate young man that he is, George rises "through all the grades from errand-boy up to chief clerk" (p. 10) and is eventually "rewarded" with his freedom. The man with picayunes in his pocket, who had forgotten to redeem his mother from slavery before she died, subsequently travels North to explore business possibilities. As he now recounts to the Garie family, he had encountered a number of economically successful blacks in Philadelphia, and had considered working and residing among them. But he rejects this possibility, the narrator reveals in the summation that ends the chapter, because "whilst . . . he would have found sufficiently refined associations amongst the people of colour to satisfy his social wants, he felt that he could not bear the isolation and contumely to which they were subjected. He, therefore, decided on leaving the United States, and on going to some country where, if he must struggle for success in life, he might do it without . . . embarrassments" (p. 14).

I spend some time on the opening chapter because it so troublingly raises the issue of Webb's moral vision in the novel. What are we to make of blacks who remain indebted to whites for their "improvement"? Of the failure of these characters, particularly Winston, to turn to other black characters for edification, love, and community? Of a black seemingly unaware of the relationship of his cotton-trading job to black exploitation? Are racism and slavery merely "embarrassments" to blacks, or something to struggle against? Moral questions such as these become less fuzzy when the narrative shifts from Savannah to Philadelphia, and we are introduced to the African American Ellis family—the family at the center of the somewhat oddly titled *The Garies and Their Friends*—who, unlike the emigrating Winston, have decided to "struggle for success" in America at the risk of great "embarrassments."

To meet the Ellises, "a highly respectable and industrious coloured family" (p. 16), is to enter the world of temperate middle-class industry envisioned by the American Moral Reform Society. The father, Charles Ellis, a friend from George Winston's days back on the Savannah plantation, is a "thrifty" (p. 26) carpenter who has managed to purchase his own house, "ground and all" (p. 49). His wife and two daughters—Esther and Caddy—sew clothes and do other odd jobs in their spare time, while his son, Charlie, attends school. In addition to working hard for their personal economic well-being, the Ellises have made a significant commitment to Philadelphia's black middle-class community and its attending institutions. Mr. Ellis, when first introduced to the reader, is not at home; he is attending a "vestry meeting" (p. 18). When Winston later visits the Ellises, he is surprised to learn that Esther and Caddy will be attending a lecture at a library. As Ellis explains to the uncomprehending Winston, "This association they speak of is entirely composed of people of colour. They have a fine library, a debating club, chemical apparatus, collections of minerals, & c." (p. 48). Winston's assertion that the Ellises must be an exception to the rule of black urban misery elicits Ellis's vociferous response that Winston has been misled by Southern and colonizationist propaganda. "Badly off, and in want, indeed! Why, my dear sir," Ellis remarks, "we not only support our own poor, but [by paying property taxes] assist the whites to support theirs" (p. 49). In short, Ellis declares, because of their commitment to hard work and mental cultivation, Philadelphia's blacks are "in advance of the whites in wealth and general intelligence" (p. 50).[14]

Though Winston (who subsequently disappears from the novel) refuses to live in Philadelphia with the social stigma that would keep him at a distance from the fashionable whites he so envies, it is his positive report on the situation of the blacks in Philadelphia that prompts the Garies to move North. For as we soon learn, Emily Garie is hardly enamored of the plantations' luxury, in large part because the luxury masks the central truth that in the eyes of the law she and her children are slaves. Relenting to her request to transplant themselves to Philadelphia, Garie warns her that Northern racism may expose them "to great inconveniences" (p. 57). But when they arrive in Philadelphia such warnings seem beside the point: Emily is beguiled by the city's "bright and fresh-looking" (p. 116) cleanliness; Garie is astonished to see black schoolchildren "skipping merrily along with their bags of books on their arms" (p. 120). And perhaps most impressive of all is the man who helps them find housing: the "jet-black" (p. 121) Mr. Walters, a real-estate mogul with holdings of approximately a half-million dollars.

More than any other character, Walters has presented a stumbling block to sympathetic readers of Webb's novel. Bernard Bell, for example, writes with respect to Walters, "Instead of Christian charity or black power, Webb's answer to racial discrimination is green power."[15] Rich and successful as he is, however, Walters seems guided primarily by conscience and a sense of obligation to Philadelphia's black community. It is significant, therefore, as Garie observes during a visit, that he displays on the wall of his parlor a portrait, not of Ben Franklin, but of the hero of San Domingo, Toussaint l'Ouverture. In the spirit of Toussaint, Walters preaches the values of hard work and industry, not simply as a way of acquiring goods but, more importantly, as a way of acquiring independence from whites who want to keep blacks in subordinate positions. Thus he counsels the Ellises against permitting their son Charlie to work as a servant for the aristocratic Thomases. Like Frederick Douglass, who warned that "free negroes must learn trades, or die,"[16] Walters argues that once a servant, always a servant, as such jobs break the spirit of the blacks who take them while reinforcing the stereotype of the "happy" black servant so central to whites' conception of blacks. As he rhetorically puts it to Mrs. Ellis (an admirer and former employee of the Thomases), "Where would I or Ellis have been had we been hired out all our lives at so much a month? It begets a feeling of dependence to place a boy in such a situation; and rely upon it, if he stays there long, it will spoil him for anything better all his days" (p. 63). Despite these warnings, Mr. and Mrs. Ellis convince Charlie to work part-time for the Thomases, though as Walters had anticipated, Charlie is too educated and ambitious to be kept in his "place." In a nice series of comic scenes, Charlie deliberately embarrasses Mrs. Thomas by "accidentally" doing his work improperly—lifting off her wig before a guest, for example—and is fired from his job.

That Charlie has the integrity to rebel against the Thomases is consistent with Webb's depiction of the pride and determination predominating among the black middle and upper classes in Philadelphia circa 1840. An approximate dating of the novel, it should be noted, can be determined in at least two ways: by the fact that at the novel's conclusion there is a generational leap forward to the present, circa mid-1850s, thereby suggesting an early 1840s setting; and by Webb's suggestive historicism. Though Webb nowhere in the novel gives us a date or particular event that would enable us precisely to determine the historical setting, his overall portrayal of the Ellises' situation—their hopes and aspirations, the pressures that will impinge upon them and their friends—allows us to hypothesize a setting in the range of 1838-42. The most serious outbreak of violence against Philadelphia's black community, as I will discuss in more detail, occurred in a major race riot of 1842—the sort of extreme violence that the characters, in their relatively upbeat relation to work and community, seem not yet to have experienced. Yet there are clear indications that racism is a feature of Philadelphia's social landscape. The Ellises, for example, "are not permitted to ride in the omnibuses or other public conveyances" (p. 64). The inclusion of this, among other details, encourages a post-1838 contextualization, in that 1838 was the year the Pennsylvania Constitutional Convention, in expanding the vote to nonpropertied citizens, made it legally the case that only whites could vote.[17] For those of the black middle class who were paying property taxes, their disenfranchisement, in favor of the enfranchisement of poorer whites (recall that Ellis had remarked to Winston that blacks were supporting poor *whites*) sent the clear signal of their marginal status within the community, and thus of an even greater need for programs of self-help and self-elevation.

The constitutional changes of 1838 legally ratified the emergent Jim Crow practices of a city that at least through the early 1830s had prided itself on its relatively progressive attitudes on race. Or, to put it another way, 1838 and the years immediately following may be taken as a moment when white authorities attempted to firm up boundaries they perceived as in danger of breaking down. Webb studies the psychopathology of such efforts in a variety of ways, focusing especially, in historicist fashion, on the heightening anti-amalgamation mood of late 1830s and 1840s Philadelphia. Thus he portrays the difficulties the Garies face, shortly after their glorious arrival in Philadelphia, in getting married. "I do not believe in the propriety of amalgamation" (p. 137), announces a minister who refuses to marry them; and the minister's words speak to larger tensions in the white community about blacks' presence in "their" workplaces and neighborhoods. As Lapsansky observes, "Nineteenth-century urban heterogeneity placed black Philadelphians house-to-house with their white contemporaries, many of whom were openly and effectively hostile to Afroamericans' achievements."[18] In Webb's novel, no one is more "hostile" than the Garies' obsessively anti-amalgamationist neighbor George Stevens, a "pettifogging attorney" known as "Slippery George" (p. 124), and no one is more intemperate.

Introduced about a third of the way into the novel, Stevens at first seems little more than a melodramatically conceived villain with the purely allegorical function of representing the evil racist. Webb corporealizes that evil, describing Stevens's efforts to cover up his spreading bald spot, for example, as producing a scalp that seems "decorated with a pair of horns" (p. 124). Such allegorical details should not obscure the fact, however, that there is a powerful social realism at work in the portrayal of Stevens. Webb presents his racism as a pathology of envy and status anxieties, and links that racism to the larger institutional power structure of antebellum Philadelphia. When he and his wife realize, for example, that an "amalgamated" family lives near them, their fears of amalgamation extend to the schools: they use their money and connections to force the Garie children out of the private school that their own children attend.[19] The plottings of Stevens and his wife anticipate the more malignant plottings of Stevens and his business associates to expel blacks from their neighborhoods—plottings that are presented as driven by Stevens's uncontrollable appetite for money and power. It is appropriate, then, that Webb should bring temperance as a motif and social issue back into prominence as Stevens's racist money-making scheme begins to command the novel's center stage.

In an attempt to extend his influence and dramatically increase his wealth, Stevens has enlisted working-class drinkers, predominantly Irish, in a plot to gain financial control of a Southern district of Philadelphia populated mainly by blacks. The central pawn in his plan is one McCloskey, who, while drunk, had killed another Irishman with a "slung shot" (p. 163). As McCloskey's counsel, Stevens pays off the one witness to the crime, the tavern owner Whitticar, and then, with Whitticar in his pocket, attempts to blackmail McCloskey into doing his dirty work. What he wants him to do is lead a mob of his fellow workers and drinkers into the district of home-owning blacks and intimidate them into selling their property at low prices. Whereupon Stevens and his fellow investors will, in Stevens's words, "reestablish order and quiet, and sell again at an immense advantage" (p. 166). As secretive speculators, Stevens and his coconspirators can display themselves as model citizens in complete control of appetite. Webb makes clear, though, that similar problems of loss of self-control and social deviancy characterize the drunkard and speculator.[20] Surreptitiously mixing with the drunks hanging out at Whitticar's tavern, Stevens, because of his intemperate desire for money, displays a similar, or analogous, lack of self-control; and like Whitticar himself, who peddles drink to these "forlorn-looking wretches" (p. 173), Stevens, in peddling his influence and payoffs to gang leaders, has sacrificed conscience to profit. As

Whitticar remarks on the "conscience," "it's a thing with very little use in the rumselling business; it interferes with trade" (p. 174).

Stevens, the metaphorical conscienceless tavern keeper, has for some time been preparing the ground for his speculative "trade," aware that in promoting a riot he would be subjecting Philadelphia to nothing out of the ordinary. As the narrator remarks, Stevens plans on taking advantage of the fact that "already several disturbances had occured, in which a number of inoffensive coloured people had been injured in their persons and property" (p. 175). One of the great achievements of Webb's novel is to offer the reader a glimpse into the sociohistorical reality of the antiblack riots recurring in antebellum Philadelphia. Though he can be accused of melodramatic overkill in making Stevens the prime generator of the riot in *Garies,* and of "classism" in presenting the Irish workers as the pawns of moneyed whites, Webb, by linking Stevens to McCloskey, challenges reductive readings of Philadelphia's riots as simply the result of ethnic, or working-class, racism. For Webb, all sectors of white society are implicated; the apparent heavy-handedness of the plotting makes the more subtle point that only in a social-institutional context of total racism could the riots have occurred in the first place.

The climactic riot of *Garies* conflates the details of several major riots in Philadelphia during the 1834-49 period, a brief overview of which would be useful before turning to Webb's harrowing representation. The first major race riot occurred in 1834, when white gangs attacked a carousel on South Street, avowedly as an act of revenge against blacks believed to have stolen equipment from the neighborhood fire company; hostilities escalated to the point that black residences were attacked over a two-day period. But once the white rioters turned their attention to the destruction of black residences, they singled out not those of the poor and working classes but of the wealthy. The riot thus revealed the limitations of the black temperance ideals put forth at the 1837 convention of the American Moral Reform Society, which suggested that the existence of a group of successful blacks would undermine racial stereotypes, thereby contributing to black elevation. If anything, the successes of blacks exacerbated white resentments, and not just among the working classes. Though there would seem to have been a certain spontaneity in the flaring of violence during this riot, whites in the various wealthier districts under attack knowingly turned off the lights of their homes in order to inform the rioters that these were whites' residences, and thus should be spared the destructiveness (which the darkness of their homes implicitly acknowledged and approved) directed against the blacks.[21]

A riot of 1838 revealed a similar measure of complicity among all classes of whites, while highlighting as well white fears of "amalgamation" and miscegenation. Soon after the Pennsylvania Anti-Slavery Society opened Pennsylvania Hall, rumors began to circulate about the "licentious" intermingling between whites and blacks behind its closed doors. Eventually the hall was attacked and burned down, with the considerable involvement of the "gentlemen of property and standing" whom Leonard Richards has argued were central participants in many of the antislavery riots of the 1830s.[22] In this riot, working-class participation took the form of silent complicity: the fire companies refused to fight the fire.

The worst of the riots, and the most significant for interpretation of temperance themes and issues in *Garies,* occurred on August 1, 1842, when members of a black temperance society sought to celebrate West Indian emancipation and, relatedly, temperance ideals (the emancipation of the black body from the slavery of drink) by parading through Philadelphia. Temperance, it should be noted, had assumed special importance for blacks during the 1838-42 period, as it was seen by many as the best possible way to address the economic difficulties brought on by the Panic of 1837. James J. G. Bias, a physician and clergyman, emerged as the leading temperance advocate within the black community, the man chiefly responsible for spearheading the construction of a black temperance hall in 1840. That hall took on special significance during the 1842 riot. Frederick Douglass, in his address "Intemperance and Slavery" (1845), describes what happened that August 1st: "A large number of colored people in Philadelphia attempted to celebrate that day by forming themselves into a temperance procession, and walking through the streets, with appropriate banners, and thus to make a temperance impression on their fellow brethren who had not yet joined their ranks. They had also 'freedom' inscribed upon their banner. Well, such was the feeling in this slave-holding city, that the display of the banner brought upon these poor colored people *an infuriated mob!* Their houses were burnt down in different parts of the city, and their churches were burned to the earth, themselves turned out of the city, and the city authorities and police did nothing to prevent it!"[23]

For Douglass, who alluded to this event numerous times during his British tour, the 1842 attack on the paraders and subsequent three-day assault on black residences revealed the hypocrisy of whites involved in the temperance movement. In Douglass's view, white temperance organizations, of which there were many, should have defended the blacks' right to march in Philadelphia; instead, so Douglass laments, they continued to be guided by their racist and proslavery proclivities. But the larger point that he makes in this and other comments on the riot, and the point that Webb will be emphasizing about the riot represented in *Garies,* is that to regard it simply as an expression of working-class whites' resentments of blacks during a period of eco-

nomic depression fails to take into account the involvement of all classes of whites in the disturbance. Not only did authorities do nothing to stop the violence (a police force was never summoned), they in fact performed their own act of violence by ordering the blacks' temperance hall destroyed lest the riots spread there and threaten the surrounding white residences. This legal sanction to destroy a building of great symbolic importance to the black community, and the related act of a grand jury "officially" placing legal blame for the riot on "the provocative nature of the Negro processions,"[24] would suggest that there was good reason for Webb to have placed the lawyer Stevens at the center of the riot in *Garies.*

Because Webb focuses so intently on Stevens's ability to manipulate various forms of power—the newspapers, real estate markets, government agencies, political figures—it could seem that Webb in a sense is undercutting the notion that there exists an ethnic community (of Irish Americans, say) capable of thinking and acting on its own. Denying the Irish community the ability even to possess its own racial hatreds smacks of condescension and would be going against the conclusions of most historians of the period. Michael Feldberg observes, for example, that the Irish, in an effort to retain their cultural ideals and pride in the face of Protestant hostilities, took some consolation in feeling superior to blacks. Moreover, expressing hostility to blacks would be a way of identifying with the very hostilities that the Protestant middle class itself expressed toward blacks; racism was a form of Americanization.[25] Yet the initial scenes involving Stevens and McCloskey work against such a conception, as McCloskey and his pals seem merely to be doing Stevens's bidding under duress. Reporting to Stevens, McCloskey tells of how he and his friends have that past night stirred up the violence Stevens had demanded: "a nagur or two half killed," McCloskey notes, "and one house set on fire and nearly burned up" (p. 176). But now Stevens wants McCloskey to do something even more audacious and much more risky: attack the Garie residence and shoot Garie himself, for which Stevens will pay him five thousand dollars. Initially resistant, McCloskey agrees to the plan for two main reasons: Stevens's threat to abandon him to the courts at the trial stage; and the news that Garie "lives with a nigger woman—and, what is more, he is married to her!" (p. 179).

As Webb well knew, central to many of the riots of 1834-49 were expressions, usually from the working class, of outrage at miscegenation. Most notably, in 1849 an Irish Catholic gang attacked California House, a black tavern and gambling hall. When the blacks resisted, the gang went on a rampage, burning at least thirty buildings and killing two blacks. California House was singled out for an attack, historian Bruce Laurie remarks, "because the proprietor, a Black man or mulatto, had recently married a white woman, presumably of Irish extraction. . . . The classic fantasy of racists, the interracial marriage was, to the Irish, sufficient cause for riot."[26] As Laurie goes on to explain in his excellent account of ethnic working-class culture in antebellum Philadelphia, central locales for the creation of this culture, and its attendant racism, were the taverns and volunteer fire companies, where manliness, camaraderie, ethnic competition, antiblack racism, and "drinking and the social rituals surrounding it"[27] were all emphasized as social values.

These are values, of course, that Webb does not much admire. In this respect, it must be said that Webb suggests yet another reason for the Irish characters' willingness to attack Philadelphia's blacks: that the Irish are a people of the baser sort. Webb thus simultaneously taps into nativist anxieties (exacerbated by the Know-Nothings) about the dangers posed to the republic by drunken, antirepublican Irish,[28] while expressing his own hostility toward the ethnic group that, for a variety of complex sociohistorical reasons, was so openly hostile to the black community. Not for nothing had Webb earlier noted that the Jim Crow regulations on a passenger train had been enforced by "Irish brake-men" (p. 111). Their enthusiastic enforcement of segregationist practices looks forward to the Irish crowd's enthusiastic embrace of Stevens's invitation to inflict violence upon blacks.

The two chapters on the riot at the heart of the novel are among the most disturbing (and spectacular) accounts of violence in antebellum literature. As readers, we are situated with the various black characters as they confront the white onslaught, and thus have a participatory relation to the self-defensive, and actually rather aggressive and heroic, actions that the blacks take to preserve their lives and community. Webb seeks to present his readers with representations of black heroism that undermine the white community's racialist stereotypes of blacks' Sambo-like passivity or unfettered (unthinking) violence. Just as the whites carefully coordinate their offense, the blacks, after having presented evidence of an impending riot to Philadelphia's unresponsive mayor, carefully tend to their own defense. Walters, the admirer of Toussaint L'Ouverture, assumes the role of guardian of his people, turning his house into a "fortress" (p. 203) and taking in the Ellis family and several other blacks. As Carla L. Peterson remarks, "The defense of Walters's house—the bastion of black capitalism—during the riot emblematizes black community interdependence as men and women of all social classes come together to protect it."[29] Playing a key role in the defense is Esther Ellis, who emerges, like her biblical progenitor, as a heroic defender of her people. As the group awaits the arrival of the mob, Walters teaches her how to shoot pistols, exclaiming at her determination to face down the whites: "You are a brave

one, after my own heart" (p. 205). She initially reveals her bravery by retrieving a piece of ignited wood that lands near their arsenal of gun powder. After being saved by Esther from a possible conflagration of their own making, the assembled group looks out the window to see that the "whole of the lower part of the city appears to be in a blaze" (p. 211).

As in Hawthorne's Revolutionary tales of the 1830s, riot is presented as a form of intemperance, a manifestation of the social body out of control. Webb makes this clear both by analogy—McCloskey is drunk on alcohol one night and drunk on malign violence the next—and by more literal representations of the rioters as intoxicated by drink. Before we actually view the rioters close up, however, all we see, from our vantage in Walters's house, is a raging crowd that appears at the house "like a torrent" (p. 211). Yet there is clearly a method to the depersonalized mob's rioting. News has reached Walters's group that the mob attempted to "fire one of the coloured churches" (p. 208), a deliberate effort at destroying a building of symbolic importance to the black community, and now the mob has singled out for destruction the home of Walters, the city's wealthiest black. "Kill the niggers!" the crowd cries. "Down with the Abolitionists!" (p. 212). Then rocks begin to break through Walters's windows.

During the 1842 riot, a mob chased blacks into a ghetto, whereupon some of the blacks, as Laurie notes, "retreated to a house on Bradford's Alley, where they held off their assailants with musket fire."[30] Though Walters lives outside of a ghetto area, the congregated blacks' defense of Walters's home would appear to be drawing on this well-documented incident of resistance. Under Walters's direction, his compatriots return stone for stone, and then, with Esther loading the guns, they fire upon the crowd. Webb's account of the violent struggle is exciting and brutal, reminiscent, in a revisionary twist, of the best of Cooper's accounts of vulnerable whites fighting off the "savage" hoards. In *Garies,* the white hoards are at their most savage when they hunt down a defenseless black, the admirable Mr. Ellis, who had left the relatively secure space of Walters's home in order to warn Garie of the crowd's intent to attack him. Spotted by the rioters on his way to the Garies', Ellis runs to the end of a dead-end street, climbs onto the roof of a building, and then realizes he is trapped. Webb keeps the point of view focused on Ellis so that the reader, along with Ellis, feels equally trapped by white savages. As Ellis desperately clings to the roof's edge, someone strikes at his hand with a hatchet, "severing two of the fingers from one hand and deeply mangling the other" (p. 219). Leaving Ellis for dead after he plummets from the roof, the mob moves on to confront Garie at his home, and eventually someone (Stevens) shoots him at close range through the head. Webb reports on the subsequent actions of the "mob of demons"

(p. 222): "For two long hours they ransacked the house, breaking all they could not carry off, drinking the wine in Mr. Garie's cellar, and shouting and screaming like so many fiends" (p. 223). As they do so, Emily Garie, hiding with her children in a freezing woodshed, dies while giving birth to a stillborn child; the children are later found by sympathetic neighbors. A subsequent coroner's inquest, we are told at the end of the chapter, fails to reveal the true cause of Emily's and her baby's deaths; Stevens served as a member of the panel.

In the immediate wake of the 1842 antiblack riot, Robert Purvis, in a letter of August 22, 1842, to the abolitionist Henry C. Wright, lamented the hopelessness of the blacks' situation in Philadelphia: "Press, Church, Magistrates, Clergymen and Devils—are against us. The measure of our suffering is full." He therefore concluded, "I am convinced of our utter and complete nothingness in public estimation."[31] Purvis's response is in some ways representative of the despair experienced among the black elite, for the riots "had undercut the elite's entire program of community improvement."[32] Not surprisingly, then, some blacks fled Philadelphia. Yet for various reasons—racist housing practices in surrounding neighborhoods, a burgeoning sense of black solidarity in the face of white racism, a continued commitment to the goals of black elevation—a significant number of blacks remained where they were.

The historical tensions between despair and hope, flight and solidarity, are addressed by Webb in his representation of the black community's response to the riot's aftermath. On one side is Clary Garie, scarred by his experiences with the Stevenses and their network of racist intimidators, who, shortly after learning of his parents' deaths, accepts an arrangement worked out for him by the family lawyer, Balch, to travel to Sudbury and attempt to "pass" for white. On the other side are Charlie Ellis and Walters, who persist in their efforts to "elevate" Philadelphia's black community. Walters may declare that "I am almost tempted to curse the destiny that made me what I am" (p. 275), but he never does make that curse, and instead attempts to live up to the responsibilities of his wealth by offering aid to the devastated Ellis family (a synecdoche for the devastated black middle class). In choosing to help the Ellises, Walters articulates a self-conscious commitment to black community that cuts across class lines: "God has blessed me with abundance, and to what better use can it be appropriated than the relief of my friends?" (p. 239). Thus, like a number of blacks in the novel, he continues to "attend to the collectivity," as Peterson puts it, "returning surplus value to the community."[33]

Black solidarity and a redoubled commitment to the temperance values of industry and restraint comes across as well in the account of Charlie Ellis's response to his family's plight. Charlie, to fill in some of the plot

details, had gone to live with the benevolent (and white) Mrs. Bird in order to recuperate from a broken arm and further his education. When he learns about his father's injuries, he immediately realizes, unlike the confused Clary (or George Winston), that he cannot separate his personal fate from the fate of his family. With his father's hands mere stumps, Charlie, his arm now healed, attempts to do for his family what his father, in one of his few lucid moments, urges him to do, "take care of them" (p. 272). But he will do so in a world in effect redefined by the antiblack riots, a world in which subtle forms of racist discrimination must be viewed on a continuum with more direct acts of racist violence. It is a world that his father's mad ravings again and again chillingly unmask: "run home quick, little boy! and tell your mother they're coming, thousands of them; they've guns, and swords, and clubs. Hush! There they come—there they come!" (p. 267).

In such a world of ever-present violence, a continued advocacy of temperate self-help could be taken as rather naive. Or, and this is where I think Webb locates himself, such an advocacy and commitment could be taken as simultaneously pragmatic and political, for it asserts to the white community, as Frederick Douglass was asserting during the 1850s, that blacks continue to lay claim to America's material resources and political ideals. Although Charlie will eventually find a job with the help of whites sympathetic to his situation (and appreciative of his talents), much more weight is given to portraying his determined resistance to white racism. A gracefully written letter of inquiry gets him an interview for a position as an office "boy," but his color proves to be, in the words of the manager who rejects him, "a *fatal* objection" (p. 293). Unlike Clary, or perhaps more significantly, unlike George Winston, Charlie, in response to this rejection, has an even stronger sense of his racial identity and pride, asserting to his equally prideful sister Esther, "I shouldn't care to be white if I knew I would not have a dear old Ess like you for a sister" (p. 293). Applying next for a job as a bank-note engraver, he is rebuffed in this pursuit as well, for the large reason that the other craftsmen and journeymen proclaim to their initially receptive boss, who happens to be an abolitionist, "No nigger apprentices!" (p. 297).[34] But in a Stowe-like scene, Mr. Burrell, a friend of the "abolitionist," describes Charlie's travails to his wife, whose transracial sympathy prompts her to charge her husband with hiring Charlie to work at his new business (p. 302), which he does. We then take leave of Charlie and his friends for what the narrator terms a "few years" (p. 308).

Actually, we leave them for a number of years—approximately fifteen—as Webb makes a historical leap forward to the present, the mid-1850s. From this new vantage point, Stevens's "intemperate" greed and quest for power can now be more literally represented in corporeal terms: he is portrayed rather conventionally, along the lines of the drunken father in T. S. Arthur's great temperance best-seller *Ten Nights in a Bar-Room* (1855), as a drunk whose body and moral principles have, over the years, wasted away. In order to assess what Webb is up to in his portrayal of Stevens's decline, we need to recall where we left Stevens before the leap forward, and to rehearse the scattered evidence of genealogical entanglement that both influenced his desire to murder Garie and contributed to his dissolution. For we learn near the end of the novel that, in attacking the Garies, Stevens attacked his own family. (So much for inviolable boundaries!) The key facts are embedded early in the narrative, when Garie, just before moving to Philadelphia, learns that his uncle's sister years ago had "made a very low marriage" (p. 102) to a "drunken and vicious" (p. 102) carpenter from New York, and was subsequently cut off from the family by her father. Though the sister eventually died, rumor has it that their son survives. That Stevens may well be that son is hinted at just prior to his act of instructing McCloskey and his companions to attack the Garies: After his coconspirator Morton informs him that Garie's Uncle John had died, leaving to Garie—because no one knows the whereabouts of the sister's son—over $100,000, Stevens soliloquizes on his desire for the Garies' wealth, "I'll have it, if I———" (p. 168), and then gazes in a mirror and declares: "I look like a murderer already" (p. 168). His words and secret actions implicitly confirm that he is indeed the "drunken and vicious" carpenter's lost son; but only after the inquest on the Garies that he helped to fix does he reveal himself as the missing heir. Despite the fact that Walters and the lawyer Balch possess evidence of Stevens's role in the death of Garie, such is Stevens's influence within the community that they can only work out a deal whereby they agree to withhold the evidence in return for $12,000 of the $150,000 inheritance for Garie's children.

The fifteen-year jump from this corrupt bargain to Stevens's dissolution makes explicit the connection between greed and drink, power and intemperance, central to Webb's thematics. In his resplendent New York City apartment on Fifth Avenue, Stevens, referred to in George Lippardian antiaristocratic terms as one of New York's "upper ten thousand" (p. 309), is revealed as a drunken wreck of a man, the fitting heir to the father's putative depravities. True to the model of generational transmission informing Arthur's temperance narratives,[35] Stevens's son, George, introduced earlier in the novel as a boy who enjoys torturing flies (p. 127), is an irresponsible dandy who is "often fearfully intoxicated" (p. 358). As is typical of Arthur, virtue remains the repository of the daughter, in this case Lizzie, who as a girl rescued flies from her brother's tortures, and now, as a young woman, acts as Stevens's moral guardian. When her father "lifts his hand to pour out another glass of li-

quor from the decanter at his side, . . . his daughter lays her hand upon it, and looks appealingly in his face" (p. 310).

The setup here—inebriate father, virtuous daughter—is ripe for melodrama, which is what we get when McCloskey, "a shabbily dressed man, bearing a strong odour of rum about him" (p. 312), enters the scene. But though melodramatic, the encounter between the two inebriates neatly summarizes the relationship that has developed between the men over the years, and points to one of the novel's key concerns as well—the dangerous connections between speculation and intemperance in a capitalist economy. Stevens may well be wasting away, but such is his addiction to gain that he continues his economic speculations. Driven by similar economic desires, McCloskey has been blackmailing Stevens for years, and has come to New York to demand additional money in exchange for his silence about Stevens's murder of Garie. Consistent with Webb's connection of intemperance to the desire spawned by the pursuit of capital, both men drink brandy as they conduct their negotiations. Eventually, McCloskey agrees to accept Stevens's offer of four thousand dollars, while unbeknownst to Stevens, Lizzie, who has been eavesdropping on the scene, faints away. When she revives, the faithful virtuous daughter journeys to Philadelphia with the intention of confronting McCloskey, but she arrives too late. The intemperate McCloskey had spent all of his money gambling and drinking, and, following "an awful attack of *delirium tremens*" (p. 362), had died of typhus fever. Just before he died, however, he gained a measure of peace of mind by revealing to legal authorities the truth about the murder of Garie, the news of which prompts Lizzie to hurry back to New York, where she once again is too late: Seeking to escape the warrant for his arrest, Stevens leaps to his death from his apartment window.

His legacy lives on, however, in his inebriated son, whose inheritance of his father's antimiscegenationist zeal leads him to wreak havoc on Clary Gary by exposing his "blackness." Years after agreeing to Balch's advice to separate himself from his family, Clary is about to reap the benefits of "passing" in the form of a marriage to the socially prominent Anne Bates. In order to protect his interests, he has for nearly a year refused to visit with his sister. Like Winston, he has become a moral coward who has fallen in love with whiteness. After his secret past is (inevitably) revealed by George Stevens and the marriage is broken off by Anne's parents, he begins making secret visits to the Bates's home so he can look in at Anne's window. "There she stood in the moonlight," he tells Charlie Ellis, "gazing upward at the sky, so pale, so calm and holy looking, in her pure white dress, that I should not have thought it strange if the heavens had opened" (p. 385). The very traditionalism of the whiteness—purity association so central to his conception here suggests the extent to which he has bought into the symbology of the racial class that does everything it can to expel him.

Clary's pathetic fate in attempting to pass for white and ending up nowhere—he dies of a broken heart—is counterpointed against Webb's larger celebration of the African American characters prospering in 1850s Philadelphia. Addison Gayle, Jr., writes that the novel's apparently happy ending expresses Webb's sense that "individuality must take preference over racial unity."[36] Yet the most visible signs of triumphant individuality depicted at the end of the novel—the continued economic power of Walters, Charlie Ellis's burgeoning career—are all predicated on the belief that the individual's hard work assumes its significance only in relation to family and friends. If there is an "individualist" at the novel's end, it is Clary, who clearly has not earned the narrator's admiration. As opposed to the kind of high-status marriage Clary was pursuing, the marriages culminating the novel—of Walters and Esther Ellis, and then of Charlie Ellis and Emily Garie—signify these characters' commitments to forging bonds that will further strengthen their community. Though white in appearance, Emily conceives of herself as a black in white society, and so she embraces her upcoming marriage to Charlie as a sign of her commitment to her fellow marginalized African Americans. As she had earlier written Clary, who had been urging her to break her ties to Philadelphia's black community: "You walk on the side of the oppressor—I, thank God, am with the oppressed" (p. 336). In putting her commitments on the side of the oppressed, she gains a family. After her marriage to Charlie, the narrator remarks, "she no longer felt herself an orphan" (p. 375).

The penultimate chapter of the novel describes the opulent festivities following Charlie and Emily's marriage ceremony. Wine and sherry are consumed at the reception, and the wedding feast itself is nothing short of luxurious (and excessive): boneless turkeys, stewed terrapin, "oysters in every variety" (p. 376), "jellies, blancmange, chocolate cream" (p. 376) are served, along with "champagne, Rhine wine, sparkling catawba, liquors" (p. 376). There is even "a man in the corner making sherry cobblers of wondrous flavor" (pp. 376-77). How can these African Americans celebrate so excessively, so intemperately, we might ask, given what they have been through, and given their continuing efforts to struggle economically in a racist society? But surely Webb's point here, in the novel's only mention of black drinking, is that a central aspect of the community's strength lies precisely in its ability and willingness, even with all of its hardships, to celebrate an event worth celebrating, and to do so in a fully corporeal fashion. It does so as well in an interracial fashion, as this utopianistic picture of happiness and good cheer includes some of the whites who, in helping the Garies

and their friends, challenged the strictures of their culture. "What a happy time they had!" (p. 377) the narrator concludes. Yet even as the narrator takes pride in the ability of this group to carve out a niche of happiness amidst racist Philadelphia, Webb is hardly naive about the larger problems that continue to face the black community. Within the larger context of the novel, the elder Ellis, mad and "paranoid," looms as the group's most prescient realist. "There they come! there they come!" (p. 342) he regularly declares from within his visionary prison. Amidst the wedding's plenty and festivity, he sees just "another mob" (p. 372).

Despite the elder Ellis's warnings, though, the happiness and economic rejuvenation of the Ellises and their friends provide the novel with a relatively happy ending, and a sense, as in Emily's self-conscious declarations of her alliance with the oppressed, that that happiness has a political dimension. But all of this is not to deny that the novel is rife with contradictions, particularly as concerns the linked issues of temperance and capitalism. One might certainly wonder, for example, about the excesses of the final wedding celebration, as the feasting and drinking can seem, when compared with the novel's opening presentation of the similarly excessive afternoon tea at the Garies' slave plantation, as portentous signs of the encroachment of luxury on the novel's black community. From this perspective, one could argue that the marginalized and oppressed black celebrants seem all too ready to enter the comfortable world of their oppressors. Yet to my mind the parallels between the novel's opening and closing feasts are deliberately intended by Webb to suggest difference more than similarity, the key difference being precisely what Emily says it is: that the blacks, despite the celebration, remain oppressed. Moreover, in portraying the blacks as drinking lustily at the celebration, Webb distances himself from the puritanical and Franklinian strain of the black temperance movement—the world, say, of the American Moral Reform Society. At the novel's conclusion, Charlie Ellis's sister, Caddy, stands as the sole representative of this extreme commitment to frugality and self-restraint, as she and her husband have a "wonderful little girl, who, instead of buying candy and cake with her sixpences, as other children did, gravely invested them in miniature wash-boards and dust-brushes, and was saving up her money to purchase a tiny stove with a full set of cooking utensils" (p. 392). In a final act of narrative mockery, Webb remarks, "Caddy declares her a child worth having" (p. 392). Clearly, from Webb's perspective, temperate self-regulation for the mere sake of temperate self-regulation will fail to do much of anything to strengthen and elevate the African American community.

But contradictions remain. For even if we read the parallel between the Garies' opening feast and the closing wedding feast as pointing to difference, what are we to make of the picture of upwardly aspiring black capitalists in relation to the picture of the intemperate Stevens? His intemperance, as we have seen, has an analogue in his rapacious capitalistic desires. Though Webb's melodramatic characterizations permit us to conceive of a relatively easy dichotomy between Stevens and the capitalists of the black community, we may nonetheless discern an ideological conflict or confusion on Webb's part. For the question that is deflected (or avoided) throughout the novel is, to put it bluntly, how to separate the good from the bad capitalists? That is to say, if participation in the marketplace is central to black self-elevation, and money is central to the ability to have lavish, sensuous feasts, how does one ensure that the pursuit of wealth does not involve the pursuer in the forms of power and intemperance typified by Stevens? Like Stevens, Walters, for example, is a speculator in real estate; and like Stevens and his business associates, Charlie Ellis proclaims that he wants money principally to provide for his family. In this respect, a sentimental aspect of the novel is Webb's seeming insistence that blacks can gain moral stature from participation in a marketplace that is otherwise shown to elicit, indeed depend upon, "intemperate" desires and actions.

This leads to a final and even larger ideological conundrum of the novel: What about the problem of slavery in America? And what about the slaves? Given that slavery remains a central reality of American cultural life, it is a troubling fact of the novel's conclusion that the black Philadelphia community seems to be working rather narrowly for its own survival. Gayle thus remarks, "Not with the slave . . . lies the sympathy of this middle-class novelist, but with those who, through hard work and initiative, seek to travel light-years from their brothers."[37] While there is no evidence in the novel to suggest that characters like Walters and Charlie Ellis want to travel "light-years from their brothers" (and sisters), there is every sense that they want to travel light-years from being enslaved, and therefore can seem self-absorbed in their quest for economic independence. In their defense, we could say that the characters clearly have enough problems of their own without having to take onto their shoulders the plight of the slaves. We could also say that in obtaining economic power, and in developing their own cultural institutions—such as the reading societies that the Ellis daughters attend at the novel's opening—the black characters are in their own ways furthering the elevation of blacks in America (and for all we know slavery *was* the central focus of these reading societies). In the spirit of the black temperance movement, which argued that black material success would refute proslavery ideology, Webb most likely regards the fortunes of Philadelphia's blacks as very much linked to the fates of the Southern slaves. That said, it must be conceded that none of the major characters explicitly participates in antislavery actions, though Walters's reverence for Toussaint l'Ouverture does suggest that he conceives of his economic pursuits in an antislavery context.[38]

In *Garies,* then, the issue of black elevation takes weight over antislavery, which can help to explain a rather chilling blind spot in the text. An important aspect of the novel's "happy" ending is that McCloskey's confession and Stevens's death allow the lawyer Balch to recover for the Garie children some of their father's legacy. Central to that legacy, we have to assume, is the money earned from his slave plantation. Have Emily and Charlie in effect received the blood money of slaveholders as their inheritance? We need to recall that when the Garies went North early in the novel, Winston, as is typical of his lack of political consciousness, urges Garie to leave behind on the plantation a trustworthy overseer, whose services Garie indeed secures. At no point while in Philadelphia does Garie order the slaves sold or freed, which means that when he died they constituted part of his legacy. When financial matters are sorted out in the end, therefore, the children, by the Northern law under which Balch is operating, are entitled to their property, which means they can now claim the slaves, or, more likely, given that slavery is still the law of the land, the money obtained by Stevens in selling them to other slaveholders. I take Webb's failure to confront these matters directly less as a sign of his lack of sympathy for antislavery, or the slaves, than as a sign of the way in which his emphasis on the Philadelphia blacks' efforts to achieve middle-class American identity leads him to fall into a trap of a number of ethnic writers with "assimilationist" aspirations: to want to make origins relatively invisible, as if origins, for those aspiring to just such an "American" identity, threaten to become shameful.[39]

As compelling as is Webb's portrayal of black middle-class life in antebellum Philadelphia, and as complex as is his treatment of the dissolving boundaries between temperate self-control and capitalist exploitation, the sense that Webb, in too uncritically aligning himself with temperance and capitalist values, has forgotten (or is shamed by) the slaves no doubt has contributed, as the various adduced comments by Bell, Jackson, and Gayle suggest, to the novel's neglect. Webb's reputation has also not been helped by the fact that his two other extant fictional works, the short stories **"Two Wolves and a Lamb"** and **"Marvin Hayle,"** which appeared in 1870 issues of *New Era: A Colored National Journal,* focus on white aristocratic characters in London and Paris and thus seem oblivious to blacks' continuing struggles in America.[40]

And yet in the issue of *New Era* immediately following the final installment of **"Two Wolves and a Lamb,"** there appeared a front-page editorial by Webb in which he addresses the debate on Reconstruction in terms that can help us to tease out a utopian dimension of *Garies* and a possible explanation of its blind spots. After accusing the Democrats in particular of a fundamental racism that keeps them "fighting now, as they fought then [before the Civil War] . . . any movement that is calculated to elevate [the African American] to his proper position and maintain him there," Webb addresses his black (male) readers on the possible end results of such elevation. "Colored men of the South," he proclaims, "what are the rash innovations, the institutions of the country have lately experienced—they are colored voters, walking manfully to the polls, depositing an intelligent vote for that party whose friendship for us has been tried. They are the governance of southern cities, by men who dared not walk their streets at night without a pass. They are colored men as state legislators, making the law by which white men are governed. They are happy-faced colored children on their way to mixed schools."[41] We should recall that when Garie first arrived in Philadelphia and saw black children on their way to school, he remarked to himself that Philadelphia "don't much resemble Georgia" (p. 120), only to learn, in his final moments, that Philadelphia in fact does resemble Georgia. Webb's dream in *Garies* and in this post-Civil War piece, similar to the dream informing Frederick Douglass's writings, is of an egalitarian, biracial America in which there *are* differences between slavery and freedom. In post-Civil War America, which he hopes will not resemble pre-Civil War America, the participation of blacks and whites in democratic institutions will dissolve boundaries between the races, providing opportunities for those who energetically pursue them. Among the opportunities for blacks would be the right to assert governance over whites. That such a right, along with unrestricted access to the market economy, would mean that blacks would have the potential to become as corrupt and intemperate as most of the whites we meet in *Garies* is a problem that, for both the visionary-utopianist and the liberal-pragmatist sides of Webb, can be addressed at such a time when these epochal changes in American society have truly occurred.

Notes

1. *Minutes and Proceedings of the First Annual Meeting of the American Moral Reform Society: Held at Philadelphia in the Presbyterian Church in Seventh Street, below Shippen, from the 14th to the 19th of August, 1837* (1837), reprinted in *Early Negro Writing, 1760-1837,* ed. Dorothy Porter (Boston: Beacon, 1971), pp. 207, 241, 235, 236.

2. On black temperance, see Benjamin Quarles, *Black Abolitionists* (New York: Oxford University Press, 1969), pp. 91-100; and Donald Yacovone, "The Transformation of the Black Temperance Movement, 1827-1854: An Interpretation," *Journal of the Early Republic* 8 (1988): 281-97. The seminal study of black elevation is Frederick Cooper, "Elevating the Race: The Social Thought of Black Leaders, 1827-50," *American Quarterly* 24 (1972): 604-25. See also Jane H. Pease and William H. Pease, *They Who Would Be Free: Blacks' Search for Freedom, 1830-1861* (New York: Atheneum, 1974). On the antebellum temperance movement generally, see Ian R. Tyrell, *Sobering Up: From Temperance to Prohibition in Antebellum America, 1800-1860* (Westport, Conn.: Greenwood, 1979); and W. J. Rorabaugh, *The Alcoholic Republic: An American Tradition* (New York: Oxford University Press, 1979).

3. Gary Nash, *Forging Freedom: The Formation of Philadelphia's Black Community, 1720-1840* (Cambridge: Harvard University Press, 1988), p. 221.

4. Emma Jones Lapsansky, "'Since They Got Those Separate Churches': Afro-Americans and Racism in Jacksonian Philadelphia," *American Quarterly* 32 (1980): 57. Blacks viewed the pursuit of wealth as a way of challenging white racialist notions of black indolence. As Lapsansky remarks in another fine article, black Philadelphians of the middle and upper classes were "molded together by a self-conscious belief that its successes and behaviors could significantly effect the life-chances of *all* Afroamericans" ("Friends, Wives, and Strivings: Networks and Community Values Among Nineteenth-Century Philadelphia Afroamerican Elites," *Pennsylvania Magazine of History and Biography* 108 [1984]: 4).

5. Blyden Jackson, for example, terms the book "pedestrian and hackneyed," "the stuff of melodrama." See his *A History of Afro-American Literature. Volume I: The Long Beginning, 1746-1895* (Baton Rouge: Louisiana State University Press, 1989), p. 344. Similarly, Vernon Loggins writes about Webb's *Garies*: "There is power in his story, but it is all but lost in melodrama and sentimentality" (*The Negro Author: His Development in America to 1900* [1931; rept. Port Washington, N.Y.: Kennikat, 1964], p. 251). And Arlene H. Elder maintains that Webb "found light touches with the satirist's brush unsatisfying and reached for the muckraker's hammer instead" (*The "Hindered Hand": Cultural Implications of Early African-American Fiction* [Westport, Conn.: Greenwood, 1978], p. 47).

6. See Carla L. Peterson's excellent "Capitalism, Black (Under)development, and the Production of the African-American Novel in the 1850s," *American Literary History* 4 (1992): 577-79.

7. Brook Thomas, *The New Historicism and Other Old-Fashioned Topics* (Princeton: Princeton University Press, 1991), p. 58. See also the discussion

of the minority hybrid text's enactment of "repetition with a difference" (p. 567) in Peterson's "Capitalism, Black (Under)development."

8. The best account of the emigration movement and debate may be found in Floyd J. Miller's *The Search for a Black Nationality: Black Emigration and Colonization, 1787-1863* (Urbana: University of Illinois Press, 1975). See also Pease and Pease, *They Who Would Be Free,* pp. 251-78.

9. "Colored Citizens of Pennsylvania," *Frederick Douglass' Paper,* April 13, 1855, p. 2. The column is anonymous, though it appears in the spot in the newspaper where Douglass usually printed his own editorials.

10. Jackson, *History of Afro-American Literature,* p. 348. Arthur P. Davis, the editor of a 1969 facsimile reprinting of *Garies,* similarly criticizes the novel's "highly contrived plot, its purple patches, its tear-jerking scenes, and its deathbed repentances." Though he argues that the book looks forward to important tropes and themes in later 19th- and 20th-Century African American writing, he terms the novel a "typical 19th-century melodrama" which uncritically portrays middle class blacks for whom "money is all important" (Introduction to Frank J. Webb, *The Garies and Their Friends* [1857; rept. New York: Arno, 1969], pp. viii, v). With Davis as its champion, it is no wonder that the book was allowed once again to go out of print!

11. Addison Gayle, Jr., *The Way of the New World: The Black Novel in America* (Garden City, N.J.: Anchor, 1975), pp. 11, 13, 14. Robert Bone also sees the "dominant tone of Webb's novel" to be, somewhat inappropriately, "that of the conventional success story" (*The Negro Novel in America* [New Haven: Yale University Press, 1965], p. 31).

12. Webb, *Garies,* p. v.

13. Webb, *Garies,* p. 1. All further page references to Webb's novel will be cited parenthetically in the text.

14. The sensationalistic urban journalist George G. Foster observed of Philadelphia's blacks in the 1840s, "The better class of colored men and women in Philadelphia are as virtuous, as cleanly, as industrious, as intelligent and in every way as worthy as the corresponding class of whites. In point of sobriety and economy they are at least equal to their white brethren." See "'Philadelphia in Slices,' by George G. Foster," ed. George Rogers Taylor, *Pennsylvania Magazine of History and Biography,* 93 (1969): 61. Foster's series of articles first appeared in the New York *Tribune,* October 21, 1848 to February 15, 1849.

15. Bernard Bell, *The Afro-American Novel and Its Tradition* (Amherst: University of Massachusetts Press, 1987), p. 43.

16. Frederick Douglass, "Learn Trades or Starve!" *Frederick Douglass' Paper,* March 4, 1853; reprinted in *The Life and Writings of Frederick Douglass. II: Pre-Civil War Decade, 1850-1860,* ed. Philip S. Foner (New York: International, 1950), p. 223. Martin R. Delany similarly warned his black readers of the degradation accompanying servile positions; see for example his essay "Domestic Economy," *North Star,* April 20, 1849, p. 2.

17. See Elizabeth M. Geffen, "Violence in Philadelphia in the 1840's and 1850's," *Pennsylvania History* 36 (1969): 386-87.

18. Lapsansky, "Friends, Wives, and Strivings," p. 22. Also emphasizing Philadelphia's heterogeneous housing patterns is Sam Bass Warner, Jr., *The Private City: Philadelphia in Three Periods of Its Growth* (Philadelphia: University of Pennsylvania Press, 1968), p. 50. Other historians have argued that, despite the apparent heterogeneity, stratification by race and class was beginning to dominate housing patterns during the 1840-60 period. For interesting discussions of these developments, see Stuart M. Blumin, "Residential Mobility Within the Nineteenth-Century City," in *The Peoples of Philadelphia: A History of Ethnic Groups and Lower-Class Life, 1790-1940,* ed. Allen F. Davis and Mark H. Haller (Philadelphia: Temple University Press, 1973), pp. 37-51; Theodore Hershberg, "Free Blacks in Antebellum Philadelphia," in Davis and Haller, *Peoples of Philadelphia,* pp. 111-33; and Bruce Laurie, *Working People of Philadelphia: 1800-1850* (Philadelphia: Temple University Press, 1980), esp. pp. 10-11. On white concerns about "amalgamation" in *Garies,* see James Kinney, *Amalgamation! Race, Sex, and Rhetoric in the Nineteenth-Century American Novel* (Westport, Conn.: Greenwood, 1985), pp. 92-97, 100-1.

19. By showing how racism can undermine blacks' efforts to gain an education, Webb makes clear that whites understood just how important education was to black efforts at self-elevation. Though Clary and Em attend a private school, what is true for that school is also true for Philadelphia's public schools: that whites for the most part successfully resist black participation. At the approximate historical period in which the bulk of *Garies* is set—the early 1840s—only 3 percent of the total public school population was white. See Harry C. Silcox, "Delay and Neglect: Negro Public Education in Antebellum Philadelphia, 1800-1860,"

Pennsylvania Magazine of History and Biography 97 (1973): 444-64.

20. Webb is also rhetorically aligned with George G. Foster, whose "Philadelphia in Slices" (pp. 48, 49) presented the gambling houses as "vile, filthy dens" of alcoholic consumption, wherein "lawyers, merchants, gentlemen of refined taste and cultivated understanding, here meet unabashed to gratify the most cruel and relentless appetite implanted in the breast of man."

21. See Julie Winch, *Philadelphia's Black Elite: Activism, Accommodation, and the Struggle for Autonomy, 1787-1848* (Philadelphia: Temple University Press, 1988), pp. 144-45. As Lapsansky notes, the blacks most bitterly resented by whites were those who "represented economic and social 'success' and 'respectability'" ("Since They Got Those Separate Churches," p. 64). On this and later race riots in antebellum Philadelphia, see also Warner, *Private City,* pp. 125-57.

22. See Leonard L. Richards, *"Gentlemen of Property and Standing": Anti-Abolition Mobs in Jacksonian America* (New York: Oxford University Press, 1970). Winch remarks on the origin of the 1838 riot in rumor: "Robert Purvis was seen accompanying his darker-skinned wife, Harriet, to a meeting of the female antislavery convention. On this occasion, as on others, Purvis was mistakenly thought to be white" (*Philadelphia's Black Elite,* pp. 146-47).

23. Frederick Douglass, "Intemperance and Slavery," in *The Frederick Douglass Papers: Series One: Speeches, Debates, and Interviews: Volume I: 1841-46,* ed. John W. Blassingame et al. (New Haven: Yale University Press, 1979), p. 57. The banner of "freedom" that Douglass referred to pictured a black slave breaking out of his chains against a backdrop of what appeared to be flames. Many whites regarded the banner as an overly assertive representation of black independence and power. In a classic case of blaming the victim, whites therefore talked of the banner as having "caused" the riot. See Winch, *Philadelphia's Black Elite,* pp. 148-50; and Warner, *Private City,* pp. 140-41.

24. Leon Litwack, *North of Slavery: The Negro in the Free States, 1790-1860* (University of Chicago Press, 1961), p. 102.

25. See Michael Feldberg, "The Crowd in Philadelphia History: A Comparative Perspective," in *American Workingclass Culture: Explorations in American Labor and Social History,* ed. Milton Cantor (Westport, Conn.: Greenwood, 1979), p. 89.

26. Laurie, *Working People,* pp. 156-57.

27. Laurie, *Working People,* p. 54. On the role of the fire companies in helping the Irish to maintain a sense of pride and identity in the face of nativist hostility, see also Dennis J. Clark, "The Philadelphia Irish: Persistent Presence," in *Peoples of Philadelphia,* pp. 135-54. In an interesting and powerful scene, Webb challenges the paternalistic reading of the working class informing most of the novel by depicting Stevens venturing into the ethnic pockets of Philadelphia and becoming the victim of the very forces he attempts to marshal. Unaware that he is wearing the clothes "in the rowdy style . . . of a notorious fire company" (p. 186), Stevens wanders into a rival neighborhood, is taken as a member of "one of the well-known and hated faction" (p. 186), the Rangers, and is viciously beaten by a gang (presumably consisting of members of that neighborhood's fire company) while others in the community look on. In the context of his own plottings, he has become a metaphorical "black," a metaphor that the gang attempts to literalize by tarring his face: "Oh! don't he look like a nigger!" (p. 188). Needless to say, Stevens learns nothing from his painful experience.

28. Historian William E. Gienapp observes, "For both Know Nothings and temperance crusaders, besotted Irish Catholics functioned as their primary negative reference group" (*The Origins of the Republican Party, 1852-1856* [New York: Oxford University Press, 1987], p. 98). In portraying the Irish so unsympathetically as intractable drinkers, Webb ignores the fact that many of Philadelphia's Irish Catholics, like many of Philadelphia's African Americans, embraced temperance as a social program of elevation during economic hard times. Father Mathew's preachings had a trans-Atlantic influence on the Irish community; the tavern culture of some Irish was not the culture of all. By 1841 there were approximately 3,000 members of the Catholic Total Abstinence Society; and in 1842, the year of the black temperance parade, approximately 8,000 Irish Catholics marched in their own temperance parade. For information on temperance in Philadelphia's Irish community, I am indebted to Edith Jeffrey, "Reform, Renewal, and Vindication: Irish Immigrants and the Catholic Total Abstinence Movement in Antebellum Philadelphia," *Pennsylvania Magazine of History and Biography* 112 (1988): 407-31.

29. Peterson, "Capitalism, Black (Under)development," p. 579.

30. Laurie, *Working People,* p. 125.

31. Cited in Winch, *Philadelphia's Black Elite,* p. 150.

32. Winch, *Philadelphia's Black Elite,* p. 151.

33. Peterson, "Capitalism, Black (Under)develop-ment," p. 578. Thus I think Bernard Bell is mis-taken when he writes of *Garies:* "Class values . . . displace color in Webb's narrative" (*Afro-American Novel,* p. 44).

34. Historians of the period have observed that segre-gation in the work force was sharply on the rise during the 1840-60 period; in fact, as Hershberg notes, by "1847 less than one-half of 1 percent of the black male work force was employed in facto-ries" ("Free Blacks," p. 117).

35. See especially the transmission of moral and cor-poreal qualities from the tavern owner to his son in T. S. Arthur, *Ten Nights in a Bar-Room* (1855; rept. New York: Odyssey, 1960).

36. Gayle, *Way of the New World,* p. 14.

37. Gayle, *Way of the New World,* p. 14.

38. Interestingly, the only explicitly antislavery activ-ity of the novel is displayed by poorer, working-class blacks—waiters at a fancy hotel who declare to Southern guests their love for slavery only to turn over their additional tips to the underground railroad. Winston, who is outraged by their fawn-ing servility, fails to see through their ruse (pp. 40-41).

39. For an excellent discussion of these issues, see Donald Weber, "Reconsidering the Hansen Thesis: Generational Metaphors and American Ethnic Studies," *American Quarterly* 43 (1991): 320-32.

40. "Two Wolves and a Lamb," for example, tells the story of a "wolfish" woman who (perhaps accidentally) kills the woman engaged to the man she loves, one Mr. Walton; the tale builds to a rather ludicrous scene in which Walton takes re-venge against the "wolf" by covering her with snakes in a remote island cabin. Why offer up such a Poe-like Gothic tale of white aristocrats to an audience of African American readers during the time of Reconstruction? No doubt an inge-nious reader could discover in the story an alle-gorical critique of white inbreeding and depravity; but with its placement on the page in *New Era* regularly devoted to "lighter" fare (p. 4), it would not be inappropriate to set ingenuity aside and conclude that Webb was simply out to entertain, and was doing so, after years abroad in predomi-nately white circles, in somewhat decadent fash-ion. See *New Era: A Colored American National Journal* 1 (January-February 1870).

41. F. J. Webb, "An Old Foe with a New Face," *New Era: A Colored American National Journal* (February 10, 1870): 1. This piece has not been noted previously in any discussions of Webb's writings and is missing from the bibliography in Gregory L. Candela, "Frank J. Webb," *Dictionary of Literary Biography. Volume 50: Afro-American Writers Before the Harlem Renaissance,* ed. Trudier Harris and Thadious M. Davis (Detroit: Gale Research, 1986), pp. 242-45.

Robert Reid-Pharr (essay date 1997)

SOURCE: Reid-Pharr, Robert. Introduction to *The Gar-ies and Their Friends,* pp vii-xviii. Baltimore: Johns Hopkins University Press, 1997.

[*In the following introduction to the 1997 edition of Webb's* The Garies and Their Friends, *Reid-Pharr dis-cusses the principles of domesticity and black ethnicity that were integral to Webb's writings and philosophy.*]

It is remarkable that, even as the study of African American literature and culture has become central to any number of projects within American intellectual life, so little attention has been given a work as signifi-cant as Frank J. Webb's **The Garies and Their Friends** (1857). The second novel to be published by an African American and one of the first American novels to deal explicitly with miscegenation and the lives of free blacks in the antebellum northeast, **The Garies** remains in relative obscurity while other early black novels— William Wells Brown's *Clotel* (1853), Harriet Wilson's *Our Nig* (1859), and Martin Delany's *Blake,* published in serial between 1859 and 1862—are all more or less regularly read, taught, and critiqued. It seems, in fact, that the work continues to be not so much forgotten as ignored. Even though it was reprinted in 1969, **The Garies** has received almost no critical attention since then and most of what it has received has been descrip-tive and encyclopedic instead of interpretive or theoreti-cal. The work's author, Frank J. Webb, has been dis-cussed, if at all, as a somewhat imitative and peripheral figure, forever lost to the vagaries of historical memory. His relation to contemporaries Frederick Douglass, Mar-tin Delany, William Wells Brown, Harriet Jacobs, Har-riet Wilson, Henry Highland Garnet, William Craft and Ellen Craft, among others, has barely been commented upon, much less contextualized. Addison Gayle does discuss **The Garies** in *The Way of the New World,*[1] cit-ing it as a relatively well-wrought example of the inte-grationist tradition in which he places both *Clotel* and Charles Chesnutt's *The House Behind the Cedars* (1900), a point to which we will return. Gayle does not, however, go much further than that. **The Garies** contin-ues, then, to languish.

In attempting to decode the riddle of **The Garies**—or rather, in attempting to understand why the work has been given so little attention by contemporary critics—I am drawn to the several problems it poses for students of African American literature. First, there is the miscegenation motif, in which a white southern planter educates, manumits, and eventually weds—ostensibly for the sake of their children—his slave concubine. Frank Webb was absolutely fascinated by the serious problem that interracialism—that is, race mixing—poses to what I call here the project of black domesticity, an ideological orientation that emphasizes family and familial life as the wellspring of black economic, political, and social development. This black domesticity is the same ideological orientation that Webb rigorously follows in both this novel and his short stories. His response to this problem is to reject interracialism in favor of integrationism, a stance in which the cultural similarity of all American people is insisted upon while racial distinctiveness is maintained. The black and the white are at once the same and different.

The second difficulty posed by *The Garies* is that most of the action in the novel takes place in "free" Philadelphia and centers on the struggle by the black population there to maintain and advance itself or, more precisely, to construct a free black domesticity. Like Harriet Wilson's *Our Nig*—another work that was largely forgotten until recently—this novel represents a serious reworking of, if not a decisive break with, much early African American writing. It was not conceived as a tool of the abolitionist movement—an accurate, transparent depiction of the realities of the slave experience—in the same ways that Frederick Douglass's *The Heroic Slave* (1853) was. Both *The Garies* and *Our Nig* traffic first and foremost in the intricacies of domestic life, with a specific and sustained emphasis on the problem of whiteness within the project of black domesticity. This does not mean, however, that we see in *The Garies* a simple avoidance of the difficult issues surrounding slavery, emancipation, and sectional strife. Instead, I believe Webb's particular genius was that he refused to recognize a clear distinction, not so much between the slave and the free, the southern and the northern, but rather, and perhaps more importantly, between the domestic and the political. Webb suggested that, at least for the African American, the domestic sphere represented a sort of ground zero in the struggle for both the liberation of the slaves and the just treatment of free black populations.

The Garies opens with a description of the refined, well-educated, and good-tempered Clarence Garie, the white father of the ill-fated interracial family. His wife, Emily, a woman whose light brown complexion suggested "the faintest hint of carmine," had been bought some ten years earlier in the Savannah slave market. Thereafter Mr. Garie treated her as his protégée, arranging for her education and lavishing her with attention. Finally they unite and produce two children, Clarence and Emily, neither of whom has any idea they are black,

much less slaves. Nevertheless it is the issue of these children and what would become of them if Mr. Garie were to suddenly die that prompts the family to leave the idyllic surroundings of their Georgia plantation for the relatively freer environment of Philadelphia. There, the Garies hope that their presence will be tolerated, if not exactly accepted.

Standing in contradistinction to the Garies are the Ellises, "a highly respectable and industrious coloured family," consisting of a tender mother, a hard-working father, and their three children: the beautiful and accomplished older daughter, Esther, the shrewish and extremely fastidious middle child, Caddy, and a rambunctious young son, Charlie. It is the Ellis family that in every particular acts as the mirror of the Garies' various identities. Whereas the Garies are masters, the Ellises are servants (Caddy Ellis takes particular pains to prepare the Garies' Philadelphia mansion for its new occupants). Whereas the Garies are rich, the Ellises are relatively poor. While the Garies seem to be always at leisure, the Ellises work constantly. Most importantly, the Garies are a "mixed" family, whereas the Ellises are "purely" black, secure in their understanding of where they stand in Philadelphia's racial economy.

Finally, there is Mr. Walters, a black real estate speculator who amasses a considerable fortune through sheer hard work and intellect, a man who stands at the pinnacle of respectable and cultured life in black Philadelphia, his taste and accomplishments rivaling those of any white man in the Americas. To his credit, he holds particular affection for both the Garies and the Ellises, harboring Mrs. Ellis, Esther, and Caddy in his home during a fateful riot scene and attempting to warn the Garies by using Mr. Ellis as an (unsuccessful) messenger of the advancing mob. After the riot is over and some level of normality returns to their lives, he invites the remnants of both families—with the one exception of Clarence Garie—to remain under his roof. Eventually he marries Esther, installing himself as the new (good) husband and father, stepping in where both Mr. Garie and Mr. Ellis have failed.

The danger one faces when attempting an interpretation of *The Garies* is to stick too closely to one of two rather well-worn paths. The first would suggest that the novel is deeply flawed because it draws rather heavily on the rhetoric and motifs of sentimentalism that typified the work of many of Webb's contemporaries, particularly Harriet Beecher Stowe's *Uncle Tom's Cabin* (1850) and Susan Warner's *Wide Wide World* (1851). The second would specifically refute this claim by pointing to elements within the novel that dramatized the realpolitik of the mid-nineteenth-century antebellum northeast—particularly the riot scene, the economic struggles of the free black population, and the difficulties surrounding education. What I would like to suggest instead is that both these paths are ultimately dead ends, since they both posit the very distinction between the domestic and the political that I argue Frank Webb specifically rejects. Webb imagines the novel of manners and domesticity as anything but frivolous or apolitical. Instead, as I have argued already, he imagines the domestic sphere as the center of black political life, the place at which community is formed and resistance is mounted. More to the point, he imagines the domestic sphere as the place at which a "pure" black community might protect itself from the dangers of an always encroaching whiteness.

We see this graphically demonstrated during the riot, when the individuals trapped in Walters' home defend themselves from the violent white mob not only with the traditional tools of political resistance—guns and ammunition—but also with those less obvious, if more effective, means found within the properly managed household. When a large cinder from the fireplace falls onto a group of cartridges resting nearby, threatening to explode the ammunition and kill the entire group, Esther Ellis, in her role as calm and level-headed household manager, gingerly plucks it from among the heap on the floor and tosses it back into the flames. (She then immediately faints and is consigned to the bosom of her mother.) Meanwhile, Caddy, the more strident and shrill younger sister, and Kinch, her somewhat disheveled counterpart and future husband, have prepared a concoction of hot water and pepper which she pours onto the offending mob below just as it threatens to break down the doors and enter the house. She engages, then, in the typically female and domestic activity of "cleaning" as the very means by which she resists white supremacy and mob violence.

The danger of whiteness does not stop, however, at the threshold of the black home. The more significant danger is not the clearly defined white mob, but the white friend and in particular, the white lover—the interloper who would disallow black purity. It is important to note here that the riot does not simply bring together the new black family under Walters' roof. It also destroys the old interracial family, the Garies. Mr. Garie is murdered. His wife, Emily, dies giving birth to a stillborn child, the very emblem of the nonviability of interracialism, of race mixing. The last turn that one must make, then, in deciphering Webb's aesthetic, is to recognize that while it is within the domestic that the civility, or the Americanness, of the black is represented, it is a peculiar domesticity that produces this effect. The *black* household produces exclusively *black* Americans. The politics of domesticity proceed, then, by both showing blackness to be similar, to be American, while also representing it as different, as black.

This explains, then, why Mr. Walters is such a significant character, one separate from and superior to the others. He is the quintessence of successful hybridiza-tion. He is in America and of America and yet his blackness remains pristine. "Mr. Walters was . . . of jet-black complexion, and smooth glossy skin. . . . His aquiline nose, thin lips, and broad chin, were the very reverse of African in their shape, and gave his face a very singular appearance." Walters is both "The Black" and its inverse. Imbedded within the skin of the Negro are the nose, the lips, the chin and, one might even argue, the "mind" of the European. He is the symbol of the African's creation of a space for himself in Western culture, a space that, however hemmed in by whiteness, remains purely black.

Once we understand this, it becomes possible to read more thoroughly the scene in which Mr. Garie makes his first visit with Walters. Mr. Garie is transfixed by a portrait of Toussaint L'Ouverture in the uniform of a general, a piece that stands among all the many markers of Walters' cultivated taste, his domesticity: the richly papered walls, the paintings of American and European masters, the rich vases and well-executed bronzes, and those "charming little bijoux which the French only are capable of conceiving." In the midst of Euro-American refinement we find the black hero, as cultivated as his surroundings, yet nevertheless separate and ready for struggle. Following the work of C. L. R. James, one might even suggest that the image of Toussaint L'Ouverture is already heavily overdetermined by the integrationist ideology that I am attempting to explicate here. Indeed, James works assiduously to demonstrate that L'Ouverture imagined the revolution in Santo Domingo not as a black nationalist revolt, but instead as an extension of the republican ethic at the center of the French Revolution itself. The former slaves on the island of Hispaniola were black, but they were Jacobins as well.[2]

We see a similar ideological stance in the life and the literature of Frank Webb. Webb was both a self conscious American and a "race man." An early agent of *Freedom's Journal* (1827-29), the first newspaper published by African Americans, Webb was clearly involved in the production of "the black aesthetic" some three decades before he published his novel. Moreover, for a time following the war Webb was a regular contributor to *The New Era: A Colored American National Journal,* published in Washington, D.C., from 1870 to 1874 with J. Stella Martin as editor and Frederick Douglass as corresponding editor. Douglass would eventually take the leading role, when the paper was continued as *The New National Era.* Webb published his two known short stories, **"Two Wolves and a Lamb"** and **"Martin Hayle"** in *The New Era,* along with the essays **"International Exhibition," "The Mixed School Question,"** and **"An Old Foe with a New Face,"** as well as a poem, **"None Spoke a Single Word to Me."**

> It was indeed a festive scene
> The hall was all agleam with light,

And stalwart men and maidens fair
      In mirth forgot times hasty flight.
I sadly wander'd midst the throng,
      To where I heard their laughter free,
And stood, a lonely looker on;
      None spoke a single word to me.

Around me men and matrons smil'd
      On the loud mirth they once could share,
And gaz'd with loving eyes upon
      Loved offspring in their places there.
And ever and anon they threw
      A quiet jest to swell the glee;
Yet whilst I sadly smil'd on them,
      None spoke a single word to me.

Young eyes were brighten'd by the tale
      Told from old Eve's time until now,
And fair cheeks flush'd and then grew pale,
      Whilst list'ning to some whisper'd vow.
And laughing children midst the throng
      Were faces, ah! so sweet to see;
Yet though my heart o'erflowed to them,
      None spoke a single world to me.

'Tis very sad to walk amidst
      A joy in which you mingle not,
And feel yourself amidst the crowd
      The only one who seems forgot.
Yes, even far above the stars
      I dull and sad of heart should be,
If, 'midst that bright angelic host,
      None spoke a single word to me.[3]

The poem clearly celebrates the domesticity and the articulation of blackness that I argue are the defining features of Webb's aesthetic. Men and matrons gaze on loved offspring while young lovers blush at the exchange of whispered vows. The unnamed and ostensibly unmarked protagonist suffers, moreover, not because of some direct assault or bitter insult but because he is denied the sign that would mark inclusion into this scene of bliss: "None spoke a single word to me."

Still, even as Webb bemoans the exclusion of the black narrator from this scene, he does not mean to suggest that there is no difference at all between the black and the white. Instead, he imagines only that there is no *public* difference, no breach in the brotherhood of citizens. There is, however, a domestic difference. There is—and I think Webb would argue necessarily so—some private space in which blackness and whiteness are incommensurable. One should remember that the setting of Webb's poem is not the bedroom, or even the parlor, but the hall, a space in which the public and the private overlap but which nevertheless does not invite absolute intimacy. Domesticity should be read in this poem, then, not as an equalizing force that breaks down racial difference, but instead as an ideological structure in which and by which questions of difference are negotiated.

Perhaps I can help clarify my argument by turning for a moment to Harriet Beecher Stowe's brief preface to *The Garies,* in which she describes Webb as a man "born and reared in the city of Philadelphia," a city where the free black population, forming "a large class—have increased in numbers, wealth, and standing—[constituting] a peculiar society of their own, presenting many social peculiarities worthy of interest and attention." What I would like to bring into focus here is the notion of this peculiar society and the positive spin given it in Stowe's preface. Again, though *The Garies* is frankly abolitionist and sentimental, Stowe is marking it as somehow different, as black. Moreover, she suggests that this blackness is deep, inevitable, penetrating into the very heart of domesticity, that space where the world's many evils crumble in the face of "right feeling." Blackness is not simply a matter of the public sphere, but also, importantly, a natural (domestic) phenomenon. The black is black even, and especially, when there is no white—or whiteness—present to reflect this reality.

Recall that Webb wrote in the *New Era,* alongside Frederick Douglass, black nationalist stalwart Martin R. Delany, as well as a number of lesser known writers and intellectuals including George Vashon, Rev. John Ogden (president of Fisk University), and George Rice—who, next to Webb's almost gothic fiction and Martin Delany's fiery and precise political rhetoric, wrote improbable articles such as "Early English Literature," "Has Literature Attained its Perfection," and "The Negro and American Literature," in which he argued that "the negro is as much American as he is a negro. He has his own marked traits of character; but surely his ideas, manners and customs are American in the full sense of the word, as much as those of his white contemporaries." Clearly, then, the production of literature was imagined as itself a form of political insurgency, one in which the Americanness of the Negro was not so much demonstrated as insisted upon. Even more significant for our purposes here, however, is the idea of the Negro's "own marked traits." For if Addison Gayle is correct in labeling *The Garies* an integrationist novel in the tradition of *Clotel,* then it is not the case, as I have argued repeatedly, that this integrationism was one and the same with interracialism—an ideological stance that would privilege and perhaps even celebrate race-mixing, or miscegenation.

In offering this brief introduction to *The Garies,* I hope to have suggested at least one way in which we might begin to reread the work. I have struggled to demonstrate that the novel can be read and studied, instead of simply genuflected toward by those who see it only as evidence of a somewhat less-than-noble black writing past. In so doing, I have harnessed the more complicated readings of "the domestic" that have been offered in recent years by scholars like Nancy Armstrong, Hazel Carby, Jane Tompkins, and Claudia Tate.[4] I believe, in fact, that Webb was clearly in conversation with a score of authors, mostly female, of the mid-nineteenth century whose sentimentalism and emphasis on the domestic helped shape the ideological structures of the antebellum American writing world. Moreover, this was not a conversation that excluded the political, but instead mitigated it through this same sentimentalism and domesticity. Still, it is important to reiterate that Webb, although he was thoroughly integrated into that world, the world of "right feeling," continued to insist upon a black distinctiveness within it. He worked to articulate a specificity, or peculiarity, that marked *The Garies* as not simply a novel about domesticity, or even abolitionism, but also—and importantly—about race, about blackness. It is past time, then, to bring this work back into the public purview in order to better understand the roots of African American literature and the relation of that literature to parallel, and perhaps even competing, traditions. This road still lies before us.

Notes

1. Addison Gayle, Jr., *The Way of the New World: The Black Novel in America* (Garden City, N.Y.: Anchor Press/Doubleday, 1975).

2. C. L. R. James, *The Black Jacobins: Toussaint L'Ouverture and the San Domingo Revolution* (New York: Vintage Books, 1963).

3. Frank Webb, "None Spoke a Single Word to Me," *New Era,* 13 January 1870.

4. Nancy Armstrong, *Desire and Domestic Fiction: A Political History of the Novel* (New York: Oxford University Press, 1987); Hazel Carby, *Reconstructing Womanhood: The Emergence of the Afro-American Woman Novelist* (New York: Oxford University Press, 1987); Jane Tompkins, *Sensational Designs: The Cultural Work of American Fiction, 1790-1860* (New York: Oxford University Press, 1985); Claudia Tate, *Domestic Allegories of Political Desire: The Black Heroine's Text at the Turn of the Century* (New York: Oxford University Press, 1992).

Robert Reid-Pharr (essay date 1999)

SOURCE: Reid-Pharr, Robert. "Clean House, Peculiar People." In *Conjugal Union: The Body, The House, and the Black American,* pp. 65-88. New York: Oxford University Press, 1999.

[*In the following excerpt, Reid-Pharr examines the methods that Webb uses in* The Garies and Their Friends *to dismiss the notion of miscegenation as a viable approach to racial integration.*]

The book which now appears before the public may be of interest in relation to a question which the late agitation of the subject of slavery has raised in many thoughtful minds; viz.—Are the race at present held as slaves capable of freedom, self-government, and progress?

—*Harriet Beecher Stowe*

THE RACE

Even though I have struggled in this study to demonstrate that (black) bodies both constitute and are constituted by domesticity, by households, I do not want to suggest a simple symbiosis between body and house. Instead, I maintain an emphasis on ambiguity and indeterminacy, arguing that corporeal existence is always and inevitably awkward and unstable, even as it is figured as transparent and natural. Thus, by collapsing notions of domesticity and corporeality into one another, by insisting that they are essentially one and the same, I do not mean to resuscitate the very conceptual rigidity that I have attempted to combat. Domesticity should not be understood, then, as a static phenomenon, the achievement of a sort of guarded peace between individual desire and communal interest. Instead, domesticity is better understood as an irregular process of regulation, of law, in which the constant flight and return of desiring bodies is negotiated. Moreover, a domesticity produced through unstable bodies must necessarily reproduce the very ambiguity by which these bodies, "its" bodies, are defined. The household, the home, must suffer the same gaping orifices—physical, ideological, and otherwise—as the "open" and "vulnerable" bodies that produce it and that it produces. The fact of this domestic instability ensures the dynamic nature of the body/household dialectic in that it guarantees the production of irregular bodies, deformed bodies, grotesque bodies, bodies that may threaten the cohesion of the very households from which they have been produced even as they help to reestablish the domestic boundaries that they traverse.

The "domestic sphere" exists, then, as a fiction at least so far as it is taken to be sociologically demonstrable, the locus of a stable set of "real" economic and social relations that exist apart from the public, particularly the market.[1] One might argue, in fact, that since the idea of the domestic is intimately tied to bourgeois articulations of an essential difference between public and private, that the marketplace, an important, if not the important, location for the production of the bourgeois, always encroaches upon domestic life. As the bourgeois patriarch leaves his home to produce wealth in an open marketplace he is always sullied. Promiscuous money dirties his hands, strangers of "alien" classes and races press upon his person, fallen women threaten his morality and health. The whole stinking miasma of the marketplace sticks to him as he returns to his presumably self-contained household, necessitating the ubiquitous scrapers, sewers, mats, and back entrances so apparent in and about the homes of bourgeois Americans.

His "cleanliness" must be understood, therefore, as a discursive strategy, one designed to affect a bourgeois individualism distinct from the sullied public market.[2] Cleaning becomes, as a consequence, a primary technology in the production of self and other. I am clean while the other is dirty. The rub is that the very act of cleaning must necessarily bring one into contact with the same discomfiting and destabilizing dirt that threatens the production of the bourgeois. As Peter Stallybrass and Allon White have argued, the bourgeois household and the bourgeois individual are produced and reproduced through the machinations of armies of outsiders who ferret out and expel foul, dangerous waste.[3] These same "extra-domestic household members" also ensure the cleanliness of that which enters both the home and the bodies that it contains. Yet they seem never to rid themselves completely of the dirt that they manage. They provide an always frightening and sometimes intriguing bridge to the dirty world that exists outside household boundaries. Indeed, the very fact that they are paid for their services brings us back to the difficulties of the sullied and sullying marketplace that the household is designed to resist. This is precisely where the fiction of the domestic sphere is produced. Somehow the conceptual difficulty of the dirty servant must be addressed. Somehow a stable, exclusive family structure must be maintained, even as this maintenance necessitates the presence of destabilizing outsiders. When we turn to Freud's notion of the family romance, then, it is important to remember, as Stallybrass and White have demonstrated, that Freud's theory is itself a fiction established to guard against the breakdown between (bourgeois) domesticity and (dirty) public life. His family, his household, even if in crisis, is always composed simply and exclusively of a father, mother, and their children. The cook who feeds them, the nurse who suckles them, the nanny who bathes them, the teacher who educates them, and the maid who manages their dirt, shit, semen, urine, and blood are nowhere in evidence.

This is the ideological structure out of which Frank Webb's 1857 novel ***The Garies and Their Friends*** was produced. The novel opens with a description of the refined, well-educated, and good-tempered Clarence Garie, the white father of the ill-fated interracial family. His wife, Emily, a woman whose light brown complexion suggested "the faintest hint of carmine," had been bought some ten years earlier in the Savannah slave market. Thereafter, Mr. Garie treated her as his protégé, arranging for her education and lavishing her with attention until finally the two become one, producing first one child, then another, Clarence and Emily, neither of whom has any idea that he or she is black, much less a

slave. Nevertheless, it is the issue of the children and what will become of them if Mr. Garie suddenly dies that prompts the family to leave the idyllic surroundings of their Georgia plantation for the relatively more free environment of Philadelphia. There the Garies hope that their presence will be tolerated, if not exactly accepted.

Immediately we see how overdetermined Webb's work is by the ideological complexities inherent in the production of families and individuals. In the logic of the novel, Garie's sin is not exclusively that he marries a black woman, though this is by no means a work that celebrates amalgamation. Instead, Garie's sin is that he has been so lax in policing the distinction between the market and the household. He buys his "wife" and owns his children and no amount of grace, good intention, or fine feeling can absolve him of this. On the contrary, as his well-meaning, aristocratic uncle warns him before he leaves for Philadelphia, the very fact that Garie treats his family well and not as his concubine and bastards furthers the dissolution of boundaries between black and white and, most important, between public and private, market and home.

> [Y]ou can't expect to live there as you do here; the prejudice against persons of colour is much stronger in some of the Northern cities than it is amongst us Southerners. You can't live with Emily there as you do here; you will be in everybody's mouth. You won't be able to sustain your old connections with your Northern friends—you'll find that they will cut you dead.[4]

The elderly gentleman pinpoints the difficulties inherent in the Garies's attempt to bring their southern, alien, unclean notions of family out of the confines of their plantation home and into the publicity of the modern North. Their narratives of self and community are raw, unworked, lacking the clear distinction between master and servant so necessary to the production of the bourgeois and the domestic.

The whole family is composed, in fact, of runaways. They attempt to escape the ideological structures out of which notions of normative individuality are constructed. They endeavor to establish a grotesque household that can produce only grotesque bodies. They strive to cross the rigid boundary between North and South without cleaning up first, shaking off the dust from their long physical and ideological journey. The tragedy of the Garie family is that all of its members, save young Emily, are divided against themselves. It is not just that they are produced out of multiple and competing desires, but that they adopt no clear logic in the negotiation of the same. Garie loves a black woman and imagines himself a natural democrat, yet he clings tenaciously to the slave culture that produced him. His "wife," moreover, plays dangerously close to the line separating the servant from the family member, creating herself more on the model of the Haitian *menagere,* the black woman who was combination household manager and live-in lover/companion for white planters and merchants in prerevolutionary Santo Domingo, than the fully established bourgeois matron.[5] Young Clarence, on the other hand, passes for white after the death of his parents. He is never, as a consequence, able to establish either a stable black or a stable white identity. He pines away not only for his white lover, Birdie, a fact to which we will return below, but also for a racial economy that would allow for indeterminacy, a racial economy that was perhaps southern but most decidedly not American.

Standing in contradistinction to the Garies are the Ellises, "a highly respectable and industrious coloured family," consisting of a tender mother, a hard-working father, and their three children: the beautiful and accomplished oldest daughter, Esther, the shrewish and extremely fastidious middle child, Caddy; and a rambunctious young son, Charlie. It is the Ellis family that in every particular acts as the mirror of the Garies's various identities. Where the Garies are masters the Ellises are servants. (Caddy Ellis takes particular pains to prepare the Garies's Philadelphia mansion for its new occupants.) Where the Garies are rich the Ellises are relatively poor. Where the Garies seem to be always at leisure the Ellises are working constantly. Most important, where the Ellises are a "mixed" family the Ellises are "purely" black, secure in their understanding of where they stand in Philadelphia's racial economy.

It would seem that the narrative should proceed along a rather obvious and well-worn path. The bad mixed-race family will be destroyed while the good black family will be strengthened, possibly acquiring some of the resources and social standing of the "bad" family in the process. Yet Webb's narrative is quite a bit more complex than this. It is true that by the end of the novel both Mr. and Mrs. Garie are dead. It is true that through a number of improbable narrative turns Charlie and Emily (now reconfigured as black) recover much of the fortune stolen from the Garies by the novel's villain, Mr. Stevens. It is also true, however, that the once virile Mr. Ellis becomes an invalid, a grotesque body, his mind wandering into and out of moments of recognition and lucidity, the fatal fall that reduces him to this state a result of the same race riot that consumes the Garies. Thus, we are left in a situation in which both of the fathers with whom the novel began are excised from the text, leaving their families to re-form themselves with whatever resources still remaining at their disposal.

In attempting to understand why Webb complicates his narrative by producing Mr. Ellis as "undead," it is important to consider just how decidedly hostile he is to the "unclean" tendencies that produce the "southernness" of the slave South. Significantly, Mr. and Mrs. Ellis, though always free, immigrate from the South as

adults. Mrs. Ellis was a childhood friend of Mrs. Garie while Mr. Ellis helped to rear a young slave boy who will reappear later in the novel as the accomplished Mr. Winston. It is difficult, therefore, not to reach the conclusion that by debilitating Mr. Ellis, Webb demonstrates a fear of "southern principles" that is so great that anyone associated with them must be tamed, if not destroyed. Indeed, Mr. Ellis is himself figured as a (southern) runaway. In his attempt to warn his fellow immigrants, the Garies, of the approaching mob he is spotted by a group of men who chase him onto a roof and attempt to throw him over the side. When he resists, clinging to the side of the building, they chop off several of his fingers, at which point he falls to the street below. The half-conscious, half-dead state in which Webb leaves him suggests the author's ambiguity in relation to a character who apparently has none of the uncleanliness of the Garies, but who is southern nonetheless. He must have imbibed, therefore, many of the old patterns, the old pre-bourgeois mores, of the southern plantocracy. Mr. Ellis is described as gray and bent even before he is attacked and positively old and dottering afterward. This is even though Webb has done him the incredible service of making him a carpenter and joiner, a powerful position in a novel obsessed with households and the construction of households. But, as I have argued repeatedly, Ellis has too much of the stench of the unreconstructed southerner about him. His household runs the risk of producing the same grotesque ideological lapses as does the Garies's. Can it be any wonder, then, that after the riot is over Mr. Ellis is not only disabled but also his home has been burned to the ground?

I will even go so far as to claim that what Webb is engaged in is a sort of domestic eugenics, one in which the goal is to produce properly socialized modern individuals who maintain proper racial and domestic distinctions. Mr. Ellis committed a grave error by allowing his son, Charlie, to be placed into service in the home of Mrs. Thomas, his wife's girlhood mistress. Mr. Walters, the nominal hero of the novel, whose virility—and modernity—are unmatched and who subsequently becomes a surrogate father for Charlie, immediately announces the novel's critique of such mixing:

> If you can't get on without the boy's earning something, why don't you do as white women and men do? Do you ever find them sending their boys out as servants? No; they rather give them a stock of matches, blacking, newspapers, or apples, and start them out to sell them. What is the result? The boy that learns to sell the matches soon learns to sell other things; he learns to make bargains; he becomes a small trader, then a merchant, then a millionaire. Did you ever hear of any one who made a fortune at service?
>
> (Webb [1857] 1997, 62-63)

The critique stems not only from purely pecuniary considerations but also from the horror that the loosening of boundaries between the household and the market enacts in the psychologies on display in the text. The servant is kept in a sort of limbo in which he sells not only his labor but also his person. Charlie is horrified at the livery that Mrs. Thomas expects him to wear, understanding all too clearly that the suit works to produce him as the woman's ornament. Moreover, the other servants in the household, Aunt Rachel and Mr. Robberts, are figured as grotesque creatures. Aunt Rachel is hysterical and violent while Robberts is sycophantic and buffoonish. Both, moreover, exist in bodies deformed by long service in the Thomas household, Aunt Rachel with her supersensitive corns and Mr. Robberts with his rheumatism and delicate shins. Mr. Ellis's mistake, then, is that he has allowed Charlie to leave his properly constituted household for an irregular, excessive, grotesque home with a history of producing grotesque bodies.[6]

Charlie does escape the Thomas home after taking advantage of the vulnerable bodies of his assailants. Mrs. Thomas's wig is knocked from her head. Mr. Robberts's shins come in for their share of abuse, and Aunt Rachel's corns are given no mercy. Still, the specter of some intangible southern "messiness" lingers about the household constructed by Mr. Ellis. Charlie, always a rambunctious and boyish youth, is sent to deliver his sister's dinner to her as she prepares the Garies's new home for their arrival. On the way he stops to play marbles with a group of boys, at which point he inadvertently exchanges the pail with his sister's dinner for that of another boy. When Caddy opens the container and finds only the remnants of someone else's meal she goes into a rage and begins to beat Charlie so viciously that he falls down a flight of stairs. In the process, he is terribly injured and must be removed to the Warmouth estate of a Mrs. Bird, a rich white woman who had been impressed some time before by Charlie's recitations at the local black public school. Again, Mr. Ellis's household is broken up and supplemented by a liberal interracialism that the novel repeatedly rejects. Yet Charlie, unlike Clarence Garie who leaves behind his family only to fall hopelessly in love with his Birdie, remains unceasingly loyal to his own (black) community and (black) household. He insists upon returning to Philadelphia the moment he receives a painfully written note from his older sister, Esther, detailing the horrors his family and community have suffered.

> My Dear Little Brother,—We are all in deep distress in consequence of the misfortunes brought upon us by the mob. Our home has been destroyed; and worse than all, our poor father was caught, and so severely beaten by the rioters that for some days his life was entirely despaired of. Thank God! he is now improving, and we have every reasonable hope of his ultimate recovery. Mother, Caddy, and I, as you may well suppose, are almost prostrated by this accumulation of misfortunes, and but for the kindness of Mr. Walters, with whom we

are living, I do not know what would have become of us. Dear Mr. and Mrs. Garie—[Here followed a passage that was so scored and crossed as to be illegible. After a short endeavour to decipher it, he continued:] We would like to see you very much, and mother grows every day more anxious for your return. I forgot to add, in connection with the mob, that Mr. Walters' house was also attacked, but unsuccessfully, the rioters having met a signal repulse. Mother and Caddy send a world of love to you. . . . Give our united kind regards to Mrs. Bird, and thank her in our behalf for her great kindness to you.—Ever yours, Esther.

(Webb. [1857] 1997, 263-264)

Here we see the novel in an act of self-reflection. The entirety of the dual logics of domesticity and corporeality has been reduced into this brief note. Mr. Ellis is all but disembodied as his home is reduced to a smoldering heap of ashes, while Mr. Walters's house remains erect (all allusions intended), a haven from the roaring crowd. The Garies, moreover, are not only removed from the narrative but also rendered literally illegible. They have been scored over and scratched out, marked as things apart, wretched and impermissible mistakes in the literature that Webb is attempting to construct.

This is, in fact, the place in the novel at which Webb most explicitly announces his project as the production of a specifically Black American literature. Webb not only summarily dismisses the unclean (southern) interracialism of the Garies but also clues the reader into the fact that his work should be read as a thing apart from the abolitionist literature with which it is clearly in dialogue. Mrs. Bird comes to us, of course, from Harriet Beecher Stowe's *Uncle Tom's Cabin,* where she assists the runaways, Eliza and Harry, in their journey toward freedom. In the process, she gives Harry the clothing of her own dead son, just as Charlie's Mrs. Bird gives him the clothing and "things" of her own long deceased "Charlie." As Gillian Brown has argued, however, this act was not an invitation for the runaways to join their respective Bird households. Instead, it is at once an act of recognition and differentiation in which the black is hailed as human and "equal" while simultaneously restricted from certain (white) modes of domestic intercourse.[7] While Harry and Charlie may receive the clothing of their respective doppelgängers, they are nonetheless never hailed as members of these white families, grotesque replacements within already barren households. Clarence attempts just this type of domestic sleight of hand, becoming the "white" child of Miss Ada and eventually the "white" lover of Birdie, but his deformed, overly desirous, disloyal body cannot forever continue the charade.

The fact that Stowe introduces Webb's novel as itself emblematic of the particularity, the blackness, of Philadelphia's black community should come, therefore, as no surprise. "In this city they form a large class—have increased in numbers, wealth, and standing—they constitute a peculiar society of their own, presenting many social peculiarities worthy of interest and attention" (Webb [1857] 1997, v). The key concept here is peculiarity, a cultural and racial ontology that is somehow equivalent to whiteness, but not exactly equal. Again, the effort in the novel is to define a modern racial identity that is distinct and peculiar, that does not bleed into whiteness thereby producing monsters like Clarence. Thus, Webb's phobic response to the "fact of southernness," particularly in relation to Mr. Ellis, is indicative of a desire for the clear, clean differentiation that Zygmunt Bauman argues is *the* distinguishing characteristic of modern thought.[8] Mr. Ellis, precisely because of the fact of his southernness, can be presumed incapable of maintaining a clean household. Charlie is always being shipped from one white elite home to another while Ellis's daughter, Caddy, is prone to such an excess of domestic feeling that she almost kills her brother. Indeed, Caddy's hysteria, her absolute fear that nothing can ever be clean enough, speaks to a dirtiness within the Ellis home, a basic ideological instability that her constant cleaning resists. I would argue, in fact, that Caddy demonstrates the same obsessiveness of other "southern" maids, among them Aunt Rachel and Stowe's Dinah, that comes from the incredibly difficult task of "cleaning" households that have been deeply, indelibly stained.

I will go further and suggest that what Webb recoils at is the "yellowness" of the South, the mixing of races and racial ideologies, a mixing that had not established an intermediate group but which made that possibility palpable. Garie's detractors accuse him of having been bewitched by a "yaller wench," a fact that made him incapable of behaving "like other men who happen to have half-white children" and "breed them up for the market and sell them" (Webb [1857] 1997, 59). Mr. Winston, a man who though once a slave could easily pass physically and socially as white, is told in no uncertain terms that, "Either you must live exclusively amongst coloured people, or go to the whites and remain with them" (Webb [1857] 1997, 41). Young Clarence Garie, meanwhile, dies an agonizing death in which fiery spots appear on his cheeks, spots that correspond to the black spots that had broken out on his body in the dream of his lover, Birdie. It is no accident that these symptoms are exactly those of yellow fever.[9] Indeed, as we will see throughout this study, yellow fever was a constantly recurring motif in the earliest fiction produced by African Americans, a motif that mimetically represents the national phobia surrounding interracialism.

The point that I am driving toward is that with *The Garies* Webb is attempting to aestheticize a process of racial modernization in which notions of racelessness and indeterminacy become untenable. The fumbling,

proto-scientific "racial" theories of early national America were being abandoned for a racial ideology that allowed the black to enter the public sphere precisely by rejecting the notion of disembodiment that so overdetermined public discourse. The black could enter, but only as a black, as an individual whose body was not peripheral to his subjectivity but constitutive of it. Moreover, that body became a factor not of biology but of ideology, of domesticity, such that even a nominally "white" body like Emily Garie's could be reconstructed as "black" within properly black homes. The argument that I am making flies directly in the face of the common sense of American racialism. The idea that the production and reproduction of the American slave state necessitated the development of forms of racial distinctiveness with which we are now familiar stems from a lingering exceptionalism in American and African-American studies that disallows the idea that racial indeterminacy was a significant and defining aspect of American culture, so much so that technologies as blunt and imprecise as Jim Crow were developed to contain it.

The truth is that Webb must have been extremely aware, as indeed the rest of the country was, of not only the fact that alternate racial economies existed in almost every other country in this hemisphere but that these alternate economies were constantly encroaching upon "U.S. territory." I have mentioned already the *menagere* and her importance, financial, racial, domestic, and otherwise, to the life of Santo Domingo. She was only one figure, however, in a pantheon of (foreign) racial interlopers who seemed bent on sullying American ideals—and bodies. We should remember that the revolution in Santo Domingo was preceded by years of unrest among the slaves in the colony, precipitating the emigration of more than 10,000 persons, many of them persons of color, who brought with them not only property, human and otherwise, but also "revolutionary" notions of race and domesticity. The residents of Hispaniola were not so particular about avoiding the touch of the tar brush. Nor did they balk at the notion of persons of African descent holding other persons of African descent in bondage. In 1792, French-speaking immigrants petitioned the Pennsylvania legislature for exemption from the newly enacted abolition laws. They were refused. The point, however, was that even though these new additions to the community were suspiciously regarded as perhaps "black" themselves, they nevertheless were far from democratic. Race mixing did not necessitate racial egalitarianism.[10]

The presence of these alien amalgamationists was even more strongly felt within the antebellum south. After 1792, many southern states forbade or seriously curtailed the immigration of slaves from (revolutionary) Santo Domingo.[11] This did nothing, however, to stop refugees from entering Louisiana, which was notorious not only for its large number of mixed-race persons but also for the liberal manumission policies of both the French and the Spanish, policies that actually encouraged white fathers to free their slave children (Berlin 1974, 109). The result was that by 1788, free Negroes composed more than one-third of the population of New Orleans (Berlin 1974, 112). When the United States purchased the Louisiana Territory in 1803, not only then did the numbers of free Negroes in the United States drastically increase but also a set of "foreign" racial ideologies became part of the national dialogue. This fact, along with the great success of the Louisiana free Negro population whose numbers increased four-fold between 1803 and 1810, drove many racially conservative Americans to distraction (Berlin 1974, 116).

It is surprising, therefore, that Webb offers such a simplistic and conservative reading of the revolution in Santo Domingo, one designed I argue to posit a particularly American politics of racial identity. Through the character of Mr. Walters, the most two-dimensional of the protagonists, Webb is able to spirit away many of the complexities surrounding race in both countries. Mr. Walters, a black real estate speculator who amasses a considerable fortune through sheer hard work and intellect, stands at the pinnacle of respectable and cultured life in black Philadelphia, his taste and accomplishments rivaling those of any white man in the Americas. To his credit he holds particular affection for both the Garies and the Ellises, harboring Mrs. Ellis, Esther, and Caddy in his home during the riot and attempting to warn the Garies, using Mr. Ellis as an unsuccessful messenger, of the advancing mob. After the riot is over and some level of normality returns to their lives, he invites the remnants of both families, with the one exception of Clarence Garie, to remain under his roof. Eventually he marries Esther, installing himself as the new (good) husband and father, stepping in where both Mr. Garie and Mr. Ellis failed.

What makes Mr. Walters superior to the other men, particularly Mr. Ellis, is the fact of his singularity. While he is not white he is certainly not a slave or a servant, he has not even a trace of that nasty southern funkiness about him. Moreover, he has no family other than the instantly produced one that comes to him after the riot. The reader is not forced to consider, therefore, the possibility that Walters's body, and thus his character, might have been polluted by a (dirty) home or (grotesque) domesticity. At the same time, even as he is aggressive within the public sphere, particularly within the market, his blackness and the constant inconvenience that it causes, forces him to remain distant from his (white) business peers. Unlike the novel's villain, Mr. Stevens, he maintains his (black) self as a thing apart from the marketplace. From the first he is described as a creature who maintains a delicate balance between the black and the white, the inside and the out, such that there is al-

ways a (black) core that remains inviolate. "Mr. Walters was . . . of jet-black complexion, and smooth glossy skin. His aquiline nose, thin lips, and broad chin, were the very reverse of African in their shape, and gave his face a very singular appearance" (Webb [1857] 1997, 121-122). Walters is both "The black" and its inverse. Embedded within the skin of the Negro are the nose, the lips, the chin, but not the mind of the European. He is the symbol of the African's creation of a space for himself in western culture, a peculiar space that, however hemmed in by whiteness, remains purely black. Indeed, it is through the characterization of Walters that Webb is able to wrench his narrative out of and away from the competing and conflicting racial ideologies represented by the revolutionary figures of Santo Domingo while nonetheless appropriating the patina of virility and modernity with which they were associated.

During Mr. Garie's first visit with Walters he is transfixed by a portrait of Toussaint L'Ouverture in the uniform of a general. The piece stands among all the many markers of Walters's cultivated taste: the richly papered walls, the paintings of American and European masters, the rich vases and well-executed bronzes, and those "charming little bijoux which the French only are capable of conceiving" (Webb [1857] 1997, 121). In the midst of Euro-American refinement we find the black hero, as cultivated as his surroundings, yet nevertheless separate and ready for struggle. Thus, Toussaint stands as the hero who produced the revolution in Santo Domingo as a black event, a great triumph of pure Africanity.[12] Moreover, Walters, as the reflection of Toussaint, is pressed to the service of guarding against the boundary crossings, the shuttling between black and white, household and market, that are the great obsessions of the novel. Walters argues vehemently against sending Clarence Garie away after the death of his parents, claiming that by passing, by producing himself as a (black) white man, Clarence can only bring himself to ruin:

> with all I have endured, and yet endure from day to day, I esteem myself happy in comparison with that man, who, mingling in the society of whites, is at the same time aware that he has African blood in his veins, and is liable at any moment to be ignominiously hurled from his position by the discovery of his origin.
>
> (Webb [1857] 1997, 276)

Again, we see an explicit disavowal of indeterminacy, this one mediated through a character heavily associated with the decidedly "black" revolution in Santo Domingo. Still, as C. L. R. James has suggested, narratives that would place Toussaint exclusively at the center of a black liberation struggle do damage to the truth of both Toussaint's life and the revolution with which his name is associated. James argues that the relationship of Toussaint to European, and in particular

French culture, was anything but detached. At no point during the revolution in Santo Domingo did Toussaint relinquish his faith in the principles of the French Revolution. Even as he languished in a French prison during the final days of the insurgency he continued to think of himself as a citizen and patriot, loyal to France and the ideals of liberty, equality, and brotherhood. Until nearly the moment of his death he continued to plead with Bonaparte to recognize him as his loyal servant.

> [A]s to fidelity and probity, I am strong in my conscience, and I dare to say with truth that among all the servants of the State none is more honest than I. I was one of your soldiers and the first servant of the Republic in San Domingo. I am today wretched, ruined, dishonoured, a victim of my own services. Let your sensibility be touched at my position, you are too great in feeling and too just not to pronounce on my destiny. . . .
>
> (p. 264)

The tragic aspect of Toussaint L'Ouverture's life and career was that even as he was feared and hated by the French and the Creoles alike, he continued to be—like the fictional Walters—one of the first men of the West. Though nearly illiterate, he maintained an impressive correspondence with a variety of the best educated and most finely cultured figures in both Europe and the New World. He sent his two sons to be educated in France with the specific intent that they should learn to emulate the fine manners of French-born citizens. Moreover, his exceptional generosity toward the family that once enslaved him and whites in general is legendary.

Toussaint was a man of crisis. Had the blacks of Santo Domingo not risen it is likely that he would have lived out his life as an anonymous individual perhaps steadily climbing out of slavery and into the ranks of free black merchant and military society. Instead, he became caught up in a set of international crises: the revolution, the counterrevolution, the quixotic campaigns of Bonaparte, and the remarkable success of the slaves in Santo Domingo. He came into the (American) public consciousness as a prominent figure on the international stage, but one who was precisely embodied as a black, a man, an exslave, a revolutionary, and a general. No sense of indeterminacy is brooked in his representation.

I will develop further the notion that (national) crises produce particularized modes of corporeal existence in the second half of this chapter. I would like to end this section, however, by lingering for a moment on James's own discussion of yellow fever as it affected the combatants in the Santo Domingo revolution.

> It seems that this sickness is that which is called Yellow fever or Siamese disease; that this sickness reigns every year in the Antilles at the time of the passage of the sun in this hemisphere. . . . This sickness is heralded in some people by symptoms which are either slight pains or pains in the bowels or shivering. In others, the sickness affects them suddenly and kills within two days or three; but of those attacked not one fifth have escaped death.
>
> (Quoted in James 1963, 331)

Again, we see this dirty, engulfing yellow fever figured as the very sign of the boundary crossings that so offended the sensibilities of bourgeois Americans. Not only did it affect a dissolution of the body, it also broke down longstanding social distinctions, attacking "equally those who are in comfortable positions and who care for themselves well, and those whose means do not permit them to take precautions necessary to their health" (quoted in James 1963, 332). The implication in James work is that even as the combatants fought against each other they had necessarily to struggle against the dreaded yellow fever. The success of the revolution can be attributed, at least in part, then, to the havoc that the fever wreaked on unseasoned European soldiers. The battles in Santo Domingo took place precisely within bodies, so much so that at the end of the revolution racially indeterminate Santo Domingo gave way to black Haiti.

I make this point only to reiterate my earlier claim that what Webb is attempting is the aestheticization of a process of racial modernization in which racial stability, a stable blackness, is produced at the expense of a racial ambiguity and indeterminacy. This process was understood by Webb, moreover, as specifically "American," as deeply resistant to the influence of foreign interlopers. By reiterating "black" distinctiveness Webb celebrates American distinctiveness, suggesting an American public sphere that was not bounded by an insurmountable whiteness, by racism, but by a racialist ideology that at once privileged racial equality and racial difference. In the next section I will suggest that it is through public crisis, the riot, that the domestic institutions necessary for the enactment of this new racial order were both established and secured.

THE RIOT

Body and household operate as constitutive elements in a dynamic process of identity formation. Moreover, the relation between the two is heterodox, promiscuous, always inviting impurity, uncleanliness. Thus, the work of Frank Webb, like the work of maids, is to clean, to produce domesticity and order in an environment constantly threatened by disorder. In making this argument I have attempted to broaden consideration of the domestic, untethering it from narratives in which the "family" becomes a hermetically sealed unit threatened by the very members, the maids, who help reproduce it. I have not, however, suggested that what we see in *The Garies* is a critique of the family romance. Instead, I believe that Webb has attempted to produce a rather remarkable rearticulation of this narrative form in a distinctly black vernacular. He is faced at the outset, however, with the problem of how to establish the fiction of (black) bourgeois stability necessary to the production of a recognizable domesticity. Slaves, servants, runaways, and amalgamationists people the romance that Webb is attempting to synthesize. And yes, he does kill them off, cripple them, and simply drop them from the text with alacrity. Still, there is something messy about his narrative, something necessitating a great, unmerciful cleansing, if the work is to be read as representative, peculiar.

I have intimated already the productive nature of the riot, suggesting that it works to reproduce (black) households in the bourgeois forms that Webb privileges. Moreover, many of the images that Webb uses to describe the event are precisely images of cleaning, easily leading one to the conclusion that the riot represents in itself a necessary act of purification. After the newly formed black family has gathered in the home/fortress of Mr. Walters, Esther Ellis undergoes a remarkable transition, becoming ardent in her desire to defend her new home, so much so that she runs the risk of slipping outside of the logic of (black) respectability and becoming monstrous herself.

> As we came through the streets to-day, and I saw so many inoffensive creatures, who, like ourselves, have never done these white wretches the least injury,—to see them and us driven from our homes by a mob of wretches, who can accuse us of nothing but being darker than themselves,—it takes all the woman out of my bosom, and makes me feel like a—" here Esther paused, and bit her lip to prevent the utterance of a fierce expression that hovered on the tip of her tongue.
>
> (Webb [1857] 1997, 205)

Esther is in danger. Like the Garies, who will shortly meet their bloody fate, she is on the verge of becoming unspeakable, illegible. She is almost a—. And yet we see unleashed in her a fury so powerful and so pure that it attracts all to her. Mr. Walters first recognizes his own desire for Esther during this scene. Thus, the protestations of her family and friends are swept aside and Esther is allowed to stay with the men to load their guns during battle.

It is not this action, however, that earns the reverential respect that will stick with her throughout the text. In a novel with such a rigid and clearly defined logic of gender hierarchy Esther could only sully herself with such manly behavior. Instead, it is when Esther reverts back to her original state, a role defined by an all-encompassing domesticity, that she gains her own presence. When a small fire is made in the war room no one takes much notice of it until one of the cinders flies from the hearth and onto the pile of cartridges laying near at hand. "Esther alone, of the whole party, retained

her presence of mind; springing forward, she grasped the blazing fragment and dashed it back again into the grate. All this passed in a few seconds, and in the end Esther was so overcome with excitement and terror, that she fainted outright" (Webb [1857] 1997, 209). Perhaps it is too much to say that Esther's act of heroism is little more than the typically domestic practice of "taking out the ashes." Still, the logic of cleanliness is altogether apparent here. Esther saves the nascent black family of which she is a part, as well as her own femininity, her own legibility within domestic ideology, by reestablishing her role as literal guardian and caretaker of the hearth.

That the reader recognizes this fact is so important to the continuation of Webb's narrative strategies that he does not allow this already heavily didactic scene to carry the entire burden of representation. Only a few pages before Esther's heroic actions Walters meets Caddy and Kinch on the stairs, carrying up a huge pot of boiling water. "Is it possible Caddy," asked Mr. Walters, "that your propensity to dabble in soap and water has overcome you even at this critical time? You certainly can't be going to scrub?" (Webb [1857] 1997, 207). Caddy assures Walters that she has no such plans and then continues about her business. At a key point in the battle, however, Caddy does indeed make her mark as an extraordinary household manager and domestic warrior. As the white mob seems certain to overtake the house, their axes already chopping at the front door, Caddy and Kinch open an upstairs window and poor a noxious combination of boiling hot water and cayenne pepper onto the heads of the assailants below, thus saving the entire household. "'We gave 'em a settler, didn't we, Mr. Walters?' asked Caddy, as he entered the room. 'It takes us; we fight with hot water. This, said she, holding up a dipper, is my gun. I guess we made 'em squeal" (Webb [1857] 1997, 214). Finally Caddy, a character whose "will to clean" has up to now bordered on the perverse, has been reintegrated into a proper domestic enterprise. She literally cleans away the white interlopers from the black household, using domesticity as a powerful—and appropriately female—mode of defense.

Still, even this process, this cleansing, is full of ambiguity, a dirtiness that is never quite resolved in the text. The riot brings to a head not only the virulent, ugly racism of white Americans but also, and importantly, the pressing questions of class and class loyalty that must necessarily perplex any person reading the novel. The representation in *The Garies* of the white working classes is, in fact, almost entirely negative. Not only is the riot described as a largely, though not exclusively, proletarian affair, but it is also these same white workers who constantly plague the lives of the protagonists. White servants insult Charlie. White workers refuse to take him as an apprentice. And white hooligans not only attack his family but also burn down his home. Moreover, this cleansing riot, this riot purported to be by and of the working classes, has its own history. It was clearly modeled on a number of violent "race" riots that took place in the antebellum Northeast, particularly the Philadelphia riot of 1834, a riot that Eric Lott maintains worked to produce a blackness distinct from the whiteness of the "white" working classes, disestablishing in particular the dirty notion of the "black" Irishman.[13] As a consequence, the riot comes to us as an already well-established character, one with a past and a contradictory present.

Webb's present (1857) was one yet marred by the ugliest practices of American slavery. So it is not just a passing observation I make when I point out the fact that the riot, and the resistance to it, are not the actions of either slaves or slavers. It is not a whipping, a fight between master and slave, a run toward freedom, nor is it the simple act of reading or writing. Indeed, incredulous responses to demonstrations of Black American literacy are all but disallowed in the text. This conflagration, though it continues the themes of violent attack so omnipresent within slave and abolitionist literature, is figured as an act that is specifically not defined by enslavement, but by the notions of freedom, individuality, race, and community that were congealing in the antebellum North-east. This (northern) violence is figured, then, as a thing apart, the demonstration not of helplessness, nor inability, but of presence and definition. The race riot is not possible without the race. The point would not have been lost on Webb's readers, all of whom were being asked to imagine not just an end to slavery but also the beginning of a Black American community and a Black American literature. Stowe points to just this fact when she asks, "Are the race at present held as slaves capable of freedom, self-government, and progress?" Can these blacks exist as anything other than slaves, can they clean up, rid themselves of the fetor from their none too distant pasts? I have asked that we reconsider the riot as a figure of cleaning, an event that finally rids the community of that sticky southernness with which it has been plagued, helping to produce it as cleanly and distinctly black. I ask now that we consider its utility in the production of a literature defined by its peculiarity, a literature that is not southern, not abolitionist, and not exactly American.

What I am suggesting is that the riot works to announce a peculiar Black American literature by bringing into play not only the antiproletarian rhetorics to which I have alluded already but also the very antiabolitionist, antislave rhetoric against which the work reacts. The phrase, "I am no abolitionist" is repeated constantly in the text. Moreover, the novel allows a fair amount of hostility to the very bourgeois communities out of which it is most often imagined that abolitionism developed. Webb suggests repeatedly that northern charity and phi-

lanthropy were but the shadows of a bald capitalism precisely attuned to the rhythms of white supremacy. The white upper classes of Philadelphia and environs are sometimes figured, as with Mrs. Bird, as wellsprings of old-fashioned domestic values that remain so pristine as to override the overwhelming (white) aversion to blacks. At the same time, Webb regularly demonstrates not simply the hypocrisy of white bourgeois characters but also the means by which codes of bourgeois domesticity enable this same hypocrisy. When Mrs. Stevens, the wife of the villain whom we will take up shortly, finds that young Clarence and Emily Garie are enrolled in the same school as her own children, she sabotages the family by expertly manipulating the discursive tools of polite society, a society that announces itself precisely through rhetorics of philanthropy and charity. First she intercepts Mrs. Kinney as she is on her way to a meeting of "a female missionary society for evangelizing the Patagonians" (Webb [1857] 1997, 154). After persuading that lady to let her use her name, she visits Mrs. Roth, a lady who "swore by Mrs. Kinney," and thus armed, confronts Mrs. Jordan, the proprietor of the small school in question.

> [I]f this matter was known to me alone, I should remove my daughter and say nothing more about it; but, unfortunately for you, I find that, by some means or other, both Mrs. Kinney and Mrs. Roth have become informed of the circumstance, and are determined to take their children away. I thought I would act a friend's part by you, and try to prevail on you to dismiss these two coloured children at once. I so far relied upon your right judgment as to assure them that you would not hesitate for a moment to comply with their wishes; and I candidly tell you, that it was only by my so doing that they were prevented from keeping their children at home to-day.
>
> (Webb [1857] 1997, 158)

It only takes a moment or two before the spinster teacher tallies her expenses and assets and sends the children packing, thereby doing her part to maintain stability in a community in which she is only marginally and tentatively a member. Honor, respect, friendship and propriety have been maintained, even as the teacher cringes at the vulgarity of her actions. Mrs. Stevens, however, might raise her head even higher in society. Again, she has acted the part of the good neighbor, giving to the young teacher the very fruits of her domestic labors: her children and her gossip. In the process she has masterfully utilized the very tools of the philanthropist and the civic activist in another successful foray against the steady efforts to establish black presence in civil society.

Webb regularly treats the reader to such scenes, allowing no ambiguity whatsoever in his articulation of bourgeois—and abolitionist—complacency in the demoralization of the free black community. After Charlie's return from Warmouth he becomes obsessed with the idea of reestablishing familial normality by taking a job and picking up where his father failed. He is met at every turn, however, by prejudice against his race that interestingly enough has taken hold precisely among the liberal whites from whom he might have expected support. Tellingly, Charlie who, unlike his father, has become an expert drawer and penman, is rebuked by whites as he attempts to enter as a fully defined agent within the field of representation. Where his father built Charlie writes. As Charlie mails his first letter to a respective employer, Webb wastes no time alerting the reader to what a powerful and propitious act this is:

> How many more had stopped that day to add their contributions to the mass which Charlie's letter now joined? Merchants on the brink of ruin had deposited missives whose answer would make or break them; others had dropped upon the swelling heap tidings which would make poor men rich—rich men richer; maidens came with delicately written notes, perfumed and gilt-edged, eloquent with love—and cast them amidst invoices and bills of lading. Letters of condolence and notes of congratulation jostled with each other as they slid down the brass throat; widowed mothers' tender epistles to wandering sons; the letters of fond wives to absent husbands; erring daughters' last appeals to outraged parents; offers of marriage; invitations to funerals; hope and despair; joy and sorrow; misfortune and success—had glided in one almost unbroken stream down that ever-distended and insatiable brass throat.

(Webb [1857] 1997, 288)

I doubt that it would be possible to represent any more graphically how writing, and "anonymous" communication generally, holds together the calculus of market and household that I have been at pains to demonstrate. Love notes and bills of lading, mothers's tender epistles, and business invoices are all literally bundled together in a standardized process of mass communication. The promiscuity of the various—and varying—discursive modes on display works, moreover, to produce none other than the grotesque body, the "distended and insatiable brass throat" with which we have been so much concerned.

More important still is the fact that by the time Charlie's letter finally reaches its destination, Charlie has himself been figured as grotesque. The fact of standardized communications removes the impress of the author's hand from his text. It separates the fact of the black's body from the necessity of his representation. Charlie's clear prose and standard script both recommend him to his potential employers and hide the fact of his peculiarity, returning him to a state of disembodiment from which the black is excluded already. When he presents his (black) body at the offices of Mr. Western, a drawling southerner, and Mr. Twining, a parsimonious Yankee, the latter objects to allowing the black

child, no matter how skilled, to apprentice in the office. When confronted with the fact that such apprentices are numerous in the South, he responds, "Ah, but New Orleans is a different place; such a thing never occurred in Philadelphia" (Webb [1857] 1997, 291). Mr. Western then counters, "You Northern people are perfectly incompwehensible. You pay taxes to have niggers educated, and made fit for such places—and then won't let them fill them when they are pwepared to do so. I shall leave you, then, to tell them we can't take him. I doosed sowwy for it—I like his looks" (Webb [1857] 1997, 292).

Here we have what seems to be a striking reversal of the anti-southern logic that has permeated the text. Mr. Western is able to see Charlie for what he is, a particularly gifted black child who is as capable, if not more so, as any of his peers. We have not gotten away, however, from the notion of (southern) uncleanliness. Instead, I would suggest that Webb allows and respects southern difference as long as that difference is clearly marked, as long as it does not pass itself off as bourgeois normality.

Mr. Western presents a particularly fine model for the relationship among body, text, and self that Webb is attempting to establish. The fact of his southernness is so omnipresent, so pressing that it is graphically represented within the text itself. "You northern people are perfectly incompwehensible," he argues, suggesting that their representations of themselves do not correspond to the fact of the peculiarities of their ethnicity. They give the black the tools to create himself as disembodied "equal," while simultaneously vigorously policing the boundaries between "black" and "white" bodies. Western's southern peculiarity screams out at every turn, however. It is anything but incompwehensible. He can accept Charlie's presence in the office because it does nothing to detract from his own clearly defined race and ethnicity. "We need not care what others say—evewybody knows who we are and what we are?" (Webb [1857] 1997, 292).

Charlie later meets a similar fate in the office of Thomas Blatchford, a prominent Philadelphia abolitionist and bank note engraver. Upon applying at Blatchford's office, Charlie is met with the instant approval of the kind-hearted gentleman. Soon thereafter Mrs. Ellis and Mr. Walters meet with Blatchford to negotiate the terms of Charlie's employment and set a time for him to begin work. When Charlie enters the shop on what is to be his first morning of gainful employment, he is met by a hostile group of journeymen who threaten to quit if Blatchford allows him to stay. "'We won't work with niggers!' cried one; 'No nigger apprentices!' cried another; and 'No niggers—no niggers!' was echoed from all parts of the room" (Webb [1857] 1997, 297). Blatchford collapses under the weight of their demands and sends Charlie on his way, explaining that he had just received several large orders for new bank notes and that a strike just then would ruin him. Again, we see a racial liberalism in which the black is tolerated, sympathized with, even championed, as long as he is not embodied, not present. Blatchford has given himself over totally to a logic of capital gain in which the will literally to produce more capital eclipses all of his vaunted claims of racial egalitarianism. Abolitionism exists in this logic only at the level of representation and fails in the presence of a single black body.

Tellingly, Charlie finally gains a position from a Mr. Burrell, Mr. Blatchford's less successful business associate, who specifically rejects abolitionism. "Now, you know, my dear, that no one would call me an Abolitionist," he says to his young wife as he relates to her the events that had taken place in Blatchford's office (Webb [1857] 1997, 300). Burrell holds, however, a set of ideals that are deeper and more genuinely felt than Blatchford's professed abolitionism. He has produced himself as a proper northern bourgeois, one who is able to manage the difficulties of maintaining a loving domestic life and an active presence in the market. His anger at Charlie's treatment is turned to action by the machinations of his young wife and infant son, who together appeal to a part of him that can never be sullied by the exigencies of the market. Moreover, when he brings the matter before the two elderly men who work for him, and had worked for his father before him, he is met with a response definitive of "proper" relations between workers and employers.

> Laws me! Colour is nothing after all; and black fingers can handle a graver as well as white ones, I expect.
>
> I thought it best to ask you, to avoid any after difficulty. You have both been in the establishment so long, that I felt that you ought to be consulted.
>
> You needn't have taken that trouble. . . . You might have known that anything done by your father's son, would be satisfactory to us. I never had anything to do with coloured people, and haven't anything against them; and as long as you are contented I am.
>
> (Webb [1857] 1997, 304)

The point is, of course, that Blatchford's establishment is run by the dictates of the market. When the workers reject Charlie they reject not only his black body but also a developing system of management in which decisions are made by a specialized set of managers and then announced to operatives who presumably respond appropriately. Burrell is certainly bourgeois, but for him this is an identity that is also produced out of (domestic) notions of loyalty and right feeling. His workers gain not only income from him but also affection and a certain intergenerational continuity that lead them to accept his direction.

Even more striking still is the fact that prior to Charlie's employment, prior to his entrance into public life,

his race is announced. Colour may be nothing at all, but this does not mean that one cannot and should not notice the obvious racial distinction displayed by those black and white fingers that have taken hold of the lathe. Webb must always reject earlier racialist notions that allow for only a nebulous (public) blackness. Thus, even as he establishes this tableau of paternalism he is careful not to allow the same domestic and racial instability that the work specifically rejects. This argument is brought into focus when one considers the fact that the story of the Garies repeats in striking detail the infamous story of Ralph Quarles, a rich, southern planter who in the early 1800s bought his slave wife, Lucy Jane Langston (Horton and Horton 1997, 105). Again, interracial domestic intimacy is allied with slavery such that the black's closeness to the white is exactly that which is understood to impede public presence, to impede liberty. That this story is eclipsed by the equally available history of the 1834 Philadelphia race riot represents, I believe, an attempt on Webb's part to refashion an older, more ambiguous discourse of blackness into the stark, binaristic notions represented by the riot while calling into question the severe divisions between (white) labor and (white) capital that allow such an event to occur.

The logic becomes quite tricky here. For while Webb insists upon a clear distinction between worker and bourgeois, market and household, black and white, he is also searching for a means by which to negotiate these divisions. The notion of right feeling comes, then, to operate as a means by which various communities can interact and communicate. Mr. Burrell is not black, not labor, and not female, but he is able to access these peculiar communities through established notions of civility. This stance is preferable in Webb's schema to a polite racial liberalism, even abolitionism, because, on the one hand, it does not necessitate mixing, the pollution of the household and the body, but on the contrary privileges traditional divisions of race and class. On the other, it does allow for some level of civility between black and white, even if it is a civility based on the mutual recognition—and celebration—of racial distinction.

The rich characterization of the novel's villain, Mr. Stevens, stems from the fact that he is responsible for advancing so much of the aesthetic project that I have just described. It is Stevens who by initiating the riot helps to stabilize the awkward project of interpellation, of hailing a Black American community into existence, that Webb is attempting. Stevens is literally and figuratively a minstrel as he walks the thin line separating classes and races. He is the consummate performer such that *The Garies*' narrative is driven by the expectation that he will be found out, revealed as a fraud, returned to an original and natural state, one that reflects the grotesque households through which he has been produced: "he was rather above than below the middle height, with round shoulders, and long, thin arms, finished off by disagreeable looking hands" (Webb [1857] 1997, 124). Stevens, as we will see below, is always engaged in a process of concealing what those "disagreeable-looking" hands demonstrate, that he is a fraud, one who cannibalizes those around him, devouring them, wrapping himself in their skins in a vain attempt to reembody himself, to wear the respectability and vigor of his victims.

Stevens, or "Slippery George," is a "pettifogging" attorney, one whose speciality is aiding the most criminally active, if legally astute, members of both the gentry and the working classes. He is totally a man of the market, one who would and does gladly give up the rituals and practices of bourgeois domesticity for the sake of economic gain. As such he actualizes the profound danger posed by individual—and individualistic—desire not mediated through properly composed households. Specifically, he demonstrates how a man like Walters, a man of the market, could be led to monstrous excess without the restraint of (black) family and (black) community. "If I was black," Stevens tells his wife in a conversation about Walters, "I would sacrifice conscience and everything else to the acquisition of wealth" (Webb [1857] 1997, 127).

Black or not, Stevens does acquire wealth and he does it the old-fashioned way. He breaks up black or ostensibly black households. The riot was, we are told, not simply the result of pent-up white working-class resentment to blacks, abolitionists, and racial liberals, but instead a well-thought-through white bourgeois conspiracy—concocted by Stevens—to snatch up property in an area of the city with a high rate of black home ownership.

> You are probably aware that a large amount of property in the lower part of the city is owned by niggers; and if we can create a mob and direct it against them, they will be glad to leave that quarter, and remove further up into the city for security and protection. Once get the mob thoroughly aroused, and have the leaders under our control, we may direct its energies against any parties we desire; and we can render the district so unsafe, that property will be greatly lessened in value— the houses will rent poorly, and many proprietors will be happy to sell at very reduced prices.
>
> (Webb [1857] 1997, 166)

Thus, we have a succinctly stated, remarkably clear articulation of the practice of redlining in American cities, a practice that has been so persistent because it has such marked utility.

The production of the black area as the riot area not only forces capital upward and inward toward a narrower conglomeration of the bourgeois but also reestablishes the blackness of the black community. As the

black runs from the privacy of her peculiar domestic sphere, she is more easily seen. Her body and the domestic arrangements through which it is figured become available for the visual consumption of the mob.

> Throughout the day parties of coloured people might have been seen hurrying to the upper part of the city: women with terror written on their faces, some with babes in their arms and children at their side, hastening to some temporary place of refuge, in company with men who were bending beneath the weight of household goods.
>
> (Webb [1857] 1997, 203)

Women, children, men under the weight of household goods, the entire tableau of black domesticity running, are on display in this passage. Even though the logic of antebellum race riots was to remove blacks and blackness, very often just the opposite was accomplished. These eruptions of violence tended to force blacks to establish firmer intraracial social ties, as well as construct more clearly defined ghettos.[14] The point is that the black, as a clearly defined agent who stands in contradistinction to the white, is made visible, legible within the public sphere. It is not lost on Webb, however, that this process takes place through the manipulation of minstrelesque performances enacted most successfully by Mr. Stevens.

Shortly after Stevens announces the plan to his associates he is revealed to be immersed even more deeply within the text's class and race masquerades than we had first imagined. The timely death of a penniless aunt and Stevens's subsequent inheritance of a set of letters that his mother had written to her estranged father reveal that Stevens is actually a long lost cousin of Mr. Garie, a first cousin, in fact. Stevens's southern mother had married below her station to an abusive northern husband. She had subsequently been cut off by her aristocratic southern family, the same family of which Mr. Garie was now the scion. The fact of his impure genealogy becomes an inescapable reality for the reader. Stevens is at once a dirty southerner and a dirty mechanic. Moreover, he compounds these sins by refusing to embrace these identities, instead using them to attack his own southern relations, the Garies, and to manipulate the workingmen who are his natural compatriots.

I repeat my claim that Stevens is always in performance. I will also go further to suggest that all of his actions leading up to the riot are designed to demonstrate his skill and alacrity as a minstrel, one who works with and through any number of media. We know already that he is an uncouth lawyer, skilled at manipulating written representations of order to further ends that always tend toward disorder. The contract, both written and verbal, is Mr. Stevens's primary mode, his most dastardly crimes always being trumped up as civil business transactions between peers.

When Stevens walks one afternoon into the old clothes shop belonging to Kinch's father and commands the young boy to array him in the worst apparel that he has to offer, he is only continuing in the performative vein out of which his character had been established already. "I never knew before, said he, mentally, "how far a suit of clothes goes towards giving one the appearance of a gentleman" (Webb [1857] 1997, 184). The point is obvious. Stevens engages as fully in the spectacle of transvestism when he is in the fine garments of a gentleman as he does in the shabby drag of the minstrel performer. Interestingly, many of the participants in the 1834 Philadelphia riot wore black masks and old clothes in order to represent a black figure that was not yet wholly available within antebellum America. The inauthenticity of these false representations is always, however, uncovered. The ostensibly white performers become so beguiled by their own masquerade that they allow all manner of clues as to their "real" identities.

While Stevens is trying on his costume he loses the slip of paper on which he had written down the targets of the riot that he was then planning. Moreover, in his rush to rendezvous with Whitticar, his underworld contact and operative, he decides not to change back into his own clothing, instead leaving his card with Kinch so that the boy can return them to his home. Kinch, or Snowball as Stevens calls him, does not, however, correspond to the image of him that Stevens has constructed, the image that he is attempting to access through his own drag performance. Instead Kinch, a character who will later establish himself in remarkably close proximity to the dandy figure that was a staple of minstrel performance, exists within the alternate (black) narrative that I have attempted to describe. After some small bit of bumbling he eventually gives both the list and the card to Mr. Walters, thereby alerting "the black community" not only to Stevens's treachery, not only to the impending riot, but also to its own existence within the public sphere. The addresses that the list contains operate collectively as a geography of the nascent Black American community. It demonstrates that which needs defending, that which can only be maintained through communal action.

Even more to the point, it demonstrates a (black) peculiarity that is not bourgeois, not abolitionist, nor even working class. Instead, the note, the card, and the revelations that they engender establish a "true" blackness that stands in contradistinction to both the farcical notions out of which Stevens produces his racist plot and the competing articulations of communal identity. The black exists as a thing unto itself and not simply as the adjunct of an already established whiteness. Indeed, the novel is always eager to ridicule any example of black presence that is produced through white racialist fantasies. In one of the most interesting scenes in the novel, Webb forces Stevens into the character of the monstrous black dandy that might have been so easily hoisted onto our good fellow Kinch. As he leaves the bar in which he has just met with Whitticar, he seems to have transformed himself, through the very double dealing at which he is expert, into the "racey" character that he presumably only represents.

> The coat that temporarily adorned the person of Mr. Stevens was of peculiar cut and colour—it was, in fact, rather in the rowdy style, and had, in its pristine state, bedecked the member of a notorious fire company. These gentry had for a long time been the terror of the district in which they roamed, and had rendered themselves highly obnoxious to some of the rival factions on the borders of their own territory.
>
> (Webb [1857] 1997, 186)

It is almost inevitable, then, that Stevens should run into one of these hostile gangs just at the moment when all of his dirty dealing has seemingly been done. They claim him as a "Ranger" (roamer, runner) and viciously beat him, ignoring the (false) protestations that his clothing does not reflect his character. Finally, they take him to a wheelwright's shop and cover his face completely with tar. Thus, Stevens becomes not only the bourgeois decked out in the trappings of the white working classes but also the very black beast that he has attempted to represent.[15] "Hallo! here's a darkey!" a group of young gentry exclaims as they encounter him on his way home. "Ha, ha! Here's a darkey—now for some fun!" they continue as they force him into a rain barrel (Webb [1857] 1997, 189). When finally Stevens recognizes Mr. Morton, one of his co-conspirators, he manages to get the intoxicated man to help him reach his house, trying (unsuccessfully) to wash the tar from his face along the way. After they reach their destination, Mr. Morton jokes to Mrs. Stevens that her husband has brought "a gentleman from Africa with him" (Webb [1857] 1997, 192). And of course this sentiment is remarkably close to the truth. Stevens has brought home the very frightening gentleman from Africa that so plagued the imaginations of white America, the very beast bent upon defiling the various domestic enterprises on which the country had been founded, the beast that as we will find below was both vicious and immensely dangerous to its neighbors. The beast that kills.

It has been established already that the attack on the Garies was successful, killing both Mr. and Mrs. Garie and their newborn child. What I have not established is that it was during this act of extinguishing the Garies that Stevens also extinguishes his last hold on bourgeois respectability. The Garies are never warned of the mob that is approaching their home. Moreover, they never know of their relation to the Stevens family, nor the fact that Stevens has committed himself to removing them as an impediment to a vast fortune. His plan is, of course, to use another to commit the actual act, preferring to keep himself clear and clean of the charge of murder. Yet when the presumed assailant, McCloskey, proves incapable of committing the crime, Stevens panics and pulls the trigger himself, killing Mr. Garie. Mrs. Garie, though she has run from the house with the children and hidden herself in the woodshed, dies at the same moment as her husband, silently giving birth to their stillborn child, the very emblem of the interracialism that the novel—and novelist—have attempted to counteract. McCloskey meanwhile secures the will of the dead gentleman, keeping it for years in order to extort money from Stevens and his children after him, until on his death bed he reveals his horrible secret and returns the will. Stevens, old and demented by the time of this final revelation, a character who has become like Mr. Ellis a grotesquely hyper-embodied creature, repeats the trauma of his counterpart and throws himself to the street below as the constable with the "keen gray eyes" comes to reveal him for what he is.

I have attempted to broaden the discussion of domestic ideology within American literature and culture to suggest that the domestic is implicated not simply in the production of class and political identity but in the production of racial identity as well. Specifically, I have nominated the "household" (versus the family) as a more accurate lens by which to bring into focus the complex manner in which individuals are rendered visible within the public sphere. In the process, I have rejected the notion that black presence was disallowed because of the "fact of blackness." Instead, I have argued that the black did enter the public sphere, but only as an already embodied individual. Moreover, the household operates as the primary means of this corporealization, producing properly black subjects from the motley and often racially indeterminate group of premodern, strange[16] figures who dotted the landscape of antebellum America and its environs. Further, I have suggested that the riot that stands at the center of *The Garies* should not be understood as distinct from the processes of domestication with which we have been concerned. Instead, even as I recognize the potential for radical destabilization within the riot, I have suggested it as part of the process of "cleansing" that was central to the production of a peculiar Black American domesticity and a peculiar Black American literature.

Notes

1. My understanding of the interplay between market and household has been greatly influenced by the work of Gillian Brown. See Gillian Brown, *Domestic Individualism: Imagining Self in Nineteenth-Century America* (Berkeley: The University of California Press, 1990).

2. For more on the trope of cleanliness within American culture, see Suellen Hoy, *Chasing Dirt: The American Pursuit of Cleanliness* (New York: Oxford University Press, 1995).

3. Peter Stallybrass and Allon White, *The Politics and Poetics of Transgression* (Ithaca: Cornell University Press, 1986).

4. Frank J. Webb, *The Garies and Their Friends,* introduced by Robert F. Reid-Pharr (1857; reprint, Baltimore: Johns Hopkins University Press, 1997), 100.

5. See Stewart R. King, "Blue Coat or Lace Collar?" Military and Civilian Free Coloreds in the Colonial Society of Saint-Domingue," Ph.D. diss., Johns Hopkins University, 1997).

6. For more on the complex interaction between notions of the grotesque and (American) notions of racial distinction, see Leonard Cassuto, *The Inhuman Race: The Racial Grotesque in American Literature and Culture* (New York: Columbia University Press, 1997).

7. See especially "Domestic Politics in Uncle Tom's Cabin," in Gillian Brown, *Domestic Individualism: Imagining Self in Nineteenth-Century America* (Berkeley: The University of California Press, 1990), 13-38.

8. Zygmunt Bauman, *Modernity and Ambivalence* (Ithaca: Cornell University Press, 1991). I discuss the phobia within certain precincts of African-American nationalism regarding third parties, or unclean interlopers, in Robert F. Reid-Pharr, "Speaking Through Anti-Semitism: The Nation of Islam and the Poetics of Black (Counter) Modernity," *Social Text* 14.4 (Winter 1996): 132-147.

9. The repeated occurrences of yellow fever in the United States during both the eighteenth and nineteenth centuries created such panic that normal modes of behavior were thrown unceremoniously by the wayside. Bodies remained unburied. The sick were not attended. More important, the social intercourse of blacks and whites was for a time radically altered. Persons of African descent were imagined to be less vulnerable to the effects of fever because of their supposedly increased ability to fight off tropical disease. As a consequence, blacks at times played prominent roles in the management of yellow fever outbreaks. This was particularly true of the infamous Philadelphia epidemic of 1793, during which African Americans volunteered to bury the dead and care for the dying while whites kept their distance for fear of becoming infected. "When the yellow fever raged in Philadelphia . . . and the whites fled . . . the colored people volunteered to do that painful and dangerous job. . . . It is notorious that many whites who were forsaken by their own relations and left to the mercy of this fell disease, were nursed gratuitously by the colored people." Thus

in this appeal to the citizens of Philadelphia directed at securing black political rights we find a writer explicitly making the connection between [a] peculiar black body (the presumed immunity to yellow fever) and the fitness of blacks for positions within social and political life. See Robert Purvis, *Appeal of Forty Thousand Citizens, Threatened with Disfranchisement, to the People of Pennsylvania* (Philadelphia: Merrihew and Gunn, 1838), 13-14. See also Absalom Jones and Richard Allen, *A Narrative of the Proceedings of the Black People. During the Late Awful Calamity in Philadelphia, in the Year 1793: and a Refutation of Some Censure Thrown Upon Them in Some Late Publications* (Philadelphia: William W. Woodward, 1793); Benjamin Banneker, *Banneker's Almanac for the Year 1795: Being the Year After the Third Leap Year Containing (Besides Everything Necessary in an Almanac.) An Account of the Yellow Fever Lately Prevalent in Philadelphia; With the Number of those Who have Died. From the Fifth of August Till the Ninth of November, 1793* (Philadelphia: William Young Bookseller, 1795); and William Coleman, *Yellow Fever in the North: The Methods of Early Epidemiology* (Madison: The University of Wisconsin Press, 1987).

10. James Oliver Horton and Lois E. Horton, *In Hope of Liberty: Culture, Community and Protest Among Northern Free Blacks, 1700-1860* (New York: Oxford University Press, 1997).

11. Ira Berlin, *Slaves Without Masters: The Free Negro in the Antebellum South* (New York: The New Press, 1974).

12. Quoted in C. L. R. James, *The Black Jacobins: Toussaint L'Ouverture and the San Domingo Revolution* (New York: Vintage, 1963), 364.

13. Eric Lott, *Love and Theft: Blackface Minstrelsy and the American Working Class* (New York: Oxford University Press, 1993). Robert Levine also points to the 1842 attack on the Moyamensing Temperance Society as an important source for the riot scene. See Robert Levine, "Disturbing Boundaries: Temperance, Black Elevation, and Violence in Frank J. Webb's *The Garies and Their Friends,*" *Prospects* 19 (1994): 349-374. See also Robert Levine, *Martin Delany, Frederick Douglass and the Politics of Representative Identity* (Chapel Hill: The University of North Carolina Press, 1997).

14. See James Oliver Horton, *Free People of Color: Inside the African American Community* (Washington, D.C.: Smithsonian Institution Press, 1993).

15. Paul Hoch's early discussion of the necessity of the black beast to the production of white male identity has yet, in my opinion, to be eclipsed. See Paul Hoch, *White Hero, Black Beast: Racism, Sexism and the Mask of Masculinity* (London: Pluto, 1979).

16. The notion of the strange figure who acts as the spoiler of modern conceptions of community and identity has been developed by a number of scholars. See especially Julia Kristeva, *Strangers to Ourselves,* trans. by Leon S. Roudiez (New York: Columbia University Press, 1991); and Rene Girard, *The Scapegoat,* trans. by Yvonne Freccero (Baltimore: The Johns Hopkins University Press, 1986).

Anna Engle (essay date spring 2001)

SOURCE: Engle, Anna. "Depictions of the Irish in Frank Webb's *The Garies and Their Friends* and Frances E. W. Harper's *Trial and Triumph.*" *MELUS* 26, no. 1 (spring 2001): 151-71.

[*In the following essay, Engle emphasizes the similar depictions of Irish Americans and African Americans in the novels by Webb and Harper to demonstrate how ethnicity was often conflated with class in nineteenth-century America.*]

In the 1991 movie *The Commitments,* Jimmy, the manager of an aspiring Dublin soul band, convinces a band member skeptical of playing African American music that the band's class background makes them black. He argues: "The Irish are the Blacks of Europe. The Dubliners are the Blacks of Ireland. And the Northside Dubliners are the Blacks of Dublin. So say it once, say it loud: I'm Black and I'm proud." In his provocative remark, Jimmy equates low class position with blackness, collapsing class and race. Jimmy draws unusually liberating results from this comparison when the Irish band is allowed to sing the powerful black music of soul, but in likening working-class Irish and African Americans, he is hardly being original. Rather, Jimmy plays upon a comparison that was first widespread in nineteenth-century America. Between 1845 and 1889, approximately three million Irish immigrated to the United States (Foner, "Class" 6). Especially during the famine decade of 1845-1855, the majority were extremely impoverished and poorly educated. Although not enslaved, in their educational and financial status Irish immigrants in this decade resembled the majority of African Americans.

This similarity posed a dilemma for other Euro-Americans who, throughout the nineteenth century, were attempting in literature and popular culture to highlight racial differences and smooth over class divisions.[1] Instead of recognizing the class similarities between Irish and African Americans, many Euro-Americans painted Irish-Americans black, attributing their low class status to their alleged physical or even racial difference from other Euro-Americans. In contrast, African American writers such as Frank Webb and Frances E. W. Harper argue against such conflations of race and class. In Webb's novel **The Garies and Their Friends** (1857) and Harper's novel *Trial and Triumph* (1888-9), these writers use Irish-American characters to demonstrate that categories of blackness and whiteness are not separate from but intricately entwined with class categories.

To comprehend the necessity and persuasiveness of Harper's and Webb's arguments, one must first understand how images of Irish-Americans circulated in nineteenth-century American culture. In the wake of Irish mass immigration to the United States at mid-century, the character of the uneducated, uncouth Irish worker cropped up everywhere in Euro-American popular culture and literature. Historian Dale Knobel, in his exhaustive study *Paddy and the Republic,* examines approximately 1600 references to Irish-Americans from 1820 to 1860, which form a composite image of the "Paddy stereotype." According to Knobel, the descriptors applied to Irish-Americans in the press, popular fiction, government documents, and pseudoscientific treatises were overwhelmingly negative, focusing on their reputed violent nature and lack of intellect (196) and increasingly depicting the Irish as physically distinct from other Euro-Americans. Popular descriptions of Irish-Americans attributed their perceived character flaws to imputed biological deficiencies. Pseudosciences such as physiognomy and phrenology emphasized the "dark eyes, florid complexion, red hair, robust figure, and simianized face (prominent cheekbones, upturned nose, and projecting teeth)" of Irish-Americans (Knobel 121). Cartoons in influential magazines such as *Harper's* illustrated Irish-Americans with extended jaws, dark faces, and beady eyes. Other print sources, including newspapers, school books, and government documents, referred to Irish-Americans as "Low-browed and savage, grovelling and bestial, lazy and wild, simian and sensual" (Roediger 133). That writers singled out Irish-Americans as behaviorally and physically substandard is evident from the fact that the same sources describe another prominent immigrant group, German-Americans, in generally positive terms (Knobel 32-33).

Nineteenth-century American literary writers also did their part to perpetuate the idea that Irish-Americans were ethnically inferior. Henry David Thoreau, Nathaniel Hawthorne, Ralph Waldo Emerson, Susan Warner, Maria Cummins, Reuben Weiser, Elizabeth Stuart Phelps, and Horatio Alger number among American mid-century authors who derided Irish immigrant workers as slovenly, dirty, and good-for-nothing.[2] Unflattering images of Irish-Americans appear not only in various genres, from Weiser's captivity narrative *Regina,*

the German Captive to Cummins's bestseller *The Lamplighter* to Thoreau's treatise *Walden,* but also among writers of differing political persuasions, from the reputedly liberal Emerson to the allegedly conservative Warner. Ironically, even writers otherwise critical of ethnic prejudice did not scruple to criticize the Irish. In Louisa May Alcott's 1872 novel *Work,* for example, the protagonist expresses sympathy with African American servants while refusing to work with Irish-American ones; the narrator describes Irish servants as "incapable" (17). Similarly, the Mexican-American writer Maria Ruiz de Burton lambastes the racism and provincialism of nativist New Englanders in her 1872 novel *Who Would Have Thought It?,* but her critique does not extend to prejudice against Irish-Americans. Instead, emphasizing the gentility and whiteness of her Spanish-American heroine Lola, Burton highlights the distinction between the high-bred Lola and the "repulsive," frightful Irish servants with whom she is forced to sleep. Even while insisting on the equality of Spanish- and Anglo-Americans, Burton, like the popular press, singles out Irish-Americans as inferior.

Other literary texts are even more explicit in depicting Irish-Americans as physically and racially distinct. In 1823, James Fenimore Cooper describes an Irish-American as "swarthy" (124), while in 1846 George Lippard portrays an Irish Philadelphian as possessing "compressed brows" and a "look of savage ferocity" (Knobel 92). A character in Maria Cummins's 1854 novel *The Lamplighter,* convinced of Irish-Americans' savagery, "would sooner admit a wild beast into her family than an Irish girl" (131). The elite Concord writers Hawthorne and Emerson also imply that Irish-Americans constitute a different breed. In the 1852 novel *The Blithedale Romance,* Hawthorne contrasts the character Priscilla, "the pale Western child," with the "innumerable progeny" of the "big, red, Irish matrons" (187). In the 1856 essay *English Traits,* Emerson describes Irishmen as "men deteriorated in size and shape, the nose sunk, the gums . . . exposed, with diminished brain and brutal form" (195). Even more sympathetic treatments, such as Rebecca Harding Davis's 1861 *Life in the Iron Mills* and later Stephen Crane's 1893 *Maggie: A Girl of the Streets* liken Irish factory workers and city dwellers to animals and devils in attempts to delineate the degrading conditions of their lives.[3] Davis's story focuses not on Irish-Americans but on factory workers generally, whose "massed, vile, slimy lives" she compares to "those of the torpid lizards" (13). However, Davis begins her story by describing a group of "drunken Irishmen," suggesting that this particular ethnic group is even more debased than their working-class counterparts of other ethnicities (11). In the first few pages of his story, Crane likens Maggie to a "tigress" and her brother Jimmie to a "demon" (1, 7); at several points in the story he compares Jimmie and his cohorts to dogs (15, 39). Like their contemporaries in the press, the schoolroom, and elsewhere, literary writers helped to construct Irish-Americans as innately depraved.

The references to Irish-Americans as physically and racially distinct from other Euro-Americans "blacken" the Irish in nineteenth-century American literature and culture. All of these descriptors operate from the illogic that blames a group's poverty on their imputed innate difference. According to this thinking, the Irish were poor, hence they must be racially different. In fact, they must be black—or at least not entirely white. The descriptions of Irish-Americans in both literature and popular culture resemble those of African Americans in the same period, suggesting that writers attempted to lump the two groups together. The stereotype of the slatternly servant, for example, applied both to Irish and African Americans. Euro-American writers described Irish-Americans as "sensual" and characterized African Americans similarly as "passionate" (Stowe 421). Both stereotypes contrast sharply with that of the ideal sensitive or sentimental heroine, who controls both her temper and her sexual desires.

Stereotypes of Irish- and African Americans not only depicted them negatively, however, but even cast doubt on their humanity. Euro-Americans described Irish-Americans in animalistic terms, and they disagreed as to whether African Americans were, in fact, entirely human. For example, pseudoscientific texts beginning with Samuel George Morton's *Crania Americana* in 1839 popularized a belief in polygenism, or the idea that races originated separately, and thus that African Americans and Euro-Americans formed different species. This view gained widespread currency by mid-century, and even a writer as sympathetic to abolition as Harriet Beecher Stowe implied that African Americans belong to a different biological group. In *The Key to "Uncle Tom's Cabin,"* Stowe writes that "it should never be forgotten that out of *this race whom man despiseth* have often been chosen of God true messengers of his grace," suggesting that the African American race is not to be included in the larger term "man" (420, emphasis mine). Hence stereotypes of Irish-Americans were a milder version of those applied to African Americans at the same time. Indeed, racist comments circulated that explicitly stated a parallel between the two groups, such as the saying that the Irish were "'niggers turned inside out'" (Ignatiev 41).

Prejudice against Irish-Americans can be traced at one level to economic factors such as labor competition. Both the number and poverty of mid-nineteenth-century immigrants from Europe, especially Ireland, were unprecedented in American experience and caused tension between immigrant and "native" workers.[4] However, the anxiety generated by Irish immigration extended far beyond the working class and can be explained more broadly as an anxiety about who was allowed to participate in the citizenry of the United States. Noel Ignatiev notes that, while the U.S. Congress of 1790 specified that only whites could be naturalized as citizens, "it was by no means obvious who was white" (41). Winthrop Jordan argues that the concept of the American citizen in the post-revolutionary era was developed hand-in-hand with the exclusion of African Americans from that definition (335). Hence the category "white," that is, potential American citizen, gained greater cohesion when placed against its opposite, "Negro," non-American, suggesting that the term "white" lacked its own identifiable, fixed content. (See Roediger, Ch. 2.) Furthermore, the varying (and varyingly negative) stereotypes applied, for example, to German immigrants, Irish immigrants, and unspecified European immigrants illustrate that regardless of legal statute, not all light-skinned folk were considered equal. (See Knobel.) If it was not obvious who was white, then neither was it obvious who could be legally American.

The ambiguity in these definitions allowed the blackening of the Irish in American literature and popular culture. For several reasons, not everyone welcomed Irish immigrants as prospective American citizens. First, definitions of whiteness, insofar as they did exist, hinged upon ideas of class. As Jordan notes, the ideal American Republican citizen was not simply a political subject but also a propertied one: "the ideas of freedom and equal rights were intimately linked with the concept of private material property," a concept that gave impetus to a rebellion not against enslavement but against taxation (350). In contrast, the Irish, particularly after the famine immigration, were generally propertyless. For this reason, they constituted a large part of the first white U.S. proletariat, and since their numbers made them visible, they threatened not only other workers but the concept of white Republican citizenry. By blackening the Irish, Euro-American writers of other backgrounds struggled to maintain the conflation of whiteness and the propertied class; in defining the Irish, they also attempted to define themselves. The Irish were also unwelcome because they constituted a practical threat to the political order. As early as 1844, they formed the most consistent white voting block in the United States, posing an ever-increasing constituency that politicians could not ignore (Ignatiev 75). By blackening the Irish, Euro-American writers figuratively erased their citizenship, thus registering resistance to their political power.

Of course, the blackening of Irish-Americans in the nineteenth-century popular imagination never translated into legal statute. In fact, Irish-Americans actively identified themselves as white and forged political and economic alliances with other Euro-Americans across class lines based on the ideology of white supremacy. (See Ignative and Roediger.) Nevertheless, the numerous descriptions of the Irish as culturally and racially different demonstrate that many Euro-Americans were unwilling or unable to admit class difference in America. Both before and after the Civil War, many Euro-Americans tenaciously insisted that class difference was racial difference.

Euro-American writers' collapse of low class status with blackness had extremely negative implications for African Americans. The idea that the poverty of generally fair-skinned Irish-Americans resulted from their "blackness" could only exacerbate Euro-American prejudice toward African Americans. As part of a general effort to explain inequalities in power as racial difference, the blackening of the Irish supported the phalanx of racist theories to justify the subjugation and enslavement of African Americans. Thus it is not an accident that nineteenth-century African American writers counter this collapse of race and class. Rather than conflating race and class, writers such as Webb and Harper "deconflate," so to speak. They expose how racial categories are intertwined with class categories and in so doing argue against racist conflations of race and class.

Webb's novel *The Garies and Their Friends* recounts the story of two families: the Ellises, an African American, middle-class, Philadelphia family, and the Garies, a family who move from the South to Philadelphia, where Mr. Garie, a white man, marries his mulatto mistress Emily and emancipates her and their children. From the first scene of the novel, Webb dissociates race and class. In the opening description, Webb troubles racial stereotypes by depicting upper-class African American characters in terms conventionally used for Euro-Americans. Webb begins by portraying the Garies' plantation home. The first lines depict the luscious tea table of a "Southern matron," words usually reserved for Euro-American, married women. Here, however, it refers to the mulatto slave Emily, whom Southern law prevents from marrying Mr. Garie (1).[5] Webb then describes Winston, a former slave, as a "dark-complexioned gentleman" (3), whose "polished manner and irreproachable appearance" compare favorably to Mr. Garie, the white hero (8). By describing African Americans in terms conventionally limited to Euro-Americans, Webb startles the reader into recognizing that these class-based words ("gentleman" and "Southern matron") have been conflated with whiteness. He also asserts that they are perfectly legitimate words with which to describe African Americans: the gentility and wealth of Emily Garie and George Winston make Emily not a slave mistress but a matron and George not a former slave but a gentleman.

Webb continues to negate any equation between blackness and subordination throughout the novel. Most of his African American characters are middle or upper class, while most of his working-class characters are white. The central event of the novel is a riot of working-class, primarily Irish, whites against African American Philadelphia neighborhoods, a riot based on actual assaults in the 1830s and 1840s.[6] Webb emphasizes that the riot, although white on black, is motivated more by class than by race. Poor whites target not only the home of the mixed-race Garies, but also the homes of the middle-class Ellises and the wealthy, African American Mr. Walters; the African Americans offend the white mob not merely because of their skin color but also because of their enviable class position.[7] Furthermore, greed is the prime motive of Mr. Stevens, the Euro-American instigator of the riots. Mr. Garie is his cousin, and Stevens wants to inherit Garie's fortune. The success of this plot transforms Stevens, the son of an aristocratic mother and a "greasy mechanic," from a corrupt, middle-class lawyer into a guilt-ridden gentryman (102). Hence Webb depicts propertied African Americans who are culturally and morally superior to their white nemeses.

Furthermore, Webb makes it impossible to draw any consistent correlations between race and class status. Webb points out throughout the book that alliances and enmities are not always divided by race but can occasionally form on the basis of class. He suggests, for example, that Stevens's ignominious associations with the Irish mob are based not so much on a shared whiteness as on a shared sense of class status stemming from Stevens's working-class roots. Conversely, while Webb celebrates the solidarity of Philadelphia's genteel African American community in his depiction of a wedding at the end of the novel, he also notes that the invited guests included several white friends (372). Webb does not simply reverse the racism and portray only working-class whites but instead presents a complicated picture in which both races can occupy a variety of class positions.

In fact, Webb argues that both whites and African Americans can achieve class mobility. In the second chapter, Webb depicts Mrs. Ellis and her daughter Caddy delivering their sewing to a rich Euro-American family and writes that they "entered upon the aristocratic quarter into which many of its residents had retired, that they might be out of sight of the houses in which their fathers or grandfathers had made their fortunes" (20). When Caddy remarks that one of the aristocracy "had been appointed an attaché to the American legation at Paris; the newspapers say he is 'a rising man,'" Mrs. Ellis replies in jest that "he ought to be . . . for his old granddaddy made yeast enough to raise the whole family" (20). In this scene, Webb mocks the class pretensions of Euro-Americans, as he does throughout the novel.

In addition, however, the idea that an upper-class generation of Euro-Americans is not far removed from their working-class ancestors can inspire a working African American family like the Ellises. Mr. Walters, an African American entrepreneur and friend of the Ellises, urges Mrs. Ellis to make her son Charlie an entrepreneur, saying, "The boy that learns to sell matches soon learns to sell other things; he learns to make bargains; he becomes a small trader, then a merchant, then a millionaire" (63). Thus Webb not only deconstructs strict class demarcations but also applies the concept of upward mobility to African Americans as well as Euro-Americans. He places both African and Euro-Americans on a flexible hierarchy, in which one's position is not fixed but subject to change. Just like the now rich Euro-Americans of Philadelphia, the Ellis family could rise to the upper class within a couple of generations.

Webb does acknowledge that class mobility is often obstructed for African Americans and can also carry a high price. While he holds out hope that African Americans can rise to the upper class, he recognizes the physical and psychological violence they often face in doing so. In the riot scene, for example, Irish and other Euro-American attackers destroy years of the Ellises' hard work by burning their house and seriously injuring their primary breadwinner, Mr. Ellis. In other scenes, Euro-American employers reject the Ellises' son Charlie for jobs because of his skin color. Webb also makes clear that he opposes light-skinned African Americans who pass as white in order to rise economically. One of the weakest characters in the novel is Clarence Garie, the Garies' son who passes for white, while the most positive character is Mr. Walters, a very dark-skinned, very rich man who is committed to the African American community. Webb hence proposes an ideal of class mobility; he does not argue that African Americans should reject their cultural heritage.

Nevertheless, Webb demonstrates repeatedly that race and class are not fixed positions. Rather, they often function as constructed masks, and one depends upon the other. Webb shows this interrelatedness most clearly in a remarkable scene in which the middle-class, Euro-American Stevens becomes first a working-class Irishman, then an African American, and then an ethnically unspecified "white" man within a couple of hours. The story runs as follows: Stevens buys some second-hand clothes in order to disguise himself and spy on the Irishmen he is inciting for the upcoming riots. After leaving the bar where the Irishmen have congregated, Stevens encounters another group of working-class Euro-Americans who, recognizing his coat as one of a rival fire company, proceed to beat him up and paint his face with tar before they finally release him. Stevens next meets a group of upper-class Euro-Americans who mistake him for African American. One of this group paints his face with lime to make him "white." This scene, with its multiple racial and class transformations, epitomizes Webb's challenge to essentialist categories of race and class.

In addition, this scene uses the racially ambiguous Irish stereotype to expose the mechanics by which nineteenth-century American culture blackens lower-class whites. Webb first suggests that Stevens, a non-Irish, middle-class, Euro-American, is transformed not simply into an unspecified member of the working class but specifically into an Irish worker. Upon entering the mostly Irish bar at the beginning of the scene, he attracts no attention in his second-hand clothes. Furthermore, the rival fire company who then attacks Stevens assaults him as an Irishman. Webb does not indicate the ethnicity of these firemen, but background on the Philadelphia fire companies sheds some light on this scene. As Bruce Laurie explains, in the first quarter of the nineteenth century, volunteer Philadelphia fire companies, originally organized by Benjamin Franklin as civic artisan associations, became ethnically integrated working-class organizations. During the 1840s, however, the period of Webb's novel, fire companies began to be increasingly segregated along ethnic lines (Laurie 158-61, 53-55). This period was also the point at which Irish stereotypes began to be increasingly racialized. Hence instead of recognizing their class similarities, members of fire companies, both in actual Philadelphia and in Webb's novel, emphasized ethnic rivalries.

In the attack on Stevens, working-class firemen express their power over him by transforming a class similarity into a racial difference, painting the supposedly working-class Stevens black. This scene illustrates and even parodies the blackening of the Irish working class occurring throughout mid-nineteenth-century American literature and culture. Not only the tar but the beating itself transforms Stevens, inflating his lips "to a size that would have been regarded as large even on the face of a Congo negro" (189). By comparing Stevens not to an actual African American but to a grotesque caricature, Webb highlights the artificiality of this blackening. He again shows how racial and class stereotypes are intertwined: black here, far from indicating cultural heritage, is a mask imposed upon Stevens because of his perceived class position.

In the next part of the scene, Stevens, still painted with tar, meets a group of upper-class Euro-Americans; he pretends to be dumb in order to avoid recognition by some of his acquaintances. This encounter illustrates Webb's point made elsewhere in the book that both upper- and lower-class Euro-Americans participate in mob violence against African Americans (or those perceived to be African Americans, in this case). However, this scene also undermines the ideology that whiteness guarantees citizenship and power. One of the upper-class men begins to "strea[k] the face of Mr. Stevens with lime," exclaiming, "I'm making a white man of him, I'm going to make him a glorious fellow-citizen, and have him run for Congress" (191). In this statement, Stevens's tormentor, not unlike the U.S. Congress of 1790, equates whiteness with citizenry. The implication, if only jokingly, is that white color will not only make this supposed mute African American a citizen but will grant him the ability to speak and participate in the political system. But as the scene makes abundantly obvious, racial identities are hardly clear-cut, and white coloring is no guarantee of being a well-respected citizen. Those with white skin color but low class status, such as Irish-Americans, can be easily blackened and hence denied political representation. Class plays a crucial role in determining not only whether one gets beat up but how one is racially categorized.

Webb wrote *The Garies* in the 1850s, a decade in which racial divisions were not only increasingly popularized through pseudo-sciences, popular fiction, and the press, but also frequently determined political coalitions and job opportunities. As Noel Ignatiev explains, the Jacksonian Democratic party had, by this time, already forged an uncommon alliance between northern white wage workers, among them Irish-Americans, and southern slave-holders based on white supremacy. To this movement came the Free Soil Party, formed in 1848, which favored not an abolitionist but rather a white separatist platform. Meanwhile, local Northern labor organizations, which Irish-Americans helped to spearhead, consciously promoted themselves as white and over time excluded free African Americans from many jobs; this process accelerated in the 1850s with the wave of foreign immigration. (See Ignatiev, Ch. 3 and 4.) At the same time, federal laws such as the Fugitive Slave Act of 1850 and state laws governing the movements of free African Americans in slave states tightened the clamps on slaves and threatened the existence of free African Americans.[8] Thus Euro-Americans during this decade institutionalized the conflation of race and class, essentializing their difference from African Americans and smoothing over class distinctions among themselves. They increasingly attempted to define white and black as two polar opposites, in which whiteness equaled access to power, citizenship, and class mobility, and blackness equaled low class status at best and slave status at worst. By exposing and discrediting the conflation of race and class, Webb powerfully argues against these attempts to essentialize racial difference.

Frances E. W. Harper, in her 1888-89 novel *Trial and Triumph,* also argues against racial essentialism. Thirty years after Webb's novel, the abolition of slavery had not succeeded in stemming the tendency to institutionalize racial difference. If anything, the color line became more entrenched, as shown by the differing fortunes of Irish-Americans and African Americans during this period. As the literary examples mentioned earlier attest, racial slurs against Irish-Americans did continue into the 1870s and 80s,[9] but historians agree that Irish-Americans had more or less stabilized their position on the white side of the color line by this point. While

Irish heroism in the Civil War did its part to decrease prejudice, more crucial factors may have been their participation in the Democratic party and the labor movement. One sign of this shift in popular feeling was that pseudoscientific theories about racial differences began as early as the 1860s to classify the Irish as members of the "white" race (Knobel 176).

More practically, because they had always been able to claim citizenship rights, Irish-Americans began gaining power before the Civil War and by the 1880s had attained considerable political and economic force. By 1888, Irish-Americans controlled political machines in six cities, Chicago, New York, San Francisco, Albany, Jersey City, and Pittsburgh (Erie 19); Boston and New York had Irish mayors and the Irish-American vote dominated politics in the key state of New York; an Irish-American headed America's largest labor union; another had established America's first newspaper syndicate; and Irish politics had influenced the American presidential elections of 1884 and 1888.[10] As the political and financial strength of Irish Americans grew, negative stereotypes against them may have had less and less bite; an unflattering cartoon of a political leader, after all, signifies differently than one of a social outcast.

In contrast, the political and economic outlook of African Americans in the 1880s was considerably less rosy. In the South, white supremacists successfully intimidated African American voters through labyrinthine voting procedures and violence; the number of recorded lynchings rose steadily over the decade. Furthermore, the U.S. Supreme Court sanctioned Jim Crow practices in 1883 by overturning the 1875 Civil Rights Act, which had forbidden racial discrimination in public places. In the North, African Americans also continued to face exclusion from Euro-American labor unions and jobs. As William Foster explains, the National Labor Union, formed in 1866, argued for inclusion of African Americans but did nothing to prevent their exclusion in practice by employers and white unionists (351). The situation worsened as the American Federation of Labor grew in the late 1880s; while the Knights of Labor, the dominant postwar labor group until 1886, sought to include all workers, the AFL focused on skilled laborers and hence ignored most African American (and many Euro-American) workers. To make matters worse, racism and competitiveness among Euro-American workers produced fifty strikes against African American workers between 1882 and 1900, in which Euro-Americans sought to bar them from skilled jobs and unions (Foster 367).

The difference between the Irish-American and African American situations gave racial essentialists further ammunition against African Americans. Irish-American poverty could formerly be attributed to their supposed blackness, but now their gradual progress could be explained as a natural result of their whiteness. Perhaps for this reason, Harper not only shows that racial stereotypes are intertwined with class stereotypes but explicitly argues that they are. Set in a postbellum northern city, *Trial and Triumph* features an orphaned African American protagonist, Annette Harcourt, who overcomes many struggles to become a teacher of African Americans in the South. Harper maintains repeatedly that contemporary African American problems result from prejudice not against their physical appearance but against their history and class position. After one African American character loses a clerk position because of his race, another tells him that this discrimination was based on "the information that you were connected by blood with a once enslaved and despised people on whom society had placed its ban, and to whom slavery and a low social condition had given a heritage of scorn" (214). In this statement, Harper contests racial essentialism by historicizing African American opportunities. Since class, or "social condition," is changeable, she implies that African Americans can have hope for the future; they were "once enslaved and despised," not forever so.

Harper compares the situation of African Americans in the South to that of Irish-Americans in order to dissociate race and class. One character describes the South as a "black Ireland," drawing a parallel between repressive political and economic policies in the two regions. What makes this comparison particularly interesting is that the situation of impoverished Ireland captured American sympathy and influenced American politics in the 1880s. As Joseph O'Grady explains, the majority of the Irish population in the 1870s suffered from repressive agricultural working conditions; they were forced to pay rent, sometimes in crops, to work land that they did not own and from which they could easily be evicted. This situation, of course, strikingly resembles that of many contemporaneous African Americans, 75% of whom lived in the South in 1880, usually under similarly disadvantageous conditions (Franklin 397).

However, Irish-American political muscle and an anti-Anglo American political atmosphere garnered sympathy in the U.S. for the Irish but not for African Americans. The Irish reformer Michael Davitt and political hero Charles Stewart Parnell toured America in support for the Irish National Land League, formed in 1879, which sought better protection for workers and fomented an uprising in Ireland through 1882 known as the Irish Land War. In enthusiastic response, Irish-Americans formed an American Land League, and the broader public came to their support as well, with state legislatures and newspapers rallying for the Irish cause in the early 1880s (O'Grady 82). Interest in Irish affairs continued throughout the 1880s, although the issue under debate switched from land reform to Home Rule for Ireland.

Furthermore, Irish-American control of the New York vote meant that they formed a crucial constituency in the delicate balance of power between Republicans and Democrats and could effectively lobby for Irish issues. For this reason, in 1884 both the Republican and the Democratic presidential candidates courted Irish-American voters by promoting their Irish origins and talking tough toward England (O'Grady 85-97). In contrast, the situation of African Americans in the South was generally ignored by politicians and the Northern public alike. With the end of Reconstruction, Northern politicians left the governance of the South to white "redeemers." African American efforts in the 1880s and 1890s to organize for better working conditions were not greeted by broad public support but rather quelled by Southern law enforcement (Foner, *Reconstruction* 251).

By comparing the American South to Ireland, Harper points out that feudalistic systems in both regions stem from class inequities. Furthermore, she reminds readers that both blacks and whites can experience class oppression and thus that one cannot blame the poverty of a particular group on their race. Harper also suggests that Euro-Americans might do well to correct oppression at home, before it blows up in their faces. For to describe the South as a "black Ireland" is also to imply that the kind of rebellion that wreaked havoc for land owners in the Irish Land War could take place in the southern American states as well. As a white character in *Trial and Triumph* remarks, "I should be sorry to know that by our Southern supineness we were thoughtlessly helping create a black Ireland in our Gulf States, that in case the fires of anarchy should ever sweep through our land, that a discontented and disaffected people in our midst might be as so much fuel to fire" (225). Harper's comparison of Irish- and African Americans warns that class oppressors will eventually reap their proper reward.

Like Webb, Harper not only separates race and class but also asserts that African Americans can achieve class mobility. She illustrates this possibility through the character Mr. Thomas, who gets a job and finds that those Euro-Americans who despised him as their subordinate willingly accept him as their superior. Harper writes, "When he was down they were ready to kick him down. When he was up they were ready to receive his helping hand" (245). As in Webb's novel, Euro-Americans' perceptions of African Americans hinge less upon their color than upon their position on the economic scale. In another scene, Harper uses the similar class position of Irish and African Americans to offer hope to African Americans struggling for upward mobility. Plagued by Mary Joseph, a racist Irish girl at her school, the protagonist Annette complains of this abuse to her mentor Mrs. Lasette and remarks in passing that "Grandmother says that an Irishman is only a negro turned wrong side out" (217). In response, her mentor Mrs. Lasette points out that the terms "Black" or "Negro" have become slurs only because of their association with "slavery, poverty, and ignorance," again arguing that race stereotypes have become conflated with class stereotypes (219). She then goes on to describe the ignorance and former poverty of Joseph's family, once more asserting the class similarities between Irish and African Americans.

Harper here takes a racist slur, that Irish are inverted African Americans, and uses it to argue that Irish-Americans and African Americans actually do resemble each other, but in terms of class, not race. Ignorance and poverty are ameliorable social conditions, not inherent qualities; hence prejudice against these conditions forms a temporary hindrance, not a permanent obstacle. Harper thus not only discredits any conflation of race and class but, against the political and economic developments of the 1880s, asserts the primacy of class instead of color. During the 1880s, this was an inspiring argument. In a decade of increasing Irish-American political and economic strength, to assert that African Americans are Irish-Americans turned inside out gave hope about their potential to gain the same kind of power. By describing the Irish in terms of class, Harper uses them to argue for African American rights.

Webb and Harper manipulate Irish-American stereotypes to expose how class similarities became transformed into racial differences in the nineteenth-century literary imagination. They were not the only African American writers to contest this transformation, nor the only ones to use Irish-Americans to make this point. Frederick Douglass, for example, also likens the class status of southern African Americans to that of the Irish. In speeches from the 1880s, he repeatedly refers to the American South as a "black Ireland" (Blassingame 17, 68, 118), and in one speech, he compares the situation of African American and Irish sharecroppers at length, writing that "the condition of the Irish tenant is merciful, tender, and just as compared to the American freedman" (367). In Pauline Hopkins's 1900 novel *Contending Forces,* her character Will Smith compares the class position of Irish-Americans and African Americans to argue against the color line in the U.S., pointing out that Irish-Americans, originally "as little welcome at the North as the Negro at the South," have used politics to gain power (265). Like Harper, Hopkins uses the rise of Irish-Americans to offer hope to African Americans; Smith calls for African Americans to agitate against disenfranchisement so that they can rise as well.

By 1921, African Americans were still asserting the fundamental class similarities between Irish and African Americans. In an editorial in *The Crisis,* W. E. B. Du Bois notes that despite the similarity between the oppression of African Americans by Euro-Americans and that of the Irish by the English, "No people in the world have in the past gone with blither spirit to 'kill niggers'" (200). However, he blames not the Irish for this situation but rather "the Universal Oppressor," who uses "the Oppressed . . . to cow and kill the Oppressed" by converting a fundamental class similarity into a racial divide. That this particular form of oppression was still happening in 1948 is noted by another article in *The Crisis* calling for Irish-American Catholics to help fight discrimination against African Americans. "The informed Negro and the informed Irishman," the author writes, "realize that, historically and sociologically, their races have felt the same burdens, prayed the same prayers, and lived upon the same hopes" (Doyle 51). Unfortunately, however, Irish-Americans generally have failed to recognize these commonalties, instead dwelling upon racial difference.

These examples show that Webb's and Harper's novels participate in a tradition. They provide a powerful reminder of class stratification in America and critique attempts to transform that stratification into racial difference. The example at the beginning of this article from the movie *The Commitments,* a movie popular in the United States as well as Ireland, suggests that this reminder is still pertinent today.

Notes

1. Throughout this chapter, I generally use the term "Euro-American" to refer to descendants of Europeans other than the Irish. As Nelson argues and I attempt to show here, the designations "white" and "black" are constructed terms whose definitions vary over historical periods. For lack of a better term, I use the term "white" in cases where I am referring simultaneously to both Irish-Americans and those of other European descent.

2. See Warner 266, 277; Thoreau 152-56; Emerson 195; Weiser 100; Hawthorne, *Passages* 47-48; Hawthorne, *Blithedale* 187; Alger 122-23. For further discussion of the Hawthorne passages, see Morgan and Renza, and Lueck.

3. Crane never directly states that his protagonist is Irish, but her name, Maggie Murphy, strongly suggests that she is. In addition, references to Ireland appear twice in the scene in which Pete takes Maggie on a date. First, a ventriloquist "made [his dolls] sing mournful ditties and say funny things about geography and Ireland," and then at the end of the program, a singer "rendered some verses which described a vision of Britain annihilated by America, and Ireland bursting her bonds" (24-25). Crane points out that ironically, the largely immigrant audience responds ardently to the singer's last line, "The star-spangled banner" (25). However, the vision the singer describes, with its anti-

British and pro-Irish sentiment, appeals not only to American patriotism but equally to Irish patriotism. Hence Crane suggests that many in the audience respond so enthusiastically because the song resonates with their own Irish-American heritage.

4. Foner estimates that half of the approximately three million Irish who immigrated to the United States between 1845 and 1889 arrived in the years 1845-1855, the decade of the Irish potato famine (*Short History* 6). Other figures include 2.6 to 2.8 million Irish between 1815 and 1885 (Ignatiev) and 4.2 million between 1820 and 1910 (Wittke). See Ignatiev for a discussion of labor competition and why it does not sufficiently account for struggles between members of different ethnic and racial groups.

5. I am indebted to Amy Lang's spring 1997 seminar at Emory University, "Social Vocabularies in Nineteenth-Century American Literature," for some of my ideas about this passage.

6. Whites attacked African American Philadelphia neighborhoods nine times between 1834 and 1849; Webb's account combines elements of the riots from 1838, 1842, and 1849. As in the riot of 1838, a leader of Webb's African American community, Mr. Walters, requests the mayor to provide their neighborhood with protection and is refused. Before the 1838 riot that burned down Pennsylvania Hall, an abolitionist meeting house, the Philadelphia mayor denied a similar request for protection from abolitionists. Like the Philadelphia riot of 1842, Webb's riot involves a large percentage of Irish participants. Also as in the riot of 1849, the rioters in Webb's novel attack the house of a mixed-race couple (the Garies) and elsewhere meet with resistance on the part of African Americans, who successfully defend Walters's house from attack. In the 1849 riot, whites attacked a tavern, California House, owned by an African American man married to a Euro-American woman; African Americans in the tavern resisted but were eventually overpowered. (See Sam Bass Warner.)

7. As Lapansky convincingly argues, the actual Philadelphia attacks were also motivated more by class than by race; rioters assaulted homes and institutions of wealthy African Americans, often passing over those of more proximate working-class African Americans (64). According to Lapansky, white, working-class rioters acted out their economic frustrations as well as their racial hatred against the wealth and gentility of a small (and hence comparatively weak) group of African Americans. Hence Webb's novel realistically portrays the actual events.

8. In Frances Harper's home state of Maryland, for example, a law was passed in 1853 allowing any African Americans entering the state to be captured, regardless of their legal status.

9. Thomas Nast's popular cartoons from the postbellum era also affirm that depictions of Irish-Americans as racially different continued to find acceptance after the Civil War.

10. O'Grady and Foner provide indepth discussions of Irish politics during this period.

Works Cited

Alcott, Louisa May. *Work: A Story of Experience.* 1873. Ed. Joy S. Kasson. New York: Penguin, 1994.

Alger, Horatio. *Ragged Dick and Mark, the Match Boy.* 1867. New York: MacMillan, 1962.

Blassingame, John and John McKivigan, ed. *The Frederick Douglass Papers.* New Haven: Yale UP, 1992.

Burton, Mariz Ruiz de. *Who Would Have Thought It?* 1872. Ed. Rosaura Sanchez and Beatrice Pita. Houston: Arte Publico, 1995.

Cooper, James Fenimore. *The Pioneers.* 1823. New York: Penguin, 1988.

Crane, Stephen. *Maggie and Other Stories.* New York: Pocket Books, 1960.

Davis, Rebecca Harding. *Life in the Iron Mills and Other Stories.* Ed. Tillie Olsen. New York: Feminist Press, 1985.

Doyle, Thomas. "A Mission for the Irish." *The Crisis* 55.2 (1948): 51-53.

Du Bois, W. E. B. "Bleeding Ireland." *The Crisis* 21.5 (1921): 200.

Emerson, Ralph Waldo. *English Traits.* 1856. Ed. Howard Mumford Jones. Cambridge: Harvard UP, 1966.

Erie, Steven P. *Rainbow's End: Irish-Americans and the Dilemmas of Urban Machine Politics, 1840-1985.* Berkeley: U of California P, 1988.

Foner, Eric. "Class, Ethnicity, and Radicalism in the Gilded Age: The Land League in Irish America." *Marxist Perspective* 1.2 (1978): 7-55.

———. *A Short History of Reconstruction 1863-1877.* New York: Harper & Row, 1990.

Foster, William. *The Negro People in American History.* New York: International, 1954.

Franklin, John Hope. *From Slavery to Freedom: A History of Negro Americans.* 3rd ed. New York: Knopf, 1967.

Harper, Frances. *Minnie's Sacrifice, Sowing and Reaping, Trial and Triumph: Three Rediscovered Novels by Frances E. W. Harper.* Ed. Frances Smith Foster. Boston: Beacon, 1994.

Hawthorne, Nathaniel. *The Blithedale Romance.* 1852. New York: Penguin, 1964.

———. *Passages from the American Note-Books of Nathaniel Hawthorne.* Vol. 1. Boston: Houghton Mifflin, 1868.

Hopkins, Pauline. *Contending Forces.* 1900. New York: AMS, 1971.

Ignatiev, Noel. *How the Irish Became White.* New York: Routledge, 1995.

Jordan, Winthrop D. *White Over Black: American Attitudes Toward the Negro 1550-1812.* Baltimore: Penguin, 1969.

Knobel, Dale T. *Paddy and the Republic: Ethnicity and Nationality in Antebellum America.* Middletown, CT: Wesleyan UP, 1986.

Lapansky, Emma Jones. "'Since They Got Those Separate Churches': Afro-Americans and Racism in Jacksonian Philadelphia." *American Quarterly* 32.1 (1980): 54-78.

Laurie, Bruce. *Working Class People in Philadelphia, 1800-1850.* Philadelphia: Temple UP, 1980.

Lueck, Beth L. "'Meditating on the Varied Congregation of Human Life': Immigrants in Hawthorne's Travel Sketches." *The Nathaniel Hawthorne Review* 14.2 (1988): 1-7.

Morgan, Jack and Louis A. Renza. Introduction. *The Irish Stories of Sarah Orne Jewett.* Carbondale: Southern Illinois UP, 1996. xix-liii.

Nelson, Dana. *The Word in Black and White: Reading "Race" in American Literature 1638-1867.* New York: Oxford UP, 1993.

O'Grady, Joseph. *How the Irish Became Americans.* New York: Twayne, 1973.

Roediger, David R. *The Wages of Whiteness: Race and the Making of the American Working Class.* London: Verso, 1991.

Stowe, Harriet Beecher. *Uncle Tom's Cabin: Authoritative Text, Backgrounds and Contexts, Criticism.* Ed. Elizabeth Ammons. New York: Norton, 1994.

Thoreau, Henry David. *Walden, or Life in the Woods and On the Duty of Civil Disobedience.* New York: Harper & Row, 1965.

Warner, Sam Bass. *The Private City: Philadelphia in Three Periods of Its Growth.* Philadelphia: U of Pennsylvania P, 1968.

Warner, Susan. *The Wide, Wide World.* 1850. New York: Feminist Press, 1987.

Webb, Frank. *The Garies and Their Friends.* 1857. New York: Arno, 1969.

Weiser, Reuben. *Regina, the German Captive; or True Piety Among the Lowly.* 1860. New York: Garland, 1977.

Wittke, Carl. *The Irish in America.* Baton Rouge: Louisiana State UP, 1956.

FURTHER READING

Bibliographies

Barbour, James and Robert E. Fleming. "Nineteenth Century Black Novelists: A Checklist." *Minority Voices* 3, no. 2 (fall 1979): 27-43.

> Provides a comprehensive listing of bibliographical, biographical, and critical studies of six African-American novelists who lived and wrote between 1850 and 1910, including Webb.

Bone, Robert. "Bibliography." *The Negro Novel In America,* pp. 255-70. New Haven: Yale University Press, 1958.

> Presents a bibliographical listing of full-length novels written by African-Americans that were published between 1853 and 1952.

Miller, Ruth and Katopes, Peter J. "Modern Beginnings: William Wells Brown, Charles Waddell Chesnutt, Martin R. Delany, Paul Laurence Dunbar, Sutton E. Griggs, Frances Ellen Watkins Harper, and Frank J. Webb." In *Black American Writers: Bibliographical Essays,* Vol. 1, edited by M. Thomas Inge, Maurice Duke, and Jackson F. Bryer, pp. 133-60. New York: St. Martin's Press, 1978.

> Includes a brief bibliographical summary of Webb's *The Garies and Their Friends.*

Biographies

Crockett, Rosemary F. "Frank J. Webb: The Shift to Color Discrimination." In *The Black Columbiad: Defining Moments in African American Literature and Culture,* edited by Werner Sollors and Maria Diedrich, pp. 112-22. Cambridge: Harvard University Press, 1994.

> Offers a detailed reconstruction of Webb's biography in order to rescue the author from "almost total literary obscurity."

Gardner, Eric "'A Gentleman of Superior Cultivation and Refinement': Recovering the Biography of Frank J. Webb." *African American Review* 35, no. 2 (summer 2001): 297-308.

Documents Webb's life and career, offering detailed biographical information and valuable insights into his literary works.

Criticism

Review of *The Garies and Their Friends. The Athenæum,* no. 1565 (24 October 1857): 1320.

Describes *The Garies and Their Friends* as an "interesting" novel about racism in the free North of the United States.

Bone, Robert. "Novels of The Talented Tenth." In *The Negro Novel In America,* pp. 29-50. New Haven: Yale University Press, 1958.

Discusses the works of early black novelists, including Webb.

Fleming, Robert E. "Humor in the Early Black Novel." *CLA Journal* 17, no. 2 (December 1973): 250-62.

Examines the satirical and humorous aspects of the works of early African-American novelists, including Webb.

Gayle, Addison, Jr. "Paradigms of the Early Past." In *The Way of the New World: The Black Novel in America,* pp. 1-24. Garden City, N.Y.: Anchor Press, 1975.

Considers *The Garies and Their Friends* as an early contribution to a now rich African-American literary tradition.

Gloster, Hugh M. "Negro Fiction to World War I." In *Negro Voices in American Fiction.* 1948. Reprint, pp. 23-100. New York: Russell & Russell, 1965.

Briefly comments on Webb's treatment of miscegenation in *The Garies and Their Friends.*

Nielsen, A. L. "Mark Twain's *Pudd'nhead Wilson* and The Novel of the Tragic Mulatto." *Greyfriar: Siena Studies in Literature* 26 (1985): 14-30.

Surveys a number of nineteenth-century melodramatic novels—including *The Garies and Their Friends*—which feature the motif of the tragic mulatto.

Additional coverage of Webb's life and career is contained in the following sources published by Thomson Gale: *Dictionary of Literary Biography,* **Vol. 50; and** *Literature Resource Center.*

How to Use This Index

The main references

> **Calvino, Italo**
> 1923-1985 .... CLC 5, 8, 11, 22, 33, 39,
> 73; SSC 3, 48

list all author entries in the following Gale Literary Criticism series:

AAL = *Asian American Literature*
BG = *The Beat Generation: A Gale Critical Companion*
BLC = *Black Literature Criticism*
BLCS = *Black Literature Criticism Supplement*
CLC = *Contemporary Literary Criticism*
CLR = *Children's Literature Review*
CMLC = *Classical and Medieval Literature Criticism*
DC = *Drama Criticism*
HLC = *Hispanic Literature Criticism*
HLCS = *Hispanic Literature Criticism Supplement*
HR = *Harlem Renaissance: A Gale Critical Companion*
LC = *Literature Criticism from 1400 to 1800*
NCLC = *Nineteenth-Century Literature Criticism*
NNAL = *Native North American Literature*
PC = *Poetry Criticism*
SSC = *Short Story Criticism*
TCLC = *Twentieth-Century Literary Criticism*
WLC = *World Literature Criticism, 1500 to the Present*
WLCS = *World Literature Criticism Supplement*

The cross-references

> See also CA 85-88, 116; CANR 23, 61;
> DAM NOV; DLB 196; EW 13; MTCW 1, 2;
> RGSF 2; RGWL 2; SFW 4; SSFS 12

list all author entries in the following Gale biographical and literary sources:

AAYA = *Authors & Artists for Young Adults*
AFAW = *African American Writers*
AFW = *African Writers*
AITN = *Authors in the News*
AMW = *American Writers*
AMWR = *American Writers Retrospective Supplement*
AMWS = *American Writers Supplement*
ANW = *American Nature Writers*
AW = *Ancient Writers*
BEST = *Bestsellers*
BPFB = *Beacham's Encyclopedia of Popular Fiction: Biography and Resources*
BRW = *British Writers*
BRWS = *British Writers Supplement*
BW = *Black Writers*
BYA = *Beacham's Guide to Literature for Young Adults*
CA = *Contemporary Authors*
CAAS = *Contemporary Authors Autobiography Series*
CABS = *Contemporary Authors Bibliographical Series*
CAD = *Contemporary American Dramatists*
CANR = *Contemporary Authors New Revision Series*
CAP = *Contemporary Authors Permanent Series*
CBD = *Contemporary British Dramatists*
CCA = *Contemporary Canadian Authors*
CD = *Contemporary Dramatists*
CDALB = *Concise Dictionary of American Literary Biography*
CDALBS = *Concise Dictionary of American Literary Biography Supplement*
CDBLB = *Concise Dictionary of British Literary Biography*

CMW = *St. James Guide to Crime & Mystery Writers*
CN = *Contemporary Novelists*
CP = *Contemporary Poets*
CPW = *Contemporary Popular Writers*
CSW = *Contemporary Southern Writers*
CWD = *Contemporary Women Dramatists*
CWP = *Contemporary Women Poets*
CWRI = *St. James Guide to Children's Writers*
CWW = *Contemporary World Writers*
DA = *DISCovering Authors*
DA3 = *DISCovering Authors 3.0*
DAB = *DISCovering Authors: British Edition*
DAC = *DISCovering Authors: Canadian Edition*
DAM = *DISCovering Authors: Modules*
    DRAM: *Dramatists Module;* **MST:** *Most-studied Authors Module;*
    MULT: *Multicultural Authors Module;* **NOV:** *Novelists Module;*
    POET: *Poets Module;* **POP:** *Popular Fiction and Genre Authors Module*
DFS = *Drama for Students*
DLB = *Dictionary of Literary Biography*
DLBD = *Dictionary of Literary Biography Documentary Series*
DLBY = *Dictionary of Literary Biography Yearbook*
DNFS = *Literature of Developing Nations for Students*
EFS = *Epics for Students*
EXPN = *Exploring Novels*
EXPP = *Exploring Poetry*
EXPS = *Exploring Short Stories*
EW = *European Writers*
FANT = *St. James Guide to Fantasy Writers*
FW = *Feminist Writers*
GFL = *Guide to French Literature,* Beginnings to 1789, 1798 to the Present
GLL = *Gay and Lesbian Literature*
HGG = *St. James Guide to Horror, Ghost & Gothic Writers*
HW = *Hispanic Writers*
IDFW = *International Dictionary of Films and Filmmakers: Writers and Production Artists*
IDTP = *International Dictionary of Theatre: Playwrights*
LAIT = *Literature and Its Times*
LAW = *Latin American Writers*
JRDA = *Junior DISCovering Authors*
MAICYA = *Major Authors and Illustrators for Children and Young Adults*
MAICYAS = *Major Authors and Illustrators for Children and Young Adults Supplement*
MAWW = *Modern American Women Writers*
MJW = *Modern Japanese Writers*
MTCW = *Major 20th-Century Writers*
NCFS = *Nonfiction Classics for Students*
NFS = *Novels for Students*
PAB = *Poets: American and British*
PFS = *Poetry for Students*
RGAL = *Reference Guide to American Literature*
RGEL = *Reference Guide to English Literature*
RGSF = *Reference Guide to Short Fiction*
RGWL = *Reference Guide to World Literature*
RHW = *Twentieth-Century Romance and Historical Writers*
SAAS = *Something about the Author Autobiography Series*
SATA = *Something about the Author*
SFW = *St. James Guide to Science Fiction Writers*
SSFS = *Short Stories for Students*
TCWW = *Twentieth-Century Western Writers*
WLIT = *World Literature and Its Times*
WP = *World Poets*
YABC = *Yesterday's Authors of Books for Children*
YAW = *St. James Guide to Young Adult Writers*

Literary Criticism Series
Cumulative Author Index

Ali, Ahmed 1908-1998 .... **CLC 69**
See also CA 25-28R; CANR 15, 34; EWL 3
Ali, Tariq 1943- .... **CLC 173**
See also CA 25-28R; CANR 10, 99
Alighieri, Dante
See Dante
Allan, John B.
See Westlake, Donald E(dwin)
Allan, Sidney
See Hartmann, Sadakichi
Allan, Sydney
See Hartmann, Sadakichi
Allard, Janet .... **CLC 59**
Allen, Edward 1948- .... **CLC 59**
Allen, Fred 1894-1956 .... **TCLC 87**
Allen, Paula Gunn 1939- ..... **CLC 84; NNAL**
See also AMWS 4; CA 112; 143; CANR
63, 130; CWP; DA3; DAM MULT; DLB
175; FW; MTCW 1; RGAL 4
Allen, Roland
See Ayckbourn, Alan
Allen, Sarah A.
See Hopkins, Pauline Elizabeth
Allen, Sidney H.
See Hartmann, Sadakichi
Allen, Woody 1935- .... **CLC 16, 52**
See also AAYA 10, 51; CA 33-36R; CANR
27, 38, 63, 128; DAM POP; DLB 44;
MTCW 1
Allende, Isabel 1942- ... **CLC 39, 57, 97, 170;
HLC 1; SSC 65; WLCS**
See also AAYA 18; CA 125; 130; CANR
51, 74, 129; CDWLB 3; CLR 99; CWW
2; DA3; DAM MULT, NOV; DLB 145;
DNFS 1; EWL 3; FW; HW 1, 2; INT CA-
130; LAIT 5; LAWS 1; LMFS 2; MTCW
1, 2; NCFS 1; NFS 6, 18; RGSF 2;
RGWL 3; SSFS 11, 16; WLIT 1
Alleyn, Ellen
See Rossetti, Christina (Georgina)
Alleyne, Carla D. .... **CLC 65**
Allingham, Margery (Louise)
1904-1966 .... **CLC 19**
See also CA 5-8R; 25-28R; CANR 4, 58;
CMW 4; DLB 77; MSW; MTCW 1, 2
Allingham, William 1824-1889 ...... **NCLC 25**
See also DLB 35; RGEL 2
Allison, Dorothy E. 1949- .... **CLC 78, 153**
See also AAYA 53; CA 140; CANR 66, 107;
CSW; DA3; FW; MTCW 1; NFS 11;
RGAL 4
Alloula, Malek .... **CLC 65**
Allston, Washington 1779-1843 .... **NCLC 2**
See also DLB 1, 235
Almedingen, E. M. .... **CLC 12**
See Almedingen, Martha Edith von
See also SATA 3
Almedingen, Martha Edith von 1898-1971
See Almedingen, E. M.
See also CA 1-4R; CANR 1
Almodovar, Pedro 1949(?)- .... **CLC 114;
HLCS 1**
See also CA 133; CANR 72; HW 2
Almqvist, Carl Jonas Love
1793-1866 .... **NCLC 42**
**al-Mutanabbi, Ahmad ibn al-Husayn Abu
al-Tayyib al-Jufi al-Kindi**
915-965 .... **CMLC 66**
See also RGWL 3
Alonso, Damaso 1898-1990 .... **CLC 14**
See also CA 110; 131; 130; CANR 72; DLB
108; EWL 3; HW 1, 2
Alov
See Gogol, Nikolai (Vasilyevich)
Al Siddik
See Rolfe, Frederick (William Serafino Aus-
tin Lewis Mary)
See also GLL 1; RGEL 2

Alta 1942- .... **CLC 19**
See also CA 57-60
Alter, Robert B(ernard) 1935- .... **CLC 34**
See also CA 49-52; CANR 1, 47, 100
Alther, Lisa 1944- .... **CLC 7, 41**
See also BPFB 1; CA 65-68; CAAS 30;
CANR 12, 30, 51; CN 7; CSW; GLL 2;
MTCW 1
Althusser, L.
See Althusser, Louis
Althusser, Louis 1918-1990 .... **CLC 106**
See also CA 131; 132; CANR 102; DLB
242
Altman, Robert 1925- .... **CLC 16, 116**
See also CA 73-76; CANR 43
Alurista .... **HLCS 1**
See Urista (Heredia), Alberto (Baltazar)
See also DLB 82; LLW 1
Alvarez, A(lfred) 1929- .... **CLC 5, 13**
See also CA 1-4R; CANR 3, 33, 63, 101;
CN 7; CP 7; DLB 14, 40
Alvarez, Alejandro Rodriguez 1903-1965
See Casona, Alejandro
See also CA 131; 93-96; HW 1
Alvarez, Julia 1950- .... **CLC 93; HLCS 1**
See also AAYA 25; AMWS 7; CA 147;
CANR 69, 101; DA3; DLB 282; LATS 1;
LLW 1; MTCW 1; NFS 5, 9; SATA 129;
WLIT 1
Alvaro, Corrado 1896-1956 .... **TCLC 60**
See also CA 163; DLB 264; EWL 3
Amado, Jorge 1912-2001 ... **CLC 13, 40, 106;
HLC 1**
See also CA 77-80; 201; CANR 35, 74;
CWW 2; DAM MULT, NOV; DLB 113;
EWL 3; HW 2; LAW; LAWS 1; MTCW
1, 2; RGWL 2, 3; TWA; WLIT 1
Ambler, Eric 1909-1998 .... **CLC 4, 6, 9**
See also BRWS 4; CA 9-12R; 171; CANR
7, 38, 74; CMW 4; CN 7; DLB 77; MSW;
MTCW 1, 2; TEA
Ambrose, Stephen E(dward)
1936-2002 .... **CLC 145**
See also AAYA 44; CA 1-4R; 209; CANR
3, 43, 57, 83, 105; NCFS 2; SATA 40,
138
Amichai, Yehuda 1924-2000 .. **CLC 9, 22, 57,
116; PC 38**
See also CA 85-88; 189; CANR 46, 60, 99;
CWW 2; EWL 3; MTCW 1
Amichai, Yehudah
See Amichai, Yehuda
Amiel, Henri Frederic 1821-1881 .... **NCLC 4**
See also DLB 217
Amis, Kingsley (William)
1922-1995 ...... **CLC 1, 2, 3, 5, 8, 13, 40,
44, 129**
See also AITN 2; BPFB 1; BRWS 2; CA
9-12R; 150; CANR 8, 28, 54; CDBLB
1945-1960; CN 7; CP 7; DA; DA3; DAB;
DAC; DAM MST, NOV; DLB 15, 27,
100, 139; DLBY 1996; EWL 3; HGG;
INT CANR-8; MTCW 1, 2; RGEL 2;
RGSF 2; SFW 4
Amis, Martin (Louis) 1949- .... **CLC 4, 9, 38,
62, 101**
See also BEST 90:3; BRWS 4; CA 65-68;
CANR 8, 27, 54, 73, 95; CN 7; DA3;
DLB 14, 194; EWL 3; INT CANR-27;
MTCW 1
Ammianus Marcellinus c. 330-c.
395 .... **CMLC 60**
See also AW 2; DLB 211
Ammons, A(rchie) R(andolph)
1926-2001 ...... **CLC 2, 3, 5, 8, 9, 25, 57,
108; PC 16**
See also AITN 1; AMWS 7; CA 9-12R;
193; CANR 6, 36, 51, 73, 107; CP 7;
CSW; DAM POET; DLB 5, 165; EWL 3;
MTCW 1, 2; PFS 19; RGAL 4

Amo, Tauraatua i
See Adams, Henry (Brooks)
Amory, Thomas 1691(?)-1788 .... **LC 48**
See also DLB 39
Anand, Mulk Raj 1905- .... **CLC 23, 93**
See also CA 65-68; CANR 32, 64; CN 7;
DAM NOV; EWL 3; MTCW 1, 2; RGSF
2
Anatol
See Schnitzler, Arthur
Anaximander c. 611B.C.-c.
546B.C. .... **CMLC 22**
Anaya, Rudolfo A(lfonso) 1937- ...... **CLC 23,
148; HLC 1**
See also AAYA 20; BYA 13; CA 45-48;
CAAS 4; CANR 1, 32, 51, 124; CN 7;
DAM MULT, NOV; DLB 82, 206, 278;
HW 1; LAIT 4; LLW 1; MTCW 1, 2; NFS
12; RGAL 4; RGSF 2; WLIT 1
Andersen, Hans Christian
1805-1875 .... **NCLC 7, 79; SSC 6, 56;
WLC**
See also CLR 6; DA; DA3; DAB; DAC;
DAM MST, POP; EW 6; MAICYA 1, 2;
RGSF 2; RGWL 2, 3; SATA 100; TWA;
WCH; YABC 1
Anderson, C. Farley
See Mencken, H(enry) L(ouis); Nathan,
George Jean
Anderson, Jessica (Margaret) Queale
1916- .... **CLC 37**
See also CA 9-12R; CANR 4, 62; CN 7
Anderson, Jon (Victor) 1940- .... **CLC 9**
See also CA 25-28R; CANR 20; DAM
POET
Anderson, Lindsay (Gordon)
1923-1994 .... **CLC 20**
See also CA 125; 128; 146; CANR 77
Anderson, Maxwell 1888-1959 .... **TCLC 2,
144**
See also CA 105; 152; DAM DRAM; DFS
16; DLB 7, 228; MTCW 2; RGAL 4
Anderson, Poul (William)
1926-2001 .... **CLC 15**
See also AAYA 5, 34; BPFB 1; BYA 6, 8,
9; CA 1-4R; 181; 199; CAAE 181; CAAS
2; CANR 2, 15, 34, 64, 110; CLR 58;
DLB 8; FANT; INT CANR-15; MTCW 1,
2; SATA 90; SATA-Brief 39; SATA-Essay
106; SCFW 2; SFW 4; SUFW 1, 2
Anderson, Robert (Woodruff)
1917- .... **CLC 23**
See also AITN 1; CA 21-24R; CANR 32;
DAM DRAM; DLB 7; LAIT 5
Anderson, Roberta Joan
See Mitchell, Joni
Anderson, Sherwood 1876-1941 .. **SSC 1, 46;
TCLC 1, 10, 24, 123; WLC**
See also AAYA 30; AMW; AMWC 2; BPFB
1; CA 104; 121; CANR 61; CDALB
1917-1929; DA; DA3; DAB; DAC; DAM
MST, NOV; DLB 4, 9, 86; DLBD 1; EWL
3; EXPS; GLL 2; MTCW 1, 2; NFS 4;
RGAL 4; RGSF 2; SSFS 4, 10, 11; TUS
Andier, Pierre
See Desnos, Robert
Andouard
See Giraudoux, Jean(-Hippolyte)
Andrade, Carlos Drummond de ..... **CLC 18**
See Drummond de Andrade, Carlos
See also EWL 3; RGWL 2, 3
Andrade, Mario de .... **TCLC 43**
See de Andrade, Mario
See also EWL 3; LAW; RGWL 2, 3; WLIT
1
Andreae, Johann V(alentin)
1586-1654 .... **LC 32**
See also DLB 164

Andreas Capellanus fl. c. 1185- .... **CMLC 45**
See also DLB 208

Andreas-Salome, Lou 1861-1937 ... **TCLC 56**
See also CA 178; DLB 66

Andreev, Leonid
See Andreyev, Leonid (Nikolaevich)
See also DLB 295; EWL 3

Andress, Lesley
See Sanders, Lawrence

Andrewes, Lancelot 1555-1626 .... **LC 5**
See also DLB 151, 172

Andrews, Cicily Fairfield
See West, Rebecca

Andrews, Elton V.
See Pohl, Frederik

Andreyev, Leonid (Nikolaevich)
1871-1919 .... **TCLC 3**
See Andreev, Leonid
See also CA 104; 185

Andric, Ivo 1892-1975 .... **CLC 8; SSC 36;**
TCLC 135
See also CA 81-84; 57-60; CANR 43, 60;
CDWLB 4; DLB 147; EW 11; EWL 3;
MTCW 1; RGSF 2; RGWL 2, 3

Androvar
See Prado (Calvo), Pedro

Angelique, Pierre
See Bataille, Georges

Angell, Roger 1920- .... **CLC 26**
See also CA 57-60; CANR 13, 44, 70; DLB
171, 185

Angelou, Maya 1928- ... **BLC 1; CLC 12, 35,**
64, 77, 155; PC 32; WLCS
See also AAYA 7, 20; AMWS 4; BPFB 1;
BW 2, 3; BYA 2; CA 65-68; CANR 19,
42, 65, 111; CDALBS; CLR 53; CP 7;
CPW; CSW; CWP; DA; DA3; DAB;
DAC; DAM MST, MULT, POET, POP;
DLB 38; EWL 3; EXPN; EXPP; LAIT 4;
MAICYA 2; MAICYAS 1; MAWW;
MTCW 1, 2; NCFS 2; NFS 2; PFS 2, 3;
RGAL 4; SATA 49, 136; WYA; YAW

Angouleme, Marguerite d'
See de Navarre, Marguerite

Anna Comnena 1083-1153 .... **CMLC 25**

Annensky, Innokentii Fedorovich
See Annensky, Innokenty (Fyodorovich)
See also DLB 295

Annensky, Innokenty (Fyodorovich)
1856-1909 .... **TCLC 14**
See also CA 110; 155; EWL 3

Annunzio, Gabriele d'
See D'Annunzio, Gabriele

Anodos
See Coleridge, Mary E(lizabeth)

Anon, Charles Robert
See Pessoa, Fernando (Antonio Nogueira)

Anouilh, Jean (Marie Lucien Pierre)
1910-1987 . **CLC 1, 3, 8, 13, 40, 50; DC**
8, 21
See also CA 17-20R; 123; CANR 32; DAM
DRAM; DFS 9, 10, 19; EW 13; EWL 3;
GFL 1789 to the Present; MTCW 1, 2;
RGWL 2, 3; TWA

Anselm of Canterbury
1033(?)-1109 .... **CMLC 67**
See also DLB 115

Anthony, Florence
See Ai

Anthony, John
See Ciardi, John (Anthony)

Anthony, Peter
See Shaffer, Anthony (Joshua); Shaffer, Peter (Levin)

Anthony, Piers 1934- .... **CLC 35**
See also AAYA 11, 48; BYA 7; CA 200;
CAAE 200; CANR 28, 56, 73, 102; CPW;
DAM POP; DLB 8; FANT; MAICYA 2;
MAICYAS 1; MTCW 1, 2; SAAS 22;
SATA 84, 129; SATA-Essay 129; SFW 4;
SUFW 1, 2; YAW

Anthony, Susan B(rownell)
1820-1906 .... **TCLC 84**
See also CA 211; FW

Antiphon c. 480B.C.-c. 411B.C. .... **CMLC 55**

Antoine, Marc
See Proust, (Valentin-Louis-George-Eugene)
Marcel

Antoninus, Brother
See Everson, William (Oliver)

Antonioni, Michelangelo 1912- .... **CLC 20,**
144
See also CA 73-76; CANR 45, 77

Antschel, Paul 1920-1970
See Celan, Paul
See also CA 85-88; CANR 33, 61; MTCW
1

Anwar, Chairil 1922-1949 .... **TCLC 22**
See Chairil Anwar
See also CA 121; 219; RGWL 3

Anzaldua, Gloria (Evanjelina)
1942- .... **HLCS 1**
See also CA 175; CSW; CWP; DLB 122;
FW; LLW 1; RGAL 4

Apess, William 1798-1839(?) .... **NCLC 73;**
NNAL
See also DAM MULT; DLB 175, 243

Apollinaire, Guillaume 1880-1918 .... **PC 7;**
TCLC 3, 8, 51
See Kostrowitzki, Wilhelm Apollinaris de
See also CA 152; DAM POET; DLB 258;
EW 9; EWL 3; GFL 1789 to the Present;
MTCW 1; RGWL 2, 3; TWA; WP

Apollonius of Rhodes
See Apollonius Rhodius
See also AW 1; RGWL 2, 3

Apollonius Rhodius c. 300B.C.-c.
220B.C. .... **CMLC 28**
See Apollonius of Rhodes
See also DLB 176

Appelfeld, Aharon 1932- ... **CLC 23, 47; SSC**
42
See also CA 112; 133; CANR 86; CWW 2;
DLB 299; EWL 3; RGSF 2

Apple, Max (Isaac) 1941- .... **CLC 9, 33; SSC**
50
See also CA 81-84; CANR 19, 54; DLB
130

Appleman, Philip (Dean) 1926- .... **CLC 51**
See also CA 13-16R; CAAS 18; CANR 6,
29, 56

Appleton, Lawrence
See Lovecraft, H(oward) P(hillips)

Apteryx
See Eliot, T(homas) S(tearns)

Apuleius, (Lucius Madaurensis)
125(?)-175(?) .... **CMLC 1**
See also AW 2; CDWLB 1; DLB 211;
RGWL 2, 3; SUFW

Aquin, Hubert 1929-1977 .... **CLC 15**
See also CA 105; DLB 53; EWL 3

Aquinas, Thomas 1224(?)-1274 ..... **CMLC 33**
See also DLB 115; EW 1; TWA

Aragon, Louis 1897-1982 .... **CLC 3, 22;**
TCLC 123
See also CA 69-72; 108; CANR 28, 71;
DAM NOV, POET; DLB 72, 258; EW 11;
EWL 3; GFL 1789 to the Present; GLL 2;
LMFS 2; MTCW 1, 2; RGWL 2, 3

Arany, Janos 1817-1882 .... **NCLC 34**

Aranyos, Kakay 1847-1910
See Mikszath, Kalman

Aratus of Soli c. 315B.C.-c.
240B.C. .... **CMLC 64**
See also DLB 176

Arbuthnot, John 1667-1735 .... **LC 1**
See also DLB 101

Archer, Herbert Winslow
See Mencken, H(enry) L(ouis)

Archer, Jeffrey (Howard) 1940- .... **CLC 28**
See also AAYA 16; BEST 89:3; BPFB 1;
CA 77-80; CANR 22, 52, 95; CPW; DA3;
DAM POP; INT CANR-22

Archer, Jules 1915- .... **CLC 12**
See also CA 9-12R; CANR 6, 69; SAAS 5;
SATA 4, 85

Archer, Lee
See Ellison, Harlan (Jay)

Archilochus c. 7th cent. B.C.- .... **CMLC 44**
See also DLB 176

Arden, John 1930- .... **CLC 6, 13, 15**
See also BRWS 2; CA 13-16R; CAAS 4;
CANR 31, 65, 67, 124; CBD; CD 5;
DAM DRAM; DFS 9; DLB 13, 245;
EWL 3; MTCW 1

Arenas, Reinaldo 1943-1990 .. **CLC 41; HLC**
1
See also CA 124; 128; 133; CANR 73, 106;
DAM MULT; DLB 145; EWL 3; GLL 2;
HW 1; LAW; LAWS 1; MTCW 1; RGSF
2; RGWL 3; WLIT 1

Arendt, Hannah 1906-1975 .... **CLC 66, 98**
See also CA 17-20R; 61-64; CANR 26, 60;
DLB 242; MTCW 1, 2

Aretino, Pietro 1492-1556 .... **LC 12**
See also RGWL 2, 3

Arghezi, Tudor .... **CLC 80**
See Theodorescu, Ion N.
See also CA 167; CDWLB 4; DLB 220;
EWL 3

Arguedas, Jose Maria 1911-1969 .... **CLC 10,**
18; HLCS 1; TCLC 147
See also CA 89-92; CANR 73; DLB 113;
EWL 3; HW 1; LAW; RGWL 2, 3; WLIT
1

Argueta, Manlio 1936- .... **CLC 31**
See also CA 131; CANR 73; CWW 2; DLB
145; EWL 3; HW 1; RGWL 3

Arias, Ron(ald Francis) 1941- .... **HLC 1**
See also CA 131; CANR 81; DAM MULT;
DLB 82; HW 1, 2; MTCW 2

Ariosto, Ludovico 1474-1533 ... **LC 6, 87; PC**
42
See also EW 2; RGWL 2, 3

Aristides
See Epstein, Joseph

Aristophanes 450B.C.-385B.C. .... **CMLC 4,**
51; DC 2; WLCS
See also AW 1; CDWLB 1; DA; DA3;
DAB; DAC; DAM DRAM, MST; DFS
10; DLB 176; LMFS 1; RGWL 2, 3; TWA

Aristotle 384B.C.-322B.C. .... **CMLC 31;**
WLCS
See also AW 1; CDWLB 1; DA; DA3;
DAB; DAC; DAM MST; DLB 176;
RGWL 2, 3; TWA

Arlt, Roberto (Godofredo Christophersen)
1900-1942 .... **HLC 1; TCLC 29**
See also CA 123; 131; CANR 67; DAM
MULT; EWL 3; HW 1, 2; LAW

Armah, Ayi Kwei 1939- . **BLC 1; CLC 5, 33,**
136
See also AFW; BW 1; CA 61-64; CANR
21, 64; CDWLB 3; CN 7; DAM MULT,
POET; DLB 117; EWL 3; MTCW 1;
WLIT 2

Armatrading, Joan 1950- .... **CLC 17**
See also CA 114; 186

Armitage, Frank
See Carpenter, John (Howard)

Barber, Benjamin R. 1939- .... **CLC 141**
See also CA 29-32R; CANR 12, 32, 64, 119

Barbera, Jack (Vincent) 1945- .... **CLC 44**
See also CA 110; CANR 45

Barbey d'Aurevilly, Jules-Amedee
1808-1889 .... **NCLC 1; SSC 17**
See also DLB 119; GFL 1789 to the Present

Barbour, John c. 1316-1395 .... **CMLC 33**
See also DLB 146

Barbusse, Henri 1873-1935 .... **TCLC 5**
See also CA 105; 154; DLB 65; EWL 3;
RGWL 2, 3

Barclay, Bill
See Moorcock, Michael (John)

Barclay, William Ewert
See Moorcock, Michael (John)

Barea, Arturo 1897-1957 .... **TCLC 14**
See also CA 111; 201

Barfoot, Joan 1946- .... **CLC 18**
See also CA 105

Barham, Richard Harris
1788-1845 .... **NCLC 77**
See also DLB 159

Baring, Maurice 1874-1945 .... **TCLC 8**
See also CA 105; 168; DLB 34; HGG

Baring-Gould, Sabine 1834-1924 ... **TCLC 88**
See also DLB 156, 190

Barker, Clive 1952- .... **CLC 52; SSC 53**
See also AAYA 10, 54; BEST 90:3; BPFB
1; CA 121; 129; CANR 71, 111; CPW;
DA3; DAM POP; DLB 261; HGG; INT
CA-129; MTCW 1, 2; SUFW 2

Barker, George Granville
1913-1991 .... **CLC 8, 48**
See also CA 9-12R; 135; CANR 7, 38;
DAM POET; DLB 20; EWL 3; MTCW 1

Barker, Harley Granville
See Granville-Barker, Harley
See also DLB 10

Barker, Howard 1946- .... **CLC 37**
See also CA 102; CBD; CD 5; DLB 13,
233

Barker, Jane 1652-1732 .... **LC 42, 82**
See also DLB 39, 131

Barker, Pat(ricia) 1943- ...... **CLC 32, 94, 146**
See also BRWS 4; CA 117; 122; CANR 50,
101; CN 7; DLB 271; INT CA-122

Barlach, Ernst (Heinrich)
1870-1938 .... **TCLC 84**
See also CA 178; DLB 56, 118; EWL 3

Barlow, Joel 1754-1812 .... **NCLC 23**
See also AMWS 2; DLB 37; RGAL 4

Barnard, Mary (Ethel) 1909- .... **CLC 48**
See also CA 21-22; CAP 2

Barnes, Djuna 1892-1982 .... **CLC 3, 4, 8, 11,
29, 127; SSC 3**
See Steptoe, Lydia
See also AMWS 3; CA 9-12R; 107; CAD;
CANR 16, 55; CWD; DLB 4, 9, 45; EWL
3; GLL 1; MTCW 1, 2; RGAL 4; TUS

Barnes, Jim 1933- .... **NNAL**
See also CA 108, 175; CAAE 175; CAAS
28; DLB 175

Barnes, Julian (Patrick) 1946- . **CLC 42, 141**
See also BRWS 4; CA 102; CANR 19, 54,
115; CN 7; DAB; DLB 194; DLBY 1993;
EWL 3; MTCW 1

Barnes, Peter 1931-2004 .... **CLC 5, 56**
See also CA 65-68; CAAS 12; CANR 33,
34, 64, 113; CBD; CD 5; DFS 6; DLB
13, 233; MTCW 1

Barnes, William 1801-1886 .... **NCLC 75**
See also DLB 32

Baroja (y Nessi), Pio 1872-1956 .... **HLC 1;
TCLC 8**
See also CA 104; EW 9

Baron, David
See Pinter, Harold

Baron Corvo
See Rolfe, Frederick (William Serafino Austin Lewis Mary)

Barondess, Sue K(aufman)
1926-1977 .... **CLC 8**
See Kaufman, Sue
See also CA 1-4R; 69-72; CANR 1

Baron de Teive
See Pessoa, Fernando (Antonio Nogueira)

Baroness Von S.
See Zangwill, Israel

Barres, (Auguste-)Maurice
1862-1923 .... **TCLC 47**
See also CA 164; DLB 123; GFL 1789 to
the Present

Barreto, Afonso Henrique de Lima
See Lima Barreto, Afonso Henrique de

Barrett, Andrea 1954- .... **CLC 150**
See also CA 156; CANR 92

Barrett, Michele .... **CLC 65**

Barrett, (Roger) Syd 1946- .... **CLC 35**

Barrett, William (Christopher)
1913-1992 .... **CLC 27**
See also CA 13-16R; 139; CANR 11, 67;
INT CANR-11

Barrie, J(ames) M(atthew)
1860-1937 .... **TCLC 2**
See also BRWS 3; BYA 4, 5; CA 104; 136;
CANR 77; CDBLB 1890-1914; CLR 16;
CWRI 5; DA3; DAB; DAM DRAM; DFS
7; DLB 10, 141, 156; EWL 3; FANT;
MAICYA 1, 2; MTCW 1; SATA 100;
SUFW; WCH; WLIT 4; YABC 1

Barrington, Michael
See Moorcock, Michael (John)

Barrol, Grady
See Bograd, Larry

Barry, Mike
See Malzberg, Barry N(athaniel)

Barry, Philip 1896-1949 .... **TCLC 11**
See also CA 109; 199; DFS 9; DLB 7, 228;
RGAL 4

Bart, Andre Schwarz
See Schwarz-Bart, Andre

Barth, John (Simmons) 1930- ... **CLC 1, 2, 3,
5, 7, 9, 10, 14, 27, 51, 89; SSC 10**
See also AITN 1, 2; AMW; BPFB 1; CA
1-4R; CABS 1; CANR 5, 23, 49, 64, 113;
CN 7; DAM NOV; DLB 2, 227; EWL 3;
FANT; MTCW 1; RGAL 4; RGSF 2;
RHW; SSFS 6; TUS

Barthelme, Donald 1931-1989 ... **CLC 1, 2, 3,
5, 6, 8, 13, 23, 46, 59, 115; SSC 2, 55**
See also AMWS 4; BPFB 1; CA 21-24R;
129; CANR 20, 58; DA3; DAM NOV;
DLB 2, 234; DLBY 1980, 1989; EWL 3;
FANT; LMFS 2; MTCW 1, 2; RGAL 4;
RGSF 2; SATA 7; SATA-Obit 62; SSFS
17

Barthelme, Frederick 1943- ...... **CLC 36, 117**
See also AMWS 11; CA 114; 122; CANR
77; CN 7; CSW; DLB 244; DLBY 1985;
EWL 3; INT CA-122

Barthes, Roland (Gerard)
1915-1980 .... **CLC 24, 83; TCLC 135**
See also CA 130; 97-100; CANR 66; DLB
296; EW 13; EWL 3; GFL 1789 to the
Present; MTCW 1, 2; TWA

Barzun, Jacques (Martin) 1907- ..... **CLC 51,
145**
See also CA 61-64; CANR 22, 95

Bashevis, Isaac
See Singer, Isaac Bashevis

Bashkirtseff, Marie 1859-1884 .... **NCLC 27**

Basho, Matsuo
See Matsuo Basho
See also PFS 18; RGWL 2, 3; WP

Basil of Caesaria c. 330-379 .... **CMLC 35**

Basket, Raney
See Edgerton, Clyde (Carlyle)

Bass, Kingsley B., Jr.
See Bullins, Ed

Bass, Rick 1958- .... **CLC 79, 143; SSC 60**
See also ANW; CA 126; CANR 53, 93;
CSW; DLB 212, 275

Bassani, Giorgio 1916-2000 .... **CLC 9**
See also CA 65-68; 190; CANR 33; CWW
2; DLB 128, 177, 299; EWL 3; MTCW 1;
RGWL 2, 3

Bastian, Ann .... **CLC 70**

Bastos, Augusto (Antonio) Roa
See Roa Bastos, Augusto (Antonio)

Bataille, Georges 1897-1962 .... **CLC 29**
See also CA 101; 89-92; EWL 3

Bates, H(erbert) E(rnest)
1905-1974 .... **CLC 46; SSC 10**
See also CA 93-96; 45-48; CANR 34; DA3;
DAB; DAM POP; DLB 162, 191; EWL
3; EXPS; MTCW 1, 2; RGSF 2; SSFS 7

Bauchart
See Camus, Albert

Baudelaire, Charles 1821-1867 . **NCLC 6, 29,
55; PC 1; SSC 18; WLC**
See also DA; DA3; DAB; DAC; DAM
MST, POET; DLB 217; EW 7; GFL 1789
to the Present; LMFS 2; RGWL 2, 3;
TWA

Baudouin, Marcel
See Peguy, Charles (Pierre)

Baudouin, Pierre
See Peguy, Charles (Pierre)

Baudrillard, Jean 1929- .... **CLC 60**
See also DLB 296

Baum, L(yman) Frank 1856-1919 .. **TCLC 7,
132**
See also AAYA 46; BYA 16; CA 108; 133;
CLR 15; CWRI 5; DLB 22; FANT; JRDA;
MAICYA 1, 2; MTCW 1, 2; NFS 13;
RGAL 4; SATA 18, 100; WCH

Baum, Louis F.
See Baum, L(yman) Frank

Baumbach, Jonathan 1933- .... **CLC 6, 23**
See also CA 13-16R; CAAS 5; CANR 12,
66; CN 7; DLBY 1980; INT CANR-12;
MTCW 1

Bausch, Richard (Carl) 1945- .... **CLC 51**
See also AMWS 7; CA 101; CAAS 14;
CANR 43, 61, 87; CSW; DLB 130

Baxter, Charles (Morley) 1947- . **CLC 45, 78**
See also CA 57-60; CANR 40, 64, 104;
CPW; DAM POP; DLB 130; MTCW 2

Baxter, George Owen
See Faust, Frederick (Schiller)

Baxter, James K(eir) 1926-1972 .... **CLC 14**
See also CA 77-80; EWL 3

Baxter, John
See Hunt, E(verette) Howard, (Jr.)

Bayer, Sylvia
See Glassco, John

Baynton, Barbara 1857-1929 .... **TCLC 57**
See also DLB 230; RGSF 2

Beagle, Peter S(oyer) 1939- .... **CLC 7, 104**
See also AAYA 47; BPFB 1; BYA 9, 10,
16; CA 9-12R; CANR 4, 51, 73, 110;
DA3; DLBY 1980; FANT; INT CANR-4;
MTCW 1; SATA 60, 130; SUFW 1, 2;
YAW

Bean, Normal
See Burroughs, Edgar Rice

Beard, Charles A(ustin)
1874-1948 .... **TCLC 15**
See also CA 115; 189; DLB 17; SATA 18

Beardsley, Aubrey 1872-1898 .... **NCLC 6**

Bodenheimer, Maxwell
See Bodenheim, Maxwell
Bodker, Cecil 1927-
See Bodker, Cecil
Bodker, Cecil 1927- .... **CLC 21**
See also CA 73-76; CANR 13, 44, 111;
CLR 23; MAICYA 1, 2; SATA 14, 133
Boell, Heinrich (Theodor)
1917-1985 ..... **CLC 2, 3, 6, 9, 11, 15, 27,**
32, 72; SSC 23; WLC
See Boll, Heinrich
See also CA 21-24R; 116; CANR 24; DA;
DA3; DAB; DAC; DAM MST, NOV;
DLB 69; DLBY 1985; MTCW 1, 2; TWA
Boerne, Alfred
See Doeblin, Alfred
Boethius c. 480-c. 524 .... **CMLC 15**
See also DLB 115; RGWL 2, 3
Boff, Leonardo (Genezio Darci)
1938- .... **CLC 70; HLC 1**
See also CA 150; DAM MULT; HW 2
Bogan, Louise 1897-1970 .... **CLC 4, 39, 46,**
93; PC 12
See also AMWS 3; CA 73-76; 25-28R;
CANR 33, 82; DAM POET; DLB 45, 169;
EWL 3; MAWW; MTCW 1, 2; RGAL 4
Bogarde, Dirk
See Van Den Bogarde, Derek Jules Gaspard
Ulric Niven
See also DLB 14
Bogosian, Eric 1953- .... **CLC 45, 141**
See also CA 138; CAD; CANR 102; CD 5
Bograd, Larry 1953- .... **CLC 35**
See also CA 93-96; CANR 57; SAAS 21;
SATA 33, 89; WYA
Boiardo, Matteo Maria 1441-1494 .... **LC 6**
Boileau-Despreaux, Nicolas 1636-1711 . **LC 3**
See also DLB 268; EW 3; GFL Beginnings
to 1789; RGWL 2, 3
Boissard, Maurice
See Leautaud, Paul
Bojer, Johan 1872-1959 .... **TCLC 64**
See also CA 189; EWL 3
Bok, Edward W(illiam)
1863-1930 .... **TCLC 101**
See also CA 217; DLB 91; DLBD 16
Boker, George Henry 1823-1890 . **NCLC 125**
See also RGAL 4
Boland, Eavan (Aisling) 1944- .. **CLC 40, 67,**
113; PC 58
See also BRWS 5; CA 143, 207; CAAE
207; CANR 61; CP 7; CWP; DAM POET;
DLB 40; FW; MTCW 2; PFS 12
Boll, Heinrich
See Boell, Heinrich (Theodor)
See also BPFB 1; CDWLB 2; EW 13; EWL
3; RGSF 2; RGWL 2, 3
Bolt, Lee
See Faust, Frederick (Schiller)
Bolt, Robert (Oxton) 1924-1995 .... **CLC 14**
See also CA 17-20R; 147; CANR 35, 67;
CBD; DAM DRAM; DFS 2; DLB 13,
233; EWL 3; LAIT 1; MTCW 1
Bombal, Maria Luisa 1910-1980 .... **HLCS 1;**
SSC 37
See also CA 127; CANR 72; EWL 3; HW
1; LAW; RGSF 2
Bombet, Louis-Alexandre-Cesar
See Stendhal
Bomkauf
See Kaufman, Bob (Garnell)
Bonaventura .... **NCLC 35**
See also DLB 90
Bond, Edward 1934- .... **CLC 4, 6, 13, 23**
See also AAYA 50; BRWS 1; CA 25-28R;
CANR 38, 67, 106; CBD; CD 5; DAM
DRAM; DFS 3, 8; DLB 13; EWL 3;
MTCW 1

Bonham, Frank 1914-1989 .... **CLC 12**
See also AAYA 1; BYA 1, 3; CA 9-12R;
CANR 4, 36; JRDA; MAICYA 1, 2;
SAAS 3; SATA 1, 49; SATA-Obit 62;
TCWW 2; YAW
Bonnefoy, Yves 1923- . **CLC 9, 15, 58; PC 58**
See also CA 85-88; CANR 33, 75, 97;
CWW 2; DAM MST, POET; DLB 258;
EWL 3; GFL 1789 to the Present; MTCW
1, 2
Bonner, Marita .... **HR 2**
See Occomy, Marita (Odette) Bonner
Bonnin, Gertrude 1876-1938 .... **NNAL**
See Zitkala-Sa
See also CA 150; DAM MULT
Bontemps, Arna(ud Wendell)
1902-1973 ..... **BLC 1; CLC 1, 18; HR 2**
See also BW 1; CA 1-4R; 41-44R; CANR
4, 35; CLR 6; CWRI 5; DA3; DAM
MULT, NOV, POET; DLB 48, 51; JRDA;
MAICYA 1, 2; MTCW 1, 2; SATA 2, 44;
SATA-Obit 24; WCH; WP
Boot, William
See Stoppard, Tom
Booth, Martin 1944-2004 .... **CLC 13**
See also CA 93-96, 188; 223; CAAE 188;
CAAS 2; CANR 92
Booth, Philip 1925- .... **CLC 23**
See also CA 5-8R; CANR 5, 88; CP 7;
DLBY 1982
Booth, Wayne C(layson) 1921- .... **CLC 24**
See also CA 1-4R; CAAS 5; CANR 3, 43,
117; DLB 67
Borchert, Wolfgang 1921-1947 .... **TCLC 5**
See also CA 104; 188; DLB 69, 124; EWL
3
Borel, Petrus 1809-1859 .... **NCLC 41**
See also DLB 119; GFL 1789 to the Present
Borges, Jorge Luis 1899-1986 ... **CLC 1, 2, 3,**
4, 6, 8, 9, 10, 13, 19, 44, 48, 83; HLC 1;
PC 22, 32; SSC 4, 41; TCLC 109;
WLC
See also AAYA 26; BPFB 1; CA 21-24R;
CANR 19, 33, 75, 105; CDWLB 3; DA;
DA3; DAB; DAC; DAM MST, MULT;
DLB 113, 283; DLBY 1986; DNFS 1, 2;
EWL 3; HW 1, 2; LAW; LMFS 2; MSW;
MTCW 1, 2; RGSF 2; RGWL 2, 3; SFW
4; SSFS 17; TWA; WLIT 1
Borowski, Tadeusz 1922-1951 .... **SSC 48;**
TCLC 9
See also CA 106; 154; CDWLB 4; DLB
215; EWL 3; RGSF 2; RGWL 3; SSFS
13
Borrow, George (Henry)
1803-1881 .... **NCLC 9**
See also DLB 21, 55, 166
Bosch (Gavino), Juan 1909-2001 ..... **HLCS 1**
See also CA 151; 204; DAM MST, MULT;
DLB 145; HW 1, 2
Bosman, Herman Charles
1905-1951 .... **TCLC 49**
See Malan, Herman
See also CA 160; DLB 225; RGSF 2
Bosschere, Jean de 1878(?)-1953 ... **TCLC 19**
See also CA 115; 186
Boswell, James 1740-1795 ... **LC 4, 50; WLC**
See also BRW 3; CDBLB 1660-1789; DA;
DAB; DAC; DAM MST; DLB 104, 142;
TEA; WLIT 3
Bottomley, Gordon 1874-1948 ..... **TCLC 107**
See also CA 120; 192; DLB 10
Bottoms, David 1949- .... **CLC 53**
See also CA 105; CANR 22; CSW; DLB
120; DLBY 1983
Boucicault, Dion 1820-1890 .... **NCLC 41**
Boucolon, Maryse
See Conde, Maryse

Bourget, Paul (Charles Joseph)
1852-1935 .... **TCLC 12**
See also CA 107; 196; DLB 123; GFL 1789
to the Present
Bourjaily, Vance (Nye) 1922- .... **CLC 8, 62**
See also CA 1-4R; CAAS 1; CANR 2, 72;
CN 7; DLB 2, 143
Bourne, Randolph S(illiman)
1886-1918 .... **TCLC 16**
See also AMW; CA 117; 155; DLB 63
Bova, Ben(jamin William) 1932- ...... **CLC 45**
See also AAYA 16; CA 5-8R; CAAS 18;
CANR 11, 56, 94, 111; CLR 3, 96; DLBY
1981; INT CANR-11; MAICYA 1, 2;
MTCW 1; SATA 6, 68, 133; SFW 4
Bowen, Elizabeth (Dorothea Cole)
1899-1973 . **CLC 1, 3, 6, 11, 15, 22, 118;**
SSC 3, 28, 66; TCLC 148
See also BRWS 2; CA 17-18; 41-44R;
CANR 35, 105; CAP 2; CDBLB 1945-
1960; DA3; DAM NOV; DLB 15, 162;
EWL 3; EXPS; FW; HGG; MTCW 1, 2;
NFS 13; RGSF 2; SSFS 5; SUFW 1;
TEA; WLIT 4
Bowering, George 1935- .... **CLC 15, 47**
See also CA 21-24R; CAAS 16; CANR 10;
CP 7; DLB 53
Bowering, Marilyn R(uthe) 1949- ... **CLC 32**
See also CA 101; CANR 49; CP 7; CWP
Bowers, Edgar 1924-2000 .... **CLC 9**
See also CA 5-8R; 188; CANR 24; CP 7;
CSW; DLB 5
Bowers, Mrs. J. Milton 1842-1914
See Bierce, Ambrose (Gwinett)
Bowie, David .... **CLC 17**
See Jones, David Robert
Bowles, Jane (Sydney) 1917-1973 ..... **CLC 3,**
68
See Bowles, Jane Auer
See also CA 19-20; 41-44R; CAP 2
Bowles, Jane Auer
See Bowles, Jane (Sydney)
See also EWL 3
Bowles, Paul (Frederick) 1910-1999 . **CLC 1,**
2, 19, 53; SSC 3
See also AMWS 4; CA 1-4R; 186; CAAS
1; CANR 1, 19, 50, 75; CN 7; DA3; DLB
5, 6, 218; EWL 3; MTCW 1, 2; RGAL 4;
SSFS 17
Bowles, William Lisle 1762-1850 . **NCLC 103**
See also DLB 93
Box, Edgar
See Vidal, Gore
See also GLL 1
Boyd, James 1888-1944 .... **TCLC 115**
See also CA 186; DLB 9; DLBD 16; RGAL
4; RHW
Boyd, Nancy
See Millay, Edna St. Vincent
See also GLL 1
Boyd, Thomas (Alexander)
1898-1935 .... **TCLC 111**
See also CA 111; 183; DLB 9; DLBD 16
Boyd, William 1952- .... **CLC 28, 53, 70**
See also CA 114; 120; CANR 51, 71, 131;
CN 7; DLB 231
Boyesen, Hjalmar Hjorth
1848-1895 .... **NCLC 135**
See also DLB 12, 71; DLBD 13; RGAL 4
Boyle, Kay 1902-1992 .... **CLC 1, 5, 19, 58,**
121; SSC 5
See also CA 13-16R; 140; CAAS 1; CANR
29, 61, 110; DLB 4, 9, 48, 86; DLBY
1993; EWL 3; MTCW 1, 2; RGAL 4;
RGSF 2; SSFS 10, 13, 14
Boyle, Mark
See Kienzle, William X(avier)
Boyle, Patrick 1905-1982 .... **CLC 19**
See also CA 127

Boyle, T. C.
See Boyle, T(homas) Coraghessan
See also AMWS 8

Boyle, T(homas) Coraghessan
1948- .... CLC 36, 55, 90; SSC 16
See Boyle, T. C.
See also AAYA 47; BEST 90:4; BPFB 1;
CA 120; CANR 44, 76, 89; CN 7; CPW;
DA3; DAM POP; DLB 218, 278; DLBY
1986; EWL 3; MTCW 2; SSFS 13, 19

Boz
See Dickens, Charles (John Huffam)

Brackenridge, Hugh Henry
1748-1816 .... NCLC 7
See also DLB 11, 37; RGAL 4

Bradbury, Edward P.
See Moorcock, Michael (John)
See also MTCW 2

Bradbury, Malcolm (Stanley)
1932-2000 .... CLC 32, 61
See also CA 1-4R; CANR 1, 33, 91, 98;
CN 7; DA3; DAM NOV; DLB 14, 207;
EWL 3; MTCW 1, 2

Bradbury, Ray (Douglas) 1920- .... CLC 1, 3,
10, 15, 42, 98; SSC 29, 53; WLC
See also AAYA 15; AITN 1, 2; AMWS 4;
BPFB 1; BYA 4, 5, 11; CA 1-4R; CANR
2, 30, 75, 125; CDALB 1968-1988; CN
7; CPW; DA; DA3; DAB; DAC; DAM
MST, NOV, POP; DLB 2, 8; EXPN;
EXPS; HGG; LAIT 3, 5; LATS 1; LMFS
2; MTCW 1, 2; NFS 1; RGAL 4; RGSF
2; SATA 11, 64, 123; SCFW 2; SFW 4;
SSFS 1; SUFW 1, 2; TUS; YAW

Braddon, Mary Elizabeth
1837-1915 .... TCLC 111
See also BRWS 8; CA 108; 179; CMW 4;
DLB 18, 70, 156; HGG

Bradfield, Scott (Michael) 1955- .... SSC 65
See also CA 147; CANR 90; HGG; SUFW
2

Bradford, Gamaliel 1863-1932 .... TCLC 36
See also CA 160; DLB 17

Bradford, William 1590-1657 .... LC 64
See also DLB 24, 30; RGAL 4

Bradley, David (Henry), Jr. 1950- .... BLC 1;
CLC 23, 118
See also BW 1, 3; CA 104; CANR 26, 81;
CN 7; DAM MULT; DLB 33

Bradley, John Ed(mund, Jr.) 1958- . CLC 55
See also CA 139; CANR 99; CN 7; CSW

Bradley, Marion Zimmer
1930-1999 .... CLC 30
See Chapman, Lee; Dexter, John; Gardner,
Miriam; Ives, Morgan; Rivers, Elfrida
See also AAYA 40; BPFB 1; CA 57-60; 185;
CAAS 10; CANR 7, 31, 51, 75, 107;
CPW; DA3; DAM POP; DLB 8; FANT;
FW; MTCW 1, 2; SATA 90, 139; SATA-
Obit 116; SFW 4; SUFW 2; YAW

Bradshaw, John 1933- .... CLC 70
See also CA 138; CANR 61

Bradstreet, Anne 1612(?)-1672 ...... LC 4, 30;
PC 10
See also AMWS 1; CDALB 1640-1865;
DA; DA3; DAC; DAM MST, POET; DLB
24; EXPP; FW; PFS 6; RGAL 4; TUS;
WP

Brady, Joan 1939- .... CLC 86
See also CA 141

Bragg, Melvyn 1939- .... CLC 10
See also BEST 89:3; CA 57-60; CANR 10,
48, 89; CN 7; DLB 14, 271; RHW

Brahe, Tycho 1546-1601 .... LC 45
See also DLB 300

Braine, John (Gerard) 1922-1986 . CLC 1, 3,
41
See also CA 1-4R; 120; CANR 1, 33; CD-
BLB 1945-1960; DLB 15; DLBY 1986;
EWL 3; MTCW 1

Braithwaite, William Stanley (Beaumont)
1878-1962 .... BLC 1; HR 2; PC 52
See also BW 1; CA 125; DAM MULT; DLB
50, 54

Bramah, Ernest 1868-1942 .... TCLC 72
See also CA 156; CMW 4; DLB 70; FANT

Brammer, William 1930(?)-1978 ...... CLC 31
See also CA 77-80

Brancati, Vitaliano 1907-1954 .... TCLC 12
See also CA 109; DLB 264; EWL 3

Brancato, Robin F(idler) 1936- .... CLC 35
See also AAYA 9; BYA 6; CA 69-72; CANR
11, 45; CLR 32; JRDA; MAICYA 2;
MAICYAS 1; SAAS 9; SATA 97; WYA;
YAW

Brand, Dionne 1953- .... CLC 192
See also BW 2; CA 143; CWP

Brand, Max
See Faust, Frederick (Schiller)
See also BPFB 1; TCWW 2

Brand, Millen 1906-1980 .... CLC 7
See also CA 21-24R; 97-100; CANR 72

Branden, Barbara .... CLC 44
See also CA 148

Brandes, Georg (Morris Cohen)
1842-1927 .... TCLC 10
See also CA 105; 189; DLB 300

Brandys, Kazimierz 1916-2000 .... CLC 62
See also EWL 3

Branley, Franklyn M(ansfield)
1915-2002 .... CLC 21
See also CA 33-36R; 207; CANR 14, 39;
CLR 13; MAICYA 1, 2; SAAS 16; SATA
4, 68, 136

Brant, Beth (E.) 1941- .... NNAL
See also CA 144; FW

Brathwaite, Edward Kamau
1930- .... BLCS; CLC 11; PC 56
See also BW 2, 3; CA 25-28R; CANR 11,
26, 47, 107; CDWLB 3; CP 7; DAM
POET; DLB 125; EWL 3

Brathwaite, Kamau
See Brathwaite, Edward Kamau

Brautigan, Richard (Gary)
1935-1984 .... CLC 1, 3, 5, 9, 12, 34, 42;
TCLC 133
See also BPFB 1; CA 53-56; 113; CANR
34; DA3; DAM NOV; DLB 2, 5, 206;
DLBY 1980, 1984; FANT; MTCW 1;
RGAL 4; SATA 56

Brave Bird, Mary .... NNAL
See Crow Dog, Mary (Ellen)

Braverman, Kate 1950- .... CLC 67
See also CA 89-92

Brecht, (Eugen) Bertolt (Friedrich)
1898-1956 ..... DC 3; TCLC 1, 6, 13, 35;
WLC
See also CA 104; 133; CANR 62; CDWLB
2; DA; DA3; DAB; DAC; DAM DRAM,
MST; DFS 4, 5, 9; DLB 56, 124; EW 11;
EWL 3; IDTP; MTCW 1, 2; RGWL 2, 3;
TWA

Brecht, Eugen Berthold Friedrich
See Brecht, (Eugen) Bertolt (Friedrich)

Bremer, Fredrika 1801-1865 .... NCLC 11
See also DLB 254

Brennan, Christopher John
1870-1932 .... TCLC 17
See also CA 117; 188; DLB 230; EWL 3

Brennan, Maeve 1917-1993 ... CLC 5; TCLC
124
See also CA 81-84; CANR 72, 100

Brent, Linda
See Jacobs, Harriet A(nn)

Brentano, Clemens (Maria)
1778-1842 .... NCLC 1
See also DLB 90; RGWL 2, 3

Brent of Bin Bin
See Franklin, (Stella Maria Sarah) Miles
(Lampe)

Brenton, Howard 1942- .... CLC 31
See also CA 69-72; CANR 33, 67; CBD;
CD 5; DLB 13; MTCW 1

Breslin, James 1930-
See Breslin, Jimmy
See also CA 73-76; CANR 31, 75; DAM
NOV; MTCW 1, 2

Breslin, Jimmy .... CLC 4, 43
See Breslin, James
See also AITN 1; DLB 185; MTCW 2

Bresson, Robert 1901(?)-1999 .... CLC 16
See also CA 110; 187; CANR 49

Breton, Andre 1896-1966 .. CLC 2, 9, 15, 54;
PC 15
See also CA 19-20; 25-28R; CANR 40, 60;
CAP 2; DLB 65, 258; EW 11; EWL 3;
GFL 1789 to the Present; LMFS 2;
MTCW 1, 2; RGWL 2, 3; TWA; WP

Breytenbach, Breyten 1939(?)- .. CLC 23, 37,
126
See also CA 113; 129; CANR 61, 122;
CWW 2; DAM POET; DLB 225; EWL 3

Bridgers, Sue Ellen 1942- .... CLC 26
See also AAYA 8, 49; BYA 7, 8; CA 65-68;
CANR 11, 36; CLR 18; DLB 52; JRDA;
MAICYA 1, 2; SAAS 1; SATA 22, 90;
SATA-Essay 109; WYA; YAW

Bridges, Robert (Seymour)
1844-1930 .... PC 28; TCLC 1
See also BRW 6; CA 104; 152; CDBLB
1890-1914; DAM POET; DLB 19, 98

Bridie, James .... TCLC 3
See Mavor, Osborne Henry
See also DLB 10; EWL 3

Brin, David 1950- .... CLC 34
See also AAYA 21; CA 102; CANR 24, 70,
125, 127; INT CANR-24; SATA 65;
SCFW 2; SFW 4

Brink, Andre (Philippus) 1935- . CLC 18, 36,
106
See also AFW; BRWS 6; CA 104; CANR
39, 62, 109; CN 7; DLB 225; EWL 3; INT
CA-103; LATS 1; MTCW 1, 2; WLIT 2

Brinsmead, H. F(ay)
See Brinsmead, H(esba) F(ay)

Brinsmead, H. F.
See Brinsmead, H(esba) F(ay)

Brinsmead, H(esba) F(ay) 1922- ...... CLC 21
See also CA 21-24R; CANR 10; CLR 47;
CWRI 5; MAICYA 1, 2; SAAS 5; SATA
18, 78

Brittain, Vera (Mary) 1893(?)-1970 . CLC 23
See also CA 13-16; 25-28R; CANR 58;
CAP 1; DLB 191; FW; MTCW 1, 2

Broch, Hermann 1886-1951 .... TCLC 20
See also CA 117; 211; CDWLB 2; DLB 85,
124; EW 10; EWL 3; RGWL 2, 3

Brock, Rose
See Hansen, Joseph
See also GLL 1

Brod, Max 1884-1968 .... TCLC 115
See also CA 5-8R; 25-28R; CANR 7; DLB
81; EWL 3

Brodkey, Harold (Roy) 1930-1996 .. CLC 56;
TCLC 123
See also CA 111; 151; CANR 71; CN 7;
DLB 130

Brodsky, Iosif Alexandrovich 1940-1996
See Brodsky, Joseph
See also AITN 1; CA 41-44R; 151; CANR
37, 106; DA3; DAM POET; MTCW 1, 2;
RGWL 2, 3

Butts, Mary 1890(?)-1937 .... **TCLC 77**
    See also CA 148; DLB 240

Buxton, Ralph
    See Silverstein, Alvin; Silverstein, Virginia
    B(arbara Opshelor)

Buzo, Alex
    See Buzo, Alexander (John)
    See also DLB 289

Buzo, Alexander (John) 1944- .... **CLC 61**
    See also CA 97-100; CANR 17, 39, 69; CD
    5

Buzzati, Dino 1906-1972 .... **CLC 36**
    See also CA 160; 33-36R; DLB 177; RGWL
    2, 3; SFW 4

Byars, Betsy (Cromer) 1928- .... **CLC 35**
    See also AAYA 19; BYA 3; CA 33-36R,
    183; CAAE 183; CANR 18, 36, 57, 102;
    CLR 1, 16, 72; DLB 52; INT CANR-18;
    JRDA; MAICYA 1, 2; MAICYAS 1;
    MTCW 1; SAAS 1; SATA 4, 46, 80;
    SATA-Essay 108; WYA; YAW

Byatt, A(ntonia) S(usan Drabble)
    1936- .... **CLC 19, 65, 136**
    See also BPFB 1; BRWC 2; BRWS 4; CA
    13-16R; CANR 13, 33, 50, 75, 96; DA3;
    DAM NOV, POP; DLB 14, 194; EWL 3;
    MTCW 1, 2; RGSF 2; RHW; TEA

Byrne, David 1952- .... **CLC 26**
    See also CA 127

Byrne, John Keyes 1926-
    See Leonard, Hugh
    See also CA 102; CANR 78; INT CA-102

Byron, George Gordon (Noel)
    1788-1824 ..... **NCLC 2, 12, 109; PC 16;
    WLC**
    See also BRW 4; BRWC 2; CDBLB 1789-
    1832; DA; DA3; DAB; DAC; DAM MST,
    POET; DLB 96, 110; EXPP; LMFS 1;
    PAB; PFS 1, 14; RGEL 2; TEA; WLIT 3;
    WP

Byron, Robert 1905-1941 .... **TCLC 67**
    See also CA 160; DLB 195

C. 3. 3.
    See Wilde, Oscar (Fingal O'Flahertie Wills)

Caballero, Fernan 1796-1877 .... **NCLC 10**

Cabell, Branch
    See Cabell, James Branch

Cabell, James Branch 1879-1958 .... **TCLC 6**
    See also CA 105; 152; DLB 9, 78; FANT;
    MTCW 1; RGAL 4; SUFW 1

Cabeza de Vaca, Alvar Nunez
    1490-1557(?) .... **LC 61**

Cable, George Washington
    1844-1925 .... **SSC 4; TCLC 4**
    See also CA 104; 155; DLB 12, 74; DLBD
    13; RGAL 4; TUS

Cabral de Melo Neto, Joao
    1920-1999 .... **CLC 76**
    See Melo Neto, Joao Cabral de
    See also CA 151; DAM MULT; LAW;
    LAWS 1

Cabrera Infante, G(uillermo) 1929- . **CLC 5,
    25, 45, 120; HLC 1; SSC 39**
    See also CA 85-88; CANR 29, 65, 110; CD-
    WLB 3; CWW 2; DA3; DAM MULT;
    DLB 113; EWL 3; HW 1, 2; LAW; LAWS
    1; MTCW 1, 2; RGSF 2; WLIT 1

Cade, Toni
    See Bambara, Toni Cade

Cadmus and Harmonia
    See Buchan, John

Caedmon fl. 658-680 .... **CMLC 7**
    See also DLB 146

Caeiro, Alberto
    See Pessoa, Fernando (Antonio Nogueira)

Caesar, Julius .... **CMLC 47**
    See Julius Caesar
    See also AW 1; RGWL 2, 3

Cage, John (Milton, Jr.)
    1912-1992 .... **CLC 41; PC 58**
    See also CA 13-16R; 169; CANR 9, 78;
    DLB 193; INT CANR-9

Cahan, Abraham 1860-1951 .... **TCLC 71**
    See also CA 108; 154; DLB 9, 25, 28;
    RGAL 4

Cain, G.
    See Cabrera Infante, G(uillermo)

Cain, Guillermo
    See Cabrera Infante, G(uillermo)

Cain, James M(allahan) 1892-1977 .. **CLC 3,
    11, 28**
    See also AITN 1; BPFB 1; CA 17-20R; 73-
    76; CANR 8, 34, 61; CMW 4; DLB 226;
    EWL 3; MSW; MTCW 1; RGAL 4

Caine, Hall 1853-1931 .... **TCLC 97**
    See also RHW

Caine, Mark
    See Raphael, Frederic (Michael)

Calasso, Roberto 1941- .... **CLC 81**
    See also CA 143; CANR 89

Calderon de la Barca, Pedro
    1600-1681 .... **DC 3; HLCS 1; LC 23**
    See also EW 2; RGWL 2, 3; TWA

Caldwell, Erskine (Preston)
    1903-1987 .... **CLC 1, 8, 14, 50, 60; SSC
    19; TCLC 117**
    See also AITN 1; AMW; BPFB 1; CA 1-4R;
    121; CAAS 1; CANR 2, 33; DA3; DAM
    NOV; DLB 9, 86; EWL 3; MTCW 1, 2;
    RGAL 4; RGSF 2; TUS

Caldwell, (Janet Miriam) Taylor (Holland)
    1900-1985 .... **CLC 2, 28, 39**
    See also BPFB 1; CA 5-8R; 116; CANR 5;
    DA3; DAM NOV, POP; DLBD 17; RHW

Calhoun, John Caldwell
    1782-1850 .... **NCLC 15**
    See also DLB 3, 248

Calisher, Hortense 1911- ..... **CLC 2, 4, 8, 38,
    134; SSC 15**
    See also CA 1-4R; CANR 1, 22, 117; CN
    7; DA3; DAM NOV; DLB 2, 218; INT
    CANR-22; MTCW 1, 2; RGAL 4; RGSF
    2

Callaghan, Morley Edward
    1903-1990 ..... **CLC 3, 14, 41, 65; TCLC
    145**
    See also CA 9-12R; 132; CANR 33, 73;
    DAC; DAM MST; DLB 68; EWL 3;
    MTCW 1, 2; RGEL 2; RGSF 2; SSFS 19

Callimachus c. 305B.C.-c.
    240B.C. .... **CMLC 18**
    See also AW 1; DLB 176; RGWL 2, 3

Calvin, Jean
    See Calvin, John
    See also GFL Beginnings to 1789

Calvin, John 1509-1564 .... **LC 37**
    See Calvin, Jean

Calvino, Italo 1923-1985 .... **CLC 5, 8, 11, 22,
    33, 39, 73; SSC 3, 48**
    See also CA 85-88; 116; CANR 23, 61;
    DAM NOV; DLB 196; EW 13; EWL 3;
    MTCW 1, 2; RGSF 2; RGWL 2, 3; SFW
    4; SSFS 12

Camara Laye
    See Laye, Camara
    See also EWL 3

Camden, William 1551-1623 .... **LC 77**
    See also DLB 172

Cameron, Carey 1952- .... **CLC 59**
    See also CA 135

Cameron, Peter 1959- .... **CLC 44**
    See also AMWS 12; CA 125; CANR 50,
    117; DLB 234; GLL 2

Camoens, Luis Vaz de 1524(?)-1580
    See Camoes, Luis de
    See also EW 2

Camoes, Luis de 1524(?)-1580 . **HLCS 1; LC
    62; PC 31**
    See Camoens, Luis Vaz de
    See also DLB 287; RGWL 2, 3

Campana, Dino 1885-1932 .... **TCLC 20**
    See also CA 117; DLB 114; EWL 3

Campanella, Tommaso 1568-1639 .... **LC 32**
    See also RGWL 2, 3

Campbell, John W(ood, Jr.)
    1910-1971 .... **CLC 32**
    See also CA 21-22; 29-32R; CANR 34;
    CAP 2; DLB 8; MTCW 1; SCFW; SFW 4

Campbell, Joseph 1904-1987 .... **CLC 69;
    TCLC 140**
    See also AAYA 3; BEST 89:2; CA 1-4R;
    124; CANR 3, 28, 61, 107; DA3; MTCW
    1, 2

Campbell, Maria 1940- .... **CLC 85; NNAL**
    See also CA 102; CANR 54; CCA 1; DAC

Campbell, (John) Ramsey 1946- ..... **CLC 42;
    SSC 19**
    See also AAYA 51; CA 57-60; CANR 7,
    102; DLB 261; HGG; INT CANR-7;
    SUFW 1, 2

Campbell, (Ignatius) Roy (Dunnachie)
    1901-1957 .... **TCLC 5**
    See also AFW; CA 104; 155; DLB 20, 225;
    EWL 3; MTCW 2; RGEL 2

Campbell, Thomas 1777-1844 .... **NCLC 19**
    See also DLB 93, 144; RGEL 2

Campbell, Wilfred .... **TCLC 9**
    See Campbell, William

Campbell, William 1858(?)-1918
    See Campbell, Wilfred
    See also CA 106; DLB 92

Campion, Jane 1954- .... **CLC 95**
    See also AAYA 33; CA 138; CANR 87

Campion, Thomas 1567-1620 .... **LC 78**
    See also CDBLB Before 1660; DAM POET;
    DLB 58, 172; RGEL 2

Camus, Albert 1913-1960 ...... **CLC 1, 2, 4, 9,
    11, 14, 32, 63, 69, 124; DC 2; SSC 9;
    WLC**
    See also AAYA 36; AFW; BPFB 1; CA 89-
    92; CANR 131; DA; DA3; DAB; DAC;
    DAM DRAM, MST, NOV; DLB 72; EW
    13; EWL 3; EXPN; EXPS; GFL 1789 to
    the Present; LATS 1; LMFS 2; MTCW 1,
    2; NFS 6, 16; RGSF 2; RGWL 2, 3; SSFS
    4; TWA

Canby, Vincent 1924-2000 .... **CLC 13**
    See also CA 81-84; 191

Cancale
    See Desnos, Robert

Canetti, Elias 1905-1994 .. **CLC 3, 14, 25, 75,
    86**
    See also CA 21-24R; 146; CANR 23, 61,
    79; CDWLB 2; CWW 2; DA3; DLB 85,
    124; EW 12; EWL 3; MTCW 1, 2; RGWL
    2, 3; TWA

Canfield, Dorothea F.
    See Fisher, Dorothy (Frances) Canfield

Canfield, Dorothea Frances
    See Fisher, Dorothy (Frances) Canfield

Canfield, Dorothy
    See Fisher, Dorothy (Frances) Canfield

Canin, Ethan 1960- .... **CLC 55; SSC 70**
    See also CA 131; 135

Cankar, Ivan 1876-1918 .... **TCLC 105**
    See also CDWLB 4; DLB 147; EWL 3

Cannon, Curt
    See Hunter, Evan

Cao, Lan 1961- .... **CLC 109**
    See also CA 165

Cape, Judith
    See Page, P(atricia) K(athleen)
    See also CCA 1

Coleridge, Samuel Taylor
1772-1834 ...... **NCLC 9, 54, 99, 111; PC 11, 39; WLC**
See also BRW 4; BRWR 2; BYA 4; CD-BLB 1789-1832; DA; DA3; DAB; DAC; DAM MST, POET; DLB 93, 107; EXPP; LATS 1; LMFS 1; PAB; PFS 4, 5; RGEL 2; TEA; WLIT 3; WP

Coleridge, Sara 1802-1852 .... **NCLC 31**
See also DLB 199

Coles, Don 1928- .... **CLC 46**
See also CA 115; CANR 38; CP 7

Coles, Robert (Martin) 1929- .... **CLC 108**
See also CA 45-48; CANR 3, 32, 66, 70; INT CANR-32; SATA 23

Colette, (Sidonie-Gabrielle)
1873-1954 .... **SSC 10; TCLC 1, 5, 16**
See Willy, Colette
See also CA 104; 131; DA3; DAM NOV; DLB 65; EW 9; EWL 3; GFL 1789 to the Present; MTCW 1, 2; RGWL 2, 3; TWA

Collett, (Jacobine) Camilla (Wergeland)
1813-1895 .... **NCLC 22**

Collier, Christopher 1930- .... **CLC 30**
See also AAYA 13; BYA 2; CA 33-36R; CANR 13, 33, 102; JRDA; MAICYA 1, 2; SATA 16, 70; WYA; YAW 1

Collier, James Lincoln 1928- .... **CLC 30**
See also AAYA 13; BYA 2; CA 9-12R; CANR 4, 33, 60, 102; CLR 3; DAM POP; JRDA; MAICYA 1, 2; SAAS 21; SATA 8, 70; WYA; YAW 1

Collier, Jeremy 1650-1726 .... **LC 6**

Collier, John 1901-1980 . **SSC 19; TCLC 127**
See also CA 65-68; 97-100; CANR 10; DLB 77, 255; FANT; SUFW 1

Collier, Mary 1690-1762 .... **LC 86**
See also DLB 95

Collingwood, R(obin) G(eorge)
1889(?)-1943 .... **TCLC 67**
See also CA 117; 155; DLB 262

Collins, Hunt
See Hunter, Evan

Collins, Linda 1931- .... **CLC 44**
See also CA 125

Collins, Tom
See Furphy, Joseph
See also RGEL 2

Collins, (William) Wilkie
1824-1889 .... **NCLC 1, 18, 93**
See also BRWS 6; CDBLB 1832-1890; CMW 4; DLB 18, 70, 159; MSW; RGEL 2; RGSF 2; SUFW 1; WLIT 4

Collins, William 1721-1759 .... **LC 4, 40**
See also BRW 3; DAM POET; DLB 109; RGEL 2

Collodi, Carlo .... **NCLC 54**
See Lorenzini, Carlo
See also CLR 5; WCH

Colman, George
See Glassco, John

Colman, George, the Elder
1732-1794 .... **LC 98**
See also RGEL 2

Colonna, Vittoria 1492-1547 .... **LC 71**
See also RGWL 2, 3

Colt, Winchester Remington
See Hubbard, L(afayette) Ron(ald)

Colter, Cyrus J. 1910-2002 .... **CLC 58**
See also BW 1; CA 65-68; 205; CANR 10, 66; CN 7; DLB 33

Colton, James
See Hansen, Joseph
See also GLL 1

Colum, Padraic 1881-1972 .... **CLC 28**
See also BYA 4; CA 73-76; 33-36R; CANR 35; CLR 36; CWRI 5; DLB 19; MAICYA 1, 2; MTCW 1; RGEL 2; SATA 15; WCH

Colvin, James
See Moorcock, Michael (John)

Colwin, Laurie (E.) 1944-1992 .... **CLC 5, 13, 23, 84**
See also CA 89-92; 139; CANR 20, 46; DLB 218; DLBY 1980; MTCW 1

Comfort, Alex(ander) 1920-2000 .... **CLC 7**
See also CA 1-4R; 190; CANR 1, 45; CP 7; DAM POP; MTCW 1

Comfort, Montgomery
See Campbell, (John) Ramsey

Compton-Burnett, I(vy)
1892(?)-1969 .... **CLC 1, 3, 10, 15, 34**
See also BRW 7; CA 1-4R; 25-28R; CANR 4; DAM NOV; DLB 36; EWL 3; MTCW 1; RGEL 2

Comstock, Anthony 1844-1915 ...... **TCLC 13**
See also CA 110; 169

Comte, Auguste 1798-1857 .... **NCLC 54**

Conan Doyle, Arthur
See Doyle, Sir Arthur Conan
See also BPFB 1; BYA 4, 5, 11

Conde (Abellan), Carmen
1901-1996 .... **HLCS 1**
See also CA 177; CWW 2; DLB 108; EWL 3; HW 2

Conde, Maryse 1937- ..... **BLCS; CLC 52, 92**
See also BW 2, 3; CA 110; 190; CAAE 190; CANR 30, 53, 76; CWW 2; DAM MULT; EWL 3; MTCW 1

Condillac, Etienne Bonnot de
1714-1780 .... **LC 26**

Condon, Richard (Thomas)
1915-1996 .... **CLC 4, 6, 8, 10, 45, 100**
See also BEST 90:3; BPFB 1; CA 1-4R; 151; CAAS 1; CANR 2, 23; CMW 4; CN 7; DAM NOV; INT CANR-23; MTCW 1, 2

Condorcet 1743-1794 .... **LC 104**
See also GFL Beginnings to 1789

Confucius 551B.C.-479B.C. .... **CMLC 19, 65; WLCS**
See also DA; DA3; DAB; DAC; DAM MST

Congreve, William 1670-1729 ... **DC 2; LC 5, 21; WLC**
See also BRW 2; CDBLB 1660-1789; DA; DAB; DAC; DAM DRAM, MST, POET; DFS 15; DLB 39, 84; RGEL 2; WLIT 3

Conley, Robert J(ackson) 1940- .... **NNAL**
See also CA 41-44R; CANR 15, 34, 45, 96; DAM MULT

Connell, Evan S(helby), Jr. 1924- . **CLC 4, 6, 45**
See also AAYA 7; CA 1-4R; CAAS 2; CANR 2, 39, 76, 97; CN 7; DAM NOV; DLB 2; DLBY 1981; MTCW 1, 2

Connelly, Marc(us Cook) 1890-1980 . **CLC 7**
See also CA 85-88; 102; CANR 30; DFS 12; DLB 7; DLBY 1980; RGAL 4; SATA-Obit 25

Connor, Ralph .... **TCLC 31**
See Gordon, Charles William
See also DLB 92; TCWW 2

Conrad, Joseph 1857-1924 ..... **SSC 9, 67, 69, 71; TCLC 1, 6, 13, 25, 43, 57; WLC**
See also AAYA 26; BPFB 1; BRW 6; BRWC 1; BRWR 2; BYA 2; CA 104; 131; CANR 60; CDBLB 1890-1914; DA; DA3; DAB; DAC; DAM MST, NOV; DLB 10, 34, 98, 156; EWL 3; EXPN; EXPS; LAIT 2; LATS 1; LMFS 1; MTCW 1, 2; NFS 2, 16; RGEL 2; RGSF 2; SATA 27; SSFS 1, 12; TEA; WLIT 4

Conrad, Robert Arnold
See Hart, Moss

Conroy, (Donald) Pat(rick) 1945- ... **CLC 30, 74**
See also AAYA 8, 52; AITN 1; BPFB 1; CA 85-88; CANR 24, 53, 129; CPW; CSW; DA3; DAM NOV, POP; DLB 6; LAIT 5; MTCW 1, 2

Constant (de Rebecque), (Henri) Benjamin
1767-1830 .... **NCLC 6**
See also DLB 119; EW 4; GFL 1789 to the Present

Conway, Jill K(er) 1934- .... **CLC 152**
See also CA 130; CANR 94

Conybeare, Charles Augustus
See Eliot, T(homas) S(tearns)

Cook, Michael 1933-1994 .... **CLC 58**
See also CA 93-96; CANR 68; DLB 53

Cook, Robin 1940- .... **CLC 14**
See also AAYA 32; BEST 90:2; BPFB 1; CA 108; 111; CANR 41, 90, 109; CPW; DA3; DAM POP; HGG; INT CA-111

Cook, Roy
See Silverberg, Robert

Cooke, Elizabeth 1948- .... **CLC 55**
See also CA 129

Cooke, John Esten 1830-1886 .... **NCLC 5**
See also DLB 3, 248; RGAL 4

Cooke, John Estes
See Baum, L(yman) Frank

Cooke, M. E.
See Creasey, John

Cooke, Margaret
See Creasey, John

Cooke, Rose Terry 1827-1892 ...... **NCLC 110**
See also DLB 12, 74

Cook-Lynn, Elizabeth 1930- .... **CLC 93; NNAL**
See also CA 133; DAM MULT; DLB 175

Cooney, Ray .... **CLC 62**
See also CBD

Cooper, Douglas 1960- .... **CLC 86**

Cooper, Henry St. John
See Creasey, John

Cooper, J(oan) California (?)- .... **CLC 56**
See also AAYA 12; BW 1; CA 125; CANR 55; DAM MULT; DLB 212

Cooper, James Fenimore
1789-1851 .... **NCLC 1, 27, 54**
See also AAYA 22; AMW; BPFB 1; CDALB 1640-1865; DA3; DLB 3, 183, 250, 254; LAIT 1; NFS 9; RGAL 4; SATA 19; TUS; WCH

Cooper, Susan Fenimore
1813-1894 .... **NCLC 129**
See also ANW; DLB 239, 254

Coover, Robert (Lowell) 1932- ...... **CLC 3, 7, 15, 32, 46, 87, 161; SSC 15**
See also AMWS 5; BPFB 1; CA 45-48; CANR 3, 37, 58, 115; CN 7; DAM NOV; DLB 2, 227; DLBY 1981; EWL 3; MTCW 1, 2; RGAL 4; RGSF 2

Copeland, Stewart (Armstrong)
1952- .... **CLC 26**

Copernicus, Nicolaus 1473-1543 .... **LC 45**

Coppard, A(lfred) E(dgar)
1878-1957 .... **SSC 21; TCLC 5**
See also BRWS 8; CA 114; 167; DLB 162; EWL 3; HGG; RGEL 2; RGSF 2; SUFW 1; YABC 1

Coppee, Francois 1842-1908 .... **TCLC 25**
See also CA 170; DLB 217

Coppola, Francis Ford 1939- ... **CLC 16, 126**
See also AAYA 39; CA 77-80; CANR 40, 78; DLB 44

Copway, George 1818-1869 .... **NNAL**
See also DAM MULT; DLB 175, 183

Corbiere, Tristan 1845-1875 .... **NCLC 43**
See also DLB 217; GFL 1789 to the Present

Dexter, Pete 1943- .... **CLC 34, 55**
    See also BEST 89:2; CA 127; 131; CANR
    129; CPW; DAM POP; INT CA-131;
    MTCW 1
Diamano, Silmang
    See Senghor, Leopold Sedar
Diamond, Neil 1941- .... **CLC 30**
    See also CA 108
Diaz del Castillo, Bernal
    1496-1584 .... **HLCS 1; LC 31**
    See also LAW
di Bassetto, Corno
    See Shaw, George Bernard
Dick, Philip K(indred) 1928-1982 ... **CLC 10,
    30, 72; SSC 57**
    See also AAYA 24; BPFB 1; BYA 11; CA
    49-52; 106; CANR 2, 16; CPW; DA3;
    DAM NOV, POP; DLB 8; MTCW 1, 2;
    NFS 5; SCFW; SFW 4
Dickens, Charles (John Huffam)
    1812-1870 .... **NCLC 3, 8, 18, 26, 37, 50,
    86, 105, 113; SSC 17, 49; WLC**
    See also AAYA 23; BRW 5; BRWC 1, 2;
    BYA 1, 2, 3, 13, 14; CDBLB 1832-1890;
    CLR 95; CMW 4; DA; DA3; DAB; DAC;
    DAM MST, NOV; DLB 21, 55, 70, 159,
    166; EXPN; HGG; JRDA; LAIT 1, 2;
    LATS 1; LMFS 1; MAICYA 1, 2; NFS 4,
    5, 10, 14; RGEL 2; RGSF 2; SATA 15;
    SUFW 1; TEA; WCH; WLIT 4; WYA
Dickey, James (Lafayette)
    1923-1997 .... **CLC 1, 2, 4, 7, 10, 15, 47,
    109; PC 40; TCLC 151**
    See also AAYA 50; AITN 1, 2; AMWS 4;
    BPFB 1; CA 9-12R; 156; CABS 2; CANR
    10, 48, 61, 105; CDALB 1968-1988; CP
    7; CPW; CSW; DA3; DAM NOV, POET,
    POP; DLB 5, 193; DLBD 7; DLBY 1982,
    1993, 1996, 1997, 1998; EWL 3; INT
    CANR-10; MTCW 1, 2; NFS 9; PFS 6,
    11; RGAL 4; TUS
Dickey, William 1928-1994 .... **CLC 3, 28**
    See also CA 9-12R; 145; CANR 24, 79;
    DLB 5
Dickinson, Charles 1951- .... **CLC 49**
    See also CA 128
Dickinson, Emily (Elizabeth)
    1830-1886 .... **NCLC 21, 77; PC 1; WLC**
    See also AAYA 22; AMW; AMWR 1;
    CDALB 1865-1917; DA; DA3; DAB;
    DAC; DAM MST, POET; DLB 1, 243;
    EXPP; MAWW; PAB; PFS 1, 2, 3, 4, 5,
    6, 8, 10, 11, 13, 16; RGAL 4; SATA 29;
    TUS; WP; WYA
Dickinson, Mrs. Herbert Ward
    See Phelps, Elizabeth Stuart
Dickinson, Peter (Malcolm) 1927- .. **CLC 12,
    35**
    See also AAYA 9, 49; BYA 5; CA 41-44R;
    CANR 31, 58, 88; CLR 29; CMW 4; DLB
    87, 161, 276; JRDA; MAICYA 1, 2;
    SATA 5, 62, 95, 150; SFW 4; WYA; YAW
Dickson, Carr
    See Carr, John Dickson
Dickson, Carter
    See Carr, John Dickson
Diderot, Denis 1713-1784 .... **LC 26**
    See also EW 4; GFL Beginnings to 1789;
    LMFS 1; RGWL 2, 3
Didion, Joan 1934- . **CLC 1, 3, 8, 14, 32, 129**
    See also AITN 1; AMWS 4; CA 5-8R;
    CANR 14, 52, 76, 125; CDALB 1968-
    1988; CN 7; DA3; DAM NOV; DLB 2,
    173, 185; DLBY 1981, 1986; EWL 3;
    MAWW; MTCW 1, 2; NFS 3; RGAL 4;
    TCWW 2; TUS
Dietrich, Robert
    See Hunt, E(verette) Howard, (Jr.)
Difusa, Pati
    See Almodovar, Pedro

Dillard, Annie 1945- .... **CLC 9, 60, 115**
    See also AAYA 6, 43; AMWS 6; ANW; CA
    49-52; CANR 3, 43, 62, 90, 125; DA3;
    DAM NOV; DLB 275, 278; DLBY 1980;
    LAIT 4, 5; MTCW 1, 2; NCFS 1; RGAL
    4; SATA 10, 140; TUS
Dillard, R(ichard) H(enry) W(ilde)
    1937- .... **CLC 5**
    See also CA 21-24R; CAAS 7; CANR 10;
    CP 7; CSW; DLB 5, 244
Dillon, Eilis 1920-1994 .... **CLC 17**
    See also CA 9-12R, 182; 147;
    CAAS 3; CANR 4, 38, 78; CLR 26; MAI-
    CYA 1, 2; MAICYAS 1; SATA 2, 74;
    SATA-Essay 105; SATA-Obit 83; YAW
Dimont, Penelope
    See Mortimer, Penelope (Ruth)
Dinesen, Isak .... **CLC 10, 29, 95; SSC 7**
    See Blixen, Karen (Christentze Dinesen)
    See also EW 10; EWL 3; EXPS; FW; HGG;
    LAIT 3; MTCW 1; NCFS 2; NFS 9;
    RGSF 2; RGWL 2, 3; SSFS 3, 6, 13;
    WLIT 2
Ding Ling .... **CLC 68**
    See Chiang, Pin-chin
    See also RGWL 3
Diphusa, Patty
    See Almodovar, Pedro
Disch, Thomas M(ichael) 1940- ... **CLC 7, 36**
    See Disch, Tom
    See also AAYA 17; BPFB 1; CA 21-24R;
    CAAS 4; CANR 17, 36, 54, 89; CLR 18;
    CP 7; DA3; DLB 8; HGG; MAICYA 1, 2;
    MTCW 1, 2; SAAS 15; SATA 92; SCFW;
    SFW 4; SUFW 2
Disch, Tom
    See Disch, Thomas M(ichael)
    See also DLB 282
d'Isly, Georges
    See Simenon, Georges (Jacques Christian)
Disraeli, Benjamin 1804-1881 ... **NCLC 2, 39,
    79**
    See also BRW 4; DLB 21, 55; RGEL 2
Ditcum, Steve
    See Crumb, R(obert)
Dixon, Paige
    See Corcoran, Barbara (Asenath)
Dixon, Stephen 1936- .... **CLC 52; SSC 16**
    See also AMWS 12; CA 89-92; CANR 17,
    40, 54, 91; CN 7; DLB 130
Djebar, Assia 1936- .... **CLC 182**
    See also CA 188; EWL 3; RGWL 3; WLIT
    2
Doak, Annie
    See Dillard, Annie
Dobell, Sydney Thompson
    1824-1874 .... **NCLC 43**
    See also DLB 32; RGEL 2
Doblin, Alfred .... **TCLC 13**
    See Doeblin, Alfred
    See also CDWLB 2; EWL 3; RGWL 2, 3
Dobroliubov, Nikolai Aleksandrovich
    See Dobrolyubov, Nikolai Alexandrovich
    See also DLB 277
Dobrolyubov, Nikolai Alexandrovich
    1836-1861 .... **NCLC 5**
    See Dobroliubov, Nikolai Aleksandrovich
Dobson, Austin 1840-1921 .... **TCLC 79**
    See also DLB 35, 144
Dobyns, Stephen 1941- .... **CLC 37**
    See also AMWS 13; CA 45-48; CANR 2,
    18, 99; CMW 4; CP 7
Doctorow, E(dgar) L(aurence)
    1931- .... **CLC 6, 11, 15, 18, 37, 44, 65,
    113**
    See also AAYA 22; AITN 2; AMWS 4;
    BEST 89:3; BPFB 1; CA 45-48; CANR
    2, 33, 51, 76, 97; CDALB 1968-1988; CN

7; CPW; DA3; DAM NOV, POP; DLB 2,
    28, 173; DLBY 1980; EWL 3; LAIT 3;
    MTCW 1, 2; NFS 6; RGAL 4; RHW;
    TUS
Dodgson, Charles L(utwidge) 1832-1898
    See Carroll, Lewis
    See also CLR 2; DA; DA3; DAB; DAC;
    DAM MST, NOV, POET; MAICYA 1, 2;
    SATA 100; YABC 2
Dodsley, Robert 1703-1764 .... **LC 97**
    See also DLB 95; RGEL 2
Dodson, Owen (Vincent) 1914-1983 .. **BLC 1;
    CLC 79**
    See also BW 1; CA 65-68; 110; CANR 24;
    DAM MULT; DLB 76
Doeblin, Alfred 1878-1957 .... **TCLC 13**
    See Doblin, Alfred
    See also CA 110; 141; DLB 66
Doerr, Harriet 1910-2002 .... **CLC 34**
    See also CA 117; 122; 213; CANR 47; INT
    CA-122; LATS 1
Domecq, H(onorio Bustos)
    See Bioy Casares, Adolfo
Domecq, H(onorio) Bustos
    See Bioy Casares, Adolfo; Borges, Jorge
    Luis
Domini, Rey
    See Lorde, Audre (Geraldine)
    See also GLL 1
Dominique
    See Proust, (Valentin-Louis-George-Eugene)
    Marcel
Don, A
    See Stephen, Sir Leslie
Donaldson, Stephen R(eeder)
    1947- .... **CLC 46, 138**
    See also AAYA 36; BPFB 1; CA 89-92;
    CANR 13, 55, 99; CPW; DAM POP;
    FANT; INT CANR-13; SATA 121; SFW
    4; SUFW 1, 2
Donleavy, J(ames) P(atrick) 1926- .... **CLC 1,
    4, 6, 10, 45**
    See also AITN 2; BPFB 1; CA 9-12R;
    CANR 24, 49, 62, 80, 124; CBD; CD 5;
    CN 7; DLB 6, 173; INT CANR-24;
    MTCW 1, 2; RGAL 4
Donnadieu, Marguerite
    See Duras, Marguerite
    See also CWW 2
Donne, John 1572-1631 ... **LC 10, 24, 91; PC
    1, 43; WLC**
    See also BRW 1; BRWC 1; BRWR 2; CD-
    BLB Before 1660; DA; DAB; DAC;
    DAM MST, POET; DLB 121, 151; EXPP;
    PAB; PFS 2, 11; RGEL 3; TEA; WLIT 3;
    WP
Donnell, David 1939(?)- .... **CLC 34**
    See also CA 197
Donoghue, P. S.
    See Hunt, E(verette) Howard, (Jr.)
Donoso (Yanez), Jose 1924-1996 ... **CLC 4, 8,
    11, 32, 99; HLC 1; SSC 34; TCLC 133**
    See also CA 81-84; 155; CANR 32, 73; CD-
    WLB 3; DAM MULT; DLB 113; EWL 3;
    HW 1, 2; LAW; LAWS 1; MTCW 1, 2;
    RGSF 2; WLIT 1
Donovan, John 1928-1992 .... **CLC 35**
    See also AAYA 20; CA 97-100; 137; CLR
    3; MAICYA 1, 2; SATA 72; SATA-Brief
    29; YAW
Don Roberto
    See Cunninghame Graham, Robert
    (Gallnigad) Bontine
Doolittle, Hilda 1886-1961 . **CLC 3, 8, 14, 31,
    34, 73; PC 5; WLC**
    See H. D.
    See also AMWS 1; CA 97-100; CANR 35,
    131; DA; DAC; DAM MST, POET; DLB
    4, 45; EWL 3; FW; GLL 1; LMFS 2;
    MAWW; MTCW 1, 2; PFS 6; RGAL 4

Eckert, Allan W. 1931- .... **CLC 17**
See also AAYA 18; BYA 2; CA 13-16R;
CANR 14, 45; INT CANR-14; MAICYA
2; MAICYAS 1; SAAS 21; SATA 29, 91;
SATA-Brief 27
Eckhart, Meister 1260(?)-1327(?) ... **CMLC 9**
See also DLB 115; LMFS 1
Eckmar, F. R.
See de Hartog, Jan
Eco, Umberto 1932- .... **CLC 28, 60, 142**
See also BEST 90:1; BPFB 1; CA 77-80;
CANR 12, 33, 55, 110, 131; CPW; CWW
2; DA3; DAM NOV, POP; DLB 196, 242;
EWL 3; MSW; MTCW 1, 2; RGWL 3
Eddison, E(ric) R(ucker)
1882-1945 .... **TCLC 15**
See also CA 109; 156; DLB 255; FANT;
SFW 4; SUFW 1
Eddy, Mary (Ann Morse) Baker
1821-1910 .... **TCLC 71**
See also CA 113; 174
Edel, (Joseph) Leon 1907-1997 .. **CLC 29, 34**
See also CA 1-4R; 161; CANR 1, 22, 112;
DLB 103; INT CANR-22
Eden, Emily 1797-1869 .... **NCLC 10**
Edgar, David 1948- .... **CLC 42**
See also CA 57-60; CANR 12, 61, 112;
CBD; CD 5; DAM DRAM; DFS 15; DLB
13, 233; MTCW 1
Edgerton, Clyde (Carlyle) 1944- ...... **CLC 39**
See also AAYA 17; CA 118; 134; CANR
64, 125; CSW; DLB 278; INT CA-134;
YAW
Edgeworth, Maria 1768-1849 .... **NCLC 1, 51**
See also BRWS 3; DLB 116, 159, 163; FW;
RGEL 2; SATA 21; TEA; WLIT 3
Edmonds, Paul
See Kuttner, Henry
Edmonds, Walter D(umaux)
1903-1998 .... **CLC 35**
See also BYA 2; CA 5-8R; CANR 2; CWRI
5; DLB 9; LAIT 1; MAICYA 1, 2; RHW;
SAAS 4; SATA 1, 27; SATA-Obit 99
Edmondson, Wallace
See Ellison, Harlan (Jay)
Edson, Russell 1935- .... **CLC 13**
See also CA 33-36R; CANR 115; DLB 244;
WP
Edwards, Bronwen Elizabeth
See Rose, Wendy
Edwards, G(erald) B(asil)
1899-1976 .... **CLC 25**
See also CA 201; 110
Edwards, Gus 1939- .... **CLC 43**
See also CA 108; INT CA-108
Edwards, Jonathan 1703-1758 ...... **LC 7, 54**
See also AMW; DA; DAC; DAM MST;
DLB 24, 270; RGAL 4; TUS
Edwards, Sarah Pierpont 1710-1758 .. **LC 87**
See also DLB 200
Efron, Marina Ivanovna Tsvetaeva
See Tsvetaeva (Efron), Marina (Ivanovna)
Egoyan, Atom 1960- .... **CLC 151**
See also CA 157
Ehle, John (Marsden, Jr.) 1925- ...... **CLC 27**
See also CA 9-12R; CSW
Ehrenbourg, Ilya (Grigoryevich)
See Ehrenburg, Ilya (Grigoryevich)
Ehrenburg, Ilya (Grigoryevich)
1891-1967 .... **CLC 18, 34, 62**
See Erenburg, Il'ia Grigor'evich
See also CA 102; 25-28R; EWL 3
Ehrenburg, Ilyo (Grigoryevich)
See Ehrenburg, Ilya (Grigoryevich)
Ehrenreich, Barbara 1941- .... **CLC 110**
See also BEST 90:4; CA 73-76; CANR 16,
37, 62, 117; DLB 246; FW; MTCW 1, 2

Eich, Gunter
See Eich, Gunter
See also RGWL 2, 3
Eich, Gunter 1907-1972 .... **CLC 15**
See Eich, Gunter
See also CA 111; 93-96; DLB 69, 124;
EWL 3
Eichendorff, Joseph 1788-1857 .... **NCLC 8**
See also DLB 90; RGWL 2, 3
Eigner, Larry .... **CLC 9**
See Eigner, Laurence (Joel)
See also CAAS 23; DLB 5; WP
Eigner, Laurence (Joel) 1927-1996
See Eigner, Larry
See also CA 9-12R; 151; CANR 6, 84; CP
7; DLB 193
Eilhart von Oberge c. 1140-c.
1195 .... **CMLC 67**
See also DLB 148
Einhard c. 770-840 .... **CMLC 50**
See also DLB 148
Einstein, Albert 1879-1955 .... **TCLC 65**
See also CA 121; 133; MTCW 1, 2
Eiseley, Loren
See Eiseley, Loren Corey
See also DLB 275
Eiseley, Loren Corey 1907-1977 .... **CLC 7**
See Eiseley, Loren
See also AAYA 5; ANW; CA 1-4R; 73-76;
CANR 6; DLBD 17
Eisenstadt, Jill 1963- .... **CLC 50**
See also CA 140
Eisenstein, Sergei (Mikhailovich)
1898-1948 .... **TCLC 57**
See also CA 114; 149
Eisner, Simon
See Kornbluth, C(yril) M.
Ekeloef, (Bengt) Gunnar
1907-1968 .... **CLC 27; PC 23**
See Ekelof, (Bengt) Gunnar
See also CA 123; 25-28R; DAM POET
Ekelof, (Bengt) Gunnar 1907-1968
See Ekeloef, (Bengt) Gunnar
See also DLB 259; EW 12; EWL 3
Ekelund, Vilhelm 1880-1949 .... **TCLC 75**
See also CA 189; EWL 3
Ekwensi, C. O. D.
See Ekwensi, Cyprian (Odiatu Duaka)
Ekwensi, Cyprian (Odiatu Duaka)
1921- .... **BLC 1; CLC 4**
See also AFW; BW 2, 3; CA 29-32R;
CANR 18, 42, 74, 125; CDWLB 3; CN
7; CWRI 5; DAM MULT; DLB 117; EWL
3; MTCW 1, 2; RGEL 2; SATA 66; WLIT
2
Elaine .... **TCLC 18**
See Leverson, Ada Esther
El Crummo
See Crumb, R(obert)
Elder, Lonne III 1931-1996 ..... **BLC 1; DC 8**
See also BW 1, 3; CA 81-84; 152; CAD;
CANR 25; DAM MULT; DLB 7, 38, 44
Eleanor of Aquitaine 1122-1204 ... **CMLC 39**
Elia
See Lamb, Charles
Eliade, Mircea 1907-1986 .... **CLC 19**
See also CA 65-68; 119; CANR 30, 62; CD-
WLB 4; DLB 220; EWL 3; MTCW 1;
RGWL 3; SFW 4
Eliot, A. D.
See Jewett, (Theodora) Sarah Orne
Eliot, Alice
See Jewett, (Theodora) Sarah Orne
Eliot, Dan
See Silverberg, Robert

Eliot, George 1819-1880 ...... **NCLC 4, 13, 23,
41, 49, 89, 118; PC 20; SSC 72; WLC**
See also BRW 5; BRWC 1, 2; BRWR 2;
CDBLB 1832-1890; CN 7; CPW; DA;
DA3; DAB; DAC; DAM MST, NOV;
DLB 21, 35, 55; LATS 1; LMFS 1; NFS
17; RGEL 2; RGSF 2; SSFS 8; TEA;
WLIT 3
Eliot, John 1604-1690 .... **LC 5**
See also DLB 24
Eliot, T(homas) S(tearns)
1888-1965 ...... **CLC 1, 2, 3, 6, 9, 10, 13,
15, 24, 34, 41, 55, 57, 113; PC 5, 31;
WLC**
See also AAYA 28; AMW; AMWC 1;
AMWR 1; BRW 7; BRWR 2; CA 5-8R;
25-28R; CANR 41; CDALB 1929-1941;
DA; DA3; DAB; DAC; DAM DRAM,
MST, POET; DFS 4, 13; DLB 7, 10, 45,
63, 245; DLBY 1988; EWL 3; EXPP;
LAIT 3; LATS 1; LMFS 1; MTCW 1, 2;
NCFS 5; PAB; PFS 1, 7, 20; RGAL 4;
RGEL 2; TUS; WLIT 4; WP
Elizabeth 1866-1941 .... **TCLC 41**
Elkin, Stanley L(awrence)
1930-1995 .. **CLC 4, 6, 9, 14, 27, 51, 91;
SSC 12**
See also AMWS 6; BPFB 1; CA 9-12R;
148; CANR 8, 46; CN 7; CPW; DAM
NOV, POP; DLB 2, 28, 218, 278; DLBY
1980; EWL 3; INT CANR-8; MTCW 1,
2; RGAL 4
Elledge, Scott .... **CLC 34**
Elliott, Don
See Silverberg, Robert
Elliott, George P(aul) 1918-1980 .... **CLC 2**
See also CA 1-4R; 97-100; CANR 2; DLB
244
Elliott, Janice 1931-1995 .... **CLC 47**
See also CA 13-16R; CANR 8, 29, 84; CN
7; DLB 14; SATA 119
Elliott, Sumner Locke 1917-1991 ..... **CLC 38**
See also CA 5-8R; 134; CANR 2, 21; DLB
289
Elliott, William
See Bradbury, Ray (Douglas)
Ellis, A. E. .... **CLC 7**
Ellis, Alice Thomas .... **CLC 40**
See Haycraft, Anna (Margaret)
See also DLB 194; MTCW 1
Ellis, Bret Easton 1964- ...... **CLC 39, 71, 117**
See also AAYA 2, 43; CA 118; 123; CANR
51, 74, 126; CN 7; CPW; DA3; DAM
POP; DLB 292; HGG; INT CA-123;
MTCW 1; NFS 11
Ellis, (Henry) Havelock
1859-1939 .... **TCLC 14**
See also CA 109; 169; DLB 190
Ellis, Landon
See Ellison, Harlan (Jay)
Ellis, Trey 1962- .... **CLC 55**
See also CA 146; CANR 92
Ellison, Harlan (Jay) 1934- ... **CLC 1, 13, 42,
139; SSC 14**
See also AAYA 29; BPFB 1; BYA 14; CA
5-8R; CANR 5, 46, 115; CPW; DAM
POP; DLB 8; HGG; INT CANR-5;
MTCW 1, 2; SCFW 2; SFW 4; SSFS 13,
14, 15; SUFW 1, 2
Ellison, Ralph (Waldo) 1914-1994 .... **BLC 1;
CLC 1, 3, 11, 54, 86, 114; SSC 26;
WLC**
See also AAYA 19; AFAW 1, 2; AMWC 2;
AMWR 2; AMWS 2; BPFB 1; BW 1, 3;
BYA 2; CA 9-12R; 145; CANR 24, 53;
CDALB 1941-1968; CSW; DA; DA3;
DAB; DAC; DAM MST, MULT, NOV;

DLB 2, 76, 227; DLBY 1994; EWL 3; EXPN; EXPS; LAIT 4; MTCW 1, 2; NCFS 3; NFS 2; RGAL 4; RGSF 2; SSFS 1, 11; YAW

Ellmann, Lucy (Elizabeth) 1956- ..... **CLC 61**
See also CA 128

Ellmann, Richard (David)
1918-1987 .... **CLC 50**
See also BEST 89:2; CA 1-4R; 122; CANR 2, 28, 61; DLB 103; DLBY 1987; MTCW 1, 2

Elman, Richard (Martin)
1934-1997 .... **CLC 19**
See also CA 17-20R; 163; CAAS 3; CANR 47

Elron
See Hubbard, L(afayette) Ron(ald)

Eluard, Paul .... **PC 38; TCLC 7, 41**
See Grindel, Eugene
See also EWL 3; GFL 1789 to the Present; RGWL 2, 3

Elyot, Thomas 1490(?)-1546 .... **LC 11**
See also DLB 136; RGEL 2

Elytis, Odysseus 1911-1996 .... **CLC 15, 49, 100; PC 21**
See Alepoudelis, Odysseus
See also CA 102; 151; CANR 94; CWW 2; DAM POET; EW 13; EWL 3; MTCW 1, 2; RGWL 2, 3

Emecheta, (Florence Onye) Buchi
1944- .... **BLC 2; CLC 14, 48, 128**
See also AFW; BW 2, 3; CA 81-84; CANR 27, 81, 126; CDWLB 3; CN 7; CWRI 5; DA3; DAM MULT; DLB 117; EWL 3; FW; MTCW 1, 2; NFS 12, 14; SATA 66; WLIT 2

Emerson, Mary Moody
1774-1863 .... **NCLC 66**

Emerson, Ralph Waldo 1803-1882 . **NCLC 1, 38, 98; PC 18; WLC**
See also AMW; ANW; CDALB 1640-1865; DA; DA3; DAB; DAC; DAM MST, POET; DLB 1, 59, 73, 183, 223, 270; EXPP; LAIT 2; LMFS 1; NCFS 3; PFS 4, 17; RGAL 4; TUS; WP

Eminescu, Mihail 1850-1889 .. **NCLC 33, 131**

Empedocles 5th cent. B.C.- .... **CMLC 50**
See also DLB 176

Empson, William 1906-1984 ... **CLC 3, 8, 19, 33, 34**
See also BRWS 2; CA 17-20R; 112; CANR 31, 61; DLB 20; EWL 3; MTCW 1, 2; RGEL 2

Enchi, Fumiko (Ueda) 1905-1986 ..... **CLC 31**
See Enchi Fumiko
See also CA 129; 121; FW; MJW

Enchi Fumiko
See Enchi, Fumiko (Ueda)
See also DLB 182; EWL 3

Ende, Michael (Andreas Helmuth)
1929-1995 .... **CLC 31**
See also BYA 5; CA 118; 124; 149; CANR 36, 110; CLR 14; DLB 75; MAICYA 1, 2; MAICYAS 1; SATA 61, 130; SATA-Brief 42; SATA-Obit 86

Endo, Shusaku 1923-1996 ..... **CLC 7, 14, 19, 54, 99; SSC 48; TCLC 152**
See Endo Shusaku
See also CA 29-32R; 153; CANR 21, 54, 131; DA3; DAM NOV; MTCW 1, 2; RGSF 2; RGWL 2, 3

Endo Shusaku
See Endo, Shusaku
See also DLB 182; EWL 3

Engel, Marian 1933-1985 .... **CLC 36; TCLC 137**
See also CA 25-28R; CANR 12; DLB 53; FW; INT CANR-12

Engelhardt, Frederick
See Hubbard, L(afayette) Ron(ald)

Engels, Friedrich 1820-1895 .. **NCLC 85, 114**
See also DLB 129; LATS 1

Enright, D(ennis) J(oseph)
1920-2002 .... **CLC 4, 8, 31**
See also CA 1-4R; 211; CANR 1, 42, 83; CP 7; DLB 27; EWL 3; SATA 25; SATA-Obit 140

Enzensberger, Hans Magnus
1929- .... **CLC 43; PC 28**
See also CA 116; 119; CANR 103; EWL 3

Ephron, Nora 1941- .... **CLC 17, 31**
See also AAYA 35; AITN 2; CA 65-68; CANR 12, 39, 83

Epicurus 341B.C.-270B.C. .... **CMLC 21**
See also DLB 176

Epsilon
See Betjeman, John

Epstein, Daniel Mark 1948- .... **CLC 7**
See also CA 49-52; CANR 2, 53, 90

Epstein, Jacob 1956- .... **CLC 19**
See also CA 114

Epstein, Jean 1897-1953 .... **TCLC 92**

Epstein, Joseph 1937- .... **CLC 39**
See also CA 112; 119; CANR 50, 65, 117

Epstein, Leslie 1938- .... **CLC 27**
See also AMWS 12; CA 73-76, 215; CAAE 215; CAAS 12; CANR 23, 69; DLB 299

Equiano, Olaudah 1745(?)-1797 . **BLC 2; LC 16**
See also AFAW 1, 2; CDWLB 3; DAM MULT; DLB 37, 50; WLIT 2

Erasmus, Desiderius 1469(?)-1536 ..... **LC 16, 93**
See also DLB 136; EW 2; LMFS 1; RGWL 2, 3; TWA

Erdman, Paul E(mil) 1932- .... **CLC 25**
See also AITN 1; CA 61-64; CANR 13, 43, 84

Erdrich, Louise 1954- .... **CLC 39, 54, 120, 176; NNAL; PC 52**
See also AAYA 10, 47; AMWS 4; BEST 89:1; BPFB 1; CA 114; CANR 41, 62, 118; CDALBS; CN 7; CP 7; CPW; CWP; DA3; DAM MULT, NOV, POP; DLB 152, 175, 206; EWL 3; EXPP; LAIT 5; LATS 1; MTCW 1; NFS 5; PFS 14; RGAL 4; SATA 94, 141; SSFS 14; TCWW 2

Erenburg, Ilya (Grigoryevich)
See Ehrenburg, Ilya (Grigoryevich)

Erickson, Stephen Michael 1950-
See Erickson, Steve
See also CA 129; SFW 4

Erickson, Steve .... **CLC 64**
See Erickson, Stephen Michael
See also CANR 60, 68; SUFW 2

Erickson, Walter
See Fast, Howard (Melvin)

Ericson, Walter
See Fast, Howard (Melvin)

Eriksson, Buntel
See Bergman, (Ernst) Ingmar

Eriugena, John Scottus c.
810-877 .... **CMLC 65**
See also DLB 115

Ernaux, Annie 1940- .... **CLC 88, 184**
See also CA 147; CANR 93; NCFS 3, 5

Erskine, John 1879-1951 .... **TCLC 84**
See also CA 112; 159; DLB 9, 102; FANT

Eschenbach, Wolfram von
See Wolfram von Eschenbach
See also RGWL 3

Eseki, Bruno
See Mphahlele, Ezekiel

Esenin, Sergei (Alexandrovich)
1895-1925 .... **TCLC 4**
See Yesenin, Sergey
See also CA 104; RGWL 2, 3

Eshleman, Clayton 1935- .... **CLC 7**
See also CA 33-36R, 212; CAAE 212; CAAS 6; CANR 93; CP 7; DLB 5

Espriella, Don Manuel Alvarez
See Southey, Robert

Espriu, Salvador 1913-1985 .... **CLC 9**
See also CA 154; 115; DLB 134; EWL 3

Espronceda, Jose de 1808-1842 ..... **NCLC 39**

Esquivel, Laura 1951(?)- ... **CLC 141; HLCS 1**
See also AAYA 29; CA 143; CANR 68, 113; DA3; DNFS 2; LAIT 3; LMFS 2; MTCW 1; NFS 5; WLIT 1

Esse, James
See Stephens, James

Esterbrook, Tom
See Hubbard, L(afayette) Ron(ald)

Estleman, Loren D. 1952- .... **CLC 48**
See also AAYA 27; CA 85-88; CANR 27, 74; CMW 4; CPW; DA3; DAM NOV, POP; DLB 226; INT CANR-27; MTCW 1, 2

Etherege, Sir George 1636-1692 . **DC 23; LC 78**
See also BRW 2; DAM DRAM; DLB 80; PAB; RGEL 2

Etheria fl. 4th cent. - .... **CMLC 70**

Euclid 306B.C.-283B.C. .... **CMLC 25**

Eugenides, Jeffrey 1960(?)- .... **CLC 81**
See also AAYA 51; CA 144; CANR 120

Euripides c. 484B.C.-406B.C. .... **CMLC 23, 51; DC 4; WLCS**
See also AW 1; CDWLB 1; DA; DA3; DAB; DAC; DAM DRAM, MST; DFS 1, 4, 6; DLB 176; LAIT 1; LMFS 1; RGWL 2, 3

Evan, Evin
See Faust, Frederick (Schiller)

Evans, Caradoc 1878-1945 ... **SSC 43; TCLC 85**
See also DLB 162

Evans, Evan
See Faust, Frederick (Schiller)
See also TCWW 2

Evans, Marian
See Eliot, George

Evans, Mary Ann
See Eliot, George

Evarts, Esther
See Benson, Sally

Everett, Percival
See Everett, Percival L.
See also CSW

Everett, Percival L. 1956- .... **CLC 57**
See Everett, Percival
See also BW 2; CA 129; CANR 94

Everson, R(onald) G(ilmour)
1903-1992 .... **CLC 27**
See also CA 17-20R; DLB 88

Everson, William (Oliver)
1912-1994 .... **CLC 1, 5, 14**
See also BG 2; CA 9-12R; 145; CANR 20; DLB 5, 16, 212; MTCW 1

Evtushenko, Evgenii Aleksandrovich
See Yevtushenko, Yevgeny (Alexandrovich)
See also RGWL 2, 3

Ewart, Gavin (Buchanan)
1916-1995 .... **CLC 13, 46**
See also BRWS 7; CA 89-92; 150; CANR 17, 46; CP 7; DLB 40; MTCW 1

Ewers, Hanns Heinz 1871-1943 ..... **TCLC 12**
See also CA 109; 149

Ewing, Frederick R.
See Sturgeon, Theodore (Hamilton)

Exley, Frederick (Earl) 1929-1992 .... **CLC 6, 11**
See also AITN 2; BPFB 1; CA 81-84; 138; CANR 117; DLB 143; DLBY 1981

Eynhardt, Guillermo
See Quiroga, Horacio (Sylvestre)
Ezekiel, Nissim (Moses) 1924-2004 .. **CLC 61**
See also CA 61-64; 223; CP 7; EWL 3
Ezekiel, Tish O'Dowd 1943- .... **CLC 34**
See also CA 129
Fadeev, Aleksandr Aleksandrovich
See Bulgya, Alexander Alexandrovich
See also DLB 272
Fadeev, Alexandr Alexandrovich
See Bulgya, Alexander Alexandrovich
See also EWL 3
Fadeyev, A.
See Bulgya, Alexander Alexandrovich
Fadeyev, Alexander .... **TCLC 53**
See Bulgya, Alexander Alexandrovich
Fagen, Donald 1948- .... **CLC 26**
Fainzilberg, Ilya Arnoldovich 1897-1937
See Ilf, Ilya
See also CA 120; 165
Fair, Ronald L. 1932- .... **CLC 18**
See also BW 1; CA 69-72; CANR 25; DLB
33
Fairbairn, Roger
See Carr, John Dickson
Fairbairns, Zoe (Ann) 1948- .... **CLC 32**
See also CA 103; CANR 21, 85; CN 7
Fairfield, Flora
See Alcott, Louisa May
Fairman, Paul W. 1916-1977
See Queen, Ellery
See also CA 114; SFW 4
Falco, Gian
See Papini, Giovanni
Falconer, James
See Kirkup, James
Falconer, Kenneth
See Kornbluth, C(yril) M.
Falkland, Samuel
See Heijermans, Herman
Fallaci, Oriana 1930- .... **CLC 11, 110**
See also CA 77-80; CANR 15, 58; FW;
MTCW 1
Faludi, Susan 1959- .... **CLC 140**
See also CA 138; CANR 126; FW; MTCW
1; NCFS 3
Faludy, George 1913- .... **CLC 42**
See also CA 21-24R
Faludy, Gyoergy
See Faludy, George
Fanon, Frantz 1925-1961 .... **BLC 2; CLC 74**
See also BW 1; CA 116; 89-92; DAM
MULT; DLB 296; LMFS 2; WLIT 2
Fanshawe, Ann 1625-1680 .... **LC 11**
Fante, John (Thomas) 1911-1983 .... **CLC 60;
SSC 65**
See also AMWS 11; CA 69-72; 109; CANR
23, 104; DLB 130; DLBY 1983
Far, Sui Sin .... **SSC 62**
See Eaton, Edith Maude
See also SSFS 4
Farah, Nuruddin 1945- ...... **BLC 2; CLC 53,
137**
See also AFW; BW 2, 3; CA 106; CANR
81; CDWLB 3; CN 7; DAM MULT; DLB
125; EWL 3; WLIT 2
Fargue, Leon-Paul 1876(?)-1947 .... **TCLC 11**
See also CA 109; CANR 107; DLB 258;
EWL 3
Farigoule, Louis
See Romains, Jules
Farina, Richard 1936(?)-1966 .... **CLC 9**
See also CA 81-84; 25-28R
Farley, Walter (Lorimer)
1915-1989 .... **CLC 17**
See also BYA 14; CA 17-20R; CANR 8,
29, 84; DLB 22; JRDA; MAICYA 1, 2;
SATA 2, 43, 132; YAW

Farmer, Philip Jose 1918- .... **CLC 1, 19**
See also AAYA 28; BPFB 1; CA 1-4R;
CANR 4, 35, 111; DLB 8; MTCW 1;
SATA 93; SCFW 2; SFW 4
Farquhar, George 1677-1707 .... **LC 21**
See also BRW 2; DAM DRAM; DLB 84;
RGEL 2
Farrell, J(ames) G(ordon)
1935-1979 .... **CLC 6**
See also CA 73-76; 89-92; CANR 36; DLB
14, 271; MTCW 1; RGEL 2; RHW; WLIT
4
Farrell, James T(homas) 1904-1979 . **CLC 1,
4, 8, 11, 66; SSC 28**
See also AMW; BPFB 1; CA 5-8R; 89-92;
CANR 9, 61; DLB 4, 9, 86; DLBD 2;
EWL 3; MTCW 1, 2; RGAL 4
Farrell, Warren (Thomas) 1943- ...... **CLC 70**
See also CA 146; CANR 120
Farren, Richard J.
See Betjeman, John
Farren, Richard M.
See Betjeman, John
Fassbinder, Rainer Werner
1946-1982 .... **CLC 20**
See also CA 93-96; 106; CANR 31
Fast, Howard (Melvin) 1914-2003 .. **CLC 23,
131**
See also AAYA 16; BPFB 1; CA 1-4R, 181;
214; CAAE 181; CAAS 18; CANR 1, 33,
54, 75, 98; CMW 4; CN 7; CPW; DAM
NOV; DLB 9; INT CANR-33; LATS 1;
MTCW 1; RHW; SATA 7; SATA-Essay
107; TCWW 2; YAW
Faulcon, Robert
See Holdstock, Robert P.
Faulkner, William (Cuthbert)
1897-1962 .... **CLC 1, 3, 6, 8, 9, 11, 14,
18, 28, 52, 68; SSC 1, 35, 42; TCLC
141; WLC**
See also AAYA 7; AMW; AMWR 1; BPFB
1; BYA 5, 15; CA 81-84; CANR 33;
CDALB 1929-1941; DA; DA3; DAB;
DAC; DAM MST, NOV; DLB 9, 11, 44,
102; DLBD 2; DLBY 1986, 1997; EWL
3; EXPN; EXPS; LAIT 2; LATS 1; LMFS
2; MTCW 1, 2; NFS 4, 8, 13; RGAL 4;
RGSF 2; SSFS 2, 5, 6, 12; TUS
Fauset, Jessie Redmon
1882(?)-1961 .. **BLC 2; CLC 19, 54; HR
2**
See also AFAW 2; BW 1; CA 109; CANR
83; DAM MULT; DLB 51; FW; LMFS 2;
MAWW
Faust, Frederick (Schiller)
1892-1944(?) .... **TCLC 49**
See Austin, Frank; Brand, Max; Challis,
George; Dawson, Peter; Dexter, Martin;
Evans, Evan; Frederick, John; Frost, Fred-
erick; Manning, David; Silver, Nicholas
See also CA 108; 152; DAM POP; DLB
256; TUS
Faust, Irvin 1924- .... **CLC 8**
See also CA 33-36R; CANR 28, 67; CN 7;
DLB 2, 28, 218, 278; DLBY 1980
Faustino, Domingo 1811-1888 ...... **NCLC 123**
Fawkes, Guy
See Benchley, Robert (Charles)
Fearing, Kenneth (Flexner)
1902-1961 .... **CLC 51**
See also CA 93-96; CANR 59; CMW 4;
DLB 9; RGAL 4
Fecamps, Elise
See Creasey, John
Federman, Raymond 1928- .... **CLC 6, 47**
See also CA 17-20R, 208; CAAE 208;
CAAS 8; CANR 10, 43, 83, 108; CN 7;
DLBY 1980
Federspiel, J(uerg) F. 1931- .... **CLC 42**
See also CA 146

Feiffer, Jules (Ralph) 1929- ...... **CLC 2, 8, 64**
See also AAYA 3; CA 17-20R; CAD; CANR
30, 59, 129; CD 5; DAM DRAM; DLB 7,
44; INT CANR-30; MTCW 1; SATA 8,
61, 111
Feige, Hermann Albert Otto Maximilian
See Traven, B.
Feinberg, David B. 1956-1994 .... **CLC 59**
See also CA 135; 147
Feinstein, Elaine 1930- .... **CLC 36**
See also CA 69-72; CAAS 1; CANR 31,
68, 121; CN 7; CP 7; CWP; DLB 14, 40;
MTCW 1
Feke, Gilbert David .... **CLC 65**
Feldman, Irving (Mordecai) 1928- ..... **CLC 7**
See also CA 1-4R; CANR 1; CP 7; DLB
169
Felix-Tchicaya, Gerald
See Tchicaya, Gerald Felix
Fellini, Federico 1920-1993 .... **CLC 16, 85**
See also CA 65-68; 143; CANR 33
Felltham, Owen 1602(?)-1668 .... **LC 92**
See also DLB 126, 151
Felsen, Henry Gregor 1916-1995 ..... **CLC 17**
See also CA 1-4R; 180; CANR 1; SAAS 2;
SATA 1
Felski, Rita .... **CLC 65**
Fenno, Jack
See Calisher, Hortense
Fenollosa, Ernest (Francisco)
1853-1908 .... **TCLC 91**
Fenton, James Martin 1949- .... **CLC 32**
See also CA 102; CANR 108; CP 7; DLB
40; PFS 11
Ferber, Edna 1887-1968 .... **CLC 18, 93**
See also AITN 1; CA 5-8R; 25-28R; CANR
68, 105; DLB 9, 28, 86, 266; MTCW 1,
2; RGAL 4; RHW; SATA 7; TCWW 2
Ferdowsi, Abu'l Qasem 940-1020 . **CMLC 43**
See also RGWL 2, 3
Ferguson, Helen
See Kavan, Anna
Ferguson, Niall 1964- .... **CLC 134**
See also CA 190
Ferguson, Samuel 1810-1886 .... **NCLC 33**
See also DLB 32; RGEL 2
Fergusson, Robert 1750-1774 .... **LC 29**
See also DLB 109; RGEL 2
Ferling, Lawrence
See Ferlinghetti, Lawrence (Monsanto)
Ferlinghetti, Lawrence (Monsanto)
1919(?)- ..... **CLC 2, 6, 10, 27, 111; PC 1**
See also CA 5-8R; CANR 3, 41, 73, 125;
CDALB 1941-1968; CP 7; DA3; DAM
POET; DLB 5, 16; MTCW 1, 2; RGAL 4;
WP
Fern, Fanny
See Parton, Sara Payson Willis
Fernandez, Vicente Garcia Huidobro
See Huidobro Fernandez, Vicente Garcia
Fernandez-Armesto, Felipe .... **CLC 70**
Fernandez de Lizardi, Jose Joaquin
See Lizardi, Jose Joaquin Fernandez de
Ferre, Rosario 1938- ...... **CLC 139; HLCS 1;
SSC 36**
See also CA 131; CANR 55, 81; CWW 2;
DLB 145; EWL 3; HW 1, 2; LAWS 1;
MTCW 1; WLIT 1
Ferrer, Gabriel (Francisco Victor) Miro
See Miro (Ferrer), Gabriel (Francisco
Victor)
Ferrier, Susan (Edmonstone)
1782-1854 .... **NCLC 8**
See also DLB 116; RGEL 2
Ferrigno, Robert 1948(?)- .... **CLC 65**
See also CA 140; CANR 125

Ferron, Jacques 1921-1985 .... **CLC 94**
 See also CA 117; 129; CCA 1; DAC; DLB
 60; EWL 3

Feuchtwanger, Lion 1884-1958 .... **TCLC 3**
 See also CA 104; 187; DLB 66; EWL 3

Feuerbach, Ludwig 1804-1872 ..... **NCLC 139**
 See also DLB 133

Feuillet, Octave 1821-1890 .... **NCLC 45**
 See also DLB 192

Feydeau, Georges (Leon Jules Marie)
 1862-1921 .... **TCLC 22**
 See also CA 113; 152; CANR 84; DAM
 DRAM; DLB 192; EWL 3; GFL 1789 to
 the Present; RGWL 2, 3

Fichte, Johann Gottlieb
 1762-1814 .... **NCLC 62**
 See also DLB 90

Ficino, Marsilio 1433-1499 .... **LC 12**
 See also LMFS 1

Fiedeler, Hans
 See Doeblin, Alfred

Fiedler, Leslie A(aron) 1917-2003 ..... **CLC 4,
 13, 24**
 See also AMWS 13; CA 9-12R; 212; CANR
 7, 63; CN 7; DLB 28, 67; EWL 3; MTCW
 1, 2; RGAL 4; TUS

Field, Andrew 1938- .... **CLC 44**
 See also CA 97-100; CANR 25

Field, Eugene 1850-1895 .... **NCLC 3**
 See also DLB 23, 42, 140; DLBD 13; MAI-
 CYA 1, 2; RGAL 4; SATA 16

Field, Gans T.
 See Wellman, Manly Wade

Field, Michael 1915-1971 .... **TCLC 43**
 See also CA 29-32R

Field, Peter
 See Hobson, Laura Z(ametkin)
 See also TCWW 2

Fielding, Helen 1958- .... **CLC 146**
 See also CA 172; CANR 127; DLB 231

Fielding, Henry 1707-1754 .... **LC 1, 46, 85;
 WLC**
 See also BRW 3; BRWR 1; CDBLB 1660-
 1789; DA; DA3; DAB; DAC; DAM
 DRAM, MST, NOV; DLB 39, 84, 101;
 NFS 18; RGEL 2; TEA; WLIT 3

Fielding, Sarah 1710-1768 .... **LC 1, 44**
 See also DLB 39; RGEL 2; TEA

Fields, W. C. 1880-1946 .... **TCLC 80**
 See also DLB 44

Fierstein, Harvey (Forbes) 1954- .... **CLC 33**
 See also CA 123; 129; CAD; CD 5; CPW;
 DA3; DAM DRAM, POP; DFS 6; DLB
 266; GLL

Figes, Eva 1932- .... **CLC 31**
 See also CA 53-56; CANR 4, 44, 83; CN 7;
 DLB 14, 271; FW

Filippo, Eduardo de
 See de Filippo, Eduardo

Finch, Anne 1661-1720 .... **LC 3; PC 21**
 See also BRWS 9; DLB 95

Finch, Robert (Duer Claydon)
 1900-1995 .... **CLC 18**
 See also CA 57-60; CANR 9, 24, 49; CP 7;
 DLB 88

Findley, Timothy (Irving Frederick)
 1930-2002 .... **CLC 27, 102**
 See also CA 25-28R; 206; CANR 12, 42,
 69, 109; CCA 1; CN 7; DAC; DAM MST;
 DLB 53; FANT; RHW

Fink, William
 See Mencken, H(enry) L(ouis)

Firbank, Louis 1942-
 See Reed, Lou
 See also CA 117

Firbank, (Arthur Annesley) Ronald
 1886-1926 .... **TCLC 1**
 See also BRWS 2; CA 104; 177; DLB 36;
 EWL 3; RGEL 2

Fish, Stanley
 See Fish, Stanley Eugene

Fish, Stanley E.
 See Fish, Stanley Eugene

Fish, Stanley Eugene 1938- .... **CLC 142**
 See also CA 112; 132; CANR 90; DLB 67

Fisher, Dorothy (Frances) Canfield
 1879-1958 .... **TCLC 87**
 See also CA 114; 136; CANR 80; CLR 71,;
 CWRI 5; DLB 9, 102, 284; MAICYA 1,
 2; YABC 1

Fisher, M(ary) F(rances) K(ennedy)
 1908-1992 .... **CLC 76, 87**
 See also CA 77-80; 138; CANR 44; MTCW
 1

Fisher, Roy 1930- .... **CLC 25**
 See also CA 81-84; CAAS 10; CANR 16;
 CP 7; DLB 40

Fisher, Rudolph 1897-1934 .... **BLC 2; HR 2;
 SSC 25; TCLC 11**
 See also BW 1, 3; CA 107; 124; CANR 80;
 DAM MULT; DLB 51, 102

Fisher, Vardis (Alvero) 1895-1968 .... **CLC 7;
 TCLC 140**
 See also CA 5-8R; 25-28R; CANR 68; DLB
 9, 206; RGAL 4; TCWW 2

Fiske, Tarleton
 See Bloch, Robert (Albert)

Fitch, Clarke
 See Sinclair, Upton (Beall)

Fitch, John IV
 See Cormier, Robert (Edmund)

Fitzgerald, Captain Hugh
 See Baum, L(yman) Frank

FitzGerald, Edward 1809-1883 .... **NCLC 9**
 See also BRW 4; DLB 32; RGEL 2

Fitzgerald, F(rancis) Scott (Key)
 1896-1940 ... **SSC 6, 31; TCLC 1, 6, 14,
 28, 55; WLC**
 See also AAYA 24; AITN 1; AMW; AMWC
 2; AMWR 1; BPFB 1; CA 110; 123;
 CDALB 1917-1929; DA; DA3; DAB;
 DAC; DAM MST, NOV; DLB 4, 9, 86,
 219, 273; DLBD 1, 15, 16; DLBY 1981,
 1996; EWL 3; EXPN; EXPS; LAIT 3;
 MTCW 1, 2; NFS 2, 19; RGAL 4; RGSF
 2; SSFS 4, 15; TUS

Fitzgerald, Penelope 1916-2000 . **CLC 19, 51,
 61, 143**
 See also BRWS 5; CA 85-88; 190; CAAS
 10; CANR 56, 86, 131; CN 7; DLB 14,
 194; EWL 3; MTCW 2

Fitzgerald, Robert (Stuart)
 1910-1985 .... **CLC 39**
 See also CA 1-4R; 114; CANR 1; DLBY
 1980

FitzGerald, Robert D(avid)
 1902-1987 .... **CLC 19**
 See also CA 17-20R; DLB 260; RGEL 2

Fitzgerald, Zelda (Sayre)
 1900-1948 .... **TCLC 52**
 See also AMWS 9; CA 117; 126; DLBY
 1984

Flanagan, Thomas (James Bonner)
 1923-2002 .... **CLC 25, 52**
 See also CA 108; 206; CANR 55; CN 7;
 DLBY 1980; INT CA-108; MTCW 1;
 RHW

Flaubert, Gustave 1821-1880 .... **NCLC 2, 10,
 19, 62, 66, 135; SSC 11, 60; WLC**
 See also DA; DA3; DAB; DAC; DAM
 MST, NOV; DLB 119, 301; EW 7; EXPS;
 GFL 1789 to the Present; LAIT 2; LMFS
 1; NFS 14; RGSF 2; RGWL 2, 3; SSFS
 6; TWA

Flavius Josephus
 See Josephus, Flavius

Flecker, Herman Elroy
 See Flecker, (Herman) James Elroy

Flecker, (Herman) James Elroy
 1884-1915 .... **TCLC 43**
 See also CA 109; 150; DLB 10, 19; RGEL
 2

Fleming, Ian (Lancaster) 1908-1964 . **CLC 3,
 30**
 See also AAYA 26; BPFB 1; CA 5-8R;
 CANR 59; CDBLB 1945-1960; CMW 4;
 CPW; DA3; DAM POP; DLB 87, 201;
 MSW; MTCW 1, 2; RGEL 2; SATA 9;
 TEA; YAW

Fleming, Thomas (James) 1927- ...... **CLC 37**
 See also CA 5-8R; CANR 10, 102; INT
 CANR-10; SATA 8

Fletcher, John 1579-1625 .... **DC 6; LC 33**
 See also BRW 2; CDBLB Before 1660;
 DLB 58; RGEL 2; TEA

Fletcher, John Gould 1886-1950 .... **TCLC 35**
 See also CA 107; 167; DLB 4, 45; LMFS
 2; RGAL 4

Fleur, Paul
 See Pohl, Frederik

Flooglebuckle, Al
 See Spiegelman, Art

Flora, Fletcher 1914-1969
 See Queen, Ellery
 See also CA 1-4R; CANR 3, 85

Flying Officer X
 See Bates, H(erbert) E(rnest)

Fo, Dario 1926- .... **CLC 32, 109; DC 10**
 See also CA 116; 128; CANR 68, 114;
 CWW 2; DA3; DAM DRAM; DLBY
 1997; EWL 3; MTCW 1, 2

Fogarty, Jonathan Titulescu Esq.
 See Farrell, James T(homas)

Follett, Ken(neth Martin) 1949- .... **CLC 18**
 See also AAYA 6, 50; BEST 89:4; BPFB 1;
 CA 81-84; CANR 13, 33, 54, 102; CMW
 4; CPW; DA3; DAM NOV, POP; DLB
 87; DLBY 1981; INT CANR-33; MTCW
 1

Fontane, Theodor 1819-1898 .... **NCLC 26**
 See also CDWLB 2; DLB 129; EW 6;
 RGWL 2, 3; TWA

Fontenot, Chester .... **CLC 65**

Fonvizin, Denis Ivanovich
 1744(?)-1792 .... **LC 81**
 See also DLB 150; RGWL 2, 3

Foote, Horton 1916- .... **CLC 51, 91**
 See also CA 73-76; CAD; CANR 34, 51,
 110; CD 5; CSW; DA3; DAM DRAM;
 DLB 26, 266; EWL 3; INT CANR-34

Foote, Mary Hallock 1847-1938 .. **TCLC 108**
 See also DLB 186, 188, 202, 221

Foote, Shelby 1916- .... **CLC 75**
 See also AAYA 40; CA 5-8R; CANR 3, 45,
 74, 131; CN 7; CPW; CSW; DA3; DAM
 NOV, POP; DLB 2, 17; MTCW 2; RHW

Forbes, Cosmo
 See Lewton, Val

Forbes, Esther 1891-1967 .... **CLC 12**
 See also AAYA 17; BYA 2; CA 13-14; 25-
 28R; CAP 1; CLR 27; DLB 22; JRDA;
 MAICYA 1, 2; RHW; SATA 2, 100; YAW

Forche, Carolyn (Louise) 1950- .... **CLC 25,
 83, 86; PC 10**
 See also CA 109; 117; CANR 50, 74; CP 7;
 CWP; DA3; DAM POET; DLB 5, 193;
 INT CA-117; MTCW 1; PFS 18; RGAL 4

Ford, Elbur
 See Hibbert, Eleanor Alice Burford

Ford, Ford Madox 1873-1939 ... **TCLC 1, 15,
 39, 57**
 See Chaucer, Daniel
 See also BRW 6; CA 104; 132; CANR 74;
 CDBLB 1914-1945; DA3; DAM NOV;
 DLB 34, 98, 162; EWL 3; MTCW 1, 2;
 RGEL 2; TEA

Freneau, Philip Morin 1752-1832 .. **NCLC 1, 111**
See also AMWS 2; DLB 37, 43; RGAL 4

Freud, Sigmund 1856-1939 .... **TCLC 52**
See also CA 115; 133; CANR 69; DLB 296; EW 8; EWL 3; LATS 1; MTCW 1, 2; NCFS 3; TWA

Freytag, Gustav 1816-1895 .... **NCLC 109**
See also DLB 129

Friedan, Betty (Naomi) 1921- .... **CLC 74**
See also CA 65-68; CANR 18, 45, 74; DLB 246; FW; MTCW 1, 2; NCFS 5

Friedlander, Saul 1932- .... **CLC 90**
See also CA 117; 130; CANR 72

Friedman, B(ernard) H(arper)
1926- .... **CLC 7**
See also CA 1-4R; CANR 3, 48

Friedman, Bruce Jay 1930- ...... **CLC 3, 5, 56**
See also CA 9-12R; CAD; CANR 25, 52, 101; CD 5; CN 7; DLB 2, 28, 244; INT CANR-25; SSFS 18

Friel, Brian 1929- .... **CLC 5, 42, 59, 115; DC 8**
See also BRWS 5; CA 21-24R; CANR 33, 69, 131; CBD; CD 5; DFS 11; DLB 13; EWL 3; MTCW 1; RGEL 2; TEA

Friis-Baastad, Babbis Ellinor
1921-1970 .... **CLC 12**
See also CA 17-20R; 134; SATA 7

Frisch, Max (Rudolf) 1911-1991 ... **CLC 3, 9, 14, 18, 32, 44; TCLC 121**
See also CA 85-88; 134; CANR 32, 74; CD-WLB 2; DAM DRAM, NOV; DLB 69, 124; EW 13; EWL 3; MTCW 1, 2; RGWL 2, 3

Fromentin, Eugene (Samuel Auguste)
1820-1876 .... **NCLC 10, 125**
See also DLB 123; GFL 1789 to the Present

Frost, Frederick
See Faust, Frederick (Schiller)
See also TCWW 2

Frost, Robert (Lee) 1874-1963 .. **CLC 1, 3, 4, 9, 10, 13, 15, 26, 34, 44; PC 1, 39; WLC**
See also AAYA 21; AMW; AMWR 1; CA 89-92; CANR 33; CDALB 1917-1929; CLR 67; DA; DA3; DAB; DAC; DAM MST, POET; DLB 54, 284; DLBD 7; EWL 3; EXPP; MTCW 1, 2; PAB; PFS 1, 2, 3, 4, 5, 6, 7, 10, 13; RGAL 4; SATA 14; TUS; WP; WYA

Froude, James Anthony
1818-1894 .... **NCLC 43**
See also DLB 18, 57, 144

Froy, Herald
See Waterhouse, Keith (Spencer)

Fry, Christopher 1907- .... **CLC 2, 10, 14**
See also BRWS 3; CA 17-20R; CAAS 23; CANR 9, 30, 74; CBD; CD 5; CP 7; DAM DRAM; DLB 13; EWL 3; MTCW 1, 2; RGEL 2; SATA 66; TEA

Frye, (Herman) Northrop
1912-1991 .... **CLC 24, 70**
See also CA 5-8R; 133; CANR 8, 37; DLB 67, 68, 246; EWL 3; MTCW 1, 2; RGAL 4; TWA

Fuchs, Daniel 1909-1993 .... **CLC 8, 22**
See also CA 81-84; 142; CAAS 5; CANR 40; DLB 9, 26, 28; DLBY 1993

Fuchs, Daniel 1934- .... **CLC 34**
See also CA 37-40R; CANR 14, 48

Fuentes, Carlos 1928- .. **CLC 3, 8, 10, 13, 22, 41, 60, 113; HLC 1; SSC 24; WLC**
See also AAYA 4, 45; AITN 2; BPFB 1; CA 69-72; CANR 10, 32, 68, 104; CD-WLB 3; CWW 2; DA; DA3; DAB; DAC; DAM MST, MULT, NOV; DLB 113; DNFS 2; EWL 3; HW 1, 2; LAIT 3; LATS 1; LAW; LAWS 1; LMFS 2; MTCW 1, 2; NFS 8; RGSF 2; RGWL 2, 3; TWA; WLIT 1

Fuentes, Gregorio Lopez y
See Lopez y Fuentes, Gregorio

Fuertes, Gloria 1918-1998 .... **PC 27**
See also CA 178, 180; DLB 108; HW 2; SATA 115

Fugard, (Harold) Athol 1932- . **CLC 5, 9, 14, 25, 40, 80; DC 3**
See also AAYA 17; AFW; CA 85-88; CANR 32, 54, 118; CD 5; DAM DRAM; DFS 3, 6, 10; DLB 225; DNFS 1, 2; EWL 3; LATS 1; MTCW 1; RGEL 2; WLIT 2

Fugard, Sheila 1932- .... **CLC 48**
See also CA 125

Fukuyama, Francis 1952- .... **CLC 131**
See also CA 140; CANR 72, 125

Fuller, Charles (H.), (Jr.) 1939- .... **BLC 2; CLC 25; DC 1**
See also BW 2; CA 108; 112; CAD; CANR 87; CD 5; DAM DRAM, MULT; DFS 8; DLB 38, 266; EWL 3; INT CA-112; MTCW 1

Fuller, Henry Blake 1857-1929 .... **TCLC 103**
See also CA 108; 177; DLB 12; RGAL 4

Fuller, John (Leopold) 1937- .... **CLC 62**
See also CA 21-24R; CANR 9, 44; CP 7; DLB 40

Fuller, Margaret
See Ossoli, Sarah Margaret (Fuller)
See also AMWS 2; DLB 183, 223, 239

Fuller, Roy (Broadbent) 1912-1991 ... **CLC 4, 28**
See also BRWS 7; CA 5-8R; 135; CAAS 10; CANR 53, 83; CWRI 5; DLB 15, 20; EWL 3; RGEL 2; SATA 87

Fuller, Sarah Margaret
See Ossoli, Sarah Margaret (Fuller)

Fuller, Sarah Margaret
See Ossoli, Sarah Margaret (Fuller)
See also DLB 1, 59, 73

Fulton, Alice 1952- .... **CLC 52**
See also CA 116; CANR 57, 88; CP 7; CWP; DLB 193

Furphy, Joseph 1843-1912 .... **TCLC 25**
See Collins, Tom
See also CA 163; DLB 230; EWL 3; RGEL 2

Fuson, Robert H(enderson) 1927- .... **CLC 70**
See also CA 89-92; CANR 103

Fussell, Paul 1924- .... **CLC 74**
See also BEST 90:1; CA 17-20R; CANR 8, 21, 35, 69; INT CANR-21; MTCW 1, 2

Futabatei, Shimei 1864-1909 .... **TCLC 44**
See Futabatei Shimei
See also CA 162; MJW

Futabatei Shimei
See Futabatei, Shimei
See also DLB 180; EWL 3

Futrelle, Jacques 1875-1912 .... **TCLC 19**
See also CA 113; 155; CMW 4

Gaboriau, Emile 1835-1873 .... **NCLC 14**
See also CMW 4; MSW

Gadda, Carlo Emilio 1893-1973 ...... **CLC 11; TCLC 144**
See also CA 89-92; DLB 177; EWL 3

Gaddis, William 1922-1998 ... **CLC 1, 3, 6, 8, 10, 19, 43, 86**
See also AMWS 4; BPFB 1; CA 17-20R; 172; CANR 21, 48; CN 7; DLB 2, 278; EWL 3; MTCW 1, 2; RGAL 4

Gaelique, Moruen le
See Jacob, (Cyprien-)Max

Gage, Walter
See Inge, William (Motter)

Gaines, Ernest J(ames) 1933- .. **BLC 2; CLC 3, 11, 18, 86, 181; SSC 68**
See also AAYA 18; AFAW 1, 2; AITN 1; BPFB 2; BW 2; BYA 6; CA 9-12R; CANR 6, 24, 42, 75, 126; CDALB 1968-1988; CLR 62; CN 7; CSW; DA3; DAM MULT; DLB 2, 33, 152; DLBY 1980; EWL 3; EXPN; LAIT 5; LATS 1; MTCW 1, 2; NFS 5, 7, 16; RGAL 4; RGSF 2; RHW; SATA 86; SSFS 5; YAW

Gaitskill, Mary (Lawrence) 1954- .... **CLC 69**
See also CA 128; CANR 61; DLB 244

Gaius Suetonius Tranquillus c. 70-c. 130
See Suetonius

Galdos, Benito Perez
See Perez Galdos, Benito
See also EW 7

Gale, Zona 1874-1938 .... **TCLC 7**
See also CA 105; 153; CANR 84; DAM DRAM; DFS 17; DLB 9, 78, 228; RGAL 4

Galeano, Eduardo (Hughes) 1940- . **CLC 72; HLCS 1**
See also CA 29-32R; CANR 13, 32, 100; HW 1

Galiano, Juan Valera y Alcala
See Valera y Alcala-Galiano, Juan

Galilei, Galileo 1564-1642 .... **LC 45**

Gallagher, Tess 1943- .... **CLC 18, 63; PC 9**
See also CA 106; CP 7; CWP; DAM POET; DLB 120, 212, 244; PFS 16

Gallant, Mavis 1922- ..... **CLC 7, 18, 38, 172; SSC 5**
See also CA 69-72; CANR 29, 69, 117; CCA 1; CN 7; DAC; DAM MST; DLB 53; EWL 3; MTCW 1, 2; RGEL 2; RGSF 2

Gallant, Roy A(rthur) 1924- .... **CLC 17**
See also CA 5-8R; CANR 4, 29, 54, 117; CLR 30; MAICYA 1, 2; SATA 4, 68, 110

Gallico, Paul (William) 1897-1976 ..... **CLC 2**
See also AITN 1; CA 5-8R; 69-72; CANR 23; DLB 9, 171; FANT; MAICYA 1, 2; SATA 13

Gallo, Max Louis 1932- .... **CLC 95**
See also CA 85-88

Gallois, Lucien
See Desnos, Robert

Gallup, Ralph
See Whitemore, Hugh (John)

Galsworthy, John 1867-1933 .... **SSC 22; TCLC 1, 45; WLC**
See also BRW 6; CA 104; 141; CANR 75; CDBLB 1890-1914; DA; DA3; DAB; DAC; DAM DRAM, MST, NOV; DLB 10, 34, 98, 162; DLBD 16; EWL 3; MTCW 1; RGEL 2; SSFS 3; TEA

Galt, John 1779-1839 .... **NCLC 1, 110**
See also DLB 99, 116, 159; RGEL 2; RGSF 2

Galvin, James 1951- .... **CLC 38**
See also CA 108; CANR 26

Gamboa, Federico 1864-1939 .... **TCLC 36**
See also CA 167; HW 2; LAW

Gandhi, M. K.
See Gandhi, Mohandas Karamchand

Gandhi, Mahatma
See Gandhi, Mohandas Karamchand

Gandhi, Mohandas Karamchand
1869-1948 .... **TCLC 59**
See also CA 121; 132; DA3; DAM MULT; MTCW 1, 2

Gann, Ernest Kellogg 1910-1991 ..... **CLC 23**
See also AITN 1; BPFB 2; CA 1-4R; 136; CANR 1, 83; RHW

Gao Xingjian 1940- .... **CLC 167**
See Xingjian, Gao

Gozzano, Guido 1883-1916 .... **PC 10**
See also CA 154; DLB 114; EWL 3
Gozzi, (Conte) Carlo 1720-1806 .... **NCLC 23**
Grabbe, Christian Dietrich
1801-1836 .... **NCLC 2**
See also DLB 133; RGWL 2, 3
Grace, Patricia Frances 1937- .... **CLC 56**
See also CA 176; CANR 118; CN 7; EWL
3; RGSF 2
Gracian y Morales, Baltasar
1601-1658 .... **LC 15**
Gracq, Julien .... **CLC 11, 48**
See Poirier, Louis
See also CWW 2; DLB 83; GFL 1789 to
the Present
Grade, Chaim 1910-1982 .... **CLC 10**
See also CA 93-96; 107; EWL 3
Graduate of Oxford, A
See Ruskin, John
Grafton, Garth
See Duncan, Sara Jeannette
Grafton, Sue 1940- .... **CLC 163**
See also AAYA 11, 49; BEST 90:3; CA 108;
CANR 31, 55, 111; CMW 4; CPW; CSW;
DA3; DAM POP; DLB 226; FW; MSW
Graham, John
See Phillips, David Graham
Graham, Jorie 1950- .... **CLC 48, 118**
See also CA 111; CANR 63, 118; CP 7;
CWP; DLB 120; EWL 3; PFS 10, 17
Graham, R(obert) B(ontine) Cunninghame
See Cunninghame Graham, Robert
(Gallnigad) Bontine
See also DLB 98, 135, 174; RGEL 2; RGSF
2
Graham, Robert
See Haldeman, Joe (William)
Graham, Tom
See Lewis, (Harry) Sinclair
Graham, W(illiam) S(idney)
1918-1986 .... **CLC 29**
See also BRWS 7; CA 73-76; 118; DLB 20;
RGEL 2
Graham, Winston (Mawdsley)
1910-2003 .... **CLC 23**
See also CA 49-52; 218; CANR 2, 22, 45,
66; CMW 4; CN 7; DLB 77; RHW
Grahame, Kenneth 1859-1932 ...... **TCLC 64,**
136
See also BYA 5; CA 108; 136; CANR 80;
CLR 5; CWRI 5; DA3; DAB; DLB 34,
141, 178; FANT; MAICYA 1, 2; MTCW
2; RGEL 2; SATA 100; TEA; WCH;
YABC 1
Granger, Darius John
See Marlowe, Stephen
Granin, Daniil .... **CLC 59**
Granovsky, Timofei Nikolaevich
1813-1855 .... **NCLC 75**
See also DLB 198
Grant, Skeeter
See Spiegelman, Art
Granville-Barker, Harley
1877-1946 .... **TCLC 2**
See Barker, Harley Granville
See also CA 104; 204; DAM DRAM;
RGEL 2
Granzotto, Gianni
See Granzotto, Giovanni Battista
Granzotto, Giovanni Battista
1914-1985 .... **CLC 70**
See also CA 166
Grass, Guenter (Wilhelm) 1927- ... **CLC 1, 2,**
4, 6, 11, 15, 22, 32, 49, 88; WLC
See also BPFB 2; CA 13-16R; CANR 20,
75, 93; CDWLB 2; DA; DA3; DAB;
DAC; DAM MST, NOV; DLB 75, 124;
EW 13; EWL 3; MTCW 1, 2; RGWL 2,
3; TWA

Gratton, Thomas
See Hulme, T(homas) E(rnest)
Grau, Shirley Ann 1929- .... **CLC 4, 9, 146;**
SSC 15
See also CA 89-92; CANR 22, 69; CN 7;
CSW; DLB 2, 218; INT CA-89-92,
CANR-22; MTCW 1
Gravel, Fern
See Hall, James Norman
Graver, Elizabeth 1964- .... **CLC 70**
See also CA 135; CANR 71, 129
Graves, Richard Perceval
1895-1985 .... **CLC 44**
See also CA 65-68; CANR 9, 26, 51
Graves, Robert (von Ranke)
1895-1985 .. **CLC 1, 2, 6, 11, 39, 44, 45;**
PC 6
See also BPFB 2; BRW 7; BYA 4; CA 5-8R;
117; CANR 5, 36; CDBLB 1914-1945;
DA3; DAB; DAC; DAM MST, POET;
DLB 20, 100, 191; DLBD 18; DLBY
1985; EWL 3; LATS 1; MTCW 1, 2;
NCFS 2; RGEL 2; RHW; SATA 45; TEA
Graves, Valerie
See Bradley, Marion Zimmer
Gray, Alasdair (James) 1934- .... **CLC 41**
See also BRWS 9; CA 126; CANR 47, 69,
106; CN 7; DLB 194, 261; HGG; INT
CA-126; MTCW 1, 2; RGSF 2; SUFW 2
Gray, Amlin 1946- .... **CLC 29**
See also CA 138
Gray, Francine du Plessix 1930- ..... **CLC 22,**
153
See also BEST 90:3; CA 61-64; CAAS 2;
CANR 11, 33, 75, 81; DAM NOV; INT
CANR-11; MTCW 1, 2
Gray, John (Henry) 1866-1934 ...... **TCLC 19**
See also CA 119; 162; RGEL 2
Gray, Simon (James Holliday)
1936- .... **CLC 9, 14, 36**
See also AITN 1; CA 21-24R; CAAS 3;
CANR 32, 69; CD 5; DLB 13; EWL 3;
MTCW 1; RGEL 2
Gray, Spalding 1941-2004 .... **CLC 49, 112;**
DC 7
See also CA 128; 225; CAD; CANR 74;
CD 5; CPW; DAM POP; MTCW 2
Gray, Thomas 1716-1771 .... **LC 4, 40; PC 2;**
WLC
See also BRW 3; CDBLB 1660-1789; DA;
DA3; DAB; DAC; DAM MST; DLB 109;
EXPP; PAB; PFS 9; RGEL 2; TEA; WP
Grayson, David
See Baker, Ray Stannard
Grayson, Richard (A.) 1951- .... **CLC 38**
See also CA 85-88, 210; CAAE 210; CANR
14, 31, 57; DLB 234
Greeley, Andrew M(oran) 1928- .... **CLC 28**
See also BPFB 2; CA 5-8R; CAAS 7;
CANR 7, 43, 69, 104; CMW 4; CPW;
DA3; DAM POP; MTCW 1, 2
Green, Anna Katharine
1846-1935 .... **TCLC 63**
See also CA 112; 159; CMW 4; DLB 202,
221; MSW
Green, Brian
See Card, Orson Scott
Green, Hannah
See Greenberg, Joanne (Goldenberg)
Green, Hannah 1927(?)-1996 .... **CLC 3**
See also CA 73-76; CANR 59, 93; NFS 10
Green, Henry .... **CLC 2, 13, 97**
See Yorke, Henry Vincent
See also BRWS 2; CA 175; DLB 15; EWL
3; RGEL 2
Green, Julian (Hartridge) 1900-1998
See Green, Julien
See also CA 21-24R; 169; CANR 33, 87;
DLB 4, 72; MTCW 1

Green, Julien .... **CLC 3, 11, 77**
See Green, Julian (Hartridge)
See also EWL 3; GFL 1789 to the Present;
MTCW 2
Green, Paul (Eliot) 1894-1981 .... **CLC 25**
See also AITN 1; CA 5-8R; 103; CANR 3;
DAM DRAM; DLB 7, 9, 249; DLBY
1981; RGAL 4
Greenaway, Peter 1942- .... **CLC 159**
See also CA 127
Greenberg, Ivan 1908-1973
See Rahv, Philip
See also CA 85-88
Greenberg, Joanne (Goldenberg)
1932- .... **CLC 7, 30**
See also AAYA 12; CA 5-8R; CANR 14,
32, 69; CN 7; SATA 25; YAW
Greenberg, Richard 1959(?)- .... **CLC 57**
See also CA 138; CAD; CD 5
Greenblatt, Stephen J(ay) 1943- ...... **CLC 70**
See also CA 49-52; CANR 115
Greene, Bette 1934- .... **CLC 30**
See also AAYA 7; BYA 3; CA 53-56; CANR
4; CLR 2; CWRI 5; JRDA; LAIT 4; MAI-
CYA 1, 2; NFS 10; SAAS 16; SATA 8,
102; WYA; YAW
Greene, Gael .... **CLC 8**
See also CA 13-16R; CANR 10
Greene, Graham (Henry)
1904-1991 .... **CLC 1, 3, 6, 9, 14, 18, 27,**
37, 70, 72, 125; SSC 29; WLC
See also AITN 2; BPFB 2; BRWR 2; BRWS
1; BYA 3; CA 13-16R; 133; CANR 35,
61, 131; CBD; CDBLB 1945-1960; CMW
4; DA; DA3; DAB; DAC; DAM MST,
NOV; DLB 13, 15, 77, 100, 162, 201,
204; DLBY 1991; EWL 3; MSW; MTCW
1, 2; NFS 16; RGEL 2; SATA 20; SSFS
14; TEA; WLIT 4
Greene, Robert 1558-1592 .... **LC 41**
See also BRWS 8; DLB 62, 167; IDTP;
RGEL 2; TEA
Greer, Germaine 1939- .... **CLC 131**
See also AITN 1; CA 81-84; CANR 33, 70,
115; FW; MTCW 1, 2
Greer, Richard
See Silverberg, Robert
Gregor, Arthur 1923- .... **CLC 9**
See also CA 25-28R; CAAS 10; CANR 11;
CP 7; SATA 36
Gregor, Lee
See Pohl, Frederik
Gregory, Lady Isabella Augusta (Persse)
1852-1932 .... **TCLC 1**
See also BRW 6; CA 104; 184; DLB 10;
IDTP; RGEL 2
Gregory, J. Dennis
See Williams, John A(lfred)
Grekova, I. .... **CLC 59**
See Ventsel, Elena Sergeevna
See also CWW 2
Grendon, Stephen
See Derleth, August (William)
Grenville, Kate 1950- .... **CLC 61**
See also CA 118; CANR 53, 93
Grenville, Pelham
See Wodehouse, P(elham) G(renville)
Greve, Felix Paul (Berthold Friedrich)
1879-1948
See Grove, Frederick Philip
See also CA 104; 141, 175; CANR 79;
DAC; DAM MST
Greville, Fulke 1554-1628 .... **LC 79**
See also DLB 62, 172; RGEL 2
Grey, Lady Jane 1537-1554 .... **LC 93**
See also DLB 132

Hawthorne, Nathaniel 1804-1864 ... **NCLC 2, 10, 17, 23, 39, 79, 95; SSC 3, 29, 39; WLC**
See also AAYA 18; AMW; AMWC 1; AMWR 1; BPFB 2; BYA 3; CDALB 1640-1865; DA; DA3; DAB; DAC; DAM MST, NOV; DLB 1, 74, 183, 223, 269; EXPN; EXPS; HGG; LAIT 1; NFS 1; RGAL 4; RGSF 2; SSFS 1, 7, 11, 15; SUFW 1; TUS; WCH; YABC 2

Haxton, Josephine Ayres 1921-
See Douglas, Ellen
See also CA 115; CANR 41, 83

Hayaseca y Eizaguirre, Jorge
See Echegaray (y Eizaguirre), Jose (Maria Waldo)

Hayashi, Fumiko 1904-1951 .... **TCLC 27**
See Hayashi Fumiko
See also CA 161

Hayashi Fumiko
See Hayashi, Fumiko
See also DLB 180; EWL 3

Haycraft, Anna (Margaret) 1932-
See Ellis, Alice Thomas
See also CA 122; CANR 85, 90; MTCW 2

Hayden, Robert E(arl) 1913-1980 ..... **BLC 2; CLC 5, 9, 14, 37; PC 6**
See also AFAW 1, 2; AMWS 2; BW 1, 3; CA 69-72; 97-100; CABS 2; CANR 24, 75, 82; CDALB 1941-1968; DA; DAC; DAM MST, MULT, POET; DLB 5, 76; EWL 3; EXPP; MTCW 1, 2; PFS 1; RGAL 4; SATA 19; SATA-Obit 26; WP

Hayek, F(riedrich) A(ugust von)
1899-1992 .... **TCLC 109**
See also CA 93-96; 137; CANR 20; MTCW 1, 2

Hayford, J(oseph) E(phraim) Casely
See Casely-Hayford, J(oseph) E(phraim)

Hayman, Ronald 1932- .... **CLC 44**
See also CA 25-28R; CANR 18, 50, 88; CD 5; DLB 155

Hayne, Paul Hamilton 1830-1886 . **NCLC 94**
See also DLB 3, 64, 79, 248; RGAL 4

Hays, Mary 1760-1843 .... **NCLC 114**
See also DLB 142, 158; RGEL 2

Haywood, Eliza (Fowler)
1693(?)-1756 .... **LC 1, 44**
See also DLB 39; RGEL 2

Hazlitt, William 1778-1830 ...... **NCLC 29, 82**
See also BRW 4; DLB 110, 158; RGEL 2; TEA

Hazzard, Shirley 1931- .... **CLC 18**
See also CA 9-12R; CANR 4, 70, 127; CN 7; DLB 289; DLBY 1982; MTCW 1

Head, Bessie 1937-1986 ...... **BLC 2; CLC 25, 67; SSC 52**
See also AFW; BW 2, 3; CA 29-32R; 119; CANR 25, 82; CDWLB 3; DA3; DAM MULT; DLB 117, 225; EWL 3; EXPS; FW; MTCW 1, 2; RGSF 2; SSFS 5, 13; WLIT 2; WWE 1

Headon, (Nicky) Topper 1956(?)- ..... **CLC 30**

Heaney, Seamus (Justin) 1939- ..... **CLC 5, 7, 14, 25, 37, 74, 91, 171; PC 18; WLCS**
See also BRWR 1; BRWS 2; CA 85-88; CANR 25, 48, 75, 91, 128; CDBLB 1960 to Present; CP 7; DA3; DAB; DAM POET; DLB 40; DLBY 1995; EWL 3; EXPP; MTCW 1, 2; PAB; PFS 2, 5, 8, 17; RGEL 2; TEA; WLIT 4

Hearn, (Patricio) Lafcadio (Tessima Carlos)
1850-1904 .... **TCLC 9**
See also CA 105; 166; DLB 12, 78, 189; HGG; RGAL 4

Hearne, Samuel 1745-1792 .... **LC 95**
See also DLB 99

Hearne, Vicki 1946-2001 .... **CLC 56**
See also CA 139; 201

Hearon, Shelby 1931- .... **CLC 63**
See also AITN 2; AMWS 8; CA 25-28R; CANR 18, 48, 103; CSW

Heat-Moon, William Least .... **CLC 29**
See Trogdon, William (Lewis)
See also AAYA 9

Hebbel, Friedrich 1813-1863 . **DC 21; NCLC 43**
See also CDWLB 2; DAM DRAM; DLB 129; EW 6; RGWL 2, 3

Hebert, Anne 1916-2000 .... **CLC 4, 13, 29**
See also CA 85-88; 187; CANR 69, 126; CCA 1; CWP; CWW 2; DA3; DAC; DAM MST, POET; DLB 68; EWL 3; GFL 1789 to the Present; MTCW 1, 2; PFS 20

Hecht, Anthony (Evan) 1923- ...... **CLC 8, 13, 19**
See also AMWS 10; CA 9-12R; CANR 6, 108; CP 7; DAM POET; DLB 5, 169; EWL 3; PFS 6; WP

Hecht, Ben 1894-1964 ..... **CLC 8; TCLC 101**
See also CA 85-88; DFS 9; DLB 7, 9, 25, 26, 28, 86; FANT; IDFW 3, 4; RGAL 4

Hedayat, Sadeq 1903-1951 .... **TCLC 21**
See also CA 120; EWL 3; RGSF 2

Hegel, Georg Wilhelm Friedrich
1770-1831 .... **NCLC 46**
See also DLB 90; TWA

Heidegger, Martin 1889-1976 .... **CLC 24**
See also CA 81-84; 65-68; CANR 34; DLB 296; MTCW 1, 2

Heidenstam, (Carl Gustaf) Verner von
1859-1940 .... **TCLC 5**
See also CA 104

Heidi Louise
See Erdrich, Louise

Heifner, Jack 1946- .... **CLC 11**
See also CA 105; CANR 47

Heijermans, Herman 1864-1924 .... **TCLC 24**
See also CA 123; EWL 3

Heilbrun, Carolyn G(old)
1926-2003 .... **CLC 25, 173**
See Cross, Amanda
See also CA 45-48; 220; CANR 1, 28, 58, 94; FW

Hein, Christoph 1944- .... **CLC 154**
See also CA 158; CANR 108; CDWLB 2; CWW 2; DLB 124

Heine, Heinrich 1797-1856 .... **NCLC 4, 54; PC 25**
See also CDWLB 2; DLB 90; EW 5; RGWL 2, 3; TWA

Heinemann, Larry (Curtiss) 1944- .. **CLC 50**
See also CA 110; CAAS 21; CANR 31, 81; DLBD 9; INT CANR-31

Heiney, Donald (William) 1921-1993
See Harris, MacDonald
See also CA 1-4R; 142; CANR 3, 58; FANT

Heinlein, Robert A(nson) 1907-1988 . **CLC 1, 3, 8, 14, 26, 55; SSC 55**
See also AAYA 17; BPFB 2; BYA 4, 13; CA 1-4R; 125; CANR 1, 20, 53; CLR 75; CPW; DA3; DAM POP; DLB 8; EXPS; JRDA; LAIT 5; LMFS 2; MAICYA 1, 2; MTCW 1, 2; RGAL 4; SATA 9, 69; SATA-Obit 56; SCFW; SFW 4; SSFS 7; YAW

Helforth, John
See Doolittle, Hilda

Heliodorus fl. 3rd cent. - .... **CMLC 52**

Hellenhofferu, Vojtech Kapristian z
See Hasek, Jaroslav (Matej Frantisek)

Heller, Joseph 1923-1999 . **CLC 1, 3, 5, 8, 11, 36, 63; TCLC 131, 151; WLC**
See also AAYA 24; AITN 1; AMWS 4; BPFB 2; BYA 1; CA 5-8R; CABS 1; CANR 8, 42, 66, 126; CN 7; CPW; DA; DA3; DAB; DAC; DAM MST, NOV, POP; DLB 2, 28, 227; DLBY 1980, 2002; EWL 3; EXPN; INT CANR-8; LAIT 4; MTCW 1, 2; NFS 1; RGAL 4; TUS; YAW

Hellman, Lillian (Florence)
1906-1984 .. **CLC 2, 4, 8, 14, 18, 34, 44, 52; DC 1; TCLC 119**
See also AAYA 47; AITN 1, 2; AMWS 1; CA 13-16R; 112; CAD; CANR 33; CWD; DA3; DAM DRAM; DFS 1, 3, 14; DLB 7, 228; DLBY 1984; EWL 3; FW; LAIT 3; MAWW; MTCW 1, 2; RGAL 4; TUS

Helprin, Mark 1947- .... **CLC 7, 10, 22, 32**
See also CA 81-84; CANR 47, 64, 124; CDALBS; CPW; DA3; DAM NOV, POP; DLBY 1985; FANT; MTCW 1, 2; SUFW 2

Helvetius, Claude-Adrien 1715-1771 .. **LC 26**

Helyar, Jane Penelope Josephine 1933-
See Poole, Josephine
See also CA 21-24R; CANR 10, 26; CWRI 5; SATA 82, 138; SATA-Essay 138

Hemans, Felicia 1793-1835 ...... **NCLC 29, 71**
See also DLB 96; RGEL 2

Hemingway, Ernest (Miller)
1899-1961 .... **CLC 1, 3, 6, 8, 10, 13, 19, 30, 34, 39, 41, 44, 50, 61, 80; SSC 1, 25, 36, 40, 63; TCLC 115; WLC**
See also AAYA 19; AMW; AMWC 1; AMWR 1; BPFB 2; BYA 2, 3, 13, 15; CA 77-80; CANR 34; CDALB 1917-1929; DA; DA3; DAB; DAC; DAM MST, NOV; DLB 4, 9, 102, 210; DLBD 1, 15, 16; DLBY 1981, 1987, 1996, 1998; EWL 3; EXPN; EXPS; LAIT 3, 4; LATS 1; MTCW 1, 2; NFS 1, 5, 6, 14; RGAL 4; RGSF 2; SSFS 17; TUS; WYA

Hempel, Amy 1951- .... **CLC 39**
See also CA 118; 137; CANR 70; DA3; DLB 218; EXPS; MTCW 2; SSFS 2

Henderson, F. C.
See Mencken, H(enry) L(ouis)

Henderson, Sylvia
See Ashton-Warner, Sylvia (Constance)

Henderson, Zenna (Chlarson)
1917-1983 .... **SSC 29**
See also CA 1-4R; 133; CANR 1, 84; DLB 8; SATA 5; SFW 4

Henkin, Joshua .... **CLC 119**
See also CA 161

Henley, Beth .... **CLC 23; DC 6, 14**
See Henley, Elizabeth Becker
See also CABS 3; CAD; CD 5; CSW; CWD; DFS 2; DLBY 1986; FW

Henley, Elizabeth Becker 1952-
See Henley, Beth
See also CA 107; CANR 32, 73; DA3; DAM DRAM, MST; MTCW 1, 2

Henley, William Ernest 1849-1903 .. **TCLC 8**
See also CA 105; DLB 19; RGEL 2

Hennissart, Martha
See Lathen, Emma
See also CA 85-88; CANR 64

Henry VIII 1491-1547 .... **LC 10**
See also DLB 132

Henry, O. ..... **SSC 5, 49; TCLC 1, 19; WLC**
See Porter, William Sydney
See also AAYA 41; AMWS 2; EXPS; RGAL 4; RGSF 2; SSFS 2, 18

Henry, Patrick 1736-1799 .... **LC 25**
See also LAIT 1

Henryson, Robert 1430(?)-1506(?) ...... **LC 20**
See also BRWS 7; DLB 146; RGEL 2

Henschke, Alfred
See Klabund

Henson, Lance 1944- .... **NNAL**
See also CA 146; DLB 175

Hiraoka, Kimitake 1925-1970
See Mishima, Yukio
See also CA 97-100; 29-32R; DA3; DAM DRAM; GLL 1; MTCW 1, 2

Hirsch, E(ric) D(onald), Jr. 1928- .... **CLC 79**
See also CA 25-28R; CANR 27, 51; DLB 67; INT CANR-27; MTCW 1

Hirsch, Edward 1950- .... **CLC 31, 50**
See also CA 104; CANR 20, 42, 102; CP 7; DLB 120

Hitchcock, Alfred (Joseph)
1899-1980 .... **CLC 16**
See also AAYA 22; CA 159; 97-100; SATA 27; SATA-Obit 24

Hitchens, Christopher (Eric)
1949- .... **CLC 157**
See also CA 152; CANR 89

Hitler, Adolf 1889-1945 .... **TCLC 53**
See also CA 117; 147

Hoagland, Edward 1932- .... **CLC 28**
See also ANW; CA 1-4R; CANR 2, 31, 57, 107; CN 7; DLB 6; SATA 51; TCWW 2

Hoban, Russell (Conwell) 1925- ... **CLC 7, 25**
See also BPFB 2; CA 5-8R; CANR 23, 37, 66, 114; CLR 3, 69; CN 7; CWRI 5; DAM NOV; DLB 52; FANT; MAICYA 1, 2; MTCW 1, 2; SATA 1, 40, 78, 136; SFW 4; SUFW 2

Hobbes, Thomas 1588-1679 .... **LC 36**
See also DLB 151, 252, 281; RGEL 2

Hobbs, Perry
See Blackmur, R(ichard) P(almer)

Hobson, Laura Z(ametkin)
1900-1986 .... **CLC 7, 25**
See Field, Peter
See also BPFB 2; CA 17-20R; 118; CANR 55; DLB 28; SATA 52

Hoccleve, Thomas c. 1368-c. 1437 ...... **LC 75**
See also DLB 146; RGEL 2

Hoch, Edward D(entinger) 1930-
See Queen, Ellery
See also CA 29-32R; CANR 11, 27, 51, 97; CMW 4; SFW 4

Hochhuth, Rolf 1931- .... **CLC 4, 11, 18**
See also CA 5-8R; CANR 33, 75; CWW 2; DAM DRAM; DLB 124; EWL 3; MTCW 1, 2

Hochman, Sandra 1936- .... **CLC 3, 8**
See also CA 5-8R; DLB 5

Hochwaelder, Fritz 1911-1986 .... **CLC 36**
See Hochwalder, Fritz
See also CA 29-32R; 120; CANR 42; DAM DRAM; MTCW 1; RGWL 3

Hochwalder, Fritz
See Hochwaelder, Fritz
See also EWL 3; RGWL 2

Hocking, Mary (Eunice) 1921- .... **CLC 13**
See also CA 101; CANR 18, 40

Hodgins, Jack 1938- .... **CLC 23**
See also CA 93-96; CN 7; DLB 60

Hodgson, William Hope
1877(?)-1918 .... **TCLC 13**
See also CA 111; 164; CMW 4; DLB 70, 153, 156, 178; HGG; MTCW 2; SFW 4; SUFW 1

Hoeg, Peter 1957- .... **CLC 95, 156**
See also CA 151; CANR 75; CMW 4; DA3; DLB 214; EWL 3; MTCW 2; NFS 17; RGWL 3; SSFS 18

Hoffman, Alice 1952- .... **CLC 51**
See also AAYA 37; AMWS 10; CA 77-80; CANR 34, 66, 100; CN 7; CPW; DAM NOV; DLB 292; MTCW 1, 2

Hoffman, Daniel (Gerard) 1923- . **CLC 6, 13, 23**
See also CA 1-4R; CANR 4; CP 7; DLB 5

Hoffman, Eva 1945- .... **CLC 182**
See also CA 132

Hoffman, Stanley 1944- .... **CLC 5**
See also CA 77-80

Hoffman, William 1925- .... **CLC 141**
See also CA 21-24R; CANR 9, 103; CSW; DLB 234

Hoffman, William M(oses) 1939- ..... **CLC 40**
See Hoffman, William M.
See also CA 57-60; CANR 11, 71

Hoffmann, E(rnst) T(heodor) A(madeus)
1776-1822 .... **NCLC 2; SSC 13**
See also CDWLB 2; DLB 90; EW 5; RGSF 2; RGWL 2, 3; SATA 27; SUFW 1; WCH

Hofmann, Gert 1931- .... **CLC 54**
See also CA 128; EWL 3

Hofmannsthal, Hugo von 1874-1929 ... **DC 4; TCLC 11**
See also CA 106; 153; CDWLB 2; DAM DRAM; DFS 17; DLB 81, 118; EW 9; EWL 3; RGWL 2, 3

Hogan, Linda 1947- ..... **CLC 73; NNAL; PC 35**
See also AMWS 4; ANW; BYA 12; CA 120; CANR 45, 73, 129; CWP; DAM MULT; DLB 175; SATA 132; TCWW 2

Hogarth, Charles
See Creasey, John

Hogarth, Emmett
See Polonsky, Abraham (Lincoln)

Hogg, James 1770-1835 .... **NCLC 4, 109**
See also DLB 93, 116, 159; HGG; RGEL 2; SUFW 1

Holbach, Paul Henri Thiry Baron
1723-1789 .... **LC 14**

Holberg, Ludvig 1684-1754 .... **LC 6**
See also DLB 300; RGWL 2, 3

Holcroft, Thomas 1745-1809 .... **NCLC 85**
See also DLB 39, 89, 158; RGEL 2

Holden, Ursula 1921- .... **CLC 18**
See also CA 101; CAAS 8; CANR 22

Holderlin, (Johann Christian) Friedrich
1770-1843 .... **NCLC 16; PC 4**
See also CDWLB 2; DLB 90; EW 5; RGWL 2, 3

Holdstock, Robert
See Holdstock, Robert P.

Holdstock, Robert P. 1948- .... **CLC 39**
See also CA 131; CANR 81; DLB 261; FANT; HGG; SFW 4; SUFW 2

Holinshed, Raphael fl. 1580- .... **LC 69**
See also DLB 167; RGEL 2

Holland, Isabelle (Christian)
1920-2002 .... **CLC 21**
See also AAYA 11; CA 21-24R; 205; CAAE 181; CANR 10, 25, 47; CLR 57; CWRI 5; JRDA; LAIT 4; MAICYA 1, 2; SATA 8, 70; SATA-Essay 103; SATA-Obit 132; WYA

Holland, Marcus
See Caldwell, (Janet Miriam) Taylor (Holland)

Hollander, John 1929- .... **CLC 2, 5, 8, 14**
See also CA 1-4R; CANR 1, 52; CP 7; DLB 5; SATA 13

Hollander, Paul
See Silverberg, Robert

Holleran, Andrew 1943(?)- .... **CLC 38**
See Garber, Eric
See also CA 144; GLL 1

Holley, Marietta 1836(?)-1926 .... **TCLC 99**
See also CA 118; DLB 11

Hollinghurst, Alan 1954- .... **CLC 55, 91**
See also CA 114; CN 7; DLB 207; GLL 1

Hollis, Jim
See Summers, Hollis (Spurgeon, Jr.)

Holly, Buddy 1936-1959 .... **TCLC 65**
See also CA 213

Holmes, Gordon
See Shiel, M(atthew) P(hipps)

Holmes, John
See Souster, (Holmes) Raymond

Holmes, John Clellon 1926-1988 ...... **CLC 56**
See also BG 2; CA 9-12R; 125; CANR 4; DLB 16, 237

Holmes, Oliver Wendell, Jr.
1841-1935 .... **TCLC 77**
See also CA 114; 186

Holmes, Oliver Wendell
1809-1894 .... **NCLC 14, 81**
See also AMWS 1; CDALB 1640-1865; DLB 1, 189, 235; EXPP; RGAL 4; SATA 34

Holmes, Raymond
See Souster, (Holmes) Raymond

Holt, Victoria
See Hibbert, Eleanor Alice Burford
See also BPFB 2

Holub, Miroslav 1923-1998 .... **CLC 4**
See also CA 21-24R; 169; CANR 10; CDWLB 4; CWW 2; DLB 232; EWL 3; RGWL 3

Holz, Detlev
See Benjamin, Walter

Homer c. 8th cent. B.C.- .... **CMLC 1, 16, 61; PC 23; WLCS**
See also AW 1; CDWLB 1; DA; DA3; DAB; DAC; DAM MST, POET; DLB 176; EFS 1; LAIT 1; LMFS 1; RGWL 2, 3; TWA; WP

Hongo, Garrett Kaoru 1951- .... **PC 23**
See also CA 133; CAAS 22; CP 7; DLB 120; EWL 3; EXPP; RGAL 4

Honig, Edwin 1919- .... **CLC 33**
See also CA 5-8R; CAAS 8; CANR 4, 45; CP 7; DLB 5

Hood, Hugh (John Blagdon) 1928- . **CLC 15, 28; SSC 42**
See also CA 49-52; CAAS 17; CANR 1, 33, 87; CN 7; DLB 53; RGSF 2

Hood, Thomas 1799-1845 .... **NCLC 16**
See also BRW 4; DLB 96; RGEL 2

Hooker, (Peter) Jeremy 1941- .... **CLC 43**
See also CA 77-80; CANR 22; CP 7; DLB 40

Hooker, Richard 1554-1600 .... **LC 95**
See also BRW 1; DLB 132; RGEL 2

hooks, bell
See Watkins, Gloria Jean

Hope, A(lec) D(erwent) 1907-2000 .... **CLC 3, 51; PC 56**
See also BRWS 7; CA 21-24R; 188; CANR 33, 74; DLB 289; EWL 3; MTCW 1, 2; PFS 8; RGEL 2

Hope, Anthony 1863-1933 .... **TCLC 83**
See also CA 157; DLB 153, 156; RGEL 2; RHW

Hope, Brian
See Creasey, John

Hope, Christopher (David Tully)
1944- .... **CLC 52**
See also AFW; CA 106; CANR 47, 101; CN 7; DLB 225; SATA 62

Hopkins, Gerard Manley
1844-1889 .... **NCLC 17; PC 15; WLC**
See also BRW 5; BRWR 2; CDBLB 1890-1914; DA; DA3; DAB; DAC; DAM MST, POET; DLB 35, 57; EXPP; PAB; RGEL 2; TEA; WP

Hopkins, John (Richard) 1931-1998 .. **CLC 4**
See also CA 85-88; 169; CBD; CD 5

Hopkins, Pauline Elizabeth
1859-1930 .... **BLC 2; TCLC 28**
See also AFAW 2; BW 2, 3; CA 141; CANR 82; DAM MULT; DLB 50

Hopkinson, Francis 1737-1791 .... **LC 25**
See also DLB 31; RGAL 4

Hopley-Woolrich, Cornell George 1903-1968
See Woolrich, Cornell
See also CA 13-14; CANR 58; CAP 1;
CMW 4; DLB 226; MTCW 2

Horace 65B.C.-8B.C. .... **CMLC 39; PC 46**
See also AW 2; CDWLB 1; DLB 211;
RGWL 2, 3

Horatio
See Proust, (Valentin-Louis-George-Eugene)
Marcel

Horgan, Paul (George Vincent
O'Shaughnessy) 1903-1995 .. **CLC 9, 53**
See also BPFB 2; CA 13-16R; 147; CANR
9, 35; DAM NOV; DLB 102, 212; DLBY
1985; INT CANR-9; MTCW 1, 2; SATA
13; SATA-Obit 84; TCWW 2

Horkheimer, Max 1895-1973 .... **TCLC 132**
See also CA 216; 41-44R; DLB 296

Horn, Peter
See Kuttner, Henry

Horne, Frank (Smith) 1899-1974 .... **HR 2**
See also BW 1; CA 125; 53-56; DLB 51;
WP

Horne, Richard Henry Hengist
1802(?)-1884 .... **NCLC 127**
See also DLB 32; SATA 29

Hornem, Horace Esq.
See Byron, George Gordon (Noel)

Horney, Karen (Clementine Theodore
Danielsen) 1885-1952 .... **TCLC 71**
See also CA 114; 165; DLB 246; FW

Hornung, E(rnest) W(illiam)
1866-1921 .... **TCLC 59**
See also CA 108; 160; CMW 4; DLB 70

Horovitz, Israel (Arthur) 1939- .... **CLC 56**
See also CA 33-36R; CAD; CANR 46, 59;
CD 5; DAM DRAM; DLB 7

Horton, George Moses
1797(?)-1883(?) .... **NCLC 87**
See also DLB 50

Horvath, odon von 1901-1938
See von Horvath, Odon
See also EWL 3

Horvath, Oedoen von -1938
See von Horvath, Odon

Horwitz, Julius 1920-1986 .... **CLC 14**
See also CA 9-12R; 119; CANR 12

Hospital, Janette Turner 1942- .... **CLC 42,**
145
See also CA 108; CANR 48; CN 7; DLBY
2002; RGSF 2

Hostos, E. M. de
See Hostos (y Bonilla), Eugenio Maria de

Hostos, Eugenio M. de
See Hostos (y Bonilla), Eugenio Maria de

Hostos, Eugenio Maria
See Hostos (y Bonilla), Eugenio Maria de

Hostos (y Bonilla), Eugenio Maria de
1839-1903 .... **TCLC 24**
See also CA 123; 131; HW 1

Houdini
See Lovecraft, H(oward) P(hillips)

Houellebecq, Michel 1958- .... **CLC 179**
See also CA 185

Hougan, Carolyn 1943- .... **CLC 34**
See also CA 139

Household, Geoffrey (Edward West)
1900-1988 .... **CLC 11**
See also CA 77-80; 126; CANR 58; CMW
4; DLB 87; SATA 14; SATA-Obit 59

Housman, A(lfred) E(dward)
1859-1936 .... **PC 2, 43; TCLC 1, 10;**
WLCS
See also BRW 6; CA 104; 125; DA; DA3;
DAB; DAC; DAM MST, POET; DLB 19,
284; EWL 3; EXPP; MTCW 1, 2; PAB;
PFS 4, 7; RGEL 2; TEA; WP

Housman, Laurence 1865-1959 .... **TCLC 7**
See also CA 106; 155; DLB 10; FANT;
RGEL 2; SATA 25

Houston, Jeanne (Toyo) Wakatsuki
1934- .... **AAL**
See also AAYA 49; CA 103; CAAS 16;
CANR 29, 123; LAIT 4; SATA 78

Howard, Elizabeth Jane 1923- ..... **CLC 7, 29**
See also CA 5-8R; CANR 8, 62; CN 7

Howard, Maureen 1930- .... **CLC 5, 14, 46,**
151
See also CA 53-56; CANR 31, 75; CN 7;
DLBY 1983; INT CANR-31; MTCW 1, 2

Howard, Richard 1929- .... **CLC 7, 10, 47**
See also AITN 1; CA 85-88; CANR 25, 80;
CP 7; DLB 5; INT CANR-25

Howard, Robert E(rvin)
1906-1936 .... **TCLC 8**
See also BPFB 2; BYA 5; CA 105; 157;
FANT; SUFW 1

Howard, Warren F.
See Pohl, Frederik

Howe, Fanny (Quincy) 1940- .... **CLC 47**
See also CA 117, 187; CAAE 187; CAAS
27; CANR 70, 116; CP 7; CWP; SATA-
Brief 52

Howe, Irving 1920-1993 .... **CLC 85**
See also AMWS 6; CA 9-12R; 141; CANR
21, 50; DLB 67; EWL 3; MTCW 1, 2

Howe, Julia Ward 1819-1910 .... **TCLC 21**
See also CA 117; 191; DLB 1, 189, 235;
FW

Howe, Susan 1937- .... **CLC 72, 152; PC 54**
See also AMWS 4; CA 160; CP 7; CWP;
DLB 120; FW; RGAL 4

Howe, Tina 1937- .... **CLC 48**
See also CA 109; CAD; CANR 125; CD 5;
CWD

Howell, James 1594(?)-1666 .... **LC 13**
See also DLB 151

Howells, W. D.
See Howells, William Dean

Howells, William D.
See Howells, William Dean

Howells, William Dean 1837-1920 ... **SSC 36;**
TCLC 7, 17, 41
See also AMW; CA 104; 134; CDALB
1865-1917; DLB 12, 64, 74, 79, 189;
LMFS 1; MTCW 2; RGAL 4; TUS

Howes, Barbara 1914-1996 .... **CLC 15**
See also CA 9-12R; 151; CAAS 3; CANR
53; CP 7; SATA 5

Hrabal, Bohumil 1914-1997 .... **CLC 13, 67**
See also CA 106; 156; CAAS 12; CANR
57; CWW 2; DLB 232; EWL 3; RGSF 2

Hrotsvit of Gandersheim c. 935-c.
1000 .... **CMLC 29**
See also DLB 148

Hsi, Chu 1130-1200 .... **CMLC 42**

Hsun, Lu
See Lu Hsun

Hubbard, L(afayette) Ron(ald)
1911-1986 .... **CLC 43**
See also CA 77-80; 118; CANR 52; CPW;
DA3; DAM POP; FANT; MTCW 2; SFW
4

Huch, Ricarda (Octavia)
1864-1947 .... **TCLC 13**
See also CA 111; 189; DLB 66; EWL 3

Huddle, David 1942- .... **CLC 49**
See also CA 57-60; CAAS 20; CANR 89;
DLB 130

Hudson, Jeffrey
See Crichton, (John) Michael

Hudson, W(illiam) H(enry)
1841-1922 .... **TCLC 29**
See also CA 115; 190; DLB 98, 153, 174;
RGEL 2; SATA 35

Hueffer, Ford Madox
See Ford, Ford Madox

Hughart, Barry 1934- .... **CLC 39**
See also CA 137; FANT; SFW 4; SUFW 2

Hughes, Colin
See Creasey, John

Hughes, David (John) 1930- .... **CLC 48**
See also CA 116; 129; CN 7; DLB 14

Hughes, Edward James
See Hughes, Ted
See also DA3; DAM MST, POET

Hughes, (James Mercer) Langston
1902-1967 ..... **BLC 2; CLC 1, 5, 10, 15,**
35, 44, 108; DC 3; HR 2; PC 1, 53;
SSC 6; WLC
See also AAYA 12; AFAW 1, 2; AMWR 1;
AMWS 1; BW 1, 3; CA 1-4R; 25-28R;
CANR 1, 34, 82; CDALB 1929-1941;
CLR 17; DA; DA3; DAB; DAC; DAM
DRAM, MST, MULT, POET; DFS 6, 18;
DLB 4, 7, 48, 51, 86, 228; EWL 3; EXPP;
EXPS; JRDA; LAIT 3; LMFS 2; MAI-
CYA 1; MTCW 1, 2; PAB; PFS 1, 3, 6,
10, 15; RGAL 4; RGSF 2; SATA 4, 33;
SSFS 4, 7; TUS; WCH; WP; YAW

Hughes, Richard (Arthur Warren)
1900-1976 .... **CLC 1, 11**
See also CA 5-8R; 65-68; CANR 4; DAM
NOV; DLB 15, 161; EWL 3; MTCW 1;
RGEL 2; SATA 8; SATA-Obit 25

Hughes, Ted 1930-1998 . **CLC 2, 4, 9, 14, 37,**
119; PC 7
See Hughes, Edward James
See also BRWC 2; BRWR 2; BRWS 1; CA
1-4R; 171; CANR 1, 33, 66, 108; CLR 3;
CP 7; DAB; DAC; DLB 40, 161; EWL 3;
EXPP; MAICYA 1, 2; MTCW 1, 2; PAB;
PFS 4, 19; RGEL 2; SATA 49; SATA-
Brief 27; SATA-Obit 107; TEA; YAW

Hugo, Richard
See Huch, Ricarda (Octavia)

Hugo, Richard F(ranklin)
1923-1982 .... **CLC 6, 18, 32**
See also AMWS 6; CA 49-52; 108; CANR
3; DAM POET; DLB 5, 206; EWL 3; PFS
17; RGAL 4

Hugo, Victor (Marie) 1802-1885 .... **NCLC 3,**
10, 21; PC 17; WLC
See also AAYA 28; DA; DA3; DAB; DAC;
DAM DRAM, MST, NOV, POET; DLB
119, 192, 217; EFS 2; EW 6; EXPN; GFL
1789 to the Present; LAIT 1, 2; NFS 5;
RGWL 2, 3; SATA 47; TWA

Huidobro, Vicente
See Huidobro Fernandez, Vicente Garcia
See also DLB 283; EWL 3; LAW

Huidobro Fernandez, Vicente Garcia
1893-1948 .... **TCLC 31**
See Huidobro, Vicente
See also CA 131; HW 1

Hulme, Keri 1947- .... **CLC 39, 130**
See also CA 125; CANR 69; CN 7; CP 7;
CWP; EWL 3; FW; INT CA-125

Hulme, T(homas) E(rnest)
1883-1917 .... **TCLC 21**
See also BRWS 6; CA 117; 203; DLB 19

Humboldt, Wilhelm von
1767-1835 .... **NCLC 134**
See also DLB 90

Hume, David 1711-1776 .... **LC 7, 56**
See also BRWS 3; DLB 104, 252; LMFS 1;
TEA

Humphrey, William 1924-1997 .... **CLC 45**
See also AMWS 9; CA 77-80; 160; CANR
68; CN 7; CSW; DLB 6, 212, 234, 278;
TCWW 2

Humphreys, Emyr Owen 1919- .... **CLC 47**
See also CA 5-8R; CANR 3, 24; CN 7;
DLB 15

Jensen, Laura (Linnea) 1948- .... **CLC 37**
See also CA 103

Jerome, Saint 345-420 .... **CMLC 30**
See also RGWL 3

Jerome, Jerome K(lapka)
1859-1927 .... **TCLC 23**
See also CA 119; 177; DLB 10, 34, 135;
RGEL 2

Jerrold, Douglas William
1803-1857 .... **NCLC 2**
See also DLB 158, 159; RGEL 2

Jewett, (Theodora) Sarah Orne
1849-1909 .... **SSC 6, 44; TCLC 1, 22**
See also AMW; AMWC 2; AMWR 2; CA
108; 127; CANR 71; DLB 12, 74, 221;
EXPS; FW; MAWW; NFS 15; RGAL 4;
RGSF 2; SATA 15; SSFS 4

Jewsbury, Geraldine (Endsor)
1812-1880 .... **NCLC 22**
See also DLB 21

Jhabvala, Ruth Prawer 1927- . **CLC 4, 8, 29,**
94, 138
See also BRWS 5; CA 1-4R; CANR 2, 29,
51, 74, 91, 128; CN 7; DAB; DAM NOV;
DLB 139, 194; EWL 3; IDFW 3, 4; INT
CANR-29; MTCW 1, 2; RGSF 2; RGWL
2; RHW; TEA

Jibran, Kahlil
See Gibran, Kahlil

Jibran, Khalil
See Gibran, Kahlil

Jiles, Paulette 1943- .... **CLC 13, 58**
See also CA 101; CANR 70, 124; CWP

Jimenez (Mantecon), Juan Ramon
1881-1958 .... **HLC 1; PC 7; TCLC 4**
See also CA 104; 131; CANR 74; DAM
MULT, POET; DLB 134; EW 9; EWL 3;
HW 1; MTCW 1, 2; RGWL 2, 3

Jimenez, Ramon
See Jimenez (Mantecon), Juan Ramon

Jimenez Mantecon, Juan
See Jimenez (Mantecon), Juan Ramon

Jin, Ha .... **CLC 109**
See Jin, Xuefei
See also CA 152; DLB 244, 292; SSFS 17

Jin, Xuefei 1956-
See Jin, Ha
See also CANR 91, 130; SSFS 17

Joel, Billy .... **CLC 26**
See Joel, William Martin

Joel, William Martin 1949-
See Joel, Billy
See also CA 108

Johann Sigurjonsson 1880-1919 .... **TCLC 27**
See also CA 170; DLB 293; EWL 3

John, Saint 10(?)-100 .... **CMLC 27, 63**

John of Salisbury c. 1115-1180 ..... **CMLC 63**

John of the Cross, St. 1542-1591 .... **LC 18**
See also RGWL 2, 3

John Paul II, Pope 1920- .... **CLC 128**
See also CA 106; 133

Johnson, B(ryan) S(tanley William)
1933-1973 .... **CLC 6, 9**
See also CA 9-12R; 53-56; CANR 9; DLB
14, 40; EWL 3; RGEL 2

Johnson, Benjamin F., of Boone
See Riley, James Whitcomb

Johnson, Charles (Richard) 1948- .... **BLC 2;**
CLC 7, 51, 65, 163
See also AFAW 2; AMWS 6; BW 2, 3; CA
116; CAAS 18; CANR 42, 66, 82, 129;
CN 7; DAM MULT; DLB 33, 278;
MTCW 2; RGAL 4; SSFS 16

Johnson, Charles S(purgeon)
1893-1956 .... **HR 3**
See also BW 1, 3; CA 125; CANR 82; DLB
51, 91

Johnson, Denis 1949- . **CLC 52, 160; SSC 56**
See also CA 117; 121; CANR 71, 99; CN
7; DLB 120

Johnson, Diane 1934- .... **CLC 5, 13, 48**
See also BPFB 2; CA 41-44R; CANR 17,
40, 62, 95; CN 7; DLBY 1980; INT
CANR-17; MTCW 1

Johnson, E. Pauline 1861-1913 .... **NNAL**
See also CA 150; DAC; DAM MULT; DLB
92, 175

Johnson, Eyvind (Olof Verner)
1900-1976 .... **CLC 14**
See also CA 73-76; 69-72; CANR 34, 101;
DLB 259; EW 12; EWL 3

Johnson, Fenton 1888-1958 .... **BLC 2**
See also BW 1; CA 118; 124; DAM MULT;
DLB 45, 50

Johnson, Georgia Douglas (Camp)
1880-1966 .... **HR 3**
See also BW 1; CA 125; DLB 51, 249; WP

Johnson, Helene 1907-1995 .... **HR 3**
See also CA 181; DLB 51; WP

Johnson, J. R.
See James, C(yril) L(ionel) R(obert)

Johnson, James Weldon 1871-1938 .. **BLC 2;**
HR 3; PC 24; TCLC 3, 19
See also AFAW 1, 2; BW 1, 3; CA 104;
125; CANR 82; CDALB 1917-1929; CLR
32; DA3; DAM MULT, POET; DLB 51;
EWL 3; EXPP; LMFS 2; MTCW 1, 2;
PFS 1; RGAL 4; SATA 31; TUS

Johnson, Joyce 1935- .... **CLC 58**
See also BG 3; CA 125; 129; CANR 102

Johnson, Judith (Emlyn) 1936- .... **CLC 7, 15**
See Sherwin, Judith Johnson
See also CA 25-28R; 153; CANR 34

Johnson, Lionel (Pigot)
1867-1902 .... **TCLC 19**
See also CA 117; 209; DLB 19; RGEL 2

Johnson, Marguerite Annie
See Angelou, Maya

Johnson, Mel
See Malzberg, Barry N(athaniel)

Johnson, Pamela Hansford
1912-1981 .... **CLC 1, 7, 27**
See also CA 1-4R; 104; CANR 2, 28; DLB
15; MTCW 1, 2; RGEL 2

Johnson, Paul (Bede) 1928- .... **CLC 147**
See also BEST 89:4; CA 17-20R; CANR
34, 62, 100

Johnson, Robert .... **CLC 70**

Johnson, Robert 1911(?)-1938 .... **TCLC 69**
See also BW 3; CA 174

Johnson, Samuel 1709-1784 .... **LC 15, 52;**
WLC
See also BRW 3; BRWR 1; CDBLB 1660-
1789; DA; DAB; DAC; DAM MST; DLB
39, 95, 104, 142, 213; LMFS 1; RGEL 2;
TEA

Johnson, Uwe 1934-1984 .. **CLC 5, 10, 15, 40**
See also CA 1-4R; 112; CANR 1, 39; CD-
WLB 2; DLB 75; EWL 3; MTCW 1;
RGWL 2, 3

Johnston, Basil H. 1929- .... **NNAL**
See also CA 69-72; CANR 11, 28, 66;
DAC; DAM MULT; DLB 60

Johnston, George (Benson) 1913- .... **CLC 51**
See also CA 1-4R; CANR 5, 20; CP 7; DLB
88

Johnston, Jennifer (Prudence)
1930- .... **CLC 7, 150**
See also CA 85-88; CANR 92; CN 7; DLB
14

Joinville, Jean de 1224(?)-1317 ..... **CMLC 38**

Jolley, (Monica) Elizabeth 1923- ..... **CLC 46;**
SSC 19
See also CA 127; CAAS 13; CANR 59; CN
7; EWL 3; RGSF 2

Jones, Arthur Llewellyn 1863-1947
See Machen, Arthur
See also CA 104; 179; HGG

Jones, D(ouglas) G(ordon) 1929- ..... **CLC 10**
See also CA 29-32R; CANR 13, 90; CP 7;
DLB 53

Jones, David (Michael) 1895-1974 .... **CLC 2,**
4, 7, 13, 42
See also BRW 6; BRWS 7; CA 9-12R; 53-
56; CANR 28; CDBLB 1945-1960; DLB
20, 100; EWL 3; MTCW 1; PAB; RGEL
2

Jones, David Robert 1947-
See Bowie, David
See also CA 103; CANR 104

Jones, Diana Wynne 1934- .... **CLC 26**
See also AAYA 12; BYA 6, 7, 9, 11, 13, 16;
CA 49-52; CANR 4, 26, 56, 120; CLR
23; DLB 161; FANT; JRDA; MAICYA 1,
2; SAAS 7; SATA 9, 70, 108; SFW 4;
SUFW 2; YAW

Jones, Edward P. 1950- .... **CLC 76**
See also BW 2, 3; CA 142; CANR 79; CSW

Jones, Gayl 1949- ...... **BLC 2; CLC 6, 9, 131**
See also AFAW 1, 2; BW 2, 3; CA 77-80;
CANR 27, 66, 122; CN 7; CSW; DA3;
DAM MULT; DLB 33, 278; MTCW 1, 2;
RGAL 4

Jones, James 1921-1977 ...... **CLC 1, 3, 10, 39**
See also AITN 1, 2; AMWS 11; BPFB 2;
CA 1-4R; 69-72; CANR 6; DLB 2, 143;
DLBD 17; DLBY 1998; EWL 3; MTCW
1; RGAL 4

Jones, John J.
See Lovecraft, H(oward) P(hillips)

Jones, LeRoi .... **CLC 1, 2, 3, 5, 10, 14**
See Baraka, Amiri
See also MTCW 2

Jones, Louis B. 1953- .... **CLC 65**
See also CA 141; CANR 73

Jones, Madison (Percy, Jr.) 1925- ...... **CLC 4**
See also CA 13-16R; CAAS 11; CANR 7,
54, 83; CN 7; CSW; DLB 152

Jones, Mervyn 1922- .... **CLC 10, 52**
See also CA 45-48; CAAS 5; CANR 1, 91;
CN 7; MTCW 1

Jones, Mick 1956(?)- .... **CLC 30**

Jones, Nettie (Pearl) 1941- .... **CLC 34**
See also BW 2; CA 137; CAAS 20; CANR
88

Jones, Peter 1802-1856 .... **NNAL**

Jones, Preston 1936-1979 .... **CLC 10**
See also CA 73-76; 89-92; DLB 7

Jones, Robert F(rancis) 1934-2003 .... **CLC 7**
See also CA 49-52; CANR 2, 61, 118

Jones, Rod 1953- .... **CLC 50**
See also CA 128

Jones, Terence Graham Parry
1942- .... **CLC 21**
See Jones, Terry; Monty Python
See also CA 112; 116; CANR 35, 93; INT
CA-116; SATA 127

Jones, Terry
See Jones, Terence Graham Parry
See also SATA 67; SATA-Brief 51

Jones, Thom (Douglas) 1945(?)- ..... **CLC 81;**
SSC 56
See also CA 157; CANR 88; DLB 244

Jong, Erica 1942- .... **CLC 4, 6, 8, 18, 83**
See also AITN 1; AMWS 5; BEST 90:2;
BPFB 2; CA 73-76; CANR 26, 52, 75;
CN 7; CP 7; CPW; DA3; DAM NOV,
POP; DLB 2, 5, 28, 152; FW; INT CANR-
26; MTCW 1, 2

Koestler, Arthur 1905-1983 ... **CLC 1, 3, 6, 8, 15, 33**
See also BRWS 1; CA 1-4R; 109; CANR 1, 33; CDBLB 1945-1960; DLBY 1983; EWL 3; MTCW 1, 2; NFS 19; RGEL 2

Kogawa, Joy Nozomi 1935- ...... **CLC 78, 129**
See also AAYA 47; CA 101; CANR 19, 62, 126; CN 7; CWP; DAC; DAM MST, MULT; FW; MTCW 2; NFS 3; SATA 99

Kohout, Pavel 1928- .... **CLC 13**
See also CA 45-48; CANR 3

Koizumi, Yakumo
See Hearn, (Patricio) Lafcadio (Tessima Carlos)

Kolmar, Gertrud 1894-1943 .... **TCLC 40**
See also CA 167; EWL 3

Komunyakaa, Yusef 1947- .. **BLCS; CLC 86, 94; PC 51**
See also AFAW 2; AMWS 13; CA 147; CANR 83; CP 7; CSW; DLB 120; EWL 3; PFS 5, 20; RGAL 4

Konrad, George
See Konrad, Gyorgy
See also CWW 2

Konrad, Gyorgy 1933- .... **CLC 4, 10, 73**
See Konrad, George
See also CA 85-88; CANR 97; CDWLB 4; CWW 2; DLB 232; EWL 3

Konwicki, Tadeusz 1926- .... **CLC 8, 28, 54, 117**
See also CA 101; CAAS 9; CANR 39, 59; CWW 2; DLB 232; EWL 3; IDFW 3; MTCW 1

Koontz, Dean R(ay) 1945- .... **CLC 78**
See also AAYA 9, 31; BEST 89:3, 90:2; CA 108; CANR 19, 36, 52, 95; CMW 4; CPW; DA3; DAM NOV, POP; DLB 292; HGG; MTCW 1; SATA 92; SFW 4; SUFW 2; YAW

Kopernik, Mikolaj
See Copernicus, Nicolaus

Kopit, Arthur (Lee) 1937- ...... **CLC 1, 18, 33**
See also AITN 1; CA 81-84; CABS 3; CD 5; DAM DRAM; DFS 7, 14; DLB 7; MTCW 1; RGAL 4

Kopitar, Jernej (Bartholomaus)
1780-1844 .... **NCLC 117**

Kops, Bernard 1926- .... **CLC 4**
See also CA 5-8R; CANR 84; CBD; CN 7; CP 7; DLB 13

Kornbluth, C(yril) M. 1923-1958 .... **TCLC 8**
See also CA 105; 160; DLB 8; SFW 4

Korolenko, V. G.
See Korolenko, Vladimir Galaktionovich

Korolenko, Vladimir
See Korolenko, Vladimir Galaktionovich

Korolenko, Vladimir G.
See Korolenko, Vladimir Galaktionovich

Korolenko, Vladimir Galaktionovich
1853-1921 .... **TCLC 22**
See also CA 121; DLB 277

Korzybski, Alfred (Habdank Skarbek)
1879-1950 .... **TCLC 61**
See also CA 123; 160

Kosinski, Jerzy (Nikodem)
1933-1991 .... **CLC 1, 2, 3, 6, 10, 15, 53, 70**
See also AMWS 7; BPFB 2; CA 17-20R; 134; CANR 9, 46; DA3; DAM NOV; DLB 2, 299; DLBY 1982; EWL 3; HGG; MTCW 1, 2; NFS 12; RGAL 4; TUS

Kostelanetz, Richard (Cory) 1940- .. **CLC 28**
See also CA 13-16R; CAAS 8; CANR 38, 77; CN 7; CP 7

Kostrowitzki, Wilhelm Apollinaris de
1880-1918
See Apollinaire, Guillaume
See also CA 104

Kotlowitz, Robert 1924- .... **CLC 4**
See also CA 33-36R; CANR 36

Kotzebue, August (Friedrich Ferdinand) von
1761-1819 .... **NCLC 25**
See also DLB 94

Kotzwinkle, William 1938- ..... **CLC 5, 14, 35**
See also BPFB 2; CA 45-48; CANR 3, 44, 84, 129; CLR 6; DLB 173; FANT; MAICYA 1, 2; SATA 24, 70, 146; SFW 4; SUFW 2; YAW

Kowna, Stancy
See Szymborska, Wislawa

Kozol, Jonathan 1936- .... **CLC 17**
See also AAYA 46; CA 61-64; CANR 16, 45, 96

Kozoll, Michael 1940(?)- .... **CLC 35**

Kramer, Kathryn 19(?)- .... **CLC 34**

Kramer, Larry 1935- .... **CLC 42; DC 8**
See also CA 124; 126; CANR 60; DAM POP; DLB 249; GLL 1

Krasicki, Ignacy 1735-1801 .... **NCLC 8**

Krasinski, Zygmunt 1812-1859 .... **NCLC 4**
See also RGWL 2, 3

Kraus, Karl 1874-1936 .... **TCLC 5**
See also CA 104; 216; DLB 118; EWL 3

Kreve (Mickevicius), Vincas
1882-1954 .... **TCLC 27**
See also CA 170; DLB 220; EWL 3

Kristeva, Julia 1941- .... **CLC 77, 140**
See also CA 154; CANR 99; DLB 242; EWL 3; FW; LMFS 2

Kristofferson, Kris 1936- .... **CLC 26**
See also CA 104

Krizanc, John 1956- .... **CLC 57**
See also CA 187

Krleza, Miroslav 1893-1981 .... **CLC 8, 114**
See also CA 97-100; 105; CANR 50; CDWLB 4; DLB 147; EW 11; RGWL 2, 3

Kroetsch, Robert 1927- .. **CLC 5, 23, 57, 132**
See also CA 17-20R; CANR 8, 38; CCA 1; CN 7; CP 7; DAC; DAM POET; DLB 53; MTCW 1

Kroetz, Franz
See Kroetz, Franz Xaver

Kroetz, Franz Xaver 1946- .... **CLC 41**
See also CA 130; EWL 3

Kroker, Arthur (W.) 1945- .... **CLC 77**
See also CA 161

Kropotkin, Peter (Aleksieevich)
1842-1921 .... **TCLC 36**
See Kropotkin, Petr Alekseevich
See also CA 119; 219

Kropotkin, Petr Alekseevich
See Kropotkin, Peter (Aleksieevich)
See also DLB 277

Krotkov, Yuri 1917-1981 .... **CLC 19**
See also CA 102

Krumb
See Crumb, R(obert)

Krumgold, Joseph (Quincy)
1908-1980 .... **CLC 12**
See also BYA 1, 2; CA 9-12R; 101; CANR 7; MAICYA 1, 2; SATA 1, 48; SATA-Obit 23; YAW

Krumwitz
See Crumb, R(obert)

Krutch, Joseph Wood 1893-1970 ..... **CLC 24**
See also ANW; CA 1-4R; 25-28R; CANR 4; DLB 63, 206, 275

Krutzch, Gus
See Eliot, T(homas) S(tearns)

Krylov, Ivan Andreevich
1768(?)-1844 .... **NCLC 1**
See also DLB 150

Kubin, Alfred (Leopold Isidor)
1877-1959 .... **TCLC 23**
See also CA 112; 149; CANR 104; DLB 81

Kubrick, Stanley 1928-1999 .... **CLC 16; TCLC 112**
See also AAYA 30; CA 81-84; 177; CANR 33; DLB 26

Kumin, Maxine (Winokur) 1925- ..... **CLC 5, 13, 28, 164; PC 15**
See also AITN 2; AMWS 4; ANW; CA 1-4R; CAAS 8; CANR 1, 21, 69, 115; CP 7; CWP; DA3; DAM POET; DLB 5; EWL 3; EXPP; MTCW 1, 2; PAB; PFS 18; SATA 12

Kundera, Milan 1929- . **CLC 4, 9, 19, 32, 68, 115, 135; SSC 24**
See also AAYA 2; BPFB 2; CA 85-88; CANR 19, 52, 74; CDWLB 4; CWW 2; DA3; DAM NOV; DLB 232; EW 13; EWL 3; MTCW 1, 2; NFS 18; RGSF 2; RGWL 3; SSFS 10

Kunene, Mazisi (Raymond) 1930- ... **CLC 85**
See also BW 1, 3; CA 125; CANR 81; CP 7; DLB 117

Kung, Hans .... **CLC 130**
See Kung, Hans

Kung, Hans 1928-
See Kung, Hans
See also CA 53-56; CANR 66; MTCW 1, 2

Kunikida Doppo 1869(?)-1908
See Doppo, Kunikida
See also DLB 180; EWL 3

Kunitz, Stanley (Jasspon) 1905- .. **CLC 6, 11, 14, 148; PC 19**
See also AMWS 3; CA 41-44R; CANR 26, 57, 98; CP 7; DA3; DLB 48; INT CANR-26; MTCW 1, 2; PFS 11; RGAL 4

Kunze, Reiner 1933- .... **CLC 10**
See also CA 93-96; CWW 2; DLB 75; EWL 3

Kuprin, Aleksander Ivanovich
1870-1938 .... **TCLC 5**
See Kuprin, Aleksandr Ivanovich; Kuprin, Alexandr Ivanovich
See also CA 104; 182

Kuprin, Aleksandr Ivanovich
See Kuprin, Aleksander Ivanovich
See also DLB 295

Kuprin, Alexandr Ivanovich
See Kuprin, Aleksander Ivanovich
See also EWL 3

Kureishi, Hanif 1954(?)- .... **CLC 64, 135**
See also CA 139; CANR 113; CBD; CD 5; CN 7; DLB 194, 245; GLL 2; IDFW 4; WLIT 4; WWE 1

Kurosawa, Akira 1910-1998 ..... **CLC 16, 119**
See also AAYA 11; CA 101; 170; CANR 46; DAM MULT

Kushner, Tony 1956(?)- .... **CLC 81; DC 10**
See also AMWS 9; CA 144; CAD; CANR 74, 130; CD 5; DA3; DAM DRAM; DFS 5; DLB 228; EWL 3; GLL 1; LAIT 5; MTCW 2; RGAL 4

Kuttner, Henry 1915-1958 .... **TCLC 10**
See also CA 107; 157; DLB 8; FANT; SCFW 2; SFW 4

Kutty, Madhavi
See Das, Kamala

Kuzma, Greg 1944- .... **CLC 7**
See also CA 33-36R; CANR 70

Kuzmin, Mikhail (Alekseevich)
1872(?)-1936 .... **TCLC 40**
See also CA 170; DLB 295; EWL 3

Kyd, Thomas 1558-1594 .... **DC 3; LC 22**
See also BRW 1; DAM DRAM; DLB 62; IDTP; LMFS 1; RGEL 2; TEA; WLIT 3

Kyprianos, Iossif
See Samarakis, Antonis

L. S.
See Stephen, Sir Leslie

Laȝamon
See Layamon
See also DLB 146
Labrunie, Gerard
See Nerval, Gerard de
La Bruyere, Jean de 1645-1696 .... **LC 17**
See also DLB 268; EW 3; GFL Beginnings to 1789
Lacan, Jacques (Marie Emile)
1901-1981 .... **CLC 75**
See also CA 121; 104; DLB 296; EWL 3; TWA
Laclos, Pierre Ambroise Francois
1741-1803 .... **NCLC 4, 87**
See also EW 4; GFL Beginnings to 1789; RGWL 2, 3
Lacolere, Francois
See Aragon, Louis
La Colere, Francois
See Aragon, Louis
La Deshabilleuse
See Simenon, Georges (Jacques Christian)
Lady Gregory
See Gregory, Lady Isabella Augusta (Persse)
Lady of Quality, A
See Bagnold, Enid
La Fayette, Marie-(Madelaine Pioche de la Vergne) 1634-1693 .... **LC 2**
See Lafayette, Marie-Madeleine
See also GFL Beginnings to 1789; RGWL 2, 3
Lafayette, Marie-Madeleine
See La Fayette, Marie-(Madelaine Pioche de la Vergne)
See also DLB 268
Lafayette, Rene
See Hubbard, L(afayette) Ron(ald)
La Flesche, Francis 1857(?)-1932 ...... **NNAL**
See also CA 144; CANR 83; DLB 175
La Fontaine, Jean de 1621-1695 .... **LC 50**
See also DLB 268; EW 3; GFL Beginnings to 1789; MAICYA 1, 2; RGWL 2, 3; SATA 18
Laforgue, Jules 1860-1887 . **NCLC 5, 53; PC 14; SSC 20**
See also DLB 217; EW 7; GFL 1789 to the Present; RGWL 2, 3
Lagerkvist, Paer (Fabian)
1891-1974 ..... **CLC 7, 10, 13, 54; TCLC 144**
See Lagerkvist, Par
See also CA 85-88; 49-52; DA3; DAM DRAM, NOV; MTCW 1, 2; TWA
Lagerkvist, Par .... **SSC 12**
See Lagerkvist, Paer (Fabian)
See also DLB 259; EW 10; EWL 3; MTCW 2; RGSF 2; RGWL 2, 3
Lagerloef, Selma (Ottiliana Lovisa)
1858-1940 .... **TCLC 4, 36**
See Lagerlof, Selma (Ottiliana Lovisa)
See also CA 108; MTCW 2; SATA 15
Lagerlof, Selma (Ottiliana Lovisa)
See Lagerloef, Selma (Ottiliana Lovisa)
See also CLR 7; SATA 15
La Guma, (Justin) Alex(ander)
1925-1985 . **BLCS; CLC 19; TCLC 140**
See also AFW; BW 1, 3; CA 49-52; 118; CANR 25, 81; CDWLB 3; DAM NOV; DLB 117, 225; EWL 3; MTCW 1, 2; WLIT 2; WWE 1
Laidlaw, A. K.
See Grieve, C(hristopher) M(urray)
Lainez, Manuel Mujica
See Mujica Lainez, Manuel
See also HW 1
Laing, R(onald) D(avid) 1927-1989 . **CLC 95**
See also CA 107; 129; CANR 34; MTCW 1
Laishley, Alex
See Booth, Martin

Lamartine, Alphonse (Marie Louis Prat) de
1790-1869 .... **NCLC 11; PC 16**
See also DAM POET; DLB 217; GFL 1789 to the Present; RGWL 2, 3
Lamb, Charles 1775-1834 ..... **NCLC 10, 113; WLC**
See also BRW 4; CDBLB 1789-1832; DA; DAB; DAC; DAM MST; DLB 93, 107, 163; RGEL 2; SATA 17; TEA
Lamb, Lady Caroline 1785-1828 ... **NCLC 38**
See also DLB 116
Lamb, Mary Ann 1764-1847 .... **NCLC 125**
See also DLB 163; SATA 17
Lame Deer 1903(?)-1976 .... **NNAL**
See also CA 69-72
Lamming, George (William) 1927- ... **BLC 2; CLC 2, 4, 66, 144**
See also BW 2, 3; CA 85-88; CANR 26, 76; CDWLB 3; CN 7; DAM MULT; DLB 125; EWL 3; MTCW 1, 2; NFS 15; RGEL 2
L'Amour, Louis (Dearborn)
1908-1988 .... **CLC 25, 55**
See Burns, Tex; Mayo, Jim
See also AAYA 16; AITN 2; BEST 89:2; BPFB 2; CA 1-4R; 125; CANR 3, 25, 40; CPW; DA3; DAM NOV, POP; DLB 206; DLBY 1980; MTCW 1, 2; RGAL 4
Lampedusa, Giuseppe (Tomasi) di
.... **TCLC 13**
See Tomasi di Lampedusa, Giuseppe
See also CA 164; EW 11; MTCW 2; RGWL 2, 3
Lampman, Archibald 1861-1899 ... **NCLC 25**
See also DLB 92; RGEL 2; TWA
Lancaster, Bruce 1896-1963 .... **CLC 36**
See also CA 9-10; CANR 70; CAP 1; SATA 9
Lanchester, John 1962- .... **CLC 99**
See also CA 194; DLB 267
Landau, Mark Alexandrovich
See Aldanov, Mark (Alexandrovich)
Landau-Aldanov, Mark Alexandrovich
See Aldanov, Mark (Alexandrovich)
Landis, Jerry
See Simon, Paul (Frederick)
Landis, John 1950- .... **CLC 26**
See also CA 112; 122; CANR 128
Landolfi, Tommaso 1908-1979 .... **CLC 11, 49**
See also CA 127; 117; DLB 177; EWL 3
Landon, Letitia Elizabeth
1802-1838 .... **NCLC 15**
See also DLB 96
Landor, Walter Savage
1775-1864 .... **NCLC 14**
See also BRW 4; DLB 93, 107; RGEL 2
Landwirth, Heinz 1927-
See Lind, Jakov
See also CA 9-12R; CANR 7
Lane, Patrick 1939- .... **CLC 25**
See also CA 97-100; CANR 54; CP 7; DAM POET; DLB 53; INT CA-97-100
Lang, Andrew 1844-1912 .... **TCLC 16**
See also CA 114; 137; CANR 85; DLB 98, 141, 184; FANT; MAICYA 1, 2; RGEL 2; SATA 16; WCH
Lang, Fritz 1890-1976 .... **CLC 20, 103**
See also CA 77-80; 69-72; CANR 30
Lange, John
See Crichton, (John) Michael
Langer, Elinor 1939- .... **CLC 34**
See also CA 121
Langland, William 1332(?)-1400(?) ..... **LC 19**
See also BRW 1; DA; DAB; DAC; DAM MST, POET; DLB 146; RGEL 2; TEA; WLIT 3
Langstaff, Launcelot
See Irving, Washington

Lanier, Sidney 1842-1881 . **NCLC 6, 118; PC 50**
See also AMWS 1; DAM POET; DLB 64; DLBD 13; EXPP; MAICYA 1; PFS 14; RGAL 4; SATA 18
Lanyer, Aemilia 1569-1645 ...... **LC 10, 30, 83**
See also DLB 121
Lao Tzu c. 6th cent. B.C.-3rd cent. B.C. .... **CMLC 7**
Lao-Tzu
See Lao Tzu
Lapine, James (Elliot) 1949- .... **CLC 39**
See also CA 123; 130; CANR 54, 128; INT CA-130
Larbaud, Valery (Nicolas)
1881-1957 .... **TCLC 9**
See also CA 106; 152; EWL 3; GFL 1789 to the Present
Lardner, Ring
See Lardner, Ring(gold) W(ilmer)
See also BPFB 2; CDALB 1917-1929; DLB 11, 25, 86, 171; DLBD 16; RGAL 4; RGSF 2
Lardner, Ring W., Jr.
See Lardner, Ring(gold) W(ilmer)
Lardner, Ring(gold) W(ilmer)
1885-1933 .... **SSC 32; TCLC 2, 14**
See Lardner, Ring
See also AMW; CA 104; 131; MTCW 1, 2; TUS
Laredo, Betty
See Codrescu, Andrei
Larkin, Maia
See Wojciechowska, Maia (Teresa)
Larkin, Philip (Arthur) 1922-1985 ... **CLC 3, 5, 8, 9, 13, 18, 33, 39, 64; PC 21**
See also BRWS 1; CA 5-8R; 117; CANR 24, 62; CDBLB 1960 to Present; DA3; DAB; DAM MST, POET; DLB 27; EWL 3; MTCW 1, 2; PFS 3, 4, 12; RGEL 2
La Roche, Sophie von
1730-1807 .... **NCLC 121**
See also DLB 94
Larra (y Sanchez de Castro), Mariano Jose de 1809-1837 .... **NCLC 17, 130**
Larsen, Eric 1941- .... **CLC 55**
See also CA 132
Larsen, Nella 1893(?)-1963 .... **BLC 2; CLC 37; HR 3**
See also AFAW 1, 2; BW 1; CA 125; CANR 83; DAM MULT; DLB 51; FW; LATS 1; LMFS 2
Larson, Charles R(aymond) 1938- ... **CLC 31**
See also CA 53-56; CANR 4, 121
Larson, Jonathan 1961-1996 .... **CLC 99**
See also AAYA 28; CA 156
La Sale, Antoine de c. 1386-1460(?) . **LC 104**
See also DLB 208
Las Casas, Bartolome de
1474-1566 .... **HLCS; LC 31**
See Casas, Bartolome de las
See also LAW
Lasch, Christopher 1932-1994 .... **CLC 102**
See also CA 73-76; 144; CANR 25, 118; DLB 246; MTCW 1, 2
Lasker-Schueler, Else 1869-1945 ... **TCLC 57**
See Lasker-Schuler, Else
See also CA 183; DLB 66, 124
Lasker-Schuler, Else
See Lasker-Schueler, Else
See also EWL 3
Laski, Harold J(oseph) 1893-1950 . **TCLC 79**
See also CA 188
Latham, Jean Lee 1902-1995 .... **CLC 12**
See also AITN 1; BYA 1; CA 5-8R; CANR 7, 84; CLR 50; MAICYA 1, 2; SATA 2, 68; YAW
Latham, Mavis
See Clark, Mavis Thorpe

Lathen, Emma .... **CLC 2**
  See Hennissart, Martha; Latsis, Mary J(ane)
  See also BPFB 2; CMW 4
Lathrop, Francis
  See Leiber, Fritz (Reuter, Jr.)
Latsis, Mary J(ane) 1927(?)-1997
  See Lathen, Emma
  See also CA 85-88; 162; CMW 4
Lattany, Kristin
  See Lattany, Kristin (Elaine Eggleston) Hunter
Lattany, Kristin (Elaine Eggleston) Hunter 1931- .... **CLC 35**
  See also AITN 1; BW 1; BYA 3; CA 13-16R; CANR 13, 108; CLR 3; CN 7; DLB 33; INT CANR-13; MAICYA 1, 2; SAAS 10; SATA 12, 132; YAW
Lattimore, Richmond (Alexander) 1906-1984 .... **CLC 3**
  See also CA 1-4R; 112; CANR 1
Laughlin, James 1914-1997 .... **CLC 49**
  See also CA 21-24R; 162; CAAS 22; CANR 9, 47; CP 7; DLB 48; DLBY 1996, 1997
Laurence, (Jean) Margaret (Wemyss) 1926-1987 . **CLC 3, 6, 13, 50, 62; SSC 7**
  See also BYA 13; CA 5-8R; 121; CANR 33; DAC; DAM MST; DLB 53; EWL 3; FW; MTCW 1, 2; NFS 11; RGEL 2; RGSF 2; SATA-Obit 50; TCWW 2
Laurent, Antoine 1952- .... **CLC 50**
Lauscher, Hermann
  See Hesse, Hermann
Lautreamont 1846-1870 .. **NCLC 12; SSC 14**
  See Lautreamont, Isidore Lucien Ducasse
  See also GFL 1789 to the Present; RGWL 2, 3
Lautreamont, Isidore Lucien Ducasse
  See Lautreamont
  See also DLB 217
Lavater, Johann Kaspar 1741-1801 .... **NCLC 142**
  See also DLB 97
Laverty, Donald
  See Blish, James (Benjamin)
Lavin, Mary 1912-1996 . **CLC 4, 18, 99; SSC 4, 67**
  See also CA 9-12R; 151; CANR 33; CN 7; DLB 15; FW; MTCW 1; RGEL 2; RGSF 2
Lavond, Paul Dennis
  See Kornbluth, C(yril) M.; Pohl, Frederik
Lawler, Ray
  See Lawler, Raymond Evenor
  See also DLB 289
Lawler, Raymond Evenor 1922- .... **CLC 58**
  See Lawler, Ray
  See also CA 103; CD 5; RGEL 2
Lawrence, D(avid) H(erbert Richards) 1885-1930 .... **PC 54; SSC 4, 19, 73; TCLC 2, 9, 16, 33, 48, 61, 93; WLC**
  See Chambers, Jessie
  See also BPFB 2; BRW 7; BRWR 2; CA 104; 121; CANR 131; CDBLB 1914-1945; DA; DA3; DAB; DAC; DAM MST, NOV, POET; DLB 10, 19, 36, 98, 162, 195; EWL 3; EXPP; EXPS; LAIT 2, 3; MTCW 1, 2; NFS 18; PFS 6; RGEL 2; RGSF 2; SSFS 2, 6; TEA; WLIT 4; WP
Lawrence, T(homas) E(dward) 1888-1935 .... **TCLC 18**
  See Dale, Colin
  See also BRWS 2; CA 115; 167; DLB 195
Lawrence of Arabia
  See Lawrence, T(homas) E(dward)
Lawson, Henry (Archibald Hertzberg) 1867-1922 .... **SSC 18; TCLC 27**
  See also CA 120; 181; DLB 230; RGEL 2; RGSF 2

Lawton, Dennis
  See Faust, Frederick (Schiller)
Layamon fl. c. 1200- .... **CMLC 10**
  See Laȝamon
  See also DLB 146; RGEL 2
Laye, Camara 1928-1980 ..... **BLC 2; CLC 4, 38**
  See Camara Laye
  See also AFW; BW 1; CA 85-88; 97-100; CANR 25; DAM MULT; MTCW 1, 2; WLIT 2
Layton, Irving (Peter) 1912- .... **CLC 2, 15, 164**
  See also CA 1-4R; CANR 2, 33, 43, 66, 129; CP 7; DAC; DAM MST, POET; DLB 88; EWL 3; MTCW 1, 2; PFS 12; RGEL 2
Lazarus, Emma 1849-1887 ...... **NCLC 8, 109**
Lazarus, Felix
  See Cable, George Washington
Lazarus, Henry
  See Slavitt, David R(ytman)
Lea, Joan
  See Neufeld, John (Arthur)
Leacock, Stephen (Butler) 1869-1944 .... **SSC 39; TCLC 2**
  See also CA 104; 141; CANR 80; DAC; DAM MST; DLB 92; EWL 3; MTCW 2; RGEL 2; RGSF 2
Lead, Jane Ward 1623-1704 .... **LC 72**
  See also DLB 131
Leapor, Mary 1722-1746 .... **LC 80**
  See also DLB 109
Lear, Edward 1812-1888 .... **NCLC 3**
  See also AAYA 48; BRW 5; CLR 1, 75; DLB 32, 163, 166; MAICYA 1, 2; RGEL 2; SATA 18, 100; WCH; WP
Lear, Norman (Milton) 1922- .... **CLC 12**
  See also CA 73-76
Leautaud, Paul 1872-1956 .... **TCLC 83**
  See also CA 203; DLB 65; GFL 1789 to the Present
Leavis, F(rank) R(aymond) 1895-1978 .... **CLC 24**
  See also BRW 7; CA 21-24R; 77-80; CANR 44; DLB 242; EWL 3; MTCW 1, 2; RGEL 2
Leavitt, David 1961- .... **CLC 34**
  See also CA 116; 122; CANR 50, 62, 101; CPW; DA3; DAM POP; DLB 130; GLL 1; INT CA-122; MTCW 2
Leblanc, Maurice (Marie Emile) 1864-1941 .... **TCLC 49**
  See also CA 110; CMW 4
Lebowitz, Fran(ces Ann) 1951(?)- ... **CLC 11, 36**
  See also CA 81-84; CANR 14, 60, 70; INT CANR-14; MTCW 1
Lebrecht, Peter
  See Tieck, (Johann) Ludwig
le Carre, John .... **CLC 3, 5, 9, 15, 28**
  See Cornwell, David (John Moore)
  See also AAYA 42; BEST 89:4; BPFB 2; BRWS 2; CDBLB 1960 to Present; CMW 4; CN 7; CPW; DLB 87; EWL 3; MSW; MTCW 2; RGEL 2; TEA
Le Clezio, J(ean) M(arie) G(ustave) 1940- .... **CLC 31, 155**
  See also CA 116; 128; DLB 83; EWL 3; GFL 1789 to the Present; RGSF 2
Leconte de Lisle, Charles-Marie-Rene 1818-1894 .... **NCLC 29**
  See also DLB 217; EW 6; GFL 1789 to the Present
Le Coq, Monsieur
  See Simenon, Georges (Jacques Christian)

Leduc, Violette 1907-1972 .... **CLC 22**
  See also CA 13-14; 33-36R; CANR 69; CAP 1; EWL 3; GFL 1789 to the Present; GLL 1
Ledwidge, Francis 1887(?)-1917 .... **TCLC 23**
  See also CA 123; 203; DLB 20
Lee, Andrea 1953- .... **BLC 2; CLC 36**
  See also BW 1, 3; CA 125; CANR 82; DAM MULT
Lee, Andrew
  See Auchincloss, Louis (Stanton)
Lee, Chang-rae 1965- .... **CLC 91**
  See also CA 148; CANR 89; LATS 1
Lee, Don L. .... **CLC 2**
  See Madhubuti, Haki R.
Lee, George W(ashington) 1894-1976 .... **BLC 2; CLC 52**
  See also BW 1; CA 125; CANR 83; DAM MULT; DLB 51
Lee, (Nelle) Harper 1926- .... **CLC 12, 60; WLC**
  See also AAYA 13; AMWS 8; BPFB 2; BYA 3; CA 13-16R; CANR 51, 128; CDALB 1941-1968; CSW; DA; DA3; DAB; DAC; DAM MST, NOV; DLB 6; EXPN; LAIT 3; MTCW 1, 2; NFS 2; SATA 11; WYA; YAW
Lee, Helen Elaine 1959(?)- .... **CLC 86**
  See also CA 148
Lee, John .... **CLC 70**
Lee, Julian
  See Latham, Jean Lee
Lee, Larry
  See Lee, Lawrence
Lee, Laurie 1914-1997 .... **CLC 90**
  See also CA 77-80; 158; CANR 33, 73; CP 7; CPW; DAB; DAM POP; DLB 27; MTCW 1; RGEL 2
Lee, Lawrence 1941-1990 .... **CLC 34**
  See also CA 131; CANR 43
Lee, Li-Young 1957- .... **CLC 164; PC 24**
  See also CA 153; CANR 118; CP 7; DLB 165; LMFS 2; PFS 11, 15, 17
Lee, Manfred B(ennington) 1905-1971 .... **CLC 11**
  See Queen, Ellery
  See also CA 1-4R; 29-32R; CANR 2; CMW 4; DLB 137
Lee, Nathaniel 1645(?)-1692 .... **LC 103**
  See also DLB 80; RGEL 2
Lee, Shelton Jackson 1957(?)- .. **BLCS; CLC 105**
  See Lee, Spike
  See also BW 2, 3; CA 125; CANR 42; DAM MULT
Lee, Spike
  See Lee, Shelton Jackson
  See also AAYA 4, 29
Lee, Stan 1922- .... **CLC 17**
  See also AAYA 5, 49; CA 108; 111; CANR 129; INT CA-111
Lee, Tanith 1947- .... **CLC 46**
  See also AAYA 15; CA 37-40R; CANR 53, 102; DLB 261; FANT; SATA 8, 88, 134; SFW 4; SUFW 1, 2; YAW
Lee, Vernon .... **SSC 33; TCLC 5**
  See Paget, Violet
  See also DLB 57, 153, 156, 174, 178; GLL 1; SUFW 1
Lee, William
  See Burroughs, William S(eward)
  See also GLL 1
Lee, Willy
  See Burroughs, William S(eward)
  See also GLL 1
Lee-Hamilton, Eugene (Jacob) 1845-1907 .... **TCLC 22**
  See also CA 117

Lynch, David (Keith) 1946- ...... **CLC 66, 162**
See also AAYA 55; CA 124; 129; CANR 111

Lynch, James
See Andreyev, Leonid (Nikolaevich)

Lyndsay, Sir David 1485-1555 .... **LC 20**
See also RGEL 2

Lynn, Kenneth S(chuyler)
1923-2001 .... **CLC 50**
See also CA 1-4R; 196; CANR 3, 27, 65

Lynx
See West, Rebecca

Lyons, Marcus
See Blish, James (Benjamin)

Lyotard, Jean-Francois
1924-1998 .... **TCLC 103**
See also DLB 242; EWL 3

Lyre, Pinchbeck
See Sassoon, Siegfried (Lorraine)

Lytle, Andrew (Nelson) 1902-1995 ... **CLC 22**
See also CA 9-12R; 150; CANR 70; CN 7; CSW; DLB 6; DLBY 1995; RGAL 4; RHW

Lyttelton, George 1709-1773 .... **LC 10**
See also RGEL 2

Lytton of Knebworth, Baron
See Bulwer-Lytton, Edward (George Earle Lytton)

Maas, Peter 1929-2001 .... **CLC 29**
See also CA 93-96; 201; INT CA-93-96; MTCW 2

Macaulay, Catherine 1731-1791 .... **LC 64**
See also DLB 104

Macaulay, (Emilie) Rose
1881(?)-1958 .... **TCLC 7, 44**
See also CA 104; DLB 36; EWL 3; RGEL 2; RHW

Macaulay, Thomas Babington
1800-1859 .... **NCLC 42**
See also BRW 4; CDBLB 1832-1890; DLB 32, 55; RGEL 2

MacBeth, George (Mann)
1932-1992 .... **CLC 2, 5, 9**
See also CA 25-28R; 136; CANR 61, 66; DLB 40; MTCW 1; PFS 8; SATA 4; SATA-Obit 70

MacCaig, Norman (Alexander)
1910-1996 .... **CLC 36**
See also BRWS 6; CA 9-12R; CANR 3, 34; CP 7; DAB; DAM POET; DLB 27; EWL 3; RGEL 2

MacCarthy, Sir (Charles Otto) Desmond
1877-1952 .... **TCLC 36**
See also CA 167

MacDiarmid, Hugh .... **CLC 2, 4, 11, 19, 63; PC 9**
See Grieve, C(hristopher) M(urray)
See also CDBLB 1945-1960; DLB 20; EWL 3; RGEL 2

MacDonald, Anson
See Heinlein, Robert A(nson)

Macdonald, Cynthia 1928- .... **CLC 13, 19**
See also CA 49-52; CANR 4, 44; DLB 105

MacDonald, George 1824-1905 .... **TCLC 9, 113**
See also BYA 5; CA 106; 137; CANR 80; CLR 67; DLB 18, 163, 178; FANT; MAICYA 1, 2; RGEL 2; SATA 33, 100; SFW 4; SUFW; WCH

Macdonald, John
See Millar, Kenneth

MacDonald, John D(ann)
1916-1986 .... **CLC 3, 27, 44**
See also BPFB 2; CA 1-4R; 121; CANR 1, 19, 60; CMW 4; CPW; DAM NOV, POP; DLB 8; DLBY 1986; MSW; MTCW 1, 2; SFW 4

Macdonald, John Ross
See Millar, Kenneth

Macdonald, Ross ..... **CLC 1, 2, 3, 14, 34, 41**
See Millar, Kenneth
See also AMWS 4; BPFB 2; DLBD 6; MSW; RGAL 4

MacDougal, John
See Blish, James (Benjamin)

MacDougal, John
See Blish, James (Benjamin)

MacDowell, John
See Parks, Tim(othy Harold)

MacEwen, Gwendolyn (Margaret)
1941-1987 .... **CLC 13, 55**
See also CA 9-12R; 124; CANR 7, 22; DLB 53, 251; SATA 50; SATA-Obit 55

Macha, Karel Hynek 1810-1846 .... **NCLC 46**

Machado (y Ruiz), Antonio
1875-1939 .... **TCLC 3**
See also CA 104; 174; DLB 108; EW 9; EWL 3; HW 2; RGWL 2, 3

Machado de Assis, Joaquim Maria
1839-1908 .... **BLC 2; HLCS 2; SSC 24; TCLC 10**
See also CA 107; 153; CANR 91; LAW; RGSF 2; RGWL 2, 3; TWA; WLIT 1

Machaut, Guillaume de c.
1300-1377 .... **CMLC 64**
See also DLB 208

Machen, Arthur .... **SSC 20; TCLC 4**
See Jones, Arthur Llewellyn
See also CA 179; DLB 156, 178; RGEL 2; SUFW 1

Machiavelli, Niccolo 1469-1527 ... **DC 16; LC 8, 36; WLCS**
See also DA; DAB; DAC; DAM MST; EW 2; LAIT 1; LMFS 1; NFS 9; RGWL 2, 3; TWA

MacInnes, Colin 1914-1976 .... **CLC 4, 23**
See also CA 69-72; 65-68; CANR 21; DLB 14; MTCW 1, 2; RGEL 2; RHW

MacInnes, Helen (Clark)
1907-1985 .... **CLC 27, 39**
See also BPFB 2; CA 1-4R; 117; CANR 1, 28, 58; CMW 4; CPW; DAM POP; DLB 87; MSW; MTCW 1, 2; SATA 22; SATA-Obit 44

Mackay, Mary 1855-1924
See Corelli, Marie
See also CA 118; 177; FANT; RHW

Mackenzie, Compton (Edward Montague)
1883-1972 .... **CLC 18; TCLC 116**
See also CA 21-22; 37-40R; CAP 2; DLB 34, 100; RGEL 2

Mackenzie, Henry 1745-1831 .... **NCLC 41**
See also DLB 39; RGEL 2

Mackey, Nathaniel (Ernest) 1947- .... **PC 49**
See also CA 153; CANR 114; CP 7; DLB 169

MacKinnon, Catharine A. 1946- .... **CLC 181**
See also CA 128; 132; CANR 73; FW; MTCW 2

Mackintosh, Elizabeth 1896(?)-1952
See Tey, Josephine
See also CA 110; CMW 4

MacLaren, James
See Grieve, C(hristopher) M(urray)

Mac Laverty, Bernard 1942- .... **CLC 31**
See also CA 116; 118; CANR 43, 88; CN 7; DLB 267; INT CA-118; RGSF 2

MacLean, Alistair (Stuart)
1922(?)-1987 .... **CLC 3, 13, 50, 63**
See also CA 57-60; 121; CANR 28, 61; CMW 4; CPW; DAM POP; DLB 276; MTCW 1; SATA 23; SATA-Obit 50; TCWW 2

Maclean, Norman (Fitzroy)
1902-1990 .... **CLC 78; SSC 13**
See also CA 102; 132; CANR 49; CPW; DAM POP; DLB 206; TCWW 2

MacLeish, Archibald 1892-1982 ... **CLC 3, 8, 14, 68; PC 47**
See also AMW; CA 9-12R; 106; CAD; CANR 33, 63; CDALBS; DAM POET; DFS 15; DLB 4, 7, 45; DLBY 1982; EWL 3; EXPP; MTCW 1, 2; PAB; PFS 5; RGAL 4; TUS

MacLennan, (John) Hugh
1907-1990 .... **CLC 2, 14, 92**
See also CA 5-8R; 142; CANR 33; DAC; DAM MST; DLB 68; EWL 3; MTCW 1, 2; RGEL 2; TWA

MacLeod, Alistair 1936- .... **CLC 56, 165**
See also CA 123; CCA 1; DAC; DAM MST; DLB 60; MTCW 2; RGSF 2

Macleod, Fiona
See Sharp, William
See also RGEL 2; SUFW

MacNeice, (Frederick) Louis
1907-1963 .... **CLC 1, 4, 10, 53**
See also BRW 7; CA 85-88; CANR 61; DAB; DAM POET; DLB 10, 20; EWL 3; MTCW 1, 2; RGEL 2

MacNeill, Dand
See Fraser, George MacDonald

Macpherson, James 1736-1796 .... **LC 29**
See Ossian
See also BRWS 8; DLB 109; RGEL 2

Macpherson, (Jean) Jay 1931- .... **CLC 14**
See also CA 5-8R; CANR 90; CP 7; CWP; DLB 53

Macrobius fl. 430- .... **CMLC 48**

MacShane, Frank 1927-1999 .... **CLC 39**
See also CA 9-12R; 186; CANR 3, 33; DLB 111

Macumber, Mari
See Sandoz, Mari(e Susette)

Madach, Imre 1823-1864 .... **NCLC 19**

Madden, (Jerry) David 1933- .... **CLC 5, 15**
See also CA 1-4R; CAAS 3; CANR 4, 45; CN 7; CSW; DLB 6; MTCW 1

Maddern, Al(an)
See Ellison, Harlan (Jay)

Madhubuti, Haki R. 1942- ... **BLC 2; CLC 6, 73; PC 5**
See Lee, Don L.
See also BW 2, 3; CA 73-76; CANR 24, 51, 73; CP 7; CSW; DAM MULT, POET; DLB 5, 41; DLBD 8; EWL 3; MTCW 2; RGAL 4

Madison, James 1751-1836 .... **NCLC 126**
See also DLB 37

Maepenn, Hugh
See Kuttner, Henry

Maepenn, K. H.
See Kuttner, Henry

Maeterlinck, Maurice 1862-1949 ..... **TCLC 3**
See also CA 104; 136; CANR 80; DAM DRAM; DLB 192; EW 8; EWL 3; GFL 1789 to the Present; LMFS 2; RGWL 2, 3; SATA 66; TWA

Maginn, William 1794-1842 .... **NCLC 8**
See also DLB 110, 159

Mahapatra, Jayanta 1928- .... **CLC 33**
See also CA 73-76; CAAS 9; CANR 15, 33, 66, 87; CP 7; DAM MULT

Mahfouz, Naguib (Abdel Aziz Al-Sabilgi)
1911(?)- .... **CLC 153; SSC 66**
See Mahfuz, Najib (Abdel Aziz al-Sabilgi)
See also AAYA 49; BEST 89:2; CA 128; CANR 55, 101; CWW 2; DA3; DAM NOV; MTCW 1, 2; RGWL 2, 3; SSFS 9

Mahfuz, Najib (Abdel Aziz al-Sabilgi)
.... **CLC 52, 55**
See Mahfouz, Naguib (Abdel Aziz Al-Sabilgi)
See also AFW; DLBY 1988; EWL 3; RGSF 2; WLIT 2

McFadden, David 1940- .... **CLC 48**
See also CA 104; CP 7; DLB 60; INT CA-104

McFarland, Dennis 1950- .... **CLC 65**
See also CA 165; CANR 110

McGahern, John 1934- ... **CLC 5, 9, 48, 156; SSC 17**
See also CA 17-20R; CANR 29, 68, 113; CN 7; DLB 14, 231; MTCW 1

McGinley, Patrick (Anthony) 1937- . **CLC 41**
See also CA 120; 127; CANR 56; INT CA-127

McGinley, Phyllis 1905-1978 .... **CLC 14**
See also CA 9-12R; 77-80; CANR 19; CWRI 5; DLB 11, 48; PFS 9, 13; SATA 2, 44; SATA-Obit 24

McGinniss, Joe 1942- .... **CLC 32**
See also AITN 2; BEST 89:2; CA 25-28R; CANR 26, 70; CPW; DLB 185; INT CANR-26

McGivern, Maureen Daly
See Daly, Maureen

McGrath, Patrick 1950- .... **CLC 55**
See also CA 136; CANR 65; CN 7; DLB 231; HGG; SUFW 2

McGrath, Thomas (Matthew)
1916-1990 .... **CLC 28, 59**
See also AMWS 10; CA 9-12R; 132; CANR 6, 33, 95; DAM POET; MTCW 1; SATA 41; SATA-Obit 66

McGuane, Thomas (Francis III)
1939- .... **CLC 3, 7, 18, 45, 127**
See also AITN 2; BPFB 2; CA 49-52; CANR 5, 24, 49, 94; CN 7; DLB 2, 212; DLBY 1980; EWL 3; INT CANR-24; MTCW 1; TCWW 2

McGuckian, Medbh 1950- .... **CLC 48, 174; PC 27**
See also BRWS 5; CA 143; CP 7; CWP; DAM POET; DLB 40

McHale, Tom 1942(?)-1982 .... **CLC 3, 5**
See also AITN 1; CA 77-80; 106

McIlvanney, William 1936- .... **CLC 42**
See also CA 25-28R; CANR 61; CMW 4; DLB 14, 207

McIlwraith, Maureen Mollie Hunter
See Hunter, Mollie
See also SATA 2

McInerney, Jay 1955- .... **CLC 34, 112**
See also AAYA 18; BPFB 2; CA 116; 123; CANR 45, 68, 116; CN 7; CPW; DA3; DAM POP; DLB 292; INT CA-123; MTCW 2

McIntyre, Vonda N(eel) 1948- .... **CLC 18**
See also CA 81-84; CANR 17, 34, 69; MTCW 1; SFW 4; YAW

McKay, Claude .... **BLC 3; HR 3; PC 2; TCLC 7, 41; WLC**
See McKay, Festus Claudius
See also AFAW 1, 2; AMWS 10; DAB; DLB 4, 45, 51, 117; EWL 3; EXPP; GLL 2; LAIT 3; LMFS 2; PAB; PFS 4; RGAL 4; WP

McKay, Festus Claudius 1889-1948
See McKay, Claude
See also BW 1, 3; CA 104; 124; CANR 73; DA; DAC; DAM MST, MULT, NOV, POET; MTCW 1, 2; TUS

McKuen, Rod 1933- .... **CLC 1, 3**
See also AITN 1; CA 41-44R; CANR 40

McLoughlin, R. B.
See Mencken, H(enry) L(ouis)

McLuhan, (Herbert) Marshall
1911-1980 .... **CLC 37, 83**
See also CA 9-12R; 102; CANR 12, 34, 61; DLB 88; INT CANR-12; MTCW 1, 2

McManus, Declan Patrick Aloysius
See Costello, Elvis

McMillan, Terry (L.) 1951- . **BLCS; CLC 50, 61, 112**
See also AAYA 21; AMWS 13; BPFB 2; BW 2, 3; CA 140; CANR 60, 104, 131; CPW; DA3; DAM MULT, NOV, POP; MTCW 2; RGAL 4; YAW

McMurtry, Larry (Jeff) 1936- .. **CLC 2, 3, 7, 11, 27, 44, 127**
See also AAYA 15; AITN 2; AMWS 5; BEST 89:2; BPFB 2; CA 5-8R; CANR 19, 43, 64, 103; CDALB 1968-1988; CN 7; CPW; CSW; DA3; DAM NOV, POP; DLB 2, 143, 256; DLBY 1980, 1987; EWL 3; MTCW 1, 2; RGAL 4; TCWW 2

McNally, T. M. 1961- .... **CLC 82**

McNally, Terrence 1939- .... **CLC 4, 7, 41, 91**
See also AMWS 13; CA 45-48; CAD; CANR 2, 56, 116; CD 5; DA3; DAM DRAM; DFS 16, 19; DLB 7, 249; EWL 3; GLL 1; MTCW 2

McNamer, Deirdre 1950- .... **CLC 70**

McNeal, Tom .... **CLC 119**

McNeile, Herman Cyril 1888-1937
See Sapper
See also CA 184; CMW 4; DLB 77

McNickle, (William) D'Arcy
1904-1977 .... **CLC 89; NNAL**
See also CA 9-12R; 85-88; CANR 5, 45; DAM MULT; DLB 175, 212; RGAL 4; SATA-Obit 22

McPhee, John (Angus) 1931- .... **CLC 36**
See also AMWS 3; ANW; BEST 90:1; CA 65-68; CANR 20, 46, 64, 69, 121; CPW; DLB 185, 275; MTCW 1, 2; TUS

McPherson, James Alan 1943- . **BLCS; CLC 19, 77**
See also BW 1, 3; CA 25-28R; CAAS 17; CANR 24, 74; CN 7; CSW; DLB 38, 244; EWL 3; MTCW 1, 2; RGAL 4; RGSF 2

McPherson, William (Alexander)
1933- .... **CLC 34**
See also CA 69-72; CANR 28; INT CANR-28

McTaggart, J. McT. Ellis
See McTaggart, John McTaggart Ellis

McTaggart, John McTaggart Ellis
1866-1925 .... **TCLC 105**
See also CA 120; DLB 262

Mead, George Herbert 1863-1931 . **TCLC 89**
See also CA 212; DLB 270

Mead, Margaret 1901-1978 .... **CLC 37**
See also AITN 1; CA 1-4R; 81-84; CANR 4; DA3; FW; MTCW 1, 2; SATA-Obit 20

Meaker, Marijane (Agnes) 1927-
See Kerr, M. E.
See also CA 107; CANR 37, 63; INT CA-107; JRDA; MAICYA 1, 2; MAICYAS 1; MTCW 1; SATA 20, 61, 99; SATA-Essay 111; YAW

Medoff, Mark (Howard) 1940- .... **CLC 6, 23**
See also AITN 1; CA 53-56; CAD; CANR 5; CD 5; DAM DRAM; DFS 4; DLB 7; INT CANR-5

Medvedev, P. N.
See Bakhtin, Mikhail Mikhailovich

Meged, Aharon
See Megged, Aharon

Meged, Aron
See Megged, Aharon

Megged, Aharon 1920- .... **CLC 9**
See also CA 49-52; CAAS 13; CANR 1; EWL 3

Mehta, Gita 1943- .... **CLC 179**
See also CA 225; DNFS 2

Mehta, Ved (Parkash) 1934- .... **CLC 37**
See also CA 1-4R; 212; CAAE 212; CANR 2, 23, 69; MTCW 1

Melanchthon, Philipp 1497-1560 .... **LC 90**
See also DLB 179

Melanter
See Blackmore, R(ichard) D(oddridge)

Meleager c. 140B.C.-c. 70B.C. ...... **CMLC 53**

Melies, Georges 1861-1938 .... **TCLC 81**

Melikow, Loris
See Hofmannsthal, Hugo von

Melmoth, Sebastian
See Wilde, Oscar (Fingal O'Flahertie Wills)

Melo Neto, Joao Cabral de
See Cabral de Melo Neto, Joao
See also CWW 2; EWL 3

Meltzer, Milton 1915- .... **CLC 26**
See also AAYA 8, 45; BYA 2, 6; CA 13-16R; CANR 38, 92, 107; CLR 13; DLB 61; JRDA; MAICYA 1, 2; SAAS 1; SATA 1, 50, 80, 128; SATA-Essay 124; WYA; YAW

Melville, Herman 1819-1891 ..... **NCLC 3, 12, 29, 45, 49, 91, 93, 123; SSC 1, 17, 46; WLC**
See also AAYA 25; AMW; AMWR 1; CDALB 1640-1865; DA; DA3; DAB; DAC; DAM MST, NOV; DLB 3, 74, 250, 254; EXPN; EXPS; LAIT 1, 2; NFS 7, 9; RGAL 4; RGSF 2; SATA 59; SSFS 3; TUS

Members, Mark
See Powell, Anthony (Dymoke)

Membreno, Alejandro .... **CLC 59**

Menander c. 342B.C.-c. 293B.C. .... **CMLC 9, 51; DC 3**
See also AW 1; CDWLB 1; DAM DRAM; DLB 176; LMFS 1; RGWL 2, 3

Menchu, Rigoberta 1959- .. **CLC 160; HLCS 2**
See also CA 175; DNFS 1; WLIT 1

Mencken, H(enry) L(ouis)
1880-1956 .... **TCLC 13**
See also AMW; CA 105; 125; CDALB 1917-1929; DLB 11, 29, 63, 137, 222; EWL 3; MTCW 1, 2; NCFS 4; RGAL 4; TUS

Mendelsohn, Jane 1965- .... **CLC 99**
See also CA 154; CANR 94

Menton, Francisco de
See Chin, Frank (Chew, Jr.)

Mercer, David 1928-1980 .... **CLC 5**
See also CA 9-12R; 102; CANR 23; CBD; DAM DRAM; DLB 13; MTCW 1; RGEL 2

Merchant, Paul
See Ellison, Harlan (Jay)

Meredith, George 1828-1909 ... **TCLC 17, 43**
See also CA 117; 153; CANR 80; CDBLB 1832-1890; DAM POET; DLB 18, 35, 57, 159; RGEL 2; TEA

Meredith, William (Morris) 1919- .... **CLC 4, 13, 22, 55; PC 28**
See also CA 9-12R; CAAS 14; CANR 6, 40, 129; CP 7; DAM POET; DLB 5

Merezhkovsky, Dmitrii Sergeevich
See Merezhkovsky, Dmitry Sergeyevich
See also DLB 295

Merezhkovsky, Dmitry Sergeevich
See Merezhkovsky, Dmitry Sergeyevich
See also EWL 3

Merezhkovsky, Dmitry Sergeyevich
1865-1941 .... **TCLC 29**
See Merezhkovsky, Dmitrii Sergeevich; Merezhkovsky, Dmitry Sergeevich
See also CA 169

Merimee, Prosper 1803-1870 ... **NCLC 6, 65; SSC 7**
See also DLB 119, 192; EW 6; EXPS; GFL 1789 to the Present; RGSF 2; RGWL 2, 3; SSFS 8; SUFW

Merkin, Daphne 1954- .... **CLC 44**
See also CA 123

Mishima, Yukio ... CLC 2, 4, 6, 9, 27; DC 1; SSC 4
See Hiraoka, Kimitake
See also AAYA 50; BPFB 2; GLL 1; MJW; MTCW 2; RGSF 2; RGWL 2, 3; SSFS 5, 12

Mistral, Frederic 1830-1914 .... TCLC 51
See also CA 122; 213; GFL 1789 to the Present

Mistral, Gabriela
See Godoy Alcayaga, Lucila
See also DLB 283; DNFS 1; EWL 3; LAW; RGWL 2, 3; WP

Mistry, Rohinton 1952- ...... CLC 71; SSC 73
See also CA 141; CANR 86, 114; CCA 1; CN 7; DAC; SSFS 6

Mitchell, Clyde
See Ellison, Harlan (Jay)

Mitchell, Emerson Blackhorse Barney
1945- .... NNAL
See also CA 45-48

Mitchell, James Leslie 1901-1935
See Gibbon, Lewis Grassic
See also CA 104; 188; DLB 15

Mitchell, Joni 1943- .... CLC 12
See also CA 112; CCA 1

Mitchell, Joseph (Quincy)
1908-1996 .... CLC 98
See also CA 77-80; 152; CANR 69; CN 7; CSW; DLB 185; DLBY 1996

Mitchell, Margaret (Munnerlyn)
1900-1949 .... TCLC 11
See also AAYA 23; BPFB 2; BYA 1; CA 109; 125; CANR 55, 94; CDALBS; DA3; DAM NOV, POP; DLB 9; LAIT 2; MTCW 1, 2; NFS 9; RGAL 4; RHW; TUS; WYAS 1; YAW

Mitchell, Peggy
See Mitchell, Margaret (Munnerlyn)

Mitchell, S(ilas) Weir 1829-1914 .... TCLC 36
See also CA 165; DLB 202; RGAL 4

Mitchell, W(illiam) O(rmond)
1914-1998 .... CLC 25
See also CA 77-80; 165; CANR 15, 43; CN 7; DAC; DAM MST; DLB 88

Mitchell, William (Lendrum)
1879-1936 .... TCLC 81
See also CA 213

Mitford, Mary Russell 1787-1855 ... NCLC 4
See also DLB 110, 116; RGEL 2

Mitford, Nancy 1904-1973 .... CLC 44
See also CA 9-12R; DLB 191; RGEL 2

Miyamoto, (Chujo) Yuriko
1899-1951 .... TCLC 37
See Miyamoto Yuriko
See also CA 170, 174

Miyamoto Yuriko
See Miyamoto, (Chujo) Yuriko
See also DLB 180

Miyazawa, Kenji 1896-1933 .... TCLC 76
See Miyazawa Kenji
See also CA 157; RGWL 3

Miyazawa Kenji
See Miyazawa, Kenji
See also EWL 3

Mizoguchi, Kenji 1898-1956 .... TCLC 72
See also CA 167

Mo, Timothy (Peter) 1950(?)- ... CLC 46, 134
See also CA 117; CANR 128; CN 7; DLB 194; MTCW 1; WLIT 4; WWE 1

Modarressi, Taghi (M.) 1931-1997 ... CLC 44
See also CA 121; 134; INT CA-134

Modiano, Patrick (Jean) 1945- .... CLC 18
See also CA 85-88; CANR 17, 40, 115; CWW 2; DLB 83, 299; EWL 3

Mofolo, Thomas (Mokopu)
1875(?)-1948 .... BLC 3; TCLC 22
See also AFW; CA 121; 153; CANR 83; DAM MULT; DLB 225; EWL 3; MTCW 2; WLIT 2

Mohr, Nicholasa 1938- .... CLC 12; HLC 2
See also AAYA 8, 46; CA 49-52; CANR 1, 32, 64; CLR 22; DAM MULT; DLB 145; HW 1, 2; JRDA; LAIT 5; LLW 1; MAICYA 2; MAICYAS 1; RGAL 4; SAAS 8; SATA 8, 97; SATA-Essay 113; WYA; YAW

Moi, Toril 1953- .... CLC 172
See also CA 154; CANR 102; FW

Mojtabai, A(nn) G(race) 1938- ..... CLC 5, 9, 15, 29
See also CA 85-88; CANR 88

Moliere 1622-1673 ..... DC 13; LC 10, 28, 64; WLC
See also DA; DA3; DAB; DAC; DAM DRAM, MST; DFS 13, 18; DLB 268; EW 3; GFL Beginnings to 1789; LATS 1; RGWL 2, 3; TWA

Molin, Charles
See Mayne, William (James Carter)

Molnar, Ferenc 1878-1952 .... TCLC 20
See also CA 109; 153; CANR 83; CDWLB 4; DAM DRAM; DLB 215; EWL 3; RGWL 2, 3

Momaday, N(avarre) Scott 1934- ...... CLC 2, 19, 85, 95, 160; NNAL; PC 25; WLCS
See also AAYA 11; AMWS 4; ANW; BPFB 2; BYA 12; CA 25-28R; CANR 14, 34, 68; CDALBS; CN 7; CPW; DA; DA3; DAB; DAC; DAM MST, MULT, NOV, POP; DLB 143, 175, 256; EWL 3; EXPP; INT CANR-14; LAIT 4; LATS 1; MTCW 1, 2; NFS 10; PFS 2, 11; RGAL 4; SATA 48; SATA-Brief 30; WP; YAW

Monette, Paul 1945-1995 .... CLC 82
See also AMWS 10; CA 139; 147; CN 7; GLL 1

Monroe, Harriet 1860-1936 .... TCLC 12
See also CA 109; 204; DLB 54, 91

Monroe, Lyle
See Heinlein, Robert A(nson)

Montagu, Elizabeth 1720-1800 .... NCLC 7, 117
See also FW

Montagu, Mary (Pierrepont) Wortley
1689-1762 .... LC 9, 57; PC 16
See also DLB 95, 101; RGEL 2

Montagu, W. H.
See Coleridge, Samuel Taylor

Montague, John (Patrick) 1929- ..... CLC 13, 46
See also CA 9-12R; CANR 9, 69, 121; CP 7; DLB 40; EWL 3; MTCW 1; PFS 12; RGEL 2

Montaigne, Michel (Eyquem) de
1533-1592 .... LC 8; WLC
See also DA; DAB; DAC; DAM MST; EW 2; GFL Beginnings to 1789; LMFS 1; RGWL 2, 3; TWA

Montale, Eugenio 1896-1981 ... CLC 7, 9, 18; PC 13
See also CA 17-20R; 104; CANR 30; DLB 114; EW 11; EWL 3; MTCW 1; RGWL 2, 3; TWA

Montesquieu, Charles-Louis de Secondat
1689-1755 .... LC 7, 69
See also EW 3; GFL Beginnings to 1789; TWA

Montessori, Maria 1870-1952 ...... TCLC 103
See also CA 115; 147

Montgomery, (Robert) Bruce 1921(?)-1978
See Crispin, Edmund
See also CA 179; 104; CMW 4

Montgomery, L(ucy) M(aud)
1874-1942 .... TCLC 51, 140
See also AAYA 12; BYA 1; CA 108; 137; CLR 8, 91; DA3; DAC; DAM MST; DLB 92; DLBD 14; JRDA; MAICYA 1, 2; MTCW 2; RGEL 2; SATA 100; TWA; WCH; WYA; YABC 1

Montgomery, Marion H., Jr. 1925- .... CLC 7
See also AITN 1; CA 1-4R; CANR 3, 48; CSW; DLB 6

Montgomery, Max
See Davenport, Guy (Mattison, Jr.)

Montherlant, Henry (Milon) de
1896-1972 .... CLC 8, 19
See also CA 85-88; 37-40R; DAM DRAM; DLB 72; EW 11; EWL 3; GFL 1789 to the Present; MTCW 1

Monty Python
See Chapman, Graham; Cleese, John (Marwood); Gilliam, Terry (Vance); Idle, Eric; Jones, Terence Graham Parry; Palin, Michael (Edward)
See also AAYA 7

Moodie, Susanna (Strickland)
1803-1885 .... NCLC 14, 113
See also DLB 99

Moody, Hiram (F. III) 1961-
See Moody, Rick
See also CA 138; CANR 64, 112

Moody, Minerva
See Alcott, Louisa May

Moody, Rick .... CLC 147
See Moody, Hiram (F. III)

Moody, William Vaughan
1869-1910 .... TCLC 105
See also CA 110; 178; DLB 7, 54; RGAL 4

Mooney, Edward 1951-
See Mooney, Ted
See also CA 130

Mooney, Ted .... CLC 25
See Mooney, Edward

Moorcock, Michael (John) 1939- ...... CLC 5, 27, 58
See Bradbury, Edward P.
See also AAYA 26; CA 45-48; CAAS 5; CANR 2, 17, 38, 64, 122; CN 7; DLB 14, 231, 261; FANT; MTCW 1, 2; SATA 93; SCFW 2; SFW 4; SUFW 1, 2

Moore, Brian 1921-1999 ... CLC 1, 3, 5, 7, 8, 19, 32, 90
See Bryan, Michael
See also BRWS 9; CA 1-4R; 174; CANR 1, 25, 42, 63; CCA 1; CN 7; DAB; DAC; DAM MST; DLB 251; EWL 3; FANT; MTCW 1, 2; RGEL 2

Moore, Edward
See Muir, Edwin
See also RGEL 2

Moore, G. E. 1873-1958 .... TCLC 89
See also DLB 262

Moore, George Augustus
1852-1933 .... SSC 19; TCLC 7
See also BRW 6; CA 104; 177; DLB 10, 18, 57, 135; EWL 3; RGEL 2; RGSF 2

Moore, Lorrie .... CLC 39, 45, 68
See Moore, Marie Lorena
See also AMWS 10; DLB 234; SSFS 19

Moore, Marianne (Craig)
1887-1972 .... CLC 1, 2, 4, 8, 10, 13, 19, 47; PC 4, 49; WLCS
See also AMW; CA 1-4R; 33-36R; CANR 3, 61; CDALB 1929-1941; DA; DA3; DAB; DAC; DAM MST, POET; DLB 45; DLBD 7; EWL 3; EXPP; MAWW; MTCW 1, 2; PAB; PFS 14, 17; RGAL 4; SATA 20; TUS; WP

Moore, Marie Lorena 1957- .... CLC 165
See Moore, Lorrie
See also CA 116; CANR 39, 83; CN 7; DLB 234

Moore, Thomas 1779-1852 .... NCLC 6, 110
See also DLB 96, 144; RGEL 2

Moorhouse, Frank 1938- .... SSC 40
See also CA 118; CANR 92; CN 7; DLB
289; RGSF 2

Mora, Pat(ricia) 1942- .... HLC 2
See also AMWS 13; CA 129; CANR 57,
81, 112; CLR 58; DAM MULT; DLB 209;
HW 1, 2; LLW 1; MAICYA 2; SATA 92,
134

Moraga, Cherríe 1952- ...... CLC 126; DC 22
See also CA 131; CANR 66; DAM MULT;
DLB 82, 249; FW; GLL 1; HW 1, 2; LLW
1

Morand, Paul 1888-1976 .... CLC 41; SSC 22
See also CA 184; 69-72; DLB 65; EWL 3

Morante, Elsa 1918-1985 .... CLC 8, 47
See also CA 85-88; 117; CANR 35; DLB
177; EWL 3; MTCW 1, 2; RGWL 2, 3

Moravia, Alberto .... CLC 2, 7, 11, 27, 46;
SSC 26
See Pincherle, Alberto
See also DLB 177; EW 12; EWL 3; MTCW
2; RGSF 2; RGWL 2, 3

More, Hannah 1745-1833 ...... NCLC 27, 141
See also DLB 107, 109, 116, 158; RGEL 2

More, Henry 1614-1687 .... LC 9
See also DLB 126, 252

More, Sir Thomas 1478(?)-1535 .... LC 10, 32
See also BRWC 1; BRWS 7; DLB 136, 281;
LMFS 1; RGEL 2; TEA

Moreas, Jean .... TCLC 18
See Papadiamantopoulos, Johannes
See also GFL 1789 to the Present

Moreton, Andrew Esq.
See Defoe, Daniel

Morgan, Berry 1919-2002 .... CLC 6
See also CA 49-52; 208; DLB 6

Morgan, Claire
See Highsmith, (Mary) Patricia
See also GLL 1

Morgan, Edwin (George) 1920- .... CLC 31
See also BRWS 9; CA 5-8R; CANR 3, 43,
90; CP 7; DLB 27

Morgan, (George) Frederick
1922-2004 .... CLC 23
See also CA 17-20R; 224; CANR 21; CP 7

Morgan, Harriet
See Mencken, H(enry) L(ouis)

Morgan, Jane
See Cooper, James Fenimore

Morgan, Janet 1945- .... CLC 39
See also CA 65-68

Morgan, Lady 1776(?)-1859 .... NCLC 29
See also DLB 116, 158; RGEL 2

Morgan, Robin (Evonne) 1941- .... CLC 2
See also CA 69-72; CANR 29, 68; FW;
GLL 2; MTCW 1; SATA 80

Morgan, Scott
See Kuttner, Henry

Morgan, Seth 1949(?)-1990 .... CLC 65
See also CA 185; 132

Morgenstern, Christian (Otto Josef
Wolfgang) 1871-1914 .... TCLC 8
See also CA 105; 191; EWL 3

Morgenstern, S.
See Goldman, William (W.)

Mori, Rintaro
See Mori Ogai
See also CA 110

Moricz, Zsigmond 1879-1942 .... TCLC 33
See also CA 165; DLB 215; EWL 3

Morike, Eduard (Friedrich)
1804-1875 .... NCLC 10
See also DLB 133; RGWL 2, 3

Mori Ogai 1862-1922 .... TCLC 14
See Ogai
See also CA 164; DLB 180; EWL 3; RGWL
3; TWA

Moritz, Karl Philipp 1756-1793 .... LC 2
See also DLB 94

Morland, Peter Henry
See Faust, Frederick (Schiller)

Morley, Christopher (Darlington)
1890-1957 .... TCLC 87
See also CA 112; DLB 9; RGAL 4

Morren, Theophil
See Hofmannsthal, Hugo von

Morris, Bill 1952- .... CLC 76
See also CA 225

Morris, Julian
See West, Morris L(anglo)

Morris, Steveland Judkins 1950(?)-
See Wonder, Stevie
See also CA 111

Morris, William 1834-1896 . NCLC 4; PC 55
See also BRW 5; CDBLB 1832-1890; DLB
18, 35, 57, 156, 178, 184; FANT; RGEL
2; SFW 4; SUFW

Morris, Wright 1910-1998 .. CLC 1, 3, 7, 18,
37; TCLC 107
See also AMW; CA 9-12R; 167; CANR 21,
81; CN 7; DLB 2, 206, 218; DLBY 1981;
EWL 3; MTCW 1, 2; RGAL 4; TCWW 2

Morrison, Arthur 1863-1945 .... SSC 40;
TCLC 72
See also CA 120; 157; CMW 4; DLB 70,
135, 197; RGEL 2

Morrison, Chloe Anthony Wofford
See Morrison, Toni

Morrison, James Douglas 1943-1971
See Morrison, Jim
See also CA 73-76; CANR 40

Morrison, Jim .... CLC 17
See Morrison, James Douglas

Morrison, Toni 1931- ..... BLC 3; CLC 4, 10,
22, 55, 81, 87, 173
See also AAYA 1, 22; AFAW 1, 2; AMWC
1; AMWS 3; BPFB 2; BW 2, 3; CA 29-
32R; CANR 27, 42, 67, 113, 124; CDALB
1968-1988; CLR 99; CN 7; CPW; DA;
DA3; DAB; DAC; DAM MST, MULT,
NOV, POP; DLB 6, 33, 143; DLBY 1981;
EWL 3; EXPN; FW; LAIT 2, 4; LATS 1;
LMFS 2; MAWW; MTCW 1, 2; NFS 1,
6, 8, 14; RGAL 4; RHW; SATA 57, 144;
SSFS 5; TUS; YAW

Morrison, Van 1945- .... CLC 21
See also CA 116; 168

Morrissy, Mary 1957- .... CLC 99
See also CA 205; DLB 267

Mortimer, John (Clifford) 1923- ..... CLC 28,
43
See also CA 13-16R; CANR 21, 69, 109;
CD 5; CDBLB 1960 to Present; CMW 4;
CN 7; CPW; DA3; DAM DRAM, POP;
DLB 13, 245, 271; INT CANR-21; MSW;
MTCW 1, 2; RGEL 2

Mortimer, Penelope (Ruth)
1918-1999 .... CLC 5
See also CA 57-60; 187; CANR 45, 88; CN
7

Mortimer, Sir John
See Mortimer, John (Clifford)

Morton, Anthony
See Creasey, John

Morton, Thomas 1579(?)-1647(?) .... LC 72
See also DLB 24; RGEL 2

Mosca, Gaetano 1858-1941 .... TCLC 75

Moses, Daniel David 1952- .... NNAL
See also CA 186

Mosher, Howard Frank 1943- .... CLC 62
See also CA 139; CANR 65, 115

Mosley, Nicholas 1923- .... CLC 43, 70
See also CA 69-72; CANR 41, 60, 108; CN
7; DLB 14, 207

Mosley, Walter 1952- .... BLCS; CLC 97, 184
See also AAYA 17; AMWS 13; BPFB 2;
BW 2; CA 142; CANR 57, 92; CMW 4;
CPW; DA3; DAM MULT, POP; MSW;
MTCW 2

Moss, Howard 1922-1987 . CLC 7, 14, 45, 50
See also CA 1-4R; 123; CANR 1, 44; DAM
POET; DLB 5

Mossgiel, Rab
See Burns, Robert

Motion, Andrew (Peter) 1952- .... CLC 47
See also BRWS 7; CA 146; CANR 90; CP
7; DLB 40

Motley, Willard (Francis)
1909-1965 .... CLC 18
See also BW 1; CA 117; 106; CANR 88;
DLB 76, 143

Motoori, Norinaga 1730-1801 .... NCLC 45

Mott, Michael (Charles Alston)
1930- .... CLC 15, 34
See also CA 5-8R; CAAS 7; CANR 7, 29

Mountain Wolf Woman 1884-1960 . CLC 92;
NNAL
See also CA 144; CANR 90

Moure, Erin 1955- .... CLC 88
See also CA 113; CP 7; CWP; DLB 60

Mourning Dove 1885(?)-1936 .... NNAL
See also CA 144; CANR 90; DAM MULT;
DLB 175, 221

Mowat, Farley (McGill) 1921- .... CLC 26
See also AAYA 1, 50; BYA 2; CA 1-4R;
CANR 4, 24, 42, 68, 108; CLR 20; CPW;
DAC; DAM MST; DLB 68; INT CANR-
24; JRDA; MAICYA 1, 2; MTCW 1, 2;
SATA 3, 55; YAW

Mowatt, Anna Cora 1819-1870 ..... NCLC 74
See also RGAL 4

Moyers, Bill 1934- .... CLC 74
See also AITN 2; CA 61-64; CANR 31, 52

Mphahlele, Es'kia
See Mphahlele, Ezekiel
See also AFW; CDWLB 3; DLB 125, 225;
RGSF 2; SSFS 11

Mphahlele, Ezekiel 1919- ... BLC 3; CLC 25,
133
See Mphahlele, Es'kia
See also BW 2, 3; CA 81-84; CANR 26,
76; CN 7; DA3; DAM MULT; EWL 3;
MTCW 2; SATA 119

Mqhayi, S(amuel) E(dward) K(rune Loliwe)
1875-1945 .... BLC 3; TCLC 25
See also CA 153; CANR 87; DAM MULT

Mrozek, Slawomir 1930- .... CLC 3, 13
See also CA 13-16R; CAAS 10; CANR 29;
CDWLB 4; CWW 2; DLB 232; EWL 3;
MTCW 1

Mrs. Belloc-Lowndes
See Lowndes, Marie Adelaide (Belloc)

Mrs. Fairstar
See Horne, Richard Henry Hengist

M'Taggart, John M'Taggart Ellis
See McTaggart, John McTaggart Ellis

Mtwa, Percy (?)- .... CLC 47

Mueller, Lisel 1924- .... CLC 13, 51; PC 33
See also CA 93-96; CP 7; DLB 105; PFS 9,
13

Muggeridge, Malcolm (Thomas)
1903-1990 .... TCLC 120
See also AITN 1; CA 101; CANR 33, 63;
MTCW 1, 2

Muhammad 570-632 .... WLCS
See also DA; DAB; DAC; DAM MST

Muir, Edwin 1887-1959 . PC 49; TCLC 2, 87
See Moore, Edward
See also BRWS 6; CA 104; 193; DLB 20,
100, 191; EWL 3; RGEL 2

Muir, John 1838-1914 .... TCLC 28
See also AMWS 9; ANW; CA 165; DLB
186, 275

Mujica Lainez, Manuel 1910-1984 ... **CLC 31**
See Lainez, Manuel Mujica
See also CA 81-84; 112; CANR 32; EWL 3; HW 1

Mukherjee, Bharati 1940- ..... **AAL; CLC 53, 115; SSC 38**
See also AAYA 46; BEST 89:2; CA 107; CANR 45, 72, 128; CN 7; DAM NOV; DLB 60, 218; DNFS 1, 2; EWL 3; FW; MTCW 1, 2; RGAL 4; RGSF 2; SSFS 7; TUS; WWE 1

Muldoon, Paul 1951- .... **CLC 32, 72, 166**
See also BRWS 4; CA 113; 129; CANR 52, 91; CP 7; DAM POET; DLB 40; INT CA-129; PFS 7

Mulisch, Harry 1927- .... **CLC 42**
See also CA 9-12R; CANR 6, 26, 56, 110; DLB 299; EWL 3

Mull, Martin 1943- .... **CLC 17**
See also CA 105

Muller, Wilhelm .... **NCLC 73**

Mulock, Dinah Maria
See Craik, Dinah Maria (Mulock)
See also RGEL 2

Munday, Anthony 1560-1633 .... **LC 87**
See also DLB 62, 172; RGEL 2

Munford, Robert 1737(?)-1783 .... **LC 5**
See also DLB 31

Mungo, Raymond 1946- .... **CLC 72**
See also CA 49-52; CANR 2

Munro, Alice 1931- .... **CLC 6, 10, 19, 50, 95; SSC 3; WLCS**
See also AITN 2; BPFB 2; CA 33-36R; CANR 33, 53, 75, 114; CCA 1; CN 7; DA3; DAC; DAM MST, NOV; DLB 53; EWL 3; MTCW 1, 2; RGEL 2; RGSF 2; SATA 29; SSFS 5, 13, 19; WWE 1

Munro, H(ector) H(ugh) 1870-1916 .... **WLC**
See Saki
See also CA 104; 130; CANR 104; CDBLB 1890-1914; DA; DA3; DAB; DAC; DAM MST, NOV; DLB 34, 162; EXPS; MTCW 1, 2; RGEL 2; SSFS 15

Murakami, Haruki 1949- .... **CLC 150**
See Murakami Haruki
See also CA 165; CANR 102; MJW; RGWL 3; SFW 4

Murakami Haruki
See Murakami, Haruki
See also DLB 182; EWL 3

Murasaki, Lady
See Murasaki Shikibu

Murasaki Shikibu 978(?)-1026(?) ... **CMLC 1**
See also EFS 2; LATS 1; RGWL 2, 3

Murdoch, (Jean) Iris 1919-1999 ... **CLC 1, 2, 3, 4, 6, 8, 11, 15, 22, 31, 51**
See also BRWS 1; CA 13-16R; 179; CANR 8, 43, 68, 103; CDBLB 1960 to Present; CN 7; CWD; DA3; DAB; DAC; DAM MST, NOV; DLB 14, 194, 233; EWL 3; INT CANR-8; MTCW 1, 2; NFS 18; RGEL 2; TEA; WLIT 4

Murfree, Mary Noailles 1850-1922 .. **SSC 22; TCLC 135**
See also CA 122; 176; DLB 12, 74; RGAL 4

Murnau, Friedrich Wilhelm
See Plumpe, Friedrich Wilhelm

Murphy, Richard 1927- .... **CLC 41**
See also BRWS 5; CA 29-32R; CP 7; DLB 40; EWL 3

Murphy, Sylvia 1937- .... **CLC 34**
See also CA 121

Murphy, Thomas (Bernard) 1935- ... **CLC 51**
See also CA 101

Murray, Albert L. 1916- .... **CLC 73**
See also BW 2; CA 49-52; CANR 26, 52, 78; CSW; DLB 38

Murray, James Augustus Henry 1837-1915 .... **TCLC 117**

Murray, Judith Sargent 1751-1820 .... **NCLC 63**
See also DLB 37, 200

Murray, Les(lie Allan) 1938- .... **CLC 40**
See also BRWS 7; CA 21-24R; CANR 11, 27, 56, 103; CP 7; DAM POET; DLB 289; DLBY 2001; EWL 3; RGEL 2

Murry, J. Middleton
See Murry, John Middleton

Murry, John Middleton 1889-1957 .... **TCLC 16**
See also CA 118; 217; DLB 149

Musgrave, Susan 1951- .... **CLC 13, 54**
See also CA 69-72; CANR 45, 84; CCA 1; CP 7; CWP

Musil, Robert (Edler von) 1880-1942 .... **SSC 18; TCLC 12, 68**
See also CA 109; CANR 55, 84; CDWLB 2; DLB 81, 124; EW 9; EWL 3; MTCW 2; RGSF 2; RGWL 2, 3

Muske, Carol .... **CLC 90**
See Muske-Dukes, Carol (Anne)

Muske-Dukes, Carol (Anne) 1945-
See Muske, Carol
See also CA 65-68, 203; CAAE 203; CANR 32, 70; CWP

Musset, (Louis Charles) Alfred de 1810-1857 .... **NCLC 7**
See also DLB 192, 217; EW 6; GFL 1789 to the Present; RGWL 2, 3; TWA

Mussolini, Benito (Amilcare Andrea) 1883-1945 .... **TCLC 96**
See also CA 116

Mutanabbi, Al-
See al-Mutanabbi, Ahmad ibn al-Husayn Abu al-Tayyib al-Jufi al-Kindi

My Brother's Brother
See Chekhov, Anton (Pavlovich)

Myers, L(eopold) H(amilton) 1881-1944 .... **TCLC 59**
See also CA 157; DLB 15; EWL 3; RGEL 2

Myers, Walter Dean 1937- .. **BLC 3; CLC 35**
See also AAYA 4, 23; BW 2; BYA 6, 8, 11; CA 33-36R; CANR 20, 42, 67, 108; CLR 4, 16, 35; DAM MULT, NOV; DLB 33; INT CANR-20; JRDA; LAIT 5; MAICYA 1, 2; MAICYAS 1; MTCW 2; SAAS 2; SATA 41, 71, 109; SATA-Brief 27; WYA; YAW

Myers, Walter M.
See Myers, Walter Dean

Myles, Symon
See Follett, Ken(neth Martin)

Nabokov, Vladimir (Vladimirovich) 1899-1977 .... **CLC 1, 2, 3, 6, 8, 11, 15, 23, 44, 46, 64; SSC 11; TCLC 108; WLC**
See also AAYA 45; AMW; AMWC 1; AMWR 1; BPFB 2; CA 5-8R; 69-72; CANR 20, 102; CDALB 1941-1968; DA; DA3; DAB; DAC; DAM MST, NOV; DLB 2, 244, 278; DLBD 3; DLBY 1980, 1991; EWL 3; EXPS; LATS 1; MTCW 1, 2; NCFS 4; NFS 9; RGAL 4; RGSF 2; SSFS 6, 15; TUS

Naevius c. 265B.C.-201B.C. .... **CMLC 37**
See also DLB 211

Nagai, Kafu .... **TCLC 51**
See Nagai, Sokichi
See also DLB 180

Nagai, Sokichi 1879-1959
See Nagai, Kafu
See also CA 117

Nagy, Laszlo 1925-1978 .... **CLC 7**
See also CA 129; 112

Naidu, Sarojini 1879-1949 .... **TCLC 80**
See also EWL 3; RGEL 2

Naipaul, Shiva(dhar Srinivasa) 1945-1985 .... **CLC 32, 39; TCLC 153**
See also CA 110; 112; 116; CANR 33; DA3; DAM NOV; DLB 157; DLBY 1985; EWL 3; MTCW 1, 2

Naipaul, V(idiadhar) S(urajprasad) 1932- .... **CLC 4, 7, 9, 13, 18, 37, 105; SSC 38**
See also BPFB 2; BRWS 1; CA 1-4R; CANR 1, 33, 51, 91, 126; CDBLB 1960 to Present; CDWLB 3; CN 7; DA3; DAB; DAC; DAM MST, NOV; DLB 125, 204, 207; DLBY 1985, 2001; EWL 3; LATS 1; MTCW 1, 2; RGEL 2; RGSF 2; TWA; WLIT 4; WWE 1

Nakos, Lilika 1903(?)-1989 .... **CLC 29**

Napoleon
See Yamamoto, Hisaye

Narayan, R(asipuram) K(rishnaswami) 1906-2001 . **CLC 7, 28, 47, 121; SSC 25**
See also BPFB 2; CA 81-84; 196; CANR 33, 61, 112; CN 7; DA3; DAM NOV; DNFS 1; EWL 3; MTCW 1, 2; RGEL 2; RGSF 2; SATA 62; SSFS 5; WWE 1

Nash, (Frediric) Ogden 1902-1971 . **CLC 23; PC 21; TCLC 109**
See also CA 13-14; 29-32R; CANR 34, 61; CAP 1; DAM POET; DLB 11; MAICYA 1, 2; MTCW 1, 2; RGAL 4; SATA 2, 46; WP

Nashe, Thomas 1567-1601(?) .... **LC 41, 89**
See also DLB 167; RGEL 2

Nathan, Daniel
See Dannay, Frederic

Nathan, George Jean 1882-1958 .... **TCLC 18**
See Hatteras, Owen
See also CA 114; 169; DLB 137

Natsume, Kinnosuke
See Natsume, Soseki

Natsume, Soseki 1867-1916 .... **TCLC 2, 10**
See Natsume Soseki; Soseki
See also CA 104; 195; RGWL 2, 3; TWA

Natsume Soseki
See Natsume, Soseki
See also DLB 180; EWL 3

Natti, (Mary) Lee 1919-
See Kingman, Lee
See also CA 5-8R; CANR 2

Navarre, Marguerite de
See de Navarre, Marguerite

Naylor, Gloria 1950- ..... **BLC 3; CLC 28, 52, 156; WLCS**
See also AAYA 6, 39; AFAW 1, 2; AMWS 8; BW 2, 3; CA 107; CANR 27, 51, 74, 130; CN 7; CPW; DA; DA3; DAC; DAM MST, MULT, NOV, POP; DLB 173; EWL 3; FW; MTCW 1, 2; NFS 4, 7; RGAL 4; TUS

Neff, Debra .... **CLC 59**

Neihardt, John Gneisenau 1881-1973 .... **CLC 32**
See also CA 13-14; CANR 65; CAP 1; DLB 9, 54, 256; LAIT 2

Nekrasov, Nikolai Alekseevich 1821-1878 .... **NCLC 11**
See also DLB 277

Nelligan, Emile 1879-1941 .... **TCLC 14**
See also CA 114; 204; DLB 92; EWL 3

Nelson, Willie 1933- .... **CLC 17**
See also CA 107; CANR 114

Nemerov, Howard (Stanley) 1920-1991 .... **CLC 2, 6, 9, 36; PC 24; TCLC 124**
See also AMW; CA 1-4R; 134; CABS 2; CANR 1, 27, 53; DAM POET; DLB 5, 6; DLBY 1983; EWL 3; INT CANR-27; MTCW 1, 2; PFS 10, 14; RGAL 4

Neruda, Pablo 1904-1973 .. **CLC 1, 2, 5, 7, 9, 28, 62; HLC 2; PC 4; WLC**
See also CA 19-20; 45-48; CANR 131; CAP 2; DA; DA3; DAB; DAC; DAM MST, MULT, POET; DLB 283; DNFS 2; EWL 3; HW 1; LAW; MTCW 1, 2; PFS 11; RGWL 2, 3; TWA; WLIT 1; WP

Nerval, Gerard de 1808-1855 ... **NCLC 1, 67; PC 13; SSC 18**
See also DLB 217; EW 6; GFL 1789 to the Present; RGSF 2; RGWL 2, 3

Nervo, (Jose) Amado (Ruiz de) 1870-1919 .... **HLCS 2; TCLC 11**
See also CA 109; 131; DLB 290; EWL 3; HW 1; LAW

Nesbit, Malcolm
See Chester, Alfred

Nessi, Pio Baroja y
See Baroja (y Nessi), Pio

Nestroy, Johann 1801-1862 .... **NCLC 42**
See also DLB 133; RGWL 2, 3

Netterville, Luke
See O'Grady, Standish (James)

Neufeld, John (Arthur) 1938- .... **CLC 17**
See also AAYA 11; CA 25-28R; CANR 11, 37, 56; CLR 52; MAICYA 1, 2; SAAS 3; SATA 6, 81, 131; SATA-Essay 131; YAW

Neumann, Alfred 1895-1952 .... **TCLC 100**
See also CA 183; DLB 56

Neumann, Ferenc
See Molnar, Ferenc

Neville, Emily Cheney 1919- .... **CLC 12**
See also BYA 2; CA 5-8R; CANR 3, 37, 85; JRDA; MAICYA 1, 2; SAAS 2; SATA 1; YAW

Newbound, Bernard Slade 1930-
See Slade, Bernard
See also CA 81-84; CANR 49; CD 5; DAM DRAM

Newby, P(ercy) H(oward) 1918-1997 .... **CLC 2, 13**
See also CA 5-8R; 161; CANR 32, 67; CN 7; DAM NOV; DLB 15; MTCW 1; RGEL 2

Newcastle
See Cavendish, Margaret Lucas

Newlove, Donald 1928- .... **CLC 6**
See also CA 29-32R; CANR 25

Newlove, John (Herbert) 1938- .... **CLC 14**
See also CA 21-24R; CANR 9, 25; CP 7

Newman, Charles 1938- .... **CLC 2, 8**
See also CA 21-24R; CANR 84; CN 7

Newman, Edwin (Harold) 1919- .... **CLC 14**
See also AITN 1; CA 69-72; CANR 5

Newman, John Henry 1801-1890 . **NCLC 38, 99**
See also BRWS 7; DLB 18, 32, 55; RGEL 2

Newton, (Sir) Isaac 1642-1727 ...... **LC 35, 53**
See also DLB 252

Newton, Suzanne 1936- .... **CLC 35**
See also BYA 7; CA 41-44R; CANR 14; JRDA; SATA 5, 77

New York Dept. of Ed. .... **CLC 70**

Nexo, Martin Andersen 1869-1954 .... **TCLC 43**
See also CA 202; DLB 214; EWL 3

Nezval, Vitezslav 1900-1958 .... **TCLC 44**
See also CA 123; CDWLB 4; DLB 215; EWL 3

Ng, Fae Myenne 1957(?)- .... **CLC 81**
See also BYA 11; CA 146

Ngema, Mbongeni 1955- .... **CLC 57**
See also BW 2; CA 143; CANR 84; CD 5

Ngugi, James T(hiong'o) . **CLC 3, 7, 13, 182**
See Ngugi wa Thiong'o

Ngugi wa Thiong'o
See Ngugi wa Thiong'o
See also DLB 125; EWL 3

Ngugi wa Thiong'o 1938- ... **BLC 3; CLC 36, 182**
See Ngugi, James T(hiong'o); Ngugi wa Thiong'o
See also AFW; BRWS 8; BW 2; CA 81-84; CANR 27, 58; CDWLB 3; DAM MULT, NOV; DNFS 2; MTCW 1, 2; RGEL 2; WWE 1

Niatum, Duane 1938- .... **NNAL**
See also CA 41-44R; CANR 21, 45, 83; DLB 175

Nichol, B(arrie) P(hillip) 1944-1988 . **CLC 18**
See also CA 53-56; DLB 53; SATA 66

Nicholas of Cusa 1401-1464 .... **LC 80**
See also DLB 115

Nichols, John (Treadwell) 1940- .... **CLC 38**
See also AMWS 13; CA 9-12R, 190; CAAE 190; CAAS 2; CANR 6, 70, 121; DLBY 1982; LATS 1; TCWW 2

Nichols, Leigh
See Koontz, Dean R(ay)

Nichols, Peter (Richard) 1927- .... **CLC 5, 36, 65**
See also CA 104; CANR 33, 86; CBD; CD 5; DLB 13, 245; MTCW 1

Nicholson, Linda ed. .... **CLC 65**

Ni Chuilleanain, Eilean 1942- .... **PC 34**
See also CA 126; CANR 53, 83; CP 7; CWP; DLB 40

Nicolas, F. R. E.
See Freeling, Nicolas

Niedecker, Lorine 1903-1970 ..... **CLC 10, 42; PC 42**
See also CA 25-28; CAP 2; DAM POET; DLB 48

Nietzsche, Friedrich (Wilhelm) 1844-1900 .... **TCLC 10, 18, 55**
See also CA 107; 121; CDWLB 2; DLB 129; EW 7; RGWL 2, 3; TWA

Nievo, Ippolito 1831-1861 .... **NCLC 22**

Nightingale, Anne Redmon 1943-
See Redmon, Anne
See also CA 103

Nightingale, Florence 1820-1910 ... **TCLC 85**
See also CA 188; DLB 166

Nijo Yoshimoto 1320-1388 .... **CMLC 49**
See also DLB 203

Nik. T. O.
See Annensky, Innokenty (Fyodorovich)

Nin, Anais 1903-1977 ..... **CLC 1, 4, 8, 11, 14, 60, 127; SSC 10**
See also AITN 2; AMWS 10; BPFB 2; CA 13-16R; 69-72; CANR 22, 53; DAM NOV, POP; DLB 2, 4, 152; EWL 3; GLL 2; MAWW; MTCW 1, 2; RGAL 4; RGSF 2

Nisbet, Robert A(lexander) 1913-1996 .... **TCLC 117**
See also CA 25-28R; 153; CANR 17; INT CANR-17

Nishida, Kitaro 1870-1945 .... **TCLC 83**

Nishiwaki, Junzaburo
See Nishiwaki, Junzaburo
See also CA 194

Nishiwaki, Junzaburo 1894-1982 .... **PC 15**
See Nishiwaki, Junzaburo; Nishiwaki Junzaburo
See also CA 194; 107; MJW; RGWL 3

Nishiwaki Junzaburo
See Nishiwaki, Junzaburo
See also EWL 3

Nissenson, Hugh 1933- .... **CLC 4, 9**
See also CA 17-20R; CANR 27, 108; CN 7; DLB 28

Nister, Der
See Der Nister
See also EWL 3

Niven, Larry .... **CLC 8**
See Niven, Laurence Van Cott
See also AAYA 27; BPFB 2; BYA 10; DLB 8; SCFW 2

Niven, Laurence Van Cott 1938-
See Niven, Larry
See also CA 21-24R, 207; CAAE 207; CAAS 12; CANR 14, 44, 66, 113; CPW; DAM POP; MTCW 1, 2; SATA 95; SFW 4

Nixon, Agnes Eckhardt 1927- .... **CLC 21**
See also CA 110

Nizan, Paul 1905-1940 .... **TCLC 40**
See also CA 161; DLB 72; EWL 3; GFL 1789 to the Present

Nkosi, Lewis 1936- .... **BLC 3; CLC 45**
See also BW 1, 3; CA 65-68; CANR 27, 81; CBD; CD 5; DAM MULT; DLB 157, 225; WWE 1

Nodier, (Jean) Charles (Emmanuel) 1780-1844 .... **NCLC 19**
See also DLB 119; GFL 1789 to the Present

Noguchi, Yone 1875-1947 .... **TCLC 80**

Nolan, Christopher 1965- .... **CLC 58**
See also CA 111; CANR 88

Noon, Jeff 1957- .... **CLC 91**
See also CA 148; CANR 83; DLB 267; SFW 4

Norden, Charles
See Durrell, Lawrence (George)

Nordhoff, Charles Bernard 1887-1947 .... **TCLC 23**
See also CA 108; 211; DLB 9; LAIT 1; RHW 1; SATA 23

Norfolk, Lawrence 1963- .... **CLC 76**
See also CA 144; CANR 85; CN 7; DLB 267

Norman, Marsha 1947- . **CLC 28, 186; DC 8**
See also CA 105; CABS 3; CAD; CANR 41, 131; CD 5; CSW; CWD; DAM DRAM; DFS 2; DLB 266; DLBY 1984; FW

Normyx
See Douglas, (George) Norman

Norris, (Benjamin) Frank(lin, Jr.) 1870-1902 .... **SSC 28; TCLC 24**
See also AMW; AMWS 2; BPFB 2; CA 110; 160; CDALB 1865-1917; DLB 12, 71, 186; LMFS 2; NFS 12; RGAL 4; TCWW 2; TUS

Norris, Leslie 1921- .... **CLC 14**
See also CA 11-12; CANR 14, 117; CAP 1; CP 7; DLB 27, 256

North, Andrew
See Norton, Andre

North, Anthony
See Koontz, Dean R(ay)

North, Captain George
See Stevenson, Robert Louis (Balfour)

North, Captain George
See Stevenson, Robert Louis (Balfour)

North, Milou
See Erdrich, Louise

Northrup, B. A.
See Hubbard, L(afayette) Ron(ald)

North Staffs
See Hulme, T(homas) E(rnest)

Northup, Solomon 1808-1863 ...... **NCLC 105**

Norton, Alice Mary
See Norton, Andre
See also MAICYA 1; SATA 1, 43

Norton, Andre 1912- .... **CLC 12**
See Norton, Alice Mary
See also AAYA 14; BPFB 2; BYA 4, 10, 12; CA 1-4R; CANR 68; CLR 50; DLB 8, 52; JRDA; MAICYA 2; MTCW 1; SATA 91; SUFW 1, 2; YAW

Norton, Caroline 1808-1877 .... **NCLC 47**
See also DLB 21, 159, 199

Paustovsky, Konstantin (Georgievich)
1892-1968 .... **CLC 40**
See also CA 93-96; 25-28R; DLB 272;
EWL 3

Pavese, Cesare 1908-1950 .... **PC 13; SSC 19;
TCLC 3**
See also CA 104; 169; DLB 128, 177; EW
12; EWL 3; PFS 20; RGSF 2; RGWL 2,
3; TWA

Pavic, Milorad 1929- .... **CLC 60**
See also CA 136; CDWLB 4; CWW 2; DLB
181; EWL 3; RGWL 3

Pavlov, Ivan Petrovich 1849-1936 . **TCLC 91**
See also CA 118; 180

Pavlova, Karolina Karlovna
1807-1893 .... **NCLC 138**
See also DLB 205

Payne, Alan
See Jakes, John (William)

Paz, Gil
See Lugones, Leopoldo

Paz, Octavio 1914-1998 . **CLC 3, 4, 6, 10, 19,
51, 65, 119; HLC 2; PC 1, 48; WLC**
See also AAYA 50; CA 73-76; 165; CANR
32, 65, 104; CWW 2; DA; DA3; DAB;
DAC; DAM MST, MULT, POET; DLB
290; DLBY 1990, 1998; DNFS 1; EWL
3; HW 1, 2; LAW; LAWS 1; MTCW 1, 2;
PFS 18; RGWL 2, 3; SSFS 13; TWA;
WLIT 1

p'Bitek, Okot 1931-1982 .... **BLC 3; CLC 96;
TCLC 149**
See also AFW; BW 2, 3; CA 124; 107;
CANR 82; DAM MULT; DLB 125; EWL
3; MTCW 1, 2; RGEL 2; WLIT 2

Peacock, Molly 1947- .... **CLC 60**
See also CA 103; CAAS 21; CANR 52, 84;
CP 7; CWP; DLB 120, 282

Peacock, Thomas Love
1785-1866 .... **NCLC 22**
See also BRW 4; DLB 96, 116; RGEL 2;
RGSF 2

Peake, Mervyn 1911-1968 .... **CLC 7, 54**
See also CA 5-8R; 25-28R; CANR 3; DLB
15, 160, 255; FANT; MTCW 1; RGEL 2;
SATA 23; SFW 4

Pearce, Philippa
See Christie, Philippa
See also CA 5-8R; CANR 4, 109; CWRI 5;
FANT; MAICYA 2

Pearl, Eric
See Elman, Richard (Martin)

Pearson, T(homas) R(eid) 1956- .... **CLC 39**
See also CA 120; 130; CANR 97; CSW;
INT CA-130

Peck, Dale 1967- .... **CLC 81**
See also CA 146; CANR 72, 127; GLL 2

Peck, John (Frederick) 1941- .... **CLC 3**
See also CA 49-52; CANR 3, 100; CP 7

Peck, Richard (Wayne) 1934- .... **CLC 21**
See also AAYA 1, 24; BYA 1, 6, 8, 11; CA
85-88; CANR 19, 38, 129; CLR 15; INT
CANR-19; JRDA; MAICYA 1, 2; SAAS
2; SATA 18, 55, 97; SATA-Essay 110;
WYA; YAW

Peck, Robert Newton 1928- .... **CLC 17**
See also AAYA 3, 43; BYA 1, 6; CA 81-84,
182; CAAE 182; CANR 31, 63, 127; CLR
45; DA; DAC; DAM MST; JRDA; LAIT
3; MAICYA 1, 2; SAAS 1; SATA 21, 62,
111; SATA-Essay 108; WYA; YAW

Peckinpah, (David) Sam(uel)
1925-1984 .... **CLC 20**
See also CA 109; 114; CANR 82

Pedersen, Knut 1859-1952
See Hamsun, Knut
See also CA 104; 119; CANR 63; MTCW
1, 2

Peeslake, Gaffer
See Durrell, Lawrence (George)

Peguy, Charles (Pierre)
1873-1914 .... **TCLC 10**
See also CA 107; 193; DLB 258; EWL 3;
GFL 1789 to the Present

Peirce, Charles Sanders
1839-1914 .... **TCLC 81**
See also CA 194; DLB 270

Pellicer, Carlos 1900(?)-1977 .... **HLCS 2**
See also CA 153; 69-72; DLB 290; EWL 3;
HW 1

Pena, Ramon del Valle y
See Valle-Inclan, Ramon (Maria) del

Pendennis, Arthur Esquir
See Thackeray, William Makepeace

Penn, William 1644-1718 .... **LC 25**
See also DLB 24

PEPECE
See Prado (Calvo), Pedro

Pepys, Samuel 1633-1703 ... **LC 11, 58; WLC**
See also BRW 2; CDBLB 1660-1789; DA;
DA3; DAB; DAC; DAM MST; DLB 101,
213; NCFS 4; RGEL 2; TEA; WLIT 3

Percy, Thomas 1729-1811 .... **NCLC 95**
See also DLB 104

Percy, Walker 1916-1990 .... **CLC 2, 3, 6, 8,
14, 18, 47, 65**
See also AMWS 3; BPFB 3; CA 1-4R; 131;
CANR 1, 23, 64; CPW; CSW; DA3;
DAM NOV, POP; DLB 2; DLBY 1980,
1990; EWL 3; MTCW 1, 2; RGAL 4;
TUS

Percy, William Alexander
1885-1942 .... **TCLC 84**
See also CA 163; MTCW 2

Perec, Georges 1936-1982 .... **CLC 56, 116**
See also CA 141; DLB 83, 299; EWL 3;
GFL 1789 to the Present; RGWL 3

**Pereda (y Sanchez de Porrua), Jose Maria
de** 1833-1906 .... **TCLC 16**
See also CA 117

Pereda y Porrua, Jose Maria de
See Pereda (y Sanchez de Porrua), Jose
Maria de

Peregoy, George Weems
See Mencken, H(enry) L(ouis)

Perelman, S(idney) J(oseph)
1904-1979 .. **CLC 3, 5, 9, 15, 23, 44, 49;
SSC 32**
See also AITN 1, 2; BPFB 3; CA 73-76;
89-92; CANR 18; DAM DRAM; DLB 11,
44; MTCW 1, 2; RGAL 4

Peret, Benjamin 1899-1959 .... **PC 33; TCLC
20**
See also CA 117; 186; GFL 1789 to the
Present

Peretz, Isaac Leib 1851(?)-1915
See Peretz, Isaac Loeb
See also CA 201

Peretz, Isaac Loeb 1851(?)-1915 ...... **SSC 26;
TCLC 16**
See Peretz, Isaac Leib
See also CA 109

Peretz, Yitzkhok Leibush
See Peretz, Isaac Loeb

Perez Galdos, Benito 1843-1920 ..... **HLCS 2;
TCLC 27**
See Galdos, Benito Perez
See also CA 125; 153; EWL 3; HW 1;
RGWL 2, 3

Peri Rossi, Cristina 1941- .. **CLC 156; HLCS
2**
See also CA 131; CANR 59, 81; DLB 145,
290; EWL 3; HW 1, 2

Perlata
See Peret, Benjamin

Perloff, Marjorie G(abrielle)
1931- .... **CLC 137**
See also CA 57-60; CANR 7, 22, 49, 104

Perrault, Charles 1628-1703 ... **DC 12; LC 2,
56**
See also BYA 4; CLR 79; DLB 268; GFL
Beginnings to 1789; MAICYA 1, 2;
RGWL 2, 3; SATA 25; WCH

Perry, Anne 1938- .... **CLC 126**
See also CA 101; CANR 22, 50, 84; CMW
4; CN 7; CPW; DLB 276

Perry, Brighton
See Sherwood, Robert E(mmet)

Perse, St.-John
See Leger, (Marie-Rene Auguste) Alexis
Saint-Leger

Perse, Saint-John
See Leger, (Marie-Rene Auguste) Alexis
Saint-Leger
See also DLB 258; RGWL 3

Perutz, Leo(pold) 1882-1957 .... **TCLC 60**
See also CA 147; DLB 81

Peseenz, Tulio F.
See Lopez y Fuentes, Gregorio

Pesetsky, Bette 1932- .... **CLC 28**
See also CA 133; DLB 130

Peshkov, Alexei Maximovich 1868-1936
See Gorky, Maxim
See also CA 105; 141; CANR 83; DA;
DAC; DAM DRAM, MST, NOV; MTCW
2

Pessoa, Fernando (Antonio Nogueira)
1888-1935 ..... **HLC 2; PC 20; TCLC 27**
See also CA 125; 183; DAM MULT; DLB
287; EW 10; EWL 3; RGWL 2, 3; WP

Peterkin, Julia Mood 1880-1961 ...... **CLC 31**
See also CA 102; DLB 9

Peters, Joan K(aren) 1945- .... **CLC 39**
See also CA 158; CANR 109

Peters, Robert L(ouis) 1924- .... **CLC 7**
See also CA 13-16R; CAAS 8; CP 7; DLB
105

Petofi, Sandor 1823-1849 .... **NCLC 21**
See also RGWL 2, 3

Petrakis, Harry Mark 1923- .... **CLC 3**
See also CA 9-12R; CANR 4, 30, 85; CN 7

Petrarch 1304-1374 .... **CMLC 20; PC 8**
See also DA3; DAM POET; EW 2; LMFS
1; RGWL 2. 3

Petronius c. 20-66 .... **CMLC 34**
See also AW 2; CDWLB 1; DLB 211;
RGWL 2, 3

Petrov, Evgeny .... **TCLC 21**
See Kataev, Evgeny Petrovich

Petry, Ann (Lane) 1908-1997 .. **CLC 1, 7, 18;
TCLC 112**
See also AFAW 1, 2; BPFB 3; BW 1, 3;
BYA 2; CA 5-8R; 157; CAAS 6; CANR
4, 46; CLR 12; CN 7; DLB 76; EWL 3;
JRDA; LAIT 1; MAICYA 1, 2; MAIC-
YAS 1; MTCW 1; RGAL 4; SATA 5;
SATA-Obit 94; TUS

Petursson, Halligrimur 1614-1674 .... **LC 8**

Peychinovich
See Vazov, Ivan (Minchov)

Phaedrus c. 15B.C.-c. 50 .... **CMLC 25**
See also DLB 211

Phelps (Ward), Elizabeth Stuart
See Phelps, Elizabeth Stuart
See also FW

Phelps, Elizabeth Stuart
1844-1911 .... **TCLC 113**
See Phelps (Ward), Elizabeth Stuart
See also DLB 74

Philips, Katherine 1632-1664 . **LC 30; PC 40**
See also DLB 131; RGEL 2

Philipson, Morris H. 1926- .... **CLC 53**
See also CA 1-4R; CANR 4

Poliakoff, Stephen 1952- .... **CLC 38**
See also CA 106; CANR 116; CBD; CD 5;
DLB 13

Police, The
See Copeland, Stewart (Armstrong); Summers, Andrew James

Polidori, John William 1795-1821 . **NCLC 51**
See also DLB 116; HGG

Pollitt, Katha 1949- .... **CLC 28, 122**
See also CA 120; 122; CANR 66, 108;
MTCW 1, 2

Pollock, (Mary) Sharon 1936- .... **CLC 50**
See also CA 141; CD 5; CWD; DAC; DAM
DRAM, MST; DFS 3; DLB 60; FW

Pollock, Sharon 1936- .... **DC 20**

Polo, Marco 1254-1324 .... **CMLC 15**

Polonsky, Abraham (Lincoln)
1910-1999 .... **CLC 92**
See also CA 104; 187; DLB 26; INT CA-
104

Polybius c. 200B.C.-c. 118B.C. ...... **CMLC 17**
See also AW 1; DLB 176; RGWL 2, 3

Pomerance, Bernard 1940- .... **CLC 13**
See also CA 101; CAD; CANR 49; CD 5;
DAM DRAM; DFS 9; LAIT 2

Ponge, Francis 1899-1988 .... **CLC 6, 18**
See also CA 85-88; 126; CANR 40, 86;
DAM POET; DLBY 2002; EWL 3; GFL
1789 to the Present; RGWL 2, 3

Poniatowska, Elena 1933- . **CLC 140; HLC 2**
See also CA 101; CANR 32, 66, 107; CD-
WLB 3; DAM MULT; DLB 113; EWL 3;
HW 1; LAWS 1; WLIT 1

Pontoppidan, Henrik 1857-1943 .... **TCLC 29**
See also CA 170; DLB 300

Poole, Josephine .... **CLC 17**
See Helyar, Jane Penelope Josephine
See also SAAS 2; SATA 5

Popa, Vasko 1922-1991 .... **CLC 19**
See also CA 112; 148; CDWLB 4; DLB
181; EWL 3; RGWL 2, 3

Pope, Alexander 1688-1744 ...... **LC 3, 58, 60,**
64; PC 26; WLC
See also BRW 3; BRWC 1; BRWR 1; CD-
BLB 1660-1789; DA; DA3; DAB; DAC;
DAM MST, POET; DLB 95, 101, 213;
EXPP; PAB; PFS 12; RGEL 2; WLIT 3;
WP

Popov, Evgenii Anatol'evich
See Popov, Yevgeny
See also DLB 285

Popov, Yevgeny .... **CLC 59**
See Popov, Evgenii Anatol'evich

Poquelin, Jean-Baptiste
See Moliere

Porter, Connie (Rose) 1959(?)- .... **CLC 70**
See also BW 2, 3; CA 142; CANR 90, 109;
SATA 81, 129

Porter, Gene(va Grace) Stratton .. **TCLC 21**
See Stratton-Porter, Gene(va Grace)
See also BPFB 3; CA 112; CWRI 5; RHW

Porter, Katherine Anne 1890-1980 ... **CLC 1,**
3, 7, 10, 13, 15, 27, 101; SSC 4, 31, 43
See also AAYA 42; AITN 2; AMW; BPFB
3; CA 1-4R; 101; CANR 1, 65; CDALBS;
DA; DA3; DAB; DAC; DAM MST, NOV;
DLB 4, 9, 102; DLBD 12; DLBY 1980;
EWL 3; EXPS; LAIT 3; MAWW; MTCW
1, 2; NFS 14; RGAL 4; RGSF 2; SATA
39; SATA-Obit 23; SSFS 1, 8, 11, 16;
TUS

Porter, Peter (Neville Frederick)
1929- .... **CLC 5, 13, 33**
See also CA 85-88; CP 7; DLB 40, 289;
WWE 1

Porter, William Sydney 1862-1910
See Henry, O.
See also CA 104; 131; CDALB 1865-1917;
DA; DA3; DAB; DAC; DAM MST; DLB
12, 78, 79; MTCW 1, 2; TUS; YABC 2

Portillo (y Pacheco), Jose Lopez
See Lopez Portillo (y Pacheco), Jose

Portillo Trambley, Estela 1927-1998 .. **HLC 2**
See Trambley, Estela Portillo
See also CANR 32; DAM MULT; DLB
209; HW 1

Posey, Alexander (Lawrence)
1873-1908 .... **NNAL**
See also CA 144; CANR 80; DAM MULT;
DLB 175

Posse, Abel .... **CLC 70**

Post, Melville Davisson
1869-1930 .... **TCLC 39**
See also CA 110; 202; CMW 4

Potok, Chaim 1929-2002 ... **CLC 2, 7, 14, 26,**
112
See also AAYA 15, 50; AITN 1, 2; BPFB 3;
BYA 1; CA 17-20R; 208; CANR 19, 35,
64, 98; CLR 92; CN 7; DA3; DAM NOV;
DLB 28, 152; EXPN; INT CANR-19;
LAIT 4; MTCW 1, 2; NFS 4; SATA 33,
106; SATA-Obit 134; TUS; YAW

Potok, Herbert Harold -2002
See Potok, Chaim

Potok, Herman Harold
See Potok, Chaim

Potter, Dennis (Christopher George)
1935-1994 .... **CLC 58, 86, 123**
See also CA 107; 145; CANR 33, 61; CBD;
DLB 233; MTCW 1

Pound, Ezra (Weston Loomis)
1885-1972 .. **CLC 1, 2, 3, 4, 5, 7, 10, 13,**
18, 34, 48, 50, 112; PC 4; WLC
See also AAYA 47; AMW; AMWR 1; CA
5-8R; 37-40R; CANR 40; CDALB 1917-
1929; DA; DA3; DAB; DAC; DAM MST,
POET; DLB 4, 45, 63; DLBD 15; EFS 2;
EWL 3; EXPP; LMFS 2; MTCW 1, 2;
PAB; PFS 2, 8, 16; RGAL 4; TUS; WP

Povod, Reinaldo 1959-1994 .... **CLC 44**
See also CA 136; 146; CANR 83

Powell, Adam Clayton, Jr.
1908-1972 .... **BLC 3; CLC 89**
See also BW 1, 3; CA 102; 33-36R; CANR
86; DAM MULT

Powell, Anthony (Dymoke)
1905-2000 .... **CLC 1, 3, 7, 9, 10, 31**
See also BRW 7; CA 1-4R; 189; CANR 1,
32, 62, 107; CDBLB 1945-1960; CN 7;
DLB 15; EWL 3; MTCW 1, 2; RGEL 2;
TEA

Powell, Dawn 1896(?)-1965 .... **CLC 66**
See also CA 5-8R; CANR 121; DLBY 1997

Powell, Padgett 1952- .... **CLC 34**
See also CA 126; CANR 63, 101; CSW;
DLB 234; DLBY 01

Powell, (Oval) Talmage 1920-2000
See Queen, Ellery
See also CA 5-8R; CANR 2, 80

Power, Susan 1961- .... **CLC 91**
See also BYA 14; CA 160; NFS 11

Powers, J(ames) F(arl) 1917-1999 ..... **CLC 1,**
4, 8, 57; SSC 4
See also CA 1-4R; 181; CANR 2, 61; CN
7; DLB 130; MTCW 1; RGAL 4; RGSF
2

Powers, John J(ames) 1945-
See Powers, John R.
See also CA 69-72

Powers, John R. .... **CLC 66**
See Powers, John J(ames)

Powers, Richard (S.) 1957- .... **CLC 93**
See also AMWS 9; BPFB 3; CA 148;
CANR 80; CN 7

Pownall, David 1938- .... **CLC 10**
See also CA 89-92, 180; CAAS 18; CANR
49, 101; CBD; CD 5; CN 7; DLB 14

Powys, John Cowper 1872-1963 ... **CLC 7, 9,**
15, 46, 125
See also CA 85-88; CANR 106; DLB 15,
255; EWL 3; FANT; MTCW 1, 2; RGEL
2; SUFW

Powys, T(heodore) F(rancis)
1875-1953 .... **TCLC 9**
See also BRWS 8; CA 106; 189; DLB 36,
162; EWL 3; FANT; RGEL 2; SUFW

Prado (Calvo), Pedro 1886-1952 ... **TCLC 75**
See also CA 131; DLB 283; HW 1; LAW

Prager, Emily 1952- .... **CLC 56**
See also CA 204

Pratolini, Vasco 1913-1991 .... **TCLC 124**
See also CA 211; DLB 177; EWL 3; RGWL
2, 3

Pratt, E(dwin) J(ohn) 1883(?)-1964 . **CLC 19**
See also CA 141; 93-96; CANR 77; DAC;
DAM POET; DLB 92; EWL 3; RGEL 2;
TWA

Premchand .... **TCLC 21**
See Srivastava, Dhanpat Rai
See also EWL 3

Preseren, France 1800-1849 .... **NCLC 127**
See also CDWLB 4; DLB 147

Preussler, Otfried 1923- .... **CLC 17**
See also CA 77-80; SATA 24

Prevert, Jacques (Henri Marie)
1900-1977 .... **CLC 15**
See also CA 77-80; 69-72; CANR 29, 61;
DLB 258; EWL 3; GFL 1789 to the
Present; IDFW 3, 4; MTCW 1; RGWL 2,
3; SATA-Obit 30

Prevost, (Antoine Francois)
1697-1763 .... **LC 1**
See also EW 4; GFL Beginnings to 1789;
RGWL 2, 3

Price, (Edward) Reynolds 1933- ... **CLC 3, 6,**
13, 43, 50, 63; SSC 22
See also AMWS 6; CA 1-4R; CANR 1, 37,
57, 87, 128; CN 7; CSW; DAM NOV;
DLB 2, 218, 278; EWL 3; INT CANR-
37; NFS 18

Price, Richard 1949- .... **CLC 6, 12**
See also CA 49-52; CANR 3; DLBY 1981

Prichard, Katharine Susannah
1883-1969 .... **CLC 46**
See also CA 11-12; CANR 33; CAP 1; DLB
260; MTCW 1; RGEL 2; RGSF 2; SATA
66

Priestley, J(ohn) B(oynton)
1894-1984 .... **CLC 2, 5, 9, 34**
See also BRW 7; CA 9-12R; 113; CANR
33; CDBLB 1914-1945; DA3; DAM
DRAM, NOV; DLB 10, 34, 77, 100, 139;
DLBY 1984; EWL 3; MTCW 1, 2; RGEL
2; SFW 4

Prince 1958- .... **CLC 35**
See also CA 213

Prince, F(rank) T(empleton)
1912-2003 .... **CLC 22**
See also CA 101; 219; CANR 43, 79; CP 7;
DLB 20

Prince Kropotkin
See Kropotkin, Peter (Aleksieevich)

Prior, Matthew 1664-1721 .... **LC 4**
See also DLB 95; RGEL 2

Prishvin, Mikhail 1873-1954 .... **TCLC 75**
See Prishvin, Mikhail Mikhailovich

Prishvin, Mikhail Mikhailovich
See Prishvin, Mikhail
See also DLB 272; EWL 3

Pritchard, William H(arrison)
1932- .... **CLC 34**
See also CA 65-68; CANR 23, 95; DLB
111

Pritchett, V(ictor) S(awdon)
1900-1997 ... **CLC 5, 13, 15, 41; SSC 14**
See also BPFB 3; BRWS 3; CA 61-64; 157; CANR 31, 63; CN 7; DA3; DAM NOV; DLB 15, 139; EWL 3; MTCW 1, 2; RGEL 2; RGSF 2; TEA

Private 19022
See Manning, Frederic

Probst, Mark 1925- .... **CLC 59**
See also CA 130

Prokosch, Frederic 1908-1989 ...... **CLC 4, 48**
See also CA 73-76; 128; CANR 82; DLB 48; MTCW 2

Propertius, Sextus c. 50B.C.-c.
16B.C. .... **CMLC 32**
See also AW 2; CDWLB 1; DLB 211; RGWL 2, 3

Prophet, The
See Dreiser, Theodore (Herman Albert)

Prose, Francine 1947- .... **CLC 45**
See also CA 109; 112; CANR 46, 95; DLB 234; SATA 101, 149

Proudhon
See Cunha, Euclides (Rodrigues Pimenta) da

Proulx, Annie
See Proulx, E(dna) Annie

Proulx, E(dna) Annie 1935- ...... **CLC 81, 158**
See also AMWS 7; BPFB 3; CA 145; CANR 65, 110; CN 7; CPW 1; DA3; DAM POP; MTCW 2; SSFS 18

Proust, (Valentin-Louis-George-Eugene)
Marcel 1871-1922 .... **TCLC 7, 13, 33; WLC**
See also BPFB 3; CA 104; 120; CANR 110; DA; DA3; DAB; DAC; DAM MST, NOV; DLB 65; EW 8; EWL 3; GFL 1789 to the Present; MTCW 1, 2; RGWL 2, 3; TWA

Prowler, Harley
See Masters, Edgar Lee

Prus, Boleslaw 1845-1912 .... **TCLC 48**
See also RGWL 2, 3

Pryor, Richard (Franklin Lenox Thomas)
1940- .... **CLC 26**
See also CA 122; 152

Przybyszewski, Stanislaw
1868-1927 .... **TCLC 36**
See also CA 160; DLB 66; EWL 3

Pteleon
See Grieve, C(hristopher) M(urray)
See also DAM POET

Puckett, Lute
See Masters, Edgar Lee

Puig, Manuel 1932-1990 .... **CLC 3, 5, 10, 28, 65, 133; HLC 2**
See also BPFB 3; CA 45-48; CANR 2, 32, 63; CDWLB 3; DA3; DAM MULT; DLB 113; DNFS 1; EWL 3; GLL 1; HW 1, 2; LAW; MTCW 1, 2; RGWL 2, 3; TWA; WLIT 1

Pulitzer, Joseph 1847-1911 .... **TCLC 76**
See also CA 114; DLB 23

Purchas, Samuel 1577(?)-1626 .... **LC 70**
See also DLB 151

Purdy, A(lfred) W(ellington)
1918-2000 .... **CLC 3, 6, 14, 50**
See also CA 81-84; 189; CAAS 17; CANR 42, 66; CP 7; DAC; DAM MST, POET; DLB 88; PFS 5; RGEL 2

Purdy, James (Amos) 1923- .... **CLC 2, 4, 10, 28, 52**
See also AMWS 7; CA 33-36R; CAAS 1; CANR 19, 51; CN 7; DLB 2, 218; EWL 3; INT CANR-19; MTCW 1; RGAL 4

Pure, Simon
See Swinnerton, Frank Arthur

Pushkin, Aleksandr Sergeevich
See Pushkin, Alexander (Sergeyevich)
See also DLB 205

Pushkin, Alexander (Sergeyevich)
1799-1837 .... **NCLC 3, 27, 83; PC 10; SSC 27, 55; WLC**
See Pushkin, Aleksandr Sergeevich
See also DA; DA3; DAB; DAC; DAM DRAM, MST, POET; EW 5; EXPS; RGSF 2; RGWL 2, 3; SATA 61; SSFS 9; TWA

P'u Sung-ling 1640-1715 .... **LC 49; SSC 31**

Putnam, Arthur Lee
See Alger, Horatio, Jr.

Puzo, Mario 1920-1999 .... **CLC 1, 2, 6, 36, 107**
See also BPFB 3; CA 65-68; 185; CANR 4, 42, 65, 99, 131; CN 7; CPW; DA3; DAM NOV, POP; DLB 6; MTCW 1, 2; NFS 16; RGAL 4

Pygge, Edward
See Barnes, Julian (Patrick)

Pyle, Ernest Taylor 1900-1945
See Pyle, Ernie
See also CA 115; 160

Pyle, Ernie .... **TCLC 75**
See Pyle, Ernest Taylor
See also DLB 29; MTCW 2

Pyle, Howard 1853-1911 .... **TCLC 81**
See also BYA 2, 4; CA 109; 137; CLR 22; DLB 42, 188; DLBD 13; LAIT 1; MAICYA 1, 2; SATA 16, 100; WCH; YAW

Pym, Barbara (Mary Crampton)
1913-1980 .... **CLC 13, 19, 37, 111**
See also BPFB 3; BRWS 2; CA 13-14; 97-100; CANR 13, 34; CAP 1; DLB 14, 207; DLBY 1987; EWL 3; MTCW 1, 2; RGEL 2; TEA

Pynchon, Thomas (Ruggles, Jr.)
1937- ...... **CLC 2, 3, 6, 9, 11, 18, 33, 62, 72, 123, 192; SSC 14; WLC**
See also AMWS 2; BEST 90:2; BPFB 3; CA 17-20R; CANR 22, 46, 73; CN 7; CPW 1; DA; DA3; DAB; DAC; DAM MST, NOV, POP; DLB 2, 173; EWL 3; MTCW 1, 2; RGAL 4; SFW 4; TUS

Pythagoras c. 582B.C.-c. 507B.C. . **CMLC 22**
See also DLB 176

Q
See Quiller-Couch, Sir Arthur (Thomas)

Qian, Chongzhu
See Ch'ien, Chung-shu

Qian Zhongshu
See Ch'ien, Chung-shu
See also CWW 2

Qroll
See Dagerman, Stig (Halvard)

Quarrington, Paul (Lewis) 1953- ..... **CLC 65**
See also CA 129; CANR 62, 95

Quasimodo, Salvatore 1901-1968 .... **CLC 10; PC 47**
See also CA 13-16; 25-28R; CAP 1; DLB 114; EW 12; EWL 3; MTCW 1; RGWL 2, 3

Quatermass, Martin
See Carpenter, John (Howard)

Quay, Stephen 1947- .... **CLC 95**
See also CA 189

Quay, Timothy 1947- .... **CLC 95**
See also CA 189

Queen, Ellery .... **CLC 3, 11**
See Dannay, Frederic; Davidson, Avram (James); Deming, Richard; Fairman, Paul W.; Flora, Fletcher; Hoch, Edward D(entinger); Kane, Henry; Lee, Manfred B(ennington); Marlowe, Stephen; Powell, (Oval) Talmage; Sheldon, Walter J(ames); Sturgeon, Theodore (Hamilton); Tracy, Don(ald Fiske); Vance, John Holbrook
See also BPFB 3; CMW 4; MSW; RGAL 4

Queen, Ellery, Jr.
See Dannay, Frederic; Lee, Manfred B(ennington)

Queneau, Raymond 1903-1976 ..... **CLC 2, 5, 10, 42**
See also CA 77-80; 69-72; CANR 32; DLB 72, 258; EW 12; EWL 3; GFL 1789 to the Present; MTCW 1, 2; RGWL 2, 3

Quevedo, Francisco de 1580-1645 .... **LC 23**

Quiller-Couch, Sir Arthur (Thomas)
1863-1944 .... **TCLC 53**
See also CA 118; 166; DLB 135, 153, 190; HGG; RGEL 2; SUFW 1

Quin, Ann (Marie) 1936-1973 .... **CLC 6**
See also CA 9-12R; 45-48; DLB 14, 231

Quincey, Thomas de
See De Quincey, Thomas

Quindlen, Anna 1953- .... **CLC 191**
See also AAYA 35; CA 138; CANR 73, 126; DA3; DLB 292; MTCW 2

Quinn, Martin
See Smith, Martin Cruz

Quinn, Peter 1947- .... **CLC 91**
See also CA 197

Quinn, Simon
See Smith, Martin Cruz

Quintana, Leroy V. 1944- ...... **HLC 2; PC 36**
See also CA 131; CANR 65; DAM MULT; DLB 82; HW 1, 2

Quiroga, Horacio (Sylvestre)
1878-1937 .... **HLC 2; TCLC 20**
See also CA 117; 131; DAM MULT; EWL 3; HW 1; LAW; MTCW 1; RGSF 2; WLIT 1

Quoirez, Francoise 1935- .... **CLC 9**
See Sagan, Francoise
See also CA 49-52; CANR 6, 39, 73; CWW 2; MTCW 1, 2; TWA

Raabe, Wilhelm (Karl) 1831-1910 . **TCLC 45**
See also CA 167; DLB 129

Rabe, David (William) 1940- .. **CLC 4, 8, 33; DC 16**
See also CA 85-88; CABS 3; CAD; CANR 59, 129; CD 5; DAM DRAM; DFS 3, 8, 13; DLB 7, 228; EWL 3

Rabelais, Francois 1494-1553 .... **LC 5, 60; WLC**
See also DA; DAB; DAC; DAM MST; EW 2; GFL Beginnings to 1789; LMFS 1; RGWL 2, 3; TWA

Rabinovitch, Sholem 1859-1916
See Aleichem, Sholom
See also CA 104

Rabinyan, Dorit 1972- .... **CLC 119**
See also CA 170

Rachilde
See Vallette, Marguerite Eymery; Vallette, Marguerite Eymery
See also EWL 3

Racine, Jean 1639-1699 .... **LC 28**
See also DA3; DAB; DAM MST; DLB 268; EW 3; GFL Beginnings to 1789; LMFS 1; RGWL 2, 3; TWA

Radcliffe, Ann (Ward) 1764-1823 ... **NCLC 6, 55, 106**
See also DLB 39, 178; HGG; LMFS 1; RGEL 2; SUFW; WLIT 3

Radclyffe-Hall, Marguerite
See Hall, (Marguerite) Radclyffe

Radiguet, Raymond 1903-1923 .... **TCLC 29**
See also CA 162; DLB 65; EWL 3; GFL 1789 to the Present; RGWL 2, 3

Radnoti, Miklos 1909-1944 .... **TCLC 16**
See also CA 118; 212; CDWLB 4; DLB 215; EWL 3; RGWL 2, 3

Rado, James 1939- .... **CLC 17**
See also CA 105

Radvanyi, Netty 1900-1983
See Seghers, Anna
See also CA 85-88; 110; CANR 82

Rae, Ben
See Griffiths, Trevor

Raeburn, John (Hay) 1941- .... **CLC 34**
See also CA 57-60

Ragni, Gerome 1942-1991 .... **CLC 17**
See also CA 105; 134

Rahv, Philip .... **CLC 24**
See Greenberg, Ivan
See also DLB 137

Raimund, Ferdinand Jakob
1790-1836 .... **NCLC 69**
See also DLB 90

Raine, Craig (Anthony) 1944- .. **CLC 32, 103**
See also CA 108; CANR 29, 51, 103; CP 7;
DLB 40; PFS 7

Raine, Kathleen (Jessie) 1908-2003 .. **CLC 7, 45**
See also CA 85-88; 218; CANR 46, 109;
CP 7; DLB 20; EWL 3; MTCW 1; RGEL 2

Rainis, Janis 1865-1929 .... **TCLC 29**
See also CA 170; CDWLB 4; DLB 220;
EWL 3

Rakosi, Carl .... **CLC 47**
See Rawley, Callman
See also CAAS 5; CP 7; DLB 193

Ralegh, Sir Walter
See Raleigh, Sir Walter
See also BRW 1; RGEL 2; WP

Raleigh, Richard
See Lovecraft, H(oward) P(hillips)

Raleigh, Sir Walter 1554(?)-1618 .... **LC 31, 39; PC 31**
See Ralegh, Sir Walter
See also CDBLB Before 1660; DLB 172;
EXPP; PFS 14; TEA

Rallentando, H. P.
See Sayers, Dorothy L(eigh)

Ramal, Walter
See de la Mare, Walter (John)

Ramana Maharshi 1879-1950 .... **TCLC 84**

Ramoacn y Cajal, Santiago
1852-1934 .... **TCLC 93**

Ramon, Juan
See Jimenez (Mantecon), Juan Ramon

Ramos, Graciliano 1892-1953 .... **TCLC 32**
See also CA 167; EWL 3; HW 2; LAW;
WLIT 1

Rampersad, Arnold 1941- .... **CLC 44**
See also BW 2, 3; CA 127; 133; CANR 81;
DLB 111; INT CA-133

Rampling, Anne
See Rice, Anne
See also GLL 2

Ramsay, Allan 1686(?)-1758 .... **LC 29**
See also DLB 95; RGEL 2

Ramsay, Jay
See Campbell, (John) Ramsey

Ramuz, Charles-Ferdinand
1878-1947 .... **TCLC 33**
See also CA 165; EWL 3

Rand, Ayn 1905-1982 ...... **CLC 3, 30, 44, 79; WLC**
See also AAYA 10; AMWS 4; BPFB 3;
BYA 12; CA 13-16R; 105; CANR 27, 73;
CDALBS; CPW; DA; DA3; DAC; DAM
MST, NOV, POP; DLB 227, 279; MTCW
1, 2; NFS 10, 16; RGAL 4; SFW 4; TUS;
YAW

Randall, Dudley (Felker) 1914-2000 . **BLC 3; CLC 1, 135**
See also BW 1, 3; CA 25-28R; 189; CANR
23, 82; DAM MULT; DLB 41; PFS 5

Randall, Robert
See Silverberg, Robert

Ranger, Ken
See Creasey, John

Rank, Otto 1884-1939 .... **TCLC 115**

Ransom, John Crowe 1888-1974 .. **CLC 2, 4, 5, 11, 24**
See also AMW; CA 5-8R; 49-52; CANR 6,
34; CDALBS; DA3; DAM POET; DLB
45, 63; EWL 3; EXPP; MTCW 1, 2;
RGAL 4; TUS

Rao, Raja 1909- .... **CLC 25, 56**
See also CA 73-76; CANR 51; CN 7; DAM
NOV; EWL 3; MTCW 1, 2; RGEL 2;
RGSF 2

Raphael, Frederic (Michael) 1931- ... **CLC 2, 14**
See also CA 1-4R; CANR 1, 86; CN 7;
DLB 14

Ratcliffe, James P.
See Mencken, H(enry) L(ouis)

Rathbone, Julian 1935- .... **CLC 41**
See also CA 101; CANR 34, 73

Rattigan, Terence (Mervyn)
1911-1977 .... **CLC 7; DC 18**
See also BRWS 7; CA 85-88; 73-76; CBD;
CDBLB 1945-1960; DAM DRAM; DFS
8; DLB 13; IDFW 3, 4; MTCW 1, 2;
RGEL 2

Ratushinskaya, Irina 1954- .... **CLC 54**
See also CA 129; CANR 68; CWW 2

Raven, Simon (Arthur Noel)
1927-2001 .... **CLC 14**
See also CA 81-84; 197; CANR 86; CN 7;
DLB 271

Ravenna, Michael
See Welty, Eudora (Alice)

Rawley, Callman 1903-
See Rakosi, Carl
See also CA 21-24R; CANR 12, 32, 91

Rawlings, Marjorie Kinnan
1896-1953 .... **TCLC 4**
See also AAYA 20; AMWS 10; ANW;
BPFB 3; BYA 3; CA 104; 137; CANR 74;
CLR 63; DLB 9, 22, 102; DLBD 17;
JRDA; MAICYA 1, 2; MTCW 2; RGAL
4; SATA 100; WCH; YABC 1; YAW

Ray, Satyajit 1921-1992 .... **CLC 16, 76**
See also CA 114; 137; DAM MULT

Read, Herbert Edward 1893-1968 ..... **CLC 4**
See also BRW 6; CA 85-88; 25-28R; DLB
20, 149; EWL 3; PAB; RGEL 2

Read, Piers Paul 1941- .... **CLC 4, 10, 25**
See also CA 21-24R; CANR 38, 86; CN 7;
DLB 14; SATA 21

Reade, Charles 1814-1884 .... **NCLC 2, 74**
See also DLB 21; RGEL 2

Reade, Hamish
See Gray, Simon (James Holliday)

Reading, Peter 1946- .... **CLC 47**
See also BRWS 8; CA 103; CANR 46, 96;
CP 7; DLB 40

Reaney, James 1926- .... **CLC 13**
See also CA 41-44R; CAAS 15; CANR 42;
CD 5; CP 7; DAC; DAM MST; DLB 68;
RGEL 2; SATA 43

Rebreanu, Liviu 1885-1944 .... **TCLC 28**
See also CA 165; DLB 220; EWL 3

Rechy, John (Francisco) 1934- ...... **CLC 1, 7, 14, 18, 107; HLC 2**
See also CA 5-8R; 195; CAAE 195; CAAS
4; CANR 6, 32, 64; CN 7; DAM MULT;
DLB 122, 278; DLBY 1982; HW 1, 2;
INT CANR-6; LLW 1; RGAL 4

Redcam, Tom 1870-1933 .... **TCLC 25**

Reddin, Keith .... **CLC 67**
See also CAD

Redgrove, Peter (William)
1932-2003 .... **CLC 6, 41**
See also BRWS 6; CA 1-4R; 217; CANR 3,
39, 77; CP 7; DLB 40

Redmon, Anne .... **CLC 22**
See Nightingale, Anne Redmon
See also DLBY 1986

Reed, Eliot
See Ambler, Eric

Reed, Ishmael 1938- ..... **BLC 3; CLC 2, 3, 5, 6, 13, 32, 60, 174**
See also AFAW 1, 2; AMWS 10; BPFB 3;
BW 2, 3; CA 21-24R; CANR 25, 48, 74,
128; CN 7; CP 7; CSW; DA3; DAM
MULT; DLB 2, 5, 33, 169, 227; DLBD 8;
EWL 3; LMFS 2; MSW; MTCW 1, 2;
PFS 6; RGAL 4; TCWW 2

Reed, John (Silas) 1887-1920 .... **TCLC 9**
See also CA 106; 195; TUS

Reed, Lou .... **CLC 21**
See Firbank, Louis

Reese, Lizette Woodworth 1856-1935 . **PC 29**
See also CA 180; DLB 54

Reeve, Clara 1729-1807 .... **NCLC 19**
See also DLB 39; RGEL 2

Reich, Wilhelm 1897-1957 .... **TCLC 57**
See also CA 199

Reid, Christopher (John) 1949- .... **CLC 33**
See also CA 140; CANR 89; CP 7; DLB
40; EWL 3

Reid, Desmond
See Moorcock, Michael (John)

Reid Banks, Lynne 1929-
See Banks, Lynne Reid
See also AAYA 49; CA 1-4R; CANR 6, 22,
38, 87; CLR 24; CN 7; JRDA; MAICYA
1, 2; SATA 22, 75, 111; YAW

Reilly, William K.
See Creasey, John

Reiner, Max
See Caldwell, (Janet Miriam) Taylor
(Holland)

Reis, Ricardo
See Pessoa, Fernando (Antonio Nogueira)

Reizenstein, Elmer Leopold
See Rice, Elmer (Leopold)
See also EWL 3

Remarque, Erich Maria 1898-1970 . **CLC 21**
See also AAYA 27; BPFB 3; CA 77-80; 29-
32R; CDWLB 2; DA; DA3; DAB; DAC;
DAM MST, NOV; DLB 56; EWL 3;
EXPN; LAIT 3; MTCW 1, 2; NFS 4;
RGWL 2, 3

Remington, Frederic 1861-1909 ..... **TCLC 89**
See also CA 108; 169; DLB 12, 186, 188;
SATA 41

Remizov, A.
See Remizov, Aleksei (Mikhailovich)

Remizov, A. M.
See Remizov, Aleksei (Mikhailovich)

Remizov, Aleksei (Mikhailovich)
1877-1957 .... **TCLC 27**
See Remizov, Alexey Mikhaylovich
See also CA 125; 133; DLB 295

Remizov, Alexey Mikhaylovich
See Remizov, Aleksei (Mikhailovich)
See also EWL 3

Renan, Joseph Ernest 1823-1892 .. **NCLC 26**
See also GFL 1789 to the Present

Renard, Jules(-Pierre) 1864-1910 .. **TCLC 17**
See also CA 117; 202; GFL 1789 to the
Present

Renault, Mary .... **CLC 3, 11, 17**
See Challans, Mary
See also BPFB 3; BYA 2; DLBY 1983;
EWL 3; GLL 1; LAIT 1; MTCW 2; RGEL
2; RHW

Rendell, Ruth (Barbara) 1930- .. **CLC 28, 48**
See Vine, Barbara
See also BPFB 3; BRWS 9; CA 109; CANR
32, 52, 74, 127; CN 7; CPW; DAM POP;
DLB 87, 276; INT CANR-32; MSW;
MTCW 1, 2

Renoir, Jean 1894-1979 .... **CLC 20**
See also CA 129; 85-88

Resnais, Alain 1922- .... **CLC 16**

Revard, Carter (Curtis) 1931- .... **NNAL**
　　See also CA 144; CANR 81; PFS 5

Reverdy, Pierre 1889-1960 .... **CLC 53**
　　See also CA 97-100; 89-92; DLB 258; EWL
　　3; GFL 1789 to the Present

Rexroth, Kenneth 1905-1982 .... **CLC 1, 2, 6,**
　　11, 22, 49, 112; PC 20
　　See also BG 3; CA 5-8R; 107; CANR 14,
　　34, 63; CDALB 1941-1968; DAM POET;
　　DLB 16, 48, 165, 212; DLBY 1982; EWL
　　3; INT CANR-14; MTCW 1, 2; RGAL 4

Reyes, Alfonso 1889-1959 .... **HLCS 2; TCLC**
　　33
　　See also CA 131; EWL 3; HW 1; LAW

Reyes y Basoalto, Ricardo Eliecer Neftali
　　See Neruda, Pablo

Reymont, Wladyslaw (Stanislaw)
　　1868(?)-1925 .... **TCLC 5**
　　See also CA 104; EWL 3

Reynolds, Jonathan 1942- .... **CLC 6, 38**
　　See also CA 65-68; CANR 28

Reynolds, Joshua 1723-1792 .... **LC 15**
　　See also DLB 104

Reynolds, Michael S(hane)
　　1937-2000 .... **CLC 44**
　　See also CA 65-68; 189; CANR 9, 89, 97

Reznikoff, Charles 1894-1976 .... **CLC 9**
　　See also CA 33-36; 61-64; CAP 2; DLB 28,
　　45; WP

Rezzori (d'Arezzo), Gregor von
　　1914-1998 .... **CLC 25**
　　See also CA 122; 136; 167

Rhine, Richard
　　See Silverstein, Alvin; Silverstein, Virginia
　　B(arbara Opshelor)

Rhodes, Eugene Manlove
　　1869-1934 .... **TCLC 53**
　　See also CA 198; DLB 256

R'hoone, Lord
　　See Balzac, Honore de

Rhys, Jean 1894(?)-1979 ...... **CLC 2, 4, 6, 14,**
　　19, 51, 124; SSC 21
　　See also BRWS 2; CA 25-28R; 85-88;
　　CANR 35, 62; CDBLB 1945-1960; CD-
　　WLB 3; DA3; DAM NOV; DLB 36, 117,
　　162; DNFS 2; EWL 3; LATS 1; MTCW
　　1, 2; RGEL 2; RGSF 2; RHW; TEA;
　　WWE 1

Ribeiro, Darcy 1922-1997 .... **CLC 34**
　　See also CA 33-36R; 156; EWL 3

Ribeiro, Joao Ubaldo (Osorio Pimentel)
　　1941- .... **CLC 10, 67**
　　See also CA 81-84; EWL 3

Ribman, Ronald (Burt) 1932- .... **CLC 7**
　　See also CA 21-24R; CAD; CANR 46, 80;
　　CD 5

Ricci, Nino (Pio) 1959- .... **CLC 70**
　　See also CA 137; CANR 130; CCA 1

Rice, Anne 1941- .... **CLC 41, 128**
　　See Rampling, Anne
　　See also AAYA 9, 53; AMWS 7; BEST
　　89:2; BPFB 3; CA 65-68; CANR 12, 36,
　　53, 74, 100; CN 7; CPW; CSW; DA3;
　　DAM POP; DLB 292; GLL 2; HGG;
　　MTCW 2; SUFW 2; YAW

Rice, Elmer (Leopold) 1892-1967 ...... **CLC 7,**
　　49
　　See Reizenstein, Elmer Leopold
　　See also CA 21-22; 25-28R; CAP 2; DAM
　　DRAM; DFS 12; DLB 4, 7; MTCW 1, 2;
　　RGAL 4

Rice, Tim(othy Miles Bindon)
　　1944- .... **CLC 21**
　　See also CA 103; CANR 46; DFS 7

Rich, Adrienne (Cecile) 1929- ... **CLC 3, 6, 7,**
　　11, 18, 36, 73, 76, 125; PC 5
　　See also AMWR 2; AMWS 1; CA 9-12R;
　　CANR 20, 53, 74, 128; CDALBS; CP 7;
　　CSW; CWP; DA3; DAM POET; DLB 5,
　　67; EWL 3; EXPP; FW; MAWW; MTCW
　　1, 2; PAB; PFS 15; RGAL 4; WP

Rich, Barbara
　　See Graves, Robert (von Ranke)

Rich, Robert
　　See Trumbo, Dalton

Richard, Keith .... **CLC 17**
　　See Richards, Keith

Richards, David Adams 1950- .... **CLC 59**
　　See also CA 93-96; CANR 60, 110; DAC;
　　DLB 53

Richards, I(vor) A(rmstrong)
　　1893-1979 .... **CLC 14, 24**
　　See also BRWS 2; CA 41-44R; 89-92;
　　CANR 34, 74; DLB 27; EWL 3; MTCW
　　2; RGEL 2

Richards, Keith 1943-
　　See Richard, Keith
　　See also CA 107; CANR 77

Richardson, Anne
　　See Roiphe, Anne (Richardson)

Richardson, Dorothy Miller
　　1873-1957 .... **TCLC 3**
　　See also CA 104; 192; DLB 36; EWL 3;
　　FW; RGEL 2

Richardson (Robertson), Ethel Florence
　　Lindesay 1870-1946
　　See Richardson, Henry Handel
　　See also CA 105; 190; DLB 230; RHW

Richardson, Henry Handel .... **TCLC 4**
　　See Richardson (Robertson), Ethel Florence
　　Lindesay
　　See also DLB 197; EWL 3; RGEL 2; RGSF
　　2

Richardson, John 1796-1852 .... **NCLC 55**
　　See also CCA 1; DAC; DLB 99

Richardson, Samuel 1689-1761 ...... **LC 1, 44;**
　　WLC
　　See also BRW 3; CDBLB 1660-1789; DA;
　　DAB; DAC; DAM MST, NOV; DLB 39;
　　RGEL 2; TEA; WLIT 3

Richardson, Willis 1889-1977 .... **HR 3**
　　See also BW 1; CA 124; DLB 51; SATA 60

Richler, Mordecai 1931-2001 .... **CLC 3, 5, 9,**
　　13, 18, 46, 70, 185
　　See also AITN 1; CA 65-68; 201; CANR
　　31, 62, 111; CCA 1; CLR 17; CWRI 5;
　　DAC; DAM MST, NOV; DLB 53; EWL
　　3; MAICYA 1, 2; MTCW 1, 2; RGEL 2;
　　SATA 44, 98; SATA-Brief 27; TWA

Richter, Conrad (Michael)
　　1890-1968 .... **CLC 30**
　　See also AAYA 21; BYA 2; CA 5-8R; 25-
　　28R; CANR 23; DLB 9, 212; LAIT 1;
　　MTCW 1, 2; RGAL 4; SATA 3; TCWW
　　2; TUS; YAW

Ricostranza, Tom
　　See Ellis, Trey

Riddell, Charlotte 1832-1906 .... **TCLC 40**
　　See Riddell, Mrs. J. H.
　　See also CA 165; DLB 156

Riddell, Mrs. J. H.
　　See Riddell, Charlotte
　　See also HGG; SUFW

Ridge, John Rollin 1827-1867 ...... **NCLC 82;**
　　NNAL
　　See also CA 144; DAM MULT; DLB 175

Ridgeway, Jason
　　See Marlowe, Stephen

Ridgway, Keith 1965- .... **CLC 119**
　　See also CA 172

Riding, Laura .... **CLC 3, 7**
　　See Jackson, Laura (Riding)
　　See also RGAL 4

Riefenstahl, Berta Helene Amalia 1902-2003
　　See Riefenstahl, Leni
　　See also CA 108; 220

Riefenstahl, Leni .... **CLC 16, 190**
　　See Riefenstahl, Berta Helene Amalia

Riffe, Ernest
　　See Bergman, (Ernst) Ingmar

Riggs, (Rolla) Lynn
　　1899-1954 .... **NNAL; TCLC 56**
　　See also CA 144; DAM MULT; DLB 175

Riis, Jacob A(ugust) 1849-1914 ..... **TCLC 80**
　　See also CA 113; 168; DLB 23

Riley, James Whitcomb 1849-1916 .... **PC 48;**
　　TCLC 51
　　See also CA 118; 137; DAM POET; MAI-
　　CYA 1, 2; RGAL 4; SATA 17

Riley, Tex
　　See Creasey, John

Rilke, Rainer Maria 1875-1926 .... **PC 2;**
　　TCLC 1, 6, 19
　　See also CA 104; 132; CANR 62, 99; CD-
　　WLB 2; DA3; DAM POET; DLB 81; EW
　　9; EWL 3; MTCW 1, 2; PFS 19; RGWL
　　2, 3; TWA; WP

Rimbaud, (Jean Nicolas) Arthur
　　1854-1891 ... **NCLC 4, 35, 82; PC 3, 57;**
　　WLC
　　See also DA; DA3; DAB; DAC; DAM
　　MST, POET; DLB 217; EW 7; GFL 1789
　　to the Present; LMFS 2; RGWL 2, 3;
　　TWA; WP

Rinehart, Mary Roberts
　　1876-1958 .... **TCLC 52**
　　See also BPFB 3; CA 108; 166; RGAL 4;
　　RHW

Ringmaster, The
　　See Mencken, H(enry) L(ouis)

Ringwood, Gwen(dolyn Margaret) Pharis
　　1910-1984 .... **CLC 48**
　　See also CA 148; 112; DLB 88

Rio, Michel 1945(?)- .... **CLC 43**
　　See also CA 201

Rios, Alberto (Alvaro) 1952- .... **PC 57**
　　See also AMWS 4; CA 113; CANR 34, 79;
　　CP 7; DLB 122; HW 2; PFS 11

Ritsos, Giannes
　　See Ritsos, Yannis

Ritsos, Yannis 1909-1990 .... **CLC 6, 13, 31**
　　See also CA 77-80; 133; CANR 39, 61; EW
　　12; EWL 3; MTCW 1; RGWL 2, 3

Ritter, Erika 1948(?)- .... **CLC 52**
　　See also CD 5; CWD

Rivera, Jose Eustasio 1889-1928 ... **TCLC 35**
　　See also CA 162; EWL 3; HW 1, 2; LAW

Rivera, Tomas 1935-1984 .... **HLCS 2**
　　See also CA 49-52; CANR 32; DLB 82;
　　HW 1; LLW 1; RGAL 4; SSFS 15;
　　TCWW 2; WLIT 1

Rivers, Conrad Kent 1933-1968 .... **CLC 1**
　　See also BW 1; CA 85-88; DLB 41

Rivers, Elfrida
　　See Bradley, Marion Zimmer
　　See also GLL 1

Riverside, John
　　See Heinlein, Robert A(nson)

Rizal, Jose 1861-1896 .... **NCLC 27**

Roa Bastos, Augusto (Antonio)
　　1917- .... **CLC 45; HLC 2**
　　See also CA 131; CWW 2; DAM MULT;
　　DLB 113; EWL 3; HW 1; LAW; RGSF 2;
　　WLIT 1

Robbe-Grillet, Alain 1922- .... **CLC 1, 2, 4, 6,**
　　8, 10, 14, 43, 128
　　See also BPFB 3; CA 9-12R; CANR 33,
　　65, 115; DLB 83; EW 13; EWL 3; GFL
　　1789 to the Present; IDFW 3, 4; MTCW
　　1, 2; RGWL 2, 3; SSFS 15

Robbins, Harold 1916-1997 .... **CLC 5**
　　See also BPFB 3; CA 73-76; 162; CANR
　　26, 54, 112; DA3; DAM NOV; MTCW 1,
　　2

Robbins, Thomas Eugene 1936-
　　See Robbins, Tom
　　See also CA 81-84; CANR 29, 59, 95; CN
　　7; CPW; CSW; DA3; DAM NOV, POP;
　　MTCW 1, 2

Robbins, Tom .... CLC 9, 32, 64
See Robbins, Thomas Eugene
See also AAYA 32; AMWS 10; BEST 90:3;
BPFB 3; DLBY 1980; MTCW 2
Robbins, Trina 1938- .... CLC 21
See also CA 128
Roberts, Charles G(eorge) D(ouglas)
1860-1943 .... TCLC 8
See also CA 105; 188; CLR 33; CWRI 5;
DLB 92; RGEL 2; RGSF 2; SATA 88;
SATA-Brief 29
Roberts, Elizabeth Madox
1886-1941 .... TCLC 68
See also CA 111; 166; CWRI 5; DLB 9, 54,
102; RGAL 4; RHW; SATA 33; SATA-
Brief 27; WCH
Roberts, Kate 1891-1985 .... CLC 15
See also CA 107; 116
Roberts, Keith (John Kingston)
1935-2000 .... CLC 14
See also CA 25-28R; CANR 46; DLB 261;
SFW 4
Roberts, Kenneth (Lewis)
1885-1957 .... TCLC 23
See also CA 109; 199; DLB 9; RGAL 4;
RHW
Roberts, Michele (Brigitte) 1949- .... CLC 48,
178
See also CA 115; CANR 58, 120; CN 7;
DLB 231; FW
Robertson, Ellis
See Ellison, Harlan (Jay); Silverberg, Rob-
ert
Robertson, Thomas William
1829-1871 .... NCLC 35
See Robertson, Tom
See also DAM DRAM
Robertson, Tom
See Robertson, Thomas William
See also RGEL 2
Robeson, Kenneth
See Dent, Lester
Robinson, Edwin Arlington
1869-1935 .... PC 1, 35; TCLC 5, 101
See also AMW; CA 104; 133; CDALB
1865-1917; DA; DAC; DAM MST,
POET; DLB 54; EWL 3; EXPP; MTCW
1, 2; PAB; PFS 4; RGAL 4; WP
Robinson, Henry Crabb
1775-1867 .... NCLC 15
See also DLB 107
Robinson, Jill 1936- .... CLC 10
See also CA 102; CANR 120; INT CA-102
Robinson, Kim Stanley 1952- .... CLC 34
See also AAYA 26; CA 126; CANR 113;
CN 7; SATA 109; SCFW 2; SFW 4
Robinson, Lloyd
See Silverberg, Robert
Robinson, Marilynne 1944- ...... CLC 25, 180
See also CA 116; CANR 80; CN 7; DLB
206
Robinson, Mary 1758-1800 .... NCLC 142
See also DLB 158; FW
Robinson, Smokey .... CLC 21
See Robinson, William, Jr.
Robinson, William, Jr. 1940-
See Robinson, Smokey
See also CA 116
Robison, Mary 1949- .... CLC 42, 98
See also CA 113; 116; CANR 87; CN 7;
DLB 130; INT CA-116; RGSF 2
Rochester
See Wilmot, John
See also RGEL 2
Rod, Edouard 1857-1910 .... TCLC 52
Roddenberry, Eugene Wesley 1921-1991
See Roddenberry, Gene
See also CA 110; 135; CANR 37; SATA 45;
SATA-Obit 69

Roddenberry, Gene .... CLC 17
See Roddenberry, Eugene Wesley
See also AAYA 5; SATA-Obit 69
Rodgers, Mary 1931- .... CLC 12
See also BYA 5; CA 49-52; CANR 8, 55,
90; CLR 20; CWRI 5; INT CANR-8;
JRDA; MAICYA 1, 2; SATA 8, 130
Rodgers, W(illiam) R(obert)
1909-1969 .... CLC 7
See also CA 85-88; DLB 20; RGEL 2
Rodman, Eric
See Silverberg, Robert
Rodman, Howard 1920(?)-1985 .... CLC 65
See also CA 118
Rodman, Maia
See Wojciechowska, Maia (Teresa)
Rodo, Jose Enrique 1871(?)-1917 .... HLCS 2
See also CA 178; EWL 3; HW 2; LAW
Rodolph, Utto
See Ouologuem, Yambo
Rodriguez, Claudio 1934-1999 .... CLC 10
See also CA 188; DLB 134
Rodriguez, Richard 1944- .... CLC 155; HLC
2
See also CA 110; CANR 66, 116; DAM
MULT; DLB 82, 256; HW 1, 2; LAIT 5;
LLW 1; NCFS 3; WLIT 1
Roelvaag, O(le) E(dvart) 1876-1931
See Rolvaag, O(le) E(dvart)
See also CA 117; 171
Roethke, Theodore (Huebner)
1908-1963 .... CLC 1, 3, 8, 11, 19, 46,
101; PC 15
See also AMW; CA 81-84; CABS 2;
CDALB 1941-1968; DA3; DAM POET;
DLB 5, 206; EWL 3; EXPP; MTCW 1, 2;
PAB; PFS 3; RGAL 4; WP
Rogers, Carl R(ansom)
1902-1987 .... TCLC 125
See also CA 1-4R; 121; CANR 1, 18;
MTCW 1
Rogers, Samuel 1763-1855 .... NCLC 69
See also DLB 93; RGEL 2
Rogers, Thomas Hunton 1927- .... CLC 57
See also CA 89-92; INT CA-89-92
Rogers, Will(iam Penn Adair)
1879-1935 .... NNAL; TCLC 8, 71
See also CA 105; 144; DA3; DAM MULT;
DLB 11; MTCW 2
Rogin, Gilbert 1929- .... CLC 18
See also CA 65-68; CANR 15
Rohan, Koda
See Koda Shigeyuki
Rohlfs, Anna Katharine Green
See Green, Anna Katharine
Rohmer, Eric .... CLC 16
See Scherer, Jean-Marie Maurice
Rohmer, Sax .... TCLC 28
See Ward, Arthur Henry Sarsfield
See also DLB 70; MSW; SUFW
Roiphe, Anne (Richardson) 1935- .. CLC 3, 9
See also CA 89-92; CANR 45, 73; DLBY
1980; INT CA-89-92
Rojas, Fernando de 1475-1541 ... HLCS 1, 2;
LC 23
See also DLB 286; RGWL 2, 3
Rojas, Gonzalo 1917- .... HLCS 2
See also CA 178; HW 2; LAWS 1
Roland, Marie-Jeanne 1754-1793 .... LC 98
**Rolfe, Frederick (William Serafino Austin
Lewis Mary)** 1860-1913 .... TCLC 12
See Al Siddik
See also CA 107; 210; DLB 34, 156; RGEL
2
Rolland, Romain 1866-1944 .... TCLC 23
See also CA 118; 197; DLB 65, 284; EWL
3; GFL 1789 to the Present; RGWL 2, 3
Rolle, Richard c. 1300-c. 1349 ...... CMLC 21
See also DLB 146; LMFS 1; RGEL 2

Rolvaag, O(le) E(dvart) .... TCLC 17
See Roelvaag, O(le) E(dvart)
See also DLB 9, 212; NFS 5; RGAL 4
Romain Arnaud, Saint
See Aragon, Louis
Romains, Jules 1885-1972 .... CLC 7
See also CA 85-88; CANR 34; DLB 65;
EWL 3; GFL 1789 to the Present; MTCW
1
Romero, Jose Ruben 1890-1952 .... TCLC 14
See also CA 114; 131; EWL 3; HW 1; LAW
Ronsard, Pierre de 1524-1585 . LC 6, 54; PC
11
See also EW 2; GFL Beginnings to 1789;
RGWL 2, 3; TWA
Rooke, Leon 1934- .... CLC 25, 34
See also CA 25-28R; CANR 23, 53; CCA
1; CPW; DAM POP
Roosevelt, Franklin Delano
1882-1945 .... TCLC 93
See also CA 116; 173; LAIT 3
Roosevelt, Theodore 1858-1919 ..... TCLC 69
See also CA 115; 170; DLB 47, 186, 275
Roper, William 1498-1578 .... LC 10
Roquelaure, A. N.
See Rice, Anne
Rosa, Joao Guimaraes 1908-1967 ... CLC 23;
HLCS 1
See Guimaraes Rosa, Joao
See also CA 89-92; DLB 113; EWL 3;
WLIT 1
Rose, Wendy 1948- . CLC 85; NNAL; PC 13
See also CA 53-56; CANR 5, 51; CWP;
DAM MULT; DLB 175; PFS 13; RGAL
4; SATA 12
Rosen, R. D.
See Rosen, Richard (Dean)
Rosen, Richard (Dean) 1949- .... CLC 39
See also CA 77-80; CANR 62, 120; CMW
4; INT CANR-30
Rosenberg, Isaac 1890-1918 .... TCLC 12
See also BRW 6; CA 107; 188; DLB 20,
216; EWL 3; PAB; RGEL 2
Rosenblatt, Joe .... CLC 15
See Rosenblatt, Joseph
Rosenblatt, Joseph 1933-
See Rosenblatt, Joe
See also CA 89-92; CP 7; INT CA-89-92
Rosenfeld, Samuel
See Tzara, Tristan
Rosenstock, Sami
See Tzara, Tristan
Rosenstock, Samuel
See Tzara, Tristan
Rosenthal, M(acha) L(ouis)
1917-1996 .... CLC 28
See also CA 1-4R; 152; CAAS 6; CANR 4,
51; CP 7; DLB 5; SATA 59
Ross, Barnaby
See Dannay, Frederic
Ross, Bernard L.
See Follett, Ken(neth Martin)
Ross, J. H.
See Lawrence, T(homas) E(dward)
Ross, John Hume
See Lawrence, T(homas) E(dward)
Ross, Martin 1862-1915
See Martin, Violet Florence
See also DLB 135; GLL 2; RGEL 2; RGSF
2
Ross, (James) Sinclair 1908-1996 ... CLC 13;
SSC 24
See also CA 73-76; CANR 81; CN 7; DAC;
DAM MST; DLB 88; RGEL 2; RGSF 2;
TCWW 2

Sachs, Marilyn (Stickle) 1927- .... **CLC 35**
See also AAYA 2; BYA 6; CA 17-20R;
CANR 13, 47; CLR 2; JRDA; MAICYA
1, 2; SAAS 2; SATA 3, 68; SATA-Essay
110; WYA; YAW

Sachs, Nelly 1891-1970 .... **CLC 14, 98**
See also CA 17-18; 25-28R; CANR 87;
CAP 2; EWL 3; MTCW 2; PFS 20;
RGWL 2, 3

Sackler, Howard (Oliver)
1929-1982 .... **CLC 14**
See also CA 61-64; 108; CAD; CANR 30;
DFS 15; DLB 7

Sacks, Oliver (Wolf) 1933- .... **CLC 67**
See also CA 53-56; CANR 28, 50, 76;
CPW; DA3; INT CANR-28; MTCW 1, 2

Sackville, Thomas 1536-1608 .... **LC 98**
See also DAM DRAM; DLB 62, 132;
RGEL 2

Sadakichi
See Hartmann, Sadakichi

Sade, Donatien Alphonse Francois
1740-1814 .... **NCLC 3, 47**
See also EW 4; GFL Beginnings to 1789;
RGWL 2, 3

Sade, Marquis de
See Sade, Donatien Alphonse Francois

Sadoff, Ira 1945- .... **CLC 9**
See also CA 53-56; CANR 5, 21, 109; DLB
120

Saetone
See Camus, Albert

Safire, William 1929- .... **CLC 10**
See also CA 17-20R; CANR 31, 54, 91

Sagan, Carl (Edward) 1934-1996 .... **CLC 30, 112**
See also AAYA 2; CA 25-28R; 155; CANR
11, 36, 74; CPW; DA3; MTCW 1, 2;
SATA 58; SATA-Obit 94

Sagan, Francoise .... **CLC 3, 6, 9, 17, 36**
See Quoirez, Francoise
See also CWW 2; DLB 83; EWL 3; GFL
1789 to the Present; MTCW 2

Sahgal, Nayantara (Pandit) 1927- .... **CLC 41**
See also CA 9-12R; CANR 11, 88; CN 7

Said, Edward W. 1935-2003 .... **CLC 123**
See also CA 21-24R; 220; CANR 45, 74,
107, 131; DLB 67; MTCW 2

Saint, H(arry) F. 1941- .... **CLC 50**
See also CA 127

St. Aubin de Teran, Lisa 1953-
See Teran, Lisa St. Aubin de
See also CA 118; 126; CN 7; INT CA-126

Saint Birgitta of Sweden c.
1303-1373 .... **CMLC 24**

Sainte-Beuve, Charles Augustin
1804-1869 .... **NCLC 5**
See also DLB 217; EW 6; GFL 1789 to the
Present

**Saint-Exupery, Antoine (Jean Baptiste
Marie Roger) de** 1900-1944 .... **TCLC 2, 56; WLC**
See also BPFB 3; BYA 3; CA 108; 132;
CLR 10; DA3; DAM NOV; DLB 72; EW
12; EWL 3; GFL 1789 to the Present;
LAIT 3; MAICYA 1, 2; MTCW 1, 2;
RGWL 2, 3; SATA 20; TWA

St. John, David
See Hunt, E(verette) Howard, (Jr.)

St. John, J. Hector
See Crevecoeur, Michel Guillaume Jean de

Saint-John Perse
See Leger, (Marie-Rene Auguste) Alexis
Saint-Leger
See also EW 10; EWL 3; GFL 1789 to the
Present; RGWL 2

Saintsbury, George (Edward Bateman)
1845-1933 .... **TCLC 31**
See also CA 160; DLB 57, 149

Sait Faik .... **TCLC 23**
See Abasiyanik, Sait Faik

Saki .... **SSC 12; TCLC 3**
See Munro, H(ector) H(ugh)
See also BRWS 6; BYA 11; LAIT 2; MTCW
2; RGEL 2; SSFS 1; SUFW

Sala, George Augustus 1828-1895 . **NCLC 46**

Saladin 1138-1193 .... **CMLC 38**

Salama, Hannu 1936- .... **CLC 18**
See also EWL 3

Salamanca, J(ack) R(ichard) 1922- .. **CLC 4, 15**
See also CA 25-28R, 193; CAAE 193

Salas, Floyd Francis 1931- .... **HLC 2**
See also CA 119; CAAS 27; CANR 44, 75,
93; DAM MULT; DLB 82; HW 1, 2;
MTCW 2

Sale, J. Kirkpatrick
See Sale, Kirkpatrick

Sale, Kirkpatrick 1937- .... **CLC 68**
See also CA 13-16R; CANR 10

Salinas, Luis Omar 1937- ... **CLC 90; HLC 2**
See also AMWS 13; CA 131; CANR 81;
DAM MULT; DLB 82; HW 1, 2

Salinas (y Serrano), Pedro
1891(?)-1951 .... **TCLC 17**
See also CA 117; DLB 134; EWL 3

Salinger, J(erome) D(avid) 1919- .. **CLC 1, 3,
8, 12, 55, 56, 138; SSC 2, 28, 65; WLC**
See also AAYA 2, 36; AMW; AMWC 1;
BPFB 3; CA 5-8R; CANR 39, 129;
CDALB 1941-1968; CLR 18; CN 7; CPW
1; DA; DA3; DAB; DAC; DAM MST,
NOV, POP; DLB 2, 102, 173; EWL 3;
EXPN; LAIT 4; MAICYA 1, 2; MTCW
1, 2; NFS 1; RGAL 4; RGSF 2; SATA 67;
SSFS 17; TUS; WYA; YAW

Salisbury, John
See Caute, (John) David

Sallust c. 86B.C.-35B.C. .... **CMLC 68**
See also AW 2; CDWLB 1; DLB 211;
RGWL 2, 3

Salter, James 1925- .. **CLC 7, 52, 59; SSC 58**
See also AMWS 9; CA 73-76; CANR 107;
DLB 130

Saltus, Edgar (Everton) 1855-1921 . **TCLC 8**
See also CA 105; DLB 202; RGAL 4

Saltykov, Mikhail Evgrafovich
1826-1889 .... **NCLC 16**
See also DLB 238:

Saltykov-Shchedrin, N.
See Saltykov, Mikhail Evgrafovich

Samarakis, Andonis
See Samarakis, Antonis
See also EWL 3

Samarakis, Antonis 1919-2003 .... **CLC 5**
See Samarakis, Andonis
See also CA 25-28R; 224; CAAS 16; CANR
36

Sanchez, Florencio 1875-1910 .... **TCLC 37**
See also CA 153; EWL 3; HW 1; LAW

Sanchez, Luis Rafael 1936- .... **CLC 23**
See also CA 128; DLB 145; EWL 3; HW 1;
WLIT 1

Sanchez, Sonia 1934- .... **BLC 3; CLC 5, 116;
PC 9**
See also BW 2, 3; CA 33-36R; CANR 24,
49, 74, 115; CLR 18; CP 7; CSW; CWP;
DA3; DAM MULT; DLB 41; DLBD 8;
EWL 3; MAICYA 1, 2; MTCW 1, 2;
SATA 22, 136; WP

Sancho, Ignatius 1729-1780 .... **LC 84**

Sand, George 1804-1876 ..... **NCLC 2, 42, 57;
WLC**
See also DA; DA3; DAB; DAC; DAM
MST, NOV; DLB 119, 192; EW 6; FW;
GFL 1789 to the Present; RGWL 2, 3;
TWA

Sandburg, Carl (August) 1878-1967 . **CLC 1,
4, 10, 15, 35; PC 2, 41; WLC**
See also AAYA 24; AMW; BYA 1, 3; CA
5-8R; 25-28R; CANR 35; CDALB 1865-
1917; CLR 67; DA; DA3; DAB; DAC;
DAM MST, POET; DLB 17, 54, 284;
EWL 3; EXPP; LAIT 2; MAICYA 1, 2;
MTCW 1, 2; PAB; PFS 3, 6, 12; RGAL
4; SATA 8; TUS; WCH; WP; WYA

Sandburg, Charles
See Sandburg, Carl (August)

Sandburg, Charles A.
See Sandburg, Carl (August)

Sanders, (James) Ed(ward) 1939- .... **CLC 53**
See Sanders, Edward
See also BG 3; CA 13-16R; CAAS 21;
CANR 13, 44, 78; CP 7; DAM POET;
DLB 16, 244

Sanders, Edward
See Sanders, (James) Ed(ward)
See also DLB 244

Sanders, Lawrence 1920-1998 .... **CLC 41**
See also BEST 89:4; BPFB 3; CA 81-84;
165; CANR 33, 62; CMW 4; CPW; DA3;
DAM POP; MTCW 1

Sanders, Noah
See Blount, Roy (Alton), Jr.

Sanders, Winston P.
See Anderson, Poul (William)

Sandoz, Mari(e Susette) 1900-1966 .. **CLC 28**
See also CA 1-4R; 25-28R; CANR 17, 64;
DLB 9, 212; LAIT 2; MTCW 1, 2; SATA
5; TCWW 2

Sandys, George 1578-1644 .... **LC 80**
See also DLB 24, 121

Saner, Reg(inald Anthony) 1931- .... **CLC 9**
See also CA 65-68; CP 7

Sankara 788-820 .... **CMLC 32**

Sannazaro, Jacopo 1456(?)-1530 .... **LC 8**
See also RGWL 2, 3

Sansom, William 1912-1976 . **CLC 2, 6; SSC
21**
See also CA 5-8R; 65-68; CANR 42; DAM
NOV; DLB 139; EWL 3; MTCW 1;
RGEL 2; RGSF 2

Santayana, George 1863-1952 .... **TCLC 40**
See also AMW; CA 115; 194; DLB 54, 71,
246, 270; DLBD 13; EWL 3; RGAL 4;
TUS

Santiago, Danny .... **CLC 33**
See James, Daniel (Lewis)
See also DLB 122

Santmyer, Helen Hooven
1895-1986 .... **CLC 33; TCLC 133**
See also CA 1-4R; 118; CANR 15, 33;
DLBY 1984; MTCW 1; RHW

Santoka, Taneda 1882-1940 .... **TCLC 72**

Santos, Bienvenido N(uqui)
1911-1996 .... **AAL; CLC 22**
See also CA 101; 151; CANR 19, 46; DAM
MULT; EWL; RGAL 4; SSFS 19

Sapir, Edward 1884-1939 .... **TCLC 108**
See also CA 211; DLB 92

Sapper .... **TCLC 44**
See McNeile, Herman Cyril

Sapphire
See Sapphire, Brenda

Sapphire, Brenda 1950- .... **CLC 99**

Sappho fl. 6th cent. B.C.- ... **CMLC 3, 67; PC
5**
See also CDWLB 1; DA3; DAM POET;
DLB 176; PFS 20; RGWL 2, 3; WP

Saramago, Jose 1922- ..... **CLC 119; HLCS 1**
See also CA 153; CANR 96; DLB 287;
EWL 3; LATS 1

Stanton, Elizabeth Cady
1815-1902 .... **TCLC 73**
See also CA 171; DLB 79; FW

Stanton, Maura 1946- .... **CLC 9**
See also CA 89-92; CANR 15, 123; DLB 120

Stanton, Schuyler
See Baum, L(yman) Frank

Stapledon, (William) Olaf
1886-1950 .... **TCLC 22**
See also CA 111; 162; DLB 15, 255; SFW 4

Starbuck, George (Edwin)
1931-1996 .... **CLC 53**
See also CA 21-24R; 153; CANR 23; DAM POET

Stark, Richard
See Westlake, Donald E(dwin)

Staunton, Schuyler
See Baum, L(yman) Frank

Stead, Christina (Ellen) 1902-1983 ... **CLC 2, 5, 8, 32, 80**
See also BRWS 4; CA 13-16R; 109; CANR 33, 40; DLB 260; EWL 3; FW; MTCW 1, 2; RGEL 2; RGSF 2; WWE 1

Stead, William Thomas
1849-1912 .... **TCLC 48**
See also CA 167

Stebnitsky, M.
See Leskov, Nikolai (Semyonovich)

Steele, Sir Richard 1672-1729 .... **LC 18**
See also BRW 3; CDBLB 1660-1789; DLB 84, 101; RGEL 2; WLIT 3

Steele, Timothy (Reid) 1948- .... **CLC 45**
See also CA 93-96; CANR 16, 50, 92; CP 7; DLB 120, 282

Steffens, (Joseph) Lincoln
1866-1936 .... **TCLC 20**
See also CA 117; 198

Stegner, Wallace (Earle) 1909-1993 .. **CLC 9, 49, 81; SSC 27**
See also AITN 1; AMWS 4; ANW; BEST 90:3; BPFB 3; CA 1-4R; 141; CAAS 9; CANR 1, 21, 46; DAM NOV; DLB 9, 206, 275; DLBY 1993; EWL 3; MTCW 1, 2; RGAL 4; TCWW 2; TUS

Stein, Gertrude 1874-1946 .... **DC 19; PC 18; SSC 42; TCLC 1, 6, 28, 48; WLC**
See also AMW; AMWC 2; CA 104; 132; CANR 108; CDALB 1917-1929; DA; DA3; DAB; DAC; DAM MST, NOV, POET; DLB 4, 54, 86, 228; DLBD 15; EWL 3; EXPS; GLL 1; MAWW; MTCW 1, 2; NCFS 4; RGAL 4; RGSF 2; SSFS 5; TUS; WP

Steinbeck, John (Ernst) 1902-1968 ... **CLC 1, 5, 9, 13, 21, 34, 45, 75, 124; SSC 11, 37; TCLC 135; WLC**
See also AAYA 12; AMW; BPFB 3; BYA 2, 3, 13; CA 1-4R; 25-28R; CANR 1, 35; CDALB 1929-1941; DA; DA3; DAB; DAC; DAM DRAM, MST, NOV; DLB 7, 9, 212, 275; DLBD 2; EWL 3; EXPS; LAIT 3; MTCW 1, 2; NFS 1, 5, 7, 17, 19; RGAL 4; RGSF 2; RHW; SATA 9; SSFS 3, 6; TCWW 2; TUS; WYA; YAW

Steinem, Gloria 1934- .... **CLC 63**
See also CA 53-56; CANR 28, 51; DLB 246; FW; MTCW 1, 2

Steiner, George 1929- .... **CLC 24**
See also CA 73-76; CANR 31, 67, 108; DAM NOV; DLB 67, 299; EWL 3; MTCW 1, 2; SATA 62

Steiner, K. Leslie
See Delany, Samuel R(ay), Jr.

Steiner, Rudolf 1861-1925 .... **TCLC 13**
See also CA 107

Stendhal 1783-1842 .. **NCLC 23, 46; SSC 27; WLC**
See also DA; DA3; DAB; DAC; DAM MST, NOV; DLB 119; EW 5; GFL 1789 to the Present; RGWL 2, 3; TWA

Stephen, Adeline Virginia
See Woolf, (Adeline) Virginia

Stephen, Sir Leslie 1832-1904 .... **TCLC 23**
See also BRW 5; CA 123; DLB 57, 144, 190

Stephen, Sir Leslie
See Stephen, Sir Leslie

Stephen, Virginia
See Woolf, (Adeline) Virginia

Stephens, James 1882(?)-1950 .... **SSC 50; TCLC 4**
See also CA 104; 192; DLB 19, 153, 162; EWL 3; FANT; RGEL 2; SUFW

Stephens, Reed
See Donaldson, Stephen R(eeder)

Steptoe, Lydia
See Barnes, Djuna
See also GLL 1

Sterchi, Beat 1949- .... **CLC 65**
See also CA 203

Sterling, Brett
See Bradbury, Ray (Douglas); Hamilton, Edmond

Sterling, Bruce 1954- .... **CLC 72**
See also CA 119; CANR 44; SCFW 2; SFW 4

Sterling, George 1869-1926 .... **TCLC 20**
See also CA 117; 165; DLB 54

Stern, Gerald 1925- .... **CLC 40, 100**
See also AMWS 9; CA 81-84; CANR 28, 94; CP 7; DLB 105; RGAL 4

Stern, Richard (Gustave) 1928- ... **CLC 4, 39**
See also CA 1-4R; CANR 1, 25, 52, 120; CN 7; DLB 218; DLBY 1987; INT CANR-25

Sternberg, Josef von 1894-1969 .... **CLC 20**
See also CA 81-84

Sterne, Laurence 1713-1768 .... **LC 2, 48; WLC**
See also BRW 3; BRWC 1; CDBLB 1660-1789; DA; DAB; DAC; DAM MST, NOV; DLB 39; RGEL 2; TEA

Sternheim, (William Adolf) Carl
1878-1942 .... **TCLC 8**
See also CA 105; 193; DLB 56, 118; EWL 3; RGWL 2, 3

Stevens, Mark 1951- .... **CLC 34**
See also CA 122

Stevens, Wallace 1879-1955 . **PC 6; TCLC 3, 12, 45; WLC**
See also AMW; AMWR 1; CA 104; 124; CDALB 1929-1941; DA; DA3; DAB; DAC; DAM MST, POET; DLB 54; EWL 3; EXPP; MTCW 1, 2; PAB; PFS 13, 16; RGAL 4; TUS; WP

Stevenson, Anne (Katharine) 1933- .. **CLC 7, 33**
See also BRWS 6; CA 17-20R; CAAS 9; CANR 9, 33, 123; CP 7; CWP; DLB 40; MTCW 1; RHW

Stevenson, Robert Louis (Balfour)
1850-1894 ...... **NCLC 5, 14, 63; SSC 11, 51; WLC**
See also AAYA 24; BPFB 3; BRW 5; BRWC 1; BRWR 1; BYA 1, 2, 4, 13; CD-BLB 1890-1914; CLR 10, 11; DA; DA3; DAB; DAC; DAM MST, NOV; DLB 18, 57, 141, 156, 174; DLBD 13; HGG; JRDA; LAIT 1, 3; MAICYA 1, 2; NFS 11; RGEL 2; RGSF 2; SATA 100; SUFW; TEA; WCH; WLIT 4; WYA; YABC 2; YAW

Stewart, J(ohn) I(nnes) M(ackintosh)
1906-1994 .... **CLC 7, 14, 32**
See Innes, Michael
See also CA 85-88; 147; CAAS 3; CANR 47; CMW 4; MTCW 1, 2

Stewart, Mary (Florence Elinor)
1916- .... **CLC 7, 35, 117**
See also AAYA 29; BPFB 3; CA 1-4R; CANR 1, 59, 130; CMW 4; CPW; DAB; FANT; RHW; SATA 12; YAW

Stewart, Mary Rainbow
See Stewart, Mary (Florence Elinor)

Stifle, June
See Campbell, Maria

Stifter, Adalbert 1805-1868 .. **NCLC 41; SSC 28**
See also CDWLB 2; DLB 133; RGSF 2; RGWL 2, 3

Still, James 1906-2001 .... **CLC 49**
See also CA 65-68; 195; CAAS 17; CANR 10, 26; CSW; DLB 9; DLBY 01; SATA 29; SATA-Obit 127

Sting 1951-
See Sumner, Gordon Matthew
See also CA 167

Stirling, Arthur
See Sinclair, Upton (Beall)

Stitt, Milan 1941- .... **CLC 29**
See also CA 69-72

Stockton, Francis Richard 1834-1902
See Stockton, Frank R.
See also CA 108; 137; MAICYA 1, 2; SATA 44; SFW 4

Stockton, Frank R. .... **TCLC 47**
See Stockton, Francis Richard
See also BYA 4, 13; DLB 42, 74; DLBD 13; EXPS; SATA-Brief 32; SSFS 3; SUFW; WCH

Stoddard, Charles
See Kuttner, Henry

Stoker, Abraham 1847-1912
See Stoker, Bram
See also CA 105; 150; DA; DA3; DAC; DAM MST, NOV; HGG; SATA 29

Stoker, Bram . **SSC 62; TCLC 8, 144; WLC**
See Stoker, Abraham
See also AAYA 23; BPFB 3; BRWS 3; BYA 5; CDBLB 1890-1914; DAB; DLB 36, 70, 178; LATS 1; NFS 18; RGEL 2; SUFW; TEA; WLIT 4

Stolz, Mary (Slattery) 1920- .... **CLC 12**
See also AAYA 8; AITN 1; CA 5-8R; CANR 13, 41, 112; JRDA; MAICYA 1, 2; SAAS 3; SATA 10, 71, 133; YAW

Stone, Irving 1903-1989 .... **CLC 7**
See also AITN 1; BPFB 3; CA 1-4R; 129; CAAS 3; CANR 1, 23; CPW; DA3; DAM POP; INT CANR-23; MTCW 1, 2; RHW; SATA 3; SATA-Obit 64

Stone, Oliver (William) 1946- .... **CLC 73**
See also AAYA 15; CA 110; CANR 55, 125

Stone, Robert (Anthony) 1937- ... **CLC 5, 23, 42, 175**
See also AMWS 5; BPFB 3; CA 85-88; CANR 23, 66, 95; CN 7; DLB 152; EWL 3; INT CANR-23; MTCW 1

Stone, Ruth 1915- .... **PC 53**
See also CA 45-48; CANR 2, 91; CP 7; CSW; DLB 105; PFS 19

Stone, Zachary
See Follett, Ken(neth Martin)

Stoppard, Tom 1937- ... **CLC 1, 3, 4, 5, 8, 15, 29, 34, 63, 91; DC 6; WLC**
See also BRWC 1; BRWR 2; BRWS 1; CA 81-84; CANR 39, 67, 125; CBD; CD 5; CDBLB 1960 to Present; DA; DA3; DAB; DAC; DAM DRAM, MST; DFS 2, 5, 8, 11, 13, 16; DLB 13, 233; DLBY 1985; EWL 3; LATS 1; MTCW 1, 2; RGEL 2; TEA; WLIT 4

Swift, Augustus
See Lovecraft, H(oward) P(hillips)

Swift, Graham (Colin) 1949- ...... **CLC 41, 88**
See also BRWC 2; BRWS 5; CA 117; 122; CANR 46, 71, 128; CN 7; DLB 194; MTCW 2; NFS 18; RGSF 2

Swift, Jonathan 1667-1745 ..... **LC 1, 42, 101; PC 9; WLC**
See also AAYA 41; BRW 3; BRWC 1; BRWR 1; BYA 5, 14; CDBLB 1660-1789; CLR 53; DA; DA3; DAB; DAC; DAM MST, NOV, POET; DLB 39, 95, 101; EXPN; LAIT 1; NFS 6; RGEL 2; SATA 19; TEA; WCH; WLIT 3

Swinburne, Algernon Charles
1837-1909 ... **PC 24; TCLC 8, 36; WLC**
See also BRW 5; CA 105; 140; CDBLB 1832-1890; DA; DA3; DAB; DAC; DAM MST, POET; DLB 35, 57; PAB; RGEL 2; TEA

Swinfen, Ann .... **CLC 34**
See also CA 202

Swinnerton, Frank Arthur
1884-1982 .... **CLC 31**
See also CA 108; DLB 34

Swithen, John
See King, Stephen (Edwin)

Sylvia
See Ashton-Warner, Sylvia (Constance)

Symmes, Robert Edward
See Duncan, Robert (Edward)

Symonds, John Addington
1840-1893 .... **NCLC 34**
See also DLB 57, 144

Symons, Arthur 1865-1945 .... **TCLC 11**
See also CA 107; 189; DLB 19, 57, 149; RGEL 2

Symons, Julian (Gustave)
1912-1994 .... **CLC 2, 14, 32**
See also CA 49-52; 147; CAAS 3; CANR 3, 33, 59; CMW 4; DLB 87, 155; DLBY 1992; MSW; MTCW 1

Synge, (Edmund) J(ohn) M(illington)
1871-1909 .... **DC 2; TCLC 6, 37**
See also BRW 6; BRWR 1; CA 104; 141; CDBLB 1890-1914; DAM DRAM; DFS 18; DLB 10, 19; EWL 3; RGEL 2; TEA; WLIT 4

Syruc, J.
See Milosz, Czeslaw

Szirtes, George 1948- .... **CLC 46; PC 51**
See also CA 109; CANR 27, 61, 117; CP 7

Szymborska, Wislawa 1923- ... **CLC 99, 190; PC 44**
See also CA 154; CANR 91; CDWLB 4; CWP; CWW 2; DA3; DLB 232; DLBY 1996; EWL 3; MTCW 2; PFS 15; RGWL 3

T. O., Nik
See Annensky, Innokenty (Fyodorovich)

Tabori, George 1914- .... **CLC 19**
See also CA 49-52; CANR 4, 69; CBD; CD 5; DLB 245

Tacitus c. 55-c. 117 .... **CMLC 56**
See also AW 2; CDWLB 1; DLB 211; RGWL 2, 3

Tagore, Rabindranath 1861-1941 .... **PC 8; SSC 48; TCLC 3, 53**
See also CA 104; 120; DA3; DAM DRAM, POET; EWL 3; MTCW 1, 2; PFS 18; RGEL 2; RGSF 2; RGWL 2, 3; TWA

Taine, Hippolyte Adolphe
1828-1893 .... **NCLC 15**
See also EW 7; GFL 1789 to the Present

Talayesva, Don C. 1890-(?) .... **NNAL**

Talese, Gay 1932- .... **CLC 37**
See also AITN 1; CA 1-4R; CANR 9, 58; DLB 185; INT CANR-9; MTCW 1, 2

Tallent, Elizabeth (Ann) 1954- .... **CLC 45**
See also CA 117; CANR 72; DLB 130

Tallmountain, Mary 1918-1997 .... **NNAL**
See also CA 146; 161; DLB 193

Tally, Ted 1952- .... **CLC 42**
See also CA 120; 124; CAD; CANR 125; CD 5; INT CA-124

Talvik, Heiti 1904-1947 .... **TCLC 87**
See also EWL 3

Tamayo y Baus, Manuel
1829-1898 .... **NCLC 1**

Tammsaare, A(nton) H(ansen)
1878-1940 .... **TCLC 27**
See also CA 164; CDWLB 4; DLB 220; EWL 3

Tam'si, Tchicaya U
See Tchicaya, Gerald Felix

Tan, Amy (Ruth) 1952- . **AAL; CLC 59, 120, 151**
See also AAYA 9, 48; AMWS 10; BEST 89:3; BPFB 3; CA 136; CANR 54, 105; CDALBS; CN 7; CPW 1; DA3; DAM MULT, NOV, POP; DLB 173; EXPN; FW; LAIT 3, 5; MTCW 2; NFS 1, 13, 16; RGAL 4; SATA 75; SSFS 9; YAW

Tandem, Felix
See Spitteler, Carl (Friedrich Georg)

Tanizaki, Jun'ichiro 1886-1965 ... **CLC 8, 14, 28; SSC 21**
See Tanizaki Jun'ichiro
See also CA 93-96; 25-28R; MJW; MTCW 2; RGSF 2; RGWL 2

Tanizaki Jun'ichiro
See Tanizaki, Jun'ichiro
See also DLB 180; EWL 3

Tanner, William
See Amis, Kingsley (William)

Tao Lao
See Storni, Alfonsina

Tapahonso, Luci 1953- .... **NNAL**
See also CA 145; CANR 72, 127; DLB 175

Tarantino, Quentin (Jerome)
1963- .... **CLC 125**
See also CA 171; CANR 125

Tarassoff, Lev
See Troyat, Henri

Tarbell, Ida M(inerva) 1857-1944 . **TCLC 40**
See also CA 122; 181; DLB 47

Tarkington, (Newton) Booth
1869-1946 .... **TCLC 9**
See also BPFB 3; BYA 3; CA 110; 143; CWRI 5; DLB 9, 102; MTCW 2; RGAL 4; SATA 17

Tarkovskii, Andrei Arsen'evich
See Tarkovsky, Andrei (Arsenyevich)

Tarkovsky, Andrei (Arsenyevich)
1932-1986 .... **CLC 75**
See also CA 127

Tartt, Donna 1963- .... **CLC 76**
See also CA 142

Tasso, Torquato 1544-1595 .... **LC 5, 94**
See also EFS 2; EW 2; RGWL 2, 3

Tate, (John Orley) Allen 1899-1979 .. **CLC 2, 4, 6, 9, 11, 14, 24; PC 50**
See also AMW; CA 5-8R; 85-88; CANR 32, 108; DLB 4, 45, 63; DLBD 17; EWL 3; MTCW 1, 2; RGAL 4; RHW

Tate, Ellalice
See Hibbert, Eleanor Alice Burford

Tate, James (Vincent) 1943- ..... **CLC 2, 6, 25**
See also CA 21-24R; CANR 29, 57, 114; CP 7; DLB 5, 169; EWL 3; PFS 10, 15; RGAL 4; WP

Tauler, Johannes c. 1300-1361 ...... **CMLC 37**
See also DLB 179; LMFS 1

Tavel, Ronald 1940- .... **CLC 6**
See also CA 21-24R; CAD; CANR 33; CD 5

Taviani, Paolo 1931- .... **CLC 70**
See also CA 153

Taylor, Bayard 1825-1878 .... **NCLC 89**
See also DLB 3, 189, 250, 254; RGAL 4

Taylor, C(ecil) P(hilip) 1929-1981 ... **CLC 27**
See also CA 25-28R; 105; CANR 47; CBD

Taylor, Edward 1642(?)-1729 .... **LC 11**
See also AMW; DA; DAB; DAC; DAM MST, POET; DLB 24; EXPP; RGAL 4; TUS

Taylor, Eleanor Ross 1920- .... **CLC 5**
See also CA 81-84; CANR 70

Taylor, Elizabeth 1932-1975 ..... **CLC 2, 4, 29**
See also CA 13-16R; CANR 9, 70; DLB 139; MTCW 1; RGEL 2; SATA 13

Taylor, Frederick Winslow
1856-1915 .... **TCLC 76**
See also CA 188

Taylor, Henry (Splawn) 1942- .... **CLC 44**
See also CA 33-36R; CAAS 7; CANR 31; CP 7; DLB 5; PFS 10

Taylor, Kamala (Purnaiya) 1924-2004
See Markandaya, Kamala
See also CA 77-80; NFS 13

Taylor, Mildred D(elois) 1943- .... **CLC 21**
See also AAYA 10, 47; BW 1; BYA 3, 8; CA 85-88; CANR 25, 115; CLR 9, 59, 90; CSW; DLB 52; JRDA; LAIT 3; MAICYA 1, 2; SAAS 5; SATA 135; WYA; YAW

Taylor, Peter (Hillsman) 1917-1994 .. **CLC 1, 4, 18, 37, 44, 50, 71; SSC 10**
See also AMWS 5; BPFB 3; CA 13-16R; 147; CANR 9, 50; CSW; DA3; DLB 218, 278; DLBY 1981, 1994; EWL 3; EXPS; INT CANR-9; MTCW 1, 2; RGSF 2; SSFS 9; TUS

Taylor, Robert Lewis 1912-1998 .... **CLC 14**
See also CA 1-4R; 170; CANR 3, 64; SATA 10

Tchekhov, Anton
See Chekhov, Anton (Pavlovich)

Tchicaya, Gerald Felix 1931-1988 .. **CLC 101**
See Tchicaya U Tam'si
See also CA 129; 125; CANR 81

Tchicaya U Tam'si
See Tchicaya, Gerald Felix
See also EWL 3

Teasdale, Sara 1884-1933 .... **PC 31; TCLC 4**
See also CA 104; 163; DLB 45; GLL 1; PFS 14; RGAL 4; SATA 32; TUS

Tecumseh 1768-1813 .... **NNAL**
See also DAM MULT

Tegner, Esaias 1782-1846 .... **NCLC 2**

Teilhard de Chardin, (Marie Joseph) Pierre
1881-1955 .... **TCLC 9**
See also CA 105; 210; GFL 1789 to the Present

Temple, Ann
See Mortimer, Penelope (Ruth)

Tennant, Emma (Christina) 1937- .. **CLC 13, 52**
See also BRWS 9; CA 65-68; CAAS 9; CANR 10, 38, 59, 88; CN 7; DLB 14; EWL 3; SFW 4

Tenneshaw, S. M.
See Silverberg, Robert

Tenney, Tabitha Gilman
1762-1837 .... **NCLC 122**
See also DLB 37, 200

Tennyson, Alfred 1809-1892 ... **NCLC 30, 65, 115; PC 6; WLC**
See also AAYA 50; BRW 4; CDBLB 1832-1890; DA; DA3; DAB; DAC; DAM MST, POET; DLB 32; EXPP; PAB; PFS 1, 2, 4, 11, 15, 19; RGEL 2; TEA; WLIT 4; WP

Teran, Lisa St. Aubin de .... **CLC 36**
See St. Aubin de Teran, Lisa

Terence c. 184B.C.-c. 159B.C. ...... **CMLC 14; DC 7**
See also AW 1; CDWLB 1; DLB 211; RGWL 2, 3; TWA

Teresa de Jesus, St. 1515-1582 .... **LC 18**

Terkel, Louis 1912-
See Terkel, Studs
See also CA 57-60; CANR 18, 45, 67; DA3; MTCW 1, 2

Terkel, Studs .... **CLC 38**
See Terkel, Louis
See also AAYA 32; AITN 1; MTCW 2; TUS

Terry, C. V.
See Slaughter, Frank G(ill)

Terry, Megan 1932- .... **CLC 19; DC 13**
See also CA 77-80; CABS 3; CAD; CANR 43; CD 5; CWD; DFS 18; DLB 7, 249; GLL 2

Tertullian c. 155-c. 245 .... **CMLC 29**

Tertz, Abram
See Sinyavsky, Andrei (Donatevich)
See also CWW 2; RGSF 2

Tesich, Steve 1943(?)-1996 .... **CLC 40, 69**
See also CA 105; 152; CAD; DLBY 1983

Tesla, Nikola 1856-1943 .... **TCLC 88**

Teternikov, Fyodor Kuzmich 1863-1927
See Sologub, Fyodor
See also CA 104

Tevis, Walter 1928-1984 .... **CLC 42**
See also CA 113; SFW 4

Tey, Josephine .... **TCLC 14**
See Mackintosh, Elizabeth
See also DLB 77; MSW

Thackeray, William Makepeace 1811-1863 .... **NCLC 5, 14, 22, 43; WLC**
See also BRW 5; BRWC 2; CDBLB 1832-1890; DA; DA3; DAB; DAC; DAM MST, NOV; DLB 21, 55, 159, 163; NFS 13; RGEL 2; SATA 23; TEA; WLIT 3

Thakura, Ravindranatha
See Tagore, Rabindranath

Thames, C. H.
See Marlowe, Stephen

Tharoor, Shashi 1956- .... **CLC 70**
See also CA 141; CANR 91; CN 7

Thelwell, Michael Miles 1939- .... **CLC 22**
See also BW 2; CA 101

Theobald, Lewis, Jr.
See Lovecraft, H(oward) P(hillips)

Theocritus c. 310B.C.- .... **CMLC 45**
See also AW 1; DLB 176; RGWL 2, 3

Theodorescu, Ion N. 1880-1967
See Arghezi, Tudor
See also CA 116

Theriault, Yves 1915-1983 .... **CLC 79**
See also CA 102; CCA 1; DAC; DAM MST; DLB 88; EWL 3

Theroux, Alexander (Louis) 1939- .... **CLC 2, 25**
See also CA 85-88; CANR 20, 63; CN 7

Theroux, Paul (Edward) 1941- ..... **CLC 5, 8, 11, 15, 28, 46**
See also AAYA 28; AMWS 8; BEST 89:4; BPFB 3; CA 33-36R; CANR 20, 45, 74; CDALBS; CN 7; CPW 1; DA3; DAM POP; DLB 2, 218; EWL 3; HGG; MTCW 1, 2; RGAL 4; SATA 44, 109; TUS

Thesen, Sharon 1946- .... **CLC 56**
See also CA 163; CANR 125; CP 7; CWP

Thespis fl. 6th cent. B.C.- .... **CMLC 51**
See also LMFS 1

Thevenin, Denis
See Duhamel, Georges

Thibault, Jacques Anatole Francois 1844-1924
See France, Anatole
See also CA 106; 127; DA3; DAM NOV; MTCW 1, 2; TWA

Thiele, Colin (Milton) 1920- .... **CLC 17**
See also CA 29-32R; CANR 12, 28, 53, 105; CLR 27; DLB 289; MAICYA 1, 2; SAAS 2; SATA 14, 72, 125; YAW

Thistlethwaite, Bel
See Wetherald, Agnes Ethelwyn

Thomas, Audrey (Callahan) 1935- .... **CLC 7, 13, 37, 107; SSC 20**
See also AITN 2; CA 21-24R; CAAS 19; CANR 36, 58; CN 7; DLB 60; MTCW 1; RGSF 2

Thomas, Augustus 1857-1934 .... **TCLC 97**

Thomas, D(onald) M(ichael) 1935- . **CLC 13, 22, 31, 132**
See also BPFB 3; BRWS 4; CA 61-64; CAAS 11; CANR 17, 45, 75; CDBLB 1960 to Present; CN 7; CP 7; DA3; DLB 40, 207, 299; HGG; INT CANR-17; MTCW 1, 2; SFW 4

Thomas, Dylan (Marlais) 1914-1953 .... **PC 2, 52; SSC 3, 44; TCLC 1, 8, 45, 105; WLC**
See also AAYA 45; BRWS 1; CA 104; 120; CANR 65; CDBLB 1945-1960; DA; DA3; DAB; DAC; DAM DRAM, MST, POET; DLB 13, 20, 139; EWL 3; EXPP; LAIT 3; MTCW 1, 2; PAB; PFS 1, 3, 8; RGEL 2; RGSF 2; SATA 60; TEA; WLIT 4; WP

Thomas, (Philip) Edward 1878-1917 . **PC 53; TCLC 10**
See also BRW 6; BRWS 3; CA 106; 153; DAM POET; DLB 19, 98, 156, 216; EWL 3; PAB; RGEL 2

Thomas, Joyce Carol 1938- .... **CLC 35**
See also AAYA 12, 54; BW 2, 3; CA 113; 116; CANR 48, 114; CLR 19; DLB 33; INT CA-116; JRDA; MAICYA 1, 2; MTCW 1, 2; SAAS 7; SATA 40, 78, 123, 137; SATA-Essay 137; WYA; YAW

Thomas, Lewis 1913-1993 .... **CLC 35**
See also ANW; CA 85-88; 143; CANR 38, 60; DLB 275; MTCW 1, 2

Thomas, M. Carey 1857-1935 .... **TCLC 89**
See also FW

Thomas, Paul
See Mann, (Paul) Thomas

Thomas, Piri 1928- .... **CLC 17; HLCS 2**
See also CA 73-76; HW 1; LLW 1

Thomas, R(onald) S(tuart) 1913-2000 .... **CLC 6, 13, 48**
See also CA 89-92; 189; CANR 30; CDBLB 1960 to Present; CP 7; DAB; DAM POET; DLB 27; EWL 3; MTCW 1; RGEL 2

Thomas, Ross (Elmore) 1926-1995 .. **CLC 39**
See also CA 33-36R; 150; CANR 22, 63; CMW 4

Thompson, Francis (Joseph) 1859-1907 .... **TCLC 4**
See also BRW 5; CA 104; 189; CDBLB 1890-1914; DLB 19; RGEL 2; TEA

Thompson, Francis Clegg
See Mencken, H(enry) L(ouis)

Thompson, Hunter S(tockton) 1937(?)- .... **CLC 9, 17, 40, 104**
See also AAYA 45; BEST 89:1; BPFB 3; CA 17-20R; CANR 23, 46, 74, 77, 111; CPW; CSW; DA3; DAM POP; DLB 185; MTCW 1, 2; TUS

Thompson, James Myers
See Thompson, Jim (Myers)

Thompson, Jim (Myers) 1906-1977(?) .... **CLC 69**
See also BPFB 3; CA 140; CMW 4; CPW; DLB 226; MSW

Thompson, Judith .... **CLC 39**
See also CWD

Thomson, James 1700-1748 .... **LC 16, 29, 40**
See also BRWS 3; DAM POET; DLB 95; RGEL 2

Thomson, James 1834-1882 .... **NCLC 18**
See also DAM POET; DLB 35; RGEL 2

Thoreau, Henry David 1817-1862 .. **NCLC 7, 21, 61, 138; PC 30; WLC**
See also AAYA 42; AMW; ANW; BYA 3; CDALB 1640-1865; DA; DA3; DAB; DAC; DAM MST; DLB 1, 183, 223, 270, 298; LAIT 2; LMFS 1; NCFS 3; RGAL 4; TUS

Thorndike, E. L.
See Thorndike, Edward L(ee)

Thorndike, Edward L(ee) 1874-1949 .... **TCLC 107**
See also CA 121

Thornton, Hall
See Silverberg, Robert

Thorpe, Adam 1956- .... **CLC 176**
See also CA 129; CANR 92; DLB 231

Thubron, Colin (Gerald Dryden) 1939- .... **CLC 163**
See also CA 25-28R; CANR 12, 29, 59, 95; CN 7; DLB 204, 231

Thucydides c. 455B.C.-c. 395B.C. . **CMLC 17**
See also AW 1; DLB 176; RGWL 2, 3

Thumboo, Edwin Nadason 1933- .... **PC 30**
See also CA 194

Thurber, James (Grover) 1894-1961 .. **CLC 5, 11, 25, 125; SSC 1, 47**
See also AMWS 1; BPFB 3; BYA 5; CA 73-76; CANR 17, 39; CDALB 1929-1941; CWRI 5; DA; DA3; DAB; DAC; DAM DRAM, MST, NOV; DLB 4, 11, 22, 102; EWL 3; EXPS; FANT; LAIT 3; MAICYA 1, 2; MTCW 1, 2; RGAL 4; RGSF 2; SATA 13; SSFS 1, 10, 19; SUFW; TUS

Thurman, Wallace (Henry) 1902-1934 .... **BLC 3; HR 3; TCLC 6**
See also BW 1, 3; CA 104; 124; CANR 81; DAM MULT; DLB 51

Tibullus c. 54B.C.-c. 18B.C. .... **CMLC 36**
See also AW 2; DLB 211; RGWL 2, 3

Ticheburn, Cheviot
See Ainsworth, William Harrison

Tieck, (Johann) Ludwig 1773-1853 .... **NCLC 5, 46; SSC 31**
See also CDWLB 2; DLB 90; EW 5; IDTP; RGSF 2; RGWL 2, 3; SUFW

Tiger, Derry
See Ellison, Harlan (Jay)

Tilghman, Christopher 1946- .... **CLC 65**
See also CA 159; CSW; DLB 244

Tillich, Paul (Johannes) 1886-1965 .... **CLC 131**
See also CA 5-8R; 25-28R; CANR 33; MTCW 1, 2

Tillinghast, Richard (Williford) 1940- .... **CLC 29**
See also CA 29-32R; CAAS 23; CANR 26, 51, 96; CP 7; CSW

Timrod, Henry 1828-1867 .... **NCLC 25**
See also DLB 3, 248; RGAL 4

Tindall, Gillian (Elizabeth) 1938- ...... **CLC 7**
See also CA 21-24R; CANR 11, 65, 107; CN 7

Tiptree, James, Jr. .... **CLC 48, 50**
See Sheldon, Alice Hastings Bradley
See also DLB 8; SCFW 2; SFW 4

Tirone Smith, Mary-Ann 1944- .... **CLC 39**
See also CA 118; 136; CANR 113; SATA 143

Tirso de Molina 1580(?)-1648 .... **DC 13; HLCS 2; LC 73**
See also RGWL 2, 3

Titmarsh, Michael Angelo
See Thackeray, William Makepeace

Tocqueville, Alexis (Charles Henri Maurice Clerel Comte) de 1805-1859 .. **NCLC 7, 63**
  See also EW 6; GFL 1789 to the Present; TWA

Toer, Pramoedya Ananta 1925- ...... **CLC 186**
  See also CA 197; RGWL 3

Toffler, Alvin 1928- .... **CLC 168**
  See also CA 13-16R; CANR 15, 46, 67; CPW; DAM POP; MTCW 1, 2

Toibin, Colm
  See Toibin, Colm
  See also DLB 271

Toibin, Colm 1955- .... **CLC 162**
  See Toibin, Colm
  See also CA 142; CANR 81

Tolkien, J(ohn) R(onald) R(euel)
  1892-1973 .... **CLC 1, 2, 3, 8, 12, 38; TCLC 137; WLC**
  See also AAYA 10; AITN 1; BPFB 3; BRWC 2; BRWS 2; CA 17-18; 45-48; CANR 36; CAP 2; CDBLB 1914-1945; CLR 56; CPW 1; CWRI 5; DA; DA3; DAB; DAC; DAM MST, NOV, POP; DLB 15, 160, 255; EFS 2; EWL 3; FANT; JRDA; LAIT 1; LATS 1; LMFS 2; MAI-CYA 1, 2; MTCW 1, 2; NFS 8; RGEL 2; SATA 2, 32, 100; SATA-Obit 24; SFW 4; SUFW; TEA; WCH; WYA; YAW

Toller, Ernst 1893-1939 .... **TCLC 10**
  See also CA 107; 186; DLB 124; EWL 3; RGWL 2, 3

Tolson, M. B.
  See Tolson, Melvin B(eaunorus)

Tolson, Melvin B(eaunorus)
  1898(?)-1966 .... **BLC 3; CLC 36, 105**
  See also AFAW 1, 2; BW 1, 3; CA 124; 89-92; CANR 80; DAM MULT, POET; DLB 48, 76; RGAL 4

Tolstoi, Aleksei Nikolaevich
  See Tolstoy, Alexey Nikolaevich

Tolstoi, Lev
  See Tolstoy, Leo (Nikolaevich)
  See also RGSF 2; RGWL 2, 3

Tolstoy, Aleksei Nikolaevich
  See Tolstoy, Alexey Nikolaevich
  See also DLB 272

Tolstoy, Alexey Nikolaevich
  1882-1945 .... **TCLC 18**
  See Tolstoy, Aleksei Nikolaevich
  See also CA 107; 158; EWL 3; SFW 4

Tolstoy, Leo (Nikolaevich)
  1828-1910 . **SSC 9, 30, 45, 54; TCLC 4, 11, 17, 28, 44, 79; WLC**
  See also CA 104; 123; DA; DA3; DAB; DAC; DAM MST, NOV; DLB 238; EFS 2; EW 7; EXPS; IDTP; LAIT 2; LATS 1; LMFS 1; NFS 10; SATA 26; SSFS 5; TWA

Tolstoy, Count Leo
  See Tolstoy, Leo (Nikolaevich)

Tomalin, Claire 1933- .... **CLC 166**
  See also CA 89-92; CANR 52, 88; DLB 155

Tomasi di Lampedusa, Giuseppe 1896-1957
  See Lampedusa, Giuseppe (Tomasi) di
  See also CA 111; DLB 177; EWL 3

Tomlin, Lily .... **CLC 17**
  See Tomlin, Mary Jean

Tomlin, Mary Jean 1939(?)-
  See Tomlin, Lily
  See also CA 117

Tomline, F. Latour
  See Gilbert, W(illiam) S(chwenck)

Tomlinson, (Alfred) Charles 1927- .... **CLC 2, 4, 6, 13, 45; PC 17**
  See also CA 5-8R; CANR 33; CP 7; DAM POET; DLB 40

Tomlinson, H(enry) M(ajor)
  1873-1958 .... **TCLC 71**
  See also CA 118; 161; DLB 36, 100, 195

Tonna, Charlotte Elizabeth
  1790-1846 .... **NCLC 135**
  See also DLB 163

Tonson, Jacob fl. 1655(?)-1736 .... **LC 86**
  See also DLB 170

Toole, John Kennedy 1937-1969 ..... **CLC 19, 64**
  See also BPFB 3; CA 104; DLBY 1981; MTCW 2

Toomer, Eugene
  See Toomer, Jean

Toomer, Eugene Pinchback
  See Toomer, Jean

Toomer, Jean 1894-1967 .. **BLC 3; CLC 1, 4, 13, 22; HR 3; PC 7; SSC 1, 45; WLCS**
  See also AFAW 1, 2; AMWS 3, 9; BW 1; CA 85-88; CDALB 1917-1929; DA3; DAM MULT; DLB 45, 51; EWL 3; EXPP; EXPS; LMFS 2; MTCW 1, 2; NFS 11; RGAL 4; RGSF 2; SSFS 5

Toomer, Nathan Jean
  See Toomer, Jean

Toomer, Nathan Pinchback
  See Toomer, Jean

Torley, Luke
  See Blish, James (Benjamin)

Tornimparte, Alessandra
  See Ginzburg, Natalia

Torre, Raoul della
  See Mencken, H(enry) L(ouis)

Torrence, Ridgely 1874-1950 .... **TCLC 97**
  See also DLB 54, 249

Torrey, E(dwin) Fuller 1937- .... **CLC 34**
  See also CA 119; CANR 71

Torsvan, Ben Traven
  See Traven, B.

Torsvan, Benno Traven
  See Traven, B.

Torsvan, Berick Traven
  See Traven, B.

Torsvan, Berwick Traven
  See Traven, B.

Torsvan, Bruno Traven
  See Traven, B.

Torsvan, Traven
  See Traven, B.

Tourneur, Cyril 1575(?)-1626 .... **LC 66**
  See also BRW 2; DAM DRAM; DLB 58; RGEL 2

Tournier, Michel (Edouard) 1924- .... **CLC 6, 23, 36, 95**
  See also CA 49-52; CANR 3, 36, 74; DLB 83; EWL 3; GFL 1789 to the Present; MTCW 1, 2; SATA 23

Tournimparte, Alessandra
  See Ginzburg, Natalia

Towers, Ivar
  See Kornbluth, C(yril) M.

Towne, Robert (Burton) 1936(?)- .... **CLC 87**
  See also CA 108; DLB 44; IDFW 3, 4

Townsend, Sue .... **CLC 61**
  See Townsend, Susan Lilian
  See also AAYA 28; CA 119; 127; CANR 65, 107; CBD; CD 5; CPW; CWD; DAB; DAC; DAM MST; DLB 271; INT CA-127; SATA 55, 93; SATA-Brief 48; YAW

Townsend, Susan Lilian 1946-
  See Townsend, Sue

Townshend, Pete
  See Townshend, Peter (Dennis Blandford)

Townshend, Peter (Dennis Blandford)
  1945- .... **CLC 17, 42**
  See also CA 107

Tozzi, Federigo 1883-1920 .... **TCLC 31**
  See also CA 160; CANR 110; DLB 264; EWL 3

Tracy, Don(ald Fiske) 1905-1970(?)
  See Queen, Ellery
  See also CA 1-4R; 176; CANR 2

Trafford, F. G.
  See Riddell, Charlotte

Traherne, Thomas 1637(?)-1674 .... **LC 99**
  See also BRW 2; DLB 131; PAB; RGEL 2

Traill, Catharine Parr 1802-1899 .. **NCLC 31**
  See also DLB 99

Trakl, Georg 1887-1914 .... **PC 20; TCLC 5**
  See also CA 104; 165; EW 10; EWL 3; LMFS 2; MTCW 2; RGWL 2, 3

Tranquilli, Secondino
  See Silone, Ignazio

Transtroemer, Tomas Gosta
  See Transtromer, Tomas (Goesta)

Transtromer, Tomas
  See Transtromer, Tomas (Goesta)

Transtromer, Tomas (Goesta)
  1931- .... **CLC 52, 65**
  See also CA 117; 129; CAAS 17; CANR 115; DAM POET; DLB 257; EWL 3

Transtromer, Tomas Gosta
  See Transtromer, Tomas (Goesta)

Traven, B. 1882(?)-1969 .... **CLC 8, 11**
  See also CA 19-20; 25-28R; CAP 2; DLB 9, 56; EWL 3; MTCW 1; RGAL 4

Trediakovsky, Vasilii Kirillovich
  1703-1769 .... **LC 68**
  See also DLB 150

Treitel, Jonathan 1959- .... **CLC 70**
  See also CA 210; DLB 267

Trelawny, Edward John
  1792-1881 .... **NCLC 85**
  See also DLB 110, 116, 144

Tremain, Rose 1943- .... **CLC 42**
  See also CA 97-100; CANR 44, 95; CN 7; DLB 14, 271; RGSF 2; RHW

Tremblay, Michel 1942- .... **CLC 29, 102**
  See also CA 116; 128; CCA 1; CWW 2; DAC; DAM MST; DLB 60; EWL 3; GLL 1; MTCW 1, 2

Trevanian .... **CLC 29**
  See Whitaker, Rod(ney)

Trevor, Glen
  See Hilton, James

Trevor, William .. **CLC 7, 9, 14, 25, 71, 116; SSC 21, 58**
  See Cox, William Trevor
  See also BRWS 4; CBD; CD 5; CN 7; DLB 14, 139; EWL 3; LATS 1; MTCW 2; RGEL 2; RGSF 2; SSFS 10

Trifonov, Iurii (Valentinovich)
  See Trifonov, Yuri (Valentinovich)
  See also RGWL 2, 3

Trifonov, Yuri (Valentinovich)
  1925-1981 .... **CLC 45**
  See Trifonov, Iurii (Valentinovich); Trifonov, Yury Valentinovich
  See also CA 126; 103; MTCW 1

Trifonov, Yury Valentinovich
  See Trifonov, Yuri (Valentinovich)
  See also EWL 3

Trilling, Diana (Rubin) 1905-1996 . **CLC 129**
  See also CA 5-8R; 154; CANR 10, 46; INT CANR-10; MTCW 1, 2

Trilling, Lionel 1905-1975 .... **CLC 9, 11, 24**
  See also AMWS 3; CA 9-12R; 61-64; CANR 10, 105; DLB 28, 63; EWL 3; INT CANR-10; MTCW 1, 2; RGAL 4; TUS

Trimball, W. H.
  See Mencken, H(enry) L(ouis)

Tristan
  See Gomez de la Serna, Ramon

Tristram
  See Housman, A(lfred) E(dward)

CANR-27; LAIT 3; MAWW; MTCW 1,
2; NFS 5; RGAL 4; RGSF 2; SATA 31;
SSFS 2, 11; TUS; YAW

Walker, David Harry 1911-1992 ...... **CLC 14**
See also CA 1-4R; 137; CANR 1; CWRI 5;
SATA 8; SATA-Obit 71

Walker, Edward Joseph 1934-2004
See Walker, Ted
See also CA 21-24R; CANR 12, 28, 53; CP
7

Walker, George F. 1947- .... **CLC 44, 61**
See also CA 103; CANR 21, 43, 59; CD 5;
DAB; DAC; DAM MST; DLB 60

Walker, Joseph A. 1935- .... **CLC 19**
See also BW 1, 3; CA 89-92; CAD; CANR
26; CD 5; DAM DRAM, MST; DFS 12;
DLB 38

Walker, Margaret (Abigail)
1915-1998 .... **BLC; CLC 1, 6; PC 20;**
TCLC 129
See also AFAW 1, 2; BW 2, 3; CA 73-76;
172; CANR 26, 54, 76; CN 7; CP 7;
CSW; DAM MULT; DLB 76, 152; EXPP;
FW; MTCW 1, 2; RGAL 4; RHW

Walker, Ted .... **CLC 13**
See Walker, Edward Joseph
See also DLB 40

Wallace, David Foster 1962- ... **CLC 50, 114;**
SSC 68
See also AAYA 50; AMWS 10; CA 132;
CANR 59; DA3; MTCW 2

Wallace, Dexter
See Masters, Edgar Lee

Wallace, (Richard Horatio) Edgar
1875-1932 .... **TCLC 57**
See also CA 115; 218; CMW 4; DLB 70;
MSW; RGEL 2

Wallace, Irving 1916-1990 .... **CLC 7, 13**
See also AITN 1; BPFB 3; CA 1-4R; 132;
CAAS 1; CANR 1, 27; CPW; DAM NOV,
POP; INT CANR-27; MTCW 1, 2

Wallant, Edward Lewis 1926-1962 ... **CLC 5,**
10
See also CA 1-4R; CANR 22; DLB 2, 28,
143, 299; EWL 3; MTCW 1, 2; RGAL 4

Wallas, Graham 1858-1932 .... **TCLC 91**

Waller, Edmund 1606-1687 .... **LC 86**
See also BRW 2; DAM POET; DLB 126;
PAB; RGEL 2

Walley, Byron
See Card, Orson Scott

Walpole, Horace 1717-1797 .... **LC 2, 49**
See also BRW 3; DLB 39, 104, 213; HGG;
LMFS 1; RGEL 2; SUFW 1; TEA

Walpole, Hugh (Seymour)
1884-1941 .... **TCLC 5**
See also CA 104; 165; DLB 34; HGG;
MTCW 2; RGEL 2; RHW

Walrond, Eric (Derwent) 1898-1966 .... **HR 3**
See also BW 1; CA 125; DLB 51

Walser, Martin 1927- .... **CLC 27, 183**
See also CA 57-60; CANR 8, 46; CWW 2;
DLB 75, 124; EWL 3

Walser, Robert 1878-1956 ..... **SSC 20; TCLC**
18
See also CA 118; 165; CANR 100; DLB
66; EWL 3

Walsh, Gillian Paton
See Paton Walsh, Gillian

Walsh, Jill Paton .... **CLC 35**
See Paton Walsh, Gillian
See also CLR 2, 65; WYA

Walter, Villiam Christian
See Andersen, Hans Christian

Walters, Anna L(ee) 1946- .... **NNAL**
See also CA 73-76

Walther von der Vogelweide c.
1170-1228 .... **CMLC 56**

Walton, Izaak 1593-1683 .... **LC 72**
See also BRW 2; CDBLB Before 1660;
DLB 151, 213; RGEL 2

Wambaugh, Joseph (Aloysius), Jr.
1937- .... **CLC 3, 18**
See also AITN 1; BEST 89:3; BPFB 3; CA
33-36R; CANR 42, 65, 115; CMW 4;
CPW 1; DA3; DAM NOV, POP; DLB 6;
DLBY 1983; MSW; MTCW 1, 2

Wang Wei 699(?)-761(?) .... **PC 18**
See also TWA

Warburton, William 1698-1779 .... **LC 97**
See also DLB 104

Ward, Arthur Henry Sarsfield 1883-1959
See Rohmer, Sax
See also CA 108; 173; CMW 4; HGG

Ward, Douglas Turner 1930- .... **CLC 19**
See also BW 1; CA 81-84; CAD; CANR
27; CD 5; DLB 7, 38

Ward, E. D.
See Lucas, E(dward) V(errall)

Ward, Mrs. Humphry 1851-1920
See Ward, Mary Augusta
See also RGEL 2

Ward, Mary Augusta 1851-1920 ... **TCLC 55**
See Ward, Mrs. Humphry
See also DLB 18

Ward, Peter
See Faust, Frederick (Schiller)

Warhol, Andy 1928(?)-1987 .... **CLC 20**
See also AAYA 12; BEST 89:4; CA 89-92;
121; CANR 34

Warner, Francis (Robert le Plastrier)
1937- .... **CLC 14**
See also CA 53-56; CANR 11

Warner, Marina 1946- .... **CLC 59**
See also CA 65-68; CANR 21, 55, 118; CN
7; DLB 194

Warner, Rex (Ernest) 1905-1986 ...... **CLC 45**
See also CA 89-92; 119; DLB 15; RGEL 2;
RHW

Warner, Susan (Bogert)
1819-1885 .... **NCLC 31**
See also DLB 3, 42, 239, 250, 254

Warner, Sylvia (Constance) Ashton
See Ashton-Warner, Sylvia (Constance)

Warner, Sylvia Townsend
1893-1978 .. **CLC 7, 19; SSC 23; TCLC**
131
See also BRWS 7; CA 61-64; 77-80; CANR
16, 60, 104; DLB 34, 139; EWL 3; FANT;
FW; MTCW 1, 2; RGEL 2; RGSF 2;
RHW

Warren, Mercy Otis 1728-1814 ..... **NCLC 13**
See also DLB 31, 200; RGAL 4; TUS

Warren, Robert Penn 1905-1989 .. **CLC 1, 4,**
6, 8, 10, 13, 18, 39, 53, 59; PC 37; SSC
4, 58; WLC
See also AITN 1; AMW; AMWC 2; BPFB
3; BYA 1; CA 13-16R; 129; CANR 10,
47; CDALB 1968-1988; DA; DA3; DAB;
DAC; DAM MST, NOV, POET; DLB 2,
48, 152; DLBY 1980, 1989; EWL 3; INT
CANR-10; MTCW 1, 2; NFS 13; RGAL
4; RGSF 2; RHW; SATA 46; SATA-Obit
63; SSFS 8; TUS

Warrigal, Jack
See Furphy, Joseph

Warshofsky, Isaac
See Singer, Isaac Bashevis

Warton, Joseph 1722-1800 .... **NCLC 118**
See also DLB 104, 109; RGEL 2

Warton, Thomas 1728-1790 .... **LC 15, 82**
See also DAM POET; DLB 104, 109;
RGEL 2

Waruk, Kona
See Harris, (Theodore) Wilson

Warung, Price .... **TCLC 45**
See Astley, William
See also DLB 230; RGEL 2

Warwick, Jarvis
See Garner, Hugh
See also CCA 1

Washington, Alex
See Harris, Mark

Washington, Booker T(aliaferro)
1856-1915 .... **BLC 3; TCLC 10**
See also BW 1; CA 114; 125; DA3; DAM
MULT; LAIT 2; RGAL 4; SATA 28

Washington, George 1732-1799 .... **LC 25**
See also DLB 31

Wassermann, (Karl) Jakob
1873-1934 .... **TCLC 6**
See also CA 104; 163; DLB 66; EWL 3

Wasserstein, Wendy 1950- ... **CLC 32, 59, 90,**
183; DC 4
See also CA 121; 129; CABS 3; CAD;
CANR 53, 75, 128; CD 5; CWD; DA3;
DAM DRAM; DFS 5, 17; DLB 228;
EWL 3; FW; INT CA-129; MTCW 2;
SATA 94

Waterhouse, Keith (Spencer) 1929- . **CLC 47**
See also CA 5-8R; CANR 38, 67, 109;
CBD; CN 7; DLB 13, 15; MTCW 1, 2

Waters, Frank (Joseph) 1902-1995 .. **CLC 88**
See also CA 5-8R; 149; CAAS 13; CANR
3, 18, 63, 121; DLB 212; DLBY 1986;
RGAL 4; TCWW 2

Waters, Mary C. .... **CLC 70**

Waters, Roger 1944- .... **CLC 35**

Watkins, Frances Ellen
See Harper, Frances Ellen Watkins

Watkins, Gerrold
See Malzberg, Barry N(athaniel)

Watkins, Gloria Jean 1952(?)- .... **CLC 94**
See also BW 2; CA 143; CANR 87, 126;
DLB 246; MTCW 2; SATA 115

Watkins, Paul 1964- .... **CLC 55**
See also CA 132; CANR 62, 98

Watkins, Vernon Phillips
1906-1967 .... **CLC 43**
See also CA 9-10; 25-28R; CAP 1; DLB
20; EWL 3; RGEL 2

Watson, Irving S.
See Mencken, H(enry) L(ouis)

Watson, John H.
See Farmer, Philip Jose

Watson, Richard F.
See Silverberg, Robert

Watts, Ephraim
See Horne, Richard Henry Hengist

Watts, Isaac 1674-1748 .... **LC 98**
See also DLB 95; RGEL 2; SATA 52

Waugh, Auberon (Alexander)
1939-2001 .... **CLC 7**
See also CA 45-48; 192; CANR 6, 22, 92;
DLB 14, 194

Waugh, Evelyn (Arthur St. John)
1903-1966 .. **CLC 1, 3, 8, 13, 19, 27, 44,**
107; SSC 41; WLC
See also BPFB 3; BRW 7; CA 85-88; 25-
28R; CANR 22; CDBLB 1914-1945; DA;
DA3; DAB; DAC; DAM MST, NOV,
POP; DLB 15, 162, 195; EWL 3; MTCW
1, 2; NFS 13, 17; RGEL 2; RGSF 2; TEA;
WLIT 4

Waugh, Harriet 1944- .... **CLC 6**
See also CA 85-88; CANR 22

Ways, C. R.
See Blount, Roy (Alton), Jr.

Waystaff, Simon
See Swift, Jonathan

Webb, Beatrice (Martha Potter)
1858-1943 .... **TCLC 22**
See also CA 117; 162; DLB 190; FW

Webb, Charles (Richard) 1939- .... CLC 7
See also CA 25-28R; CANR 114
Webb, Frank J. .... NCLC 143
See also DLB 50
Webb, James H(enry), Jr. 1946- ...... CLC 22
See also CA 81-84
Webb, Mary Gladys (Meredith)
1881-1927 .... TCLC 24
See also CA 182; 123; DLB 34; FW
Webb, Mrs. Sidney
See Webb, Beatrice (Martha Potter)
Webb, Phyllis 1927- .... CLC 18
See also CA 104; CANR 23; CCA 1; CP 7;
CWP; DLB 53
Webb, Sidney (James) 1859-1947 .. TCLC 22
See also CA 117; 163; DLB 190
Webber, Andrew Lloyd .... CLC 21
See Lloyd Webber, Andrew
See also DFS 7
Weber, Lenora Mattingly
1895-1971 .... CLC 12
See also CA 19-20; 29-32R; CAP 1; SATA
2; SATA-Obit 26
Weber, Max 1864-1920 .... TCLC 69
See also CA 109; 189; DLB 296
Webster, John 1580(?)-1634(?) ...... DC 2; LC
33, 84; WLC
See also BRW 2; CDBLB Before 1660; DA;
DAB; DAC; DAM DRAM, MST; DFS
17, 19; DLB 58; IDTP; RGEL 2; WLIT 3
Webster, Noah 1758-1843 .... NCLC 30
See also DLB 1, 37, 42, 43, 73, 243
Wedekind, (Benjamin) Frank(lin)
1864-1918 .... TCLC 7
See also CA 104; 153; CANR 121, 122;
CDWLB 2; DAM DRAM; DLB 118; EW
8; EWL 3; LMFS 2; RGWL 2, 3
Wehr, Demaris .... CLC 65
Weidman, Jerome 1913-1998 .... CLC 7
See also AITN 2; CA 1-4R; 171; CAD;
CANR 1; DLB 28
Weil, Simone (Adolphine)
1909-1943 .... TCLC 23
See also CA 117; 159; EW 12; EWL 3; FW;
GFL 1789 to the Present; MTCW 2
Weininger, Otto 1880-1903 .... TCLC 84
Weinstein, Nathan
See West, Nathanael
Weinstein, Nathan von Wallenstein
See West, Nathanael
Weir, Peter (Lindsay) 1944- .... CLC 20
See also CA 113; 123
Weiss, Peter (Ulrich) 1916-1982 .. CLC 3, 15,
51; TCLC 152
See also CA 45-48; 106; CANR 3; DAM
DRAM; DFS 3; DLB 69, 124; EWL 3;
RGWL 2, 3
Weiss, Theodore (Russell)
1916-2003 .... CLC 3, 8, 14
See also CA 9-12R; 189; 216; CAAE 189;
CAAS 2; CANR 46, 94; CP 7; DLB 5
Welch, (Maurice) Denton
1915-1948 .... TCLC 22
See also BRWS 8, 9; CA 121; 148; RGEL
2
Welch, James (Phillip) 1940-2003 ..... CLC 6,
14, 52; NNAL
See also CA 85-88; 219; CANR 42, 66, 107;
CN 7; CP 7; CPW; DAM MULT, POP;
DLB 175, 256; LATS 1; RGAL 4; TCWW
2
Weldon, Fay 1931- . CLC 6, 9, 11, 19, 36, 59,
122
See also BRWS 4; CA 21-24R; CANR 16,
46, 63, 97; CDBLB 1960 to Present; CN
7; CPW; DAM POP; DLB 14, 194; EWL
3; FW; HGG; INT CANR-16; MTCW 1,
2; RGEL 2; RGSF 2

Wellek, Rene 1903-1995 .... CLC 28
See also CA 5-8R; 150; CAAS 7; CANR 8;
DLB 63; EWL 3; INT CANR-8
Weller, Michael 1942- .... CLC 10, 53
See also CA 85-88; CAD; CD 5
Weller, Paul 1958- .... CLC 26
Wellershoff, Dieter 1925- .... CLC 46
See also CA 89-92; CANR 16, 37
Welles, (George) Orson 1915-1985 .. CLC 20,
80
See also AAYA 40; CA 93-96; 117
Wellman, John McDowell 1945-
See Wellman, Mac
See also CA 166; CD 5
Wellman, Mac .... CLC 65
See Wellman, John McDowell; Wellman,
John McDowell
See also CAD; RGAL 4
Wellman, Manly Wade 1903-1986 ... CLC 49
See also CA 1-4R; 118; CANR 6, 16, 44;
FANT; SATA 6; SATA-Obit 47; SFW 4;
SUFW
Wells, Carolyn 1869(?)-1942 .... TCLC 35
See also CA 113; 185; CMW 4; DLB 11
Wells, H(erbert) G(eorge) 1866-1946 . SSC 6,
70; TCLC 6, 12, 19, 133; WLC
See also AAYA 18; BPFB 3; BRW 6; CA
110; 121; CDBLB 1914-1945; CLR 64;
DA; DA3; DAB; DAC; DAM MST, NOV;
DLB 34, 70, 156, 178; EWL 3; EXPS;
HGG; LAIT 3; MTCW 1, 2;
NFS 17; RGEL 2; RGSF 2; SATA 20;
SCFW; SFW 4; SSFS 3; SUFW; TEA;
WCH; WLIT 4; YAW
Wells, Rosemary 1943- .... CLC 12
See also AAYA 13; BYA 7, 8; CA 85-88;
CANR 48, 120; CLR 16, 69; CWRI 5;
MAICYA 1, 2; SAAS 1; SATA 18, 69,
114; YAW
Wells-Barnett, Ida B(ell)
1862-1931 .... TCLC 125
See also CA 182; DLB 23, 221
Welsh, Irvine 1958- .... CLC 144
See also CA 173; DLB 271
Welty, Eudora (Alice) 1909-2001 .. CLC 1, 2,
5, 14, 22, 33, 105; SSC 1, 27, 51; WLC
See also AAYA 48; AMW; AMWR 1; BPFB
3; CA 9-12R; 199; CABS 1; CANR 32,
65, 128; CDALB 1941-1968; CN 7; CSW;
DA; DA3; DAB; DAC; DAM MST, NOV;
DLB 2, 102, 143; DLBD 12; DLBY 1987,
2001; EWL 3; EXPS; HGG; LAIT 3;
MAWW; MTCW 1, 2; NFS 13, 15; RGAL
4; RGSF 2; RHW; SSFS 2, 10; TUS
Wen I-to 1899-1946 .... TCLC 28
See also EWL 3
Wentworth, Robert
See Hamilton, Edmond
Werfel, Franz (Viktor) 1890-1945 ... TCLC 8
See also CA 104; 161; DLB 81, 124; EWL
3; RGWL 2, 3
Wergeland, Henrik Arnold
1808-1845 .... NCLC 5
Wersba, Barbara 1932- .... CLC 30
See also AAYA 2, 30; BYA 6, 12, 13; CA
29-32R, 182; CAAE 182; CANR 16, 38;
CLR 3, 78; DLB 52; JRDA; MAICYA 1,
2; SAAS 2; SATA 1, 58; SATA-Essay 103;
WYA; YAW
Wertmueller, Lina 1928- .... CLC 16
See also CA 97-100; CANR 39, 78
Wescott, Glenway 1901-1987 .. CLC 13; SSC
35
See also CA 13-16R; 121; CANR 23, 70;
DLB 4, 9, 102; RGAL 4

Wesker, Arnold 1932- .... CLC 3, 5, 42
See also CA 1-4R; CAAS 7; CANR 1, 33;
CBD; CD 5; CDBLB 1960 to Present;
DAB; DAM DRAM; DLB 13; EWL 3;
MTCW 1; RGEL 2; TEA
Wesley, John 1703-1791 .... LC 88
See also DLB 104
Wesley, Richard (Errol) 1945- .... CLC 7
See also BW 1; CA 57-60; CAD; CANR
27; CD 5; DLB 38
Wessel, Johan Herman 1742-1785 .... LC 7
See also DLB 300
West, Anthony (Panther)
1914-1987 .... CLC 50
See also CA 45-48; 124; CANR 3, 19; DLB
15
West, C. P.
See Wodehouse, P(elham) G(renville)
West, Cornel (Ronald) 1953- .... BLCS; CLC
134
See also CA 144; CANR 91; DLB 246
West, Delno C(loyde), Jr. 1936- .... CLC 70
See also CA 57-60
West, Dorothy 1907-1998 .. HR 3; TCLC 108
See also BW 2; CA 143; 169; DLB 76
West, (Mary) Jessamyn 1902-1984 ... CLC 7,
17
See also CA 9-12R; 112; CANR 27; DLB
6; DLBY 1984; MTCW 1, 2; RGAL 4;
RHW; SATA-Obit 37; TCWW 2; TUS;
YAW
West, Morris
See West, Morris L(anglo)
See also DLB 289
West, Morris L(anglo) 1916-1999 ..... CLC 6,
33
See West, Morris
See also BPFB 3; CA 5-8R; 187; CANR
24, 49, 64; CN 7; CPW; MTCW 1, 2
West, Nathanael 1903-1940 .. SSC 16; TCLC
1, 14, 44
See also AMW; AMWR 2; BPFB 3; CA
104; 125; CDALB 1929-1941; DA3; DLB
4, 9, 28; EWL 3; MTCW 1, 2; NFS 16;
RGAL 4; TUS
West, Owen
See Koontz, Dean R(ay)
West, Paul 1930- .... CLC 7, 14, 96
See also CA 13-16R; CAAS 7; CANR 22,
53, 76, 89; CN 7; DLB 14; INT CANR-
22; MTCW 2
West, Rebecca 1892-1983 ... CLC 7, 9, 31, 50
See also BPFB 3; BRWS 3; CA 5-8R; 109;
CANR 19; DLB 36; DLBY 1983; EWL
3; FW; MTCW 1, 2; NCFS 4; RGEL 2;
TEA
Westall, Robert (Atkinson)
1929-1993 .... CLC 17
See also AAYA 12; BYA 2, 6, 7, 8, 9, 15;
CA 69-72; 141; CANR 18, 68; CLR 13;
FANT; JRDA; MAICYA 1, 2; MAICYAS
1; SAAS 2; SATA 23, 69; SATA-Obit 75;
WYA; YAW
Westermarck, Edward 1862-1939 . TCLC 87
Westlake, Donald E(dwin) 1933- . CLC 7, 33
See also BPFB 3; CA 17-20R; CAAS 13;
CANR 16, 44, 65, 94; CMW 4; CPW;
DAM POP; INT CANR-16; MSW;
MTCW 2
Westmacott, Mary
See Christie, Agatha (Mary Clarissa)
Weston, Allen
See Norton, Andre
Wetcheek, J. L.
See Feuchtwanger, Lion
Wetering, Janwillem van de
See van de Wetering, Janwillem

Wetherald, Agnes Ethelwyn
1857-1940 .... **TCLC 81**
  See also CA 202; DLB 99

Wetherell, Elizabeth
  See Warner, Susan (Bogert)

Whale, James 1889-1957 .... **TCLC 63**

Whalen, Philip (Glenn) 1923-2002 .... **CLC 6, 29**
  See also BG 3; CA 9-12R; 209; CANR 5, 39; CP 7; DLB 16; WP

Wharton, Edith (Newbold Jones)
1862-1937 ... **SSC 6; TCLC 3, 9, 27, 53, 129, 149; WLC**
  See also AAYA 25; AMW; AMWC 2; AMWR 1; BPFB 3; CA 104; 132; CDALB 1865-1917; DA; DA3; DAB; DAC; DAM MST, NOV; DLB 4, 9, 12, 78, 189; DLBD 13; EWL 3; EXPS; HGG; LAIT 2, 3; LATS 1; MAWW; MTCW 1, 2; NFS 5, 11, 15; RGAL 4; RGSF 2; RHW; SSFS 6, 7; SUFW; TUS

Wharton, James
  See Mencken, H(enry) L(ouis)

Wharton, William (a pseudonym) . **CLC 18, 37**
  See also CA 93-96; DLBY 1980; INT CA-93-96

Wheatley (Peters), Phillis
1753(?)-1784 ... **BLC 3; LC 3, 50; PC 3; WLC**
  See also AFAW 1, 2; CDALB 1640-1865; DA; DA3; DAC; DAM MST, MULT, POET; DLB 31, 50; EXPP; PFS 13; RGAL 4

Wheelock, John Hall 1886-1978 .... **CLC 14**
  See also CA 13-16R; 77-80; CANR 14; DLB 45

Whim-Wham
  See Curnow, (Thomas) Allen (Monro)

White, Babington
  See Braddon, Mary Elizabeth

White, E(lwyn) B(rooks)
1899-1985 .... **CLC 10, 34, 39**
  See also AITN 2; AMWS 1; CA 13-16R; 116; CANR 16, 37; CDALBS; CLR 1, 21; CPW; DA3; DAM POP; DLB 11, 22; EWL 3; FANT; MAICYA 1, 2; MTCW 1, 2; NCFS 5; RGAL 4; SATA 2, 29, 100; SATA-Obit 44; TUS

White, Edmund (Valentine III)
1940- .... **CLC 27, 110**
  See also AAYA 7; CA 45-48; CANR 3, 19, 36, 62, 107; CN 7; DA3; DAM POP; DLB 227; MTCW 1, 2

White, Hayden V. 1928- .... **CLC 148**
  See also CA 128; DLB 246

White, Patrick (Victor Martindale)
1912-1990 ...... **CLC 3, 4, 5, 7, 9, 18, 65, 69; SSC 39**
  See also BRWS 1; CA 81-84; 132; CANR 43; DLB 260; EWL 3; MTCW 1; RGEL 2; RGSF 2; RHW; TWA; WWE 1

White, Phyllis Dorothy James 1920-
  See James, P. D.
  See also CA 21-24R; CANR 17, 43, 65, 112; CMW 4; CN 7; CPW; DA3; DAM POP; MTCW 1, 2; TEA

White, T(erence) H(anbury)
1906-1964 .... **CLC 30**
  See also AAYA 22; BPFB 3; BYA 4, 5; CA 73-76; CANR 37; DLB 160; FANT; JRDA; LAIT 1; MAICYA 1, 2; RGEL 2; SATA 12; SUFW 1; YAW

White, Terence de Vere 1912-1994 ... **CLC 49**
  See also CA 49-52; 145; CANR 3

White, Walter
  See White, Walter F(rancis)

White, Walter F(rancis) 1893-1955 ... **BLC 3; HR 3; TCLC 15**
  See also BW 1; CA 115; 124; DAM MULT; DLB 51

White, William Hale 1831-1913
  See Rutherford, Mark
  See also CA 121; 189

Whitehead, Alfred North
1861-1947 .... **TCLC 97**
  See also CA 117; 165; DLB 100, 262

Whitehead, E(dward) A(nthony)
1933- .... **CLC 5**
  See also CA 65-68; CANR 58, 118; CBD; CD 5

Whitehead, Ted
  See Whitehead, E(dward) A(nthony)

Whiteman, Roberta J. Hill 1947- ...... **NNAL**
  See also CA 146

Whitemore, Hugh (John) 1936- .... **CLC 37**
  See also CA 132; CANR 77; CBD; CD 5; INT CA-132

Whitman, Sarah Helen (Power)
1803-1878 .... **NCLC 19**
  See also DLB 1, 243

Whitman, Walt(er) 1819-1892 .. **NCLC 4, 31, 81; PC 3; WLC**
  See also AAYA 42; AMW; AMWR 1; CDALB 1640-1865; DA; DA3; DAB; DAC; DAM MST, POET; DLB 3, 64, 224, 250; EXPP; LAIT 2; LMFS 1; PAB; PFS 2, 3, 13; RGAL 4; SATA 20; TUS; WP; WYAS 1

Whitney, Phyllis A(yame) 1903- .... **CLC 42**
  See also AAYA 36; AITN 2; BEST 90:3; CA 1-4R; CANR 3, 25, 38, 60; CLR 59; CMW 4; CPW; DA3; DAM POP; JRDA; MAICYA 1, 2; MTCW 2; RHW; SATA 1, 30; YAW

Whittemore, (Edward) Reed, Jr.
1919- .... **CLC 4**
  See also CA 9-12R, 219; CAAE 219; CAAS 8; CANR 4, 119; CP 7; DLB 5

Whittier, John Greenleaf
1807-1892 .... **NCLC 8, 59**
  See also AMWS 1; DLB 1, 243; RGAL 4

Whittlebot, Hernia
  See Coward, Noel (Peirce)

Wicker, Thomas Grey 1926-
  See Wicker, Tom
  See also CA 65-68; CANR 21, 46

Wicker, Tom .... **CLC 7**
  See Wicker, Thomas Grey

Wideman, John Edgar 1941- ... **BLC 3; CLC 5, 34, 36, 67, 122; SSC 62**
  See also AFAW 1, 2; AMWS 10; BPFB 4; BW 2, 3; CA 85-88; CANR 14, 42, 67, 109; CN 7; DAM MULT; DLB 33, 143; MTCW 2; RGAL 4; RGSF 2; SSFS 6, 12

Wiebe, Rudy (Henry) 1934- .. **CLC 6, 11, 14, 138**
  See also CA 37-40R; CANR 42, 67, 123; CN 7; DAC; DAM MST; DLB 60; RHW

Wieland, Christoph Martin
1733-1813 .... **NCLC 17**
  See also DLB 97; EW 4; LMFS 1; RGWL 2, 3

Wiene, Robert 1881-1938 .... **TCLC 56**

Wieners, John 1934- .... **CLC 7**
  See also BG 3; CA 13-16R; CP 7; DLB 16; WP

Wiesel, Elie(zer) 1928- .... **CLC 3, 5, 11, 37, 165; WLCS**
  See also AAYA 7, 54; AITN 1; CA 5-8R; CAAS 4; CANR 8, 40, 65, 125; CDALBS; DA; DA3; DAB; DAC; DAM MST, NOV; DLB 83, 299; DLBY 1987; EWL 3; INT CANR-8; LAIT 4; MTCW 1, 2; NCFS 4; NFS 4; RGWL 3; SATA 56; YAW

Wiggins, Marianne 1947- .... **CLC 57**
  See also BEST 89:3; CA 130; CANR 60

Wiggs, Susan .... **CLC 70**
  See also CA 201

Wight, James Alfred 1916-1995
  See Herriot, James
  See also CA 77-80; SATA 55; SATA-Brief 44

Wilbur, Richard (Purdy) 1921- ..... **CLC 3, 6, 9, 14, 53, 110; PC 51**
  See also AMWS 3; CA 1-4R; CABS 2; CANR 2, 29, 76, 93; CDALBS; CP 7; DA; DAB; DAC; DAM MST, POET; DLB 5, 169; EWL 3; EXPP; INT CANR-29; MTCW 1, 2; PAB; PFS 11, 12, 16; RGAL 4; SATA 9, 108; WP

Wild, Peter 1940- .... **CLC 14**
  See also CA 37-40R; CP 7; DLB 5

Wilde, Oscar (Fingal O'Flahertie Wills)
1854(?)-1900 ..... **DC 17; SSC 11; TCLC 1, 8, 23, 41; WLC**
  See also AAYA 49; BRW 5; BRWC 1, 2; BRWR 2; BYA 15; CA 104; 119; CANR 112; CDBLB 1890-1914; DA; DA3; DAB; DAC; DAM DRAM, MST, NOV; DFS 4, 8, 9; DLB 10, 19, 34, 57, 141, 156, 190; EXPS; FANT; LATS 1; RGEL 2; RGSF 2; SATA 24; SSFS 7; SUFW; TEA; WCH; WLIT 4

Wilder, Billy .... **CLC 20**
  See Wilder, Samuel
  See also DLB 26

Wilder, Samuel 1906-2002
  See Wilder, Billy
  See also CA 89-92; 205

Wilder, Stephen
  See Marlowe, Stephen

Wilder, Thornton (Niven)
1897-1975 .. **CLC 1, 5, 6, 10, 15, 35, 82; DC 1; WLC**
  See also AAYA 29; AITN 2; AMW; CA 13-16R; 61-64; CAD; CANR 40; CDALBS; DA; DA3; DAB; DAC; DAM DRAM, MST, NOV; DFS 1, 4, 16; DLB 4, 7, 9, 228; DLBY 1997; EWL 3; LAIT 3; MTCW 1, 2; RGAL 4; RHW; WYAS 1

Wilding, Michael 1942- ...... **CLC 73; SSC 50**
  See also CA 104; CANR 24, 49, 106; CN 7; RGSF 2

Wiley, Richard 1944- .... **CLC 44**
  See also CA 121; 129; CANR 71

Wilhelm, Kate .... **CLC 7**
  See Wilhelm, Katie (Gertrude)
  See also AAYA 20; BYA 16; CAAS 5; DLB 8; INT CANR-17; SCFW 2

Wilhelm, Katie (Gertrude) 1928-
  See Wilhelm, Kate
  See also CA 37-40R; CANR 17, 36, 60, 94; MTCW 1; SFW 4

Wilkins, Mary
  See Freeman, Mary E(leanor) Wilkins

Willard, Nancy 1936- .... **CLC 7, 37**
  See also BYA 5; CA 89-92; CANR 10, 39, 68, 107; CLR 5; CWP; CWRI 5; DLB 5, 52; FANT; MAICYA 1, 2; MTCW 1; SATA 37, 71, 127; SATA-Brief 30; SUFW 2

William of Malmesbury c. 1090B.C.-c. 1140B.C. .... **CMLC 57**

William of Ockham 1290-1349 ..... **CMLC 32**

Williams, Ben Ames 1889-1953 ..... **TCLC 89**
  See also CA 183; DLB 102

Williams, C(harles) K(enneth)
1936- .... **CLC 33, 56, 148**
  See also CA 37-40R; CAAS 26; CANR 57, 106; CP 7; DAM POET; DLB 5

Williams, Charles
  See Collier, James Lincoln

Literary Criticism Series
Cumulative Topic Index

This index lists all topic entries in Gale's *Classical and Medieval Literature Criticism* (CMLC), *Contemporary Literary Criticism* (CLC), *Drama Criticism* (DC), *Literature Criticism from 1400 to 1800* (LC), *Nineteenth-Century Literature Criticism* (NCLC), *Short Story Criticism* (SSC), and *Twentieth-Century Literary Criticism* (TCLC). The index also lists topic entries in the Gale Critical Companion Collection, which includes the following publications: *The Beat Generation* (BG), and *Harlem Renaissance* (HR).

Topic Index

NCLC Cumulative Nationality Index

Nationality Index

NCLC-143 Title Index